Introduction

to

Psychology

4th edition

Introduction
to
Psychology

Under the general editorship of
JEROME KAGAN
Harvard University

ERNEST R. HILGARD
STANFORD UNIVERSITY

RICHARD C. ATKINSON
STANFORD UNIVERSITY

4th edition

HARCOURT, BRACE & WORLD, INC.

New York / Chicago / San Francisco / Atlanta

For permission to adapt the copyrighted material below, grateful acknowledgment is made to the following publishers:

American Association for the Advancement of Science. For Figure 8–2 on page 193, copyright © 1960. For Figure 11–8 on page 278, copyright © 1965. For Figure 13–8 on page 349, copyright © 1961. American Association for the Advancement of Science.

The Bobbs-Merrill Company, Inc. For Table 4–1 on page 98, copyright © 1957, by H. H. Remmers.

Harcourt, Brace & World, Inc. For Figure 15–4 on page 402, copyright © 1965. Harcourt, Brace & World, Inc. New York.

Holt, Rinehart and Winston, Inc. For Table 7–4 on page 171, copyright 1938 © 1966. For Table 8–1 on page 189, copyright © 1962. For Figure 11–17 on page 293, copyright © 1965. For Table 14–2 on page 390, copyright © 1965. For Figure 22–2 on page 557, copyright © 1964. All rights reserved. Holt, Rinehart and Winston, Inc. New York.

McGraw-Hill, Inc. For Figure 14–9 on page 382, copyright © 1963. For Figure 14–10 on page 383, copyright © 1968. McGraw-Hill, Inc. New York.

W. W. Norton & Company, Inc. For Table 3–3 on page 74, copyright © 1963. For Table 17–6 on page 456, copyright 1953. W. W. Norton & Company, Inc. New York.

Prentice-Hall, Inc. For Table 14–2 on page 390, copyright © 1962. All rights reserved. Prentice-Hall, Inc. Englewood Cliffs, New Jersey.

Random House, Inc. For Table 7–1 on page 164, copyright © 1962. Random House, Inc. New York.

The Ronald Press Company. For Figure 11–6 on page 276, copyright © 1963. The Ronald Press Company. New York.

Scientific American, Inc. For Figure 8–5 on page 196, copyright © 1961. All rights reserved. Scientific American, Inc. New York.

Photographs not accompanied by a credit line are from the following sources:

page   1 NASA, Ames Research Center
       59 Ann Zane Shanks
      117 Alan C. Shane, University of Pittsburgh
          from Scientific American, June, 1964
      187 Museum of Modern Art, Philip C. Johnson Fund
      268 Fred Kaplan, Black Star
      395 Fritz Goro, Black Star
      503 C. Bernstein, Black Star
      573 Associated Press

Charts: Harry Lazarus, George Kelvin
Physiology drawings: Lorelle Raboni

Editor's Foreword

Psychology is today experiencing a vitality and growth that is at once exhilarating to its practitioners and beneficial to the larger community. Parents, teachers, physicians, and legislators are pressing the psychologist for counsel, and the urgency of their appeal demands a reply that reflects the complexity of the issues and presents a balanced account of current theories and facts.

Introduction to Psychology, one of the preeminent introductory textbooks of this generation, constitutes such a reply. It blends classic material with the most recent developments in theory, presenting in this Fourth Edition new findings that are both representative of contemporary psychology and appropriate to the needs of the student. The newly added sections, on topics ranging from consciousness to behavior pathology, are highlights of this edition.

Professor Richard C. Atkinson, who has joined Professor Hilgard as a collaborator in the Fourth Edition, has taught introductory psychology both at the University of California, Los Angeles, and at Stanford University. He brings to his task not only the background of his original research in the fields of learning and perception, but his expertness in programed learning and computer-based instruction in public schools.

In surveying the broad and demanding field of psychology, Professors Hilgard and Atkinson skillfully pit data against hypotheses, speculating where appropriate but always allowing the empirical realities to settle the argument. They have produced that combination of scholarship and comprehensive coverage that marks a truly distinguished introductory textbook. It is a high privilege to have served as General Editor for this book.

JEROME KAGAN

Harvard University
January 1967

Preface

To prepare a book that represents contemporary psychology without becoming encyclopedic requires the exercise of considerable arbitrary judgment in the selection of material. While this edition, like the earlier ones, is abundantly documented (with some 1,200 citations of books and journal articles), such a selection merely scratches the surface of the literature, the magnitude of which can be estimated from the appearance of 16,000 new titles in a single year's *Psychological Abstracts*.

In deciding what to report from this massive production of scholarly materials we have been guided mainly by three criteria: *First*, we wish to represent fairly the residue from psychology's history, so that we do not discard classical studies merely because they are old. *Second*, we wish to represent the changing front of modern psychology; thus we do not include older topics merely because they conventionally have been included in textbooks. *Third*, we wish to acquaint students with the frontiers of contemporary psychology (for example, information-processing with the aid of modern high-speed computers); so fast has psychology been growing that over 40 percent of the citations in this edition, five years after the last edition, are new to it.

We might list as a *fourth* criterion in the choice of material our desire to meet the concerns of that large fraction of the students in our colleges and universities who find themselves, for various reasons, taking a first course in psychology. We know these students well through our association with them both inside and outside of class. They are not motivated primarily by the desire to learn the stock and trade of psychologists: instead they want to know what is relevant to their own lives, and to find answers to the questions raised by their own interests. To satisfy student interests is compatible with the scientific aspects of psychology; a course that arouses student interest can fulfill the twin goals of being both pertinent and scholarly. The potential relevance of basic psychology to human problems can be shown; it is this eventual relevance that justifies the investment society makes in scientific endeavors. For example, one of our new chapters—Chapter 10, entitled "States of Awareness"—represents the renewed attention of contemporary psychologists to cognitive processes, and at the same time provides some answers to the student who is faced by a variety of claims on subjects ranging from consciousness-expanding drugs to sleep-learning courses. Our emphasis on developmental psychology—including adolescence and early adulthood—goes beyond that in most beginning textbooks because we know that the student is trying to find and define his own identity in this period between recent adolescence and the adult world.

Among topics that reflect the current areas of excitement among psychologists we may select a few to give something of the flavor of new emphases in this edition: the problem of critical periods versus stages in development; the distinction within theories of identification between sex-role and non-sex-role identification; local versus central determiners of hunger and thirst; distinctively human motivation according to three viewpoints (behavior theory, the theory of unconscious determination, and cognitive theory that includes the approaches of humanistic psychology); threshold psychophysics versus detection theory; sleep, dreams, drugs, and hypnosis; information-processing models of learning, including computer-based instruction; new developments in neurophysiological and related theories of memory, including the topics of short-term memory and the "tip-of-the-tongue" phenomenon; adjustive coping mechanisms recognized alongside defense mechanisms; expanded treatment of behavior disorders and psychotherapy, with attention to the behavior therapies.

The newer materials to which reference has just been made are but a few specimens of topics that have been integrated within a book that follows essentially its old outline—an outline that has been based in no small part on the replies to questionnaires submitted by teachers who have used the earlier editions. It is clear from these questionnaires that no one chapter order will please all instructors; some have in the past preferred to select certain chapters, omitting others, and to teach these selected chapters in an order according to individual choice. Instructors report that this works out satisfactorily so long as they provide a few transitions to chapters that are assigned in novel order.

For those who teach shorter courses, we recommend selecting a few chapters and treating them more fully. The obligation to "cover the ground" should never be allowed to interfere with a better coverage of those topics that are carefully considered. Additional suggestions on instruction are included in the accompanying *Instructor's Manual*.

Critical discussions have been included again because they provide an opportunity for examining areas of uncertainty and conflict within psychology without unduly cluttering the free flow of the text. Some instructors may prefer to omit these, others to expand upon them. References at the ends of chapters often contain more material of an advanced nature than it would be feasible to assign. They are there as aids to the reader who may wish to delve further into a topic. If the course calls for one or more term papers, these lists are valuable as aids to scholarship of greater depth on a specified topic.

We owe debts of gratitude to many people who have helped make this edition possible: To those whose patient scientific work has advanced psychology and whose efforts lie behind it all, and to those many colleagues who have counseled us and aided us through the reading of particular chapters. Persons listed in the earlier editions will not be mentioned again, though much of their help has been of abiding value. This edition has been particularly helped by Professor Jerome Kagan of

Harvard University, who as editorial adviser read every chapter and made many useful comments and suggestions. The work of our wives deserves more than the usual courteous mention: Josephine R. Hilgard, M.D., has contributed a number of unpublished cases from her psychiatric experience, and Rita L. Atkinson, Ph.D., has worked very closely with us throughout, contributing new writing in those chapters reflecting her special competency in abnormal and clinical psychology. Our secretaries, Thelma E. Weeks and Myrna E. Valdez, have shown unusual patience and care in seeing this large book through the many stages involved before it was finally ready for the printer.

ERNEST R. HILGARD
RICHARD C. ATKINSON

Stanford University
January 1967

Contents

x

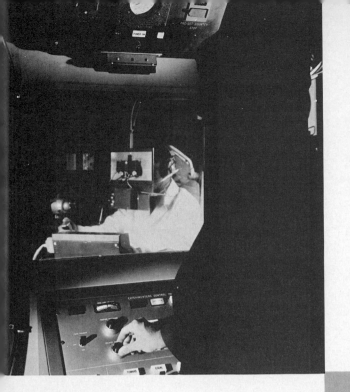

THE SCIENCE OF PSYCHOLOGY

In seeking to understand man and the lower animals, psychology falls among the behavioral sciences that include sociology, anthropology, and those aspects of social science concerned with the individual in relation to his environment. Man's interest in himself began before recorded history, but psychology as a science is a product of the last hundred years. The natural science approach to psychology lays heavy emphasis upon the flesh-and-blood organism—its anatomical equipment, its growth, its processes of integration and interaction. The comparative method, as in other biological sciences, studies the interrelationships among organisms at different stages in evolutionary development.

1 Psychology as a Behavioral Science

Because he can reflect upon the past, take account of present experiences, and make plans for the future, man has always sought to understand himself and the world around him. When he found occurrences beyond his comprehension, he at first tended to attribute them to divine intervention or to some sort of magic, perhaps practiced upon him by his enemies. The roots of science began when he started to find some sort of order in natural occurrences that made them comprehensible: when, for example, he found that he could control his food supply by domesticating animals or by planting crops.

Science leads to understanding of natural events; it leads to predictions about their course and therefore to some control over what takes place. Psychology is like other sciences in seeking to comprehend, to predict, and to control, taking as its special subject matter the behavior of man and the lower animals. Psychology is interested in the ways in which behavior develops in the evolution of the species and in the growth of the individual, in learning and problem-solving, in the motives that initiate, sustain, and guide behavior. As in the case of other sciences, psychology has its "pure" and its "applied" aspects; as an applied science it proposes ways in which psychological knowledge can be used in child rearing, in education, in industrial production, in government, and in international relations.

The student will naturally ask whether a course in psychology will help him in his human relationships and personality difficulties. Will he be able to form better judgments of other people? Will he be able to plan more wisely for himself? Will he make friends more easily? Will he be less likely to lose his temper when he becomes angry?

The answer to these questions is both "Yes" and "No." The "Yes" part of the answer is that, after studying psychology, you should be better able to understand human motives, better able to appraise your own and others' interests and abilities, and better prepared to get along with those about you. The "No" part of the answer is that it is not easy to apply psychological knowledge to the solving of your personal problems. If you have had difficulties in getting along up to now, a single course in psychology is not going to teach you suddenly to overcome all your difficulties. A course in psychology is not a course in self-help, and a psychology textbook is not a manual on the art of handling people.

Psychological science, furthermore, is in an early stage of development. Many of its facts are not yet firmly established, and theoretical interpretations are often controversial. Sometimes we shall be studying more about how psychologists seek answers than about the results they have found.

If, however, you do not expect that one course in psychology will teach you all there is to know about human behavior, you may properly look forward to learning many things that will be useful to you in your ordinary life. In fact, you will gain more from your study of psychology if you make an effort throughout to apply what you are learning to yourself and to those around you. Psychological science is not to be thought of as something mysterious and remote.

The Definition of Psychology

Psychology may be defined as *the science that studies the behavior of man and other animals.*[1] For this definition to be useful, it is necessary to specify more clearly what psychologists mean by behavior. We can get some idea of what *behavior* means to the psychologist if we look briefly at the organization of this book, pausing occasionally to glance at an illustration of what it is that psychologists do. Later in the chapter we can return to a more detailed definition of behavior and a consideration of the relationship of psychology to other sciences.

The topics covered in this book

1. *The behaving organism.* As a science rooted in biology, psychology is interested in the bodily processes that make activity possible. Thus psychologists often refer to the *stimuli* (singular *stimulus*) that impinge upon sense organs, and to the *responses* that occur because of the way the organism operates. Stimuli include the lights, sounds, odors, pinpricks, and other physical energy sources that are the external (and sometimes internal) occasions for what the organism does, goading it to action, interrupting what it is doing, directing its choices. The responses (in man) are what he does when his brain is active, his muscles move, and his glands secrete. We therefore touch briefly on the operation of the *skeleton* and the *muscles,* moving on to glance at the varied functioning of the *endocrine* (ductless) glands, such as the

[1] At the end of the book there is a glossary which defines technical terms appearing in the text and also common words that have special meanings in psychology.

thyroid or the sex glands. But psychologists are particularly interested in the *nervous system* and especially in the *central nervous system,* whose most complex portion is the *brain.*

It has been found, for example, that there are centers deep in the brain (in a part of the brain, old from an evolutionary standpoint, called the hypothalamus) that appear to produce the equivalent of pleasure or of pain when these centers are electrically stimulated (Olds and Olds, 1965).[2] Psychologists not only participated in the original experiments in which this discovery was made, but have since carried out a number of further experiments to determine how similar the responses to electrical stimulation of the brain are to the effects of external pain or food reward. For example, studies have been made of the reaction to conflict when a thirsty rat receives an electric shock as it attempts to drink. The rat at once approaches the water and withdraws from it in fear, assuming a characteristic posture. When the shock is received through an implanted electrode in the brain, the rat behaves just as if a shock had been received on its snout (see Figure 1–1). Thus it appears plausible that the shock through the electrode is equivalent to painful stimulation.

2. *Growth and development.* The child is indeed "father of the man." We can understand much of adult behavior only through a knowledge of the course of its development in the child. Two principles stand out as we study human development. One is that the growth of the body and the nervous system follows certain patterns rooted in biology. These are reflected in the concept of *maturation* of the organism along built-in (inherited) lines. The other is that a mature organism is also a product of *learning.* In man, this learning is in part a product of *social living,* a product of his *culture.* Hence in studying human development, we are interested in the processes of

[2] Throughout this book you will find references to studies which document or expand on the statements made here. Detailed bibliographical information on these studies appears in the list at the end of the book.

Conflict between thirst and pain in the rat

A rat that has learned to drink from the spout (*left*) is given an unpleasant stimulation through the electrode implanted in his brain when he approaches the spout.

This produces the typical conflict position shown: the rat's neck is stretched out toward the water, but he is ready to back away because of the threatened shock. The conflict between thirst and the pain produced by brain stimulation is indistinguishable from that between thirst and the pain produced by an external electric shock.

Martin Iger

socialization, that is, the ways in which the infant turns into a civilized person.

3. *Motivation and emotion.* The newborn infant is aroused to activity by his bodily needs—the needs for air, food, elimination, a comfortable temperature, sleep. All such needs are the physiological roots of what psychologists call *motivation.* But motives become complex as the individual grows up, and psychologists study how they are acquired, how strong they are, and how people differ in their motives. Some individuals conform readily to their cultures, others rebel; some develop good work habits and have high motives to achieve, others are more shiftless; some

are competitive and aggressive, others self-effacing. Emotions and motives are closely related, for the excitement of highly motivated activity has its emotional coloring; aggressive behavior may be accompanied by deep feelings of anger, flight from danger by strong fear.

4. *Perception.* We perceive the world through our eyes or ears or by way of our other senses. But what is perception? How is it that we recognize a given color as red, or hear one sound as music and another as noise, or "sense" that one facial expression is friendly and another hostile? From its earliest days psychology has devoted a great deal of attention to such questions.

It is clear that perception depends not only on our equipment of sense organs, but also on the structures in our nervous system which enable us to say "This is hot" or "That tastes salty." We shall meet a number of the problems posed by perception in this book.

We shall be concerned too with problems of consciousness. How does our physiological state when alert and awake differ from conditions of sleep? We shall see that there is no sharp distinction between conscious and unconscious states; rather there are degrees of awareness in which we may be more or less receptive to stimuli in the environment. Even during the stage of sleep where dreaming occurs we may be affected by events that take place around us.

5. *Learning and thinking.* Because of its importance learning is a topic of special interest to psychologists, both in its theoretical aspects and in its practical aspects. The theoretical problems of learning include the answers to such puzzling questions as how rewards and punishments operate; what goes on when we remember and when we forget, or when we acquire skills; how learning one thing affects the learning of others. The answers to these questions have important practical consequences, for much social effort goes into learning and teaching—of the young by parents and teachers, of apprentices on the job, of members of industrial and business organizations as they face new tasks.

A new interest in "programed" learning, often using so-called teaching machines, illustrates the practical consequences of experimental studies of learning. A *program* is an attempt to apply what we know about the essential features of learning to the task of individual instruction, using a technique in which each step of the process is carefully planned to provide the best conditions for learning. We shall consider later on the detailed ways in which such programs make use of learning theory; for the present we may merely indicate that there have been promising successes in their use. For example, it has been reported that elementary school children who

studied their mathematics by using a program presented by a computer-controlled teaching machine did much better than those who learned it in the conventional way (Suppes, 1967).

Thinking and problem-solving make use of what we have learned, and thereby provide the occasions for new learning. The interrelations between learning and thinking, including the role of language, furnish plenty of problems for investigation.

6. *Individuality and personality.* Individual uniqueness is a product of the hereditary and environmental influences that have shaped the person: the accidents of his birth and upbringing, what he has perceived and learned, what he has thought about. Psychologists have developed various ways of assessing or measuring many kinds of differences among people. Perhaps the most familiar of these devices is the intelligence test.

But intelligence is only one aspect of individuality. All of us know people of whom we say "He's a real person" (or, regrettably, "He's got quite a personality"). What is personality? What is it that conclusively distinguishes one individual from another? And what do we mean when we speak of the "self"? These are questions of much concern to psychology.

7. *Conflict, adjustment, and mental health.* For many readers, this aspect of psychology may seem the most important. How does a person meet frustration and conflict? What happens when he can no longer cope with his problems in ordinary ways? Is "adjustment" an ideal, or not? What, indeed, is mental health? While psychology has no final answers to these questions, it has at least been able to shed some light on them. There have been some successes in applying the methods of the experimental laboratory to these fields, and much has been accomplished in developing new techniques for treating mentally ill individuals.

8. *Social aspects of psychology.* The old saw, "Two's company and three's a crowd," familiar as it may seem in one context, illustrates a number of basic psychological questions. What is the difference

between the response of an individual to his physical environment and his response to that same environment in the presence of another individual? What do we mean by a group, and how does group behavior differ from and affect individual behavior? The final section of this book tackles these questions, concluding with a discussion of the ways in which psychologists as professionals address themselves to these and all the other aspects of human behavior touched on in this introductory text.

Behavior as defined by psychology

With the preceding illustrations of psychology before us, we are now prepared to state more precisely what the psychologist means when he says that psychology is the study of the behavior of man and other animals.

Behavior. By *behavior* we mean those activities of an organism that can be observed by another person or by an experimenter's instruments. A child eats breakfast, rides a bicycle, talks, blushes, laughs, and cries. All these verbs describe forms of behavior. Observations of behavior may be made unaided, as in watching a child at play, or they may be aided with instruments, as in giving a lie-detection test.

Though our primary interest in this book is the understanding of man, we shall also have something to say about the behavior of lower animals, because what we learn from studying the lower animals is often helpful in understanding man. We can control the lives of lower organisms in the laboratory from the moment of their birth. In those of short life span we can study inheritance through several generations. We can do brain surgery on animals (as in the illustration of implanted electrodes, Figure 1-1), while such experiments are possible with human beings only under special conditions of illness or injury. Sometimes the fact that animals learn less rapidly than human beings is an advantage in that the details of the process are spaced out for study. While caution is always needed in applying the results of animal experimentation to man, study of lower animals con-

tributes to knowledge in psychology just as it does in biology and medicine.

A point of disagreement among some psychologists exists over the relative emphasis to be placed upon lower organisms and man in a science of psychology. The disagreement leads to two interpretations of *comparative psychology,* the name given to the study of the behavior of lower organisms in their interrelationships with each other and to man. One interpretation is that any specimen of behavior is worth studying in its own right, yielding such generalizations as it may, without regard to its relationship to man. Thus a comparative psychologist studying why salmon return to lay their eggs in the river in which they were hatched may not want to be asked what this has to do with human behavior. The other interpretation is that we seek to understand man, and in order to do so we study the evolution of the processes that we find at work in him. This kind of interest is similar to that of the medical investigator who works with animals in order to find the drugs or other treatment procedures that may prove useful in treating human disease. As long as one remains within the framework of natural science, the issue is not a divisive one, for there is plenty of investigatory work to be done by those who accept either one of the alternatives.

Another form of the issue with regard to emphasis upon man is a more important one. Some psychologists hold that man is so different from the lower organisms that human psychology is something entirely different from animal psychology, and the behavior of lower animals can therefore be disregarded. This point of view finds its expression in forms of psychology more prevalent in Europe than in America, going by such names as "understanding"—psychology, character-psychology, phenomenology, existentialism. These psychologies make much of man's ability to foresee the future,

[3] Critical discussions are introduced from time to time, especially to point up controversial issues in contemporary psychology. They may be omitted at the discretion of the instructor.

of his knowledge that he will die, of his ability to understand directly the feelings of another human being and to find meaning in human suffering. These intuitive, moral qualities are said to be distinctly human, without parallels in animal psychology. Such a point of view deserves acknowledgment and is not to be lightly dismissed. While it is affiliated more with philosophy and religion than with a naturalistic psychology, it has become influential in psychiatry and clinical psychology, that is, in the treatment of human emotional and mental illness (e.g., Bugental, 1965; Severin, 1965).

The emphasis in this book will reflect the general orientation of American psychology today, which seeks to place the study of behavior in the context of natural science, recognizing man's affiliation with other biological organisms, and hence tracing continuities between man and other animals. Such an orientation need not deny man's uniqueness where such uniqueness is demonstrable.

Conscious processes. Each of us knows what it feels like to be hungry, to have a headache, to burn a finger. Each of us knows what it feels like to be praised or reproved. Each of us is aware of his own anger and fear, excitement and fatigue; no one else has full access to this awareness. An individual's perception of his world, his memories, his flights of imagination, his dreams, his pleasures and pains belong to a private world, the world of his own *consciousness*. By conscious experiences we mean simply those events of which only the person himself is fully aware. Psychology is interested in this world, even though access to it is necessarily by way of *inference*.[4] We may learn

[4] Our observations almost always include inferences that go beyond the data given. If I see a man waving his hand on a street corner in New York, I *observe* merely the hand-waving, though I may *infer* that he is trying to hail a taxicab. I may be wrong; he may be trying to catch a friend's attention or he may be making a meaningless drunken gesture. Inferences are thus always somewhat uncertain; the scientific task is to see that our inferences from data are made in such a manner as to have a high probability that they are correct.

by external signs that a man is suffering pain and we may even arrive at a satisfactory judgment of its intensity, but the conscious process—the actual awareness of the pain—is his alone.

Psychologists are by no means unanimous as to the place of private experience (conscious processes) in a science of psychology. Some extremists believe that private experiences have no place in science; a consistent science, they say, must be built with objective data open to observation by any unbiased observer. Most psychologists, however, hold that private experiences are just as much a part of the real world as more observable activities, and, while insisting that data must be objective, they accept the *verbal report* of these experiences as data for science. Suppose, for example, you tell me that you had a dream of flying with wings. Then what you have told me about your dream is part of your observable behavior. I can record it on tape and play it back to anyone who wishes to know exactly what you said when you reported your dream. I do not have full access to your dream, although I may be able to make some inferences about its meaning from other things that I know about you and your behavior. By including verbal reports in the study of behavior, psychologists can restrict their data to overt activities but include in their *inferences* statements about conscious processes.

Unconscious processes. An even more difficult problem is raised when we infer the presence of *unconscious processes*. This term is not usually applied to the "nonconscious" physiological processes, such as the circulation of the blood or the reflex constriction of the pupil of the eye. Rather, by unconscious processes we mean thoughts, wishes, and fears of which the person is unaware but which still influence his behavior. Can the existence of such processes legitimately be inferred, and can they be classified as behavior? The answer is yes: most psychologists grant that we can infer unconscious motives from speech, gestures, and other behavioral signs. For example, if a person acts in a conceited manner it may be that he is actually boasting in order to conceal an *unconscious* fear of being thought inferior. As we shall see in Chapter 10, there is no sharp distinction between conscious and unconscious; it would perhaps be better to speak of degrees of awareness. For example, we may be only dimly aware of the clock's striking, yet be able later to count the strokes; we may catch ourselves humming a tune we did not know we had started to hum. The conceited person is not wholly unaware of his need to hide his fears; he may simply be unaware of the extent to which he goes to "cover up." By making inferences from observations, we are then able to include unconscious as well as conscious processes within our science of behavior.

Psychology and other sciences

The family of sciences to which psychology belongs is coming to be known as the *behavioral sciences*. Other members of the family are *anthropology,* which deals largely with nonliterate (primitive) human societies, and *sociology,* which is concerned with man's social life and the institutions he creates. Other social sciences (e.g., economics, history, political science) are classifiable as behavioral sciences to the extent that they are committed to the study of man by the methods of science.

Psychology, as a behavioral science, touches and overlaps the other behavioral sciences. But psychology leans also toward physiology and the physical sciences. In relation to *physical science* it is chiefly a borrower. Many of the instruments used in the psychological laboratory, such as galvanometers, amplifiers, time-measuring instruments, and electronic computers, come out of physics or engineering laboratories. The methods of chemical analysis are borrowed when waste products in the blood are studied under conditions of fatigue or when the effects of hormone injection are analyzed.

During World War II, with the elaboration of many new observational devices such as direction finders and radar screens,

the importance of man's ability to respond to complex instruments came into focus. There developed a branch of applied science known as *human factors research.* This new study is only one illustration of the blending of sciences—in this case, engineering and psychology.

The affiliation between psychology and *physiology* has always been very close. Much of early experimental psychology was concerned with sensory problems and hence with the sense organs and related nervous structures. Many of the developments in the study of animal psychology depended upon correlations between brain damage and learning. Studies of the effects of drugs and hormones also cross the border between psychology and physiology or pharmacology. Other aspects of biology, such as embryology, genetics, and ecology, have their significance for psychology because of the psychologist's interest in growth, in heredity, and in the adaptation of the organism to its environment.

Within medicine, psychology finds its closest affiliation with *psychiatry*. Psychiatry, in its broadest sense, can be defined as a medical psychology. The field of *psychosomatic medicine* recognizes the part that emotional and other psychological disturbances play in organic ailments such as ulcers and asthma. The interests of psychology and medical science overlap in studying the effects of drugs on behavior or special conditions such as aphasia (loss of speech or language), amnesia, hallucinations, or hypnosis.

These brief suggestions of the interplay between psychology and other fields of study open up fascinating possibilities for collaboration between those whose expertness lies in one or another of these studies and those whose expertness lies within psychology. An interesting question arises as to how much the related expertnesses can be combined in the same person, or whether the collaboration can be better achieved through joint efforts. That is, it may be that a good legal psychology will be forthcoming only when a lawyer trains himself in psychology or when a psychologist trains himself in the law, rather than when a lawyer and a psychologist get together. Perhaps a compromise is possible; the collaborators may need to know something of the other person's specialty, but they may not need to be equally expert in both specialties.

The Methods of Psychological Science

Above all else, the aim of science is to discover new and useful information in the form of verifiable data, that is, data obtained under conditions such that other qualified people can make similar observations and obtain the same results. This calls for orderliness and precision in uncovering relationships and communicating them to others. The scientific ideal is not always reached, but as a science becomes better established it rests upon a large body of relationships that can be taken for granted because they have been so often validated.

Methods of the experimental laboratory

The term *experimental psychology* was once applied only to a particular subject matter of general psychology inherited from the earliest nineteenth-century laboratories, chiefly sensory processes, perception, and learning. While there are still some psychologists who define experimental psychology in this limited way (usually adding today physiological studies and studies with lower animals), it is preferable to think of experimental psychology as psychology grounded in the laboratory method, whatever the content of the experiment may be. The distinguishing characteristics are those of the laboratory, not of the subjects used or the topics covered. Thus child psychology and social psychology may be amenable to experimental study, and to the extent that they are they belong within experimental psychology.

The relationships the psychologist seeks to discover are *regular* ("lawful") *relationships among variables*. By a variable we mean something that can occur with different values. For example, in an experiment seeking to discover the relationship between learning ability and age, both learning ability and age can take on different values, learning being either slower or faster and the learner being younger or older. To the extent that learning changes systematically with increasing age, we can discover a lawful relationship between them. In this case, learning ability and age are the variables.

We distinguish the methods of the experimental laboratory from other forms of observation and description by the degree to which the experimenter is able to *control the variables* that determine the experimental outcome. If he seeks to discover whether learning depends upon age, he can control the age variable by selecting groups of children of different ages. If he then sets for each group the same learning task, such as memorizing a sequence of numbers, he can determine whether the older children do indeed master the task more rapidly than the younger ones. In this situation the various age levels are the *antecedent* conditions; the learning performance is the *result* of these conditions (among others, presumably). We call the antecedent condition the *independent variable;* the variable that changes as a result of change in the antecedent condition is called the *dependent variable*.

The experimenter controls the value of the independent variable; the circumstances of the experiment determine the value of the dependent variable. These terms may be confusing, but the distinction can best be remembered if it is noted that the value of the *dependent* variable *depends* upon what happens in the experiment—it is the outcome variable. The distinction between the two kinds of variables will become clearer if we follow an actual illustrative experiment.

Experiments often begin with hunches coming from ordinary experience. For example, the hunch that there is a relationship between ease of learning and muscle tension (some students prefer to study in an upright, alert position, others lying down) may have led to the study of this relationship in the laboratory. The following experiment by Courts (1939) illustrates his attempt to reduce the uncertainty about this relationship through the control and measurement of variables.

Sixty college students learned nonsense syllables (consisting of two consonants with a vowel between, such as *geb*) while exerting muscular effort by squeezing an instrument known as a *dynamometer* (Figure 1–2). Each subject participating in the experiment was first asked to squeeze the dynamometer as hard as he could for 30 seconds. The reading at the end of this time was used to assign his maximum grip. He then learned different lists of syllables both under normal conditions (without the dynamometer) and while squeezing with a grip representing various fractions of the maximum grip. The amount learned under each tension condition was tested by the number of syllables recalled after five trials through the list. Meaningless com-

1–3

Effects of tension on learning

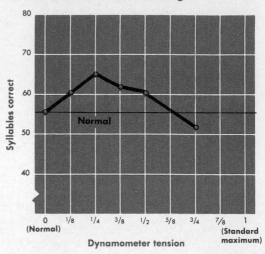

Muscular tension improves learning of nonsense syllables up to one-fourth of the maximum tension possible; greater tension decreases learning. (From Courts, 1939)

binations were used so that the several lists could all be made alike in difficulty. The results show that learning increased with the strength of grip up to one-fourth the maximum grip; from that point on an increase in tension was accompanied by reduced learning, until at three-fourths the maximum grip the learning was below normal (Figure 1–3).

Note that the experimenter had worked out a careful *plan* before he brought the subjects to the laboratory. First of all, he had planned to hold many conditions constant: the general setting for the experiment, the measuring instruments used, the nature of the materials to be learned, the length of each list, the number of trials allowed for learning, and the method of testing learning. Then he carefully established *tension* as the *independent variable* by assigning a maximum value according to the subject's strength of grip. He obtained this value by having the subject squeeze as hard as he could. Then he set the lower values as fractions of the maximum value. The *dependent variable* became the amount of *learning* associated with each step of tension. To do a quantitative experiment the experimenter had to

1–2

A dynamometer

Lafayette Instrument Co.

This version of the instrument measures strength of grip.

have scales of measurement for both kinds of variables. The *tension* was measured by the units of the dynamometer (kilograms) and then converted to fractions of the maximum. The *learning* was measured by the number of nonsense syllables recalled. The experimenter could plot the results as a relationship between two variables, in the form of Figure 1–3. Finally, he used enough subjects (60) so that he could count on similar results if he repeated the experiment with other subjects.

Psychological laboratories, like other scientific laboratories, are specially equipped places in which experimentation is carried on. Precision instruments are usually necessary to control the experiment and obtain exact data. We may need to produce colors of known wave lengths in studies of vision or sounds of known frequency for studies of audition. Or we may wish to expose a pattern in the aperture of a viewing screen for a fraction of a second. Thus, to control stimuli we often require apparatus. In measuring response, we may also need precision instruments. We may wish to have an accurate measure of time in thousandths of a second or to amplify slight electrical currents from the muscles or from the brain. The psychological laboratory has its audiometers, photometers, oscilloscopes, mazes, precision timers, and many other instruments for presenting controlled stimuli and for accurate registration of responses.

The value of an experiment is not determined, however, by the amount of apparatus used. Fundamentally, arrangements for experimentation are a matter of logic. If the logic of experimentation requires precision apparatus, then such apparatus is used; if it does not, then good experimentation may be done by means of pencil and paper procedures.

The degree of control possible in the laboratory makes a laboratory experiment the preferred scientific method when it can be used appropriately. However, for psychology to develop as a science, it is not essential that all its problems be brought into the laboratory. Some other sciences, such as geology and astronomy,

are experimental only to a very limited extent. Recognizing the great value of the laboratory approach, we shall now turn to some of the other methods used in psychological investigations.

Naturalistic observation

In the early stages of a science it is necessary to explore the ground, to become familiar with the relationships that will later become the subject of more precise study. Careful observation of animal and human behavior (including the study of our own conscious processes) is the starting point for psychology. A study of gibbons in their native environment of Thailand may tell us things about their social organization that will help us to direct our laboratory investigations. Nonliterate tribes will help us to see ranges of variation in human institutions that would go unrecognized if we confined our study to men and women in our own culture. We learn from observing a mother cat caring for her kittens something about the uniformities of innate animal behavior. Motion pictures of a newborn baby can reveal the details of movement patterns shortly after birth. Such observations of natural phenomena gradually merge into experiments as the conditions of observation are standardized through laboratory control (see Figure 1–4).

The value of naturalistic observations is limited by the fact that anecdotes may be substituted for genuine observations and that interpretation may be substituted for description. Thus we might be tempted to say that a hungry animal is "looking for food" when all we have observed is heightened activity. Investigators must therefore be trained to observe and record accurately in order to avoid reading their own wishes or biases into what they report. With proper precautions, however, naturalistic observations can be important not only in the early stages of a science but later on, as correctives to incomplete theories.

Case histories

Psychologists are often interested in the individual. For that reason scientific biog-

Naturalistic observations merge into experimental ones when made under controlled conditions, as, for example, in this one-way vision dome used in studying child behavior.

Edmund B. Gerard, Life Magazine © Time, Inc.

raphies of individuals become important sources of data. A scientific biography is known as a *case history*. Case histories originally were developed largely in connection with social work. The workers found it helpful in making recommendations about an individual to know something of his family background, the circumstances of his mother's pregnancy, ease or difficulty of childbirth, health history, school history, social history, any unusual emotional episodes, and the circumstances surrounding the present complaint. When case histories are organized for purposes of scientific study, items have to be included that are relevant to the theories being tested. If, for example, someone is studying the difference between bottle-fed children and breast-fed children, it is important that he have additional details about how the child was fed, who did the feeding, the nature of the weaning, and so on.

Two methods can be used for constructing the case history. One method is that of *the diary of development*, in which the case history is constructed as the individual grows up. Some long-term studies have selected groups of children at birth or in early childhood and then followed their development for years. The second method is to prepare the case history by *reconstructing the biography* according to recollections by the individual, his parents, or others who knew him in his earlier days. This method is, of course, the usual way of obtaining a case history when a juvenile gets into trouble or an adult enters a mental hospital. There are disadvantages in this retrospective method because of distortions or oversights, but it is often the only method available.

The interview

The interview as a means of obtaining the data that go into the case history has itself become a research device. The hazards of the interview are many: accurate replies depend upon questions that are clear and unambiguous, an unbiased interviewer, a good relationship between the interviewer and the person interviewed. The interview is now widely used in studies of voting behavior, opinions on public issues, and market research. With advances in techniques of interviewing, selecting the sample, and treating the data, the interview has become an important tool.

Test methods

The *test* as an instrument of research has an important place in contemporary psychology. We use it to measure all manner of abilities, interests, attitudes, and accomplishments. By means of tests, large quantities of data can be obtained from people in factories or hospitals or schools, with a minimum of disturbance of their living routines and without elaborate laboratory equipment. Test construction and use are no simple matters; later chapters will explore the problems of testing in some detail.

The Roots of Modern Psychology

Although psychology as a science has developed in recent times, thoughtful men in all periods of history have attempted to find explanations for human behavior. Books on the history of psychology discuss the views of early Greek philosophers, especially those of Plato and Aristotle. After the Greeks, St. Augustine (354–430) is considered the next great precursor of the modern psychologist because of his skill in introspection [5] and his great curiosity about psychological phenomena, including the behavior of young infants and of crowds at chariot races. Descartes (1596–1650) left his mark on the history of psychology through his theory that animals are machines to be studied much as other machines are studied. He introduced the concept of reflex action, which has had a significant place in both physiology and psychology. Many prominent philosophers of the seventeenth and eighteenth centuries—Leibniz, Hobbes, Locke, Hume, to name only four—grappled with questions of concern to psychologists today. Thus psychology grew out of philosophy, and its history is intermingled with the history of philosophy and of other sciences.

Two early approaches

In the nineteenth century, before experimental psychology proper began, two theories of the mind competed for psychologists' support. The one, known as *faculty psychology*, was a doctrine of mental powers. According to this theory, the mind had a few principal faculties, such as thinking, feeling, and willing, that accounted for its activities. These faculties were further broken down into several dozen mental subfaculties, such that we remembered through the subfaculty of memory, imagined through the subfaculty of imagination, and so on. It was faculty psychology that encouraged early nineteenth-century anatomists such as Franz Gall to try to localize special faculties in parts of the brain. Gall and his colleagues developed an elaborate system (*phrenology*) that proposed not only that such complex mental subfaculties as memory, love, curiosity, numerical ability, etc., could be precisely located in the brain, but that the convolutions of the skull gave evidence of the strength of the faculties located beneath. Thus a bump above the ear signified musical talent, one on the forehead indicated mathematical ability, one toward the back of the head, cautiousness, and so on. Although phrenology had enormous popular appeal, research did not support its claims and it was soon discredited among scientists. Theorists also became dissatisfied with the doctrine of faculties because it explained nothing; it merely classified mental activities.

The *association psychologists* held a second, opposing theory. They denied inborn

---

[5] Introspection is a term used in psychology to refer to the description of one's own conscious processes. It is not to be confused with morbid introspection, in which one is preoccupied with one's inner life in an unhealthy way.

TABLE 1–1

Important dates in the history of psychology

B.C.

400 Hippocrates relates personality characteristics to body types and proposes a physiological (as opposed to demonological) theory of mental illness.

350 Aristotle stresses the objective observation of man's behavior and proposes three principles to account for association of ideas.

A.D.

400 St. Augustine makes careful introspections in his *Confessions;* influenced by Platonic ideas.

1650 René Descartes characterizes the mind-body relation as one of interaction.

1651 Thomas Hobbes foreshadows associationism by declaring that all ideas come from sensory experience.

1690 John Locke carries Hobbes' notion a step further by declaring that the mind at birth is a blank slate (*tabula rasa*).

1749 David Hartley formalizes doctrine of associationism and suggests a neurological basis for memory.

1809 Franz Gall and Johann Spurzheim give prominence through phrenology to the study of mental faculties and brain function.

1811 Sir Charles Bell and François Magendie discover anatomical and functional discreteness of sensory and motor nerves.

1821 Pierre Flourens performs first significant experiments in localization of brain functions.

1822 Friedrich Bessel measures individual differences in reaction time for astronomical observations.

1838 Johannes Müller formulates doctrine of specific nerve energies.

1846 Ernst Weber derives the first quantitative law in psychology.

1850 Hermann von Helmholtz measures the rate of conduction of nerve impulses.

1860 Gustav Fechner publishes *Elements of psychophysics*, in which he presents various methods for measuring the relationship between physical stimuli and experienced sensations.

1869 Sir Francis Galton studies individual differences and applies Darwin's concept of selective adaptation to the evolution of races.

1870 Gustav Fritsch and Eduard Hitzig discover specific sensory and motor areas in brain.

1879 Wilhelm Wundt opens the first formal psychological laboratory in Leipzig.

1883 G. Stanley Hall establishes first psychology laboratory in America at Johns Hopkins University.

faculties of the mind; instead, they limited the mind's content to ideas coming by way of the senses, which then became associated through principles such as similarity, contrast, and contiguity. They explained all mental activity through this *association of ideas*. Both faculty psychology and association psychology have their counterparts at the present time, but with notable differences between the old and the new. The search for primary abilities underlying scores on psychological tests, which we will meet later, is related to faculty psychology, but it differs in its careful quantitative approach. Much of learning theory, especially the theory of conditioned responses, is similar to earlier association theory, except that now we believe that stimuli and responses rather than ideas are associated. Very often, thinking men of earlier centuries anticipated later developments.

Wundt's laboratory

Wilhelm Wundt (1832–1920) is commonly called the "founder of modern experimental psychology," for it was he who opened the first formal psychological laboratory, in Leipzig in 1879. The largest part of his work was devoted to the senses, especially to vision. But Wundt and his coworkers also did a good deal of work on measuring the time of mental processes through the study of reaction time. In addition, they studied attention, emotional processes, and associative processes in memory.

Wundt's psychology was *introspective* (i.e., it relied heavily on the subject's report of his own experiences), but at the

1885	Hermann Ebbinghaus publishes the first experimental studies of memory.
1890	William James's *Principles of psychology* is published in the United States.
1892	Edward Titchener at Cornell University establishes "structuralism" as a major influence in American psychology.
1898	Edward Thorndike performs some of first controlled experiments on animal learning at Columbia University.
1900	Sigmund Freud publishes *The interpretation of dreams* which presents many of his basic ideas on psychoanalysis.
1905	In France, Alfred Binet and Theodore Simon devise the first intelligence test.
1906	In Russia, Ivan Pavlov publishes results of his studies on classical conditioning.
1912	Max Wertheimer publishes the first formulation of Gestalt psychology.
1913	John Watson has major impact on the course of American psychology with paper on behaviorism.
1916	Lewis Terman at Stanford University revises the Binet Intelligence Test for use in the United States (now called the Stanford-Binet).
1917	Wolfgang Köhler publishes results of studies in problem-solving in primates.
1921	Hermann Rorschach, a Swiss psychiatrist, devises projective technique for assessing personality.
1922	Edward Tolman presents his initial ideas on purposive behaviorism.
1929	Karl Lashley publishes *Brain mechanisms and intelligence*.
1935	Louis Thurstone develops factor analysis.
1938	B. F. Skinner publishes *The behavior of organisms*, which summarizes research on operant conditioning.
1943	Clark Hull presents his mathematico-deductive theory of learning in *Principles of behavior*.
1949	Donald Hebb in *Organization of behavior*, presents a general behavior theory that attempts to bridge the gap between neurophysiology and psychology.
1950	William Estes lays the foundations for current developments in mathematical learning theory.
1950	Events since 1950 are not listed here because there has not been enough time to judge their long-term impact on the field.

same time it was devoted to laboratory methods, including the use of various kinds of precision instruments. An illustration of the early experiments from Wundt's laboratory is one on *reaction time*, performed in 1888. Reaction time is the time that elapses between a stimulus and the response to the stimulus. Wundt found that if a subject who is prepared to lift a finger from a telegraph key when a light comes on pays careful attention to *seeing the light,* it takes him longer to respond than if he directs his attention to *moving his finger.* This seems a little strange, especially since he reacts very promptly in either case, but the difference, as reported somewhat inexactly in the early experiment, was about 0.1 second. To what was it attributed? Wundt distinguished between *perception* and *ap-perception,* a distinction that is now chiefly of historical interest. He said that when the attention was on the movement, there was simple perception, and the light triggered the movement very promptly. When, however, the attention was on the stimulus, there was the additional activity of apperception, which we may think of as a richer, "conscious" perception of the light. Wundt decided that this apperception required about 0.1 second. His interpretations are no longer accepted, for the processes intervening between the stimulus and the response are organized in more complex ways than he proposed. But such experiments helped to tie theory to observations, familiarized psychologists with the use of laboratory instruments, and introduced quantitative measurements.

Galton whistle

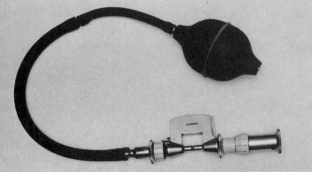

David Linton, courtesy N.Y.U.

This whistle, used to measure sensitivity to tones of high pitch, was one of Sir Francis Galton's contributions to the psychological laboratory. It has a modern counterpart in the dog-calling whistles that make use of tones too high for the human ear to hear.

Wundt's laboratory is important to us because so many pioneers in American psychology went there to study. Although William James had a small demonstration laboratory at Harvard as early as 1875, the first formal laboratory in America was that established in 1883 at Johns Hopkins University by G. Stanley Hall, one of those who went to study with Wundt. Before the end of the 1890s, Wundt's students were to be found at such universities as California, Catholic University, Clark, Cornell, Harvard, Iowa, Minnesota, Princeton, Stanford, and Yale. It is not surprising, therefore, that the new laboratories in America were founded largely on the pattern of Wundt's laboratory.

Other roots of contemporary psychology

Although the impetus for the founding of laboratories and suggestions for problems to be dealt with at first came largely from Germany, especially from Wundt, other influences soon began to be felt. One set of influences came from England, especially from Sir Francis Galton (1822–1911). Galton pioneered in a measurement psychology in Great Britain which was devoted mainly to a study of the problem of individual differences, including inherited abilities. Hence he had an important influence on the development of intelligence tests and other kinds of tests that have become prominent in American psychology. He also had his influence upon the laboratory (Figure 1–5). It was he who invented the statistical technique of correlation and developed the index later to be named the *coefficient of correlation*. We shall meet that coefficient often in the pages of this book.

Also from England came the influence of the theory of evolution, as propounded by Charles Darwin (1809–82). Because Darwin's theory established the continuity between animal and man, it made *comparative psychology* important. American psychologists have closely studied lower animals, especially white rats, monkeys, and chimpanzees, not only in order to understand their behavior but also to learn principles important in the understanding of man. The notion of adaptation to environment, inherent in the evolutionary theory, led also to a psychology of adjustment. That is, following Darwin, some psychologists believed that we could understand consciousness, emotions, and other psychological processes if we knew how they served the adjustment of man to his environment.

Another body of influence upon psychology came from medicine and psychiatry, especially from the treatment of the mentally ill. We need think only of the long history of hypnotism, dating especially from Anton Mesmer (1734–1815). And at every turn today we meet the influence of another Viennese physician, Sigmund Freud (1856–1939), the founder of that branch of psychology known as *psychoanalysis*.

Once the laboratories of psychology were in operation and trained psychologists became available to man them, new problems in increasing numbers were made the subject of experimental attack. Animal psychology, child psychology, social psychology—all have provided material for experimental study. As new problems have entered psychology, they have been studied in the spirit of scientific inquiry. Since the establishment of their first laboratories, psychologists have been intent upon making the methods of psychology conform to those of science in general.

The Role of Theory in Psychology

It was once thought that a science would emerge if facts were carefully collected, and generalizations were made by induction from these facts. Few people now hold this simple a view. Sciences are often helped to take form when the search for facts is guided by *theories,* and when the theories are modified or expanded to encompass the range of newly discovered facts.

When psychology broke off from philosophy and began to establish itself as an independent science, some of the thought patterns of the philosophers persisted, and psychologists soon found themselves developing competing *systems* or *schools* of psychology. The period of schools in psychology is passing, but these systematic schools have served their purposes in providing rallying points for enthusiastic workers, in correcting faulty emphases within opposing schools, and in giving some measure of unity to the complex fragments of psychology, even though the unity achieved may in some instances have been ill-founded. Without reviewing the many systematic positions that have flourished for a time and then faded away, it is worthwhile to consider several systematic positions which are recent enough to help us to understand some contemporary controversies within psychology.

Behaviorism and S-R psychology

A system known as *behaviorism* has been very influential, especially in America. Its founder, John B. Watson (1878–1958), reacted against the tradition of his time that the introspective study of conscious experience was the province of psychology, and he boldly proposed a psychology that would get along *without* introspection. He felt no need to make assertions about consciousness when he studied the adjustive processes, the various muscular movements and glandular secretions of animals and infants. He decided that the results of animal psychology and child psychology could not only stand on their own as science, but that they set a pattern that adult psychology might well follow (Watson, 1913, 1925).

In order to make psychology a science, Watson said, its data must be open to public inspection like the data of any other science. When a rat runs a maze you can take a motion picture of its movements, and any competent person can check your statement about the order in which it entered the blind alleys. As long as you study what the animal or the person *does,* or what he accomplishes (his behavior or the products of his behavior), then you can have an *objective science* distinct from the *subjective science* to which introspection limits you. Behavior is public; consciousness is private. Science should deal with public facts.

Watson had to meet many objections. How about a man buried in thought? If he is not moving, is he not thinking? Watson had his reply: he is moving if you make careful enough measurements. Particularly, his vocal cords may be active. One of Watson's favorite theories was that silent thinking consists essentially in talking to yourself. So he made the distinction between *explicit* movements (the kind easily open to observation and measurement) and *implicit* movements (the kind to be detected only by sensitive instruments). Whatever the circumstances, all that the psychologist as behaviorist is interested in is responses of the muscles and of the glands. And, according to Watson, this limitation of interest will prove to be no limitation whatever to the progress of psychology as a science.

How about the richness of emotional experiences? Here again Watson had his answer. The chief characteristic of emotions (for purposes of science) is not their conscious coloring but the stirred-up state of the organism. Nobody doubts that a dog has emotions such as fear or anger or de-

Entrance

1–6

A laboratory maze
and data processing room

Behaviorism produced many experimental studies of animals, similar to this one. Here the rat in the Y-maze, *above*, is learning a behavior pattern which results in a reward of food, delivered by the mechanism at the end of the arm of the "Y." His maze is connected electronically to the control room, *below*, where his behavior is automatically recorded. The use of modern automation equipment allows massive quantities of data to be processed in such studies. (After D'Amato and Jagoda, 1960)

David Linton, courtesy N.Y.U.

jection, yet nobody has ever examined a dog's consciousness. Visceral responses, prominent in emotion, can be studied as such. Many of the processes involved in emotion are unconscious or unverbalized—to the behaviorist they are visceral tension states for which we have no words.

Because many psychologists were growing impatient with introspection, the new behaviorism caught on very rapidly in America, particularly in the 1920s, and for a time most of the younger psychologists liked to think of themselves as behaviorists. As enthusiastic supporters of such systems tend to do, they went to extremes, but gradually the excitement about behaviorism subsided. There are still a few ardent behaviorists, but most contemporary psychologists are not extreme about it.

The heir to behaviorism in contemporary psychology is the *stimulus-response psychologist*, or S-R psychologist, as the position is often abbreviated. Many contemporary psychologists, particularly in America, find it congenial to discuss psychological events as beginning with a *stimulus* and ending with a *response*. For example, if a light is flashed in your eye and your pupil constricts, the light is a stimulus and the pupillary constriction is a response. Stimulus-response theory (or S-R theory) asserts that all behavior is in response to stimuli, whether the behavior is overt (as in running or shouting) or covert (as in thinking and dreaming).

The advantage of the S-R formulation is that it repeatedly reminds the psychologist that he must anchor his explanations of behavior in the real world—the world of stimuli, at the beginning of the causal chain, and the world of responses, at the end of the chain. He thus shares with behaviorism the desire to relate psychological principles to the same sorts of events that are studied in other sciences. The present S-R psychologist goes beyond the earlier behaviorist, however, in his willingness to infer all sorts of processes between the stimulus and the response, processes that he calls *intervening variables*. The nature of the organism, its aroused motives, its previous experiences—all help to determine the response. Because various S-R psychologists prefer and deal with different kinds of intervening variables, not all S-R psychologists have the same theory. They agree only in viewing a psychological event as something that always involves a stimulus-response relationship.

The men who had most to do with establishing a stimulus-response psychology in America were Robert S. Woodworth (1869–1962) and Edward L. Thorndike (1874–1949), both professors at Columbia University. Neither of them was ever a behaviorist, strictly speaking, though they can of course be thought of as behavioral scientists.

The more precise meaning of stimulus is that of a restricted source of energy impinging upon a sense organ, and the more precise meaning of a response is the activation of a muscle or a gland. Both Thorndike and Woodworth broadened the concepts of stimulus and response beyond their original meanings, so that a stimulus often became a total situation and a response could mean an outcome made up of fairly complex movements. The problems of how to delimit the stimulus and the response have not yet been fully resolved in S-R theory. If very broad definitions are used, so that stimulus refers to a whole class of antecedent conditions, and response to a whole class of outcomes in the way of movements and products of behavior, then S-R psychology becomes merely a psychology of independent and dependent variables. That is, we can remain within the general logic of S-R psychology if we can clearly specify and measure the antecedents of behavior (the independent variables) and then study the results or outcomes associated with these conditions as consequents (the dependent variables). The mediating processes that go on between the specified antecedents and the measured consequents may also be studied, or they may simply be inferred. Viewed in this way, S-R psychology is not a particular theory, but rather a *language*

that can be used to make psychological information clear and communicable (e.g., Mandler and Kessen, 1959). As such, the S-R outlook is widely prevalent in American psychology today.

Gestalt psychology and cognitive theory

At about the same time that Watson announced behaviorism in America a "new" psychology going by the name of Gestalt psychology was appearing in Germany. The word *Gestalt* is sometimes translated from the German as *form* or *configuration*, and the psychology announced by Max Wertheimer in 1912 was one concerned with the organization of mental processes. The position came to be identified most closely with Wertheimer (1880–1943) and his colleagues Kurt Koffka (1886–1941) and Wolfgang Köhler (1887–), all of whom migrated to America. An influential variation of Gestalt psychology was developed by Kurt Lewin (1890–1947). His version, often known as *field theory*, laid greater stress than did other Gestalt psychologies upon motivation and social psychology.

The earliest Gestalt experiments dealt with perceived motion, the *phi phenomenon* (Wertheimer, 1912). When two separated lights are flashed in succession, provided the timing is proper, what one sees is a single light moving from the position of the first light to that of the second. This illusion of motion is familiar in lighted signs, and of course lies at the basis of the motion picture. The phenomenon of such motion was familiar (a child's toy, known as a stroboscope, has a long history), but the Gestalt psychologists sensed the theoretical importance of the patterning of stimuli in producing the effect. Another illustration of patterning or organization is that of *figure and ground,* a tendency to see part of pattern as an object in the foreground, against an unstructured background. The tendency is clear in reversible figure-ground patterns (see Figure 1–7).

According to the Gestalt psychologists, then, our experiences depend on the *patterns* that stimuli form, on the *organization*

1–7

**The vase
and the faces**

A reversible
figure-ground effect.

of experience. What we see is relative to background, to other aspects of the whole. The whole is different from the sum of its parts: the whole consists of parts in relationship.

While the Gestalt psychologists did not like the typical introspective psychology of their day any more than Watson did, they were vigorous opponents of behaviorism. They did not wish to give up a kind of free introspection that goes by the name of *phenomenology*. They wanted to be free to ask a child what something looked like, what it meant to him. They were interested in seen movement, in judged sizes, in the appearance of colors under changes in illumination.[6]

The importance of perception in all psychological phenomena led those influenced by Gestalt psychology to a number of perception-centered interpretations of learning, memory, and problem-solving. These interpretations were spoken of as forms of *cognitive theory* and were contrasted with S-R interpretations. Cognitive theorists combined influences from sources other than those of Gestalt psychology, just as S-R theorists have in their background influences other than those from behaviorism. A psychologist influential upon cognitive theorists was Edward C. Tolman (1886–1959), who called himself a "purposive behaviorist," but incorporated a number of notions from Gestalt psychology. Tolman argued that a stimulus-response analysis

[6] While early behaviorists would have thought of such phenomenology as improper science, the later incorporation of *verbal report* as a legitimate source of data makes the issue no longer a real one. For historical reasons, however, an ardent behaviorist is less likely to interest himself in these problems.

was not sufficient to explain behavior; purpose and a cognitive perception of the environment were essential elements. For example, a rat learning the correct pathway from the start of a maze to food in the goal box does not learn simply a chain of movement responses associated with the stimuli of the maze; instead, he learns a cognitive map or pattern which tells him the location of the goal. Thus if one path to the goal is blocked he will take another; if the pathway is flooded he will swim to the goal even though he has never used these particular responses before in the maze. Cognitions and purpose would, of course, play an even more important role in human behavior.

Integration of S-R
and cognitive viewpoints

In the past these two theoretical orientations led to quite different types of experimentation. The S-R theorists tended to concentrate on relatively simple learning situations, such as a rat learning to press a bar or run a maze to obtain food, a human subject learning to discriminate between two stimuli or to rote memorize a set of verbal materials. The cognitive theorists, on the other hand, devoted most of their attention to experiments concerned with problem-solving or concept formation—situations where the nature of the stimuli and responses are more difficult to specify. However, the division in viewpoint between S-R and cognitive psychologists has been progressively diminishing over recent years until now many psychologists would not consider themselves as belonging solely to either viewpoint. Most contemporary psychologists feel that it is now possible to investigate the more complex cognitive processes—thinking, language, and problem-solving—with the same degree of rigorous experimental control that was previously possible only in situations involving simpler responses. The development of high-speed electronic computers has provided one important tool for the study of such cognitive processes. A computer model of human thinking incorporates the S-R notion of input (stimulus) and output (response) but at the same time allows for an internal control system that consists of stored memories and rules for operating on these memories to produce new responses. It is now possible for psychologists to program a computer to simulate the thought processes a human being engages in when he solves a difficult mathematical problem or plays chess. (We will have more to say about computer simulation of complex behavioral processes in later chapters.)

Thus, within the past 50 years, the focus of psychology has completed a full circle. Initially rejecting the study of conscious experience as ill-suited for scientific investigation and turning to psychological phenomena more easily described in terms of overt behavior, psychologists are once again considering some of the earlier problems of thinking and motivation in the light of new and more powerful techniques. The gain from behaviorism is an emphasis upon objectivity and reproducibility of findings—an emphasis that has not been lost in the newer integration of S-R and cognitive viewpoints.

Psychoanalysis

The psychoanalytic psychology of Sigmund Freud was presented in lectures before leading American psychologists as early as 1909, before behaviorism and Gestalt psychology came on the scene. The lectures were given at Clark University upon the invitation of the psychologist G. Stanley Hall. Thus the first scholarly and scientific recognition of the importance of Freud's work came from professional psychologists, although for many years any recognition of Freud was grudging, if not hostile. Freud's influence, direct and indirect, is now so pervasive that those who know nothing else about psychology have at least a nodding acquaintance with Freud.

If we are to single out any one of Freud's theories for consideration along with behaviorism and Gestalt psychology it is his interpretation of the *unconscious*. Basic to Freud's theory of the unconscious is the conception that the unacceptable (forbidden, punished) wishes of childhood get driven out of awareness. They become part of the active unconscious where, while out of awareness, they remain influential. The active unconscious presses to find expression in dreams, slips of speech, unconscious mannerisms, as well as through such socially approved behavior as artistic, literary, or scientific activity. The method of psychoanalysis—free association under the guidance of the analyst—is itself a way of helping unconscious wishes find verbal expression. In classical Freudian theory the unconscious wishes were almost exclusively sexual. This emphasis upon childhood sexuality was one of the barriers to the acceptance of Freud's theories by the medical and psychological professions. But a consequence of his emphasis upon early childhood has been the encouragement of numerous studies of the effects of child-rearing practices, and a new emphasis upon the motives or drives that initiate or regulate behavior.

The development of child psychology and clinical psychology has brought Freud's views increasingly to the fore in psychology. After World War II academic psychologists became more open to his teachings than they were earlier, but this does not mean that they became disciples, and there are now many trenchant criticisms of Freud's views. The general position is that there is much to be learned from psychoanalysis, but that its concepts need to be translated into those of general psychology and experimentally verified wherever possible.

Scientific models

One can be interested in psychological theories without subscribing to any one of the major psychological systems or schools. Many psychologists refuse to give their loyalty to any closed or final system while the data of their science are being constantly revised and while many relationships have not yet been satisfactorily studied. Some psychologists have turned their backs upon theory, saying in effect that theory can wait until more facts are known. What is needed first, they say, are the kinds of lawful relationships that are pictured in our graphs or described by our equations summarizing the results of experiments done under standardized conditions. Others prefer to go at theory construction just as they go at the planning of experiments. That is, they build theories appropriate to the limited topics upon which they are working, just as they design experiments appropriate to these topics. So, instead of proposing major systems of psychology, they propose theories of forgetting, theories of attitude formation, or theories of hearing. These much more limited theories lead to smaller systems that take into account a restricted set of facts and relationships. Such systems may be called *miniature systems* or *models* to distinguish them from the more ambitious systems that lead to schools of psychology.

When models for psychological phenomena are formulated in terms of mathematical equations they are referred to as *mathematical models;* when formulated in terms of information processing concepts they are called *information processing models;* when formulated in terms of physiological or neurological concepts they are called *neurophysiological models.* We will consider examples of each of these types of models in later chapters.

At this time it would take us too far afield to examine in any detail the models of contemporary psychology. We mention them here to emphasize our previous statement that an interest in psychological theory does not require adherence to a general system or school. The miniature system or more limited model saves science from becoming an unwieldy mass of scattered facts without forcing it prematurely into a mold that might warp its development. Until many smaller systems are securely established, a comprehensive system of psychology may be some distance away.

Developmental and interactive explanations

The foregoing discussion of the points of view of behaviorism and S-R theory, of Gestalt psychology and cognitive theory, and of psychoanalysis, with a mention also of scientific models, is enough to make the beginner in psychology wonder how psychologists are able to communicate with each other. The problem does not turn out to be very great, particularly when attention is turned to the results of experimental investigations. Then everyone understands everyone else, regardless of preferences for one kind of explanation over another. We shall be able to get along with a minimum of system in this book because so many of the references will be to concrete, factual relationships. When there are important alternative ways of formulating an explanation, particularly if the alternatives are a source of controversy, these will be pointed out, for only so will the student appreciate how psychology develops.

There are, however, two modes of explanation that will recur enough for attention to be called to them at this point. One of them is *developmental,* the other *interactive.*

A developmental explanation stresses the historical roots of present behavior, focusing on individual experiences as the individual grows and learns. This mode of explanation has its origins in association psychology, which generally tries to explain what happens in the present according to associations built up in the past. Modern S-R psychology, because of its strong emphasis upon learning, is also very largely a developmental psychology. Psychoanalysis, with its emphasis upon early childhood, also favors such explanations.

An interactive explanation deals with the arousal and control of behavior in the present, according to motives and needs that are active, stimuli that are perceived, and possibilities of action that are open. Gestalt theory and the forms of cognitive theory related to it have been emphatic in stressing present "configurations" as determiners of behavior. All psychological positions, however, including S-R theory and psychoanalysis, are concerned with present behavior as well as with residues from the past. All must deal, for example, with the way individuals resolve conflicts, since the conflicting tendencies are simultaneously present no matter what their origins may have been in the past. The two explanations, developmental and interactive, belong together, because development always provides the potential that is capitalized on in the present. It is a matter of convenience at some points to stress explanations that are largely developmental, at other points explanations that are largely interactive. This never means that one explanation excludes the other.

An example may make the distinction clearer. Suppose we are studying how a chimpanzee retrieves a stick from outside its cage to be used to pull in a banana. We can find out, first of all, his prior experience with using sticks as tools. We will learn that if he has had previous experience, he will do much better. This is to take a *developmental* approach, that is, explaining the present in terms of earlier behavior. We can also find out what difference it makes if we present the problem in different ways. For example, we may find that if the stick is on the same side of the cage as the banana, he will use the stick as a tool much more promptly than if the stick is out of view on the other side of the cage, though equally accessible to him. In that case we become interested in the *interactive* aspects of his problem-solving behavior. The interaction is important, because sufficient past experience does not lead to prompt solution unless the present display of the problem is appropriate and makes the past experience accessible in the present.

It is important to keep both aspects in mind in order to avoid explaining too much according to the past or too much according to the present. Thus we may learn that delinquent youths have alcoholic fathers more frequently than nondelinquent youths, and so become tempted to say that this youth is delinquent *because* he had an alcoholic father. He does not become delinquent because he had an alcoholic father but because he shows some inadequacy *at the present time* in relation to specific temptation and opportunities for delinquent acts. It is this inadequacy that must be understood for what it is now, if it is to be corrected. It may help us to understand this present inadequacy if we know both what kind of early history produces delin-

quent boys and what reaction the boy had to his alcoholic father. It is not illogical to accept both a developmental and an interactive explanation at the same time.

Measurement in Psychology

Whatever methods psychologists use, sooner or later they find it necessary to make statements about *amounts* or *quantities*. Variables have to be assessed in some clear manner, so that investigations can be repeated and confirmed by others and results can be appropriately applied. Occasionally variables can be grouped into *classes* or *categories*, as in separating boys and girls for the study of sex differences. Sometimes the variables are subject to ordinary *physical measurement:* height, weight, age, illumination. Sometimes they have to be *scaled* in a manner that places the values of the variables in some sort of order: for example, from least preferred to most preferred. Usually, for purposes of precise communication, *numbers* are assigned to objects or events; then we can say that we are dealing with *quantitative* values. There are a number of problems that arise in using quantities in psychology, but we may speak of *measurement* in a somewhat general sense whenever we mean that we have assigned numerical values to independent and dependent variables, or indeed to any variables entering into some sort of systematically studied relationship.

Experimental design

When an experimenter plans his experiments, he has in mind the ways in which he will gather his data and how he will treat the data in order to discover the relationships involved and make inferences from what he finds. The expression *experimental design* has come to be used for any of the more formal patterns according to which experiments are planned. The same design might be used for an experiment in vision, one in learning, and perhaps one in psychotherapy. The total plan includes more than the design, for it involves the substance of the particular experiment.

The designs that are most easily understood are those in which one variable is manipulated (the independent variable) and its effects on another variable (the dependent variable) studied. The ideal is to hold everything else constant, so that one comes out with an assertion of the form: "With everything else constant, when X increases, Y also increases." (Or, in other cases, "When X increases, Y decreases," etc.) This form of statement implies *concomitant variation*, the two variables being linked together by some demonstrable relationship. Note that almost any content can be fitted into this kind of study: the amount of change in illumination that can be perceived in relation to the standard illumination with which you start, the rate of learning as related to the age of the learner, the fear of snakes as related to prior experience with snakes. The method of *graphical representation* of the results is a very convenient one to use, with the independent variable plotted along the horizontal axis (the abscissa) and the dependent variable plotted on the vertical axis (the ordinate). In Figure 1–8 the latency of response (the

1–8

Shock as independent variable; latency as dependent variable

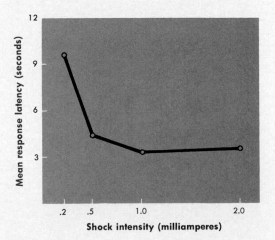

Rats could avoid an electric shock by turning a wheel. The latency of the rat's response gets shorter (i.e., the response occurs more quickly) as the shock increases. (After Kimble, 1955)

1–9

Experimental and control groups

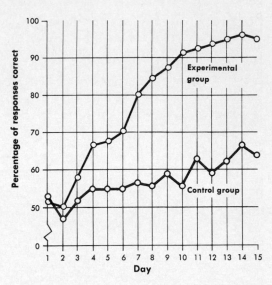

The response called for was a discrimination between a circle and a triangle; the experimental animals had seen circles and triangles in their living cages, the control animals had not. (After Gibson and Walk, 1956)

delay between the stimulus and the start of the response) is related to the intensity of a shock that the response can prevent.

Sometimes we are interested only in the influence of a single condition, which can be either present or absent. (Such a condition is simply a variable with only two values, one representing its presence and the other its absence.) In such a case the experimental design commonly calls for an *experimental* group in which the condition is present and a *control* group in which the condition is absent. The results of an experiment designed in this way are presented in Figure 1–9. It is clear that the experimental group made a higher percentage of correct responses than the control group, the differences being more marked as the experiment proceeded. What accounts for the difference? From the point of view of experimental design we can infer that *something* has been related to the difference; from the point of view of a particular experiment we are of course interested in the content. In this case the something was prior experience with the stimuli to be responded to. Laboratory rats were tested on their ability to discriminate (i.e., distinguish) between a circle and a triangle, one or the other being a "sign" on a door that led to food. The experimental group was already familiar with circles and triangles from having had them on the walls of their living cages; the control group lacked this experience. Apparently familiarity with the forms made it easier for the rats to use them in the later portions of the experiment.

Sometimes it is necessary to study the simultaneous effects of several variables at once. Suppose, for example, that we are studying plant growth and wish to study the effects of moisture, temperature, and illumination. We could hold two of these variables constant and study the effect of one, but a little reflection would show us how limited this design would be: unless *favorable* levels of the other variables were chosen, the plant would not live, and the experiment could not be performed at all. But *how* favorable would they have to be? A better procedure would be some way of varying in different combinations, moisture, temperature, and illumination. Then the effect of one variable would be studied not against a *constant* value of other variables, but against an array of values of the other variable. The statistical problems of such a design are more complex than a design involving changes in only one independent variable at a time, but the yield in information is often greater for the same amount of experimental effort, and hence such designs are increasingly popular in psychology.[7]

The use and interpretation of correlation coefficients

Although the experimental ideal is to have things so under control that one can specify the variables under study and produce changes in them as called for in the experimental design, there are circumstances when this is not possible. For exam-

---

[7] The statistical methods appropriate to such designs involve *analysis of variance*, now met very frequently in the reports of psychological investigations. The details need not concern us at this point.

ple, the experimenter who is interested in the human brain is not free to remove portions at will, as he does with lower animals, but can only take advantage of naturally occurring brain damage through disease, injury, or gunshot wounds. He can still use the method of *concomitant variation*, but now the related variables are *correlated* rather than experimentally controlled. For example, a relationship may be reported between the amount of damage in some region of the brain and the amount of difficulty in seeing. This is not very different from producing the damage in an experimental animal and noting the changes, except that other factors cannot be as well controlled; that is, other kinds of damage may also be present, kinds of treatment may have varied following the accident, the intellectual level prior to the accident may be important in interpreting the results, and so on. Because of its greater precision of control, the experimental method is preferred where it is applicable, but where it is not applicable, the general logic of experimentation can still be approximated through the use of the correlational method.

When large masses of data are available, the method of correlation is often the best available for discovering relationships. For example, we have records of the high school grades of students entering college. The best way to get at the relationship between high school and college grades is to *correlate* them, that is, to find out if those who did well in high school generally do well in college, and vice versa.

The unit of measurement in correlation is the *coefficient of correlation,* signified by the letter r. (Psychologists often omit the word "coefficient" and speak only of the "correlation.") The methods of calculating the coefficient of correlation are described in Chapter 15; at this point we can only set forth some rules of thumb that will help you interpret the coefficients of correlation used in some of the tables and graphs in this book.

1. A correlation of $r = +1.00$ means a perfect *positive* relationship (a one-to-one correspondence) between two variables. If

weight corresponded exactly to height, so that you could state a person's weight precisely if you knew his height, then height and weight would be perfectly correlated. (The circumference of a circle and its radius are perfectly correlated, but the perimeter of a triangle and its height are not.) When the correlation is positive, the plus sign is often omitted.

2. A correlation of $r = -1.00$ means a perfect *negative* relationship. For example, if the price of a used car decreased as its age increased so that one could specify the price precisely if the age were known, then the relations between the car's age and price would be expressed by a correlation of $r = -1.00$.

3. A correlation of $r = .00$ signifies no relation. Thus one would expect a zero correlation between the number of freckles and the score on an intelligence test. Knowing the value of one variable in no way helps predict the value of the other variable when their correlation is zero.

4. A correlation between $r = .00$ and either $+1.00$ or -1.00 indicates an imperfect relationship. The *degree of relationship* is specified by the extent to which the value of the correlation (ignoring the $+$ or $-$ sign) approaches 1.00. The closer the correlation is to 1.00, the greater the degree of the relationship; that is, as the correlation approaches 1.00, knowing the value of one variable makes prediction of the other more accurate. Negative and positive correlations of the same size represent the same degree of relationship, and the sign simply indicates whether the relation is positive (as one variable increases so does the other) or negative (as one variable increases the other decreases).[8]

5. A correlation is *not* a percent, so that a correlation of $r = .25$ cannot be interpreted as being half as great as one of $r = .50$. We shall have some rules later for

[8] The sign of a correlation is often arbitrary. For example, if the number of classes missed correlated $-.50$ with the course grade, then the correlation between number of classes attended and the course grade would be $+.50$. The change of sign would not change the meaning of the relationship.

interpreting correlations. Some typical correlations found by researchers include the following:

(a) a correlation of $r = +.50$ between the height of a parent and the adult height of a child of that parent; (b) correlations of about $+.40$ between scholastic aptitude tests and freshman grades in college; (c) correlations of about $+.75$ between grades in the first semester of the freshman year and those in the second semester.

6. Some supplementary information is needed to indicate whether or not a given correlation is *significant*, that is, whether or not the implied relationship is to be counted on. This depends both upon the size of the coefficient of correlation and upon the number of cases entering into the computation of the coefficient of correlation. Most dependable, of course, is a high correlation (either positive or negative) based on many cases; least dependable, as an indication of relationship, is a low correlation based on a few cases. Even a high correlation based on few cases is not to be trusted because it might arise by chance even though no true relationship exists.[9]

The relationships brought out by a coefficient of correlation will become clearer if we look at a diagram of actual results (Figure 1–10). Forty-nine subjects were given a test of their susceptibility to hypnosis on two separate days. Each tally in the diagram represents the *combined* score of one subject on the two tests. Thus two subjects made scores of 1 on both days, and two other subjects made scores of 13 on both days. But one subject (see the lower right-hand portion of the diagram) made a score of 11 on the first test but only 5 on the second one.

If all the subjects had repeated their original scores on the second test, all the plotted tallies would have fallen in the shaded area indicated. The majority of

[9] The correlations just described involve only two variables. For problems involving relations among many variables more complex correlational methods are required, but we shall take these up later.

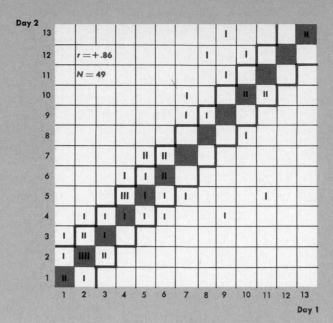

1–10

**A scatter diagram
illustrating correlation**

Each tally indicates the combined scores of one subject on two separate days of testing hypnotic susceptibility. Tallies in the shaded area indicate identical scores on both tests; those between the solid lines indicate a difference of no more than one point between the two scores. The correlation of $r = +.86$ means that the performances were fairly consistent on the two days. (After Hilgard, 1961)

tallies are reasonably close to this area, however; all the tallies within the solid lines represent scores in which one day's score differed from the other by no more than one point. This indicates a high degree of correlation between the two pairs of test results; the coefficient of correlation as actually calculated was +.86, which is considered to show a substantial relationship.

Before concluding this section, we should emphasize an important distinction between experimental and correlational studies. In an experimental study one variable (the independent variable) is systematically manipulated to determine its effect on some other variable (the dependent variable). However, similar cause-effect relationships cannot be inferred from correlational studies. The fallacy of interpreting high correlations as implying cause-effect is best illustrated with a few examples. The softness of the asphalt in the streets of a

city may correlate with the number of sunstroke cases but this does not mean that the asphalt when soft gives off some kind of poison that sends people to hospitals. We understand the cause in this example—a hot sun both softens the asphalt and produces sunstroke. Another example, which is frequently used as an illustration, is the high positive correlation obtained for the number of storks seen nesting in English villages and the number of child births recorded in the same community. We shall leave it to the reader's ingenuity to figure out possible reasons for such a correlation without postulating a cause-effect relationship between babies and storks. These examples provide sufficient warning against giving a causal interpretation to a correlation coefficient. When two variables are correlated, variation in one variable may *possibly* be the cause of variation in the other, but in the absence of experimental evidence no such conclusion is justified.

SUMMARY 1. Psychology is defined as the science that studies the *behavior* of man and other animals.

2. In practice, the definition of behavior implied by psychology is a very broad one. By including within the science the *inferences* that are

made from verbal behavior, it is possible to study both *conscious* and *unconscious* processes without sacrificing the objectivity of the data on which these inferences rest.

3. Psychology, like other *behavioral sciences,* has overlapping interests with many neighboring sciences, chiefly with biology on the one hand and with social sciences on the other. There are affiliations with the physical sciences as well. Many promising opportunities for studies lie ahead in areas where psychology blends with other sciences.

4. Among the methods of psychology as a science the *methods of the experimental laboratory* are preferred where they are applicable. These methods have the advantage that variables can be brought under control and subjected to measurement, both the *independent variables,* whose values the experimenter sets, and the *dependent variables,* which take on different values depending on the outcome of the experiment.

5. Other methods of psychology include *naturalistic observations, case histories, the interview,* and *test methods.*

6. Psychology inherited from the pre-experimental period the opposing viewpoints of *faculty psychology* (proposing that the mind consisted of separate mental powers that accounted for mental activity) and of *association psychology* (proposing that everything could be explained through the association of ideas, ideas coming originally by way of sensory experience). The association theory really set the background for the new psychology, and the first experiments were concerned with sensory processes.

7. The first formal laboratory was established by Wundt at Leipzig in 1879. The spurt in experimental psychology in America can be attributed largely to his influence, for many of his students came to hold important positions in American universities. Other important figures were Galton and Darwin in England.

8. Efforts to provide a theoretical orientation for modern psychology have led to the formulation of a number of competing systems, three of which have important residual influence in contemporary psychology. The first of these, *behaviorism,* a psychology that did not involve *introspection,* is now represented by *stimulus-response* (S-R) psychology, a somewhat broader position. The second, earlier known as *Gestalt psychology,* later the *cognitive viewpoint,* gave increasing prominence to perception and thought. The third influence, *psychoanalysis,* has made psychology more dynamic, that is, more concerned with motivational problems, especially with *unconscious motivation* and with motivational conflicts.

9. An alternative to all-inclusive systems is the more modest miniature system or *model.* Such models take into account a restricted set of facts and are not intended to provide a general theoretical framework within which to view all of psychology.

10. Two modes of explanation occur frequently within psychology, modes that are related to some of the past systematic emphases but are not in themselves controversial. These are *developmental* explanations

and *interactive* explanations. Developmental explanations attempt to account for present behavior on the basis of what has gone before, relying on the *history* of the present behavior. Interactive explanations are contemporary and nonhistorical, trying to account for behavior on the basis of what is currently going on in the way of stimuli, bodily condition, aroused conflicting tendencies, and so on. The two kinds of explanation are not contradictory because the past provides the potentiality for response in the present. However, it is occasionally convenient to emphasize one kind of explanation over the other; often a full account of behavior requires propositions reflecting both varieties of explanation.

11. The *coefficient of correlation* is a convenient way of expressing the relationship between two variables. However, a high correlation does not imply a cause-effect relation. When two variables are correlated one may possibly be the cause of the other, but in the absence of experimental evidence such a conclusion is not warranted.

SUGGESTIONS FOR FURTHER READING

To follow up on the early history of psychology or to find the history of a particular topic, four very useful books are Boring, *A history of experimental psychology* (2nd ed., 1950), Murphy, *Historical introduction to modern psychology* (rev. ed., 1949), Herrnstein and Boring, *A sourcebook in the history of psychology* (1965), and Postman (ed.), *Psychology in the making* (1962). Postman's volume presents in historical context important research problems that have constituted stepping stones in the progress of psychology as a science.

A number of books describe the larger systems of psychology that have influenced contemporary developments. To the standard text by Woodworth and Sheehan, *Contemporary schools of psychology* (3rd ed., 1964), have been added Chaplin and Krawiec, *Systems and theories of psychology* (1960), and Wolman and Nagel (eds.), *Scientific psychology* (1965).

For the methods of psychology, see Sidowski (ed.), *Experimental methods and instrumentation in psychology* (1966), and Underwood, *Experimental psychology* (2nd ed., 1966). For an overview of the tactics and strategies involved in psychological research, see Helson and Bevan, *Contemporary approaches to psychology* (1967). Rosenthal, *Experimenter effects in behavioral research* (1966), calls attention to some of the special hazards in psychological research.

2 The Behaving Organism

Man is a flesh-and-blood organism related to other organisms through an evolutionary history. Man's habits, thoughts, and aspirations are centered in his brain and nervous system, and whenever we study him we study something he does or expresses through his bodily processes.

We may examine man as a vertebrate, a mammal, and a primate—as one who shares an evolutionary background with the rest of the biological world. Our emphasis here will be on the evolution of man's nervous system; by discovering how the nervous system in the lower animals has evolved we will learn a good deal about the significance of the various nervous structures for the behavior of man. The nervous system and the related structures of sense organs, muscles, and glands provide for man's responsiveness to the environment and his immediate adjustment to it; they also provide for the storing up of experiences and the development of habits and attitudes that make the past serve the present and the future. Again we confront the distinction between present interactions and developmental history; the nervous system is important in whichever viewpoint we are emphasizing.

The areas of behavior in which we can hope to achieve enlightenment through the study of bodily processes (particularly the action of the brain) are: first, sensory discrimination, because the brain makes use of the information that comes to it by way of the senses; second, regulatory, need-serving, and emotion-laden behavior (eating and sleeping, fighting, escaping, sexual behavior), the impulsive processes that we share with the rest of the animal world; third, the processes of learning, language, thought, appreciation, and creativity, which at best establish man's high place in the evolutionary scheme; and, finally, those aspects of individual differences in ability, temperament, or style of life, which we call "personality." In each of these areas we are interested both in normal functioning and in what happens when the bodily processes go awry. It is too much to ask of present-day neurophysiology to give us clear answers in all of these areas, but it is important to know where we now stand, and to be clear about the relevance to psychology of new knowledge about the nervous system.

Integration Within the Organism

The word "organism" implies organization. The body is not only a collection of cells but an arrangement of cells as organs and organ systems. The psychologist is interested in knowing how the bodily machinery works, for he is concerned with the skilled acts of which the individual is capable, the hierarchical nature of controls which permits voluntary acts to be carried out smoothly with the cooperation of involuntary reflexes, the effects of emotional arousal, and the manner in which information is retained. However mind and body are conceived, it is through the body that mental activity finds its expression. The character of the body as a unitary organism is determined by the manner in which parts fit together so that the whole operates with reasonable smoothness.

Integration through skeleton and muscles

What does the psychologist need to know about the skeleton and the related structures of muscles and tendons that tie it together and make it operate? The answer depends upon his purposes. If, for example, the psychologist becomes interested in the limits of possible human performance, he may wish to know about the maximum weight a muscle can support, or about the maximum speed with which it can contract, or about the effects of practice upon it. If he is interested in muscular fatigue, he may wish to learn something of the chemical by-products of muscular action. Of course, we cannot go into such details here; we will merely call attention to the importance of the skeleton and the muscles as mechanical integrators of the body.

The body operates as an effective machine partly because of the way in which it is fitted together around a jointed skeleton of rigid bones. This *mechanical integration* makes possible the maintenance of posture, locomotion, skilled action, facial expression, and speech.

When a muscle contracts, it commonly produces a movement at the joints, as in walking or lifting. But if the joint is prevented from moving, the muscle may still contract. In an alert but quiet state the muscles are bombarded by an irregular barrage of nervous impulses that maintain a normal amount of contraction called *muscle tone.* The tone of muscles varies with the condition of the individual: an energetic, athletic person tends to have high tone, a weak, listless person low tone. If tone is reduced too far, the person collapses; if tone is too high, his movements are interfered with, as in the condition known as *spastic paralysis.* Spastic paralysis, with muscle tone so high that smooth

movement is impossible, is not infrequently a result of birth injury.

Although muscle tone is maintained automatically through reflex mechanisms, we can increase the tension in our muscles voluntarily, as in "making a muscle" without moving the arm. Some people habitually tense their muscles and are unable to relax. Such a high tension state is fatiguing, and may carry with it signs of mild personality disturbance. The voluntary increase of muscular tension, without movement, comes about through increasing the tension of *antagonistic muscles.* Such muscles are arranged in pairs; the contraction of one member of the pair tends to stretch the other member of the pair. Thus the *biceps* of the upper arm is a *flexor* muscle, bending the arm at the elbow, while the *triceps* is an *extensor* muscle, antagonistic to the biceps and tending by contraction to straighten the arm at the elbow (Figure 2–1). The nervous control of muscles is such that when one of a pair of antagonists contracts the other ordinarily relaxes. This principle is known as *reciprocal innervation,* and is very important in the free movements of, say, walking along and swinging the arms. When we move muscles voluntarily, we can either take advantage of this reciprocal relationship to produce free movement or contract both antagonists at once and raise tension.

With reciprocal innervation we meet a principle that is very important to the organization of bodily controls: the interplay between *facilitation,* leading to increased activity, and *inhibition,* leading to decreased activity. By their appropriate balancing we are able to maintain coordinated action, distribute attention appropriately, and in many other ways manage our affairs more smoothly.

Integration via the blood stream

A second system that maintains the body as a smoothly operating machine is the circulatory system: the heart, the blood vessels, and the other closely related structures that feed into the system. Because the system contributes to integration by sending chemical substances throughout the body,

Antagonistic muscular action

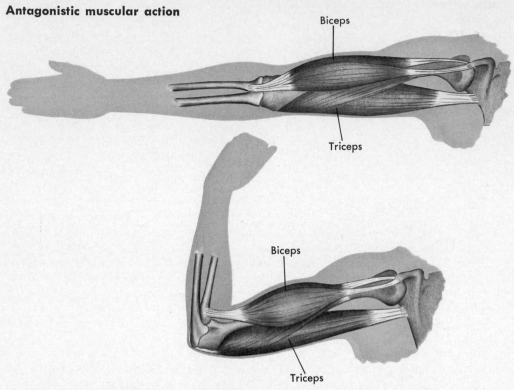

When the triceps muscle contracts to extend the forearm, the biceps is relaxed and extended. The pattern is reversed when the forearm is pulled toward the body.

we may think of it as *chemical* in its action, supplementing the mechanical integration of muscles and joints. We shall pass over the normal metabolic role of the circulatory system and turn instead to certain special substances the blood stream carries, the substances being called *hormones,* a word derived from the Greek root meaning "activators."

The glands of internal secretion (the *endocrine* or *ductless* glands) discharge their secretions (hormones) directly into the blood stream, with effects upon growth, behavior, and personality. These glands are distinguished from the *duct* glands, such as tear glands or salivary glands, which secrete their products on the surface of the body or into the body cavities but not into the blood stream. Seven sets of endocrine glands produce hormones whose actions are fairly well understood, although new evidence about their activity is still

being collected: (1) the thyroid gland, (2) the parathyroids, (3) the thymus, (4) the pancreas, (5) the adrenal glands, (6) the sex glands or gonads (ovaries in the female and testes in the male), and (7) the pituitary gland. In Figure 2–2 their locations are pictured in a schematized human body; their functions are summarized briefly in Table 2–1.

As one illustration of the psychological relevance of the endocrine glands we may consider the role of the *adrenal* glands. These glands have two major parts, each secreting its own hormones. The *medulla* of the gland secretes *adrenalin* and *noradrenalin.* The *cortex* of the gland secretes a number of hormonal products collectively called *adrenocortical* hormones.

The adrenal medulla is active in emotion. Secretion of the hormone adrenalin produces many of the symptoms found in excited emotion: tremor in the striate muscles increases; smooth muscles relax; the blood distribution of the body changes; the liver releases blood sugar into the blood and thereby makes available a ready supply of energy; blood pressure increases; the blood clots more quickly in case of injury. The discovery of noradrenalin, another secretion of the adrenal medulla, has furthered knowledge of the action of the adrenal glands. Adrenalin and noradrenalin occasionally produce similar consequences and occasionally opposite ones. Whereas adrenalin may dilate blood vessels, noradrenalin constricts them. There is as yet no simple formula by which to describe their interrelated actions.

The products of the adrenal cortex are so important to the maintenance of life that destruction of the adrenal cortex invariably produces death unless the missing products are continuously replaced from outside—a very difficult process. These life-maintaining regulators, which are concerned with salt and carbohydrate metabolism, have been identified as complex chemical substances known as *steroids*. The steroids have become useful agents for the treatment of many health disturbances, such as shock, allergy, and arthritis. Their possible role in mental disturbance is suggested by the occasional appearance of symptoms similar to those of mental illness among mentally normal patients being treated with adrenal steroids, such as cortisone.

Neural integration

The nervous system controls the muscles as they make use of the skeletal apparatus; it controls the beating of the heart, respira-

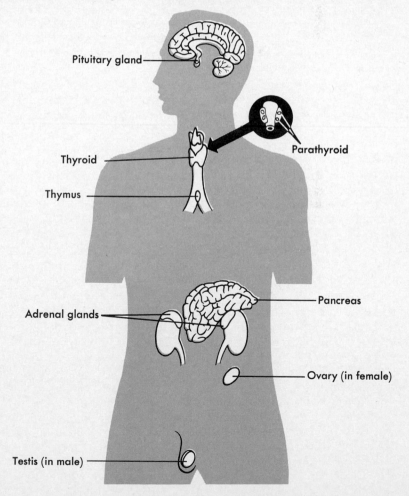

2–2

The endocrine glands

The location of the endocrine glands in the body.

Pituitary gland

Parathyroid

Thyroid

Thymus

Adrenal glands

Pancreas

Ovary (in female)

Testis (in male)

TABLE 2–1

Some typical functions of the endocrine glands

Gland	Activities regulated
Pituitary—anterior	Growth (dwarfism, giantism); as "master gland" influences secretions of thyroid, pancreas, adrenal glands, and gonads.
—posterior	Water metabolism, etc.
Thyroid	Metabolic rate; hence activity and fatigue; body weight.
Thymus	Important in regulation of the lymphoid system, and in the development of immune reactions of the body.
Parathyroid	Calcium metabolism; maintenance of normal excitability of the nervous system.
Pancreas	Via insulin controls sugar metabolism; excess insulin leads to state of shock.
Adrenal—cortex	Secretes life-maintaining regulators; control of salt and carbohydrate metabolism; may be important in mental illness.
—medulla	Active in emotion through the effects of adrenalin and noradrenalin.
Gonads*	Secondary sex characteristics distinguishing the male and female at maturity; maintenance of a functional condition in male and female reproductive apparatuses.

* As glands of internal secretion; to be distinguished from their reproductive functions.

tion, and circulation of the blood; it regulates the secretions of the glands. Therefore this third system, the *neural mechanism,* rules over the mechanical and chemical integrators that we have just considered. Because it possesses a nervous system, the organism is capable of complex and modifiable action, of learning as a result of experience, and of increased adaptability to variety in the environment. So important is the nervous system that most of the remainder of this chapter will be devoted to it.

Evolution of the Nervous System

We need not concern ourselves here with the details of evolutionary theory, which belong to the science of biology. The basic assumptions, since Darwin, are that living organisms are not all alike, and that some of the variations among them are more adaptive than others. An adaptive variation gives the organism a competitive advantage in the environment in which it finds itself (or perhaps helps it to seek a more favorable environment). Thus protective coloration may develop, so that the white polar bear is less visible against the snow of its natural habitat and the brown bear less visible in the dark woods where he lives. Among man's nearest relatives (the primates) there has been a striking change in the size of the jaw relative to the size of the brain. As man's ancestors came to use tools to secure game and to fight off enemies, the size of the jaw was less important than the size of the brain, and hence the course of evolution of man moved in this direction by capitalizing on variations that made him craftier rather than stronger of tooth.

Both adaptive and maladaptive (unfavorable) variations are transmitted by heredity, and differences become accentuated through time as organisms continue to vary and to adapt to their special environments, the successful ones surviving, the unsuccessful ones dying off. Modern genetic theory has helped show how variation and selection can occur not only by way of mutations but by way of shifts in the available hereditary determiners (genes) as populations of individuals become isolated from each other. In time, as species develop that can no longer mate successfully with each other, families of organisms develop along these branching lines. The branching lines along which man has developed include, far back, the earliest vertebrate, but specialization continued through the mammalian line and the primate line until now the genus to which man belongs contains only one species: *Homo sapiens sapiens.* The so-called races of man are all variants of the one species.

Because of our interest in behavior, the aspect of evolution that is of primary importance for us is the evolution of the brain and nervous system, those parts of the body that interpret the sensory inputs from the environment, coordinate the organism's responses, and, in general, serve memory and thought.

Nerve net and synaptic nervous system

One-celled animals, such as the amoeba, get along without a nervous system. The cell body is responsive to stimulation, so that the amoeba moves about, avoids noxious stimuli, engulfs food. There must be some sort of conduction within the cell body, for movement often takes place at a distance from the point of stimulation. The sponge is a multicellular organism without a nervous system; its cells conduct individually. Muscle fibers have already evolved in the sponge, so that we have here the beginning of muscular contraction but without a nerve supply to the muscles. Some coordination is provided by one cell influencing a neighboring cell, but the influence is not by way of any connecting nerve fibers.

The real beginning of a nervous system is in the *nerve net* as found in coelenterates, such as the polyps (Figure 2–3). Here individual specialized cells, called *neurons,* are spread rather evenly through the outer layers of the body. When any part of the nerve net is stimulated, impulses diffuse from that point and produce local contraction of muscles in the areas where the neurons are activated. Nothing very complex is controlled by such a nervous system.

In certain jellyfishes, such as the umbrella-shaped medusa, some of the fibers of the nerve net are concentrated in a ring

2–3

Nerve net in coelenterates

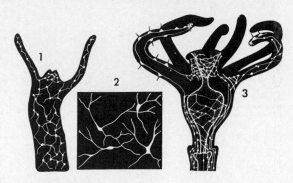

The nerve net in *Hydra* (1) is enlarged in (2) to show the arrangement of neurons. The nerve net of the polyp *Obelia* (3) shows a concentration in the mouth region. (After Simpson and Beck, 1965)

at the margin of the umbrella (Figure 2–4). This led to some interesting experiments years ago by Harvey (1922). He cut from a medusa a doughnut-shaped ring of tissue. He then started an impulse around the ring, its course being mapped by the contractions of the muscles around the ring as the impulse passed along. The impulse kept traveling for 11 days, until the growth of new tissue replacing that cut away produced antagonistic impulses. One by-product of the observation was that the muscle fatigued much earlier than the nerve net.

A characteristic of the nerve net is that the impulses can travel in either direction, although, as the foregoing experiment shows, they may occasionally continue only in the direction in which they get started. Modern research on coelenterates has shown that there is some differential responsiveness based on the number of nervous impulses per second reaching a particular muscle, and that there is some facilitation when impulses converge at a junction between nerve cell and nerve cell (Pantin, 1952). Even with these additions, the processes are relatively simple.

The flatworms (planaria) show a further stage in the evolution of the nervous system, in which the nerve net is combined with a nervous system much more like that of man. In its ladder-like nervous system,

Nerve ring of a medusa

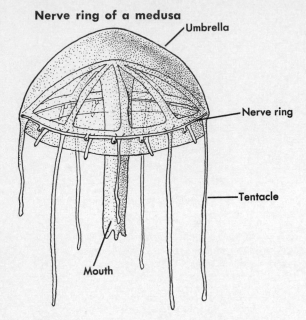

This jellyfish also has a diffuse nerve net on the under surface, but its details are not shown. The nerve ring provides an integration of movement in response to impulses originating in the sensitive tentacles. The swimming movement (pulsations of the whole body) may be set off by a stimulus applied to a single tentacle. (From Herrick, *Neurological foundations of animal behavior,* 1924, p. 93)

neurons are arranged in bundles called *nerve cords* (a kind of primitive spinal cord); moreover, the cell bodies of the neurons concentrate in the head to form something similar to a brain (Figure 2–5). This nervous system is of the *polarized synaptic* variety. A *synapse* is a junction between neurons. A polarized synapse is a junction at which there is conduction of the impulse in only one direction; it is characteristic of all higher nervous systems.[1] The cells making up the eyes at the front end of the flatworm are connected to the collection of neurons that we may call a brain; this pattern is continued in higher forms.

As we move beyond the primitive synaptic nervous system of the flatworms, the lines of evolution divide between inverte-

[1] Higher organisms may display residues of earlier forms. The human intestine, for example, contains a nerve net in its wall.

brates, such as insects, and vertebrates. Since man is a vertebrate, it is the development of the vertebrate nervous system, and particularly the vertebrate brain, that is of primary interest to us here.

Basic units of the nervous system

The specialized cells called *neurons* are the basic units of the nervous system. It is important that we should understand them, for they probably hold the secrets of learning and memory and mental functioning generally. We know their role in the transmission and coordination of nervous impulses, but their more complex functioning in learning and retention and thought remains to be unraveled. We shall meet with some evidence and some speculation as we go along; if there is rather more emphasis here on structural detail than seems necessary, it is only because we want to know what we are talking about when we later assign some duties to these parts.

Each neuron is a living cell with a nucleus and other parts common to all cells. As a specialized structure it consists of three main parts: the *cell body,* containing the nucleus; the *dendrites;* and the *axon.* Nerve impulses normally move in this one direction—from dendrites, through the cell

2–5

Nerve net and ladder nervous system in flatworms

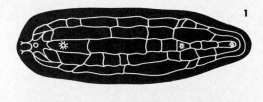

In some flatworms (1) the nervous system is still of the simple net type, while others (2) show the beginning of a central nervous system in the ladder-like structure of cords with a concentration of cell bodies at the head end, constituting a primitive brain. (After Simpson and Beck, 1965)

The many synapses at the cell body of a neuron

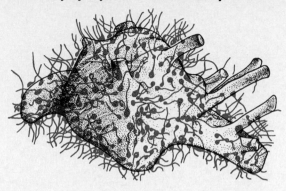

This diagram of a neuron of the cerebral cortex suggests the multiple interconnections with other neurons. Axon fibers from other neurons (in color) connect with the cell body and its dendrites via synaptic knobs (indicated by the enlarged areas at the ends of the axons). The stumps of the neuron's dendrites are shown at the right, the stump of its axon at the left. (After Eccles, 1958)

body, along the axon to the dendrites or cell body of the next neuron, or to a muscle or gland. Closely interwoven among the neurons are a large number of cells, called *glia* cells, which until recently were considered to serve only a supportive and nutritive function. New evidence suggests that the glia cells may be actively involved in the conduction of nerve impulses, but their exact role is as yet unknown.

Nerves and synapses. A nerve is not a single fiber, but a bundle of elongated dendrites or axons, belonging to hundreds of neurons. The axons from a great many neurons (perhaps of the order of 1000) may make synaptic junctions with the dendrites and cell body of another neuron. The synapse is not a direct connection; there is always a slight physical separation across which the nervous impulse is transmitted, probably by a chemical intermediary. A neuron of the cerebral cortex, with axons of other neurons making synapses with it, is shown schematically in Figure 2–6.

Transmission of neural impulses. While a nerve impulse moves along a nerve fairly rapidly, its motion should not be strictly compared to that of an electrical current through a wire. Electricity travels at the speed of light, while a nerve impulse moves along at about 60 to 100 feet per second in a frog's motor nerve and perhaps at 300 feet per second in the fastest fibers of warm-blooded animals. The analogy to a fuse has sometimes been used: when a fuse

is lighted, one part of the fuse lights the next part, the impulse being regenerated along the way. The details are much more complex than this, though they are now fairly well understood. The action is electrochemical: when a nerve fiber is stimulated, there is an interchange between potassium (K) ions and sodium (Na) ions through the surface of the fiber, thereby changing its electrical characteristics so as to produce a small electrical current that can be recorded with a sensitive instrument (see Figure 2–7).

Electrochemical basis of the nervous impulse

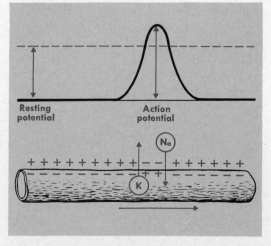

Resting potential   Action potential

Transmission of the nervous impulse is made possible by an interchange of charged particles, or ions, through the membrane of the nerve fiber. (After Katz, 1952)

Some nerve fibers have an insulating sheath called a *myelin* sheath; such fibers are known as *myelinated* fibers. In these fibers the impulse travels 10 times faster and with much less energy expenditure than in a nonmyelinated fiber. It is not surprising to learn that the myelin sheath was a late development in evolution and is characteristic of the nervous systems of higher animals.

Synaptic transmission. The synaptic junction between neurons is of tremendous importance because it is here that switching of impulses takes place, making possible facilitation, inhibition, coordination, and integration of impulses through the way in which groups of neurons act together. A single neuron transmits an impulse, or "fires," when the impulses reaching it become strong enough. Because its axon does not transmit at all prior to this, the neuron has been said to follow an "all-or-nothing" principle of action. The neuron fires in a single brief and transient burst and then is temporarily inactive (in what is called a *refractory phase*) for a few thousandths of a second. This is not, however, the complete story of neuron action. Further work has shown enduring activity in dendrites, lasting 15- to 30-thousandths of a second (Bishop and Clare, 1952; Li, Cullen, and Jasper, 1956). Thus there has come about a new interest in graduated activity, as supplementing all-or-nothing activity, but the work in this field is still in progress and its implications have not yet been fully understood.

It is now believed that some kind of chemical substance is released when the impulse reaches the end of the axon, and that it is this substance that activates the next neuron. Convergence of many impulses (at least more than one) is necessary to cause a neuron to fire; this complexity may account for the fine adjustments that must occur in learning, memory, and thought. These chemical processes go on at a minute scale. The energy involved in firing a neuron is something like a billionth of a watt; with 10 billion neurons in the human brain, and assuming every neuron is active simultaneously (which is hardly likely), the whole brain can operate on a power supply of about 10 watts. This is a remarkably low energy requirement for such a complex operating mechanism.

2–8

A primitive vertebrate brain

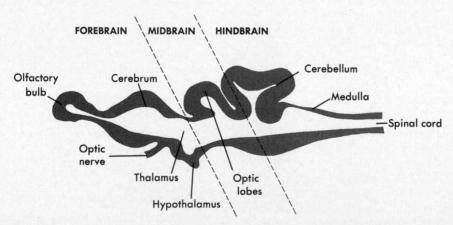

The basic structure of a tube with various bends, folds, and outpouchings is clearly visible in this schematic drawing of the dogfish brain. The three main portions (forebrain, midbrain, hindbrain) are distinguishable, but a "between-brain" (thalamus and hypothalamus) is also present, and the hindbrain has developed a cerebellum distinguishable from the medulla. The forebrain and midbrain are paired structures (see Figure 2–9).

Evolution of the vertebrate brain

The general characteristics of the brain reveal a common pattern throughout the vertebrate series, beginning with primitive fishes and moving through the reptiles; the brains of birds and mammals follow somewhat different directions from this common background. The basic pattern is that of a single hollow cord made up of partially interconnected neurons running along the back of the body, with various more complicated areas of interconnections forming enlargements at the forward (head) end. There are, in most primitive brains, three such enlargements, the *forebrain, midbrain,* and *hindbrain,* and these three are still identifiable in man.

The main parts of a primitive vertebrate brain help us to understand the pattern upon which the much more complex human brain is built. A schematic representation of a dogfish brain is shown in Figure 2–8. At this stage the *forebrain* consists of the *olfactory bulb* (connected with the sense organs of smell), the *cerebrum* (chiefly at this stage a "nose brain," using the information coming from the sense of smell to guide the behavior of the fish), the *thalamus* (a way station for impulses coming up from the spinal cord and down from the cerebrum), and the *hypothalamus* (concerned with many of the internal regulatory processes). The *midbrain* consists chiefly of the *optic lobes,* connected with the eyes and regulating behavior by way of stimuli affecting the eyes. The *hindbrain* includes the *cerebellum* (controlling balance, among other things) and the *medulla,* the enlargement of the spinal cord that is important in maintaining the vital functions, such as respiration and circulation of the blood.

The evolution of the brain structures is related, of course, to the kinds of lives the various organisms lead. Fishes, with their large olfactory lobes, rely heavily on their chemical senses to detect food; birds, with their complex flight patterns, have highly developed cerebellums, related to equilibrium and fine muscular coordination. As mammals developed their more complex

sensory systems and came to rely more on learning, memory, and problem-solving, a new brain developed in the form of an outpouching or cover over the cerebrum, which has come to be called the "neocortex" ("new cortex") or simply the *cerebral cortex,* as we know it in higher forms, including man.

The gradual changes in proportionate size of the cerebrum and midbrain are shown in Figure 2–9. The cerebral cortex becomes highly wrinkled or *convoluted,* so

2–9

Development of the forebrain in vertebrate evolution

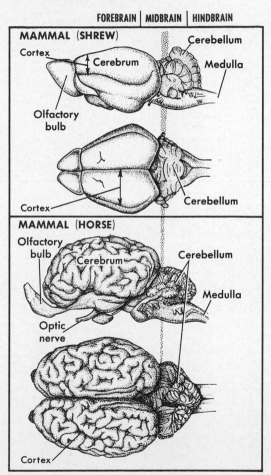

The cortex is still small and unconvoluted in the shrew, a primitive mammal; the convoluted surface of the horse cerebrum is made up entirely of cortex. Top and side views are shown. (After Simpson and Beck, 1965)

that its actual surface area is far greater than it would be were it a smooth covering of the surface of the brain.

Hierarchical organization of the human brain

The human brain consists essentially of the structures of the primitive vertebrate brain, preserved in similar anatomical rela- tions but of course modified in detail, plus the enormously developed cerebral cortex built upon the older brain. It helps to think of the human brain as composed of three concentric layers: a primitive core, an older brain evolved upon this core, and an outer layer of new brain evolved in turn upon the second layer (Figure 2–10). All three layers are, of course, interconnected

2–10

The human brain

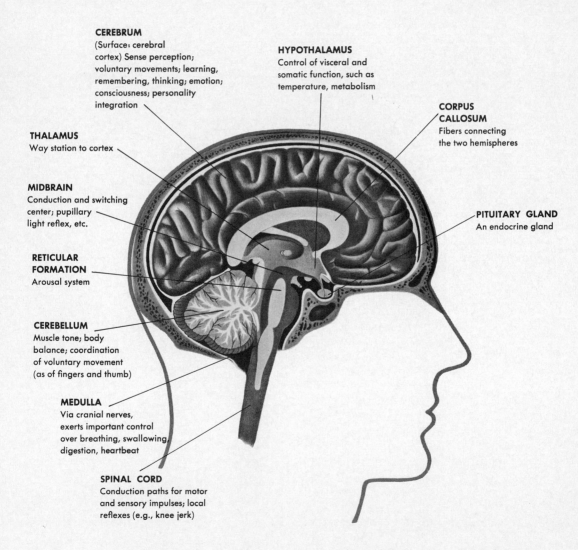

CEREBRUM
(Surface: cerebral cortex) Sense perception; voluntary movements; learning, remembering, thinking; emotion; consciousness; personality integration

HYPOTHALAMUS
Control of visceral and somatic function, such as temperature, metabolism

CORPUS CALLOSUM
Fibers connecting the two hemispheres

THALAMUS
Way station to cortex

MIDBRAIN
Conduction and switching center; pupillary light reflex, etc.

PITUITARY GLAND
An endocrine gland

RETICULAR FORMATION
Arousal system

CEREBELLUM
Muscle tone; body balance; coordination of voluntary movement (as of fingers and thumb)

MEDULLA
Via cranial nerves, exerts important control over breathing, swallowing, digestion, heartbeat

SPINAL CORD
Conduction paths for motor and sensory impulses; local reflexes (e.g., knee jerk)

This schematic drawing shows the main subdivisions of man's central nervous system and their functions. (Only the upper portion of the spinal cord, which is also part of the central nervous system, is shown here; for further detail, see Figure 2–18.)

in a complex fashion, and a new layer cannot evolve without changing the conduction of impulses to and from the earlier and more central layers of the brain (Pribram, 1960).

The central core. The central core includes parts of the hindbrain, midbrain, thalamus, and hypothalamus, that is, much of the *brain stem,* or stalk upon which the other brain structures are attached. It functions in such life-maintaining processes as respiration and metabolism, in the regulation of endocrine gland activity, and in maintaining *homeostasis.* The term "homeostasis" refers to the general level of functioning characteristic of the healthly organism, such as a normal body temperature, a standard concentration of salt in the blood, and normal heart rate and blood pressure. Under stress the usual equilibrium is disturbed, and processes are set under way to correct the disequilibrium and return the body to the normal level of functioning. Thus if we are too warm we perspire and if we are too cool we shiver—both processes tending to restore the more usual temperature. If we think of temperature control by a thermostat as providing a convenient analogy, we may say that the body has the equivalent of *homeostats* for detecting changes in various systems that can get out of balance. These control mechanisms, the details of which are unknown, are located in the hypothalamus, near the midline of the ventricles (hollow portions) at the center of the brain. The homeostats are conceived as structures sensitive to chemical and other changes that represent a feedback from the rest of the body. Their action is closely related to that of the neighboring *reticular formation,* a collection of neurons with short connections to other neurons lying in the brain stem, forming a structure about the size of the little finger. The reticular formation has to do with controlling the state of arousal of the organism, as in changing from sleep to waking, or from diffuse awareness to alert attention. It may have other regulatory functions as well (Magoun, 1963). We thus see how this central core of the brain provides for very important life-maintaining functions.

Much of the information about the homeostats and about the reticular formation is quite recent, and the developments provide an exciting field of inquiry in contemporary neurophysiology and physiological psychology. We may take as an illustration the control of perspiration as a result of temperature change in the region of the hypothalamus (Benzinger, 1961). In this experiment the investigator placed a thermocouple (a heat-measuring instrument) on the eardrum, in order to measure temperature as near as possible to the hypothalamus where the "thermostat" or "homeostat" is located. He then placed the subject in a calorimeter, where heat loss from the body could be measured to indicate the amount of perspiration. The subject's body (internal) temperature was changed by control of the external temperature and by the subject's exertion. A very clear relationship was found between the internal temperature and the rate of sweating (Figure 2–11). The sharp break point in the curve is at 36.9° C (98.4° F). It is as if the thermostat were set for this temperature. Below it no sweating occurred; above it sweating began. A change in temperature of .01° C was enough to increase the dissipation of heat through sweating by a measurable amount.

The old brain. Around this central core are older parts of the brain that serve somewhat more complex functions. These lie along the innermost edge of the cerebral hemispheres, that is, the earlier evolved parts of the cerebrum. These structures are now commonly referred to as the *limbic system.* Because the system is related to some of the internal controls that occur in digestion and circulation, it has sometimes been called the *visceral brain* (McLean, 1950). But it has other "higher" functions also, as in some aspects of memory. Pribram (1958) suggests that if all the data are combined, we would find that the limbic system is concerned with *sequential activities,* that is, with activities that proceed for some time and involve a number of move-

2–11

The hypothalamus as a thermostat

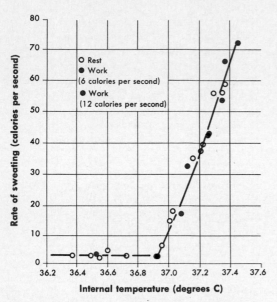

The graph shows the relation between internal head temperature and heat dissipation by sweating. A thermocouple giving a precise temperature measurement was placed on the eardrum to be near the hypothalamus; heat loss was measured by a calorimeter in which the subject worked or rested. (After Benzinger, 1961)

ments before they are completed. These include the activities of feeding, attacking, fleeing from danger, mating—kinds of activities that have often been called "instinctive" because they are so characteristic of the members of a species. Milner (1958) has shown dramatically that human patients with lesions in parts of the limbic system are particularly helpless in carrying out an intended sequence of actions. That is, a small distraction makes them forget what they have set out to do. The evidence from both lower animals and human studies suggests that the limbic system builds upon the homeostatic mechanisms, regulating the dispositions of the organism to engage in sequences of activities related to the basic adaptive functions mentioned above.

Finally, as the outer core is reached, we come to the cerebral cortex. This portion of the brain is so important in behavior that it will be given separate treatment.

Treating the brain in this way, as three concentric structures—a central core, an old brain, and an outer core—must not lead us to think of these interrelated structures as being independent. We might use the analogy of a bank of interrelated computers. Each has specialized functions but they still work together to produce the most effective result. Similarly, the analysis of information coming from the senses requires one kind of computation and decision process, for which the cortex is well adapted, differing from that which maintains a sequence of activities (limbic system). The finer adjustments of the muscles (as in writing or in playing a musical instrument) require another kind of control system, in this case mediated by the cerebellum. All these activities are ordered into complex subordinate and superordinate systems which maintain the integrity of the organism.

CRITICAL DISCUSSION

How the brain is studied

The brain is a very complex structure, and great ingenuity has been required to discover how it operates. The information already given, and that to follow, has been derived from painstaking research over the years. We may usefully note five methods that psychologists, in conjunction with neurophysiologists and neuroanatomists, use to study the brain.

1. *Study of the evolution of the brain.* By comparative study we find that parts of man's brain are very similar to the brains of lower animals. The parallels found in structure between man's brain and simpler brains lead us to infer similar functions, which need to be verified by further investigation. Another way to study the evolution of the brain is through observation of its embryological development, for in its early stages of development the brain of the human embryo reveals its relation to the brains of organisms lower in the evolutionary scale.

2. *Study through disease, injury, or extirpation.* Some forms of tumor and disease injure circumscribed areas of brain tissue.

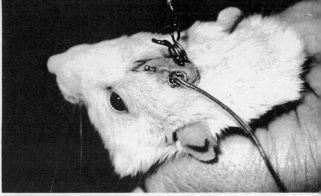

2–12

Electrodes implanted in the brain

Courtesy N. E. Miller;
photos by Martin Iger.

Similarly, gunshot wounds and other accidents may injure specific parts of the brain or spinal cord. By noting the symptoms produced by the injury (paralysis, loss of sensation, or other disturbances), it is often possible to infer what role a given part of the brain serves.

Instead of waiting for disease or accidents, it is possible to perform systematic *extirpation* experiments to determine by surgical removal of parts of the brain what kinds of defects are produced by their loss. Surgery of this kind is done primarily upon animals, although surgeons have performed extirpations of parts of the brains of human beings when they expected the operation to benefit the patient.

3. *Study of nerve degeneration.* When an area of the brain is destroyed, nerves connecting with the area may degenerate. The pathways of these connecting fibers, which in a normal brain would be lost in a mass of other fibers, can therefore be traced through microscopic study.

4. *Study through stimulation.* Stimulating parts of the brain with mild electrical currents produces effects on behavior. Surgical patients with their brain surfaces exposed under local anesthetics have assisted in such studies by reporting their experiences when different points are stimulated. Some rather satisfactory "maps" of the cortex have resulted from these studies.

More recently, animal investigators have used permanently implanted electrodes to produce repeated stimulation in a local part of the brain (Figure 2–12). Studies done with the aid of such electrodes help determine where sensory effects occur in the brain, and where various types of muscular activity are controlled.

For some purposes, however, we wish to know what is happening in the elementary parts of the nervous system, as in specific neurons or glia cells. Some progress has been made in studying these in a culture outside the brain, also using stimulation methods (Hild, 1964).

5. *Study of electrical effects of nervous action.* When neural action goes on, slight electrical currents are always produced. By inserting electrodes at appropriate places, connected in turn to measuring devices, one can detect whether impulses starting at, say, the ear reach the part of the brain where the electrodes are inserted.

Rat being weighed before operation to determine the proper dose of anesthetic.

Anesthetized rat under the stereotaxic instrument which implants the electrodes through tiny holes in the skull.

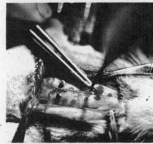

Insertion of screws which help to anchor dental cement to skull.

Electrodes are cemented and connected to pins which project from the cement.

The brain as a whole also produces rhythmical electrical discharges. The record of these total brain discharges, known as an *electroencephalogram* (EEG), plays its part in the study of central nervous activity. For example, if a particular kind of stimulation gives rise to changes in the rhythmic discharges picked up from one part of the brain and does not affect those discharges from another part, we can assume that the stimulation affected that particular region (see Figure 2–13).

A more recent method of brain study, made possible by the development of the modern computer, is the study of *evoked potentials*. The method averages a large number of EEG records, each of which follows a given type of stimulus. Thus the random EEG activity is averaged out, and the more uniform consequences of stimulation can be detected, consequences that would ordinarily be lost in the complex EEG pattern. An example is given in Figure 2–14.

These methods are merely noted here; later on in the book there will be more specific indications of how results obtained by these methods further our psychological understanding.

The Cerebral Cortex in Man

The two large hemispheres at the top of the human brain represent man's "new brain." The convoluted layer of gray matter—the cerebral cortex—that covers them controls man's most distinctively human behavior.

Our clearest knowledge of the cortex has to do with those functions that are related to specific areas of the brain. We speak of these as the *localized functions*, the ones that can be mapped; the places where they appear on a map of the cortex are called *projection areas*. Some areas of the cortex

2–13

Electrical action of the brain

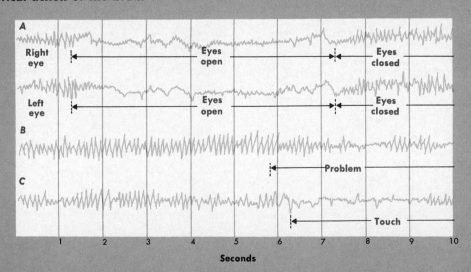

Through electrodes attached to the outside of the skull, the electroencephalograph measures the pattern of electrical activity within the brain. When the brain is at rest, the basic pattern is a large-amplitude "alpha" wave of about 10 cycles per second, as shown in the extreme left column. When the brain responds to sensory inputs, such as vision or touch, or when it is engaged by a mental problem, the alpha waves give way to irregular waves which are higher in frequency and lower in amplitude. (After Eccles, 1958)

Visually evoked potential from the human cortex

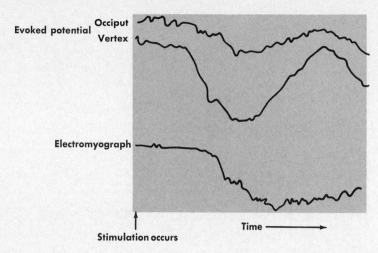

Evoked potential Occiput
Vertex

Electromyograph

↑
Stimulation occurs

Time ⟶

Visually evoked potential precedes muscular response to the evoking stimulus. The curves are obtained by averaging 100 of these responses with the aid of a computer, the responses being time-locked to the moment of stimulation so that random activity is averaged out and only events related in time to the stimulus show. The top curve (evoked potential) represents responses from the occiput (rear of the head), the next from the vertex (top of the head), corrected for visual responses occurring when no movement is called for. The bottom curve (electromyograph) is from the responding muscle, and shows that there is a delay between the time that the cortex responds to the light and the time that the movement (a flexion of the foot) begins. (From Vaughan and others, 1965)

when stimulated electrically will produce known and specifiable kinds of *motor responses* (those involving motion or activity in parts of the body) or *sensory effects* (those involving sensation, feeling, awareness). When tumors exert pressure on these areas, there are disturbances in the responses. When, through disease or injury, these areas are destroyed, the same functions are altered or obliterated. Yet we would be making an error in logic if we assumed that these functions are *controlled* by these areas alone. Even though an area is *essential* to a function, it may not be *sufficient* to control that function. With this warning, let us turn to some illustrations of localization of function.

Before beginning with the illustrations of localization, we need a few landmarks by which to describe areas of the *cerebral hemispheres.* The two hemispheres are symmetrical, one on the right and one on the left, with a deep division between

them, running from front to rear. So our first classification is into *right* and *left hemispheres.* For the most part, functions of the right side of the body are controlled by the left hemisphere, functions of the left side by the right hemisphere. Each hemisphere is divided into four *lobes:* the *frontal* lobe, the *parietal* lobe, the *occipital* lobe, and the *temporal* lobe. The landmarks dividing these lobes are shown on Figure 2–15. The frontal lobes are separated from the parietal lobes by the central *fissure,* or *fissure of Rolando,* running down from the part of the cerebrum near the top of the head sideways toward the ears. The division between the parietal lobe and the occipital lobe is not as clear-cut; it suffices for our purpose to know that the parietal lobe is at the top of the brain, behind the fissure of Rolando, while the occipital lobe is at the very rear of the brain. The temporal lobe is well set off by a deep fissure at the side of the brain, the *fissure of Sylvius.*

Localization of function in the human cortex

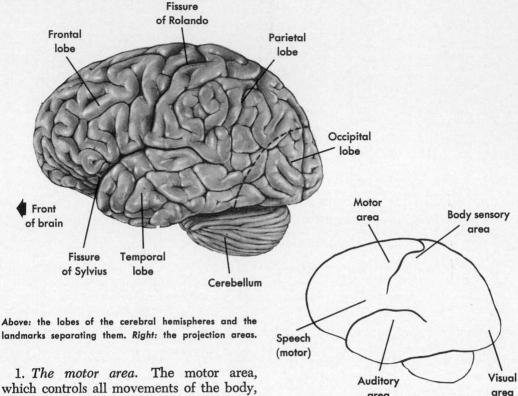

Above: the lobes of the cerebral hemispheres and the landmarks separating them. *Right:* the projection areas.

1. *The motor area.* The motor area, which controls all movements of the body, lies just in front of the fissure of Rolando, half of the body being represented on each side. When stimulated electrically, parts of the motor area cause movements in the extremities, and when these areas are injured the same extremities are paralyzed. The body is represented in approximately upside-down form, movement of the toes being mediated by the part near the top of the head, and tongue and mouth movements by the part near the bottom of the area toward the side of the brain (Figure 2–16). Movements on the right side of the body originate through stimulation of the motor area of the left hemisphere, movements on the left side through stimulation of the right hemisphere.

2. *The body-sense area.* In the parietal lobes, separated from the motor area by the fissure of Rolando, lies an area which if stimulated electrically gives rise to sensory experiences, as though a part of the body were being touched or moved. Again the lower extremities are represented high on the area of the opposite hemisphere, the face represented low on the area.

Disease or injury in the body-sense area produces disturbances of sensory processes but seldom produces complete absence of sensation (*anesthesia*). The injured person may lose the ability to tell the positions of his arms or hands when his eyes are closed or to recognize objects by touch. While he may still be able to detect extremes of temperature, he may be at a loss to judge finer gradations of warmth and coolness.

3. *The visual area.* At the very back of each cerebral hemisphere, in the part of the occipital lobe known as the *striate area*, lie centers important in vision.

New knowledge of the functioning of the visual cortex has come through studies of the electrical responses of single cells in the cortex, chiefly in cats, either unrestrained and mobile or lightly anesthetized (Hubel and Wiesel, 1959, 1963, 1965). When spots of light, or slits of light, are presented in different positions, the responses from cells within the visual cortex differ in orderly ways, showing that the sensory system is organized to perceive aspects of form and movement, and not simply points of light.

4. *The auditory area.* An area for audition is found on the surface of the temporal lobes at the sides of the hemispheres. There is some spatial distribution, a part sensitive to high tones being different from one that is sensitive to low tones. In the auditory areas, both ears are totally represented on both sides, so that the loss of one temporal lobe has very little effect upon hearing.

5. *The speech area.* One of the very earliest findings in localization is still under dispute. As early as 1861 the neurologist Paul Broca examined the brain of a patient with speech loss and found damage in an area on the side of the left hemisphere. This area has since been known as Broca's speech area, and it has been assigned the functions of motor speech, that is, control of the tongue and jaws in speaking. The conventional interpretation is that the area is located in the left hemisphere of right-handed people (those whose left hemisphere is dominant), while it is found in the right hemisphere of left-handed people (those whose right hemisphere is dominant).

Speech is far too complex to be localized in this simple manner, and psychological disorders of speech and language (*aphasias*) have defied simple classification and therefore precise localization. In a careful study of ten left-handed people, half with lesions on the right sides of their brains and half with lesions on the left sides, all

2–16

Localization of function within the motor and sensory areas

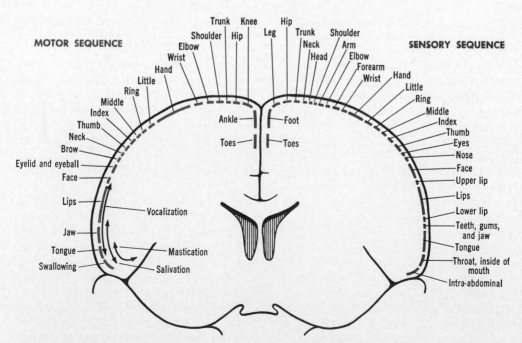

In this cross section of the cerebrum through the sensorimotor region, the motor sequence is indicated on the left and the sensory sequence on the right. Both hemispheres have both functions (see Figure 2–15). (After Penfield and Rasmussen, 1950)

but one showed disturbances of speech; this one had a lesion on the right side, which, according to convention, should be more severe for a left-handed person (Humphrey and Zangwill, 1952).

6. *The association areas.* The many large areas of the cerebrum not accounted for when maps of localized areas are assembled have often been called *association areas* (as distinguished from the primary projection areas), on the assumption that they must serve to bring together phenomena involving more than one sense and must also be involved in learning, memory, and thinking.

The evidence for this assumption is, in fact, quite fragmentary and, such as it is, very puzzling. Electrical stimulation of various parts of these association areas will produce disturbances of speech. Epileptic patients (but not nonepileptic ones) produce hallucinatory experiences and occasionally recount specific memories under electrical stimulation, especially of areas near certain points that produce convulsions when stimulated. For example, when a given point is stimulated, the patient may report a phonograph playing a recognizable and remembered tune. The record can be "turned on" or "turned off" through electrical stimulation (Penfield and Jasper, 1954; Penfield, 1958). These results are interesting, but their interpretation is baffling. Why are such findings limited to epileptic patients? Is the memory of this experience really localized in this small spot? When the spot is surgically excised (as part of an operation to relieve epilepsy), it is of course no longer possible to secure the effect formerly produced by stimulating that spot. But the excision does not destroy the subject's ability to tell what the record sounded like when that spot was earlier stimulated. Evidently other parts of the brain are involved in the total memory experience.

Evidence from extirpation experiments and other studies makes clear that the areas of the brain not concerned with sensory projection are not "silent" or nonfunctional. Such areas may serve distinguishable functions. Thus the frontal lobes may appear to be especially important in *sequential tasks,* in which events must be kept in order. In this they supplement the limbic system (p. 41). Other areas appear to cooperate with the primary projection areas whenever complex tasks are involved.

While we do not yet know in detail how the association areas serve, modern methods, both surgical and electrical, are telling us a number of things about the gross functions of these parts that were once described as "silent" because their functions were unknown. According to Pribram (1960) the "association areas" have their own specialized functions, even though their specializations are of a different order than those of the projection areas. For example, the primary visual projection area (at the rear of the brain) is inadequate for discrimination unless another area (in the temporal lobes) is intact. This secondary area is thus specialized for discrimination. Other parts, such as the forebrain, may serve kinds of memory that the limbic system does not serve. Still other parts serve for learning and problem-solving and, in man, for language. Because each of the brain regions appears to have some special function of its own that is independent of learning, Pribram would substitute the term "intrinsic system" for "association area" because the latter term does not suggest the specialized ways in which the various areas contribute to integration.

The Autonomic Nervous System

The outgoing nerves, running from the central nervous system to the response mechanisms, can be classified into two groups: those running to the striate muscles and those running to smooth muscles and glands. Those going to the striate muscles are usually grouped with the central nervous system, while those going to smooth muscles and glands are grouped together as the *autonomic nervous system.* An anatomical basis for the distinction is that the nerve fibers of the autonomic system always have a junction with another neuron (i.e., a synapse) *outside* the brain or spinal cord on the way to a muscle or gland, while such outside synapses are not found for nerves running to striate muscle. The autonomic nervous system derives its name from the fact that many of the activities it controls are "autonomous" or "self-regulating" activities, such as digestion and circulation, which go on even when a person is asleep or unconscious.

There are two divisions of the autonomic system, often antagonistic in their action. These are the *sympathetic* and the *parasympathetic* divisions.

The sympathetic division

On either side of the spinal column, closely connected with it through the spinal nerves, lie chains of nerve fibers and masses of cell bodies (*ganglia*) from which fibers extend to the various visceral organs. These are known as the *sympathetic chains*. The fibers coming from the spinal cord to the sympathetic chain arise in the thoracic and lumbar portion of the spine, between the cervical (neck) and the sacral (lower spine) regions. All the fibers and ganglia together constitute the *sympathetic division* of the autonomic system (Figure 2–17).

The sympathetic division tends to act as a unit. In emotional excitement it simultaneously speeds up the heart and dilates the arteries of the muscles and heart, while constricting those of the skin and digestive organs; its action leads also to perspiring and to secretion of adrenalin. In fact, the responses to adrenalin (see p. 32) and to the action of the sympathetic system are very much alike, and these chemical and neural actions support each other in strong emotion.

The parasympathetic division

The parasympathetic division falls into two parts, some of its fibers originating in the cranial region, above those of the sympathetic system, and others originating in the sacral region, below those of the sympathetic system.

Unlike the sympathetic system, the parasympathetic system tends to act in a more piecemeal fashion, affecting one organ at a time. If the sympathetic system is thought of as dominant in violent and excited activity, the parasympathetic system may be thought of as dominant in quiescence. It participates in digestion and, in general, maintains the functions that conserve and protect bodily resources. (It is worth noting that there is no parasympathetic connection to the adrenal gland, which is dominant in excitement.)

Competition and cooperation between the two autonomic divisions

When both sympathetic and parasympathetic fibers are connected to the same muscle or gland, the usual rule is that they act in opposite manner. Thus the sympathetic system speeds the heart rate, the parasympathetic system slows it; the sympathetic system inhibits digestive processes, the parasympathetic system facilitates them. A list of the functions of the two systems is given in Table 2–2.

There are some exceptions to the principle that the two systems are antagonistic. Both divisions may be active at once, and in some cases they act together in sequence. While the sympathetic system is usually dominant in fear and excitement, a not uncommon parasympathetic symptom in extreme emotion is the involuntary discharge of the bladder or bowels. Another example is the complete sex act in the male, which requires erection (parasympathetic) followed by ejaculation (sympathetic). Thus, while the two divisions are often antagonistic, they interact in more complex ways, and their interaction even today is not fully understood.

Levels of Functioning

Thus far we have considered both the finer features of integrated nervous action (neuron, nervous impulse, synapse) and some gross aspects of anatomical localization of function. Now we shall consider some further aspects of integrated action as represented in reflex patterns and in responsiveness to under- and overstimulation.

The autonomic nervous system

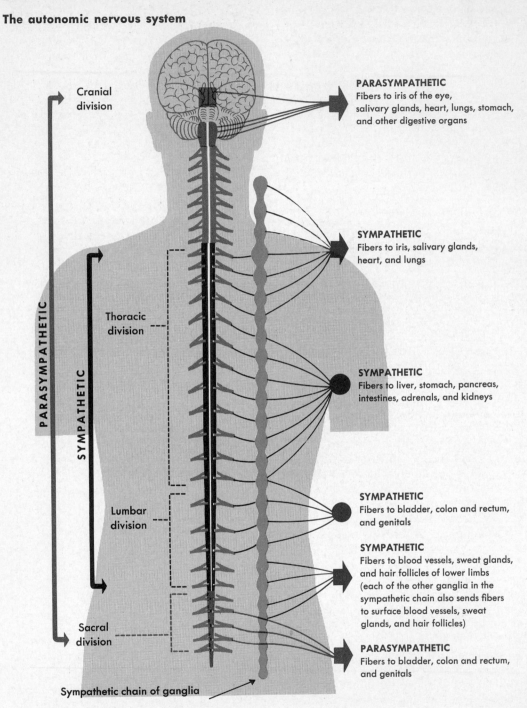

Cranial division

PARASYMPATHETIC
Fibers to iris of the eye,
salivary glands, heart, lungs, stomach,
and other digestive organs

SYMPATHETIC
Fibers to iris, salivary glands,
heart, and lungs

PARASYMPATHETIC

SYMPATHETIC

Thoracic division

SYMPATHETIC
Fibers to liver, stomach, pancreas,
intestines, adrenals, and kidneys

Lumbar division

SYMPATHETIC
Fibers to bladder, colon and rectum,
and genitals

SYMPATHETIC
Fibers to blood vessels, sweat glands,
and hair follicles of lower limbs
(each of the other ganglia in the
sympathetic chain also sends fibers
to surface blood vessels, sweat
glands, and hair follicles)

Sacral division

PARASYMPATHETIC
Fibers to bladder, colon and rectum,
and genitals

Sympathetic chain of ganglia

The diagram represents only one-half of the system, which is duplicated on the other side of the spinal cord. The *sympathetic* system (in black) is characterized by chains of ganglia on either side of the cord and by other large ganglia (represented by large circles). The *parasympathetic* system (in color) has its ganglia (not shown) nearer the organs stimulated so that it acts in a more piecemeal fashion.

TABLE 2-2

Functions of the two divisions of the autonomic nervous system

Organ	Sympathetic function	Parasympathetic function
Heart	Acceleration	Inhibition
Blood vessels		
In skin	Constriction	None
In striate muscle	Dilation, constriction	None
In heart	Dilation	Constriction
In abdominal viscera	Constriction	None
Pupil of eye	Dilation	Constriction
Tear glands	(Possibly a secretory function)	Secretion
Sweat glands	Secretion	None
Hair on skin	Hairs erected	None
Adrenal glands	Secretion	None
Liver	Sugar liberated	None
Salivary glands	Secretion (?)	Secretion
Stomach	Inhibition of secretion and peristalsis (some excitation)	Secretion, peristalsis (some inhibition)
Intestines	Inhibition	Increased tone and motility
Rectum	Inhibition	Feces expelled
Bladder	Inhibition	Urine expelled
Genital organs (male)	Ejaculation	Erection

SOURCE: Data from Best and Taylor (1955), p. 1097, and other sources.

The reflex pattern

The basic pattern of stimulation by the environment and response to stimulation is that of the *reflex circuit*. Irritability and contractibility are primitive properties of protoplasm, as found in single-celled organisms, but when nervous systems develop, response to stimulation becomes divided into the processes of *reception of stimuli, transmission and integration of nervous impulses,* and *activation of muscles and glands.* Specialized *receptors* convert the energy from the environment into nervous impulses; the nerves and central nervous system provide the *connectors;* the nervous impulses are converted back into action by the *effectors.* The reflex circuit provides the terminology for S-R psychology, as discussed in Chapter 1.

The truly simple reflex is a convenient fiction. It would represent a simple receptor which, when activated, would transmit impulses through a single neuron to a waiting muscle. Actual reflexes consist in the stimulation of numerous nerve fibers, which in turn make junctions with other neurons, often supplemented by bursts of impulses coming from other sources, and resulting in impulses transmitted along numerous fibers before reaching a muscle or gland, or several muscles and glands. Some reflexes operate relatively mechanically, despite these complications of the simple reflex circuit. Thus a tap on the

TABLE 2-3

Man's receptors

Bodily organ or tissue	Location of sensitive portion	Sensory experience or discrimination
Eye	Retina	Black, white, color; visual perception of objects, space, motion
Inner ear	Cochlea	Tones, noises; speech, music, location of sounds in space
	Saccule, utricle	Static position of the body in reference to gravity; accelerated motion
	Semicircular canals	Rotation of the head
Nose	Olfactory epithelium (in upper part of right and left nasal cavities)	Smell
	Sensitive nerve endings (in membranes of nose)	Irritation
Tongue, mouth, and throat	Taste buds (on surface and edges of tongue; in lesser numbers in other tissues of mouth and throat)	Sweet, salt, sour, bitter
Skin	Various end organs (organs and nerve endings of differential sensitivity, distributed unevenly through the superficial and deeper layers of the skin)	Light touch, deep pressure, warmth, coolness, pain
Internal organs	Various	Pain from distention (also, in some parts of some organs, touch, warmth, coolness, pressure)
Muscles, tendons, and joints	Muscle spindles (stimulated by stretching of muscle)	Position and movement of parts of the body
	Endings in tendons (stimulated when muscles contract)	
	Pressure-sensitive end organs in tissues around joints	

patellar tendon will ordinarily produce a knee jerk; light flashed into the eye will be followed by constriction of the pupil. Even in these cases, however, other processes may accentuate (facilitate) or diminish (inhibit) the response. For example, one way of obtaining a more pronounced knee jerk is to grip the hands together just before the tendon is tapped. Evidently what is happening in the leg is affected by what is happening elsewhere. When we consider more complex processes, such as memory and imagination, the notion of a reflex is continued with greater difficulty, yet it is convenient to assume that the same principles can be applied.

Receptors. Man's equipment of *receptors* is very inadequately indicated by the traditional five senses. Not only do some of these (e.g., touch) break down into several senses, but receptors related to bodily position and to muscular movements are totally unaccounted for in the traditional scheme. A catalogue of human receptors and their functions is given above in Table 2–3.

A receptor is an energy-converter, what the engineer calls a *transducer*. That is, it converts energy from the environment into chemical processes that in turn produce electrochemical nervous impulses (Loewenstein, 1960).

Effectors. The *effectors* which carry out the responses to stimuli are the muscles and the glands. They mediate the smooth muscle and glandular responses within the body as well as responses to the environment.

Connectors. Between the receptors and the effectors lie the *connectors,* or what we call "the nervous system." These may be grouped into three classes:

1. Incoming or *afferent* nerves. The receptors all over the body are connected to nerve fibers over which impulses come into the *central nervous system.* A nerve is a bundle of individual nerve fibers.
2. *Centers.* The internal connections and interconnections of nerve cells, made across their endings at *synapses,* occur chiefly within the brain and spinal cord, although there are some junctions between neurons (synapses) outside the brain and spinal cord in col-

lections of nerve cells, or *ganglia.* We may group all these complex switching places together as *central processes,* or, simply, *centers.*

3. Outgoing or *efferent* nerves. From the centers, nerve fibers lead out, again through bundles called nerves, to connect with effectors. (It is easy to recall which nerves are called *a*fferent and which *e*fferent by remembering that *e*fferent nerves are connected with *e*ffectors.)

This simple picture of afferent and efferent nerves, supported both by the anatomy of nerves and by the physiology of reflex action, is another one of the oversimplifications that has recently been corrected. The oversimplification lies not in the direction of movement of impulses, but in their purposes (Figure 2–18). It has been assumed that afferent nerves were sensory nerves and efferent nerves motor nerves, that is, that afferent nerves served purposes of signaling changes at the sense organ and effer-

2–18

Spinal cord and spinal roots

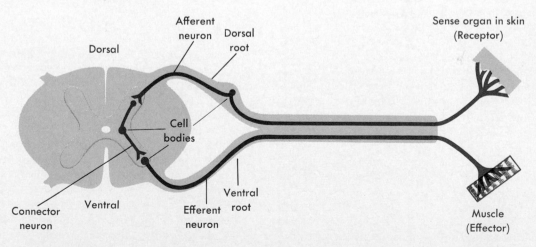

Nerves enter and leave the spinal cord through the dorsal (upper) and ventral (lower) roots. The H-shaped portion is gray matter at the center of the cord, consisting largely of cell bodies and their interconnections. An oversimplified three-neuron reflex circuit is illustrated. The cell bodies (greatly enlarged) for each of the three kinds of neurons are shown. The efferent fibers are not, however, all motor fibers; see text. Note that this is a cross section; much of the cord (the matter surrounding the central gray, called "white matter" though shown in color in the diagram) consists of ascending and descending fibers connecting the various segments with each other and with the brain.

ent nerves purposes of movement and secretion. It is now known, however, that the
efferent fibers also regulate the amount of
sensory input, thereby selectively allowing
more or fewer afferent impulses to be transmitted. As many as one-third of the fibers
in the *efferent* ventral roots to muscles
serves this purpose of regulating the *afferent* impulses from muscle receptors (Livingston, 1958). Similar efferent modification of afferent processes has been reported
for the visual and auditory mechanisms in
the brain.

Stimulation

The simple reflex as the unit of behavior
tends to picture the organism as passive,
waiting like a calculating machine to be
stimulated from without. If nothing trig-
gers a reflex, nothing happens. This is not,
of course, a true picture of a living organism. There are internal sources of stimulation that keep many reflex mechanisms
active: circulatory, respiratory, digestive,
postural. Any new stimulus is received into
a stream of activity, so that reflex activity
always takes place in a context. Some of
this context can be described according to
general levels of stimulation, varying between understimulation and overstimulation.

It was pointed out earlier that the body
tends to preserve a normal state of equilibrium, or homeostasis, from which behavior departs in response to stimulation.
Once there is effort or change of any sort,
homeostasis is temporarily disturbed, and
mechanisms are aroused that tend to restore it. Despite the importance of homeostasis and the stresses that are implied
when it is upset, the normal life of the
organism is not one of quiescence, but one
of action.

The fact that a healthy organism seeks
stimulation and activity is evident to anyone who has watched children and animals
at play. As adults we know that solitary
confinement is the cruelest form of punishment, reducing as it does opportunities for
physical stimulation and eliminating social
stimulation and response.

Our level of activity can vacillate between complete quiescence and an overactive, stressful level. In the normal cycle
of sleep and wakefulness, the vacillation is
between moderate limits of quiet and action. The harmful effects of extreme overactivity are obvious (exhaustion, collapse),
but extreme inactivity can also have serious
consequences.

Understimulation. Experiments have
shown that even a relatively short period
of inactivity will disturb the adaptive responses of a person. In one such experiment, college students were paid to remain in bed in isolated cubicles for two
to three days under conditions of very restricted stimulation. Not only were the
rooms free of pictures and other centers of
interest, but the students wore special cuffs
to reduce the stimulation from their own
movements as they lay quietly in bed.
They were interrupted occasionally for
psychological testing. During the isolation
period scores on a number of intelligence
test items decreased markedly. Some disturbances in perception were noted as the
students left the cubicles. Occasionally during the period of isolation hallucinations
appeared, not dissimilar to those found in
some cases of mental illness (Bexton,
Heron, and Scott, 1954; Doane, Mahatoo,
Heron, and Scott, 1959).

These experiments show in rather striking fashion that the normal level of psychological functioning depends upon active
participation with the environment. Workers in mental hospitals have found that
some gains are produced merely by keeping patients active, as in sports and hobbies. Some minimum level of active stimulation and response is necessary to keep us
operating as human beings.

Overstimulation: stress. When conditions place the organism under great strain,
the homeostatic mechanisms no longer
operate smoothly; if the stresses continue,
the organism may suffer injury, even as a
consequence of its own efforts to meet the
stress. Agents and events that can place
the organism under stress include infections, nervous strain, physical injury, ex-

cessive heat or cold, muscular fatigue. Conditions of modern life place some people under stress for long periods of time. The physiological mechanisms of adaptation to stress become significant as we try to understand what is happening to such people.

A number of investigators have been concerned with a response pattern that develops under extreme and long-continued stress. This pattern, known as the *general adaptation syndrome*, moves through three stages:

1. An *alarm-reaction,* in which adaptation has not yet been acquired. This commonly includes a stage of reduced activity (a state of shock), followed by excessive mobilization of forces within the organism to meet the threat (counter-shock).
2. The stage of *resistance,* in which adaptation to threat is adequate.
3. The stage of *exhaustion,* in which the acquired adaptation is again lost (Selye, 1956).

The organism's attempts to meet continued stress may lead, according to Selye, to "diseases of adaptation." Of particular interest psychologically are the *psychosomatic disorders,* in which psychological stress in the form of worry or anxiety may produce tension states resulting, for example, in stomach ulcers. Such a condition would fit Selye's idea of diseases of adaptation.

Optimal levels of functioning. Between the understimulation that produces less than human functioning and the stress conditions that produce disease and exhaus-

tion, there is a wide range within which normal functioning goes on. Man can live an active life or a sedentary life and still be healthy.

W. B. Cannon, who introduced the notion of homeostasis, is often misunderstood as proposing that the condition of homeostasis represents the optimal level of activity. On the contrary, he stated the position that homeostasis merely protects the body so that a person can go about his enterprises, motivated by goals unrelated to maintaining the equilibrium of processes within the body. According to Cannon, bodily homeostasis liberates the nervous system

from the necessity of paying routine attention to the management of the details of bare existence. Without homeostatic devices we should be in constant danger of disaster, unless we were always on the alert to correct voluntarily what normally is corrected automatically. With homeostatic devices, however, that keep essential bodily processes steady, we as individuals are free from such slavery—free to enter into agreeable relations with our fellows, to enjoy beautiful things, to explore and understand the wonders of the world about us, to develop new ideas and interests, and to work and play untrammeled by anxieties concerning our bodily affairs.[2]

Homeostasis, then, does not define the appropriate level of human functioning; it is merely a protective device. Among man's highest attainments are those that homeostasis permits him to accomplish without his giving thought to the condition of his body.

[2] Cannon (1939), p. 323.

SUMMARY
1. The human body is a complex sensitive and responding organism, capable of functioning harmoniously because of its mechanical structure of bones and muscles, its blood stream that carries hormones throughout its body, and its nervous system that rules over all the rest.

2. Among the mechanisms that permit fine muscular coordination are those of *reciprocal innervation* whereby the interaction of *antagonistic*

muscles is provided for, and the slight but constant action in resting muscles that yields *muscle tone.*

3. The *endocrine glands* by way of the *hormones* secreted into the blood stream are important for aspects of behavior concerned with emotion, motivation, and personality. Among those most relevant to behavior are the *pituitary, thyroid,* and *adrenal glands* and the *gonads,* but the *parathyroids, thymus,* and the *pancreas* are also important.

4. Because of its intimate relationship to behavior, the evolution of the *brain* and *nervous system* is of primary interest. One-celled animals react directly to the environment, without a specialized nervous system; even a multicellular animal such as a sponge has no nerves. The beginning of the nervous system is seen in the *nerve net* found in coelenterates such as jellyfishes. This is a network of nerve cells called *neurons.* Muscles contract locally where the nerves are stimulated; conduction spreads in all directions from the point of stimulation. One form of coelenterate, the jellyfish medusa, achieves some coordination of its swimming movements by having some of the nerves concentrated in a ring at the margin of its "umbrella," but there is no central coordination, nothing corresponding to a "brain." In the flatworms (planaria) we have the beginnings of the kind of nervous system found in higher forms. The nerve net is combined with a *polarized synaptic* nervous system, in which conduction is in one direction only across the junction between neurons, this junction being called the *synapse.* In some flatworms there is a ladder-type nervous system with nerve cords and a primitive brain.

5. The nervous system is composed of cells called *neurons.* They receive stimulation by way of their *dendrites* and *cell body* and transmit impulses via their *axons.* Two types of propagation of the nerve impulse are of importance: that along nerve fibers and that across the synaptic junction between the neurons. Propagation along fibers is by way of an electrochemical process involving the interchange of sodium and potassium ions across the fiber membrane; the conduction is much more rapid for myelinated fibers, reaching a rate of about 300 feet per second in some mammalian nerves. The activation of a neuron across a synapse is also by way of a chemical intermediary; any one axon discharge does not provide enough of the activating substance to fire the neuron, so that several impulses must arrive close together to produce a response. This makes possible a kind of complex switching at the synapse, undoubtedly important in the integration of behavior. The neuron tends to fire in all-or-nothing fashion, followed by a brief *refractory phase.* However, longer lasting and graduated reactions within the dendrites probably influence the electrical activity of the brain in some manner other than by the axon-discharge of the neuron.

6. The vertebrate brain evolved about a single hollow cord of nerves running along the back of the body, with some enlargements at the forward (head) end. The three enlargements became the *forebrain, midbrain,* and *hindbrain,* connecting in turn with the *spinal cord.* This basic pattern is preserved in man's brain.

7. Even a primitive vertebrate such as the dogfish has developed more specialized parts of the forebrain such as *olfactory lobes, cerebrum,*

thalamus, and *hypothalamus.* The midbrain consists at this stage chiefly of optic lobes, connected with the visual apparatus. The hindbrain includes *cerebellum* and *medulla.*

8. While other changes of course occur, the most notable change in the brain in higher vertebrate forms is the development of the new brain, the *cerebral cortex,* the large convoluted portion of the brain that is about all one sees when he looks at the brain of a higher animal such as a horse or dog or at a human brain. The midbrain has decreased a great deal in relative size.

9. The organization of the human brain can be comprehended as composed of three concentric layers: a *primitive core,* an *older brain* evolved upon this core, and a third or outer layer of *new brain,* evolved in turn upon the second layer. The primitive core within the *brain stem* serves life-maintaining processes such as respiration and metabolism and keeps the level of body functioning near a steady equilibrium state through *homeostatic* processes. These homeostatic processes operate by way of *homeostats* within the hypothalamus, analogous to thermostats in maintaining constant temperature. An activating system, the *reticular formation,* lies within the brain stem and helps control waking and sleeping, alertness and attention. At the next level are structures lying along the innermost edge of the cerebral hemispheres, the older or more primitive cortex, now referred to as the *limbic system.* These regulate the *sequential activities* such as feeding, attacking, fleeing from danger, mating—essential activities that include interaction with the environment and take place in sequences somewhat spread out in time. Finally, the outer core of new brain, the *cerebral cortex,* controls discrimination, choice, learning, and thinking—the "higher mental processes," the most flexible, least stereotyped aspects of behavior. The *projection areas* represent specific sensory inputs or centers for control of specific movements; the remainder of the brain consists of *association areas* or *intrinsic systems.*

10. The *autonomic nervous system* is made up of two parts, a *sympathetic* and a *parasympathetic* division. Its fibers mediate the action of the viscera and of the glands, and hence the autonomic system is particularly important in emotional reactions. The sympathetic division is usually involved in excited action and the parasympathetic in quiescent states, but the antagonism between the two divisions is not universal, and they cooperate in complex fashion.

11. In considering the way in which the nervous system works, psychologists find it convenient to build upon the notion of the *reflex circuit,* beginning with the stimulation of a sensitive organ (*receptor*) where the energy of the stimulus is converted into a *nervous impulse* (or a train of such impulses) which travels to the spinal cord and brain via incoming (*afferent*) nerves; switching and integration take place in *centers* of the nervous system; then impulses are propagated along outgoing (*efferent*) nerves to the responding organs, muscles, and glands (*effectors*). While a simple reflex is a convenient fiction, the pattern of the reflex circuit permits discussion of action in terms of input from the environment, central coordination and elaboration, and output in the form of response.

12. Studies of the consequences of under- and overstimulation show the radical effects of extreme departure from the equilibrium state of homeostasis. Understimulation may produce in adult human beings extreme symptoms of loss of adaptive response and the development of hallucinations. The *general adaptation syndrome,* found under conditions of extreme stress, may lead to disease. But the normally functioning organism has enough protective devices to engage in widely varied activities without threatening its survival.

SUGGESTIONS FOR FURTHER READING

For a general introduction to neurology and neuroanatomy, see Stevens, *Neurophysiology: a primer* (1966), or Ochs, *Elements of neurophysiology* (1965). A speculative account, giving various possibilities for accounting for behavior on the basis of brain action, can be found in Hebb, *The organization of behavior* (1949). Another account, with a good deal of physiology but also a good deal of speculation, is Eccles, *The neurophysiological basis of mind* (1953); see also Eccles, *Synaptic transmission* (1964), and Eccles, *The physiology of synapses* (1964).

A careful account of the methods and results of electrostimulation as a means of studying brain function is that of Sheer, *Electrical stimulation of the brain* (1961).

For a summary on stress see Selye, *The stress of life* (1956). On the effects of sensory deprivation (understimulation), see Solomon and others, *Sensory deprivation* (1961).

For physiological psychology in general, see Morgan, *Physiological psychology* (3rd ed., 1964), and Milner, *Physiological psychology* (1966). Isaacson in *Basic readings in neuropsychology* (1964) and Landauer in *Readings in physiological psychology* (1967) republish many of the more important papers of the last few years which already are considered "classics" in the field.

GROWTH
AND
DEVELOPMENT

The developmental point of view within psychology suggests that present behavior can often best be understood if we know something of its history, for the child is indeed "father of the man." The human infant, like other animals, is born with a wide range of possible behavior. His maturation depends upon his physiological growth potential and the characteristics of his species. He becomes an individual through his experiences as he grows up—experiences in interacting with both the physical and the social environment. The process of socialization—the training for group living given by the cultural environment in which an individual happens to be born—has much to do with adult behavior.

3 Infancy and Childhood

We are now prepared to look at the functioning of the individual from the point of view of his development. The human infant is helpless for a longer time than any other mammal. If we consider only man's nearest relatives in the animal world, we find that we can make a scale of dependency from the more primitive lemur through the more highly evolved primates to man. The newborn lemur can move himself from place to place within a few hours; the monkey is dependent for a few days or weeks; the infant chimpanzee remains with his mother three to six months. The human infant is dependent for a far longer period; despite (or because of!) this long slow start he has had a highly diversified career by the time he becomes adult.

The slow development of the human infant means that he is subjected to a long period of learning and interaction with other people before he is fully "on his own." We are therefore interested in how what he becomes is shaped by his early experiences, so that we may be wiser in our child-care practices.

The Developmental Viewpoint

We have distinguished the developmental and interactive viewpoints in a general way, the developmental point of view emphasizing the historical antecedents of present behavior. What we can learn from taking this viewpoint should become clearer as we study the development of the human infant in relation to some more general aspects of biological development.

Why we study development

Any topic in psychology can be studied both in its basic science aspects and in its applied aspects. The development of the human organism is interesting as a basic scientific problem, but it is of course a practical problem for parents, educators, and others responsible for the management of human lives. The main assumption of the developmental point of view is that there is continuity from the past to the present, so that the present can be understood in terms of its history; this is so obvious that it would not lend much theoretical interest in development except for some more puzzling and controversial aspects of this continuity. One possibility is that there may be *critical periods* in development, where both favorable and unfavorable outcomes may have lasting and well-nigh irreversible consequences. For example, it has been hypothesized that a person's basic trust in other people is a characteristic developed in the first year of life through the warmth and affection of those who care for him (Erikson, 1963). If this hypothesis is true, and the child who lacks such early affectionate care grows up to be inadequate and mistrustful in social relationships, then the first few months of life would represent a critical period with respect to the development of basic trust.

Another possibility is that growth proceeds in definable *stages,* so that behavior and personality become somewhat restructured (in definable ways) as growth proceeds. The shifts in interest with the onset of adolescence would be one of the familiar aspects of such restructuring, but there are others of less obvious kind. The concepts of critical periods and of stages suggest that there are aspects of the developmental process inherent in growth, and not the result solely of learning. Hence the issue between inherent growth aspects, or *maturation,* and the result of experience, or *learning,* is one that has to be faced.

Embryological development as maturation

In all the higher forms of life a good deal of development takes place before birth, so that much hereditary potential has already manifested itself by the time the infant is born. At the same time, the infant is so relatively helpless at birth that we may think of development in the early months after birth as being an extension of the same sort of process that went on in the fetus, that is, an orderly development whose timing is determined more by the nature of the organism than by how it is handled. This is the assumption that *maturation* is important, which means that the timing and patterning of changes, beyond birth, are relatively independent of exercise and experience, and they go on despite wide variations in the environment, assuming, of course, that these variations occur within limits favorable to survival and growth. If birds whose wings have been restrained from birth learn to fly as quickly as birds that have fluttered their wings many days before they fly, we may reasonably say that flying is controlled more largely by maturation than by learning.

In its earliest stages the human embryo resembles that of other animals, but by the eighth week of existence it has acquired rudimentary human characteristics; from then until birth it is known as a *fetus.* Fetal development goes on in the uniform environment of the mother's body according to a relatively fixed time schedule. Fetal behavior, such as turning and kicking, also follows an orderly sequence, depending on the growth stages of the fetus. Studies have been made of the responsiveness to outside stimulation of the human fetus born prematurely, and more systematic studies have been made of fetal behavior in animals such as the guinea pig and cat. When the fetus is surgically removed from the mother in animal studies, the circulation of the blood in the fetus is maintained through the umbilical cord, which is not severed. Then the fetus is placed in a salt solution at body temperature. Now the response of the fetus to stimulation can be studied at successive stages, with the physiological condition of the fetus essentially normal (Figure 3–1). Such studies show the appearance of behavior patterns in a developmental sequence depending upon growth (i.e., fetal age) rather than upon prior external stimulation (Carmichael, 1954).

Transplantation experiments with simpler forms of life, such as sea urchins and salamanders, have helped biologists to understand the nature of the developmental processes in the embryo. At an early stage of the salamander's development a small group of cells known as "the organizer"

3–1

Maturation prior to birth

Since the guinea pig fetus has just been removed from the mother's body, it has not previously experienced stimulation from external stimuli. With mild stimulation above the eye the only response is closing of the eye (left), but with stronger stimulation the forepaw is raised to the stimulated spot. Fetal age, 51 days; birth is normally at 68 days. (After Carmichael and Smith, 1939, p. 432)

becomes very important. The *organizer* determines which will be the head end and which the tail end of the growing embryo. Previously undifferentiated cells begin to differentiate appropriately to their location, so that the embryonic salamander develops properly.

As development proceeds, subregions, such as the mouth region or eye region, are also "organized" by the environment of cells around them. That is, tissue from the belly region, if transplanted to the eye region or the mouth region at the appropriate stages, will conform to the new environment of cells and form an eye or a mouth.

Because the transplantation experiments work only when the developing organism is young enough, they also provide an illustration of *critical periods*. We find in embryological development many of the problems that will have to be considered in the study of development generally: species characteristics, internal and external environmental influences, critical periods and stages.

Orderly behavior patterns in infant development

As we have noted, the orderly development of the human organism begins long before birth. The regulation of fetal development lies within the organism's own tissues, although normal development requires the continuing protection and sustenance provided by the mother's body. Evidence that the timing of development is internally regulated can be found in prematurely born infants who, kept alive in an incubator that simulates the intra-uterine environment, develop at much the same rate as infants remaining in the uterus full term. The regularity of development before birth provides a clear picture of what is meant by maturation, for growth goes on in regular and predictable ways.

Postnatal maturation is regulated much like growth before birth. That is, many kinds of behavior follow orderly sequences little affected by environmental influences, provided only that the environment is sufficiently favorable to support the necessary growth. Such sequences are found in stand-

ing, walking, using hands and fingers, and talking. For example, every infant goes through such regular sequences of crawling and creeping before he walks upright that a uniform growth pattern is evidently responsible for the behavior.

Maturation of structure continues into adult life. Some of the growth changes at adolescence are internally regulated in a sequence not unlike the regulation of fetal development. To the extent that adolescent behavior corresponds to bodily changes, maturational principles apply. The changes associated with aging also go on at their own rates. While maturation is thus a lifelong process, its nature is most readily understood through observing infants and young children, in whom behavioral changes dependent upon growth are rapid and apparent.

Long before learning to walk, the infant goes through a number of movement stages related to this later and more complex behavior. An early form of "locomotion" is learning to roll over (Figure 3–2). Again this regularity of sequence suggests that a growth process determines the order of behavior. The alternative conclusion would be that all parents go through a training ritual which leads to this uniformity of performance from one child to another. We know, of course, that *all* parents do nothing of the sort. Not all children go through the sequence at the same rate; in general, the *order* in which they go from one stage to the next is more alike from infant to infant than the *age* at which they reach each stage. An idea of the range of variation from child to child is given in Figure 3–3, showing the age zones within which 95 percent of a group of infants reached a stated level of performance. Some of the zones spread over four or five months, indicating that some infants are four or five months ahead of others in reaching the stage of standing alone or walking alone.

The sequences of normal behavior lead to the conviction that growth lies beneath the development of behavior, and further evidence of the influence of maturation comes from experiments in which the en-

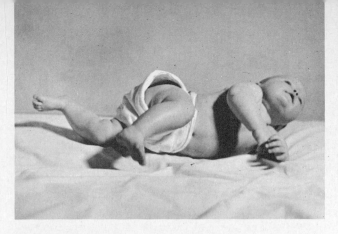

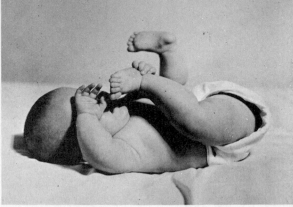

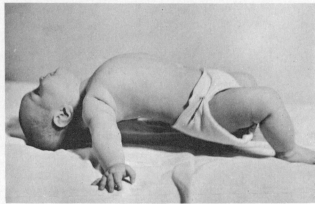

3–2

Muscular activity of babies at the rolling stage

This six-month-old baby discovers for itself movements that prepare it for further development and lead to its ability to walk later on.

3–3

Babies develop at differing rates

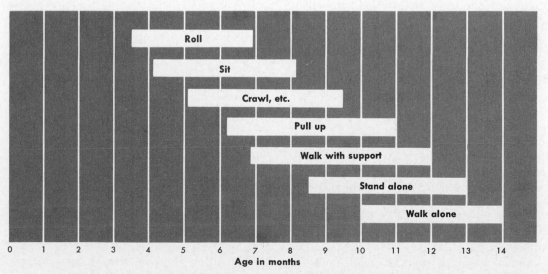

Although development is orderly, some infants reach each stage ahead of others. The bars show the zones of age within which 95 percent of infants in a well-baby clinic achieved the stated performances. (After Aldrich and Norval, 1946)

vironment is either restricted or enriched. If environmental variations produce little change in the rate of change of behavior, then it becomes clearer that the process is determined by growth *within* rather than by influence from *without*.

Observations of the effects of restricted movements have been made on human infants. Hopi Indians, for example, have traditionally kept their infants bound to a board carried on the mother's back. Some Hopi mothers continue to follow the custom, while others, because of contact with white American culture, do not. Although the cradleboard markedly restricts movements of the infant's arms and legs during the early months, children raised on it began (on the average) to walk at the same age as those who were never bound on it (Dennis and Dennis, 1940).

A similar study, made with a pair of fraternal twins (twins developed from separate eggs), provided similar results. The twin girls were kept in their cribs from the age of one month until the age of nine months. They were given no training of any kind and only a minimum of handling. They spent most of the time lying on their backs, their hands and feet under the bedclothes. Despite this marked restriction of activity, they developed normally in such behavior as putting their hands to their mouths, grasping objects, playing with their hands, and sitting up when propped. They did, however, fall slightly behind the norms for other children in the age at which they were able to walk holding onto furniture and that at which they were able to stand alone. There was no report of any permanent effect upon the ability to walk or upon other muscular skills (Dennis, 1935). Maturation thus appears to be an important influence, but too severe restrictions may cause some delay in development.

Maturation and readiness to learn

The practical (and theoretical) importance of recognizing the influence of maturation lies in the relation of maturation to the results of training at different ages. The idea here is that maturation may provide a *readiness to learn.* Most behavior is developed by *both* maturation and learning. Language provides a useful illustration. The child learns to talk only when he has *grown* old enough to learn (maturation), but the language he learns to talk is the one he *hears* (learning).

Imprinting. The manner in which inborn readiness affects what is later learned is well illustrated by the process of *imprinting,* a kind of learning that capitalizes upon an inherited tendency when the time is ripe. The clearest example is given by the tendency of a young duckling to start following its mother shortly after it is hatched, and then to follow only this particular female duck. Incubator-hatched ducklings can be imprinted upon artificial models, both inanimate and human. For example, mallard ducklings exposed to a moving model for 10 minutes between 12 and 17 hours after hatching will continue to treat that model as though it were the "mother" and will remain with it against the attraction of live mallard ducks (Figure 3–4). Once imprinting has occurred, the response of following will be elicited only by the imprinted object (Ramsay and Hess, 1954; Hess, 1959).

Critical periods. The discussion of imprinting suggests that this is a learned bit of behavior, but that it can be learned only at the right age. Later experiments have shown that the results are not quite as simple as this. Part of the reason that imprinting is difficult when the ducks are older is that they have developed fear responses which interfere with the imprinting; when they are given tranquilizers to reduce the fear, then they can be imprinted later (Hess, 1957). Still, in the normal course of events, we find one period much more favorable for this kind of learning than other periods in the life of the organism.

It has been noted in the training of seeing-eye dogs that the handling has to be adjusted very carefully to produce a faithful dog. In an experiment to test when human handling best produced a tame dog, Freedman, King, and Elliott (1961) raised puppies in a large field with tame mothers

3–4

Imprinting in ducklings

The newly hatched duckling learns to follow the model duck around a circular track.

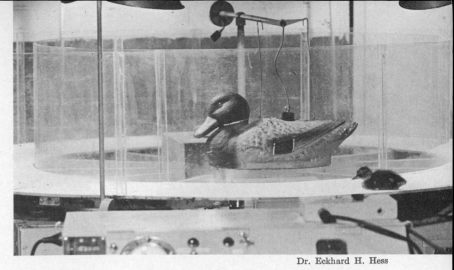

Dr. Eckhard H. Hess

but without human handlers. They were then removed at various ages to spend 10 minutes a day with a human handler who was passive, that is, who waited for them to approach him. If this was delayed as long as 14 weeks the puppies had become wild dogs, frightened and timid with human beings. The best time for taming was shown to be between five to seven weeks of age; when tamed at these ages, the dogs remained tame, as was seen when they were tested again 14 weeks later. Thus we have evidence for another critical period. Whether or not such critical periods occur for human infants is a matter of some dispute, but we need to be prepared to find evidence for them.

Some generalizations about maturation and learning in infancy and childhood

Studies of efforts to train young infants at different ages permit us to make a few generalizations about learning and maturation. Although most of these apply to muscular skills rather than to more subtle aspects of personal and social behavior, it may be that in the long run we will discover that critical periods have more to do with such matters as anxiety and self-confidence than with skills such as typing or bicycle riding.

1. *Skills that build upon developing behavior patterns are most easily learned.* In almost all languages there are words for

mother and father with sound patterns similar to *pa-pa* and *ma-ma*. The words which the infant usually acquires first are words like these which fit in most readily with his natural babbling. He can be taught words like *ma-ma, pa-pa, da-da, ba-ba, bye-bye,* because these words are like the sounds that he makes spontaneously.

2. *The rate of development remains uniform within wide ranges of stimulation.* The maturation of performance often requires environmental support, since growth alone is not enough to account for the resulting behavior. But maturation may still be fundamental in accounting for the *rate* of development. A study of stair-climbing by a pair of twins bears this out.

Twins T and C were identical twins, that is, twins developed from a single egg and with identical heredity. Because of their common heredity and similarity in development, they made an ideal pair for purposes of study. At the age of 46 weeks, the two twins showed no discernible difference in their behavior when placed at the bottom of a small staircase consisting of four treads and a platform that formed the fifth tread. As an initial test, the experimenter placed each twin before the staircase, while holding both hands. Each twin stepped forward and lifted one foot, but neither was able to place a foot or knee on the first tread.

Twin T was then given a daily 10-minute practice period in stair-climbing, while twin C (the "control" twin) was given no practice on stairs. At the end of six weeks,

T could climb the steps in a little over 25 seconds, while C had not progressed further than putting the left knee on the first tread. Now T's training was discontinued, and a week later C began a two-week period of training. In these two weeks she caught up with and surpassed T's performance at the end of six weeks of training. Twin C had the advantage because she was older when she began her practice. One week later, when both T and C were 56 weeks old, their performances on the experimental stairs were essentially alike. It did not matter at the end that one twin had had three times the specific training of the other (Gesell and Thompson, 1941).

Within very wide limits of encouragement and exercise (i.e., environment), the child learns to walk and talk only when old enough and continues to improve at his own rate (i.e., maturation).

3. *The more mature the organism, the less training is needed to reach a given level of proficiency.* Many experiments point to the faster gains of older children over younger, with the same amount of directed practice. Maturation thus produces a certain *readiness* for specific kinds of learning. The generalization applies only within the period of growth; after adult status is achieved, a decline in learning rate may set in.

An experiment on typing was conducted in the first five grades of a school. After one year of practice, children in the second grade were typing at an average rate of less than five words per minute, while those in the fifth grade were typing at an average rate of 10 words per minute. In each grade the average gain with one year's practice was greater than in any lower grade.

The experiment went on for two years. It was then found that children who had had two years of typing experience were typing no faster than children in the same grade who had only one year of experience (Wood and Freeman, 1932).

The results of this experiment show that the final rate of typing depends more upon the level of maturation than upon the amount of typing experience, thus conforming to the stated principle that the more

mature organism learns more readily. This principle would be limited were "critical periods" the rule for most kinds of learning.

4. *Training given before maturational readiness may bring either no improvement or only temporary improvement.* In an experiment in training in bladder control, conducted with two pairs of twins, an effort to train *one* member of each pair was begun shortly after birth, while no effort was made to train the other member of each pair. Training was ineffective until the infants were old enough; at that time the other two babies, previously untrained, learned very promptly. Although the two pairs of twins differed by some months in the time at which control was achieved, the trained and untrained member of each pair acquired control at the same time (McGraw, 1940). The necessary understanding awaited maturational readiness, and premature training was wasted. Any gains made under premature training are short-lived.

The temporary nature of improvements made beyond the natural maturational level is shown in some additional experiments done with the pair of identical twins who participated in the stair-climbing experiment.

When twins T and C were four years old, they participated in a number of experiments in which one was trained while the other received no training. The experiments included learning to cut with scissors, reciting digits, learning a ring-toss game, and maintaining balance while walking on boards of various widths. The experiments were so arranged that after a pretest of both twins only one was trained. Then there was a retest of both twins, followed by a period in which the second twin was trained. When training was stopped, both twins were retested three additional times at approximately 10-week intervals.

The typical result was that both twins profited by training, but that the one trained second gained more than the one trained first. After training was discontinued, there was loss in skill in both twins, as the performance dropped back to the level typical for children of their maturational

3–5

Temporary effects of training beyond maturational level

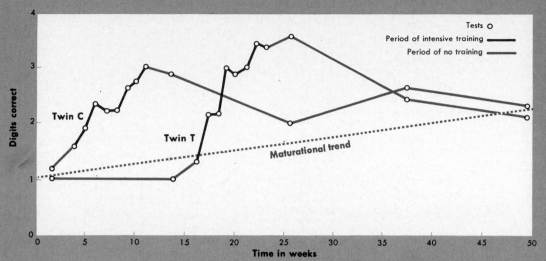

Both twins profited from intensive training in digit memory, the one trained when older gaining more rapidly than the one trained when younger. Without continued training, both fell back to the maturational trend level. (After J. R. Hilgard, 1933)

development. One of the tasks, digit memory, called for repeating numbers of several digits, spoken slowly by the experimenter. Results for digit memory are plotted in Figure 3–5 (J. R. Hilgard, 1933).

There was thus no evidence of permanent gain from training that had taken place too near the ceiling of ability for these twins.

5. *Premature training, if frustrating, may do more harm than good.* Although lack of training delays development, the lack appears to do no harm, for the retardation is overcome when practice begins. What is the effect of overstimulation, that is, premature training, before maturational readiness? May it also retard development?

The child who has been exposed too early to an activity for which he is not ready may lose his natural enthusiasm for the activity when he reaches the stage of development appropriate for it. This loss was noted in an experiment in which there was a daily effort to teach a one-year-old to ride a tricycle. The experimenter observed, after the experiment was over, that the child's seven months of futile effort to

ride the tricycle curtailed the interest that he would have shown later had the training been delayed (McGraw, 1943).

Experiments concerned with methods of drilling in arithmetic suggest that pressure for speed before the child is ready may actually interfere with learning. When tested after two years of speed drill, children who had been able to master arithmetic in the first grade when taught without pressure for speed did not do as well as they had in the first grade (Myers, 1928).

CRITICAL DISCUSSION

Generalizations from maturation and problems of educational readiness

Considerable interest has developed recently among educators in the improvement of educational practices, especially in regard to the teaching of more "advanced" subjects at earlier ages. Previously the maturational concepts had led to the postponement of some subjects until the learner was "ready," according to the principles that premature training is wasteful or even harmful (the last two principles stated in the foregoing discussion). The concept of postponement, of waiting for development, has come under particular attack (Tyler, 1964). The questions that arise are these: (1) Are the generalizations from the earlier studies of maturation wrong? (2) Do the desires of the educators to get the more difficult subjects taught earlier fly in the face of developmental facts? (3) Is there some way of accepting both the maturational facts and the proposed educational practices?

The maturational facts are indeed quite well established, and, as we shall see, new support is given to them by the interpretations of stages in cognitive growth coming from Piaget (see p. 71). At the same time, we have many convincing demonstrations of the teaching of difficult subject matters early, when new methods are used. Teaching reading to children of age three and four by means of an electric typewriter that "speaks" the name of the letter as it is typed is a case in point (Moore, 1965). On a larger scale, teaching the reading of English by using a more purely phonetic alphabet (the Initial Teaching Alphabet, or ITA) appears to get much quicker result than older methods and with younger children (Harrison, 1964).

The contradiction between the maturational principles and the educational facts can be resolved by the recognition that successful educational practices rest on more than maturation alone. Successful teaching depends as well upon (1) the structuring of the material to be learned in suitable form for the learner, (2) the arousal of appropriate motives, and (3) the acquisition of the necessary prior learning. If the maturational stage is appropriate, then learning can run smoothly if the other conditions are also met. There is some circularity involved, for the conditions cannot be met if the child is not far enough along to have acquired the necessary experience, and if the material is not presented appropriately to the developmental level. Hence we see that there is no basic conflict at a theoretical level; the uncertainties are at a practical level. One way of stating this is to use a hypothesis suggested by Bruner (1960) that "any subject can be taught in a manner that is intellectually honest to a child at any stage of development." While he does not propose that there should be postponement, he does propose adapting the material to the level of understanding of the child. Hence the practical problem is one of this matching of material to be learned with the learner; no contradiction to maturational principles is involved.

There is an issue of efficiency, however, which will eventually have to be answered. No doubt many difficult subjects can be taught early (e.g., symbolic logic) but there is still the question whether or not such early teaching is a mere "stunt" with little in the way of cumulative gains to recommend it, as in the case of the typing experiments reported. Just because something *can* be taught earlier does not mean that it *should* be taught earlier.

Evidence for remote consequences of early developmental experiences

The developmental point of view stresses the continuity between early and later development. To the extent that this is a matter of maturation it is characteristic of the species, and (unless there has been severe deficit with stunting of development) we merely wait for the interactions with the environment to produce their expected effects. But this is by no means the whole story, and we wish to know how individual experience, of either deprivation or unusual stimulation, is reflected in later years.

Infant chimpanzees were reared in the dark for seven months. When removed from the dark, they failed to show the normal blinking response to an object moving toward their eyes. Even when a large yellow- and black-striped disk was connected repeatedly with electric shock, they showed no signs of recognizing (and avoiding) it, although normal animals develop avoidance responses after one or two mild shocks. Three such animals were used in this part of the experiment; a fourth, of the same age, had been in the light for one and a half hours each day. His reactions to light after seven months were entirely normal. Being raised in the dark may cause some injury to the eyes, but in addition there are behavioral defects that are gradually removed by practice, such as the inability to converge the eyes upon an object. These results led to more careful study of normal chimpanzee infants, and it was found that their visual development was rather slow, with blinking in response to moving objects in the visual field not appearing until the age of two months. The animals raised in the dark took about two weeks to acquire the response after they had been brought into the light. Thus fully adequate use of vision in the chimpanzee depends both upon internal growth factors continuing after birth and upon practice in the use of vision (Riesen, 1950).

In another experiment, dogs reared in confined quarters so that they did not have the opportunity to explore the environment were perfectly healthy, but in some respects appeared stupid (Melzack and Scott, 1957). For one thing, they seemed quite insensitive to pain. They did not respond to a pin prick or to having their tails stepped on. They would investigate a lighted match by putting a nose into the flame; this would be repeated time after time, without any of the avoidance reaction expected from a normal dog. Whatever the felt experience may have been to the dog, certainly the pain stimulus did not evoke the compelling responses found in the normal dog.

A curious effect of early experience upon emotional responsiveness, and development generally, has been reported, based on experiments with white rats. The experimenter subjected one group of young rats to mild electric shocks, expecting to produce some abnormalities in behavior later on. As controls he had two other groups of young rats, one handled as the shocked rats were, but without shocks, the other merely left in the nest and not handled at all. The result of the experiment was unexpected: the shocked rats after they grew up were not distinguishable from those handled but not shocked; it was the non-handled rats that showed the abnormalities! They were particularly timid when placed in a new environment, crouching in the corner rather than exploring the open cage as normal rats do. Other lines of evidence showed that the handled (or shocked) rats devel-

oped more rapidly in many respects, opening their eyes sooner, gaining weight more rapidly, growing larger. Later, under stress, the handled animals were found to have a more rapid response from the adrenal glands than the nonhandled ones. Thus the handling produced profound changes in development, reflected in changes of the regulatory systems within the body as well as in overt behavior (Levine, 1962).

We may well ask whether or not we can find comparable evidence in human growth for the effects of stressful experiences in early infancy. One place to look might be for effects on adult height, for the experiments on animals showed pronounced changes in size as a result of infantile stress. Two investigators set out to find what evidence they could for stress in infancy and adult height in men (Landauer and Whiting, 1964).

For many years anthropologists have been gathering information on nonliterate cultures all over the world. A cooperative enterprise has resulted in the depositing of relevant information on all available cultures in a collection known as the Human Relations Area Files, originating at Yale University but with copies now deposited in many libraries. Evidence on both infant care and adult size exists for many cultures in these records. Landauer and Whiting found 80 cultures for which the evidence seemed adequate, and then they proceeded to classify these cultures separately for (a) stressful treatment of infant boys, and (b) adult male size. The stressful events that were selected for study were *piercing* (piercing the nose, lips, or ear to receive an ornament; circumcision, innoculation, scarification, or cauterization) and *molding* (stretching the arms or legs or shaping the head, usually for the sake of some preferred appearance). The study was repeated on two separate samples of cultures for whom the evidence was clear, with the usual care to avoid bias through having the classification into stressed and nonstressed childcare practices done by persons not familiar with the hypothesis being tested. The results for the two samples are given in Table 3–1. The somewhat surprising result for

TABLE 3–1

Adult male height in inches as related to infant stress

| | *Piercing or molding during first 24 months of life* | |
	Present	Absent
First sample	65.2 ($N = 17$)	62.7 ($N = 18$)
Second sample	66.1 ($N = 19$)	63.4 ($N = 11$)
Combined sample	65.7 ($N = 36$)	63.0 ($N = 29$)

Significance of difference between combined means, by *t*-test, $P < .001$.*

SOURCE: After Landauer and Whiting (1964), pp. 1101–12.

* Significant statements of this kind will appear in tables from time to time. The statement ("$P < .001$") can be interpreted as follows: "The probability that a difference of the magnitude found would arise through chance is less than 1 in 1,000." The letter N refers to the number of cases in a sample. See Chapter 15.

both samples was that the males stressed in infancy averaged 2.7 inches taller than those not so stressed.

This finding is in accordance with the animal studies, but it is, of course, subject to some reservations. The authors themselves looked for any confounding factors that they could find, such as different racial stock, different amounts of available food, or different climates, but they were not able to find any alternate explanation. The Spartan explanation that those cultures which treated their infants more harshly had only the fittest and strongest survive cannot be completely ruled out, for these practices may have gone on for many generations. A supplementary finding, which is of some interest in relation to the animal work, is that the adult stature appears to be affected when the stress occurs within the first two years rather than later in childhood. This has to do with the problem of "critical periods" in human development. It may be that the first two years are critical for the stresses affecting physical size.

These investigations, taken together, suggest that early experiences are very important in both higher animals and man in providing the background for coping with the environment when they are older. The implications for child-rearing practices are not firm, but they suggest that a certain amount of fondling and stimulation are important for development, and that neglect may be more harmful than some degree of stress. The parents who are so proud of the "good" baby who lies quietly in the crib may not in fact be giving to that baby what is best for him.

Stages in Development

Another problem to be faced in assessing the continuities between early and later life is whether or not there are definable stages through which the individual goes as he grows up, with their special problems to be surmounted. Perhaps growth is not actually at a steady rate but is instead somewhat steplike, as one stage is left and another one entered. We define such crude stages as a matter of common practice, as we distinguish between successive periods such as infancy, childhood, adolescence, and adulthood. This may, however, be in part a matter of age-grading, a practice very common in our culture: some behavior is recognized as less mature than other behavior, and we compliment a child by telling him that he is acting like a "big boy" or a "big girl." We have to look more carefully at the evidence to see whether or not there are, in fact, distinct stages.

The relationship between critical periods and stages is close but the two concepts are not identical. The critical period principle assumes that at a given stage of development some kinds of influences are unusually important. If they are lacking there will be later stunting of development, while if they are favorable there may be a promising later fulfillment. Failures at this period can only be made up, if at all, with great difficulty. The notion of stages is related, in that a failure to deal adequately with the developmental problems or tasks at that stage will somewhat cripple the development at the subsequent stage. However, the organism might still have definable stages in development, even though the stages were not tightly hierarchical with respect to many important abilities; thus a child goes through adolescence whether or not he has been taught to read as a preadolescent, and he can still learn to read as an adult. Learning to read is thus not stage-dependent in the critical period sense. What is critical, and what is stage-related, can be found out only by study.

Stages in cognitive development

The one who has done the most to make the stage concept plausible in human development is the Swiss psychologist Jean Piaget. He has been interested for many years in the development of individual children, with a primary focus on their cognitive or intellectual development. Although his work has been known to American psychologists for three decades, it has recently been receiving renewed attention. The

main stages of intellectual development according to Piaget are presented in somewhat simplified form in Table 3–2.

In careful observations of infants in the first months after birth, Piaget has noted the close interplay between action and perception, hence the designation *sensorimotor* period. One consequence of the manipulations that the infant makes and of his "playing" with the environment is what is called *object-attainment*, that is, the awareness that an object, seen from different angles, is an enduring something, the "same" object that it was before. For example, when the infant has learned to hold a bottle and nurse from it, if the bottle is presented in reversed form, he will try to suck the glass bottom. Later, however, when he recognizes the bottle for what it is as an enduring object, he will turn it around in order to suck on the nipple.

TABLE 3–2
Piaget's stages of intellectual development

Stage	Approximate ages	Characterization
I. Sensorimotor period	Birth to 2 years	Infant differentiates himself from objects; seeks stimulation, and makes interesting spectacles last; prior to language, meanings defined by manipulations, so that object remains "the same object" with changes in location and point of view.
II. Preoperational thought period		
Preoperational phase	2–4	Child egocentric, unable to take viewpoint of other people; classifies by single salient features; if A is like B in one respect, must be like B in other respects.
Intuitive phase	4–7	Is now able to think in terms of classes, to see relationships, to handle number concepts, but is "intuitive" because he may be unaware of his classification. Gradual development of *conservation* in this order: mass (age 5), weight (age 6), and volume (age 7).*
III. Period of concrete operations	7–11	Able now to use logical operations such as *reversibility* (in arithmetic), *classification* (organizing objects into hierarchies of classes), and *seriation* (organizing objects into ordered series, such as increasing size.)
IV. Period of formal operations	11–15	Final steps toward abstract thinking and conceptualization; capable of hypothesis-testing.

SOURCE: After Piaget, modified from Sigal (1964).

* Ages for 50 percent passing, according to Kooistra (1963).
The ages given by Piaget and Inhelder (1941) are generally higher.

Other evidence that the infant has formed an object concept comes when he removes a cloth concealing an object or searches for hidden or lost objects. These events, so much taken for granted, in Piaget's hands have become a source of developmental principles.

The kinds of evidence that Piaget and his co-workers have used in studying thought problems of children in a slightly later stage (intuitive stage of preoperational thought) can be illustrated by the development of what he calls *conservation*, during the ages of four to seven, approximately. As adults we take the conservation principle for granted: the amount (mass) of a substance is not changed when its shape is changed or when it is divided into parts; the total weight of a set of objects will remain the same no matter how they are packaged together, and liquids do not change volume by being changed from a container of one shape to that of another. But not so for children: to attain these concepts of conservation is an important aspect of intellectual growth that requires several years.

To study the conservation of mass, a child is given some plastic clay to make into a ball equal to another ball of the material; he declares them to be "the same." Now, leaving one for reference, the other is rolled out into a long sausage shape. If the child is about four years old, the two objects do not now (for him) contain the same amount of clay: the longer one contains more. Not until five years can we expect half the children to have reached the stage where the clay in five balls made from one larger one is perceived to be the same amount of clay as that in the original large ball (Piaget and Inhelder, 1941; Kooistra, 1963).

The same kind of experiment can be used to study the conservation of weight and volume. For example, the child who knows that equal things will balance on a scale (he can test this with the two balls to begin with), is then asked whether the sausage-shaped ball will keep the scale arm straight out the way the original ball did. This is a harder task of conservation than conservation of mass or amount, and comes about a year later in development. To do the experiment with volume, the child first sees that the equal-sized balls will raise the water level in a graduated cylinder an equal amount. Now asked whether the sausage shape will raise the water a like amount the child doubts it until still older—typically another year.

Conservation has not been fully attained when mass, weight, and volume are seen as conserved; there are other problems of horizontality, length, area, number, and duration. We shall meet some of the issues of concept formation later on (Chapter 14). At this point we are interested in the developmental theory that is involved.

We may ask: Are the sequences that are found to be understood as a result of inherent development (maturation) rather than as a result of prior experience? Can training speed up the transition to a higher stage?

The answers to such questions cannot be given with assurance at this time, although there are many kinds of evidence bearing upon the answers. The evidence in answer to the first of these two questions is consistent, coming as it does from many studies that show the *sequences* of stages to be similar to those that Piaget describes (e.g., conservation of mass, weight, and volume, in that order). Answers to the second question come from the effort to train children in a later stage when they are not quite there according to tests at the earlier stage. Some experiments of Smedslund (1961) are instructive in this respect. In the first place, he was able to show that children of five and a half to six and a half were able to acquire the principle of conservation of mass (amount), especially if taught in the presence of conflict. For example, when the plastic clay was rolled into an elongated shape (to make it appear longer), some of it was at the same time removed (to make it appear smaller). This made the child reflect on what was happening, and he was thus able to learn the principle of conservation without the use of any special rewards. Of interest from the viewpoint of the developmental significance of stages of learning, children who had acquired a conservation concept naturally rather than by training held on to it against challenging experimental conditions, in which, for example, the experimenter removed a bit of clay without their seeing it. When they said that the two pieces should weigh alike (by balancing on a scale) and he proved they no longer weighed alike (by demonstrating this on the scale), those who had come by the conservation of weight naturally said that some must have fallen on the floor, while those who had been trained experimentally went back to their nonconservation explanations (Smedslund, 1961).

Taken together, these experiments bring conservation into line with other experiments on maturation, showing that special training is effective but that there tends to be a reversion to the developmental level that has been gradually acquired over time.

It is to Piaget's credit that his stages of intellectual growth have some genuine elements of discovery within them. So much of scientific evidence in the area of child growth is merely an elaboration of what we already know, such as making our knowledge more precise about the increase of vocabulary with age. But Piaget has pointed out what we did not know on a common sense basis, such as the difficulty in achieving the concept of conservation of mass, weight, and volume (and in that order of increasing difficulty). Because of Smedslund's work showing how difficult it is to teach children to gain the concepts beyond their developmental stages and of the tendency to revert to an earlier stage even after training, we may interpret Piaget's findings as essentially coherent with a maturational viewpoint. Of course, appropriate learning must take place at the earlier stage before the next stage can be mastered, but this is equally true of other processes that exhibit some internal (maturational) regulating mechanism. Thus Piaget's work gives support to a restructuring that goes on at certain periods in development, breaking a mere steady accumulation of changes. This is the essence of a stage theory.

Psychosexual and psychosocial stages

Another type of stage theory was proposed by Sigmund Freud. In some respects it is a more comprehensive theory than Piaget's because it is concerned with the whole personality in its emotional and motivational aspects; it is like Piaget's, however, in assuming rather clearly definable stages.

Freud considered the childhood stages as having to do with deriving pleasure from different zones of the body at different ages, leading up to the gratifications of adult sexuality. By using a very broad definition of sexuality, these stages came to be known as *psychosexual* stages, of which the chief ones were *oral* (gratification through stimulation of the lips and mouth region, as in nursing or thumbsucking), *anal* (gratification through withholding and expelling feces), *phallic* (gratification through fondling the sex organs), *Oedipal* (a sexual desire for the parent that is said to be concurrent with the phallic phase, the name deriving from Oedipus who, in the Greek tragedy, fell in love with his mother and was punished for it), *latency* (in which sexual interests are no longer active, so that the child of elementary school age turns his interests to the environment), and, finally, *genital*, at which point normal heterosexual interests arise. Each of the earlier stages is normally outgrown, but there may be arrested development ("fixation"), in which event some of the problems associated with an earlier stage persist beyond their normal time; in this respect the theory is also a critical period theory. This classification of stages, while it has been influential and is still adhered to by some practicing psychoanalysts, is not generally accepted by psychologists as a precise statement of development, whatever partial truths there may be within it.

A later psychoanalyst, Erikson (1963), has proposed another way of looking at stages of development. He describes a progression of *psychosocial* stages in which the child faces a wider range of human relationships as he grows up and has specific problems to be solved at each of these

TABLE 3–3

Eight stages of psychosocial development

Stages (with approximate ages)	Psychosocial crises	Radius of significant relations	Psychosocial modalities	Favorable outcome
I. Birth through first year	Trust vs. mistrust	Maternal person	To get To give in return	Drive and hope
II. Through second year	Autonomy vs. shame, doubt	Parental persons	To hold (on) To let (go)	Self-control and willpower
III. Third year through fifth year	Initiative vs. guilt	Basic family	To make (going after) To "make like" (playing)	Direction and purpose
IV. Sixth to onset of puberty	Industry vs. inferiority	"Neighborhood"; school	To make things (competing) To make things together	Method and competence
V. Adolescence	Identity and repudiation vs. identity diffusion	Peer groups and outgroups; models of leadership	To be oneself (or not to be) To share being oneself	Devotion and fidelity
VI. Early adult	Intimacy and solidarity vs. isolation	Partners in friendship, sex, competition, cooperation	To lose and find oneself in another	Affiliation and love
VII. Young and middle adult	Generativity vs. self-absorption	Divided labor and shared household	To make be To take care of	Production and care
VIII. Later adult	Integrity vs. despair	"Mankind" "My Kind"	To be, through having been To face not being	Renunciation and wisdom

SOURCE: Erikson (1959), p. 166; Erikson (1963), p. 274; slightly modified from original.

stages. Again, as with Freud, how well the child solves his problems at any one stage may determine how adequate a person he will become later and how well he will be able to cope with new problems as they arise.

Erikson's psychosocial stages of development are listed and characterized in the table above. There is enough plausibility to the issues raised within Erikson's stages to make his scheme a useful one in calling attention to problems of social development. It lacks, however, the rigor of a strictly scientific delineation of stages, and its appeal must be thought of as literary unless more precise evidence in support of it is forthcoming.

Conclusions on stages and critical periods

The evidence on stages of development and on critical periods in human development is far from conclusive. Overlapping of one "stage" with another appears more common than a sharp transition, and seldom is there a deficiency from an earlier period that cannot be corrected later. Thus, while it is doubtless advantageous to learn to read early in life, many persons learn to read as adults, with some of them going on to careers as writers and scholars.

Some of the evidence favoring critical periods and stages is promising, however, and the issues involved are important enough to deserve investigation.

Personality Development in Early Childhood

We shall now turn from the more general problems of development to some specific problems, both practical and theoretical, that arise out of child-care practices, particularly as these affect the personality and social behavior of the growing individual. Different peoples use different child-care practices, and even within one country the many social groups may raise their children in different ways. We wish to discover how these practices mold the child's personality and how they prepare him for life in the society of other people.

Early socialization

Cultural influences begin at birth; from the very first day of life we begin to civilize the child. Among the important early influences are those concerned with feeding and with toilet training.

Psychological accompaniments of feeding. What goals does a civilized mother have in mind when she begins to feed her baby? She wishes to do two things: to nourish him and to train him to eat properly. Good nourishment is primarily a matter of physiology, although cultural standards may enter—some cultures insist on fat babies, while others prefer them sturdy. "Proper" eating, then, depends upon practices within the culture. For example, in American middle-class culture, the mother looks forward to raising a three-meal-a-day child who will eat noiselessly and without spilling, who will consume everything on his plate, and who will use knife, fork, and spoon correctly. The expectations of the mother may cause a great many difficulties both for her and for the child before these ends are accomplished.

The infant-feeding practices of the last few decades in America give us an instructive example of the way in which cultural expectations determine what we ask of the infant. Between 1920 and 1940, nearly all pediatricians recommended for the newborn child a regular feeding schedule which had the goal of a three-meal-a-day child distantly in view. The infant wards in most hospitals adopted the four-hour schedule: 6 A.M., 10 A.M., 2 P.M., 6 P.M., 10 P.M., and 2 A.M. Parents wished their child to learn to eat at mealtimes normal to the usual routine of adult life (and to disturb that routine as little as possible!), and so they tried to eliminate the 2 A.M. feeding as soon as they could. The four-hour feeding schedule thus represented a compromise between the needs of the child and parental desires in our middle-class culture. Not all babies conformed well to this schedule, and in the attempt to hold to it many parents had to tolerate an inordinate amount of crying before feeding their infants.

In the early 1940s the pendulum began to swing away from a fixed feeding schedule to a "self-demand schedule." According to this practice, whenever the infant cried the nurse picked him up, patted him to expel air, changed his diaper, and replaced him in his crib. If he did not stop crying, the nurse fed him. In one experiment using this method the only restriction imposed was that the feedings could not occur at intervals of less than one hour (D. P. Marquis, 1941). The natural feeding rhythm, as judged from this study, appears to be somewhat variable, usually three hours or more between feedings, but seldom as long as four hours within the first week after birth. Even during these first days the length of time between feedings at night was longer (3.6 hours) than during the day (2.9 hours). The preferred schedule was subject to fluctuation as the infant grew older.

The enthusiastic adoption of the self-demand schedule perhaps went too far, and there is now a tendency to return to a regulated schedule adapted to the infant, thus achieving the advantages of both regularity and respect for the individuality of the infant.

It has been conjectured that in order to have satisfying feeding experiences an infant needs to suck; that is, an infant can be emotionally "starved" from too little sucking just as he can be nutritionally starved from too little food. Those who

3-6

Breast-feeding and increased vigor of sucking

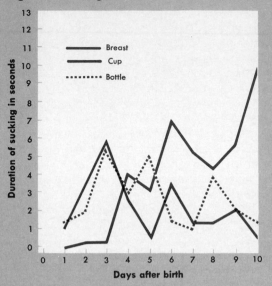

Sucking on a finger guard shows an increase following breast-feeding, but no corresponding increase with cup- and bottle-feeding. Twenty infants in each group. (After Davis, Sears, Miller, and Brodbeck, 1948)

receive their food supply too rapidly and easily through large holes in the bottles' nipples are said to make up for the lack of sucking during eating by sucking their hands or bedclothes or other objects accessible to their lips. According to one study, from the first week until the fourth month of life infants require two hours of sucking per day, either during the eating period or at other times (Ribble, 1943).

Another possibility exists, however—that the need to suck is derived from the experience of sucking. Infants fed from a cup from birth show much less evidence of a need to suck than those who are breast-fed from birth (Davis, Sears, Miller, and Brodbeck, 1948). The increased vigor of sucking by those breast-fed over those fed from a bottle or a cup is shown in Figure 3-6. A later study has shown that infants whose sucking was much encouraged showed resistance to weaning. When they were four or five years old, if given a choice

between a suckable food (lollipop) and a nonsuckable one (a piece of chocolate), they more often chose the lollipop (Bernstein, 1955).

The emotional consequences of weaning, like those of bottle-feeding, are harsh only if weaning is harshly handled. If the child suddenly loses the comfort of his mother's caresses, if he ends the mealtime hungry because of his dislike for new food or his lack of skill with new eating instruments, he will be physically unsatisfied and emotionally disturbed. The result may well be feelings of insecurity which may have later psychological consequences.

Closely related to the fact that sucking serves more than a nutritive purpose is the widespread practice of thumb sucking among infants. Habitual thumb sucking is found to occur in roughly 25 to 50 percent of children, with a slightly higher incidence among girls than among boys (Caldwell, 1964). The pattern is fairly durable, once it starts, with some 80 percent of those who ever get started still sucking their thumbs at age two; the average age for abandoning the habit is just under four years (Traisman and Traisman, 1958). Two opposing theories are used to account for the relationship between feeding and non-nutritive sucking: (1) that too rapid feeding produces a need to suck that has to be supplied by non-nutritive sucking; (2) that prolonged sucking (delayed weaning) establishes the sucking habit. Yarrow (1954) suggests that both theories may be true, but specific to phases of development, the first applying to the early months of life, when the habit may be established through frustration, the second applying to the later months when it is prolonged through strengthening by practice.

Toilet training. Training for cleanliness, like training for feeding, has first of all a hygienic purpose. By teaching the infant to keep his diapers dry and clean, the mother protects him from skin irritation produced by waste products from his body, and from the dangers of infection. In addition, the training leads to conduct which in our culture is considered proper and admirable and, of course, saves trouble for the mother once training is successful. A mother in our culture is proud when her baby achieves the ability to stay dry and unsoiled and when he confines elimination to the places provided for it.

It may be that the child experiences primitive emotional satisfactions from the relief of tension in the bladder or the bowels, corresponding to the satisfactions he gets from the relief of hunger tension when he eats. He may experience annoyance and conflict if there is excessive pressure to make him conform to adult demands. Control comes slowly, and, as we saw earlier (p. 66), experiments show that efforts to train yield little success if they are begun too soon. Instead of learning to control his bladder and bowels, the child is perhaps dimly aware of not coming up to expectations, and the parent, too, has a sense of disappointment and of failure which may be communicated to the child. Generally a child is not ready for control until he can take the initiative in indicating his desires by means of word or gesture.

Closely related to remaining dry and unsoiled are the properties we know as modesty. (Modesty has sexual connotations as well, but in the beginning the distinctions between toilet functions and sexual functions are either not made or are unclear.) The toilet functions are private; they go on behind closed doors and are not supposed to be talked about to strangers. Similarly, the parts of the body involved in these performances are private, not to be exposed to view, not to be played with. It is in connection with these parts of the body that the child becomes sensitive to taboos.

Highly conventionalized ways of acting are so familiar by the time we become adults that they appear to be "natural." But the child often is unable to meet the standards expected of him because these "natural" ways are in part artificial, and sometimes contradictory. After he begins to learn about modesty and privacy at home, he may go to a nursery school where the bathroom doors remain open. He is usually told not to undress before other people, yet he is expected to let the new maid give him a bath or to strip for examination by a nurse or physician. If he undresses before the doctor, he is a good boy; if he undresses in the front yard, he is a bad boy. If he goes to the bathroom "all by himself," he is praised and told that he is really a big boy now; but if he urinates against a tree in pleased imitation of a dog, he is scolded, perhaps spanked. Modesty, as our society interprets the word, is not at all "natural," and long and patient training is needed before it can seem so to a child. Those discriminations between what is permitted, and where, and what is not permitted are hard for a child to understand.

The accepted methods of infant feeding and cleanliness training are designed to maximize the child's sense of comfort, well-being, and security, and to minimize his feelings of annoyance and anxiety, within the limits of parental convenience and social convention.

The processes of infant care and child rearing are incompletely described according to feeding schedules, disciplinary practices, and the like, because the process is a subtle, social one involving the interaction between the helpless and sensitive infant and the available adult caretakers. Attitudes of acceptance and warmth (or their opposites of rejection and coldness) may be communicated despite variations in specific training methods. Hence we turn now to consider the development of social attachments, intimately related to methods of handling the child.

The development of social attachments. Much of child-care literature in the past has focused almost exclusively upon the mother, partly because of an emphasis upon nursing, weaning, and toilet training, in which she is likely to be the central figure. More recent studies have shown that other human beings in the environment (father, brothers and sisters, other caretakers) enter the picture in important ways.

In a careful study of 60 normal infants (31 males and 29 females) from the earliest months through the age of 18 months, Schaffer and Emerson (1964) studied the

The development of attachments during the first year of life

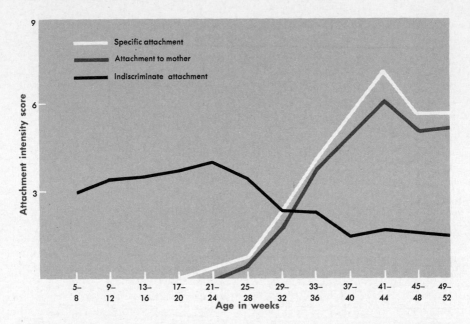

Attachment was measured by the amount of protest made by the infant when separated from the person to whom he was then close. Attachments are indiscriminate during the first six months or so, then become specific to recognized persons, with a peak at seven months. As specific attachments develop, indiscriminate ones weaken. (After Schaffer and Emerson, 1964)

development of attachment to the mother, specific attachments to other discriminated persons, and fear of strangers. While there were some individual differences, specific attachments to the mother and to other persons began at about seven months, and fear of strangers developed a little later, with usually about a month between the showing of specific attachment and fear. It is of interest that the specific attachments to the mother were commonly accompanied by specific attachments to others, usually, but not exclusively, the father (Figure 3–7). Attachment was measured by the amount of protest shown when separated from the person with whom the infant was then comfortable and close.

Other lines of evidence show also that social discrimination between those who are strange and those who are familiar begins during the second half of the first year. For example, the infant tends to smile at a strange face between the ages of two and six months, but thereafter, as detection of strangers begins, the smiling tends to be confined to those familiar (Spitz, 1946). Schaffer and Emerson propose a three-stage theory of the development of attachments. In the first stage the infant seeks stimulation of any kind from the environment, whether or not it is social. In the second stage he begins to find people the most interesting and satisfying agents in the environment, and seeks closeness to them, without expressing much preference among them. Finally, he narrows his interests to selected people; at this stage his reactions are truly social.

It was formerly thought that the beginning of social attachment came about because the mother, as a source of food, met the infant's needs, reduced tensions, and hence was satisfying. It is now felt, however, that the source of attachment may

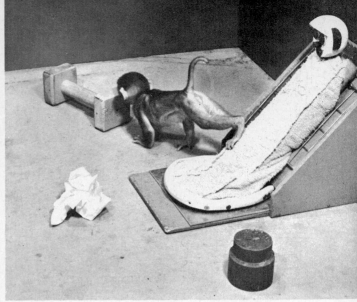

Gordon Coster from *Scientific American*

3–8

A monkey's response to an artificial mother

Left: Although fed via the wire "mother," the infant spends more time with the terry-cloth mother. *Right:* The inert "mother" is a safe base from which to explore the world. Experiments of Harlow (1958); Harlow and Zimmerman (1959).

have nothing particularly to do with the mother as a source of food. This was indicated in the foregoing account by the fact that attachments occurred equally well to other people. Experiments with animals have also borne out this suggestion.

Some species of animals, such as young ducklings, feed themselves from birth, yet they follow their mothers around closely and spend a great deal of time in contact with their mother; the comfort they derive from the mother cannot come from the mother's role in feeding.

More dramatic are some experiments with young monkeys reared in isolation from their true mothers but permitted to feed from and cling to artificial mothers (Harlow and Zimmerman, 1959). Two "laboratory mothers" were provided with arrangements permitting the young monkeys to obtain milk by sucking. Both "mothers" were immobile and, although they had torsos, heads, and faces, they did not much resemble monkey mothers (see Figure 3–8). One of the laboratory mothers was constructed of wire, so that, while the

young monkey could cling to it, it could scarcely be described as "cuddly." The other, covered with terry cloth (of Turkish towel type) was more "cuddly" than the wire model.

The experiment consisted in seeing whether, if one "mother" was always the source of food, that mother would be the one to which the young monkey would cling. The results were dramatic: no matter which mother was the source of food, the infant monkey spent his time clinging to the terry-cloth "cuddly" mother. This purely passive but soft-contact mother served as a source of security for the monkey. For example, when the infant monkey was placed in a strange environment in which he showed great signs of fear, the fear was allayed if the infant could make contact with the cloth mother. While holding to her with one hand he was willing to explore objects that were otherwise too terrifying to approach.

More recent experiments show that in monkeys inadequate experience with other monkeys (particularly other young monkeys) in early life makes mating difficult when they become adult; females without such contact will make very poor mothers (Harlow and Harlow, 1966). While contact with artificial mothers is an important contribution of "mothering," it is not sufficient to produce satisfactory development.

During the air raids of World War II in England, many young children became separated from their parents, and a series of studies were made as to the consequences of such separation. Children whose parents were alive and available were often sent to residential nurseries because of the conditions under which the parents were forced to live—for example, spending their nights crowded into an underground shelter.

The case of Patrick, a boy of three years and two months, is illustrative (Freud and Burlingham, 1943). He was first evacuated to a country home but "fretted" so much that he was returned, and—after hospitalization for measles—came to live at the Hampstead Nursery, a residential center for children. He gradually developed a kind of ritual in which he would nod his head compulsively and repeat over and over again: "My mother will put on my overcoat and take me home again." Every effort to reach him with understanding words, affection, and sympathy failed; a visit from his father did not help. Only having his mother come and stay in the house helped; he clung to her much as the baby monkeys clung to the terry-cloth mother. An interesting feature of the case was that after this restoration he came gradually to accept his mother's absence, although the transition required three or four weeks. The authors of this account believe that the suddenness of the separation is often the cause of the most serious reactions by the children.

Residential treatment in such nurseries, as contrasted with life in a single-family home, had varying effects upon development. Such adjustments as good eating habits and the development of muscular control seem to favor the residential children, while those adjustments of more emotional significance, such as the social responsiveness to people (in the ages of five

months to 12 months), cleanliness training, and acquiring language, place the residential child at a disadvantage (Freud and Burlingham, 1944).

The human being is, however, resilient, and a poor beginning does not "doom" a child for the rest of his days; his subsequent experiences are important. Maas (1963) studied 20 adults who had been evacuated during World War II from London to small residential nurseries in the country. He found that most of them were getting along satisfactorily in their adult roles, although those separated from home under one year of age seemed to show somewhat more personality disturbance.

Language and socialization

Learning to talk reveals another aspect of development that can be understood only in the light of the interplay of biological potentialities and the molding effect of culture. Biological development (i.e., maturation) accounts for the ability to talk; the culture (i.e., the language heard) accounts for what the child actually says. Because language is such an important tool of interacting with other people, we can appropriately consider it an aspect of socialization.

It is not enough for the child to know the meaning of words, to understand sentences, and to make himself understood. He must conform to what society expects of him; he must not only make himself understood, but he must speak *properly*. In many languages, speaking properly means that he must learn to address those of a different status with different words or different phraseology. The German child learns to say *Sie* (deferential form of the word meaning *you*) when addressing superiors and strangers, and to say *du* (familiar form of *you*) to those with whom he is intimate. The Japanese child has to learn several degrees of deferential expression.

The child born in an English-language culture escapes a good many difficulties because the language is relatively free of many changes in word forms, such as are found in the declensions of the more inflected languages. But he must learn to speak properly, just as he has to learn to eat properly. He has problems of irregularities in grammar and of courtesy words such as "please" and "thank you," which have little to do with literal meanings. Once he knows these expressions, he uses them when he wishes to conform, and he may refuse to use them when he wishes to defy. They become a way for him to exercise power. Then there are the forbidden words, some of which he may use in the privacy of the family, some of which he may not use at all—even though his father or mother occasionally does in emotional moments. Thus the child learns about certain prohibitions, social taboos. While he is learning to talk *properly,* he is also learning the ways of his culture.

Adherence to or deviation from the proprieties in language is one standard on which social class distinctions are based. The choice of words or of pronunciation is often a giveaway of one's social position. The cockney speech of the lower-class Londoner is an extreme example. In America certain grammatical errors are associated with the uneducated ("them things"; "I come home" for "I came home"). Distinctions are also made on the basis of troublesome variations in usage, as between "I feel bad" and "I feel badly" (sometimes deliberately avoided by the more elegant "I do not feel well"). Those who have risen in social position and attempt to improve their language may reveal the lack of early training in good usage by such efforts at refinement as "between you and I," an overcorrection for faulty lower-class use of "me." Students of language call such occurrences "hyperurbanisms"—an exaggerated effort at upper-class urban speech.

As the child learns the language, he learns much more than the words and grammar. He learns to control other people through words, he learns courtesy, he learns taboos, and he learns social distinctions. He also acquires an instrument that permits him to think and reflect.

Disciplinary practices and later behavior

In order to produce a child who obeys the demands of society in which he grows up and who internalizes these values so that he becomes a self-controlling person, parents find it necessary to exert control in the form of discipline, approving some kinds of behavior, disapproving others. Discipline may take various forms, and it is not simply a matter of choosing between rewards and punishments. All parental discipline is an interaction between the parent and the child, and such matters as parental affection and warmth may be as important as the particular kinds of discipline used.

One classification of discipline techniques by Sears, Maccoby, and Levin (1957) groups together the *love-oriented techniques* (praise as reward, withdrawal of love as punishment) and the *object-oriented techniques* (tangible rewards, deprivation of privileges, physical punishment). Which of these is favored in child training makes a difference in the kind of child that results.

If we think first of effectiveness in producing socially conforming behavior, such as good eating habits, we find that those mothers who report the regular use of physical punishment have more feeding problems with their young children than those who use punishment rarely or occasionally; in turn, those mothers who show affectionate warmth toward their children have fewer feeding problems than those who tend to be cold and hostile. Some of the findings are shown in Table 3–4.

If, instead of looking at the behavior itself, we think of self-control or a developed conscience, we also find a relationship to the kind of training the parents have given. The children rated highest on conscience were those whose mothers were not only relatively warm but used withdrawal of love as a means of control (Table 3–5).

It is evident that home training is an important factor in the socialization of the child. The subtleties are such that it is difficult to give cookbook recommendations as to how parents should treat children, but some of the preferred directions appear clear enough from the results of research. Whatever the method used, it should be used with consistency and firmness. Punitive methods, especially if used erratically,

TABLE 3-4

Children's feeding problems and the training practices of their parents

	Number of cases	Children having feeding problems
Extent of use of physical punishment:		
Rarely or never used	58	17%
Occasionally to fairly often	293	20
Regularly used	25	36
Mother's affectional warmth toward child:		
Exceptionally warm	36	11%
Warm and quite warm	233	19
Matter-of-fact	63	22
Cold, some hostility	46	35

SOURCE: Sears, Maccoby, and Levin (1957), p. 521.

TABLE 3-5

Conscience as related to mother's warmth and use of withdrawal of love *

	Children rated high on conscience
Mother relatively warm and uses withdrawal of love fairly often	42%
Mother relatively warm and uses little or no withdrawal of love	24
Mother relatively cold and uses little or no withdrawal of love	25
Mother relatively cold and uses withdrawal of love fairly often	18

SOURCE: Sears, Maccoby, and Levin (1957), p. 388.
* Number of cases not stated in original table. Total cases in four groups 188.

appear notably unsuccessful, whereas love-oriented techniques, including affectional warmth but also withdrawal of love to enforce conformity, appear to be successful in producing not only desirable behavior but the kind of conscience that internalizes control.

Identification and achieved identity

The child has to establish his place in the society of people about him and eventually to take his place as a man or a woman. Very important to him in finding his place are the members of his own family: mother, father, brothers, and sisters.

Because parents are the dominant figures and the primary sources of both satisfactions and prohibitions, the child's attitudes toward them are mixtures of wishes to please and wishes to protest. In our culture there is often between the ages of two and three a period characterized by defiant or *negativistic* behavior. It may be that with his new-found freedom of locomotion and with the increase of manipulative skills, the child asserts his individuality and tests his powers by his refusals to respond to parental requests. His favorite word becomes "No!" The negativistic stage is not an inevitable one; it is not found in all children. It is common, however, and parents and nursery school teachers must be prepared for it.

Although a kind of tug of war between children and parents goes on, with children exhibiting occasional negativism and defiance, the long-run influence of parents is that of models, or *identification figures,* for the children to copy. The process of identification is a very important one in the development of personality.

Sex-role identification. Each culture sets certain approved ways in which men and women are expected to behave; these may be called the *sex-role standards* for that culture (Kagan, 1964). The role that the boy will eventually play in society is that of a man, and the man he knows best is his father. Similarly, the girl learns the woman's role from her mother. Both mother and father, through their attitudes toward each other, help the child of either sex to acquire an appropriate role.

The play activities of boys and girls gradually diverge, especially after the age of five years. By that age they are aware that their roles in society differ, and they begin to try out in play the roles that they will assume some day in fact. The individual gradually comes to see himself as appropriately masculine or feminine; this self-perception we may call his *sex-role identity*. It is based for the young child on his perception of himself as similar to the like-sexed parent, and as capable in adopting the games and doing the things encouraged for his sex. When this self-image is inappropriate, anxiety is often aroused.

In a test devised to assess sex-type preferences, Brown (1957) chose as materials a figure ambiguous with respect to sex and a number of different toys and objects. In selecting the toys that the figure would like to play with, the child gave indication of what he preferred. Boys as early as three show some preference for sex-appropriate games, and this preference increases with age. Many girls show an early preference for male games (being a "tomboy" not being frowned upon as much as being a "sissy"), so that at the age of five more boys show a preference for masculine toys than girls do for feminine toys. By 9 or 10 years of age the preferences have clearly diverged for both sexes. There are some class differences because lower-class mothers insist on sex typing for girls more than middle-class mothers do (Kohn, 1959).

The development of identification would seem to be straightforward enough. The child knows his or her sex, and imitates the like-sexed parents. This sex-appropriate behavior is rewarded, and sex-inappropriate behavior punished. Except where there has been some interference with this process, because the appropriate parent is either inadequate or missing through divorce or death, or because parents reject their own roles as parents, there seem to be no special mysteries about the process. When, however, careful studies are done to investigate the development of identification, the situation does not turn out to be as simple as this account would suggest.

It is usually supposed that the parent the child models himself after is the one who is nurturant, that is, responsive to the needs of the child. Because this is commonly the mother early in life, the girl can continue this modeling of her, but the boy must shift to his father later on. The fact that nurturant models are imitated has been demonstrated experimentally by Bandura (1962), and evidence shows that kindergarten boys tend to imitate and identify more with fathers who are nurturant (Mussen and Distler, 1959); corresponding results have been found with junior and senior high school boys (Payne and Mussen, 1956). The circumstances producing identification are usually assumed to include (a) perceiving the like-sexed model as supportive, (b) perceiving the model as exercising power, commanding love, and being competent in valued areas, and (c) finding some objective basis (size, appearance) for being similar to the model. An inadequate parent can fail as a model according to (a) or (b), in which case (c) will produce a poor self-identity (Kagan, 1958).

Personal (non-sex-role) identification. While making the proper sex-role identification is very important, not only for the kinds of behavior most readily perceived as sex-related but also in respect to schooling and vocational aspiration, it must not be overlooked that there are other kinds of identification as well (Slater, 1961). Many personal qualities are not strongly sex-typed, such as enthusiasm, sense of humor, personal warmth; and many moral qualities such as integrity and considerateness are shared by both men and women. The child may thus learn and imitate qualities of *either* parent in these areas without violating the adoption of an appropriate sex standard of behavior. That is, there are many areas of life in which a male and a female can act similarly without going against any cultural taboos.

Personality, temperament, and attitudes toward work and play can come from either parent, even for the fully masculine boy or the fully feminine girl. Thus a mother's standards of housekeeping may be reflected in the son's work, even though he models after his father and enters his profession;

a daughter, gracefully accepting the woman's role in imitation of her mother, may still tell a story the way her father does. Less is known in detail about these subordinate aspects of identification because of the unresolved puzzles in respect to sextyping. Yet it takes little reflection or observation of one's friends to see how important both parents are in determining what a boy or girl will become.

The place of siblings and peers. While the parents are the primary identification figures, a child comes to conceive of himself as someone distinctive and valuable (or, contrariwise, someone inadequate) through his relations with brothers and sisters and age mates (peers) outside the home. Hence any discussion of identification with others, and the achievement of an identity for oneself, would be incomplete if these other important influences were ignored. It will be recalled that in Erikson's discussion of psychosocial development (Table 3–2) he noted the gradually enlarging radius of significant relations, from the parents to the immediate family, to the neighborhood, and beyond.

Birth order affects the ease with which a child finds a place for himself. One study of personality roles of children in large families identified eight different roles, three of which showed some relation to birth order. These three were (1) the responsible child (often the first-born), (2) the sociable, well-liked child (often the second), and (3) the spoiled child (often the youngest). Other roles that made for individuality in large families were (4) the social butterfly, who places a high value on social activities, (5) the studious child, (6) the isolate, who minds his own business, (7) the irresponsible child, and (8) the sickly child (Bossard and Ball, 1955). The contrast between the first-born and the second in two-child families has often been reported, the first-born tending to have stronger consciences than the second, and showing more intellectual interests and less aggressive behavior (Koch, 1956a; McArthur, 1956).

In addition to order of birth, sex of the other siblings affects the child's interests and behavior: girls with older brothers are likely to be more masculine (tomboyish) than girls with older sisters. Similarly, boys with older sisters are less aggressive than boys with older brothers (Koch, 1956b). The growing child learns from the siblings as well as from the parents.

In trying to retain his share of attention from parents, a child often shows jealousy of brothers and sisters, especially at the time of the birth of a sibling. The phrase *sibling rivalry* has been used to describe this condition and its resulting behavior. Apparently a two- to four-year difference is most threatening to the older child; earlier than this how he sees himself is still diffuse enough that the appearance of a rival does not disturb him; when he is older than four he is already somewhat independent and hence less threatened. Parents may minimize rivalry by preparing the older child for the birth of the baby and by taking care that the new baby does not completely absorb their affection. However, some signs of sibling rivalry are almost inevitable in our competitive culture. Parents may unwittingly produce rivalries among their children, based on rivalry problems persisting from their own childhoods (J. R. Hilgard, 1951). The solution is to handle the relationships among children so that these relationships will induce maturing rather than become the causes of insecurity and ill will.

The school continues the process of preparing the child for life in our kind of society. It gives him the necessary tools (such as the three R's) and teaches him how to cooperate with his peers, how to maintain standards of work, how to set goals and strive toward them. What his playmates expect of him becomes very important to the child of school age. He must dress as they do and must be good at the games they play. If he is teased for awkwardness or called a "sissy," he will feel deeply hurt. So important is the opinion of the age mates that parents whose standards for their children differ from those of other parents may find their authority lessening or their child emotionally upset.

Moral development

An important aspect of identification with parents is taking over their standards of conduct, so that the child learns how to react to other people in terms of accepted standards of what is good and proper and to resist the temptation to transgress the rules of acceptable behavior. Many studies have been directed to the moral development of children. Because of conceptual difficulties, however, widespread agreement has not yet been reached and some uncertainties persist. Piaget, whose scheme for intellectual development was presented earlier (p. 71), has proposed some stages in moral development (Piaget, 1932); these stages have provided the background for much later work. For example, Kohlberg (1963), using a related type of analysis, distinguished six types of morality, classified into three levels, and proceeded to study their development between ages 7 to 16. The stages are given in Table 3–6, with illustrative behavior at each stage. In the table the illustrations have to do with motivation for moral action; other dimensions of morality could have been listed, as, for example, the basis for respecting human life or the basis of respect for social morality. The assumption is that moral development falls roughly into these stages; earlier in life conduct is controlled according to the principles of earlier stages, later according to the more mature principles. For the purposes of Figure 3–9 the statements made by children when commenting on various acts of morality have been combined to reflect the three levels of Table 3–6. It will be seen that at the age of seven nearly all statements are at Level I; by age 13, half the statements are at Level II; at age 16 the Level II statements continue at a high level, but more of Level III statements appear, and those from Level I continue to drop off.

The two chief interpretations of these data are (1) that the results are a result of *social learning*, the child gradually coming to accept the norms of the culture as he becomes old enough both to have the necessary experiences and to make the neces-

---

TABLE 3–6

Stages in the development of moral character

Stage	Illustrative behavior
Level I. Premoral	
Stage 1. Punishment and obedience orientation	Obeys rules in order to avoid punishment
Stage 2. Naive instrumental hedonism	Conforms to obtain rewards, to have favors returned
Level II. Morality of conventional role-conformity	
Stage 3. "Good-boy" morality of maintaining good relations, approval of others	Conforms to avoid disapproval, dislike by others
Stage 4. Authority maintaining morality	Conforms to avoid censure by legitimate authorities with resultant guilt
Level III. Morality of self-accepted moral principles	
Stage 5. Morality of contract, of individual rights, and of democratically accepted law	Conforms to maintain the respect of the impartial spectator judging in terms of community welfare
Stage 6. Morality of individual principles of conscience	Conforms to avoid self-condemnation

SOURCE: After Kohlberg (1963), p. 400.

3–9

Age changes in moral statements according to three levels of moral development

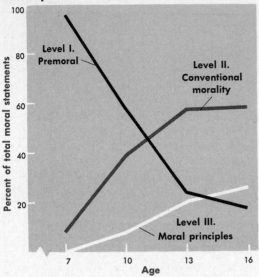

(From the data of Kohlberg, 1963)

sary discriminations, or (2) that the developmental process has large *maturational* components, so that the stages are more nearly spontaneous products of development, each stage arising in sequence from the one before. Kohlberg (1964) accepts the second of these interpretations because he believes that each stage depends upon the earlier one. If the statements of any one child are studied, it is found that if most of his moral statements come from one stage, the rest of the statements will usually come from the neighboring stages. If an effort is made to move the child ahead, it is found that he can more readily learn moral reasoning one level above his stage than two levels above it (Turiel, 1966).

In their investigation of identification, Sears, Rau, and Alpert (1965) included some ingenious experimental arrangements for studying the development of conscience and guilt in preschool children, presumably related to the later internalizing of moral principles, as in Kohlberg's Level III. Among the experimental measures were five situations calling for resistance to

temptation: resistance to eating appetizing candy when left alone in the room with it; violation of the rules of a ring-toss game after the experimenter leaves; playing with a forbidden toy in the absence of an adult; a "quoting rules" drama in which the child is expected to urge another child to obey the restrictive rules under which he is acting; and, finally, being left alone for 20 minutes to watch carefully that a hamster does not escape from his box. In the last situation, the box has a false bottom; if the child fails in his vigilance, the unobserved experimenter can trip a switch and cause the hamster to disappear. This somewhat diabolical procedure made it possible to observe a child's failure and his reaction to it; in the end he always found the "escaped" hamster somewhere on the floor, felt better about it, and no permanent harm was done (Figure 3–10).

Experimenters always hope that some consistencies will show up in their measures, so that, say, a child who shows resistance in one experiment will also show resistance in another. This was achieved to a degree in this experiment, as shown by Table 3–7. Only the candy temptation failed to correlate with the hamster experiment; while the other correlations are not all significantly high, they are all positive, and when the scores were added together

TABLE 3–7

Resistance to temptation: correlation of five other measures with seriousness of response in the disappearing hamster situation

	BOYS (N = 21)	GIRLS (N = 19)
Candy temptation	−.09	−.02
Ring-toss game	.35	.72*
Toy temptation	.24	.29
Quoting rules	.40	.48*
Disappearing hamster: latency	.55*	.75*

SOURCE: After Sears, Rau, and Alpert (1965), p. 215.

* Significant at the level of $P < .05$.

they formed a composite "resistance to temptation" score.

In general, the older children (even in this limited range of from four years and one month to five years and nine months) showed more capacity for resistance to temptation, and the girls slightly more than the boys. The girls were slightly more upset than the boys by their transgression with the hamster. Both boys and girls who were able to resist temptation showed high impulse control in other ways, for example, in avoiding the kind of negative behavior that seeks attention from adults.

Durability of personality as continuous from childhood

To say that the "child is father of the man" is to imply that the adult personality will reflect the kind of child the adult had been. This conjecture is subject to direct study. We have already noted some results of early experience as bearing upon adult height (pp. 69–70).

Some direct data comparing child and adult characteristics come from an investigation by Kagan and Moss (1962). During the 10 years between 1929 and 1939, a number of children were studied at the Fels Research Institute, Yellow Springs, Ohio, with careful records kept from birth through adolescence. Of these, 71 (36 males and 35 females) were brought back for interviews and ratings as young adults, in the age range of 19 to 29 years.

Correlations were arrived at between ratings in the various age ranges: 0–3, 3–6, 6–10, 10–14, and early adulthood. While some continuities were found from the earliest years on, the most striking findings showed how predictive the ages 6–10 were for young adult years. Representative findings are summarized in Figure 3–11.

The various behaviors are arranged in the figure according to the heights of the correlations for males, although the correlations for females are shown also. For both males and females there are relatively high correlations for intellectual achievement as shown in the early school years and in early adult life, and for sex-typed activity. Spontaneity of behavior shows moderate corre-

3–10

An experimental test of conscience and guilt

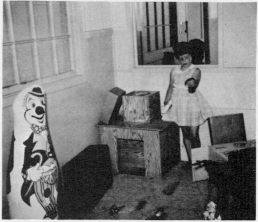

John C. Wright

The girl is holding a pet hamster that she is to guard when it is placed in the box. If she is distracted by the interesting things in the room, it will disappear and she will have failed in her responsibility. How will she react? (Sears, Rau, and Alpert, 1965)

lations for both sexes. Apparently, the cultural pressures on boys and girls are similar in these respects. For the other items the sex differences are striking. It is fairly clear that the overt expression of sex and anger is less controlled in boys than in girls, while girls are freer to continue their passive and dependent behavior from childhood.[1]

The fact that there are a number of significant correlations between behavior in the early school years (6 to 10) and in early-adult life strengthens the conviction that early socializing experiences in school and among peers are very important for further development. Kagan and Moss believe that the sex-role identification plays a major governing role in this development.

[1] In the foregoing discussion the assumption has been made that socialization practices, hence learned behaviors, account for a large fraction of the differences between the sexes. There may also be physiological and biological factors that result in greater male aggressiveness and greater female submissiveness. Cultures often support natural tendencies, in part to suppress deviations from the expected standards; hence socialization pressures and innate tendencies may agree.

Correlation between child and adult behavior

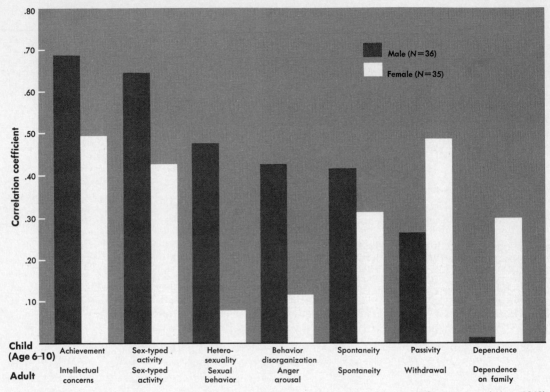

	Child (Age 6-10)	Adult
	Achievement	Intellectual concerns
	Sex-typed activity	Sex-typed activity
	Hetero-sexuality	Sexual behavior
	Behavior disorganization	Anger arousal
	Spontaneity	Spontaneity
	Passivity	Withdrawal
	Dependence	Dependence on family

(After Kagan and Moss, 1962)

SUMMARY   1. The course of development in man, as in other organisms, is shaped by *maturation* and *learning*. The study of maturation shows that development goes on at its own rate, relatively independent of the environment, although an essential minimum of environmental stimulation and support is needed. Embryological development clearly illustrates the meaning of maturation within a relatively uniform environment.

2. *Imprinting*, whereby at the right time the young duckling follows whatever appropriately moving object is nearest, shows the interplay between maturational readiness and environmental opportunity.

3. Imprinting and other evidence suggests that there may be *critical periods* in development when the organism is most plastic and ready to acquire some of the behavior essential for optimal development later.

4. Studies of the human infant and child suggest a number of relationships between maturation and readiness to learn. (1) Skills that build upon developing behavior patterns are most easily learned. (2) The rate of development remains uniform within wide ranges of stimulation.

(3) The more mature the organism, the less training is needed to reach a given level of proficiency. (4) Training given before maturational readiness may bring either no improvement or only a temporary improvement. (5) Premature training, if frustrating, may do more harm than good.

5. There is a growing body of evidence that early deprivation or early stimulation (including stress) may have consequences for later development. The possibility that this applies to man is exemplified by a study on adult stature related to stress within the first two years.

6. An unsolved problem of development is whether or not it is essentially *continuous* or consists in a series of definable *stages*. Among the theories stressing stages, one of the better substantiated is that of Piaget having to do with stages in cognitive or intellectual growth, moving from the sensorimotor period through the period of preoperational thought to the period of concrete operations and finally to the period of formal operations. The psychosexual stages of Freud and the psychosocial stages of Erikson are attempts to place the whole personality development in the context of a theory of stages. Critical periods and stages are still to some extent controversial.

7. Personality development of the child begins through the early practices of feeding, toilet training, and social attachments, because he is learning to conform to the demands of a culture. Even though the demands upon the infant must be limited to what he can do, his feeding schedules move in the direction of the three-meal-a-day person he is expected to become. The accompaniments of feeding may be psychologically as important as nutrition. The need for appropriate body contact has been dramatically illustrated by experiments using monkeys with artificial mothers. They support the results obtained in studies of humans, according to which children separated too early from their mothers show signs of disturbance.

8. The gradual development of language provides an important tool for social interaction. It serves purposes of status and power that go beyond mere communication.

9. Disciplinary practices are important not only in the control of specific behavior, but in the development of conscience and later social conduct.

10. The processes of identification and identity formation are particularly important in personality development. Some distinctions can be made between *sex-role standards* and *sex-role identity*, in which modeling after the like-sexed parent is central, and *personal (non-sex-role) identification*, in which temperament and other traits are learned from the parent of either sex and from siblings and peers. The siblings and peers are important in relation both to sex-role and non-sex-role identifications.

11. The composition of the family by sex and order of birth affect individual development, occasionally giving rise also to *sibling rivalries*.

12. Personality characteristics formed by the ages of 6 to 10 are often predictive of later personality, particularly when the behavior is congruent with sex-role standards. Thus passive and dependent characteristics are more stable in girls than in boys, and aggression and expressed sexuality are more stable in boys than in girls.

SUGGESTIONS FOR FURTHER READING

There are many textbooks on child development, of which the following are representative: Martin and Stendler, *Child development: the process of growing up in society* (2nd ed., 1959), and the accompanying book of readings, Stendler, *Readings in child behavior and development* (2nd ed., 1964); Mussen, Conger, and Kagan, *Child development and personality* (2nd ed., 1963). A useful short paperback is Mussen, *The psychological development of the child* (1963). For historical background see Kessen, *The child* (1965).

There are now a number of substantial books with chapters for the specialist. These include Mussen, *Handbook of research methods in child development* (1960); Stevenson, *Child psychology* (1963); Hoffman and Hoffman, *Review of child development research*, vol. I (1964); Lipsitt and Spiker, *Advances in child development and behavior*, vol. I (1963).

For the embryological basis of development a useful source is Willier, Weiss, and Hamburger, *Analysis of development* (1955). A good summary of the work on imprinting is Sluckin, *Imprinting and early learning* (1965). On the effects of early experience, see Fiske and Maddi, *Functions of varied experience* (1961). The problem of durability of various characteristics important in development is reviewed in Bloom, *Stability and change in human characteristics* (1964).

4 Adolescence and Adulthood

Adolescents have a bad reputation. Parents feel that troubles double when their children enter adolescence; policemen are caustic about the mischief adolescents get into. Someone is always talking about the "youth problem" and the prevalence of juvenile delinquency. When a hot rod goes by, packed full of noisy youngsters, its horn blowing and the tires squealing as it turns the corner, one adult turns to another and says with disdain or disgust, "a bunch of teen-agers."

The foregoing picture is, of course, incomplete and unfair to youth, but there is some truth in it. The transition from childhood to adult life is not always smooth. As the youth breaks his emotional dependence upon his parents, he may embrace his new-found freedom with excessive exuberance. But he may also be shy and sensitive. He has many adjustments to make within the next few years: he must choose his lifework and make preparation for it; he must find ways to manage his new interest in members of the opposite sex; he must look ahead to selecting a mate and establishing a home of his own. And he faces these social problems and decisions at the very time that striking changes in his physical appearance and physiological functioning may often make it hard for him to understand and accept himself.

The importance of puberty (the transition to sexual maturity, which is the chief physical development in adolescence) is signalized in many nonliterate societies by initiation ceremonies through which the adolescent is inducted into adulthood. Anthropologists have described such ceremonies in societies all over the world, in places as remote from each other as Africa, Indonesia, Polynesia, and North and South America. However, the rites are not universal among nonliterate groups; some groups in each area mentioned above have no such ceremonies.

While rites of initiation often force the adolescent of nonliterate cultures to undergo ordeals of starvation, sleeplessness, and pain, once the initiation is over he is honored by new status and responsibilities. The more gradual transition to adult life in our society and in nonliterate societies which do not have rites has some advantages, but it also produces in the adolescent a period of conflict and vacillation between dependence and independence. Such vestigial remains of ceremonial introduction into adult life as are seen in the confirmation ceremonies of some religious groups, the "coming out" parties of debutantes, and the fraternity initiation form no sharp break with the past, nor do they confer the status of full adulthood.

The adolescent period is only a phase in the stream of growth, and it is a mistake to emphasize too sharply its discontinuities with other phases. A number of studies (e.g., Elkin and Westley, 1955; Bandura and Walters, 1959) have pointed out that there is a certain amount of mythology about adolescence, so that parents wait in fear and trembling for their teen-age children to show the expected defiance and

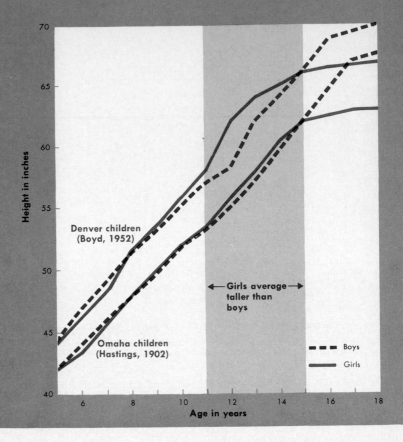

4-1

Growth in height

The average height of American boys and girls has increased several inches in the 50-year period separating these two studies, but the differences in height between boys and girls remain much the same. The beginning of puberty at an earlier age for girls is reflected in the years between 11 and 15, when their height exceeds that of boys. (Data from Hastings, 1902, and Boyd, 1952, reproduced by Hathaway, 1957)

rebellion; when some issue comes up, they say to themselves "Here it is!" and perhaps make more of the incident than they should. For many adolescents the transition to adult life runs smoothly; for others, the problems and conflicts have a long history, and troubles in adolescence are but further manifestations of earlier troubles. Furthermore, as the adolescent becomes stronger, a problem that once could have been handled easily may get out of hand.

Bodily Changes During Adolescence

Everyone is aware of the striking changes that take place in the body during adolescence. Changes take place in *primary sex characteristics*, that is, in the reproductive organs, both internal and external, which make possible sexual union and reproduction. Modifications also occur in the *sec-*

ondary sex characteristics, those physical features distinguishing a mature man from a mature woman in ways not directly related to the sexual apparatus. Some of these modifications, such as the development of the breasts, appear only in girls; some, such as the marked change in voice and the growth of a beard, appear only in boys; others, such as the appearance of pubic hair, are common to both boys and girls. These physical changes are of psychological interest because of the behavioral changes that accompany them—changes in attitudes, in emotional responsiveness, and in social behavior.

The definition of adolescence

The developments of adolescence take place over several years. Students of adolescence have found it difficult to demarcate both the whole period and its phases exactly, because the first signs of puberty appear very gradually, and bodily changes continue after the sexual apparatus has matured. The onset of pubescence (or puberty) has commonly been assigned to that stage of development in which pigmented hairs appear in the pubic region. The period of *prepubescence* is then all of life before this, and *postpubescence* is the period marked by the development of more advanced sexual characteristics.

The growth pattern as reflected in height

In infancy the child grows very rapidly in height, so that half the adult height is reached between the ages of two and three. Then the rate of growth slows until the new spurt toward the end of the prepubescent period. Figure 4–1 shows the rate of growth from age five to age 18.

Annual gains in height (growth increments) for boys and for girls are plotted in Figure 4–2. The maximum growth rate is achieved by girls at an average age of 12.6 years, by boys at an average age of 14.8 years. The patterns of growth in height for boys and girls are very similar, both showing a striking spurt in the prepuberal period and a gradual decline as adult stature is approached.

Some kind of plot other than that used in Figure 4–2 is needed to show the variations from one boy or girl to another in the age of maximum growth. While the general pattern of growth is common to all individuals, some individuals mature early, some late. How the ages of maximum growth spread out over the years from 10 to 18 is shown in Figure 4–3. The girls as a group mature earlier than the boys as a group, but the graph shows that there is considerable overlap. Two-thirds of the girls achieve their maximum growth within a year before or after the average of 12.6 years; two-thirds of the boys achieve their maximum growth within a year before or after the average age of 14.8 years. The differences between the averages (2.2 years) correspond to the differences in ages of maturing. But the overlap cannot be ignored. For example, at age 13.5 about one-sixth of the girls have not reached their maximum growth rates, while about one-sixth of the boys have already reached

Annual increments in height

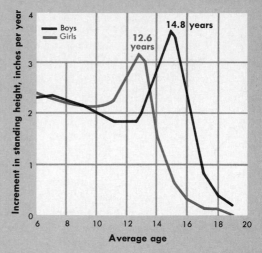

The peak growth period comes earlier for girls than boys. (After Shuttleworth, 1939)

Age of maximum growth rates

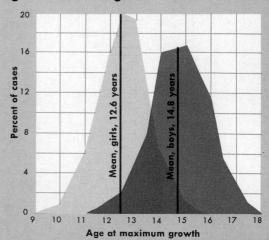

The age at which growth increment was most rapid (see Figure 4–2) was determined for each boy and for each girl, and these results were then plotted to make this figure. Note that a very few boys and a very few girls developed very early and very late, the largest numbers falling around the average of 12.6 years for girls and 14.8 years for boys. (After Shuttleworth, 1939)

theirs. For these boys and girls of age 13.5, the usual differences are reversed: the boys are ahead and the girls are behind.

The question is often asked whether the early maturer tends to grow taller than the late maturer. The answer is that there is very little relationship between time of onset of puberal changes and adult height. There is, however, a positive correlation between prepubescent height and ultimate adult height at all ages (Figure 4–4). When the correlations between earlier height and adult height are plotted, it is found that these correlations begin to drop for girls at age nine and for boys at age 11. This merely reflects the out-of-step development, so that some girls at this early age are already entering their growth spurt, and some boys are entering theirs a little later. Thus the preferred time to estimate adult height is before the adolescent spurt begins. While such predictions satisfy individual and parental curiosity, they may also have some practical values. For example, as Tanner (1962) points out, the Royal Ballet selects

girls at the age of nine, and yet has very strict limits upon the mature height of its ballerinas; prediction tables can therefore save time and disappointment for girls likely to grow too tall.

While the time of maximum growth rate has come to be accepted as a convenient index of maturing, reaching adulthood is much more complex than this. For example, the fact that a girl has menstruated does not necessarily indicate that she has become fertile. In fact, most girls menstruate before their ovaries can produce ripe eggs (Ford and Beach, 1951). One major study of child bearing showed that of 700 women who married between the ages of 15–19, 44 percent bore children within two years of marriage, while of 1835 who married between the ages of 20–24, 91 percent bore children within the next two years (Duncan, as reported by Montagu, 1946). The inference is that many of the younger women may not yet have been mature enough to bear children at the time of their marriage. A period of sterility in early ado-

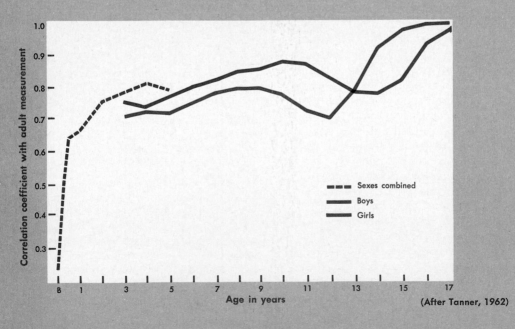

4–4

Correlation of adult height with height of same individuals as children

Correlation coefficient with adult measurement

Age in years

- - - Sexes combined
— Boys
— Girls

(After Tanner, 1962)

lescence is very common among many mammals, including primates (Ford and Beach, 1951). For the male the best index of sexual maturity is the ability to produce fertile spermatozoa, but this index is difficult to apply.

Sexual maturity is not the whole story of becoming adult, and merely because a man or woman has become fertile does not mean that the maturing process has been completed. With these reservations, we may still take the maximum growth rate as a convenient milestone by which to compare different individuals as to their relative levels of maturity.

Early and late maturers

Growth curves for height during adolescence (e.g., Figure 4–3) show that not all adolescents follow the same pattern of growth. A boy once relatively tall may find himself short by comparison to his friends; a girl once considered small may later find herself unusually large for her age. Too much may be expected of those who mature early, while anxiety may be created among those who mature late and are left behind by their companions. Among the adolescents in one study, the *early-maturing girls* and the *late-maturing boys* found that their out-of-step growth caused them problems of adjustment (Bayley and Tuddenham, 1944).

Further studies have shown that late-maturing boys have higher drives for social acceptance and more tendencies toward aggression than the early-maturing ones (Mussen and Jones, 1958). The aggression of the late maturers appears to be related to their feelings of inadequacy, rejection, and dependence.

Results for girls are less striking. While some early-maturing girls are at a disadvantage because they are too "grown-up" for their age groups, the late maturers are sometimes at a disadvantage also. Like the boys, the late-maturing girls may have less adequate self-concepts than the early maturers, have poorer relations with parents, and resent their dependency (Jones and Mussen, 1958).

There is another way in which adoles-

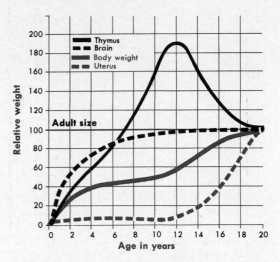

The brain approaches adult size very early; tissues related to reproduction (e.g., uterus) wait until later for rapid growth. (After Jackson, 1928)

cent growth may be out of step: the body does not grow as a unit, and one part may be out of step with another. Metabolism has to be adjusted to a rapidly growing skeleton and musculature and a new glandular balance reached. The relative sizes of different bodily tissues at different periods, plotted in Figure 4–5, show most rapid fluctuation during the early teens. No wonder there are occasional disturbances in the balance of physiological processes within the body as these shifts take place. Adolescent acne is a commonly occurring symptom of these internal disharmonies.

Adolescent awkwardness

The idea is common that during adolescence boys and girls go through an "awkward stage." Such awkwardness might conceivably result from the out-of-step growth just described. But to some extent the "awkward stage" is more illusion than fact.

If adolescents are genuinely awkward, they ought to show muscular incoordination or loss of athletic prowess. Careful studies indicate that adolescents improve steadily at athletics; at no point is there loss of skill for boys; any fluctuations downward for girls are minor. Figure 4–6 shows the results of such a study. The Brace Motor Skills Test, named after its originator, consists of a set of tasks measuring the kinds of muscular coordinations characteristic of good athletics. While boys, according to the tests used, surpass girls athletically, both boys and girls improve throughout the teen years, when awkwardness might be expected.

If we accept this evidence that adolescents are not *in fact* awkward, how can we account for the general *impression* that they are?

The first reason for the false impression of awkwardness is the *size-age confusion* during adolescence. Because of the out-of-step nature of some growth, muscular skill and size do not keep pace, and muscular skill depends more on age than on size. A 12-year-old boy who looks like a 14-year-old is expected to act like a 14-year-old, but he has the movement patterns characteristic of a 12-year-old. He therefore looks awkward, although he has not really *become* so; he has not yet outgrown whatever awkwardness younger boys have.

The size-age confusion is not limited to adolescence. Even in nursery school, the two-year-old who looks like a three-year-old will be considered awkward. The confusion is emphasized in adolescence because of the rapidity of growth over short periods of time.

The second source of the impression of muscular awkwardness is the very real *social* awkwardness of some adolescents. Self-consciousness is often intensified during the adolescent years, and an adolescent boy who is highly skilled on the tennis court may spill the punch at an afternoon party. Even for a poised adult, it is not easy to acknowledge an introduction while holding a cup in one hand and a sandwich in the other. For the inexperienced adolescent, the cup and the sandwich become unsolvable problems when he is expected to shake hands. He certainly looks awkward—and he is awkward, *socially*

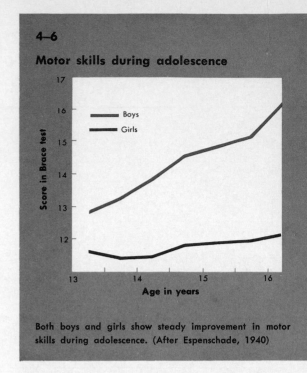

4–6

Motor skills during adolescence

Both boys and girls show steady improvement in motor skills during adolescence. (After Espenschade, 1940)

awkward, but not necessarily physically awkward. He may be able to dance in perfect rhythm or swim with a smooth, sure stroke.

The Role of the Adolescent

The adolescent commonly becomes a problem to his parents or to the community because he is a problem to himself. The transition from childhood to adulthood brings with it both the strains accompanying physical growth and physiological change and the conflicts associated with adopting the roles transitional to achieving the social behavior characteristic of adults in our culture.

Sexual development and the adolescent role

Adolescents are keenly aware of changes in their bodies, changes that are at once a source of pride and of embarrassment. The boy, secretly proud of his budding mustache, may find teasing about his "lip fuzz" or "pinfeathers" humiliating. The girl, pleased with the development of a more womanly figure, may feel overly conspicuous in her bathing suit. But adolescent self-consciousness is due to invisible changes as well as visible ones. There are new wishes, desires, and fantasies stirred by sexual maturing. Because of the taboos on sexual matters in our culture, the new intense awareness of sex can become a source of embarrassment.

That physiological changes do bring with them distinct changes in outlook is shown by a study of girls of the same age, some of whom had reached sexual maturity and some of whom were still in the pre-puberal period. Of two groups of 175 girls, matched for age and socioeconomic status, the postmenarcheal girls (those who had begun to menstruate) were found to differ significantly from the premenarcheal girls in their responses to the questions of a personality inventory. They reported more interest in boys, more interest in their own physical appearance, less desire for vigorous physical exercise, a stronger tendency to daydreaming, and greater concern over conflicts in family life (Stone and Barker, 1937).

Sexual emotions are not a new experience to the adolescent, but his intensified sexual motivation makes the taboos against sexual expression more frustrating than in childhood. Our culture imposes taboos on sexual relationships before marriage, and the circumstances of modern life lead to the postponement of marriage for several years beyond the attainment of sexual maturity. There is a theory that the "storm and stress" of adolescence is due more to cultural conflicts arising from sexual restrictions than to biological development. This theory receives support from studies of nonliterate cultures in which greater sexual freedom is permitted. Some of these cultures may be called *permissive* in contrast to cultures, like ours, that are *restrictive*. In permissive cultures adolescence is relatively uneventful, and the transition from childhood to adulthood is reported to be smoother than in ours.

The Trobriand Islanders, for instance, are tolerant of premarital sexual relationships. Sexual experimentation goes on freely among preadolescents, and an easy transition from childhood to adulthood ensues (Malinowski, 1929). Anthropological studies of several New Guinea and Samoan groups indicate that the period of adolescence is less trying in the tribes that have the less restrictive sex taboos (Mead, 1935).

To examine one aspect of a culture apart from its other aspects may be misleading, however, for cultures that permit greater sexual freedom than ours may also permit greater freedom for the adolescent in other ways. The adolescent may be relieved of "stress and strain" in problems of wider scope as well as in sexual problems.

Just as sexual restrictions vary from one culture to another, they also vary in the subcultures of a complex society such as ours. Studies suggest that in American society young men from lower educational and occupational levels are more likely to find sexual outlets in actual intercourse than are those from upper educational and social levels, who are more likely to find their outlets in masturbation and petting to climax (Kinsey, Pomeroy, and Martin, 1948). Among those who accept the cultural taboos, any form of sexual interest (even sexual fantasy) brings with it feelings of apprehension that generally accompany experimentation with the forbidden. Under these circumstances sex becomes a source of adolescent conflict, even though biological demands alone would not make such conflict inevitable.

Emancipation from home

Emancipation from parental authority and from emotional dependence upon parents begins in childhood, but the process of emancipation is greatly accelerated during adolescence. Some independence is achieved in the nursery school years, and the child's spheres of independence and responsibility are extended throughout his childhood. The ease of transition to fuller independence in later adolescence depends largely upon the attitudes parents take during the preceding years. Some parents who have insisted upon close supervision of the child in his early years attempt to continue their control through his adolescence. One result for the child is likely to be the continuance through adolescence of childish dependence and obedience, which may make him an adult who never becomes fully mature.

The "parent problem" as seen by teenagers has been the subject of inquiry among girls and boys of high school age (grades 9 through 12) by the Purdue Opinion Poll, a survey receiving replies from several thousand students representative of the nation at large (Remmers and Radler, 1957). Apparently there is little ground for alarm in their findings, for in no specific problem did more than one in five high school students voice a complaint about parents (Table 4–1). On the whole,

there is no evidence of a very high parent-child conflict. Even so, the areas of conflict reported are of interest. Many of the problems revolve around restrictions on grown-up behavior (dates, use of the family car, use of money); in these, as in other ways, the teen-ager sees the parents as treating him (or her) too much like a child. The differences in replies of boys and girls represent in part a sex typing in our culture: the boy is troubled about having the car and about spending the money he earns, while the girl is troubled about her freedom in choosing friends, about strictness concerning dates, and about favoritism (which, one may guess, she feels is demonstrated in her brother's greater freedom). Concealed in the figures may be the fact of the girl's earlier maturing, so that her desire for dates in the ninth grade may produce parental opposition, while a ninth-grade boy may not yet care very much about dating.

Resentment of parental control is not limited to adolescence. The negativism of the preschool child has already been referred to. Defiance of parental authority is not something that appears at only one stage of growth, but may increase during adolescence, as shown by the data of Figure 4–7. In this study, done in Europe, girls of ages nine to 17 reported poor, moderate, and good social relations with other members of their own family. The number of reports of bad relations increased gradually until a peak was reached near age 13, and then it declined. While the exact ages would undoubtedly vary from one culture to another, the close relationship between the peak of family difficulties and the puberal period suggests an important connection between the two (after Buseman, reported by Bühler, 1933).

The relationships of parents to adolescent children can create problems for both. The differences in age and the circumstances of the parents' remembered youth are likely to make the parents seem old-fashioned to their children. The adolescent's vacillation between childish dependence and the desire for independence and privacy makes it hard for the parent to

TABLE 4–1

The "parent problem" as seen by high school students

Problem	Replies acknowledging this problem *		
	BOYS	GIRLS	TOTAL
Afraid to tell parents what I've done wrong	18%	19%	19%
Parents too strict about my going out at night	16	19	18
Parents too strict about family car	24	9	16
Family always worried about money	15	15	15
Parents too strict about dating	8	17	13
Parents interfere in my choice of friends	10	15	13
Parents nag about studying	16	10	13
Parents hate to admit I'm sometimes right	13	13	13
Parents too strict about dates on school nights	10	13	12
Wish parents would treat me like a grown-up	10	14	12
Parents interfere with spending money I earn	15	7	11
Parents play favorites	8	12	10

SOURCE: Remmers and Radler (1957), pp. 117-18.

* The percentages are not additive, because one student may make several complaints.

4-7

Adolescent difficulties with social relations

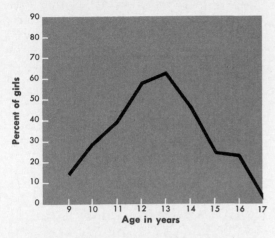

Percentage of girls at each age between nine and 17 reporting poor social relations with members of their families. (After Buseman, reported by Bühler, 1933)

know how he should treat his child at any given time. Emancipation from home and parents does not come all at once, and the unevenness of the transition may baffle both the parents and the adolescent youth.

The adolescent subculture

If the adolescent can find secure relations with others of his own age, he is freer to emancipate himself from home ties. Adolescents place great importance on being accepted by their own group. Ample evidence of this need is offered by the emphasis they place upon conformity. If the fashion in junior high school is to wear tight pants and loafers, almost all the boys will insist that they have to wear tight pants and loafers. To differ would be to risk criticism and rejection.

The need for the security that comes from the group leads to the formation of in-groups, such as gangs among boys and cliques among girls. Members of an in-group feel especially close to others within the group and are very much aware of the distinction between "in" and "out," between those who belong and those who do not. The nature of these closely knit groups depends very much upon the opportunities that the neighborhood provides. Close

friendship with a few of his fellows is important to the adolescent, and the isolated child does suffer.

So important are the relationships with peers that some observers perceive that the way in which the adolescents look to each other creates a distinctive subculture, considerably removed from that of adults (Coleman, 1961). High school students are deeply involved in "dating and rating," and the ingrown cliques that develop have little to do with the larger society outside. Among boys the adolescent subculture values athletics and car ownership; among girls what counts is attractiveness, social success, and clothes. While parents are concerned over the competition for grades, worried lest their children not be accepted by the college of their choice, the adolescent generally is more concerned about being "in."

Juvenile delinquency

Enough adolescents engage in antisocial behavior to make juvenile delinquency a serious social problem, apparently an increasingly serious one (Figure 4-8). The circumstances that lead adolescents into antisocial behavior, if understood, can throw light on the more general problem of adolescent development.

We can distinguish between two kinds of delinquency: *social delinquency* and *individual delinquency*. Social delinquency expresses itself in gang behavior in which large numbers of young people conform to a neighborhood pattern that may include car stealing, fighting, sexual indulgences, the use of illegal drugs, or other forms of behavior frowned upon by the adult culture. Individual delinquency, by contrast, crops up anywhere, in "good" families and neighborhoods as well as "bad" ones, and can be best understood as an attempt by the young person to solve some sort of problem of his own.

The circumstances that lead to social or gang delinquency and the kind of subculture that leads the gang members to conform to its standards have been well stated by Cohen (1955). One explanation he offers is that children from lower-class

4–8

Number of juvenile delinquency cases per population 10–17 years of age, 1940–60

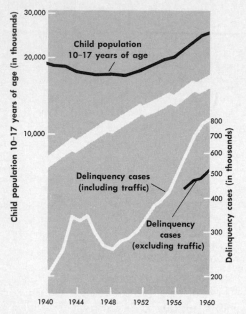

(From Sherif and Sherif, 1964; based on data from U.S. Department of Health, Education, and Welfare)

homes meet a great deal of frustration and humiliation in schools, which tend to value middle-class standards. Hence those who suffer together tend to draw together in little groups, and they express their defiance by attacking or assaulting the middle-class status system. The problem is a complex one, accentuated by poverty, broken homes, cruelty, and rejection, although antisocial gangs may also be found among middle-class youth. The main point is that youths with common backgrounds find in the gang and its rewards a basis for mutual support.

Individual delinquency, not associated primarily with bad neighborhoods or cultural conflict, is in some ways more puzzling. That it has something to do with the subtle influences of child-rearing practices is indicated by some data pertaining to the influence of childhood discipline on later aggression and crime (Table 4–2). The fact that the tendency toward delinquent careers starts early has been pointed out in several studies in which delinquent or criminal careers have been foreshadowed between the ages of six and 10 (Glueck and Glueck, 1964; McCord, McCord, and Zola, 1959).[1]

Self-perception, ideals, and values

If the adolescent is to achieve any consistency in his social behavior, he has to

[1] These studies are subject to some criticisms, for example, Gough (1962).

TABLE 4–2
Parental discipline and later crime convictions and incarcerations

Type of discipline	Number of cases	Convicted of crimes	Sentenced to penal institutions
Punitive	14	21%	7%
Love-oriented	60	27	5
Erratic A (love-lax)	40	35	5
Erratic B (love-lax-punitive)	41	49	19
Lax	52	50	19
Erratic C (punitive-lax)	43	56	30
TOTAL GROUP OF BOYS	250	41	15

SOURCE: McCord, McCord, and Zola (1959), p. 77.

TABLE 4–3

Parental interest and the adolescent's self-esteem

| Adolescent's self-esteem | Parental interest | |
	No evidence of lack of interest	Some evidence of lack of interest
High	49%	29%
Medium	25	26
Low	26	44
	N = 945	N = 241

SOURCE: Rosenberg (1965), p. 10. (By permission of the American Sociological Association.)

arrive at certain standards of conduct. He must decide for himself the kind of person he wishes to be and ascertain for himself what things are worthwhile. Such standards are known as *ideals,* or *values.* When he becomes independent of home, shall he continue to accept the standards that his parents approve? In making himself acceptable to his age mates, does he have to do everything they urge or dare him to do? He has to choose whether to conform or to defy, whether to respect conventional taboos or to see what he can "get by" with, whether to seek immediate pleasures or to set his sights on distant goals. He arrives at some sort of image of the ideal self he would like to become and then judges himself according to this ideal.

The adolescent does not always find it easy to attain stable standards and guiding values. His parents are the most natural source for his standards, but he does not always agree with his parents. The younger generation faces certain problems the older generation did not have to face, such as television and the drive-in theater. New rules have to be made, and debate with parents over the rules may become a source of conflict.

The desire of the adolescent to amount to something, to do what adults do, but on his own initiative, leads to an uncertain relationship to adult models. He wants to be like the adults he knows and at the

same time to break away from them. As he struggles for a satisfying self-image, parental influences are strongly in evidence despite his conflicts with respect to them. For example, in a study of high school juniors and seniors in New York, Rosenberg (1965) found that parental interest, as shown by interest in the adolescent's friends and school work and in dinner conversations, was associated with self-esteem; lack of parental interest was associated with low self-esteem (Table 4–3).

But regardless of the conflict between generations, adolescents turn to parents or other adults for advice on matters of greater long-range importance, while relying on their peers for matters having to do with present social participation (Table 4–4).

The problem of finding a set of values by which to regulate conduct is made difficult because the values of society itself are in a state of flux. Furthermore, the adolescent's own values change as he grows older (Figure 4–9). Some indication of changing standards between older and younger contemporaries over a 30-year period are given by a study of the attitudes of adolescents, a study that also shows how the standards of society itself changed during the period.

4–9

Increasing tolerance in later years

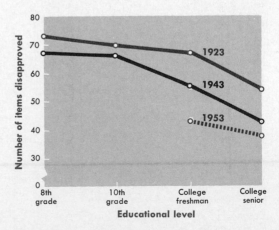

Shifts in attitude between the eighth grade and the senior year in college, and between 1923, 1943, and 1953. (After Pressey and Jones, 1955)

TABLE 4–4

Peer group vs. adults as source of advice on various matters, as reported by high school students

	Peers	Parents (or other adults)	Equally important
Peers more important:			
What to wear to a party	72%	17%	11%
The clubs you join	64	22	14
Personal grooming (how to comb your hair, dress, etc.)	58	21	21
How to act when out with the gang	57	29	14
Adults more important:			
Advice on personal problems or troubles	16	75	9
Your political feelings	21	54	25
How you spend your money	31	49	20
How you feel about people of other races or nationalities	30	32	38

SOURCE: Remmers and Radler (1957), pp. 234–35.

The time span of the study was from 1923 to 1953.

Eighth-grade, high school, and university students checked a set of 375 behavior items in 1923. Each item could be marked as "disapproved," "worried about," or "liked." The study was repeated at 10-year intervals. The present account is based on the replies of 1734 students in 1923, 1706 in 1943, and 842 (college freshmen and seniors only) in 1953. Results for items dis-approved (thought "wrong") are charted in Figure 4–9. Two trends can be noted. (1) In both 1923 and 1943 college students disapproved of fewer items than did contemporary eighth-grade pupils or high school sophomores. (2) Between 1923 and 1943 and again between 1943 and 1953, there was a decrease in the number of disapproved items, at least by college students.

The over-all trend is toward a relaxing of

TABLE 4–5

Social class and self-values among adolescent boys

Social class	Self-values			
	A good student in school	Well-respected, looked up to by others	Tough, not afraid to fight	Good at working with hands
High ($N = 31$)	71%	46%	15%	17%
High middle ($N = 295$)	56	30	25	28
Low middle ($N = 164$)	51	21	28	32
Low ($N = 54$)	39	16	39	53

SOURCE: Rosenberg, (1965), p. 257. (By permission of the American Sociological Association)

standards, both with increasing age at any one time and in our society generally as the years go by. Similar age trends have been found in the attitude toward religion. With increasing age (from 12 to 18 years) those studied showed increasing tolerance toward others' religious beliefs and practices and more doubt about such beliefs as the infallibility of the Bible or the existence of God (Kuhlen and Arnold, 1944).

What the adolescent values and the way in which he sees himself are, of course, the results of many background factors that determine what he has experienced and what he expects of himself. Some of the influences are a result of the social and economic background in which he has grown up. It is not surprising that a high value on education and self-respect is associated with higher socioeconomic status, and willingness to be tough and a high value on manual skill are associated with the lower class (Table 4–5). It should be noted, however, that even among those of the lowest class, being a good student is stressed by a number equal to those who value being tough; it is important not to characterize all members of a class by some differences in percentages between the classes.

CRITICAL DISCUSSION
Is adolescence changing?

A provocative book appeared in 1959 entitled *The vanishing adolescent* (Friedenberg). It was followed only a little later by one entitled *The adolescent society* (Coleman, 1961). The first implies that adolescence is losing its uniqueness; the second that adolescents are forming a subculture distinct from that of the adults around them. Is one of these right and the other wrong, or do they both express some measure of truth about adolescence today?

Friedenberg says: "I believe that adolescence, as a developmental process, is becoming obsolete. The kind of personal integration which results from conflict between a growing human being and his society is no longer the mode of maturity our society cultivates. We expect—indeed, we usually

demand—from adults quite a different sort of behavior than that which exemplifies a well-defined and well-established self." [2] He thus assigns to the adult the responsibility for the disintegration of the process according to which an adolescent should establish his own individual identity or selfhood.

While Friedenberg deplores the lack of open conflict between the adolescent and his society because, for all his defiance, the adolescent permits himself to be manipulated, Coleman goes to the other extreme by saying that the gulf between the adolescent society and the adult society is widening, with the adolescent culture becoming better defined.

It is possible to find some common ground between these views. To the extent that Coleman's adolescent society is a mass society, insisting upon conformity, it is defeating to the opportunity for finding individual identity. In this respect Coleman's conclusions agree with Friedenberg's. That Western culture is in some sort of identity crisis is asserted by many observers; the adolescent problems are probably not isolated from the general puzzlement over values that is so widespread in our time.

The Adult Years

It is possible to think of the life span as divided into a number of periods such as infancy, childhood, adolescence, early adulthood, middle age, later maturity, and old age. Such a classification into "stages" need not imply sharp boundaries, yet it is clear that the opportunities and problems change from one period to the next. As we move beyond adolescence into the adult years, problems of adjustment continue.

Adult responsibilities and satisfactions

Early adult years are for most men and women the years of greatest energy and productivity. The adjustment problems of young adults, as distinct from those of adolescents, are often problems of choice (vocational choice, marital choice, decisions

[2] Friedenberg (1959), pp. 133–34.

Range of free movement (behavioral settings) in which age subgroups are performers.

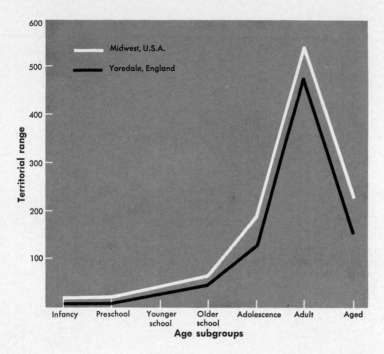

(After Barker and Barker, 1963)

as to family size) rather than primarily problems of emotional conflict and insecurity. This does not mean that young adults do not have such personal problems, for choices stir up whatever problems of dependency and insecurity remain unresolved from the preceding years.

One reason that the early adult years are generally full of opportunity is that the community gives young adults access to areas of life that permit significant participation. By careful study of where people of different ages go in their daily lives in small communities and what they do when they get there, Barker and Barker (1963) showed clearly that it is the adults who have the widest participation (what they describe as "territorial range") of any age group. The study done originally in a small town in midwestern United States was repeated in a small town in England, with

very similar results (Figure 4–10). The adolescents have not yet achieved that full access, and restrictions come again with advancing age.

It is not altogether surprising that young adulthood is looked back upon by most older people as their time of greatest happiness (Table 4–6). In the studies cited, women often reported satisfaction in housekeeping and raising their children; men, while also referring to happy family life, mentioned interest in their work during those years. It is worth noting that in the Iowa group studied, two-thirds of those who had not been married selected the childhood years as the time of greatest happiness, while only a third of the married ones chose the years of childhood and youth in preference to the years of early adult life (Landis, 1942).

For many men and women life becomes

somewhat stabilized during the early adult years. Satisfactory adjustments in these years occur when the preparation for a career has been successfully accomplished, when marriage has led to the establishment of a home, and when children are coming along and finding their places in school. Friendships are established with congenial families; opportunities are found for participating in the civic life of the community; and there is enough energy to enjoy what leisure remains. But this picture of the settled young family in the community is, unfortunately, not the only picture; in fact, it is perhaps a rare one.

Each of the areas of satisfaction is also an area of risk. Vocational adjustment is not easy: military careers may delay fulfilling a plan, and many young adults face from time to time the demoralization of unemployment. The young wife who wishes to devote herself to her children finds that she must go to work in order to supplement the meager income of her husband, or, conversely, the wife who wishes to continue to work finds her children a burden and an interference. Marriage entered upon with romantic enthusiasm may end in the divorce court. Prolonged ill-

nesses may upset well-laid plans. The young man who pictured himself as a contented husband and father may find himself a disgruntled bachelor, a divorced man, or a widower. The young woman similarly may end up single, divorced, or widowed.

There are no sharp transitions from young adulthood to middle age, but the years of 45 to 65 bring a number of shifts. There is often something of a plateau in vocational accomplishment: the man has either arrived or is well on his way or must content himself with a station in life that is likely to persist with little advancement. The woman's life is changed by her menopause, which marks the end of her child-bearing years. By the age of 50 half the parents have seen the departure of the last child from the home. Future orientation becomes more difficult as awareness gradually comes that life is more than half over.

The years of later maturity are commonly thought of as beginning around age 65 or 70, when those in employed positions commonly face retirement, often with reduced income and other attendant dislocations. By the middle sixties, because men die younger than women and women tend to marry men older than they, the majority of married women have become widows.

We tend now to think of old age as setting in when there is a general decline in abilities, restriction of activities, often the abandonment of independent living. Some people, even of advanced years, really never reach this stage, for they remain active and involved until overtaken by death.

Each of these periods in life has its attendant problems. Instead of considering the whole gamut of adjustments that people make, we shall illustrate some of the characteristics of adult life by considering a few specimen topics: adjustment to the sex role of being a man or a woman, marital happiness, productive work, and successful aging.

Masculine and feminine roles

In the adult years we find the culmination of the differences between the sexes that have resulted in part from biological

TABLE 4–6 Years which appeared happiest in retrospect		
Years which appeared happiest	Resident in New York *	Resident in Iowa †
Childhood (5-15 years)	15%	11%
Youth (15-25 years)	19	19
Young adulthood (25-45 years)	49	51
Middle age (45-60 years)	12	6
Later life (60 and up)	5	5
Undecided or no data	—	8
TOTAL	100	100
Number of persons reporting	370	450

* SOURCE: Morgan (1937). Subjects from age 70 into the 90s.
† SOURCE: Landis (1942). Subjects from ages 65–98.

differentiation and in part from the roles assigned the sexes in our culture.

Because the sexes are physiologically unlike, it would be easy to infer that as adults the differences in behavior between them correspond simply to their different biological organizations. Actually the situation is much more complex. Whether it is the man or the woman who wears lace, long hair, or brightly colored clothes depends upon the styles current at the time. A series of historical accidents determined that until recently men became bank clerks and women cashiers in stores; men telegraph operators and women telephone operators. Now, as women are increasingly taking over some of the jobs men alone formerly held, the problem becomes one of determining whether the behavioral distinctions between men and women are to be attributed to biological differences or to cultural influences.

Masculinity and femininity in nonliterate societies. Studies of cultures very unlike our own dramatically reveal the wide range of possibilities in the behavior of the two sexes. Reports on sex roles in three New Guinea tribes illustrate well how those roles differ in various cultures (Mead, 1935, 1949).

1. In a mountain-dwelling tribe known as the Arapesh, men and women were more alike than in our culture. Their similarity lay in their passivity, gentleness, mildness, and domesticity—traits predominantly "feminine" in our culture. Men and women shared the care of the children and other home duties with less division of labor than that with which we are familiar.

2. Among a river-dwelling people called the Mundugumor, men and women also were more nearly alike than in our culture. But the Mundugumor similarity was "masculine." Both sexes tended to be ruthless, aggressive, and violent.

3. The lake-dwelling Tchambuli offer the most dramatic contrast to our culture. While the sexes had dissimilar roles, as ours do, the pattern was largely reversed. The Tchambuli woman was the aggressive partner, the manager of business affairs. The man was emotionally responsive to the feelings of his children, and he was subordinate to and dependent upon his mate. The psychological reversal was so real that the Tchambuli interpreted it as biologically natural—even to the extent that the man went into confinement and suffered while his wife had the baby!

What these contrasting cultures tell us is that sex roles are subject to a variety of different patternings. The difference does not mean that anatomical and physiological differences between the sexes have nothing to do with behavior, but it does mean that culture has to be taken into account.

It is certainly true that the common division of labor between the sexes in nonliterate cultures is determined in part by physical differences between men and women. Study of 224 tribes throughout the world shows that, in general, men gravitate toward work requiring muscular strength (warfare, metalworking, hunting, mining and quarrying, boat-building). Women tend toward occupations centering around the home and children (basketry, gathering fruits and nuts, water-carrying, grain-grinding, pottery-making, and clothes manufacture and repair) (Murdock, 1937). Bearing and nursing children provide a biological reason for keeping women at home; man's greater muscular strength makes possible his participation in more strenuous activities. Once the division of labor is established, however, complex regulation by social pressure sets in, and familiar ways of doing things are enforced by taboo, ritual, superstition, prejudice, and other forms of social control. After the patterns have been set, members of one sex may do exclusively what members of the other sex could do equally well.

Masculinity and femininity in American culture. The differences between men and women on ability tests are slight. Yet on the basis of recognized achievements, women tend to fall far behind men. An early list of the 1000 most eminent persons in the world included only 32 women (Cattell, 1903). Lehman's list of 116 noteworthy young creative workers, those in all fields who did significant work before age 22, included only three women, and no woman appeared on his list of older achievers. In a few fields, however, women workers represent a substantial proportion of the recognized experts (i.e., those whose names appear in biographical dictionaries or in chronological lists of important achievements). Leaving aside the acting profession, where feminine roles are required, we note that the most striking field is that of children's literature: 46 percent of the recognized authors are women. Women represent a fifth or more of American authors in other literary fields and a fifth of the recognized sculptors, but women do not represent even 5 percent of the eminent people in any of the scientific fields (Lehman, 1953).

How can we explain the relatively poor showing of women? One reason may be that our culture offers men greater opportunities for achievement, so that, for equal ability, the man tends to be encouraged more than the woman. There is also greater social pressure motivating men toward achievement. All men, for example, are expected to earn a living, and for them marriage provides an added incentive to earn it; women, on the other hand, often expect a professional career to be ended by marriage and child rearing. What our culture expects of men and women may be more important than any differences in abilities.

Ability tests are designed to be "fair" to men and women—tests of general muscular ability do not use knitting or crocheting, which would give advantage to women, or the assembling of electrical devices, which would give advantage to men. It is possible to reverse this approach by selecting tests which seek to discover exactly those items within our culture on which men and women are most likely to differ, and thereby to arrive at a *social* definition of masculinity and femininity. Such a test has been devised (Terman and Miles, 1936). It contains only items that men and women would tend to answer differently. When

any one person takes the test, it can be determined whether he answers the questions predominantly as a man would or as a woman would. He thus receives a score characterizing the masculinity or femininity of his interests.

By *social masculinity* and *social femininity* we mean only the tendencies for men in general and for women in general to differ in the relative frequencies with which they answer questions one way or another. Social masculinity and femininity so defined must be distinguished from certain other concepts of maleness and femaleness.

The extremes of social masculinity and social femininity do not yield pictures of the personalities most generally *admired* in men and women. For example, chewing tobacco, spitting on the floor, and hanging around pool halls are extremely masculine characteristics as judged by the fact that those activities are engaged in by many more males than females. However, men who engage in such activities are not necessarily more admired merely because they are socially more masculine.

One ideal of masculinity and femininity is based on sexual attractiveness, with attendant considerations of youthfulness and vigor. This ideal also is not identical with social masculinity and femininity. The young woman at the height of her sexual attractiveness is likely to have many socially masculine interests, such as an interest in sports or politics. This fact accounts for the somewhat unexpected ranking of the 20-year-old women in Table 4–7. By the criteria of social femininity she is only moderately feminine; women over 60 are more feminine in their interests because they tend to be more domestic than 20-year-olds, and domestic interests are associated in our culture with social femininity.

The kinds of items yielding differences between men and women help us to see the importance of cultural roles in the determination of interests. Men tend to express interest more frequently than women in science, mechanics, and sports; women more often than men express interest in religion, art, domestic arts, and music. Tests of information bear out these dif-

TABLE 4-7

Social masculinity and femininity of interests of representative groups of men and women

Groups of men	Groups of women
Most socially masculine: Male college athletes Engineers and architects	**Most socially feminine:** Domestic employees Stenographers Dressmakers and hair- dressers Women over sixty
Moderately socially masculine: Men in *Who's Who* Farmers Policemen and firemen	**Moderately socially feminine:** Twenty-year-old women Teachers Nurses
Less socially masculine: Journalists, artists, clergymen Men over sixty	**Less socially feminine:** *Who's Who* women Women with Ph.D.'s and M.D.'s Superior women athletes

SOURCE: Terman and Miles (1936), pp. 160, 181.

ferences in interests. Men are able to give the correct answers more frequently when the subject matter is science, mechanics, or sports; women give the correct answers more often when the subject matter is flowers, dress fabrics, color combinations, precious stones, or household furnishings.

The results of such a test show us that masculine and feminine interests are largely determined by custom and that they are only moderately influenced by the native endowments of men and women.

CRITICAL DISCUSSION

Alternatives to a social definition of masculinity and femininity

While it is convenient to determine how men and women differ in a given culture by the ways in which they characteristically act, this may tell us more about the culture than it does about the masculinity or feminity of a given man or woman within that culture. By cultural standards a young woman may be much too interested in sports and politics to score high on the Terman-Miles femininity test; yet, in terms of her femininity as judged by appearance, dress, and attractiveness to the opposite sex, she might be rated highly feminine. Similarly, a young man interested in music and religion will by these interests lower his score on a social masculinity test, yet he, too, might rate highly masculine by physical appearance, strength, interest in and attractiveness to women. It would evidently be possible to construct a masculinity-femininity scale that would not exaggerate the differences in answers by men and women, but would use other criteria, such as prominence of the appropriate secondary sex characteristics or interest in and capacity to elicit favorable responses from the opposite sex.

Other interesting pencil-and-paper tests of masculinity and femininity tend to resemble the Terman-Miles test in construction, although at least one of these, a scale on the California Psychological Inventory (Gough, 1957), attempts to eliminate extreme items (such as attendance at pool halls or beauty parlors) as *too* social to deserve inclusion in a test based purely on the differences in the way most men and women answer.

A radically different kind of test, devised by Franck and Rosen (1949), is based on the assumption that men and women differ in their fantasies and hence in their imaginative productions. They prepared a test consisting of simple arrangements of lines or geometrical forms. The subject is asked to draw a picture to complete the form in any way he wishes. Because men and women tend to complete the forms differently, it is possible to score the productions of any one subject with respect to the agreement or disagreement with the productions typical of his sex. The scores on this test, while meeting satisfactory standards of consistency, do not correlate with scores on the previously described question-and-answer tests. The presumption is that scores on the Franck test reveal certain latent or "unconscious" aspects of masculinity and femininity not revealed in the more superficial, social

Marital happiness

As we follow the development of the child through adolescence into adult life, we may naturally inquire as to his or her suitability for marriage and likelihood of making a happy marriage. The increasing divorce rate (now about one divorce for every five marriages) is only one indication of the amount of unhappiness in marriage, for many unhappy marriages do not end in divorce. We may well investigate the factors in early life that make one person better suited for marriage than another.

Two large-scale studies, carried on at about the same time and with similar techniques, provided useful information which has been followed up by later investigators. One study was based on the replies of 792 couples, primarily from the Los Angeles area (Terman and others, 1938), the other on the replies of 526 couples located in the Chicago area (Burgess and Cottrell, 1939).

The logic of both studies was similar. First the investigators tried to establish a reasonably satisfactory index of happiness in marriage; then they examined the background of each person to find certain factors, present before marriage, from which a scale predictive of happiness could be made. Each couple was asked to supply information of two sorts: information about the happiness of the present marriage and information about his or her experiences before marriage. By relating the two sorts of information, one can predict what kind of person is likely to have a happy marriage and what kind is likely to have an unhappy marriage.

Later studies have shown that the original investigations were valid by taking the essential next step: testing engaged couples *before* marriage and then studying their happiness *after* marriage. Kelly (1939) tested 82 couples before marriage on background-personality items and then tested them on marital-happiness items after they had been married for two years. He found correlations of +.26 for husbands and +.30 for wives, showing a low but positive relationship.

Burgess and Wallin (1953) report a study in which they tested 1000 engaged couples and followed up 666 of them after they had been married three to five years. They found correlations of +.31 for husbands and +.27 for wives, values similar to those found by Kelly. The significance of these studies is that they show some people to be better marital risks than others. Whether or not a person is a good risk can perhaps be determined from the kind of person he is and the kinds of experiences he has had before marriage. The correlations are too low for much weight to be given to these tests, however, for purposes of individual guidance.

The continuity of personality is well illustrated by the fact that characteristics most predictive of happiness have their origins in early childhood: [3] the happiness of the parents' marriage, lack of conflict with the mother or father, attachment to the parents and to brothers and sisters, attractiveness of the opposite-sexed parent. Any of these increases the likelihood of a happy marriage when this child grows up.

One item found in the California study to be related to marital happiness scores was happiness in childhood. Those who remembered their childhoods as being generally happy made higher marital happiness scores than those whose childhoods were remembered as less happy.

It is a favorable omen for the success of a marriage if husband and wife had a happy childhood. According to our data, no other item of information relating to background is more significant. . . . It far outweighs such items as adequacy of sex instruction, religious education, adolescent "petting," or even premarital intercourse.[4]

[3] Recall the earlier discussion of continuity from childhood to adult personality, Chapter 3, p. 87.
[4] Terman and others (1938), p. 228.

Childhood discipline and marital happiness

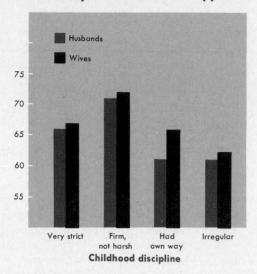

Reports by husbands and wives of the kind of childhood discipline they experienced show its effects on marital happiness. (After Terman and others, 1938)

Discipline in the home is another item predictive of later happiness or unhappiness. As we might have expected from the discussion in Chapter 3, the favorable type of discipline is that which is *firm but not harsh* (Figure 4–11), whereas the most unfavorable kind is that which is irregular and unpredictable. The relationships hold equally well for men and for women. It is noteworthy that the kind of discipline predictive of happy marriage is also predictive of nondelinquency (p. 100).

Productive work

As we shall see in later chapters, self-esteem and mental health often are influenced by seeing oneself as a productive person. The years in school and in preparation come to fruition in the work-life of the adult, and we may well inquire as to the changes in ability throughout the life span and when the most productive work can be expected.

So far as ability is concerned, we can expect some slowing down with age. Fisher and Birren (1947) gave a strength test to men at various ages and found a progressive decline after a peak in the late twenties. The reasons for this are somewhat complex, however, for many men are in sedentary occupations and do not exercise enough to keep up their muscular strength; at least some of the men in their seventies were as strong as some in their thirties. More complex skills, involving mental ability rather than muscular speed and precision, can be retained well into the sixties and seventies. A study of chess masters showed that they reached their peaks in tournament play in the thirties and that there was little decline until the fifties. The chess master Blackburne in nine exhibitions between the ages of 76 and 79 played an average of 21 games at a time, and won 86 percent of the games played. Although he had declined in ability, as measured against other champions, it is evident that the amount of residual ability was of a high order (Buttenwieser, 1935). It is because of the retention of abilities of this kind that many people doubt the wisdom of setting fixed ages for retirement.

It is still of interest to ask: From which years can we expect man's best work? The answer is important in case we are prolonging dependency by continuing students in education too long, when they ought to be producing on their own.

Performers who depend upon strength, speed, or precision of movement tend to reach their peaks of skill in the years from 25 to 29. It may be assumed that champion performers are always well trained and eager to do their best, so that a study of the ages at which the championship is reached furnishes useful evidence of age as an element in skill. The ages at which championships were won in a number of sports are plotted in Figure 4–12. The sports which make less demand upon stamina and more upon precision (rifle and pistol shooting, billiards) do not show the rapid falling off with age characteristic of the more strenuous sports, such as tennis or boxing. The leisure-time interests of adults correspond in part to these age changes in skill: as adults grow older, they turn to sports that can be played at a pace

How old are champions?

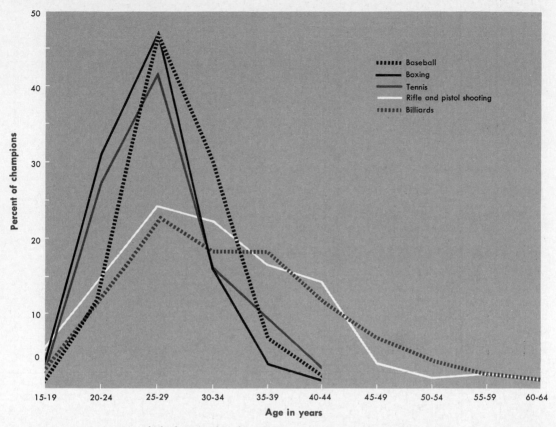

Ages at which championships have been won in sports. (After Lehman, 1938)

suited to the age of the participant, such as golf.

How about productive efforts in science, literature, and the arts? When are men at their best in creative work?

The results of a prodigious amount of work by Lehman (1953) are summarized in Table 4–8. Here we find the ages at which men tend most frequently to make superior contributions to the fields specified in the table. Lehman produced the data by going to bibliographies and historical summaries of the various fields and by getting the cooperation of experts in sorting out the superior from the pedestrian performance. By then finding out the age of each man at the time of his discovery or creative work, Lehman was able to chart the most productive years in each of the fields. In

this way he avoided the bias that comes from looking either for very young producers or very aged ones. For most of the fields the age of maximum productivity is between 30 and 40; for a few it is earlier, for a few later. Within each field productivity begins before 30 and continues after 40; a generalized curve for the fields of science, mathematics, and invention is plotted in Figure 4–13. Although distinguished contributions are made throughout life, the rapid rise to the peak and the gradual decline thereafter are striking.

Eminent scientists, whether they achieve eminence early or late in life, continue to be productive throughout their lives, so that a relationship can be established between eminence and productivity (Dennis, 1954a). Not only in the sciences but in

TABLE 4-8

Age of maximum rate of very superior contributions

General field of creative work	Age at time of maximum rate of contribution			
	25-30	30-35	35-40	40-45
Physical sciences, mathematics, inventions	Chemistry	Mathematics Physics Electronics Practical inventions Surgical techniques	Geology Astronomy	
Biological sciences and medicine		Botany Classical descriptions of disease	Bacteriology Physiology Pathology Medical discoveries	
			Genetics Entomology Psychology	
Philosophy, education, and social sciences		Economics and political science		
			Logic Ethics Esthetics "General philosophy" Educational theory and practice	Metaphysics
			Social philosophy	
Musical compositions	Instrumental selections	Vocal solos Symphonies	Chamber music Nonsymphonic orchestral music Grand opera	Cantatas Light opera and musical comedy
Literary compositions	Lyrics and ballads (German) Odes Elegies Pastoral poetry Narrative poetry Sonnets Lyric poetry	Satiric poetry Short stories Religious poetry (hymns) Comedies	Tragedies "Most influential books" Hymns by women	Novels "Best books" Best sellers Miscellaneous prose writings
Painting and sculpture		Oil paintings	American sculpture	Modern architecture Oil paintings (contemporary artists)

SOURCE: Lehman, 1953.

Age at which superior works were produced

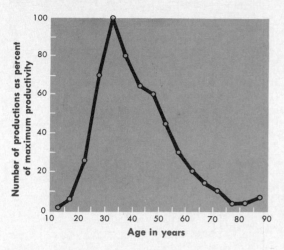

Ages at which 933 scientists, mathematicians, and inventors produced 1359 superior contributions. (After Lehman, 1953)

other fields as well (e.g., music, general books, linguistics), between one-third and two-thirds of the material is produced by only 10 percent of those active in the respective field (Dennis, 1955). These data raise fascinating but elusive problems. Do very productive people have a better chance to hit upon something important? Do people who happen to attract prominence early become motivated to remain productive? Further research is needed to obtain answers to these questions. We do know that people who are productive early are more likely than the less productive to continue to create in their later years. This is true whether or not they attain eminence (Dennis, 1954a, b).

There are two major lessons to be learned from this massive data on the productivity of creative persons. The first is that the early adult years are important ones, and that it would probably be a good idea to place able people on their own at the youngest feasible age. The second is that some means should be found for continuing the creativity of those who show early promise. Equally impressive as the early age of major contributions is the very

rapid fall-off in contributions, beginning, as shown in Figure 4–13, immediately beyond the high peak in the early 30s. It may be that society's rewards for early success are antithetical to creative work: shifting to "better" jobs with loss of continuity of effort, taking on administrative duties, excessive demands for lecturing at a distance from the workbench; one observer after a study done many years ago felt that in his field (history) it appeared that historians of promise were being paid *not* to do research (Jernegan, 1927).

CRITICAL DISCUSSION

Life-history data vs. laboratory data; advantages and hazards

The work of both Lehman and Dennis calls attention to the possibility of using existing historical data for quantitative purposes. Hypotheses can be tested with such data as well as with data freshly gathered in the laboratory and (as in these studies) can provide information that could not be obtained in the laboratory. Historical data have other advantages over laboratory data, in that the people studied represent an ability level that could not be matched in the laboratory and are more highly motivated in their work than laboratory subjects generally are. The laboratory has the advantage of more stringent control, but the disadvantage of more restricted subjects.

Dennis (1958) points out certain hazards in the use of historical data. He has argued that one reason Lehman's scientists seem more eminent when they are younger than when they are older is that the number of scientists increases very rapidly, so that on the basis of numbers alone scientists are losing their competitive advantage. That is, if the same famous man had been a young man 25 years later, his chances of fame, with the same amount of creativity, would have been much less. Perhaps Lehman has been plotting an increase in competition rather than a decrease in productivity with age. This is an interesting point, but Lehman (1960) appears to have shown that the amount of this effect as a distortion of his findings would not be very great.

Successful aging

Some changes with age are inevitable; successful aging does not mean retaining youth, but achieving satisfaction in the later years through wise choices. There are two main theories of how successful aging is achieved. The one stresses *activity,* the other *disengagement.*

The activity theory assumes that society often forces retirement when a person is still energetic and capable of productive participation in the life of the community. Hence he should make plans for his retirement, so that he can turn to other interests, and find ways in which to see himself as continuing to be significant. The extreme of this is that a person wishes "to die with his boots on," that is, while still in the midst of things. This theory can of course be modified to take into account the lessened energies of older people, so that plans are proposed, for example, for "partial retirement," in which the person remains active but on a part-time basis (Breckinridge, 1953). This is familiar in university circles, where the emeritus professor, no longer conducting classes, commonly continues his research and writing.

The disengagement theory assumes that as a person gets older he views himself differently, and can make a good adjustment through a gradual withdrawal from active participation and responsibility. This withdrawal is not forced upon him, but is at least in part a matter of his own choosing (Cummings and others, 1960). Instead of being preoccupied with what he is doing now, the disengaged person is reflective about what he was and what he accomplished in the past.

Doubtless there are both kinds of people: those who will find their satisfactions through continuing activity and those who will take comfort in disengagement. The fact that disengagement is not merely a response to lessened capacity for social interaction, and to society's isolation of the older person, comes from some studies of changes over the years 40 to 65. Gross measures of social competence show no changes over these years that can be associated directly with age (Havighurst, 1957). Careful personality studies, however, show that there are indeed significant personality changes associated with age within these years, particularly as bearing on the image of the self and outlook to the future (Neugarten and others, 1964). It appears, then, that there may be processes looking toward disengagement that start as early as the 40s, even though full social competency is maintained during the next 20 or more years.

The problems of the later years of life have many facets. The person who has suffered a heart attack or some other debilitating illness is often demoralized by the experience, and he may require a period of psychological as well as physical rehabilitation. Loneliness due to death of family members, children moving away, or the inability to travel has to be confronted. Various activity centers for older people are being developed to meet these needs. The present scale of the problem is aggravated by the fact that there is a larger

4–14

The aged in the United States

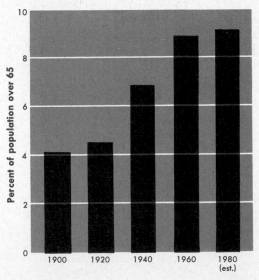

The percentage of the total population aged 65 or over has more than doubled in the last half-century, though the trend shows signs of slackening. (U.S. Bureau of Census)

fraction of older people in the population (Figure 4–14). With more research and inventiveness being directed toward the solution of these problems, it is certain that new and sounder policies can be proposed.

SUMMARY

1. Puberal changes bring the greatest modifications in physiological processes during the lifetime of the individual. These changes differ between boys and girls, but there are similarities in the pattern of changes both undergo. Girls enter upon the puberal changes earlier and on the average reach maturity about two years before boys do, but because of individual differences some boys go through puberal changes earlier than some girls.

2. The different rates of bodily growth have their psychological consequences. The late-maturing boy has adjustment problems aggravated by his falling behind the early maturers, while the early maturer has corresponding advantages. The early-maturing girl may have some problems associated with being too advanced for her age mates. Other out-of-step changes are responsible for the idea that adolescence is an awkward age, which is true enough of some adolescent social behavior but not of physical coordination.

3. Specific problems arise in the areas of sex, emancipation from home, relation to age mates, and arriving at standards of value. The peer-culture becomes very important and is in some sense a distinctive subculture.

4. Adolescent conflicts may result in juvenile delinquency. *Individual delinquency,* based on personal problems, is distinguished from *social delinquency,* expressed in gang behavior.

5. The problems familiar in adolescence do not end with the attainment of adulthood. Problems of adjustment in early adult life are continuous with those in adolescence except for the lesser importance of growth changes.

6. Sex roles become differentiated in adult life. Study of nonliterate cultures (as well as our own) shows that the differences depend only in part upon the biological roles of the two sexes. Cultural arrangements determine many of the differences that we find.

7. Studies of marital happiness point up the fact of continuity of development, for the most important predictors of marital happiness go back to childhood: the happiness of parents, a happy childhood, affectionate relations with parents and siblings, and a firm but not harsh discipline.

8. The years of greatest proficiency and productivity center in the ages between 20 and 40. Although productivity may continue until late in life, the later rate can generally be predicted from productivity in the 30s.

9. Increased longevity creates new problems for those who pass the retirement age. There appears to be an important choice between *activity* and *disengagement* as approaches to successful aging.

SUGGESTIONS FOR FURTHER READING

The physical and physiological changes in adolescence, along with their correlates in social behavior, are dealt with in Tanner, *Growth at adolescence* (1962). There are a number of textbooks on adolescent psychology, such as Jersild, *The psychology of adolescence* (1963), Douvan and Adelson, *The adolescent experience* (1966), and Hurlock, *Adolescent development* (3rd ed., 1966).

For many ways of viewing the adolescent, see Muuss, *Theories of adolescence* (1962).

A useful book of readings on adolescent psychology is Grinder (ed.), *Studies in adolescence* (1963).

For a general overview of development, including the problems of the older years, see Pressey and Kuhlen, *Psychological development through the life span* (1957).

For some of the problems of aging, see Kleemeier, *Aging and leisure* (1961), Neugarten and others, *Personality in middle and late life* (1964), and Williams and others, *Processes of aging* (1963).

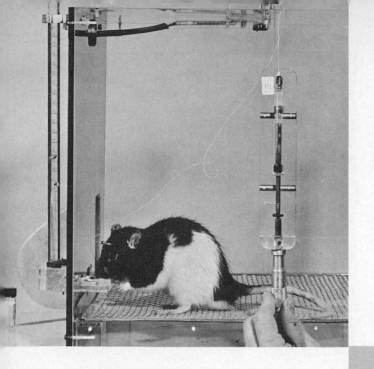

MOTIVATED AND EMOTIONAL BEHAVIOR

To understand behavior we must know how it is aroused and directed; these aspects of energetic and goal-directed behavior fall within the province of motivational psychology. Because pleasures and pains, hopes and fears, satisfactions and annoyances are closely related to the successes and failures of motivated behavior, there is an intimate connection between motivation and emotion.

5 Physiological Background of Motivation

Although organisms are occasionally quiescent, as in sleep or hibernation, it is much more characteristic of them to be active. In order to understand the active organism—why it does what it does when it does it—we search for motives, for springs of action. By a *motive* we mean something that incites the organism to action or that sustains and gives direction to action once the organism has been aroused. A dog buries a bone, a child practices on the piano, a task force sends a rocket to the moon. When we ask why these actions take place, we are inquiring about motives.

There are two main aspects of motivated behavior: the *activating* or *energizing* aspect and the *directional* aspect. By activation we mean the change that occurs between sleeping and waking, between being relaxed and being tense, between "taking it easy" and putting forth effort. Motivational activation produces a state of readiness for behavior, as in the horse's change from standing quietly in the stall to his champing at the bit when ready for the race. The same act engaged in by a less activated organism will be done less vigorously than by an aroused one. In addition to producing a state of readiness for behavior, an activated motive also tends to set off behavior in a particular direction. The hungry animal is ready to run to food and to eat, the thirsty one to drink, the one in pain to escape the painful stimulus.

We may well ask whether or not *all* behavior is motivated. The answer is not easy, for even such reflex behaviors as the heartbeat and digestion serve purposes in the life of the organism and are responsive to various kinds of motivational activation. Simple reflex behavior is not usually thought of as motivated, although there is no easy rule by which it is excluded, but all more complex behavior, especially all learned behavior, is clearly responsive to motivational activation and control.

The most dramatic human motives are revealed in daring and heroic action: when determined men explore new lands, when one man sacrifices his life to save another, when a man withstands the pains of torture rather than renounce an ideal. We might begin by trying to give a psychological account of such noble human motives, but we would soon find our tools inadequate to the task. So we start much more modestly by studying need-satisfying behavior, as represented by the commonplace motives of hunger and thirst. Man never outgrows these basic biological needs, for he needs food and water to survive. If we first try to understand these simpler, more elemental motives, we may hope eventually to understand more about the bolder, more complex motives that characterize man at his best; there may, indeed, be some important bridges between them. Hence in this chapter we shall consider chiefly motives for which the bodily needs are obvious, which are commonly called *organic* or *physiological* motives. Much of the behavior of the newborn baby can be explained on a physiological basis. He is primarily occupied with satisfaction of the needs for food, water, sleep, excretion of wastes, and avoidance of pain and discomfort. These are all motives that man shares with the lower animals; we shall be concerned here primarily with this common biological ancestry.

In the next chapter we shall examine human motivation more directly, not on the assumption that there is any sharp break between motives with a physiological basis and other human motives, but because man is a social animal capable of planning and foresight.

Physiological Needs as Determiners of Behavior

We use a great many words to describe motivation: needs, urges, impulses, desires, goals. They all refer in some way to the forces that energize behavior and give it direction. While the vocabulary of psychology has not settled down, it is convenient to treat some physiological motives in terms of *needs* and *drives*.

Needs and drives

If a rat that has been deprived of food for several hours is placed in a checkerboard maze, such as the one illustrated in Figure 5–1, it will be active. We may keep track of its movements and find how many squares it covers. A well-fed rat placed in the same maze may move about a little, but it will cover less ground than the hungry rat. We may say that a food-deprived rat is an *active* rat. Now, if the same rat is placed in a maze consisting of several alleys, one of which leads to food, it will run about until it happens to reach the food. Then it will eat. We may say now that a food-deprived rat is also a *hungry* rat. After eating it is no longer restless. If returned to its cage, it is likely to curl up and go to sleep. When it is hungry again, its activity cycle will begin again.

How shall we talk scientifically about the behavior of the rat just described? We may refer to the food-deprived state as a state of *need*. The organism needs food,

Checkerboard maze

Differences in amount of exploratory behavior of hungry and well-fed rats can be recorded by counting the squares entered. Although no food is present, the hungry animals are more restless and active than the well-fed ones. (After Dashiell, 1925)

and when the rat has not eaten for a while there are chemical changes in its blood which are indicators of its need. The need for food is physiological, not psychological, but a state of physiological need has psychological consequences. The psychological consequences of a need we call a *drive*. Thus the food-need in the rat leads, through processes which we shall investigate, to the hunger drive.

While need and drive are parallel, they are not the same. Drive does not necessarily get stronger as need gets stronger. A starved organism may be so weakened by its great need that drive is weakened (Figure 5–2). Men who have fasted for a long time report that their hunger pangs (a subjective representation of hunger drive) come and go, though, of course, their need for food persists.

Typical deprivation drives based on physiological needs are those for air, food, and water. Other physiological drives (sex, maternal activity, pain avoidance) are somewhat differently related to deprivation. It is here proposed that each of the needs, as it becomes sufficiently intense owing to deprivation, leads to a corresponding drive.

Strength of hunger drive

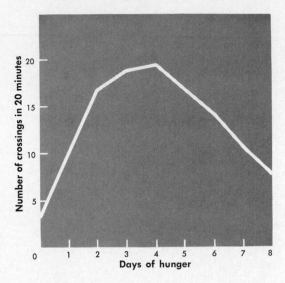

Determination of the point at which the hunger drive is at a maximum, by the obstruction method. Each day the rat was permitted to cross an electrified grill in order to be fed. Strength of drive was measured by the number of crossings in 20 minutes, under standardized conditions. (After Warden, 1931)

Measuring drives

A good deal of ingenuity has been used in finding ways to measure drives, since psychologists often want to know the "drive level" in order to relate it to other behavior, such as learning. We may consider four such methods: measures of general activity level, the rate of performing learned acts, the obstruction method, and the choice method.

1. *Measures of general activity level.* It is assumed that heightened drive leads to restlessness, so that restless behavior will increase as drive increases. Thus speed of running in an activity cage (Figure 5-3) can be related to hours of food deprivation. Another form of activity measurement is that of the living cage suspended on springs with markers, so that the amount of restless activity is recorded.

It has been found that these measures, while useful, have to be used with some

sophistication. For example, the cage activity of unfed rats is not higher than that of well-fed rats *unless* some external source of stimulation is provided, in which case the differences become marked (Campbell and Sheffield, 1953).

2. *Rate of performing learned acts.* If a rat has learned to press a lever in order to receive a food pellet but the pellets come only occasionally, the rat will press the lever more rapidly when hungry. Thus rate of lever-pressing may be used as a measure of drive. Alternate behavior measures are the delay of starting a run down an alley (latency of response) or the running speed itself. Care has to be taken not to depend upon one measure only. Thus rate of lever-pressing and amount of water ingested may not be equivalent as measures of the thirst drive (Miller, 1961).

3. *Overcoming an obstruction.* A number of years ago a method of drive meas-

Activity measurement

Lafayette Instrument Co.

In the activity cage the distance that the rat runs is recorded by a revolving drum.

Obstruction box (floor plan)

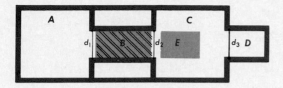

A, entrance compartment; B, charged grill giving access to C. A release plate E opens a door (d_3), which permits access to an incentive in D. Other doors (d_1 and d_2) are manually operated. (After Warden, 1931)

urement was devised in which drive strength could be assessed by seeing how much punishment the organism would take in order to satisfy the drive. An *obstruction box* (Figure 5–4) provided a passageway with a grid floor through which the animal received a shock in crossing. The aroused animal was placed at the starting point and allowed to run across the uncharged grid to the chamber in which the goal-object (food, water, etc.) was placed. Then, with the shock turned on, a record was kept of the number of crossings that the animal would make in a given 20-minute period.

4. *The choice method.* Occasionally more than one drive is active at a time. In the case of two simultaneously aroused drives, the relative strengths of the drives may be determined by permitting the animal to choose one goal-object if he turns in one direction, another goal-object if he turns in the other direction.

Of the four methods, the most used today are the first two, in one or another variation. The first method relies on the general restlessness associated with heightened drive; the second depends upon the intensification of a well-learned act under appropriate drive.

Hunger drive

Studies of hunger permit us to understand some of the components of motivation. The need for food rests upon the depletion of food substances in the blood.

This condition leads to restless activity in animals and, in man, to the awareness of a craving for food. When food substances are depleted in the blood, the need to replenish them causes an increase in stomach contractions. These stomach contractions produce internal stimuli that are part of the aroused state: they make the organism active and they are the source of hunger pangs.

A person who has gone without food for some hours does not feel hungry all the time. The aching or gnawing feelings described as hunger pangs occur irregularly. In experiments designed to discover the basis for these pangs, the food-deprived subject swallowed a rubber balloon, which was then inflated until it was firm against the walls of the stomach. A small tube from the balloon was connected to a recording instrument, so that a pointer moved whenever the walls of the stomach contracted (see Figure 5–5). The subject, who could not see the pointer, was given a telegraph key to press whenever he felt the pangs of hunger. It was found that his pressing of the key was almost simultaneous with the contractions of his stomach.

The relationship of food deprivation to stomach contractions suggests that the hunger drive may be identified with stimuli from the contracting stomach. The explanation is not so simple, however, for hunger can occur in the absence of stomach contractions. The hunger drive to which food deprivation gives rise is dependent on more than these contractions. For example, a man whose stomach had been removed surgically and whose esophagus was then connected directly to his intestine reported periodic desires for food much the same as those of persons with stomachs (Hoelzel, 1927). And rats whose stomachs were removed for experimental purposes showed hunger behavior like that of normal rats, except that they tended to show it more frequently. The more frequent hunger undoubtedly was due to the reduced food-storage capacity (Tsang, 1938).

Hunger stirs a rat to activity. If we assume that its hunger is due to stomach

Hunger pangs and stomach contractions

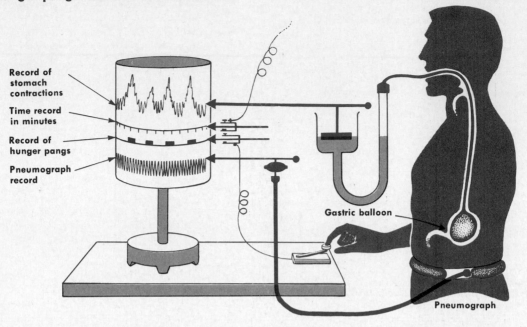

Record of stomach contractions

Time record in minutes

Record of hunger pangs

Pneumograph record

Gastric balloon

Pneumograph

Note that the reported hunger pangs correspond closely to the periods when stomach contractions are at their maximum. (After Cannon, 1934)

contractions, we must also assume that its activity is the result of sensory messages from the stomach to the brain; but the fact is that when the sensory nerves from the stomach to the brain are cut, a rat still exhibits hunger behavior (Morgan and Morgan, 1940).

We have sufficient evidence to indicate that the chemical state of the body influences the hunger drive in ways other than by stomach contractions. The complexity of hunger is further indicated by the presence not only of a general hunger drive but of specific hungers, that is, drives toward specific food incentives.

Specific hungers. A child who is no longer hungry for spinach may still be hungry for ice cream. Foods differ in their attractiveness to different people. Differences in food preferences are sometimes due to cultivated tastes. They may, however, arise from specific bodily needs. A diet that is deficient in some essentials

causes special drives. Experiments with animals have shown that such specific drives are satisfied only by the foods appropriate to them.

Rats on a fat-free diet, when offered a choice among fat, sugar, and wheat, exhibit a marked preference for fat. Similarly, rats deprived of either sugar or wheat will prefer the food of which they have been deprived. Other experiments have shown that rats have specific hungers for sugar, fat, protein, thiamine, riboflavin, salt, phosphorus, sodium, and calcium (see Figure 5–6).

Still other experiments have shown that barnyard animals as well as laboratory animals will commonly select a well-balanced diet if given a wide range of foods from which to choose. Experiments on the self-regulation of diet have been carried out on pigs, dairy cows, and chickens as well as on laboratory rats and mice. The results of these experiments show that animals demand in their food something more than the requisite number of calories; they hunger for the necessary chemical constituents of a balanced diet.

It is not clear how specific hungers are regulated, but it is assumed that the needed foods must taste better to the animal or child choosing from a variety of foods. That taste does influence choosing is indicated by the fact that rats with their taste nerves cut failed to select a balanced diet (Richter, 1943).

Whatever may be the origin of appetite and food preference, it is evident from ordinary observation that the preferences can be distorted by learning. The deficiency disease beriberi is found among peoples whose diet consists largely of polished rice. This preference for polished rice instead of whole-grain rice is contrary to needs of the body. Animal experiments have also shown that preference can be established for poor diets, so that the animal may continue for some time to choose the poor food to which it has become accustomed, even though a more balanced food is accessible. We need neither carry "naturalness" too far nor be alarmed by the harmful results of learning. Modern dietitians can provide more nutritious diets for both animals and human beings, and organisms can learn to like better diets as well as poorer ones.

Thirst drive

Dryness of the mouth and throat is one condition of thirst; when the tissues are relatively dry, we are aware of being thirsty. But the craving for water can be satisfied only in part through stimulating salivation by chewing gum, wetting the mouth, or anesthetizing the skin of mouth and throat. Just as stomach contractions provide only one component of the hunger drive, so dryness in the mouth and throat provides only one component of the thirst drive. Experiments with dogs bear out the

5–6

Self-selection of diet

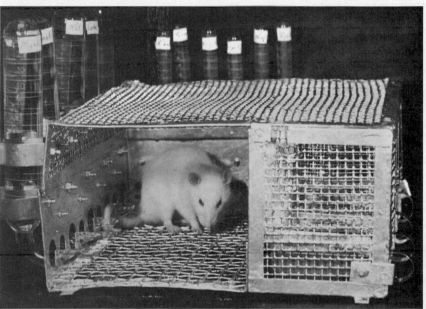

Dr. Curt Richter

The cage above shows the apparatus used in studies in which rats are allowed to select their own diet from 15 to 18 different substances. Under these conditions, rats select a healthful, nutritious diet.

fact that water intake is regulated by the amount of water that the body needs, not merely by the dryness of the mouth.

Dogs whose normal daily intake of water had been computed were placed on a schedule limiting the amount of water they were given, so that the water deficit could be known and systematically varied. When later tested, the dogs showed an accurate "ability to estimate" the amount of water needed to make up the deficit; that is, they drank the same amount of water of which they had been deprived (Adolph, 1939).

In another experiment, water equal to the deficit was placed directly in the dog's stomach either through a surgical opening or by means of a tube. Thus the water entered the stomach without affecting the dryness of the mouth and throat tissues. If allowed to drink before the water had been assimilated, the dog drank as much as he would have if no water had been artificially placed in his stomach. If, however, a 15-minute wait was introduced, so that the water could be assimilated into his system, the dog did not drink at all, showing that thirst had been relieved without any direct wetting of the mouth and throat tissues (Adolph, 1941).

How can we explain results such as these? There must be some regulator within the nervous system that acts to control the thirst drive much as a thermostat regulates the temperature of a room. Experiments have located a region in or near the hypothalamus where such regulation may occur. The first experiments testing this theory were done with goats, although the results have since been confirmed with other animals. If a slight amount of salt solution is injected into the third ventricle (a fluid-filled cavity inside the brain in the region of the hypothalamus), the goat drinks an excessive amount of water. Injection of pure water does not lead to such drinking (Andersson, 1953). The conclusion is that there must be some "brain center," sensitive to the body's need for liquid, that controls thirst, and the speculation arises that there may be such "centers" for other drives.

An ingenious suggestion has been made by Deutsch (1960) that the act of drinking (and tasting) sends some sort of "thirst-quenching" messages to the brain, thereby regulating the amount drunk. A thirsty animal requires more such "messages" and hence drinks more. As a specific test of this theory Deutsch studied the drinking of saline solution by rats. The assumption is that one unit of saline solution will not be as thirst-quenching as one unit of ordinary water: it is as though the salt "dilutes" the water.[1] If a thirsty animal is permitted to drink all it wishes of both salty water and ordinary water, it will actually drink more of the water with salt in it (Deutsch and Jones, 1959). However, if the amount is limited, so that it can drink only a given amount, it will prefer to drink ordinary water, as the theory would predict.

CRITICAL DISCUSSION
Local vs. central determiners of hunger and thirst

In the discussion of hunger and thirst drives, attention was called to both local and central sources for the activated drive. By "local sources" is meant, for hunger, sources near the stomach, as in stomach contractions, and, for thirst, sources near the mouth and throat, such as dryness of tissues. By "central sources" is meant portions of the brain that monitor chemical substances in the blood.

Rosenzweig (1962) has given a very illuminating history, beginning with the ancient Greeks, of preferences for one or another of these interpretations. Until quite recently the local theories have been the most widely accepted, despite a great deal of contradictory evidence that has been available for a century. The preference for the local theories illustrates a kind of sociology of science whereby in one climate of opinion a position is favored over another because of prevailing common-sense views, the testimony of authorities, and an occasional dramatic experiment that over-

---

[1] If salt "dilutes" water, can anything "concentrate" it? Yes, water is more thirst quenching per unit amount if it is cold or slightly acid.

shadows equally good observations made on the other side.

The testimony of authorities from the time of Plato, Aristotle, and Galen through Erasmus Darwin (Charles's grandfather) was on the side of local theories, and the beginning of modern experimental work also favored this position. In the period from 1824 to 1833, William Beaumont, an army surgeon, studied a man who as a result of gunshot had a fistula in his stomach, so that what went on in his stomach could be observed. Beaumont reported that when he placed food directly through the aperture the motions of the stomach subsided and the hunger also ceased immediately. This was the beginning of the kinds of observations later made impressive by the experiments of Carlson and Cannon (see Figure 5–5). Thus the stomach as the source of the sensations of hunger seemed well established.

Actually this theory had been questioned for many years. Adults questioned by Schiff (1867) as to where they felt hunger failed to localize it in the stomach (only two of some 30 designating the stomach region at all). A number of experiments with animals were critical of the local hypothesis, but it prevailed until more modern methods of brain study have now shown very clearly that a large fraction of hunger and thirst behavior, as reflected in eating and drinking, is indeed controlled by the brain, particularly in the region of the hypothalamus.

Sex as a drive

The male mammal can typically live out his life without sexual activity; he is not in pain because of being deprived of sex and his health does not suffer. His sexual motivation is very much incentive-related rather than need-related: the odor of a female in heat or, in some animals, changes in coloring or size of the genital areas cause intense approach reactions, leading to the remainder of the sexual cycle. In many species there is no special cycle of sexual activity for the male, so that he is hormonally prepared for mating at any time, except, perhaps, when depleted by too much sexual activity. In some males there is a particular time for mating. In the Virginia deer, for example, there is a fall rutting season, and prior to this the male gonads grow in size. If this growth is associated with tension, then the female may indeed serve as an incentive to reduce this aspect of sex drive.[2]

The cycle of sexual receptivity in female animals, known as the *estrus cycle*, demonstrates the influence of sex hormones upon sex drive. The estrus cycle in the rat is between four and five days in length. Every fourth or fifth day of her life the mature female rat is in the receptive state known as *estrus*, or, as we say colloquially, she is *in heat*.

The sexually aroused state in the female rat leads to tension and restless activity, and hence may be treated similarly to hunger and thirst drives. An illustration of the increase in the rate of a female rat's running in an activity cage during estrus is given in Figure 5–7. At the height of estrus the female rat is sexually receptive as well as physically active; when placed with a

[2] The drive-incentive relationship is treated in greater detail later in this chapter (pp. 128–29).

5–7

Estrus cycle and activity

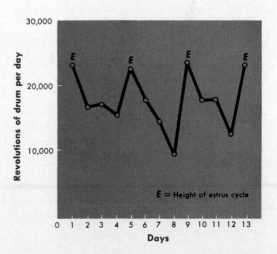

Specimen record showing the effect of the estrus cycle in the female rat. Note that activity tends to be at its maximum near the peak of estrus. (After Wang, 1923)

male rat, she actively seeks copulation by presenting herself appropriately.

Sexual receptivity and appropriate mating behavior can be made to appear (or reappear) in female rats through the injection of ovarian hormones. If young female rats receive injections of ovarian hormones, they develop mature mating patterns well in advance of the time when such patterns would normally appear. Mature female rats whose sexual activity has ceased after removal of the ovaries will again engage in normal sexual behavior if treated with ovarian hormones. Mating patterns appear whether the ovaries were removed before or after sexual maturity had been reached.

Immature male rats engage in incomplete sexual behavior while they are still incapable of complete copulation. In this they differ from young female rats, which do not indulge in sexual behavior until they are sexually mature. Castration does not completely abolish mating behavior in the male as it does in the female. This persistence of sexual behavior of the castrated adult male contrasts with the immediate cessation of sexual responsiveness in the female after loss of ovaries (Beach, 1944).

These studies suffice to indicate the important role played by hormones in the sexual behavior of lower animals. There is a hint, however, in the conduct of the castrated adult male rat, of controls other than hormones. Hormonal control, although significant, is less important in sexual behavior among higher animals, including primates and man (Beach, 1956).

The results of castration in the male human and ovarian removal in the female are variable. In a high proportion of women whose ovaries have been surgically removed, sexual desire and capacity are little changed. While castration of the male may result in gradual diminution of sexual interest, sex drive and the capacity for sexual intercourse may persist undiminished for several decades.

Maternal drive

A mother rat is strongly motivated to care for her newborn offspring. She will return them to the nest if they are placed outside it. If she is separated from them, she will overcome barriers and suffer pain in order to reach them.

The physiological states that activate this maternal behavior are complex. The hormone *prolactin,* associated with milk secretion, is one influence, for if it is injected into virgin female rats or even into males, they begin to build nests and take care of young rats as a mother does. Nest-building among rats appears to be regulated in part by temperature. The hormonal condition may reduce the body temperature, and the mother rat perhaps builds a nest not so much because of the needs of her young as to make herself comfortable.

Although the human mother shares with the lower animals the bodily changes associated with pregnancy and lactation as well as some aspects of maternal drive, her care of children differs from culture to culture and is largely regulated by learning. It is a general rule that human motives can never be fully explained on the basis of physiological influences alone.

CRITICAL DISCUSSION

Instinctive tendencies as explanations of motivated behavior

The complex behaviors of various animal species, such as nest-building in birds, swarming in bees, migration of birds and fishes, mating rituals, caring for the young, have defied explanation on any simple drive-incentive basis. The word "instinct" was widely used in the past to characterize such behavior. Instinct referred to unlearned, patterned, goal-directed behavior characteristic of a species. The word was often used in reference to human behavior as well, a mother's love illustrating a parental instinct, warfare an aggressive instinct, social behavior a gregarious or herd instinct.

The presence or absence of instincts in man was a source of intense controversy in the 1920s. The controversy became part of an argument over the relative contribution of heredity and environment, those believing in instincts attributing the major developmental influence to heredity. Those who did not believe in them won the victory because the believers failed to agree with each other on either the number or the kinds of instincts man possessed. Because of man's prolonged infancy and the great importance of learning in all that he does, the concept of instinct has not proved helpful in studying or understanding human behavior.

The problems raised by the study of instincts are genuine ones, and have taken on renewed interest under the influence of a group of European zoologists who call themselves "ethologists" (see reports by Tinbergen, 1961; Thorpe, 1963; Hinde, 1959). Several of their concepts have attained widespread adoption. One of them, *imprinting*, was discussed in Chapter 3 (p. 64). Another is that of a *releaser*, a particular environmental stimulus that sets off a kind of behavior characteristic of a species. Thus a spot on the mother's beak "releases" pecking in some young gulls, causing the mother to regurgitate the food that the infant will eat; the swollen abdomen of the female of a small fish (the three-spined stickleback) initiates courtship behavior by the male; owl-like figures initiate mobbing behavior—a kind of feigned attack—by some birds for whom the owl is a natural enemy. The highly specific nature of some releasers shows a primacy for particular incentives. In a very fundamental sense, some motivated behavior is under control of the *environment*, and not merely under the control of internal drives.

While these studies have called attention to the importance of studying organisms in their natural environments, the concept of instinct has again not proved very helpful and has been abandoned by the ethologists in favor of the more neutral expression, *species-specific* behavior. The difficulty with instinct is that it tends to become an *explanation* for what is found, when in fact it is a mere label for species-specific behavior. The return of the homing pigeon is explained because it has a homing instinct, but this tells us no more than that it came home. The label is not entirely inappropriate, for not all pigeons have this tendency, but the tendency for the label to become an explanation has led to the discard of the term "instinct" in most discus-sions of behavior of this kind. The *explanation* of instinctive behavior turns out to be very complex, and depends upon breaking up the total "instinctive" behavior into its component parts. For example, there is now good evidence on the use of the sun in "navigation" by both bees and birds; this explains in part some of the success of bees in foraging and of birds in their migrations, but it does not tell the whole story of other features of foraging and migrating.

Pain as a drive

The drive to avoid pain arises from the organism's need to escape damage through tissue injury and is created by the discomfort and intolerability of the painful state. It illustrates the fact that physiological drives are aversive, that they are states from which the organism is led to escape. Just as the hunger drive leads to escape from hunger pangs and the thirst drive leads to escape from a parched throat, so the pain-avoidance drive leads to whatever behavioral sequence will reduce the organism's discomfort—running off a charged grid, taking off a shoe that pinches, placing an ice pack on a feverish brow, escaping to a safe place.

Pain differs from hunger and thirst in that it is not a result of deprivation, but is based on a readiness that is always present though inactive unless a painful (noxious) stimulus is encountered. Thus pain is *episodic*, while other drives tend to be *cyclical*, depending as they do upon the body's metabolism.

Other drives with physiological bases

Many other conditions serve as drives. We have a drive to avoid extremes of temperature; a drive to avoid suffocation; a drive against accumulating waste products in the body; a drive against excessive fatigue and exhaustion. Note that these operate as subordinate pain-avoidance drives; all are aversive states.

Sometimes the physiological basis of a drive is acquired. Drug addiction provides an example, for a person who habitually takes morphine originally had no need for it. Continued use, however, creates an imperative need; morphine then becomes necessary for him. He has become an addict and, deprived of the drug, is driven by his craving for it; without it he becomes restless and develops symptoms of acute illness that are relieved only by the drug.

The Need-Drive-Incentive Formulation

Thus far we have talked about the drives that goad the organism into activity, but we have touched only lightly on the rest of the motivated behavior sequence. The full pattern of goal-directed activity, as formulated in terms of need, drive, and incentive, moves from the drive to the goal in a number of steps:

1. The condition of *need* is established either through deprivation or through noxious stimulation (need for sustenance; need to avoid damage to the tissues).
2. The need comes to be represented as an active, directed state of *drive*, characterized by tension, energy, and (usually) goal-directedness.
3. The first phase of the motivated behavior sequence, initiated and sustained by drive, is *preparatory activity*, such as going to the place where food or water or a receptive animal can be found. This activity, particularly if on the part of an experienced animal, shows marks of being *goal-directed* or *goal-seeking*.
4. The preparatory activity, if successful, leads the organism to an environmental object called a *positive incentive*, that is, an object that can typically reduce the drive through satisfying the conditions of need. When we bait a trap we place a positive incentive in it. The words "lure," "reward," "goal-object," "reinforcement" [3] all refer to positive incentives. Food as an incentive satisfies the hunger drive; water as an incentive satisfies the thirst drive. In the case of the pain drive the positive incentive is anything that brings relief.

[3] "Reinforcement" is a technical word for incentive used in connection with learning theory (Chapter 11).

5. The incentive arouses *goal-activity* or *consummatory behavior*. The animal eats the food, drinks the water, or jumps from the charged grid. The reduction of drive through consummatory behavior ends the motivated behavior sequence.

Positive incentives

While we consider a positive incentive first as something that can satisfy a drive condition, we find that incentives have other characteristics as well. Limiting incentives to their drive-reducing properties places too much importance upon need satisfaction and avoidance of discomfort. A full definition of a positive incentive must recognize two possible roles:

1. Any object or circumstance that can reduce a drive through satisfying a need classifies as a *positive incentive*.
2. Any object or circumstance that when perceived or anticipated directs behavior toward itself also classifies as a *positive incentive*, regardless of its need-satisfying qualities. For example, good music as a positive incentive attracts behavior toward itself, but the behavior does not satisfy a physiological need based on deprivation.

Thus, all objects or circumstances that reduce drives or satisfy needs are positive incentives, but not all positive incentives satisfy drive conditions.

Complexity of the drive-incentive relationship

In the uncomplicated form of the drive-incentive pattern, the drive results in activity of a preparatory sort, leading the organism eventually to the incentive. The incentive then reduces the drive, and the organism is less tense and restless.

We have already met a few complications. Experience with incentives may lead to changes in the attractiveness of incentives and in drive arousal (as in specific food preferences or in drug addiction). Changes occur also in the preparatory activity: with practice the random activity of the hungry animal becomes learned goal-seeking activity, as in looking for the food where it was found before. In other words there is an interrelatedness among drive, preparatory activity, incentive, and goal-activity, so that the whole cycle of behavior becomes modified as the organism engages repeatedly in a motivated sequence. Three illustrations of such modifications follow.

Positive incentives may enhance drives. A person who is not especially hungry may have his hunger drive aroused by seeing pastries in a bakery window or by smelling the odor of freshly baked bread. The incentive (i.e., fresh bakery goods) can activate the hunger as well as reduce it.

An old experiment with chickens illustrates this point. A hen that has not eaten for 24 hours will eat more from a larger pile of grain than from a smaller pile; the *total amount* of incentive enhances drive. If the remainder of the pile is brushed away as soon as she has stopped eating, she will start again if a new pile of grain is placed before her. With some hens this process was repeated as often as eight times, and each time the hens would eat from the new pile. They ate as much as 67 percent more from the new piles than they had eaten up to the first point of ceasing to eat. Here *renewal* of incentive reactivated the drive (Bayer, 1929; see Katz, 1937, pp. 160–62).

Drive-incentive relationships may become specific. The well-fed child who wants a candy bar he sees is not hungry for a piece of bread and butter. Only the candy bar will do. Rats that have learned to run a maze for bran mash will make errors again if sunflower seeds are substituted, though they can learn to run the maze as well with sunflower seeds as the incentive as with bran mash (Elliott, 1928). Apparently when they have learned to work for one incentive the drive-incentive relationship becomes specific and they do not work as well when some other incentive is substituted.

Drive-incentive relationships in a free responding situation become very complexly interrelated. Logan (1964) studied the cycle of eating, drinking, and sleeping behavior of rats that were on their own to choose their periods of eating, drinking, and sleeping, but were under some constraints with respect to what the environment offered. For example, if their intake of water was limited, they ate less, as though they regulated the food consumed by the amount that could be "washed down" or digested. Food drive, at least as shown by behavior, had to come into some sort of equilibrium with thirst drive. The periods of eating and drinking also had cyclical qualities, so that eating and drinking did not necessarily occur when deprivation was greatest, particularly if the deprivation coincided with a sleep cycle. These findings are not in themselves surprising, but they warn against too strict adherence to a simple need-drive-incentive formula, even when dealing with such activities as eating and drinking.

Basic Motives with Unspecified Physiological Correlates

As we have noted, the theory of need-drive-incentive based upon deprivation and aversive stimulation (hunger, thirst, pain) takes a little forcing to make it fit other obviously physiological motives such as sexual and maternal ones. Some other motives which appear to be basic ones because they are found among young organisms and can be counted upon in many species fit even less well the ordinary conceptions of needs and drives. We shall therefore simply use the more neutral term *motive* in describing them. They include such motives as *activity, manipulation,* and *investigation.*

Activity as a motive

It is the nature of animals to be in active interchange with the environment, and to some extent this activity has a tonic effect apart from the specific needs that are being served. We noted in Chapter 3 that development of the organism proceeds normally only if there is sufficient stimulation, so that the need for stimulation has its own biological basis. Impressed by the need of animals to be active, Woodworth (1958) proposed a *behavior-primacy* theory of motivation, which is opposed to the *need-primacy* theory we earlier considered. According to his theory, the organism must learn to deal with the environment, and he is challenged by the opportunities to do so. Once this point of view is accepted we can more readily account for play (in animals as well as in children), for curiosity, and for strenuous kinds of adventure that serve only slightly to satisfy the needs of the body. A related position has been taken by White (1959) who believes organisms are motivated by a desire for *competence*, that is, for effective functioning.

It is possible to set up experiments to test whether or not activity serves as a motive with some of the characteristics of a drive. Hill (1956) did this by limiting the activity of rats and then seeing whether or not the opportunity to be active would have incentive properties. He found that animals would learn in order to be rewarded by the opportunity to be active, thus appearing to enjoy activity for its own sake.

The manipulation motive

Activity readily takes the form of manipulation. We give babies rattles and other toys early because we know that they like to hold them, shake them, pull them. We are aware that monkeys do this sort of thing, so much so that the word "monkey" serves as a verb to describe casual manipulation for whatever satisfaction it brings. That monkeys do indeed like to "monkey" is illustrated by a number of experiments. If various mechanical devices are placed in the monkey's cage (Figure 5–8) he will begin to take them apart, becoming more skilled with practice, without any evident reward other than the satisfaction of some sort of manipulation drive (Harlow, Harlow, and Meyer, 1950). If he is fed each time that he takes the puzzle apart the behavior changes: the interest in manipulation is reduced in favor

H. F. Harlow

5–8

Manipulation motive

The monkey takes the latches apart, even though there is no "incentive" or "reward" except that deriving from the manipulation itself.

of finding in the puzzle a means to food. It appears, therefore, that manipulation is a motive in its own right.

Investigation as a motive

That animals can be motivated by curiosity has been shown in a number of experiments in which the incentive was the opportunity to open a window and see what was going on outside; this opportunity operates as a positive incentive (Butler, 1953). Interest in such behavior has been growing, and the experiments may be subdivided into those dealing with orienting responses, locomotor exploration, and investigatory responses.

Orienting responses. The orienting reaction has been given particular attention by Russian investigators (e.g., Sokolov, 1963). When a novel or striking stimulus appears, the organism responds by changes in posture and sense-organ adjustments that have widespread physiological consequences. The reaction tends to disappear gradually if the novel stimulus is presented repeatedly at intervals of a few seconds or a few minutes.

The determinants of the orienting reaction are those that we associate with attention: intensity, color, novelty, surprisingness, complexity. For example, when Berlyne (1966) showed the patterns of Figure 5–9 to three- to nine-month-old infants, most frequently their eyes turned first to the patterns on the right.

Locomotor exploration. Locomotor exploration refers to the tendency of animals to run about when in a new place, investigating and inspecting the environment— the kind of behavior folklore attributes to the house cat when taken to a new house. Such behavior is readily demonstrated in the laboratory. For example, hungry rats well trained through 80 trials to select an arm of a Y-shaped maze for food, selected a new arm on the 81st trial when this opportunity for exploration was opened to them (Thiessen and McGaugh, 1958). When the rear walls of otherwise empty goal boxes at the end of a runway contained either familiar or novel visual figures, rats spent more time in the goal box exploring the novel figures than the familiar ones (Berlyne and Slater, 1957). That this may be a variety of complexity-seeking, rather than novelty alone, is shown in later experiments reported by Walker (1964), in which rats spend more time in rooms with greater complexity than in more monotonous ones, regardless of familiarity.

Investigatory responses. By investigatory responses Berlyne means those that involve some sort of manipulation that changes the unfamiliar object: picking it up, tearing it apart, and so on. This is not too different from the manipulation motive previously described, except that the aim is to gain new information.

Piaget has made a number of observations on children, bearing on investigatory responses early in life. Within the first few months of life the human infant learns to pull a string to activate a hanging rattle— a form of manipulation that must be considered merely entertaining. Between five and seven months the infant will remove a cloth covering its face, anticipating the

5–9

Complexity and curiosity

Three- to nine-month-old infants looked first at the right-hand figures, presumably because they were more complex. (Berlyne, 1966)

peekaboo game. At eight to 10 months the infant will begin to look for things behind or beneath other things. By 11 months he will "experiment" with things, varying the reaction each time (Piaget, 1952). Thus inquisitive behavior is a dependable characteristic of the growing child.

The explanation of the kinds of behavior discussed here that is most coherent with the one used to describe hunger and thirst is that the lack of activity, and the limitation of opportunity to explore, produces a kind of boredom, that is, a sort of deficiency which the organism seeks to overcome. The deficiency must not be simply a state of understimulation, however, or we would expect the organism to be quiescent or to sleep; apparently the restriction of activity leads eventually to a state of arousal that induces the organism to do something about it, just as the polar bear, restricted to his cage, engages in his endless march back and forth in the cage.

Appetites and Aversions: Alternatives to Need, Drive, and Incentive

Because a number of motives do not fit very well the need-drive-incentive pattern, some other basis for formulating relationships is desirable, without losing the information that we gained in studying the motivational significance of deprivation and noxious stimulation.

The need-drive-incentive formulation of motivation was at its height of acceptance some years ago, and many other theories seemed translatable into its terms. A prominent supporter of it was Clark L. Hull, who based his learning theory on the notion that learning took place when an incentive reduced a drive; this was, as we shall see later, his interpretation of the mechanism of reinforcement or reward (Hull, 1943). A very basic idea was that homeostasis (Chapter 2, p. 41) is a desirable state to which the organism seeks to return when its equilibrium has been disrupted. It was believed that the incentive reduced the

drive and returned the organism to a more homeostatic state, thus pointing to a general biological basis for motivation. Activity was found to be manipulable by depriving the animal of food or water or by subjecting it to pain. That aspect of psychoanalytic theory which stated that much behavior is motivated to escape anxiety and guilt had a similar biological basis. With this basis in observed relationships securely established, there were many speculations about how other motives were derived from the basic drives. The infant was said to become dependent upon the mother, for example, because she is the source of food and becomes a token for satisfaction, like any other reward-object. Her absence arouses a tension state, or anxious state, which is relieved when she returns. Hence attachment to the mother is explained according to the theory. Actually, many doubts were later thrown upon this plausible derivation, as we noted earlier (Chapter 3, pp. 78–79).

Criticisms of the theory were made all along, but they began to mount in the 1950s. A strong attack by Harlow (1953) on the deprivation theory of drive came at a time when many others who were dissatisfied with the theory had begun to express their doubts and turn their attention to such motives as activity, manipulation, and curiosity, which did not fit the drive-incentive pattern. Even Hull, who had done so much to popularize the theory, began to see that too little attention had been paid to the motivational significance of the incentive and too much to the condition of drive, so that he added a concept of incentive motivation to that of drive, giving incentive a role paralleling that of drive (Hull, 1952). This was carried forward by his follower, Spence (1956), who now attributed additive value to drive and incentive motivation, thus making what happens in the presence of the incentive (or in anticipation of it) a component of drive. Thus even those who saved the need-drive-incentive formula began to pay much more attention to the incentive.

While deprivation and aversive drives exist, and are highly motivating, we need to find some way of talking about those motives that do not fit very well into the drive pattern. One way to begin is by adding a category of *negative incentives.* In the theory of deprivation and noxious drives, all incentives are positive, that is, they are sought in order to reduce the drive through satisfying the need or through eliminating the noxious stimulation. We already noted (p. 128) that there may be positive incentives which do not reduce any readily definable drive; some incentives are defined as directing behavior toward themselves. We may define a *negative incentive* as any object or circumstance that when perceived or anticipated directs behavior *away* from itself. Note that by this definition a source of pain which is a source of *drive* in the need-drive-incentive formulation may now serve as a *negative incentive* when it is perceived as an object to be avoided. This permits us to study the differences in motivational effect between promised reward and threatened punishment, treating reward as a positive incentive and punishment as a negative incentive.

When we distinguish between positive and negative incentives we are at the same time pointing out a fundamental dichotomy in motivated behavior. A positive incentive is one for which the organism has an appetite, such as tasty food; a negative incentive, such as a repugnant odor, is one for which the organism has an aversion.

Appetite and pleasure seeking

The need to satisfy hunger is based upon the chemistry of the body, but the appetite for a particular food depends upon the chemistry of the food. The two are related in that appetite is increased by hunger, even though a hungry person may have no appetite for a food that is extremely distasteful for him. Some Chinese, for example, are said to find cheese so distasteful that they may starve before eating it. Appetite thus calls attention to the quality of the positive incentive; an appetizing food is something sought, not merely something accepted to relieve hunger pangs.

Support for an interpretation that some goal-activity may be pleasurable apart from conditions of need has been given by experiments involving electrical stimulation of parts of the central nervous system.

Electrodes were planted in the brains of rats, and a healing period was allowed so that the rats appeared to suffer no discomfort. Shocks could be administered through these electrodes to specific portions of the brain. A bar placed in the rat's cage permitted the rat to control the current, so that when he pressed the bar the current was turned on. Unless the bar was pressed the current would not pass through the electrodes. Under these circumstances rats gave appetitive responses to the current; that is, they positively sought the stimulation through repeated bar-pressing. When the stimulating devices were disconnected, the bar-pressing no longer produced excitation, and bar-pressing ceased. The result was found only for certain centers of the brain, particularly in the septal area lying deep in the midline between the two hemispheres (Olds and Milner, 1954; Olds, 1956).

The most plausible interpretation of these results is that the electrical stimulation produces in the rat a state equivalent to what we would call "pleasure." An interpretation in terms of satisfaction through drive reduction is pretty well ruled out.

Aversion and pain avoidance

Experiments similar to those on appetitive centers in the brain have been done on aversive centers. When the electrodes are placed in such centers, the rat will press the bar or perform other learned acts in order to *turn off* the current (Delgado, Roberts, and Miller, 1954). While fully as important as the other experiments they seem less striking because we are familiar with headaches and might suppose that an electric shock to the rat's brain has some sort of painful consequence.

When pain is a continuing state of annoyance, it has all the properties of a drive, producing tension, activity, and relief seeking. The headache, stomach ache, or frostbite acts as a drive but not as an incentive.

A negative incentive is something else; it is something to be avoided because of the pain which it might cause. Thus the negative incentive is always perceived or anticipated or it would have no effect; the incentive exists in the environment, and not (as a drive) within the organism.

Another reason for recognizing a class of negative incentives is that environmental objects may have at once appetitive and aversive qualities. The bitter medicine that cures an ailment is at once desirable and forbidding. Mixed incentives lead to a conflict between the desire to approach and the desire to avoid. We shall return in a later chapter (Chapter 20) to a consideration of motivational conflicts and their handling.

Summary on appetites and aversions

Because incentives may be either positive, negative, or mixed, their relationships to behavior can be understood only if they are more fully specified. The following outline summarizes the relationships of perceived incentives to the enhancement of goal-related behavior.

1. Appetitive behavior (approach behavior) is enhanced by the appearance of a positive incentive and by the withdrawal of a negative incentive. A house-to-house salesman enters a house because he hopes to make a sale (positive incentive), but he hesitates to enter when there is a barking dog unless the dog is on a leash (withdrawal of the negative incentive).

2. Aversive behavior (avoidance behavior) is enhanced by the appearance of a negative incentive and by the withdrawal of a positive incentive. The eye of the teacher may inhibit the whispering schoolchild (appearance of a negative incentive), the lack of ice cream in the refrigerator may reduce the bedtime search (withdrawal of positive incentive).

3. Conflict behavior is induced by a forced choice among incentives, either positive or negative, or by confrontation by an incentive that has at once positive and negative characteristics. A choice between two bitter pills or two attractive desserts can be conflictual, as is the choice of being pained by the dentist or of enduring the pain of the toothache.

These relationships are what we would expect from our familiarity with rewards and punishments. Satisfaction can come either from a reward or from relief from threatened punishment; annoyance can come either from punishment or withheld reward.

Derived Motives

Whatever inventory of basic drives and motives we accept, actual motivation as we find it will not be completely describable in terms of these drives and motives alone. It may be, however, that new motives are derived from a basic few, and this possibility we wish to examine.

Acquired drives

One might make a case for acquired drives on the basis of cultivated appetite or perhaps drug addiction, but these appear to be rather close to the more basic drives for food in general and for avoidance of discomfort. The most carefully studied acquired drive is that of fear. In the chapter on emotion (Chapter 7) we shall have additional things to say about emotions in relation to motivation, but fear serves well to show what can be meant by an acquired drive.

Miller (1948a) conducted an experiment in which he placed rats one at a time in the left compartment of the box shown in Figure 5–10. Each rat received an electric shock in the closed compartment, with no means of escape. Each reacted to the shock with all the signs of pain and fright —jumping about, squealing, defecating. After a few repetitions of shocking in this compartment, each rat became emotionally agitated when placed in it without any shock. They had all acquired a conditioned fear of the compartment.

Next the rats learned to use a trap door as a means of escape into the second compartment, in which it had never received

Apparatus used in studying fear
as an acquired drive

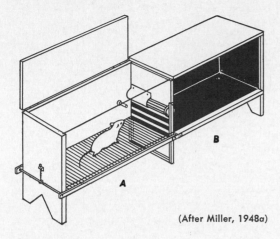

(After Miller, 1948a)

a shock. For several hundred trials, whenever a conditioned rat was placed in compartment A, it went through the trap door to compartment B, although it received no additional shocks in compartment A. When the trap door was locked and a second escape device substituted, the rat learned to use the new device as a means of escape.

This experiment shows not only that the rats acquired a fear of the compartment in which they were shocked, but that the fear became an acquired drive. The animals went from the compartment in which they were tense and agitated to the one in which they were relaxed and comfortable. The "safe" compartment served as an incentive to relieve the fear. Thus aroused fear and the impulse toward fear reduction are not unlike aroused hunger and the impulse to reduce hunger pangs. Many psychologists believe that such acquired fears and related states of anxiety and apprehension account for much of human motivation.

Once a fear is acquired, it leads to strong avoidance of those situations in which the feared object or event is likely to appear. Fear motivates the organism both to escape from the feared object and to avoid contact with it. Extreme or pathological fears, known as *phobias,* strongly affect the conduct of those who suffer from them. The fears may be of high places, closed spaces,

open spaces, animals, dirt, or diseases. This list is, of course, not complete; almost anything can become the object of a phobia. A striking case history of such a phobia was given by William Ellery Leonard, in his autobiography, *The locomotive god.* His fear of a locomotive, based on a childhood incident, led to fear of leaving home, until he virtually imprisoned himself. He dared go only a short distance away. Fear was for him a very powerful motive greatly affecting his movements, and hence the very course of his life.

While fear acquired on the basis of previously experienced pain thus operates as a drive, it is not easy to demonstrate that other motives could be acquired in the same way. Miller, who did the experiments on fear, attempted in collaboration with Myers to demonstrate an acquired drive based on hunger, using the same apparatus as that illustrated in Figure 5–10. By having the animals always hungry in the white compartment and going to be fed in the black compartment, the question was whether or not the white compartment would arouse an acquired hunger drive in satiated rats, corresponding to our earlier illustration of bakery goods arousing appetite in our nonhungry person. To test this, satiated rats trained in the box, and satiated rats, not trained in the box, were given the opportunity to move from the white to the black compartment by operating a new mechanism. If the parallel with fear had held, the trained group should have learned more promptly to go to the black box, where there had been food. No such differences were found, and the investigators concluded that they had failed to show an acquired drive based on hunger (Myers and Miller, 1954).

Acquired incentives

Although the acquiring of a new drive based on hunger was not demonstrated, many experiments have shown that objects can acquire incentive value. The simple illustration is the value of money, which acquires its incentive value because of the things it can buy. That something of the same sort occurs with animals below man

5-11

The Chimp-o-mat

Yerkes Laboratories of Primate Biology

The poker chips that can be used to obtain food have acquired incentive value.

is shown in *token-learning* experiments conducted with chimpanzees (Cowles, 1937). Chimpanzees were taught to work for poker chips as incentives rather than for food. The chimpanzee could later use the poker chip to obtain food from a vending machine called a "Chimp-o-mat" (Figure 5-11). After learning, the animal would work as hard for a poker chip as for the food itself, occasionally saving up a few

poker chips before converting them into the food reward.

Notice here that the drive has remained the same—hunger—but something other than food has acquired incentive value. There is little doubt that the number of things that can come to serve as both positive and negative incentives becomes greatly increased by experienced satisfactions and dissatisfactions in the past.

Transformed motives

Still another possibility exists with respect to the derivation of new motives from more basic ones. This is the possibility that the motives become greatly transformed, so that their roots are scarcely recognizable. One of the first to propose such a theory was Sigmund Freud, who attempted to account for most of human motivation on the basis of sex and aggression. According to the theory, in civilized men and women these basic drives seldom appear in their original raw form but are more likely to be expressed in *sublimated* forms, that is, transformed so as to be socially acceptable and proper. Thus creative art, religion, or hard work might turn out to be derivatives of the basic sexual and aggressive drives, but so disguised and altered that only an elaborate process of analysis would uncover the threads linking the original motives with their social expression. Another proposal was that of Allport (1937) that motives become so far removed from their original sources as to be *functionally autonomous*, that is, no longer dependent upon their original drives to sustain them. Thus the miser might come to value money merely for the sake of piling it up, depriving himself of the things money can buy. We shall deal with some of these possibilities in the next chapter, when the many varieties of human motivation are under review.

SUMMARY   1. Behavior is in part regulated by drives that are the consequences of needs. Among the deprivation drives are hunger and thirst. Pain as a noxious drive is a special case: it acts as a drive because the pain typically indicates a danger to the organism, so that it is related to the need for protection or safety.

2. While there is some evidence favoring *local* theories of the origin of hunger and thirst drives (hunger related to stomach contractions, thirst to dryness of the mouth and throat), more recent experimentation increasingly favors *central* theories, that is, control of drive by way of centers in the brain (chiefly in the hypothalamus) sensitive to changes in the blood.

3. The need-drive-incentive formulation is that the total motivated behavior sequence moves from *drive* through *preparatory activity* to *goal-activity,* which takes place when a *positive incentive* is encountered. The result of the goal-activity is usually to reduce the drive through satisfying the need, thus producing a more relaxed state.

4. Positive incentives are environmental objects or circumstances that act upon motivated behavior as follows: (a) some positive incentives bring an end to the motivated behavior sequence by reducing the drive through satisfying the need; (b) other positive incentives when perceived or anticipated lead the motivated organism toward themselves and further goal-activity, whether or not they satisfy a need.

5. Perceived incentives may arouse or intensify drives, and, through learning, the drive-incentive relationship may become more specific. In free environments the interactions between need, drive, and incentive become very complex.

6. Some basic motives (basic in the sense that they are found widely in the animal world and early in the life of human infants) are without clearly specified physiological correlates. Among these are activity, manipulation, and investigation motives. Investigation or curiosity motives may be subdivided into orienting responses, locomotor exploration, and investigatory responses.

7. *Appetites* and *aversions* parallel the distinction between positive and negative incentives. With increased dissatisfaction with the total need-drive-incentive formulation, more attention has turned to the influence of incentives—a positive incentive being one toward which the motivated organism tends to approach, a negative incentive one which it tends to avoid or withdraw from. Appetitive behavior tends to be associated with pleasure; experiments on self-stimulation of the brain suggest that there are centers in the brain which, if stimulated, give experiences corresponding to a pleasurable state. There are also centers in the brain which self-stimulation experiments show give painful experiences.

8. The possibility exists that more complex motives may be derived from a few basic drives. Fear provides a convenient illustration of an acquired drive based on pain, but it has been difficult to demonstrate a corresponding acquired drive based on hunger. Acquired incentives are more readily demonstrated, as in the token-learning experiments. In addition to the possibility of acquiring new drives and new incentives, which will then operate according to the drive-incentive pattern, there is the further possibility that the motivational system may operate through transformed motives, in which the final motive bears little resemblance to the drive out of which it originated. This was early suggested by Freud, who felt that much of human behavior could be accounted for on the basis of two main drives (sex and aggression), but,

according to him, social behavior as we find it is regulated by these drives in highly transformed ways through *sublimation,* the original drive being disguised so that it serves in socially acceptable ways. Another possibility is that the drive eventually becomes disconnected from its original source and operates in a manner that is described as *functionally autonomous.*

SUGGESTIONS FOR FURTHER READING

Some shorter summaries on motivation, taking somewhat the position of this chapter are Fuller, *Motivation: a biological perspective* (1962), and Murray, *Motivation and emotion* (1964).

More extensive accounts can be found in a number of advanced books on motivation, of which the following are representative: Atkinson, *An introduction to motivation* (1964); Cofer and Appley, *Motivation: theory and research* (1964).

For collections of readings on motivation close to the topics of this chapter, see Haber, *Current research in motivation* (1966), and Teevan and Birney, *Theories of motivation in learning* (1964a).

6 Human Motivation

A large part of the experimental work on motivation reviewed in the previous chapter was concerned with hunger, thirst, pain, and sex as these motives are aroused through deprivation and noxious stimulation as well as by external incentives. Human motivation is continuous with that of animals; this is, of course, one reason for paying attention to the bodily correlates of motivated behavior. At the same time we noted complexity of drive-incentive relationships in animals, and these complexities become even more striking in man. Men differ so much in their learned behavior, and they operate under complex social rules which determine, at least in part, what is permitted and not permitted; consequently a great deal of information is usually needed before we can infer clearly a man's motives from what he is doing. Let us consider a few aspects of human motivated behavior that set problems for motivational theory.

Problems Posed for a Theory of Human Motivation

Why men behave as they do has intrigued thinkers from earliest times; much of the thematic material in literature, art, and drama is concerned with goal-striving, ambition, jealousy, heroism, sacrifice, love, hostility—all intensely motivated human behavior. Because of the variety and richness of these themes, it is no wonder that a psychology of motivation has difficulty achieving a simple and orderly theory of human motivation that will be adequate to the subject matter. Some of the difficulties will be noted, and then a few of the major theories that have attempted to give some order to what we know will be considered. Representative motives will be discussed to illustrate each of the theories, but no attempt will be made to give a scientific inventory of the totality of human motivated behavior.

Motivational dispositions

Not all motives that can incite an organism to action are operative at the same time. A student who spends long hours studying during the week because of his motivation to do well on his examinations may be seen howling with excitement at the Saturday afternoon football game for quite different motives. He carries many possibilities of motivated action within him, even when they are not being expressed. These are called *motivational dispositions* because they are persistent tendencies to express particular motives when the conditions are appropriate. To the extent that these are universal (tendencies to eat when hungry, to drink when thirsty) the motivational disposition can be inferred from the behavior, but even with such basic motives as hunger and thirst there are large individual differences in behavior. In the satisfaction of hunger drives we distinguish between the voracious eater and the one with a moderate appetite. Moreover, at any one time the voracious eater may be well fed and not ready to eat more, while the person with a moderate appetite at times may be very hungry indeed. In making these statements we are calling attention to two important points: (1) people differ in the strengths of their motivational dispositions, and (2) at any one time the relevant behavior may not correspond to the strengths of the persisting dispositions.

Motivational arousal

Motivational dispositions that are not evident in behavior become evident when the conditions are appropriate: for example, when a state of need is created through deprivation, or when an incentive stirs the organism to action. If we were able to equate the conditions of arousal, then the one who engaged most strongly in the motivated activity would be said to be the one with the stronger disposition.

To illustrate how behavior is affected jointly by motivational dispositions and conditions of arousal, we may consider a study by French (1958). She selected two groups of subjects, 128 found to be high in achievement motivation but low in affiliative motivation, and 128 high in affiliative motivation but low in achievement motivation, according to a test which she had earlier devised. These are both enduring motivational dispositions, achievement motivation referring to a tendency to work toward some standard of excellence, affiliative motivation referring to the tendency to work in such a way as to belong to and be accepted by a group of others. These enduring tendencies were capitalized upon by setting tasks for the subjects under different conditions of motivational arousal. The task consisted in assembling a story from phrases or short sentences printed on separate cards. The subjects had to get the information from others in order to complete the story, but were not permitted to show each other their cards. The members of each group worked in teams of four. The experimenter aroused one or the other kind of motive by interrupting the task to record scores and to give a progress report, or "feedback," telling the subject how he was doing. One kind of feedback aroused achievement motivation by emphasizing how well the team was doing in completing the task: "This team is working very efficiently." The other feedback aroused affiliative tendencies by emphasizing the feeling of belonging: "This team works very well together." The results (Figure 6–1) were in the direction predicted: the group performance of those with high achievement dispositions was better when achievement feedback capitalized on these tendencies, and the group performance of those with high affiliative tendencies was better when these tendencies were aroused through feedback. Thus when conditions of arousal favor those with a given motivational disposition, their performance of the required task is superior to those lacking (or lower) in this motivational disposition. What is being emphasized here is interaction between the more enduring motivational disposition and the aroused motive.

The main point is that motivational dispositions persist and may be thought of as enduring personality characteristics, while aroused motives affect the present ongoing behavior.

How behavior reflects motives

There is a tendency to infer motives directly from behavior, on the assumption that all behavior is motivated. Hence a classification of motives becomes a classification of behavior: nest-building motive, mothering motive, fighting motive, and so on. When examined closely this approach is found to be unsatisfactory, for the inference from behavior to motive is somewhat more complex. It is not a bad starting point to assume that incentive behavior indicates that some relevant motive is active, but some provisos have to be added. For example, a person may eat an unappetizing food not because he is hungry for it but because he does not wish to offend his hostess; he may pass up something he would very much wish to eat at a cafeteria because he cannot afford it or because he is on a diet. In other words, actual behavior is often the result of a cer-

6–1

Effect of appropriate motivation on performance

For the groups high in achievement motivation, arousal of this motive ("achievement feedback") leads to superior performance; for those high in affiliation, its arousal ("affiliation feedback") leads to superior performance. (Plotted from the data of French, 1958)

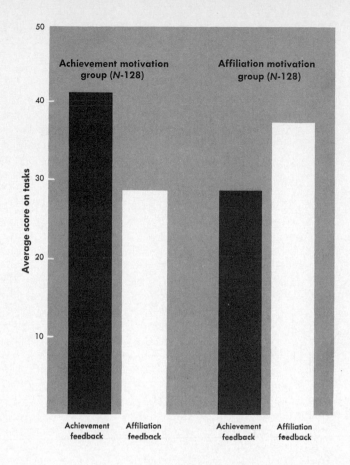

tain resolution between conflicting motives, and the motive that on the surface may seem to be the relevant one is not necessarily the strongest one.

Behavior often is carried out in long sequences, so that the given bit of behavior must also be seen in context. In the case of human motivated behavior we have to consider not only the general attractiveness of the activity, but the expectation by the behaving person of what the consequences may be. He may enjoy a particular sport but refuse to enter a contest with someone he knows will beat him unmercifully. We cannot infer that his motivational disposition is lacking, nor that there is no arousal (for he has been invited to play); we have to consider his expectations as well.

The following statements help call at-

tention to the impossibility of inferring a motive directly from behavior:

1. The expression of human motives differs from culture to culture and from person to person within a culture. This difference arises because many motives are learned as a result of specific experiences; in any case, these motives are expressed through learned behavior.
2. Similar motives may be manifested through unlike behavior. A motive to assert antagonism to another person may be expressed either by an attack upon him or by withdrawal from his presence.
3. Unlike motives may be expressed through similar behavior. Thus two people may take up oil painting, one

to please a parent, the other to annoy a parent.

4. Motives may appear in disguised forms. Boys have been known to steal because of sexual conflicts. Here the motive for stealing was not a "motive to acquire" but a disguised sexual drive.

5. Any single act of behavior may express several motives. A scientist at work in his laboratory may be motivated by a yearning to search for truth, by a desire for fame, by the necessity of increasing his earning power to support his family. All these as well as other motives may be active at the same time. The principle of multiple determination of behavior is an important one, but it makes difficult the description of the motives active at any given time.

Difficulties in making an inventory of motives

The above considerations indicate that an inventory of behavior will not be an inventory of motives, because the motive has to be inferred by a somewhat complex process. There is a strong temptation, however, to prepare classifications of motivational dispositions closely related to human behavior in all its variety. This is coherent with the tendency within any science to sort out its objects of investigation as a starting point (animal, vegetable, mineral; solid, liquid, gas; bird, beast, fish; cirrus, cumulus, and other clouds). Very often the science in its advanced stages abandons the earlier sorting, but it has at least helped to define the subject matter of the science. The present lists of human motives have this status of a preliminary sorting, and for that reason are not agreed upon as appropriate final categories. For example, Thomas (1923) reduced human motives to four "wishes": security, recognition, response from one's fellows, and new experience. Maslow (1954) listed the basic "needs" (i.e., motivational dispositions) as physiological needs, safety needs, belongingness and love needs, esteem needs, and the need for self-actualization. Others have preferred much longer lists. Murray (1938) listed 12 "viscerogenic" (i.e., physiological) and 28 "psychogenic" needs (Table 6–1).

A long list, such as that of Murray's, helps us to see the kinds of behaviors that a complete theory of human motivation will have to comprehend, although it does not deny the possibility of some eventual simplification with respect to the number of basic underlying motives.

Theories of human motivation

The differences in motivational dispositions, and how they come about, the circumstances of arousal, both internal and environmental, and the type of behavior that results, are all matters for theoretical discussion. Motivational theory has not, in fact, settled down in contemporary psychology; some even argue that the concept of motive is so unclear that it had better be dispensed with altogether. The concept is probably here to stay, however, and we may examine three theories as representative of the efforts to deal with the perplexing problems. In presenting these three theories it will be noted that they are actually not very far apart; they accept many of the same relationships within data. It cannot be inferred that we know nothing about human motivation merely because we do not agree on the best way of talking about it.

The three approaches that we shall discuss are *behavior theory,* the *theory of unconscious motivation,* and *cognitive theory.* Behavior theory takes off originally from the need-drive-incentive interpretation of the last chapter and makes learning a central concept. It uses the derived motivation interpretation and attempts to apply it specifically to human behavior. The theory of unconscious motivation was brought forward by Freud in the interpretation of irrational, neurotic behavior, and then extended to account for much ordinary socially acceptable behavior. The main point is that motives are not clear to the person who is expressing them, and actual behavior often must be understood as some form of conversion or symbolic representation of a hidden or unconscious motive.

TABLE 6-1

A list of psychogenic needs

A. Needs associated chiefly with inanimate objects

1. **Acquisition:** the need to gain possessions and property.
2. **Conservation:** the need to collect, repair, clean, and preserve things.
3. **Orderliness:** the need to arrange, organize, put away objects, to be tidy and clean; to be precise.
4. **Retention:** the need to retain possession of things; to hoard; to be frugal, economical, and miserly.
5. **Construction:** the need to organize and build.

B. Needs expressing ambition, will power, desire for accomplishment, and prestige

6. **Superiority:** the need to excel, a composite of achievement and recognition.
7. **Achievement:** the need to overcome obstacles, to exercise power, to strive to do something difficult as well and as quickly as possible.
8. **Recognition:** the need to excite praise and commendation; to demand respect.
9. **Exhibition:** the need for self-dramatization; to excite, amuse, stir, shock, thrill others.
10. **Inviolacy:** the need to remain inviolate, to prevent a depreciation of self-respect, to preserve one's "good name."
11. **Avoidance of inferiority:** the need to avoid failure, shame, humiliation, ridicule.
12. **Defensiveness:** the need to defend oneself against blame or belittlement; to justify one's actions.
13. **Counteraction:** the need to overcome defeat by restriving and retaliating.

C. Needs having to do with human power exerted, resisted, or yielded to

14. **Dominance:** the need to influence or control others.
15. **Deference:** the need to admire and willingly follow a superior; to serve gladly.
16. **Similance:** the need to imitate or emulate others; to agree and believe.
17. **Autonomy:** the need to resist influence, to strive for independence.
18. **Contrariness:** the need to act differently from others, to be unique, to take the opposite side.

D. Needs having to do with injuring others or oneself

19. **Aggression:** the need to assault or injure another; to belittle, harm, or maliciously ridicule a person.
20. **Abasement:** the need to comply and accept punishment; self-depreciation.
21. **Avoidance of blame:** the need to avoid blame, ostracism, or punishment by inhibiting unconventional impulses; to be well behaved and obey the law.

E. Needs having to do with affection between people

22. **Affiliation:** the need to form friendships and associations.
23. **Rejection:** the need to be discriminating, to snub, ignore, or exclude another.
24. **Nurturance:** the need to nourish, aid, or protect another.
25. **Succorance:** the need to seek aid, protection, or sympathy; to be dependent.

F. Additional socially relevant needs

26. **Play:** the need to relax, amuse oneself, seek diversion and entertainment.
27. **Cognizance:** the need to explore, to ask questions, to satisfy curiosity.
28. **Exposition:** the need to point and demonstrate; to give information, explain, interpret, lecture.

SOURCE: Murray (1938). The psychogenic needs are distinguished from viscerogenic, or physiological, ones. In the listing, changes of wording have been made to avoid some of the neologisms coined by Murray.

Finally, cognitive theory places more attention upon man's awareness of what is going on, his deliberate tendency to anticipate the future, to plan, to take risks. The theories do not fall into quite as clear separation as this brief description indicates, but it helps first to see them as somewhat different and then to note their overlaps.

Behavior Theory: The Concept of Behavior Systems

Behavior theory is that interpretation of psychology which emphasizes stimulus-response relationships and learning (habit formation) in accounting for the development of behavior and its present manifestations. The motivational theory is not uniformly stated by all behavior theorists; here we shall follow a developmental scheme proposed by Whiting and Child (1953). They proposed that we can classify adult behavior appropriately into a few *behavior systems*, each system consisting of a set of habits or customs motivated by a common innate or early acquired motive and leading to common satisfactions. They selected five behavior systems for consideration: oral, anal, sexual, dependency, and aggression. The first three are developed from motives with evident physiological bases (hunger, elimination, and sex), while the final two (dependency and aggression) are assumed to be motives acquired universally in early childhood as a result of the infant's helplessness, on the one hand, and inevitable frustrations, on the other. The following steps are implied in this approach to human motivation:

1. The motive that defines a behavior system can be identified in early childhood.
2. The methods of "socializing" the motive can be identified and studied. The motive is satisfied in each culture by rewarding the "approved" methods of satisfaction and punishing the attempts to satisfy the motive in other ways. Diverse methods of child training, whether the differences are from one culture to another or within the culture, produce differentiated social behavior within the particular behavior system under study.
3. The "causal" connections between the early manifestations of the motive and social behavior of adult life can be studied to find out whether the later practices are to some extent continuous with and predictable from the early experiences. We

expect to find some general theme common to behavior within the selected system and also variations on it. The variations between cultures will depend in part on the differences within those cultures, but even within a culture there will be variations due to individual experience.

Social behavior related to the hunger drive

As an illustration of this approach we may consider the complex outcomes of the hunger drive, as it is ramified in various ways in relation to food-related behavior, and as it is related to dependency because of the infant's helplessness as its needs are satisfied by others.

The hunger drive as such is rewarded by food, and leads to all manner of food-related behavior, as shown in the upper portion of Table 6–2. Obviously the behavior of the people engaged in the activities suggested in the right-hand column involves a good deal more than the drive for food: the complex motivations of farmers and entrepreneurs; chefs, grocers, and night club operators; priests, policemen, and doctors. In other words, as social behavior proliferates we can trace some aspects of it back to a common source, but we must also be reminded that food-related behavior is not motivated by the hunger drive alone.

The second main point in Table 6–2 is that feeding in early infancy is done by another person (usually the mother) and leads to dependency on that person. Such dependency later becomes extended to other persons. This need has come to be called a "dependency motive," an unfortunate expression but one widely enough used to have become a recognizable technical term. The dependency motive begins with individuals and then leads to affiliation with clubs and organizations; some people become habitual joiners. We have already noted that it may not be true that dependency (or social attachment) comes about in just this way (Chapter 3, pp. 78–79); however it may begin, its spread can be traced from dependency on one or a

TABLE **6–2**

The complex outcome of social behavior related to the hunger drive

Basic organic background	Primary drive	Early drive differentiation	Social behavior, customs, and institutions related to these motives
Infant's helplessness and need for nutrients	Hunger drive	Food-related behavior ("oral drive")	1. **Food production and conservation** (Hunting, fishing, agricultural crops, dairying, etc.; drying, salting, canning, storage, refrigeration) 2. **Meal preparation and social eating** (Food preparation and cooking, staple foods and varied menus, appetites and aversions, eating habits, table manners, etc.) 3. **Food ceremonies little related to satisfying hunger** (Fasts, food taboos, food sacrifices to the gods, Communion) 4. **Other symbolic and nonfood consequences of deriving satisfaction through the mouth** (Alcoholism and drug addiction; chewing gum and tobacco; smoking; oral interpretation of illness) 5. **Resistance to overeating** (Dieting, neurotic loss of appetite)
		Behavior related to dependence on other people ("dependency motive")	1. **Relations with individuals** (Parents and immediate family, "homesickness" if separated, dependence on teachers, friends, spouse, physician) 2. **Relations with groups and social organizations** (Social organizations, such as religious fellowships, catering especially to dependency needs; social clubs and organizations of all kinds, designed for other purposes but also satisfying the need to belong) 3. **Resistance to overdependence** ("Autonomy motive," "achievement motive," etc.)

limited number of people to social relations in general.

The concept of behavior systems is promising because it allows us to trace a limited number of social motives forward throughout life, rather than to begin with a catalogue of adult behavior and work back to a few underlying motives. But the program has limitations. Because we continue to acquire some social motives beyond early infancy, and perhaps throughout life, we have no assurance that a set of behavior systems based on the motives of early infancy will be adequate; in fact, we can be confident that they will not be. Even if the behavior-system approach does not carry us all the way in the study of human motives, it can tell us enough about the natural history of *some* motives and their transformations to make the effort of

following a few such systems worthwhile. As further illustrations of behavior systems we will examine some of the behavior related to early dependency and aggression.

Behavior related to the dependency motive

Whatever its origin, the early dependency of the infant upon the adults who care for him can be interpreted as providing a foundation for various sorts of later affiliative behaviors. A number of these have been indicated in the lower part of Table 6–2. Such behaviors are motivated at least in part by the support that comes from the presence of other people. Affiliative behavior in man, which may be interpreted as beginning with the infant's dependency upon the mother, moves through ordinary companionship and friendship in childhood to enduring adult friendships and group memberships, and is represented also by the closely knit loyalty and devotion within marriage and family. Obviously other motives enter as well, but multi-determination is inevitably the nature of adult motivated behavior.

As representative studies within the dependency behavior system we may consider two studies, one of young children and one of college students under experimental arousal.

Sources of dependent behavior in young children. Although, as noted earlier, children form early attachments to persons other than the mother, the mother's special role in feeding and handling may make the relationship to the mother of special importance in the development of the dependency motive. In an attempt to test this assumption, 40 preschool children were studied. First an attempt was made to determine their present disposition to show dependent behavior when the opportunity presented itself. Teachers rated their dependency, and research workers derived dependency scores based on observing the reactions of the children to other children and to the teacher in the nursery school, and under controlled conditions in which the child played with dolls representing his family. A single dependency score was arrived at, best characterizing the child at the nursery school age.

These same children received separate ratings on infancy experiences, based upon interviews with their mothers. Scales were designed to get at *nurturance* (i.e., the mother's care in feeding), and *frustration* (i.e., the infant's helplessness in the face of insoluble problems). The feeding practices of the mothers who used the self-demand schedule were scored as high nurturance, those based on rigidly scheduled feeding as low nurturance. The abruptness and harshness of weaning determined the score on feeding frustration. The resulting correlations between infant experiences and later dependent behavior are given in Table 6–3.

Contrary to initial expectations, the most

TABLE 6–3

Correlations between infancy experiences and dependent behavior in preschool

Infancy experiences	Correlations with total dependency measures *	
	GIRLS	BOYS
Self-demand feeding	−.38	−.08
Weaning severity	.54	.40

SOURCE: Sears and others (1953).

* With the number of children (*N*) between 18 and 21 in the different comparisons, correlations must reach at least .35 to approach significance.

carefully nurtured children (on the self-demand schedule) showed *less* dependent behavior than those strictly scheduled. Apparently feeding *frustration* is the variable that results in later dependent behavior, if we interpret rigid scheduling as well as severe weaning as being frustrating (Sears and others, 1957).

In view of the theory that the mother's rewarding role in feeding causes the infant to depend on her, thereby giving rise to the dependency motive, the somewhat unexpected result of the foregoing experiment calls for explanation. In order to survive at all, the infant must have his basic needs met. Hence *all* infants have their hunger drives satisfied in a social context, and they all develop a normal amount of dependency motive. If the mother's behavior in scheduling or weaning produces frustration, something happens in addition to this normal drive satisfaction. The infant's troubled and helpless protests are eventually responded to by the mother, so that she probably gives *additional* satisfaction to dependent forms of behavior. In any case, the infant who has experienced a great deal of frustration with accompanying feelings of helplessness is the one who later on turns to others for support.

Affiliative behavior in young adults when anxiety is aroused. Schachter (1959) placed women college students in a situation that they saw as threatening. If we accept the above interpretation of the origin of dependency behavior, we may assume that under anxiety-producing conditions those who have developed a dependency drive in early life will manifest it in some socially approved form as adults. This at least is the developmental inference from the behavior system approach that we are now examining. When Schachter had shown the subjects the threatening nature of the experiment in which they were about to participate he asked them to wait for their turn to be called as subject. The experimental problem was to predict, on the basis of their early history, whether or not, given the choice, they would prefer to wait alone or with others. It was assumed that those who wished to have company while waiting for the threatening experiment had the stronger affiliative tendencies, and, in line with the theory we are discussing, that this preference would have its roots in early dependency behavior.

University women were shown, as part of this experiment, some forbidding-looking apparatus that they were made to believe could deliver severe electric shocks. Another group, similarly reporting for an experiment, were shown nothing threatening and were assured that the experimental procedures were mild and nonpainful.

When both groups were given the choice of waiting alone or waiting together, a larger proportion of the threatened group preferred to wait together (Table 6–4). The general interpretation is that the more threatened ones turned to company because affiliative needs were aroused. (In the end, neither group had to undergo any painful experiences.)

Another analysis of the same kind of behavior showed that some individuals, under threat of pain, were more eager to have company than others. When the data from only children and first-born children were considered separately from the later-born ones, it was found that the only and first-born children showed higher tendencies toward affiliation in this situation. Schachter interprets this result to mean that the first-born child probably experienced more adult responsiveness to his uneasiness in early childhood than later-born children, whom parents may have taken more for granted.

Although Schachter's interpretation of the way in which parents rewarded dependency in first-born and later-born children is conjectural, it is at least coherent with the origins of dependency motive as described in the earlier study of young children. Hence the two studies, taken together, illustrate the point that adult affiliative behavior may have a historical connection with early childhood experiences related to dependency. Furthermore, they show that the motivational disposition becomes more evident when aroused by threat, so that those who do very well alone under ordinary circumstances will seek companionship when their anxieties are raised.

These illustrations of attempts to bring dependent or affiliative tendencies under experimental observation do not, of course, exhaust the kinds of things men do in seeking companionship of other people or in participating in group life. They indicate, however, that it is possible to make some measurements even in a field as complex as this, with the kinds of results that will eventually add up to a science of human motives.

TABLE 6–4

Relationship between anxiety and the affiliative tendency among college women

	Waiting conditions chosen			
Experimental manipulation	TOGETHER	DON'T CARE	ALONE	TOTAL
High anxiety	20	9	3	32
Low anxiety	10	18	2	30

SOURCE: Schachter (1959), p. 18.

Aggression

The problem of human cruelty is a baffling one, but the history of human behavior abounds with man-imposed suffering upon other men. The fact that man's potential aggressiveness has an evolutionary basis may explain why he is capable of cruel and destructive behavior, but it does not necessarily *justify* his aggressiveness. The study of motivated behavior in lower animals often helps us to understand man's behavior, but it does not in itself tell us how man can control what he does.

In line with the behavior-system approach, we may appropriately look for the origins of human aggression in infancy. It is partly related, no doubt, to the need for activity. A growing child is active, and activity may sooner or later lead the child to destroy something or to injure someone. At that point adults will judge his behavior as aggressive, although it may not yet have any hostile quality in it. In the same study referred to in relation to dependency, Sears and others (1953) also studied aggression. They found, as one might expect, a high correlation between the general activity level and aggression as rated by teachers: .86 for boys and .66 for girls. From these figures alone it is not possible to tell which is cause and which is effect. An active child may stumble into aggressive acts; an aggressive child may become active in expressing his aggression; or, of course, the rater himself may confuse activity with aggression.

A suggestion, deriving from Freud and widely accepted by others, is that aggression is one of the consequences of frustration (Dollard and others, 1939). The measures used by Sears and others (1953) of experienced frustration in early infancy did not correlate significantly with rated or observed aggressive activity in preschool. These authors suggest that the learning involved in true hostile aggression (making another person experience pain) develops slowly. The kinds of aggression shown by the very young infant are mere obstacle-removing activities, often violent

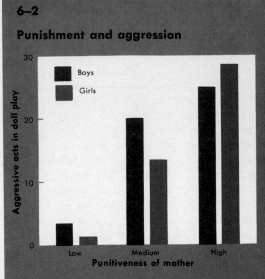

6–2

Punishment and aggression

The relationship between punitiveness of the mother and aggression by the child as revealed in doll play. (After Sears and others, 1953)

or strenuous but not really oriented toward a goal response of inflicting pain upon another. If this suggestion is correct, the true motive for aggression develops late and is not directly correlated with the experiences of very early infancy.

If we accept a slow development of the aggressive motive, we might expect a correlation with later parental encouragement of, or punishment of, aggression. Davis and Dollard (1940) studied the behavior of Negro children raised in underprivileged groups in the deep South. It was very clear that among many of these children aggressive behavior was often rewarded by the parents; where the behavior was rewarded, the amount of aggression increased.

Punishment of aggression also has its consequences. A parent who punishes a child excessively tends to set up in the child some sort of wish to punish in return. This is clearly revealed in the "doll play" of children grouped according to the punitiveness of their mothers (Figure 6–2). The more punitive the mother, the more aggressive are the acts shown in doll play.

There is a continuity, especially in boys,

between the early expression of aggression and its later expression; this is what the behavior system interpretation would lead us to expect (Sears, 1961). The relationship is complicated by anxiety over aggression, especially for girls who, having been permitted to express unladylike aggression in the early years, tend to repress the tendency to aggression later on because of the anxiety associated with it. The behavior-system interpretation allows for such failures to find a positive correlation for the expression of a motive at two ages.

Aggression can take many forms: angry attacks, verbal insults, and even self-punishment. There is also the form called prosocial aggression, in which right and order are strongly defended, in this case by aggression against the one who violates prohibitions. We have to be careful in the case of aggression to distinguish between aggression as a means to an end and aggression as a motive in its own right. That is, does one have some sort of *need* to inflict pain on another person, as he may, perhaps, have a need for affection? This is a matter of some dispute, but in the behavior theory interpretation the answer is that aggressive behavior, having been in some way rewarding and satisfying in early childhood, comes to be a motive in its own right. Freud was one of the first to accept the interpretation that aggression was a fundamental human tendency, ranking for him along with sex as one of the two basic human drives.

However the aggression comes about, some children and some adults develop strong tendencies to injure themselves or others. The extreme forms have been given names: *sadism* for the extreme motive to pain others; *masochism* for the extreme motive to inflict pain upon oneself. In some forms of sadism and masochism the satisfaction to the aggressive person appears to be sexual in nature. This fact merely illustrates how the strands from different motivational dispositions become intertwined.

This completes our illustrations of the behavior system approach, calling attention to hunger, dependency, and aggres-

sion as illustrative of tendencies strongly developed in the early years and then manifesting themselves in various kinds of proliferated behavior in later years. This developmental approach appears to be a profitable way of studying human motivation.

Unconscious Motives and Their Derivatives

The behavior system approach can sidestep the person's own awareness of his motives by inferring his motives from his overt behavior. This does not tell us whether his motives are clear to him or not. It was commonly assumed historically that man was rational, and made his plans with foresight; this is reflected in our laws about criminal responsibility for acts unless a person is mentally ill. But even the man who is not mentally ill behaves irrationally at least some of the time; he is often driven by impulses of which he is unaware or that he denies, and he often does things that upon reflection he wishes he had not done.

Behavior from which unconscious motives are inferred

While literary men long recognized some unconscious controls over human conduct, it remained for Freud to call to the attention of the public the powerful role of unconscious motives in human behavior. He pointed to several forms of behavior through which unconscious motives express themselves:

1. The dreamer often expresses in his dreams wishes of which he is unaware.
2. Unconscious mannerisms and slips of speech "let the cat out of the bag" and reveal hidden motives.
3. Symptoms of illness (especially the symptoms of neurotic illnesses) often can be shown to serve the unconscious needs of the person.

Following Freud's lead, most psychologists now accept the existence of unconscious motives, although they differ from one another in their ways of talking about them. Sometimes a person is aware of certain motives in himself but unaware of how important they are. He may know that he works hard and likes to succeed, but he may not realize how overweening his ambition is and how incapable he is of accepting defeat.

Calling attention to the impulsive unconscious aspects of human motivation need not lead to pessimism about human nature. On the contrary, the only hope of rational control of conduct lies in the frank facing of the unconscious springs of action. It is a triumph of rationality that we have been able to discover how much of our behavior is irrational. If we are to behave reasonably, we must be ready to unmask our own unreasonableness.

The possibility that Freud is right, or at least has hit on important partial truths, makes theorizing about unconscious motives a significant contribution to the explanation of human motives. Like the behavior-system approach, the psychoanalytic approach is developmental also, with the assumption that many of our unconscious motives have their roots in childhood, so that adult actions are derivative from them.[1]

Sex as a social motive and source of unconscious motivation

The fundamental social institution, the family, is based upon a sexual union in which, under ideal conditions, an enduring relationship of affection binds the parents together and gives them a feeling of security. As a physiological drive, sexual behavior leads to sexual pleasure and the release of tension, but as a social motive it leads

[1] Historically, the psychoanalytic theory came first, and to some extent the behavior-system theory as expounded by Whiting and Child (1953) is a translation of aspects of Freudian theory into behavioral and learning terms. Of their primary motivational systems, the oral, anal, sexual, and aggressive ones could hardly have been selected except for the corresponding emphases within psychoanalysis, and the dependency system reflects the psychoanalytic interest in the infant's attachment to his mother.

also to abiding personal attachments. The sexual partner becomes highly prized, and jealousy of rivals becomes motivationally important. In the social aspects of sex we have a clear illustration of a motive with a physiological basis in the sex drive, yet with a central role in the evolution of acquired social behavior.

The theory of unconscious motivation asserts that sexual motivation has many ramifications that are not directly sexual, as in literature, painting, sculpture, and religion. The earlier Freudian theory found sexual motivation behind nearly all of human behavior, though later psychoanalysts have tended to reduce somewhat the emphasis upon the pervasiveness of the sex drive by paying more attention to what they call the ego—the part of the person that copes realistically with the environment in all its aspects.

How suppression of sexual expression leads to symbolic derivatives of sexual interest was illustrated in some experiments of Clark (1952). (See also Clark and Sensibar, 1956.) Clark studied the stories written by male college students as they viewed some pictures of neutral content after they had been sexually aroused through the viewing of pictures of attractive nude females under two conditions: in the classroom and at a fraternity beer party when the students were under the influence of alcohol. The results may be summarized as follows:

1. Direct arousal under classroom conditions did *not* increase the *overt sexual imagery* appearing in the stories. This suggests that under these conditions whatever sexual fantasies were aroused led to some anxiety and hence to suppression.

2. Direct arousal under classroom conditions *did* increase the *indirect* or *symbolic* expression of sex, thus conforming to the above conjecture that sexual fantasy was indeed aroused.

3. Under the alcoholic condition there *was* an increase in *overt sexual imagery*, indicating less anxiety and suppression under alcohol.

4. Under the alcoholic condition there was *no* increase in *indirect* or *symbolic* ex-

pression. Thus with direct expression there was less resort to disguised representation.

Much behavior in our culture is sex-typed, so that the importance of appropriate sex-role identification is very great indeed (Kagan, 1964). A concern with sex only in relation to the sex act itself would be a very incomplete description of the part sex plays in human motivation.

This is a very brief specimen of the theory of unconscious motivation, but it illustrates the main point that suppressed motives find indirect, symbolic, or disguised expression. We shall have further illustrations later on, particularly in the discussion of mechanisms of defense in which the person deceives himself and others in order to deny or transform his motives (Chapter 20).

Cognitive Theory of Motivation

We should not conclude from our discussion so far that *all* motives must be inferred from observing action or from interpreting behavior in the light of unconscious impulses. There are many aspects of individual motivation that are represented in awareness. To the extent that an individual makes clear plans, knows what he is doing, is guided by his expectations and the risks involved, and moves steadfastly toward his goals, he is motivated according to his *cognitions* (a word with the root meaning of "to know"), and it is possible to formulate a theory of human motivation in these terms. This does not mean that impulsivity and irrationality are denied, or that behavioral systems rooted in childhood have not developed; all that has been said already can be accepted as true, but there is still another way at looking at some of the facts of human motivation.

Goals, purposes, and plans

When an individual knows what he wants, knows the effort that will be involved in overcoming obstacles along the way, and knows what satisfaction the end state will bring he can put his goals into

words. If there are risks, he is prepared to face them. Such behavior is clearly *purposeful*, in that an intention is carried out according to an announced goal. The student who enters college to train himself to become an engineer knows in general what the profession of engineering is and what courses he must pursue in order to achieve his goal. He may see mathematics as an obstacle to overcome, but he assumes the risk.

There is no doubt that an individual can make *plans* and carry them out. He knows what he wants to do, where he wants to be at a particular time, and he arranges things so that he gets there.[2] He can leave word where he can be found, and (except for unforeseeable circumstances) there is often a high probability that the plan will materialize. By a person of "strong will" we mean one who can adopt a plan and commit himself so firmly to it that he will show resistance to distractions and resourcefulness in finding ways to continue toward the intended goal. A person of "weak will" is one who is unable to stick to a plan, no matter how clearly he may be able to formulate it; he gives up easily in the face of obstacles or distractions. There is no deep philosophical issue over "freedom of the will" here; the matter is complicated but does not lie outside of empirical science. People differ in their capacities to announce and fulfill plans just as they differ in their capacities to solve intellectual problems or to perform acts of skill.

Plans are of various kinds and lengths, including not only the seeking of certain goals but also *stop-plans* to avoid fatigue or danger. A stop-plan, for example, is not taking too many cups of coffee before retiring or determining to leave the card game in order to have enough sleep. The more that a person is able to formulate plans, even short-term ones, and carry them out, the greater sense of self-control he develops.

[2] Miller, Galanter, and Pribram (1960) use the word "Image" to refer to the organized knowledge and values that serve as the occasion for a "Plan." Thus the intended goal is part of the Image, while the steps along the way are part of the Plan. We shall not follow their interesting theoretical treatment further.

Level of aspiration

Goal-setting has been studied in experiments on the *level of aspiration*. In these experiments level of aspiration refers to a fairly immediate goal, that is, something almost within reach, a possible success near at hand. The goal-setting in the experiments parallels what the high jumper does when he sets the bar between the posts. Where he sets it is his momentary goal, a measure of his level of aspiration. He expects to succeed, but he sets it high enough that he might fail. He would take no satisfaction in setting it so low that he could jump successfully every time. Satisfaction comes when he is able to clear the bar at a new height.

Experiments on level of aspiration help to define a person's goal, because in these experiments (as in the high jump illustration) success is determined by what the person himself is trying to do.

In the first experiment definitely concerned with these problems (Hoppe, 1930) it was revealed that the person's feeling of success or failure depends upon the difficulty of the task. As shown in Figure 6–3, a task may be "much too easy." Then the person experiences no sense of success, even though he accomplishes the task. A person who can play chess is not satisfied to win at dominoes. Or a task may be "much too difficult." Because he has no *ego involvement*, a person who makes no pretense of knowing Russian grammar will not have a sense of failure if he is unable to answer questions about it; he does not expect himself to know the answers. Success and failure experiences come in the in-between range: between the point at which success is highly probable, but failure possible, and that at which failure is highly probable, but success possible. This is the range in which the high jumper in the example will set his bar. Experiments on level of aspiration have been concerned with a number of problems, among them the effect of group standards on individual behavior.

In one experiment, by Hilgard, Sait, and Magaret (1940), college students worked together in small groups (usually four students at a time). The task consisted of simple arithmetic problems, the score being the time required to complete a page. Public announcement of the finishing time was made, so that each student knew what the others were doing. Each student recorded privately his level of aspiration, that is, the score he expected to make on the next test. It was found that these private expectations were modified by the group performances: those whose groups had scores above average tended to lower their estimates; those with scores below average tended to expect to gain. The same tendency was found whether the score differences were due to differences in arithmetic ability on tests of equal difficulty or due to hidden differences in test difficulty for students of equal ability.

In another experiment with college students, by Festinger (1942), shifts in aspiration level were studied when (1) the student knew only his own previous scores, and (2) he was told that his score was above or below that of one of three reference groups: high school, college, and graduate students. The results are shown

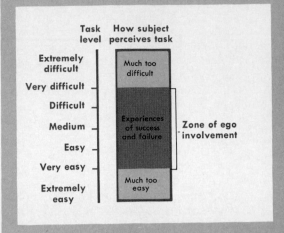

The subject tends to set his own goal (level of aspiration) within the shaded area in which he can experience success or failure. (After Hoppe, 1930)

in Figure 6–4. If the score was below that of the low-prestige group (high school students), the aspiration level increased most; if it was above that of the high-prestige group (graduate students), aspiration level decreased most.

Thus individual goal-setting is modified by prestige-seeking, self-protection, and other goals that reflect the setting in which motivated behavior occurs.

Studies of aspiration level illustrate cognitive-type motivation because the individual becomes involved in a task, estimates his own level of achievement, sets his goals, and is elated or chagrined by what happens.

Achievement motivation

The level of aspiration experiments provided the background for a later and much more extensive series of experiments on achievement motivation. Man is a doer, and observers all along have found a place for some sort of achievement motive, whether in the form of an "instinct of workmanship" or in the desire to master nature or to be a leader of men. Achievement motivation, as defined in the experiments to be reported, refers to a tendency to define one's goals according to some standard of excellence in the product or performance attained.

McClelland and his associates (1953) developed a method by which fantasy productions are used for measuring achievement motivation. It may be noted that there is an influence here from the theory of unconscious motivation as well, for the assumption is made that if there is a strong motivational disposition toward achievement it will be revealed in fantasy without the subject's knowing that he is telling something about himself. The following account illustrates the method.

The experimenter showed male college students three pictures with the instructions to write brief five-minute stories about each. The pictures suggested a work situation (two men working at a machine), a study situation (a boy seated at a desk with a book in front of him), and a father-son situation. The stories were written around the following four questions printed on the answer sheet: "What is happening?" "What has led up to this situation?" "What is being thought?" "What will happen?"

The stories were examined for notions emphasizing the importance of achievement, of getting things done, of success. Subjects who wrote into their stories many such ideas were scored as having a high motive for achievement, those with few such ideas a low one. There were 19 in the high group and 21 in the low group.

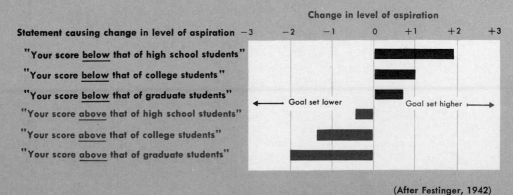

6–4

Effect of prestige of reference groups on level of aspiration

(After Festinger, 1942)

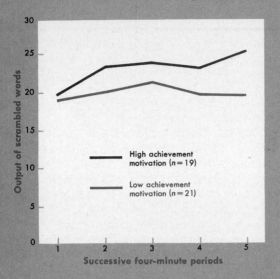

6–5

Achievement motivation and performance

Mean output of scrambled words for subjects above and below the mean in the achievement motive score. (After Lowell, 1950; McClelland, 1955)

Following this test the experimenter asked the subjects to work on a 20-minute scrambled-words test, in which they had to rearrange an anagram such as WTSE into a meaningful word such as WEST. Results for those high and low in achievement motive are given in Figure 6–5. Similar results were found for problems in addition, with output higher for those with strong achievement motivation. Evidently the results in the test of fantasy did measure a motive having to do with success in laboratory tasks (Lowell, 1950, as reported in McClelland, 1955).

Later studies of achievement-oriented behavior soon began to note a complication that had appeared in earlier studies of level of aspiration: some individuals appeared to be more motivated by *pleasure in success* and others by *fear of failure*. It had been found much earlier that children with a history of success tended to set realistic goals that they had a chance of reaching and enjoying, while children with histories of failures either set goals very low, so as

to avoid the repeated experience of defeat, or very high, so that they would not feel degraded by failure (Sears, 1940).

One way to put this is that people whose fantasy scores show them to be imagining success are usually those who have realistic confidence in themselves, while those whose fantasy scores show low achievement motivation are those who are anxious about failure. Raphelson (1957) tested achievement motivation in the usual way through using the storytelling cards, but he measured the same subjects for their test anxiety and a physiological correlate of anxiety, the galvanic skin response (GSR). He found under achievement-oriented conditions a correlation of −.43 between achievement motivation and anxiety, whether measured by the verbal test of anxiety or by the GSR measure. It appears that the more testlike and competitive a situation is, the better the high-achievement subjects do, while those in the low-achievement and high-anxiety category do less well under such pressure (Moulton and others, 1958). It thus turns out that a low score on achievement motivation does not necessarily mean a lack of desire for success but reflects a fear of failure, so that the subject does not risk setting his sights too high.

The achievement theme is a prominent one in western culture, and it appears to be inculcated early in life. Mothers of high-achievement boys tend to make demands for achievement of their sons at an earlier age than do mothers of low-achievement sons (Winterbottom, 1958).

use of money as an index of achievement, it is surprising how little reference is made to this motive by psychologists.

The reasons for this neglect of the profit motive are several. For one thing, the concept of profit as used by economists has a very special meaning, as a return on capital, and does not cover, strictly speaking, the wages or salaries for which men work. Hence if a psychologist talks about profits he has to define profits in the light of economists' discussions, and all anticipation of monetary return is not from that point of view an interest in profits. Another problem is that the motives of the capitalist are not single, and have tended to change as managerial capitalism has developed with its separation of ownership from control. While management seeks to please stockholders through dividend payments (recognizing that the stockholders are in this sense motivated by expected profits), the managers themselves are often more interested in the growth of the corporation, its diversity, and its stability rather than in profits as such. Hence it is a great oversimplification to say that the managers who are responsible for our corporate enterprises are working only, or even chiefly, for profits; for them, achievement motivation takes other forms. Furthermore, there are large sectors of our economy in which nonacquisitive tendencies are more prominent than acquisitive ones, as in government service, education, the professions, and the artistic world. Men work at economically important tasks for prestige, for power, for self-satisfaction in ways not measured by a profit index.

To be sure, property is a symbol of prestige in our culture, as it is in less developed ones, so that in acquiring property one is acquisitive, but the motives may be mixed. Among some of the herders of South Africa a man's status depended upon the size of his flock. As a result, individuals devoted great effort to acquiring flocks many times larger than required to supply their families' needs (Goldenweiser, 1937). Among the Trobriand Islanders, food was collected and placed in warehouses where others could see how much the owner had been able to acquire. In that society a man without stored food was a man without status (Malinowski, 1935).

The institution of the potlatch among the Indians of the Northwest Coast exemplifies the acquisition of property largely for prestige. If two men quarreled, one of them gave a feast at which he gave away or destroyed as much property as possible. This feast was called a "potlatch." The other lost status unless he could reply in kind (Benedict, 1934). It is evident that the need to keep or give up property is less a "need for acquisition" than a need for prestige.

Despite these complexities in the interpretation of the profit motive, the psychologist McClelland believes that growth of the profit-system economy is based on a high level of the achievement motive. By arousing the motive in groups of businessmen in the United States, Mexico, and India, he showed that such men were encouraged to engage in more entrepreneurial behavior than they would if they had not had their achievement motives aroused (McClelland, 1965). If his theory is correct, then the studies of achievement motivation make up in part for the neglect of the profit motive by psychologists.

A formulation of cognitive motivational theory

One way of looking at a cognitive theory of motivation is to see that it is a theory of preferential choice or of decision-making. That is, the decision to engage in a given activity in preference to alternatives, and how deeply to become involved in it, is made on the basis of cognitive considerations.

Some types of decision theory have been developed by economists to account for the purchase of one kind of goods over another. In simplest terms, the economist assumes that the individual can assign *utility* to possible incentives, and that he makes his decision according to the utility and the *risk* involved. He is willing to take more risk for something that he prefers. Such a theory can be expressed in mathematical terms, in simplest form:

$$\text{Choice} = f(\text{Utility} \times \text{Probability of attainment})\ [3]$$

[3] The f in an equation of the form $y = f(x)$ means "function of" or "depends upon."

A type of formulation, somewhat similar to that of the economists, has been put in motivation terms by J. W. Atkinson (1964). His formula, modified somewhat to conform with the vocabulary of this book, is as follows:

$$\text{Motive arousal} = f(\text{Motivational disposition} \times \text{Incentive} \times \text{Expectation})$$

This formula is much like the preceding one, substituting incentive for utility and expectation for probability of attainment. The "motivational disposition" term recognizes the existence of individual differences —something the economists have occasionally overlooked in their concept of "economic man."

Atkinson's own experimental tests of his formula have been concerned with two main conjectures derived from it. The first conjecture is that the success-oriented subject should work hardest at a task of intermediate difficulty when the outcome has a 50/50 chance of success or failure. This follows because a task of very high probability of success has low incentive value, while the task of low probability of success discourages effort even though its incentive value is high. The maximum product of probability of success (expectation) and of incentive (see formula above) is at intermediate values; hence the greatest motivational arousal will be at the 50/50 value. The second conjecture is that the anxiety-ridden (fear of failure) subject will show the reverse reaction; his anxiety will be highest at the 50/50 point, so he will avoid tasks of intermediate difficulty, preferring those very easy or very hard. A further assumption is that for any one person achievement (success) tendencies and anxiety (fear of failure) tendencies can be added algebraically.

In one experiment designed to test these predictions, male college students participated in a ring-toss game in which the subject was given the choice of making his shots at any distance from one to 15 feet from the peg (Atkinson and Litwin, 1960). The presumption was that some middle distance would be preferred (as corresponding roughly to the 50/50 likelihood of success as predicted by the theory), and that this would be most preferred by those with high-achievement motivation and low-anxiety. In fact, the order expected would be: high-achievement plus low-anxiety, high-achievement plus high-anxiety, low-achievement plus low-anxiety, and, finally, low-achievement plus high-anxiety. The experiment depends of course on adequate measures of achievement motivation and test anxiety and makes the assumption that achievement motivation was aroused in the ring-toss game. The arousal was enhanced by having other subjects standing around and by the goading instructions "See how good you are at this." The results were in the predicted direction (Figure 6–6), with the high-achievement plus low test-anxiety subjects selecting an intermediate task in 77 percent of their choices, while the low-achievement plus high test-anxiety subjects selected this range in only 31 percent of their shots. The other groups fell between.

The studies of achievement motivation and fear of failure give indication of the usefulness of cognitive theory in the approach to motivation.

Summary note on motivational theories

The specimens of motivational theory selected for discussion (behavior theory, the theory of unconscious motivation, and cognitive theory) represent selections from among current efforts to find some orderly way in which to deal with human motivation. Each has sufficient success to its credit to make it of value. The overlaps have been noted; each theory, for example, has its developmental aspects. In behavior theory this development is usually described according to a specific learning theory, while in the psychoanalytic theory more is made (as we saw in Chapter 3) of a maturational theory of stages. Cognitive theory also looks for childhood influences upon the development of motivational dispositions. The role of the unconscious is not denied in any of the theories. In behavioral theory the unconscious is usually associated with habits that operate outside the

6–6

Performance according to varying degrees of achievement and anxiety motivation

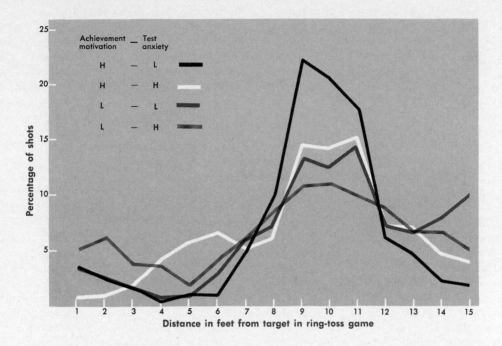

Percentage of shots taken from each distance by male college students in a ring-toss game. Each student took 10 shots from any distance he chose. Subjects classified as high or low in achievement motivation and in test anxiety. (After Atkinson and Litwin, 1960)

system of verbal behavior, in psychoanalysis the concept of some sort of active unconscious is a central feature of the theory, while in cognitive theory unconscious influences are noted to affect the fantasy behavior that is widely used in its measurements. No one of the theories has gained universal acceptance among psychologists as a satisfactory account of the complexity of human motivation.

Self-Reference in Human Motivation

Most experimental studies of motivation are concerned with rather specific, somewhat isolated fragments of behavior, as in the choices between two alternatives or in the behavior elicited under specific conditions of arousal. One of the difficulties in such studies is that they do not come to grips with the organization of motives in the individual and with the *hierarchical* nature of motives. That is, some things are more important to the person than others, and some activities are engaged in merely because they contribute to long-range goals. When one attempts to deal with motivational hierarchies, he often finds that they turn upon the way in which the individual sees himself, what he expects of himself, how confident he is, what ideal he sets before himself. Many motives can be understood in relation to some sort of self-image: self-assertion, self-abnegation, the desire for power or for recognition.

Self-consistency and the reduction of cognitive dissonance

One likes to think that one's attitudes, beliefs, and related behavior form a consistent pattern. Incongruity that is detected results in a sense of imbalance or dissonance, which the person then seeks to correct. The motivating effects of the need to correct incongruity, imbalance, or dissonance has been the occasion for several theories (Brown, 1962). We may select for consideration the theory proposed by Festinger (1957) which treats of *cognitive dissonance* and its reduction. The kind of disagreement or disharmony with which Festinger has been chiefly concerned is that which occurs after a decision has been made, after one is committed to a course of action; under such circumstances there is often some lack of harmony between what ones does and what one believes, and there is pressure to change either one's behavior or one's beliefs. For example, if a regular smoker reads about the relationship between smoking and lung cancer, the habitual action and the new information are dissonant. If the decision is made to continue smoking, the dissonance will be reduced by disbelieving the information about the relationship between smoking and lung cancer; if the decision is made to give up smoking, the information on the linkage between smoking and lung cancer will be accepted. The fact that this information also affected the decision is not important here. As Festinger and others (1964) have shown, the weighing of alternatives is more realistic prior to the decision; after the decision the pressure is great to bring belief and action into balance. The results plotted in Figure 6–7 support this interpretation. (These results were obtained before the case for a linkage between lung cancer and smoking was as well established as it is now.)

The theory goes on to make some nonobvious predictions: for example, in some cases failure of expectations instead of destroying belief may strengthen it. This was illustrated by the study of a group of people who expected to be saved from a prophesied disastrous flood by the intervention of a heavenly being. The theory predicted that when the long-awaited day arrived and the prophecy failed (no flood), those who had the social support of the other believers would indeed proselyte for their beliefs with new enthusiasm; while those who had to face the crisis alone would have their faith weakened. These predicted results did indeed occur, the rationalization for the group of disappointed believers who faced failure together being that God had postponed his vengeance because of their faith (Festinger, Riecken, and Schachter, 1956).

Motives toward self-actualization

The tendency to be consistent is but one aspect of how self-perception influences motivation. Earlier illustrations of human motivation might also be reinterpreted in these terms. For example, the success motivation and the avoidance of failure are also concerned with how a person sees himself. R. W. White, for example, reinterprets many motives concerned with curiosity, desire for knowledge and for achievement,

6–7

Cognitive dissonance reduced by change in belief

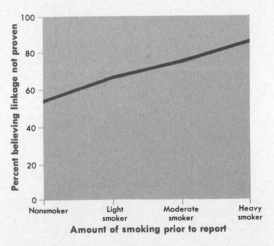

Belief in lack of linkage between smoking and lung cancer on the part of those who smoke. (Data from Minneapolis *Sunday Tribune*, March 21, 1954, as reported by Festinger, 1957)

as though they are all concerned with one's sense of *competence* as a person who is effective in relation to the environment (White, 1959). In another sense, the person likes to develop his potentials to the full, to be as complete a person as he can. For such a pervasive type of motive the expression *self-actualization* was coined, originally by Carl Jung, one of Freud's followers who later developed a system of his own. By self-actualization he meant the development of full individuality, with all parts somehow in harmony. The term and closely related ones (productive orientation, creative becoming, etc.), have been used by many psychologists who criticize contemporary motivational theory as being too narrow, concerned with short episodes of choice and behavior rather than with the more profound and pervasive aspects of individual hopes and aspirations. The term has been widely used by Maslow, and the present discussion will be based on his conjectures and experiments (Maslow, 1954, 1962).

In addition to his general motivational hierarchy (physiological needs, safety needs, belongingness and love needs, esteem needs, and the need for self-actualization), Maslow has come to distinguish between the lower and the higher motives as *deficiency motives* (D-motives) and *being motives* (B-motives). In general, motives lower in the hierarchy are aroused through deficiency and they are indeed urgent determiners of behavior when their satisfaction is lacking. The higher motives (B-motives) come into play chiefly when the D-motives have been taken care of. For man to function at his highest level his survival needs and his normal social requirements have to be taken care of; after that we have the opportunity to see him at his best.

In order to give some empirical support to his position, Maslow set out to find people who appeared to him to be *self-actualizing persons;* he later described some of the *peak experiences* associated with their kind of motivation.

The selection of self-actualizing persons for study did not follow the ordinary methods of choosing a sample and then sorting those within it according to scores on some kind of test. Instead, a great many people were reviewed, and a few of them studied as best representing what Maslow had in mind as self-actualizers (Maslow, 1954, pp. 199–234). In general, he felt that the students in his group represented the healthiest one percent of the college population (absence of neurotic or psychotic trends; presence of full use of their talents, capacities, and potentialities); the eminent cases studied included such persons as Abraham Lincoln, Thomas Jefferson, Albert Einstein, Eleanor Roosevelt, William James, and a number of others. After an impressionistic study of these lives, of both famous people and contemporaries, Maslow arrived at a kind of composite picture of self-actualizing people. His characterizations included 15 items such as the following: more efficient perception of reality and more comfortable relations with it, acceptance of self and others, spontaneity and continued freshness of appreciation, sense of humor, creativeness, resistance to enculturation (while not especially unconventional, they get along in their culture but are relatively independent of it).

While these qualities are on the whole admirable, it takes a good deal of analysis (possibly along the lines of the motivational theories treated earlier) to see how these qualities come about. Indeed some empirical studies of narrower focus support many of Maslow's ideas. For example, Kaplan and Singer (1963) report that people who score high on a dogmatism scale (who would be classified as nonactualizers because of their inflexibility) are less perceptive in some respects than others, as indicated by a correlation of $-.61$ between dogmatism and sensory acuity as measured in the laboratory. This would support Maslow's notion that self-actualizers are more efficient in the perception of reality. In another study a personality-orientation inventory was developed based essentially on the characteristics of self-actualizers; results of this were then correlated with a personality inventory scoring both neurotic and extravert-introvert tendencies (Knapp, 1965). The results showed a negative correlation between the personality orientation in the direction of self-actualization and the neuroticism scores, which would support Maslow's contention that he was describing mentally healthy people.

In looking for some other aspects of self-actualizers, Maslow (1959) turned to what he called *peak experiences*. A peak experience is one of happiness and fullfilment. In his terms it is an experience of *being*, which means for him a temporary, nonstriving, nonself-centered, purposeless, self-validating end experience, a state of perfection and goal-attainment. By asking some 190 college students to describe any experience that came near to such an experience, he attempted to categorize what they said. He came out with a list of values found in such experiences—"B-values," as he called them. They include wholeness, perfection, aliveness, uniqueness, effortlessness, self-sufficiency, and the standard values of beauty, goodness, and truth.

As a result of the study of peak experiences, Maslow has somewhat modified his conception of the self-actualizer. It appears now that nearly everyone may at some time or other have had a peak experience, during which he was, for a time, a self-actualizer. The consistent self-actualizers whom Maslow earlier sought differ only in that they have these satisfying peak experiences more frequently, intensely, and perfectly.

CRITICAL DISCUSSION

Self-actualization and existentialism

There is a robust, optimistic flavor to the concept of self-actualization, often reflected in the writings of others who take similar positions, such as Rogers, who says, for example, "It has been my experience that persons have a basically positive orientation." [4]

Existentialism, the closely related view that has come out of the writings of philosophers, theologians, and humanists, tends to take a somewhat more pessimistic position, or at least a position more oriented toward the tragic in life. Consider, for example, the theologian Paul Tillich's *The courage to be* (1952). In this the three great anxieties that all men must face are those of fate and death, of emptiness and meaninglessness, and of guilt and condemnation. The thesis is that it takes courage to overcome the despair that all reflective men share. One finds little of this in Maslow or Rogers.

These are views which are all concerned with man at his most reflective, as well as man at his moral best. Psychologists have paid little attention to the fact that the great literature and great dramas tend to be tragic; somehow the basic human problems seem to be reflected in these tragic themes. For some inherent weaknesses in the optimistic "positive thinking" emphases so frequent in America, a useful review is that of Meyer (1965).

[4] Rogers (1961), p. 26.

SUMMARY   1. Because man shares a common mammalian ancestry with other animals many of his motives are based on the satisfaction of basic needs and are expressed in the form of drives or other physiologically based motives, as discussed in the preceding chapter. However, the prominence of learning in the expression of human motives, the expression of motives in a social context, and man's capacity for resourcefulness and reflection make some of the problems of human motivation unique.

2. The complexity of human motivation is evident when we think of persistent *motivational dispositions* in which men differ; these may be quiescent or become evident under conditions of appropriate *motivational arousal*. A given type of arousal, say, of achievement motive, will be more effective for those whose motivational dispositions include high-

achievement motivation, while another type of arousal may be more effective for those who are higher in some other disposition, such as affiliative tendencies. Finally, *overt behavior*, while motivated and hence expressive of motives, cannot be used to infer motives directly because the same behavior may represent different motives.

3. The difficulties in inferring motives directly from behavior lead to arbitrariness in the listing of human motives, although such lists may be useful in a preliminary way by calling attention to the range of motivated behavior in which man engages.

4. Three theories of motivation were selected to illustrate the nature of theories of human motivation: *behavior theory,* the *theory of unconscious motivation,* and *cognitive motivational theory.*

5. Behavior theory as proposed by Whiting and Child makes the assumption that a few basic motives acquired in early infancy proliferate into *behavior systems* in later life, in which many kinds of behavior are influenced by this common motive. The mechanism is assumed to be that of learning and habit formation. As illustrative motives, three are considered: *hunger,* with its derivatives in all sorts of food-related behavior, but with some derivatives not readily recognized as food-related; *dependency,* with its derivatives in all sorts of behavior involving attachment to and affiliation with other people; and *aggression,* which finds expression in many situations where there is some need or motive to inflict harm on another (or to turn it against the self).

6. The theory of unconscious motivation, prominent in the theories coming from Freud and psychoanalysis, uses as evidence for unconscious motivation the motivational relevance of dreams, the indications through mannerisms and slips of speech, and the form that symptoms of neurosis take. In the Freudian theory sex and aggression are particularly prominent as impulses that find indirect or symbolic expression. The experimental illustration used was that of the effects of sexual arousal on fantasy when conditions favored repression and when they favored open expression.

7. The cognitive theory of motivation, accepting the essential findings of the other theories, combines with other theories an interest in resourcefulness, goal-setting, and decision-making in which the subject is often aware of the risks involved and controls his behavior accordingly. Two sets of experiments were considered, one on *level of aspiration,* in which goal-setting is determined in part by difficulty level, the involvement of the person in the task, and prior experiences of success and failure. The second set concerned *achievement motivation;* that is, behavior oriented around successful performance according to some standard of excellence.

8. In the formulation of cognitive motivational theory by John W. Atkinson it was essential to take into account the fact that some people are more highly motivated by hope of success and others by fear of failure. Depending on the task, a person may of course have some of each type of motivation. The theory states that *motive arousal* can be expressed as a product of *motivational disposition, incentive,* and *expectation.* Derivations from this theory predict that people high in achieve-

ment motivation and low in anxiety (fear of failure) will tend to choose tasks of moderate difficulty, so that they can take moderate risks in the hope of building up their stock of success experiences, while those with low achievement motivation and high anxiety tend to choose either very easy tasks (so that they do not risk failure) or very difficult tasks (so that failure will not be held against them). Experimental evidence gives some support for these implications of the theory.

9. When motives are not studied piecemeal but instead in relation to their organization within the individual, we often find some sort of *self-reference* in the motive, having to do with the way in which the individual sees himself, what he hopes to become, what values he treasures. One aspect of this pattern is the desire of the person to see himself as consistent, so that he is uneasy when he detects a lack of consistency between what he believes and what he does, or between two belief systems. This discordance is called *cognitive dissonance* (Festinger), and it has motivational power in causing the individual to make some maneuvers in order to reduce the dissonance.

A broad approach to the problem is by way of the conception of *self-actualization*. As proposed by Maslow, the self-actualizing tendency has full play only when the lower motives are satisfied. He introduces the concept of a *hierarchy* of motives, with deficiency motives (D-motives) lower in the hierarchy and "being" motives (B-motives) higher. These conceptions challenge the present experimentation on human motivation chiefly by asserting that present approaches are too fragmentary, and do not represent man at his best or highest.

SUGGESTIONS FOR FURTHER READING

The problems basic to human motivation have been well treated in a number of books, among which may be mentioned Atkinson, *An introduction to motivation* (1964), Atkinson and Feather (eds.), *A theory of achievement motivation* (1966), Cofer and Appley, *Motivation: Theory and research* (1964), Lindzey (ed.), *Assessment of human motives* (1958), McClelland (ed.), *Studies in motivation* (1955), Murray, *Motivation and emotion* (1964), Rethlingshafer, *Motivation as related to personality* (1963), Stacey and De-Martino (eds.), *Understanding human motivation* (rev. ed., 1963).

For convenient access to shorter articles covering much of the material in this chapter, the following readings are recommended: Birney and Teevan (eds.), *Measuring human motivation* (1962); Teevan and Birney (eds.), *Theories of motivation in personality and social psychology* (1964b); Haber (ed.), *Current research in motivation* (1966).

For Maslow's views, see his *Toward a psychology of being* (1962). Its bibliography can serve as a guide to views congenial to his, often little represented in the books above.

7 Emotion

Life without emotion would be drab. If there were no joys and sorrows, no hopes and dismays, no thrills or triumphs, the warmth and color would go out of human experience.

Men prefer to have pleasurable states endure and do things to make them recur; men also prefer to have unpleasant, painful, or annoying states end promptly and do what they can to avoid them. But is this a sufficient statement of the relation between emotion and motivation? We need to look more closely into pleasant and disturbing emotional states to see how they are related to goal-directed behavior.

Affective States

The range of affectively toned experience

The *mild* states of feeling that accompany many of our activities can be described as states of pleasantness or unpleasantness. We may find a warm test tube pleasant to touch and a piece of sandpaper unpleasant to touch. In a restaurant we may find a cup of hot coffee pleasant, but waiting for it unpleasant. When we call attention to the pleasantness or unpleasantness of experiences, we are referring to their *affective tone*. When psychologists were more given to making fine introspective distinctions than they are today, they called these mild affective states *feelings* and reserved the term *emotion* for the more profound, widespread, and stirred-up states

suggested by such words as terror, grief, rage, or exultation. However, the stirred-up character is not enough to distinguish between emotions and other states, for the body is stirred up when we chop wood or saw a board; it is really the intensity of the affective toning that makes the state emotional. To be sure, such a full-fledged emotion will be reflected in characteristic behavior and diffuse changes in body physiology—the kinds of behavior that permit us to detect emotions in others or in animals. We may recognize, however, many intermediate states between the very mild experiences of pleasantness and unpleasantness and the violent, intense emotions: states of excitement or quiescence, of appreciation of beauty or dislike of ugliness. We shall therefore not attempt to define "an emotion," but instead will be concerned with a variety of affective states.

Virtually all psychologists who have classified emotions divide them into those that are *pleasant* (e.g., joy, love) and those that are *unpleasant* (e.g., anger, sadness). This classification suggests the primacy of pleasantness and unpleasantness, of acceptance and rejection, of approach and avoidance as the very basis of emotion. Beyond the classification into pleasant and unpleasant states, many of our emotional terms express the *intensity* of the experience. The differences in intensity are carried by word pairs such as the following: anger-rage, fear-horror, pain-agony, sadness-grief. By grouping together the whole family of experiences from mild satisfactions and annoyances at one end of the scale through weak emotional states up to the most intense emotions at the other end, we emphasize the continuities among these emotional states.

In an experiment to see how our language reflects differences in emotional intensity, Plutchik (1962) presented lists of synonyms for various emotions to 30 college students, asking them to rate the intensity of emotion that the emotional word signified, using a scale from 1 to 11, with 1 being very low and 11 very intense. Representative of his results are the ratings found for six classes or "dimensions" of emotional experience (Table 7–1). Note that at a quite high level (rated between 9 and 10 on the 11-point scale) are *rage, ecstasy, astonishment, panic, grief,* and *loathing,* while (for the same emotional

classes or dimensions) the corresponding terms at a lower level (rated 7 to 8 on the 11-point scale) are *anger, joy, surprise, fear, sorrow,* and *disgust.*

Once we recognize the gradation from the less intense to the more intense experiences, the old distinction between feeling and emotion loses its force. In discussing the emotional aspects of behavior and experience, we shall include all our affectively colored activity regardless of intensity. In summary, we shall define as an *emotional state* the condition of the organism during affectively toned experience, whether the affective toning is mild or intense.

Bodily changes in emotion

The symptoms of fear reported by fliers on missions in World War II (Table 7–2)

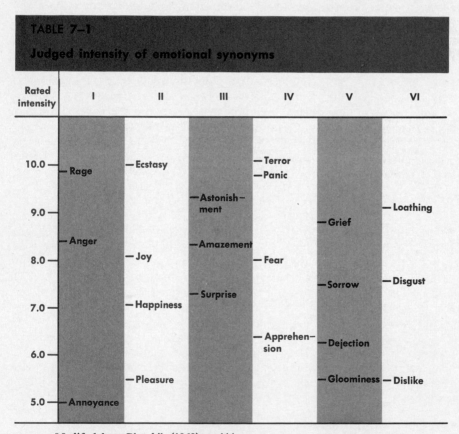

TABLE 7–1

Judged intensity of emotional synonyms

Rated intensity	I	II	III	IV	V	VI
10.0	Rage	Ecstasy		Terror / Panic		
9.0			Astonishment		Grief	Loathing
8.0	Anger	Joy	Amazement	Fear	Sorrow	Disgust
7.0		Happiness	Surprise			
6.0				Apprehension	Dejection	
5.0	Annoyance	Pleasure			Gloominess	Dislike

SOURCE: Modified from Plutchik (1962), p. 114.

TABLE 7–2
Symptoms of fear in combat flying

"During combat missions did you feel"	*"Often"*	*"Sometimes"*	*Total*
A pounding heart and rapid pulse	30%	56%	89%
That your muscles were very tense	30	53	83
Easily irritated, angry, or "sore"	22	58	80
Dryness of the throat or mouth	30	50	80
"Nervous perspiration" or "cold sweat"	26	53	79
"Butterflies" in the stomach	23	53	76
Sense of unreality that this couldn't be happening to you	20	49	69
Need to urinate very frequently	25	40	65
Trembling	11	53	64
Confused or rattled	3	50	53
Weak or faint	4	37	41
Right after a mission, unable to remember details of what happened	5	34	39
Sick to the stomach	5	33	38
Unable to concentrate	3	32	35
That you have wet or soiled your pants	1	4	5

SOURCE: Based on reports of 1985 flying officers and 2519 enlisted fliers of World War II. After Shaffer (1947).

well illustrate the complexity of the bodily processes in an emotional state. The symptoms at the top of the list, the ones most frequently mentioned, are the milder ones (pounding heart, tense muscles), while the less frequent symptoms, near the bottom of the list, are more severe (confusion, faintness, loss of memory, nausea).

The symptoms of emotion, especially of intense emotion, include profound changes throughout the body, changes regulated in a complex way by the central nervous system, by both divisions of the autonomic system, and by the endocrine glands. Out of the mass of these physical changes, psychologists have studied a number of selected indicators, some of which follow:

1. *Galvanic skin response.* Whenever emotions are aroused, detectable electrical changes take place on the skin. Electrodes attached to the skin (e.g., on the palms of the hands) are connected with a recording galvanometer. The *galvanic skin response* (GSR) is a sensitive indicator of changes in emotional state. Demonstrations such as the following are commonly used in psychology classes: a male student, with the electrodes attached to his palms, recites the alphabet aloud slowly while thinking of the name of his girl friend. The class tries to judge from the swing of the galvanometer needle when he has come to her initial. His slight embarrassment or excitement or concern about being detected is commonly revealed through an unusually wide swing of the needle to the appropriate letter. This is the principle used in the operation of the lie detector (see p. 184).

2. *Blood distribution.* Changes in blood pressure and changes in the distribution of the blood between the surface and the interior of the body occur in emotion. We are familiar with blushing in embarrassment or a flushed face and neck in anger ("hot under the collar"). These changes occur because blood vessels in the skin dilate, and more blood is found near the surface of the skin. The opposite symptom is the blanching of the face under some conditions of fright. In this case the blood vessels constrict.

3. *Heart rate.* The pounding of the heart in emotional excitement is so familiar that the heart has long been a symbol of emotion.

4. *Respiration.* The rate and depth of breathing as well as the relative amount of time spent in inspiration compared to expiration provide useful indicators, especially in emotional conflict. The relative times determine the "inspiration-expiration ratio" (I/E ratio). Gasping for breath and sighing are the kinds of changes that affect the I/E ratio.

5. *Pupillary response.* The pupil of the eye tends to dilate in moments of anger and pain or emotional excitement, and to constrict in times of quiescence.

6. *Salivary secretion.* Experimental evidence supports the common observation that emotional excitement often produces a dryness of the mouth because of a decrease in saliva or a change in its consistency.

7. *Pilomotor response.* This is the technical name for "goose pimples," which appear when hairs of the skin stand on end.

8. *Gastrointestinal motility.* Investigators have used X-ray methods and the stomach-balloon technique (the method described in connection with the study of hunger, p. 121) to determine that the movements of stomach and intestine are affected by strong emotion. Emotional excitement may lead to nausea or diarrhea. Persistent emotional or mood states may be responsible, through the tensions set up in the walls of the stomach or intestines, for the ulcers that some people get when under stress for long periods of time.

9. *Muscle tension and tremor.* We sometimes say of a person, "If only he could relax. He's too tense." Muscular tension is a symptom of emotion. Tensed muscles may tremble when opposing muscles are contracted simultaneously (see Chapter 2, p. 31). The tremor may also occur when a person experiences a conflict of desires, as, for example, a powerful desire to slap an irritating smart aleck conflicting with an equally powerful desire to retain one's dignity and self-respect.

10. *Blood composition.* Because the endocrine glands are active during emotion and pour hormones into the blood stream, chemical analysis reveals actual changes in blood composition. There are changes in blood sugar, acid-base balance, and adrenalin content. In Chapter 2, adrenalin and noradrenalin were described as hormones of the adrenal medulla, important agents in emotional excitement.

These ten emotional indicators suffice to dramatize the profound and widespread changes that go on in the body when one is emotionally aroused.

Physiological mechanisms in emotion

The many bodily changes that occur during emotion are not unrelated phenomena; they fit together into patterns organized under the influence of the nervous system and the endocrine glands. W. B. Cannon, the physiologist, noted that one large group of symptoms prominent in anger and rage prepare the organism to face emergencies and to defend itself against attack and injury (Cannon, 1929).

If a cat, quietly digesting its meal, is confronted suddenly by a barking dog, the following physiological changes (among others) take place: (1) digestive movements of the stomach cease; (2) blood pressure increases; (3) heart rate accelerates; (4) adrenalin is secreted into the blood stream.

Each of these reactions is regulated through the sympathetic division of the autonomic nervous system. The secretion of adrenalin has the effect of: (1) raising the blood pressure; (2) increasing the sugar in the blood, making it available for energetic action and counteraction of fatigue; (3) making the blood clot more quickly.

The cat arches its back and hisses (these particular activities are *not* mediated by the sympathetic system, although they are part of the emotional activity). Its hair stands on end. It is now ready to fight. The additional sugar in its blood gives it energy and increased endurance. If it is wounded, its blood will clot more quickly. If the cat is bitten, the dog is likely to get a mouthful of hair instead of a chunk of flesh.

Because these physical responses fit together and prepare the organism for action, Cannon called them *emergency reactions.*

He interpreted intense emotional excitement as a method of preparing the organism to meet emergencies. Reactions that at first seemed independent and unrelated, he found, form a pattern serving the common purposes of protection.

Most of the reactions demonstrated in the cat are found in man also. When we get angry we may have stomach aches due to changes in stomach movements: our hearts beat faster, our adrenalin flows, and our blood, like the cat's, clots more quickly. The bloody nose of the athlete is less of a problem when he is excited because the blood flow stops more readily.

The sympathetic and parasympathetic divisions often have nerve connections to the same organs, but, as we learned in Chapter 2 (p. 49), they usually produce opposite effects. Stimulation over the sympathetic system accelerates the heart rate; stimulation over the parasympathetic system slows the heart rate. Stimulation over the sympathetic system inhibits the muscular contractions of the stomach in digestion, while stimulation over the parasympathetic system enhances contractions.

The antagonism between the two systems suggests that the sympathetic system is active in excited emotional states, the parasympathetic in quiescent emotional states. This idea is true to some extent; for example, pleasant tastes and smells stimulate the gastric secretions, which are under parasympathetic control. But the parasympathetic system participates in unpleasant and excited states as well. It is responsible for vomiting in disgust as well as for salivation in anticipation of pleasure. The parasympathetic system may excite discharge of the bladder and the bowels in moments of extreme fright. One series of studies of rats used amount of defecation as an index of emotionality; the increase in amount was highly correlated with other evidences of emotional excitement (Hall, 1934).

The central nervous system is also active in emotion. Through its control of skeletal muscles, it is responsible for frowning, grimacing, muscular tension, trembling, moaning, whining, purring, snarling. The central and autonomic systems thus cooperate in producing organized patterns of emotional expression such as laughing, weeping, and sexual excitement, patterns which are incomplete without this cooperation. The tears in laughter and weeping are controlled by the autonomic system, the vocal and facial muscles by the central nervous system, the changes in breathing by both systems.

How are these patterned states regulated? There are many theories and much fragmentary evidence, but we need to know more before we fully understand the physiological patterning of emotional expression.

There is evidence that the hypothalamus plays a central role in the organization and activation of many types of emotional and motivational behavior (Stellar, 1954). For example, it exerts control over the pattern described as "rage." A restricted surgical lesion in part of the hypothalamus may make a cat that formerly welcomed friendly petting and caressing turn savagely upon the person who tries to handle it in a gentle manner (Wheatley, 1944).

Some emotional expressions clearly involve the cerebral cortex, the highest level of the brain. For example, after cortical injury, one side of a patient's face may be affected. He may be unable to laugh voluntarily except with the "good" side of his face, though an involuntary laugh will spread over both sides. Another line of evidence comes from patients who have undergone brain surgery in order to relieve or reduce the intractable pain suffered in the last stages of cancer. The frontal lobe operation, even when it is successful in relieving suffering, does not produce total insensitivity to pain. A pin prick still feels painful. The pain that disappears is the overwhelming one that most disturbed the patient, best described as a kind of anguish (Landis, Zubin, and Mettler, 1950).

What we do know with assurance is that intense emotions involve profound changes throughout the body, which are regulated in a complex way by the central nervous system, by both divisions of the autonomic system, and by the endocrine glands.

Distinguishing among emotions

Psychologists and physiologists have tried unsuccessfully for many years to differentiate among human emotional states according to characteristics of the bodily indicators of emotion. The reasons for the difficulty are not hard to find:

1. Intense emotions (such as anger and fear) are highly activated, disturbed states, and have many bodily responses in common. The specific responses do not serve to define a particular emotion: one may turn pale or start to run when either afraid or angry.

2. A person can express any one emotion in a variety of ways. In fear, he may freeze to the spot or he may run away from danger. In anger, he may bite his lip, turn on his heel, or attack the person who has aroused him.

3. The *name* of the emotion depends commonly on supplementary information about the stimuli that aroused the emotion or about the nature of the goal-directed activity that follows the stimuli. That is, the emotional response to a dangerous animal will be called *fear,* especially if the person tries to escape; an emotional response to an insult will be called *anger,* especially if the person retaliates against the one who insulted him. The bodily state might be alike in the two cases, even though the emotions have different names.

4. The *conscious* or *introspective* differentiation of the emotions is not free of influence by external circumstances.

A number of years ago Cantril and Hunt (1932) injected adrenalin into adult subjects and questioned them about their emotions resulting from the symptoms (trembling, increased breathing, disturbed pulse and heartbeat) that the drug produced. Several of the subjects gave responses such as: "I feel as if afraid or angry, but I am not afraid or angry." One of them put it: "I feel that during the whole reaction I should be readily subject to any kind of emotional suggestion."

Thirty years later Schachter and Singer (1962) carried forward the corresponding experiment by injecting the drug and manipulating the environmental conditions in such a way as to test some conjectures about the way in which emotions become labeled. Instead of thinking about difficulties in the way of differentiating emotions according to physiological states, they proposed that, in man at least, an emotional state depends *both* on the state of physiological arousal *and* on a cognition appropriate to this state of arousal; the cognition determines what label will be assigned to the emotion. More specifically, they proposed and tested the following three propositions:

1. If a person is in a physiological state for which he has no immediate explanation, he will label this state according to the environmental circumstances determining his cognitions.

2. If the person has an appropriate explanation for his state ("I feel this way because I just received a drug injection"), then the environmental circumstances will have less influence on the label he assigns because he has no need for a further evaluative label.

3. Given the same environmental circumstances that led to assigning an emotional label appropriate to the subject's cognitions when he was physiologically aroused, no such emotional label will be assigned when he is not aroused.

In order to test propositions regarding the adequacy of explanation of the aroused state, physiological adrenalin was administered to the following three groups of subjects: (1) adrenalin-informed, in which the subject was told what physiological changes to expect after the drug was injected (accelerated heartbeat, involuntary tremor of hands, arms, or legs); (2) adrenalin-ignorant, in which no information was given about expected symptoms; (3) adrenalin-misinformed, in which the subject was told to expect the wrong symptoms (numbness, itching, headache). Finally, a placebo group was treated with neutral saline solution that would not produce any physiological arousal; they received the same instructions as the adrenalin-ignorant group. Note that the conjecture is that the cognitive influences on the labels assigned to the emotion should *increase* in the order of the three adrenalin groups because the physiological symptoms are fully explained for the first group, unknown for the second, and completely puzzling for the third. The placebo group, without arousal, should have a low level of emotional labeling.

To test the cognitive influences, two opposite cognitions were created by the use of a trained companion subject who had presumably been given the same drug and was participating under the same circumstances. This subject acted either "euphoric," that is, playful and gay, doodling, making paper airplanes, playing "basketball" by throwing wads of paper into the wastebasket (and encouraging his partner to join him), or "angry," that is, complaining about the experiment, resenting a questionnaire that he and his partner had to fill out, and so on. The prediction is that the subject most confused about his physiological arousal would interpret his mood according to that of the companion, and would feel euphoric in the one condition and angry in the other. A subject given the placebo, with no physiological arousal, should show relatively little emotion.

The conditions and the experimental predictions are summarized in Table 7–3. The results based both on the observed behavior of the subjects and on their self-reports were essentially in agreement with the conjectures, although they were somewhat more pronounced for the euphoria condition than for the anger condition.

Physiological psychologists have not permitted these difficulties in the symbolic interpretation of states of arousal to prevent their search for some response differences underlying the major emotional states. Ax (1953) attached various devices to his subjects so that he could record at once seven different physiological indicators of emotional response (pulse rate, heart stroke, breathing, face temperature, hand temperature, galvanic skin response, and muscle action currents just over the eyes). He then frightened his subjects on some occasions and angered them on others. In doing this, he made very clever use of the technicians in his laboratory whose clumsiness invoked fear and whose remarks induced anger; the emotional arousal was thus more natural than is usually the case when a person is strapped up with instruments. Each of the 43 subjects was angered once and frightened once (about half in one order, half in the reverse) and then questioned about the reality of the emotion as experienced.

The experimenter developed 14 indexes or scores, based on the seven physiological indicators, to use in describing the emo-

---

TABLE 7–3

Physiological arousal and cognitive influence upon the labels assigned emotional states

	Emotional state reported	
	Euphoria cognition	*Anger cognition*
Placebo	Little euphoria	Little anger
Adrenalin-informed	Little euphoria	Little anger
Adrenalin-ignorant	More euphoria	More anger
Adrenalin-misinformed	Much euphoria	*not tested*

SOURCE: Based on Schachter and Singer (1962).

Differential reactions in anger and fear

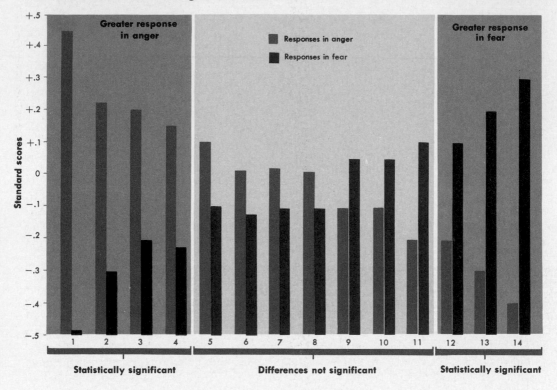

Physiological responses in anger and fear. The chart plots changes from the normal (zero) level for 14 indicators all simultaneously recorded. The indicators are numbered to correspond to the numbers at the base of the chart. (After Ax, 1953)

More responses in anger

1　Galvanic skin responses (increases in number).
2　Heart rate decreases.
3　Muscle tension increases.
4　Diastolic blood pressure rises.

Responses not significantly different

5　Face temperature decreases.
6　Heart-stroke volume decreases.
7　Heart-stroke volume increases.
8　Hand temperature decreases.
9　Systolic blood pressure increases.
10　Face temperature increases.
11　Heart rate increases.

More responses in fear

12　Muscle tension peaks.
13　Skin conductance increases.
14　Respiration rate increases.

tional responses of the subjects. Half of these were common to both fear and anger. But the other half (seven of the indexes) showed significant differences in the degree to which they were displayed in anger and in fear (Figure 7–1). The differences more prominent in fear correspond to the action of adrenalin; those more prominent in anger correspond to the action of both adrenalin and noradrenalin (see pp. 32–33).

These findings on the differences be-

tween fear and anger gain support from studies of the adrenal medullas of wild animals. Rabbits, which depend for survival on the ability to run away quickly (as in fear), show a predominance of adrenalin; lions and other aggressive animals (whose responses resemble behavior in anger) show a relatively high amount of noradrenalin (Funkenstein, 1955).

Funkenstein and his collaborators have extended the type of study done by Ax to include heart responses and chemical studies of the blood (Funkenstein, King, and Drolette, 1957). Under experimental circumstances designed to arouse anger or apprehension, some subjects openly expressed their anger, others felt angry but turned the anger inward against themselves, still others became severely anxious. The open expression of anger and the anxiety reaction were associated with the secretion of noradrenalin in the blood; the controlled, inward-directed anger was associated with the secretion of adrenalin.

It is difficult to differentiate human emotions on the basis of bodily changes and easier to differentiate them by the conventionalized expressions humans learn to use to convey emotional meanings. (These are superimposed upon the "natural" expressions resulting from maturation, which will be discussed shortly.) Psychologists have photographed the faces of actors portraying various emotions and have then asked subjects to try to identify the emotions from the photographs. While some confusion results, identification is well above chance. If six broad classes are used, subjects can assign the posed emotions reasonably well (Table 7–4). The percentage of

correspondence between the posed and judged emotion varies from a high of 93 percent for love, happiness, and mirth to a low of 60 percent for anger and determination. The list of six classes can be arranged in a scale; that is, items often confused are placed nearer together; those less often confused are placed farther apart. Such an arrangement (used in Table 7–4) works only because there is some systematic relationship among the pictured emotions.

Subjects asked to name the emotions represented in unposed candid camera shots do quite well also, even when the facial expression is presented alone, with the background masked out. They do better, of course, when the whole context of the picture is included (Munn, 1940).

Schlosberg (1952, 1954) attempted to refine the scaling of posed emotions. When a very large number of pictures were used, showing all manner of expressions (he used 72 pictures of the same face expressing various emotions), he noted that in some sortings the ends of the scale were confused; that is, some subjects interchanged expressions intended to show mirth with those intended to show contempt. This re-

TABLE 7–4

Success in judging posed emotions from photographs

	Emotions intended in the posed photographs					
Emotions as judged from the photographs	(1) Love, happiness, mirth	(2) Surprise	(3) Fear, suffering	(4) Anger, determination	(5) Disgust	(6) Contempt
(1) Love, happiness, mirth	93	5	1	2	0	0
(2) Surprise	1	77	3	4	0	0
(3) Fear, suffering	0	7	79	24	3	1
(4) Anger, determination	0	1	10	60	22	4
(5) Disgust	0	0	2	1	63	7
(6) Contempt	0	0	0	3	12	86
Other	6	10	5	6	0	2
	100	100	100	100	100	100

SOURCE: Woodworth (1938), p. 251. Data from Feleky (1922). Results with 100 subjects.

A simplified version of Schlosberg's surface of emotions

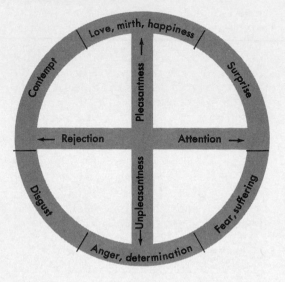

study of the organization and description of emotional states was taken by Block (1957), who investigated how men and women tended to interpret emotional states from the *names* of these states. He asked a group of college students (40 male, 48 female) to rate each emotion according to 20 scales based on pairs of adjectives, such as weak-strong, active-passive, tense-relaxed, happy-sad, loud-soft. Block arrived at a series of typical connotations for the different emotions and was thus able to determine by correlational methods which emotions grouped together. It turned out that the three main dimensions of emotion, as revealed by this method, bore a family resemblance to those found by Schlosberg's study of facial expression, although they are not exactly equivalent. Block named the dimensions *pleasantness-unpleasantness, level of activation,* and *interpersonal relatedness.*

These factors will perhaps be clearer if a few examples are cited. Emotional names opposite on the pleasantness-unpleasantness dimension include contentment as pleasant and guilt as unpleasant; on the activation dimension, anger is high and boredom is low; on interpersonal relatedness, sympathy is high and envy is low. Of course, an emotion is defined by its position on all three dimensions; anger is not only active but it is also unpleasant and low in social relatedness to another person. Men and women within American culture appraised the emotions very similarly; an intercorrelation of the whole set of correlations between pairs of emotional descriptions, known as a matrix intercorrelation, yielded an $r = .93$, which shows the two sets of correlations, for men and for women, to be essentially equivalent.

sult led him to arrange his scale into a circular surface into which all of the pictured emotions can be made to fit. A simplified version of his arrangement is presented in Figure 7–2. Note that there are two main axes, the familiar *pleasantness-unpleasantness* one and another at right angles to it, which he calls *rejection-attention*. In addition to their generally pleasant or unpleasant aspects, some emotions are associated with avoidance or turning away, as in disgust (rejection dimension), while others are associated with fascination, as in rapture (attention dimension). Any pictured emotion can be placed on this surface, depending upon how it is judged in accordance with these two dimensions.

Other studies have shown some success in judging emotions from gestures of the hands alone (Carmichael, Roberts, and Wessel, 1937) or from the recorded speaking voice (Dusenbury and Knower, 1939). We do not know how successful such judgments would be if the materials came from an alien culture. Success in recognizing emotions from face, gesture, and voice depends greatly upon the conventions of the society in which one has been reared.

A somewhat different approach to a

CRITICAL DISCUSSION

Physiological differentiation of emotions

The effort to find a physiological basis on which to differentiate the emotions, to state just how many emotions there are and what their bodily responses are, has not proved to be a very fruitful quest. With shifts in the nature of the problems that interest psychologists, the question has tended to decrease in importance.

More attention is now being paid to the general state of emotional excitement rather than to the fine distinctions between the several emotions. A favorite theory today goes by the name of the *activation theory* (Lindsley, 1951; Schlosberg, 1954). It suggests that there is an intensity scale or dimension in emotion, from sleep at the one end to diffuse excitement at the other. A related theory, stressing energy mobilization (Duffy, 1962), makes it difficult to distinguish between drive and emotion; but drive and emotion are in fact closely related, no matter how we try to define them. There are certain to be difficult borderline cases; behavioral phenomena always resist tight compartmentalization, and perhaps emotion and drive need not be differentiated at all.

Present interest in psychosomatic medicine has, however, led to renewed effort to distinguish among the physiological *consequences* of fear, anger, and anxiety. For example, using a patient with a *gastric fistula* (an artificial passage to the surface of the abdomen) through which food could be placed directly into his stomach, experimenters were able to observe that his stomach showed differences in reactions associated with fear and hostility, thus indicating a physiological differentiation of these states (Wolf and Wolff, 1942). But psychosomatic medicine is concerned more with chronic, persistent, or recurrent emotional states than with the emotional crises that have been the subject matter of psychological studies of emotional expression.

Theories of emotion

The foregoing discussion of attempts to differentiate emotions on the basis of bodily responses, facial expression, or meanings of descriptive terms suffices to indicate that it will not be easy to develop a theory of emotional expression. There have been several historically important theories, however, and some contemporary ones.

A classical theory of emotions, the *James-Lange theory* named after the two men who originated it in the 1880s, stressed the importance in felt emotion of the reper-

cussion of the bodily responses. William James stated this in the form of seeming paradoxes which apparently put the cart before the horse: "We are afraid because we run." "We are angry because we strike." What gives the theory some plausibility is that our awareness of bodily states involves not only a judgment of the situation (e.g., as a dangerous or frightening one), but also what today we call a *feedback* from the bodily responses released in emotion. Thus if I stumble on the stairs, I automatically grasp the handrail before I have time to recognize my emotional state; my felt emotion, after the crisis is over, includes the perception of my pounding heart and exaggerated breathing. Because this recognition comes after the bodily responses, the theory has some plausibility; at the same time, in view of the fact that recognition comes after the circumstances have already been judged (as dangerous, etc.), it is doubtful if the felt bodily responses are entirely responsible for the quality that differentiates one emotion from another.

The James-Lange theory came under severe attack by the physiologist Cannon (1927), whose views on the effects of the sympathetic system were earlier discussed (p. 166). As an alternative he proposed a theory which because of some similar proposals by Bard has come to be called the *Cannon-Bard theory*. This theory states that the incoming impulses from the event that excites the emotion are filtered through the thalamus, where the distinctive quality of the emotional experience is added; the impulses then go both to the cortex where the intellectual aspects are integrated and to the viscera and musculature. The feedback from the responses is not the essential feature, as it was in the James-Lange theory. But the thalamic theory itself has come under attack because other areas of the brain may be as active in emotion as the thalamus, and it is unclear that the thalamus acts just the way Cannon and Bard said it did (Arnold, 1960).

It should be noted that both the James-Lange and the Cannon-Bard theories were trying to account for the differences between the various emotional states on the basis of bodily processes. Recent theorists have usually tried to bring in somewhat more of the environment and of the expectations of the subject, as the Schachter and Singer experiment would require. Thus Arnold (1960) believes that too little attention has been given to the perceptual analysis of the situation that gives rise to the emotion and too much to the so-called expression of the emotion. Surely the tears that flow when a letter bringing bad news is read must be based on some kind of judgment of the content of the letter. The sequence of events as she puts it is perception-appraisal-emotion-expression-action.

Perhaps one reason for the unsatisfactory state of theories of emotions is that the more precise theories attempt to account for limited aspects of what is a very broad and complex field, and that the more general theories attempt to cover the whole range but get bogged down in the complexity of human motivation as it is related to emotion.

Emotional Development

Emotional expression, like other complex behavior, develops through maturation and learning. The infant cries at birth; as he grows older, his laughter is as spontaneous as his crying. He is born with the capacity to cry; the capacity to laugh comes through maturation. However, some aspects of his emotional behavior are acquired. As the child grows older, he learns to cry for a purpose—to gain parental attention or sympathy—and he learns to withhold his tears sometimes when he feels like crying. He learns, too, that there are times when it is proper to laugh and times when laughter is frowned upon. The child has to learn not only the occasions for emotion, but how to control emotional expression according to the patterns considered proper in his culture. He may laugh and cry softly or loudly, with or without restraint. He learns to distinguish between a pleasant smile, a gentle laugh, and a loud guffaw.

The maturation of emotional patterns

The newborn infant has a very limited repertory of emotional responsiveness. Most contemporary students of infant behavior agree that at birth the only distinguishable emotion is excitement. Besides this emotion there is only quiescence, probably not an emotional state at all. The state of excitement (crying, straining, thrashing about) appears to the observer to be an emotionally unpleasant one. The resting or quiet state of the newborn child is emotionally neutral, without the positive qualities of the later cheerful, cooing, delighted state. Thus, in the beginning, the one emotional state is a rather unpleasant departure from quiescence. How then does emotional responsiveness develop?

Recalling the Schachter and Singer study (p. 168), we may note that in the adult the labeling of the emotion depends very much upon the environmental context that provides cognitive cues for the chosen label. We cannot expect this in the young infant; in the early months the behavior—smiling and laughing, crying, yelling, thrashing about—is no doubt more a reflection of the infant's internal state of arousal. The adult is likely to name these states as pleasure, fear, or rage, but in the infant they are merely fairly direct responses to the environmental stimulation (caressing, restricting movements, etc.) and to the internal states, and only gradually become recognizable to the child, with an appropriate label. There are both maturational and learning aspects to this development, as we noted in connection with the reaction to strangers (Chapter 3).

That the process of differentiation of emotional responsiveness through maturation goes on beyond early infancy is supported by a study of emotional expression in a 10-year-old child, deaf and blind from birth, whose opportunities to learn from others were greatly restricted. This child had had scarcely any opportunity to observe the expression of emotions by other children, since her only observations came through touch. Yet under conditions that would tend to provoke fear, anger, or pleasure, her facial expressions of crying or laughter and her accompanying postures and gestures all accorded very well with the typical descriptions of emotional behavior (Goodenough, 1932). It appears that characteristic forms of emotion as well as many of the actions that indicate emotion to us develop through maturation.

Learning how to express emotion

Learning modifies the manner in which emotion is expressed. Anger, for example, may be expressed by fighting, by using abusive language, or by leaving the room. Unlike crying, leaving the room is not an expression of emotion that is known at birth; and certainly the abusive language has to be learned.

Studies of emotional expression in different cultures demonstrate impressively how much of that expression is developed by learning. One psychologist reviewed several Chinese novels in order to determine how a Chinese writer conveyed to his readers pictures of various human emotions. He found many of the bodily changes in emotion (flushing, paling, cold perspiration, trembling, goose pimples) used as symptoms of emotion in Chinese fiction much as they are in Western writings. There are, however, among the Chinese many other and quite different ways of expressing emotion.

The following quotations from Chinese novels would surely be misinterpreted by an American reader unfamiliar with the Chinese (Klineberg, 1938):

"Her eyes grew round and opened wide." (This means that she became angry.)
"They stretched out their tongues." (They showed signs of surprise.)
"He clapped his hands." (He was worried or disappointed.)
"He scratched his ears and cheeks." (Now we know that he was happy.)

Such evidence indicates that cultures teach conventionalized or stereotyped forms of expression, which become a kind of "language of emotion" recognized by others within the culture. Skilled actors are able to convey to their audiences any intended emotion by using facial expression, tone of voice, and gesture according to the patterns an audience recognizes. In simulating emotion, those of us who are less skilled actors can convey our intent deliberately by exaggerating the conventional expressions: gritting our teeth and clenching our fists to indicate anger, turning down the corners of our mouths to look sad, raising our eyebrows to express doubt or disapproval.

The child growing up in a culture gradually learns to interpret the signs of emotion used by those about him, just as he learns also to express his feelings as they do. Experiments have shown that the ability to judge emotions from posed pictures increases with age (Gates, 1923).

Learning the occasions for emotion

Emotional behavior occurs in response to objects or situations that are the *occasions* for emotion. While there are doubtless some innately frightening stimuli (e.g., loud sounds, sudden strange stimuli, etc.), our fears tend to become more specialized as we grow older. We fear something, are angry at someone, are worried about some possible turn of events. Though we may not have to learn how to fear, we learn what to be afraid of.

Ordinary observation shows many learned occasions for emotions. In American culture, for example, men seldom weep, whether the occasion be a wedding, a funeral, or failure to pass an examination in college, although American women commonly weep on such occasions. French men, however, weep much more freely than American men. Sending a loved one off on a trip may be the cause for weeping by the whole French family. How to weep is not learned, but when and where to weep are learned.

As the infant grows he learns to distinguish between what is familiar, and therefore "safe," and what is unfamiliar, and therefore perhaps "dangerous" or "threatening."

In the course of giving psychological tests to 61 infants during their first year of life Bayley (1932) noted the occasions

Infants' reasons for crying change with age

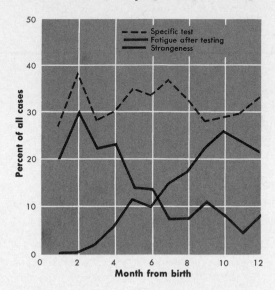

- - - Specific test
—— Fatigue after testing
━━ Strangeness

Percent of all cases

Month from birth

The relative amount of crying to be attributed to strangeness increases as contrasted with other causes of crying. (After Bayley, 1932)

on which the infants cried. As the infants grew older the causes of crying shifted, as shown in Figure 7–3 which is plotted as the percentage of total crying to be attributed to the specific tests, to fatigue after testing, and to strangeness. Strangeness of places and persons produces the largest increase in relative frequency of crying as the child gets older. A possible interpretation is that the older the child is, the better he is able to discriminate between the familiar and the strange, and hence the more often he reacts to strangeness by crying (see Figure 7–4).

An experiment was designed by Hebb (1946) to study the kinds of objects that provoked fear in chimpanzees that had been born and reared in captivity, so that the history of their previous experience with objects was known. These chimpanzees tended to show fear of many strange objects seen for the first time: a skull, a painted wax snake, a disembodied chimpanzee head. They showed marked fear of strangers and were disturbed by slight changes in the clothing of familiar attend-

ants. Thus learning enters, in that it is the unfamiliar that arouses fear.

Learning may enter in other ways. One explanation of the manner in which emotions become associated with new objects or occasions is through *conditioning*. Conditioning (discussed in detail in Chapter 11) is a process of association whereby something present at the time an emotion is experienced takes on the capacity for arousing that emotion. For example, a song heard during an unhappy experience may always thereafter arouse in the hearer an emotion of unhappiness.

A famous experiment in which a child learned to fear a white rat serves as the prototype of emotional conditioning (Watson and Rayner, 1920). The infant boy, Albert, when shown a white rat reached for it and showed no signs of fear. While he was paying attention to the rat, he was suddenly frightened by a loud sound. Thereafter he was afraid of the rat. The originally neutral rat became a "conditioned stimulus" to fear. Albert now also showed fear of his mother's fur neckpiece and of other soft and furry objects. He showed no such fear of rubber balls or blocks that were entirely un-ratlike in appearance.

It is supposed that many irrational fears are acquired in this relatively automatic way. Because lightning precedes thunderbolts, the child comes to fear the lightning as much as the thunder, although the loud sound of the thunder is the primary reason for fright. But many children (and adults) experience fear when they are aware of impending danger; their fear of lightning is probably less related to its association with thunderclaps than to the real danger of being struck by lightning. One must be careful not to explain too much by conditioning; fear of real danger is rational and arises in part, at least, through understanding.

Preferences, attitudes, and prejudices

As we grow older, we become predisposed to experience emotion in relation to persons, objects, and ideas that have be-

7-4

Fear of strangers at eight months

At about eight months, the child's ability to discriminate among people leads to increasing uneasiness with strangers.

Dr. René Spitz

Alone, but calm and attentive.

Apprehension and screaming at approach of stranger.

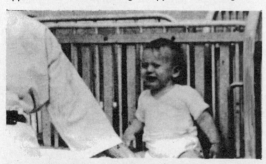

Stranger turns away; screaming subsides.

Infant reaches for hand of motionless stranger.

come important to us through our individual experiences. Emotions aroused by our own parents are different from and more intense than emotions aroused in us by parents in general; our country's flag stirs us, while the flag of another country may leave us unmoved. These are learned tendencies to experience emotion, and they are learned with individual discrimination so that one person's emotional attachments are not quite like those of another.

The mildest form of affective coloring is aroused by simple *preferences*, such as likes and dislikes for one geometrical pattern over another or for one food over another. Because nearly all our experiences fit into a pattern of likes and dislikes, most of them are affectively colored, if ever so mildly. That people vary markedly in their preferences is indicated by the old adage, "There's no accounting for tastes."

Simple preferences become organized into patterns of preference called *attitudes*. A person may have a favorable or unfavorable attitude toward labor unions, the Republican party, churchgoing, or smoking. If the attitude is favorable, the person, object, situation, or idea produces pleasant or favorable emotional response; if the attitude is unfavorable, the response is unpleasant, unfavorable, possibly hostile. The attitude is more than a statement or judgment that something is good or bad, desirable or undesirable, for the judgment is accompanied by affective response.

An attitude that is firmly fixed and not open to free discussion is known as a *prejudice*. Some cooks prefer cane sugar to beet sugar. This preference can be called a prejudice if the cook is unwilling to try beet sugar where sugar is required in a recipe. Fixed social beliefs—that members of one race are inferior to those of another, that women cannot think as keenly as men—are also prejudices, because the people holding them are not capable of change through the examination of evidence bearing on them.

Whether we speak of preferences, attitudes, or prejudices, we are calling attention to the fact that, through learning, particular persons, objects, institutions, and ideas arouse in an individual emotional responses different in kind or intensity from those aroused in other persons by the same stimuli.

Emotions and Motivated Behavior

No arguments are needed to establish the close relationship between emotion and motivation. Think of the stirring scenes in drama or literature, in which emotions provoke men to violent or desperate action and in which resolute, heroic, or shameful actions are accompanied by an intensification of emotion. These examples, reflecting as they do what goes on in real life, suggest that emotion acts both as a *drive* and as an *accompaniment to motivated action*. The triangle theme of love and jealousy is at once a story of motivation and of emotion. Sex is not only a powerful motive; it is a source of vivid emotional experience as well. Moreover, the emotional experience itself may become an incentive.

Emotion as drive

Emotional states are aroused states. If the emotional state is an unpleasant one, the organism seeks to terminate it. This unpleasant emotional state corresponds to the tension state in aroused drive. The organism, if frightened, tries to escape exactly as it attempts to escape from pain. The person with fear of high places will learn to avoid such places or, if he finds himself on a height, will be restless until he gets away. Reduction of the tension aroused in unpleasant emotion is equivalent to the reduction of drive tension; in this situation emotion *is* drive.

Earlier (Chap. 5, p. 135) we considered the problem of fear as a drive, and the possibility that fear is derived from experienced pain. Anxiety may perhaps in some cases be derived from pain and fear, but there may be independent origins also (Kessen and Mandler, 1961). However it comes about, anxiety is an important motivator of behavior, and it illustrates how emotion acts as drive in human behavior.

Anxiety. Anxiety is a state closely related to fear and, like fear, has motivational consequences. The vocabulary of emotion, having come from the language of ordinary life and of literature, lacks scientific precision. Anxiety is a word from this vocabulary, and psychologists are not consistent in the way they use it.

Anxiety is first of all a state of apprehension, of concern, of uneasiness. It is a special kind of fear. While ordinary fear always has an object, anxiety is fear with only a vague object or with no object at all. One meaning of anxiety is, then, a *vague fear* which is perhaps the commonest meaning for psychologists.

A state of anxiety, like that of fear, is an unpleasant state, a tension state from which we yearn to escape. Hence anxiety, too, can be considered a drive. An individual is often made to conform to social expectations by threats to his security; that is, the threats make him anxious if he does not conform. If he breaks the law, he may be punished by a fine or by imprisonment. Society hopes that the punishment will not only control his conduct in the future but also stand as a warning to others, intensifying their anxieties if they violate the code. Not all nonconformity is serious enough to require punishment, but the nonconformer may find himself teased or ridiculed. Ridicule puts him apart, makes him feel ostracized, and so arouses anxiety about his status and puts pressure upon him to behave like those about him.

Jealousy. Jealousy, a special form of anxiety based on insecurity, involves *fear of loss of affection to a rival*. That it has strong drive properties is evident enough from the frequent occurrence of the triangle theme in dramatic literature. The husband who is jealous of another man believes that the man is stealing his wife's affection; even when there is no rival, the jealous husband guards his wife lest one appear. The reactions of the jealous person may be violent. If there is a genuine rival, the jealous person may attack him. If there is only the fear of a rival, the jealous person may go to great pains to protect and keep informed about the loved one whose faithfulness he is afraid of losing.

Emotions such as jealousy and envy are distinguished more by their motivational aspects than by the states of arousal that accompany them. A careful effort to distinguish between envy and jealousy as *states* that could be described introspectively or according to bodily responses led to failure (Ankles, 1939). As *motives*, however, useful distinctions can be made between jealousy as fear of a rival and envy as wishing for something possessed by another. For example, a person may *envy* another person his car without bearing any ill will toward that person. In jealousy, however, attitudes toward the rival are always hostile. These illustrations point up the importance of considering emotions as motives and not merely as stirred-up states of the organism.

While the definition of anxiety as a vague fear, as in "free-floating" anxiety, covers many instances of anxiety, several other conjectures have found some support.

A second use of anxiety restricts it to a more limited kind of vague fear: the *fear of insecurity*. According to the concept on which this use is based, anxiety is social in its origin, beginning in infancy while the child is dependent upon the adults who care for him. Deprivation, neglect, and loss of affection arouse the feelings of insecurity that the infant comes to fear. This fear of insecurity is considered the basic anxiety, and it is a fear always associated with other people. What is feared is isolation, lack of affectionate responses by other people. When anxiety is used with this meaning, it is distinguished from fear: *things* can cause fear; only *people* can cause insecurity (Sullivan, 1949).

Anxiety is used in a third way to mean *concern over our own conduct*, that is, feelings of guilt. We are uneasy about forbidden impulses or past misdemeanors. We fear that if they come to light, our guilt will be uncovered. Children, for example, have learned to show love and respect for their parents, yet are often resentful of parental authority. Fear of blurting out their hidden resentments may be a source of anxiety. The adolescent may fear to reveal his intensified interest in sex. Fear of being afraid or of showing fear may give rise to anxiety, especially if the accepted code (as in some military groups) is to appear fearless. Concern about our own feelings is undoubtedly one important form anxiety takes.

Modern existentialists, concerned with man's concept of himself, identify other aspects of anxiety, but these are described in half-mystical ways making it difficult to incorporate them in science. Anxiety in this usage is said to arise in part because of the contemplation of the inevitability of death and in part because of a sense of man's unrealized possibilities. These views derive from Søren Kierkegaard (1813–55), an early existentialist philosopher (Kierkegaard, 1844; tr. by Walter Lowrie, 1944). While Kierkegaard's translator uses the word "dread," the word "anxiety" can be substituted for it (May, 1950; Tillich, 1952).

Anxiety came to be emphasized as a drive state at the time when the notion of aversive drives was at its height of popularity. Now that there is a tendency to turn to more positive aspects of motivation, a number of authors have begun to introduce the concept of hope as a counterpart to anxiety when an uncertain future is faced (e.g., French, 1952; Mowrer, 1960). This position was anticipated by Kierkegaard, who felt that only when one had faced anxiety could he find faith, that is, hope.

Emotions as incentives

Parents and other adults sometimes tear their hair over the seemingly deliberate efforts of young boys to generate and enjoy excitement, trouble, danger. The emotion appears to be a kind of end in itself. Commercial amusements and the entertainment and recreation industries in general play on people's wishes to experience emotion. Some people go to the theater or the movies for a good laugh or cry.

While emotions can serve as motives, they can thus also serve as incentives. We are reminded again of hedonism, the belief that men *seek* pleasure and *avoid* pain. Can we specify the incentives in these situations? The incentives sought are not disembodied emotions, but *activities* that have emotional coloration. If the specific nature of the activity is less important than the excitement, thrill, delight, or joy it provides, the emotion itself can be said to define the incentive; thus the semi-danger and gravity-changes of the various thrilling devices in an amusement park determine the excitement, and it does not matter too much just what sort of roller coaster or crack-the-whip one rides. But once these emotions have been aroused by particular activities or particular people (e.g., a favorite comedian as a source of laughter), such activities or people become sought-after sources of stimuli and hence positive incentives.

Emotion as an accompaniment of motivated behavior

Motivated behavior tends to be tinged with emotion in all its stages; that is, affective coloration is not confined only to the drive state or to the responses in the presence of the incentive, but also accompanies the intervening activity. It is unpleasant to be hungry and pleasant to eat when hungry, but there is pleasure also in food-seeking, in anticipating a good meal. We feel elated when we overcome obstacles on the way to a goal, even though we have not yet arrived at the goal. Because we are on the way to the goal, obstacles create a problem; overcoming them brings the satisfaction of problem-solving. On the other hand, serious blocking or delaying of action on the way to a goal arouses in us annoyance and anger—or anxiety lest the goal not be reached.

The emotional accompaniment of activity toward a goal is a kind of comment on the progress. Words such as "encouragement," "suspense," "surprise," "worry," and "hope" indicate the emotional significance of motivated behavior that takes a new turn, that is fraught with uncertainty, that has high or low probability of success. The pleasure of goal achievement is modified or enhanced by the struggle to attain success. When a man goes trout fishing, he enjoys the preparations and anticipation and tolerates getting out of bed at dawn, hiking through underbrush, and struggling against the cold current in the stream. The fish he catches taste much better than those purchased at the market. But the emotional accompaniment is not a *mere* by-product without motivational significance; it serves to sustain and reinforce (or weaken and disrupt) the ongoing activity.

We will consider next three common emotional responses in their roles as accompaniments of motivated behavior: laughter, weeping, anger. At times these responses may also serve as drives or incentives, but here we consider their roles in relation to sequences of behavior defined independently of them and to which they are incidental.

Laughter. The child who jumps up and down in joyous laughter at the announcement that he is going to the circus well illustrates an emotional accompaniment of motivation. The laughter is not here an end in itself, for laughter as a goal has not been substituted for the desire to go to the circus. While psychologists are by no means in agreement as to all the occasions for laughter, two aspects are commonly recognized:

1. Most occasions arousing laughter are social. One investigator found that in 223 situations in which preschool children laughed, 209 (or 94 percent) of the laughing episodes occurred in the presence of a second person (Kenderdine, 1931). Another investigator, studying 240 college students, found their laughter attributed to social situations in 98 percent of the instances (Young, 1937). Even something as physiological as response to tickling has a large social component. The child does not laugh when he tries to tickle himself; that is no tickle. He laughs only when someone else tickles him (Leuba, 1941).
2. Most occasions for laughter have in them an element of surprise. Tickling

—one of the most primitive and universal sources of laughter—usually has in it an element of surprise. The tickling is usually threatened before it begins, and the moment of beginning is uncertain. Children's games that call forth laughter, such as "peek-aboo," have both social and surprise elements.

The preliminary stages of the laughter-provoking sequences are usually tension-producing, so that the laughter comes as an expression of relief. We may assign as one of the motivational aspects of laughter this relief from certain tension-producing situations in the presence of other people. The excitement of mild tension is not damaging, the social attention is welcome, and the resolution through laughter provides a happy ending. Adults as well as children seek such sequences of events; under such circumstances laughter becomes an incentive. It is these sequences that produce laughter in plays, on radio and television, and in stories; their popularity sufficiently attests to their appeal.

Weeping. Laughter and tears are often close together, and although we associate laughter with joy and tears with sadness, there are also tears of joy. The writer Arthur Koestler has noted a failure in textbooks of psychology to treat weeping, and he has attempted to supply this lack by an analysis of his own. He notes five kinds of situations in which weeping accompanies motivated behavior (Koestler, 1965, p. 273):

1. Raptness. Listening to an organ in a cathedral, looking at a majestic landscape from a mountaintop, watching an infant hesitatingly return a smile—instances such as these may be touching and may moisten the eyes.

2. Mourning. When nothing can be done on the occasion of loss one "gives in to grief."

3. Relief. A mother's reaction to her son's returning from the battlefield may be one of joyful relief, yet she may weep, perhaps saying: "How silly of me to cry."

4. Sympathy. Sharing another's sorrow or joy may bring forth tears.

5. Self-pity. A little boy who is attacked by bullies may cry, not so much out of helplessness as out of impotent rage.

These illustrations show how emotions provide a kind of commentary on ongoing motivated behavior. The weeping is neither a drive nor an incentive, but it is a sign that something motivationally important is occurring.

Anger. Just as laughter is representative of pleasant emotional concomitants of motivated behavior and weeping may accompany either joy or sorrow, anger is representative of unpleasant emotional accompaniments. The primary occasion for anger is the thwarting of goal-seeking activity. Hence anger may be the by-product of any interrupted motivational sequence regardless of the motivational content of that sequence. Although anger may in turn acquire drive properties and lead to retaliatory action against the person or object held responsible for the thwarting, anger *begins* as an emotional accompaniment of something else.

Fifty-one college women kept records of the occasions on which they experienced anger or extreme irritation and of the impulses which resulted (Gates, 1926). The period of observation covered one week. The annoyances that produced anger or irritation included such matters as unjust accusations and insults, contradictions, scoldings, loss of a fountain pen, breaking of glasses. The impulses to which the anger or irritation led were reported as follows:

Impulses following anger	Number of reports
To make a verbal retort	53
To do physical injury to offender (slap, pinch, shake, strike, choke, push, step on, scratch, shoot, beat, throw out of window, kill, tear to pieces, throw something at, spank)	40
To injure inanimate objects	20
To run away, leave the room	12
To cry, scream, swear	10

Both laughter and anger originate as by-products of behavior sequences otherwise motivated. But when occasions for laughter are sought, and when anger, once aroused, starts sequences of retaliatory action, they become translated into goal-seeking behavior as drives and incentives. They then function as motives, not only as motivational accompaniments.

Emotional States as Adaptive and Disruptive

What is the role of emotions in civilized life? Do they help organisms to survive or are they chiefly sources of disturbance, of maladjustment? When we consider whether or not emotions hinder living in civilized society, we first have to inquire about the intensity of the emotional experience.

Intensity of emotion and adaptive significance

Affective responses vary from the mildest satisfaction to the most complete panic. Mild emotions have a tonic influence. We work better when we are interested and when we have some enthusiasm for what we are doing. One consequence of mild emotion is a moderate increase in normal physiological functioning, possibly due to a slight increase in general tension. We know that a moderate increase in tension aids learning. This principle has been demonstrated in experiments in which the subject had to lift a weight or squeeze a dynamometer while memorizing. We noted earlier that the subject memorized best under mild tension, when neither too relaxed nor under too much strain. If mild emotion produces similar tensions, it may also aid learning. A second consequence of mild emotion, provided it is relevant to the task, is to make the task more important and meaningful. Without affective coloring, activity becomes dull and meaningless and soon takes on a monotonous tone. Therefore, a mild emotional state, generated by interest in a task, is serviceable.

Intense emotions play a more ambiguous role. They vary from the unpleasant states of anger, fear, and grief to the pleasant ones of joy and affection. When intense emotions are free to run their course, they may do no harm and may increase one's zest for living. Excitement may be followed by relaxation, fear by relief, despair by satisfaction. But situations may arise in which intense emotions cannot run their course. Then worry, anxiety, and heightened tension develop and become distractions that interfere with smooth performance. In the experiments on the role of tension in memorizing, it was found that there was an optimum point beyond which tension interfered with memorization.

The adverse effects of intense emotion on problem-solving have been demonstrated in a number of experiments. In one, grade-school boys participated one at a time in an experiment consisting of three steps. As his first step, each boy took a short form of the Stanford-Binet Intelligence Test. Then he engaged in a problem-solving task for which success led to reward and failure to no reward. As a possible reward, he selected one of several attractive packages containing candy, money, or a model airplane. The task was so arranged that half the boys succeeded and half failed. Those who succeeded were jubilant over their rewards; those who failed were downcast. As the third step, each boy repeated the intelligence test. The experiment showed very definite loss of score on the second test by those boys who had experienced the upset of failure in the intervening problem-solving situation (Lantz, 1945).[1]

Consequences of enduring emotional states

Some individuals react more strongly to mild emotional stimuli than do others; we consider such people "emotional." The characteristic level of emotional reactivity of a person is called his *temperament*. A more temporary state of emotional reactiv-

[1] That such changes in score can occur as a result of frustration indicates the need of skill on the part of those who do intelligence testing (see Chapter 14).

ity is called a *mood*. When we find a person who is usually cheerful, we say that he is of cheerful temperament; when we find a person of unpredictable temperament who is in a cheerful state, we say that he is in a cheerful mood. Either temperament or mood tends to arouse emotions congruent with it; that is, events otherwise more or less neutral became affectively colored according to the prevailing mood. If a person is in a gay mood, he may see minor setbacks as amusing challenges and take them in his stride; if he is in a troubled mood, he may see the same minor setbacks as occasions for anger or despair.

Moods sometimes represent the aftereffects of an emotional shock, as when a person goes around somewhat depressed for a time after having received bad news. The mood may linger on, even if the emotion has been overtly expressed; occasionally the mood continues as a state of tension because the feelings were not freely expressed when the occasion for them arose. Both internal conditions and external events may determine moods. A study of the time of day when children are most likely to show anger revealed that the peak of irascibility was just before meals and just before retiring. Hunger and sleepiness undoubtedly had some influence in arousing the irritable mood (Goodenough, 1931).

Medical men today are aware of a group of illnesses which they call *psychosomatic disorders:* although the symptoms themselves are "somatic," that is, symptoms of damage or disturbance in bodily organs or tissues, the circumstances that give rise to these symptoms appear to lie in the emotional life of the person. Prominent among these psychosomatic illnesses are ulcerative disorders of the digestive tract. It is supposed that ulcers of the stomach, for example, may be caused by the changes in muscular tension and in blood distribution in the walls of the stomach resulting from often-repeated or long-continued emotional states. Excessive digestive secretions, which are aroused by intense emotion, may have chemical effects accentuating the damage. Although the details concerning these effects are still somewhat in question, the association of organic ailments with prolonged emotional states of certain kinds appears now to be reasonably well established (Dunbar, 1955).

We have seen, then, that emotional intensity affects the role of emotion in furthering or hindering man's adaptation to his environment. Mild emotions are tonic, intense emotions sometimes disruptive. More enduring emotional states, as in temperament and mood, may also make adjustment to life's demands easier or more difficult and may lead to actual illness.

Emotional suppression and release

If some features of emotional behavior are adaptive and other features disruptive, we need a hygiene of emotions so that mature people can enjoy emotional expression without suffering the damage due to emotional excesses. The hygiene of emotions largely involves the question of emotional control. Does maturity consist primarily in suppressing emotional expression so that life can be conducted more rationally? Or is emotional expression a kind of safety valve essential to healthy living?

Civilization requires us to suppress much overt emotional expression. To be civilized is to be moderate in behavior, not to "lose one's head," not to "fly off the handle." We consider imperturbability, the ability "to take it," a virtue. While we admire emotional sensitivity in the form of social warmth and tenderness, we think it should be exercised with restraint. In all things we admire temperance over free indulgence.

Psychologists doubt the desirability of a general suppression of emotional expression. While some emotional control is no doubt essential for adults as well as for children, there are two qualifications concerning the *amount* of control, and these should be kept in mind. (1) Emotional suppression is not always successful; instead of being eliminated, the emotion may express itself in distorted form or in illness. (2) The beneficial results of appropriate emotional release can be demonstrated.

Many of the physiological aspects of emotional expression—say, muscular tension or blushing—are not under voluntary control. Hence voluntary suppression does not completely suppress, nor does it always succeed in eliminating, the emotional state. Sometimes, however, the suppression goes on so long and so successfully that one is no longer consciously aware of any need to suppress. Under such circumstances, the emotion is said to be repressed. We will return to the problems of repression and suppression in Chapter 20. But even repressed emotions are not lost; by appropriate means it is possible to find signs that they are still active. Some evidence of the impossibility of fully suppressing emotional expression is found in studies making use of the lie detector, an instrument designed to determine whether or not an accused person is telling the truth.

The lie detector is based on the principle that a person accused of crime will be apprehensive and therefore will involuntarily make characteristic emotional responses to stimuli related to the crime. When he is asked questions that he can answer without any feeling of guilt, his responses will show his general relief. When he is asked questions which he must answer with a lie in order to conceal his crime, he will usually experience an inner disturbance over which he has little if any control. In the lie-detector test, the person's words are recorded along with his bodily changes, for example, changes in breath-ing, blood pressure, and electrical responses from the skin (Reid and Inbau, 1964).

As we shall learn in Chapter 22 in the discussion of psychotherapy (i.e., the treatment of personal maladjustments by psychological means), many patients early in treatment yield an outpouring of statements heavily loaded with pent-up emotion. This outpouring has been called an "emotional catharsis." Such a purging or cleansing is often the first and necessary step toward a reorientation for the disturbed person. In work with children in need of help as a result of emotional disturbance it has been found useful to permit them great freedom of emotional expression. This "release therapy," as it is called, often results in better emotional control at a more healthful level.

It is not healthful to deny expression to emotional impulses that are genuine or natural. This does not mean that free play should be given to each and every impulse; emotional control is possible without emotional denial. If you lose a student election or fail a course, you may legitimately feel disappointed and unhappy. It is not necessary to toss the failure off as of no consequence or to deny that you feel dejected. But the disappointment need not turn to bitterness, to attacks upon the rival who won the election or upon the teacher who assigned the grade. You have proper control if you accept the naturalness of your

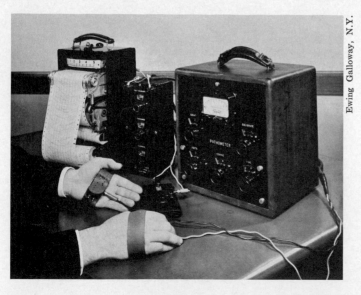

Ewing Galloway, N.Y.

7–5

The lie detector

The galvanic skin response (GSR) is measured by electrodes placed on the palms. The changes in the electrical resistance of the skin are an indication of emotional response as a result of interrogation.

own feelings and do not feel guilty because you are emotionally upset, and if at the same time you do not become the victim of your emotions. When a person can experience emotionally charged impulses without anxiety and guilt and can achieve a proper balance between expression and control, he is then emotionally healthy. He finds it possible to accept his emotional impulses as natural and to handle their expression in ways that are socially acceptable. In this way he has achieved emotional control without emotional denial.

We must recognize, however, that while it is easy to make generalizations about emotional expression and emotional control, the generalizations are often difficult to apply. For one thing, their application may depend upon circumstances peculiar to a particular culture or subculture (e.g., how would they apply to a Buddhist monk?). For another, in applying them to oneself, one runs up against tendencies to self-deception that make self-regulation of emotion particularly difficult. We shall return to these topics in Chapters 20–22.

SUMMARY   1. Emotional states range from the *mild affective states* of pleasantness and unpleasantness that accompany virtually all behavior to the more *intense affective states,* usually known as emotions. The more intense states can be classified into those that are pleasant (joy, affection) and those that are unpleasant (anger, fear, grief).

2. Emotional states as experienced in ordinary life are complex, and little is to be gained by trying to distinguish sharply among them. A state of arousal may be given one label under some circumstances, another under other circumstances. Studies of the bodily processes in emotion show that widespread changes are common to all intense emotions, although some physiological differentiation has proven possible. For example, one study showed responses in *fear* to be those predictable from the action of adrenalin, those in *anger* to be predictable from the action of adrenalin combined with noradrenalin.

3. Interpretation of emotional expression from the face, gesture, and voice is somewhat easier than interpretation from the state of physiological arousal, because added to the natural expressions are the conventional ones the culture uses as its language of emotion.

4. Among the theories of emotion is the classical *James-Lange* theory that the quality of the emotion is determined by the feedback from the bodily responses, a theory that is objected to by the *Cannon-Bard* theory, which assigns the quality of the emotion to additions by the thalamus to the sensory input to the cortex, so that the quality of the emotion may register at the same time that the bodily reactions are being released. A more recent theory (by Arnold) places the events in order from perception to action with the part usually designated as emotion lying somewhere in between, as a felt tendency toward stimuli judged as good and away from stimuli judged as bad. No one theory of emotion commands wide support, partly because the various theories deal with different aspects of very complex processes.

5. Emotional development takes place through maturation and learning. That maturation is involved is suggested both by the pattern of emotional development in normal infants and by the similarities of expression of emotion in deaf-blind children to those in physically normal

children. Learning is involved both in determining the *occasions* upon which emotions can be safely expressed and in shaping the *form of expression* to conform to patterns approved within the culture. Emotional tendencies become associated with persons, objects, and ideas. These tendencies include *attitudes, preferences,* and *prejudices.* Each individual's particular tendencies become important in his behavior.

6. When emotional states are considered in relation to motivation, it is found that emotions may serve as *drives,* as *incentives,* or as *accompaniments of motivated behavior.* Emotions such as fear and anxiety function as drives because they are tension states that we seek to relieve by appropriate behavior in relation to an incentive. When the goal of motivated behavior is excitement or thrill, emotion serves as an incentive.

7. Emotions as accompaniments of motivated behavior arise in the course of goal-seeking activity when that activity is blocked or thwarted. The study of *laughter* provides a convenient introduction to the nature of pleasant emotional accompaniments; *weeping* may signify various outcomes from rapture to grief or relief; *anger* provides an illustration of the unpleasant emotional accompaniments of blocked behavior sequences.

8. Emotions may be both useful and harmful: they may serve the purposes of smooth adjustment and problem-solving, but they may also interfere with these purposes. Certain physiological changes accompanying excited emotion energize the organism for action and thereby serve as aids to survival for animals struggling in combat. While these "emergency reactions" may have been useful for primitive man, they are of little use in our culture where violent emotion is frowned upon. The question may be a matter of intensity, *mild* emotional states being tonic and helpful, *strong* emotional states being debilitating and disruptive.

9. More enduring emotional states, known as *mood* and *temperament,* may under some circumstances maintain internal tension with harmful bodily consequences. These difficulties are studied as *psychosomatic disorders.*

10. Modern civilization may have gone too far in the direction of seeking to suppress emotional expression. For one thing, the effort to be rid of emotion through suppression or repression is relatively unsuccessful, as shown by the signs of residual emotional effects registered on a lie detector or manifested in psychosomatic illnesses. Emotional expression may be beneficial to health. Emotional control need not mean emotional denial. It is possible to accept emotions as normal and natural, while directing emotional expression into channels that are socially acceptable.

SUGGESTIONS FOR FURTHER READING

The following accounts, all relatively brief, give a good introduction to contemporary thinking about emotion: Mandler, "Emotion," in *New directions in psychology* (1962), 269–343; Murray, *Motivation and emotion* (1964); Plutchik, *The emotions: facts, theories, and a new model* (1962).

An interesting multiple-author book on human emotional expression is that edited by Knapp, *Expression of the emotions in man* (1963).

PERCEPTION

*All organisms discriminate among
stimuli that impinge upon them by
way of sensitive tissues, which in the
higher organisms take the form of
sense organs. The senses are thus the
channels for information about the
world. To understand behavior we
need to know something of how the
sensory mechanisms are constructed
and how they mediate the sensations
of light, sound, touch, taste, and so
forth. But perception goes beyond the
discrimination of single stimuli; the
human organism must be able to interpret and react to patterns of stimuli. We will consider first the role of
the specific sense organs in perceiving
and then turn to the factors involved in
our perception of objects and events.
Finally, our attention will be directed
to various states of awareness.*

8 The Sensory Basis of Perceiving

At one time the study of sensory psychology was the chief preoccupation of experimental psychologists. Even early in the development of their new science psychologists could arrange laboratory investigations of the senses, in which they achieved precise control of the stimulating conditions and could measure changes in the stimuli and record the responses of the subjects to them. Scientific interests show swings of the pendulum just as do other human pursuits, and with the upsurge of interest in learning and adjustment there was for a time a decline in the interest of psychologists in the sensory mechanisms.

These early studies of the sensory processes were predominantly of the "basic science" variety; that is, they were efforts to understand the details of the relationships among stimuli, the sense organs, the nerve tracts, and the brain areas, as well as the conscious processes associated with the stimulation of the sense organs and their connections. More recent sensory studies have continued in this direction but have moved also into the area of applied psychology. During World War II there was much interest in what was at first called *human engineering,* now known as the study of *human factors* in relation to machine operation. As modern military equipment becomes more precise and automatic, it depends more and more on the accurate discriminations of the human operator. An operator picks up visual signals on the radar screen and discriminates auditory signals from underwater sound-detection

devices. The pilot has to watch the dials of countless instruments and make appropriate adjustments. Instructions coming over earphones have to be heard above the surrounding noise and, sometimes, against intentional "jamming." After the war, sensory psychology began to find uses in industry as well as in the military services—and, of course, in dealing with the problems of the space age.

We will consider first some general characteristics of the senses that indicate the limits of the human operator's capacity to discriminate and interpret sensory stimuli. If we are designing a complex system to be controlled by a human being, we need to know whether the discriminations required of him can be performed with accuracy and consistency.

Some General Characteristics of the Senses

Absolute thresholds

A certain minimum of sense-organ stimulation is required before any sensory experience will be evoked. For example, a spot of light appearing in a dark room must reach some measurable intensity before it can be distinguished from darkness, and a sound emitted in a soundproof room must reach a certain intensity level before it can be heard. The minimum physical energy necessary to activate a given sensory system is known as the *absolute threshold.* One method for determining the

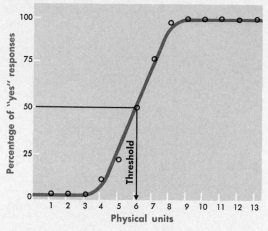

Psychophysical function

Plotted on the ordinate is the likelihood that the subject will respond "Yes, I detect the stimulus"; on the abscissa is the measure of the physical energy of the signal. Psychophysical functions can be obtained for any sensory modality; when vision is involved the function is sometimes called the "frequency-of-seeing curve."

absolute threshold is simply to present the subject with a stimulus of given intensity and ask whether or not he detects it. On the next trial a different stimulus intensity is used, and so on through a wide range of intensities. When such a procedure is used the term *absolute* threshold is somewhat inappropriate because we do not arrive at a *single* intensity value below which the subject never detects the stimulus and above which he always reports detecting it. Instead we find a range of intensities over which the physical energy of the stimulus gradually moves from having no effect to having a partial effect (i.e., is sometimes detected and sometimes not) to having a complete effect.

This region of partial effect is illustrated in Figure 8–1. The curve depicted in the figure is called a *psychophysical function* because it expresses the relationship between a "psychological" variable (experience of perceiving the stimulus) and a "physical" variable (the intensity of the stimulus). It plots the percentage of times the subject says, "Yes, I detect a stimulus,"

against a measure of the physical energy of the stimulus. Without worrying about the scale used in Figure 8–1 for measuring physical energy, note that whenever the stimulus is below an energy level equal to three units the subject never reports the presence of a stimulus, whereas above nine units he always reports it. Between three and nine units the relative frequency of reporting the presence of a stimulus gradually increases.

How do we define the threshold for a particular stimulus dimension when the performance can be characterized by a psychophysical function of the type presented in Figure 8–1? Is it the point where the subject's curve first breaks away from zero (in this case at about three physical units) or where it finally reaches 100 percent responding (in this case at about nine units)? Obviously, the definition of a threshold must be somewhat arbitrary. However, on the basis of certain theoretical and statistical considerations, psychologists have agreed to define the *absolute threshold* as that value at which the stimulus is perceived 50 percent of the time. Thus, for the data displayed in Figure 8–1, the absolute threshold would be at six units.

TABLE 8–1

Some approximate values for absolute thresholds

Sense modality	Threshold
Vision	A candle flame seen at 30 miles on a dark, clear night
Hearing	The tick of a watch under quiet conditions at 20 feet
Taste	One teaspoon of sugar in two gallons of water
Smell	One drop of perfume diffused into the entire volume of a six-room apartment
Touch	Wing of a fly falling on your cheek from a distance of 1 centimeter

SOURCE: Adapted from Galanter (1962), p. 97.

Table 8–1 presents some estimates of absolute thresholds for various sense modalities in terms of physical measures that are intuitively meaningful. Of course, the absolute threshold varies considerably from one individual to the next. And the threshold for a particular individual will also vary from time to time depending on his physical condition, his motivational state, and the conditions under which the observations are made. In the case of vision, for example, the absolute threshold depends on the color of the light used, the duration of the light flash, and also on the state of adaptation of the sensory system.

Difference threshold

In the same sense that a certain minimum amount of stimulation is required to evoke a sensory experience, there must also be a certain amount of difference between two stimuli before one can be distinguished from the other. The minimum amount of stimulation necessary to tell two stimuli apart is known as the *difference threshold.* Two reds must differ in wave lengths by some finite amount before they can be discriminated from each other; two tones must differ in decibels by a measurable amount before one can be heard as louder than the other. Thus, thresholds are identified at the transitions between no experience and some experience (the absolute threshold) and between no difference and some difference (the difference threshold).

As in the case of absolute thresholds, the difference threshold is defined as a statistical quantity. Specifically it is the amount of change in physical energy necessary for a subject to detect a *just noticeable difference* between two stimuli 50 percent of the time. (The term *just noticeable difference* is frequently used by psychologists and is abbreviated as j.n.d.)

One remarkable feature of the human organism and, for that matter, most animals, is that the difference threshold tends to be a constant fraction of the stimulus intensity. To illustrate, suppose we estimate the difference threshold for a subject judging weights. If we give him a 100 gram weight we note that his difference threshold is 2 grams; that is, the 100 gram weight must be compared to a weight of at least 102 grams in order for him to detect a noticeable difference. Similarly, if we give him a 200 gram weight the difference threshold is 4 grams. For a 400 gram weight, the difference threshold is 8 grams; and for an 800 gram weight, the difference threshold is 16 grams. The absolute value of the difference threshold increases in direct proportion to the increase in weights; for weights of 100, 200, 400, and 800 grams, the difference thresholds are 2, 4, 8, and 16 grams, respectively. Thus, the difference threshold relative to the weight being judged is constant; specifically:

$$\frac{2}{100} = \frac{4}{200} = \frac{8}{400} = \frac{16}{800} = .02$$

The above observation has come to be known as "Weber's law," named after Ernst H. Weber who first explicitly pointed out the relationship. Stated mathematically, if I is the amount of stimulation taken as a referent, and ΔI is the increase in stimulation necessary for a j.n.d., then:

$$\frac{\Delta I}{I} = k$$

where k is a constant that does not depend on I. In our example of weights, $k = .02$. The quantity k varies from one sense modality to the next and is called "Weber's constant."

We may observe the operation of something similar to Weber's law in everyday experience: a 20-minute increase in air-travel time from Los Angeles to San Francisco may be detected as a "just noticeable difference," but a similar increase in travel time from San Francisco to Paris may not; an increase of five dollars in the cost of a shirt is quite noticeable, whereas a similar increase in the cost of a suit may be of little concern.

Table 8–2 presents values of Weber's constant for various sense modalities. We see that there is a tremendous range in values, reflecting the fact that some sensory

TABLE 8–2

Weber's constant

Values of Weber's constant obtained under ideal laboratory conditions for various sensory discriminations. The smaller the fraction, the greater the differential sensitivity.

Sense modality	Weber's constant
Pitch of a tone	1/333
Deep pressure, from skin and subcutaneous tissue	1/77
Visual brightness	1/62
Lifted weights	1/53
Loudness of a tone	1/11
Cutaneous pressure	1/7
Taste for saline solution	1/5

SOURCE: Adapted from Stevens (1957).

systems are much more responsive to changes in the physical environment than are others.

It is interesting to conjecture about the aspects of the sensory system that make Weber's law hold. A number of theories have been proposed, some of which have been based on very specific speculations regarding the structure and function of certain parts of the nervous system. We shall not be able to discuss these theories here, but the research initiated by them has made it clear that matters are more complex than indicated by Weber's law. Weber's law holds fairly well in the middle range of sensory dimensions but is somewhat in error at the extremes, particularly at very low levels of stimulation.

While Weber's law applied only to thresholds, it was early extended by Fechner (1860) to the development of scales for measuring sensory experiences. By summing successive j.n.d.'s, he developed a psychological scale for measuring how far a given stimulus was above threshold; this procedure in turn permitted him to measure the distance between any two stimuli. His formulation of the relationship, commonly called the Weber-Fechner law, is that the sensory response (R) bears a logarithmic relationship to the intensity of the physical stimulus (I). The simplest statement is that $R = C \cdot \log I$, where C is a constant. Modern workers in the study of sense distances have modified his law somewhat in order to fit empirical results more closely (Stevens, 1966). Relationships of this kind have proved useful, for example, to telephone engineers in specifying scales for loudness and pitch. They have also been used to scale complex stimulus dimensions such as consumer attitudes toward prices (Webb, 1961), stock market analyses (Osborne, 1959), and court penalties for crimes (Stevens, 1966).

Sensory adaptation

While thresholds are always changing, their changes are not entirely haphazard. One consistent type of change, found within several senses, is called *sensory adaptation*. It refers to the reduction in sensitivity to stimulation as stimulation persists through time and to the increase in sensitivity with lack of stimulation. It is a familiar phenomena in vision, smell, and temperature, though not limited to these senses. When we have been in sunlight, our eyes become much less sensitive, so that if we enter a dimly lighted room we cannot see the objects about us until our eyes have become adapted to the dark. The person working in a fish store or a paint store soon becomes unaware of the odors about him. A room that feels hot to someone coming in from the cold may feel cold to someone emerging from a bathtub. The range of sensory adaptation possible varies from one sensory system to the next and in some cases can be quite large. For example, the longer the eye is in total darkness the more sensitive it is to visual stimuli. As a rough indication of the magnitude of the adaptation effect, the eye in its most sensitive state (after a long period in total darkness) will respond to a stimulus 1/100,000 as intense as that required when the eye is least sensitive (after a sustained exposure to bright light).

A wide array of theories have been proposed to describe threshold phenomena. We cannot review them here, but a few remarks are appropriate concerning the two major developments. One formulation has been labeled the *neural quantum theory* (Békésy, 1930), and the other, *signal detectability theory* (Swets, Tanner, and Birdsall, 1961). In the neural quantum theory, the sensory system is assumed to be activated in discrete steps called *quanta*. Thus, although the stimulus input may be continuous, it is recorded by the sensory mechanism as a countable sequence of discrete events. As an analogy we can think of the sand-dumping toy popular with young children. Sand is poured continuously into the funnel-shaped top compartment. When a certain weight is reached a lever is tripped dumping the sand into the truck below; the input is continuous but the output occurs in discrete steps. In contrast, the signal detectability theory rejects the concept of a steplike function and assumes that the output of the sensory system is a continuous function of the stimulus input. It recognizes also that detection is always against some distractions ("noise") in the sensory system. Superficially it appears that the two theories would lead to quite different consequences and that it therefore might be easy to choose between them. However, the resolution of this issue is not simple. Both theories account for certain aspects of the data, but the facts handled well by one theory are dealt with less adequately by the other (Luce, 1963; Green and Swets, 1966).

Because of the problems of determining any exact point for the absolute threshold, it is not surprising that arguments have arisen as to whether or not undetected (hence, subthreshold) stimuli may influence the organism. The problem became accentuated a few years ago over the possible use of subthreshold stimuli in advertising. The question remains interesting in itself (apart from advertising); it appears quite likely that in some cases a stimulus might *register* in the nervous system without being represented in awareness, that is, not consciously *detected*. There are many controversial issues remaining to be resolved (e.g., Goldiamond, 1958; Eriksen, 1962; Hilgard, 1962).

The Visual Sense

In the course of evolution, a number of mechanisms have evolved to permit the organism to respond to light or to visual patterns; the "eyes" thus developed by the various organisms often bear little resemblance to each other. The invertebrate eye (as in the octopus) is constructed on a pattern very different from the vertebrate eye. Insects display both simple (one-lens) and compound eyes. Many fish and other aquatic animals have light-sensitive skin, as well as eyes. A third eye on the top of the head (a parietal eye) is found in certain lizards and other reptiles and in fish. What these evolutionary "experiments" signify is that sensitivity to changes in illumination has had important adaptive usefulness; the organisms that have developed various kinds of light-sensitive mechanisms tend to be among those that have survived.

The human eye

Light enters the eye through the transparent *cornea,* the amount of light being regulated by the *pupil,* which is an opening in the pigmented *iris;* the *lens* then focuses the light on the sensitive surface, the *retina.* Constriction and dilation of the pupil is under control of the autonomic nervous system (see p. 48): the parasympathetic division of the autonomic nervous system controls the change in pupil size as a function of changes in illumination (in much the same way as we increase the shutter opening of a camera to admit more light on a dark day and decrease the opening under conditions of bright illumination). The sympathetic division of the autonomic nervous system acts to dilate the pupil under conditions of strong emotion, either pleasant or unpleasant. Even under conditions of mild emotional arousal or interest systematic changes in pupil size can be detected by means of sensitive photographic equipment (see Figure 8–2).

The most sensitive portion of the eye in normal daylight vision is a small part of the retina called the *fovea*, on which is focused light that comes from the center of the *visual field*. (By *visual field* we mean what the subject looks at.) Since the single convex lens in the eye reverses the image, the right visual field is represented on the left of the retina, and the lower field is represented at the top of the retina. (Just as the image on the film of a single lens camera

is an upside-down and reversed version of the scene being photographed.)

Figure 8–3 shows the optic nerve fibers leading from each eye to the cortical areas where vision is represented (*occipital lobes*). Notice that some of the fibers go to the occipital lobe of the corresponding cerebral hemisphere (i.e., from the right eye to the right cerebral hemisphere and from the left eye to the left) whereas other fibers cross over at a junction called the *optic chiasma* and go to the opposite or contralateral hemisphere. Fibers from the right sides of both eyes go to the right hemisphere of the cerebral cortex and fibers from the left sides of both eyes go

8–2

Changes in pupil size as a response to pictures

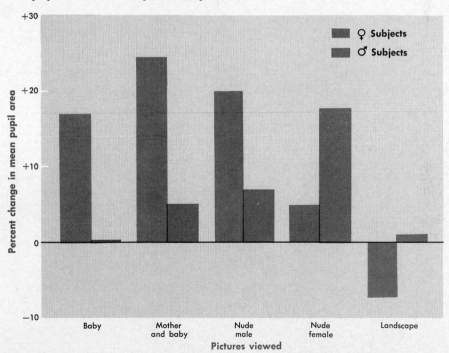

Changes in pupil size were recorded on film and later measured. The figure shows the percentage of increase or decrease in pupil area (as compared with size during viewing of control patterns) in response to various pictures for both male and female subjects. Amount of light entering the eye is constant for all pictures. The sexes differ quite markedly with regard to the interest value of these particular pictures. A later study showed that homosexuals could be distinguished from normal males on the basis of pupilary responses to pictures of female pinups. (After Hess and Polt, 1960)

Visual pathways

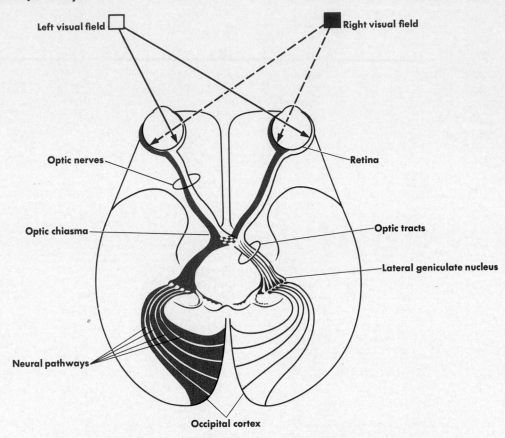

Light waves from objects in the right visual field fall on the left half of each retina; light waves from the left visual field impinge on the right half of each retina. The optic nerve bundles from each eye meet at the optic chiasma where the nerve fibers from the inner, nasal half of the retina cross over and go to opposite sides of the brain. Thus stimuli impinging on the right side of each retina are transmitted to the occipital cortex of the right cerebral hemisphere and stimuli impinging on the left side of each retina are transmitted to the left cerebral hemisphere. In terms of the visual field this means that objects in the right visual field are projected to the left cerebral hemisphere, while objects in the left visual field are projected to the right hemisphere. Damage to the occipital cortex of one hemisphere will result in blind areas in both eyes. (Adapted from Sheppard, after Polyak, 1957)

to the left hemisphere. Consequently, damage to the occipital lobe of one hemisphere (say, the left) will result in blind areas in *both* eyes (the left sides of both eyes). This fact is sometimes helpful in pinpointing the location of a cerebral tumor or injury.

The eye is a very imperfect optical system. The light waves not only have to pass through the lens and liquids that fill the eyeball, none of which is a perfect transmitter of light, but they have to penetrate the network of blood vessels and the nerve fibers that lie on the *inside* of the eye before they reach the sensitive cells—the *rods* and *cones* in the retina—where light is converted into nervous impulses (Figure 8–4). The retina is composed of at least 10 distinct layers of tissue with the rods and

Rods and cones and their connections

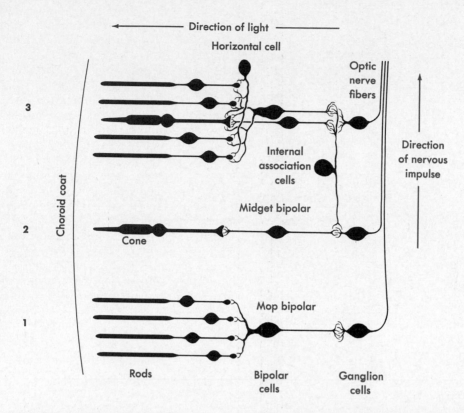

Direction of light

Horizontal cell

Optic nerve fibers

3

Choroid coat

Internal association cells

Direction of nervous impulse

Midget bipolar

2

Cone

Mop bipolar

1

Rods

Bipolar cells

Ganglion cells

Shown here are the main layers of the retina: rods and cones, bipolar cells, and ganglion cells. The bipolar cells receive impulses from one or more rods or cones and transmit the impulses to the nerve fibers, whose cell bodies are shown as the ganglion cells. In (1) is a typical arrangement of several rods connected by one "mop" bipolar cell, in (2) an arrangement of one cone attached to a single "midget" bipolar cell, while in (3) some (but not all) of the more complex patterns are shown. Integration across the retina is accomplished by horizontal cells connecting rods and cones, and by internal association cells at the ganglion cell level, as well as by the mop bipolar cells. (Simplified, after Polyak, 1941)

cones comprising the bottom layer (note "direction of light" arrow in Figure 8–4). Even when the light finally reaches the rods and cones it has to strike them at an angle because the photosensitive area of these cells is pointed toward the back of the eye rather than the front. From the standpoint of efficient optics it is surprising that we can see at all!

Under some conditions, particularly when our eyes are tired from excessive use, it is possible to actually see the movement of blood through the retinal blood vessels that lie in front of the rods and cones. The

blood vessel walls appear as pairs of narrow lines in the periphery of our field of vision, and the disk-shaped objects which appear to move between these lines are the tiny platelets of the blood as it flows through the vessel.

The rods and the cones in the retina are not uniformly distributed. The fovea contains only *cones*—some 50,000 of them packed together in its small area. Outside the fovea there are both rods and cones, with the cones decreasing in number from the center of the retina to the periphery. As we shall find out in more detail later,

Method for producing a stabilized image on the retina

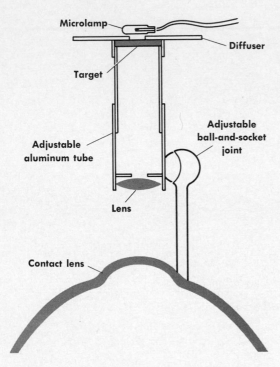

A tiny projector mounted on a contact lens is worn over the subject's cornea. With each minute movement of the eyeball the lens and projector also move so that the projected image always falls on the same area of the retina. (After Pritchard, 1961)

the cones are active in daylight vision. They permit us to see both *achromatic* colors (white, black, and the intermediate grays) and *chromatic* colors (red, green, blue, etc.). The rods, by contrast with the cones, function especially during vision under reduced illumination (night vision), and they permit us to see only achromatic colors.

As indicated in Figure 8–4 the rods are connected together in units with each unit having a single "wire" running to the optic nerve. Each of the cones in the fovea, however, has its own "private wire" to the brain (although in the periphery of the retina they are grouped together in units as are the rods). Hence our vision is much more

acute when light waves strike the fovea. It is for this reason that we turn our head to look directly at an object when we want to see it clearly. The fovea, equivalent in area to a photographic film of one square millimeter, is able to detect a telephone wire at a distance of a quarter of a mile. At its best the eye can detect a wire the thickness of which covers only 0.5 seconds of arc, about one two-millionth of the arc of a circle. This discrimination is all the more remarkable because a single cone fills an angular part of the retina 60 times as large as the thickness represented by the image of the wire. The fine discrimination takes place while the eye is in constant motion through an arc larger than the size of the minimum visible object (Ratliff and Riggs, 1950). In fact, such fine *visual activity* is probably possible only because the eye is constantly in motion, and it may be the result of stimulating many neighboring cones as the eye moves back and forth over the object.

The course of dark adaptation

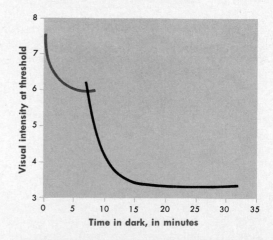

The subject stares at a bright light until the retina has become light-adapted. When he is then placed in darkness, he becomes increasingly sensitive to fainter lights as the retina becomes dark-adapted. The first part of the curve is for cones, the second for rods. The units of visual intensity are logarithms of micromicrolamberts (a very small unit of visual intensity). (After Hecht and Shlaer, 1938)

The importance of these minute eye oscillations (which occur at a rate of 30 to 100 times per second) is demonstrated by experiments which essentially eliminate movement of the retinal image by means of a projector mounted on a contact lens, as diagramed in Figure 8–5. Since the lens and projector move with the subject's eye, a stabilized image is presented to the retina; that is, the retinal image impinges on the same retinal receptors regardless of eye movements. Initially the subject sees the projected figure with normal, or slightly better than normal, visual acuity. Within a few seconds, however, the image begins to fade and within a minute disappears altogether (Riggs, Ratliff, Cornsweet, and Cornsweet, 1953; Pritchard, 1961). These phenomena are not artifacts caused by the attachment of the projector to the eye, because if the image that has disappeared is flickered or moved on the retina it immediately reappears. Apparently the sensory cells of the retina become easily fatigued, and under normal conditions our ability to view an object for a prolonged period of time is due to minute eye movements which change the particular retinal elements under stimulation.

Dark adaptation

When you go from daylight into a darkened motion-picture theater, the usher may use a flashlight to escort you to your seat. You are unable to locate an empty seat unaided because your eyes are unaccustomed to the darkness. After a while, however, you can see people around you even though the lighting has not changed, for you have undergone *dark adaptation.*

The course of dark adaptation (see Figure 8–6) provides indirect support for the difference in action between the rods and the cones. The first part of the curve shows that the *cones* gradually become sensitive to fainter lights, but after five minutes in the dark their sensitivity has increased as much as it will, as measured by the absolute threshold. Then the *rods* continue to adapt and become appreciably more sensitive for about half an hour.

The difference in function between rods and cones was discovered in part by studies on limited areas of the retina. As mentioned earlier, the center of the retina (the fovea) is rod-free. This means that in this area we can study the cones alone, which adapt according to the first part of Figure 8–6. When we realize that the cones are not very sensitive in the dark, we can understand why at night we detect a faint stimulus, such as a dim star, better if we do not look directly at it. The rods, in the peripheral parts of the retina, are more sensitive in the dark-adapted eye than are the cones.

Color

When sunlight is sent through a prism it breaks into a band of varicolored light, such as we see in the rainbow. The colors correspond to wave lengths, the *red* end of the rainbow being produced by the *long* waves, the *violet* end by the *short* waves. A band produced by sending sunlight through a prism of known characteristics is described as a *solar spectrum* (Figure 8–7). The wave lengths corresponding to the various portions of the spectrum are indicated below the chart. They are expressed in millionths of a millimeter—a unit called the *millimicron* and abbreviated $m\mu$. For the human subject the spectrum fades into invisibility at the red end at about 780 $m\mu$ and at the violet end at about 380 $m\mu$. We are able to see some vivid colors that do not exist in the spectrum at all, although they can be produced by mixing spectral lights. These are the purples redder than the violet end of the spectrum and the red that looks "purest" to most normal eyes. The reddest part of the solar spectrum looks a little yellowish.

An interesting relationship among colors was discovered by Sir Isaac Newton. He found that the spectral colors can be wrapped in their natural order around the circumference of a circle, allowing room between the red and violet ends of the spectrum for the purples and reds not found on the spectrum. If properly spaced, colors opposite each other on the circle will be *complementary,* that is, if lights of these colors are mixed in proper proportions, they disappear to a neutral gray. Such a color circle is presented in Figure 8–7, with specimen complementary colors pictured. For convenience in remembering the positions, we usually name the main complementary pairs as blue-yellow and red-green, although the yellow complementary to blue is slightly orange and the green complementary to red is really a blue-green (see Figure 8–8).

Those familiar with painting will object to the naming of yellow and blue as complementaries because those pigments when mixed give green, not gray. We are here talking about mixing *lights,* not pigments. The principles of mixture in the two cases are not contradictory, though the explanation of the difference is somewhat involved. Without going into detail, it is worth noting that the mixture of lights is an *additive* mixture, while the mixture of pigments is in part a *subtractive* mixture because of the way in which pigments selectively absorb some of the light. (It is never possible to be sure from the color of the components what the result of subtractive mixture will be.) Additive mixtures may be studied by the use of colored lights or the color wheel; subtractive mixtures, by transmitting light through colored filters (see Figures 8–8 and 8–9).

Some of the colors on the color circle appear to us to be more elementary than others; that is, they appear to be composed of a single hue. These elementary colors are called *psychological primaries,* and usually four primary colors are named: *red, yellow, green,* and *blue.* Between them are "secondary" colors in which the components are still identifiable: orange between red and yellow, yellow-greens between yellow and green, blue-greens between green and blue, and purples and violets between blue and red. Another set of primaries is called *color-mixture primaries.* Any three widely spaced colors on the spectrum can be used to provide all the other colors by additive mixture. The three colors usually chosen are a *red,* a *green,* and a *blue.* For this purpose, the red and green are so chosen that mixing them together will yield yellow.

Hue, brightness, and saturation

The circumference of the color circle describes one *dimension* of color experience: *hue*—the technical term for the quality of redness, blueness, yellowness, or greenness that differentiates one color from another and results from stimulation by light of a certain wave length. By *dimension* we mean simply some characteristic according to which items can be placed in an order, along some sort of scale. Hues are placed in the order in which they are found along the circumference of the color circle, proceeding from the shortest to the longest visible wave length.

Another dimension along which colors can be scaled is *brightness.* The achromatic colors have only the dimension of brightness from very dark (black) to very bright (white). But chromatic colors can vary in brightness, too, depending upon the extent to which they appear to approach black or white. Two blues may be of exactly the same hue (wave length), but they may differ noticeably in brightness. The physical basis of brightness is primarily the energy of the light wave which essentially corresponds to the amplitude (height) of the wave.

A third dimension along which colors can be scaled is *saturation,* which refers to the apparent purity of the color. Many chromatic colors look as though they are mixed with gray. Near the extreme are grays with a mere touch of color; the limit is pure gray. Highly saturated colors appear to be pure hue, without any gray, while colors of low saturation appear close to gray. The primary physical correlate of saturation is the complexity of the light wave. A light wave composed of only one or a few different wave lengths will produce the most highly saturated color. Light waves composed of many components result in colors of low saturation. However, saturation is dependent to some extent upon brightness too. As colors become brighter (merge into white) or darker (merge into black) they begin to lose the apparent purity of their hue and thus reduce their saturation.

The color solid

The relationship between the three dimensions of hue, brightness, and saturation will become clearer if we look at the color solid (Figure 8–10), which represents all three simultaneously. The dimension of hue is represented by points around the circumference; saturation, by points along the radius going from a pure or highly saturated color on the outside to a gray or unsaturated color in the center; and brightness, by points along the vertical axis going toward black at the bottom and toward white at the top. (The color plate does not show the actual gradations of gray going from black to white along the central axis.) You can see that the reds and purples become pink as light gray is added; the oranges and yellows become variations of brown as they become less saturated. On any vertical slice taken through the center of the color solid, all the colors are the same hue (wave length) but vary in brightness and saturation.

The color solid helps in our understanding of the relationship between brightness and saturation. The most highly saturated colors are of medium brightness. The color solid tapers to a point at both top and bottom. Consequently, as colors increase or decrease in brightness from the medial circumference they become less saturated, approaching at the extremes either black or white, which are by definition without hue and therefore of zero saturation.

Color blindness

We may conveniently think of the normal eye as discriminating three pairs of colors: light-dark and the complementaries yellow-blue and red-green. All other combinations can be derived from these. Color blindness may show as a deficiency in one or two of these systems, the light-dark system remaining if the person can see at all. The normal eye sees all three, and the person with such vision is called a *trichromat*. If a person lacks one system but has use of the two others, he is called a *dichromat*. A dichromat is partially color-blind. Finally, if only the light-dark system remains, the person is a *monochromat* and totally color-blind.

By far the commonest form of color blindness is red-green blindness, with the blue-yellow and light-dark systems intact. It is much more common among men than among women, affecting some seven percent of men (if we count color weakness along with the more extreme deficiencies), but less than one percent of women. There are different forms of red-green blindness—named "red blindness" and "green blindness"—but these names are inaccurate, for both the red-blind and the green-blind form lack both red and green; their differences lie in the regions where they see gray instead of blue and yellow. Total color blindness, in which the person sees merely black, white, and gray, is extremely rare; yellow-blue blindness, in which red-green discrimination is preserved, is rarer still.

Many color-blind persons are unaware of their defect because they are able to make such skillful use of their remaining color discrimination, combining it with the learned colors of familiar objects. Because our color vocabulary is unclear for unsaturated colors, the color-blind person can make some mistakes on these most troublesome colors without being noticed.

Many tests are available for the detection of color blindness. They usually require the subject to read a figure composed of colored dots on a background of other colored dots (Figure 8–11). The colors were chosen so as to confuse subjects who have the various forms of color deficiency.

Is there any way of telling what color the color-blind person actually sees? We can be sure of the colors that look alike to him because he will confuse them when, for example, he attempts to sort out colored yarns. But we can go farther than that, thanks to a few cases of people who are color-blind in only one eye (Sloan and Wollach, 1948; Hsia and Graham, 1965). We know that for the red-green blind, blues and yellows (as hues) look very much the same as they do to those with normal eyes, and these, in combinations with gray, are all that he sees. There are other words in his color vocabulary, however, so that he will call "green" the yellow of low saturation (i.e., a grayish yellow) that he sees when he looks at a lawn, and he will call "red" the grayish yellow that he sees when he looks at a fire engine.

Nothing can be done to cure congenital color blindness, although such aids as colored filters can be provided to help the color-blind person make more accurate color discriminations. Some forms of color blindness are the result of disease or injury (poisoning by carbon disulfide, lead poisoning, optic neuritis, etc.). Recovery from color blindness may be possible in such cases.

Afterimages and color contrast

If you stare at a *red* circle and then look at a plain gray rectangle, you are likely to see a *green* circle on it; that is, you experience a *negative afterimage,* negative because green is the complementary color of red. Not all afterimages are in the complementary color—after staring at a very bright light you are likely to see a whole succession of colors—but seeing the complementary color is very common.

The complementary color pairs are also found in *simultaneous contrast.* The shadow cast by chromatic light upon a surface dimly illuminated by achromatic light is vividly colored in the hue complementary to that of the chromatic light. It is hard to convince yourself that the shadow is not actually tinted, but you can prove this by viewing it through a tube that cuts off the chromatic light from your vision. Then the shadow will be seen as gray. This contrast effect enhances the borders between complementary colors and is one reason for making pennants of such complementary pairs as red and green and yellow and blue.

The facts of vision are enormously complex, and until our knowledge is more precise we must be prepared for exceptions to many of our generalizations. It was mentioned above that the afterimage need not always be in the complementary color. Another exception is worth noting. Usually dark surroundings make a light area seem lighter, and light surroundings make the enclosed area seem darker. But under some conditions there is what is called a *spreading effect,* so that dark areas make neighboring portions appear darker and light areas make neighboring portions appear lighter. We lack explanations of these seemingly contradictory effects, and they set problems for future investigators.

Spreading effect, afterimage, and a contrast phenomenon are illustrated in Figures 8–12 to 8–14.

The physiology of vision

The distinction between the function of the rods and that of the cones noted in the differences between foveal vision and peripheral vision and in the nature of dark adaptation has been well confirmed in the physiological laboratory. At least for the *rods* their distinctive function seems to be clearly established. A light-sensitive substance called *visual purple* or *rhodopsin* can be extracted from the rods and its properties studied. It is found to be bleached by lights of different wave lengths in a manner that corresponds to the sensitivity of the dark-adapted eye to these wave lengths (Figure 8–15). Furthermore its bleaching *rate* corresponds to the rate of light adaptation (Hsia, 1965). These correspondences suggest that visual purple represents an intermediary process between the light entering the eye and the activation of the sensory nerves which leads to seeing.

Each attempt to explain how the eye sees color has taken as its starting point one of the three bodies of facts about color that we have just discussed: color mixture, color contrast and afterimages, and color blindness.

The classical theory starting with the facts of *color mixture* goes by the name of the Young-Helmholtz theory, after the physicist Young and the physiologist Helmholtz. Being impressed by the fact that three colors were enough to produce all combinations, they proposed that three kinds of sensitive elements in the eye might serve to explain color phenomena (one sensitive to red wave lengths, one to blue, and one to green). The modern form of the theory attempts to search out three

| | (480) | (521) | (573) | |
| | Blue | Green | Yellow| |

| 400 mμ | 500 mμ | 600 mμ | 700 mμ |

Violet   Blue-green   Yellow-green   Orange   Red
(380-450)   (650-780)

8-7

The solar spectrum

The colors are in the order of the rainbow, as seen when sunlight is sent through a prism.

A color circle showing complementary colors

The colors opposite each other, if in proper proportions, will mix on a color wheel to yield the neutral gray at the center. Wave-lengths are indicated around the circle in mμ. Note that the spectral colors lie in their natural order on the circle, but their spacing is not uniform by wave-length and the circle includes the nonspectral reds, purples, and violets.

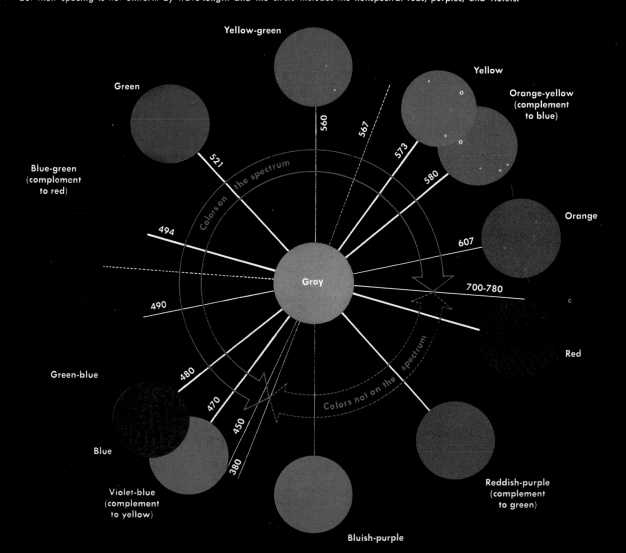

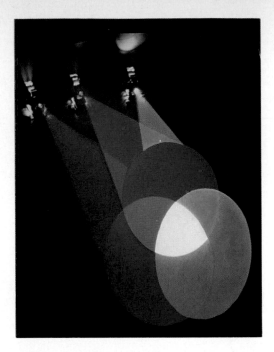

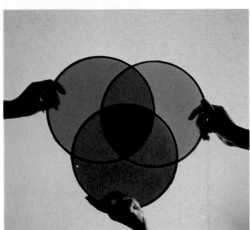

8-8

Additive and subtractive color mixtures

Additive color mixture (illustrated by the top figure) takes place when lights are mixed or when sectors of colored papers are mixed by rotation on a color wheel. Red and green lights combine to give yellow, green and bluish-purple to give blue, etc. The three colors overlap in the center to give white. Mixture of any two of the colors produces the complement of the third, as shown in the triangular portions.

Subtractive color mixture (illustrated by the bottom figure) takes place when pigments are mixed or when light is transmitted through colored filters placed one over another. Usually, blue-green and yellow will mix to give green and complementary colors will reduce to black, as in the example given. Unlike with additive mixture, one cannot always tell from the color of the components what color will result. For example, blue and green will commonly yield blue-green by subtractive mixture, but with some filters they may yield red. Note that in the diagram the triangular portions are the original complementary colors used in the additive mixture, but here they appear as a result of subtractive mixture.

8-9

The color wheel

Disks with sectors of different colors are fastened to a metal plate. When the plate rotates, the colors fuse to yield an additive mixture. The wheel in the left-hand picture is stationary; on the right the rotating red and green half-circles have fused to produce the effect of yellow.

8-10

The color solid

The three dimensions of color can be represented on a double cone: hue is represented by points around the circumference, saturation by points along the radius, and brightness by points on the vertical axis. A vertical slice from the color solid shows differences in saturation and brightness of a single hue.

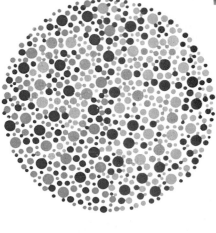

8-11

Tests for color blindness

Two plates from the Dvorine Pseudo-Isochromatic series of color-blindness tests. In the top plate, individuals with certain kinds of red-green blindness see only the number 5; others see only the 9; still others, no number at all. Those with normal vision see 95. Similarly, in the bottom plate, the person with normal vision sees the number 28, whereas those with red-green blindness see no number at all. (From I. Dvorine, Dvorine Pseudo-Isochromatic Plates, 1953, reproduced by permission of the author)

8-12

The spreading effect

The same red is used throughout the strip. But the red with black looks darker than the red with white. (After Evans, 1948)

  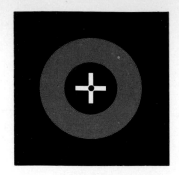

8-13

Negative afterimages

Look steadily for about 20 seconds at the dot inside the blue circle; then transfer your gaze to the dot inside the gray rectangle. Now do the same with the dot inside the yellow circle. What do you see? (After Evans, 1948)

8-14

Simultaneous contrast

Note the darkening effect on the gray patch when it is against white; the same patch of gray against black looks much lighter. A gray patch against a colored background tends to take on the complementary hue; the effect is much increased if a piece of thin tissue paper is placed over the colors. With colors that are approximately complementary (as in the red and green patches), there is an enhancement through contrast. Pennants are often red and green or yellow and blue.

8–15

The chemical basis for rod vision

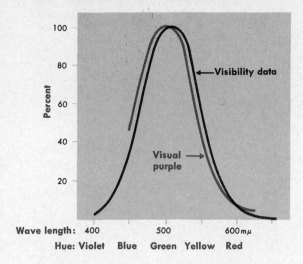

Wave length: 400   500   600 mμ

Hue: Violet Blue Green Yellow Red

The black line represents the relative visibility of the different wave lengths to the dark-adapted human eye; the colored line represents the rate at which visual purple (rhodopsin) is bleached by light of different wave lengths. The two curves are superimposed by using arbitrary units so that the maximum of each curve is at 100 percent. Because the curves so nearly coincide, it is plausible to suppose that visual purple (which is obtained from rods) is the chemical substance that mediates rod vision. (After Hecht and Williams, 1922–23)

kinds of cones or three kinds of cone substances.

A second theory, which starts with the facts of *color contrast* and *afterimages,* is attributed to Hering, another physiologist. He was impressed by the appearance of color pairs under so many circumstances: a black-white pair, a red-green pair, and a blue-yellow pair seemed to be the fundamental units of visual activity. He proposed three processes that in their building-up phase (anabolic) would yield one member of the pair and in their tearing-down phase (catabolic) would yield the other. Hence when stimulation is withdrawn, as in the afterimage experiment, the contrasting color appears because the anabolic-catabolic process is reversed.

A third theory was proposed by the psychologist Ladd-Franklin, who was impressed by the facts of *color blindness* and

had an evolutionary theory to account for them. She assumed that monochromatism was the most primitive form of seeing, followed by the addition of blue and yellow (equivalent to red-green color blindness), this in turn followed by trichromatism. Hence the person with red-green color blindness has regressed one step; blue-yellow color blindness would constitute a second regressive step and would be only one step removed from complete color blindness. The fact that blue-yellow blindness is rarer than total color blindness makes her theory less plausible than it otherwise would be.

Even this brief sketch shows how theorists tend to build their theories around a limited set of facts. Of course they go on to try to explain the other facts as well, but the nature of the theory often shows its origin in a specific starting point. Actually, no one of the theories is yet satisfactory, and newer theories have been proposed.

CRITICAL DISCUSSION

Color theories

Great advances have been made in the specifications of color and in reference standards, necessitated in part by such developments as color photography and colored motion pictures and television. The use of color in mass-produced objects such as automobiles and radios, to say nothing of its use in interior decoration, calls for precise designation of colors. Theories of the Young-Helmholtz type have remained popular because three colors are enough to serve the purposes of precise specification. Hence a three-color theory is called *parsimonious,* that is, it gets along with as few variables as possible. But the fact that three colors can produce all combinations does not prove that the eye is constructed on a three-color system. At this time, there is no unequivocal data for the existence of three specific photopigments in human cone cells, although some absorption spectra, differing from those in the rods, have been found for individual cones (Brown and Wald, 1964;

Marks, Dobelle, and MacNichol, 1964). The weight of psychophysical and physiological evidence suggests that color vision is not based on three cone photopigments, but rather on a combination of variation in the physical characteristics of cone cells and their connections to bipolar cells. This in turn suggests that both the Young-Helmholtz three-pigment theory and the Hering opponent-colors theory may each contain some element of truth, but that neither individually is capable of providing an adequate explanation of color perception (Sheppard, 1966).

Considerable interest was aroused by Land (1959), the developer of the Land Polaroid camera, who, in seeking to develop color photography for his camera, fell upon an interesting method of producing a variety of colors by mixing only two wave lengths (instead of the usually required three). He found that he could photograph any array of colored objects in black and white using colored filters so that the resulting black-and-white transparencies would differ according to the filters used. Now, regardless of the filters used, he could project *two other colors* through these transparencies, and by their overlap reproduce a colored scene rather like the one originally photographed. While this finding apparently calls for a new theory of color vision, critics have shown how the effects can be harmonized with existing theories if sufficient play is given to contrast effects, as in Hering's theory (Walls, 1960). However the discussion turns out, the complexity and richness of contrast effects can no longer be ignored in considering how we actually perceive a colored display.

8–16

A cross section of the ear

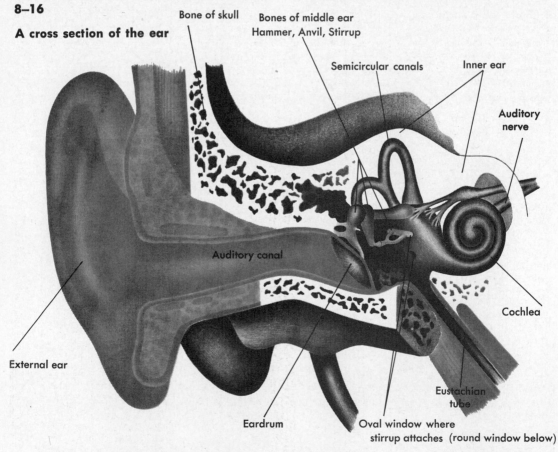

Bone of skull
Bones of middle ear
Hammer, Anvil, Stirrup
Semicircular canals
Inner ear
Auditory nerve
Auditory canal
Cochlea
External ear
Eustachian tube
Eardrum
Oval window where stirrup attaches (round window below)

This drawing shows the general structure of the ear. For the detailed neural connections, see Figure 8–17.

The Auditory Sense

The human ear

The external ear connects with an auditory canal leading to the *eardrum,* a movable diaphragm activated by sound entering the ear (Figure 8–16). On the inner side of the diaphragm is a cavity housing the bony transmitters of the *middle ear* (hammer, anvil, and stirrup). The pressure inside and outside the eardrum is equalized by way of the *Eustachian tube* that leads into the mouth cavity. When pressure changes rapidly (as in an airplane), yawning, coughing, or chewing gum employs the Eustachian tube in making the pressure inside the ear change to correspond with the pressure outside. The hammer is attached firmly to the eardrum, and the stirrup to the *oval window* that conducts the sounds to the *cochlea,* the auditory portion of the *inner ear.* Small movements at the eardrum are condensed into a magnified pressure on the oval window, an increase in pressure per unit area of about 30 to 1.

Pressure at the oval window sets into motion the fluid inside the cochlea. This pressure is relieved at the *round window,* which also lies between the cochlea and the inner ear, at the other end of the fluid-filled channel through the cochlea. The pressure on the fluid in the cochlea stimulates the true auditory receptors lying in the *organ of Corti,* the portion of the cochlea that contains the auditory equivalent of the retina (Figure 8–17). Pressure changes in the fluid displace the *basilar membrane* upon which the organ of Corti rests, and this displacement stimulates the sensitive elements in the *hair cells* of the organ of Corti, connected with the auditory nerve. The inner ear also contains other sensitive (nonauditory) portions that we shall consider later.

The pathways of the auditory nerves resemble those of the optic nerves (see Figure 8–3) in that nerve fibers from each ear travel to both cerebral hemispheres (terminating in the temporal lobes). Thus, destruction of one temporal lobe will not cause complete deafness in either ear.

8–17

Receptors for hearing

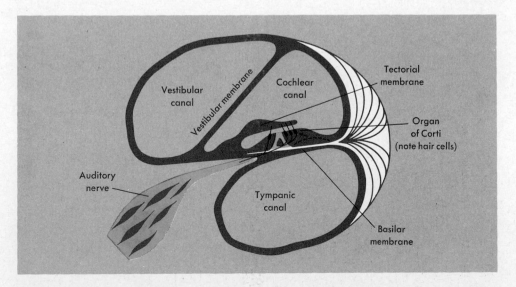

A section through the snail-shaped cochlea. The true auditory receptors lie in the organ of Corti, which rests upon the basilar membrane. Deflection of the basilar membrane activates the hair cells and produces impulses in the auditory nerve.

Single cycle of a sound wave

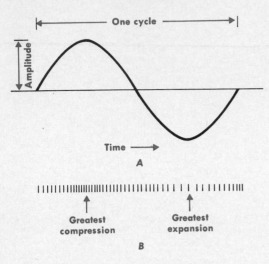

A shows the cycle as usually represented by a sine wave; B shows the state of compression and expansion at each part of the cycle.

Pitch and loudness

The stimuli for pure tones are sound waves—physical vibrations in the air (or in other substances such as water or metal). For example, at one end of a speaking tube, the vibrations compress the air molecules in front; this "push" is transmitted from air molecule to air molecule, alternately causing compressions and expansions of the air; these compressions and expansions cause "sound" to be heard at the other end of the tube when the ear is placed against it.

Sound waves can be graphically represented as transverse *sine waves* (Figure 8–18). The figure shows how a single complete cycle represents the successive compression and expansion of the air as the sound wave moves along. The two main characteristics of such a wave are its *frequency* and its *amplitude*. Frequency refers to number of vibrations per second, that is, the number of times per second

8–19

Range of frequencies of the piano and other musical instruments

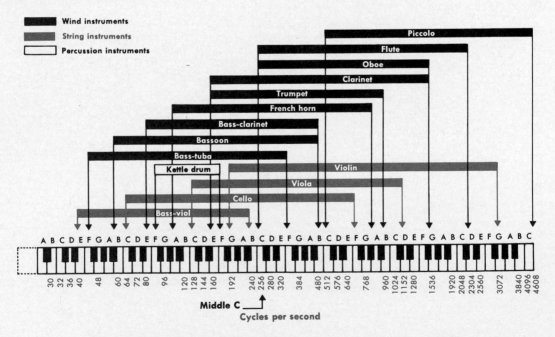

Note that each octave represents a doubling in frequency. (After Henney, 1938)

Loudness in decibels

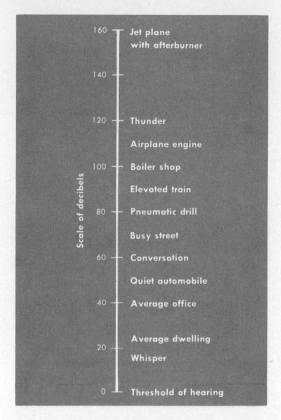

The loudness of various common sounds is indicated. (After Stevens and Davis, 1938; jet plane added)

that the whole wave is repeated. Amplitude refers to the amount of compression and expansion, as represented by the amount by which the curve is displaced above or below the base line. The psychological correlate of frequency is *pitch:* the higher the vibration frequency, the higher the pitch we hear. The corresponding correlate of amplitude is *loudness:* the greater the amplitude, the louder the tone (provided pitch remains constant).

The range of frequencies that we can hear runs from about 20 to 20,000 cycles per second (abbreviated cps). The piano produces frequencies up to a high of 4096 cps, and the piccolo goes somewhat higher (Figure 8–19).

As for amplitude, while we all know the

difference between a loud sound and a soft one, assigning scale values to loudness is not so easy. Engineers from the Bell Telephone Laboratories have contributed to the measurement of sound intensity by formulating a convenient unit by which to convert the physical pressures at the eardrum into an understandable scale. The unit is called a *decibel* (one-tenth of a *bel,* named in honor of Alexander Graham Bell). The rough meaning of a decibel is indicated in the scale of familiar sounds given in Figure 8–20.

Absolute threshold for hearing. As mentioned earlier, human beings are only sensitive to tones between about 20 and 20,000 cps. Moreover, the threshold for hearing varies with the frequency of the source (Figure 8–21). Tones between about 800 and 6000 cps require less than 10 decibels to reach threshold, whereas a tone of 40 cps requires about 70 decibels, and one of

8–21

Limits of hearing

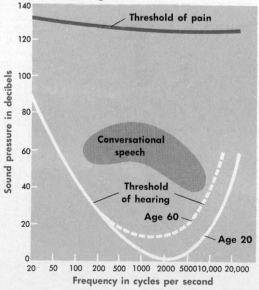

The curve across the top is the threshold of pain. The convex curves below are the threshold of hearing for age 20 and age 60. Note that with increase in age, hearing is primarily affected in the range of frequencies above 500 cps (approximate, from various determinations).

10,000 cycles requires 20 decibels. Our ears are most sensitive at about 2000 cps.

Above threshold the same relationships hold. That is, with equal amplitudes well above threshold, tones in the middle ranges continue to sound louder than either very low or very high tones. This fact explains why high-fidelity amplifiers provide adjustments for increasing the amplitude of the bass and treble sounds on a recording. (In fact, it has long been standard practice for recording engineers to incorporate such an adjustment in the recording itself.)

Complex tones and noises

Just as the colors we see are seldom pure hues produced by a single wave length of light, so the sounds we hear are seldom pure tones represented by a sound wave of a single frequency. Even the musical tone produced by striking middle C on the piano has, in addition to its fundamental tone of 256 cps, *overtones,* which are multiples of that frequency. The overtones result from the fact that the piano wire vibrates not only as a whole, producing a fundamental tone of 256 cps, but also vibrates in halves, thirds, quarters, fifths, and so on, with each partial vibration producing its own frequency. If the vibrating wire is *damped* by being touched lightly in the middle we hear the first overtone at 512 cps (double the fundamental of 256 cps). This overtone is one octave higher than the fundamental (i.e., at C above middle C). The second overtone, produced by damping the wire at one-third the distance from either end, has a frequency three times higher than the fundamental (768 cps). For any fundamental tone the overtones stand in the ratio of 1:2:3:4:5 and so on. Since amplitude decreases as the partial vibrations involve shorter lengths of string, the successive overtones become progressively more difficult to hear. But a trained listener can distinguish as many as six or seven overtones.

The tones of one musical instrument differ from those of another in the number of overtones produced and in the way in which the construction of the instrument enhances (resonates) certain overtones and deadens others. This characteristic quality of a musical tone is called *timbre*. It is the timbre of a tone that tells us whether it is being played by a piano or a clarinet.[1] Instead of the regular sound wave pictured at the top of Figure 8–22, a tone from any instrument has a complex wave form, preserving only the peaks and troughs that help to define the fundamental pitch.

If one compares the dimensions of tone with those of color, the following correspondences hold approximately:

Dimensions of color	*Dimensions of tone*
Hue	Pitch
Brightness	Loudness
Saturation	Timbre

Hue and pitch are functions of wave frequency; brightness and loudness are functions of amplitude (or other measure of intensity); saturation may be a result of mixture, just as timbre is. But these are only analogies and are limited as all analogies are.

What happens when two tones are sounded together? They do not lose their identity as colors do when mixed, although they may lead to a fusion that is heard as *consonant* (pleasant) or as *dissonant* (unpleasant). One reason some combinations of tones are preferred to others is that the two tones create a third tone based on the difference in their frequencies. This *difference tone* may or may not harmonize with the fundamental tones that are sounded. Musical harmony depends in part on the complex interaction between fundamental tones, overtones, and difference tones that combine to make up the complex tonal stimulus.

A *noise* is a very complex sound, composed of many frequencies not in harmonious relation to each other. Acoustical experts sometimes speak of "white noise" when referring to a noise composed of all frequencies in the sound spectrum, analogous to white light, which is composed of all frequencies in the light spectrum. The

[1] If all overtones are eliminated by the use of sound filters, it is difficult to determine what instrument is being played.

The wave forms of complex tones

Dr. Hugh Linebach

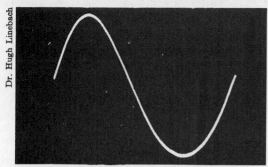

Pure tone—fundamental

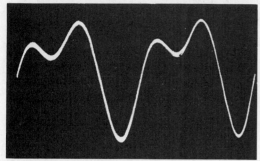

Combination of fundamental and second harmonic

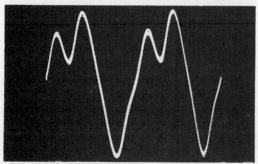

Tone of French horn

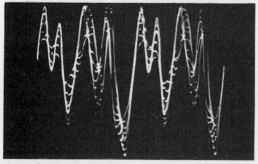

Tone of trumpet

Each illustration is of the tone of A above middle C (440 cps).

sound of a hissing steam radiator approximates the sound of white noise.

A noise may have a characteristic pitch. For example, we may legitimately use the musical term "bass" to characterize drum, even though a drum is more noisy than tonal. Speech sounds make use at once of tonal qualities and of noise qualities: *vowels* are tonal, and *consonants* are noisy.

The physiology of hearing

We know that the organ of Corti within the cochlea contains the sensitive cells that connect with the fibers of the auditory nerve, over which the impulses travel to the brain and lead to our experiences of hearing. Under the organ of Corti lies the *basilar membrane,* which somehow detects the changes transmitted through the oval window and converts them into appropriate auditory signals.

Helmholtz, whose theory of color vision we studied, made the brilliant suggestion that the basilar membrane acts like a series of resonators, responding at its narrow end to high tones and at its wide end to low tones, just as the strings of a piano or a harp will vibrate in resonance with tones that are sounded at the natural resonant frequency of the instrument. The nerve fibers connected with the different parts of the membrane signal to the brain whether the tone is high or low, each fiber (or group of fibers) transmitting stimuli of a specific frequency. This type of hearing theory has come to be called a *place theory* because it associates pitch with the *place* on the basilar membrane where auditory stimulation occurs.

The opposite type of theory interprets the membrane more nearly as though it were the diaphragm of a microphone, vibrating as a whole at the frequency of the incoming sound. This second theory is called a *frequency theory* because it assumes that nervous impulses are initiated by the basilar membrane in accordance with the frequency at which tonal vibrations reach it. There are many compromises between these two theories, and a final theory, as in vision, has not yet been agreed upon.

Some aspects of the *place theory* are by now so well established that any final theory will surely incorporate them. We know from several lines of evidence that tones of given frequencies have their maximum influence on the basilar membrane at well-defined places. The evidence comes from electrical and mechanical measurements made within the normal-functioning ear and from the tonal gaps produced when portions of the basilar membrane are damaged by prolonged exposure to loud tones of a given frequency. This evidence agrees sufficiently to permit a map of the basilar membrane such as that in Figure 8–23.

Evidence for some kind of *frequency theory* comes from the representation within the auditory nerve of the actual frequencies of sounds sent into the ear, particularly for sounds not over 4000 or 5000 cps. The early experiments on frequency were faulty in that the electrical impulses picked up from the nerve were not true signs of activity within the auditory nerve but were effects from the cochlea as a whole acting as a microphone. Later experiments have sought to correct these defects, however, and there does appear to be some representation of frequency in the auditory nerve.

8–23

Sound map of the basilar membrane

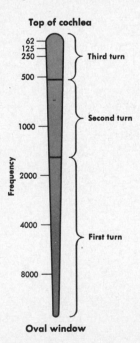

This diagram shows the location on the basilar membrane, within the coils of the cochlea, of maximum sensitivity to sounds of different frequency. (After Stevens, Davis, and Lurie, 1935)

Modern *place* theories have moved far from the theory that the basilar membrane is composed of fibers that resonate like piano strings. Because the ear is filled with a viscous fluid, the membrane is not free to vibrate like strings. The most promising of place theories, worked out by Békésy (1960) along hydrostatic lines, is known as the *traveling-wave theory*. When a sound of a given frequency enters the ear, a wave travels along the basilar membrane and displaces it a maximum amount at a certain point, depending on the frequency of the wave. Békésy's beautifully precise experiments on both animal and human ears strongly support his interpretations.

Similarly, earlier *frequency* theories have undergone changes. The chief objection to the original theory was that although the basilar membrane could conceivably vibrate as a whole to produce the experience of low frequency tones (e.g., at 256 cps for middle C) it is difficult to conceive of it vibrating at the rate of 14,000 cps to produce a more high-pitched tone. And even if the basilar membrane were capable of such rapid responding, we know that a single neuron can conduct only about 1000 impulses per second. To overcome these objections Wever (1949) proposed the *volley theory*, which assumes that frequency is represented by groups of fibers firing in turn in a sort of squad system. Different squads fire at each condensation of the sound wave. One group may fire at the first condensation, remain in a refractory phase while another group discharges, and then be ready to fire again at the third condensation. Thus, although no one fiber responds at each condensation, all respond synchronously with the frequency of the sound wave. For a 2000 cps tone there would be a spurt of activity in the auditory nerve every two-thousandths of a second with different groups of neurons firing each time. Pitch therefore depends on the frequency of the volleys and not on the frequency of the individual nerve fibers.

Even with the help of the volley theory, however, it is difficult to apply the frequency notion to account for frequencies above 5000 cps. Consequently, most experts agree that a two-process theory of pitch is necessary: the frequency principle is used to account for frequencies up to about 5000 cps and a place theory takes over at higher frequencies.

So far we have been concerned only with the problem of accounting for the experience of pitch. Loudness is usually explained by the number of impulses produced, either through the increase in the number of fibers stimulated as loudness increases or through more frequent impulses in the same fibers. Thus an increase in amplitude of the sound wave might activate 100 fibers instead of 50, and fibers that had been firing only 400 times per second may now discharge 700 times per second—the effect would be to produce more impulses per volley without changing the frequency or temporal spacing of the volleys.

Other Senses

Man's senses other than vision and audition are very important for him, but they lack the richness of patterning and organization that have led men to call vision and audition the "higher senses." Our symbolic experiences are expressed largely in visual and auditory terms. Our spoken language is to be *heard;* our written language is to be *seen.* Musical notation permits music to be read or played on an instrument. Except for Braille (the raised form of printing that permits the blind to read) we do not have any comparable symbolic coding of odors, tastes, or touches. These "lower senses" are important insofar as survival is concerned, but they are lower in the richness and variety of experiences they mediate.

Smell

From an evolutionary point of view, smell is one of the most primitive and most important of the senses. The sense organ for smell has a position of prominence in the head appropriate to a sense intended to guide behavior. The receptors high in the nose, in the *olfactory epithelium* of each nasal cavity, are connected without synapse directly to the olfactory bulbs of the brain, lying just below the frontal lobes (see Chapter 2). Thus smell has a more direct route to the brain than any other sense. The olfactory bulbs are in turn connected with the olfactory cortex on the inside of the temporal lobes and extend to the neighboring cortex. The exact neural connections are still a matter of some uncertainty.

In fishes the olfactory cortex makes up the entire cerebral hemispheres. In the dog, the olfactory cortex represents about one-third of the area of the side of the brain, as contrasted with one-twentieth of this area in man. The dog's well-known abilities to make discriminations on the basis of odor have been demonstrated under controlled conditions (Becker, King, and Markee, 1962). In man, odor has become of relatively little adaptive significance, but serving its purpose in warning of danger by fire or gas, in the discrimination of foods, and in the enjoyment of pleasant odors.

The nature of the olfactory stimulus has been the source of a great deal of speculation. Some theorists assume that smell is due to a chemical reaction between the odorous substance and the receptor (Davies, 1962), while some assume a kind of radiation activity, such as the differential absorption of infrared radiant energy corresponding to the gas being smelled (Wright, 1964). But the whole matter is far from settled and remains a promising field for research.

Taste

We know that the primary taste qualities are *sweet, sour, salt,* and *bitter.* Everything else in taste experience is contributed by fusions of these qualities and other senses. Smell, texture, temperature, and sometimes pain (judging from the pleasure some diners derive from highly spiced Mexican food) all contribute to the sensations we experience when we taste a food. When we drink a glass of lemonade we enjoy its odor and its coolness by senses other than taste; the taste sense provides only for its sweet-sour-bitter components. With our nostrils clamped tight, we cannot distinguish between the taste of a raw apple and a raw potato.

The taste receptors are found in the *taste buds* on the edges and toward the back of the tongue, with a few elsewhere in the soft palate, the pharynx, and the larynx. It is known that the number of taste buds decreases with age, so that older people are less sensitive to taste than children. Some taste buds at the tip of the tongue react only to sweet, salt, and sour, while others react to some or all of these in combination. In general, sensitivity to *sweet* is greatest at the tip of the tongue, to *salt* on the tip and the sides, to *sour* on the sides, and to *bitter* on the back.

Each of the approximately 10,000 taste buds in the human adult has 15 to 20 taste cells arranged in budlike form on its tip, much like the segments of an orange. These taste cells are continuously reproducing themselves at the rate of a complete turnover for each taste bud every seven days (Pfaffmann, 1964). Consequently, the taste cells we kill when we scald our tongue with a cup of hot coffee provide no cause for concern; they are quickly replenished. Recordings from microelectrodes implanted in single cells show that even the individual cells vary in their response to the four basic taste stimuli; that is, some cells may respond only to sugar and salt while others on the same taste bud may respond only to salt and acids, and so forth.

The initial step in the taste process is a chemical one. We do not understand this process completely, but it appears that stimulation by a taste solution depolarizes the taste cell and a weak bond is formed between the ion or molecule of the taste substance and the molecular structure of the taste-cell surface. This depolarization in turn excites the nerve fibers and gives rise to a nerve impulse. It is hypothesized that differences in the configuration of the cell surface account for the selective absorption of a particular chemical (Beidler, 1961).

In contrast to the exclusive nerve tracts for audition, vision, and olfaction (the auditory, optic, and olfactory nerves), sensations from the taste buds are carried to the central nervous system by three different cranial nerves (the facial, glossopharyngeal, and vagus nerves), which also carry nerve fibers related to other functions such as chewing, swallowing, and tactile sensation and movement of the tongue. The area of the cortex where taste is represented lies behind the central fissure at the lower part of the side of the brain.

It is interesting to note that although bitter, salt, sweet, and sour are the primary taste sensations in man, other animals differ in the receptivity of their taste buds (as determined by measurement of impulses from the taste nerve fibers as well as behavioral evidence of ability to discriminate among taste substances). Cats and chickens, for example, appear to have no taste receptors that respond to sweet, whereas dogs, rats, pigs, and most other vertebrates do. (This fact explains the observation of pet owners that dogs are usually fond of desserts, while cats generally ignore them.) For man, distilled water is a tasteless liquid that elicits no response from his taste buds; many animals, however, including monkeys, dogs, and cats, apparently have taste receptors that respond specifically to water (Zotterman, 1961).

CRITICAL DISCUSSION
Physiology and sensory quality

The general agreement that taste qualities include only sweet, salt, sour, and bitter led initially to a search for taste buds that mediated these qualities. This rather simple notion that the experienced quality would be closely related to underlying physiology goes back to the doctrine of *specific nerve energies* formulated early in the nineteenth century by Sir Charles Bell and Johannes Müller (Carmichael, 1926). This doctrine states that we are aware of the state of our nerves, rather than of external stimuli: that is, any stimulation of the eye gives rise to experiences of light and of the taste buds to experiences of taste. It was thus simple to infer that some taste buds should produce the experience of sweet, others of salt, sour, or bitter.

We now know that there is not a specific receptor for each of the taste qualities; although some receptor cells may respond only to a certain chemical, others respond to several of the primary tastes. Advances in electrophysiology have made it possible to record the nerve impulses from a single taste nerve fiber (isolated from the bundles of such fibers that make up a nerve). As a solution, such as salt, increases in concentration there is a corresponding increase in the number of impulses fired by the nerve fiber. Other taste substances will also produce impulses in the same fiber but at different thresholds. In the rat, for example, thresholds based on the minimum concentration of the substance that can be detected can be arranged in order from low to high for the following substances: quinine, hydrochloric acid, sodium chloride, potassium chloride, and sucrose. That is, the taste mechanism reacts most readily to quinine (bitter) and is least sensitive to sucrose (sweet).

Since impulses in the taste nerve fiber taken alone do not indicate which of several substances was applied to the tongue, how are we to account for the fact that different substances do taste differently? The answer must lie in some sort of "code," which includes the frequency of stimulation in neighboring fibers and the relative amounts of parallel activity in units that happen to be more sensitive to one kind of stimulation than to another (Pfaffmann, 1964). While something like the doctrine of specific nerve energies is still appropriate, the doctrine must not misguide us into oversimplified theories of the relationship of phenomenal experience to what goes on in our nervous systems.

The skin sensations

The familiar sense of touch is not one sense but at least four: *touch, pain, warm,* and *cold*—all of which are felt through distinct kinds of sensitive spots on the skin surface. If the skin is explored with appropriate instruments (fine hairs, needle points, heated or cooled pointed hammers), it is found that these sensitive spots are unevenly distributed. This *punctiform distribution* is not alike for the four qualities; the separate sensitive spots are not equally numerous nor are they found at the same locations. On most parts of the skin the relative frequencies are, in descending order: pain spots, touch spots, cold spots, and warm spots. All other skin sensations that we commonly describe, such as itch, tickle, quick-pricking pains, and dull, long-lasting pains, are considered to be variations of the four basic sensations. An itching sensation, for example, can be produced by stimulating pain spots by a light, repeated needle prick; tickle is experienced when adjacent touch spots on the skin are touched lightly in rapid succession.

The precise receptors for the various skin senses have been the subject of much study and dispute. At one time histologists identified a number of quite different nerve-end structures in the skin, each of which was thought to be the specific receptor for one of the four sensations. Psychology texts of some 20 years ago contained detailed drawings of these cutaneous receptors. Subsequent studies, however, failed to substantiate such claims: when heroic investigators "mapped" cold, warm, touch, and pain spots on their skin, excised the underlying tissue, and examined it microscopically, there was no consistent relationship between the type of sensation experienced and the type of underlying nerve-end structures. About all that can be stated with some degree of certainty is that (1) nerve fibers at the base of hair follicles serve as receptors for touch or light pressure (but not the only receptors since the lips, which are hairless, are quite sensitive to pressure), and (2) free nerve-endings that terminate in the epidermis (as opposed to those nerves that end in certain encapsulated structures) are involved in pain reception.

It is important to note that in everyday experiences the four sensations are usually mingled; we seldom feel pain without touch, or warm or cold without touch. And stimulation by extreme heat or cold activates the pain receptors too, usually at about the point where the thermal stimulation begins to produce destructive changes in the tissue surrounding the pain receptors.

Temperature. The thermometer scale is continuous—it is not divided into a part called "cold" and another part called "warm." Yet our skin senses are so divided. The experiences of "warm" and "cold" depend upon a *level of adaptation,* this level providing a kind of zero point. A very old experiment demonstrates this. You prepare three pails of water, one containing ice water, one containing hot water, and one containing water at room temperature. Then you place your right hand in the hot water and your left hand in the ice water, and leave them there for a few minutes. Now plunge both hands into the water at room temperature. To the left hand the water feels warm; to the right hand, it feels cool.

This experience is familiar. Another fact, however, is unlikely to be discovered without special experimentation. The experience of "hot" is distinct from the experience of "warm"; it results from the simultaneous stimulation of "warm" and "cold" spots. This can be demonstrated with a device consisting of intertwined coils that allows two streams of water to be passed through alternate coils (Figure 8–24). Pass cold water through both coils; of course they feel cold when you grasp them with one hand. Pass warm water through both and they feel warm. Now pass cold water through one set of coils and warm water through the other. When you grasp the coils they now feel hot! This is not the way the experience of "hot" is usually produced, but it is the way the receptors respond. Cold spots have two thresholds. They respond to stimuli of

"Hot" as simultaneous stimulation of warm and cold spots

When cold water (0–5° C) is circulated through one coil and warm water (40–44° C) through another intertwining coil, the subject experiences a hot, burning sensation on grasping the coils. This experiment demonstrates that the sensation of "hot" is produced by the simultaneous stimulation of warm and cold spots in the skin. (After Hainer, Emslie, and Jacobson, 1954)

low temperature, do not respond to stimuli of intermediate temperature, but respond again to stimuli of high temperature. Hence with high temperatures there is an activation of *both* warm and cold spots, and the felt experience of "hot" depends upon this double effect.

Local signs. If someone touches your arm while your eyes are closed, you can tell whether he touched your right or left arm and approximately where he touched it. Thus the sensory effect is accompanied by some sort of sign of location, known as a *local sign.*

The problem of what is inborn and what is acquired runs through all the topics concerned with capacity for discrimination and response. This is also true with local signs. It has been argued that local signs arise through learning. When you prick yourself on your right hand, you make a reflex withdrawal and look for the sharp object that caused the pain. Through many experiences of this kind, you learn to know when (and where) something touches your right hand; by then the touch has acquired a local sign. The argument is used to explain, for example, why it is so hard to guide someone to scratch an itch located high on your back. As the argument runs, localization on the back is poor because there are few opportunities to learn the necessary discriminations.

The other side of the argument is supported by skin transplants in animals, as illustrated in the following experiment done with frogs. Frogs are quite accurate in localizing disturbing stimuli on their skin; when they wipe off an irritant from their skin, they aim very well with their feet. If skin flaps from a tadpole are transplanted across the midline (Figure 8–25) before any localization of touch has developed, the tadpole will develop unharmed into a frog. Now, however, if the

8–25

Local signs

Transplant
in tadpole

Location
in frog

Transplantation of skin in a frog made in study of localization of stimuli. (After Sperry, 1951)

frog is stimulated at A it will try to wipe off something at B (Sperry, 1951). This experiment shows that for the frog, at least, the local signs are laid down in the nervous system without any necessary learning.

Kinesthesis

Our ordinary vocabulary lacks a word for the sensory system that informs us of the position and movement of parts of the body. In technical language this is *kinesthesis*—the muscle, tendon, and joint sense. Position and movement are detected by sense organs in the joints, while sense organs in the muscles and tendons tell us whether a muscle is stretched or contracted and help to adjust muscular tension to the load upon it.

Without kinesthesis we would have great difficulty in maintaining posture, in walking and climbing, and in controlling voluntary movements such as reaching, grasping, manipulating. Whenever we act, we make somewhat tentative movements and then adjust them according to their environmental effects. If something turns out to be heavier than expected, we brace ourselves and lift with greater effort. If we slip or stumble as we walk, we make prompt corrective movements. The kinesthetic sense gives us a feedback from the environment that keeps telling us how things are going. We take this for granted until a foot "goes to sleep" and we realize how strange it is to walk without any information as to the foot's contact with the floor.

The joints are surprisingly sensitive to position and movement. If the arm is strapped to a tilting board so that the experimenter can move it through a very small angle, the threshold for perception of movement turns out to be less than 0.5 degree of arc (Laidlaw and Hamilton, 1937). In an arm that stretches two feet from the shoulder to the finger tip, this represents a movement of about one-fifth of an inch at the finger tip. Some systems of handwriting once required control of the pen by the shoulder joint, a demand that would be impossible were it not for the high degree of discrimination at the joint.

Equilibratory senses

Cooperating with kinesthesis are the *equilibratory senses* dealing with total body position in relation to gravity and with motion of the body as a whole. The relation of bodily parts to each other and to external objects is the responsibility of kinesthesis; the orientation of the body in space is the responsibility of the equilibratory senses.

The sense organs for equilibrium are located in the bony labyrinth of the inner ear, in the parts other than the cochlea. There are two systems: the semicircular canals and the vestibular sacs.

The *semicircular canals* of each labyrinth lie in three planes, so that bodily rotation in any one of the planes will have maximum effect on one of the canals and rotation at an angle to the planes will affect more than one. The canals are filled with a liquid called *endolymph,* which is displaced when the body rotates. The nerve elements connect with hair cells embedded in a gelatinous mass known as the *cupula.* When the endolymph brings pressure on the cupula, it bends the hair cells and produces the nervous impulses that lead to the responses to rotation.

When rotation is slow and of moderate amount, the chief consequence is information that we are moving. When it is more extreme, the responses are also more extreme. Most of us as children played games in which we whirled our bodies until we lost balance, were dizzy, and watched the visual world spin around us. The eye movements following rotation, which are responsible for the spinning world, are known as *nystagmus.* They show how complex, yet orderly, some of our reflex processes are. Adults find getting dizzy less amusing than children, because they tend to become nauseated as well. Motion sickness is brought about, in part at least, through sensations from the semicircular canals (Wendt, 1951).

The *vestibular sacs* (the utricle and saccule) lie in the vestibule proper, between the base of the semicircular canals and the cochlea. They provide for our perceptions of bodily position when the body is at rest. The sensitive portion is again a gelatinous mass with hair cells and granules known as *otoliths* (literally, "ear stones") embedded in it. The normal pressure of the otoliths in the hair cells gives us the sense of upright position, and any distortion tells us that the head is tilted.

How the otoliths can control reflexes of position is illustrated by an old experiment done with lobsters. The lobster's equilibratory organ lies in a cavity open to the outside. When the lobster outgrows its shell, it loses its equilibrium until it has collected a new batch of small stones in the cavity serving the equilibratory organ in its new shell. Iron filings substituted for the stones work as well until a strong magnet is placed above the lobster. Now the lobster turns over on its back, because the attraction of the magnet has substituted for gravity. While the lobster is on its back, the iron filings press against the equilibratory organ as the stones ordinarily would when the animal is upright.

The equilibratory senses also signal accelerated motion in a straight line, but sometimes they produce illusions that distort the true path of motion. These illusions occur in flying because of changes in speed and the banking and climbing of the plane, occasionally under conditions of poor visibility. For example, when a plane is increasing its speed gradually, a blindfolded subject may feel sure that the plane is climbing; if its speed is decreasing gradually, he may feel equally sure that it is diving (Clark and Graybiel, 1949). Under conditions of poor visibility a flyer does better to trust his instruments than his equilibratory senses! Other illusions beset him also. There are, for example, visual illusions of movement as a consequence of involuntary eye movements (nystagmus) while a plane is banking. These can easily produce trouble in night maneuvers, when the movement of another plane in formation is misjudged.

SUMMARY

1. All sense experiences have their *thresholds* (both *absolute* and *difference* thresholds). Weber's law expresses the fact that difference thresholds tend to be a constant fraction of the stimulus intensity. Thresholds fluctuate, as illustrated by *sensory adaptation*—the modified sensitivity (altered threshold) after prolonged exposure to a stimulus, or an absence of stimulation.

2. Some of the main features of the *visual sense* are:

a. The eye receives light waves by way of the *cornea, pupil, lens,* and *retina.* The receptors proper are the *rods* and *cones* of the retina. The cones, concentrated in the *fovea* but scattered throughout the retina, mediate experiences of both black and white and hue (*chromatic* colors). The rods, in the periphery of the eye, mediate experiences only of black and white (the *achromatic* colors). In night vision the rods are more sensitive than the cones.

b. The distinctive roles of the rods and the cones can be inferred from *dark adaptation,* in which the cones reach their maximum sensitivity in about five minutes, while the rods continue to become more sensitive for about half an hour.

c. The *chromatic colors* can be arranged in the form of a *color circle,* following the order of wave lengths (i.e., the order seen in the rainbow or solar spectrum) but allowing space for the nonspectral purples. When properly spaced, the colors opposite each other are *complementaries.* When complementary colors are mixed as lights (additive mixture), they cancel each other and result in a neutral gray. Although four *psychological primaries* can be identified (red, yellow, green, blue), three *color primaries* are enough to produce the range of hues by additive mixture (red, green, and blue). The chief dimensions of color are *hue, brightness,* and *saturation,* which can be represented on the color solid.

d. *Afterimage* and *contrast effects* further emphasize the pairing of colors, for very often (though not always) the withdrawal of stimulation produces the complementary hue, and the contrast effect is maximum between complementaries.

e. *Color blindness* also calls attention to color pairs as well as to the primacy of certain colors. The most common form, red-green blindness (a form of *dichromatism*), is much more frequently found among men than among women. Total color blindness (*monochromatism*) is rare, while yellow-blue blindness, the alternate form of dichromatism, is rarer still.

f. *Color theories* take these facts as their starting point and attempt to give them physiological explanation. The Young-Helmholtz theory begins with color mixture; the Hering theory starts with afterimages and contrast; the Ladd-Franklin theory stresses evidence from color blindness.

3. Some of the facts and principles arising from study of the *auditory sense* are:

a. The auditory apparatus consists of the *external ear,* leading by way of the auditory canal to the *eardrum,* giving access to the *middle ear.* The bones of the middle ear transmit the sound waves to the *oval window,* leading to the *inner ear.* The *cochlea* houses the receptors of the inner ear, found in the *organ of Corti.* The *basilar membrane* has played a special role in auditory theories. The auditory nerve leads off from the organ of Corti.

b. The chief dimensions of auditory experience are *pitch,* correlated with the *frequency* of vibration of the sound waves that constitute the stimulus, and *loudness,* correlated with the *amplitude* of these waves. The absolute threshold for hearing depends on the frequency of the tone; very low- or very high-pitched tones must be louder to be heard than tones in the middle range of frequencies.

c. Most tones are not pure, that is, composed of only a single frequency. The distinguishing quality of musical instruments, while sounding a tone of a given pitch and loudness, is called *timbre* and depends on the *overtones* and other impurities differing from one instrument to another. Complex sounds composed of many frequencies not in harmonious relation to each other are called *noise.*

d. Theories attempting to give a physiological explanation of pitch fall into two groups: the *place theories,* which emphasize the place on the basilar membrane where a particular frequency produces its effect; and *frequency theories,* which assume that the effect on the basilar membrane corresponds in some direct fashion to the frequency of the stimulus. While the clearest present evidence favors some form of place theory, because of the agreement between various methods of "mapping" the basilar membrane, some compromise between the two types of theory may be necessary in order to explain all the facts of hearing.

4. The other senses, important as they are, do not enter as much into man's symbolic behavior and so are thought of as "lower senses." They include *smell, taste,* the four *skin senses* (touch, pain, warm, cold), *kinesthesis* (muscle, tendon, and joint sense), and the *equilibratory senses.*

SUGGESTIONS FOR FURTHER READING

For a general introduction to the various senses, see Mueller, *Sensory psychology* (1965). A useful reference work, now somewhat outdated, is Stevens, *Handbook of experimental psychology* (1951), with 12 chapters on the sensory mechanisms and sensory processes written by experts.

There are many sources on visual perception, including Graham, and others, *Vision and visual perception* (1965), Gregory, *Eye and brain* (1966), Evans, *An introduction to color* (1948), and Judd, *Color in business, science, and industry* (1952). An authoritative volume on color and color standards is that by the Optical Society of America, *The science of color* (1953). Teevan and Birney's *Color vision* (1961) provides a convenient source of readings.

On audition, there are Békésy, *Experiments in hearing* (1960), by the leading contemporary investigator of the physiological basis of hearing, awarded a Nobel prize in 1961 for his contributions, and Hirsh, *The measurement of hearing* (1952). The history of the several theories of hearing, and a defense of the author's own volley theory, can be found in Wever, *Theory of hearing* (1949).

A survey of mathematical theories in sensory psychology is found in the *Handbook of mathematical psychology,* vol. I (1963) and vol. III (1965), edited by Luce, Bush, and Galanter. See also Swets, *Signal detection and recognition by human observers* (1964), and Green and Swets, *Signal detection theory and psychophysics* (1966).

9 The Perception of Objects and Events

Life goes on in a world of things and other people. Were the individual not sensitive and responsive to his environment, he would be unable to satisfy his needs, communicate with his fellows, or enjoy his surroundings. The individual learns to know his world through the data that come to him by way of his sense organs, but what he perceives depends also on what he brings along with him from his past experiences and what his present needs and wishes are as he faces the world. Thus, as in all the topics of psychology, perception has its developmental as well as its interactive aspects; perception depends upon more than the stimuli now impinging upon sense organs. It involves the selective interpretation of sensory input.

Usually the objects of which we are aware are sources of multiple stimuli and are embedded in surroundings providing additional stimuli. We see signs or pictures instead of spots of light; we hear words or music instead of single pure tones. We react to *patterns* of stimuli, usually with little awareness of the parts composing the pattern. When we put a jigsaw puzzle together, the colors and sizes of figures in the individual pieces often look entirely different from the way they look when embedded in the whole picture. An oil painting, viewed close up, may appear to be a meaningless collection of daubs of paint. The total impression from organized stimuli has properties not predictable from the parts in isolation.

All experiences of objects and events take place within a framework of space and time. Vision and audition provide the most complex patterns of these perceptual experiences. Vision is our preferred spatial sense, giving us variegated patterns of form and color in three dimensions, but it is also a good time sense because we see succession, movement, and change. Audition is a spatial sense also, though its spatial patterns are much more limited than those of vision; it is primarily a time sense, for its primary patterns are those of succession, change, and rhythm. Because of vision's preeminence as a spatial sense, much discussion of perception goes on in terms of vision. Of course many perceptual experiences depend at once on several senses; then the prominence of one sense over another becomes a matter for study.

Object Perception and Perceptual Constancies

If you look around the room and ask yourself what you see, your answer is likely to be, "a room full of people and things." You may pick out specific people or things instead of making such a general statement, but you are not likely to report that you see a mosaic of light and shadow. Perception is oriented toward things rather than toward the sensory qualities that describe things. Detached sensory qualities ("blueness," "redness") can be perceived, but they are usually perceived as the qualities of objects. You see the yellow flowers

217

or the soft pillow or the hot radiator, not "yellowness," "softness," or "hotness."

Object constancy

Our perceptual experiences are not isolated; they build us a world of identifiable things. When you turn your head away, you think of the objects as remaining where you saw them. Objects endure, so that you meet the same object over and over again. When an object has been constituted perceptually as a permanent and stable thing, we perceive it as such, regardless of the illumination on it, the position from which it is viewed, or the distance at which it appears. The tendency to see it as of normal color regardless of light and shadow is called *brightness constancy* and *color constancy*. The tendency to see it as of standard shape regardless of the viewing angle is called *shape constancy*. The tendency to see it as of measurable size regardless of distance is called *size constancy*. Finally, the fact that objects retain their "same" positions, even as we move about,

is known as *location constancy*. The word "constancy" is an exaggeration, but it dramatizes our relatively stable perception of objects.

Brightness and color constancy

Black velvet looks just as black to us in bright sunlight as in shadow. We refer to this fact as *brightness constancy*. Although this effect holds under ordinary circumstances, a change in the structure of the surroundings can destroy it. Attach the black velvet to a board and throw a bright light on both it and the board. It still looks black. Now place an opaque screen between you and the velvet, with a small opening in the screen, so that you can see only a small patch of the velvet (Figure 9–1). Such a screen is called a *reduction screen,* for it reduces what you see to the actual light reflected from a surface, independent of the setting. Now the velvet looks *white* because the light coming through the reduction screen is brighter than the screen itself. In natural settings we some-

9–1

Effects of surroundings on brightness constancy

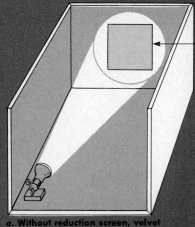

a. Without reduction screen, velvet looks black

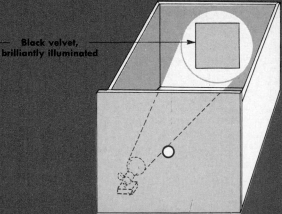

Black velvet, brilliantly illuminated

b. With reduction screen, so only velvet is visible, velvet looks white

Even though the square of velvet is brilliantly illuminated, it still looks black, provided the illuminated background is also visible. However, when only the velvet is visible through the reduction screen, it looks white, even though the illumination on it is the same.

how take into account the total illumination and are thereby able to maintain constancy.

Similar considerations apply for color constancy. Colored objects may be perceived as retaining their original colors not only when the intensity of light changes but even when illuminated by colored light, provided there are sufficient contrasts and shadows (Wallach and Galloway, 1946).

Shape constancy

When a door swings open toward us, its rectangular shape goes through a series of distortions. It becomes a trapezoid, with the edge toward us looking wider than the hinged edge; then the trapezoid grows thinner, until all we can see is a vertical line the thickness of the door. We can readily distinguish these changes, but what we *perceive* is an unchanging door swinging on its hinges. The fact that the door does not seem to change its shape is called *shape constancy*. We see the top of a milk bottle as round whether we view it from the side or from the top.

The distortions that occur when a familiar object rotates are used by us as cues to its rotation rather than as indications that the object is changing. This principle is well illustrated by some demonstrations with a rotating trapezoidal window, as pictured in Figure 9–2. No matter what the position of the window, our experiences with shape constancy suggest that edge *a* is nearer than edge *b*. Hence as the window rotates in space, to the observer it appears to vacillate back and forth, with edge *a* always in front. Because we continue to see the window as a familiar rectangle, we are led into illusory perception.

Size constancy

When we see an object at a distance, we might conceivably judge its size in one of three ways:

1. *Perspective size.* We might judge it according to the geometry of perspective, seeing it as smaller the farther away it is, the size inversely proportional to distance. This size would correspond to the size of the image on the retina. The retinal projection of an object at 20 feet is half the retinal projection at 10 feet.
2. *Object size.* If object constancy were perfect, we might judge an object by its known (measurable) size and hence not see it any smaller at a distance.
3. *Compromise between perspective size and object size.* We might compromise and see the object somewhat smaller at a distance, but not as much smaller as the geometry of perspective indicates.

Of the three alternatives described, the last one is usually correct. Our size perceptions represent compromises between perspective size and object size. Experiments can tell us more exactly the nature of these compromises.

Although we distort perspective, we do of course see things as smaller the farther they are from us. As we look through a row of arches, each fits inside the preceding one. The farthest arch may look about half the size of the nearest one, even though it is 10 times the distance away and ought to look only one-tenth as large. It certainly looks smaller, but, if asked whether it *is* a smaller arch, we may unhesitatingly say, "All the arches look the same size." The distant arches look both *smaller than* and *equal to* the near ones! (See Figure 9–3.) When we speak of *size constancy*, we refer to the ability to see the far object as equal in size to a near object of the same size.

The development of size constancy depends on experience. A child of three years, watching cars on a roadway below a lookout point, will see the cars as miniatures and often insist that they cannot be full-size. He may even beg for them as toys. His size constancy is not yet developed for this new viewing angle. Adult size constancy commonly breaks down also when objects are viewed from a height, but the adult makes an intellectual correction that the young child does not make.

The effect of limited experience on the development of size constancy is further

Illusion created by rotating trapezoidal window

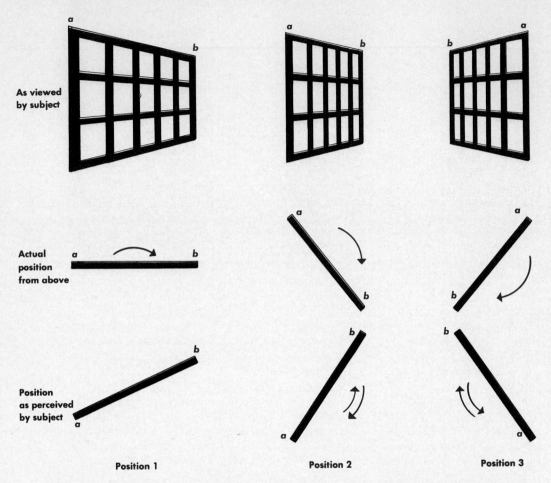

As viewed by subject

Actual position from above

Position as perceived by subject

Position 1   Position 2   Position 3

The window is so constructed that in Position 1 it looks like a rectangular window with the left edge closer to the subject. Actually the left edge (a) and the right edge (b) are equally distant from the observer. As the window rotates clockwise (as viewed from above), the left edge remains larger to the subject than the right edge; hence it still seems nearer, even though it is moving away (Position 2). Even when the window rotates completely—goes through what would be twelve o'clock on a clock and begins to come closer again (Position 3)—a is still seen as closer than b. The viewer then tends to see the window as waving back and forth rather than as going around. (After Ames, 1951)

illustrated by an incident concerning a pygmy who was taken for the first time from his home in the forest into open country. When he spotted a herd of buffalo grazing several miles away the pygmy asked what kind of "insects" they were. He refused to accept the fact that they were buffalo, actually larger in size than the forest buffalo with which he was familiar. As the car in which he was traveling ap-proached the animals the pygmy became alarmed because the animals appeared to be growing in size; he suspected that he was the victim of some sort of magic. Later he perceived a boat with several men in it sailing some distance from the shore of a lake as a scrap of wood floating on the water. Just as the small child's limited experience with viewing objects from a great height causes him to err in his perceptions,

Stanford University

Here there is no difficulty in perceiving that the arches on the right receding in perspective are all of the same size, and that they are the same as the three arches in the background. The conditions are thus good for size constancy. Now measure on this page the reproduced height (perspective size) of the nearest arch and compare it with the reproduced height of the distant arches. You will find that the near arch is more than four times as high (in perspective size) as the distant arch.

the pygmy's inexperience with distance viewing on a horizontal plane created similar misperceptions (Turnbull, 1961).

We are now ready to consider more carefully the nature of the compromise between perspective size and object size that we make in actual perception. It is safe to say that as more information is available, the more the perceived size approaches the actual size; to the extent that information is lacking or ambiguous, the more closely perceived size approaches perspective size.

The effect of reducing the number of environmental supports for maintaining size constancy is well demonstrated in Figure 9–4. When we look with both eyes, there is overconstancy; that is, we see the distant object as being somewhat larger than object size. When we use only one eye, there is nearly perfect size constancy, a relation holding also for observers who have only one eye. When the surroundings are cut off, first with an artificial pupil (a

9–4

Size perception as influenced by conditions of viewing

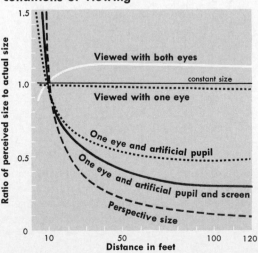

The objects judged for size were circular cardboard disks viewed in dimly illuminated hallways. (After Holway and Boring, 1941)

reduction screen worn near the eye, with a small hole corresponding to the pupil of the eye but of fixed size) and then with an additional screen, the compromise falters and the reported size approaches more nearly perspective size. The compromise between object size and perspective size thus depends upon the environmental surroundings in which the judgment is made.

Location constancy

Our world has perceptual stability for us because we perceive objects as enduring, as being the same as when we last looked. We also perceive these objects in a setting that remains essentially fixed, despite the fact that we see a kaleidoscopic world which sends us a myriad of changing impressions as we move about in it. We take the general background of perception so for granted that we have difficulty in realizing that there are psychological problems in it.

But why doesn't the world whirl by us in the opposite direction when we move our heads? Why don't we get the same kind of blurred movement that occurs in motion pictures taken by the beginner who moves the camera as he ordinarily moves his head? One reason is the way our eyes move as we look about. They *jump* from one resting spot to another, and we do not perceive whatever registers while they are in motion. When the eyes drift, as they do when we are dizzy from spinning, the world does appear to whirl in front of us. But constancy is not simply a result of the way our eyes operate; it is also learned.

The role of learning in location constancy has been demonstrated by some interesting experiments that rearrange the visual environment by the use of special glasses. In a classic study conducted 70 years ago, Stratton fitted himself with lenses that not only inverted the visual field so that he saw the world upside-down, but also reversed it so that objects perceived on the left were actually on the right and vice versa. Stratton reports that at first the world seemed to lose its stability: "When I moved my head or body so that my sight swept over the scene, the movement was not felt to be

solely in the observer, as in normal vision, but was referred both to the observer and to objects beyond. . . . I did not feel as if I were visually ranging over a set of motionless objects, but the whole field of things swept and swung before my eyes." [1] After a few days this swinging or swirling sensation decreased, indicating some regaining of location constancy. Another sign of regained location constancy was that a fire was again heard to crackle in the fireplace where it was seen, a harmony of location that was at first lost because only the eyes, and not the ears, were perceiving in reverse. Although the distortion provided by the lenses made even the simplest task extremely difficult and laborious, Stratton found that as the experiment progressed he became progressively more skillful in dealing with his mixed-up perceptual world. He bumped into objects less frequently and was able to perform such tasks as washing himself and eating, which had initially been very difficult. When the glasses were removed some adjustment was required before the old visual-motor habits were regained.

Experiments similar to Stratton's have been repeated with comparable results (Snyder and Pronko, 1952; Kohler, 1962). Human subjects have shown a remarkable ability to adjust to a visually rearranged world. Animal subjects, however, exhibit less adaptability. Monkeys who were fitted with lenses that produced inversion and reversal of the visual field adapted much more slowly and less efficiently than human subjects (Foley, 1940). Newly hatched chickens fitted with lenses that displaced vision so that objects appeared slightly to the right of where they actually were made no adjustment in learning how to peck at grain particles and would have died of starvation had the experiment continued (Hess, 1956). Human subjects equipped with this type of lens (even with a much greater angle of displacement) are able to achieve accurate localization with a few days' practice. Displaced-vision studies with lower vertebrates suggest that, as is

[1] Stratton (1897), p. 342.

true with other aspects of behavior, learning plays a more important role in visual-motor control as we ascend the phylogenetic scale.

A newer technique for studying displaced vision, and one that has fewer disturbing side effects (such as nausea) for the subject, involves the use of closed-circuit television. The subject performs tasks such as handwriting, tracing geometrical figures or mazes, tracking a moving target, or assembling an object and views his performance not directly but by means of a television screen. The television camera can be adjusted so that the subject's view of his movements is inverted, reversed, or rotated to any desired angle. The apparent size of the television image can be increased or decreased and delayed feedback can be introduced by means of video tape. These techniques permit more variety of the visual image as well as greater control than the use of glasses with special lenses. For example, in one experiment it was possible to compare the effects of inversion, reversal, and a combination of both on a series of manual tasks. The results showed that inversion of the visual image definitely produced more difficulty in performance than reversal and usually more than combined inversion and reversal (Smith and Smith, 1962).

CRITICAL DISCUSSION
Sensorimotor feedback in perception

Recent experiments have indicated that the ability to adjust to visual rearrangement depends to a large extent on feedback from the muscles and motor parts of the nervous system (Held, 1965). If a subject wearing distorting lenses is allowed to move freely, he gradually makes adjustment for the distortion. Another subject wearing the same lenses whose movements are passive (for example, he is pushed in a wheelchair instead of walking) achieves virtually no adaptation. Both subjects encounter the same visual stimuli but one is able to correlate his movements with the sensory information from his eyes while the other is not.

Held offers experimental evidence to support the proposition that the development of normal space and pattern perception in the young organism also requires active movement on the part of the perceiver. Kittens were reared in the dark with their mother and litter-mates; their only exposure to visual stimulation occurred when they were placed in the apparatus shown in Figure 9–5 for three hours each day. One kitten could move more or less normally; his gross movements were transmitted by a system of gears and pulleys to a second kitten who was transported in a gondola. Both kittens received essentially the same visual stimulation because the pattern on the walls and the center post of the apparatus was unvarying. Eight pairs of kittens were raised in this manner. After an average of 30 hours in the apparatus the active member of each pair showed normal behavior in a series of visual tests: it blinked at an approaching object, put up its paws to avoid collision when carried toward a surface, and avoided the deep side of a visual cliff (see Figure 9–21). The passive kittens, on the other hand, failed to show this type of behavior; they did develop appropriate behavior, however, after being allowed to run freely for several days.

In an extension of this study a blindfold was placed over one eye of each kitten during his daily exposure, and the blindfolds and training conditions were shifted so that each kitten had an "active" and a "passive" eye. That is, one eye viewed the scene while each kitten was actively moving about; the other eye viewed the same scene while he was being passively conveyed in the gondola. In subsequent visual tests the active eye responded normally while the passive eye showed the same lack of appropriate response displayed by the passive kittens in the earlier experiment. The sensory feedback accompanying active movement appears to play a vital role in the development of visual-motor control in the young, as well as in the adjustment to changes in the visual environment as an adult.

While movement doubtless helps to correlate vision and position sense, recent experimentation has shown vision to be remarkably stable, with position sense often proving to be the more flexible (Harris, 1965).

Apparatus for determining effect of active vs. passive movements on spatial orientation

Photo by Ted Polumbaum; courtesy of *Life*

The gross movements of the "active" kitten, who moves about more or less freely, are transmitted by means of the chain and bar to the "passive" kitten who is conveyed in a gondola. Both kittens are reared in the dark, except for their daily experience in the apparatus, and are subsequently tested for visual-motor coordination.

Organization in Perception

The perceptual constancies imply *organization* within perception. We are now ready to be somewhat more analytical and to see if we can find principles of perception that help us to explain the perception of objects.

Figure and ground

Geometrical patterns are always seen against a background and thus appear object-like, with contours and boundaries. We may think of such *figure-ground* organization as basic to stimulus patterning. Patterns do not have to contain identifiable objects to be structured as figure and ground. Patterns of black and white and many wallpaper designs are perceived as figure-ground relationships, and very often

figure and ground are reversible (Figure 9–6). Note that the part seen as *figure* tends to appear as slightly in front of the background, even though you know it is printed on the surface of the page. You seem to look *through* the spaces in and around the figure to a uniform background behind, whether the background is in white (or a light color) or black (or a dark color).

As we shall note in the next section, studies of what people see when they suddenly recover from blindness show that the figure-ground organization is found when other features of perception are missing (Senden, 1932; Hebb, 1949). Adults seeing for the first time have no difficulty in seeing *a something* as a figure on a background, although they are unable to identify familiar forms by sight.

9-6

Reversible figure and ground

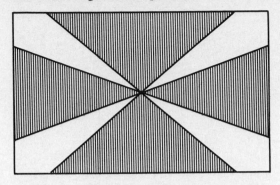

Note that either the light portions or the dark portions can be perceived as figures against a background.

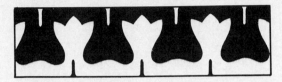

Perceptual grouping and patterning

Even simple patterns of lines and dots fall into ordered relationships when we look at them. In the top part of Figure 9–7 we tend to see three *pairs* of lines, with an

9-7

Patterning and perceptual structuring

The proximity of the lines that appear to be in pairs leads us to see three pairs and an extra line at the right.

The same lines as above, but with extensions, lead to the opposite pairing: three broken squares and an extra line at the left.

extra line at the right. But notice that we could have seen three pairs beginning at the right and an extra line at the left. The slight modification shown in the lower part of the figure causes us to do just that. These tendencies to *structure* what we see are very compelling; what we see in figures seems to be forced upon us by the patterns of stimulation (Wertheimer, 1923).

Under some circumstances the tendency toward a stable organization may *destroy* one figure perceptually in order to favor a more stable one. The principle is capitalized on in *camouflage,* which seeks to hide something by incorporating it into a dominant pattern that destroys the original contours. In Figure 9–8 we see the concealing of originally stable figures by a superimposed organization.

9-8

How organization conceals parts

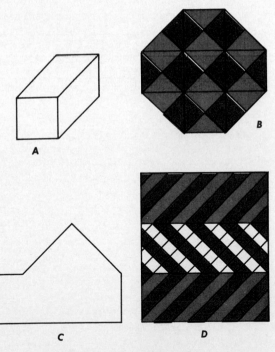

A stable organization of superimposed figures may destroy the organization of an original figure. It is difficult to see that A is contained in B and that C is contained in D. (After Witkin, 1959)

Effect of the whole on the parts

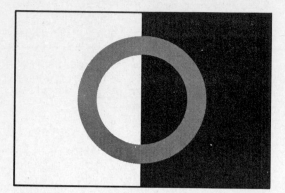

Separating the ring into two parts produces a contrast effect (see text). (After Osgood, 1953)

The properties of wholes affect the ways in which parts are perceived. For that reason we may say that the whole is different from the sum of its parts—a favorite slogan of Gestalt psychology.

The gray circle of Figure 9–9 is a stable whole, and hence tends to be seen as a uniform gray. If, however, there had been two circles cut from the same gray, one mounted on black and one on white, they would have appeared very different as a result of contrast with the two backgrounds. The contrast effect can be restored by dividing the gray circle into halves. Placing a pencil across the circle between the black and white areas will do. The left half-circle suddenly looks distinctly darker than the right half. Move the pencil slowly to the right or to the left, and the darker (or lighter) portions of the gray circle will seem to follow it, retaining uniformity within each segment. Thus we see that wholeness characteristics affect the perception of the parts.

Effect of experience on figure-ground perception

Although the features of stimulus organization are clearly important in determining what we see, perception is also influenced by previous experience. This can be shown to be true even for the organization of patterns into figure and ground.

Ambiguous figure-ground effects

A

The wife and mother-in-law ambiguity.

Figure 9–10A can be perceived either as an attractive young woman ("the wife") or as an old hag (facetiously referred to as the "mother-in-law"). An experiment was performed to compare the ways in which this picture would be seen by three different groups of people: those who had had no prior experience with the picture, those who had first been shown an unambiguous picture of a wife (10B), and those who had first seen an unambiguous picture of a mother-in-law (10C). When shown the ambiguous picture 60 percent of those in the first group saw the wife; 40 percent the mother-in-law. When those in the second group saw the ambiguous picture, 100 per-

9–10 (cont.)

Dr. Robert Leeper

B

C

cent saw the wife. In the third group, 95 percent saw the mother-in-law in the ambiguous picture (Leeper, 1935).

The main point about figure-ground relationships is that a figure is perceived as "thinglike." In our ordinary commerce with objects, we perceive things against their backgrounds, and these things maintain their identity as they move on the background.

Problems created by visual illusions

For the most part our perceptions serve us very well. Most of the time seeing is believing. Many problems are raised by the fact that perception is so satisfactory (the constancy tendencies, for example), but it is easy to take the accuracy of perception for granted. Hence in the study of perception psychologists have turned to illusions, in which perceptions are obviously misleading, in order to find out how perception works.

Geometrical illusions have been studied for many years, but their explanations have never been fully agreed upon. Sometimes the illusion is due to some feature of *embeddedness*, so that the part being judged is improperly isolated. The familiar arrow-head illusion and its variations (Figure 9–11) illustrate the difficulty of isolating the lines to be judged from the areas in which the ends are embedded. Other illusions are based on *relative size* due to contrast with surroundings (Figure 9–12). The many illusions depending upon *angles* usually can be explained if we suppose the figures to be projected in the third dimension (Figure 9–13). If the lines in figures A and B were drawn as they are on the surface of a solid double cone, or on a system of wires meeting at the horizon, they would have to be curved in order to be parallel as viewed. The lines in figure C are as though drawn on a set of steps moving off in the distance. If that is what they were, the long lines (drawn parallel) would *not* be parallel in the frontal plane of the stairs. We tend to view these figures as though they were perspective drawings, and the tendency to "constancy" previously discussed is now misleading. Occasionally two factors act together, as in Figure 9–14. Here the line that looks longer appears to be the diagonal of a larger rectangle. This is the influence of embeddedness. But if you think of the picture in perspective, the line would also have to be longer to look as it does.

The fact that there are cross-cultural differences in susceptibility to some of these illusions suggests that their perception may be related to experience with a particular visual environment. Europeans and Americans are more susceptible to the arrow and parallelogram illusions (Figures 9–11 and 9–14) than are rural Africans. This difference may be attributed, in part, to the prevalence of rectangularity in the environ-

9–11

Illusions based on embeddedness of lines

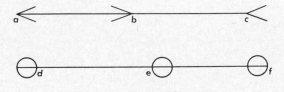

Distances *ab, bc, de,* and *ef* are all equal.

9–12

Illusions based on size contrasts

The two figures in A are identical. The center circles of B are the same size.

A

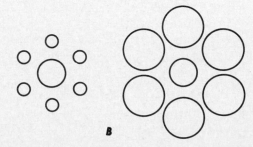

B

Illusions based on intersecting lines

The horizontal lines in A and B are parallel. The long diagonal lines in C are parallel. The spirals of D are actually concentric circles.

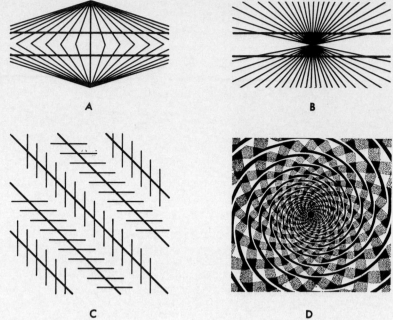

A

B

C

D

ment of the former groups (carpentered buildings and fences as opposed to round huts and enclosures), a factor which seems related to the tendency to interpret acute or obtuse angles on a two-dimensional surface as though they were actually three-dimensional. On the other hand, certain African tribes are more susceptible to the horizontal-vertical illusion (the fact that a vertical line drawn at right angles to a horizontal line of the same length appears longer ⊥) than are urban Americans. This finding is not easily explained but may be related to living in a flat open terrain as opposed to a city (Segall, Campbell, and Herskovitz, 1963).

Movement perception

Events are organized in time as well as in space; the pattern of a melody is an organization in time, just as a geometrical figure is an organization in space. When we perceive movement, we sense action in space taking place in time. We usually explain the perception of real movement according to the stimulation of successive

9–14

Illusions based on falsely implied perspective

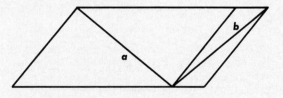

If the figure is seen as a perspective drawing of a rectangle, the diagonal a would have to be longer than b. Check the actual length.

parts of the sensory surface. Trace a path on the skin and you feel movement as successive local signs come into play. Perhaps a similar stimulation takes place on the retina. While these suggestions are a little glib, they are probably in the direction of a true explanation.

Illusions of movement are harder to explain. Some of them depend upon relative motion, as when the train on the next track moves and you believe your own train to

Device for studying the aftereffects of perceived movement

be in motion because you see through the window what you would see if you were moving. If you keep looking at the passing track when your train runs along, and then look at the track when your train stops, the track will seem to be moving in the opposite direction. A laboratory device for producing such aftereffects of movement is pictured in Figure 9–15. If the spiral is rotated so that it appears to be contracting, whatever you look at after watching it for a while appears to be expanding. While this effect has been known for a great many years, we have no fully satisfactory explanation of it.

Another kind of illusion of motion has been much more thoroughly studied, so that we know its conditions even though its explanation also eludes us. This is *stroboscopic motion,* the illusion of movement created when separated stimuli, not in motion, are presented in succession. Stroboscopic motion is the basis of the motion picture. Pictures blend into smooth motion, with little or no flicker, if the frames occur rapidly enough. Alternating light and dark stimuli give rise to flicker until the rate gets high enough for fusion to take place; the point at which flicker changes to fusion (called the *critical flicker frequency*) varies with light intensity, but for ordinary motion pictures lies at about 15–20 frames per second.

In an attempt to get at the basic condi-

tions for seeing motion, experimenters have devised apparatus such as that of Figure 9–16. Four lights at the ends of the cross-bars can be turned on in any order. When one light blinks on and then off, followed shortly by another, there is the illusion of a single light moving from the position of the first to the position of the second. This simple illustration of stroboscopic motion is called the *phi phenomenon,* and its conditions have been much studied. When the four lights of Figure 9–16 flash on and off in proper sequence, you see a rotating circle, but the diameter of the circle is *less* than that of a circle that would actually pass through the four lights. Whatever "attracts" the light to the position of the next light operates also to "attract" it to cut across the diameter of the circle toward the opposite light, thereby making the circle smaller. The two tendencies (to form a circle and to cut across the circle) result in the compromise that is seen as a circle too small to pass through the actual position of the lights.

Even though the phi phenomenon is illusory, it tends to preserve the perceptual structure that would be possible in real motion. For example, in Figure 9–17A the perceived motion is through an arc but in the plane of the paper, while in Figure 9–17B the motion is seen in the third dimension, the figure turning over as it moves across.

Depth perception

We cannot conclude our study of the organization of perception without considering the problems of perceiving the third dimension, that is, distance and depth. The retina is essentially a two-dimensional surface. How, then, is it possible for us to perceive things as filling a space of three dimensions?

Stereoscopic vision. Many of the facts of vision can be treated by considering phenomena that can be registered with only one eye. A man with one eye can have most of the visual experiences of a man with two eyes. He sees colors, forms, and space relationships, including third-dimen-

Adjustable distance

Adjustable distance

Adjustable turntable makes and breaks current to lights

Adjustable aperture

Adjustable motor

sional configurations. We might suppose that two eyes have evolved merely to give man a "spare" in case of injury, just as he has two kidneys although one is enough.

A man with two eyes does have two visual advantages over a man with one eye: his total visual field is larger, so that he can see more at once, and he has the benefit of stereoscopic vision. In *stereoscopic vision* the two eyes cooperate to yield the experience of solidity and distance. That the experience does indeed depend upon the cooperation of the two eyes is clear enough from the effects that can be produced with a *stereoscope*. In this device two flat pictures, presented one before each eye, combine to yield an experience of depth very different from that received from a single flat picture. The depth appears real, as though the objects pictured were actually set up on a stage or in their true relations of depth and distance.

The difference between the stereoscopic experience and the experience of the third

9–17

Special cases of phi movement

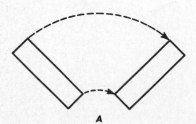

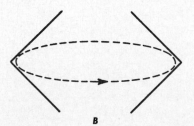

A

B

When the bars of A are lighted in succession, motion is seen through an arc, but two dimensional as in the plane of the paper. When the halves of B are lighted in succession, motion is seen in the third dimension, the figure turning over as it moves across.

dimension in flat pictures is by now rather familiar because of the prevalence of stereoscopic cameras for amateur use. The stereoscopic effect depends on presenting a slightly different picture to the right eye from that presented to the left, thereby duplicating what normally happens when we view objects. Because our eyes are separated in our heads, the left eye does not get exactly the same view as the right eye. You can easily demonstrate the fact of *retinal disparity* [2] for yourself. With one eye closed hold a pencil about a foot in front of you and line it up with some vertical edge on the opposite wall. Open that eye and close the other. The pencil will appear to have moved a considerable distance from its original alignment. If you line up the pencil with both eyes open and then close each eye alternately, you can determine which is your dominant eye; that is, if the pencil shifts when you close the right eye, your right eye is dominant (which is usually the case with right-handed individuals).

The facts of stereoscopic vision are clear enough, but just how the process works is not so clear. Because of the way in which the nerve fibers from the eyes are separated in passing to the brain (see Figure 8–3, p. 194), the combination cannot take place in the eyes. The images from the two eyes must somehow be combined in the brain, probably at the level of the visual cortex. It seems reasonable to suppose that the tendency to use our two eyes for stereoscopic vision is inherited. We lack direct evidence, though some studies of the chick indicate strongly that for the chick, at least, stereoscopic vision does not have to be learned (Hess, 1956).

Stereophonic hearing. A single good ear, like a single good eye, can provide nearly all possible hearing experiences. Having both ears helps, however, because (1) we hear better with two ears than with one, and (2) there is a stereophonic effect in hearing which corresponds in a way to the stereoscopic effect in seeing.

[2] Sometimes referred to as *binocular disparity.*

By the *stereophonic effect* we mean the location of sound sources by the use of two ears, much as position is determined visually by the two eyes. How such "auditory perspective" is obtained in stereophonic phonographs or "hi-fi" systems is diagramed in Figure 9–18.

What is the basis of this ability to locate the direction of sounds by the use of the two ears? By testing a blindfolded person, you can easily show the importance of the position of the ears. Using an ordinary "snapper" such as children play with, you can show that your blindfolded subject has no trouble locating sounds at ear level if they are to the right or to the left. If, however, you present the sound in a plane dividing the body vertically, equidistant from the two ears (e.g., just over his head), he is helpless in locating the direction of the source. More careful experimentation shows that the differences in stimulation primarily responsible for locating the direction of sounds are (1) *intensity* differences (louder in the nearer ear), and (2) *time* differences (reaching the nearer ear first). In these experiments the subject with his head in a fixed position wears a pair of headphones, so that we know what comes to each ear. If tones alike except for loudness are sent to the two ears, we can move the localization from right to left merely by changing the relative loudnesses. If we send two clicks very close together, one to the right ear and one to the left, the clicks will be heard as one (if they are given at very short intervals, below 0.0025 seconds), but the single click will be heard as coming from the side receiving the first click. These two experiments illustrate intensity and time differences in localization.

The localization on the basis of time differences turns out to be remarkably accurate; an interval between clicks of 0.00003 to 0.0003 seconds (for different subjects) is all that is needed to permit localization of the apparent single sound on one side or the other (Woodworth and Schlosberg, 1954, p. 355). When the interval is extremely short, the sound is placed just slightly off center, but when the differences reach about 0.001 seconds, the single sound

Producing stereophonic sound effects

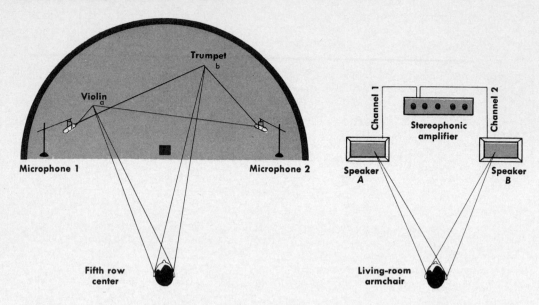

The listener in the concert hall will perceive a violin solo (a) as coming from the left side of the stage, a passage on the trumpet (b) coming from the right. Microphone 1 will pick up more from the violin than it will from the trumpet; for microphone 2 the reverse will be true. If the recordings from the two microphones are channeled via the stereo amplifier to speakers A and B, the armchair listener will hear the violin from speaker A, the trumpet from B.

that is heard is localized well to one side or the other.

We may ask, as we did for stereoscopic vision, where this interaction takes place. It cannot take place in the ears, for it depends on their separate stimulation. Hence it must take place at some common point in the nervous system reached by the impulses from the two ears, probably in the auditory cortex.

One experimenter has shown, for example, that there is more electrical activity in a cat's *left* auditory cortex when time differences would favor placing the sound on the *right* and more activity in the *right* cortex when time differences would favor placing the sound on the *left*. These are the results we would expect if analysis of stereophonic effects does occur at the cortical level (Rosenzweig, 1954).

Monocular cues to distance. Although having two eyes and two ears helps us to perceive depth and distance, we are by no

means limited to these binocular and binaural effects. If you close one eye the world does not suddenly collapse, and if you close one ear the origins of sounds do not become completely ambiguous. Some precision is lost, but there is much left to go on.

An artist is able to give depth to his picture because he can make use of the many *monocular cues* that tell us the distance of objects. Except for those cues that depend upon movement, the artist can use all the following cues:

1. *Superposition of objects.* If one object appears to cut off the view of another, the presumption is strong that the first object is nearer (Figure 9–19A).

2. *Perspective.* When you look down a railroad track, the rails appear to converge in the distance. Most of us have been taught how to prepare perspective drawings making use of the fact that parallel lines apparently come together at the horizon. This

geometry of perspective, or *linear perspective*, is one of the familiar signs of distance. The facts of perspective are carried in many subtle ways, however, not all immediately evident. *Decreasing size* with distance is, of course, related to the geometry of perspective, so that the telegraph poles alongside the railroad track appear to grow smaller in the distance, just as the track becomes narrower. Even a series of scattered circles of different sizes are viewed as spheres of common size at varying distances (Figure 9–19*B*). Another hint of perspective is *height in the horizontal plane*. As we look along a flat plane, objects farther away appear to be higher, so that we can create the impression of depth for objects of the same size by placing them at different heights (Figure 9–19*C*). (If the plane is above us, e.g., a ceiling, something higher in the field of vision appears closer.) Even for irregular surfaces, such as the waving surface of the ocean or a rocky desert, there is a *gradient of texture* with distance, so that the "grain" becomes finer as distance becomes greater. This is also a form of perspective (Figure 9–19*D*). Finally, there is an *aerial perspective* ("the purple of distance") that produces changes in brightness and saturation of distant objects, some changes in hue, and a blurring of detail.

3. *Light and shadow.* Light and shadow help to define the contours of three-dimen-

sional objects. One curious consequence of the prevalence of light sources from above is that convex and concave surfaces are sometimes reversed when a photograph is turned upside-down. It is difficult to believe that Figure 9–20*A* is 9–20*B* upside-down.

4. *Movement.* If you move in one direction, distant objects at the side appear to move with you, while near objects appear to move in the opposite direction. The relative movement provides a basis for judging distance. In attempting to judge distance, a person will often move his head back and forth even though he is unaware of the reason for doing so.

The Role of Learning in Perception

Nativist and empiricist viewpoints

The phenomena of perceptual organization, depth perception, and the various constancies lend themselves to simple and convincing experimental demonstrations, so that by now there is general agreement over what the subject perceives. There are disagreements, however, over how to *explain* what happens. One of the traditional problems of visual perception has been the question of whether our abilities to perceive the spatial aspects of our environment are learned or innate. This is the old nature-

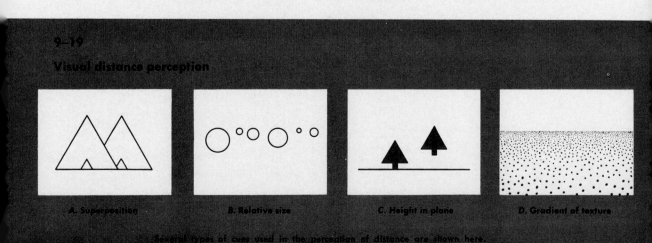

9–19

Visual distance perception

A. Superposition   B. Relative size   C. Height in plane   D. Gradient of texture

Several types of cues used in the perception of distance are shown here.

Effect of light and shadow

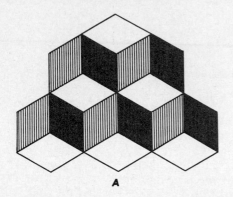

A

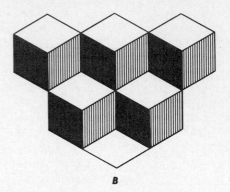

B

Turn the book upside-down. Note the transformation when the pictures are reversed. (After Kahn, 1943)

nurture problem that we have encountered in discussing other areas of behavior. Its origin as related to perception began with the seventeenth-century philosophers. The *nativists* (Descartes, Kant) argued that we are born with the ability to perceive the way we do. The *empiricists* (Berkeley, Locke) maintained that we learn to perceive as we do through experience with objects in the world about us. Among the early sensory psychologists, Hering and Helmholtz (whose theories of color vision we discussed in Chapter 8) held opposing viewpoints. Hering pointed to the fact of retinal disparity as evidence for the view that our eyes are innately designed to perceive depth; he developed a theory of distance vision based on the experience of "double images." Helmholtz argued that visual perceptions were too variable (e.g., the reversible figures, p. 225) to be explained on the basis of fixed receptor mechanisms, and must therefore be learned.

Most contemporary psychologists believe that a fruitful integration of these two traditions is possible. No one today really doubts that practice and experience affect perception. The question is whether we are born with some ability to perceive objects and space in our environment or whether these abilities are completely learned. Let us examine some of the areas of research that shed light on the role of learning in perception.

Restored vision

As far back as the seventeenth century Locke quotes a letter received by him from a Mr. Molineaux in which the problem is posed: "Suppose a man *born* blind, and now adult, and taught by his *touch* to distinguish between a cube and a sphere of the same metal, and nighly of the same bigness, so as to tell, when he felt one and the other, which is the cube, which the sphere. Suppose that the cube and the sphere placed on a table, and the blind man be made to see . . . (could he) now distinguish and tell which is the globe, which the cube?" Locke, supporting the empiricist viewpoint, concluded that he could not.

A partial answer to this question is provided by studies of individuals who were blind from birth with cataracts on both eyes and whose vision was restored by surgical means when they were adult (Senden, 1932). When the bandages are removed for the first time from the eyes of such a patient he is confused by the bewildering array of visual stimuli. He is able, however, to distinguish figure from ground (apparently perceiving figure-ground relationships in much the same way as normally sighted people), to fixate figures, scan them, and follow moving figures with his eyes. These abilities then appear to be innate. He cannot, as Locke correctly surmised, identify objects by vision alone, not even objects very familiar from the sense of touch such as faces, knives, and keys. He cannot distinguish a triangle from a square without counting the number of corners or tracing the outline with a finger. He cannot tell which of two uneven sticks is longer without feeling them, although he may report that the two sticks look somehow different. It often takes several weeks of training for such patients to learn to identify simple objects well from sight, and even after identification has been learned in a specific situation, there is little evidence of generalization or perceptual constancy; a white triangle may not be recognized when it is turned over to its red side, or when viewed under altered illumination, or when turned upside-down. His poor performance under these circumstances cannot be attributed to difficulty in discriminating colors; the restored-vision patient can distinguish between colors (although he does not at first know which name to attach to which color) long before he can distinguish between shapes.

These studies of previously blind adults who are suddenly able to see for the first time suggest that our perceptions develop gradually from primitive visual experiences in which figure-ground relationships and color predominated and become more accurate and more detailed with practice. However, they cannot be taken as conclusive evidence of the innate visual ability of the infant; we do not know what deteriorative changes may have occurred over the years the adult subject was blind, nor do we know what compensating processes this adult may have developed to overcome his handicap.

Visual deprivation with animals

In an attempt to provide a more controlled situation similar to restored vision in human subjects animals have been raised in various degrees of darkness and then tested for visual ability. Riesen (1950, 1961) studied the effects of visual restriction in infant chimpanzees. He found that chimpanzees who had been reared in the

dark until they were 16 months old or who had worn translucent goggles so that they received light stimulation but could not perceive forms showed serious perceptual deficiencies. Although their eyes were sensitive to light, they showed no visual responses to complex patterns of light, did not blink at threatening motions toward their faces, showed no reaction when objects were brought slowly toward their faces until the objects actually touched them, and were not well coordinated in visual motor activities. Another animal who was allowed one and a half hours of normal visual experience per day evidenced no deficiencies. Unfortunately, the animals who were raised totally in the dark were later found to have defective retinas. Apparently a certain amount of light stimulation is necessary for normal anatomical development of the eye. We noted, however, that kittens raised in the dark except for their passive experience in the kitten carousel (see p. 223) did manifest some of the same deficiencies and their retinas were found to be normal.

We can conclude that experience plays a relatively important role in the development of most visual abilities in mammals. The visual development of birds, however, seems to be more innately determined. We noted in the Hess study (p. 222) that chickens who wore prismatic goggles from birth onward never did learn to correct their aim in pecking.

The visual cliff

One of the areas that has been investigated most thoroughly is the perception of height, which is a special case of distance perception. The apparatus shown in Figure 9–21 has been used with human infants and a wide variety of infant animals in an attempt to determine whether the ability to perceive and avoid a brink is innate or must be learned by the experience of falling off and getting hurt. Most parents, mindful of the caution they exerted to keep their offspring from falling out of the crib or down the stairs, would assume that the ability to appreciate height is something the child must learn. However, observations

William Vandivert from *Scientific American*

Infants and young animals show an ability to perceive depth as soon as they can move about. The visual cliff consists of two surfaces, both displaying the same pattern, which are covered by a sheet of thick glass. One surface is directly under the glass; the other is dropped several feet. In the photo the infant when placed on the center board refuses to cross the "deep" side, although he will readily move off the board onto the "shallow" side. (After Gibson and Walk, 1960)

of the human infant's susceptibility to such accidents does not tell us whether he fails to discriminate depth or whether he can indeed respond to depth cues but does not possess the motor control to keep from falling off.

Gibson and Walk (1960) tested some 36 infants ranging in age from six to 14 months by placing them on the center board of the visual cliff. The mother then called to the child from the cliff side and the shallow side successively. Almost all of the infants crawled off on the shallow side and refused to crawl on the deep side. Their dependence on vision was demonstrated by the fact that they frequently peered through the glass on the deep side and then backed away. Some of the infants patted the glass with their hands but still remained unassured that it was solid and refused to cross.

Since the infants could not be tested until they were old enough to crawl, the experiment does not prove that depth perception is present at birth. The results with other organisms, however, indicate that depth perception is present at least as soon as the animal is able to locomote. Chickens tested when less than 24 hours old never made a mistake and stepped off on the deep side. Goats and lambs placed on the center board as soon as they could stand (some only a day old) always chose the shallow side. When placed on the deep side such animals characteristically froze in a state of immobility. Rats, who respond more to smell and to tactile cues from their whiskers than to visual cues, will move off the center board on either side provided they can feel the glass with their whiskers. But if the center board is raised several inches so that the glass is out of reach of their whiskers and they are forced to rely on visual cues, they will consistently descend on the shallow side. Kittens also possess whiskers, but they seem to respond more to visual cues and will invariably choose the shallow side when they are old enough to be tested, at about four weeks of age.

Numerous experiments have been designed to isolate the specific visual depth cues (e.g., retinal disparity, or monocular cues such as relative motion parallax or retinal image size) to which the organism responds in its performance on the visual cliff. The research findings to date have been contradictory, leaving the question unanswered (Eichengreen, Coren, and Nachmias, 1966).

Influences upon Perception

Attention

Our perceptions are selective. We do not react equally to all the stimuli impinging upon us; instead we focus upon a few. This perceptual focusing is called *attention*. Through attentive processes we keep in focus selected stimuli and resist distracting stimuli.

Even as you sit reading this, stop for a moment, close your eyes, and attend to the various stimuli affecting you. Notice, for example, the tightness of the heel of your left shoe, the pressure of clothing on your neck or shoulders, the sounds coming from outside the room. We are constantly bombarded by stimuli to which we do not attend. While reading a book, we may be unaware of the music on the radio and we may not notice the ticking of the clock. As the following experiment shows, even while attending to a given source of stimulation, we may note only certain details.

Cards containing pictures of a number of objects differing in color and in size were exposed briefly in an instrument known as a *tachistoscope* (Figure 9–22). When asked to report what they saw, some subjects reported the number of things, some the colors, some the sizes. When questioned about the other details of the stimuli, they were often relatively helpless. If they were prepared in advance to report one detail or another, their success in reporting the specified detail was greater (Chapman, 1932).

There is competition among stimuli; which specific stimuli will gain our attention depends upon a number of external factors inherent in the stimulus pattern as well as internal factors having to do with motivation and expectancy. The advertiser is concerned with discovering these factors so that he can direct attention to his product. Of two stimulus patterns competing for our attention the advantage generally rests with the one of greatest *size*, strongest *intensity*, most frequent *repetition*, and most *vivid* contour, contrast, or color. The attention-getting qualities of stimuli depend in part upon other stimuli that the observer has lately experienced. It is exciting to come upon a green lawn after riding through the Arizona desert, but who notices a particular lawn in the lush green of a New England village? Yet in any given place and at any given time, the compelling quality of a stimulus pattern may be fairly well predicted. The advertiser counts on this fact. He counts too on internal factors such as needs and interests that will draw our attention to his product. In our culture appeal to the sex drive has proven such a satisfactory attention-getter that pictures of scantily clad females are used to advertise everything from frozen foods to car tires.

Individuals vary greatly in their responses to the same stimuli because of habitual or momentary interests that prepare them for certain kinds of stimuli. The naturalist will hear sounds in the woods that the ordinary picnicker would miss because of his different habits of attention. A mother will hear her baby's cry above the conversation of a living room full of people. These two illustrations represent

Apparatus for producing brief visual exposures

David Linton, courtesy N.Y.U.

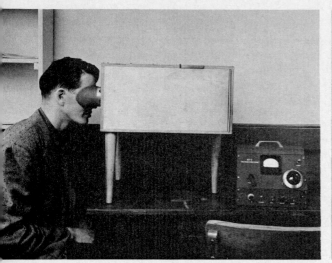
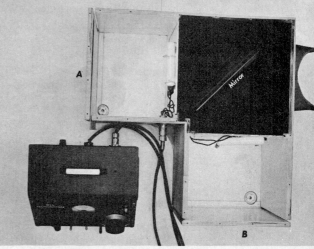

Left: the New York University model of the Dodge mirror tachistoscope in use. *Right:* as seen from above. A mirror tachistoscope operates on the principle that a sheet of smoked glass placed at an angle to the subject's line of vision will act as a mirror if lighted from the front but is transparent if lighted from the rear. When the light is on at A, subject sees the picture presented at the back of the box at A. When the light is on at B, the diagonal smoked glass acts as a mirror and the subject sees the picture presented on the wall of B. A mirror tachistoscope can present a more rapid exposure than a tachistoscope that depends upon a mechanical device, such as a shutter, for exposure.

abiding interests. Sometimes momentary interest controls attention. When you page through a book looking for a map or diagram that you know to be there, what you see depends on what you are looking for. Only pages with illustrations cause you to hesitate; others you ignore. Emotional states, especially moods, may affect the ways in which attention is directed. In a hostile mood, personal comments are noticed that might go unremarked in a more friendly mood.

The neurophysiology of attention

Experiments have provided a possible neurophysiological explanation for our ability to selectively focus attention. In one study electrical activity in the auditory nerve of the cat was measured by means of permanently implanted electrodes. When a click was sounded at regular intervals the recording from the auditory nerve

appeared as illustrated in the upper portion of Figure 9–23. Each click is accompanied by an increase in electrical activity in the auditory nerve. When a glass jar containing mice is introduced, the neural response to the click practically disappears, indicating that when the cat's attention is focused on something else the auditory response is suppressed. Removal of the mice produced a return of the electrical response to the clicks (Hernández-Peón, Scherrer, and Jouvet, 1956). Other attention-getting stimuli, such as fish odors or a shock to the forepaw, produced similar results.

It thus appears that attention involves a screening process such that at any given moment only certain sensory impulses reach the brain while others are filtered out. Recent evidence indicates that the *reticular formation* (a region of the brain stem where impulses from all sense modalities converge, see p. 41) is the control center where much of this screening takes place (Hernández-Peón, 1961). The same process appears to be involved in the organism's adaptation to continuing stimulation. The initial sounding of a tone produces electrical activity in the cat's auditory nerve, but after prolonged exposure to the same tone the neural impulses diminish markedly.

Preparatory set

Some of the selectivity in perception is present before the stimulus appears. We can prepare ourselves to perceive and to act upon stimuli that we expect to appear. Such a preparation goes by the name of *set*, and it has the same meaning here as in the situation of a runner who gets *set* to run at the sound of a gun. His set includes both the readiness to hear the gun and the readiness to leap forward into the race. When a person is set, the actual stimulus that initiates his action, like the sound of the shot for the runner,

is merely an occasion for action that was largely prepared in advance.

Momentary set is an anticipatory adjustment holding certain kinds of responses in readiness. How such a set influences what we perceive may be illustrated by an experiment in which, because of readiness, the subject perceives nonsense words as meaningful. By means of a projection tachistoscope short words were flashed on a screen. Among the words presented were six nonsense words, as listed in Table 9–1. Each word appeared for 0.10 second, followed by a pause long enough for the subject to write down what he thought the word was. The 160 subjects taking part in the experiment were divided into two groups, one of which was told that the words to appear would have to do with animals or birds, the other that they would have to do with travel or transportation.

The group instructed to expect animals or birds gave animal or bird responses to

9–23

Tuning out a stimulus

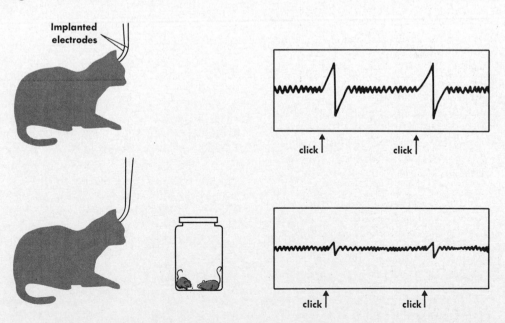

The sound of a click produces a marked increase in electrical activity in auditory nerve of the cat. When a jar of mice is placed in front of the cat the neural response to the click practically disappears, indicating that the auditory response is suppressed or tuned out when attention is directed elsewhere. (After Hernández-Peón, Scherrer, and Jouvet, 1956)

Stimulus as presented	Common interpretation as animal or bird	Common interpretation as travel or transportation
chack	chick	check
sael	seal	sail
wharl	whale	wharf
pasrort	parrot	passport
dack	duck	deck
pengion	penguin	pension

SOURCE: Siipola (1935).

the nonsense words 63 percent of the time, travel or transportation responses only 14 percent of the time. The remaining responses were in other categories. By contrast, the second group gave travel or transportation responses 74 percent of the time and animal or bird responses only 11 percent. Thus the subjects interpreted the ambiguous stimuli according to their preparatory sets (Siipola, 1935).

Perceptual readiness may be created by instructions (as in the foregoing experiment), by immediately prior experience (as in the perceived young woman or her mother-in-law in the picture on p. 226), or by a general tendency to assimilate unclear or novel experience to the familiar. The following experiment illustrates the influence of the familiar upon what we perceive.

Playing cards were exposed briefly in a tachistoscope, and the subject was asked to name the card exposed. Among the cards exposed were some unusual ones, such as a black six of hearts or a red four of spades.

1. On first meeting an incongruous card, the subjects assimilated it into their prior knowledge of playing cards. That is, 27 out of 28 subjects called the red four of spades either a red four of hearts or a black four of spades (ignoring either the incongruous color or the incongruous form).
2. Once the subjects had identified a card as incongruous, their perceptual readiness changed so that they expected incongruous cards. After that, they made fewer false identifications (Bruner and Postman, 1949).

What a person perceives depends in part upon what he is ready for. This is the meaning of preparatory set as it affects perceiving.

Needs and values

What a person perceives may be determined to some extent by his needs and personal values. The value an individual places on an object may affect such direct impressions as those of size. For example, children from poorer homes tend to overestimate the size of coins more than do children from well-to-do homes (Bruner and Goodman, 1947). The following experiment attempted to subject this process to direct laboratory control.

The experiment was performed with nursery school children, a total of 54 in the experimental group and 17 in the control group. The experimental subjects learned to turn a crank in order to receive a poker chip. When the subject inserted the poker chip in a slot, he automatically received a piece of candy. The conjecture was that the candy would enhance the value of the poker chip and that this increased value would result in overestimation of size, as in the coin experiments. The method used for estimating size involved having each child adjust a variable spot of light so that it appeared equal to the poker chip when viewed from a few feet away. Both control and experimental subjects overestimated the size by five or six percent in a pretest, but after 10 days of rewarded learning with poker chips the experimental group increased its overestimation to 13 percent, a statistically significant gain. During the same period the overestimation of the control group had not increased significantly.

As further evidence of the importance of

learning, the values of the experimental group underwent extinction through nonreward. Then the size estimation returned to normal. After reinstatement of the value of the poker chip through reconditioning, the size was again overestimated (Lambert, Solomon, and Watson, 1949).

Extrasensory Perception

If there are so many influences upon perception other than those coming from the presented stimuli, are there perhaps perceptions that require no sense-organ stimulation whatsoever? The answer to this question is the source of a major controversy within contemporary psychology over the status of *extrasensory perception* (ESP). Although some psychologists believe that the evidence for the existence of certain forms of ESP is now incontrovertible (e.g., Murphy, 1949*b*; Rhine and Pratt, 1957; Soal and Bateman, 1954; Thouless, 1950; Forwald, 1961), most remain unconvinced.

The phenomena under discussion are of four main kinds:

1. Extrasensory perception (ESP)
   a. Telepathy, or thought transference from one person to another.
   b. Clairvoyance, or the perception of objects or events not influencing the senses (e.g., stating the number and suit of a card that is in a sealed envelope).
   c. Precognition, or the perception of a future event.
2. Psychokinesis (PK), whereby a mental operation affects a material body or an energy system (e.g., wishing for a number affects what number comes up in the throw of dice).

The experimenters go at their work in accordance with the usual rules of science and generally disavow the connection between this work and spiritualism, supernaturalism, mediumistic phenomena, and other occult effects. Yet the phenomena with which they deal are so extraordinary and so similar to the superstitious beliefs of nonliterate people that many scientists disavow even the legitimacy of their inquiries. Such a priori judgments are out of place in science, however, and the real question is whether or not the empirical evidence is acceptable by ordinary scientific standards. Many psychologists who are not convinced would find it congenial to accept evidence that they found satisfactory. For example, the possibility of some sort of influence from one brain to another, other than by way of the sense organs, would not be inconceivable within the present framework of science were the facts of telepathy to be established in some orderly fashion. Some of the other phenomena are more difficult to find believable (precognition, for example), but if the evidence were firm, previous beliefs would have to yield to the facts.

The case for ESP is based largely on experiments in card-guessing, in which, under various conditions, the subject attempts to guess the symbols on cards randomly arranged in packs. The usual pack consists of 25 cards with five symbols, so that a chance performance would be 5 hits per pack. Even very successful subjects seldom reach as high a level as 7 hits, but they may score above 5 often enough to meet acceptable standards of statistical significance. If the experimenter or "sender" thinks of the symbol at the time the subject makes his record, the experiment is one on telepathy; if the experimenter does not perceive the card at all (it may be face down on the table before him or sealed in an envelope), then the experiment is one on clairvoyance. The kind of evidence used in support of the nonchance nature of the findings can be illustrated by the successive runs of one "sensitive" subject, Mrs. Gloria Stewart, studied in England over a long period (Table 9–2). If the evidence is viewed in the same spirit as that from any other experiment, it would be clear that Mrs. Stewart responded above chance on the telepathy trials but not on the clairvoyance ones. This fact also meets certain objections about card arrangements sometimes used against such experiments, for her chance performance on the clairvoyance trials shows that above-chance scores are not an inevitable result of something having to do with the shuffling of the cards. The telepathy results are above the expected level in 11 of the 13 runs of 200, and the average scoring level of 6.8 hits (instead of 5) per pack of 25 is well above chance.

The complaint has been voiced that ESP results are not subject to systematic variation through ordinary experimental control. This also is not entirely fair to the findings. For example, there are some order effects reported, in which early trials are more successful than later ones (Rhine and Humphrey, 1944; McConnell, Snowdon, and Powell, 1955), and there is re-

ported evidence that an attitude favorable to ESP, noted in advance, leads to positive results, while an unfavorable attitude leads to scoring below chance levels (Schmeidler and McConnell, 1958).

Thus empirical findings are offered in support of ESP and PK, which meet ordinary statistical standards. Why, then, do not the results become a part of established psychological science? Many arguments have been used against the work, but they usually boil down to a few, such as the following: (1) the fact that many claims of extraordinary phenomena in the past have turned out to be false when investigated; (2) certain problems in statistical inference that arise when very large numbers of trials are used to establish the significance of small differences; (3) the failure of improved methods to yield better results than crude methods; (4) general lack of orderliness in the phenomena, without which rational theorizing cannot replace the highly irrational theories now used to account for what occurs.

These arguments are not, in fact, decisive, and it is desirable to keep an open mind about issues that permit empirical demonstration, as the ESP phenomena do. At the same time it should be clear that the reservations of the majority of psychologists are based on more than stubborn prejudice. The following critical discussion is provided for those who might care to look a little further into these issues.

TABLE 9–2

Results of interspersed telepathy and clairvoyance trials with one subject *

Chronological order of successive groups of 200 trials	Hits per 200 trials (Expected = 40)	
	TELEPATHY TRIALS	CLAIRVOYANCE TRIALS
1945	65	51
	58	42
	62	29
	58	47
	60	38
1947	54	35
	55	36
	65	31
1948	39	38
	56	43
1949	49	40
	51	37
	33	42
Total hits	707	509
Expected hits	520	520
Difference	+187	−11
Hits per 25 trials	6.8	4.9

SOURCE: Soal and Bateman (1954), p. 352.

* Each group of 200 trials consisted of alternating blocks of 50 telepathy and 50 clairvoyance trials.

We may expand a little upon the objections that psychologists have to the ESP and PK experiments and to *psi,* the special ability attributed to the "sensitive" subject.

1. *General skepticism about extraordinary phenomena.* Throughout history there have always been reports of strange happenings, of ghosts, little men, poltergeists (noisy spirits who engage in throwing things about), dreams foretelling the fu-

ture. The continuing appearance of these stories does not make them true, any more than reported flying saucers establish the visits of men from Mars. Painstaking investigation by the U.S. Air Force yields no "flying saucers"; nobody ever traps the Loch Ness monster. A famous mediumistic case (still mentioned favorably by Soal and Bateman, 1954, p. xiv) is a case in point. Eusapia Palladino was a medium who was able to make a table move and produce other effects, such as tapping sounds, by the aid of a "spirit" called John King. Investigated repeatedly between 1893 and 1910, she convinced many distinguished scientists of her powers, including the distinguished Italian criminologist Lombroso and the British physicist Sir Oliver Lodge. She was caught in deceptive trickery as early as 1895, and the results were published. Yet believers continued to support her genuineness, as some do today, even though in an American investigation in 1910, her trickery was abundantly exposed (Jastrow, 1935; Rawcliffe, 1959). Two investigators, dressed in black, crawled under the table unobserved and were able to see exactly how she used her foot to create the "supernatural" phenomena. When, therefore, those most convinced about ESP are also convinced about already disproven phenomena, their testimony carries less weight than if they were more critical.

2. *Problems of statistical inference with large numbers and small effects.* One of the major contributions of ESP research to scientific psychology may turn out to be the attention it has drawn to the circumstances that make a scientific finding believable. It is commonly supposed that tests of statistical significance are sufficient guarantees of objectivity, and hence a satisfactory statistical outcome should lead to acceptance of a hypothesis as plausible. This turns out not to be the case in ESP experiments, and it is probably not the case in other experiments either. Statistical tests merely tell us how well measurement seems to establish something that is already plausible; if it is not plausible, we search for some contaminating factor that has produced the nonchance result. For example, in a major attempt to produce random digits by an electronic roulette wheel (The RAND Corporation, 1955), it proved very difficult to eliminate bias; in fact, a sample of 125,000 digits

tested after the machine had been running a month departed from a random distribution by an amount that was statistically significant. One does not argue that some devilish scientist was using PK to foul the machine; one assumes that the machine somehow ran down with continuous use.

Let us compare this example with an experiment performed in Rhine's Duke University laboratory (Rhine, 1942). He was trying to detect whether or not a subject might, through some combination of ESP and PK, influence the positions of cards in a mechanical shuffler. In all, 51 persons wrote down their predictions of the orders in which cards would come out of a mechanical shuffler two to 10 days later, the order of cards emerging from the shuffler being further complicated by having the cards cut by hand at a random trial. The experiment was carefully performed, and in a total of 57,550 trials the results were at chance level—just 11 hits in excess of expectation. But was this plausible result accepted? No—further statistical analyses were made. Two more of these, based on the division of the trials into segments, failed to yield nonchance results. Finally, a fourth analysis, based on a complex effect called a "covariance of salience ratio," gave a nonchance effect, with odds of 625 to 1 in its favor. When belief in bizarre effects is carried this far, it is no wonder that the unconvinced begins to suspect the statistics, even though the rules are followed and all computations are accurate.

There is a scientific problem here. A phenomenon may be rare and still important; hence large numbers of subjects or experiments may be needed if its existence is to be established. But the "good" or "sensitive" ESP subjects are rare. Those few that are found tend to reach a level of about 7 of 25 hits, instead of the 5 expected; such an ability is not very significant from a social point of view, no matter how established it may be statistically. The possibility of some undetected bias, as was found in the electronic roulette wheel, is real enough to temper belief.

3. *Failure of improved methods to increase the yield.* In most scientific fields, the assay from the ore becomes richer as the methods become more refined. But the reverse trend is found in ESP experiments; it is almost a truism in research in the field

of telepathy and clairvoyance that the poorer the conditions the better the results. In the early days of the Duke experiments subjects yielding high ESP scores were rather common, one virtuoso averaging, in the course of 650 trials, 10.7 hits in 25 instead of the 5 expected. As the experiments have become better controlled, however, these high-scoring subjects have disappeared. PK studies have showed a similar decrease in significant results with improved experimental control (Girden, 1962).

4. *Lack of systematic consistency in the phenomena.* Sensitive subjects in the Rhine laboratory appear to be equally successful at clairvoyance and telepathy, but the English subjects appear to be good at telepathy and not at clairvoyance. Other peculiarities emerge. In a famous series of experiments in England, one subject gave no evidence of either telepathy or clairvoyance when scored in the usual way against the target card. Instead he was shown to be successful in *precognition telepathy,* that is, in guessing what was *going to be* on the experimenter's mind in the next trial. He was unsuccessful in clairvoyance, no matter how scored (Soal and Bateman, 1954). Why, the sceptic asks, does the direct telepathy fail with this subject in favor of something far more mysterious than the telepathic success of Mrs. Stewart?

Because the psi ability does not follow the ordinary rules, explanations of its operation can be produced with the greatest of freedom. It need not be affected in any ordinary way by space or time, so that success over great distances is accepted as a sign of its extraordinary power rather than something to cause a search for artifacts. Similarly, the precognition experiments are merely evidence that it is as easy to read what is *about* to be on someone else's mind as what is on it now. The PK effects, which require the sorting of cards or the rolling of dice by mental effort ("mind over matter"), are nevertheless said to occur without any transfer of physical energy, thus presumably violating the usual belief in the conservation of energy. But in any experimental work *some* aspects of time and space have to be respected, such as spatial form and order of succession in time. Unless some restraint is shown, one might invent such hypotheses as that the subject was sometimes perceiving the cards in reverse order, sometimes in a place-skipping order, and so on: with such hypotheses no significant test could be applied.

The believer in *psi* is impatient with this kind of criticism. He says that we ask more of him than we do of other experimenters. In fact, we do ask more. To demonstrate something highly implausible requires better evidence than to demonstrate something plausible. The reason is that supporting evidence for the plausible finding comes from many directions, while the implausible one must hang upon the slender thread of nonrandomness until certain systematic relationships are found that tie it firmly to what is known.

SUMMARY   1. We mainly perceive *things,* and we perceive environmental objects as "thinglike," that is, as stable and enduring. The stability of perceived objects depends on various *constancies:* color and brightness constancy, shape constancy, size constancy, and location constancy. In the choice between perspective size and object size, perception usually tends to conform more nearly to object size unless the contextual cues are greatly reduced. When they are, perception comes close to perspective size (i.e., it corresponds to the size suggested by the image on the retina).

2. The basic organization of visual perception appears to be that of *figure and ground,* so that we recognize patterns as figures against a background whether or not the patterns are familiar. Something of the same organization is found in hearing, with groupings in time rather than space.

3. Geometrical visual illusions present problems for interpretation. The results can in part be explained by the failure to isolate clearly lines that are embedded in compelling areas, by *size contrasts* with the surroundings, and by the misleading interpretation of lines intersecting at *angles*. The *phi phenomenon,* an illusion of movement, illustrates *stroboscopic motion,* the principle underlying the motion picture.

4. Visual depth is perceived binocularly with the help of *stereoscopic vision,* the fusion of slightly unlike images of the two eyes. A somewhat comparable effect within audition is *stereophonic hearing,* the localization of sounds depending on the intensity and time relation of sounds reaching the two ears.

5. Visual depth is perceived monocularly with the aid of a number of *cues: superposition* of objects, *perspective* (whether geometric or given through relative size, height in the frontal plane, gradients of texture, or aerial perspective), *light* and *shadow,* and *movement.*

6. Both learning and innate factors contribute to our abilities to perceive aspects of our environment. Perception of figure-ground relationships, color, and depth appear to be largely innate, while perceptions of form are built up through experience.

7. Perception is *selective,* so that we *attend* at once to only part of the influx of sensory stimulation. Factors of advantage, favoring attention to one pattern of stimuli over another, reside partly in the stimuli themselves but also on both the habitual and momentary interests of the individual. *Preparatory set* is one condition for perception.

8. When the objects of perception are ambiguous, the perceiver tends to give them more meaning than the stimulating conditions alone demand. What he perceives may be determined to some extent by his own needs and personal values.

9. *Extrasensory perception* (ESP) in its various forms (telepathy, clairvoyance, precognition) and *psychokinesis* (PK), the influencing of physical events by mental operations, are the sources of controversy in contemporary psychology. There are many reasons for reserving judgment, but an a priori condemnation of the experiments is unjustified. The experiments raise interesting issues about the criteria by which scientific credibility is established.

SUGGESTIONS FOR FURTHER READING   Textbooks covering the kinds of problems dealt with in this chapter: Dember, *The psychology of perception* (1960); Graham and others, *Vision and visual perception* (1965); Hochberg, *Perception* (1964); and Forgus, *Perception* (1966). Allport's *Theories of perception and the concept of structure* (1955) is valuable for its review and critical analysis of the major theories of perception. A collection of original articles, many translated from German sources, can be found in Beardslee and Wertheimer, *Readings in perception* (1958).

An excellent introduction to the psychology of seeing with emphasis on illusions, movement perception, perspective, and related topics is Gregory, *Eye and brain* (1966); this book also discusses some of the perceptual problems man may experience as he moves into outer space and explores alien planets.

The viewpoint that learning is important in perception is well represented in Solley and Murphy, *Development of the perceptual world* (1960), and in Kilpatrick, *Explorations in transactional psychology* (1961).

For a scholarly review and criticism of extrasensory perception experiments, see Hansel, *ESP: a scientific evaluation* (1966).

10 States of Awareness

By studying the perception of the world through our senses—the substance of the preceding two chapters—we have already gained much information on the conditions of awareness. However, some problems remain to be discussed, such as the nature of consciousness (the mind-body problem, for example), the nature of unconscious processes, and considerations arising from the numerous states in which awareness is distorted, clouded, or even expanded (ranging from deep sleep to ecstatic experiences). Experimental psychology in the recent past did not concern itself very much with these states because they were often too difficult to formulate in clear stimulus-response terms. Now, however, with modern electrophysiological and biochemical methods, new scientific approaches have opened, and in cases where these new approaches are not satisfactory we are at least ready to acknowledge that there are interesting problem areas to be explored.

Consciousness as a Problem

At one time psychology was thought to be the study of consciousness, and consciousness was accepted as open to immediate observation. If you drop a brick on your toe you know whether or not it hurts, and you can say where the pain is felt. This requires no knowledge of physiology and no recording device other than the human brain. Similarly, if you look at a bright light and then close your eyes you will see a succession of colored images, and you can describe them as you see them. The question of whether or not there are "facts of consciousness" in this sense can be answered readily enough: of course there are. But at least two other kinds of questions can be asked. First: What is the relationship of this conscious experience of which you are aware, and which you can report, to underlying physiological processes? If we take awareness as evidence of mind and let physiology represent bodily process, then this question asks, in essence: What is the relationship between body and mind? Second: What is the scientific status of consciousness as subject matter for a scientific psychology?

The mind-body problem

The historical answers to the mind-body problem were often given by philosophers who had other problems to solve about the nature of man and his destiny. Although their answers were not proposed to satisfy psychologists, it is worth our while to review some of the classical positions on this problem.

The clearest answers were formulated either as dualisms or monisms. The *dualistic* answer is most prevalent in our ordinary thought about mind and body; mind and body are different, so that the problem is to characterize their interaction. A typical common-sense view is that the body, for example, takes orders from the mind and the bodily condition in turn limits what the mind can do. This sensible view is more or less implied in what we call psychosomatic medicine, in which bodily illnesses are considered in some instances to be brought about by mental disturbances. The expression "sound mind in sound body" implies such interaction. Historical figures who held such a view include the philosophers Descartes and Locke, and in more modern times, the psychologist James. There are, however, a great many difficulties with this view, particularly if we accept the notion of the conservation of energy. Then the only energy available to the body is physical energy, and the only causes can be somehow within this energy system. If the mind is not material, it is difficult to see how it can be a cause of energy changes, such as occur in willed movements.

Those who are troubled by the difficulties inherent in the interaction view tend to adopt a *monistic* answer, which says that the basic substance of the universe is essentially of one kind—either like mind (*idealism*), or like matter (*materialism*), or some neutral substance which viewed from one point of view appears mental and from another point of view appears material (*double-aspect theory*). The double-aspect theory originated with the philosopher Spinoza, who said that reality is one, but that it can be known from either aspect. When we engage in thinking we can consider this from the point of view of the mental activity or from the point of view of the functioning of the brain. In modern dream research, as we shall see, we try to find evidence of dreaming through physiological processes while at the same time we ask the dreamer about the content of his dream. This view of the mind-body problem is sometimes called a double-language position, in which one talks either the language of observable events (physiology or behavior) or the language of mental activities (private experience, intentions, and so on). A double-language position of this kind does very well in permitting the investigator to carry on his scientific enterprises without committing him to a fixed position on some of the larger and more controversial philosophical problems. Thus the first of our two questions is given a provisional answer that recognizes conscious experience and mental activity without denying a continuous chain of energy interchanges at the physiological level.

Consciousness in a scientific psychology

The second question stated above had to do with the place of consciousness in a scientific psychology. Granting some form of the double-language theory, we may accept the facts of consciousness as falling within the mental language. If, however, one denies the scientific validity of this second language, then some other disposition has to be made of the problem of consciousness.

The *behaviorist* answer, at least in its classical form, is a clear one. Either the facts of consciousness are denied altogether, or they are considered to be such poor materials out of which to construct a science of psychology that they had better be ignored so far as science is concerned. Edward C. Tolman, a broad-minded behaviorist, said that "raw feels" (by which he meant facts that could be got at by introspection) were materials for the artist, not for the scientist. One reason that the behaviorist was so outspoken against consciousness was that, at first, he was reacting against a view of psychology that considered psychology to be concerned with the facts of consciousness, and nothing else. Such a psychology could not get very far in studying lower animals, the human infant, or pathologically disturbed adults, because their "introspections" either are not available or cannot be trusted. Yet the behaviorist was able to show that good and useful studies could be done ignoring the facts of consciousness, and in this reaction against consciousness as the *only* topic of study, he tended to ignore consciousness entirely.

Even though one does not commit himself to a behavioristic position, there is a community of knowledge that is created by accepting verbal behavior as behavior, so that the words recorded on electromagnetic tape are subject to counting and to sorting, and thus become data for hypothesis-testing. It turns out that the psychologist, in order to go about his business, does not have to take a stand on the scientific value of the study of consciousness any more than he has to take a stand on the mind-body problem. This must seem evasive to someone studying psychology for the first time, and perhaps it is; in the light of history, however, it is clear that this view has made it possible for psychologists to work without getting into arguments that are not very important from a scientific standpoint, no matter how important they may be from the viewpoint of one's personal value system.

Various states of awareness

The normal waking consciousness, in which we can report accurately what is happening in the environment about us, is not the only state of awareness. The dreams that we remember are not unconscious, or we could not remember them; they occur in a state of awareness in which events go on that can often be described just as if they were events in the everyday world. Other states must also be considered—those of excessive fatigue, delirium, intoxication, and ecstasy.

The complexity of waking consciousness. It must not be assumed that waking consciousness is a simple state of receptivity to stimuli in the environment. We know that we may be attentive or inattentive, that we may be looking, listening, talking, planning, all at once. When in conversation we are listening to what a spokesman is saying, we may also be preparing our reply, and even while replying we may be thinking of further arguments to use. We have long known that when we try to do too many things at once they tend to interfere with each other, though the details are not readily formulated. Thus, while it is not hard for a man to talk while driving a car along a busy highway his conversation may give way as traffic gets snarled.

Among the experiments that test some of these interferences are some ingenious ones concerned with the ability to listen to two conversations at once. By having these carefully prepared on electromagnetic tape it is possible to arrange them in several ways: sending one conversation to one ear, one to the other; sending both simultaneously to both ears; alternately sending one to one ear and one to the other. Complications may be introduced by having different voices, different loudnesses, and different difficulties occur in the two messages. The main findings of such experiments are (Broadbent, 1958):

1. There is some truth to the belief that we can attend clearly to only one message at a time. Most people are amazingly successful at choosing *which* ear they will listen to (or which message source, if they are spatially separated), even though, with conditions remaining the same, they can equally well use the other ear or other source. This presumably makes possible intelligible cocktail conversation, where the elimination of all but the intended message is achieved. Even under these circumstances there is usually something recognized from the second message, such as whether or not the voice is that of a male or female or whether the voice changes during the course of the listening.

2. Under some circumstances there is a good deal of information from both messages. If the messages are easy, then there is a better chance that both will be understood; if one is easy and one difficult, it is usually the easier one that is heard. If the rate of presentation permits shifting back and forth, samples can be taken from both messages, and the gaps "filled in." While the exact times depend on circumstances, it takes about two seconds to shift attention from one message to the other.

These relationships have been studied in considerable detail and have been accounted for in part by the capacity of the human being to process information; there is limited capacity, and when there is an information overload some incoming information has to be discarded. As the above statements indicate, this discarding of information is not random, but selective. We shall return in a later chapter to further considerations of information processing (Chapter 14).

The split of attention between two or more simultaneous sources of information is only one of the "splits" that occurs in ordinary waking consciousness. Others are the splits between the receptive and responding function and between immediate responding and the planning of future responses. It is possible, for example, to listen and talk at the same time: Cherry (1953) had subjects repeat a message that was coming so fast that they were listening and speaking simultaneously. Under laboratory conditions the subjects tended to do this without expression, like a parrot repeating words it has been taught. That good performances of this kind can be given is indicated by the success of the simultaneous translators who repeat a speech being delivered in one language simultaneously in another, a feat now common at international conferences. The planning function that goes on while we are listening and talking has been commented upon by Miller, Galanter, and Pribram (1960). They note that during almost all of our waking consciousness we talk to ourselves about our plans as a kind of silent commentary on what is going on. ("How long shall I talk to him before moving on?" "Shall I take another helping?" "When can I get to the library?" "Is this worth putting down in my notebook?") Plans to stop activities, to enter upon others, to accept or refuse invitations, to drift or to schedule—there are many different styles for different people—this stream of extra self-talk, beyond listening and speaking, is part of waking consciousness. Some writers of the stream-of-consciousness school—Gertrude Stein, James Joyce, Virginia Woolf—have attempted to capture such self-talk as a literary device.

Not all waking states are alert. Sometimes we find ourselves or others just "staring"—not examining anything, but looking rather blankly at nothing at all. We know the difference between our minds being very active and being almost free of thought; hypnotic subjects often report that they can sit for a time with their minds practically blank, passively waiting for something to be suggested to them. Observation of newborn babies suggests that the more alert and more inert states begin very early in life. Babies in the first five days of life tend to be mostly asleep, disturbed, or eating; when in these states they pay little attention to sights and sounds about them. However, there are occasional quiet alert states in which their eyes are wide open and the eyeballs are "bright" and appear to focus. These states last for a short time (the longest observed being seven minutes at this age), and the total of the alert inactive periods does not exceed 30 minutes in a 24-hour period. Only during these alert inactive periods will the newborn baby turn his head and eyes to follow a visual object or turn toward a source of sound (at intensities too low to yield startle responses) (Wolff, 1966).

The readiness for new stimuli is sometimes called a state of *vigilance,* and is tested by responses to the occasional appearance of a stimulus on a screen or to some change within regular stimuli. Mackworth (1950) used a clock with a pointer that jumped regularly once a second, but at rare intervals the pointer gave a jump of double the length. The subject had to pay close attention in order to report these double jumps by pressing a key when they occurred. He found that a subject could do pretty well for half an hour, but tended to make many more errors after that when set to work for a longer period. In view of the tendency for attention to shift, what devices are there for holding attention within a narrow domain of stimuli, or, in other words, maintaining vigilance?

Mackworth found that he could reduce errors by reporting to the subject that he had responded correctly when he had, or by saying "You missed one there" when he had failed, or even by calling over the telephone and asking him to do better. The point is that there are techniques by which a subject is kept alert, and indeed we use such techniques on ourselves all the time. To keep from falling back into states of vacant staring we keep orienting ourselves to our tasks, reminding ourselves where we are and what time it is: we squirm, scratch, adjust clothing, tap with our fingers, chew a pencil. These are not mere nervous habits to discharge tension; they keep us from going to sleep, from becoming inattentive. Recent physiological studies suggest that we are keeping the reticular formation active (p. 41).

These remarks on the complexity of the waking consciousness are intended merely to break the stereotyped belief that we know what the alert waking state is and that only other states are interesting or puzzling. The ordinary alert waking state may be the most puzzling of all, but we are less troubled by it because it is so familiar.

Sleep as an altered state. The state that is most commonly contrasted with waking is sleeping, because it is a state of lessened awareness and of lessened activity. Biologically, we think of it as a restorative state. Again, however, the sleep state is not simple. We know that it is not just the result of accumulated waste products, for with our bodies in a given condition we can often choose either to sleep or to remain awake. We know that it is not altogether unconscious, because when we awaken we sometimes remember that we have had one or more dreams. It is not entirely quiescent, because some people walk in their sleep. It is not entirely insensitive, because a mother may be selectively awakened by the cry of her child. It is not altogether planless, because some people can set themselves to awaken at a given time, and the plan is fulfilled while they are asleep. We distinguish between lighter and deeper stages of sleep, troubled and untroubled sleep. Despite these difficulties in specifying just what sleep is, we can readily classify it as something which, on the whole, differs from waking.

Other states of awareness. Waking and sleeping do not exhaust the kinds of states people find themselves in. There are some definitely abnormal states induced by disease or by drugs and other chemical substances. *Delirium* refers to a state, com-

monly brought on by high fever or drugs, in which there is a departure from reality, with both hallucinations and delusions. Hallucinations are senselike perceptions with a minimum of sensory supports, as in the animals often seen in the hallucinations of some alcoholics. By delusions we mean faulty thought systems, in which sense perception may be accurate but events are misinterpreted, as if the nurse is seen as planning to poison the patient or visitors seen as enemy agents. *Intoxication,* as with alcohol, produces its own symptoms. Distorted awareness is also associated with mental illness.

It must not be supposed that all altered awareness is a symptom of derangement. Experiences under hypnosis and under some drugs represent kinds of distortions that are temporary; those who experience them often find the experiences extremely pleasant. Then there are experiences of *ecstasy,* as in religious mysticism, which defy categorization. William James (1902) called mystical experiences "noetic but ineffable," by which he was saying that the mystic had a sense of gaining knowledge (noetic aspect), but the experience was essentially indescribable and therefore not communicable (ineffable aspect). Experiences short of ecstacy, but with somewhat similar meanings for those who have them, have been called *peak experiences* by Maslow (1959; see p. 159 of this text). These experiences are sustaining, enrich life's meaning, and are treasured in memory by those who have had them.

Unconscious states. To round out our inventory of states of awareness we must raise the question of unconscious states. One interpretation by Freud was that we could consider three levels of awareness: the conscious level, the preconscious level, and the unconscious level. The preconscious level consists of those thoughts and wishes that are not now conscious but may readily become so, while the unconscious, as its name implies, cannot be experienced as such but must be inferred from the thoughts that come to consciousness, usually by way of the preconscious. When we say that there are unconscious determiners of a dream we infer this from the fact that the dreamer is as puzzled by his dream as the person to whom he recounts it. In telling his dream, however, he tells what actually entered his consciousness, even though he was asleep at the time. Hence the concept of unconscious processes is not rendered untenable because we cannot be aware of unconscious processes, for we are free to make inferences from the data that are accessible to us. The Freudian division into conscious, preconscious, and unconscious is helpful in defining the problem, although many do not believe in any sharp division between the various degrees of awareness.

This, then, is the rough terrain of awareness—waking, sleeping, unusual states, unconscious processes. It is our purpose in this chapter to look at some of the evidence that bears upon these states.

Sleeping and Dreaming

The most obvious change in states of awareness is that between waking and sleeping, for most of us experience the transition at least twice a day.

Sleep rhythms, depth of sleep, and signs of dreaming

The newborn baby tends to alternate rather frequently between sleeping and waking; gradually one period of sleep is lengthened, although there are still naps, and eventually the night-and-day rhythm tends to be established (Figure 10–1).

Because tired organisms tend to go to sleep, the sleep state might be looked upon as the extreme form of relief from fatigue. If lying down relieves fatigue, surely going to sleep can relieve it even more. However, this is not necessarily true, for you can go to sleep under appropriate circumstances even if you are not at all fatigued; on the other hand, you can be so fatigued that you find it difficult to sleep at all. One theory of sleep proposes that sleep, like fatigue, depends upon the accumulation of waste products resulting from activity. However, observations on Siamese twins (i.e., twins

10–1

Development of the sleep pattern

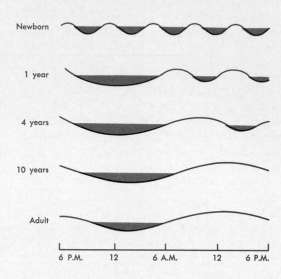

The baby's short cycles of sleep and waking gradually become the single night-day cycle of the adult. (After Kleitman, 1963)

attached to each other, with a common circulation) deny that sleep can be so simply explained. Because such twins accumulate the same fatigue products in their blood, they should sleep simultaneously if sleep depends upon the accumulation of these products. However, one twin may be sound asleep while the other remains wide awake (Figure 10–2).

10–2

Siamese twins

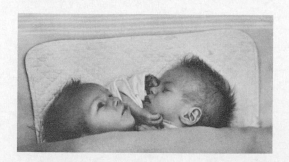

One head of this two-headed infant is asleep, indicating that sleep is not regulated by chemical changes in the blood since both share the same blood supply. (*Life Magazine* © Time, Inc.)

Another theory attributes sleep to the activity of a "sleep center" located at the base of the brain in the hypothalamus. Electrical stimulation of this center can produce sleep in cats, but because surgical removal of this center puts the animal to sleep it can perhaps be better called a "wakefulness center." However, additional experiments have shown that there is another center, slightly forward in the hypothalamus, which, if removed, keeps the animal awake. A rat with this center removed will be active and eat and drink, but after a few sleepless nights it falls into a coma from which it does not recover.

Human adults establish a rhythm of sleep that may persist through internal regulation. Some travelers, for example, find it very hard to adapt to the new time schedules that jet travel can produce within a few hours; it may take them several days to adjust to new bedtime and rising hours. An interesting experiment on adult sleep

rhythms was performed some years ago by the leading authority on sleep, Nathaniel Kleitman, and his associate. They set up temporary "housekeeping" for a month in the very uniform conditions of Mammoth Cave, Kentucky, and attempted to adapt to a 28-hour day, 19 hours under artificial illumination and 9 hours in the dark. By good fortune the two men differed sufficiently for the results to be highly instructive: one of them adapted to the new schedule in such a way that, when averaged for the last three weeks in the cave, his daily temperature changes showed the six peaks characteristic of the six lengthened (28-hour) days; the other continued to have the seven peaks characteristic of the precave rhythm (Figure 10–3).

Stages of sleep. It is easy enough for the layman to tell that someone is asleep. The scientist, however, is interested in the stages of sleep. The preferred method these

10–3

Physiological adaptation of two subjects to a changed length of day

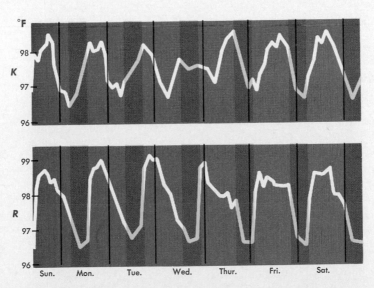

The two men lived on a 28-hour schedule in Mammoth Cave. The results are for the last three weeks in the cave. Subject K continued to have seven peaks of temperature corresponding to the days of the week (based on the 24-hour day). Subject R had adapted to the new schedule of six days, each of 28 hours. The dark bands are the hours spent in bed, mostly in sleeping. (After Kleitman, 1939, p. 261)

days (for scientific purposes) is to use evidence from the *electroencephalogram* (EEG) recorded from the scalp. We have already met this method of studying the electrical action of the brain (p. 44). When the EEG is used, four stages of sleep are recognized, as shown in Figure 10–4. Stage 1 sleep is characterized by low voltage and relatively fast patterns of changes; Stage 2 is recognizable by the presence of sleep spindles, with some complex responses with a low-voltage background; Stages 3 and 4 are identified by low-voltage slow waves known as delta waves. These distinctions are unimportant to the nontechnical reader; the main point is that there are changes associated with deepening of sleep (Dement and Kleitman, 1957).

A whole new era in the investigation of sleep and dreaming began with an observation by Aserinsky and Kleitman (1953) that eye movements tend to occur during dreams. Such eye movements can be recorded even though the eyes remain closed. By waking subjects when their eyes had been moving they found that 74 percent reported dreams, while very few reported dreams if awakened when their eyes had not been moving. Presumably the eyes move as the subject looks at the hallucinated visual presentations in his dreams. This method has now become standard in the study of dreams; hundreds of studies have been conducted in the last 10 years and a new society (Association for the Psychophysiological Study of Sleep) has been formed to serve as a clearinghouse for those engaged in this exciting new research.

When subjects are awakened from sleep by noises of graded intensity, we find that ease of waking does not always correspond to the EEG stage. In general, there is a sleep continuum through these four stages, and it is easier to arouse a person from Stages 1 or 2 than from 3 or 4. However, something else happens within Stage 1. It is only in this stage that dreaming commonly occurs, and dreaming is usually associated with *rapid eye movements* (REMs). When these rapid eye movements are occurring in Stage 1 sleep, it is very difficult to arouse the sleeping subject.

10–4

The four stages of sleep, as indicated by EEG records

(After Dement and Kleitman, 1957)

This dreaming state is sometimes known as "paradoxical sleep," because the subject is near to being awake by one criterion (EEG) but hard to arouse by another (e.g., increased arousal threshold) (Williams, Agnew, and Webb, 1964).

How much time is spent in each of the sleep stages? Studies show that this varies from person to person, but for any one person the sleep pattern is often consistent night after night. Rough percentages for the four stages are for Stage 1, 25 percent; for Stage 2, 50 percent; and for Stages 3 and 4, 25 percent of the night (Williams, Agnew, and Webb, 1964). The distribution is not even throughout the night. While all stages are found during the first third of the night, little dreaming occurs in the first hour; Stages 3 and 4 are mostly concentrated in the first few hours; Stage 2 is more evenly distributed throughout the night; and most dreaming (Stage 1-REM sleep) occurs in the last third of the night.

The most important distinction has come

to be the one between Stage 1-REM sleep and the remaining sleep, so much so that workers in the field now think of three main physiological states succeeding each other every day—wakefulness, non-REM (NREM) sleep, and REM sleep.

The discovery that most human dreaming occurs in EEG-Stage 1-REM sleep has led to a great increase in the study of human dreaming, because dream samples can now be collected in a much more satisfactory way, without waiting for recall in the morning and without futile waking when there has been no dreaming.

But the additional information about the Stage 1-REM-sleep state as a result of experiments with animals and newborn children has opened up new territories of exploration not just related to dreaming. It is found that the REM-sleep and NREM-sleep states are different in many respects, of which the occurrence of rapid eye movements is but one. For example, animal studies (chiefly with rats and cats) have shown that the neck muscles may remain somewhat tensed during ordinary NREM sleep but become very relaxed in REM sleep. Reflex responses may be much more readily evoked in NREM sleep than in REM sleep. Paradoxically, there is a good deal of spontaneous twitching that occurs in REM sleep. (The notion that the dog who kicks while sleeping in front of the fire is dreaming of chasing a cat may not be so far-fetched.) It appears that the brain is indeed much more active in REM sleep: even though the musculature is very relaxed, the neural excitement is so great that some of it spills over into spontaneous activity of the muscles (Dement, 1965).

The connection between REM sleep and dreaming, and between the physiological experiments and psychological interpretations of the nature of dreams, is made less clear than it otherwise would be because of the prominence of REM sleep in lower animals and in very young—even premature—infants. This has led some of the authorities on sleep to look for some other reason for REM sleep than can be explained by dreaming. Perhaps the dreams come about because the state is right and the eye movements are occurring, and it is not the need for dreams that is essential but the need for REM sleep. The prominence of REM sleep in early life is indicated in Figure 10–5, which combines the data from various studies. This stage of sleep is most prevalent very early, when it is doubtful that the infant consciousness is well enough equipped with structured memories to have the hallucinations that we think of as dreams. At the same time, this prevalence of REM sleep early in life suggests that very primitive processes must be associated with REMs, and, by analogy, it is not surprising that the dreams later associated with REMs may be driven in part by illogical primitive impulses.

New knowledge about dreams and dreaming

The investigation of dreams and dreaming opened up by the new psychophysiological methods has given us the answer to some age-old questions, although of course many new questions have also come up. To illustrate these findings, we shall consider those answers given for a few familiar questions.

Is Stage 1-REM a satisfactory indicator that a subject is dreaming? Occasionally a subject awakened from NREM sleep reports a dream, but it is usually more like the images that sometimes occur in the initial onset of sleep (without REMs) or described as more like "thoughts" than like "dreams." Monroe and others (1965) collected reports from both REM and NREM sleep, and then had judges sort these into piles, not knowing which kind of sleep had produced the dream. Judges were better than 90 percent successful in determining which dreams had in fact been produced under REM conditions; there is little doubt that they are more "dreamlike" than those produced under NREM conditions.

Are dreams instantaneous, or do they occupy appreciable time? A few experiences,

Decrease in REM time with increasing age

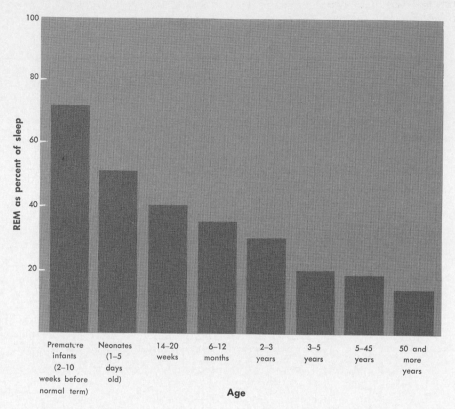

The figure has been drawn from data accumulated from various sources by Fisher (1965). While the data are limited, the trends appear unmistakable.

such as dreaming an elaborate dream about fire engines during the brief time that an alarm clock sounds, have led to the notion that dreams occur with great rapidity. Dement and Wolpert (1958) introduced external cues that could be located in the reported dream, so that they knew the time from that point to the moment of waking. When they reproduced the activities (in a kind of play-acting of the dream) they found that the time involved was about that which the dream had in fact occupied. The evidence from REMs is that most dreams last from several minutes to more than an hour.

Does everyone dream? Many people do not recall dreams in the morning, while others do. However, "recallers" and "non-recallers" appear to dream equally frequently, if we accept the Stage 1-REM evidence (Goodenough and others, 1959). It is of interest that the difficulty in recall shows up even when awakened at night, following the REM period. The nonrecallers tend to recall fewer dreams and shorter ones than the recallers (Lewis, 1963). On the whole, however, the evidence is that everyone dreams.

Can the sleeper react to the environment without awakening? Sleep is a relatively inert state, and it is sensible to suppose that dreams are determined largely by what goes on within the sleeper. Still it is an interesting question to ask how reactive the sleeper is. Williams, Morlock, and Morlock (1963) showed that subjects could discriminate auditory signals during sleep, better during Stage 1-sleep onset and Stage 2 than during REM phases. This bears, of course, on the possibility of sleep-learning, for which many claims have been made but laboratory substantiation is lacking (Emmons and Simon, 1956). When signals occur during REM sleep, they may be incorporated into the dream rather than awaken the dreamer. Thus Berger (1963) showed that spoken personal names were incorporated into dream events when presented within REM sleep.

Do sleeptalking and sleepwalking go on within REM sleep? It has been found that sleeptalking occurs primarily during NREM sleep and probably not in relation to ordinary dreaming (Kamiya, 1961; Rechtschaffen, Goodenough, and Shapiro, 1962). Essentially the same applies for sleepwalking (Jacobson and others, 1965). Subjects usually forget what they did while sleepwalking, and the dreams they remember in the morning bear no resemblance to what they did while walking about.

Sleeptalking has been seized upon as a new method for studying dream content. Through posthypnotic suggestions planted in the waking state it is possible to instruct the subject to talk about his dream while it is occurring, without awakening, and to sleep comfortably and silently when the dream is over (Arkin, Hastey, and Reiser, 1966). The remembered dream in the morning may be a fragmentary version of the full dream reported while it was happening.

Dream theory

The most influential theory of dreams within the last half-century has been that of Freud, the founder of psychoanalysis, who announced his theory in the book that he considered to be his most important work, *The interpretation of dreams* (1900). He believed that unconscious impulses were responsible for the dream, that the aim of the dream was the gratification of some drive (in the older terminology, the fulfillment of a wish). The real meaning

of the dream, called its *latent content,* is not directly expressed, but is instead dramatized in disguised form, the remembered aspects of the dream being its *manifest content.* The construction of the dream, the so-called dream work, consists in the representation of the impulse-provoked ideas in acceptable form, commonly in the form of visual imagery. The manifest content often picks up materials that were in the thoughts of the previous day (*day-residues*), and combines these with thoughts and emotions from the past. The main mechanisms are condensation, displacement, and symbolization. Condensation refers to the combining of ideas into more abbreviated form, so that a single word or figure may have multiple meanings within the dream; *displacement* permits one thing to stand for another, as one part of the body standing for another; *symbolization* is the more general term for representing ideas or events by something else. These may be private symbols, related to the individual experience of the dreamer, or more universal symbols, of which the sexual symbols are the best known. Since to Freud much of the impulsive life centers around sexual wishes, the representation of the male organ by a snake or other long or pointed object is to be expected; the female is more often represented by some kind of container, box, basket, or vessel.

Why, according to Freud, was all this disguise necessary? His reply was that by using these disguises the dream became the guardian of sleep; it got rid of the unfulfilled impulses, which might otherwise disturb the sleep, without bringing them so strongly to the attention of the sleeper as to disturb him. If the raw meaning of the dream were open to the dreamer, his impulses would often be found to be of a kind that he would not find tolerable. The dream does often fail in its work; for instance, when the dreamer awakens frightened, anxiety having been aroused within the dream. Freud acknowledged these failures of the dream work in his later writings (e.g., Freud, 1933).

If one of the purposes of the dream is to protect sleep, this purpose should be reflected in some sort of "need to dream." To test this possibility, Dement (1960) introduced the method of depriving a subject of his normal quota of dreams by arousing him whenever dreaming began, as indicated by REMs. He was able to reduce the amount of dreaming by some 70 percent, and applied this method for several nights. This dream deprivation produced some sort of deficit, for when the subject was allowed to sleep freely for several nights he dreamt much more than usual, perhaps 40 to 80 percent more than he did before deprivation. Controls are run, of course, to see that this is not merely a matter of having lost sleep through so many arousals during the night; if the same number of arousals are made from NREM sleep, no such increase in dreaming occurs on later nights.

The experiments on dream deprivation are consistent with the role of the dream as the guardian of sleep, particularly as it might be disturbed by instinctual drives seeking discharge (Fisher, 1965, p. 285). It is interesting to note in this connection that it has been found more difficult to arouse the sleeper from Stage 1 sleep if REMs are occurring, and that external stimuli, if incorporated in the ongoing dream, do not arouse him as they do if not incorporated. This is in line with the idea that the dream prevents waking.

Other aspects of Freud's dream theory are the subject of a good deal of controversy. Freud seems to have established the fact that dreams may have some genuine significance in the life of the dreamer, and their interpretation is often a useful tool in psychotherapy. Some writers, generally sympathetic with this position, feel that Freud made too much of the primitive, regressive nature of the dream and did not give enough attention to the dream as an effort to provide a solution to the dreamer's problems. When the many dreams of a series are studied, a theme may be found running through the series that does indeed reflect some of the preoccupations of the dreamer (French and Fromm, 1963). Others have felt that Freud overemphasized the disguised and hidden meanings of the dreams, for in some dreams the direct references appear to be combined with metaphorical references, somewhat as the two types of communication are used in poetry. According to this view, dream metaphors are a kind of literary device, rather than a device of concealment (Hall, 1953).

The controversies within the interpretation of dreams have greater chance of being resolved now that the new methods of investigation permit us to obtain better samples of dreams under controlled conditions and more detailed reports of the dreams themselves. It is to Freud's credit that he brought dreams back as objects of scientific inquiry; it remains to others to build theories based on sounder knowledge than was available to him.

Hypnosis as an Altered State

The word *hypnosis* is derived from the Greek word for sleep (ὕπνος), and the metaphor of sleep is commonly used in inducing the hypnotic trance. Pavlov, the famous Russian physiologist, became interested in sleep and hypnosis during his later years, and he conceived of hypnosis as a partial sleep. Now that EEG evidence is available, we can say with some assurance that hypnosis is not ordinary sleep, for the EEG of hypnosis is not that of any of the four stages of sleep. Whether or not it is some special kind of partial sleep is at present an open question.

Hypnotic induction

In order to hypnotize a willing and cooperative subject (the only kind that can be hypnotized under most circumstances), the hypnotist creates the conditions for entering hypnosis by any of a number of methods that relax the subject, exercise his imagination, and thus lead him to relinquish some control to the hypnotist and accept some reality distortion. A common method is for the hypnotist to suggest that the subject fix his eyes upon some small target, such as a thumbtack on the wall, concentrate on the target, detach his thoughts from other things, and gradually become relaxed or sleepy. The suggestion of sleep is a convenient one because it is familiar as both relaxed and out of touch with ordinary environmental demands, but it is a metaphor, and the subject does not really go to sleep. The subject continues to listen to the hypnotist and, if susceptible, finds it easy and congenial to do what the hypnotist suggests and to experience what he invites the subject to experience. In its modern form, hypnosis does not involve authoritarian commands on the part of the hypnotist; with a little training a subject can hypnotize himself, using what he has learned from the hypnotist. In other words, the subject enters the hypnotic states when the conditions are right; the hypnotist has merely helped set these conditions. The transition from the waking state to the hypnotic state takes a little time, but with practice this time tends to be shortened. It is not as clear that the person becomes more deeply hypnotized with repetition, but he reaches the state familiar to him more quickly.

Characteristics of the hypnotic state

The hypnotic state or trance recognized today is essentially as it was described in the nineteenth-century heyday of hypnosis. Some of its characteristics, as shown by subjects who illustrate a high degree of susceptibility, are as follows:

1. *The planning function subsides.* The subject does not like to initiate activity; he waits for the hypnotist to tell him what to do.
2. *Attention is redistributed.* While attention is always selective, within hypnosis it becomes more selective than usual. The hypnotist may tell the subject to listen to his voice only; he will not then hear the voices of others in the room.
3. *Reality testing is reduced and reality distortion accepted.* Ordinarily one checks up on things to see that he is awake, not suffering from illusions, and so on. Under hypnosis one may uncritically accept hallucinated experiences (petting the imaginary rabbit in his lap) or other distortions that would usually be rejected.

4. *Suggestibility is increased.* Of course one has to accept suggestions in order to be hypnotized at all, but the question is whether or not normal suggestibility is *increased* under hypnosis. This is a matter of some dispute, but careful studies do find some increase in suggestibility, though perhaps less than might be supposed (Hilgard and Tart, 1966).
5. *The hypnotized subject readily enacts acceptable roles.* When told to adopt a role, such as being someone other than himself, the hypnotized subject will commonly do so and will carry out complex activities related to that role. There may be something of the actor in each of us, and the permissiveness of the hypnotic situation, in which ordinary behavior is set aside, makes this role-behavior congenial. Impressed by this kind of behavior, Sarbin (1950; 1965) has been led to a role-enactment theory of hypnosis, affirming that those who become hypnotized have a high order of role-enactment ability and have attitudes appropriate to role-enactment.
6. *Posthypnotic amnesia is often present.* Some, but not all, susceptible hypnotic subjects will react to the suggestion that they will forget events within hypnosis after they are aroused from it, until a prearranged release signal is given; following such instructions they will forget all or most

10–6

Distribution of posthypnotic amnesia, showing bimodality

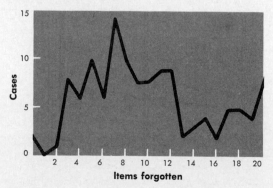

The scores are plotted according to items forgotten, with a possible of 20 (N = 124). (After Hilgard and others, 1961)

of what has transpired. When the release signal is given, the memories are restored. How this varies from one person to another in a college population is shown in Figure 10–6. Most subjects forget a few of the things they did within hypnosis, just as they forget what they have done in ordinary psychological experiments. But some subjects are extremely forgetful: it is these we think of as demonstrating posthypnotic amnesia.

Although the hypnotic state resists precise definition, the behaviors of hypnotized subjects, of which the above six are representative, are sufficiently consistent to serve as an approximate definition of the state.

Who can be hypnotized?

There is no disagreement that some people can be hypnotized more readily than others, but there is some uncertainty whether there are any persons who cannot be hypnotized at all, given the most favorable circumstances. Occasional reports have been given of heroic attempts in which the same person was hypnotized unsuccessfully for hundreds of trials until, finally, hypnosis was achieved. The record, a case report by Vogt in the last century, took 600 trials! Under ordinary circumstances, a person's hypnotizability can be determined quite well from the first attempt to hypnotize him. In a study of 25 selected subjects, chosen to represent the range of hypnotic ability (as measured on the first trial of attempted hypnosis by means of a standardized scale, the Stanford Hypnotic Susceptibility Scale, Form A), the individuals were hypnotized over and over again with varied techniques until it was quite clear that they had yielded about all they could in the way of hypnotic responsiveness. Their estimated hypnotic susceptibility at the end correlated .75 with their initial measurement of susceptibility (Shor, Orne, and O'Connell, 1966). Hypnotic susceptibility is shown to be a relatively stable personal characteristic, even though some few who are originally refractory may later become hypnotizable.

The availability of scales for measuring susceptibility to hypnosis permits more precise statements about the distribution of hypnotizability than were formerly possible. The scales that have been found most satisfactory are based on the hypnotic performances given by a subject following a standard form of hypnotic induction: the subject who responds most like a hypnotized person is expected to respond is scored as most susceptible. The items of one such scale are listed in Table 10–1.

The exact percentage of people who can be hypnotized has been variously estimated by different authorities, but the development of standardized measures now permits more precise statements. The distribution of susceptibility among university students is shown in Figure 10–7. The distribution, based on scores from 533 students, shows that the majority of students are only moderately susceptible to hypnotic influences, scores of 0 to 4 on this 12-point scale indicating responses to suggestion readily made in the waking state: falling in response to the suggestion of swaying backward from a standing position, closing the eyes after staring at a target while being told that you are getting sleepy and your eyes are closing, lowering an outstretched arm when the suggestion is that it is getting heavy, or moving the outstretched arms

10–7

Distribution of first-session scores, Form A or Form B

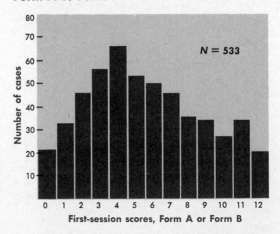

(After Hilgard, 1965)

TABLE 10–1

Items of the Stanford Hypnotic Susceptibility Scale, Form A

Item	*Criterion of passing* (Yielding score of +)
1. Postural sway	Falls without forcing
2. Eye closure	Closes eyes without forcing
3. Hand lowering (left)	Lowers at least six inches by end of 10 seconds
4. Immobilization (right arm)	Arm rises less than one inch in 10 seconds
5. Finger lock	Incomplete separation of fingers at end of 10 seconds
6. Arm rigidity (left arm)	Less than two inches of arm bending in 10 seconds
7. Hands moving together	Hands at least as close as six inches after 10 seconds
8. Verbal inhibition (name)	Name unspoken in 10 seconds
9. Hallucination (fly)	Any movement, grimacing, acknowledgment of effect
10. Eye catalepsy	Eyes remain closed at end of 10 seconds
11. Posthypnotic (changes chairs)	Any partial movement response
12. Amnesia test	Three or fewer items recalled

SOURCE: Weitzenhoffer and Hilgard (1959), p. 49.

together or apart. Sometimes these mild responses are accompanied with some feelings of being in the hypnotic state, but this is usually reserved to those who make scores of 5 to 12. Within this range, those scoring higher are usually more deeply hypnotized, and the full range of hypnotic phenomena are given only by those few who score near the top. A rough figure is that about one-fourth of unselected university students achieve a quite satisfactory hypnotic state, which includes such phenomena as posthypnotic amnesia. Fewer than this, perhaps 5 to 10 percent, can give more advanced phenomena, such as posthypnotic visual hallucinations with the eyes open.

Despite the wide differences within hypnotic susceptibility and the consistency with which subjects respond to hypnotic susceptibility tests, it is surprisingly difficult to determine just what kinds of people are more susceptible and what kinds less susceptible. Most studies have found either no correlations or very low ones with personality characteristics other than those related to hypnosis itself. Hypnotic-like experiences outside hypnosis are somewhat predictive of hypnotic susceptibility, favorable attitudes toward hypnosis have sometimes been found helpful, ideational interests are more favorable than highly competitive athletic ones (though many athletes are hypnotizable). The correlations reported in many studies are disappointingly small (Hilgard, 1965, p. 335), but a picture of the hypnotizable person begins to emerge.

When the replies on tests are examined, along with data from interviews, it becomes clearer that the hypnotizable person is one who has rich subjective experiences in which he can become deeply involved, that he reaches out for new experiences and thus welcomes the opportunity to become hypnotized, that he is interested in the life of the mind, rather than being chiefly interested in competitive muscular performances, that he is willing to accept impulses from within and is not afraid to relinquish reality testing for a time. He does not appear to be a weak or dependent person; evidence indicates that more troubled, withdrawn, or neurotic individuals do not generally make as good subjects as the normal outgoing ones.

Theoretical and practical significance of hypnosis research

Interest in hypnosis has fluctuated over the years, in part because of its use as an entertainment technique and its associations with the occult and mysterious. When it is permitted to take its place as a legitimate field of scientific inquiry, along with dreams, drug states, and other altered states of awareness, its potential usefulness within scientific psychology is easy to demonstrate. In recent years there has been a resurgence of interest in hypnosis from this point of view, and there are now scientific societies devoted to sharing experiences in its study and journals in which the results of experimental and clinical studies are reported. Both the British Medical Association and the American Medical Association have in recent years passed resolutions indicating the desirability of teaching hypnotic techniques in medical schools (Marcuse, 1964).

Within experimental psychology, hypnosis permits the study of some of the important problems of planning, of self-control, and of circumstances in which control is relinquished. The problems of voluntary and involuntary action are important ones that have been somewhat neglected in recent experimental psychology; hypnosis provides a method for reintroducing them. The features of the hypnotic state itself and of responsiveness to suggestions provide topics of interest not only for understanding hypnosis but for understanding broader aspects of the modification and control of behavior.

These uses of hypnosis—for the study of the state itself and its correlates or as a control method in connection with other problems—qualify as essentially basic science uses. There are also direct applications of hypnosis, as in dentistry, obstetrics, and psychotherapy.

A growing use of hypnosis in dentistry and obstetrics is based on two practical features of hypnosis: (1) that it is a relaxed state and can be used to reduce anxiety; (2) that it is possible to relieve pain through suggested anesthesia or analgesia. There are many other medical and surgical situations, such as burns, in which the control of pain and discomfort is important.

Burns that cover large areas of the body are often corrected by transplanting skin from other parts of the patient's body; to preserve the original circulation while the transplanting goes on may require, for example, immobilizing an arm that is attached to an ankle by way of a skin flap. The discomfort of retaining this awkward position may be relieved through hypnosis. Kelsey and Barron (1958) report a case in which an awkward posture was retained in connection with a skin graft, the posture persisting for three weeks with the help of hypnosis, the subject reporting no discomfort at the time or after freedom of movement was eventually restored. Intractable pains, as in terminal cancer, may also be relieved by hypnosis. Thus one of the large areas of usefulness of hypnosis is in the relief of pain or of the anxieties associated with anticipated pain.

Hypnosis also plays several roles in psychotherapy. If it is used to provide symptomatic relief through direct posthypnotic suggestion, then the therapeutic result belongs directly to the hypnotic technique. Often, however, hypnosis is used as an aid to other kinds of psychotherapy, such as those to be described in Chapter 22.

As our scientific knowledge of hypnosis increases, its practical applications will be better understood and managed. With the attention being given to the phenomena in recent years, we may expect increased use of hypnosis and its gradual dissociation from entertainment and pseudoscience.

CRITICAL DISCUSSION
Skepticism about hypnosis

Most investigators of hypnosis would find nothing unacceptable in the foregoing account of hypnosis, except perhaps for minor aspects of terminology or emphasis. This does not mean that the field is free of controversy. Several investigators have wittingly or unwittingly led readers to doubt the reality of hypnosis. This comes about in part because hypnosis lends itself to extreme statements, and those who claim too much for hypnosis are its scientific enemies as well as those who claim too little. We may briefly consider the views of four men who have left strong doubts about hypnosis in the minds of their readers: Sutcliffe, Orne, Sarbin, and Barber.

Sutcliffe, himself an able hypnotist and investigator of scientific hypnosis, has made a point of distinguishing between the "credulous" and "skeptical" views of hypnotic phenomena (Sutcliffe, 1960, 1961). Sutcliffe showed, for example, that subjects who reported no pain after hypnotic suggestion continued to give the physiological responses normally associated with pain. The skeptical view is that the physiological responses are the dependable ones; the hypnotic subject must therefore be deluding himself that he does not feel pain—even though he is willing to have an impacted tooth extracted or an arm amputated under hypnosis! Sutcliffe's findings are indeed puzzling ones, but they do not discredit the phenomena of hypnosis.

Orne, also an active investigator of hypnosis and a practicing hypnotherapist, has emphasized that many of the responses of the hypnotized subject depend upon what he thinks the hypnotist expects, hence on the "demand characteristics" of the situation (Orne, 1959, 1962). This gives the impression that there is some kind of faked quality about hypnotic performances. But of course all hypnotic performances have within them the quality of response to suggestion; Orne is not denying this but is merely trying to specify what is inherent in hypnosis and what is imposed by the tradition in which the hypnotist works. He is not a disbeliever in the reality of hypnosis, but he is easily misinterpreted to be.

Sarbin's interpretation of hypnosis as role-enactment has been mentioned earlier (p. 259). The expression he uses gives the impression that he thinks of hypnosis as some sort of sham behavior. He does not believe this; for him the difference between someone who is hypnotizable and someone who is not is a matter of the degree to which he can lose himself in the role the hypnotist suggests; it is *not* just a matter of voluntary cooperation with the hypnotist (Sarbin, 1956, 1965).

Of the investigators mentioned, Barber is the one who is most outspoken in denying the separateness of hypnotic phenomena from other psychological phenomena (Barber, 1965). His main point, however, is that most of the things that susceptible hypnotic subjects can do *after* hypnotic induction can be done *without* induction. Thus "waking suggestibility," as it is often called, is for him really the same as hypnotic susceptibility, provided the motivational circumstances are made the same. The individual differences that he finds within hypnosis and the age differences are essentially the same as others find. Others, too, find a high correlation between responsiveness in the waking state and after hypnotic induction. The argument is then over relatively small increases in suggestibility produced by the induction and over subjective characteristics of the established hypnotic state. These differences remain to be resolved.

Some genuine issues exist, but when the arguments are carefully examined no issue as to the legitimacy of hypnosis as a field of scientific inquiry is involved.

Hallucination-Producing and Consciousness-Expanding Drugs

Because man can think and dream, he can transcend the mundane everyday world and contemplate visions of unthought-of worlds. Like the drug addict, he can recognize that some of the distortions that he finds through drug intoxications and related experiences are a kind of escape into a world of illusion; or, like the religious mystic, he may be in earnest about his quest for a reality that lies beneath and beyond the world as we know it. Because these are in some respect polar opposites, we have "decent people" fighting the drug habit, while at the same time we have other "decent" or "enlightened" people urging the beneficent results of selected drug experiences. At the present time there is a heated controversy over drug use. Without hastening to join one or the other of the opposing camps, it behooves the student of psychology to know what is going on, both from the point of view of the individual experiences that are indeed reported while under the influence of drugs and from the point of view of the social psychology of those who find satisfaction through these experiences.

History of drug usage for psychological effects

Drugs have been used from ancient times to poison or to cure, to relieve pain, to produce sleep or hallucinations. We are particularly interested in the hallucination-producing drugs, such as opium (made from poppies), hashish and marijuana (from hemp), mescaline or peyote (from a variety of cactus), and psilocybin (related to the Mexican hallucination-producing mushroom). Each of these has been used for many years either as a form of self-indulgence or for ceremonial or religious purposes.

An upsurge of interest in *psychoactive drugs*—drugs that affect man's behavior and consciousness—began in the 1950s. First in importance were the *tranquilizers*, which reduced anxiety and made otherwise disturbed persons more serene. One of these, reserpine, had been known for years in India, a derivative of a plant known as Indian snake root or rauwolfia. Soon many other tranquilizers came on the market, initially only for use in mental hospitals, but presently widely used by the general public on a physician's prescription. Then came the *energizers*, which tended to overcome fatigue and lassitude; these drugs tried to improve upon caffeine, which in coffee had long been serving this purpose. Finally there appeared a group of drugs called at first *psychotomimetic* because they appeared to mimic in the normal the states of mentally ill (psychotic) persons; the chief of these was a drug known as LSD-25 (lysergic acid diethylamide). Although this parallelism with mental illness has not been found to be very close, the fact that this family of drugs produced such interesting effects in altering consciousness opened a whole new history of drug use. It is that history with which we are here concerned.

Current interest in hallucination-producing and consciousness-expanding drugs

There are three main uses to which drugs of the family of LSD, mescaline, and psilocybin are put. The first is best described as self-indulgence, in which the drugs are used for "thrills" or "kicks," as alcohol is used for intoxication or as other drugs are used for sought-after pleasure. A second is in connection with psychotherapy, that is, in the treatment of mental or emotional disturbance. The third use is for philosophical, religious, or social benefits by serious-minded people who believe in this method of achieving valued ends.

The first use is the kind assumed to be dangerous because drugs used in this way have tended in past history to cause injury: (1) they may have dangerous side-effects; (2) they may be habit-forming, leading to addiction; and (3) they are usually taken in the company of alienated and non-conforming people, who, in defying law and convention, commonly get the user into trouble with the police.

The second use is, of course, one to be encouraged if the research findings recommend it. One of the more promising uses of LSD, for example, appears to be in the treatment of alcoholism (Jensen and Ramsey, 1963). There are also some reports of generally therapeutic effects in cases of mild neurotic disturbances (Savage, Savage, Fadiman, and Harman, 1964).

The third use is in some ways the most controversial, because it treads upon issues of value that go beyond ordinary legal conventions with respect to the use of drugs. Those who favor this use commonly refer to the drugs as *psychedelic*, literally "mind-manifesting," because of their subjective, perception-modifying aspects.

The nature of the psychedelic experience

What happens when a person takes one of these drugs (LSD, mescaline, psilocybin) depends partly upon the person's preparation, expectancies, and "set," for the drug state appears to be a highly suggestible one. Sjoberg (1965), for example, has shown that taking LSD and mescaline (but not psilocybin) leads to about the same increase of responsiveness to a set of suggestions as a standard set of hypnosis-inducing instructions. A number of observers have given quite careful accounts of their experiences. One, for example, is Aldous Huxley in the book *Doors of perception* (1954). From such accounts one can conclude that the following kinds of experiences are fairly frequently reported:

1. Visual hallucinations, commonly of vivid colors. These may consist in a kind of play of unstructured colors or a kind of pageantry of actual observed scenes.

2. A sense of separateness from the body, of moving about independent of the body or of seeing one's own body from some other vantage point.

3. A sense of euphoria or well-being, which may be without specific content.

Not all experiences are pleasant; some may actually be terrifying. When a leader prepares those about to take the drug and creates particular expectations, these are likely to be fulfilled; thus if the leader prepares for a mystical-type experience, this is likely to occur (Savage, Terrill, and Jackson, 1962; Downing and Wygant, 1964).

A comparison of users of LSD who had been offered and accepted the drug outside traditional medical care with a corresponding group of subjects who had been offered the drug under like circumstances but had refused to take it permits some statements about those who use the drug and what personality effects they attribute to it (Blum and others, 1964). The life situations of those in both groups appeared to be about the same prior to taking the drug; when questioned later a larger fraction of the drug-users who had felt unhappy before taking the drug now felt happier, compared with the number of previously unhappy nonusers whose condition had improved. Some of the LSD-users said that before LSD they were striving and pursuing, but now they were "drifting with the current." How one interprets this is a matter of personal values; while the users are generally optimistic about their im-

provement, more objective criteria such as improved occupational status showed that the controls (nonusers) fared better than the users. The authors of the study felt that LSD-users tended toward overly positive self-descriptions because of "euphoria, denial, and selective amnesia."

While enthusiasts will report that there is no danger in the taking of LSD, experience suggests otherwise. There are a few people who become extremely disturbed, and are hospitalized with the diagnosis as psychotic. Blum and others (1964) estimate that at least 2 in 100 users would have such reactions, and perhaps as many as 5 in 100. Their conclusion is that the reaction is not predictable on the basis of personality disturbance prior to taking the drug.

The social psychology of the desire to achieve serenity or happiness through drugs and various other self-reorienting devices other than through problem-solving and committed effort is itself interesting as a topic for investigation. In his book *The positive thinkers* (1965), Meyer has traced the appeal of various inspirational writers in America from Mary Baker Eddy to Norman Vincent Peale. While the picture of healthy-mindedness created by the inspirational writers is one of heartiness and contentment, their appeal, as Meyer points out, is mostly to those who are sick. Even William James, so often quoted by such writers, called attention to the danger of trying to seek happiness through false beliefs. In considering some revivalist movements of his day, he said, in his preface to *The will to believe* (1897),

I quite agree that what mankind at large most lacks is criticism and caution, not faith. Its cardinal weakness is to let belief follow recklessly upon lively conception, especially when the conception has instinctive liking at its back. . . . Were I addressing . . . a miscellaneous popular crowd it would be a misuse of opportunity to preach the liberty of believing. . . . What such audiences most need is that their faiths should be broken up and ventilated, that the northwest wind of science should get into them and blow their sickliness and barbarism away.

SUMMARY   1. Psychology was once defined as the study of consciousness, but with the rise of behaviorism the problems of consciousness were permitted to recede and were to some extent ignored. The problems are, however, genuine ones, and modern objective psychologies are again concerning themselves with them.

2. Traditional solutions of the mind-body problem have been *dualisms*, such as the view that mind and body are different but interact, and *monisms*, in which there is only one substance, either mindlike (idealism) or bodylike (materialism). The *double-aspect theory* asserts that the common substance can be viewed from one vantage point as mental, from another as material. Psychologists, not committed to behaviorism, sometimes refer to this as a double-language position. The committed behaviorist prefers a physicalist language throughout, though he may bring in much of what is ordinarily considered to be conscious contents by reducing these to language behavior. In any case, whatever the position on the philosophical issues, contemporary psychologists are prepared to deal scientifically with problems of awareness as these are reflected in hallucinations, dreams, drug states, and the like.

3. Although considerable interest resides in the study of altered states of awareness, other than the awareness of the ordinary waking consciousness, careful examination of *waking consciousness* shows it to be complex too. In the studies concerned with doing two things at once, such as listening to two conversations, it is found that there is a limit to the capacity to process information, and so some of it has to be discarded if too much comes at once. Still, some division of attention occurs. One of the "splits" in waking consciousness is the planning function, a sort of silent talking to oneself that goes on even though we are engaged in listening and overt talking. Attention tends to shift, and alert (vigilant) states may be followed by less alert ones. This begins in early infancy, the newborn infant orienting to sound or pursuing with head and eyes a visual object only in the alert state, which endures only a few minutes per day in the first few days of life. Later in life we maintain alertness by all sorts of devices of fidgeting and irrelevant responding that prevent our drifting off into vacant staring or sleep.

4. Sleep is a familiar altered state of awareness, interesting for itself but particularly interesting in relation to awareness because of the fact of dreaming. Studies using the electroencephalogram (EEG) and the study of rapid eye movements (REMs) during sleep have now shown two main kinds of sleep, that at EEG—Stage 1, accompanied by REMs, and the remainder, occurring within all four EEG stages of sleep, which may be called nonrapid-eye-movement (NREM) sleep. It is during REM sleep that the characteristic dreaming takes place. Since the discovery of REM sleep numerous studies have been done to use this method of detecting when the subject is dreaming, and hence to study the frequency and duration of dreams. Because of this ability to spot the dream, studies of dream recall have become better grounded. Studies have also been made of the reactivity of the dreamer to outside influences and of such spontaneous behaviors as sleeptalking and sleepwalking, which seem not to be related directly to REM sleep.

5. Freud's dream theory is that dreams express wishes in disguised form; the purpose of the dream (and of the disguise) is to protect sleep. The new physiological studies are coherent with this theory in that it is very difficult to waken a sleeper while dreaming, and the need for dreams is shown by the dream-deprivation studies. The new approach is quite recent, and many investigators are at work to settle some of the points at issue.

6. Hypnosis, sometimes identified as a partial sleep, yields an EEG pattern unlike sleep, but at present there are no clear physiological indicators by which to define the state. Highly susceptible hypnotic subjects yield similar enough phenomena that the hypnotic state can be characterized by some of the things they do.

7. People vary in their susceptibility to hypnosis, with about one-fourth of college students being able to experience relatively satisfactory hypnotic states upon their first hypnotic induction. Efforts to find out why some people are more readily hypnotizable than others have not proved very conclusive. The susceptible subject does not turn out to be weak, passive, or dependent; normal outgoing subjects are more likely to be susceptible than troubled, anxious, or withdrawn ones. However, at the present time, nobody is able to say prior to attempted hypnosis whether or not a given person is hypnotizable.

8. Drugs tend to be used either for the gratification that the drug state is supposed to bring (thus leading to addiction) or for some beneficial results in psychotherapy or personality orientation that the drug experience is supposed to enhance, as in psychiatric or religious or philosophical contexts. Advances in biochemistry and pharmacology have brought a whole new set of drugs into existence, along with the familiar ones. Among these are the *tranquilizers*, the *energizers*, the *psychotomimetics*, and the *psychedelics*. The last two names are sometimes applied to the same drugs, depending on the person's interpretation of them, psychotomimetic describing their symptoms as being those of mentally ill (psychotic) persons and psychedelic describing them as consciousness-expanding.

9. The so-called psychedelic experience commonly consists of visual hallucinations, either of unstructured colors or of a kind of visual pageantry, sometimes a feeling of the person as moving out from his body or watching his body from a distance and sometimes a feeling of awe or grandeur that gives a sense of well-being, with little communicable content. The experiences are not always pleasant ones. The particular experiences received seem to depend in part upon the expectations aroused in preparation for the experience. Studies of those who have used LSD for purposes of self-help have generally reported optimistic outcomes, but when compared with control groups their actual social or work-oriented behavior has not shown the gains of their self-reported internal adjustments.

10. The current interest in drugs can be seen against a background of self-help recommendations to which Americans have been subjected and which portions of the population have received enthusiastically over the last century.

SUGGESTIONS FOR FURTHER READING

For the more general problems of the nature of mind and its place in the world of science, see the collection of essays edited by Scher, *Theories of the mind* (1962).

The problems of awareness, including subliminal processes, are treated in Eriksen (ed.), *Behavior and awareness* (1962). For some additional light on complexity of waking experience, see Singer, *Daydreaming: an introduction to the experimental study of inner experience* (1966).

The literature on sleep and dreams is moving ahead rapidly. The standard reference work is Kleitman, *Sleep and wakefulness* (1963). Two useful books are Luce and Segal, *Sleep* (1966), and Foulkes, *The psychology of sleep* (1966). For a psychologist's account, with special reference to motivation, see Murray, *Sleep, dreams, and arousal* (1965).

Recent books on hypnosis include Hilgard, *Hypnotic susceptibility* (1965), Gordon (ed.), *Handbook of hypnosis* (1966), and Shor and Orne (eds.), *The nature of hypnosis* (1965).

For an introduction to the psychological effects of drugs, see Uhr and Miller (eds.), *Drugs and behavior* (1960), and Blum and others, *Utopiates* (1964).

LEARNING AND THINKING

While modification through learning is a rule throughout the animal kingdom, the higher organisms, with prolonged infancy, depend more upon learning for their adjustment to the environment than do those lower in the evolutionary scale. Man is a learner par excellence. He not only learns muscular habits and skills but also acquires and remembers information coming to him in various forms. He is also a thinker and a problem-solver, often inventing tools and methods that help him overcome the obstacles in the way of getting the answers that he seeks.

11 The Nature of Learning

In the preceding chapters we have presented many examples of learning. We have noted how children learn food preferences, increase their vocabularies, acquire social motives, and learn to perceive the environment. However, in presenting these examples we did not discuss the details of the learning process. This chapter will be devoted to examining the dependent variables used to measure learning, and to determining the effects of important independent variables on the learning process. Many psychologists regard learning as the most significant process in understanding human behavior. In view of its importance we will devote special attention both to the methods of studying learning and to some of the theories that have been proposed to explain the process.

We may define learning as a *relatively permanent change in behavior that occurs as the result of practice*. The phrase *relatively permanent* excludes from our definition changes in behavior that result from temporary or transient conditions such as fatigue, the influence of drugs, or adaptation. By specifying that learning is the result of *practice* we exclude behavioral changes that are due to maturation of the organism, disease, or physical damage. Not all changes in behavior can be explained as learning, and hence our definition has to be qualified to exclude them. Learning could be defined more simply as profiting from experience, were it not that some learning does not "profit" the learner: useless and often harmful habits are learned as well as useful ones.

The task before an *applied* psychology of learning is clear. If psychologists can offer suggestions for improving the efficiency of learning, they may help us avoid wasteful methods in our own learning and in directing the learning of others. The task before *general* and *systematic* psychology in the study of learning is related to that of applied psychology because the more we know about the fundamentals of learning, the more soundly we can make recommendations for practice. But the scientific understanding of learning has a wider scope. Not only does it help us to understand the most evident kinds of learning, such as memorizing a poem or learning to drive a car; it also bears upon the most fundamental problems of individual development, motivation, social behavior, and personality.

Learning can be seen from the point of view of *development*, in that our knowledge and skills accumulate throughout our lives: what we are able to do today depends not only upon our natural capacities and maturational level but also upon what we have learned in the past. Learning is also *interactive*, in that it comes about through active interchange with the environment (either in movement and manipulation or in observation and discrimination), and the manner in which we are able to use our past learnings depends upon circumstances active in the present. We shall find the developmental-interactive distinction useful if we think of the accumulation of habits and knowledge as a developmental problem and their utilization in recall, in new settings, and in problem-solving as an interactive problem.

Because learning is basic to an analysis of behavior, a number of controversies within theoretical psychology revolve about it. Most psychologists who prefer to emphasize stimulus-response relationships interpret learning as *habit formation,* by which they mean *associative learning*—that is, acquiring a connection between a stimulus and a response that did not exist before. Thus the naming of objects in English depends upon a set of *verbal habits* according to which, for example, certain objects made of wood and graphite serve as stimuli for the associated response of "pencil." Riding a bicycle illustrates a set of *sensorimotor habits* appropriate to that complex stimulus. It is possible to go beyond these obvious habits and interpret *all* learned behavior as of essentially the same kind, including habitual attitudes, habitual ways of thinking, habitual emotional expression. According to this interpretation all our learning is associative learning: we learn only habits.

Within the concept of associative learning, we shall distinguish three sources of data about habits and the principles governing them: *classical conditioning, operant conditioning,* and *multiple-response learning.* We shall wait to define these until they are under discussion.

Other psychologists, not convinced that it is most profitable to treat all learning as habit formation, are impressed by the role of *understanding* in learning, or, in more technical vocabulary, the role of *cognitive processes.* Examples of cognitive processes are our ability to follow maps over routes we have never taken before and to reason our way to conclusions previously unfamiliar to us. At the end, have we learned something new, or have we merely exercised old habits? To be sure, we have *used* old habits, and herein arises disagreement among psychologists. Some psychologists are satisfied that the results of cognitive learning, or learning with understanding, can be *predicted* from knowledge of earlier habits and the principles of habit formation, while others believe that some new principles have to be added to account

for what the learner does when he makes sophisticated use of his earlier habits in novel situations. We shall return to this problem after considering the case for learning as habit formation; it is worth noting here, however, that the issue of associative learning vs. learning with understanding hàs been the source of lively controversy within contemporary psychology.

Classical Conditioning

Pavlov's experiments

The study of associative learning can be carried on in the *conditioned-response* experiment. This experiment was originated by the Russian physiologist and Nobel prize winner, Ivan Pavlov (1849–1936). While studying the relatively automatic reflexes associated with digestion, Pavlov noticed that the flow of saliva in the mouth of the dog was influenced not only by food placed in the dog's mouth but also by the sight of food. He interpreted the flow of saliva to food placed in the mouth as an unlearned response, or, as he called it, an *unconditioned response.* But surely, he thought, the influence of the *sight* of food has to be learned. Hence this is a learned or conditioned response. Pavlov experimented to find out how conditioned responses are formed. He taught the dog to salivate to various signals, such as a rotating disk or the sound of a metronome, thereby proving to his satisfaction that a new stimulus-response association could be formed in the laboratory.

Under Pavlov's method a dog is prepared for experimentation by having a minor operation performed on its cheek, so that part of the salivary gland is exposed to the surface. A capsule attached to the cheek measures salivary flow. The dog is brought to the soundproof laboratory on several occasions and is placed in a harness on a table where the experiment is to be conducted. This preliminary training is needed so that the animal will stand quietly in the harness as the experiment proceeds.

Classical-conditioning apparatus

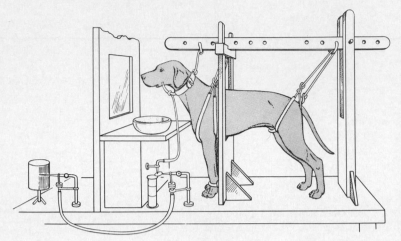

Arrangements used by Pavlov in classical salivary conditioning. Mechanical arrangements (not shown) permit the light as a conditioned stimulus to appear in the window, and the meat powder (as the unconditioned stimulus) to appear in the food bowl. (After Yerkes and Morgulis, 1909)

The laboratory is so arranged that meat powder can be delivered to a pan in front of the dog by remote control. Salivation is recorded automatically. The experimenter can view the animal through a glass panel, but the dog is alone in the experimental room (see Figure 11–1).

A light (the *conditioned stimulus*) is turned on. The dog may make some exploratory movements, but it does not salivate. After a few seconds, the meat powder (*unconditioned stimulus*) is delivered; the dog is hungry and eats. The recording device registers copious salivation. A few more trials are given in which the light is always followed by the meat, the meat by salivation. (This following of the conditioned stimulus by the unconditioned stimulus and response is called *reinforcement*.) After several reinforcements, the

11–2

A diagram of classical conditioning

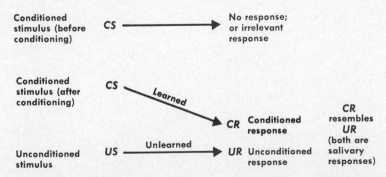

The association between the unconditioned stimulus and the unconditioned response exists at the start of the experiment and does not have to be learned. The association between the conditioned stimulus and the conditioned response is a learned one. It arises through the pairing of the conditioned and unconditioned stimuli followed by the unconditioned response (i.e., reinforcement). The conditioned response resembles the unconditioned one (though they need not be identical).

dog salivates when the light is turned on, even though food does not follow. When this happens, a *conditioned response* has been established.

The usual order of events (conditioned stimulus – unconditioned stimulus – response) can best be remembered if the conditioned stimulus is thought of as a *signal* that the unconditioned stimulus is about to appear; in the foregoing example the light is a signal that food is coming. The conditioned response may be considered a simple habit because (1) an association is demonstrated to exist between a stimulus and a response, and (2) this association is a learned one.

With this introduction we are ready for a definition of the process of *classical conditioning* as it is represented by the model of Pavlov's experiment. (We shall presently meet another variety of conditioning, called *operant conditioning;* hence the adjective "classical" is applied to Pavlov's model.) *Classical conditioning* may be defined as the formation (or strengthening) of an association between a conditioned stimulus and a response through the repeated presentation of the conditioned stimulus in a controlled relationship with an unconditioned stimulus that originally elicits that response. The original response to the unconditioned stimulus is called an *unconditioned response;* the learned response to the conditioned stimulus is called a *conditioned response.*

The arrangement described in this definition is diagramed in Figure 11–2. Because the conditioned response resembles the unconditioned response, classical conditioning is sometimes referred to as learning through *stimulus substitution,* the conditioned stimulus eventually "substituting" for the unconditioned one in eliciting the response.

Reinforcement, extinction, and spontaneous recovery

Because classical conditioning represents an extremely simple form of learning, it has been regarded by many psychologists as an appropriate starting point for the investigation of the learning process. Varia-

tions of Pavlov's techniques have been used with many different organisms (ranging from flatworms to human subjects) and many responses other than salivation in an attempt to discover, under the controlled conditions of the laboratory, the laws that govern learning. We will now consider some of the laws that characterize classical conditioning.

Each paired presentation of the conditioned stimulus (*CS*) and the unconditioned stimulus (*US*) is called a *trial,* and the period during which the organism is learning the association between the *CS* and the *US* is the *acquisition* stage of conditioning. The time interval between the *CS* and the *US* may be varied. In *simultaneous conditioning* the *CS* (in Pavlov's experiment, the light) begins with the onset of the *US* (presentation of food) and continues along with it until the response occurs. In *delayed conditioning* the *CS* begins a short time before the onset of the *US* and then continues with it. And in *trace conditioning* the *CS* is presented first and then removed before the *US* starts. These three situations are illustrated in Figure 11–3. In delayed and trace conditioning we can look for the conditioned response on every trial because there is sufficient time for it to appear before the presentation of the *US*. Thus if salivation occurs before the delivery of food we consider it a conditioned response to the light. In simultaneous conditioning the conditioned response does not have time to appear before the presentation of the *US* and it is necessary to include test trials (trials on which the *US* is omitted) to determine whether conditioning has occurred. If salivation occurs to the *CS* when it is presented alone we consider that conditioning has occurred. Experiments designed to investigate the most effective *CS-US* time interval indicate that presenting the *CS* about 0.5 seconds before the *US* usually produces the fastest learning.

With repeated paired presentations of the *CS* and *US* the conditioned response appears with increasingly greater strength and regularity. We call the procedure of pairing the *CS* and *US* *reinforcement* be-

Temporal relations in conditioning

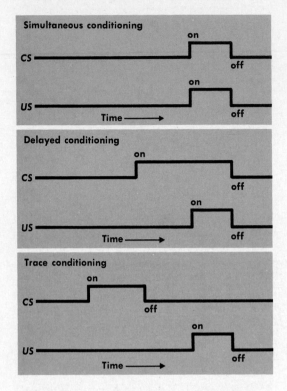

Simultaneous conditioning

CS ——— on / off

US ——— Time ——→ on / off

Delayed conditioning

CS ——— on / off

US ——— Time ——→ on / off

Trace conditioning

CS ——— on / off

US ——— Time ——→ on / off

Inflections stand for stimulus onsets; deflections represent terminations. The advantage of the delay and trace methods is that the experimenter can measure the strength of the conditioned response on every trial and not use test trials as is necessary in simultaneous conditioning.

cause any tendency for the conditioned response to appear is facilitated by the presence of the unconditioned stimulus and the response to it. Figure 11–4 shows the dog's acquisition of the salivary response to the conditioned stimulus of a light. By the third trial the animal is responding to the CS with seven drops of saliva. By the seventh trial the amount of saliva secreted has leveled off and continues (with minor variations) at the same strength for the next nine trials. We call this level or stable rate of responding the *asymptote* of the learning curve; further acquisition trials will not result in any greater strength of responding. One of the problems that in-

terests the psychologist is how various independent variables (such as intensity of the CS or amount of the US) affect the asymptotic response level.

The number of drops of saliva secreted is one measure of the strength of conditioning in Pavlov's experiment. There are a number of quantitative measures that may be used to demonstrate that one method of conditioning is more successful than another, or that one subject conditions more readily than another. Some of these measures, which may be used to plot the course of conditioning, are given below:

1. Amplitude of conditioned response. (Drops of saliva, extent of muscular movement, etc.)
2. Latency of conditioned response. (Promptness with which the conditioned response follows the conditioned stimulus)
3. Trials to a criterion of conditioning. (Number of reinforcements needed before the first measurable conditioned response appears or before some other criterion is met, e.g., before the first five conditioned responses have been given.)
4. Probability of conditioned responses. (Percentage of trials in which a detectable conditioned response appears. Even after considerable conditioning has been demonstrated, conditioned responses are not necessarily elicited on every presentation of the conditioned stimulus.)

If the unconditioned stimulus is repeatedly omitted, so that there is no reinforcement, the conditioned response gradually diminishes. Repetition of the conditioned stimulus without reinforcement is called *extinction*, and its effect on the animal's performance is shown in Figure 11–5. Notice that at the start of the fourth nonreinforced trial the amount of salivation has decreased to about three drops; by the ninth extinction trial the CS is eliciting no salivation at all. Studies have shown that the decrease in response during extinction is not a mere passive disappearance of response but is instead an active *inhibition*,

11-4

Acquisition of a conditioned response

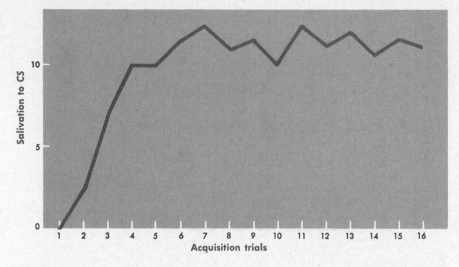

The curve depicts the acquisition phase of an experiment employing the trace-conditioning procedure. Drops of salivation to the conditioned stimulus are plotted on the ordinate and trials on the abscissa. The conditioned response gradually increases over trials and approaches an asymptotic response level of about 11 to 12 drops of salivation. (After Pavlov, 1927)

that is, a tendency against responding that may spread to other responses not included in the original conditioning. Thus extinction of a conditional response to a bell may also weaken the conditioned response to a flickering light.

Extinction does not actually destroy the conditioned response, for following a period of rest by the subject the conditioned response returns, even though no reinforcements have intervened. This return without reinforcement is called *spontaneous recovery* and is illustrated in Figure 11-6. The phenomenon of spontaneous recovery lends support to the interpretation of the consequences of extinction as some sort of active inhibition or suppression of the conditioned response, as opposed to a forgetting or permanent disappearance of the response.

Additional examples
of conditioning experiments

Before going further in our discussion of the phenomena of classical conditioning we might do well to consider a few more ex-

11-5

Extinction of a conditioned response

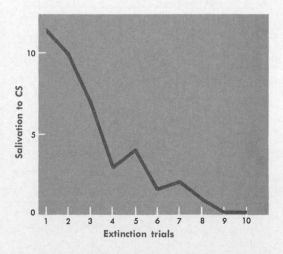

The conditioned response gradually decreases when food reinforcement is no longer paired with the conditioned stimulus. (After Pavlov, 1927)

Acquisition, extinction, and spontaneous recovery

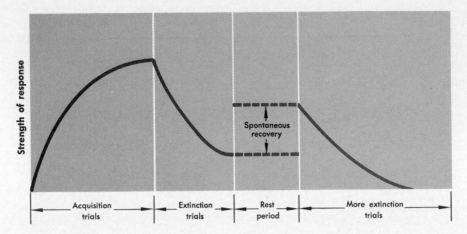

A schematic diagram of the course of acquisition, extinction, and spontaneous recovery. Within limits, the longer the rest period, the greater the degree of spontaneous recovery.

amples of the basic procedure. A wide variety of responses (ones we would not ordinarily consider capable of being learned) have been successfully conditioned both with animals and human subjects. In one study with rats an insulin reaction was conditioned (Sawry, Conger, and Turrell, 1956). Insulin is a hormone that controls the blood-sugar level. A manufactured form of insulin is used in treating diabetics and an overdose of this hormone causes a severe physiological reaction known as "insulin shock," which is often accompanied by unconsciousness. In the experiment the rats were exposed to a bright light and at the same time injected with an overdose of insulin. The bright light and the hypodermic needle served as the conditioned stimuli; the insulin was the unconditioned stimulus. After several pairings of the CS and US, a saline solution (which has no physiological effect) was substituted for the insulin. The animals continued to evidence a shock reaction that was almost indistinguishable from the reaction produced by insulin. We can thus say that the shock reaction had become a conditioned response.

We should note that in the experiment

above the conditioned response is not a single, easily measured response such as salivation, but a complex pattern of physiological and motor responses that constitutes the insulin shock reaction. A more quantitative physiological measure of conditioning was obtained in the following well-known experiment using human subjects (Menzies, 1937). When the human body is exposed to cold, one of the automatic, physiological reactions is the constriction of the small blood vessels close to the body surface; this reaction serves to maintain the warmth of the body. Although this is a reaction of which we are totally unaware, it can be conditioned. To do so a buzzer (CS) is sounded and at the same time the subject's left hand is immersed in a container of ice water (US). Since vasoconstriction of the left hand automatically results in some constriction of the blood vessels in the right hand, the degree of vasoconstriction can be accurately measured by means of a small, air-filled rubber tube (*plethysmograph*) placed around the subject's right hand. After a number of paired presentations of the buzzer and water immersion, vasoconstriction occurs in response to the buzzer alone.

To carry the procedure one step further, a word can be used as the *CS* in place of the buzzer (Roessler and Brogden, 1943). The experimenter simply says the word aloud as he plunges the subject's hand in the ice water and eventually the word alone will elicit vasoconstriction. There is some evidence that conditioning can be obtained when the subject is instructed to "think" the word instead of having the experimenter say it aloud.

The fact that automatic physiological reactions to specific stimuli can be learned has important implications for the study of emotions. As we shall see in the chapter on psychotherapy, conditioning procedures have been used to bring the physiological symptoms of anxiety under control.

Generalization

When a conditioned response to a stimulus has been acquired, other similar stimuli will evoke the same response. If a dog learns to salivate to the sound of a tuning fork producing a tone of middle C, he will also salivate to higher or lower tones without further conditioning. The more nearly alike the new stimuli are to the original, the more completely they will substitute for it. This principle, called *generalization,* accounts for our ability to react to novel situations in accordance with their similarities to familiar ones.

Careful study shows that the amount of generalization falls off in a systematic manner as the second stimulus becomes more and more dissimilar to the original conditioned stimulus. The reference experiment on this topic was done by Hovland (1937), who conditioned the galvanic skin response, abbreviated GSR (see p. 165), of human subjects to a pure tone of a specific frequency (pitch) using mild shock as the *US.* After the GSR had been conditioned, he tested for the amount of response to tones of higher and lower frequency than the original training tone. Figure 11–7 shows his results plotted in terms of the amplitude of the GSR (ordinate) and tones of varying frequencies (abscissa). The high point of the curve represents the amplitude of the GSR to the *CS;* the points to the left show

the GSR amplitudes to tones lower than the *CS,* and those to the right the amplitudes to tones higher than the *CS.* As you can see, the GSR amplitude decreases as the tones become progressively more dissimilar to the *CS* in frequency. This plotted relationship is called the *gradient of generalization.*

Stimulus generalization need not be confined to a single sense modality. For example, with human subjects a GSR conditioned to the sound of a bell may also appear (although in a lesser amount) to the sight of a bell or to the spoken word "bell." The conditioning of a response to the meaning of a word (as opposed to the configuration or sound of a word) is called *semantic conditioning.* An interesting example of semantic conditioning and generalization is provided by the work of a Russian psychologist (Volkova, 1953). She used a modification of Pavlov's salivary conditioning method with young children. The *US* was cranberry purée delivered to the subject's mouth via a chute; the response recorded was salivation. The *CS* was the Russian word for "good" pronounced aloud by the experimenter.

11–7

Gradient of generalization

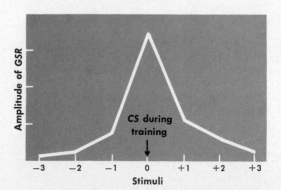

Stimulus 0 denotes the tone to which the galvanic skin response (GSR) was originally conditioned. Stimuli +1, +2, and +3 represent test tones of increasingly higher pitch; stimuli −1, −2, and −3 represent tones of lower pitch. Note that the amount of generalization decreases as the difference between the test tone and the training tone increases. (After Hovland, 1937)

After conditioning had been established the experimenter tested for generalization by pronouncing some Russian sentences that could be construed as possessing a "good" meaning and some that could not. She found, for example, that the children would salivate to sentences like "The pioneer helps his comrade" and "Leningrad is a wonderful city," but not to ones like "The pupil was rude to the teacher" and "My friend is seriously ill."

Discrimination

A process complementary to that of generalization is *discrimination*. Generalization is reaction to similarities, while discrimination is reaction to differences. Conditioned discrimination is brought about through selective reinforcement and extinction, as shown in Figure 11–8. In the experiment illustrated, two clearly different tones, CS_1 and CS_2, served as the discriminative stimuli. On some trials CS_1 was presented followed by a mild electric shock; on other trials CS_2 occurred, not followed by shock. The two tones were presented equally often but in a random

order. Initially the conditioned response (in this case, the GSR) occurred with about the same amplitude to the onset of both CS_1 and CS_2. However, during the course of the experiment the amplitude of the conditioned response to CS_1 gradually increased, while the amplitude of its response to CS_2 gradually decreased. Thus conditioned discrimination between CS_1 and CS_2 was demonstrated.

Classical conditioning and other instances of habit formation

The precise relationships studied in the Pavlovian experiment require restrictions of ways in which the subject can react and careful recording of both stimuli and responses. Since such restrictions cannot be used outside the laboratory, there appears to be a certain artificiality about conditioning. However, it is not necessary to reproduce the conditioning experiment in order to make use of *principles* derived from conditioning. We have already illustrated, for example, how conditioning principles help us to understand one form of acquired emotional behavior—conditioned

11–8

The course of conditioned discrimination in man

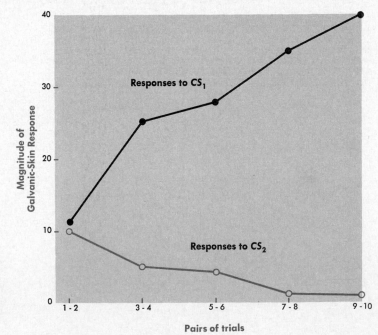

Conditioned stimuli: two tones of clearly different pitches (700 cps and 3500 cps). Unconditioned stimulus: an electric shock applied to the left forefinger. Conditioned response: amplitude of GSR. (After Fuhrer and Baer, 1965)

Magnitude of Galvanic-Skin Response

Responses to CS_1

Responses to CS_2

Pairs of trials

fear (p. 176). It is not difficult to make inferences from generalization and discrimination to ordinary behavior. When a young child has learned to say "bow-wow" to a dog, it is understandable that a similar stimulus, such as a sheep, will elicit the response "bow-wow." When the child first learns the name "Daddy," he uses it for all men. By differential reinforcement and extinction the response is finally narrowed to a single appropriate stimulus or class of stimuli.

We shall postpone further discussion of the extension of conditioning principles until we have considered operant conditioning.

Operant Conditioning

Operant conditioning is another approach to the study of habit formation. When you teach a dog a trick, such as playing dead or rolling over, it is very difficult to specify the unconditioned stimuli that could produce such behavior before conditioning. Actually, you "got him to do it" as best you could and *afterwards* rewarded him either with food or approval. The food or approval did not *produce* the behavior in the first place.

In Pavlov's experiment the conditioned salivation resembles the response elicited by the unconditioned (reinforcing) stimulus, but in operant training the behavior that is reinforced bears no resemblance to the behavior that is normally elicited by the reinforcing stimulus (i.e., salivation is a dog's normal response to food but rolling over is not). Still, the learning that takes place corresponds in some respects to classical conditioning: it can be shown to exhibit such principles as extinction and spontaneous recovery, generalization and discrimination.

Skinner's experiments

To provide a better model for this kind of conditioning, B. F. Skinner introduced the concepts of *operant behavior* and *operant conditioning*. Operant conditioning supplements classical conditioning; many of the same principles apply to both kinds of conditioning. The arrangements for the experiments differ, however, as do some of the measures of strength of conditioning.

Skinner proposed a distinction between two kinds of behavior that he called *respondent* and *operant* behavior. Respondent behavior is directly under the control of the stimulus, as in the unconditioned reflexes of classical conditioning: the flow of saliva to food in the mouth, the constriction of the pupil to a flash of light on the eye, the knee jerk to a tap on the patellar tendon. The relation of operant behavior to stimulation is somewhat different. The behavior often appears to be *emitted*; that is, it appears to be *spontaneous* rather than a response to stimulation. The gross movement of the limbs of a newborn baby can be classified as emitted behavior in this sense; most so-called voluntary behavior is emitted rather than respondent. When operant behavior becomes related to a stimulus (as when I answer the ringing telephone), the ringing telephone is a *discriminated* stimulus, telling me that the telephone is answerable, but it does not force me to answer. Even though the ringing telephone is compelling, the response to it is operant and not respondent behavior.

The word *operant* derives from the fact that operant behavior "operates" on the environment to produce some effect.[1] Thus going to where the telephone is and raising the receiver from the hook are *operant* acts that lead to the telephone conversation.

To produce operant conditioning in the laboratory, a hungry rat is placed in a box of the sort diagramed in Figure 11–9 (called a "Skinner-box"). The inside of the box is plain, except for the protruding bar with the food dish beneath it. A small light bulb above the bar can be lighted at the experimenter's discretion.

Left alone in the box, the rat moves about restlessly and occasionally presses its

[1] For the same reason such behavior is sometimes called *instrumental* behavior, because it produces effects just as a tool or other instrument does. Hence operant conditioning is also known as instrumental conditioning.

Apparatus for operant conditioning

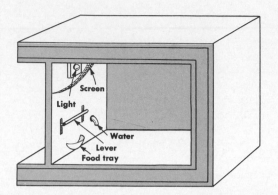

Will Rapport

The diagram shows the interior arrangement of the box used in operant conditioning of the rat. The space behind the panel at the left contains additional apparatus. This box has been named a "Skinner-box" after its developer. Photo shows an actual box in operation. (From Skinner, 1938)

paws upon the bar. The rate at which it pushes on the bar defines its preconditioned *operant level* of bar-pressing.

Now the experimenter attaches the food magazine, so that every time the rat presses the bar a pellet of food falls into the dish. The rat eats, and soon presses the bar again. The food *reinforces* bar-pressing, and a graph of the rate of bar-pressing plotted against time furnishes a record of the course of operant conditioning.

If the food magazine is disconnected, so that pressing the bar no longer delivers food, the rate of bar-pressing will fall off. That is, the operant response undergoes *extinction* with nonreinforcement, just as a classical-conditioned response does.

The experimenter can set up a *discrimination* by presenting food only if the bar is pressed while the light is on. Thus the bar-press response is reinforced if the light is on, not reinforced if the response is made in the dark. This selective reinforcement leads to the rat's pressing the bar only in the presence of the light.

With this illustration before us, we are ready to consider the meaning of conditioned *operant* behavior. As indicated above, it "operates" on the environment; the rat's bar-pressing *produces* or *gains*

access to the food. In classical conditioning the animal is passive; it merely waits until the conditioned stimulus is presented and is followed by the unconditioned stimulus. In operant conditioning the animal has to be active; its behavior cannot be reinforced unless it does something.

Now for a definition. *Operant conditioning* refers to the strengthening of a stimulus-response association by following the response with a reinforcing stimulus. Usually the reinforcing stimulus is the kind that can satisfy a drive, but it need not be. *It is reinforcing if it strengthens the response that precedes it.*

A large part of human behavior may be classified as operant—turning a key in a lock, driving a car, writing a letter, carrying on a conversation. Such activities are not elicited by an unconditioned stimulus of the Pavlovian type. But once the behavior occurs it can be reinforced according to the principles of operant conditioning.

Measures of operant strength

Because the bar is always present in the Skinner box, the rat can respond to it as frequently or infrequently as he chooses. Hence *rate of response* is a useful measure of operant strength. The more frequently the response occurs during a given interval of time, the stronger it is. This measure cannot be used for classical conditioning because rate there depends upon how often the experimenter presents the conditioned stimulus.

The rate of response in operant conditioning is usually portrayed graphically by means of a *cumulative curve*. Figure 11–10 shows how a cumulative curve is obtained. The bar of the Skinner box is attached to a recording pen that rests on a slowly moving strip of paper. Each time the animal presses the bar the pen moves upward a short distance and then continues on its horizontal path. Because the paper

11–10

Cumulative recorder

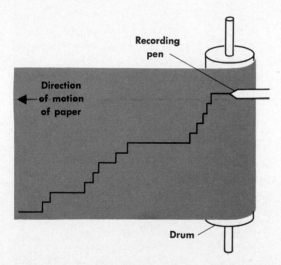

Above is a schematic representation of a cumulative recorder. The axis of the drum is fixed, and as the drum rotates the recording paper moves from left to right under the head of a writing pen. The pen is rigged so that it can only move upward, never downward. Each time the animal makes a response, the pen moves upward a fixed amount. When no responses are being made the pen moves in a straight line across the paper. Since the paper is moving at a fixed rate the slope of the cumulative curve indicates the response rate. When the animal is responding at a very high rate the slope of the cumulative curve will be quite steep; whereas when the animal is responding very slowly there will be hardly any slope at all.

moves at a fixed rate the slope of the cumulative curve is a measure of response rate. A straight horizontal line indicates that the animal is not responding. Figure 11–11 presents cumulative curves for two rats during acquisition of a bar-pressing response. Rat A had been deprived of food for 30 hours and rat B for 10 hours. As you can see from the steepness of the curves, the hungrier rat is responding much more rapidly.

Another measure of operant strength is *total number of responses during extinction*. As Figure 11–12 illustrates, a single reinforcement can produce considerable strength according to this measure.[2]

Partial reinforcement

Operant conditioning shows a high degree of orderliness or lawfulness. One illustration of this orderliness is the behavior controlled by *partial reinforcement,* that is, behavior taking place when the response is reinforced only a fraction of the time it occurs.

A pigeon learns to peck at a spot and receives access to a small quantity of grain as its reinforcement. Once this conditioned operant is established, the pigeon will continue to peck at a high and relatively uniform rate, even if it receives only a few reinforcements. The pigeon whose remarkably regular pecking is illustrated in Figure 11–13 was reinforced on the average of once every five minutes, that is, 12 times an hour, and yet it pecked at a rate of some 6000 responses per hour.

The practical significance of partial reinforcement is very great. A child's mother is not always present to reward him for looking both ways before crossing the street. But the influences of reinforcements are such that they persist against many nonreinforcements. A long straight drive will keep a golfer at his game despite many balls lost in the rough.

[2] Note that the leveling off of these curves does *not* indicate an asymptotic level of responding as was true in Figure 11–4, but rather an absence of response. We are plotting cumulative number of responses against time here rather than amplitude of response against trials.

11–11

Cumulative curves during acquisition

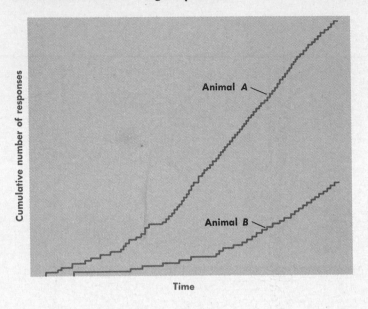

A comparison of the cumulative response curves for two rats during acquisition of a bar-pressing response. Rat A had been deprived of food for 30 hours and Rat B for 10 hours prior to the experiment. This difference in the hunger level of the two rats is reflected in the rate of responding.

11–12

Cumulative curves during extinction

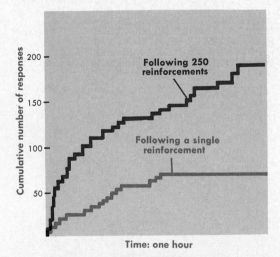

Curves of extinction of operant responses in the rat are plotted following a single reinforcement and following 250 reinforcements. The response is that of bar-pressing to obtain food. The plot shows the cumulative number of responses; every response raises the height of the curve, and the curve levels off when responses cease. (After Skinner, 1938)

CRITICAL DISCUSSION

Schedules of reinforcement

Partial reinforcement procedures have been studied extensively by psychologists. They are of interest because they represent the type of reinforcement regime that most organisms operate under in nature. In addition, under partial reinforcement schedules an animal's response rate tends to be extremely sensitive to changes in the stimulus environment (both internal and external); hence these procedures provide a natural barometer for assessing the effects of fatigue, drugs, diet, temperature, and other variables on performance. In the early exploration of space, American scientists frequently housed rats, pigeons, and other animals in the space capsule and placed them on a partial reinforcement schedule. Then, by observing changes in response rate during actual flight they were able to determine the effects of acceleration, weightlessness, and the like on learning. It is interesting to note that while American scientists used operant methods in early space probes with many different ani-

Operant responses sustained by partial reinforcement

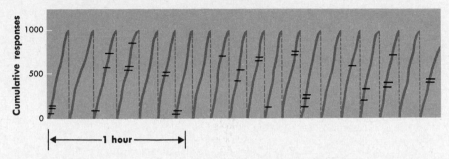

The curves are of the pecking responses of a single pigeon which are reinforced irregularly, but at an average interval of five minutes. The reinforcements are represented by horizontal dashes. Each of the sloping lines represents 1000 responses; the pen resets after each 1000. (After Skinner, 1950)

mals, the Russians employed Pavlovian procedures using dogs.

Many different reinforcement schedules have been studied by psychologists but basically they all can be categorized in terms of the following two dimensions: (1) the period between successive reinforcements is determined either by the number of intervening nonreinforced responses or by the elapsed time, and (2) the period between successive reinforcements is either regular or irregular (Ferster and Skinner, 1957). In terms of these two dimensions we can define the following four basic schedules:

1. *Fixed ratio* (*FR*). For this schedule reinforcement occurs after a fixed number of nonreinforced responses; if it occurs every 20 responses, for example, the ratio of nonreinforced to reinforced responses is 20 to 1.

2. *Fixed interval* (*FI*). Reinforcement follows the first response emitted after some fixed-time period measured from the last reinforcement. For example, on a fixed-interval schedule of one minute, no further reinforcement will occur following a reinforced response until the one minute has passed; once the time period has elapsed the first response made will be reinforced. The interval during which responses are not reinforced is sometimes referred to as the "dead period."

3. *Variable ratio* (*VR*). Like the fixed-ratio schedule, reinforcement occurs after

a specified number of nonreinforced responses. However, for this schedule the number of responses intervening between reinforcements varies from one reinforcement to the next. For example, a 20-to-1 variable-ratio schedule might be produced by requiring that the number of intervening responses be randomly selected from the numbers 11 to 29; on the average this schedule yields an interreinforcement period of 20 responses but with a wide range of values.

4. *Variable interval* (*VI*). In this schedule, reinforcement occurs after a specified period of time that varies from one reinforcement to the next. A simple variable-interval schedule of one minute might be generated by randomly setting the time period between reinforcements in a range of values from 10 to 110 seconds; this schedule yields an average time period of one minute but with a range of plus or minus 50 seconds.

These four reinforcement schedules produce characteristic modes of responding. On an *FI* schedule the animal's pattern of responding suggests that he is keeping careful track of time. Immediately after a reinforcement his rate of responding drops to near zero and then increases at an accelerating pace as the end of the dead period is approached. On *VI* schedules the response rate tends to be quite steady and does not fluctuate noticeably during the dead period.

Of course, this is what one would expect on a *VI* schedule, for the animal cannot predict the end of the dead period, and to receive reinforcement promptly when it is available he must respond at a fairly steady rate.

In contrast to the interval schedules, both the fixed- and variable-ratio schedules tend to produce extremely rapid rates of responding. If the ratio is small, responding begins immediately after a reinforcement; when the ratio is large there may be a brief pause after each reinforcement followed thereafter by steady bursts of responding. On ratio schedules the animal responds as though he knows that the next reinforcement depended on his making a certain number of responses, and he bursts forth with them at as fast a rate as possible.

Secondary reinforcement

Pavlov noted that, once a dog had learned to respond to a conditioned stimulus in a dependable way, the conditioned stimulus could be used to reinforce a conditioned response to a new stimulus. Suppose the animal learns to salivate to a tone as a conditioned stimulus. This is a first-order conditioned response. If a flashing light is then presented along with the tone, the flashing light when presented alone will come to give the conditioned response. Pavlov called this process *second-order conditioning*. The conditioned stimulus of first-order conditioning (tone) has become a *secondary reinforcer*. While second-order conditioning can thus be established within classical conditioning, it is much more easily demonstrated within operant conditioning, and for that reason its consideration has been postponed until now. The general principle, holding within both classical and operant conditioning, can be stated as follows: *any stimulus can be made reinforcing through association with a reinforcing stimulus.* Higher-order responses (third-order, fourth-order conditioning) are possible, but they tend to be established with greater difficulty the more remote they are from primary reinforcement.

When a rat in a Skinner box presses a lever, a light comes on momentarily, followed shortly by a pellet of food in the tray.

After several groups of animals are conditioned in this way, some receiving more reinforcements than others, the response is extinguished in the dark. That is, when the rat presses the lever, neither the light nor the food appears, and presently the animal almost ceases to press the lever.

Now the light is connected again, but without the food. When it is discovered that pressing the lever turns on the light, the rate of pressing increases, overcoming the extinction, even though no food follows. Hence the momentary onset of the light has acquired secondary reinforcing qualities. The number of responses in a 45-minute period corresponded to the prior number of light-and-food trials, showing that the strength of secondary reinforcement depended upon the frequency with which the light had been associated with the primary reinforcer, food (Bersh, 1951).

The *token learning* experiment discussed in Chapter 5 (p. 136) is an example of second-order conditioning that is a little closer to familiar habitual behavior. Chimpanzees learned to work for poker chips which they could later use to obtain food from a vending machine called a "Chimp-o-mat" (Figure 5–11, p. 136). The poker chips thus became secondary reinforcers.

After the chimpanzees had learned to use the Chimp-o-mat, they were introduced to another device that consisted of a lever attached by strong springs which the chimpanzees could move forward only by great exertion. The effort was rewarded by a grape attached at the end of the lever. After the chimpanzees had learned to obtain grapes in this manner, a poker chip was substituted for the grape. Three of four chimpanzees would strain as hard at the instrument for the poker chip as for the grape, using the chip later on to get grapes from the vending machine.

The value of secondary reinforcement derives originally from association with the primary reinforcer. In token learning the secondary reinforcer is a subgoal, a sort of milestone along the road to drive satisfaction, for it *assures* such satisfaction even if it does not itself *provide* it.

A feature of secondary reinforcement that

is very important for human social behavior is its wide degree of generalization.[3] The principle can be stated: *once established, a secondary reinforcer can strengthen responses other than the response used during its original establishment and can do so with motives other than the motive prevailing during the original training.* We know from ordinary observation that such reinforcers as social approval can be effective over a wide range of behavior, but there is also *experimental* evidence in support of the principle that secondary reinforcers have wide generality. In an experiment demonstrating this principle, Estes (1949), using water-deprived rats, associated an auditory stimulus with bar-pressing reinforced by water. When the rats were later deprived of food rather than water, the same auditory stimulus evoked bar-pressing. If enough drive of any kind is present to instigate activity, a secondary reinforcer is effective, even though it derived its strength while another drive prevailed.

Secondary reinforcement greatly increases the range of possible conditioning. If everything we learned had to be reinforced in unlearned stimulus-response sequences, the occasions for learning would be very much restricted. As it is, however, any habit once learned can have other habits built upon it. A verbal promise of food can reinforce behavior that would otherwise require the food itself; mere praise (without the promise of a primary reinforcer) itself becomes reinforcing.

Shaping behavior

As we noted earlier, classical conditioning is sometimes called the *method of stimulus substitution,* because the conditioned stimulus substitutes for the unconditioned stimulus in evoking the response appropriate to the unconditioned stimulus. The substitution principal fails, however, to account for *novelty* in behavior—for

[3] Long chains of responses can be sustained by a single reinforcement at the end, because the sign posts along the way, as secondary reinforcers, sustain the learned movements in approach to the goal.

the learning of totally new movement patterns. Operant conditioning, however, can be seen to play an important role in such situations.

How is novel behavior produced by operant conditioning? The experimenter takes advantage of random variations in the operant response, reinforcing only those responses that are in the desired direction. For example, he can make a pigeon hold her head ever so high as she walks around by reinforcing with grain, at first when her head is at average height, then when slightly above average, and finally only when her neck is stretched high. Or if he wants to train a dog to press a buzzer with his paw he can *shape* the dog's behavior by giving a food reinforcement each time the animal approaches the area of the buzzer, requiring closer and closer approximations to the desired spot for each reinforcement until finally the dog is touching the buzzer. This technique is called *shaping* behavior, reinforcing only responses that meet the experimenter's specifications and extinguishing all others (see Figure 11–14). In the case of the dog and the buzzer the experimenter may hasten the process by placing a bit of food on the buzzer so that the animal's attention is directed to the correct spot early in the training.

One psychologist and his psychologist wife developed a large-scale business teaching animals elaborate tricks and behavior routines by means of this shaping method. Using these relatively simple techniques, they and their staff trained thousands of animals of many species for television shows and commercials, country fairs, and various tourist attractions, such as the famous whale and porpoise shows at "Marine Studios" in Florida and "Marineland of the Pacific" in California. For example, one popular show involved a pig called "Priscilla, the Fastidious Pig." Priscilla turned on the radio, ate breakfast at a table, picked up dirty clothes and put them in a hamper, ran a vacuum clearer over the floor, picked out her favorite food (from among foods competing with that of her sponsor!), and took part in a quiz program, answering

Shaping behavior

Yale Joel from *Life*, © Time, Inc.

By reinforcing only the desired responses, the experimenter taught the pigeon to tap the correct sign when light of a certain color was turned on.

questions from the audience by flashing lights indicating "Yes" or "No." She was not an unusually bright pig; because pigs grow so fast a new "Priscilla" was trained every three to five months (Breland and Breland, 1966). The ingenuity was not the pig's but the experimenters', who used operant conditioning and shaped the behavior to produce the desired result.

In all of these training techniques the behavior is shaped by means of reinforcement; reinforcement is contingent upon the proper response. The importance of reinforcement in strengthening behavior is demonstrated by what happens when we introduce noncontingent reinforcement, that is, reinforcement that is not contingent upon a specific response. In one experiment Skinner placed hungry pigeons, one at a time, in a Skinner box and at random intervals turned on a light that was immediately followed by a food reinforcement. The effect on the behavior of the pigeons

was quite amazing. Each bird tended to select and repeat whatever behavior he was engaged in just before the reinforcement occurred. If one pigeon was pecking at his right wing just prior to reinforcement, this behavior tended to increase in frequency. The increased frequency made it more likely that this bit of behavior would occur about the time of the next food delivery and so would be reinforced again. Soon right-wing-pecking dominated the bird's behavior. Thus for each bird some particular act or mannerism gained dominance because it occurred at the time of reinforcement regardless of the fact that the act was in no way instrumental in producing the reinforcement.

Skinner has noted the similarity between the pigeons' behavior and the superstitions people develop as the result of the chance occurrence of an act and a reinforcement together. The gambler who blows on the dice before throwing them and the baseball pitcher who habitually tugs at his cap and shakes his left foot before throwing the ball are reinforced often enough by a successful performance that the behavior is strengthened and becomes a part of their repertoire. They certainly are not successful every time. But, as we noted earlier, partial reinforcement is more resistant to extinction than continuous reinforcement.

Escape and avoidance procedures

Another method of studying operant conditioning uses a negative **rather than** a positive type of reinforcement. Instead of a food tray the Skinner box is equipped with an electric grid on the floor which delivers a shock to the paws of the rat. The rat can terminate the shock by pressing a bar. On the first trial the rat may exhibit a variety of agitated and disturbed behaviors—running, squealing, jumping. Eventually he will accidentally hit the bar and the shock is terminated. On the next trial he will press the bar more rapidly following the onset of shock; after several trials he will respond within a fraction of a second. The procedure is essentially the same as in the food-reward situation except that the reinforcement is the *termination* of shock rather than the presentation of food. This type of operant conditioning is termed *escape conditioning* because the response (bar-pressing) brings about escape from a noxious or pain-producing stimulus. Escape conditioning generally proceeds at a faster rate than reward conditioning.

Avoidance conditioning is similar to escape conditioning except that the onset of the shock is preceded by a signal (such as a light or buzzer), and the animal can avoid the shock entirely by making the appropriate response. The response may be pressing a bar as in the escape example, jumping a hurdle into an adjacent compartment, or turning a wheel. Once the response has been learned the animal will perform faithfully for many trials without receiving a shock. This resistance to extinction is not unlike human avoidance behavior; we may avoid such things as poison ivy, snakes, hot stoves, and other potentially harmful stimuli for years without requiring a second exposure to their noxious qualities.

For experimental purposes avoidance conditioning may often have advantages over reward conditioning. For example, if we wish to train an animal for long periods at a time he may become satiated and stop responding if we are using food or water as reinforcement. Or if we wish to determine the influence of a certain drug on the course of learning we might prefer that the drug's effects on the body not be confounded by the ingestion of food or water.

Operant conditioning of human behavior

Analogies between operant conditioning of animals and human learning are easy to find. For example, a child's spontaneous babbling is differentially reinforced so that he begins to "talk," that is, to yield operant utterances recognizable to the parents. Though plausible, such an analogy should be supported by experimental evidence that the laws of learning we find in our animal experiments also apply to human behavior.

In the following experiment the subject did not know that he was being experimented upon, and the experimenter thereby avoided the artificiality of many condi-

tioning experiments. The experimenter carried on an informal conversation with the subject, but behaved according to a plan, kept his eye on the clock, and tallied responses inconspicuously in the "doodles" that he drew while he and the subject were talking together.

The experimenter determined in advance to reinforce, by means of agreeing with the subject, all statements of opinion, such as sentences beginning "I think," "I believe," "It seems to me," and the like. *Reinforcement* through agreement was expressed by saying, "You're right," "I agree," "That's so." *Extinction* was carried out in another portion of the experiment by mere nonreinforcement—silence—following a statement of opinion. Other conditions of the experiment included extinction by disagreement. Following verbal reinforcement, statements of opinion increased in frequency; following extinction, they decreased (Verplanck, 1955).

Operant conditioning principles have also been used to modify problem behavior in children. In one instance nursery school teachers, with the help of some psychology students from a neighboring university, used social reinforcement to change the behavior of a three-and-a-half-year-old girl who was very shy and withdrawn upon first entering school, spending most of her time crawling about the floor and resisting all attempts to encourage her to talk, play, or join in group activities. On the assumption that getting the child to spend more time on her feet was the first step toward increasing participation in school activities, a reinforcement schedule was set up whereby the teachers and student assistants gave attention to the child only when she was standing and ignored her completely the rest of the time. (At first her behavior was shaped by reinforcing any response that even approximated standing.) Careful recording of the child's minute-by-minute activity showed that she progressed from an initial rate of 93 percent of the day on the floor to the point where after two weeks her behavior was indistinguishable from that of the other children in terms of talking, smiling, and vigorous use of the school equipment (although she still did not initiate contacts with other children). To determine whether the reinforcement schedule was the causative factor (as opposed to simply adapting to the school situation over time) the procedure was reversed so that now only on-the-floor activity was reinforced. Within two days the child was back to spending 82 percent of her time on the floor. (Interestingly enough, she did not revert to her earlier behavior in other respects, but managed to play happily while sitting or crawling on her knees and for the first time began to initiate contacts with the other children.) A second reversal procedure (i.e., again giving the child steady attention when she was on her feet and none when she was on the floor) reinstated her vigorous on-the-feet participation in school activities within a few hours, and her behavior in the days that followed seemed adequate in every way (Harris, Johnston, Kelley, and Wolf, 1965). This study demonstrates the application of learning principles developed in the laboratory to life situations. We will have more to say about the use of operant-conditioning techniques in modifying human behavior in Chapter 22.

The Principle of Reinforcement

In our discussion of classical conditioning we used the term *reinforcement* to refer to the paired presentation of the unconditioned stimulus and the conditioned stimulus. In operant conditioning reinforcement referred to the presentation of food (or termination of shock) following the occurrence of the desired response. Put in other terms, in classical conditioning reinforcement *elicits* the response, and in operant conditioning reinforcement *follows* the response. Although the operation we designate as reinforcement is quite different in the two situations, in both instances the result is an increase in the likelihood of the desired response. We can therefore define reinforcement as *any event whose occur-*

rence increases the probability that a stimulus will on subsequent occasions evoke a response. We customarily distinguish between two types of reinforcers: *positive reinforcers* (such as food), whose presentation increases the probability of a response, and *negative reinforcers* (such as shock), whose termination increases response probability.[4]

Parameters of reinforcement

Psychologists have systematically investigated the effect of a number of reinforcement variables on the course of learning. Not surprisingly, the *amount of reinforcement* has been found to be an important parameter. Within limits the greater the amount of reinforcement the more rapid the rate of learning. This relationship is nicely illustrated by the following experiment (Clayton, 1964). The apparatus used was a T-maze, the simplest type of maze consisting of a start box, straight runway, and a cross bar with a goal box at both ends. A rat is placed in the start box, runs to the cross bar, and then must choose between a right or left turn to reach the food placed in one of the goal boxes. In this experiment there were three groups of rats, the groups differing in the amount of food received for a correct turn: one group received four food pellets, one group two food pellets, and one group one pellet. Each rat ran four trials a day for 13 days of acquisition training and five days of extinction (where no food was given in either goal box). The results in terms of proportion of correct responses per day are shown in Figure 11–15. Note that the curves start at 0.5; since there are only two response choices the animal would make the correct turn approximately 50 percent of the time by chance alone prior to training. All three groups reached approximately the same asymptotic level (close to perfect respond-

[4] These terms are synonymous with the terms positive and negative incentives used in our discussion of motivation in Chapter 5. Both are used interchangeably in the psychological literature but it is customary to use the word reinforcer rather than incentive in discussing learning.

Amount of reinforcement

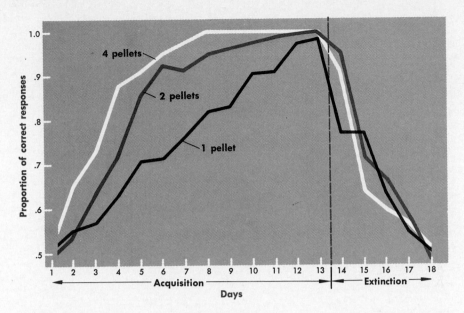

Acquisition and extinction curves for three groups of rats run in a T-maze experiment. During acquisition the groups were distinguished by the number of food pellets a rat received when he entered the correct goal box. Half the animals were trained with the left side of the maze designated as the correct response, half with the right side as the correct response. During extinction neither goal box contained food. (After Clayton, 1964)

ing) by the 13th day, but the rate at which they approached this asymptote differed. The group with the largest amount of reinforcement learned at the fastest rate and was responding with 100 percent accuracy by the eighth day. The group that received two pellets learned somewhat more slowly, and the one-pellet group showed the slowest learning rate. Interestingly enough, when we look at the extinction data the curves for the three groups are almost identical, indicating that resistance to extinction was not affected by amount of reward during acquisition.

The *delay of reinforcement* is another important parameter of reinforcement. It has been a common assumption that in training animals or young children it is most effective to reward or punish the organism immediately after he responds. The spanking given by father when he returns home from work is less effective (other variables

being equal) in reducing junior's aggressive behavior toward baby brother than punishment delivered immediately following or during the act.

The effectiveness of immediate reinforcement in a laboratory learning situation is demonstrated by the following experiment. The apparatus involved a T-maze whose goal boxes were equipped with food dispensers that could be set to delay the presentation of food pellets. One group of rats received their food immediately upon entering the correct goal box (zero-seconds delay); another group was fed following a five-second delay; and a third group was delayed 30 seconds before receiving their food. Each rat was run 10 trials per day for 10 days of acquisition training and six days of extinction. Figure 11–16 shows the proportion of correct responses per day for each of the three groups. The zero-second group and the five-second group have both

Delay of reward

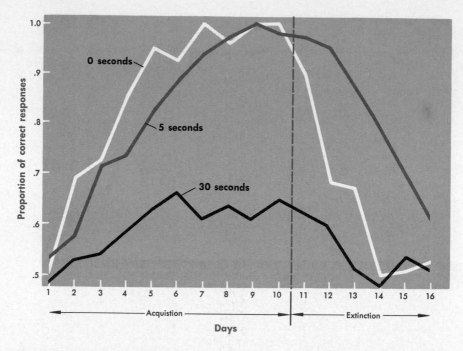

Acquisition and extinction curves for three groups of rats run in a T-maze experiment. During acquisition the three groups were distinguished by the time interval between entering the correct goal box and receiving a pellet of food. During extinction the food reward was discontinued. (Atkinson, unpublished data)

reached the same asymptotic level of responding (100 percent correct responses) by the ninth day of the experiment, but the zero-second group learned at a faster rate. The 30-second delay group is markedly inferior both in rate of learning and in its final asymptotic level during acquisition; the animals in this group never achieved better than 65 percent correct responses. Note also that the five-second delay group which learned more slowly than the zero-second group also extinguishes more slowly (is more resistant to extinction). This result is in contrast to the results of the preceding study on amount of reinforcement where all three groups extinguished at the same rate. Thus, we see that delay of reinforcement affects extinction, but amount of reinforcement does not. This result illustrates the complexity involved in the study of learning: one reinforcement variable influ-

ences both acquisition and extinction, another affects only acquisition.

That animals are able to learn when reinforcement is delayed is attributed, in part, to the role of secondary reinforcers which serve to bridge the time gap between the response and the primary reinforcement. For example, the sight of the empty food cup in the goal box can provide reinforcement (by virtue of its past association with food) even though the appearance of the pellets is delayed. It has been demonstrated that reduction in the number of secondarily reinforcing cues (e.g., by having a food cup in both the correct and incorrect goal boxes so that food cup is associated with nonreinforcement as well as reinforcement) greatly reduces the amount of delay that can be tolerated. For example, using rats as subjects, some studies (where the design of the apparatus has provided many secondarily reinforcing cues) indicate that learning can take place with a delay of 15 to 20 minutes between response and reinforcement; other studies, which have attempted to eliminate all secondarily reinforcing cues, report no learning after a delay of two seconds.

The nature of reinforcement

Why do reinforcing events increase the probability of a response? What is the nature of reinforcement? Why are certain events effective reinforcers while others are not? These questions, which have been the subject of intense interest and debate among psychologists, are obviously closely involved with the whole problem of motivation. The most prevalent hypothesis has been the *drive-reduction theory* of reinforcement. As we saw in Chapter 5, when an organism is in a state of physiological need (as the result of deprivation or some injury to the tissues) there exists a concurrent state of tension known as *drive*. Drive serves to energize the organism and to produce certain internal stimuli that are associated with the drive. An animal deprived of food exhibits restless activity and the stimuli associated with the hunger drive (such as stomach contractions and low blood-sugar level) lead to food-seeking behavior. With the ingestion of food the hunger drive is reduced and the associated stimuli disappear. According to this theory then, any event that is drive-reducing is reinforcing. All primary reinforcers are drive-reducing; secondary reinforcers are not drive-reducing in themselves but provide reinforcing effects by virtue of their previous association with primary reinforcers.

The drive-reduction theory of reinforcement does seem to be a reasonable explanation in many instances. Food, water, and shock termination (which reduce the drives of hunger, thirst, and pain) are among our most effective reinforcers. And several studies have shown that learning does take place when drives are reduced by direct physiological intervention rather than by externally administered reinforcement. For example, Miller and Kessen (1952) provided a group of rats with stomach fistulas so that milk could be injected directly into the stomach. The rats were run in a simple T-maze with milk introduced into the stomach for correct responses and saline solution introduced for incorrect responses. Although learning was faster for another group of rats that received milk by mouth, the milk-injected rats learned also and reached an asymptotic level of perfect responding by the 35th trial. In a related study food-deprived rabbits showed learning when the reinforcement was an intravenous injection of glucose which reduced the hunger drive by raising the blood-sugar level (Coppock and Chambers, 1954).

There have been a number of experimental results, however, that are difficult to explain in terms of drive-reduction theory. Some of these were mentioned in Chapter 5. Hungry rats will learn to press a bar or to choose the correct path in a maze when reinforced by a non-nutritive substance, such as saccharine; male rats will learn to jump a barrier to copulate with females in heat even though no ejaculation is permitted. In both instances no drive was reduced—in fact, one might consider the latter situation drive-increasing— yet learning to make the necessary movements to approach the incentive occurred. We have seen (p. 130) that animals as well as human subjects will learn in a variety of situations where the only reinforcement is the opportunity to see or to explore a new environment or to manipulate new or novel objects.

Other theories have been proposed as alternatives to the drive-reduction concept of reinforcement. One viewpoint is that reinforcement is more a matter of the nature of the reinforcing activities than of the reinforcing stimuli (Premack, 1962, 1965). According to this view, if activities fall in the preferential order *A-B-C-D* from low to high, then activity *B* can reinforce activity *A*, activity *C* can reinforce either *A* or *B*, and activity *D* can reinforce any one of the other three activities. Note that an activity can reinforce only some other activities— those of lower preference but not those of higher preference. It is possible to use the eating of dessert to reinforce the eating of vegetables, but the reverse order has no reinforcing value. A good deal of experimental evidence with both animals and human subjects has given support to this position.

Still another viewpoint proposes that reinforcement is not essential for learning to occur. According to this theory, *temporal contiguity* between a stimulus and a response is the only necessary condition for learning. If a response occurs in the presence of a specific stimulus, then the S-R association is strengthened and the probability that the stimulus will evoke the same response on subsequent occasions is increased. Reinforcement according to this position is important in *motivating* the organism to perform the response, but it is not necessary for learning (Guthrie, 1940; Sheffield, 1965).

CRITICAL DISCUSSION

Brain stimulation and reinforcement

One area of research which is currently of great interest stems from the rather startling discovery that electrical stimulation of certain regions of the brain can be reinforcing. In 1953 Olds was investigating the reticular formation of the rat's brain (see p. 41) by means of microelectrodes. These tiny electrodes can be implanted permanently in very specific brain areas without interfering with the rat's health or normal activity and, when connected with an electrical source, can supply stimulation of varying intensities. By accident an electrode was implanted in an area near the hypothalamus. Olds discovered that after he had delivered a mild current through the electrodes the animal repeatedly returned to the location in the cage where he had been when stimulated. Further stimulations at the same cage location caused the animal to spend most of his time there. Later Olds found that this same animal could be pulled to any spot in a maze by giving electrical stimulation after each response in the appropriate direction. And other animals with electrodes implanted in the same brain region learned to press a bar in a Skinner box to produce their own electrical stimulation (see Figure 11–17); each bar-press closed a circuit that automatically provided a brief current. These animals were bar-pressing at a phenomenal rate: a not unusual record would show an average of over 2,000 responses an hour for 15 or 20 hours, until the animal finally dropped from exhaustion.

Since the initial brain stimulation discovery, experiments have been carried out using rats, cats, and monkeys in a wide variety of tasks with microelectrodes implanted in many different areas of the brain and brain stem. The reinforcing effects of stimulation in certain areas (primarily the hypothalamus) is a powerful one: hungry rats will endure a more painful shock while crossing an electric grid to obtain brain stimulation than they will to obtain food (Olds and Sinclair, 1957); when given a choice between food or electric brain stimulation in a T-maze, rats who have been on a starvation diet for as long as 10 days will invariably choose the path leading to stimulation (Spies, 1965). In some instances brain stimulation is a more powerful reward than water or sexual activity (Olds, 1956). On the other hand, stimulation of some areas of the brain stem has been found to serve as a *negative* reinforcer; when the electrodes were moved to a different brain area, rats who previously bar-pressed at a rapid rate to receive stimulation suddenly stopped responding and avoided the bar area entirely, indicating that the new stimulation was unpleasant. And other animals have learned various responses to avoid stimulation in these areas, for example, pressing a lever or turning a wheel to turn *off* the current (Delgado, Roberts, and Miller, 1954).

Much progress has been made in mapping out the neutral, negatively, and positively reinforcing areas of the brain, and theories have been developed relating the function of these areas to avoidance and approach behavior (Olds and Olds, 1965). In addition to placement of the electrodes, two important variables determining whether brain stimulation is positively or negatively reinforcing are the intensity and duration of the stimulation. Up to a point increasing the intensity of stimulation is increasingly reinforcing; beyond that higher

Brain-stimulation experiment

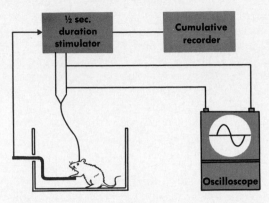

The animal's bar-press delivers a 60-cycle current for one-half second, after which the animal must release and press again for more current. The animal's response rate is recorded on the cumulative recorder, and the experimenter can monitor the delivery of the current by means of the cathode-ray oscilloscope. Rats respond with rates up to 100 per minute with electrodes in the medial-forebrain region of the hypothalamus. (After Olds and Olds, 1965)

intensities become less effective and may, if intense enough, become aversive (possibly because the stimulation spreads to negatively reinforcing areas). There is evidence too that while brief stimulation is reinforcing, prolonged stimulation in the same area becomes aversive. Both of these facts are compatible with the general notion that an intermediate level of stimulation is experienced as most pleasant while deviations to either extreme are frequently not pleasant at all.

Psychologists are not yet agreed on the significance of the brain-stimulation studies. It would be nice to think that we had discovered the anatomical location of reinforcement, that when we stimulate one brain stem area in a rat, for example, the sensations are similar to those experienced when reinforced with food to assuage hunger, or that the sensations in another area are similar to those experienced when reinforced with water for thirst. Unfortunately, the rat cannot describe his sensations. What little data we have from human subjects undergoing electrical exploration of the brain during treatment for Parkin-

son's disease indicates that the sensation is not clear-cut, but rather a vague state of "feeling good" (Semm-Jacobsen and Torkildsen, 1960).

In some respects learning with brain stimulation as reinforcement does not follow the same rules as learning with food or other external rewards. The extinction of the bar-press response for brain stimulation is much more rapid than extinction for food or water rewards. If the current is turned off the animal's responses stop quite abruptly, but he will start responding again at a rapid rate if he is given one or two stimulations. And while partial reinforcement can be used quite effectively with food or water reinforcement (animals will learn even though the ratio of nonreinforced to reinforced trials is very high) it is much less effective when the reinforcement is brain stimulation (Brodie and others, 1960). These and other data suggest that brain stimulation operates differently from other reinforcers; it seems to create a temporary sensation that does not increase in strength during deprivation.

Multiple-Response Learning

Thus far we have considered the strengthening or weakening of single identifiable responses. Although some of these are complex (such as a statement of opinion), they are still identifiable as unitary acts. But much of our learning consists in acquiring patterns or sequences of movements or words, as in learning skills or in memorizing a poem. These patterns illustrate *multiple-response learning*, a kind of learning involving more than one identifiable act, with the order of events usually fixed by the demands of the situation. Psychologists have designed a number of laboratory tasks by which to study this kind of learning. Among them are maze learning (used with both animals and men and involving much more complicated mazes than the simple T-maze), mirror drawing, pursuit learning, and rote memorization. The first three tasks are forms of *sensorimotor skill*, while the last is largely verbal. Tasks such as these approximate the learning of common skills with the tools and language of our physical and social environment. We shall discuss sensorimotor skills and rote memorization as examples of multiple-response learning. It is assumed, to be sure, that such principles as reinforcement, extinction, and generalization will apply, but perhaps new principles will emerge because of the complex patternings involved.

Sensorimotor skills

By a *sensorimotor skill* we mean one in which muscular movement is prominent, but under sensory control. Riding a bicycle, turning a flip from a springboard, playing a piano, and operating a lathe are sensorimotor skills. They are not simply patterns of skilled movements. The bicycle rider has to watch the traffic and the bumps in the road, and be guided by them; the diver must adjust his timing to the height of the platform; the musician reads notes and attempts to play with feeling; the lathe operator must follow a blueprint and stay within the tolerances allowed. These considerations call attention to the *sensory control* of skill, and are the reason for the somewhat awkward name of sensorimotor skill.

In studying skills, psychologists have not limited themselves to laboratory tasks; the pioneer study was, in fact, a practical one on learning to send and receive telegraphic messages, done by Bryan and Harter in 1897. Many of the best-established principles are first worked out on laboratory skills, however, and later validated in more complex practical situations. A convenient laboratory illustration is given by the mirror-drawing experiment. We learn something of the importance of eye-hand coordination in developing skills by studying what happens when our usual eye-hand coordinations are inappropriate, and we have to reorient accordingly.

In a typical mirror-drawing experiment, the subject is required to trace a path around a geometrical figure, such as a six-pointed star, while viewing it in a mirror. The subject knows what the correct performance is—a smoothly traced line within the path around the figure. The subject starts out by using familiar habits. These of course get him into trouble, for if he uses the visual cues of a mirror as he uses cues in direct vision, his pencil will not go where he wishes it to go. He therefore attempts to correct and gradually approximates a good performance, although at first he draws a very jagged line. He may have special trouble at the corners, where old and new habits again interfere. With practice, however, his lines smooth out, and he can achieve a rapid tracing of the figure (Figure 11–18).

Learning curves for skill. Experimenters typically keep track of progress in skill learning by plotting a learning curve similar to those used to depict the course of classical conditioning. *Proficiency,* in terms of correct responses, errors, or time scores, is plotted on the ordinate (the vertical axis) and *practice,* number of trials, is plotted on the abscissa (the horizontal axis). Two learning curves for mirror draw-

11–18

Mirror drawing

Dr. Lester Beck

The subject attempts to follow with his pencil the outlines of the stars on the paper shielded from direct view. Because in the mirror the usual right-left relationships are reversed, he has to learn a new eye-hand coordination.

11–19

Learning curves for mirror drawing

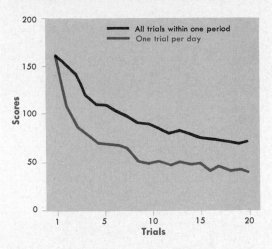

The scores that constitute the curves are related to the amount of time required to trace a figure in the mirror, and hence decrease as skill goes up. The top curve is for massed practice, all trials within one period. The bottom curve is for trials spaced one trial per day. (After Lorge, 1930)

ing are plotted in Figure 11–19, one where practice trials follow each other consecutively within one period (*massed practice*) and one with practice trials spaced at one trial per day (*distributed practice*). Note that distributed practice is more efficient. We shall return to the problem of distributed practice later, but this comparison shows how learning curves can be used to display a relationship.

The general form of a learning curve depends upon the units of measurement. In Figure 11–19 the measure of proficiency is a score related to the time required to trace a figure seen in the mirror. Improvement shows a decrease in time required and yields a falling curve.

If the measure of proficiency is a score that increases with practice, then the learning curve rises. Scores in *pursuit-rotor* learning are of this kind. For instance, the subject attempts to hold the tip of a metal stylus on a small spot revolving on a turntable similar to that of an ordinary phonograph (Figure 11–20). His score depends on the amount of time his stylus remains

in contact with the spot. Proficiency gain will be represented in this case by a rising curve, for the longer the subject stays on the target, the better his score (Figure 11–21).

Whether the curve falls or rises, we can describe its curvature according to the way in which the amount of gain varies with successive trials. The curves of both Figure 11–19 and Figure 11–21 are curves of *decreasing gains*. By decreasing gain we mean that the change in performance from the current trial to the next is always less than the change that took place on the previous trial. Such curves are by all odds the most common in studies of sensorimotor skill.

11–20

Subject following the target of a pursuit rotor

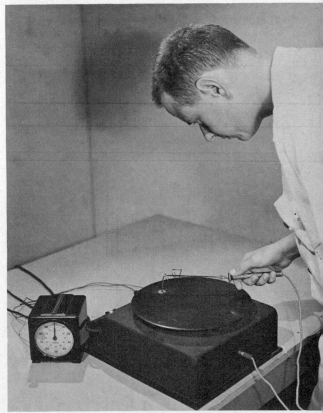

David Linton

The task is to keep the stylus on the small target as the turntable revolves.

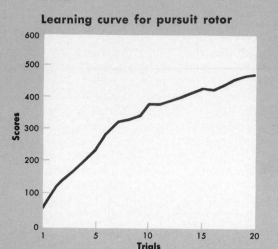

11–21

Learning curve for pursuit rotor

Each trial lasts for one minute with a brief rest period between trials. The scores that make up the curve are for successive trials and represent the time on target during the trial. A maximum possible score for a given trial is 600; that is, a possible score of 10 per second if the stylus remains on the target. (After Bell, 1950)

They tell us one reason why the learning of a skill is often discouraging to the learner, for gains are visible and satisfying at first, but the slowing down of improvement after the first few trials may easily become disappointing.

Qualitative changes with practice. A learning curve plots proficiency as though the subject followed the same pattern of activity at the end as at the beginning and improved only in efficiency. But it is quite possible that in the course of improvement he has changed his task. For example, in studying the learning of typewriting, some investigators have detected a shift from a *letter habit* (learning the location of the individual keys associated with each letter) to a *word habit* (learning to write familiar words with a single burst of movement, embedding the letters in a total pattern). Occasionally these higher-order learnings and the lower-order learnings conflict, and there is a period of no improvement in the learning curve, described as a *plateau* be-

cause it has been **preceded** by improvement and will be followed by improvement when the higher-order learning wins out. The plateau is not universally found in skill learning, and explanations other than the one given here have been offered for it. One, for example, is that it is caused by a temporary decrease in motivation related to discouragement with the decreasing gains in the typical learning curve.

Rote memorization

By *rote memorization* we mean verbatim learning by repetition, as contrasted with substance memorizing. Hermann Ebbinghaus (1850–1909), a distinguished German psychologist, performed a pioneer study of memorization in 1885. He used nonsense syllables in order to avoid the influence of previous learning that would be found in using ordinary words. The nonsense syllables consisted of two consonants with a vowel between, such as "pov" or "juk." Other materials have also been used in rote memorization, such as meaningful words or lists of numerals.

Experiments on rote memorizing take one of two chief forms, corresponding to the kinds of things learned verbatim in ordinary experience. One form is *serial memorization,* as in the memorizing of poetry or lines of a play. In the laboratory, a series of words is memorized from beginning to end, so that each word is in some sense the stimulus for the word to follow. The second form is *paired-associate* learning, which is comparable to the method sometimes used in learning the words of a foreign language. That is, the words are learned in pairs, such as *prepared-afraid, careless-vacant, hungry-quiet;* a stimulus word is presented, and the response word has to be learned. The pairs are not learned in any special order and may or may not be meaningfully related.

The experimenter usually presents the material to the subject by means of an **ex-**posure device called a *memory drum* (Figure 11–22). The items to be learned appear one at a time in the aperture of the memory drum. After the first presentation of the items, the subject tries to state in advance

A memory drum

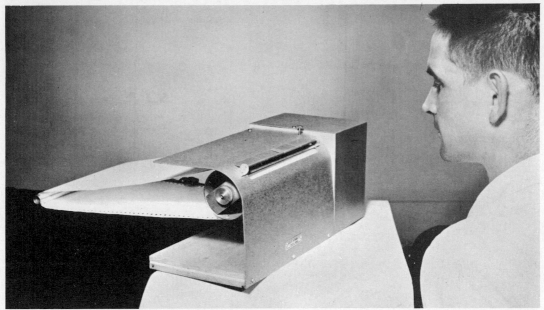

Lafayette Instrument Co.

The material to be memorized appears in the aperture as the drum revolves.

the next item to appear in the aperture. By keeping score of the subject's hits and misses throughout memorizing, the experimenter can plot a learning curve from his record.

Because the subject tries to state what lies immediately ahead, the method is called the *anticipation method*. It can be used for either serial memorization or paired-associate memorization. In the serial method the item anticipated, once it appears in the aperture, becomes the stimulus for the next anticipation; it is both a response item and a stimulus item. In the paired-associate method the stimulus item is used only as a stimulus, not as a response. When the anticipation method is used in paired-associate learning the stimulus is presented alone, the subject tries to anticipate the response item, and then the stimulus-response pair appears in the window and remains there until the next stimulus item is presented. The paired-associate method is closely analogous to conditioning, the stimulus word corresponding to the conditioned stimulus to which a response is to be learned. When the response word appears in the aperture, it "reinforces" what the subject has just said (if his anticipation was correct) or "extinguishes" a faulty anticipation. It can be shown that paired-associate learning does in fact exhibit principles in common with conditioning.

To illustrate the paired-associate procedure we shall briefly describe a study on second-language learning. The equipment used in this experiment was more elaborate than the typical memory drum, for reasons that will soon be obvious. The task was to learn the correct English translation for a list of Russian words. The subject, who had no previous knowledge of Russian, wore a set of earphones while seated before a projection screen. A Russian word was pronounced over the earphones and, at the same time, three English words were projected onto the screen, one of which was the correct translation. The subject was required to press one of three buttons to indicate which word he thought was the correct translation. After he made his response the button corresponding to the

Paired-associate learning curves

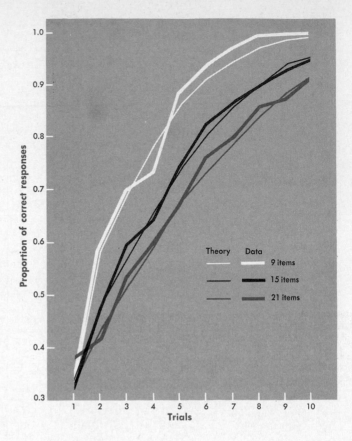

Proportion of correct anticipation responses over successive trials of a paired-associate learning experiment. The figure compares observed proportions with those predicted from a theory of verbal learning. (After Crothers and Suppes, 1967)

correct answer lighted briefly. The subject noted whether he was correct and, after a brief pause, the procedure was repeated; the next Russian word was presented and a new set of English words was projected onto the screen. After the entire list of Russian words had been run through the experimenter rearranged the items in a new random order and again presented the list to the subject. Each run through the list constituted a trial.

Three groups of subjects were run using different list lengths: one group learned to recognize nine words, another 15 words, and a third 21 words. The proportion of correct responses over successive trials of the experiment is plotted in Figure 11–23. We can see by inspecting the curves that the shortest list was learned most quickly. For example, on the third trial subjects on the nine-word list were making about 70 percent correct responses, while subjects on the 21-word list were correct only about

50 percent of the time. These results, of course, are what one would expect; the longer the list, the slower the rate at which individual stimulus items are learned. The reason for conducting the experiment, however, was to test a mathematical model of how paired associates are formed. The smooth curves in Figure 11–23 are those predicted on the basis of theoretical considerations. (We will have more to say about mathematical models for learning later. To the extent that the theoretical curves "fit" the data, the model is successful.)

In recent years a controversial issue has arisen concerning the manner in which simple paired-associate responses are formed.

In the past it generally had been assumed that stimulus-response connections were formed in a gradual fashion, with each successive reinforcement adding to the strength of the association. Because associative strength increases by small amounts, this is called the *incremental* position. More recently the view has been advanced that a stimulus-response association is formed in an *all-or-none* fashion, that is, in jumps rather than gradually.

The new position was given dramatic impetus by the experiments of Rock (1957). He set up a situation in which a number of paired items were to be memorized; any pair not learned in one trial was replaced by a new pair, so that nothing but one-trial (i.e., all-or-none) learning was possible. He found that it took the same number of trials to learn a list in this manner, where gradual learning was not possible, as in the conventional experiment in which the same

pairs are repeatedly reinforced until all are learned.

While there were some difficulties in the design of Rock's experiments, the experiments called attention to the possibility of all-or-none learning, and later experimenters and theoreticians have shown both the possibilities and limitations of this model. Estes (1960, 1964a), Bower (1961, 1966), and others have shown that in many experimental situations the all-or-none model does indeed yield a good fit to the data.

The assumptions of the all-or-none model are illustrated in Figure 11–24. Each of the small graphs on the left side of the figure represent the probability of a correct response as a function of the number of reinforcements for an individual subject. Each subject begins at the same initial level, and following each reinforcement there is some chance that his response probability will jump from its initial level to unity. Because

11–24

All-or-none learning curves

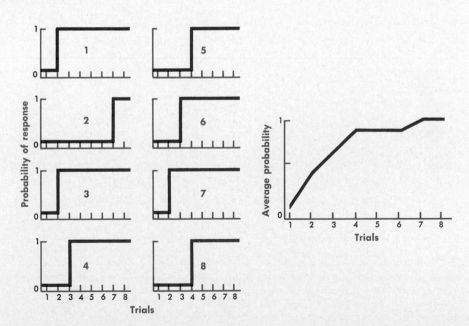

The small graphs represent the probability of a response as a function of the number of reinforcements for each of eight hypothetical subjects. The learning is all-or-none because response probability changes on a single trial from an initial level to unity (i.e., perfect responding). Because the curves for individual subjects jump to unity on different trials, the learning curve averaged over all eight subjects (plotted to the far right) displays a gradually increasing function. Thus, the average learning curve does not reflect the nature of the learning process for individual subjects.

of the probabilistic nature of the process, different subjects learn (i.e., jump to unity) on different trials; reinforcement was effective on trial two for subject one, but not effective for subject eight until trial four. If data are averaged for a large group of subjects, all behaving in an all-or-none way, a curve representing the proportion of correct responses per trial would average out to approximate a smooth increasing function. The graph in the far right of Figure 11–24 shows that even for our sample of eight subjects, the probability of a correct response averaged over these subjects is a gradually increasing function.

Figure 11–25 presents some predictions from the all-or-none model for data from a large group of hypothetical subjects. In the figure we assume that all subjects start from an initial level of 0.5. The initial level depends upon the experimental situation. For example, in a T-maze where the animal has to choose between a right or a left turn

the initial probability of a correct response would be approximately one in two, unless for some reason the animal had an initial preference for one side. For learning tasks involving a number of alternative responses the initial probability of the correct response would be lower, approaching zero as the number of response alternatives increased. In Figure 11–25 we assume also that the probability of forming the association between the stimulus and the correct response on any trial is one in 10. This probability, called the *conditioning parameter,* is essentially a measure of how quickly the subject will learn and depends on such variables as degree of deprivation, amount of reinforcement, and so forth. When the conditioning parameter is large (close to one) learning will occur rapidly; when the parameter is close to zero learning proceeds slowly. We would expect the parameter to vary, for example, with the brightness of the learner. The curve labeled $P(R_n)$ in the figure gives the proportion of correct responses per trial averaged over all subjects and is a smooth increasing function; $P(R_n)$ indicates the probability of a correct response on trial n. Another prediction of the all-or-none model is indicated by the horizontal broken line labeled $P(R_n|\overline{R}_{n-1})$.[5] This line represents the probability that a correct response will occur on any trial, given that the subject made an incorrect response on the preceding trial, and, as you can see, the probability according to the all-or-none theory is constant.

The way in which to choose between two quantitative theories is to find which one agrees better with experimental data. It happens that both the all-or-none model and the incremental (gradual-learning) model predict the same course of learning, as represented by an average curve like the $P(R_n)$ function in Figure 11–25. However, other predictions are quite different. Thus the incremental position would predict that the $P(R_n|\overline{R}_{n-1})$ function should be exactly like that for $P(R_n)$. This follows because

11–25

Predictions for all-or-none model

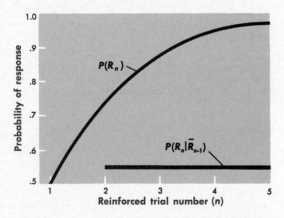

The curve marked $P(R_n)$ is the average probability of a correct response on the nth trial (where n represents any trial from one through five). It is obtained by assuming that individual subjects learn in an all-or-none fashion and that the probability that learning will occur on any given trial is .10. The curve labeled $P(R_n|\overline{R}_{n-1})$ is the probability that a response will be made on trial n conditionalized on the fact that no response occurred on trial n − 1. Note that this curve does not show any improvement as a function of the number of previously reinforced trials. (After Estes, 1964a)

[5] In probability theory a vertical bar is used for writing conditional probabilities. The expression $P(R_n|\overline{R}_{n-1})$ is read as "the probability of a response on trial n conditional upon the event of no response on trial n −1," or "the conditional probability of R_n given $\overline{R}_{n-1}$."

the probability of correct response has been increasing gradually, and whether or not a particular response was correct on the preceding trial is not an indication of its strength; the whole record up to that trial is more important, and this record is that of a rising curve of probability. For the all-or-none model, however, all responses that are incorrect are in exactly the same state of learning, so that their gains on the next trial will depend solely on the conditioning parameter and not on how far along in practice the trial is. That is why the $P(R_n|\bar{R}_{n-1})$ curve is a straight line according to the all-or-none model. When an analysis is made to see whether the function is that predicted by the incremental model or the all-or-none model, results very commonly favor the all-or-none assumption (Bower, 1966), although some experiments favor the incremental model. Thus learning appears at times to be essentially continuous and at times a sharply discontinuous process. At present the challenging tasks confronting the learning theorist are: (1) to identify those experimental conditions where the all-or-none model works and those where it does not, and (2) to construct a more general model that reduces to the all-or-none model in the former cases, but accounts for the discrepancies in the latter cases.

Some current research efforts are yielding support for the position that complex forms of learning can be broken down into constituent all-or-none processes. Theios and Brelsford (1966) have shown that avoidance conditioning with rats, which appears to be essentially continuous, can be well accounted for by assuming two all-or-none processes acting simultaneously. Bower and Trabasso (1964) have shown similar results for concept learning, and Restle (1965) has given an all-or-none account of complex behaviors involving learning rules and strategies on the part of human subjects. It is too early to give a final evaluation of the controversy over all-or-none vs. incremental learning. It may well be that certain types of learning even in their most elementary form are basically continuous in nature, but the evidence is still incomplete. Defenders of the incremental position (Underwood and Keppel, 1962; Postman, 1963) have taken issue with

the all-or-none assumption, and it appears that this fundamental question will loom large in theoretical developments for some time to come.

Learning as the Achievement of Understanding

The kinds of learning that we have thus far emphasized (classical conditioning, operant conditioning, and multiple-response learning) all stress the organization of behavior into *habits* or *associations*, learned stimulus-response sequences of greater or less complexity. Those who treat learning as habit formation do not deny the role of understanding; they recognize, for example, the effects of meaningfulness of materials and the significance of knowledge of results. But they emphasize features other than understanding—a kind of fumbling trial and error until success is reached. Some psychologists prefer to place the emphasis elsewhere, with more attention to the roles of perception and knowledge, or *cognitive processes*. They fear that emphasis upon habit formation may lead to too much concern for piecemeal activities and too little attention to organized relationships and meaning. In school, for example, the teacher impressed by habit formation may use rote memorization and drill excessively, without caring enough about whether the child understands what he learns.

Köhler's insight experiments

Partly in protest against too much study of the kinds of learning that result in improvement by trial and error, Wolfgang Köhler (1887–   ), a German psychologist who later came to America, performed some dramatic experiments with chimpanzees. At some point in working on a problem, chimpanzees appeared to grasp its inner relationships through *"insight"*; that is, they solved the problem not through mere trial and error but by perceiving the relationships essential to solution. The following experiment by Köhler is typical.

Using the shorter sticks, the chimpanzee pulls in a stick long enough to reach the piece of fruit. He has learned to solve this problem by understanding the relationship between the sticks and the piece of fruit.

Yerkes Regional Primate Center

Sultan [Köhler's most intelligent chimpanzee] is squatting at the bars but cannot reach the fruit which lies outside by means of his only available short stick. A longer stick is deposited outside the bars, about two meters on one side of the objective and parallel with the grating. It cannot be grasped with the hand, but it can be pulled within reach by means of the small stick. [See Figure 11–26 for an illustration of a similar multiple-stick problem.] Sultan tries to reach the fruit with the smaller of the two sticks. Not succeeding, he tears at a piece of wire that projects from the netting of his cage, but that, too, is in vain. Then he gazes about him (there are always in the course of these tests some long pauses, during which the animals scrutinize the whole visible area). He suddenly picks up the little stick once more, goes up to the bars directly opposite to the long stick, scratches it towards him with the "auxiliary," seizes it, and goes with it to the point opposite the objective (the fruit), which he secures. From the moment that his eyes fall upon the long stick, his procedure forms one consecutive whole, without hiatus, and although the angling of the bigger stick by means of the smaller is an action that could be complete and distinct in itself, yet observation shows that it follows, quite suddenly, on an interval of hesitation and doubt—staring about—which undoubtedly has a relation to the final objective, and is immediately merged in the final action of the attainment of the end goal.[6]

[6] Köhler (1925), pp. 174–75.

A moderate degree of insight is so common in human learning that we tend to take it for granted. Occasionally insight comes dramatically, and then we have what has been appropriately called an "aha" experience. The solution of a problem becomes suddenly clear, as though a light had been turned on in the darkness. This experience usually comes with types of puzzles (or riddles) that make good parlor tricks, precisely because people enjoy the experience of insight when (and if) it comes. One illustration is furnished by the problem presented in Figure 11–27.

If we use the ordinary methods of problem-solving to solve the problem of Figure 11–27 and rely heavily on past experience, we may set up some sort of algebraic equation to determine, step by step, how far the bird flies on each trip. For example, we know that on the first trip the bird flies east at 80 mph while the train coming west toward it is running at 40 mph. It can be determined without too much difficulty that the bird will go twice as far as the train by the time they meet. Hence when they meet, the train will have gone 33⅓ miles from its starting point while the bird has flown 66⅔ miles. For the bird's return flight it will be necessary to take account of the movement of the first train during the time the bird flew the 66⅔ miles. Then, knowing the rate of flight of the bird and of the train coming to meet it, the second trip can be computed just as the first one was. We continue these computations until the trains have met.

What is meant by solving this kind of problem with insight? Instead of trying to determine, first of all, how far the bird flies on each of its trips, we can make a different try. The clue comes from the question: How long will the bird have been flying by the time the trains meet? When this question is answered, the rest of the solution comes quickly. If you now have the answer, having first been puzzled and then suddenly having "caught on," you know what the experience of insight means.

Insight, like other multiple-response learning, depends upon the capacity of the learner. Older children, for example, can learn things that younger children cannot learn. Insight is also influenced by past experiences. A chimpanzee who has retrieved food with one stick is better able to learn to retrieve food with a second stick. The student who has solved many mathematical problems does better on similar new problems. Also, the moment at which the first success will occur is unpredictable because it comes about partly as a result of varied activity. But, in spite of what it has in common with all other learning, there are several characteristics of the insight experiment that suggest that

it can be explained on the basis of the understanding of relationships.

1. *Insight depends upon the arrangement of the problematical situation.* Appropriate past experience, while necessary, does not guarantee problem solution. Insight will come easily only if the essentials for solution are arranged so that their relationships can be perceived. For example, a chimpanzee solves the stick problem more readily if the stick is on the same side of the cage as the food. He has more difficulty if he must turn away from the food to see the stick (Jackson, 1942).

2. *Once a solution occurs with insight, it can be repeated promptly.* Gradual solution appears to be the rule in trial-and-error learning. Sudden solution is the rule in insight. Once the chimpanzee has used a stick for pulling in a banana, he will seek out a stick on the next occasion.

3. *A solution achieved with insight can be applied in new situations.* What is learned in the insight experiment is not a specific movement habit, but a cognitive relationship between a means and an end. Hence one tool may be substituted for another. In Figure 11–27 boats could replace trains without confusing the problem.

A good learner is a resourceful, adaptable person, one who is able to use what

11–27

The bird and the locomotives: an insight problem

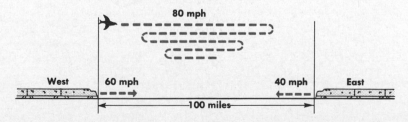

Two locomotives, now 100 miles apart, are moving toward each other. The east-bound locomotive is traveling at the rate of 60 mph. The west-bound one is traveling at the rate of 40 mph. An energetic bird, starting from the east-bound locomotive, flies back and forth between the two locomotives, without stopping or losing any speed on the turns. The bird flies at the uniform rate of 80 mph. Problem: How far does the bird fly from the start to the moment that the two trains meet? The problem can be solved by those without mathematical training (see text).

he knows in new situations and one who is able to discover for himself solutions to problems that he has never faced before. Emphasis upon insightful learning, rather than upon rote learning or mechanized skills, encourages such problem-solving behavior.

Tolman's sign learning

It is possible that some learning classified as conditioned response may actually be a learning of the signs of "what leads to what." This was the contention of Edward C. Tolman (1886–1959), who believed that much learning is *sign learning* (Tolman, 1948). A rat running through a maze may be learning a kind of map of the maze instead of merely a set of running and turning habits. If a familiar path is blocked, he can adopt another route based on this understanding of spatial relationships.

Sign learning may be defined as an acquired expectation that one stimulus will be followed by another provided a familiar behavior route is taken. Note that what is acquired is an expectation (i.e., a cognitive structure) rather than a chained sequence of movement responses. Although the expectation may lead to movement, the movement responses are not completely stereotyped; that is, one movement may be readily substituted for another, provided both movements lead to the same end point where the expected stimulus will be encountered. Because what is learned is a set of expectations or a cognitive map of the environment rather than specific responses, sign learning classifies as learning with understanding rather than as conditioning.

We will describe two kinds of experiments that Tolman cited as providing evidence for the importance of sign learning.

Place learning. Habit-formation theories assume that what the organism learns is movements or responses to stimuli. Sign learning proposes that under some circumstances the organism learns the *location* of paths or places rather than movement habits. Place learning can be demonstrated

11–28

Place learning

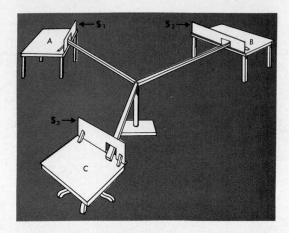

Arrangement used by Maier in studying place learning in rats. (After Maier and Schneirla, 1935)

in a number of experiments, one of which is given in the following example. A rat is allowed to explore the system of trestles and tables illustrated in Figure 11–28. The tables and runways are different in various ways (color, roughness of surface, and so forth). Following his exploration of the entire apparatus the rat is fed on one of the tables (say, table A) and at a later time is then placed on one of the other tables, B or C. (The screens S_1, S_2, and S_3 prevent the rat from seeing which table the food is on.) The rat is now able to choose the appropriate path back to the food on Table A, despite the fact that in his explorations he may never have taken this particular path in this order before. That is, the rat appears to be guided by spatial relationships rather than by reinforced movement sequences (Maier, 1932; Oakes, 1956).

Latent learning. Another experiment, that on latent learning, supports the theory that spatial orientation rather than specific responses are learned. Latent learning, broadly conceived, refers to any learning that is not demonstrated by behavior at the time of the learning. Typically, such learning goes on under low levels of drive or in the absence of reward. When drive is heightened or appropriate reinforcement appears, there is a sudden use of what is learned. In the experiment three groups of rats were run daily in a maze consisting of a series of 14 T-shaped parts, as diagramed in Figure 11–29. One group was given a food reinforcement when it reached the goal box at the end of the maze. A second group was allowed to explore the maze but, when it reached the goal box, was removed with no reinforcement. And a third group was treated in the same way as the second group for the first 10 days, and then given reinforcement for the remainder of the trials. As we can see on the chart in Figure 11–29, all groups showed some learning in that they made fewer errors in reaching the goal box as the number of trials increased. But the reinforced group clearly learned more rapidly than the two nonreinforced groups. With the introduction of food on the 11th day, however, the error scores of the third group dropped markedly and they were soon performing as well as, or even better than, the reinforced group. Evidently the rats were learning something about the spatial orientation of the maze prior to the time that they were rewarded (Tolman and Honzik, 1930).

Although at present there is some controversy over the exact circumstances under which latent learning occurs, the fact of latent learning is a familiar one in human experience. Through mild curiosity we note the location of a store selling goods in which we are not interested at the moment. When, however, we want something that the store sells, we can head directly for the store even though it was never before a goal situation. The reinforcement which comes through a purchase is not necessary to evoke the approach behavior once the appropriate motive is aroused.

Both the place-learning and the latent-learning kinds of experiment favor an explanation of learning that goes beyond mere habitual-movement sequences. Both require some recognition of what leads to what and hence lend support to a sign-learning explanation.

11–29

Latent learning in rats

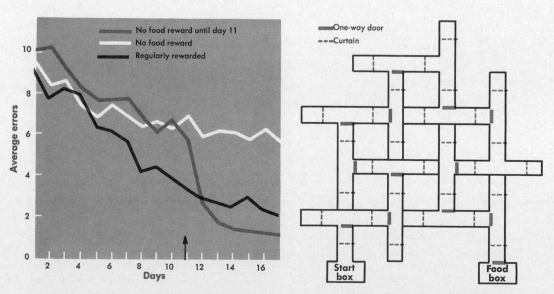

Note that after reward is introduced, on the 11th day, the rats represented by the color line perform as well as, or even a little better than, those regularly rewarded (black line). To the far right is a diagram of the maze used in this study. (After Tolman and Honzik, 1930)

CRITICAL DISCUSSION
Learning responses vs. learning cognitive structures

There is a controversy among learning theorists over the question whether the subject learns *responses* (which conditioning theories imply) or *cognitive structures* (which sign-learning theories imply). By cognitive structure psychologists mean an idea or knowledge, the root meaning of *cognition* being "knowledge." Does the rat learn a chain of movements in running from the start of an alley to the food box at the end, or does it learn the location of the food? Response learning emphasizes the movement patterns; sign learning emphasizes the knowledge of location. If the rat learns a maplike representation of the environment, so that it can take new paths and short cuts, then it has acquired a cognitive structure.

The conflicting theories are too abstract for further discussion here. For our purposes it is possible to look on habit formation (associative learning) and understanding (cognitive learning) as complementary, neither complete in itself as an explanation of learning but each helping to explain some of the features of learning that the other neglects or explains with greater difficulty.

A provisionally satisfactory position is that any given illustration of learning can be graded on a crude scale, with the most automatic kind of learning (explained best as conditioning) at the one end and the most rational (explained best as involving cognitive structures) at the other. We may picture such a scale by the diagram of Figure 11–30. At the left are the habits learned automatically (i.e., without awareness and with a minimum of understanding) by conditioning mechanisms. Learning to secrete gastric juice in our stomachs when we see food before us illustrates such conditioning. Toward the right of the diagram are the tasks learned with full awareness but still in a somewhat conventional manner, such as using a map to select the route we will follow on a motor trip. At the extreme right fall tasks that require reasoning about many facts in complex relationships. Most learnings fall somewhere be-

Automatic vs. insightful learning

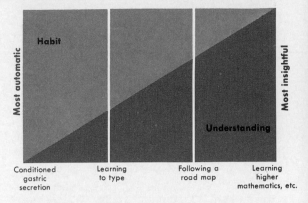

The scaling of learning tasks according to degree of understanding involved. Most learning involves a mixture of habit and insight.

tween, as a kind of mixture between habit formation and understanding. Learning to operate a typewriter competently, for example, includes both the automatic habits of finger action as well as the insights involved in inserting bond paper and carbon paper or in changing a ribbon.

This kind of "mixture" theory is considered too eclectic for many psychologists who would rather commit themselves to one or the other position and then attempt to "derive" the behavior that the opposing theorists find critical of the adopted position. Through such efforts at consistency uniform theories arise.

Mathematical Models of Learning [7]

The experimental study of learning has progressed far enough that a number of psychologists have attempted to formulate the lawful relationships within learning in the language of mathematics. In this, psychology repeats the history of other sciences that have become more mathematical as they have become more advanced in their

[7] This section may be regarded as optional by instructors, depending upon the mathematical preparation of their students.

theories and more precise in their measurements. While the details of mathematical theories of learning must be left for more advanced study, the student is not fully aware of the contemporary developments within psychology if he does not know something of the direction of these developments. A knowledge of high school algebra will enable him to follow the thread of the description that follows, though the mathematical techniques used in developing the models discussed are considerably more complex.

The Hull-Spence theory

While there were earlier attempts to fit mathematics to the course of learning and forgetting, going back at least to Ebbinghaus (1885), one of the most thorough attempts at systematizing was undertaken by Clark L. Hull (1884–1952) at Yale University. A number of psychologists were influenced by him, one of whom, Kenneth W. Spence, is considered to be in some sense Hull's intellectual heir. Hence the theory that Hull proposed and that Spence and his students have moved forward has come to be known as the *Hull-Spence theory* (Logan, 1959).

Hull recognized two sets of components in any learned performance: (1) habit strength ($_sH_R$), a result of *associative learning* under reinforcement; (2) *nonassociative* components, of which drive (D) is the most important. He set up this fundamental formula: [8]

$_sE_R$(excitatory potential)
   $= D$(drive) $\times\ _sH_R$(habit strength).

The term $_sE_R$ represents the tendency for the animal to make response (R) to stimulus (S). What the equation says is that

[8] Hull (1951), p. 35. Hull used the subscripts S and R in writing habit strength ($_sH_R$) and excitatory potential ($_sE_R$) to serve as reminders that what was symbolized was an association between a particular stimulus and response (in the case of habit) and a tendency for a particular stimulus to evoke that response (in the case of excitatory potential). The subscripts serve no mathematical purpose; they are merely descriptive labels on the symbols.

$_sE_R$ is simply the product of habit strength ($_sH_R$) times the current level of drive (D). Thus a hungry rat having learned its way through the maze, will run the maze faster than a well-fed rat equally experienced in the maze. This fundamental formula becomes complicated with other nonassociative factors in addition to drive—such as the intensity of the stimuli which evoke responses and the size of the incentive used in reinforcement. The basic idea of the system can be learned, however, from the fundamental equation in its uncomplicated form.

To move from the very simple equation to something that fits the data from experiments, Hull had first to develop a formula to express the *law of habit formation*, that is, the most typical form of the learning curve for the acquisition of a simple response reinforced on each trial. He expressed this formula as follows:

$$_sH_R = 1 - 10^{-aN}.$$

Here N is the number of reinforced trials and a is a constant that specifies the learning rate. The law states that, other things being equal, habit strength increases regularly with reinforcement to a maximum of strength 1.00 (in arbitrary units). The resulting curve is one of decreasing gains (see p. 295).

Let us see how this law of habit formation combines with the fundamental formula under consideration. Hull selected data from experiments by Perin (1942) in which rats learned the habit of bar-pressing. During acquisition the rats were given varying numbers of reinforced trials ranging from $N = 5$ for some animals to $N = 90$ for others. At a later time the animals were placed on extinction; for some rats extinction was carried out under a low drive level (three hours of food deprivation) and for others under a high drive level (22 hours of deprivation). The equation for $_sE_R$ was then used to predict the number of responses the rat would make during the course of extinction. Using standard statistical procedures, an estimate was made of the learning-rate parameter, a; similarly, estimates of drive (D) were made for each of the two drive levels.[9]

For 22 hours of hunger the equation was

$$_sE_R = 66(1 - 10^{-.02N}),$$

and for three hours of hunger it was

$$_sE_R = 25(1 - 10^{-.02N}).$$

The portions of the equations representing the acquisition of $_sH_R$ are identical as they should be according to the theory; but the multiplying quantities (66 and 25), reflecting the contribution of drive, differ in size, higher drive being associated with greater food deprivation.

Substituting the appropriate values of N into the above equations yields predictions for the number of responses emitted during extinction. These predicted values are given by the smooth curves in Figure 11–31.

If the ratio of 66 to 25 represents the drive contributions from 22 hours of hunger and from three hours of hunger, we already have some hint as to how hunger varies with hours of food deprivation; we are ready then to test this relationship in new situations. The advantage of having a strictly quantitative system is that there eventually develops a network of relationships that must be self-consistent if the theory is to be considered satisfactory.

Hull and his followers have been both painstaking and ingenious in accounting for more and more data within the system. They have, of course, found it necessary to revise the system when inconsistencies were uncovered. This is not a sign of weakness but is the very nature of quantitative science. All science is unfinished, and to the extent that it is self-correcting it is good science.

Estes' stimulus sampling theory

Some psychologists have developed mathematical models of learning, starting with assumptions quite different from those of Hull and Spence, but often arriving at theoretical expressions not so different from theirs. As an illustration we shall use *stimulus sampling theory*. This theory was first formalized in a series of important papers by Estes (1950, 1955, 1959), Estes and Burke (1953), and Estes and Suppes (1959). A survey of the current status of the theory can be found in later papers by Estes (1964b) and Atkinson and Estes (1963). It is appropriate that we include this particular development in our discussion of mathematical models since much of the current theoretical work in learning theory is formulated within this general framework.

Stimulus sampling theory begins with some assumptions about the nature of the stimulus and the nature of associative learning. The stimulus situation is represented conceptually as a set of stimulus elements, and the effective stimulation on any trial is conceived of as a sample drawn from the total set of stimulus elements. In common-sense terms, we may think of the subject as paying attention to only part of the stimuli arrayed before him at any point in time; this limitation on his attentiveness to the stimulus situation is expressed theoretically in terms of a sample of stimulus elements from the total set. As an illustrative analogy we might think of a person looking into a hardware store window containing a wide variety of items. His attention may be drawn to a display of fishing tackle, and he may fail to note the adjacent array of kitchen utensils. Stimulus sampling theory supposes that only a sample of the possible stimuli impinging on the receptor system affects the individual on any one trial.

At any time each stimulus element is conditioned to exactly one response. As a first approximation Estes assumes that all stimulus elements are equally likely to be sampled on any trial and the probability of a response at any time is equal to the proportion of stimulus elements in the sample that are conditioned to the response. By convention the Greek letter θ (theta) is used to designate the probability that any particular stimulus element will be sampled.

[9] The role of parameters in psychological theories and methods for their estimation are discussed by Atkinson, Bower, and Crothers (1965).

Hullian analysis of influence
of drive on excitatory potential

In the experiment from which the plotted data were obtained, rats were given varying numbers of reinforcements during acquisition, and then tested for the number of nonreinforced responses required to produce complete extinction. Extinction was carried out under two drive levels (22 hours and 3 hours of deprivation). As we see from the graph, (1) the more reinforcements during acquisition, the greater the number of responses during extinction, and (2) the higher the drive level, the greater the number of responses during extinction. The number of responses emitted during extinction served as an estimate of excitatory potential ($_sE_R$). According to Hull's theory the difference in drive level should multiply the effects due to number of reinforcements. If the expression $(1 - 10^{-.02N})$ is taken as a measure of $_sH_R$ it is seen that the curves do indeed conform to the formula $_sE_R = D \times {_sH_R}$ with the values of D represented by 66 and 25 for 22 hours and 3 hours, respectively. The curves using Perin's data are reproduced by Hull (1951), p. 34.

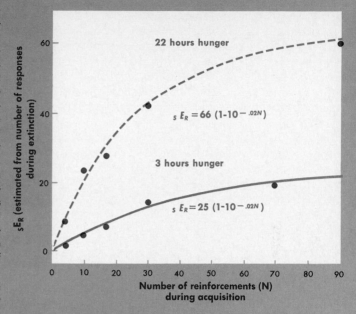

Figure labels:
- $_sE_R$ (estimated from number of responses during extinction) — vertical axis
- 22 hours hunger — $_sE_R = 66 (1\text{-}10^{-.02N})$
- 3 hours hunger — $_sE_R = 25 (1\text{-}10^{-.02N})$
- Number of reinforcements (N) during acquisition — horizontal axis

As we indicated above, the likelihood that a response will occur is simply the proportion of stimulus elements in the sample attached to it. If none is attached, the stimulus situation on that trial will not evoke the response at all; if all stimulus elements are attached the response will occur with probability one.

Estes assumes that learning occurs on an all-or-none basis; that is, any stimulus element sampled on a trial becomes conditioned to the reinforced response. Thus, over a series of trials response probability changes in discrete steps as a function of the number of stimulus elements conditioned to the response; if there are a large number of stimulus elements in the set, with elements being conditioned at different points in time, the learning curve will tend to be a smoothly increasing function. In fact, the mean probability of a response often will turn out to be as simple in form as that arising from a continuous growth function of the sort postulated by Hull for $_sH_R$.

For extinction of a response, it is necessary for the stimulus elements to become separated from the response and conditioned to some other response (or, what is the same thing, to nonresponding). Thus when a stimulus elicits a response which is not reinforced, as during extinction, the sample of stimulus elements effective on that trial becomes unhooked from the response and conditioned to some other response. This notion that extinction of a response is nothing more than conditioning the stimulus to some other response is generally referred to as *counter-condition-ing*.

Although learning is defined in terms of the probability of a response to a stimulus situation, it does not follow that probability is the only experimental measure that can be used to test the theory. Mathematical expressions can be derived relating probability to rate of responding, to latency of response, to magnitude of response, and so on. Hence the theory can be tested with the use of any of the standard measurements that one may make in the learning laboratory.

Beginning with these assumptions, the mathematical development of the theory is straightforward. The basic equation for the change in probability of a response from trial n to trial $n + 1$ of the experiment is:

$$p_{n+1} = p_n + \theta (1 - p_n)$$

Put into words, this equation says that the probability of a response on the next trial (denoted p_{n+1}) will equal the probability on the previous trial (p_n) plus a fraction (θ) of the remaining possible increase which is $(1 - p_n)$. As we indicated before, θ is simply the probability that any particular element in the stimulus set will be sampled on a given trial. The above equation expresses in mathematical form the assumptions described in the preceding discussion. An equation of this type is known as a *difference equation* because it expresses the change in probability from one trial to the next.

It is possible by mathematical methods which need not concern us here to develop a mathematical expression for what happens when the difference equation is applied over and over again, beginning with the probability at trial 1 and ending at any trial n. The expression that results is:

$$p_n = 1 - (1 - p_1)(1 - \theta)^{n-1},$$

where p_1 is the probability of the response on the initial trial of the experiment, and p_n is the probability of any arbitrary trial n. The learning curve is an exponentially increasing function which starts out at p_1 and over time approaches one as an asymptote. The rate of approach to one is determined by θ; the larger the value of θ the faster the rate at which learning proceeds.

The above equation is a general learning function, playing the same role as Hull's law of habit formation (p. 307). In fact, the two expressions are really very much alike. Both equations state that the process of learning can be described in terms of the limit of learning, minus a constant raised to a power n (the number of reinforced trials). Both equations specify that the gain per trial is some constant fraction of the amount of possible gain to occur in the remainder of learning.

In Figure 11–31 we saw how Hull used his theory in relation to data. Let us now examine some simple applications of Estes' equation. In Figure 11–32 we have four illustrations of equations fitted to actual data. The forms of the equation differ from the one given because transformations have been made to convert probability to responses per minute, to duration of response, to cumulative errors, and to running time. It is evident from inspection that the theoretical curve (the solid line in each case) fits quite well the points that represent the data from experiments.

Conclusions on mathematical models

Only the early steps in model-building have been described for the Hull-Spence model and the Estes model. In both cases many further steps have been taken in order to account for what happens in extinction, in discrimination learning, in generalization, and in various forms of multiple-response learning. Independent of these specific theoretical developments, the general notion of learning as a probabilistic process that can be described in mathematical terms has been taken up by so many investigators that it is likely to be one of the dominant features of future theoretical development in psychology. This does not mean that there will not continue to be other lines of inquiry and theorizing, but the serious student of learning theory cannot now ignore these mathematical developments.

Mathematical transformations of response-probability function

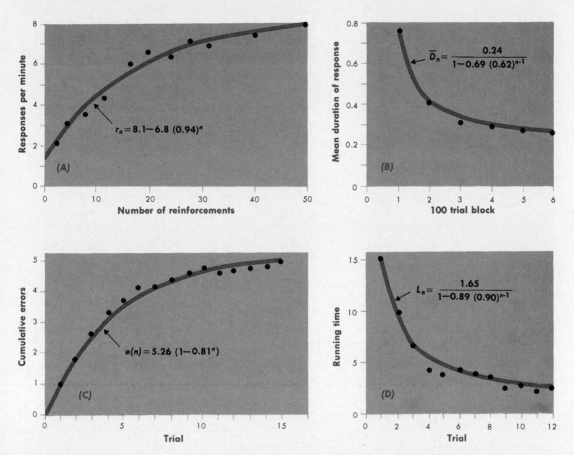

The response-probability function, derived from stimulus-sampling theory, has been transformed to a form allowing it to be tested empirically according to four measures: responses per minute, mean duration of a response, cumulative errors, and running time. The first two curves (A and B) are from a bar-pressing experiment, the last two (C and D), from a T-maze experiment. The solid line represents the theoretical curve in each case, while the black dots represent the data from experiments. (The precise meaning of the formulas for each curve, and the way they were derived, are beyond the scope of this text.) (From Estes, 1959, p. 402)

SUMMARY   1. Pavlov's experiments on *classical conditioning* in the dog brought to light several principles useful in the understanding of habit formation. These include reinforcement, extinction, spontaneous recovery, generalization, and discrimination.

2. Skinner's experiments on *operant conditioning* have extended conditioning principles to kinds of responses that cannot be elicited by recognized unconditioned stimuli. Operant behavior acts upon the environment to produce or gain access to reinforcement and becomes strengthened by reinforcement.

3. Rate of responding is a useful measure of operant strength, with applicability to practical behavior. *Partial reinforcement* illustrates the orderliness of operant behavior, since long and regular runs of responses can be sustained by occasional reinforcement. *Secondary reinforcement,* the fact that a stimulus associated with a reinforcing stimulus acquires reinforcing properties, increases the possible range of conditioning and explains the reward value of such incentives as social approval and money.

4. An animal trainer can *shape behavior* by reinforcing those variations in the operant response that move in the desired direction and by extinguishing those that do not. Thus operant conditioning can account for the learning of novel movements. Recent experiments have shown that some aspects of ordinary daily behavior can be brought under control through operant conditioning.

5. *Reinforcement* refers to any event whose occurrence increases the probability that a stimulus will, on subsequent occasions, evoke a response. *Amount* and *delay* of reinforcement are important variables which affect learning. The *drive-reduction* hypothesis is one of several theories that have been proposed to explain the effects of reinforcement.

6. Conditioning is most directly applicable to single identifiable responses, but much habit formation is more complex than this. These more complex instances are classified as *multiple-response learning.* Two examples are sensorimotor skills (such as mirror drawing and pursuit learning) and rote memorization (including serial learning and paired-associate learning).

7. The experimenter plots the results of multiple-response learning in the form of *learning curves,* indicating changes in proficiency with practice. These curves usually show *decreasing gains* over trials. Shifts from lower-order to higher-order learning habits may result in a period of no improvement called a *plateau.*

8. Emphasis within conditioning and multiple-response learning is upon the acquiring of movements or verbal habits. Some psychologists warn against an overemphasis on the automatic nature of learning which comes from exclusive concern with movement. They stress instead situations in which understanding comes to the fore. Köhler's *insight* experiments pointed out how the arrangements of the problem make the solution easy or hard, and how a solution once achieved with insight can be repeated or applied to novel situations.

9. Tolman's *sign-learning* experiments also emphasize the role of knowledge or understanding. Two kinds of experiment (place learning and latent learning) are opposed to theories that lay stress upon the reinforcement of particular movements without taking into account the subject's understanding of the relationships involved.

10. Something can be learned from each of these emphases. Learning goes on in part through automatic processes with little rational direction from the learner and in part through processes in which the learner perceives relationships and acts with knowledge.

11. As learning experimentation has become more precise, theorists have begun to develop *mathematical models* to provide a more detailed account of the learning process. The models are formulated in terms of certain basic assumptions, and then mathematical equations are derived from these assumptions and fitted to the data from experiments. If the equations fit the data, the assumptions have greater plausibility than if they do not fit. Starting with rather simple assumptions, the models are gradually extended to cover more complex instances of learning. The Hull-Spence and the Estes models illustrate some of these developments.

SUGGESTIONS FOR FURTHER READING

Pavlov's *Conditioned reflexes* (1927) is the classical work on conditioned salivary reflexes in dogs. Skinner's *The behavior of organisms* (1938) is the corresponding statement of operant conditioning. The later developments in conditioning theory and experiment are reviewed in Kimble, *Hilgard and Marquis' conditioning and learning* (1961), Prokasy (ed.), *Classical conditioning* (1965), and Honig (ed.), *Operant behavior: areas of research and application* (1966).

Cognitive theories also have their classics: Köhler's *The mentality of apes* (1925) describes the famous insight experiments with chimpanzees; Tolman's *Purposive behavior in animals and men* (1932) is the major statement of his cognitive (sign-learning) position.

The major points of view toward learning, in their historical settings and with some typical experiments to which they have led, are summarized in Hilgard and Bower, *Theories of learning* (3rd ed., 1966). Some useful original papers dealing with various approaches to learning theory have been collected by Birney and Teevan (eds.), *Reinforcement* (1961).

For substantive approaches, emphasizing the contributions of the learning laboratory, there are a number of textbooks on learning, such as Bugelski, *The psychology of learning* (1956), Deese and Hulse, *The psychology of learning* (3rd ed., 1967), and Hall, *The psychology of learning* (1966).

The literature on mathematical models for learning is growing rapidly. An elementary account of this work is presented in Atkinson, Bower, and Crothers, *An introduction to mathematical learning theory* (1965). More advanced reviews can be found in Luce, Bush, and Galanter (eds.), *Handbook of mathematical psychology*, vols. I and II (1963), vol. III (1965).

12 Remembering and Forgetting

All learning implies retaining, for if nothing were left over from previous experience, nothing would be learned. When we have studied the nature of learning, we have already begun to study remembering, because many of the same principles apply. But remembering and forgetting are far too important to dismiss merely as continuous with learning. We think and reason largely with remembered facts; the very continuity of our self-perceptions depends upon the continuity of our memories. We are able to deal with the concept of time as no other animal can, relating the present to the past and making predictions about the future, because of the strength, flexibility, and availability of our memories.

Kinds of Remembering

To remember means to show in present responses some signs of earlier learned responses. We need a set of words to distinguish among several ways in which our memories appear.

One way of remembering is to *recollect* or *redintegrate* an event and the circumstances surrounding it, as when you remember going with a "date" to your first dance. The word *recollect* is from the ordinary vocabulary; *redintegrate* is a technical word meaning to reintegrate or to reestablish an earlier experience on the basis of partial cues. For example, you redintegrate that first dance only if something "reminds" you of it. The stimuli to

redintegration are in a literal sense souvenirs, remembrances or reminders of a total, personal experience, which occurred at a given time in the past. In your recollection you conjure up the band playing the popular songs of that time, the cool breeze as you stepped outside, perhaps your aching feet when you finally got home. While such redintegrative memories are often quite detailed and complete, they need not be. They are distinguished from other kinds of remembering because they reconstruct a past occasion from your personal autobiography with its setting in time and place.

Many signs of earlier experience lack this reconstruction of the past. For example, you may *recall* a poem by reciting it, even if you do not remember the circumstances under which you learned it. You can remember how to climb stairs or ride a bicycle or sing a song without any direct reference to the past. This kind of remembering, shown through recall, is easier to measure than the redintegration of earlier experiences, and it is the kind usually studied in the laboratory.

A third kind of remembering is the indication of memory merely by *recognizing* someone or something as familiar. "That tune is familiar. What is it?" "Someone I used to know had a copy of that picture on the wall, but I can't place it now."

Finally, you may show that you once learned something by now *relearning* it more rapidly than you could if there were no retention of the earlier learning.

Redintegration, recall, recognition, and relearning all give evidence of memory, but each of these terms implies a different aspect of remembering.

Redintegrative memory

Experimental psychologists have paid relatively little attention to redintegrative memory, partly because it is difficult to check details of the recovery of events in the personal past of the subject. A few studies have been done under hypnosis; one of these, for example, has shown that memories of schoolroom experiences at ages seven and 10 can be more accurately recovered by adults under hypnosis than in the waking state (Reiff and Scheerer, 1959). These memories, of other pupils in the class, of the teacher's name, were subject to confirmation.

Studies of testimony are concerned with the reinstatement of scenes witnessed in the past. A class may unexpectedly witness a staged crime and then report what happened. The reports are often distorted, even when a student insists his recollections are vivid and dependable. One of the authors once engaged in a staged argument with a workman who interrupted his lecture. The workman spoke with a German accent. Although the assistant who acted the part of the workman in this little drama had blond hair and dark brown eyes, a substantial proportion of the students reported confidently that they had seen his *blue* eyes—the color falsely inferred from his Nordic appearance and German accent. Such experiments have bearing on the reliability of witnesses in courtrooms.

Studies of personal memories have been carried on more by those engaged in psychotherapy than by experimental psychologists. In psychoanalysis the recall of childhood memories is one of the bases of treatment and cure. A curious problem, not yet fully understood, is created by the paucity of very early memories, from the very time that the child is having many exciting new experiences. This is the problem of "childhood amnesia," early noted by Freud. One conjecture is that the child perceives the world so differently from an adult that the adult's effort to recall what registered for the child fails because of this difference (Schachtel, 1959). It may be too that the storage of memories depends upon language development.

Recall

The kind of remembering most easily tested in the laboratory is active *recall* of some performance learned in the past. You may show that you remember how to ride a bicycle by climbing on one and riding away. You may show that you know Hamlet's soliloquy on death by reciting it. What you are demonstrating is that present performance is different from what it would be if there were no residue from the past. You ride the bicycle. If there were no residue from the past, you could not ride it.

To get a quantitative measure of recall in the laboratory, the investigator allows time to elapse after a subject has memorized some material, usually by the serial method or the paired-associate method described in Chapter 11 (p. 296). Then the subject returns to the laboratory and attempts to anticipate the items *the first time* the stimulus item appears in the aperture of the memory drum, that is, before there is any new learning. The percentage correct is the *recall score*.

Recognition

When we recognize something, we mean that it is familiar, that we have met it before. Recognition is a common experience, but it is a rather complex and, in a sense, mysterious process. The entire process takes place quite automatically. We meet someone and say, "I'm sure we have met before, though I cannot recall your name or just where or when it was."

We learn a little about recognition from faulty recognition, from a deceiving sense of familiarity. The French expression *déjà vu* ("previously seen") is often used to describe the sense of familiarity that is sometimes aroused in otherwise strange surroundings. So important and convincing was this experience that Plato, the Greek philosopher, made it part of the basis for his belief in a previous existence. What may happen is that a pattern of buildings along a street is actually somewhat like one seen in earlier experience, or that in a strangely familiar garden the scent of a flower permeating the air is one met on an earlier occasion but since forgotten. Then the present, though actually strange, seems vaguely familiar. This is a form of generalization from past experience.

To study recognition in the laboratory we have to distinguish between correct and faulty recognition. We do this by presenting to the subject a series of items, such as a set of 25 photographs, with which he then becomes familiar. Now we test his recognition by mixing these 25 with 25 additional ones of the same general kind, and have him sort out those he saw before. We can obtain a score as we do for a true-false examination corrected for guessing. The formula is:

$$\text{Recognition score} = 100\left[\frac{\text{Right} - \text{Wrong}}{\text{Total}}\right]$$

That is, if all the original pictures are sorted in the "familiar" pile and all the new or misleading ones in the "unfamiliar" pile, the subject gets a score of 100. If he sorts by chance, getting half right and half wrong, his score drops to zero, as it should. If he gets 40 right and 10 wrong (neither perfect recognition nor chance sorting) then his recognition score would be 60 percent.

Relearning

Another way to show that there is some residue from the past is to demonstrate that previously familiar material can be learned more rapidly than it could be learned if it were unfamiliar. Even though something may seem to be completely "forgotten," it may be easier to learn a second time because it was once learned in the past. A dramatic illustration of how this may occur is given by a study in which a child was read selections from Greek and then learned those same selections years later.

The experimenter read three Greek selections a day to a boy of fifteen months, repeating the same selections daily for

three months. Each selection consisted of 20 lines of iambic hexameter material. At the end of three months another set of three selections was repeated daily for three months. The procedure was continued until the subject was three years old and 21 selections had been read.

The residual influence of this early experience was studied through memorization experiments conducted with the boy at the ages of 8, 14, and 18. He had not studied Greek in the meantime. At each of these ages he learned selected passages from the early experience along with equivalent but unfamiliar passages. The results indicated a substantial saving in learning the familiar material at the age of 8. About 30 percent fewer repetitions were required than for equivalent new material. By the age of 14, however, the saving was only 8 percent, and by 18 years no saving could be demonstrated. The main point is that there was demonstrable saving in learning five years after the original reading took place, even though the material to which the child had listened was classical Greek, a language that to him was without meaning (Burtt, 1941).

To use the relearning method in the laboratory, the experimenter proceeds as in the study of recall; after the initial learning he allows a time period to elapse over which retention is to be tested in a second learning. The subject, having previously learned by one of the standard methods well enough to meet some *criterion of mastery* (e.g., one perfect recitation), learns the material again *to the same criterion*. If the second learning requires fewer trials than the first, we may express this saving as a percentage by using the formula:

Saving score =

$$100\left[\frac{\text{Original trials} - \text{Relearning trials}}{\text{Original trials}}\right]$$

If the relearning criterion is reached on the first trial, then the saving is 100 percent; if it takes as much time as original learning, there is zero percent saving.

To clarify the notion of a saving score let us take an example. Suppose we ask a subject to learn a list of paired associates to a criterion of one perfect trial. On initial learning he reaches this criterion on, say, the 13th trial; that is, on this trial he gives correct responses to all of the stimuli in the list for the first time. On relearning the same list a week later, he reaches the criterion on the fourth trial. Thus, on initial learning 12 trials occurred before the criterion trial, and on relearning three trials occurred. Applying the formula, the saving score is

$$100 \left[\frac{12 - 3}{12} \right] = 75\%$$

When standard learning and relearning methods are used, it is possible to secure recall and saving scores at the same time. The recall score is computed from the degree of success on the first relearning trial and the saving score from the number of trials required to reach the criterion.

Varieties of memory processes

The processes underlying redintegration, recall, recognition, and relearning are not distinct. Each kind of memory, however, makes a somewhat different demand upon the subject, so that his retention of earlier learning might be detected by one method and not by another. For example, the retention of a past experience completely unavailable to redintegrative memory or to direct recall might be detected by recognition or relearning. The response to stimuli is easier for recognition than for recall: with the stimuli of a face before you, you are asked only to *recognize* these stimuli as familiar, while you are expected to *recall* a name from the stimuli the face provides.

There does seem to be an important difference between a memory dated in one's personal past (what we have called *redintegration*) and the kind of undated memory shown in, say, memory for a familiar vocabulary word (what we have termed *recall*). If one remembers having looked up an unusual word, then the memory is a recollection of a concrete experience, but most words are not tied in such a way to a personal history. In cases of amnesia, it is usually the personal memories that are lost; the amnesia victim is still able to speak his familiar language, buy a theatre ticket, count his change, and do many other things that indicate that his undated or impersonal memories are not lost. Recognition has some features of redintegration (having been experienced before), whereas recall can be automatic, without any personal reference whatever.

The Course of Forgetting

We know that our memories are not perfect. There are songs we once sang whose words we have now forgotten. There are childhood playmates whose names we no longer remember. There are skills that have diminished or grown rusty. These processes of fading of memories or loss of skill with disuse are open to study.

Curves of retention

The effects of an interval of no practice after learning can be plotted in the form of *curves of retention,* based upon tests introduced at set periods following learning. A typical curve falls rapidly at first and then gradually tapers off. This pattern was discovered by Ebbinghaus, a pioneer investigator in the study of retention, who first published a curve showing the course of forgetting (Figure 12–1). Ebbinghaus invented the nonsense syllable (see p. 296) in order to have a quantity of equivalent materials in constructing lists to be memorized. His curves were for the retention of such nonsense syllables after they had been barely memorized, as tested by the relearning method.

Later investigators have found that the course of forgetting is usually similar to that found by Ebbinghaus, but that the rate at which forgetting occurs varies enormously with the materials used and with the circumstances under which memorization occurs. In general, meaningful material is retained much longer than nonsense syllables.

A retention curve

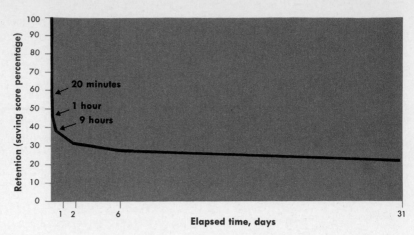

Curve of retention for lists of nonsense syllables. Retention was measured in terms of relearning, and the dependent variable is the saving score. (After Ebbinghaus, 1885)

Retention as measured by recognition, recall, and relearning

Our everyday experiences tell us that recognition is usually easier than recall. And we can easily see that relearning is a very sensitive measure of retention, because it can show some residue of past learning even when there is no evidence from either recognition or recall. A frequently quoted study by Luh (1922) tested these separate aspects following nonsense syllable memorization, under circumstances as closely comparable as he could make them (Figure 12–2). Over a two-day period of testing he found highest scores for recognition, next highest for relearning, and lowest scores for recall. The flattening of the curve for relearning suggests the possibility that in the long run relearning scores might exceed those for recognition, but the retention intervals were not long enough to find this out. In exceptional circumstances these relationships may be reversed. For example, we sometimes correctly recall the spelling of a word, only to fail to recognize that it is correct. Then recall is better than recognition.

Tip-of-the-tongue phenomenon

All of us have been in a situation where we were certain we knew a specific name or word yet were unable to recall it immediately. The word seemed to be on the tip of our tongue and we felt tormented until an active search of our memory, dredging up and then discarding words that seemed close but were not quite right, revealed (or sometimes failed to reveal) the correct word. This failure to recall a word of which one has knowledge has been called the "tip-of-the-tongue" (TOT) state. The fact that one does know the word is demonstrated either by an eventual successful recall or by recognition when the word is presented.

In an experimental investigation of the

12–2

Three measures of retention

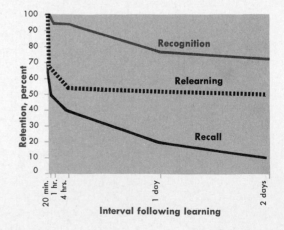

Retention curves for nonsense syllables by three methods of measurement. Luh actually used five methods, but the other two are not standard and need not concern us. (After Luh, 1922)

TOT state Brown and McNeill (1966) demonstrated that the words that come to mind when one is searching for the correct word (called the "target word") do have certain characteristics in common with the target word. In their study college students were read the definitions of words that are used infrequently in the English language. These were words such as *cloaca, ambergris,* and *sampan,* which were likely to be in the passive or recognition vocabulary of the subjects but not in their active-recall vocabulary. Whenever a subject felt that he knew a word but was unable to recall it immediately (i.e., whenever he was in a typical TOT state), he was asked a number of questions concerning the words he was thinking of in his attempt to arrive at the correct word. The results of the study demonstrated quite clearly that while a subject is in the TOT state prior to recall he has information about a number of characteristics of the target word, and the closer he is to successful recall the more accurate his information. Although some of the words that came to mind could be classed as similar in *meaning* to the target word, the majority of words were similar in *sound* to the target word. For example, if the target word is *sampan,* then similar-sounding words would be *Saipan, Siam, Cheyenne, sarong,* and *sympoon,* whereas similar-meaning words would be *barge, houseboat,* and *junk.* An analysis of the similar-sounding words showed that while in a TOT state the subject, even though he has not yet recalled the target word, can state with a high degree of accuracy the number of syllables in the word and the initial letter. He can also frequently specify, although with less accuracy, the final sound or suffix and the syllable that receives the primary accent or stress.

Thus it is apparent that recall is not a simple all-or-none process; we can forget certain characteristics of a word while still retaining other relevant information. Studies of this type have led to interesting speculations (some of which we will consider later) as to the manner in which information is stored in memory and subsequently retrieved.

The Nature of Forgetting

There are four traditional explanations of forgetting, and each plausibly accounts for some of the known facts. Because the explanations are not contradictory, each may help us to understand the nature of what we remember and why we forget. The four are: (1) *passive decay* through disuse, (2) *systematic distortions of the memory trace,* (3) *interference effects* (retroactive and proactive inhibition), and (4) *motivated forgetting.* We will see that no one explanation by itself can account for all the facts of forgetting, and consequently a number of psychologists are currently arguing for a two-process, or duplex, theory of forgetting. We will go on to consider duplex theories in the next section.

Passive decay through disuse

One of the oldest explanations of forgetting, and perhaps the one still most widely held by the layman, is that forgetting takes place simply through the passage of time. This explanation assumes that learning leaves a "trace" in the brain or nervous system; the *memory trace* involves some sort of physical change that was not present prior to learning. With the passage of time the normal metabolic processes of the brain cause a fading or decay of the memory trace so that traces of material once learned gradually disintegrate and eventually disappear altogether.

The experience of rapid fading of barely learned material lends credence to this view of forgetting. Even as you try to write down verbatim a definition given in a lecture you may find it fading away. Our forgetting of pictures or stories also suggests a process of fading with the passage of time. When first perceived, a story or picture may reveal a wealth of detail. But as time passes the details are rapidly forgotten and only the main outlines are remembered.

Plausible as is the disuse, or organic-decay, theory of forgetting, there is no direct evidence for it, and there is much evidence that it is a dubious or at least incomplete explanation. The form of the retention curve can be accounted for on other grounds. There are many instances where learning is retained over long intervals of time with no intervening practice. Most motor skills are not easily forgotten. We do not forget how to swim or drive a car even though we may not have used these skills for many years. And some verbal material may be retained over long periods while other material is forgotten. We may be able to recall quite accurately a poem we memorized in sixth grade yet be unable to remember the part in a play we learned as a high school freshman. Why should the decay process affect the second material but not the first?

Another argument against the passive-decay theory rests on the recovery of memories supposedly lost. People approaching senility often recall vividly events of their youth when they can barely remember the events of the day. Occasionally in delirium a patient speaks a language unused since childhood. Unavailable memories have not necessarily "decayed." It cannot be denied, however, that some forgetting may occur through the organic changes taking place in the nervous system with the passage of time. All we can be sure of is that this explanation does not account for all the facts about forgetting.

Systematic distortions of the memory trace

The theory of forgetting through disuse suggests that change with time is chiefly a blurring of memories, a fading, a falling away of items. But this is only one aspect of forgetting. Later recollections differ from earlier ones in other ways. Experiments on testimony have shown that many things are remembered that never happened at all or that actually happened in ways very different from those recalled (e.g., our staged argument with the workman, p. 315). Forgetting through *distortion* has to be accounted for, too.

The theory of systematic distortion of the memory trace, like the theory of passive decay, attributes the changes in recall to changes in the brain tissue. Whereas the decay theory emphasizes fading and loss,

the theory of systematic distortion attempts to account for *qualitative* changes in memory. These qualitative changes have been attributed to spontaneous changes taking place in the memory trace.

Although this theory was designed to account for an important aspect of forgetting—the fact that memories are frequently distorted—more recent evidence suggests that much of the distortion takes place *at the time the event is perceived* rather than with the passage of time. Evidence for spontaneous change comes chiefly from experiments on memory for visually perceived forms. Earlier experimenters (e.g., Wulf, 1922) had found that when subjects were presented with line drawings of simple geometric figures and asked to recall them at a later date the reproductions showed certain characteristic distortions when compared with the original figures. These changes tended to be in one of three directions: (1) the figures became more symmetrical; (2) any irregularity in the figure became accentuated; or (3) if the figure resembled some common object, its reproduction moved in the direction of looking more like that object (the effect of labeling an object is well illustrated in Figure 12–3). Such changes were attributed to gradual modifications of the memory trace. However, subsequent studies showed that, to a large extent, the distortions take place at the time the figures are first seen and reproduced (Bruner, Busiek, and Minturn, 1952); a reproduction made after greater elapsed time does not show a more striking distortion than one made almost immediately after the figure has been perceived (Hebb and Foord, 1945; Riley, 1962). Some progressive changes do take place with successive reproductions of the figure, but such changes probably occur only because the later reproductions reflect distortions made in the earlier one.

In everyday life we often have occasion to recall an experience over and over again so that opportunity for progressive distortion arises in the retelling. Experiments paralleling those on memory for form have been made with the retelling of short tales; the results show that marked distortions do

Systematic distortion of memory

Reproduced figure	Word list 1	Stimulus figure	Word list 2	Reproduced figure

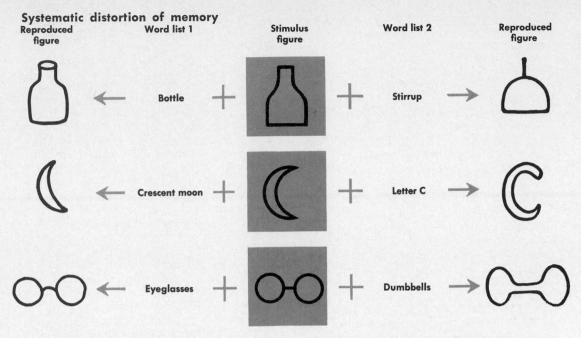

When stimulus figures like those in the boxes were presented along with words in either list 1 or list 2, the reproduced figure tended to be distorted in the direction of the object named, as shown. (After Carmichael, Hogan, and Walter, 1932)

indeed occur, some of which follow fairly predictable forms.

There is no doubt that the activity of recalling is productive (in the sense of changing or adding to the original material) as well as reproductive. But the distortions found in the recalled material need not be attributed to changes in the memory trace. The manner in which we perceive events has an important influence on our recall. Although both the theory of decay and the theory of systematic distortions of the memory trace lack convincing positive evidence, we cannot completely rule out the possibility that some changes of both types may occur in the memory trace with the passage of time.

CRITICAL DISCUSSION

RNA and the memory trace

The use of the expression *memory trace* in connection with the two foregoing theories

requires a word of explanation. The memory trace is purely hypothetical; it is not something known or understood or something we can point to in the brain. It refers to whatever representation persists in our nervous systems of an experience that is subject to recall. We must somehow carry a representation of the experience around with us when we are not recalling it, for someone who has not had the experience cannot recall it as we can. When we say that a memory trace fades or that something else happens to it, all we are really saying is that what emerges when we attempt to recall is something different from the experience that was originally registered.

When the psychologist postulates a hypothetical mechanism to explain his experimental results, he makes what is known as a *hypothetical construct*. This particular hypothetical construct means that the memory trace does exist and that we may some day discover its nature and perhaps learn thereby the physical processes responsible for remembering and forgetting. Hydén has proposed the theory that ribonucleic acid (RNA) might well be the complex molecule that serves as a chemical mediator for memory (Hydén, 1959; Hydén and Egyhâzi, 1963).

It has been known for some time that deoxyribonucleic acid (DNA) is the substance that is primarily responsible for genetic inheritance; that is, the genes are comprised chiefly of DNA, and the genetic code is literally written in a sequence of bases along the DNA molecule. In this rather unique package DNA crams the information needed to create a full-blown man—a man with blue eyes and a tendency to baldness, a man with a heart that can beat and a brain that can think. The genetic instructions contained on a single DNA molecule, if spelled out in English, would require several 24-volume sets of the Encyclopaedia Britannica. In a certain sense, this genetic code can be regarded as a "racial memory"; that is, a male and female have offspring of a certain type because the DNA molecules contained in the fertilized ovum remember what the parents were like.

DNA never leaves the cell's nucleus but directs the cell's activities by manufacturing its own assistants to which it then delegates responsibilities. These assistants are various forms of RNA which (after being produced in the nucleus) move out to the cytoplasm where they control cellular functions. Hydén reasoned that if DNA, which is exceptionally stable, encodes "racial memory," then perhaps RNA, which is known to be more malleable, could act to encode the organism's individual memories. There are a number of experimental studies that give tentative support to this idea. For example, it has been shown that if animals are given a particular type of training, the RNA found in certain cells of the nervous system is altered, presumably by the training experience. Also, it has been found that if the chemicals that block the formation of RNA are injected into the animals during training, the animals learn very poorly, if at all.

Work by McConnell and his associates (McConnell, 1966; Zelman, Kabat, Jacobson, and McConnell, 1963) has created a great deal of interest because their results appear to give direct evidence for the role of RNA in memory. The experiments involved training planaria (see Figure 2–5, p. 36), using classical-conditioning procedures. The planaria were housed in a trough of water; when a brief electrical current was passed through the water, the planaria responded with a vigorous muscular contraction. The onset of the shock was paired with the onset of a light, employing a typical Pavlovian-conditioning paradigm. After repeated pairings of the light onset with the shock, test trials with light alone were able to elicit the contraction response. The planaria that had previously not responded to the light now generated a muscular contraction when the light was turned on. A substance containing RNA was then extracted from the bodies of the trained planaria and injected directly into the body cavities of untrained animals. The latter animals were then given the same classical-conditioning routine, along with control animals that had been injected with RNA taken from untrained planaria. The results of the study showed that the planaria injected with RNA extracted from previously trained planaria learned the conditioned response more rapidly than those animals injected with the RNA from control animals.

While the results with planaria have been found difficult to repeat (Bennett and Calvin, 1964), excitement over the role of RNA was further enhanced by experiments which seemed to show that RNA injected from trained rats reproduced the learned responses in untrained rats (Babich, Jacobson, Bubash, and Jacobson, 1965; Fjerdingstad, Nissen, and Røigaard-Petersen, 1965). The evidence also appeared to indicate that the RNA transfer effect was specific to the stimulus used in the learning task rather than simply a generalized improvement in learning (Jacobson, Babich, Bubash, and Jacobson, 1965). Unfortunately, efforts to repeat these experiences in a number of different laboratories have thus far been unsuccessful (Byrne and others, 1966; Luttges and others, 1966).

If these rather amazing results were to be substantiated by further research, they would suggest that learning may well be coded onto the RNA molecule and consequently may be capable of transfer from one organism to another. From a science-fiction viewpoint the speculations are intriguing; for example, students in the distant future may be able to avoid the rigorous study involved in learning calculus, receiving their knowledge instead by injection of RNA extracted from their mathematics instructor! Even if it were demonstrated conclusively that RNA serves as the chemical mediator for memory, we have no clear idea as to how learning is coded onto the RNA molecule or how injections of RNA extract affect the behavior of the recipient animal (Landauer, 1964).

Interference effects

A third explanation of forgetting maintains that it is not so much the passage of time that determines the course of forgetting but what we do in the interval of time between learning and recall; new learning may interfere with material we have previously learned. A story told about Stanford University's first president illustrates this theory of interference. David Starr Jordan was an authority on fishes. As the president of a new university, he began to call the students by name, but every time he learned the name of a student he forgot the name of a fish. Hence, it is said, he gave up learning the names of students. Although the story lacks foundation in fact, it illustrates how new learning may interfere with the recall of old learning. The theory that the *new* learning may interfere with the *old* is known as *retroactive inhibition*.

A companion interference theory, based on the same principles, is that prior learning may interfere with the learning and recall of new material. This aspect of the theory is called *proactive inhibition*. We shall postpone consideration of it until the discussion of retroactive inhibition is completed.

Retroactive inhibition. Retroactive inhibition can easily be demonstrated by experiment. The subject learns one list of items (list *A*) and then learns a second list (list *B*). After an interval he attempts to recall list *A*. If a control group (that has not learned list *B*) recalls list *A* better than the group that has learned the new list, we infer that the new learning has interfered with the recall of list *A*. The experimental arrangement can be diagrammed as follows:

Arrangement for testing retroactive inhibition			
	Phase 1	Phase 2	Phase 3
Experimental group	Learn A	Learn B	Recall A
Control group	Learn A	Rest or unrelated activity	Recall A

If the control group's recall of *A* is significantly better than the experimental group's recall of *A*, we attribute the difference to *retroactive inhibition;* the *later* learning of *B* interfered with the recall of the *earlier* learning of *A*. By varying the amount or nature of the interpolated activity (corresponding to list *B*), the experimenter can control the amount of forgetting of list *A* which will occur over a given interval of time.

If recall is tested after an interval of rest, without any interpolated activity corresponding to list *B*, some forgetting of course occurs. Can this, too, be accounted for according to the theory of retroactive inhibition? Perhaps, but only if we think of the ordinary processes of waking life as corresponding in some respects to active learning between original learning and recall. This extension of the theory of retroactive inhibition can be tested by comparing retention after periods of sleep and waking. If waking activity interferes with recall, then retention should be better after sleep, when less intervening activity has occurred. And it has been found, as shown in Figure 12–4, that you do forget more when awake than when asleep. You lose a little during the first hour or two of sleep, but after that you forget very little more during the night (Jenkins and Dallenbach, 1924). These results have been confirmed by other experimenters. Newman (1939) found that the results of Figure 12–4 can be confirmed for rote materials but do not hold as well for organized materials. A subject who read a story before going to sleep could remember both the plot and many nonessential details when he was awakened. When he remained awake after reading a story he remembered

12–4

Retroactive inhibition

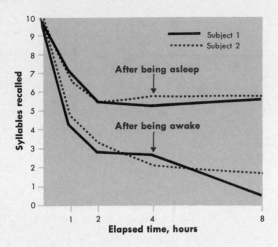

Forgetting during waking and sleeping. (After Jenkins and Dallenbach, 1924)

the plot as well as he did after sleep, but he forgot more of the details.

We may therefore accept the demonstration that retroactive inhibition occurs, not only when formal learning occurs between initial learning and recall but also when ordinary waking life intervenes. Hence retroactive inhibition has a secure place as one phenomenon of forgetting. Can we go further and say that it is a *sufficient* theory of forgetting and that the disuse, or passive-decay, theory is disproved?

It would be very difficult indeed to disprove a disuse theory. The nearest we can come is to look for a state close to suspended animation, and then try to show that no forgetting occurs while the learner is in that state. One of the more successful experimental attempts has been made with cockroaches.

The cockroach in this experiment learned to avoid a given corner of the cage; if it went there, it received an electric shock. The experimenters sought to find out whether it would remember what it had learned, and how its retention would be affected by its activity between the original learning and the test of retention. A very satisfactory rest condition was dis-

covered. If the cockroach was placed in a dark, damp passageway, it would remain immobile for as long as 24 hours. Placed in a dry, lighted cage, it was fairly active; activity was increased by placing it on a small treadmill. Results were similar to those obtained in the sleep experiments with humans. When moderate activity intervened, forgetting occurred, with an increase in forgetting as the length of time since learning increased. (Forgetting was measured by the trials required to relearn the avoidance of the corner where shocks were received.) When the roach was immobilized, its retention lessened over the first hour or two, and then there was little further drop over 24 hours (Minami and Dallenbach, 1946).

The experiment gives additional support to the retroactive-inhibition theory of forgetting, but it does not, of course, disprove the possibility of some passive decay.

Proactive inhibition. Another kind of interference occurs when material that we have previously learned now interferes with the recall of something newly learned. We may think of the following experimental arrangement for comparison with that used in the study of retroactive inhibition:

Arrangement for testing proactive inhibition

	Phase 1	Phase 2	Phase 3
Experimental group	Learn A	Learn B	Recall B
Control group	Rest or unrelated activity	Learn B	Recall B

Experiments using the above design have demonstrated results similar to those found for retroactive inhibition; the control group does indeed recall better than the experimental group. The prior learning of the experimental group apparently interferes with their recall of list B.

Underwood (1957) has shown, by reviewing a large number of experiments on retention, that proactive inhibition plays a very important role when "experienced"

12–5

Interference of previous learning with recall

Each dot represents an average from one study of learning. In those studies in which the subject had less previous practice, the amount retained after an interval of a day was greater than in those studies in which the subject had learned many prior lists. Thus a proactive inhibition is demonstrated. (After Underwood, 1957)

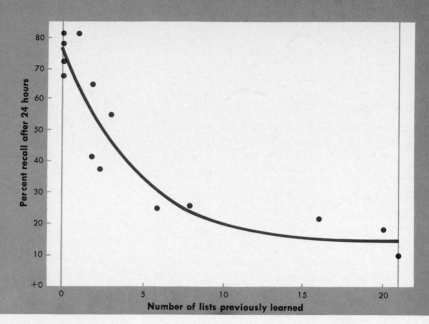

subjects are used in an experiment. As we can see from Figure 12–5 the more lists a subject has previously learned the poorer his retention. There is something of a paradox here because a number of studies have shown that the more practice a subject has in learning word lists the more quickly he learns; now we find that the more lists he learns the less well he retains. This failure of retention is interpreted as a result of interference due to prior learning, hence a form of proactive inhibition. When the subject is asked to recall the nonsense syllables he learned yesterday, the more nonsense syllables he knows from the past, the harder it will be for him to select those he recently learned. The effect is so great that a typical practiced subject after 24 hours may recall 25 percent and forget 75 percent, whereas if the subject has learned only the list he is now asked to recall, the figures are reversed, and he will recall 75 percent and forget 25 percent.

Lest the reader become too discouraged and decide that it is fruitless to learn anything new, we should hasten to point out the effects of proactive inhibition (as well as retroactive inhibition) are much less striking when the material to be learned is meaningful as opposed to nonsense syl-

lables. In addition, the further a person learns beyond the point of bare mastery, the less susceptible he is to interferences of either the proactive or retroactive type. Nevertheless, studies have indicated (e.g., Postman, 1962a; Underwood and Postman, 1960) that much of the forgetting that takes place in our daily lives is the result of processes similar to proactive inhibition.

The interference theory then emphasizes the role of competing responses in forgetting; both prior responses and subsequent responses interfere with the responses we are currently learning. We will discuss the problem of competing responses further when we consider the question of *transfer of training* in the next chapter.

Motivated forgetting

The preceding explanations of forgetting emphasize it as a matter either of physiological processes affecting the memory trace or of interference between new and old material. Neither theory gives much attention to a person's motives in remembering and forgetting. This omission is a serious one; a complete theory of forgetting cannot ignore what the person is trying to do —both when he remembers and when he forgets.

Repression. According to the principle of repression, some of our memories become inaccessible to recall because of the way in which they relate to our personal problems. The inaccessibility is due neither to faded traces nor to disruptive learnings, for the memories are still there and can be revealed under appropriate conditions. The theory of repression holds that the memories are not recalled because their recall would in some way be unacceptable to the person—because of the anxiety that they would produce or the guilt that they might activate. While psychologists are not fully agreed upon the nature of repression, the facts are as acceptable as, and no more obscure than, many of those cited in other discussions of remembering and forgetting.

The nature of the forgetting that takes place in dramatic instances of amnesia aids in the understanding of repression. The amnesia victim does not forget everything. He evidently uses a rich store of memories and habits as he conducts his present social life. What he forgets are items of personal reference—his name, his family, his home address, his personal biography. The beginning of the amnesia is often to be traced to some severe emotional shock which the individual suffered and from which the amnesia provides an escape.

Occasionally cases in psychotherapy give rather convincing evidence of repressed memories and recovery from the repression, of which the following is a dramatic, if unusual, illustration, for the memory is recovered in a dream.

Richard C., a skilled worker 40 years old, came to a mental hospital with serious depression and haunting ideas about death. As a child he had lost his mother under traumatic circumstances. About the actual death he could remember only being awakened from sleep in order to be taken to the hospital some distance away. When he and his sisters arrived there, his mother was dead. The mother's death had been very disturbing to him, and it was evident to the psychiatrist who treated him that some of his present symptoms dated from it. In order to help him recall specific events of that period, the psychiatrist asked, among other questions, whether he recalled the time of night in which the events happened. He could not remember. That these memories were repressed is suggested by the information that came in a dream the night following this interview.

The patient dreamt that he saw two clocks. One was running and one had stopped. The one that was running said twenty minutes to three, and the one that had stopped said twenty minutes to five. He was mystified by the dream.

Because of the possibility that those clocks represented the repressed childhood memories, the man's older sister was located and asked about the circumstances of the mother's death. She said that they had been roused from sleep in their farmhouse about 2.30 A.M. and had driven to the distant hospital. When they arrived there about 4:30, their mother had just died.

Whether we accept the sister's version or the patient's, it is quite convincing that the times dreamed of were close to reality. Yet this memory was not consciously accessible to the patient, even when the psychiatrist pressed him for it. But the probing by the supportive therapist in the midst of treatment may have facilitated the recall in the dream.[1]

A number of experimental attempts have been made to determine whether or not repression can be demonstrated in the ordinary experiences of people who do not show dramatic symptoms of memory disturbance. Psychoanalytic studies suggest that repression is a very general phenomenon (Rapaport, 1950). If it is, it should be possible to demonstrate it in the laboratory, and a number of laboratory studies have been directed to the problem.

A study by Clemes (1964) may serve to illustrate the laboratory approach. He found for each subject words that led to difficulties in a word-association test, as evidenced by unusual and delayed responses; these he called "critical" words, compared to the nontroublesome "control" words to which usual responses were given at normal reaction times. He then constructed

[1] Case courtesy of Josephine R. Hilgard.

lists individually for his subjects to memorize, each list containing half critical and half control words in random order. The subjects learned the lists while hypnotized. The test of repression then came when he suggested under hypnosis that, in the attempt to recall, the subject would forget half the words. He conjectured that the critical words would serve as "targets" for repression, and hence would be selected (unconsciously) as the ones to be forgotten. This he found to be the case, a statistically larger proportion of the critical words being forgotten than the noncritical control ones.

Motivation to complete unfinished work. A set of experiments that deals with motivational aspects of forgetting has been devised to test the memory for finished and unfinished tasks. A number of simple tasks are presented—making clay models, solving Chinese puzzles, doing arithmetic problems. Some of the tasks are carried to completion; others are interrupted by the experimenter after the subject has become absorbed in them but before he has completed them. After some 20 such tasks have been attempted and the materials are out of sight, the experimenter asks the subject to list everything he has worked on. There is a tendency to name more of the unfinished than of the finished tasks (Zeigarnik, 1927).

The results show that absorption in a task sets up a motivation toward completion. The unresolved motive to complete heightens memory for the uncompleted task.

The importance of motivation is shown by reversal of results when the experiment is somewhat modified (Marrow, 1938). The task was set up so that the subject thought he was helping to standardize materials for an intelligence test. The experimenter explained that if he saw the subject was getting along well he would stop him and give him a new task. Only if the subject took unusually long or was having trouble would the experimenter let him continue, so that he could be sure how long such a task would take. Under these conditions,

interruption became a mark of success and noninterruption a mark of failure. When the subject had completed several of these tasks, he was asked to list what he had done. Now he remembered best those tasks that were completed!

These contradictory results are best reconciled if we think of the selective retention as fitting in with the motives of the subject. In both cases the tasks remembered were unsuccessful, so that an achievement-motivated subject might wish to have another chance at them. This conclusion suggests that with high achievement motivation more incomplete tasks would be remembered than with lower motivation. A later experimenter found this to be true. Atkinson (1953) tested subjects with high drive for achievement and with low drive in an experiment similar to Zeigarnik's. Under conditions favoring involvement in the tasks, those with high drive for achievement remembered more of the incompleted tasks than those with low drive for achievement. Thus it is evident that a theory of remembering and forgetting must take account of motivation.

Some comments on theories of forgetting

Now that we have examined several different explanations of forgetting, what can we conclude? Each explanation highlights something important about the memory process, but each is incomplete in itself. There may be some forgetting due to passive decay; at least it is difficult to prove that there is not. However, the experimental evidence indicates that passive decay is assuredly an incomplete theory. There may be some memory distortion due to spontaneous changes in the memory trace, but again the direct evidence is thin, the objections many, and the theory incomplete. The evidence that some forgetting takes place as the result of interference by both prior and subsequent learning (i.e., retroactive and proactive inhibition) is unrefutable. And, finally, motivational and emotional factors, as implied in the theory of repression, have to be taken into account as genuine influences upon forgetting.

Obviously none of these explanations by themselves is adequate to account for the full range of phenomena that fall under the general topic of forgetting. Consequently the current interest is in the direction of multiprocess theories of forgetting.

Duplex Theories of Forgetting

As a result of the failure of any single process to give an adequate account of forgetting, in recent years a number of theorists have argued for a duplex theory of memory. They propose that one type of storage mechanism is involved in remembering events just recently perceived and that a different type is involved in the recall of information established by repeated practice over trials. These two storage mechanisms have been labeled short-term memory (STM) and long-term memory (LTM). For example, to recall a telephone number just given to you is viewed as a different process from recalling your own phone number which you have used repeatedly. Figure 12–6 presents a retention curve obtained in a short-term memory experiment where rehearsal was eliminated. The rapidity of the memory loss is striking when you compare recall under these conditions with the retention curves for nonsense syllables learned with practice presented in Figure 12–2 (p. 318).

Long- and short-term memory

To give the reader some feeling for the details of theories that postulate a distinction between LTM and STM we shall sketch out a model that encompasses many of the ideas proposed by current theorists (Atkinson and Shiffrin, 1967; Bower, 1966; Broadbent, 1963; Waugh and Norman, 1965), but as it stands it is not a faithful representation of any one of these theorists' viewpoints. Their theories are too complex to present here, but the simplified model that we shall describe captures most of the central ideas of their respective positions.

Two storage mechanisms are postulated,

12–6

Retention curve for short-term memory

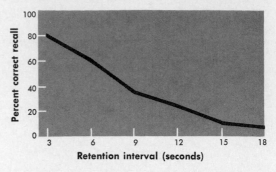

Subjects attempted to recall a single trigram of three consonants (e.g., X-J-R) after intervals of 3, 6, 9, 12, 15, and 18 seconds. The trigram was presented auditorily; during the next second a number was presented and the subject counted backward by three's from that number until he received a cue to recall the trigram. This counting procedure eliminated rehearsal of the trigram. Percentage of correct recall is plotted for the various time intervals (Peterson and Peterson, 1959). Subsequent experiments using familiar words and three-word units yielded similar results except that single words were retained longer than either trigrams or three-word units.

one for short-term memory and the other for long-term; the interaction between the two processes is characterized by the flow chart in Figure 12–7. Incoming information is fed into a short-term storage mechanism, and remains there for a period of time. During its stay in STM it can be retrieved perfectly. However, the short-term storage mechanism has a limited capacity, and an item stays in STM only until it is displaced or bumped out by new, incoming information. As an analogy we can think of STM as a box of fixed size that can hold only so many blocks. Each block represents a stimulus input. When new blocks are added to the box, old ones have to be removed to make room for them. Thus information is temporarily stored in STM until new incoming information replaces it. During this storage period it may be coded and transferred to long-term storage; if such a transfer does not occur while the information is in STM, then it will be permanently lost.

In contrast, LTM is assumed to be virtually unlimited, so that any information that is transferred from STM to LTM will have a place for permanent storage. In essence, once information has been transferred into long-term storage it is never forgotten. This statement obviously needs some clarification, for we know that we frequently fail to recall an item once known well. Retrieval of information from long-term memory may fail because the cues needed to identify the information to be retrieved may be incomplete. With incomplete cues a search of LTM may bring forth an incorrect recall or may fail to find any appropriate information. The tip-of-the-tongue state provides an excellent example of a situation where an individual has inadequate cues to find the desired information. He feels sure he knows the item but cannot recall it immediately. He has enough cues to narrow down the area of search and retrieves some words that are similar in certain characteristics to the target word; these similar words may provide additional cues that may enable him to eventually find the target word.

Long-term memory storage is analogous to a filing cabinet of large capacity. As any file clerk knows, it is one thing to toss items into various file drawers; it is a more difficult task to retrieve a desired item. For example, Mr. Johnson's letter to the city council complaining about sewerage and sanitation may have been filed under "Johnson," "complaints," "sanitation," or "sewerage." It is also possible that initially only part of the desired information was coded into long-term memory and, hence, complete retrieval is not possible.

Duplex theories thus regard forgetting as a two-process mechanism. Immediate recall may fail because subsequent inputs to STM have bumped out the information. Long-term recall may fail because the information was never transferred to LTM or because not enough cues are available at the time of recall to locate the information in LTM. The student who complains that he "knew the material backwards and forwards" but could not recall it for the examination may simply have stared at the textbook with his mind on other things and never rehearsed the material so that it could be encoded into LTM. Or the material may be stored in LTM but the examination questions did not provide sufficient cues to permit retrieval.

12–7

Flow chart for a duplex theory of memory

Schematic representation of short-term and long-term storage mechanisms. All incoming sensory information enters STM where it is rehearsed and either successfully coded for storage in LTM or forgotten. (After Waugh and Norman, 1965)

This is a rather rough sketch of a theory that does a fairly adequate job of accounting for much of the data on memory. Of particular interest are conjectures about the mechanism involved in transferring information from short-term to long-term memory. One conjecture is that the transfer involves a *coding process*. The information temporarily stored in STM is being rehearsed and translated into smaller "chunks" of information that can be more readily stored in LTM. An example of such a coding process is a person's use of a *mnemonic* (any system of coding information to make it easier to remember) to facilitate recall. For example, the telephone number 149-1625 is hard to remember with a single reading, but it can be remembered more easily if it is coded as consisting of the successive squares of the numbers 1, 2, 3, 4, and 5.

If the input of stimulus information occurs at a slow rate, then it will remain in short-term memory for a longer time and hence will have a higher probability of being encoded and transferred into LTM. If the information rate is high, less encoding will occur and thus more information will be forgotten.

How do our earlier explanations of forgetting fit into this conceptual scheme? Although the information stored in STM is a fairly faithful representation of the stimulus input, some fading and/or distortion is possible in this state before the information is encoded and transferred to LTM. Once coded and stored in LTM, however, the code is assumed to be relatively fixed over time and not susceptible to fading or distortion. However, other items of information with similar codes may be stored in LTM so that upon recall we have difficulty retrieving the correct item. The phenomena of retroactive and proactive inhibition can demonstrate their effects in this manner.

Items of information that we use frequently may be coded in such a way that many different cues lead to them. In terms of our file drawer analogy, they may be cross-indexed. Such items are thus readily available and require no searching. Or at times, when the recall of certain information is painful to us, we may set our "retrieval mechanism" to ignore the information; it is not lost, however, and can be retrieved once the need for repression is gone.

Although such speculations as the latter are somewhat far-fetched, some of the duplex theories of forgetting have proved quite successful in giving detailed accounts for much of the data of memory.

Consolidation theory

Theories of the sort we have been describing are frequently called *information-processing models*. Such models are highly schematized representations of the flow of information in the nervous system and do not venture into any of the physiological details. There is clearly a large gap between the study of complex behavior and that of neurophysiology, and many psychologists feel that the use of simplified diagrams to describe the flow of information from the initial stimulus input to the response output forms a useful bridge between the two areas (Broadbent, 1965).

One attempt to relate the hypothetical processes of long-term and short-term memory to physiological states is found in *consolidation theory* (Glickman, 1961; McGaugh, 1966). This theory proposes that the change in the nervous system produced by learning is time-dependent; the nature of the change is not specified, the neural residue of the experience being simply referred to as a memory trace. The theory assumes that the memory trace undergoes a consolidation phase after learning; during this phase (equivalent to short-term memory) it is in an unstable state and vulnerable to obliteration by interfering events. If the memory trace is in any way disrupted during this period memory loss occurs. However, if no disruption occurs (in the short period of time following the learning experience), then the memory trace consolidates and becomes a relatively permanent part of long-term memory, resistant to future destruction.

Certain clinical observations give tentative support for the consolidation notion.

For example, people who sustain injuries frequently have a loss of memory for events occurring during the period of time immediately preceding the accident, but have no loss of memory for earlier events. This phenomenon is called *retrograde amnesia*. In terms of the consolidation theory, the accident interrupts brain processes that are necessary for consolidating memories.

There have been a large number of experimental studies with animals using electroconvulsive shock (ECS) to produce retrograde amnesia. The typical experiment is roughly as follows. An animal is trained on some learning task and shortly thereafter is given an electroconvulsive shock, which produces temporary unconsciousness. The animal is then tested at a later time and the retention of the learned response is measured as a function of the interval between initial learning and the administration of ECS. The general experimental paradigm can be diagramed as follows:

In one study rats were given ECS at intervals of either zero seconds, 20 seconds, 30 minutes, or one hour following the termination of a learning task. When the animals were retested the next day, it was found that retention of the learned response increased with the length of the interval between training and the administration of ECS; the animals with a zero-second interval showed virtually no retention, whereas animals with a one-hour interval showed almost perfect retention (Hudspeth, McGaugh, and Thompson, 1964).

CRITICAL DISCUSSION

An alternative explanation for ECS results

There are now a large number of studies that indicate conclusively that ECS administered a brief time after original training

does interfere with the retention of the learned response, whereas administered later in time it has no effect. However, concurrent with the development of interest in the phenomenon of retrograde amnesia has been the development of alternative theories to that of consolidation for explaining these results. For example, Lewis and Maher (1965, 1966) interpret the literature on electroconvulsive shock and retrograde amnesia quite differently. They argue that ECS produces a generalized inhibitory response which becomes conditioned, by Pavlovian means, to the environmental stimuli present at the time the coma was induced. They assume that this inhibitory response—conditioned to environmental stimuli associated with the learning situation—will interfere with performance of any other response that was previously learned. Their explanation is based on learning notions, and argues that when comas are induced at short intervals following training, stimuli associated with the experimental task become conditioned to inhibitory responses. Consequently when the animal is reintroduced into the learning situation later to test for retention, the conditioned inhibitory response will tend to interfere with his performance and give rise to a poor recall score.

For many of the studies on retention and ECS either consolidation theory or the conditioned-inhibition hypothesis of Lewis and Maher provide a satisfactory explanation of the data. There is one area of experimentation, however, that seems to provide a crucial differentiation between the two theories. As noted above, the conditioned-inhibition hypothesis assumes that inhibition is conditioned to the stimuli present at the time the coma was induced. Hence, one would predict that ECS administered in a stimulus situation quite different from that in which the initial learning took place would have less amnesic effect than ECS administered in the apparatus where the initial learning occurred (given that the time interval was the same in both conditions). In contrast, consolidation theory predicts that variations in the stimulus environment in which ECS is given should have no significant effect. In recent tests of this prediction the amount of retrograde amnesia produced by ECS has been found to be unaffected by variations in the stimulus environment in which the treatment is administered (McGaugh and Petrinovich, 1966). This evidence is difficult to explain in terms of the conditioned-inhibition hypothesis, and argues strongly for consolidation theory. However, before the issue can be resolved more research will be necessary.

Circumstances Affecting Recall

We may arbitrarily divide the whole course of learning and memory into three major steps: *fixating* the material, *retaining* it over a period of disuse, and *reinstating* it at the time of recall. At which of these three points can we most easily effect an improvement in memory? Improving our general ability for retentivity seems the least likely possibility for major improvement—unless we want to try to improve retention by inserting long periods of sleep or inactivity between fixation and recall. But the circumstances surrounding the acts of fixation and recall can certainly affect our memory. Of the two, fixation (the act of memorization) seems the most important and we shall consider it again when we discuss learning efficiency in Chapter 13. Here we shall consider some aspects of both fixation and recall.

Recall during practice

Recall during practice usually takes the form of reciting to oneself. Such self-recitation increases the retention of the material learned. Suppose, for example, a student has two hours to devote to the study of an assignment that he can read through once in 30 minutes. Rereading the assignment four times is likely to be much less effective than reading it once and asking himself questions about the material he has read. He can then reread to clear up points that were unclear as he attempted to recall them. The generalization that it is efficient to spend a good fraction of study time in attempting recall is supported by experiments with laboratory learning as well as by experiments with school learning.

A well-known laboratory experiment

dramatized the value of self-recitation by showing greatest efficiency in recall when as much as 80 percent of the study time was devoted to active self-recitation. The materials used consisted of nonsense syllables and short biographies. The results for nonsense syllables are given in Table 12–1; the results for biographies were similar (Gates, 1917).

When the same kind of experiment was conducted with the learning of French vocabulary, the kind of task often confronted in school, the self-recitation method was found much superior to merely reading over the words and their definitions (Seibert, 1932). Similar results have been found for spelling and arithmetic (Forlano, 1936).

One reason for the advantage of the self-recitation method in ordinary learning is that it forces the reader to define and select for himself what it is that he wishes to remember. In addition, recitation represents practice in the recall of the material in the form likely to be demanded later on. That is, the learner tries to outline a history chapter or provide illustrations of a secondary reinforcer, as he may have to do on an examination. The rule is to begin an active process of recall early in a study period. Time spent in active recall, with the book closed, is time well spent. When the material to be learned is already clear, as in learning lists of nonsense syllables or

TABLE 12–1

The value of self-recitation in memorizing nonsense syllables

Percent of time devoted to self-recitation (remainder to reading)	Percent of 16 nonsense syllables recalled	
	Immediately	After 4 hours
0	35	15
20	50	26
40	54	28
60	57	37
80	74	48

SOURCE: Gates (1917).

vocabulary words, the recitation method, by demanding active participation from the learner, helps to sustain both his attention and his motivation.

Effects of overlearning on retention

Something to be long retained must be overlearned, that is, learned beyond the point of bare recall. A classical study by Krueger (1929) illustrates the advantage of overlearning. The subjects were required to memorize a list of 12 nouns by the serial-anticipation method (p. 297), using three degrees of overlearning. For subjects in the group of zero-percent overlearning, practice was terminated at a criterion of one perfect recitation of the list. For the group of 50-percent overlearning, practice was continued beyond the point of mastery for half as many trials as had been required to reach criterion; for the group of 100-percent overlearning, the number of trials was doubled. The same list was then relearned either 1, 2, 4, 7, 14, or 28 days later. The results of the experiment are shown in Figure 12–8 where the dependent variable is the *saving score* on relearning. This score is computed by the formula given earlier (p. 316). The curves in Figure 12–8 indicate that the greater the degree of overlearning, the greater the retention at all time intervals. Further, the improvement in retention going from zero- to 50-percent overlearning is quite large, compared with a much smaller improvement going from 50- to 100-percent overlearning.

More recent research generalizes these results and permits us to conclude that successive increases in the amount of overlearning yield diminishing returns. As one would expect, the rate at which increments in retention diminish with overlearning depends on the type of material being learned (Postman, 1962a).

The retention of skills learned in childhood, even after years of disuse, is not so surprising when we consider the amount of overlearning involved in such skills as swimming, skating, or riding a bicycle. The skill is not learned only to bare mastery, but is repeated far beyond the point of original learning. Overlearning may not suffice to account for all the difference in retention between skills and information, but it is assuredly a strong contributing influence.

Periodic reviews

The advantages of periodic reviews are similar to those of self-recitation, for self-recitation is in fact an early review. Experiments have been made on both the most effective spacing of reviews and the advantages of one kind of review over another.

In one extensive study of learning of sixth-grade children, one group of students was tested on its recall of a selection immediately after learning, while other groups had their first recalls (i.e., tests) after 1, 7, 14, 21, 28, or 63 days. In most cases a second test was given later on. The first recalls showed the decrease of remembered

12–8

Effects of overlearning on retention

Retention curves for three amounts of overlearning. Subjects learned a list of 12 nouns to varying degrees of mastery. Then they were tested for retention at later points in time. Retention is measured as a saving score on subsequent relearning. (After Krueger, 1929)

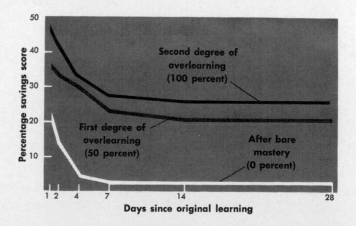

Second degree of overlearning (100 percent)

First degree of overlearning (50 percent)

After bare mastery (0 percent)

Days since original learning

material with passing of time, a phenomenon that was expected from our knowledge of curves of retention. But the main point of the experiment was that active recall markedly slowed down the forgetting process, as measured by the second recall some days or weeks later (Spitzer, 1939).

Rote vs. logical memory

In the earlier discussion of curves of retention, the implication was that forgetting consists in the mere dropping out of items, so that retention was scored as the percentage of original material retained. But memory is not merely a collection of items, some of which escape with time. Memories are of *patterns of items,* woven together with varying degrees of organization, and the success in retention depends upon how much organization is present. Meaningful materials, even though arranged in random lists, are retained better than nonsense materials because of their greater richness of associative organization. When meaningful materials are tied together in logically related patterns, retention is further improved.

It is obvious that a relationship or rule is easier to remember than the detailed illustrations of that rule. It is certainly easier to remember that the square of a number is the number multiplied by itself than it is to remember the table of squares. The student who understands his courses needs to rely a great deal less on rote memory than the student who sees the course as merely a collection of unrelated facts.

SUMMARY 1. When we remember something we may show the marks of earlier memory in several ways. *Redintegrative memory,* or the recollection of a personal event, reconstructs a past occasion not only in terms of its content but also of its setting in time and place. Such rich memories have been little studied in the psychological laboratory. Much easier to test are *recognition,* requiring only a sense of familiarity, and *recall,* requiring a reinstatement of something learned in the past. *Saving in relearning* is another test for the influence of prior learning.

2. The course of forgetting has been studied chiefly for material learned by rote, or, as we say, committed to memory. The most usual form of the *curve of retention* is that of rapid forgetting at first, followed by decreasing losses. The form holds true for different sorts of materials, but the time axis differs.

3. Four traditional explanations of forgetting include: (1) *passive decay* through disuse, (2) *systematic distortions of the memory trace,* (3) *interference effects* (retroactive and proactive inhibition), and (4) *motivated forgetting,* illustrated by repression and the effects of goal-seeking (i.e., motivation to complete unfinished work) on retention. These four theories are supplementary rather than contradictory, and each calls attention to important features of forgetting. But because no one of them can account for all the facts of forgetting, several two-process or duplex theories of forgetting have been proposed.

4. *Duplex theories* of forgetting distinguish between *short-term* and *long-term memory* and postulate different storage mechanisms for each. The results of retrograde-amnesia studies support the notion that a *consolidation* or coding period is necessary following learning if the material is to be retained in long-term memory.

5. Most of the improvement in retention comes about in part through improved methods of *fixating* the material in the first place and in part through *practice in recall*.

6. The rapidity of memory loss is lessened by *active recall* during learning, by *overlearning* beyond bare mastery, and by *periodic reviews*. Logically understood material is retained much better than material learned by rote.

x

SUGGESTIONS FOR FURTHER READING

The classical study that introduced the experimental study of memory is Ebbinghaus, *Memory* (1885; tr., 1913), now available in paperback (1964). The experiments carried out in the tradition of Ebbinghaus are well summarized in McGeoch and Irion, *The psychology of human learning* (2nd ed., 1952). Many pertinent sections can be found in Hilgard and Bower, *Theories of learning* (3rd ed., 1966), Underwood, *Experimental psychology* (2nd ed., 1966), Osgood, *Method and theory in experimental psychology* (1953), and Woodworth and Schlosberg, *Experimental psychology* (rev. ed., 1954).

A group of papers focused on controversial issues in learning and memory (some of which are appropriate to the current chapter and some to the previous one) are found in Cofer and Musgrave (eds.), *Verbal behavior and learning* (1963). Also of interest are the proceedings of a series of conferences edited by Kimble, *Learning, remembering, and forgetting*, vol. I (1966), vol. II (1967*a*), vol. III (1967*b*). See also John, *Mechanics of memory* (1967).

13 The Management of Learning

Most of the principles of learning and retention suggest practical applications, but it is seldom possible to move directly from general principles to applications. Usually it is necessary to take account of the setting, to try out the principles in practical contexts, and to make adjustments to fit the demands of special conditions. A drug may be found to kill the bacteria causing a given disease, but before this knowledge can be put to use, the dosage of the drug must be decided upon as well as the most appropriate way to administer it. In this chapter we shall examine the laboratory findings that bear most directly upon the problems of efficient learning and that yield suggestions for the management of learning. We will be concerned with such problems as the spacing of the learning sessions (concentrating on the material to be learned for a continuous period or dividing the study session into shorter periods with rest intervals interspersed); the method of attack (memorizing material as a whole vs. breaking it up into shorter segments); the importance of knowledge of results; the manner in which learning one subject transfers to learning a new subject; and the motivational and emotional conditions which may affect learning efficiency.

Economy in Acquiring Skill and in Rote Memorization

The many experiments on multiple-response learning have led to the discovery of circumstances favorable to rapid learning. When these laboratory findings are confirmed in more practical situations, they help the teacher to teach and the student to learn with maximum efficiency.

Massed vs. distributed practice

One problem that has received considerable experimental investigation involves the spacing of learning sessions. If we have a week in which to memorize the lines of a play or to learn a new motor skill but can only spend 14 hours of that week in practice, what practice schedule would produce the greatest improvement? Should we practice two hours each day for a week, concentrate for a steady seven hours a day on the two days prior to the deadline, or adopt some intermediate schedule? The two extremes represent respectively *massed practice* (in which the practice sessions or trials are crowded together) and *distributed practice* (which implies rest intervals between sessions or trials). The preponderance of experimental evidence indicates that, for the same amount of practice, learning is better when practice is distributed rather than massed, although there are exceptions to this generalization. Let us first examine the evidence that distributed practice is advantageous.

We have already seen this principle demonstrated in the experiment on mirror drawing (Figure 11–19, p. 295), where greater gains were made with one trial per day than with all trials in one day. The generalization holds for the intertrial inter-

13–1

Distributed practice in eyelid conditioning

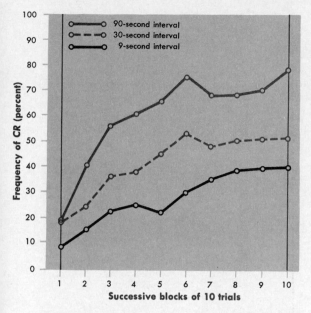

The longer the interval between trials, the greater the frequency of conditioned eyelid responses for a given number of reinforced trials. (After Spence and Norris, 1950)

vals within a single session as well (Figure 13–1). In this experiment, the number of conditioned eyelid responses emitted in 100 trials varied directly with the interval of time between trials (Spence and Norris, 1950).

It is appropriate to review at this time the major theories used to explain the advantage of distributed practice, when such advantage is found.

1. *Recovery-from-work theory.* The recovery-from-work theory assumes that continuous practice is fatiguing, so that the subject cannot show all that he has learned and his scores are therefore lower than they would be if he were rested. With rest all the learning that occurred has a chance to show itself in the actual scoring. An experimental illustration of this possibility is shown in Figure 13–2 (Bourne and Archer, 1956). The subjects were required to perform a tracking response on a pursuit rotor (see p. 295). The target was a small metal

disk mounted near the edge of a rotating turntable which the subject tracked with a stylus. Whenever the stylus was in contact with the moving target, an electric circuit was completed through a clock so that time on target was recorded automatically. Each subject received 21 trials of 30-second duration. The intertrial interval (rest period between trials) was 15, 30, or 45 seconds for different groups of subjects. After the 21st trial all subjects were given a five-minute rest period and then continued the task for an additional nine trials with no rest interval between trials. Figure 13–2 shows the results in terms of percentage of time on target per trial. As in the eyelid conditioning study, performance clearly improves as the intertrial interval is increased. However, in the final phase of the experiment when all three groups had a zero intertrial interval (massed practice) the initial benefits of the spaced practice gradually disappeared, thus supporting the recovery-from-work theory.[1]

The superiority of the distributed practice group seems to be primarily a superiority of *performance* rather than *learning* and tends to disappear when the distributed group is subjected to massed conditions. However, other theories have been proposed to account for the same results.

2. *Differential forgetting theory.* This theory assumes that the subject learns both the correct performance and some irrelevant performances that interfere with it.

[1] The improvement of performance for all groups on the first trial after the five-minute rest gives added support to the recovery-from-work theory. The fact that performance is better on the second trial after the rest period than on the first illustrates a phenomenon we have not mentioned thus far: a rapid increase in performance early in practice after a rest is called *warmup*. *Warmup* is typically found in motor skills and is assumed to depend upon a number of factors such as getting in the proper position, getting the stiffness out of the muscles, securing the proper grip on the stylus, etc. The need for warmup prior to peak performance is recognized in a number of activities requiring motor skills: the tennis player and the baseball batter take a few practice swings, the football player does some deep knee bends before going onto the field, the concert pianist flexes his fingers before going on stage.

The effects of distribution of practice on performance

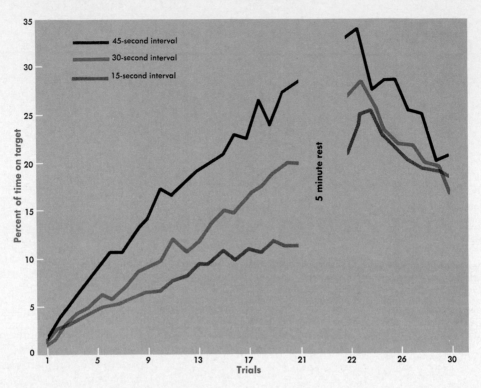

Subjects were required to perform a tracking response on a pursuit rotor. In the first phase of the experiment each subject received 21 trials, but with either 15, 30, or 45 seconds of rest between trials. After the 21st trial all subjects were given a five minute rest, and then continued the task for nine more trials with no rest between trials. The dependent variable is percentage of time on target per trial. (After Bourne and Archer, 1956)

But the irrelevant performances are likely to be less well practiced and so may be forgotten more rapidly than the correct and better-learned performances. If the interfering performances fall off rapidly enough, so that the original learning shows up before much of it has been forgotten, then there will be a rise in the performance curve between trials. Plausible as this theory sounds, most of the evidence for it is very indirect and unsatisfactory (Buxton and Ross, 1949).

3. *Consolidation theory.* In Chapter 12 we discussed the theory that the changes produced in the nervous system by learning need time to consolidate or "set" in order to be stored as permanent memories. Con-

solidation theory also provides an explanation for the superiority of distributed practice. If the physiological process that underlies learning is time-dependent, then distributed practice would provide a better opportunity for these changes to take place than massed practice.

An experiment by McGaugh and Hostetter (1961) provides additional support for a consolidation theory. They argued that if the interferences of waking activity prevent the consolidation of what was learned, then material tested after a period of sleep should be better retained than material tested after waking, as had been found by earlier investigators (see p. 323). But they add another step to the argument: if sleep comes only after a period of new waking activity that is long enough to interrupt consolidation, it should not be of any benefit in retention; conversely, if waking activity follows a sleep period that is long enough to consolidate learning, then the waking activity should no longer be disruptive. Their results are entirely in line with their predictions (Figure 13–3), thus giving support to a consolidation theory.

The above theories all assume that distributed practice is advantageous over massed practice; if they were fully satisfactory, they would also have to account for the exceptions. The puzzling questions raised by massed and distributed practice have been studied in a long series of investigations by Underwood and his students (e.g., Underwood, 1961, and references cited there). Most of the experiments are on rote memorizing, sometimes using the serial-anticipation method, sometimes the method of paired associates (p. 296).

Usually distributed practice led to more rapid learning, but seldom, in these experiments, did it lead to better retention. Hence the generalization that distributed practice is a favorable condition of learning has to be stated with extreme caution, especially if it cannot be shown to have advantages for retention.

Other reservations over distribution of practice arise when more difficult materials are learned. In some kinds of hard puzzles or other "thought" problems there seems to be an advantage in staying with the problem for a few massed trials at first, rather than spending a day or more between trials (Garrett, 1940; Ericksen, 1942). This kind of learning calls for a varied attack, rather than a smooth-running skill or rote performance. It may be that massed practice leads to such variability, which is possibly an advantage in problem-solving but a disadvantage in serial-learning.

In practical situations the distribution of study time depends on a number of factors.

13–3

Evidence for a consolidation period in learning

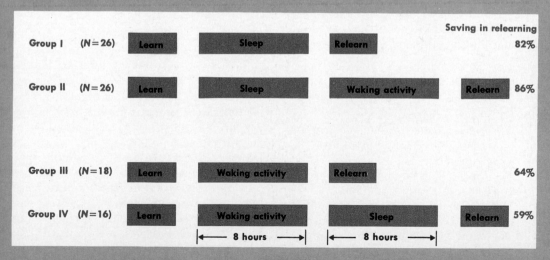

When sleep follows immediately after learning, retention is high (82–86 percent), regardless of whether the sleep is followed by waking activity before relearning. When learning is followed by waking activity, retention is less (64–59 percent), regardless of whether sleep intervenes before the test of retention. The results show Group I to have higher savings (i.e., retention) than Group III, and Group II to have higher savings than Group IV, with equal elapsed time in each comparison. These results are statistically significant. (After McGaugh and Hostetter, 1961)

If a fairly elaborate amount of preparation is required before the learning task can be started (e.g., gathering materials or equipment, organizing one's thoughts), then obviously if the practice sessions are too brief a lot of time is wasted in getting "warmed up." On the other hand, if the task requires considerable physical or mental exertion, then the rest periods provided by distributed practice allow for the dissipation of fatigue. And with tasks that are particularly boring, distributed practice helps to maintain motivation.

Learning by wholes and by parts

Suppose you have a long poem to memorize. Is it better to learn one stanza at a time or to learn the poem as a whole? Early studies of this problem favored the generalization that it is better to learn by the *whole method* rather than by the *part method.* Later studies have often turned out ambiguously, with neither method uniformly better than the other. The problem remains an important one, at least for those people who have to memorize the lines of a play or a musical selection.

One analysis of the whole/part problem proposes that all the following factors have to be considered, because they have all proved important in one or more experiments:

1. The more intelligent the subject, the more likely that the whole method will prove advantageous.
2. The advantage of the whole method increases with practice in using it.
3. When practice is distributed rather than massed, the whole method becomes increasingly favorable.
4. Material that is meaningful and unified tends to favor the whole method.
5. The total length of the material, the actual sizes of the parts, and the number of parts making up the whole must be considered. (There is no simple rule here, for it is quite possible that very short and very long passages will profit from the whole method, with in-between ones favoring the part method.)

6. A disadvantage of the part method is the time required to connect the separately learned parts. Methods that get around this difficulty will reduce the advantages of the whole method.
7. Following the separate learning of the parts, attempted recall may reveal more mutual interference among the parts with some materials than with others. Hence the disadvantage of the part method may depend upon the material to be learned.[2]

What conclusion emerges from this? In general, the whole method is probably advantageous, but slavish adherence to it cannot be recommended. In the learning of rote material there is a well-known *serial-position effect,* which means that the ends are learned most readily and that the hardest part to learn is the middle (Figure 13–4). Slavish following of the whole method leads to overlearning of the beginning and end material in order to achieve bare mastery of the material in the middle. It seems only sensible, therefore, for the learner to select for special practice the parts that are most difficult to learn. Remembering that the recombining of parts is a disadvantage of the part method, the learner should make a running start in practicing the more troublesome parts; that is, he should start *just before* a transition to the difficult material and should run *beyond the next transition.* Thus he will have practice in maintaining the whole while giving special attention to the part.

If the part is naturally separable from the whole, there is no reason why part learning should be disadvantageous. For example, in the game of golf, driving and putting are such separable activities that it makes good sense to practice them separately. But in swimming, the arm and leg movements and the breathing represent such a closely interrelated whole that one would expect a gain from the whole method. Thus the advantage of the whole method over the part method depends

[2] These seven points are paraphrased from McGeoch and Irion (1952), pp. 501–07.

The serial-position effect

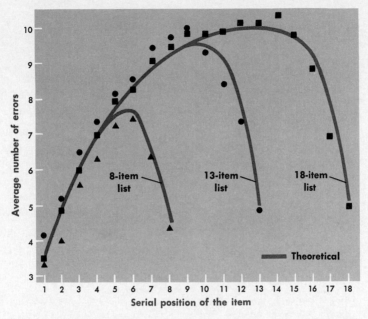

Subjects were required to learn a list of 8, 13, or 18 nonsense syllables by the method of serial anticipation. The syllables were presented one at a time in the window of a memory drum. When the first syllable appeared, the subject was asked to anticipate the syllable that followed the one he was looking at. A moment later the next syllable appeared telling him whether or not he was correct and also giving him the cue for anticipating the next syllable. And so on. After each trial (a complete run through the list) there was a brief rest period before the start of the next trial. Of course, on the first trial the subject had no chance of getting any of the items correct because he had not seen the list before; on subsequent trials he began to make increasingly more correct anticipations. The curves plot the number of errors made at each serial position over the course of learning. Note that, for all three lengths of list, the initial items were mastered most easily, the last items were the next easiest, and the middle items were the most difficult ones. The bow-shaped curve is typically obtained in learning lists by the serial-anticipation method. (After Atkinson, 1957)

somewhat on how we define wholes and parts.

Knowledge of results

We learn many things by paying attention to outcomes. When we shoot at a target we try to aim a little higher if the last shot was too low. But learning is not quite as rational as this; we do not always use all the information available to us, and sometimes we use it without being aware of it. In one experiment, for example, subjects were asked to say as many words as they could think of. One specific category of words, plural nouns, was rewarded; the type of reward varied for different groups but included the "mmm-hmm" spoken by the experimenter or the onset of a light or buzzer following each plural noun mentioned by the subject. The frequency of plural nouns increased significantly with the use of each of the rewards even though the subject, when questioned afterward, indicated he was quite unaware of the relationship between his responses and the reward. The subjects had learned to give plural nouns, but without knowing what it was that they had learned (Greenspoon, 1955).

In the pursuit-rotor task the subject

knows fairly well when his stylus is on the target, because he watches the target as it goes around and makes corrective movements when he loses it. Hence he is constantly influenced by knowledge of results. Even so, if he hears an audible click when he has successfully remained on the target for an appreciable time, he improves more rapidly (Reynolds and Adams, 1953).

The promptness with which the individual is given knowledge of results is also important. In one study subjects were blindfolded and instructed to draw a three-inch line along the edge of a metal strip every 30 seconds. The experimenter could measure the length of the line and told the subject whether his response was "long," "short," or "right" (a "right" response was one between 2¾ and 3¼ inches). Information concerning the accuracy of the line was delayed for zero, 10, or 20 seconds for different groups of subjects. A control group was given no information concerning results. Figure 13–5 presents the results. Increasing the delay interval clearly reduces the rate of learning (Greenspoon and Foreman, 1956). These results parallel those we found for delay of reinforcement (see p. 289) where rate of learning was directly related to the speed with which reward was delivered.

The importance of providing knowledge of results promptly has been demonstrated in the classroom too. Students in a freshman chemistry class who learned their right and wrong answers immediately after they took their hour quizzes during the term did significantly better on the final examination than students in a matched group who waited until the next class session to find out their results (Angell, 1949).

Knowledge of results does two things: (1) it furnishes information according to which mistakes can be corrected and performances improved, and (2) it makes a task more interesting to the learner and thus has incentive or reward value. As we shall see in a later section, one of the advantages of instruction by means of an automatic device such as a teaching machine is that knowledge of results is immediate.

13–5

Promptness of feedback

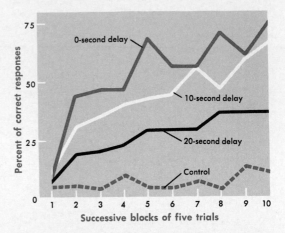

The effect of delay of feedback information on the accuracy of line drawing. The figure displays the percentage of correct responses in successive blocks of five trials; delay intervals of 0, 10, and 20 seconds were used. In addition, a control group was run with no feedback. Note that the more prompt the information feedback, the more rapidly the subject learns the desired response. (After Greenspoon and Foreman, 1956)

Transfer of Training

An important problem in the economy of learning is the extent to which the learning of one thing helps in the learning of something else. If every response we learned were specific to the situation in which it was learned (i.e., if there were no transfer from one situation to another), the amount of learning one would have to cram into a lifetime would be phenomenal. Fortunately, most learned behaviors are readily transferable, with some modification, to a number of different situations. We may have learned to drive in a car of specific make and vintage, but we can drive other cars with little difficulty even though there may be differences in the arrangement of the dashboard, the drag of the clutch, and so on. In an emergency we could probably drive a truck or a bus without further training. The influence that learning one task may have on the subsequent learning or performance of another task is called *transfer of training*.

The simplest experimental design for studying transfer of training is as follows:

Group	Phase I	Phase II
Experimental	Learn task *A*	Learn task *B*
Control	Unrelated activity	Learn task *B*

If the experimental group performs better than the control group on task *B*, then we can assume there has been *positive transfer* from the learning of *A* to *B*. If, on the other hand, the experimental group is inferior to the control on task *B*, *negative transfer* has occurred. And if there is no difference between the performance of the two groups, we assume zero transfer.

We encountered a design similar to the above in Chapter 12 (p. 324) when we discussed the role of proactive inhibition in forgetting. Actually, proactive inhibition is a special case of negative transfer. But in studying transfer of training we are more interested in how the prior task influences *acquisition* of the present task rather than its influence on the *retention* of task *B* once learned.

We can think of numerous examples of negative transfer in everyday life. When we first drive a car with automatic transmission after having been accustomed to one with a stick shift we may find ourselves often depressing a nonexistent clutch pedal. When we change from a pedal-brake to a hand-brake bicycle we may still try to press back on the pedal when we have to stop quickly. And the transition from the American custom of driving on the right-hand side of the street to the English custom of driving on the left is a difficult one for many American visitors to Great Britain. The original habit is so overlearned that even after the individual has been driving successfully on the left for some time he may revert to right-side driving when required to act quickly in an emergency.

Doctrine of formal discipline

The problem of transfer of training has been historically of great concern to people working in the area of education. For them it constitutes the very important practical question of how the school curricula should be arranged to ensure maximum positive transfer. Does learning algebra first help in the learning of geometry? Which of the sciences should be taught first to ensure maximum transfer to other scientific courses?

Among educators one of the earliest notions of transfer of training, prevalent around the turn of the century, maintained that the mind was composed of faculties that could be strengthened through exercise much as muscles are strengthened. This notion, known as the *doctrine of formal discipline*, was advanced in support of keeping in the high school curriculum such studies as Latin and Greek whose content is little used in everyday life. The argument that these subjects provided the discipline necessary to strengthen the mental faculties was advanced in statements such as: "The study of Latin trains the reason, the powers of observation, comparison, and synthesis."

The doctrine of formal discipline has been largely discredited by experiments. Some transfer takes place, but it depends much more on learning to use for a specific purpose the specific thing learned than on formal mental training. For example, the study of Latin does indeed improve the understanding of English words, but only those with Latin roots. It does not improve the understanding of words of Anglo-Saxon origin (Thorndike and Ruger, 1923). And the extent to which improvement occurs depends upon the way the Latin is taught: the gain in English vocabulary is much greater when the course is taught with emphasis on word derivation than when taught by more conventional methods.

The notion that reasoning ability is improved by the study of mathematics also has been pretty much discredited. An investigation of 13,500 high school seniors (Thorndike, 1924) found that those who had taken courses in mathematics and language tested somewhat higher in reasoning ability than those who had taken cooking and stenography. The difference was slight, however, and was readily explained by the fact that the students who chose the more abstract courses were brighter to begin with.

Stimulus and response factors affecting transfer

When we compare a previously learned task with a new one in an attempt to determine what the transfer effects will be we need to analyze both the stimulus and response variables in the two situations. If we think of a task as consisting of a specific stimulus-response pair $(S_1 - R_1)$, then we can conceive of transfer situations where the stimulus changes from the old task to the new while the response remains constant (first task, $S_1 - R_1$; second task, $S_2 - R_1$); where the response changes while the stimulus remains the same $(S_1 - R_1 : S_1 - R_2)$; and where both change $(S_1 - R_1 : S_2 - R_2)$. This conceptualization has made it possible to bring together a number of diverse results, such as the negative transfer implied in retroactive inhibition and positive transfer through generalization (Bruce, 1933; Osgood, 1949; Atkinson and Estes, 1963).

Stimulus changes. What will happen if we change the stimulus from the first to the second task but keep the response constant? In this case we are learning to give a familiar response to a new stimulus $(S_2 - R_1)$. An example would be learning the Spanish-English pair *"amigo*-friend" after having learned the French-English pair *"ami*-friend." Studies have shown that learning to make an old response to a new stimulus generally results in positive transfer. And, as we would expect from the principle of stimulus generalization, the greater the similarity between the stimuli in the two situations, the more the positive transfer. In the above example the transfer would be quite easy because the stimuli *"ami"* and *"amigo"* are highly similar. We would expect somewhat less transfer with the French and Spanish equivalents for the English word "black" (*noir* and *negro*) and little if any transfer with the equivalents for "boy" (*garçon* and *muchacho*).

In most situations, however, even if the new stimuli are quite dissimilar to the old ones and the responses remain the same we will still get some positive transfer. The practical meaning of this is that if we already have a response in our repertory of learned behavior, it is easier to attach it to a new stimulus than to learn both a new response and a new stimulus.

Response changes. What will happen if we change the response from the first to the second task but keep the stimulus constant $(S_1 - R_2)$? The general finding for this situation is that learning a new response to an old stimulus results in negative transfer. But the experimental results are not clear-cut, and there appear to be a number of exceptions to this rule. If the response in the two situations are clearly incompatible or antagonistic, then we have conflicting response tendencies and the transfer is negative. An example would be learning to "go" in response to a red light after having learned over many years of driving that red means "stop." The new response in this case would be difficult to learn and undoubtedly there would be a soaring increase in traffic accidents were such a ruling to become part of the motor vehicle code.

As the new response becomes more and more similar to the old one, negative transfer decreases and in cases where the stimuli are identical and the responses similar but not identical we may get slight positive transfer.

General factors affecting transfer

Many examples of transfer are far too complex to be analyzed in terms of either stimulus or response similarity. In these cases more general factors operate to produce transfer between tasks that appear at first glance to be dissimilar.

Mediated transfer. Sometimes the learning of a new response to an old stimulus is facilitated by the presence of a previously learned intervening response which serves as a cue to mediate between the two tasks. Much of the advantage that human beings have over lower organisms in ease of learning is due to the fact that we can use language as a mediating response. For example, in one experiment (Gagné and Baker, 1950) subjects learned to associate a different letter of the alphabet with each of four different lights. They were later required to respond to each of the same four lights by pressing one of four switches. These subjects learned the second task much faster than another group which had not had the letter training. The verbal responses served as cues which helped the subjects discriminate between the four lights when the motor response was required. (This is an example of a situation where learning a new response to an old stimulus results in positive rather than negative transfer because the responses are in no way incompatible; the original response is verbal and the new response is motor. If the second task involved learning a *different* verbal response to the original stimulus we would have interference.)

An experiment by Russell and Storms (1955) illustrates mediated transfer in a task involving paired-associate learning. The investigators, by referring to a list that specifies the words most frequently associated with certain other words, selected a series of three-word chains that were known to be closely associated.[3] For example, by checking the list they determined that the word most frequently associated with "stem" was "flower," and the word most frequently given in response to "flower" was "smell." They hypothesized that because of these associations, subjects who had learned to respond with the word "stem" to the nonsense syllable "cef" ("cef-stem") would learn the new stimulus-response pair "cef-smell" more readily than subjects whose second pair was "cef-joy" because "joy" has no easy association to "stem." The lists presented to the two groups of subjects are shown in Table 13–1. The results confirmed the experimenters' hypothesis: Group I learned their second list much faster than Group II. The chain of associations, for example, "stem-flower-smell," mediated the transfer between List 1 and List 2 for Group I; Group II had no such helpful cues.

[3] This list, known as the Kent-Rosanoff List, was compiled by obtaining associations to a large number of words from more than 1000 subjects and arranging the responses in order of frequency of occurrence to the test words.

TABLE 13–1

Word lists for the study of mediated transfer in a paired-associate learning task

Group I				Group II			
List 1		List 2		List 1		List 2	
Stimulus	*Response*	*Stimulus*	*Response*	*Stimulus*	*Response*	*Stimulus*	*Response*
CEF	Stem	CEF	Smell	CEF	Stem	CEF	Joy
DAX	Memory	DAX	Matter	DAX	Memory	DAX	Afraid
YOV	Soldier	YOV	Navy	YOV	Soldier	YOV	Cheese
VUX	Trouble	VUX	Good	VUX	Trouble	VUX	Music
WUB	Wish	WUB	Need	WUB	Wish	WUB	Table
GEX	Justice	GEX	War	GEX	Justice	GEX	House
JID	Thief	JID	Take	JID	Thief	JID	Sleep
ZIL	Ocean	ZIL	Drink	ZIL	Ocean	ZIL	Doctor
LAJ	Command	LAJ	Disorder	LAJ	Command	LAJ	Cabbage
MYV	Fruit	MYV	Red	MYV	Fruit	MYV	Hand

By supplying your first association to the response words in List 1 you can probably guess most of the words from the Kent-Rosanoff List that mediated between the response words of List 1 and the response words of List 2 in Group I. In order they are: flower, mind, army, bad, want, peace, steal, water, order, and apple.
SOURCE: Adapted from Russell and Storms (1955).

In the Gagné and Baker study the mediating cues (alphabet letters) were provided by the experimenters, while in this experiment the cues came from the subject's own previously acquired associations.

Learning to learn. We noted in Chapter 12 that subjects who practiced learning successive lists of nonsense syllables over a period of days were able to increase the speed with which they learned subsequent lists. This positive transfer occurred even though there was no similarity between the lists. The subjects apparently learned a technique or an approach to the task which facilitated their performance on later tasks of the same sort. Positive transfer of this type is called "learning to learn."

Another example of learning to learn involves presenting monkeys with a series of discrimination problems. For each problem the animal is shown two objects, for example, a red triangle and a green circle, and is reinforced by food if he selects the correct object (see Figure 13–6). The position of the two objects is alternated in a random order from trial to trial so that sometimes the triangle is on the right and sometimes on the left. The animal must learn to ignore positional cues and select the correct object regardless of whether it appears on the right or the left. After the monkey has learned consistently to select the correct object he is given a problem involving a different pair of objects.

In one experiment monkeys were each presented with a total of 344 such problems, each problem using a new and different pair of stimulus objects. The learning curves over the first six trials for problems 10, 20, 150, and 300 are presented in Figure 13–7. All the curves begin at the 50 percent level, since on the first trial of each problem the objects are new, the animal must guess, and consequently will be correct half the time by chance. On the 10th problem the monkeys are making only about 75 percent correct choices by the sixth trial. On the 300th problem they are responding at the 98 percent level on the second trial. Whereas in the beginning the animals make little

use of the information provided by the first trial, by the 300th problem they utilize this information to obtain almost perfect responding on the second trial (Harlow, 1949). That is, they now know that if the object they select on the first trial is rewarded they should pick the same object on the second trial regardless of its position; if the first trial choice is not rewarded they should select the other object on the second trial. The monkeys have learned how to learn or, to use the term proposed by Harlow, they have formed a *learning set* for this particular class of problems and can now proceed on the basis of "insight" as opposed to trial-and-error behavior.

Harlow and others have done extensive investigation of learning sets with monkeys and young children (Levinson and Reese, 1963). Their findings indicate that the formation of learning sets or learning to learn occurs only after fairly extensive practice on a particular type of problem. If practice is discontinued too soon there is little transfer to the next series of problems. The implications for education are significant: basic skills must be well learned before proceeding to more complex ones. As we shall see in the next section, one of the advantages of programed instruction is that the learner is led through a graded series of related problems toward the development of principles and concepts.

Learning to learn is a general phenomenon which involves a number of different factors. One factor may be learning to relax in the experimental situation, another to ignore irrelevant noises and other stimuli. Most important is learning to distinguish the relevant cues in the situation; for example, the monkey learns that the important cue is the quality (form or color) of the object, not its position on the display board. In a sense this involves learning a principle. And as we shall see learning principles, as opposed to specific responses, is one of the most important ways in which learning transfers.

Transfer through principles

One factor that makes transfer possible is the appropriate application of principles

13–6

Wisconsin General Test Apparatus

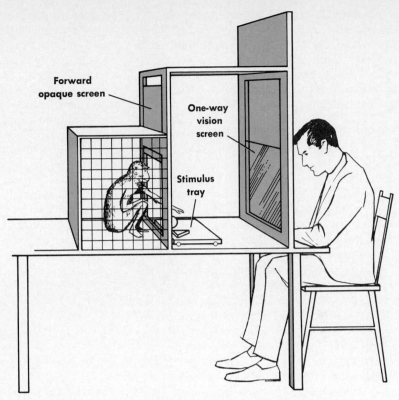

This apparatus is used for discrimination training with monkeys. When the experimenter changes the stimulus objects, the forward opaque screen is lowered, blocking the monkey's view of the stimulus tray. (Adapted from Harlow, 1951)

learned in old situations to new situations. The principles learned by the Wright brothers in flying kites were applied by them in building an airplane. Principles of reasoning learned in logic are equally applicable in mathematics. The following experiment demonstrates the advantage of learning principles (Hendrickson and Schroeder, 1941; replicating the classic study by Judd, 1908).

Two groups of boys shot with air rifles at a target submerged under water. Prior to the target practice the experimental group studied an explanation of the theory of refraction of light so that they understood the apparent displacement of objects viewed under water. The control group received no explanation. The experimental group learned to hit the target in fewer trials than the control group but the difference was not statistically significant. However, after the boys had become proficient at hitting the target the depth of the water was changed. Both groups

13–7

Learning curves from the same subjects in a series of discrimination problems

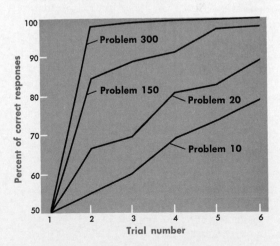

Plotted here is the probability of a correct response over the first six trials on the 10th, 20th, 150th, and 300th discrimination problem. (After Harlow, 1949)

showed positive transfer from the first to the second task, but the experimental group evidenced the greatest amount of transfer. Their knowledge of the principle of refraction enabled them to master the new task in significantly fewer trials than the control group.

Application to education

So far we have talked about transfer primarily in laboratory experiments and in situations where the stimulus and response changes can be fairly clearly specified. But a large number of studies have also been carried out in the classroom. What practical implications do they provide for the field of education?

It seems quite clear that the extent of transfer of an academic subject depends upon the method of teaching. As we mentioned earlier, Latin can be taught so as to improve understanding of English vocabulary. It is equally true that history can be taught in a manner that provides understanding of current political and economic problems, and arithmetic in a way that provides some positive transfer to the study of algebra. To teach for transfer involves emphasizing the similarities between the current subject and the situations to which the new learning will transfer. If the two subject areas are similar in general principles or concepts rather than in stimuli and responses, then transfer depends upon the extent to which the principles and their broad application are stressed. Studies have shown, too, that principles transfer more readily when the student (1) has practiced the basic problem to a high degree of mastery and (2) has experience on a variety of similar problems to insure generalization of the principle. If he is presented with a wide variety of problems but does not have time to learn any one to a moderate degree of mastery, there will be little transfer (Morrisett and Hovland, 1959).

Improvement in learning how to learn (in the sense of learning efficient study habits) provides another important opportunity for transfer. One classic study demonstrated that college students who were taught certain principles of efficient learning (e.g., use of the whole method, active recall, and attention to meaning) showed marked improvement in their ability to retain a variety of memorized materials (poetry, prose, miscellaneous facts, vocabulary, and history dates) as compared with students who simply practiced memorizing without any specific instructions (Woodrow, 1927). Other studies have shown that introducing lessons on study skills in one high school course (teaching such skills as learning to use reference books, interpret charts, summarize, and outline) results not only in substantial gains in that specific course but also transfers to other courses (Leggitt, 1934).

CRITICAL DISCUSSION

Bilateral transfer and the cerebral hemispheres

Skills learned with one hand usually show some positive transfer to the other hand even though there is no specific practice with that hand. If you learn to throw darts with the right hand there is usually some positive transfer to the left hand. If you normally write with your right hand you can also write with the left, although with much less skill. This transfer from one limb to its opposite member is called *bilateral transfer*.

Recent studies have provided some very interesting information concerning the neurological basis of bilateral transfer. You will recall from our discussion of the brain in Chapter 2 that there are two symmetrical cerebral hemispheres; the left hemisphere controls movements on the right side of the body and the right hemisphere, those on the left. Communication between the two hemispheres takes place through a bundle of nerve fibers called the *corpus callosum*.

Experiments have shown that under normal conditions when a task is learned by the right hand information is stored not only by the hemisphere receiving sensory information from that hand (the left hemisphere) but also by the opposite hemisphere. The information crosses over by way of the corpus callosum and leaves some type of memory trace in the opposite hemisphere, thus providing the possibility for bilateral transfer of learning.

The role of the corpus callosum in conducting information between the two hemispheres has been studied in a series of experiments where the corpus callosum fibers have been cut so that there is no connection between the two hemispheres. Animals surgically treated in this way are known as *split-brain* animals. In one study split-brain cats were trained to discriminate with the right paw between the tactile sensations of two different pedals. Pressing a pedal with raised horizontal lines was rewarded by food; pressing a pedal with raised vertical lines was not rewarded. The animals were prevented from seeing the pedals so that they received no visual cues (see Figure 13–8). After the discrimination had been well learned the cats were tested with the left paw. There was no transfer of training. The discrimination had to be learned all over again (Sperry, 1961). Normal animals make the transfer to the untrained paw readily.

Split-brain cats can also learn to make one discrimination with one paw and the opposite discrimination with the other paw with no apparent conflict. Normal animals would find this task very difficult because the pedal-pushing response learned by one paw would transfer to the other, thus producing negative transfer. Similar results have been found with split-brain monkeys (Ebner and Myers, 1960; Sperry, 1964).

To provide further proof that bilateral transfer takes place by means of the corpus callosum normal cats were trained to make a tactile discrimination with one paw and then had the corpus callosum severed. When tested with the opposite paw following recovery from surgery they showed good retention of the discrimination. The information had apparently been transferred from one hemisphere to the other prior to surgery.

These findings using animals have been supported by studies of human subjects who have had their corpus callosum severed as treatment for intractable epileptic seizures (Gazzangia, Bogen, and Sperry, 1965).

13–8

Tactile discrimination apparatus

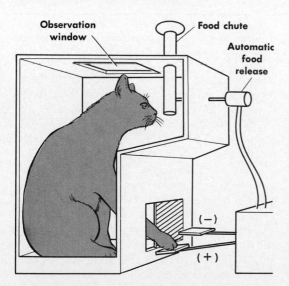

One pedal has a surface with raised horizontal lines (rewarded), and the other with raised vertical lines (not rewarded). The cat cannot see the pedals and makes his choice via tactile cues. During any part of the experiment the cat is permitted to use only his right or left paw. (After Sperry, 1961)

Teaching Machines and Programed Instruction

A great deal of society's energy is spent upon learning—upon instruction in schools, upon teaching workers their jobs, and upon persuading people to adopt one or another point of view toward the solution of social problems. The aim of an applied psychology of learning is to produce the highest possible quality of learning with the greatest possible efficiency. In recent years there have been many public discussions of the issues involved in the preferred methods of teaching reading, arithmetic, and social behavior. All of these concern the appropriate applications of the principles of learning in the field of instruction.

In the course of promoting learning a number of teaching aids, in the form of both methods and materials, have been developed. Among the time-honored methods is the recitation, whether in rote fashion by the group or in individual question-and-answer sessions. Among the traditional aids are the blackboard, the slate, the notebook, charts and maps, the textbook, and the workbook. With the development of modern technology, motion pictures, audio records, tapes, and, more recently, closed-circuit TV have become important adjuncts to instruction. Many investigations have been conducted to determine the effectiveness of these aids. The usual finding is that there is instructional benefit from the appropriate use of each of them, but the benefit is not as great as enthusiasts would wish it to be.

Some examples of teaching machines

A relative newcomer on the scene is the so-called teaching machine. Although still largely in the developmental stage, such devices are worth considering because of the way in which they illustrate principles of the management of learning.

The earliest of these machines was developed more than forty years ago by S. L. Pressey at Ohio State University (Pressey, 1926). While originally developed as a self-scoring machine for giving examinations, it was soon applied as a self-instructional device. The student read the question and chose the correct answer; he then pressed the button corresponding to this answer. If he was correct, the next question appeared in the slot; if he was incorrect, the original question remained until he pressed the right button. Because he knew he was right when the question moved, he had immediate information that told him which answer was correct, and he learned this while testing himself. The machine counted the number of errors that he made, so that his total score on the test could be read off as soon as he was finished.

Pressey's machine did not catch on, although a number of studies by him and by his students showed it to be effective as a teaching device. A new forward push was given to the idea of automatic self-instruction by the publication of an important paper in 1954 by B. F. Skinner of Harvard University (Skinner, 1954), whose experiments on operant conditioning we studied earlier (pp. 279–88). Skinner and his students have prepared several differ-

13–9

A Skinner-inspired machine

Will Rapport

A statement with a fill-in blank is presented in the open space at the left of the machine. The student writes the appropriate answer in the right-hand space.

ent models of machines; one inspired by Skinner's work is shown in Figure 13–9. The items to which the student makes his responses are presented in the form of statements with a fill-in blank (see the space at the left of the machine). The student writes the appropriate word in the answer space at the right of the machine, then moves a lever which covers his answer with a transparent window and simultaneously exposes the correct answer for him to compare. He now decides whether he is right or wrong and then moves the knob at the left to present the next item in the sequence.

Not all automated-instruction devices are restricted to the presentation of simple linear sequences of questions and answers. Some are far more versatile and often make use of high-speed computers to keep track of the students' progress and to decide from moment to moment what should be done next in the instructional sequence. Figure 13–10 displays some of the components of a computer-based instructional system used for research purposes at Stanford University. Located at each student's station is a cathode-ray tube, a microfilm-display device, and audio earphones. Each of these devices is under computer control. The computer sends out instructions to the terminal to display a particular image on the microfilm projector—to write a message of text or construct a geometric figure on the cathode-ray tube—and simultaneously plays an auditory message. The student sees the visual display, hears the auditory message, and then is required to make a response. The student responds by operating the typewriter or by touching the surface of the cathode-ray tube with an electronic pencil. This response is fed back to the computer where it is evaluated. If the student is correct the computer moves him on to the next instructional item; if he is incorrect the computer evaluates the type of error made and then branches him to appropriate remedial material. A complete record on each student is stored in the computer and is continually updated with each new response. The record is checked periodically to evaluate the student's rate of progress and to determine what particular difficulties he may be having. If the student is making exceptionally good progress he may be branched ahead in the lesson sequence, or branched out to special materials designed to enrich his understanding of the curriculum. If he is having difficulties then he may be branched back to review earlier materials or to a remedial sequence of instructional items. Thus, in a very real sense, the computer-based instructional system simulates the human tutorial process. With such highly individualized instruction and completely flexible branching it is possible to adjust the instructional sequence to each student's particular needs and abilities.

So far computer-based instructional sys-

13–10

**Student station
under computer control**

An individual student's station in a computer-based instructional system. (By permission of the Stanford University Computer-Based Learning Laboratory)

tems have had only limited development, but enough experience and research is already available to support the claim that they will have a broad range of applications in the near future. For example, researchers (Suppes, 1966; Atkinson and Hansen, 1966) have developed and tested computer-based instructional programs for the early grades in mathematics and initial reading. To date the findings have been extremely encouraging. The students have progressed through the material at a rapid rate and have demonstrated an unusually good grasp of these materials. Further, both the students and the teachers involved in the program have been enthusiastic about this method of instruction.

Programing

The essence of learning by means of a teaching machine lies, of course, in the material to be learned, arranged in such a form as to be most readily mastered. Such a body of material is called a *program*,[4] and the advantages of a program can be obtained without a machine. The program is not intended as a review or testing device, as in some older forms of testing machines or workbooks; it is intended to do the teaching, that is, to do the sorts of things textbooks and teachers do prior to an examination. Hence a program takes the place of a tutor for the student, and leads him through a specific set of instructional materials designed and sequenced to optimize the likelihood of his learning the information. The basic unit of a program has come to be called a *frame*, for it represents material that is exposed at one time. The frame may contain a question, a statement, or a problem to be solved; the frames introduce new material a little at a time and review old material as needed to make sure the student will remember it. The student is usually required to make a response to each frame. His response may be to fill

[4] In discussions of computer-based instructional systems the terms *instructional program* or *teaching program* are often used, rather than simply the term *program*, to distinguish them from the *computer program* which is a sequence of commands that controls the computer.

in a word left blank, to answer a question, to select one of a series of multiple-choice answers, or to list his solution to a problem. As soon as he has made his response, he is given immediate feedback as to whether or not he was correct.

Samples of actual teaching programs are given in Figures 13–11 and 13–12. These examples illustrate two basic formats that are used; the *linear* program and the *branching* program. In the linear program (Figure 13–11) the subject progresses along a single track from one frame to the next; each time he answers an item he moves on to the next quite independently of whether or not his response was correct. In the branching program (Figure 13–12) the learner is given alternative answers to select from, and where he goes next depends on the one selected; if he chooses a wrong answer, his error is pointed out to him, and he is given help to avoid making that error again. If he has done very well on a number of questions, he may be given an opportunity to jump ahead, or, if he has made a number of mistakes, he may retrace his steps or take an alternative route in an effort to clear up his difficulties.

Learning programs that are written in a linear format do not need to be presented and sequenced by an automated device and therefore, for reasons of economy, are often printed in textbook form. In the programed textbook the answers to each frame usually are listed at the side of the page (see Figure 13–11). The student covers the answer column with a slider (strip of cardboard) and reads one frame at a time. After reading the frame he writes down the appropriate answer and then moves his slider down to uncover the answer and see if he was correct. He then goes on in the same way to the next frame, checking his answer to each frame before going on to the next.

The program is, of course, the important ingredient of programed instruction. Whether the program is housed in an automated device or in a textbook will depend on its complexity. If the program is a simple linear sequence of frames it can often be presented as well in a program text format as in a teaching machine. However, if the

Example of a linear program

rest	1. By *massed* practice we mean putting *trials,* or practice sessions, close together, that is, having a subject continue with one trial right after the other without any _____ periods in between.
massed	2. If we have a subject learning a list of nonsense syllables (a common experiment in learning) and we tell him to proceed to the next trial each time he gets to the end of the list, without resting in between, we have instructed him to use _____ practice.
trials	3. *Distributed* practice, on the other hand, implies *rest* periods in between _____, or sessions.
distributed	4. If we ask the subject who is learning nonsense syllables to rest for one minute between each trial, we are using _____ practice.
distributed	5. It has been found in many experiments that the rest period between trials seems to improve the efficiency of learning. Therefore it is stated that, in general, the _____ practice method is the better one to use.
distributed massed	6. In spite of the fact that _____ practice is, in general, better than _____ practice, there are some conditions under which the latter is the better method to use. These exceptions to the general rule are pointed out in the text.

Here are the opening steps of a section of a program on the psychology of learning. The student covers the answer column with a slider, reads one frame at a time, writes his answer in the blank, and then moves the slider to uncover the correct answer.

program involves branching operations it will usually require implementation in terms of some automated device, and if the branching operations are very intricate then implementation in terms of a computer-based system. Some investigators have argued that all programs should be linear in form, whereas others have argued for complex branching programs. However, recent research makes it clear that the issue cannot be resolved in such a simple fashion. Some instructional materials can often be formulated quite nicely in a linear format whereas other subject matters virtually require a branching scheme. Undoubtedly the successful programs of the future will involve both linear and branching segments; the particular format adopted in any given segment of the curriculum being a function of the nature of the material being taught.

As yet, not enough research has been done to prescribe a definite set of rules for developing a successful program. By and large the development of a good teaching program is still very much an art in the same sense as writing a good textbook or preparing an effective lecture. However, a person who constructs a program has to have in mind the *organization of knowledge,* both its *logical* organization (what has to be known before something else can be understood) and its *psychological* organization (how attention can be directed to significant parts, generalizations made from prior information, and so on). Because these tasks are elusive, actual programers try their programs out on intended learn-

Flow chart for a computer-based instructional program

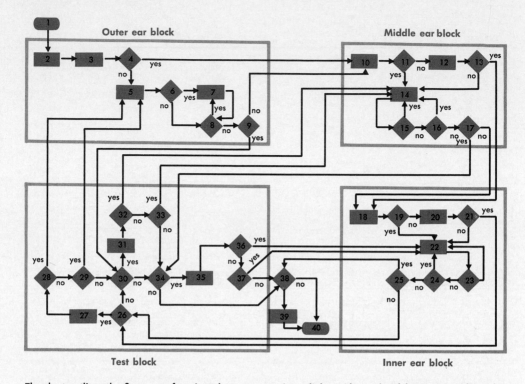

The chart outlines the first part of an introductory course in audiology (the study of hearing) taught under computer control. The student attends class only one hour per week for lecture and orientation and spends as much additional time as necessary during the remainder of the week at the computer terminal. He communicates his answers by means of an electric typewriter connected with the computer. Each large block on the flow chart (marked in dashed lines) represents a section of the course to be covered plus a test section. Each small rectangle represents a series of instructional frames with related audio messages. The diamonds indicate choice points in the instructional sequence where a decision is made as to what the student should do next, depending on the responses he made to the previous material. The large number of alternative paths between the initiation of the section at box 1 and its termination at box 40 indicates the flexibility of the program; it can accommodate both very fast and very slow learners, as well as those students who may have covered some of the material in previous courses. Thus each student can progress entirely at his own pace. (By permission from the Pennsylvania State University Computer-Assisted Instruction Laboratory)

ers. This is ordinarily done by trying it out on one group of students, revising the program to take care of the difficulties they experience, trying it on a second group, revising it again, and so on until it seems to be adequate. This process of successive revisions and improvement of a program is very important. It focuses attention on the individual learning process and helps the programer isolate for more careful analysis those aspects of the instructional sequence that cause particular difficulties.

Principles illustrated by teaching machines

What principles of the management of learning do these machines illustrate? Lumsdaine (1959) has called attention to the following three features:

KEY TO FLOW CHART

1. Student enters name on electric typewriter to start program
2. Introduction to procedures of computer-assisted instruction
3. Overview of outer ear
4. "Do you want to skip outer ear?"
5. Outer ear subprogram
6. Did student make $\geq$ 33% errors on pinna?
7. Remedial subprogram on pinna
8. "Do you want to cover pinna again?"
9. Did student come from Test Block (outer ear)?
10. First question on middle ear
11. Did student make $\geq$ 33% errors on pinna?
12. Overview of middle ear
13. "Do you want to skip middle ear?"
14. Middle ear subprogram
15. Did student make $\geq$ 50% errors on middle ear?
16. "Do you want to cover middle ear again?"
17. Did student come from Test Block (middle ear)?
18. First question on inner ear
19. Did student make $\geq$ 25% errors on the last time through middle ear subprogram?
20. Overview of inner ear and temporal bone
21. "Do you want to skip inner ear and temporal bone?"
22. Inner ear and temporal bone subprogram
23. Did student make $\geq$ 50% errors on inner ear and temporal bone?
24. "Do you want to cover inner ear and temporal bone again?"
25. Did student come from Test Block (inner ear and temporal bone)?
26. Did student skip outer ear subprogram?
27. Test on outer ear
28. Did student make $\geq$ 33% errors on outer ear test?
29. "Do you want to take outer ear subprogram?"
30. Did student skip middle ear subprogram?
31. Test on middle ear
32. Did student make $\geq$ 33% errors on middle ear test?
33. "Do you want to take middle ear subprogram?"
34. Did student skip inner ear and temporal bone subprogram?
35. Test on inner ear and temporal bone
36. Did student make $\geq$ 33% errors on inner ear and temporal bone test?
37. "Do you want to take inner ear and temporal bone subprogram?"
38. "Do you want to ask any questions?"
39. "Type your questions"
40. On with the course. Proceed to Chapter 2: "Detailed Anatomy of Ear"

1. The learner is actively responding, practicing and testing each step of what is to be learned. The old adage of "learning by doing" is well exemplified, in contrast to the passive learning that sometimes takes place in the lecture hall.

2. The learner finds out with a minimal delay whether or not his response is correct, leading him either directly or indirectly to correct his errors. This we know to be significant whether we refer to the importance of immediate reinforcement of operant responses or to the importance of knowledge of results in learning. In most of the devices the last response made to the question is the correct one, a condition that is also favorable to learning.

3. The learner moves ahead at his own rate. The rapid learner can bounce through the steps, while the slower learner can plod his way until he too completes the right answers.

There are a number of unsolved problems about teaching machines. Skinner believes that there is real advantage in having the learner provide his own responses (as in the machine of Figure 13–9) because this simulates more nearly the manner in which problem-solving occurs in real life, where recall has to be made appropriately with minimal cues rather than with the aid of alternatives of which one has to be recognized as correct. (This is the distinction between the short-answer question and the multiple-choice question, or, in the terminology of Chapter 12, the distinction between recall and recognition.) An advantage of the multiple-choice arrangement is, however, that the student has the right answer before he moves on, and this may be a help to learning. This kind of issue is resolved only by experiment; undoubtedly it will turn out that one kind of program will be better for one purpose while another kind of program will be better for another purpose.

Another problem is that of size of step in learning. Whoever prepares the material for a program has to decide how fast to move. Smaller steps tend to take more time but to lead to fewer errors (Evans, Glaser, and Homme, 1960; Coulson and Silberman, 1960). In fact, the very small size of step that may be required for efficient learning is one of the "findings" of teaching machine studies; few teachers (or tutors) would have the patience to proceed at such a slow rate, and textbook writers often assume that once an assertion has been made it has registered with the student. In practice, the size of step to be used in a program depends on many complex factors related to the specific learning situation, involving the kinds of learners as well as the kinds of materials.

There is a gain to be expected from the programed-learning devices beyond their practical utility: that is their contribution to psychological theory. There are already suggestions that individual differences between slow learners and rapid learners (as shown by other criteria) are reduced when they use these devices; if this should turn out to be the case, it will make a contribution to our understanding of individual differences. Many principles from the theoretical analysis of learning in the laboratory are put to the test in programing: time interval in reinforcement, partial reinforcement, distribution of practice, reward vs. punishment, stimulus and response generalization, and so on. Because most of the teaching devices provide an item-by-item measure of choices by the subject (whether correct or incorrect), the research possibilities are very great. Many laboratory learning devices have deliberately slowed up learning by using unfamiliar material (e.g., nonsense syllables), and by using time pressure (e.g., two seconds between exposures in a memory drum). Heretofore we have been little concerned about the amount of frustration that these devices have engendered. The teaching machine, by contrast, seeks a high level of success, and by reducing frustration may enhance learning for those very pupils who have had the greatest tendency to give up in the earlier kind of laboratory study. It may be that new interpretations of learning will arise because of changes in the situation brought about by advances in programed learning (Groen and Atkinson, 1966).

Motivational Control of Learning

Learning and motivation are inseparable. Any arrangement designed to encourage learning must provide for motivation as well.

Reward and punishment in the control of learning

Parents are responsible for training their children, teachers their pupils. Anyone who finds himself responsible for training or instruction, whether in home, school, government, or industry, has to decide which motivational techniques to use. Through his position of responsibility he usually has access to both rewards and punishments, and part of his success will depend upon his skill in using them to encourage and guide the learning he wishes, with a minimum of the by-products he wants to avoid.

Intrinsic and extrinsic rewards. In choosing the goals that are to be set before the learner, it may be possible to select those *intrinsically* related to the task rather than those *extrinsically* related. The relation is *intrinsic* if it is natural or inevitable. For example, the boy who assembles a radio in order to communicate with a friend across town derives a satisfaction inherent in the task when he completes the instrument and finds that it works. The relation between a task and a goal is *extrinsic* if it is arbitrarily or artificially established. For example, a father may promise to *buy* his son a radio if he cuts the grass each week. The radio is an incentive extrinsically related to grass-cutting; there is no natural relationship between grass-cutting and radio ownership or operation.

The distinction between intrinsic and extrinsic motivation is not clear-cut, and in most learning situations both types of motivation may be involved. A child learning to ride his new bicycle is usually intrinsically motivated by the pleasure he derives from mastering this new skill. But he may also be motivated by fear of derision from his peers if he does not succeed, which would be a form of extrinsic motivation.

Whenever possible, it is advantageous to use goals that are intrinsically related to the learning task. A child whose interest in music has been stimulated at an early age will persevere at practicing the piano longer than one whose motivation stems solely from promised rewards and threats of punishments. But even the intrinsically motivated child may require some extrinsic rewards at times when the drudgery involved in mastering technique outweighs the satisfactions of making music. However, if the person who guides and controls the learning situation can capitalize on intrinsic motives, his battle is half won.

While all that we know about the role of reinforcement in learning tells us that rewards are effective, extrinsic rewards—such as prizes for excellence—may have some objectionable by-products, two of which are worth specifying:

1. A reward planned by an adult (parent or teacher) and arbitrarily related to the activity is a kind of bribe. It leads to docility and deference to authority rather than to originality and self-initiated activity. It engenders in the child an attitude of "What do I get out of this?"—the activity becomes worthwhile only for the remuneration it brings in praise, attention, or financial gain. Some of the problems of cheating on examinations arise when desire for the external reward outweighs regard for the processes by which the reward is achieved.

2. Rewards are often competitive, so that while one or a few learners may be encouraged by the reward, many are doomed to frustration. If there is only one prize and many contestants, the problems of the losers must be faced. Is the gain to the winner worth the price in disappointment to the losers?

Controlling learning through punishment. Our folklore leads us to believe that punishment is an effective way of controlling learning. "Spare the rod and spoil the child" is not an isolated epigram. Social control by way of fines and imprisonment is sanctioned by all governments. Arguments have gone on for many years over the relative advantages and disadvantages of kind treatment (emphasizing reward for good behavior) and stern treatment (emphasizing punishment for error). The preference has shifted slowly from punishment to reward, so that the paddle is used less today than formerly in home and school and the whipping post has disappeared from penal institutions. It is worth asking whether this shift has come about solely on humanitarian grounds or whether punishment has been found less effective than reward. Evidence from psychological experiments indicates two important conclusions: (1) in many instances punishment is less effective than reward because it temporarily suppresses a response but does not weaken it; and (2) when punishment is effective it accomplishes its purpose by forcing the individual to select an alternative response which may then be rewarded.

Let us consider first the temporary effects of punishment as illustrated by an often quoted study of Estes (1944). In this experiment two groups of rats learned a bar-press response to obtain a food reward. After the response had been well learned both groups were given extinction trials where food was withheld. In addition, for the first few trials of extinction one group received electric shock through the floor of the Skinner box every time they pressed the bar. During the remaining extinction trials no shock was administered, food was simply withheld. The results showed that although the punished group did make fewer responses during the first stage of extinction, later they resumed their previous rate of bar-pressing and by the end of the experiment had made as many bar-press responses as the nonpunished animals. Punishment succeeded in temporarily suppressing the response but did not weaken it. As soon as punishment ceased the response reappeared at full strength.

Subsequent experiments have shown that the strength and duration of the suppression effect depends on the intensity and duration of the punishment and the degree of deprivation (Karsh, 1962; Azrin, Holz, and Hake, 1963). Obviously, if the punishment is severe and long enough it may effectively stop a particular response, but the important point is that the response has only been suppressed (not unlearned) and may eventually reappear with the cessation of punishment if motivation becomes strong enough to overcome the aversive qualities of the punishment. In addition, severe punishment of a strongly motivated response (e.g., intense shock every time an acutely hungry rat presses a bar for food) places the organism in such a conflict situation that grossly maladaptive behavior may result. As we shall see in Chapter 21, it is possible that a great deal of abnormal human behavior is due to the repressive nature of punishment, so that response tendencies are inhibited but remain active in indirect or disguised ways because they are not unlearned.

Some further objections to punishment as a means of controlling behavior are:

1. The results of punishment, although they may include altered behavior, are not as predictable as the results of reward. Reward says: "Repeat what you have done." Punishment says: "Stop it!" Punishment by itself fails to tell you what to do. The organism may substitute an even more undesirable response for the punished one.

2. Punishment under some circumstances tends to fix the behavior rather than to eliminate it, perhaps as a consequence of the complex acquired motives (fear, anxiety) based on punishment.

3. The by-products of punishment may be unfortunate. Punishment often leads to dislike of the punishing person—whether parent, teacher, or top sergeant—and to dislike of the activity that led to punishment.

These cautions about the use of punishment do not mean that punishment is never serviceable in learning and teaching. It may be for the following reasons:

1. Punishment can be an effective way of eliminating an undesirable response if alternative responses are available that are not punished or, better yet, that are rewarded. If there are two bars in the Skinner box, only one of which provides shock, the animal will quickly learn to press the nonshock bar. Rats who have learned to take the shorter of two paths to reach food in a goal box will quickly switch to the longer path if they are shocked in the shorter one. In fact, they will learn the new response more quickly than animals who were simply extinguished on the shorter path or who encountered a newly placed barrier in the shorter path (Whiting and Mowrer, 1943).

2. We have been talking so far about the difficulty of using punishment to eliminate an established response or habit. But punishment can be quite effective when all we want the organism to do is respond to a signal to avoid punishment. People learn to come in when they hear thunder, to seek shade when the warmth of their skin tells them that additional sun may produce an uncomfortable sunburn, and so on. Avoiding a threatened punishment can be rewarding. The policeman is seldom a punishing person; he is much more usually a symbol of *threatened* punishment. How does a policeman control us if he has never struck us with his stick or placed us under arrest? We can explain his control over us by anxiety. If we drive too fast and see a police car in the rearview mirror, we become anxious lest we get a ticket, and we feel reassured when we have slowed down and it has driven past without stopping us. This reduction in anxiety is rewarding, for by conforming to the law we reduce our apprehension. The threat of punishment is increased by occasional punishment; we drive more slowly on roads where we have been arrested or where we have seen others stopped by policemen.

Experiments show that intermittent punishment (which parallels partial reinforcement) controls behavior more effectively than regular punishment (Estes, 1944). The reasons are not clear; perhaps occasional punishment makes even the nonpunished situation threatening and so regulates behavior through fear and anxiety. Fear and anxiety conceivably may control behavior more effectively than direct punishment.

3. Punishment may be informative. If the child handles electrical appliances and gets shocked, he may learn which connec-

tions are safe, which hazardous. A teacher's corrections on a student's paper are punishing (because they reduce the grade received), but they are also informative about erroneous answers and thereby provide an occasion for learning if the student understands and corrects his errors. When punishment is an informative cue, mild punishment is as effective as (or even more effective than) intense punishment. Informative punishment can redirect behavior so that the new behavior can be rewarded. In the language of conditioning, mild punishment provides discriminatory stimuli rather than arousing a drive state such as anxiety. When the teacher says, "No, not that way," the student may be directed into doing the work correctly and receive a reward, "Yes, that's it."

Parents are often puzzled about how much they should punish their children, and yet most of them find that they resort to some sorts of deprivation if not to the actual inflicting of pain. The most effective use of punishment is the informative one, so that the child will know what is and is not allowed. Children occasionally "test the limits" to see what degree of unpermitted behavior they will be able to get by with. When they do, it is advisable to use discipline that is firm but not harsh and to administer it promptly and consistently. Nagging at the child for his nonconforming behavior may in the end be less humane than an immediate spanking. The child who is threatened with some kind of vague but postponed punishment ("What kind of person do you think you will grow up to be?") may suffer more severely than one who pays a consistent penalty for infringement but then is welcomed back into the family circle.

Anxiety and Learning

The apprehensiveness and uneasiness raised by school tasks are familiar to most of us. Examinations are threatening, and often a student does less well than he might have done had he not panicked during the examination. Young children occasionally develop school phobias; they may become nauseated every school morning yet escape all symptoms on Saturdays and Sundays. While these are extreme cases, most people in Western culture carry some burden of anxiety. What can we say about the effect of the individual's general anxiety level on his learning?

College students were chosen for a high-anxious group and a low-anxious group on the basis of a questionnaire that was given to a large number of students (Sarason, Mandler, and Craighill, 1952). The 36 subjects in each group represented extremes on the questionnaire, which asked the student about his subjective experiences in testing situations: uneasiness, accelerated heartbeat, perspiration, worry before and during a test session.

The subjects received two types of instructions. Half of each group received "expected-to-finish" instructions: they were told the task would be easy enough to finish in the time allowed, and the instructions put some pressure on them to finish. The other half were given "not-expected-to-finish" instructions; they were told that the test was too long to finish. (As it was, no one finished in the time allowed.) Hence the "expected-to-finish" subjects fell behind what they thought they ought to be doing, while the "not-expected-to-finish" subjects were reminded (after failing to finish) that they need not worry because nobody could finish.

The results for one of the tests, which required the subjects to learn a code for substituting digits in place of geometrical symbols, are plotted in Figure 13–13. The conclusions that can be drawn from this experiment are (1) that low-anxious subjects generally do better than high-anxious subjects, and (2) pressure to finish results in improved scores for low-anxious subjects but not for high-anxious subjects.

The study reported above is but one of a number showing that anxiety level affects performance in learning tasks. These studies are so numerous that they have been the subject of several reviews (e.g., Sarason, 1960; Spence, 1964). Some of the major findings are:

Anxiety and learning

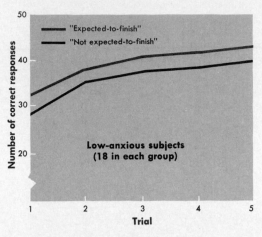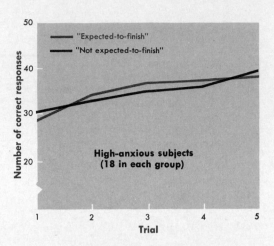

Left: digit-symbol learning by low-anxious subjects under two sets of instructions. *Right:* digit-symbol learning by high-anxious subjects under two sets of instructions. (After Sarason, Mandler, and Craighill, 1952)

1. High-anxious subjects learn a simple conditioned response (e.g., eye blink to an air puff) more rapidly than low-anxious subjects.
2. Results for conditioned discrimination are somewhat contradictory, some studies having found better discrimination among the more anxious subjects, others no difference.
3. With more complex tasks, high-anxious subjects do less well than low-anxious subjects.

CRITICAL DISCUSSION

Complications in the relation between anxiety and learning

While the foregoing account summarizes the main results of the anxiety studies in relation to learning, there are some further complications. For example, interrupting the learning with reports of either success or failure tends to depress the scores for high-anxious subjects but to raise the scores for the low-anxious subjects (Mandler and Sarason, 1952). Also, high motivation conditions result in *poorer scores* for high-anxious

subjects than for the same subjects under low motivation conditions (Sarason and Palola, 1960). There is a thread of coherence through all these studies: high-anxious subjects cannot tolerate any pressure at all, even interruption, without losing ground on complex learning tasks.

The studies relating anxiety to laboratory learning prove important not only because of their practical significance for the management of learning but because of the testing ground they provide for theories of learning. Three interpretations have been offered for the relationship between anxiety and performance on learning tasks.

The first of these is *enhanced drive*. High anxiety is interpreted as high drive level, corresponding to hunger or thirst, and thus results in high performance levels on simple tasks such as conditioning where output varies directly with drive level (Farber, 1954; Spence, 1964). On more complex tasks (such as serial learning), where there are a number of competing responses, the enhanced drive increases the strength of incorrect responses as well as the correct response and hence leads to poorer learning for high-anxious subjects.

The second interpretation involves *irrelevant learning*. Under high anxiety, subjects certainly learn, but they learn some distracting things (e.g., worries) that interfere with their making good scores on the complex task. The overt signs of emotional activity while under pressure may be indicators of such irrelevant learning, which conflicts with high scores (Mandler and Sarason, 1952; Child, 1954).

The third interpretation calls upon *inferior perceptual discrimination*. Perceptual discrimination may be poorer under threat, as implied in the expression "blind with rage" (Hilgard, Jones, and Kaplan, 1951). Some support is given to this interpretation by the breakdown of both auditory and visual discrimination in schizophrenics under threat of punishment (Garmezy, 1952; Dunn, 1954).

The second and third interpretations may overlap if it can be shown that the irrelevant learning is what interferes with discrimination. However these issues may eventually be resolved, the studies point up significant relationships for further investigation.

Anxiety and academic performance

The effect of anxiety on the academic achievement of college students has been demonstrated by Spielberger (1962). A group of high-anxious and a group of low-anxious freshmen were selected by means of a questionnaire similar to the one used by Sarason, Mandler, and Craighill. Both groups were subdivided into five levels of scholastic ability on the basis of college entrance examination scores. The investigator then evaluated the joint effects of anxiety and scholastic ability on (1) the grade-point average at the end of the freshman year and (2) the dropout rate due to academic failures by the end of the senior year. The grade-point averages for high- and low-anxious students of different ability levels are shown in Figure 13–14. In the broad middle range of ability, high-anxious students obtained poorer grades than low-anxious students. At the extremes of ability, anxiety had little effect on academic performance: the dull students did poorly regardless of their anxiety level; the most able students apparently were bright enough to overcome the detrimental effects

Grade-point averages for high- and low-anxious college students

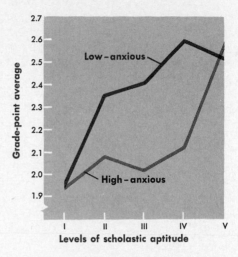

Students, in the middle range of ability, who score high on an anxiety questionnaire do less well scholastically than students of comparable ability who score low. At the extremes of ability (Level I = lowest ability, V = highest ability) degree of anxiety does not affect grade-point average. Ability level is measured by college entrance examination scores. (After Spielberger, 1962)

of anxiety. In fact there is some indication that at the highest level of ability anxiety may facilitate performance by providing increased motivation.

Analysis of dropouts due to academic failure gives further evidence of the destructive effect of anxiety on academic performance. More than 20 percent of the 129 high-anxious students selected for this study left college because of academic failure; less than 6 percent of the 138 low-anxious students left for the same reason. We must conclude that some students who have the ability to obtain a college degree fail to do so because they are hampered by the effects of anxiety.

A follow-up study (Spielberger, Weitz, and Denny, 1962) attempted to remedy this situation by providing group counseling for high-anxious students. All freshmen who scored high on the anxiety questionnaire were invited to participate in the experiment, and those who accepted were divided into two groups matched for college entrance examination scores and a number of other variables related to academic achievement. Students in one of the two groups met with a counselor (in small groups of six to eight students) for a series of about 10 sessions. Many topics were discussed during the counseling sessions, ranging from personal problems to efficient study habits. Counseling for the second group was postponed until the next semester. At the end of the first semester a comparison of the grade-point average of the counseled group with those who had not yet received counseling indicated that the program was quite successful. The counseled group showed a significantly greater improvement over their midsemester grades (the point at which counseling began) than the noncounseled group. The degree of improvement was related to the frequency of attendance at the counseling sessions: those who attended frequently improved significantly more than those whose attendance was infrequent.

Concluding comments

Whether we are grade school or college students our emotional attitudes and anxieties can have a profound effect on our learning efficiency. Personal problems unrelated to the learning situation may interfere with concentration and sap the energy required for effective work. Although a certain level of anxiety may facilitate performance by increasing motivation, excessive concern over grades and test performance may be similarly self-defeating. While no one can deny that in this day of specialization grades are important for entrance into graduate school and our chosen profession, the student who studies because he wants to improve his skills and widen his fund of information will be less anxious in a test situation than one whose sole concern is an extrinsic reward, the grade he obtains. The former knows he has achieved something of value and has progressed toward his goal regardless of his test grade; the latter feels that his efforts have been wasted should he not get the desired grade.

SUMMARY

1. Experiments on sensorimotor learning and rote memorization suggest a number of arrangements leading to more economical learning.

2. *Distributed practice* is usually to be favored over *massed practice*, except for certain difficult problem-solving tasks.

3. The *whole method* cannot be said to be universally better than the *part method* because of the puzzling problems of defining wholes and parts in relation to each other. A satisfactory compromise is to favor the whole method but to use the part method on portions of the task that cause special difficulty.

4. *Knowledge of results* is beneficial, and the more promptly the knowledge is received, the better the learning.

5. The influence that learning one task may have on the subsequent learning of another task is called *transfer of training*. Learning to give a familiar response to a new stimulus generally results in *positive transfer*, whereas learning a new response to an old stimulus may result in *negative transfer*, especially if the two responses are antagonistic.

6. Other, more general factors that produce transfer of training include *mediating responses, learning to learn* (learning to relax in the situation, ignore irrelevant stimuli, and distinguish the relevant cues), and learning general *principles*.

7. Transfer occurs best in classroom situations when there is a clearly designed effort on the part of teachers to emphasize similarities between the current subject and the situations to which the new learning will transfer and to stress the broad application of principles.

8. Among the many mechanical teaching aids, the automatic self-instructional device ("teaching machine") is a promising newcomer. Combined with proper programing, it is an important aid to learning. *Linear programs* in which the student progresses along a single track from one frame to the next may be presented in textbook form. More complicated *branching programs,* where the material to be presented next depends upon the adequacy of the student's answers to the previous frame, usually require implementation by means of a high-speed electronic computer.

9. Programing makes use of three learning principles: active participation, knowledge of results (or immediate reinforcement), and rate of learning adjusted to individual differences.

10. In attempting to guide the learning of another person, reward is generally favored over punishment. Reward strengthens the rewarded behavior, whereas punishment may not lead to unlearning of the punished behavior; instead the behavior may be merely suppressed, reappearing again when the threat of punishment is removed or perhaps appearing in disguised form. Punishment may be effective, however, when it forces the individual to select an alternative response which may then be rewarded or when it serves as an informative cue to *avoid* a certain response. Arbitrary rewards and punishments both have some unfavorable consequences because of the authoritarian control they often imply.

11. Subtle emotional factors, based on personal experiences of the individual, play a central role in learning. When college students are separated into high-anxious and low-anxious groups, the high-anxious ones often do less well on complex learning tasks than do the low-anxious ones; pressure on them to do better may actually impede their performance, while such pressure spurs the low-anxious students to improve. High-anxiety is also significantly related to lowered grade-point averages and dropout rates among college students.

SUGGESTIONS FOR FURTHER READING   Many of the standard experiments on economy in learning and on transfer of training are treated in McGeoch and Irion, *The psychology of human learning* (2nd ed., 1952), and Melton (ed.), *Categories of human learning* (1964). The relation of learning theory to problems of education and instruction is discussed from many different viewpoints in Hilgard (ed.), *Theories of learning and instruction* (1964); in this regard, see also Bruner, *Toward a theory of instruction* (1966), and Hilgard and Bower, *Theories of learning* (3rd ed., 1966).

Practical suggestions for the college student concerned with improving his study skills and exam-taking techniques may be found in Voeks, *On becoming an educated person* (2nd ed., 1964).

The literature on programed instruction and computer-based instruction is rapidly expanding. Leading surveys are Lumsdaine and Glaser (eds.), *Teach-*

ing machines and programmed learning (1960), Coulson (ed.), *Programmed learning and computer-based instruction* (1962), Glaser (ed.), *Teaching machines and programed learning, II: data and directions* (1965), and Taber, Glaser, and Schaefer, *Learning and programmed instruction* (1965).

An excellent survey of research on anxiety in relation to learning is presented in Spielberger (ed.), *Anxiety and behavior* (1966). Some interesting observations on obstacles to learning (chiefly in the age range of 7 to 16, but with a few cases at college level as well) are reported in Harris, *Emotional blocks to learning* (1961).

14 Thinking, Language, and Problem-Solving

There are many forms of behavior that can be classified as thinking. We think as we woolgather while waiting for a bus. We think as we solve a problem in mathematics or write a poem or plan a trip. Much of our thinking is highly practical, and we are more likely to think when we cannot operate by old habits alone, when thinking helps us to get where we want to go and do what we want to do. While thinking represents man's most complex form of behavior, his highest form of "mental activity," it is not so different from the other activities he engages in that one must stand in awe of it. We proceed to study it as we do any other behavior, examining its antecedents (the conditions that facilitate and impede it) and its outcomes.

The Nature of Thinking

Thinking may be viewed as a cognitive form of behavior that is characterized by the use of *symbols* as "inner representations" of objects and events. When you eat an apple or walk across the room, you do not necessarily engage in thought (although of course you may), but if you try to make reference to the eating of something that is *not* present or to walking that is not now going on, then you must use some form of *symbolic* reference. Such symbolic reference characterizes thought. Thought can deal with remembered, absent, or imagined things and events (as well as with those that are currently im-

pinging on the sensory system); because thought is symbolic, it can range more widely in its content than other kinds of activity. It incorporates present perceptions and activities into its topics, but deals with their *meanings* in a way that goes beyond the given present; hence thought reflects upon and elaborates what is given in perception and movement.

Though familiar, such a complex and wide-ranging activity is not easily characterized, for it penetrates all other forms of activity. Although we may picture thinking as the kind of process that goes on while the philosopher sits in meditation with his eyes closed and his hands folded, most thinking occurs in the course of active manipulation and exploration of the environment. In this chapter we will not cover the entire range of thinking. We will be concerned primarily with *directed thinking* —thinking that is aimed at some goal or end point—as opposed to the relatively uncontrolled and purposeless thinking (called *associative thinking*) that goes on in reveries, dreams, or when we "free associate" according to the psychoanalyst's instructions. Directed thinking includes the kind of *critical thinking* that takes place when we scrutinize a mathematical proof to determine whether or not it is correct or when we make judgments about propositions. It also includes *creative thinking* which attempts to discover new relationships, achieve new solutions to problems, invent new methods or devices, and produce new artistic forms.

We have said that thinking is characterized by the use of symbols as "inner representations" of objects, events, and relationships. How symbols acquire their meaning and how we learn to manipulate them is thus an important aspect of the study of thinking. Since language provides a rich source of the symbols used in thinking we will also want to consider the acquisition and use of language. In this chapter we first examine symbols and their meaning, then the use of language, and finally some more complex cognitive processes.

Symbols and Concepts

Symbols and meaning

A *symbol* is anything that "stands for" or refers to something other than itself. The word "book" is a symbol that stands for printed pages within a firm cover—the object called a book—but of course the symbol is not the book. When we say what "book" means or signifies, we imply that it refers to something not itself. We can think about the real books on the shelves, and talk about them through the use of language symbols, among which the word "book" is one. Words are thus very important components of our *symbol system.* When something has a name, it is much easier to refer to it in language. Language symbols can refer to all manner of things, with various degrees of concreteness; but they always refer to something else, even though the something else may not be a thing, such as a book, but perhaps an action, such as rising, or an evaluation, such as beautiful.

Symbols are not limited to the familiar language of words. There are other symbolic languages, such as the language of logic or of mathematics. There are also many concrete symbols: a stop sign, a cross on a church, a musical note, a red flag, a paper dollar. Symbols always convey meanings through reference beyond themselves; that is, as symbols, they stand for something else. Of course we can talk about the symbols themselves. We can talk about the spelling of a word or the painting of a sign.

When we do, we use symbols to refer to other symbols.

We think in symbols. Because language is a rich symbolic process, much thinking goes on in terms of language. But it is possible to think without the aid of language. Some composers claim that they "hear" the music they are composing before they actually write it down or play it on an instrument. We could mentally visualize or plan a dance routine, a series of tennis strokes or some other athletic maneuver without resorting to language. But most of the time our thinking is in linguistic terms.

A symbol conveys *meaning.* It provides information about some object or event to which it refers and thereby suggests appropriate action to the person who perceives it. Symbolic stimuli differ from stimuli in general in that the symbolic stimuli produce reactions appropriate to some stimulus *other than themselves.* The sign **POISON** alerts to danger, but the danger does not reside in the sign itself. A sign **STOP** arrests movement, without itself being a barricade or hazard. The fact that signs and words carry meaning is so familiar that it is a little surprising to find many theoretical disputes over what constitutes meaning and over the relationship between the symbol and its meaning.

The problem of meaning would not be very difficult if all symbols pointed only to specific things or actions, such as names of objects (table, pencil) or specific directions (turn right, no parking). Such meanings are called *denotative;* they specify something to which you can point and are alike to all who can comprehend them. But there are other kinds of meaning, called *connotative,* which accompany the denotative meanings of many words; connotations are emotional, usually expressing some kind of evaluation or preference and varying from one person to another. The word "beatnik" may refer to a specific group of nonconformists in our culture, but it adds the connotative meanings of *beaten down* and *alien.* The problems of connotative meaning are harder to get at than those of denotative meaning and are more interesting psychologically. Quarrels and misunder-

Osgood's semantic differential

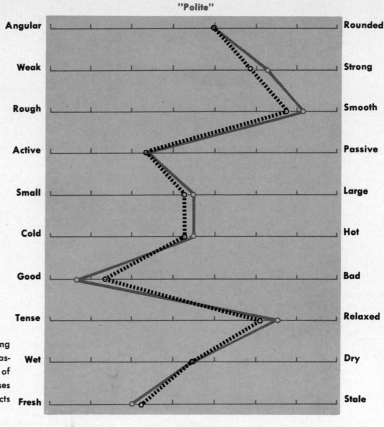

"Polite"

Profiles of ratings used in arriving at a semantic differential for measuring the connotative meaning of the word "polite." Median responses from two groups of 20 subjects each. (After Osgood, 1952)

○────○ Group 1
○ııııı○ Group 2

standings often arise because different words have different connotations for one person than for another.

In order to pin down connotative meanings somewhat more precisely, Osgood (1952, 1954) developed a method of measurement that he called the *semantic differential*. He called it "semantic" because it has to do with meaning and "differential" because the method provides several different dimensions of meaning.

Despite individual differences in connotations, a fairly homogeneous group of people tend to have similar connotations for familiar words. For example, what distinctions in connotation do the words "good" and "nice" have for American college students? By using his method, Osgood found that good had slightly male overtones and nice female ones. To express simple approval the nearly equivalent statements for

the two sexes would be "He's a good man" and "She's a nice girl." It does not seem rational to assign sex overtones to simple words such as good and nice, but connotative meanings are not strictly rational.

To go about finding the connotations of a word, Osgood asked the subject to rate the word according to a number of bipolar adjective pairs; an example is the pair "strong-weak." One member of the adjective pair was placed at one end of a seven-point scale, the other member at the opposite end. Then the subject indicated the direction and intensity of his judgment by rating the word under study at some point along this scale. In Figure 14–1 are illustrations of the way such scale values were assigned by students judging the word "polite." Pooled judgments of two groups appear on the plot, and their interpretations of the meaning of polite turn out to be very

Cultural differences reflected in the semantic differential

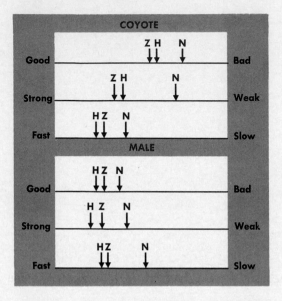

Two examples of word ratings made by Hopi (H), Zuni (Z), and Navaho (N) Indians. Note that the connotative meanings given by the Zuni and Hopi to these words are closer together than are those given by the Navaho. (After Maclay and Ware, 1961)

much alike, even though the adjectives used have little to do with the denotative meaning of politeness.

Initially Osgood used some 50 dimensions (adjective pairs) in determining the semantic differential for various words. But after analyzing a large number of English words he concluded that the connotative meaning of most words could be expressed in terms of three basic dimensions: an *evaluative* dimension (good-bad, clean-dirty, sacred-profane), a *strength* dimension (strong-weak, large-small, light-heavy), and an *activity* dimension (fast-slow, active-passive, sharp-dull). These three dimensions account for a good share of connotative meanings, with the evaluative factor carrying the most weight. Subsequent studies have found that these same dimensions characterize connotative meaning in all the other languages that have been studied (Suci, 1960).

The semantic differential has also proved to be a promising method for distinguishing between cultural groups. Figure 14–2 shows two examples from a number of words rated by Hopi, Zuni, and Navaho Indians. Although anthropologists regard these three tribes as distinct cultures, the Hopi and Zuni cultures are more similar to each other (both being classified as Western Pueblo) than they are to the Navaho. We can see this cultural similarity reflected in the semantic differential profiles. Although there are exceptions, in most instances the connotative meanings given by the Zuni and Hopi to the words are closer together than are those given by the Navaho (Maclay and Ware, 1961).

Concept formation

When a symbol stands for a class of objects or events with common properties, we say that it refers to a concept. *Girls, holidays, vegetables,* and *round objects* are examples of concepts based on common elements; *equality, longer,* and *smoother* are concepts based on common relations. By means of concepts we are able to order and classify our environment. Most single words (with the exception of proper nouns) represent concepts in that they refer not to a single object or event but to a class. "The house on the corner of 10th and Market Streets" specifies a particular object; the word "house" is a concept that refers to a building that has certain features in common with a large number of other buildings. Concepts possess varying degrees of generality: the concept *building* is more general than the concept *house,* which in turn is more general than the concept *cottage.*

Man's superior position in the animal kingdom is based largely on his ability to use language and to learn concepts. But concepts can be learned without the use of language. Rats can learn the concept of triangularity: by being rewarded for selecting triangles of various shapes and sizes and not rewarded for responding to other geometrical forms, they can learn to respond consistently to triangles (Fields, 1932). Since the triangles vary in shape

Monkey solving the oddity problem

Courtesy of Harry Harlow

A monkey will learn to select the odd member of three objects if there is a bit of food or something else of interest in the well under it.

and size they are not responding to a specific object but to the concept of triangularity. Monkeys can learn the concept of *oddity* (see Figure 14–3). They can learn to select the odd stimulus object from a set of three objects, two of which are identical (Moon and Harlow, 1955; Gunter, Feigenson, and Blakeslee, 1965). Here again the stimuli vary from trial to trial, for example, two circles and a square on one trial and two squares and a triangle on the next, so that the animal is not responding to a specific object but is learning to abstract a common property—oddity—as the situation changes from trial to trial.

The learning of concepts involves the two psychological processes of generalization and discrimination. In learning the concept of triangularity, a monkey generalizes the response initially to other geometrical forms, but since these responses are never rewarded they extinguish, and he eventually narrows his discrimination to triangles. When a child is learning the concept *dog* he may generalize the term initially to include all small animals. He soon learns from his parents' corrections the instances when he is in error and gradually makes finer discriminations until his concept approximates our conventional conception of dog. He may refine the concept further

and distinguish between "friendly or good dogs" whose wagging tails indicate that approach is safe and "unfriendly or bad dogs" whose growls signify that avoidance is the best response; he eventually learns to distinguish among breeds.

Human beings, because of their language ability, are able to deal with all sorts of concepts from fairly concrete ones such as *dog* to highly abstract ones such as *gravity, justice,* and *God.* The processes involved in forming these more abstract concepts are obviously too complex to be explained by a simple analysis, but the principles of generalization and discrimination still appear to play the major role.

What kinds of concepts are attained most readily? A series of studies by Heidbreder 1946, 1948) indicated that concrete characteristics are generally easier to conceive than the more abstract relationships of form and number. These studies used the paired-associate technique with the type of material illustrated in Figure 14–4. On each trial several stimuli were presented one at a time and the subject was required to anticipate the response paired with each stimulus. The experimenter arbitrarily assigned a different nonsense syllable as the response for each concept. Thus, SILM might refer to the object concept of birds,

Concept	Stimuli			Concept name
	Trial 1	Trial 2	Trial 3	
Circular				FARD
4				PERG
Birds				SILM

Examples of stimuli used in studies of concept formation. (After Heidbreder, Bensley, and Ivy, 1948.)

FARD to the spatial concept of circular patterns, and PERG to the number concept of four objects. On the second trial *new* stimuli were paired with the original responses. For example, Figure 14–4 shows three stimuli that might be given on trial 1, three stimuli for trial 2, and three for trial 3. The experiment continued until the subject could give the correct response to all of the stimuli on one trial.

The results of a series of such experiments showed that object concepts (shoe, book, bird) were the easiest to learn, spatial forms the next easiest, then colors, then numbers. Subsequent studies by other investigators, however, have not consistently found the same order of difficulty for the last three concepts; Grant and Curran (1953), for one, found color concepts more difficult to learn than number or spatial form. But in all cases object concepts were the easiest to attain. Our thinking apparently tends to run to *things* rather than to *abstractions*. We saw earlier in Piaget's stages of intellectual development (p. 71) that the child first learns object concepts and only develops more abstract concepts as he grows older. Interestingly enough, with certain types of brain damage the individual may lose his ability to deal

with abstract concepts, and can respond only in terms of concrete ideas. For example, he can use a key to open a door but is unable to demonstrate how to use the key unless the door is present. Or he can throw balls into three boxes located at different distances from him, performing with a high degree of accuracy, but cannot state which box is nearest and which farthest or explain his procedure in aiming (Goldstein and Scheerer, 1941). This decline of ability to think in abstract terms is so marked in certain types of brain damage that some of the tests designed to detect brain damage use performance on concept-learning tasks as a basis for diagnosis.

Language and Thought

Structure and acquisition of language

Language serves two major functions: (1) it allows us to communicate with one another—provided the speaker and listener share a common meaning of words, and (2) it provides a system of responses that facilitates our thinking and behavior. By supplying us with verbal symbols so that we can represent the past in the present it allows us to profit from past experience. As we have seen, many of our verbal responses represent concepts, and therefore can serve as stimuli for manipulating concepts. A kindergarten child might use his fingers to determine that there are 10 children in his class room. A third grader can arrive at the same answer more easily by noting that there are two tables with five children at each table and manipulating the verbal concept two times five equals 10.

Descriptive linguistics. The science that studies the form and structure of language—units of sound (*phonemes*), units of meaning (*morphemes*), and rules of order (*grammar*)—is called *descriptive linguistics.* All languages are based on a certain number of elementary sounds called *phonemes.* The English language is composed of about 45 phonemes which correspond roughly to the different ways we pronounce the vowels and consonants of our alphabet. Some languages work with as few as 15 phonemes while others make use of as many as 85. The smallest *meaningful* units in the structure of a language are called *morphemes.* Morphemes may be root words, prefixes, or suffixes and may consist of from two to six phonemes. The words *talk, rug,* and *strange* are single morphemes; strangeness consists of two morphemes, *strange* and *ness,* both of which have meaning (the suffix *ness* implies "being" or "having the quality of").

Although there are well over a hundred thousand morphemes in the English language, many more would be possible if each of the 45 phonemes were used in every possible combination. But every language has certain restrictions on the way phonemes can be sequenced and combined. In English, for example, we seldom use more than two (and never more than three) consonants to begin a morpheme, and even then only certain consonants can be combined in an initial cluster. We have words that start with *str* or *spl* but none beginning with *zb* or *vg* as is common in some Slavic languages. One function of the restrictions a language places on phoneme sequencing is to prevent errors of interpretation. If morphemes used all possible combinations of phonemes then a change in

a single phoneme would produce a new morpheme. A language based on such a system would be highly susceptible to communication errors. As it is, when we come across the typographical error *fwice* we know that an *fw* beginning is not permissible English so we guess at the nearest permissible morpheme (with help from the context of the sentence) and come up with *twice.* Studies have shown that nonsense words which follow the lawful sequence of phonemes (i.e., *prall, throop, skice*) are easier to remember than nonsense words composed of unlawful sequences (i.e., *tlib, zdrall, pshoop*) (Brown and Hildum, 1956).

Just as there are rules for sequencing phonemes, there are rules of *grammar* which specify (1) how words are formed from morphemes (e.g., add "s" to form the plural of nouns) and (2) how sentences are formed from words (e.g., the subject precedes the verb).

This brief description of the fascinating and complex structure of language is sufficient to indicate the enormity of the task confronting the child as he learns to speak his native language. He must learn not only the proper pronunciation and sequencing of words but also their meaning. It is indeed remarkable that the average six-year-old child has a vocabulary of 7000 to 8000 words and has mastered the essential grammatical structure of his language. How the human organism acquires and uses language has received a great deal of attention in recent years from psychologists and linguists; this area of research has come to be called *psycholinguistics.*

Learning theory and language. One group of theorists have argued that language acquisition can be explained in terms of the principles of learning discussed in Chapter 11. According to their view, sounds acquire meaning through a process similar to classical conditioning, and the motor responses used in the production of speech are learned through a process similar to operant conditioning.

Long before he is able to speak the child has learned to recognize and to identify many features of his environment. Certain faces, toys, items of clothing, foods, sounds, and motor responses are recognized as familiar. When a word is paired with one of these familiar objects or experiences, as when the mother repeats "doll" every time she hands the child his favorite doll, a conditioned response is established between the word and the object. Just as Pavlov's dog learned that the bell was a signal that food was coming, so we can tell from the child's reactions that he anticipates the appearance of the object doll when he hears the word "doll." An example that is more readily observable in terms of the child's behavior is the parent saying "No" and simultaneously slapping the child's hand whenever he reaches for a forbidden object. The hand-withdrawal response, which was originally elicited by the slap, is soon elicited by the word alone. An observer would say that the child has learned the meaning of the word "no."

At a later stage the child learns to produce the appropriate speech sounds through a process similar to operant conditioning. But the production of recognizable words is preceded by a long period of development during which the child's vocal responses undergo progressive modification. In the early months of his life an infant can produce all of the phonemes that form the basis of any language, including German gutturals and French trills. (This is in contrast to the common notion that an infant gradually learns to make the sounds necessary for speech.) It has been demonstrated experimentally that the frequency of vocalization can be increased in infants as young as three months if each vocalization is followed by a "social" reward such as smiling, patting, or clucking on the part of an experimenter (Rheingold, Gewirtz, and Ross, 1959).

Infants of different races emit the same speech sounds initially. However, as the child develops, his vocalizations become increasingly like the vocal behavior of the adults in his environment. Sounds that occur in his native language increase in frequency, whereas sounds that do not occur in his native language drop out (Irwin, 1952). Thus by six months of age the child is repeating syllables that resemble those used in adult speech. This type of verbal behavior is known as *babbling*. The fact that deaf children can initially produce all of the speech sounds but do not progress to the babbling stage indicates that feedback from the environment (hearing his own vocalizations as well as those of others) is essential for even this initial progress toward speech. One explanation for the development of speech, advocated by Skinner (1957), is that the child's vocalizations are "shaped" by reinforcement in much the same way as an animal's behavior can be shaped in an operant-conditioning situation; he is reinforced when he makes sounds similar to those his parents use in their language and not reinforced when he makes other sounds.

When the child produces a sound that approximates a word, the reinforcement he receives is usually strong and immediate (judging from the delight most parents express when their baby says his first word!). And we can observe many instances during the child's daily activity where verbal responses are reinforced. Sometimes a sound produced at random by the child is sufficient to cause the parent to provide an object that satisfies some need of the child. For example, the random sound "bahta" is close enough to "bottle" that the parent may think the child is asking for his bottle and hurry to provide it. Such a sequence repeated several times increases the probability that "bahta" or something similar will be repeated by the child whenever he is hungry.

There is no doubt that some verbal learning occurs as the result of specific response-reinforcement sequences, but this may not be the total explanation. For one thing, the child is capable of a good deal of imitation that may shorten the shaping process (Bandura, 1965). It would be difficult to teach the word "Philadelphia" by a step-by-step shaping of free babbling, though shaping might be involved in correcting a first attempt such as "Philadelphia."

Associating vocal responses with visual stimuli is only a small part of the total language-learning process. In addition the child has to comprehend long and complicated sentences, many of which he may never have heard before, and must produce phrases and sentences of his own using the proper form of the words and the proper grammatical sequence. This is a vastly more complicated problem than learning to use single words, and some theorists doubt that grammatical learning can be accounted for by the operant conditioning of word sequences. They question whether even a more elaborate application of conditioning concepts than we have outlined here (e.g., Crothers and Suppes, 1967; Osgood, 1963) can adequately explain our ability (as a hearer or speaker) to cope with an infinite number of speech utterances.

Those who reject Skinner's view of language acquisition propose that what we learn are not strings of verbal responses but *rules* for specifying or generating acceptable sequences of words. The individual may not be able to formulate these rules explicitly, but he knows whether or not an utterance he is producing or hearing is correct. He knows, for example, that the utterance "ran handsome rapidly boys" is not a sentence because the words do not follow the adjective-noun-verb-adverb sequence characteristic of English sentences. He recognizes this sequence as unacceptable, not because it has never been heard and reinforced before but because it does not match the rules his system employs for generating sentences. Those who espouse a *generative theory* of language acquisition feel that the learning-theory approach places too much emphasis on external stimulation and the reinforcement history of the individual and fails to recognize that human beings possess certain unique (and possibly innate) "information-processing" capabilities which operate largely independent of feedback from the environment. Thus the child not only *learns* sentences but he *produces* (generates) them. They question whether a careful shaping of vocal responses is necessary for the development of speech, noting, for example, the ease and rapidity with which the child of immigrant parents is able to

learn a second language in the streets simply from exposure to other children (Chomsky, 1964; Fodor, 1965; Miller, Galanter, and Pribram, 1960).

It is obvious that we need to know much more about the structure of language and the process of communication before we can construct a satisfactory theory of language acquisition. It seems likely that in the long run both approaches may be combined to account for the process of language acquisition. Reinforcement may play the major role not only in the learning of individual words but also in the gradual development of grammatical rules. The child may try out various word forms and sequences, keeping only those that have been reinforced as correct. Once a rule has been learned, however, it can serve to generate a wide variety of responses without the aid of additional reinforcement.

Language in children's thinking

There is a close correspondence between the child's ability to use language and his ability to deal with concepts and relationships. This correspondence is illustrated by an experiment in which preschool and kindergarten children were taught to select the smaller of a pair of squares, each mounted on the lid of a box. If the child chose the smaller square, he found the box open and an attractive toy inside. If he mistakenly chose the larger square, he found the box locked. The child began by learning to choose a six-inch square in preference to an eight-inch one. When he had learned to choose the six-inch square regularly, he was ready for the crucial tests with smaller squares.

He was now confronted with two test pairs, all pairs being smaller than the original ones. Of these smaller pairs, one (known as the "near pair") was close to the original squares in size (4.5 inches and 6 inches), the other (known as the "remote pair") was much smaller (1.4 and 1.9 inches). If the child had learned to "transpose," that is, to choose the smaller square regardless of absolute size, he should succeed in choosing the smaller square for both the near and the remote pairs. The results

Language and the perception of relationships

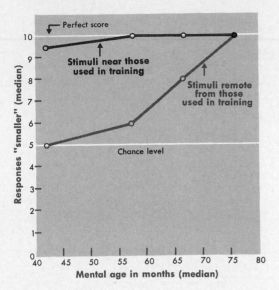

The older children, who were better able to state a test relationship in the form "The smaller one is always right," were able to transpose what they had learned from one pair to another remote pair, while the younger children could transpose only pairs close to those used in training. (After Kuenne, 1946)

are plotted in Figure 14–5. While all children did well with the near pair, on the remote pair there was a striking increase in success with age.

The reason that the older children did better with the remote pair was quite clearly related to their use of language. If a child could say the equivalent of "The smaller one is always right," he could succeed with the remote pair. Of the 13 children who failed to express in words the principle of correct choice, none transposed on the test with the remote pair; of the 31 children who stated the correct solution in words either spontaneously or upon questioning, 73 percent transposed successfully with the remote pair.

Of course the older children were more developed as problem-solvers, whether or not they relied upon language; the younger children, although able to use language to some extent, were not able to use it well

enough to serve as a tool for thinking in the transposition. We can recognize that language and thought are related, without making the assumption that they are identical. Studies comparing the performance of deaf-mute and hearing children indicate that although language may facilitate the thought processes necessary for solving problems of relationships and concept formation, it is by no means essential for the development of such cognitive abilities (Furth, 1966).

Language and forms of thought

Most of us assume that reality as we know it exists independently of the ways in which we talk about it. We believe, for example, that any idea expressed in one language can be translated into another language. This statement seems so obvious that to question it is rather startling. But a student of American Indian languages (Whorf, 1950, 1956) found such direct translation often impossible: one of the languages he studied makes no clear distinction between nouns and verbs; another blurs the distinctions of past, present, and future; a third uses the same name for the colors gray and brown. These differences led Whorf to two conclusions:

1. The world is conceived very differently by those whose languages are of completely unlike structure.
2. The structure of the language is a cause of these different ways of conceiving the world.

Whorf's thesis (known as the *linguistic-relativity hypothesis* because it proposes that thought is relative to the language in which it is conducted) has been the subject of active debate among psychologists and linguists. Most of them accept a correspondence between the language and the ways of conceiving the world, but they tend to turn things around and try to show that the experiences significant to the people affect the way things are expressed in language. Thus some Eskimos have different words for different kinds of snow that we would scarcely be able to tell apart, and the Hanunóo of the Philippine

Islands have names for 92 varieties of rice. For us, the important part of Whorf's conjecture is that there is this close correspondence between language and thinking. Experimenters interested in his theory have tested it, for example, in an experiment on the recognizing and naming of colors by English-speaking college students (Brown and Lenneberg, 1954; Lenneberg, 1961).

The color names most common in English are red, orange, yellow, green, blue, purple, pink, and brown. Preliminary to the experiment, five judges picked from 240 color patches the ones best representing these names. They agreed remarkably well. To these eight colors the experimenters added 16 more to provide a fairly even representation of all colors. The 24 subjects who served in the next part of the experiment first saw all 24 colors mounted on a chart in random order. Then they saw the colors one at a time and were asked to name them.

The experimenters called the ease with which a color was named its *codability*. The colors that were easiest to code were those described by a single word of a single syllable (e.g., "red"), given with short reaction time and with high consistency by all subjects. The hardest to code were colors that were described with many words, after hesitation, and with little agreement among the subjects. These measures were converted to quantities, so that each of the 24 colors had a *codability score*.

The *recognition* part of the experiment was carried out with new subjects. Each saw only four of the original 24 colors, but by dividing the colors among the subjects all colors were used. The new subject then had as his task picking out these four colors among 120 mounted on a chart. Most subjects said that they were able to keep the colors in mind by naming them and then "storing" the names while doing the recognition task. Based on the success of these subjects, a recognition score was assigned to each of the original colors.

The hypothesis that ease of naming and ease of recognition have something in common could be tested by correlating the codability score with the recognition score. This correlation turned out to be .42, thus agreeing with the hypothesis.

This experiment has been repeated with Zuni Indians with the same general result: codability and ease of recognition were positively correlated. However, some of the colors that were easy to code in English were not always highly codable in Zuni, and vice versa. The Zuni had difficulty remembering and recognizing colors that were poorly coded in Zuni but well coded in English; conversely, he was better able to recognize colors that were easily coded in Zuni but not in English (Lenneberg and Roberts, 1956). The general implication is that the regions of experience in which a society makes careful discriminations are likely also to be represented in linguistic discriminations. These differences among cultures will show up in the ease or difficulty of particular tasks, of which recognition is a rather simple variety.

A further example is provided by a study of two groups of Navaho children, both living on the reservation; one group spoke only English and the other only Navaho. A special characteristic of the Navaho language is that certain verbs of handling —the Navaho equivalents of to pick up, to drop, to hold in the hand, and so on— require special forms depending on the nature of the object being handled. There are 11 different forms, one for round spherical objects, one for round thin things, one for long flexible objects, and so forth. Even the very young Navaho-speaking children knew and used these forms correctly. These children were compared to English-speaking Navahos, matched for age, with respect to how often they used shape, form, or material as a basis for sorting objects, rather than color. The tasks used were those usually sorted by very young children on the basis of color. The Navaho-speaking children tended to sort on the basis of form at significantly younger ages than the English-speaking children. The fact that the Navaho language required attention to shapes, forms, and materials of things presumably made the Navaho-speaking child pay more attention to this aspect of his environment (Carroll, 1964).

Thought and the brain

While no one doubts that we use our brains when we think, beyond that we can say very little with confidence. There is no localized "thought center" in the brain, as there are localized centers for muscular action or vision.

Two main approaches to thinking pose somewhat different problems for students of brain physiology. Those who take the *peripheralist position*—that all thinking goes on in action (speech or other movements) —see the problems of thinking as essentially the same as those dealing with other aspects of movement control. According to this position all that psychology requires is a stimulus-response analysis of thinking; then a physiology of conditioned responses would also provide a physiology of thinking. For those who take the *centralist position*—that thinking goes on inside the brain and nervous system, with the muscular movements merely accompaniments (or facilitators) of the "central" process—a physiological explanation of thinking requires a theory of what goes on in the brain when we think; a stimulus-response analysis does not suffice.

CRITICAL DISCUSSION
Peripheralist vs. centralist theories

The extreme form of the peripheralist position on thought was advocated by John B. Watson, usually regarded as the founder of behaviorism. His main point was that *movements* were the substance of thought, chiefly those movements that we make in talking to ourselves. To put it another way, thought consists merely in *implicit language habits,* including within language not only speech but also such other movements as may be involved in gesture, writing, or other language accompaniments. The habits are implicit because they cannot be observed without the aid of instruments. Young children, having just learned to talk, often talk aloud as they solve their problems. As they grow older, they learn to talk silently to themselves. At that point,

according to Watson, they have learned to think.

When you think you make other muscular movements besides those involved in the process of speech. Suppose you permit an experimenter to attach electrodes to your arms so that he can measure the electrical response (action currents) from your muscles. Now, while your arms are quiet, he tells you to think of hammering twice with your right hand. His instrument will often show two bursts of impulses from your right arm muscles which correspond to your imagined hammering (Figure 14–6). When you imagined hammering, you moved your muscle slightly, even though your arms remained in resting position (Jacobson, 1932). Deaf-mutes, who use their arm muscles in talking a sign language, show more activity in these muscles when they dream than normal subjects do (Max, 1935). The presence of eye movements in dreaming is also consonant with the importance of muscular movement in thinking (Dement and Kleitman, 1957).

While these peripheral indicators of thought make plausible a theory such as that of Watson, the centralist answers that a movement *accompaniment* of thinking is not the thinking itself. Thus the slight muscular movements in the arms result from the subject's *thinking about* hammering, just as the movements themselves might result if he had decided actually to hammer. The crux of the issue is that the decision to hammer need not have been made in the muscles.

The assumption that thinking is a central process does not exclude the possibility that under some circumstances peripheral activities may interact with the central processes either to facilitate or to interfere with them. Speech, for example, depends to a large extent upon feedback from peripheral receptors (auditory receptors in the ear and kinesthetic receptors in the vocal apparatus). If while a subject is speaking his voice is fed back to him through earphones, not simultaneously but with a half-second time lag, there is marked disruption of speech. The person begins to stutter and may eventually become completely confused and speechless. The lip movements made by a beginning reader as he reads silently apparently serve a facilitative function. Expert adult readers can read fairly difficult material without any detectable activity of the speech musculature, but if the material becomes too difficult they will start subvocal speech movements. Such movements appear to aid comprehension.

The desire to hold to the stimulus-response interpretation of behavior lies behind the peripheralist position. The centralist argues that the stimulus-response analysis is not essential. Groups of nerve cells, and even the brain as a whole, appear to be spontaneously active, and there is nothing in the physiology of the brain to require that everything that happens must be a stimulus-response circuit from sense organs to muscles or glands.

Some evidence of the role of the brain in thinking comes through studies of the results of injury. As we noted earlier (p. 368) in our discussion of concept formation, some brain-injured patients lose their ability to deal with the abstract, even though they can manage very well when dealing with concrete things.

Electrical stimulation of portions of the sensorimotor area of the human cortex, exposed under local anesthetic, results in spontaneous vocalization—speech sounds without words. If the patient is talking at the time of the stimulation, his speech is interrupted. Surgical removal of the tissue in these areas is likely to produce a form of aphasia (Penfield and Roberts, 1959).

While these studies show us the importance of the brain in thinking and give us some hints about the processes of thought, they do not resolve the issue between the peripheralist and the centralist.

14–6

Muscular movements in thinking

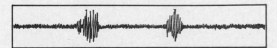

Although the subject's arms and hands were resting quietly, the thought of hammering twice with the right arm resulted in the two bursts of electrical impulses shown in the record. (After Jacobson, 1932)

Problem-Solving

What is a problem? Whenever goal-oriented activity is blocked, whenever a need re-

mains unfulfilled, perplexity unresolved, a person faces a problem. Solving a problem usually involves discovering a correct response to a new situation. We have met examples of problem-solving in the earlier chapters on learning: Köhler's monkeys solved the problem of the fruit that was beyond their reach by learning to use two sticks as tools (p. 302); Harlow's monkeys learned to find the hidden peanut in a minimum number of trials (p. 346). We noted that such apparently insightful solutions to problems depend upon prior experience or habits and upon the arrangement of the problem situation, as well as the intellectual ability of the learner.

At the human level problem-solving is obviously a much more complex process involving the appropriate combination of concepts, ideas, and skills. But even at this level previously acquired conceptual habits play a major role in the manner and ease with which problems are solved. The importance of prior conceptual habits is illustrated by experiments on (1) *habitual set*—the tendency to persist in applying a solution that was once efficient but is no longer—and (2) *functional fixedness*—the inability to see alternative uses for a tool or object whose familiar use-meaning has become entrenched.

Habitual set

The type of thinking necessary for problem-solving requires alertness to new possibilities and to the possibility of doing things differently from the way they were done before. Sometimes our previous habits may be so firmly fixed (overlearned) that they interfere with our ability to conceive of a problem in a new and unfamiliar way. They bias our thinking before we have even begun to work on a solution. The following experiment illustrates this possibility.

Fifteen members of a graduate seminar took part in a problem-solving experiment. All the problems involved measuring a given amount of water through the use of jars of different sizes. For example, with a 29-quart jar and a three-quart jar, it is possible to measure 20 quarts by first filling

TABLE 14–1

Comparing habitual solution with thoughtful search

Problem	Given the following empty jars as measures			Measure the required amount of water D	Habitual solution	Easier solution to be discovered
	A	B	C	D		
1	21	127	3	100	$D = B - A - 2C$	
2	14	163	25	99	$D = B - A - 2C$	
3	18	43	10	5	$D = B - A - 2C$	
4	9	42	6	21	$D = B - A - 2C$	
5	20	59	4	31	$D = B - A - 2C$	
		Subjects are told "Don't be blind"				
6	23	49	3	20	$D = B - A - 2C$	$D = A - C$
7	15	39	3	18	$D = B - A - 2C$	$D = A + C$

SOURCE: Modified from Luchins (1942).

the 29-quart jar and then filling the smaller jar from the larger jar three times. This illustration was shown to the group as an explanation of how their answers were to be written. Then they were given the seven problems listed in Table 14–1. The first five of these problems can be most simply solved in one way—first by filling the middle jar *B*, then by subtracting the first jar *A*, then by subtracting the last jar *C* twice. In abstract form, we may write the solution as $D = B - A - 2C$. Because all these solutions are alike, the students developed a set to use that formula.

Eleven subjects, without special instructions, went through the seven problems using the standard solution throughout. Because they followed the habitual set, they did not notice that there was an easier way of solving problems 6 and 7. After the fifth problem, four subjects were instructed to write the words "Don't be blind," as indicated in the table. These subjects were the only ones who used the easier methods. They were not entirely consistent, but they used the easier method for five of their eight answers to problems 6 and 7. Reducing the number of practice trials and

separating the first five problems from the last two also served to reduce the number of blind or habitual solutions (Luchins, 1942).

One of the problems faced by mathematics (and statistics) teachers is that of teaching students to avoid overdependence upon memorized proofs and formulas and to understand the essence of what they are trying to do. Overdependence upon habitual solutions may be an enemy of understanding.

Habitual set, as interfering with problem-solving, turns out to have two components: susceptibility to set and the ability to overcome a set once established. Guetzkow (1951) found that with the jar problem there was no sex difference in susceptibility to set; however, once set was established men were able to overcome it more easily than women.

Habitual set may result from immediately preceding experiences (as in the jar problem) or from long-established ways of approaching problems. We may be blind to the possibility of other solutions, or we may simply find it more comfortable to use old habits than to try something new.

Functional fixedness

Many objects have clearly defined uses, but they may also serve in other ways. A hammer is normally used to drive nails, but it may be used as a weapon as well. A knife is designed to cut, but it will also serve as a screwdriver or as a pry to lift the lid of a jar. The use-meaning of an object, while it often appears to inhere in the object as perceived, is determined by the relationship between the object and the other objects, and so is subject to change. The following experiment bears upon the problem of the use-meaning of an object in problem-solving.

Five tasks were arranged, each in two versions. One version of the task required that a tool be used first in its normal way and then in some new way. The second version required only the novel use. The conjecture being tested was that use of the tool in a normal way would then make it more difficult to perceive the use-meaning of the tool in the new way required for problem-solving. The five problems were as follows:

Tool	Normal use	Novel use
Gimlet	To bore holes	To support a hanging cord
Box	As a container	As a platform
Pliers	To unfasten wire	To support a board
Weight	As a pendulum bob	As a hammer
Paper clip	To fasten papers	As a hook (un-bent)

The two versions of the pliers problem will help to show how the experiment was arranged. The task was to make a board firm on two supports (as a "flower stand or the like") (Figure 14–7). In front of the subject were two iron joints, a wooden bar, and the crucial object: the pliers. The problem was to be solved by using the wooden bar as one support and the pliers as the other. In one version, the bar to be used as a support was nailed to the board. It had to be freed by using the pliers. Hence the pliers were used first in

their normal function. In the other version, the bar was tied to the board so that it was easily removed without the use of the pliers.

From seven to 15 subjects worked on each of the problems, each subject having some tasks in one version, other tasks in the second version. Those working on tasks in which they first used the tool in its normal way found more difficulty in perceiving a novel use for the tool than did those who used the tool only for the novel purpose. Success was easy when the only use required was the new one. There were 50 successes out of 51 tries, or 98 percent success, when the tool entered the novel solution without having first been used normally. But, following normal use, successes fell down to 30 out of 49 tries, or 61 percent success (Duncker, 1945). This same kind of experiment has been repeated by other experimenters with similar results, for example, Birch and Rabinowitz (1951), Adamson and Taylor (1954).

This tendency for normal use to make new use more difficult is known as *functional fixedness*. That the effects of such normal use may persist for some time is

14–7

Overcoming functional fixedness

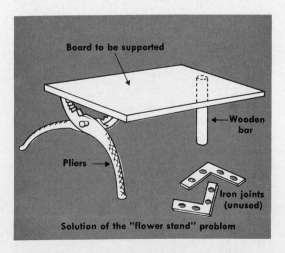

Solution of the "flower stand" problem

Presented with the object shown, the problem is to construct a flower stand using any of the items given, not necessarily all. The best result is obtained by using the pliers in an unusual way, as shown.

Persistence of functional fixedness

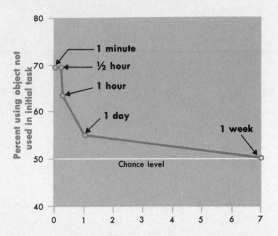

Using an object in its normal way lessens the probability of finding a novel use for it. This effect disappears over time. (After Adamson and Taylor, 1954)

shown by Figure 14–8, in which the effects last for at least a day but are gone in a week. These results imply an advantage in leaving a task for a while and then coming back to it for a fresh attack. The necessity of overcoming functional fixedness may be one of the background conditions for the observation that after turning away from a problem for a while we return to it with a fresh approach and achieve a solution.

How are we to avoid getting into the ruts of either persistent set or functional fixedness? One way is to train for flexibility. Schroder and Rotter (1952) trained four groups of 26 subjects each on a card-grouping task, similar to the typical concept-formation experiments. The groups received varying amounts of experience with changed concepts, so that the group with most experience of change came most to expect change. When tested in a novel problem-solving situation where change leads to easier solution, the groups trained for flexibility adopted the changed solutions earlier.

Group or individual?

Much thinking these days goes on in groups—in conferences, among teams of research workers—and the question naturally arises as to whether the group is better at problem-solving than the individual, or vice versa. Our earlier discussion would lead us to expect that one advantage of group problem-solving might be flexibility of approach since, hopefully, no two individuals would have the same habitual set.

The question is not easily answered, however, because any one group (say, of five people) is likely to arrive at an answer to a problem sooner than any one individual of equal ability and background. But this might be due merely to the group's capitalizing on the best thinker. Thus if the group were split into five groups of one man each and results compared, the group might not do better than the best man working alone. In analogy with fishing, the more lines there are in the water, the more likely that a fish will be caught, even though the group process contributes nothing to the art of fishing. We therefore must really ask whether or not the group is *more effective* than the best person in the group. Experiments lead to rather ambiguous results.

Earlier experimenters tended to find group solution superior, but they did not generally make the corrections needed to allow for the advantage the group has in using its most superior members, while an average performance for one-man groups counts everybody. More recent experiments have shown little superiority for randomly chosen groups, although this does not, of course, deny the effectiveness of groups composed of experts bringing different information to bear on the problem (Restle and Davis, 1962).

Group solutions will be superior to individual solutions under the following conditions:

1. One or more members of the group must possess the essential information needed for solution, such as relevant knowledge and past experience.
2. The more varied these requirements are, so that no one member possesses all the relevant background, the more

advantage the group will have over an individual.

3. The group requires leadership, so that its deliberations are focused on the objective.

In order to answer the question of whether or not groups "think better" than individuals one must specify what kind of group, composed of what kinds of people, working on what kinds of problems.

A technique of group thinking known as "brainstorming" has been used by business and industrial establishments (Osborn, 1963). The main principle is that in a first session the group members should produce ideas in rapid succession, not considering their worth but thinking "wildly and freely." The point is that the members, through relinquishing criticism, might overcome functional fixedness and bring fresh light upon the solution of the problem under consideration. Then the ideas could be sorted out soberly in a later session, and the valuable ones retained. William James had earlier recommended that an author write in haste and revise at leisure; modern brainstorming thus appears to be based on some sound psychological advice.

Careful test of the brainstorming method in the laboratory failed to show, however, that any more original ideas were created than if individuals sat alone thinking up new ideas (Taylor and others, 1958). These results do not necessarily condemn the brainstorming method under some circumstances, but they show that dramatic expectations from it are unwarranted.

Information-Processing Models of Thinking

With the development of high-speed electronic computers shortly after World War II it became apparent that many tasks that previously could be handled only by human beings could now be quite easily performed by the computer. We are all familiar with these developments. Today computers balance bank accounts, figure payrolls, check tax returns, control manufacturing plants, translate foreign-language material, play reasonably good games of chess, and so forth. In fact, many of the tasks that 20 years ago we would have all agreed involved thinking can now be done by computers. Does this mean that computers can indeed "think"? An immediate answer in the negative—that they can do only what they have been programed to do—is too glib. Perhaps a human thinker can do only what he has been programed to do also, either by inheritance or training. What is clear is that there is a wide continuum of intellectual behavior that describes human organisms; it is an open question just how far out on this continuum we can push the computer.

Computer programs and flow charts

Before we examine the role of computers as a tool for studying cognitive processes, it will be necessary to describe briefly the basic features of a computer program. The computer cannot figure out how to solve a problem by itself; it is helpless until it has been given a detailed set of instructions. These detailed instructions make up what is called the *computer program*. It is first necessary to analyze the problem to be solved and to break it down into its component parts. One of the best ways to do this is to construct a *flow chart*, which is similar to the diagram of a football play that a coach might draw on a blackboard. It shows component aspects of the problem just as the coach's diagram indicates each player's assignment. The flow chart also shows how the various parts are to be fitted together. Once the problem has been mapped out in a flow chart, each part of the chart must be broken down into simpler instructions telling the computer how to handle each operation. One part of a flow chart might require a hundred or more individual steps in the program.

The flow chart illustrated in Figure 14–9 deals with a fairly simple information-processing problem but illustrates the main points. The problem depicted in the flow chart is to find the distribution of word lengths for the words in a passage of

14–9

Flow chart

Flow chart for tallying distribution of word lengths. (After
Green, 1963)

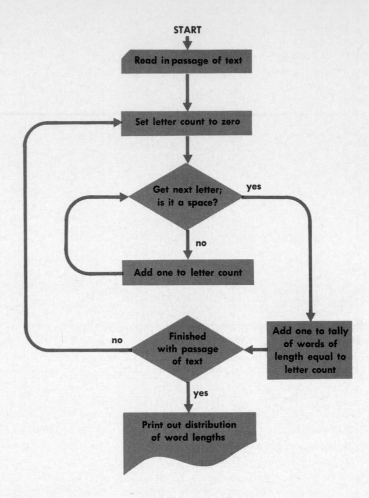

English text. The input to the program is the text material which has been punched on cards with numerical codes for the letters and space and with all other punctuation ignored. The boxes in the flow chart represent work to be done and the diamonds, choices to be made. This flow chart by itself is not very impressive, but when many of these charts are cascaded one onto another into a hierarchy of operations the output of a program does indeed perform in a truly intelligent fashion.

The flow chart of a computer program is a convenient way of picturing the flow of information through a system. Of course, the human organism can be conceptualized as an information-processing system, and it is quite natural sometimes to use flow charts as models of psychological processes. Models based on flow charts have come to

be called information-processing models.[1] Many psychologists now argue that information-processing models are well suited for theorizing about psychological processes and particularly for theorizing about complex cognitive processes.

Simulation models

When information-processing systems are used to mirror the cognitive activity of human beings, they are called *simulation models*. The first significant attempt to simulate complex cognitive processes was made by Newell and Simon (1956), who developed an information-processing model to prove theorems in symbolic logic. Their program, which was dubbed the Logic Theorist, did not try to prove theorems

[1] Information-processing models for memory were discussed in Chapter 12, p. 330.

by a brute-force technique of searching through all possible, permissible sequences of logical operations until one was found that yielded a proof. Rather, the approach taken in the Logic Theorist was to incorporate heuristic methods for proving theorems of the type used by human beings. A *heuristic* is a strategy, trick, simplification, gimmick, or any other device that drastically limits search for solution in difficult problems. Heuristics do not guarantee that a solution will be found, but when they do work they greatly reduce the search time required to obtain a solution. Human thinking obviously involves the use of heuristic procedures. A good chess player solves his problem heuristically; he could not possibly see the consequences of every possible move (see Figure 14–10). In solving a geometrical problem, we often add a line here or there, hoping that by forming a new triangle we may perceive relations that were previously not evident. This new construction may help but there are no guarantees implied.

The eminent mathematician, Polya, has described a number of heuristics that, although they were first developed with regard to problems in mathematics, are relevant to a broad range of problem-solving tasks (Polya, 1945, 1954). One of these is the heuristic of "working backwards": we begin with the result we wish to prove and then attempt to work backwards step by step to that which is initially given. Another is the "make-a-plan" heuristic: we think of another problem that is similar to the one we are trying to solve but to which the solution is already known; this method of solution is then used as a guide for solving the more difficult problem. A third heuristic described by Polya is the "means-end" procedure; here we compare the current state of affairs with that which we wish to obtain, find a difference between the two states, seek an operation that will reduce the difference, and repeat the operation until we obtain the desired effect.

The Logic Theorist, with its various heuristic methods, is an extremely impressive process. For example, Newell, Shaw, and

14–10

Brute-force solutions

One method of problem-solving in chess and related games is to enumerate exhaustively all possible sequences of moves, and then select one that is guaranteed to lead to a win. Part of the "tree of possibilities" for a chess game is illustrated in this figure: the complete tree would follow each branch out to a conclusion, and the end of each branch would be labeled win for white, win for black, or draw. The white player would then inspect the complete tree and select a move which would lead eventually to checkmate of black's king no matter how black played. In principle, this enumerative approach to chess could be programed on a computer and would make the computer an unbeatable opponent. However, in actual practice such an approach is not feasible for it has been estimated that there are 10^{120} (give or take a few trillion) different paths through a complete chess tree. If this procedure of exhaustive search were employed it is unlikely that a single game could be completed within a lifetime, even if the enumeration were carried out at the speed of the fastest computer now in existence. Instead, to develop a chess-playing computer we must program it to behave intelligently—to make use of such heuristics as "try to control the center of the board," "protect your king," etc. That is, it must search the problem maze in a selective fashion, exploring paths of the tree that look promising and ignoring those that do not. (After Feigenbaum and Feldman, 1963)

Simon (1958) set the task for the Logic Theorist of deriving the 52 theorems in the second chapter of Whitehead and Russell's famous treatise, *Principia mathematica* (1910–13); whenever a theorem was proved, it was stored in memory and was available, together with the original axioms, for use in proving subsequent theorems. The Logic Theorist succeeded in giving adequate proofs for 38 of the theorems, and some of the proofs were more elegant than those which had been originally offered by Whitehead and Russell.

Since the development of the Logic Theorist, many investigators have formulated simulation models for an array of complex behavioral processes. There are models for concept formation (Hunt, 1962; Feldman and Hanna, 1966), for attitude change (Abelson, 1964), for verbal learning (Feigenbaum, 1959, 1967), for music composititon (Reitman, 1965), and even for neurotic personality processes (Colby and Gilbert, 1964)—to name a few. These rather exciting developments are of great importance in unraveling the problems of human thinking. However, the development of these models is clearly a two-way street, for one has to know something about how creative problem-solving goes on in order to program it on a computer. Because the computer will do only what it is instructed to do, the steps have to be clearly and completely specified in the computer program. If the psychologist has made any errors in his interpretation of the steps involved in problem-solving, when he programs these for the computer the program will not succeed or at least will not display outputs that accurately simulate the behavior of human subjects. Thus, the machine serves to check the adequacy of the theoretical notions that the psychologist believes will give an account of the psychological process under study. The chief advantage that the machine has over a human theorist is its perfect memory and its attention to all details of what it is programed to do.

CRITICAL DISCUSSION

The General Problem-Solver

The ability to simulate complex cognitive processes is a major accomplishment in itself. However, what is more significant is that information-processing models developed for quite different problems (e.g., a model to prove theorems in geometry vs. a model to describe neurotic-personality processes) turn out to have many component processes in common. This commonality of processes among models suggests that a general theory of complex cognitive processes may not be too far away. Simon and Newell (1964) were the first to isolate some of the components common to many information-processing models and pull them together into a single model, which they dubbed the General Problem-Solver. They propose that one should be able to combine the special information of any particular task (chess playing, theorem proving, music composition, etc.) with the General Problem-Solver and come up with a composite program that can solve the task using strategies and tactics of the type employed by human beings.

The General Problem-Solver simulates in a formal manner what the individual does when he attacks a problem. The programs that have to be written to instruct a computer to carry out the essential steps are very complex and can be characterized here only in the barest outline. The actual program for the General Problem-Solver is built around two basic processes that follow each other in repeated cycles until the problem is solved, or until it is abandoned as too difficult or insoluble. The first process, part of what is called the *problem-solving organization*, is to set subgoals that might be appropriate to the solution of the problem. These subgoals are then evaluated and one that looks promising is selected to explore. Note that this is a kind of "executive" or "decision-making" function, including both a search and an evaluation phase. A subgoal, for example, might be the solution of a simplified version of the more general problem. Once the executive routine selects a subgoal, the process known as the *means-end analysis* applies relevant heuristics to reach the subgoal. This requires that the information-processing mechanism begin with data that are given and follow permissible transformations as in ordinary problem-solving. Because the heuristic approach does not guarantee a solution, if the initially selected approach does not succeed, the executive routine then searches for other subgoals that appear more promising.

The approach to complex cognitive processes exemplified by the General Problem-

Solver is quite promising. If it turns out that information-processing models based on only a few basic methods of symbolic representation and a small number of elementary information processes can simulate complex human behavior, then we have indeed advanced our understanding. The development of these models is still in an early stage, but the results have been encouraging. There is now substantial evidence that we can explain many of the processes of human thinking in terms of a few basic processes, arranged and ordered into an appropriate hierarchy to yield outputs which appear incredibly complex. Thus the modern high-speed computer, as a mode for implementing information-processing models, is more than an elaborate machine for carrying out mathematical operations; it is an important instrument for discovering and verifying principles of human problem-solving and creativity.

Creativity

Scientific discovery

Knowledge verified by the methods of science has made possible many of man's most conspicuous achievements: we dam rivers; irrigate and fertilize land; improve seed; harvest, store, and ship food; extract minerals; prevent and cure diseases; illuminate dwellings and factories; print books and newspapers; send and receive telephone, radio, and television messages; and travel on land and sea, through the air, and even into space. Through science we not only have achieved these practical ends but also have obtained many answers to our questions and speculations about the universe—about the nature of matter, energy, and electricity; about distant stars and subatomic particles. Because scientific activity is problem-solving organized according to the best rules that man has so far been able to invent or discover, we will do well to study the behavior of scientists as they work at their problems.

The testimony of scientists about their own work is hard to interpret, for the distinguished scientist can tell little more about how he arrives at his insights than can anyone else. However, the particular insight which leads to a notable advance is a striking experience and can therefore often be identified and dated. It is a unique event marking a turning point in thought, and we can look for the circumstances surrounding it.

One student of creative thought has suggested that thinkers, whether scientists or artists, reach their solutions through four steps: *preparation, incubation, illumination,* and *verification* (Wallas, 1921). These are not the formal steps of orderly scientific method; they are, instead, the steps in the germination of the ideas we call original, inventive, or occasionally, revolutionary. Let us examine in more detail some of the testimony of scientists to see whether or not this analysis is justified.

Preparation. Even though an idea may seem to come to us suddenly in final form, we usually can discover that we have made a great deal of preparation for it. Einstein as a student of 16 began to be troubled by certain basic problems in physics, centering around the meaning of the speed of light, and he grappled with these problems for seven years. When he saw that his problem could be solved by questioning the ordinary concept of time, it took him only five weeks to write his famous paper on relativity, even though he was then employed full time in the Swiss patent office. We cannot ignore the years of preparation when we marvel at the speed with which he produced his remarkable paper.

The scientist prepares himself for discoveries by his study of what has gone before, by willingness to disagree with what he has been taught, and by readiness to follow leads directed by observation or conjecture, whether his own or those of other scientists. Sometimes an inquiry is started by what is called a stroke of "luck." For example, A. H. Becquerel (1820–91) discovered radioactivity when he found that a uranium compound had affected a covered photographic plate on which he had left it. Would we say, however, that his discovery was complete luck and that there was no preparation for it? We would have to ask ourselves how he happened to be working with uranium compounds, how he happened to have photographic plates lying around, and what prior knowledge made him ready to infer the process of radioactivity. Alexander Fleming (1881–1955) discovered the usefulness of penicillin by accident. He was working with staphylococci (pus-forming bacteria) on a culture plate on which penicillin mold was present as a troublesome impurity. He noticed that the staphylococci were dissolving near the penicillin mold. He asked himself why, and the experiments he made to find an answer led eventually to the use of penicillin in the treatment of disease. But without Fleming's training as a bacteriologist, this discovery could not have been made.

Incubation and illumination. The stage of scientific discovery or invention in which things suddenly become clear is prepared for, as we saw with Einstein, by an understanding of the problem, a strong orientation toward its solution, and an acquaintance with the relevant facts. When the solution will come, if it comes at all, is unpredictable. This uncertainty has led to the notion of some sort of incubation process that goes on after the preparation has taken place, even though at a conscious level the thinker may not be actively engrossed with the problem.

Something of the sort happened with the formulation of the emergency theory of emotions, a theory which served to clarify a number of apparently unrelated physiological processes found present in strong emotion (p. 173). The account is by Walter B. Cannon, who proposed the emergency theory.

These changes [bodily changes that occur as a result of great emotional excitement]—the more rapid pulse, the deeper breathing, the increase of sugar in the blood, the secretion from the adrenal glands—were very diverse and seemed unrelated. Then, one wakeful night . . . the idea flashed through my mind that they could be nicely integrated if conceived as bodily prepara-

tions for supreme effort in flight or in fighting. . . .[2]

What is the nature of the incubation process that goes on before such an integrating idea? One possibility is that it is *unconscious thinking*. The number of acceptable reports of conclusions appearing in dreams or immediately upon awakening is very small, but some of these reports are sufficiently striking to have some claim as evidence.

Descartes reported that he first encountered the basic notions of analytic geometry in two dreams, but he did not clearly describe the circumstances. Friedrich Kekule (1829–96) solved the problem of the arrangement of carbon and hydrogen in benzene through a dream (among a number of similar dreams) in which he saw the atoms dancing in a ring. The dreams led him to the concept of the benzene ring, one of the most important steps in organic chemistry.

In 1865 Kekule, then professor of chemistry at Ghent, was engaged one evening in writing his textbook, but his thoughts were elsewhere.

I turned my chair to the fire and dozed. . . . Again the atoms were gamboling before my eyes. This time the smaller groups kept modestly in the background. My mental eye, rendered more acute by repeated visions of this kind, could now distinguish larger structures, of manifold conformation; long rows, sometimes more closely fitted together; all twining and twisting in snakelike motion. But look! What was that? One of the snakes had seized hold of its own tail, and the form whirled mockingly before my eyes. As if by a flash of lightning I awoke. . . .

The picture Kekule had seen of the snake which had seized its own tail gave him the clue to the most puzzling of molecular structures—the structure of the benzene molecule—for which Kekule suggested a closed ring of six carbon atoms, to each of which a hydrogen atom is attached.[3]

[2] Cannon (1945).
[3] Findlay (1948), pp. 36–38.

Another well-known experience is that of Hermann Hilprecht (1859–1925), the archeologist who solved a Babylonian inscription in a dream. In each of these experiences the dream work was of the kind for which the expert was prepared. The fact that the solution appeared in a dream is dramatic, but actually no more mysterious than if it had appeared suddenly in a waking state.

Henri Poincaré (1854–1912), the distinguished French mathematician, tells how the solution to a difficult mathematical problem came to him while he was traveling and giving no thought to mathematics. As he put his foot on the step of a bus, the idea came to him with perfect certainty. He went on with the conversation already begun before he entered the bus, and waited for his return to Caen to verify the solution at his leisure (Poincaré, 1913).

Sudden solutions in dreams or in waking states are not necessarily the results of unconscious thinking. Rest from strenuous attention to the problem provides a fresh look, and rejected alternatives are seen in a new light. Some thinkers have insisted that the suddenly occurring solution was one completely different from any previously entertained (Hadamard, 1945). The tricks of memory are such, however, that even competent testimony has to be accepted with caution. We need more evidence for safe conclusions.

Verification. After the illuminating idea has come, the scientist must verify it. Modern scientific method always ends in such steps of verification. Poincaré went home and wrote down the proof that verified the solution. Einstein finally presented his theory as a formal argument from certain basic principles or axioms. The general theory dramatically predicted that rays of light would be bent in the gravitational field of a large object. The prediction was verified during the solar eclipse of 1919. This kind of physical verification indicated enough agreement between Einstein's theory and the known facts that the theory could no longer be dismissed as a mathematical fantasy.

We know a great deal about techniques of verification and about the logic of proof. What we know least about is how preparation starts the processes that ripen through incubation to culminate in an illumination that can be verified. We need to guard against the kind of preparation that will stultify thinking and destroy creativity, leading instead to routine, pedantic, and unimaginative approaches to problems. Creative, inventive insights often mark the steps in scientific advance; we need to discover, if we can, how best to prepare a mental climate for them.

The creative person

Creative thinking goes on both in artistic production and in scientific discovery. Whereas the scientist is bent upon the discovery of facts and principles (and the invention and applications of theories), the artist seeks to interpret imaginatively things, relationships, or values as he perceives them. Some individuals are more original, inventive, and creative than others, and it is pertinent to inquire whether there are common characteristics among such persons. Although the discussion somewhat anticipates our consideration of personality appraisal (Chapter 18), some of the major approaches to this problem are worth citing at this point.

There is considerable evidence to support the conclusion that *quality* and *quantity* of creative productions are positively correlated. Although there are certainly exceptions to the rule, an outstanding creative contribution is seldom a one-shot affair. Historically, individuals who have produced highly creative ideas, inventions, or works of art—for example, Edison, Da Vinci, Beethoven, Pasteur, Faraday, and Darwin—have made a large number of important contributions. Even today, when a high degree of specialized training is required for competency in most fields, the majority of published works within any field of endeavor are written by a small minority of individuals. Dennis (1955) has estimated, after surveying seven diverse fields (including music, geology, and chemistry) that 50 percent of the published work is produced by less than 10 percent of those engaged in each field. A survey of the work produced by Ph.D.'s from the University of Chicago eight years after obtaining their degrees showed similar results: 75 percent of the published research was produced by less than 10 percent of the Ph.D.'s. Those rated in graduate school as "highly creative" were the ones that later showed high productivity (Bloom, 1956).

We are not suggesting that volume of published work and creativity are synonymous. There are some individuals who contribute one or two outstanding publications in their lifetime while others may produce reams of trivia. But ratings of creativity do tend to be highly correlated with ratings of productivity, whether the subjects are scientists in a laboratory or college freshmen (Taylor, 1964; Skager, Schultz, and Klein, 1965).[4] These findings point up the importance of determining how creative individuals differ from those less creative and what environmental factors predispose to creativity. We should be particularly concerned with the manner in which educational practices contribute to producing creative individuals.

One approach is to study the characteristics of outstandingly creative persons. A number of superior groups have been studied at the Institute for Personality Assessment Research at the Berkeley campus of the University of California (e.g., MacKinnon, 1962, 1965; Barron, 1963). The groups have included writers, artists, architects, mathematicians, and research scientists. Each individual was carefully selected as one of the most outstanding in his field. They were studied by a variety of techniques, including assessment by psychologists who lived with them for a period of days, and by a large number of tests sampling various aspects of personality and

ability. Although there were significant differences among the occupational groups, the following traits were found to characterize creative individuals regardless of occupation:

1. Independence of thought and action —not interested in group activities that demand conformity and not easily influenced by social pressure when convinced their own opinions were correct.

2. Tendency to be less dogmatic and more relativistic in their view of life than those rated as not creative.

3. Willingness to recognize their own irrational impulses.

4. Preference for complexity and novelty —favored paintings and line drawings that were complex and asymmetrical and introduced these features in their own drawings. (Barron hypothesizes that these preferences reflect a desire on the part of creative individuals to create order where none appears.)

5. Value humor and have a good sense of humor.

6. High emphasis on both theoretical and esthetic values.

If we were to pick a dominant theme underlying all of these characteristics it would be that creative persons are more flexible than those who are less creative. Certainly this characteristic would obviate some of the obstacles to problem-solving (e.g., functional fixedness and habitual set) noted in the previous section.

The reader may now be wondering why we have not listed intelligence as the prime characteristic of creative individuals. Certainly a basic level of intelligence is necessary, and the creative persons studied at the Berkeley Institute were a highly select group in terms of measured intelligence. But beyond a certain level there is little correlation between scores on standard intelligence tests and creativity and productivity. Some of the most intelligent persons are rated lowest on creativity. Some subject matters require high intelligence for mastery of the fundamentals (e.g., mathematics and physics), but within these fields the correlation between measured intelli-

[4] Some experts (e.g., Maltzman, 1960) distinguish between *originality* and *creativity: originality* is the ability to produce unusual ideas that are relevant to the situation; *creativity* refers to those products of original behavior that are viewed as valuable by society. Some individuals may have brilliant, original ideas that they never publish or verify by the necessary research.

gence and creativity tends to be positive but quite low. Among artists such as sculptors, painters, and designers, the correlation between quality of work and measures of intelligence is zero, or slightly negative. Barron has estimated that over the total range of intelligence and creativity the correlation between the two is probably about .40. Beyond an I.Q. of about 120, however, the influence of intelligence is negligible and personality variables and motivation are the more important determiners of creativity (Barron, 1963).

Another approach is to study a more general population by means of the usual methods of psychological testing in order to determine what kinds of abilities or personal characteristics appear among those who score high on tests of creativity or problem-solving. Unfortunately, the results from this type of approach have not been very consistent or definitive, partly because investigators differ in the type of tasks they consider to be measures of creativity. A sample of the tasks that have been used to measure creativity are presented in Table 14–2.

Several studies have indicated that social nonconformity is one of the traits associated with a high order of problem-solving ability (Nakamura, 1958). High school students who score high in creativity prefer less conventional careers and tend to value personal characteristics they see as *not* leading to adult success and *not* representative of the characteristics they think their teachers prefer (Getzels and Jackson, 1962). Grade school children (particularly in the first three grades) who score high on creativity tests often have a reputation among the other children for having "silly" or "naughty" ideas, or are considered "wild" by their teachers (Torrance, 1965). That these reputations diminish by the later elementary grades suggests that peer disapproval and teacher devaluation may be important factors in suppressing creative ideas.

When the methods of factor analysis (see Chapter 16) are used, such traits as fluency (the ability to produce a large number of ideas), flexibility (the ability to produce a variety of ideas or use a variety of approaches), originality (the ability to produce ideas that are off the beaten track), elaboration (the ability to fill in the details), and redefinition (the ability to define or perceive in a different way from the usual or established way) emerge as important aspects of creative ability and planning (Guilford, 1963).

Although studies that attempt to determine the characteristics of children or older students who score high on creativity tests provide interesting information concerning individual differences in abilities and attitudes, we still do not know how the types of ability measured by creativity tests relate to creative productivity as an adult. Longitudinal studies, now underway, tracking the progress of youngsters who score high on creativity tests should provide some valuable data concerning this question. In the meantime the research on creativity and problem-solving has made teachers more aware of the need for providing opportunities for creative behavior in the classroom. Such techniques as making assignments that require original work, encouraging self-initiated projects, and rewarding creative ideas rather than expecting total conformity and a sterile memorization of facts are but a few ways to further this aim.

The issue is often raised about the relationship of emotional stability and neuroticism to creative ability. It is easy to think of distinguished artists and writers who were tormented by personal problems and whose creative abilities may therefore have sprung from their internal conflicts. There is a division of opinion on this topic, even among psychoanalysts who have had considerable experience in dealing with disturbed artists and other creative people. Kris (1952) sees some contribution of neuroticism to art, whereas Kubie (1958) believes that neuroticism, while it can be found among artists as among all people, is essentially a handicap to their artistic fulfillment. Cattell (1963) concludes from his study of the biographies of famous men in the arts and sciences that the incidence of neurosis among creative persons is con-

TABLE 14–2

Examples of items used in tests of creativity

1. Ingenuity (Flanagan, 1963)

a. A very rare wind storm destroyed the transmission tower of a television station in a small town. The station was located in a town in a flat prairie with no tall buildings. Its former 300-foot tower enabled it to serve a large farming community, and the management wanted to restore service while a new tower was being erected. The problem was temporarily solved by using a _____.

b. As part of a manufacturing process, the inside lip of a deep cup-shaped casting is machine threaded. The company found that metal chips produced by the threading operation were difficult to remove from the bottom of the casting without scratching the sides. A design engineer was able to solve this problem by having the operation performed _____.

2. Unusual uses (Guilford, 1954*a*)

Name as many uses as you can think of for:
    a. a toothpick
    b. a brick
    c. a paper clip

3. Consequences (Guilford, 1954*a*)

Imagine all of the things that might possibly happen if all national and local laws were suddenly abolished.

4. Fable endings (Getzels and Jackson, 1962)

Write three endings for the following fable: a moralistic, a humorous, and a sad ending.

THE MISCHIEVOUS DOG

A rascally dog used to run quietly to the heels of every passerby and bite them without warning. So his master was obliged to tie a bell around the cur's neck that he might give notice wherever he went. This the dog thought very fine indeed, and he went about tinkling it in pride all over town. But an old hound said . . . .

5. Product improvement (Torrance, 1962*b*)

The subject is presented with a series of objects such as children's toys or instruments used in his particular occupation and asked to make suggestions for their improvement.

6. Pattern meanings (Wallach and Kogan, 1965)

The subject is shown a series of patterns of geometric forms (like the samples shown below) and asked to imagine all the things each pattern could be.

7. Remote associations (Mednick, 1962)

Find a fourth word which is associated with each of these three words:
    a. rat—blue—cottage
    b. out—dog—cat
    c. wheel—electric—high
    d. surprise—line—birthday

8. Word association (Getzels and Jackson, 1962)

Write as many meanings as you can for each of the following words:
    a. duck
    b. sack
    c. pitch
    d. fair

siderably lower than among the general population; although literary geniuses may tend to be somewhat unstable, the emotional stability of creative scientific researchers is considerably above that of the general population. Roe (1963), after studying the personality characteristics of famous scientists, concludes that creative men in the physical sciences, although emotionally stable, tend to withdraw from interpersonal relationships (perhaps because their superior ability caused them to be socially isolated as children) and hence are able to devote all their interests and energies to their work.

For some artists and writers the themes that form the content of their creative efforts are in a large measure autobiographical and in that sense may reflect their own unresolved conflicts. This was apparently the case with Eugene O'Neill, whose "conscious" autobiography appears in the play *Long day's journey into night,* whereas his "unconscious" autobiography is perhaps revealed in *Desire under the elms* (Weissman, 1957). But more often the creative person tends to be one who has resolved major difficulties and conflicts in his early life and has gone on to apply his abilities with renewed strength and sensitivity.

There are undoubtedly many facets to creative activity; some creative efforts must have simply followed Carlyle's dictum "genius . . . means the transcendent capacity for taking trouble" or Edison's famous statement "genius is one per cent inspiration and ninety-nine per cent perspiration."

SUMMARY 1. Thinking is behavior that uses symbols as "inner representations" of objects and events. It thus can go beyond perceptual solution of problems, or solution through manipulation, by having reference to events not present—to remembered, absent, or imagined things.

2. A symbol *stands for* something else. Some symbols are concrete objects, such as a stop sign; *words* are especially powerful symbols, and thus language is an important agent in the thinking process. A symbol conveys *meaning;* but the precise relation between the symbol and the object it stands for (i.e., its meaning) is a subject on which psychologists are not agreed.

3. A useful distinction can be made between *denotative* meanings, which are fixed and specific, and *connotative* meanings, which express evaluation or preference. One attempt to measure connotations is by the *semantic differential.*

4. When a symbol stands for a class of objects or events with common properties, we say that it refers to a *concept.* Studies of *concept formation* show that object concepts are usually attained more easily than abstract concepts such as spatial forms, color, and number.

5. Language provides a major source of symbols used in thinking. Some theorists explain language acquisition in terms of the principles of classical and operant conditioning. The meaning of a word is established by a process similar to Pavlovian conditioning; appropriate speech sounds are *shaped* by the reinforcement of operant babbling. Other theorists stress the importance of *rule learning* (rather than specific verbal responses) for generating speech responses.

6. Language and thought are intimately related. Thus children are able to solve some kinds of transposition problems only when they are old enough to state the solution in words. Even man's way of conceiving

the world is reflected in the language forms he uses. The cause-and-effect relationships here are confusing and are now becoming the subject of experimental study.

7. The way in which we use our brains in thinking is still a matter of conjecture. Two theories of thinking suggest differing functions of the brain: the *peripheralists* hold that all thinking goes on in muscular movements and the *centralists* hold that thinking goes on inside the brain and nervous system and that muscular movements merely accompany the "central process."

8. Skill in problem-solving depends on an ability to think about situations in new ways. Experiments on *persistence of habitual set* and *functional fixedness* (based on the normal use-meaning of a tool or other object) show how previous habits may interfere with efficient problem-solving.

9. There are difficulties in stating a generalization about group thinking compared with individual thinking. The group has advantages only under specified circumstances such as the possession of more relevant information by the group as a whole than by any one member.

10. Information-processing models of thinking utilize *flow charts* that comprise the program (set of instructions) delivered to an electronic computer to *simulate* the processes of human problem-solving. *Heuristic* methods (such as the means-end analysis) are valuable aids in reducing the search time required to solve a problem. The General Problem-Solver incorporates heuristic methods common to a number of information-processing models in an attempt to devise a general theory of complex cognitive processes.

11. Scientific discovery is a complex process illustrating the best rules man has devised so far for problem-solving. Scientists report in their own work a period of *preparation*, followed occasionally by sudden *illumination* after a period of *incubation*. They finally *verify* their work by making logical deductions from accepted principles and by checking their predictions through experiment.

12. Studies of creative persons, whether based on samples of unusually creative individuals or on general population studies, show a number of characteristics, such as independence of thought and action, preference for complexity and novelty, flexibility, fluency, and capacity to elaborate. While a certain level of intelligence is necessary for creative productivity, the correlation between scores on creativity tests and measures of intelligence is not high. No easy statement can be made about the relationship between neurotic symptoms and creativity; sometimes neurotic conflicts may provide the themes for creative efforts, sometimes these conflicts may hamper creativity. On the whole, however, creative persons have a higher level of emotional stability than the general population.

SUGGESTIONS FOR FURTHER READING

A useful summary of contemporary views held by a number of authors who participated in a conference on thinking can be found in Harms (ed.), *Fundamentals of psychology: the psychology of thinking* (1960). Anderson and Ausubel in *Readings in the psychology of cognition* (1965) provide a wide variety of articles, both theoretical and experimental, concerning many of the topics discussed in this chapter.

Concept formation is dealt with extensively in Bourne, *Human conceptual behavior* (1966), and Hunt, *Concept learning: an information processing problem* (1962). An excellent summary of theory and research in language acquisition is presented in Osgood and Seboek (eds.), *Psycholinguistics* (1965). *The structure of language* (1964), by Fodor and Katz, is a more difficult work concerned with current linguistic theory. The development of thinking in the child is reported by Inhelder and Piaget, *The growth of logical thinking from childhood to adolescence* (1958).

Information-processing models of thinking are discussed in Feigenbaum and Feldman, *Computers and thought* (1963), in Reitman, *Cognition and thought* (1965), and in survey articles by Simon and Newell (1964) and Broadbent (1965). *Digital computers in research* by Green (1963) presents the major uses of computers in psychological research.

The opposite of flexibility in problem-solving is, of course, rigidity, reported more extensively in Luchins and Luchins, *Rigidity of behavior* (1959), and Rokeach, *The open and closed mind* (1960).

A number of authors have contributed their views on creativity in *Scientific creativity: its recognition and development,* edited by Taylor and Barron (1963). Wallach and Kogan, *Modes of thinking in young children* (1965), provide a rigorous evaluation of the distinction between intelligence and creativity and elucidate possible psychological correlates of individual differences in creativity. Studies of outstandingly creative individuals are reported in MacKinnon (ed.), *The creative person* (1962), and the question of identifying and encouraging creativity in the school years is discussed by Torrance in *Guiding creative talent* (1962a).

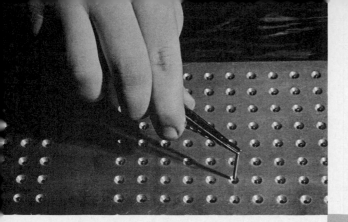

INDIVIDUALITY AND PERSONALITY

While there are general principles of psychology that apply to all men everywhere, the individual differences among men (and among other organisms) are of great interest—not only because of the desire to understand individual uniqueness, but also because a complex society demands specialized roles for its members, and problems arise in finding those individuals most suited for the various requirements of a differentiated community. The introduction of statistical methods into psychology came very largely through the attempts to measure individuality and to find interrelationships among individual characteristics. Among the aspects of individuality that we need to understand are basic abilities, such as intelligence, the influence of heredity and of environment upon such abilities, and, in general, the unique personality as an end product of all the influences within and upon the individual.

15 Statistical Methods and Measurement

Before we turn to the problems of human differences and their measurement, we shall digress a little to consider the tools used in such measurement. The basic tools come from *statistics*—the science that deals with collecting and handling numerical data and with making inferences from such data. In preceding chapters we have met many statistical statements, such as statements regarding correlation coefficients and statements that certain variables had statistically significant effects. We are now ready to consider more fully what such statements mean.

This chapter is written on the assumption that the problems of statistics are essentially problems of logic, that is, problems of clear thinking about data, and that an *introductory* acquaintance with both descriptive statistics and statistical inference is *not* beyond the scope of the student who can use a little arithmetic and understands enough algebra to use plus and minus signs and to substitute numbers for letters in equations.

Even a little acquaintance with statistics, however, requires time and exercise in applying what has been learned. Because in a beginning psychology course the amount of time that can be devoted to these problems is limited, the treatment that follows states the essential relationships first in words and in simple numerical examples that require little computation. For understanding the more complex processes there follow (in separate sections that can be omitted if necessary) specimen computa-

tions for each statistical measure under consideration. These illustrations use a minimum of data, artificially selected to make the operations clear even to the student who is mathematically unskilled. Because of the scantiness and artificiality of the data, these specimen computations violate an important principle in the use of statistics, namely, that a formula should be used only on appropriate data. But this violation can be justified, because the purpose is to provide examples easy to master and because the knowledge necessary to judge the appropriate uses and limitations of the formulas requires advanced study.

Averages and Measures of Variation

Statistics can serve, first of all, to provide us with a shorthand description of large amounts of data. Suppose that we wish to study the ages of 5000 students recorded on cards in the registrar's office. These ages are the *raw data*. If we thumb through the cards, we will get some idea of the ages of the students, but it will be impossible to keep all of them in mind. So we make some kind of statistical summary, counting the number of students of each age, and from this summary we find it easier to talk about the ages of the students. It will be still easier if we find the average age and also the age of the youngest and the oldest student. Such simplifying or summarizing statements are *descriptive statistics*.

Frequency distributions

Items of raw data become comprehensible if they are ranked in numerical order or grouped in a *frequency distribution*. To group these items of data, we must first divide the scale along which they rank into intervals and then count the number of cases that fall into each interval. To go back to our example, if we group together all students of ages 16 and 17, those of 18 and 19, and those of 20 and 21, we have combined the data into orderly groups. The two-year interval in which the students are grouped is called a *class interval* and represents a portion of our scale. The choice of the interval depends upon the problem we are studying.

A simple set of artificial data is given in Table 15–1, and the data are accumulated into a frequency distribution in Table 15–2.

TABLE 15–1
Raw scores

*Number of boxes packed in one hour
by 15 beginners in a factory*

10	34	50
20	34	26
31	46	38
34	38	42
36	43	28

TABLE 15–2
Frequency distribution

Raw scores of Table 15–1, accumulated
with class intervals of 10

Boxes packed in one hour	Number of persons achieving this score
10-19	1
20-29	3
30-39	7
40-49	3
50-59	1

The class intervals are chosen so as to include 10 scores (10–19, 20–29, 30–39, etc.). It is much easier to see what is happening by looking at Table 15–2 than Table 15–1. We can easily pick out the more extreme performances and those that are more nearly representative of the group.

A frequency distribution can often be better understood by presenting it graphically. The most widely used form of graphic presentation is the *frequency histogram*, an example of which is shown in the left panel of Figure 15–1. Histograms are constructed by drawing rectangles, whose bases are given by the class intervals and whose heights are determined by the corresponding class frequencies. An alternative way of presenting frequency distributions in graph form is to use a *frequency polygon*, an example of which is shown in the right panel of Figure 15–1. Frequency polygons are constructed by plotting the class frequencies at the center of the class interval and connecting the points thus obtained by straight lines. In order to complete the picture one extra class is usually added at each end of the distribution, and since these classes have zero frequencies, both ends of the figure will come down to the horizontal axis. Thus the frequency polygon gives the same information as the frequency histogram, the polygon by lines instead of bars.

In practice one would want far more cases than those plotted in Figure 15–1, but all our illustrations use a minimum of data so that the reader can easily check all the steps in tabulating and plotting.

Averages

By an average we mean merely some representative point on our scale, a central point with scores scattering on either side.[1] Three such measures are in common use: the *mean*, the *median*, and the *mode*.

The *mean* is the familiar arithmetic average obtained by adding the scores and dividing by the number of scores. The sum

[1] An average has been called a *measure of central tendency*, but there is little point in using the more cumbersome expression when the single word *average* will do.

Frequency diagrams

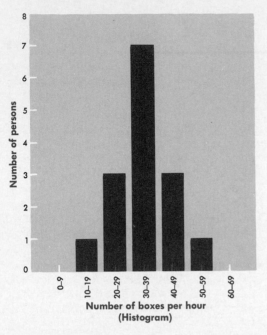

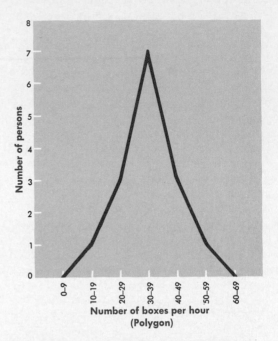

The data plotted are those from Table 15–2. A frequency histogram is on the left, and a frequency polygon on the right.

of the raw scores of Table 15–1 is 510. Divide this by 15 (the number of scores), and the mean turns out to be 34 boxes per hour.

The *median* is the score of the middle case, obtained by arranging the scores in order and then counting in to the middle from either end. The median case in Table 15–1 is the eighth from either end of the group of 15, and turns out to be 34 boxes per hour. If the number of cases is even, one may simply average the two cases on either side of the middle. For instance, with 10 cases, the median can be taken as the arithmetic average of the fifth and sixth cases.

The *mode* is the most frequent score in a given distribution. In Table 15–1 you will note that the most frequent score is 34; hence the mode of the distribution is 34.

In a *symmetrical distribution,* in which the scores distribute evenly on either side of the middle (as in the example of Figure 15–1), the mean, median, and mode all fall

together. This is not true for distributions that are *skewed,* that is, unbalanced. Suppose one were analyzing the starting times of a morning train. The train is usually on time in leaving; occasionally it starts late, but it never starts early. For a train with a scheduled starting time of 8:00 A.M., one week's record might be:

M	8:00	Mean starting time:	8:07
Tu	8:04	Median starting time:	8:02
W	8:02	Modal starting time:	8:00
Th	8:19		
F	8:22		
Sat	8:00		
Sun	8:00		

The distribution of starting times in this example is skewed because of the two late departures; they raise the mean departure time but do not have much effect on either the median or the mode. Skewed distributions are named by the direction in which the *tail* of the distribution falls—the direction of the most extreme scores (Figure

15–2). In our example, the skew is toward the late departure.

Skewness is important because, unless it is understood, the differences between the median and mean may sometimes prove misleading. Suppose that two political parties are arguing about the prosperity of the country. It is quite possible (though not common) for the mean and median incomes to move in opposite directions. Suppose, for example, that a round of wage increases was combined with a reduction in extremely high incomes. The median income might go up while the mean went down. The party wanting to show that incomes were getting higher would choose the median; the one that wished to show that incomes were getting lower would choose the mean.

The mean is the most widely used of the averages but, as we will see later, there are times when the mode or median are more appropriate.

Measures of variation

Usually we need more information about a distribution than we can get from an average. For example, we need a measure to tell us whether scores cluster closely around their average or whether they scatter widely. A measure of the spread or dispersion of scores around the average is called a *measure of variation*.

Measures of variation help us in at least two ways. First, they tell us how representative the average is. If the variation is small, we know that individual cases are close to it. If the variation is large, we can make use of the mean as a representative value with less assurance. Suppose, for example, we are designing clothing for a distant people, say, the Eskimos. Knowing their average size would help us, but it would be very important to also know the spread of sizes. The second measure gives us a "yardstick" by which we can decide how far a single score is above or below the mean. For example, if you have a grade of 85 on an examination, you want to know not only what the mean was but how high the scores went. Without some measure of variation you do not know *how far* 85 is from the mean.

Distributions of scores from two classes of 20 students showing the same mean but with different variation are pictured in Figure 15–3. It is evident that some sort of measure is required to specify more exactly how these two classes differ. Three measures will be considered: *range, mean deviation*, and *standard deviation*.

Why so many measures? The choice is in part a matter of convenience. We shall see that the range is the easiest to compute, that the mean deviation is easily understood, and that the standard deviation (even though it is the most complex) has some mathematical properties that make it a preferred measure.

In order to simplify our example still further for ease in arithmetical computation, let us suppose that five students from each of these classes seek entrance to college, and their entrance examination scores are as follows:

Student scores from Class I:
73, 74, 75, 76, 77 (mean = 75)

Student scores from Class II:
60, 65, 75, 85, 90 (mean = 75).

15–2

Skewed distribution curves

Note that skewed distributions are named by the direction in which the tail is found. Also note that the mean, median, and mode are not identical for a skewed distribution; the median commonly falls between the mode and the mean.

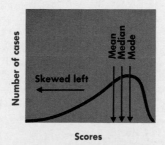 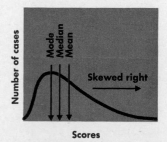

15-3

Distributions differing in variation

It is easy to see by inspection that the scores of Class I cluster closer to the mean than those of Class II, even though the means for the two classes are alike. Computations (by the methods to be discussed in this chapter) show these comparisons of measures of variation for the two classes: range, 20 and 30; mean deviation, 3.0 and 5.5; standard deviation, 4.5 and 7.2. Class II thus has the larger variation no matter how variation is measured.

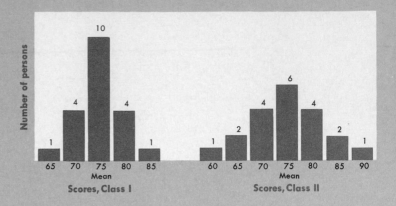

Scores, Class I

Scores, Class II

Let us now compute the measures of variation for these two small samples, one from Class I, the other from Class II.

The *range* is the spread between the highest and the lowest score. The range for the five students from Class I is 4 (from 73 to 77); for those from Class II it is 30 (from 60 to 90).

The *mean deviation* is the average amount by which each score departs from the sample mean. For this purpose we disregard the sign of the difference, that is, whether the score is above or below the mean. Then our formula for the mean deviation becomes:

$$\text{Mean deviation} = \frac{\text{Sum of } |D|}{N}$$

where $|D|$ is the absolute value of the deviation from the mean and N the number of cases entering into the determination. The advantage of the mean deviation is that it is so easily understood; anyone who can understand a mean can comprehend a mean deviation from the mean. It is not much used because of certain advantages of the standard deviation, but it is included here, along with a specimen computation, in order to show the rough similarity between it and a standard deviation.

Specimen computation of mean deviation. In Table 15-3 the scores from the samples from the two classes are arranged for a separate computation of the mean deviation for each class. In order to avoid minus signs, the mean (75) is subtracted from all scores equal to or above it; scores below the mean are subtracted from it. The deviations from the mean are then added and divided by the number of cases (5) in order to obtain the mean deviation. Class I's mean deviation of 1.2 is much less than Class II's 10.0, as we would expect from inspection of the raw data.

The *standard deviation,* for which we use either the initials (SD) or the lower-

TABLE 15-3

Computation of mean deviation

From Class I (mean = 75)	From Class II (mean = 75)
77 − 75 = 2	90 − 75 = 15
76 − 75 = 1	85 − 75 = 10
75 − 75 = 0	75 − 75 = 0
75 − 74 = 1	75 − 65 = 10
75 − 73 = 2	75 − 60 = 15
—	—
Sum of deviations = 6	Sum of deviations = 50
Mean deviation = 6/5 = 1.2	Mean deviation = 50/5 = 10.0

TABLE 15–4

Computation of standard deviation

From Class I (mean = 75)			From Class II (mean = 75)		
	D (deviation from mean)	D^2 (deviation squared)		D (deviation from mean)	D^2 (deviation squared)
$77 - 75 =$	2	4	$90 - 75 =$	15	225
$76 - 75 =$	1	1	$85 - 75 =$	10	100
$75 - 75 =$	0	0	$75 - 75 =$	0	0
$74 - 75 =$	−1	1	$65 - 75 =$	−10	100
$73 - 75 =$	−2	4	$60 - 75 =$	−15	225
Sum of $D^2 = 10$		10	Sum of $D^2 = 650$		650
Mean of $D^2 = 10/5 = 2.0$			Mean of $D^2 = 650/5 = 130$		
Standard deviation $(\sigma) = \sqrt{2.0} = 1.4$			Standard deviation $(\sigma) = \sqrt{130} = 11.4$		

case [2] Greek letter *sigma* (σ), is also based upon the deviation from the mean. However, instead of averaging the deviations directly, as in the mean deviation, each deviation is first squared; then the average of these squares is obtained. The standard deviation is the square root of this result, according to the formula:

$$\sigma = \sqrt{\frac{\text{Sum of } D^2}{N}}$$

Specimen computation of the standard deviation. The data used in Table 15–3 for the computation of the mean deviation are arranged in Table 15–4 for the computation of the standard deviation. In Table 15–4 we subtract the mean from the score regardless of the size of score. We therefore get minus scores, but these disappear when we square the deviations. Note that the two standard deviations show the same order of difference as the mean deviations. For this example, the two measures tell much the same story, although we note that they are not equivalent.

The reasons for a general preference for the standard deviation over other measures

[2] For this introductory treatment we shall use sigma (σ) throughout. However, in the psychological literature the lower-case letter s is frequently used, especially when dealing with standard deviations of small samples. In this case the formula involves dividing by $N - 1$ rather than N. For an explanation of this see Hays (1963).

of variation lie, first, in the fact that it shows a greater stability than other measures when new samples of data are gathered and, second, it has certain characteristics that make it useful in the scaling of data and in further computations, such as the product-moment coefficient of correlation. We shall meet both these topics later in the chapter.

Statistical Inference

Now that we have become familiar with averages and measures of variation as ways of describing data, we are ready to turn to the processes of interpretation, to the making of inferences from data.

Populations and samples

We need first of all to distinguish between a *population* and a *sample* drawn from the population. The U.S. Census Bureau attempts to get in touch with everyone in the country, to describe the whole population, obtaining descriptive material on age, marital status, and so on. The word "population" is appropriate to the Census, because it represents *all* the people living in the United States.

The word "population" in statistics is not limited to people or animals or things. The population may be all the possible temperatures registered on a thermometer, all the words in the English language, or all of any other specified supply of data.[3] Usually we do not have access to the total population, and so we try to represent it by a sample drawn in some *random* (unbiased) fashion. We may ask some questions of a random fraction of the people, as the U.S. Census Bureau has done as part of recent censuses; we may derive average temperatures by reading the thermometer at specified times, without taking a continuous record; we may estimate the words in the encyclopedia by counting the words on a random number of pages. These illustrations all represent the selection of a *sample* from a larger population. If we repeat any of these processes, we will come out with slightly different results, owing to the fact that a sample does not fully represent the whole population and hence has within it *errors of sampling*. This is where statistical considerations enter.

We gather data from samples and study them in order to make inferences. We may examine the census data to see whether the population is getting older, or whether the trend of migration away from the center of the city to the suburbs is continuing, and so on. Similarly, we study our experimental results to find out what effects our experimental manipulations have had upon behavior, whether or not the threshold for pitch is affected by loudness, whether child-rearing practices have detectable effects later on. In order to make *statistical inferences* from data we have to evaluate carefully the relationships revealed by our sample of data. These inferences are always made under circumstances where there is some degree of uncertainty because of sampling errors and measurement errors (to be discussed below). If our statistical tests

show us that the magnitude of the **effect** we find in our sample is fairly large relative to the estimate of the sampling error, then we can have confidence that the effect observed in the sample also holds for the population at large.

Thus, statistical inference deals with the problem of making an inference or judgment about some feature of a population when the inference must be based solely on information obtained from a sample of

15–4

A device to demonstrate a chance distribution

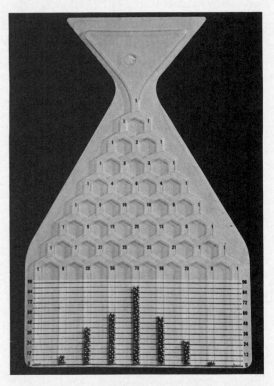

First hold the board upside-down until all of the small steel balls fall into the reservoir. Then turn the board over and hold it vertically with the bottom edge against the table until the balls fall into the nine columns at the bottom. The precise number of balls falling into each column will vary from one demonstration to the next. However, on the average the heights of the balls in the vertical columns approximate a normal distribution, with the greatest height in the center column and gradually decreasing heights in the outer columns. (Hexstat Probability Demonstrator, Harcourt, Brace & World, Inc.)

[3] Sometimes the supply of data (the total population) is not so easily specified, as when we sample a subject's speed of reaction by taking 100 measurements among all those he might possibly yield if we continued the experiment endlessly. As long as the total supply of data is many times that of the sample (whether finite, e.g., all students studying Latin at College X, or indeterminate, as in the case of all possible reaction times), we are able to use statistical theory in treating the results.

that population. As an introduction to statistical inference we shall first consider the normal distribution and its use in interpreting standard deviations. Then we shall turn to problems of sampling errors and the significance of differences.

The normal distribution

Thus far we have mentioned symmetrical and skewed distributions that result when we gather data into frequency distributions. When large amounts of data are collected, tabulated, and plotted on a graph, they often fall into a symmetrical distribution of roughly bell shape, known as the *normal distribution* and plotted as the *normal curve*. Most cases fall near the mean, thus giving the high point of the bell, and the bell tapers off sharply with very high or very low scores. This form of curve is of special interest because it also arises when we plot *chance* events—hence our assertion that it is the "normal" curve.

What do we mean by "chance" events? We mean only that the causal factors are very complex and numerous, yielding results of the sort found in tossing dice or spinning a roulette wheel. The demonstration device displayed in Figure 15–4 illustrates how a sequence of chance events gives rise to a normal distribution. The chance factor of whether a steel ball will fall left or right each time it encounters a point where the channel divides or branches results in a symmetrical distribution, more balls falling straight down the middle, but an occasional one reaching the end compartments. This is a useful way of visualizing what is meant by a chance distribution closely approximating the "normal" curve.

The normal curve (Figure 15–5) can be defined mathematically to represent the idealized distribution approximated by the device shown in Figure 15–4. It gives the likelihood that cases within a normally distributed population will depart from the mean by any stated amount. It is convenient to remember that roughly two-thirds of the cases (68 percent) will tend to fall between plus and minus one standard deviation of the mean; 95 percent of the cases within plus and minus 2σ; and virtually

15–5

The normal curve

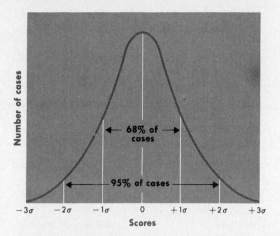

The normal distribution curve can be constructed provided we know the number of cases, the mean, and the standard deviation.

all the cases (99 percent) within 3σ. Thus if we understand the properties of the normal curve, we can interpret any statistic expressed in units of the standard devia-

TABLE 15–5

Area under normal curve as ratio of total area

Standard deviation	(1) Area to the left of this value	(2) Area to the right of this value	(3) Area between this value and mean
-3.0σ	.001	.999	.499
-2.5σ	.006	.994	.494
-2.0σ	.023	.977	.477
-1.5σ	.067	.933	.433
-1.0σ	.159	.841	.341
-0.5σ	.309	.691	.191
0.0σ	.500	.500	.000
$+0.5\sigma$	.691	.309	.191
$+1.0\sigma$	.841	.159	.341
$+1.5\sigma$	.933	.067	.433
$+2.0\sigma$	.977	.023	.477
$+2.5\sigma$	.994	.006	.494
$+3.0\sigma$	.999	.001	.499

tion, provided the cases on which the statistic is based are normally distributed. The percentages marked on Figure 15–5 represent the *percentage of the area* lying under the curve between the indicated scale values, with the total area representing the whole population. A more detailed listing of areas under portions of the normal curve is given in Table 15–5; we shall have a number of uses for the values in this table.

First let us see where the 68 percent and 95 percent values of Figure 15–5 come from. We find from column 3 of Table 15–5 that between -1σ and the mean there lies .341 of the total area, and between $+1\sigma$ and the mean also .341. Adding these, we get .682, which has been expressed in Figure 15–5 as 68 percent. Similarly, we can find the area between -2σ and $+2\sigma$ to be $2 \times .477 = .954$, which has been expressed as 95 percent.

We shall have two uses for these percentages in this chapter. One of them is in connection with the interpretation of standard scores, to which we turn next. The other is in connection with tests of the significance of the differences between means and other statistical measures. Both of these uses make an important assumption, namely, that the scores being considered are sampled from a normal distribution. It is fortunate that a great many score distributions do fit the normal curve or come very close to it, so that this basic assumption does not cause us much trouble. Since we are aware, of course, of skewed distributions, we know that the normal distribution is not always found. Fortunately, some skewness in the data does not prevent us from using most of the ordinary statistical methods.

Scaling of data

In order to interpret a score we often want to know whether it is high or low in relation to other scores. If I take a driver's test and find that I need 0.500 seconds to put my foot on the brake after a danger signal, how can I tell whether my performance is fast or slow? If I get a 60 on my physics examination, do I pass the course? To answer questions of this kind

we have to derive some sort of *scale* against which we can compare the scores.

Ranked data. By placing scores in rank order from high to low we derive one kind of scale. We interpret an individual score by telling where it ranks among the group of scores. For example, the graduates of West Point know where they stand—perhaps 35th or 125th among a class of 400.

Standard scores. The standard deviation is a very convenient unit for scaling because we know how to interpret how far away 1σ or 2σ is from the mean (Table 15–5). A score based on some multiple of the standard deviation is known as a *standard score*. Many scales used in psychological measurement are based on the principle of standard scores, with modifications often being made to eliminate negative signs and decimals. Some of these scales, derived from standard scores, are given in Table 15–6.

Specimen computations of standard scores and transformation to arbitrary scales. In Table 15–4 we had 10 scores on an entrance examination, five each from two classes. Without more information we do not know whether these are representative of applicants from other classes or not. Let us make an assumption that the Class I and Class II students have a mean score corresponding to an assumed national average of 75 on the examination and that the national standard deviation is 10. What then is the *standard score* for the student from Class II who made 90 on the examination? We must express how far this score lies above the mean in multiples of the standard deviation.

$$\text{Standard score for grade of } 90 = \frac{90 - 75}{10}$$

$$= \frac{15}{10} = 1.5\sigma$$

Suppose we wish to convert the standard score computed above to a score on the scale used in the Navy General Classification Test, as shown in Table 15–6. This scale has a mean of 50 and a standard deviation of 10. Therefore the standard score of 1.5σ for our student from Class II becomes $50 + (10 \times 1.5) = 50 + 15 = 65$.

TABLE 15–6

Some representative scales derived from standard scores *

Standard score	Graduate Record Examination	Army General Classification Test	Navy General Classification Test	Air Force Stanine †
-3σ	200	40	20	—
-2σ	300	60	30	1
-1σ	400	80	40	3
0σ	500	100	50	5
$+1\sigma$	600	120	60	7
$+2\sigma$	700	140	70	9
$+3\sigma$	800	160	80	—
Mean 0	500	100	50	5
Standard deviation 1.0	100	20	10	2

* After many scores are accumulated, the actual means and standard deviations sometimes depart widely from the intended ones. For example, the Army General Classification Test (AGCT) proved to have a mean of 97.0 and a standard deviation of 24.0 after many thousands of inductees had been tested. The norms of the Graduate Record Examination also depart from the intended scale.

† The word "stanine" was coined by the Air Force to refer to a scale known originally as "standard nine," a type of standard score with mean of 5 and standard deviation of 2, with scores ranging from 1 to 9.

Using column 1 of Table 15–5, we find beside the value for a standard score of $+1.5\sigma$ the figure .933. This means that 93 percent of the scores of a normal distribution will lie *below* a person whose standard score is $+1.5\sigma$. Thus a score of 65 on the Navy General Classification Test, 650 on a Graduate Record Examination, or 8 on the Air Force Stanine (each score being equivalent) is above that achieved by 93 percent of those on whom the test was calibrated. Scores representing any other multiple of the standard deviation can be similarly interpreted.

How representative is a mean?

When we ask about the representativeness of a mean, we are really implying two questions. First, what are the *errors of measurement?* Second, what are the *errors of sampling?* Two people measuring the same length with a rule or timing an event with a stopwatch may not get exactly the same results. These differences are errors of measurement, which we may assume to be small. The second kind of error, the sampling error, interests us now. Suppose we were to select two random samples of the same size, make the necessary measurements, and compute the mean for each sample, what differences between the first and the second mean could be expected by chance?

Successive random samples drawn from the same normally distributed population will have different means, forming a distribution of *sample means* around the *true mean* of the population. These sample means are themselves measures for which one can compute their own standard deviation. We call this standard deviation the *standard error of the mean*, or σ_M, and can make an estimate of it on the basis of the following formula:

$$\sigma_M = \frac{\sigma}{\sqrt{N}}$$

where σ is the standard deviation of the distribution of scores and N is the number of cases from which each sample mean is computed.

According to the formula, the size of the standard error of the mean decreases with increase in the number of cases; thus, a mean based on a large sample is more trustworthy (i.e., more likely to be close to the actual population mean) than one based on a smaller sample. This agrees with what common sense would lead us to expect. Computation of the standard error of the mean permits us to make clear assertions about the degree of uncertainty in our computed mean. The more cases in the sample, the more we have reduced uncertainty.

Specimen computation of the standard error of the mean. In order to estimate the standard error of the mean, all we need is the number of cases in the *sample* and the standard deviation of the *sample*. Suppose we take the mean and standard deviation computed in Table 15–4 for Class II but assume that the sample was larger. The mean is 75, and the standard deviation is 11.4. Let us assume sample sizes of 25, 100, and 900 cases; the standard errors of the mean would be, respectively:

$$N = 25: \quad \sigma_M = 11.4/\sqrt{25}$$
$$= 11.4/5 = 2.28$$
$$N = 100: \quad \sigma_M = 11.4/\sqrt{100}$$
$$= 11.4/10 = 1.14$$
$$N = 900: \quad \sigma_M = 11.4/\sqrt{900}$$
$$= 11.4/30 = 0.38$$

We can see that the standard error of the mean goes down as the sample size goes up. How can we interpret these differences? We can again go back to Table 15–5, because the standard error can be interpreted as any other standard deviation. Now we may ask, how much variation can we expect among newly obtained means if we repeat measurements on samples of 25, 100, and 900? We know from Table 15–5 that 68 percent of the cases in a normal distribution lie between -1σ and $+1\sigma$ of the mean. Our obtained mean of 75 is our best estimate of the population mean. We know the size of σ_M, so we may infer that the probability is .68 that the population mean lies between the following limits:

$N = 25$: 75 ± 2.28, or between 72.72 & 77.28
$N = 100$: 75 ± 1.14, or between 73.86 & 76.14
$N = 900$: 75 ± 0.38, or between 74.62 & 75.38

Significance of a difference between means

The conclusions of many psychological experiments are drawn from the difference or lack of difference between two means, obtained from measurements taken under two conditions. The standard error of the mean therefore poses an important problem for the experimenter: Does the difference in means reflect a true difference, or is it simply the result of sampling errors?

Although we can never be sure that error has been eliminated entirely, we can test the significance of the difference and state with some confidence the likelihood that the obtained difference might have occurred by chance. The computation will obviously depend on two sets of facts: (1) how precise the sample means themselves are (standard error of the mean), and (2) how great the difference is between them. When put in this way, the statistical problem is clear enough. If the individual scores in each sample are highly variable and the difference between the sample means is small, we have little reason to expect the population means to differ; if the individual scores in each sample show little variability and the difference between the sample means is large, we have more confidence that the population means differ.

Let us consider some examples. In a reaction-time experiment the subject lifts his finger from a key when a stimulus signal comes on, and the time between the stimulus and his response is measured. His responses constitute a *sample* of his reaction times, for he does not respond with equal promptness on every trial. If the stimulus is a *light* instead of a *sound,* most of the reaction times are longer, but the times of the two responses overlap. Now we have an opportunity to test whether the difference between the mean reaction time to light and the mean reaction time to sound is *statistically significant.* Obviously we need to take into account both the spread of scores to light and sound and the size of the difference between the two means.

As a second example, let us consider the scores of a sample of Spanish-American children in Los Angeles on reading tests, compared with the scores of a sample of other school children in Los Angeles. The Spanish-American children score higher than the others, as far as mean differences are concerned, but again there is a great deal of overlap, some Spanish-American children doing very well and some of the others doing very poorly. Hence we cannot accept the obtained differences in mean scores without making a test of significance. Only then can we tell whether the population means differ by an amount that is statistically significant.

Suppose that in an experiment to determine whether right-handed men are stronger than left-handed men the results shown in the first table had been obtained.

Strength of grip in kilograms, right-handed men	Strength of grip in kilograms, left-handed men
40	40
45	45
50	50
55	55
100	60
Sum 290	Sum 250
Mean 58	Mean 50

Our sample of five right-handed men averaged eight kilograms stronger than our sample of five left-handed men. What can be inferred about left-handed and right-handed men in general? Can we argue in terms of our sample of data that right-handed men are stronger than left-handed men? Obviously not, for the averages derived from most of the right-handed men would not differ from averages derived from the left-handed men; the one very deviant case (score of 100) tells us we are dealing with an uncertain situation.

Suppose that, instead, the results had been those shown in the second table.

Strength of grip in kilograms, right-handed men	Strength of grip in kilograms, left-handed men
56	48
57	49
58	50
59	51
60	52
Sum 290	Sum 250
Mean 58	Mean 50

Again the same mean difference of eight

kilograms is found, but we are now inclined to have greater confidence in the results because the left-handed men were consistently lower than the right-handed men. What we ask of statistics is that it provide us with a more precise way of taking into account the reliability of the mean differences, so that we do not have to depend solely on intuition that one difference is more reliable than another.

As already noted, the significance of the difference will depend both on the size of the obtained difference and upon the variability of the means being compared. We shall find below that from the standard error of the means we can compute a *standard error of the difference between two means* (σ_{D_M}). We can then evaluate the obtained difference by using a *critical ratio*, which is the ratio of the obtained difference between the means (D_M) to the standard error of the difference between the means:

$$\text{Critical ratio} = \frac{D_M}{\sigma_{D_M}}$$

This ratio helps us to evaluate the significance of the difference between the two means.[4] As a rule of thumb, a critical ratio should be 2.0 or larger in order for the difference between means to be accepted as significant. Earlier statements, accompanying tables in this book, that the difference between means was "statistically significant" meant that the critical ratio was at least that large.

Why is a critical ratio of 2.0 selected as significant? Simply because a value this large or larger can occur by chance only 5 in 100 times. Where do we get the 5 in 100? We can treat the critical ratio as a standard score, for it is merely the difference expressed as a multiple of its standard error. Referring to Table 15–5, column 2, we ascertain that the likelihood of a standard deviation as high as or higher than +2.0 occurring by chance is .023. Because

[4] Care must be taken in interpreting a critical ratio when the computations are based on small samples. With small samples the ratio should be interpreted as a *t*-test. For large samples *t* and the critical ratio are equivalent.

the chance of deviating in the opposite direction is also .023, the total probability is .046. This is 46 times in 1000, or about 5 in 100, that a critical ratio as large as 2.0 would be found by chance if the population means were identical.

Specimen computation of the critical ratio. The computation of the critical ratio calls for finding the *standard error of the difference between two means.* Let us consider first the case in which the data are *uncorrelated.* If we are comparing the mean height of Korean girls with that of Chinese girls, the data would be uncorrelated. There is no reason for pairing one Chinese girl with one Korean girl in determining the two means. The formula for the standard error of the difference between two means (σ_{DM}) for uncorrelated data is:

$$\sigma_{DM} = \sqrt{(\sigma_{M_1})^2 + (\sigma_{M_2})^2}$$

In this formula, σ_{M_1} and σ_{M_2} are the standard errors of the two means being compared.

As an illustration of uncorrelated data, suppose we were to compare the school achievement test scores in two cities with scores on an arbitrary scale. Scores in city *A* have a mean of 70 and a standard error of the mean of 0.40. Scores in city *B* have a mean of 72 and a standard error of 0.30. We want to know if the mean of 72 of city *B* is significantly higher than the mean of 70 of city *A*.

$$\sigma_{DM} = \sqrt{(\sigma_{M_1})^2 + (\sigma_{M_2})^2}$$
$$= \sqrt{.16 + .09} = \sqrt{.25}$$
$$= .5$$

$$\text{Critical ratio} = \frac{D_M}{\sigma_{DM}} = \frac{72 - 70}{.5} = \frac{2.0}{.5} = 4.0$$

Because 4.0 is above 2.0, we may assert that the mean difference between the two schools meets our test of significance. Thus we conclude that there is a reliable difference in school achievement between cities *A* and *B*.

When the measurements whose means we are testing occur in pairs and are *correlated* (e.g., if we were comparing the strength of right and left hands of the same right-handed men), the procedure for obtaining the standard error of the difference has to be modified to take the correlation into account. Once the standard error of the difference has been computed, taking the correlation into account by a formula that need not concern us, the same procedure is followed as above for obtaining the critical ratio and for testing the significance.

Statements about statistical significance

The rule of thumb that says that a critical ratio should be at least 2.0 is just that—an arbitrary but convenient rule. Instead of relying on this one arbitrary figure, our knowledge of the normal curve permits us to make other probability statements from our data.

Confidence limits. We know that an interval extending two standard deviations above and below the mean of a normal distribution will include about 95 percent of the cases (Figure 15–5). With these values in mind we can state *confidence limits* within which a population mean will fall. For example, if we assume as values for right-hand strength a mean of 50.0 and a standard error of 1.5, as determined from a single sample, we can say that the chances are 95 in 100 that the population mean for right-hand strength will fall between 47 [i.e., $50 - 2(1.5)$] and 53 [i.e., $50 + 2(1.5)$]. Were we to repeat the experiment a number of times, each time we would get a different mean and a different set of confidence limits. But of these sets of confidence limits, 95 percent would include the population mean.[5] With the aid of Table 15–5 we can also set other confidence limits.

Probability values. We use the critical ratio in order to evaluate the *null hypothesis.* That is, we assume that no difference exists between the two populations being sampled (i.e., the null hypothesis), and then evaluate our sample results against this hypothesis. The higher the critical ratio, the less plausible the hypothesis that *no* difference exists between the population means. Because the critical ratio

[5] This statement has to be read with care. It does *not* say that if the experiment were repeated 100 times, the means of the *samples* would fall within the stated confidence limits 95 percent of the time.

has to be interpreted by a table, it is customary to give the probability values of a finding directly in the form of a statement. Instead of saying that the critical ratio is 2.0, we say, "the probability (P) is .05 or less that the observed difference might have occurred, assuming that the population means were the same." Or this statement might be made: "Only those differences are considered significant for which P is .05 or less."

The Coefficient of Correlation and Its Interpretation

We have already met the *coefficient of correlation* in several places.[6] Correlation refers to the concomitant variation of paired measures, so that when one of the paired measures rises, so does the other, or (in negative correlation) as one rises, the other falls.

We meet correlation very often in the study of psychological tests. Suppose that a test is designed to predict success in college. If it is a good test, high scores on it will be related to high performance in college and low scores will be related to poorer performance. The coefficient of correlation gives us a way of stating more precisely the *degree* of relationship.

Product-moment correlation (r)

The most frequently used method of determining the coefficient of correlation is the *product-moment method,* which yields the index conventionally designated r. Such an r varies between perfect positive correlation ($r = +1.00$) and perfect negative correlation ($r = -1.00$). Lack of relationship is designated $r = .00$.

The formula for computing the product-moment correlation is:

$$r = \frac{Sum\ (dx)\,(dy)}{N\sigma_x\sigma_y}$$

[6] This topic was first discussed in Chapter 1 (pp. 25–27). The reader may find it helpful to review that material.

Here we have labeled one of the paired measures the *x*-score and the other the *y*-score. The dx and dy refer to the deviations of each score from its mean, N is the number of paired measures, and σ_x and σ_y are the standard deviations of the *x*-scores and the *y*-scores. The name "product-moment" comes from the fact that for each pair of values dx is multiplied by dy, and these products are then summed over the N cases. It is evident that the higher the sum of the $(dx)(dy)$ products, the higher will be the correlation.

The computation of the coefficient of correlation requires the determination of the sum of the products of the deviation of each of the two scores (x and y) from its respective mean, that is, the sum of the $(dx)(dy)$ products for all of the subjects entering into the correlation. This sum, in addition to the computed standard deviations for the *x*-scores and *y*-scores, can then be entered into the formula.

Specimen computation of product-moment correlation. Suppose that we had the following pairs of scores, the first being a score on a college entrance test (to be labeled arbitrarily as the *x*-score) and the second being freshman grades (the *y*-score).

Names of students	Entrance test (x)	Freshman grades (y)
Adam	71	39
Bill	67	27
Charles	65	33
David	63	30
Edward	59	21

Looking at these data, we can easily detect that there is some positive correlation between *x*- and *y*-scores. Adam makes the highest score on the entrance test and also the highest freshman grades; Edward makes the lowest score on both. The others are a little irregular, so we know that the correlation is not perfect; hence r is less than 1.00. We shall proceed to compute the correlation to illustrate the method, though no researcher would consent, in practice, to determining a correlation with so few cases.

All the details are given in Table 15–7. Following the procedure outlined in Table 15–4, we compute the standard deviation of the *x*-scores and then the standard deviation

TABLE 15–7

Computation of a product-moment correlation

Subject	x-score	y-score	(dx)	(dy)	(dx)(dy)
Adam	71	39	6	9	+54
Bill	67	27	2	−3	−6
Charles	65	33	0	3	0
David	63	30	−2	0	0
Edward	59	21	−6	−9	+54
Sum	325	150	0	0	+102
Mean	65	30			

$\sigma_x = 4$

$\sigma_y = 6$

$$r = \frac{\text{Sum } (dx)(dy)}{N\sigma_x\sigma_y} = \frac{+102}{5 \times 4 \times 6} = +.85$$

of the y-scores. The obtained values are 4 for the x-scores, and 6 for the y-scores; the reader should check that these are correct. Next we compute the $(dx)(dy)$ products for each subject and then total up the five cases. Entering these results in our equation yields an r of +.85.

Rank correlation (ρ)

When computers are not available and calculations must be done by hand, a simpler method for determining correlations makes use of ranked scores. While the resulting correlation is an estimate of r, it is not an exact equivalent of r, so that the coefficient obtained by the rank method is designated by the lower-case Greek letter *rho* (ρ). The formula for the rank-correlation coefficient is:

$$\rho = 1 - \frac{6(\text{Sum } D^2)}{N(N^2 - 1)}$$

where D is the difference in ranks for the scores of any one subject and N is the number of subjects whose scores are being correlated.[7]

[7] The formula for *rho* is derived as an approximation of r by a method that need not concern us. Those interested can find a derivation in Hays (1963).

Specimen computation of rank-correlation coefficient. We shall use the same data employed in the previous example. All the details are given in Table 15–8. The procedure is to rank both sets of scores, obtain the differences in ranks for each subject on the two tests, square and sum these differences, and enter them into the formula. The value of ρ for our example turns out to be +.70. As we indicated earlier ρ may be viewed as an estimate of r. The fact that in our example the values of r and ρ are not close together is due to the small number of cases $(N = 5)$. When larger samples are taken, ρ and r generally are quite close. Whether the researcher chooses to use r or ρ in computing a correlation coefficient is a technical matter beyond the scope of this book. The important point to remember is that both r and ρ have similar properties and, for reasonably large samples, will closely approximate each other. Once the data are ranked, the calculations for ρ are simpler, and the reader without a computing machine will undoubtedly prefer to use the rank method in future examples.

When is a coefficient of correlation significant?

A coefficient of correlation, like other statistical measures, has a standard error. That is, if a second sample were taken, the correlations computed from it would not be exactly the same as that obtained from the first sample. The *standard error of r*, which can be used to determine whether or not r differs significantly from zero, is given by the following formula:

$$\sigma_r = \frac{1}{\sqrt{N - 1}}$$

where N is the number of pairs entering into the correlation.

If we then divide r by σ_r, we get a critical ratio which can be interpreted just like the critical ratios given above. If the value of r/σ_r is greater than 2.0, we may be fairly confident that the "true" value of r is greater than zero and that there is a real correlation between the scores in the population from which the sample was drawn.

Specimen computation of the significance of a correlation coefficient. In the study of Brown and Lenneberg (1954), cited on p. 375, a correlation of r = .42 between codabil-

TABLE 15–8

Computation of rank-correlation coefficient

Subject	Entrance test	Freshman grades	Rank, entrance test	Rank, freshman grades	Difference in rank (D)	Squared difference (D^2)
Adam	71	39	1	1	0	0
Bill	67	27	2	4	−2	4
Charles	65	33	3	2	+1	1
David	63	30	4	3	+1	1
Edward	59	21	5	5	0	0
	$N = 5$					Sum $D^2 = 6$

$$\rho = 1 - \frac{6(\text{Sum } D^2)}{N(N^2 - 1)} = 1 - \frac{6 \times 6}{5 \times 24} = 1 - \frac{36}{120} = +.70$$

ity of colors and their ease of recognition was mentioned as supporting a contention of the authors. The study was done with 24 subjects. How significant, we may ask, was the correlation of .42?

Standard error of r: $\sigma_r = \dfrac{1}{\sqrt{N-1}} = \dfrac{1}{\sqrt{24-1}}$

$$= \frac{1}{\sqrt{23}} = \frac{1}{4.8} = 0.21$$

Critical ratio: $\dfrac{r}{\sigma_r} = \dfrac{.42}{.21} = 2.00$

This critical ratio just meets our arbitrary value of 2.0, corresponding to $P = .05$. Hence, we may conclude that the observed correlation is statistically significant, for a correlation as high as .42 (with 24 subjects) would be expected to occur very infrequently (less than 5 times in 100) if the correlation coefficient for the entire population were zero.

Interpreting a coefficient of correlation

It is not always enough to know that a correlation is significantly greater than zero. Sometimes we wish to make use of correlations in prediction. For example, if we have an entrance test that we know from past experience correlates with freshman grades, we can predict the freshman grades for beginning college students who have taken the test. If correlation were perfect, we could predict their grades without error.

Because r is usually less than 1.00, we make errors in prediction; the closer r is to zero, the greater the sizes of the errors in prediction based on it.

While we cannot go into the technical problems of predicting freshman grades from entrance examinations or of making other similar predictions, we can consider the meanings of coefficients of different sizes. It is evident that with a correlation of zero between x and y, knowledge of x will not help us to predict y. If weight is unrelated to intelligence, it does us no good to know weight when we are trying to estimate intelligence. At the other extreme, a perfect correlation would mean 100 percent predictive efficiency—knowing x we can predict y without error. What of intermediate values of r?

Because correlation coefficients vary from between 0 and ±1.00, there is a temptation to interpret the correlation as a percent, which would imply that a correlation of .50 was twice as large as one of .25. This is not correct; a more appropriate interpretation is based on the square of the correlation. The squared correlation (r^2) multiplied by 100 provides an estimate of the percentage of the variance that the distribution of x-scores and y-scores have in common. If in an experiment $r = .50$, then $100(.5)^2$ or 25 percent of the variation of

Scatter diagrams illustrating correlations of various sizes

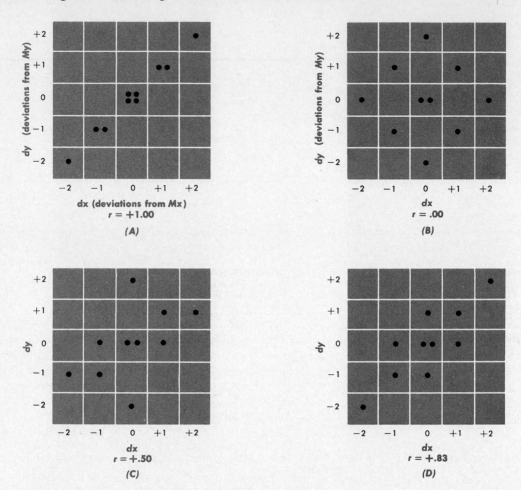

Each dot represents one individual's score on two tests, x and y. In A, all cases fall on the diagonal; the correlation is perfect (r = +1.00). If you know a subject's score on x, you know that it will be the same on y. In B, the correlation is zero. When you know a subject's score on x, you cannot predict whether it will be at, above, or below the mean on y. For example, of the four subjects who score at the mean of x (dx = 0), one makes a very high score on y (dy = +2), one a very low score (dy = −2), and two remain average. In both C and D, there is a diagonal trend to the scores, so that a high score on x is associated with a high score on y, and a low score on x with a low score on y, but the relation is imperfect. The interested student will discover that it is possible to check the value of the correlations by using the formulas given in the text for standard deviation (p. 401) and the coefficient of correlation (p. 409). The computation has been very much simplified by presenting the scores in the deviation form that permits entering them directly into the formulas.

the y's is accounted for by differences in x; similarly, if r = .40, 16 percent of the variation of the y's is accounted for by the relation with x. In the sense of "percentage of variation accounted for" we can thus say

that a correlation of r = .70 is *twice as strong* as a correlation of r = .50, and that a correlation of r = .50 is *25 times as strong* as a correlation of r = .10.

Some appreciation of the meaning of

correlations of various sizes can be gained from a careful study of the *scatter diagrams* in Figure 15–6. Note that each dot represents the score of two tests (an *x*-score and a *y*-score) for the same individual. If the correlation is one, then all the points in the scatter diagram fall on a straight line. When the correlation is zero, the points in the scatter diagram are randomly distributed and do not line up in any particular direction. By inspection of these scatter diagrams we see that the points can be encompassed by an ellipse that is long and narrow for high correlations and that approaches the form of a circle as the correlation goes to zero.

In the preceding discussion we did not emphasize the sign of the correlation coefficient since this has no bearing on the strength of a relationship. The only distinction between a correlation of $r = +.70$ and $r = -.70$ is that for the former increases in *x* are accompanied by increases in *y* and for the latter increases in *x* are accompanied by decreases in *y*.

Finally, we should also note that while the correlation coefficient is one of the most widely used statistics in psychology, it is also one of the most widely misused statistical procedures. It is misused in the sense that (1) it is often overlooked that *r* measures only the strength of a linear (i.e., straight-line) relationship between *x* and *y*, and that (2) it does not necessarily imply a cause-and-effect relation between *x* and *y*. If *r* is calculated, for example, for the data in Figure 15–7, a value of *r* close to zero will be obtained, but this does not mean that the two variables are not related. The white curve of Figure 15–7 provides an excellent fit even though a straight line does not; knowing the value of *x* we could predict very precisely what *y* would be. Let us therefore emphasize that the correlation coefficient measures only the strength of a linear (straight-line) relationship between two variables. When the psychologist believes that nonlinear relations hold between two variables *x* and *y*, then other statistical procedures must be adopted to assess the degree of relationship (Hays, 1963).

Correlation does not yield cause. When two sets of scores are correlated, we may assume that they have some causal factors in common, but we have to be careful not to state that *one* of them causes the *other*. For example, the softness of the asphalt in the streets of a city may correlate with the number of heat prostration cases, but this does not mean that the asphalt when soft gives off some kind of poison that sends people to hospitals. We understand the cause in this example—a hot sun both softens the asphalt and produces sunstroke. Hence a correlation may lead us to *search* for a cause, but alone it does not *explain* the relationship it *describes*.

Correlations sometimes appear paradoxical. For example, the correlation between time in study and college grades often has been found to be slightly negative (perhaps $-.20$). If a causal interpretation were assumed, one might suppose that the best way to raise grades would be to stop studying! The negative correlation arises because some students have advantages over others in grade-making (possibly because of native ability or better precollege preparation), so that often the students who study the hardest are those who have difficulty earning barely passing grades. This example provides sufficient warning against giving a causal interpretation to a coefficient of correlation.

However, when two sets of data are

15–7

Hypothetical scatter diagram

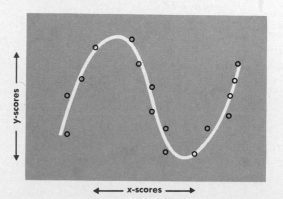

correlated, the first set may *possibly* be the cause of the other. The search for causes is a logical one, and correlations can help. Alone they do not tell us whether one variable is the cause of another, or whether what they have in common is a result of some third variable.

Statistics in Psychology

Statistical methods are becoming increasingly important in all sciences, but they are particularly important in psychology because of the complexity and variability of the phenomena psychology studies.

The earliest demand upon statistics was made when psychologists began to use psychophysical methods for *threshold measurement.* A weight that is slightly heavier than another is not always judged as heavier, even though the judgment "heavier" is made more frequently than judgments of "lighter" and "equal." Hence the threshold requires a statistical definition. It has both an average value and a standard deviation.

The most widespread development of statistical methods came in connection with *tests of individual differences.* This chapter on statistics has been introduced at this point because we shall make references to statistical concepts in the following chapters on individuality.

More recently statistical considerations have entered increasingly into the *design of experiments* in all branches of psychology. While some statistical considerations have long been important (e.g., in computing the significances of differences between performances of *experimental* and *control* groups), newer methods permit the economical treatment of a number of variables at once. These methods not only save in the time and costs of experimentation but yield kinds of information that earlier experimental comparisons could not produce.

Another field, that of *attitude and opinion surveys* (of which election polls are one illustration), relies very largely upon sampling methods to determine how many people and which people to interview. The results must meet acceptable statistical standards if they are to be appropriately interpreted.

Modern computational aids, including statistical tables, computing machines (from simple hand-operated calculators to electronic computers), punched-card methods, and test-scoring machines, permit the rapid handling of masses of data. Modern psychology as we know it would be impossible without these developments.

SUMMARY   1. *Statistics* is the science that deals with the collection and handling of numerical data and with the inferences made from such data.

2. *Descriptive statistics* provide shorthand descriptions of large numbers of observations.

3. *Averages* include the *mean,* the *median,* and the *mode.* Because of its mathematical properties, the mean is the most favored of these measures and is the ordinary arithmetical average.

4. The *measures of variation* include the *range,* the *mean deviation,* and the *standard deviation.* The standard deviation, although possibly the hardest to understand, is the most useful measure.

5. *Statistical inference* deals with the problem of making an inference or judgment about some feature of a population when the inference must be based solely on information obtained on a sample from the population. The accuracy of such inferences depend upon two factors: the size of the sample and the faithfulness with which the sample represents the popu-

lation. *Random sampling* procedures are most frequently used in order to insure a representative sample.

6. In the *scaling* of data, raw scores may be converted into *ranks*, or *standard scores*. Standard scores, which are based on distance from the mean expressed as multiples of the standard deviation, have many advantages and are widely used. Some of the better-known scales based on the assumptions of standard scores are the scale used in the Graduate Record Examination and the scales used in classification tests by the Armed Services.

7. The mean of a sample has a *standard error* that is smaller than the standard deviation of the sample, its size decreasing as the number of cases in the sample increases.

8. It is possible to compute a *standard error of a difference* (σ_{D_M}) between two means from the standard error of each mean. The *critical ratio* (D_M/σ_{D_M}) expresses the obtained difference in multiples of the standard error of the difference. If the critical ratio is 2.0 or above, we have confidence that a true difference between the means exists, that is, that the difference is unlikely to be the result of chance factors.

9. The *coefficient of correlation* is a convenient method for expressing a relationship between two variables. The *product-moment correlation* (r) is the one favored in psychological measurements. A convenient approximation is provided by the *rank correlation coefficient* (ρ). A product-moment correlation is regarded as statistically significant if its value is different from zero and if the critical ratio between r and the standard error of r is 2.0 or more.

10. Statistics as an important tool has found its place in all branches of psychology. It is especially important in tests of individual differences, and more recently it has found a place in the design of experiments and in attitude and opinion surveys.

SUGGESTIONS FOR FURTHER READING
Because of the importance of statistical methods in psychology a number of textbooks are available for the teaching of statistics to students of psychology, of which Hays, *Statistics for psychologists* (1963), and McNemar, *Psychological statistics* (3rd ed., 1962), are excellent examples.

Quantitative methods in general, including the fitting of theoretical curves to data are discussed in Guilford, *Psychometric methods* (2nd ed., 1954), Lewis, *Quantitative methods in psychology* (1960), and Atkinson, Bower, and Crothers, *An introduction to mathematical learning theory* (1965).

The role of statistics in the design of psychological experiments is explained in Winer, *Statistical principles in experimental design* (1962), and Edwards, *Experimental design in psychological research* (rev. ed., 1960).

16 Ability Testing and Intelligence

We know from our study of growth, motivation, and learning that one man will differ from another because he inherits individual characteristics and also because he experiences his culture through home, school, and community in unique ways, thereby acquiring habits, attitudes, and understandings that are distinctively his own. We are now interested in the individual as a unique person, the product of all these influences. We wish to know in what ways men are unlike, the extent of their differences, and how to judge the differences.

This is not a task of idle curiosity, for our society requires individuals to be appraised, classified, and given responsibilities on the assumptions both that they differ and that their differences will suit them better for one social role than for another. We decide by examination to send some boys into active military service and to let others remain in college. Within a college we try to assess individual differences in order to help students choose their majors or their vocational objectives. In offices and factories we test adults in order to place them in the jobs best suited to them.

Testing Aptitudes and Achievements

We shall be concerned in this chapter with *ability testing*—the study of individual differences in knowledge and skills and in aptitudes and achievements in the area of general competency.

When we are confronted with the problem of appraising a person's abilities, we make a distinction between what that person can do now and what he might do if he were trained. For example, John is an excellent premedical student who some day will be a fine physician, but we would not ask him to remove an appendix before he had completed his medical training. James is a young recruit who some day will be a good aviator, but we do not trust him with an airplane before he has learned to fly. This distinction between a *capacity to learn* and an *accomplished skill* is important in our appraisal devices. Tests designed to measure capacities, that is, to *predict* what one can accomplish with training, are known as *aptitude tests*. Tests that tell what one can do now are *achievement tests*. Intelligence tests that predict how well you will do in college are aptitude tests; examinations given at the end of the term to see how much you have learned are achievement tests. Both are ability tests.

The relation between aptitude and achievement tests

Aptitude tests, by definition, predict performances not yet attained. But the *items* in the tests must consist of samples of achievements, that is, of what can be accomplished *now*. How, then, is it possible to construct anything but achievement tests? This difficulty does not become an impasse because it is possible to derive our tests from performances other than those being predicted. For example, one of the abilities contributing to success in typing is good spelling. Because spelling can be tested before experience with typewriters, the typing *aptitude* test may include a spelling test—even though from another point of view the spelling test is an achievement test. The distinction between an aptitude test and an achievement test is not based on the content of the items, but upon the *purposes* of the two kinds of test.

Aptitude tests

Aptitude tests are sometimes classified according to the breadth or generality of the abilities they predict. Thus there are tests of abilities used in a wide range of performances, the best known being those testing *general intelligence,* to be treated more fully later in this chapter. There are also a number of tests for *mechanical aptitude,* because so much work is done either by hand or with mechanical devices.

Many tests are given to discover *special aptitudes.* For example, tests of *musical aptitude* measure discrimination of pitch, rhythm, and other aspects of musical sensitivity that might be predictive of musical performance with training. Another such test measures *clerical aptitude;* a test in simple number checking proves predictive of an individual's later achievement as an office clerk. Many aptitude tests have been constructed for the purpose of predicting success in specific jobs or vocations. Since the beginning of World War II the armed forces have continued to devise tests to select aviators, radio technicians, submarine crews, and other specialists for the various skilled jobs within the services.

In attempting to measure aptitude, it is usually necessary to use a number of different tests in combination. Earlier we used the illustration of present ability in spelling as a test for predicting typing ability. But spelling is not the only ingredient in typing skill; a good typing aptitude test must also include tests of finger dexterity and other skills. A combination of tests used for prediction is known as a *test battery.* A well-planned battery is composed only of tests that contribute to the final prediction. Scores from the individual tests are *weighted* in such a way as to get the best possible prediction; that is, scores on the tests that predict well count more in the prediction than scores on the tests that do not predict so well. For instance, if a finger-dexterity test predicts typing success better than a spelling test, scores in finger dexterity will count more than scores in spelling.

A useful test battery was developed during World War II for the selection of aircrew specialists for the U.S. Army Air Forces. Many tests were tried, and only those found by experience to aid in the prediction of success were kept. By making use of the weights appropriate to each of the specialties, officials could assign a candidate to the duty in which he was most likely to succeed. The battery of tests that remained in use at the end of World War II, is listed in Table 16–1, with an "X" marking those tests that received weights for predicting success as bombardier, navigator, bomber pilot, fighter pilot, and flight engineer.

This set of tests classifies as an aptitude battery because its aim was to *predict* success in the different specialties. Some of the individual tests listed in Table 16–1 reflect basic capacities, such as speed of identification, judgment, or finger dexterity; others seem to reflect training, such as instrument comprehension, general information, reading comprehension, and knowledge of mechanical principles. But all these capacities can be assessed *before* the candidate has had his training in any one of the air-crew specialties. We shall return a little later to the question of how successful this battery was in predicting who was likely to succeed as an air-crew specialist.

Achievement tests

Although the most widespread use of achievement tests is as school examinations and civil service tests, they are also used to test what has been learned in preparation for the practice of a specialty, such as law, medicine, or accounting. The consequences of all these achievement tests are highly important to the person who takes them. If he succeeds, he will receive a de-

TABLE 16–1

Tests composing classification battery for air-crew specialists

	Specialties for which tests predicted success *				
	Bombardier	Navigator	Bomber pilot	Fighter pilot	Flight engineer
Printed tests					
Dial and table reading	X	X	X		X
Biographical data		X	X	X	
Spatial orientation I	X	X	X		
Spatial orientation II	X	X	X	X	
Reading comprehension	X	X	X		X
Instrument comprehension			X	X	
Mechanical principles			X	X	X
Speed of identification				X	
Numerical operations	X	X			
Mechanical information					X
General information			X	X	
Judgment			X		
Arithmetic reasoning	X	X			X
Apparatus tests					
Rotary pursuit with divided attention			X		
Rudder control			X	X	
Finger dexterity	X				
Complex coordination	X		X	X	
Two-hand pursuit	X	X		X	
Discrimination reaction time	X	X		X	X

SOURCE: Adapted from DuBois (1947), p. 109.

* Two additional tests were included in the battery, applicable only to other specialties. These were a printed test of coordinate reading, used only in the battery for radar operators, and an apparatus test of pedestal sight manipulation, weighted only for the aerial gunner. For the sake of simplicity, not all the specialties are shown in this table.

gree or a license to practice or an opportunity to enter the diplomatic service. If he fails, many paths may be blocked for him. Therefore it is crucial that examinations be well conceived so that they measure what they are intended to measure and that their scores represent fairly the relative abilities of the candidate who takes the tests.

Two reasons have led psychologists to take an interest in the development of achievement tests. First, there is much demand for tests, especially in education and civil service. Second, *achievement tests furnish a standard on which aptitude tests are based.* To prepare and try out an aptitude test for typing, you first need a standard of good typing against which to meas-

ure the aptitude. Otherwise you have no way of checking your predictions. Thus, achievement tests furnish one standard, or *criterion,* for the prediction of aptitudes. If professors assigned college grades whimsically instead of on the basis of the student's achievement in the course, it would be futile to try to predict grades from an aptitude battery. With improved achievement examinations predictions can be made more efficiently. Of course, other criteria, such as success on a job, can be used. Then the measure of success serves as a measure of achievement.

Reliability and validity

In order that test scores may be used for scientific purposes, they must be trustworthy. In terms used by psychologists, this means that they must meet two requirements: *reliability* and *validity*.

Scores are *reliable* when they are dependable and reproducible, and when they measure *consistently* whatever they measure. Tests may be confusing, misleading, unclear, or tricky, and thus may mean different things to different subjects, or even to the same subject at different times. Tests may also be too short to be reliable or scoring may be too subjective. If a test is inconsistent in its results when measurements are repeated, or when it is scored by two people, it is unreliable. A simple analogy is a rubber yardstick; if we didn't know how much it stretched each time we made a measurement, the results would be unreliable, no matter how carefully we had marked it. We need stable and consistent tests if we are to use the results with confidence.

In order to measure *reliability*, we must secure two independent scores for the same individual from the same test, either by treating halves of the test separately, by repeating the test, by giving it in two forms, or by deriving some sort of statistical measure equivalent to having two such scores. We can then compare the first and second set of scores. If the same relative ranks are preserved on the two scores, the test is reliable. Some departures from identity of score are to be expected, owing to errors of measurement and sampling errors, so that a measure of *degree of relationship* between the two sets of scores is needed. This relationship is provided by the *coefficient of correlation*, already familiar to us as a measure of degree of correspondence between two sets of scores. The coefficient of correlation between the two sets of scores, adjusted according to statistical conventions, is in this case a *reliability coefficient*. Well-constructed psychological tests of ability usually have reliability coefficients of $r = .90$ or above.

Tests are *valid* when they measure what they are supposed to measure. A college examination in economics full of clever questions might turn out to be a test of student intelligence rather than of the eco-

nomics that was to have been learned in the course. Such an examination might be reliable, but it would not be a valid test of achievement for the course. A test of sense of humor, for example, might be made up of jokes whose points were very hard to catch unless one were both very bright and very well-read. Hence it might turn out to be a *reliable* test of something (intelligence? educational achievement?) but still not be *valid* as a test of the sense of humor.

To measure *validity*, we must also have two scores for each person. One of these is the test score, the reliability of which we have just been discussing. The other is some measure of what it is that the test is supposed to be measuring. This measure is called a *criterion*. Suppose that a test is designed to predict success in learning to receive telegraphic code. To determine whether or not the test is valid, it is given to a group of men beginning to study code. Later on, each man is tested on the number of words per minute he can receive. This later measure furnishes an additional set of scores which can serve as a criterion. Now we can obtain a coefficient of correlation between the early test scores and the scores on the criterion. This correlation coefficient is known as a *validity coefficient*, and it tells something about how valuable a given test is for a given purpose. The higher the coefficient, the better the prediction that can be made from an aptitude test, and the greater the confidence that can be placed in an achievement test.

High validity coefficients are essential if test scores are to be used to help an individual with such choices as those of vocation. But even relatively low validity coefficients may prove useful when large numbers of people are tested. For example, the battery of tests for the selection of aircrew specialists (Table 16–1) proved effective in predicting job success, even though some of the validity coefficients were of very moderate size. Some illustrative validity coefficients from this battery are shown in Table 16–2. Although no single test shows a validity above .49, the "stanine" score (see Chapter 15, p. 405) derived

TABLE 16–2

Validity coefficients for prediction of success in pilot training

Tests among those in classification battery	Validity for completed pilot training (N = 1275) Validity coefficient *
Printed tests with highest validity coefficients	
General information	.49
Instrument comprehension	.46
Mechanical principles	.42
Dial and table reading	.40
Spatial orientation II	.38
Apparatus tests with highest validity coefficients	
Complex coordination	.42
Discrimination reaction time	.41
Rudder control	.36
Two-hand pursuit	.35
Rotary pursuit	.31
Pilot stanine (a composite score)	.64

SOURCE: Modified from DuBois (1947), p. 190.

* In the group studies, pilot selection was not based upon test scores, because the success of the tests was still under study. Because the criterion was simply that of passing or failing in pilot training, a special kind of correlation coefficient (called biserial r) was computed; the usual r requires scaled values for both variables.

The pilot stanines gave each candidate a pilot-prediction rating from 1 to 9. Figure 16–1 shows that during the experimental period those with low stanines were eliminated much more frequently than those with high stanines. After experience with the tests, the examiners rejected those with low stanines from further training. In November, 1943, for example, a candidate had to receive a stanine score of 5 or better to be accepted for pilot training. Thus a stanine of 5 became a critical score. Had this been adopted before carrying all the candidates of Figure 16–1 through their training, the result would have been that only 17 percent of those accepted would have failed to complete training. Those dropped would have been the group of low scorers of whom 44 percent failed elementary pilot training.

The critical score is but one way in which to use data of this kind for prediction. The data of Figure 16–1, expressed in correlational terms, represent a correlation between stanine and completion of training of $r = .51$ for the total group of 166,507 trainees. People trained in statistics are able to estimate from the size of a validity coeffi-

16–1

The basis for a critical score

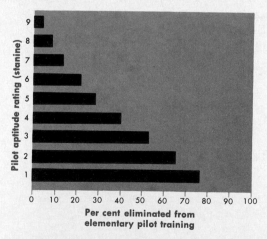

The graph shows the percentage of failures in pilot training at each stanine level. At one point the Air Force established a stanine score of 5 as a requirement for further pilot training. (After DuBois, 1947)

from the battery of tests correlates .64 with the criterion.

Test scores as a basis for prediction

With high enough reliability and validity coefficients we know that we have satisfactory tests, but the problem of using the tests in prediction still remains. The method of prediction most easily understood is the one based on *critical scores*. By this method, a critical point on the scale is selected after experience with the tests. Only those candidates with scores above the critical scores are accepted—for training, for admission to college, or for whatever purpose the testing may serve.

The pilot-selection program of the air force illustrates this use of critical scores.

cient just how successful their predictions are likely to be by appropriately interpreting the correlation. For our present purposes it suffices to know that with a validity coefficient of about .50 we can have the degree of success represented in Figure 16–1. This is appreciable success and represents substantial savings when the costs of training are considered.

Tests of General Intelligence

Intelligence tests are designed to measure the abilities that distinguish the bright from the dull. Because these distinctions are significant for school success, vocational success, and social adjustment generally, the intelligence test is one of the major tools psychology has developed. In our study of individuality, therefore, we will do well to scrutinize more carefully the nature of intelligence tests and the findings that have resulted from their development.

Alfred Binet (1857–1911), a French psychologist, invented the intelligence test as we now know it. In 1904 the French government asked him to devise a test to detect those children who were too dull to profit from ordinary schooling. In collaboration with Théodore Simon (1873–1961), another French psychologist, Binet published a scale in 1905, which he revised in 1908 and again in 1911. These Binet scales are the direct ancestors of contemporary intelligence tests.

Binet's method: a mental-age scale

Binet assumed that a dull child was like a normal child but retarded in his mental growth, that the dull child would behave on tests like a normal child of younger age. This assumption need not have turned out to be so. For example, subnormal children might have excelled at rote memorization, while being incapable of reasoning or of abstract behavior. But Binet's original conjecture, while not entirely correct, has proved serviceable as a guide in test construction. Binet decided to scale intelligence as the kind of change that ordinarily comes with growing older. Accordingly,

16–2

Totally novel items used in intelligence tests

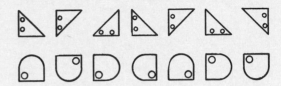

The following instructions accompany the test: "Here are some cards for you to mark. In each row mark every card that is like the first card in the row." (After Thurstone and Thurstone, 1941)

Binet devised a scale of units of *mental age*. Average *mental-age* (M.A.) scores correspond to *chronological age* (C.A.), that is to the age determined from the date of birth. A bright child's M.A. is above his C.A.; a retarded child has an M.A. below his C.A. The mental-age scale is thus easily interpreted by teachers and others who deal with children differing in mental ability.

Item selection

Because the intelligence test is designed to measure brightness rather than the results of special training, it must consist of items that do not assume any specific preparation. In other words, the intelligence test is designed to be an *aptitude* test rather than an *achievement* test, and it must be constructed accordingly.

There are two chief ways to find items on which success is uninfluenced by special training. One way is to choose *totally novel items* upon which an unschooled child has as good a chance to succeed as one who has gone to school. Figure 16–2 illustrates a totally novel item. In this particular case the child is asked to choose figures that are just alike; the assumption is that the designs as such are unfamiliar to all children. The second way is to choose *assuredly familiar items*, so that all those for whom the test is designed will have had the requisite prior experience to deal with the item. The following problem provides an example of an assuredly familiar item:

Mark F if the sentence is foolish; mark S if it is sensible.

S   F   Mrs. Smith has had no children, and I understand that the same was true of her mother.[1]

This item is "fair" only for children who know the English language, who can read, and who understand all the words in the sentence. For such children, detection of the fallacy in the statement becomes a valid test of intellectual ability.

Many of the items on an intelligence test of the Binet type are of the second sort, that requiring the assumption of general familiarity. A vocabulary test, for example, appears in almost all the scales. Familiarity with the language is necessarily assumed.

The intelligence test is in some respects a crude instrument, for its assumptions cannot be strictly met. The language environment of one home is never exactly that of another, the reading matter available to the subjects differs, the stress upon intellectual goals varies. Despite the difficulties, however, items can be chosen that work reasonably well in practice. The items of contemporary intelligence tests are those that have survived in practice after many others have been tried and found defective.

CRITICAL DISCUSSION

Culture-fair intelligence tests

As indicated, items for an intelligence test are often selected on the assumption that the substance is assuredly familiar to all those being tested. This assumption is extremely difficult to satisfy, because rural and urban children have few common experiences, the vocabulary levels of homes of different social strata vary, and accuracy of discrimination may be rewarded in some environments and ignored in others.

Based on findings of this kind, serious efforts have been made to construct tests that will be less dependent on the specific culture than the more familiar tests of the

[1] L. L. Thurstone and T. G. Thurstone (1941), p. 47.

Binet type. Among these are the tests constructed by Cattell (1949), called a "culture-free" test, and by Davis and Eells (1953), called a "culture-fair" test. Both attempt to provide tests that will not penalize the child from a lower-class home.

Consider the following question:

Pick out ONE WORD that does not belong with the others

cello   harp   drum   violin   guitar

This question was used by Eells and others (1951, p. 306) to illustrate how experience can bias vocabulary. Eighty-five percent of children from homes of high socioeconomic status underlined "drum," the correct answer, while only 45 percent of the children from homes of low socioeconomic status answered correctly. The low-status children most commonly made the mistake of answering "cello," the word on the list least likely to be familiar to them and hence likely to be the word that they think does not belong. Children in homes of high socioeconomic status are more likely to be acquainted with cellos or at least more likely to have heard the word than children from poorer homes.

There were, however, many other questions in this study showing class differences for which the effects of differing experience would be hard to demonstrate. For example, the following question was also answered correctly more often by those from higher than by those from homes of lower socioeconomic status:

Find the THREE THINGS which are alike in each list

store banana basket apple seed plum

This question (Eells and others, 1951, p. 316) requires noting that banana, apple, and plum are fruits and that store, basket, and seed are nonfruits. It is hard to believe that nine- and 10-year-old children, even from underprivileged homes, would be unacquainted with the six words or would lack acquaintance with the fruits. Such an item may be "culture-fair," even though it shows class differences in its answer; the classes may actually differ in intelligence as measured by items that are "fair."

While high hopes were expressed for such tests by those who developed them, the subsequent results have not been very encouraging. In some cases class differences in scores have been reduced, but for the most part the class differences found with these tests are very similar to the differences found with the more usual tests (Coleman and Ward, 1955; Hess, 1955; Marquart and Bailey, 1955; Knief and Stroud, 1959). Moreover, as predictors of scholastic achievement the newer tests are inferior to the more conventional ones, perhaps because of a middle-class bias in the schools. Hence, with all their difficulties, the ordinary Binet-type tests serve their predictive purposes as well or better than these substitute tests.

Item testing

How did Binet know that he had hit upon a good item? He and those who have come after him developed ways of testing the individual items to be sure that they serve their intended purposes. It is not enough to look at an item and to decide that it requires intelligence to reply successfully to it. Some "tricky" or "clever" items, which seem to put the test taker on his mettle, turn out to be poor because of chance successes or failures. Somewhat "pedestrian" items, such as matters of common information, sometimes turn out to be most useful. These are items that are "fair," because all have had a chance to learn the answers.

How can the assertion be made with assurance that one item is better than another? One method of testing an item is to study the *changes in proportions of children answering it correctly at different ages.* Unless older children are more successful than younger ones in answering the item, the item is unsatisfactory in a test based on the concept of mental growth. The curves in Figures 16–3A and 16–3B show increases in the percentage of children passing some representative items at different ages. These data were obtained in a later revision of a Binet-type scale.

A second method of testing an item is to find out whether or not the results for it *correspond to the results on the test as a whole.* This can be done by correlating success and failure on the item with the score

16–3

Intelligence-test items: percent passing should increase with age

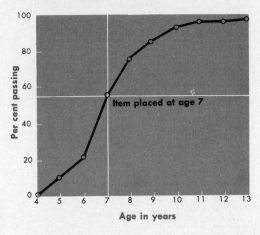

A. This item, Opposite Analogies 1, comes from the Revised Stanford-Binet. At age seven just over half the subjects are successful. The question is of the form: "Brother is a boy; sister is a _____." (After Mc-Nemar, 1942)

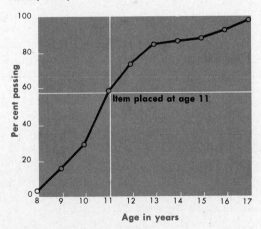

B. Placed at age 11 on the scale, this item is more difficult than the one shown in A. The item is Abstract Words 1. The question asked is: "What do we mean by _____?" (After McNemar, 1942)

made on the remaining items. If all items measure something in common, then every single item ought to contribute a score that correlates with the total score. The two items charted in Figure 16–3 met the first test of increase in percentage passing with age. They also met the second test of correlating with the total score. The correlation between the Opposite Analogies item (16–3A) and the total score at age 7 was $r = .65$; that for the Abstract Words item (16–3B) and the total score at age 11 was $r = .89$.

These two requirements for an acceptable item (increase in percentage passing with age and correlation with total score) reflect both validity and reliability. The first of these requirements is an indirect way of guaranteeing validity (based on the inference that what we mean by intelligence should distinguish an older child from a younger one), while the second requirement is a guarantee of reliability through internal consistency of the measures.

By choosing items that meet these requirements and by arranging them in a convenient form for the person giving the test, a self-consistent and useful test of intelligence results.

The definition of intelligence

The definition of intelligence has been postponed until we learned how intelligence tests were made. Now that the processes and purposes of making the tests have been explained, we can give the following practical definition of intelligence: *Intelligence is that which an intelligence test measures.* Although the statement sounds empty, it is not, for it takes in all the careful steps that have gone into the construction of the tests. All the tests constructed by different workers distinguish the dull from the bright and lead to scores with high intercorrelations; therefore they are measuring something in common. What they measure in common defines intelligence.

Of course, the testers had something in mind as they constructed the tests. Suppose that the tests did not exist. What kind of definition of intelligence could we give someone to furnish specification for the test he should construct? Although Binet did not give a formal definition of intelligence, he made many detailed studies of the processes that appeared to distinguish between the bright and the dull. He emphasized the active nature of intelligence: making attempts, groping one's way, choos-

ing between alternatives. Three characteristics of the thought processes impressed him: (1) the tendency to take and maintain a direction, without becoming distracted or sidetracked; (2) the capacity to adapt means to ends; (3) the capacity for self-criticism, dissatisfaction with a partial solution that does not really solve the problem. We imply such a definition when we say that intelligence is what an intelligence test measures.

Contemporary Binet tests

The tests originally developed by Alfred Binet underwent several revisions in this country, the first by Goddard in 1911. For many years the best-known and most widely used revision was that made by Terman at Stanford University in 1916, commonly referred to as the Stanford-Binet. The test was later revised by Terman and Merrill in 1937 and again in 1960.

An item is age-graded at the level at which a substantial majority of the children pass it, as we saw in connection with the items of Figure 16–3. In the present Stanford-Binet there are usually six tests of varied content assigned to each year, each test when passed earning a score of two months of mental age.

The procedure for testing is first to establish the *basal mental age,* the mental-age level at which (and below which) all tests are passed. Two months of mental age are then added for each test passed at higher ages. Consider, for example, the child who passes all tests at the mental-age level of six years. If he then passes two tests at the seven-year level, four months are added to his mental age; if he passes an additional test at the eight-year level, two more months are added. The earned mental age for this particular child will be six years and six months, whatever his chronological age. The test allows for some unevenness in development, so that two children can earn the same mental age by passing different items on the test.

The intelligence quotient (I.Q.)

Terman adopted a convenient index of brightness that was suggested by the German psychologist William Stern (1871–1938). This index is the *intelligence quotient,* commonly known by its initials I.Q. It expresses intelligence as a ratio of the mental age to the chronological age:

$$I.Q. = 100 \frac{\text{Mental age (M.A.)}}{\text{Chronological age (C.A.)}}$$

The 100 is used as a multiplier to remove the decimal point and to make the average I.Q. (when M.A. = C.A.) have a value of 100. It is evident that if the M.A. lags behind the C.A., the resulting I.Q. will be less than 100; if the M.A. is above the C.A., the I.Q. will be above 100. Thus the brightness scale has about the same meaning from one age to another.

How is an I.Q. to be interpreted? The distribution of I.Q.'s follows the normal curve rather closely (Figure 16–4). For the group upon which the Stanford-Binet was standardized (after adjustment for sampling), the I.Q. had a mean of 100 and a standard deviation (σ) of 16. From our knowledge of the normal distribution, we know that we may expect about 68 percent of the I.Q.'s to fall between 100 ± 16, or between 84 and 116, and 95 percent between 68 and 132. The adjectives com-

16–4

A normal distribution curve of I.Q.'s

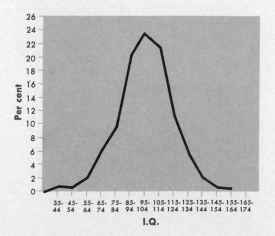

Distribution of I.Q.'s for 2904 children and youths, ages two to 18. This is the group upon which the Revised Stanford-Binet was standardized. (After Terman and Merrill, 1937)

TABLE 16–3

Interpretation of intelligence quotients on the Stanford-Binet

I.Q.	Verbal description	Percent falling in each group (among 2904 subjects, ages 2 to 18)
140 and above	Very superior	1
120-139	Superior	11
110-119	High average	18
90-109	Average	46
80-89	Low average	15
70-79	Borderline	6
Below 70	Mentally retarded or defective	3
		100

SOURCE: Merrill (1938).

monly used to describe the various I.Q. levels are given in Table 16–3, along with a frequency distribution of I.Q.'s for those tested in the standardization of the 1937 revision of the Stanford-Binet.

It is well also to have some reference points by which to judge the general level of competence of children and adults with various I.Q.'s. Persons with low I.Q.'s can succeed at many socially useful tasks. Some typical levels of competence represented by I.Q.'s of various levels are given in Table 16–4.

In their 1960 revision of the earlier Stanford-Binet the authors introduced a method of computing the I.Q. from tables. The meaning of an I.Q. remains essentially the same as before, but the tables permit some corrections so that at any age the I.Q. can be interpreted somewhat more exactly. It is now arranged so that for each age the I.Q. averages 100 and has a standard deviation of 16. The I.Q. is thus a kind of *standard score* (see p. 404), with a fixed mean and standard deviation. This kind of I.Q. is known as a *deviation* I.Q., and was earlier used in the Wechsler Adult Intelligence Scale, to be considered presently.

TABLE 16–4

Interpretation of intelligence quotients according to levels of social competence

I.Q.	Competence represented
130	Mean of persons receiving Ph.D.
120	Mean of college graduates
115	Mean of freshmen in typical four-year college
	Mean of children from white-collar and skilled-labor homes
110	Mean of high-school graduates
	Has 50-50 chance of graduating from college
105	About 50-50 chance of passing in academic high school curriculum
100	Average for total population
90	Mean of children from low-income city homes or rural homes
	Adult can perform jobs requiring some judgment (operate sewing machine, assemble parts)
75	About 50-50 chance of reaching high school
	Adult can keep small store, perform in orchestra
60	Adult can repair furniture, harvest vegetables, assist electrician
50	Adult can do simple carpentry, domestic work
40	Adult can mow lawns, do simple laundry

Summarized by Cronbach (1960), p. 174, from various sources.

The Stanford-Binet tables run only through age 18, and the test is no longer recommended for use with adults.

Diagnostic Tests of Intelligence

Tests following the pattern originated by Binet use a great assortment of items to test intelligence, and a pass or a fail on one kind of item is scored the same as a pass or a fail on another item. But those who are skilled in the use and scoring of the tests learn much more from them than appears in the final I.Q. They may note special strengths and weaknesses; tests of vocabulary, for example, may be passed at a higher level than tests of manipulating form boards. These observations lead to the conjecture that what is being measured is not one simple ability but a composite of abilities.

Tests with more than one scale

One way to obtain information on specific kinds of abilities, rather than a single mental-age score, is to separate the items into more than one group and to score the groups separately. The Wechsler Adult Intelligence Scale and the Wechsler Intelligence Scale for Children are composed of items similar to those in the familiar Binet tests, but the total test is divided into two parts according to the content of the items, and two scales result—a *verbal scale* and a *performance* scale. A *performance* item is one that requires manipulation or arrangement of blocks, beads, pictures, or other materials in which both stimuli and responses are nonverbal. Both verbal and performance items also appear in Binet tests, but the separate scaling of the items within one test is a convenience for diagnostic purposes. The tests comprising the two scales are listed in Table 16–5.

The names of the tests in most cases suggest their content, though some of them require a word of explanation. The *digit span* test calls for reciting back to the tester a series of numerical digits that he repeats aloud, such as 7–5–8–3–6, first in a forward direction, and then other series in a backward direction. The score de-

TABLE 16–5

Tests comprising the Wechsler Adult Intelligence Scale and the Wechsler Intelligence Scale for Children

Verbal	Performance
Information	Digit symbol*
Comprehension	Picture completion
Arithmetic	Block design
Similarities	Picture arrangement
Digit span†	Object assembly
Vocabulary	Coding‡
	Mazes§

SOURCE: Wechsler (1949, 1958).

* Adult scale only.

† Adult scale; alternate test for children.

‡ Scale for children only.

§ Alternate test for children.

An intelligence test requiring nonverbal performance

Harbrace Photo

An item in the Wechsler object assembly test.

pends upon the length of the series that the subject gets correct. The *digit symbol* test requires following a sample in which marks of various shapes appear in squares under other squares containing numerals. The subject then fills in blank squares below other numerals according to the code provided. The *object assembly* test calls for putting together parts to complete a figure such as a manikin, human profile, hand, or elephant (Figure 16–5).

In general, the full scale (verbal and performance) and the verbal scale of the Wechsler Scale yield scores most nearly corresponding to those of the Stanford-Binet. In one study of 52 young adults (Wechsler, 1955), the following correlations were obtained between scores on the Stanford-Binet and the Wechsler Adult Intelligence Scale: with the full scale, .85; with the verbal scale, .86; with the performance scale, .69.

Tests based upon factor analysis

Statistical methods have been devised that give much more precise information about the component parts of intelligence. These methods, known collectively as *factor analysis,* make it possible to construct tests that detect patterns of underlying abilities. Factor analysis as a tool of test

construction is still in a developmental stage, even though the first steps were taken as early as 1904 (by Charles Spearman), before Binet's test appeared. The method of multiple factor analysis developed by L. L. Thurstone (1947), although but one of several similar methods, was until recently the one most widely used, and our discussion will be based upon it.

As an illustration of tests constructed with the aid of factor analysis, let us consider a battery of intelligence tests developed by Thurstone. This battery is known as tests for Primary Mental Abilities (L. L. Thurstone, 1938). Thurstone set himself to find a few clusters of abilities that made up the composite tested by familiar intelligence tests. In other words, he wished to find some reliable method of grouping items that earlier item-sorting had grouped crudely.

Thurstone's method is to give a large number of tests to the same children. As many as 60 tests can be used (L. L. Thurstone and T. G. Thurstone, 1941). Each single test is composed of items very much alike, so that the test content is easily described. One test is for verbal comprehension, another for arithmetical computations, etc. The scores of all the tests are intercorrelated. Obviously those tests whose scores show high correlations with one another have much in common; those tests whose scores yield low correlations with one another have little in common. The method of factor analysis is merely a systematic way of finding what few common factors may account for the many obtained correlations.

The factors discovered are purely mathematical, explaining in mathematical terms what the test correlations show. But the presumption is that the factors represent some underlying "traits" or "unitary abilities" that produce the test results. Thus the name assigned a factor is really an educated guess as to the kind of trait that would reasonably yield the scores obtained.

The result of a number of studies of this kind led Thurstone to identify seven factors as the *primary abilities* revealed by the items on intelligence tests. These seven are:

1. Verbal comprehension (V). Vocabulary tests represent this factor.
2. Word fluency (W). This factor calls for the ability to think of words rapidly, as in solving anagrams or in thinking of words that rhyme.
3. Number (N). Simple arithmetic tests, especially those calling for computations, represent this factor.
4. Space (S). Tests of this factor deal with visual form relationships, as in drawing a design from memory.
5. Memory (M). This ability is found in tests requiring that pairs of items be recalled.
6. Perception (P). This factor calls for the grasping of visual details and of the similarities and differences between pictured objects. (Tests for P are omitted from some forms of the Primary Mental Abilities batteries.)
7. Reasoning (R). Tests for this ability call for finding a general rule on the basis of presented instances, as in finding how a number series is constructed from a portion of that series.

Once the several factors have been identified, it is possible to construct tests that are truly diagnostic for each factor, so that a test profile for the individual will indicate how well he performs on tests that demand each of the several abilities.

The practical question remains whether or not primary abilities tests are more efficient predictive instruments than the earlier general intelligence tests. At present, both are equally successful. But the possibility of gaining more fundamental information on patterns of ability through tests of known structure is so great that tests constructed with the aid of factor analysis will undoubtedly become more and more widely used.

The factors comprising intelligence

Thurstone's method and his results gave hope that there might indeed be a small number of *primary abilities* discovered by factor analysis, so that we could satisfactorily break intelligence down into its fundamental elements. This hope has not been realized, for two reasons: the so-called primary abilities turn out not to be independent, and the number of factors can be multiplied by an appropriate choice of items out of which to construct the tests.

The tendency to multiply factors rather than to reduce their number is represented in the work of Guilford. In a model of intellectual ability that he has been developing over a number of years, he proposes the domain of intelligence as shown graphically in Figure 16–6. The three edges of the cube illustrate five kinds of operations, six kinds of products, and four kinds of contents, resulting in $5 \times 6 \times 4 = 120$ "cells" defining specific intellectual factors. This is a conceptual scheme, but Guilford and his associates have carried on a vast amount of empirical work in designing tests which, through factor analysis, can be shown to fit the specifications for many of the 120 predicted factors. In 1966, some 82 were known (Guilford and Hoepfner, 1966). It should be noted that Guilford's definition of intelligence is much broader than that implied in Binet-type tests.

It does not appear now that there will be agreement on the number and nature of primary abilities as a result of factor analysis, but this does not mean that factor analysis has been useless. It is a technical aid in the purification of tests, making known their factor structure. Also it permits us to obtain answers to a number of interesting questions about ability, such as the change in ability patterns with increasing age. Advances in methods of factor analysis, which take advantage of modern high-speed computers, may change some of the present conclusions about the nature of intelligence.

Adult Intelligence

In the late teens intelligence as measured by tests grows so slowly that good mental-age scales can no longer be constructed. That is, it is difficult to find tests that 18-year-olds will consistently pass and 17-year-olds will fail. Without such tests we cannot continue our mental-age scale; hence, for adults, I.Q. has to be determined on some basis other than a ratio between mental age and chronological age. Some method is desirable for producing an I.Q. score for adults that can be interpreted similarly to the familiar I.Q. The simplest method is to adopt a mean of 100 and a standard deviation corresponding to that of I.Q.'s obtained in the earlier years. This is just what has been done in the Wechsler Adult Intelligence Scale.[2] The average score for any one adult age is interpreted as an I.Q. of 100, regardless of any change that may be taking place with age. Then the I.Q. is computed on the basis of the obtained standard deviation of scores near this mean value, one standard deviation being interpreted as 15 I.Q. points.

Changes during adult years

Although it is desirable for comparative purposes to assign a mean of 100 to the I.Q. at all ages, there is, in fact, some decline over the years in intelligence as measured by the ordinary tests. By using the mean scores for the years 25–34 as a reference point and scoring subjects at other ages as though they were from the same age population, the curves of Figure 16–7 result. The peak of verbal intelligence comes in the 25–34 age range and falls off slowly, while the peak for performance scores comes a little earlier, and the performance scores fall off more rapidly with age. The greater handicap of older people on the performance tests may be a result of the emphasis on speed of performance in those tests.

[2] This "deviation I.Q." was adopted for children in the 1960 Revised Stanford-Binet. Note, however, that the Wechsler test uses a standard deviation of 15 instead of the 16 used in the Stanford-Binet.

16–6

Cubical model of the structure of intellect

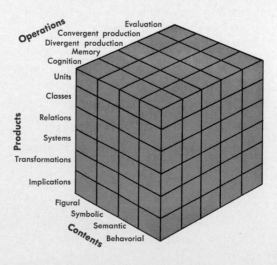

Each of the small cubes in the solid represents a primary ability to be specified by factor analysis. (Guilford, 1961)

Decline of adult intelligence over the years

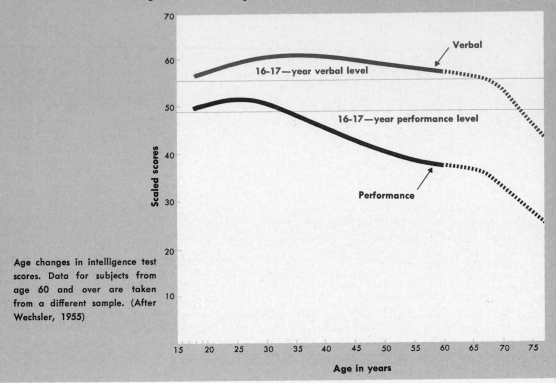

Age changes in intelligence test scores. Data for subjects from age 60 and over are taken from a different sample. (After Wechsler, 1955)

The differences in rate of decline of the actual verbal and performance scores with age correspond to the findings of others and indicate that not all adult abilities decline at the same rate. In general, items related to *information* hold up best, while those having to do with *cleverness* and *speed* show the greatest decline (Jones and Conrad, 1933; Vernon, 1961). Thus some arbitrariness enters into using any one score as an index of the intelligence of an adult.

The decline of measured intelligence in one's fourth decade does not signify that the mature adult is less competent to play his role in life. He may be accumulating new experiences less rapidly than he once did, but he has not forgotten all that he has accumulated in the past. If we think of *wisdom* as an accumulation from past experience and of intelligence as the ability to apply that experience to problems in the present, we may see how an older person may be more competent than a brighter younger person who lacks his experience. Intelligence tests weight heavily items demanding cleverness, alertness, and adaptability to novel situations. They do not weight as strongly the background of experience which permits the older person to meet wisely the familiar situations in his own life and work.

The Extremes of Intelligence

The mentally subnormal

Intelligence tests were developed, first of all, to discover those children least likely to profit from ordinary schooling. There is no sharp break between the subnormal and the normal, and many borderline cases exist. Furthermore, when a child is classified as retarded, the classification tells us very little about him. There are many kinds and degrees of retarded children; because they are not alike, calling them by a common name such as "feeble-minded" is misleading.

CRITICAL DISCUSSION
Some rejected labels for the subnormal

The mentally subnormal child suffers a number of handicaps, but he is able to overcome many of them and live a useful and satisfying life. One of the most difficult handicaps to overcome is the stigma of being classified as subnormal. The terms that society uses sooner or later become terms with negative connotations. Such terms as "half-wit" and "simpleton," familiar to an earlier generation, became replaced by the then less offensive term "feeble-minded," but this has since come to have unfavorable connotations. The classification of the retarded into a high group (moron), intermediate group (imbecile), and low group (idiot) has also outlived its usefulness, as the adjectives "moronic," "imbecilic," and "idiotic" have become terms of reproach.

The more modern approach recognizes that there are mentally subnormal children with a variety of handicaps, and general terms of classification are avoided. Descriptive expressions such as more severely defective, less severely retarded, trainable, or educable have come into use to avoid the stigma of harsh labels. One main distinction, supported by the World Health Organization and encouraged by the National Association for Retarded Children, has been made between the individual who is organically damaged, classified as "mentally defective," and the individual whose problems lie in a learning disability, classified as "mentally retarded" (Masland, Sarason, and Gladwin, 1958). This distinction will be observed in what follows.

The prevalence of subnormality. The classification of a child as mentally subnormal or retarded depends primarily upon social competence, and a child can be classified by what he can do without re-

course to an intelligence test. Any classification runs into difficulty with borderline cases. The distinction between dull normal and subnormal depends on an interpretation of "marginal social success under favorable conditions." The farm hand who was unable to finish school but lives his own life as a hired man on the farm, is economically independent and is normal in his environment, even though he may be recognizably dull; the same man might find difficulty in living successfully in the city. The distinction between the dull normal and the subnormal depends upon the complexity of the social conditions under which independence must be maintained. By social criteria, an individual might change his classification by moving from one place to another, even though his tested intelligence does not change.

The importance of social demands in determining retardation is well illustrated by the detection of retardation as related to age. Surveys of the number of retarded children at each age show that the highest percentage of retardation is found between the ages of 10 and 14, when the competitive demands of academic performance become emphasized in judging retardation (Figure 16–8). There is no other good explanation of this kind of change in the proportion of retarded individuals with age.

Examination of the distribution curve of I.Q.'s (Figure 16–4, p. 425) shows that the slope is very steep in the region of 70 to 80, where the boarderline cases tend to fall. Hence any change in the criterion of subnormality will readily produce a change in the proportion of individuals estimated to be retarded.

Because of these uncertainties, it is hard to make an accurate assessment of the prevalence of mental subnormality. It is usually asserted that about 1 or 2 percent of the population can be classified as subnormal, but as indicated in Table 16–6, the potentially retarded may constitute as much as 3 percent of the population. Because of favorable circumstances, many of these "potentially retarded" are not recognized as retarded; on the other hand, some

16–8

Incidence of mental retardation

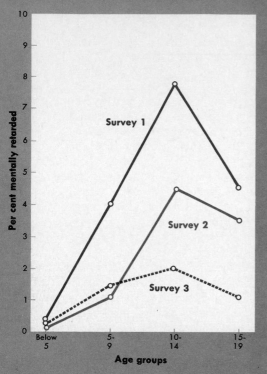

Three different surveys disagree on the total incidence, but agree in finding a larger proportion of children classified as retarded when in the 10- to 14-year-old bracket. (After Masland, Sarason, and Gladwin, 1958)

individuals with higher intellectual potential, through unfavorable aspects of health or experience, may become classified as subnormal. It is easier to count the more

TABLE 16–6

Estimated prevalence of retardation in the total population

Potentially retarded, but educable (ultimate M.A. under 12)	3.0 percent
Moderately severe retardation, trainable (ultimate M.A. from 4 to 7)	0.3 percent
Most severely retarded, helpless (ultimate M.A. under 4)	0.1 percent

SOURCE: Masland, Sarason, and Gladwin (1958), p. 3.

severely retarded because a large fraction of them are found in institutions.

Causes of subnormality. As already indicated, a useful distinction is now made between the individual who is *mentally retarded* and the one who is *mentally defective.* A child is classified as belonging to the *mentally retarded* group if he is essentially sound physically and if there is no history of disease or injury that might have caused intellectual impairment. He suffers from a general deficiency rather than an identifiable specific defect. With such a child there is often a history of retardation in the family, so that the possibility of inherited mental weakness is not ruled out. A child is classified as belonging to the *mentally defective* group if his mental impairment is due to brain injury, disease, or accidents of development that preclude normal intellectual growth. The causes may occur during fetal life, childhood, or even adult life. Such individuals crop up in any family or socio-economic group, regardless of any family history of retardation.

The brain-injured child shows kinds of intellectual impairment that differ from those of the merely retarded child. Among the differences that show up on tests is defective perception of pictures with confusion between figure and background. When presented with pictures like that of Figure 16–9, the brain-injured but not the retarded child has difficulty in picking out the figure from the background.

Now and then we come upon a child who is apparently subnormal but actually is not. He reacts emotionally to his environment by withdrawal and negativism, so that his learning of language is delayed and his test performances are poor. Only a skilled test administrator can discover that the test score is misleading. Such a child can be aided by psychotherapy.

Treatment of the subnormal. From time to time there appear dramatic reports of remarkable achievements in raising the I.Q. scores of subnormal children. Headlines in newspapers and articles in magazines raise hopes of countless parents who have retarded children. This publicity is unfortunately misleading because the overall evidence we have today is not encouraging. It gives little promise of dramatic improvement in the mentally subnormal, although this does not mean that the retarded or defective child cannot be helped. There is a difference between doing all that one can to provide a favorable opportunity for the backward child to develop and giving optimistic promises of change that are unlikely to be fulfilled.

A great deal can be done for the backward child. He can be taught social habits; he can learn vocational skills appropriate to his intellectual level; in some instances he may learn to take his place in the community outside an institution. Social aid for the mentally defective must not be confused, however, with raising the I.Q. In many subnormal individuals a small increase in I.Q. comes with better social adjustment, but there is little reason to expect striking changes as a result of bettered environment (Kirk, 1958).

Many persons of low intelligence get along satisfactorily in the community. Several follow-up studies have been made of children whose I.Q.'s during school age rated them as mentally retarded. The investigators all found a substantial proportion of these individuals maintaining themselves vocationally in the community when they became adults.

16–9

Distinguishing the mentally defective

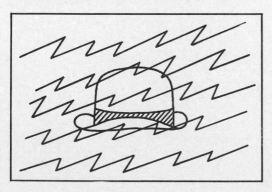

This figure-ground problem is difficult for brain-injured but not for retarded children. (After Werner and Strauss, 1941)

The mentally gifted

At the other end of the scale from the mentally retarded lie those who are intellectually gifted. With the development of intelligence tests it has become possible to select for study large groups of superior children and then to follow their careers. One of the best-known of these studies, started in September, 1921, by Terman and his associates, covers more than 1500 gifted children from their early school years through the middle years of adult life. Although the study continues, the latest report appeared in 1959 (Terman and Oden, 1959).

The group was chosen on the basis of I.Q.'s of 140 or above. About 10 or 11 out of every 1000 children in the public schools have I.Q.'s that high. Less than 1 out of every 1000 has an I.Q. above 160.

What do Terman's findings reveal about the gifted child? So far as parental backgrounds were concerned, the children came mostly from homes of professional people (about one-third of the group) and of those in higher business classes (about one-half). Less than 7 percent came from semiskilled or unskilled laboring classes, despite the fact that these classes constitute a higher proportion of the population. The home environment probably contributed to the gifted children by way of both heredity and environment. The brighter parents are found for the most part in superior occupational groups, and they provide more stimulating environments for their children.

Terman's gifted children were better than average physical specimens. They averaged more than an inch taller than others of the same age in elementary school. Their birth weights were above normal. They talked early and walked early. When the tests started, seven out of eight were in grades ahead of their age group in school; none was retarded. They were unusual in the kind and number of books they read, but reading did not interfere with their superiority in leadership and social adaptability.

These characteristics of the gifted children gave the lie to the notion that the very bright child is a weakling and a social misfit. The evidence is all to the contrary. Superior intelligence turned out to be associated with good health, social adaptability, and leadership.

Gifted children as young adults. The extent to which early promise was fulfilled by the gifted children of Terman's group can be estimated from their performances in early adult life. While the group on the whole gave a superior account of itself, it should be noted, first of all, that not all the subjects had a history of success. Some failed in college, some were vocational misfits, some ran afoul of the law. But the less successful differed little in their adult intelligence test scores from the more successful. The comparative scores are given in Table 16–7. The average I.Q. difference between the most and least successful is only six points. The slight difference in intellectual level as measured cannot account for the differences in achievement. We must therefore conclude that nonintellectual qualities are very important in success.

What does "successful" and "unsuccessful" mean in these comparisons? The subjects whose test scores are reported in Table 16–7 were all men from the gifted group selected many years earlier on the basis of a childhood I.Q. of 140 or higher. These were classified into three success groups: *A*, the most successful; *B*, the in-termediately successful; and *C*, the least successful. The criterion of success was primarily "the extent to which a subject made use of his intellectual ability." Listing in *Who's Who in America* or *American Men of Science*, representation in literary or scholarly publications, responsible managerial positions, outstanding achievement in any intellectual or professional calling— all entered into the judgments. Earned income was taken into account but was given relatively little weight in grouping the subjects.

The *A* and *C* groups differed significantly on many of the 200 items in the case histories, trait ratings, and test records. Among the most important of these were social and mental adjustment, family background, and ratings previously made on three traits: perseverance, self-confidence, and integration toward goals. In other words, the *A*'s differ from the *C*'s most of all in general adjustment and in motivation to achieve. These are personality and motivational traits rather than intellectual ones. The *A* and *C* groups began to diverge educationally in high school. Fewer of the *C* group went to college; of those who did, 31 percent averaged grades of *C* or lower, compared with but 7 percent of the *A* group.

To illustrate the extreme contrasts sometimes found between the most and least successful, the authors have summarized

---

TABLE 16–7

Adult intelligence of most successful and least successful men among a group with high I.Q.'s as children

Group	N	Mean score on concept mastery test	Estimated equivalent I.Q. as adults
A Most success as adults	79	112	139
B Intermediate success	322	99	134
C Least success as adults	116	94	133

SOURCE: Terman and Oden (1947), pp. 132, 144, 323.

briefly the achievement records of two of the men to 1950.

A SUCCESSFUL SUBJECT

Subject A792 graduated from high school at 16, from college at 20, with Phi Beta Kappa honors, and received his Ph.D. in science at 23. In his undergraduate college years he earned a quarter of his expenses and in his graduate years supported himself entirely. He was then awarded a National Research Fellowship for postdoctorate study, after which he was appointed to a position in a leading university. By the age of 40 he was nationally eminent and director of a great scientific laboratory. He is listed in *American Men of Science* and *Who's Who*.

AN UNSUCCESSFUL SUBJECT

Subject C49 had almost exactly the same I.Q. rating as A792, also had a superior record through high school, and in college earned about the same proportion of his expenses. There the similarity ends, for C graduated from college well below the average of his class. After graduation he drifted for several years, then returned to college and managed to complete his work for a master's degree. His occupations since then have ranged from semiskilled labor and clerical jobs to positions of minor responsibility in business organizations. His chief handicaps have been inferior social adjustment, uncertainty with respect to life goals, and lack of drive or persistence. As a result he has accomplished less than the average college graduate.[3]

Men of the A group who have attained national or near-national eminence are found in a great variety of work, including law, medicine, surgery, pharmacology, physiology, physics, astrophysics, oceanography, engineering, psychology, psychiatry, literature, business management, and government service. Men in the C group are more commonly found in semiprofessional pursuits or in the upper clerical and ordinary business levels. In the 10 years after the A and C ratings were made, the success of a few of the A men was lessened

[3] Private communication, courtesy of the late Lewis M. Terman and Melita H. Oden.

by physical or mental illness, and the success of a few of the C's changed for the better. For the most part, however, the two groups remained about as widely separated as ever.

The latest follow-up (Terman and Oden, 1959) showed that the distinctive abilities of the gifted were becoming more fully recognized as they grew older. The 1955 edition of *American Men of Science* listed 70 men and seven women, while the 1944 edition had listed only 19 of the men and none of the women. Listings in *Who's Who* grew from five in 1946 to 33 in 1958. It takes time to achieve recognition, and this group, picked in childhood, has given a good account of itself.

Our social responsibility to guide and assist those of high ability is no less pressing than our responsibility to provide for those handicapped by low ability. The need for highly trained specialists already comes close to tapping our available talent (David, 1965). If much of this talent is dissipated through poor social and personal adjustment or through inadequate motivation, as the C group in Terman's study suggests, one place to begin developing our supply to better advantage is with promising youth in their early years. We need to do what we can to create the atmosphere in which they will be stimulated to use their creative abilities in socially productive ways.

How Stable Is Measured Intelligence?

If intelligence tests measure some aspects of a person's fundamental and persistent abilities, such tests ought to yield comparable results when they are repeated at different times. It is not essential, however, that the I.Q. should be stable in order for the tests to be of value. For example, if the I.Q. were to change—whether because of seasonal fluctuation, adolescence, or simply training—the usefulness of the intelligence test as an instrument for describing what goes on would not decrease.

Relative stability of the I.Q. during the school years

Although intelligence, as measured by tests, does not begin to settle down until about the third year of school, when language is fairly well developed, there is an appreciable consistency throughout the school years. If a group of children is tested at age five, and the children are then sorted into groups on the basis of their test scores, those with higher mental ages tend to make more rapid growth in intelligence than those with lower mental ages. As a result, *for groups of children* the average intelligence quotient remains fairly constant. The consistency of growth in average scores is shown in Figure 16–10.

The consequence of such consistency is, of course, to produce a positive correlation between test scores at one age and those at another. Many studies have been made of the correlation between successive tests given either in immediate succession or spaced at intervals of a year or more. There is a trend toward lower correlations as the time between tests becomes greater—a trend one would naturally expect (Table 16–8).

Individual changes during the school years

The fact that repeated tests yield positive correlations can easily be misinterpreted to mean that IQ's are more constant than they

16–10

Consistency of mental age differences

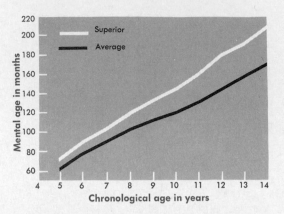

Two groups of boys were selected at age five, one scoring high, one average. The superior group gained in mental age more rapidly than the average one, thus approximating a constant I.Q. difference between the groups as they grew older. (Baldwin and Stecher, 1922)

really are. For some individuals there are very striking changes. In one study, when many repeated measures were used, it was found that 62 percent of the 140 children in the study had I.Q. differences of as much as 15 points between two scores at some point in the study. For a few of them the score trends were consistently toward a gradually increasing I.Q. or toward a gradually decreasing one (Sontag, Baker, and Nelson, 1958). The successive scores for two of their cases are plotted in Figure 16–11.

Efforts to relate changes in I.Q. of individual children to events happening in their environment have not proved very satisfactory. However, some relationships have been noted. For example, those children whose I.Q.'s increased during the early years (between ages three and six) were less emotionally dependent upon their parents than those whose I.Q.'s failed to increase. In later years (up to age 10) the changes in I.Q. appeared most closely related to high achievement motivation (see Chapter 6, p. 153). Of course, from these relationships alone it is not possible to infer whether the rising intelligence

TABLE 16–8				
Inter-age Stanford-Binet correlations *				
Age	4	6	8	10	12
3	.83	.73	.60	.54	.46
5		.87	.79	.70	.62
7			.91	.82	.73
9				.90	.81
11					.90

SOURCE: Sontag, Baker, and Nelson (1958), p. 28.
* Table entries give correlations between I.Q.'s obtained for the same individual at different ages. Data based on 50 cases.

Progressively changing I.Q.'s on repeated tests in individual cases

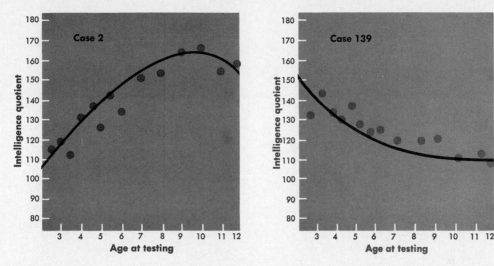

Note that for Case 2 the initial I.Q. was about 115 at age two and a half, but the last five tests were in the range of 150 to 170. The opposite trend was found for Case 139. With early tests in the range of 130 to 150, the final test scores were in the range of 110 to 120. (After Sontag, Baker, and Nelson, 1958)

produced school successes that enhanced achievement motivation, or whether a rise in I.Q. was the result of achievement motivation that was enhanced independently.

Living in city or country

Children from rural areas in America tend to make poorer scores on intelligence tests than children from cities. In the standardization of the Stanford-Binet, for example, farm children within the school ages of six to 18 scored about 10 I.Q. points lower than city children (McNemar, 1942, p. 37). Similar results have been found in Europe by testing children in several large cities and in rural areas (Klineberg, 1931).

We have two main theories to explain the differences in scores obtained in farm and city. One is *selective migration*. People who are attracted to the cities may represent a disproportionate number of those who score high on intelligence tests. They may go to cities because they have the kinds of numerical and verbal abilities that are of special value in cities. The second conjecture is that city life provides *environ-*

mental stimulation in educational and other opportunities. There is evidence to support each of these conjectures. The migration hypothesis is supported by evidence that in more remote rural areas, where the pull of the city is less directly felt, intelligence scores remain high (Thomson, 1921; Jones, Conrad, and Blanchard, 1932). If the tests favored city dwellers, such isolated people would seem to be at unusual disadvantage, but they are not. The stimulation hypothesis is supported by the well-known poverty of rural schools in many parts of America. In Scotland, where rural teachers are as well trained as city ones, the differences are not found.

A more conclusive test of the stimulating effects of life in the city is to ask the question directly: What happens to intelligence when a child moves from a less favored to a more favored environment?

Negro children born in Philadelphia took repeated intelligence tests at intervals of a year or more. The mean I.Q. did not change significantly between Grade 1A and 9A for 424 children who took the tests

Increase in mean I.Q. with years in a large city

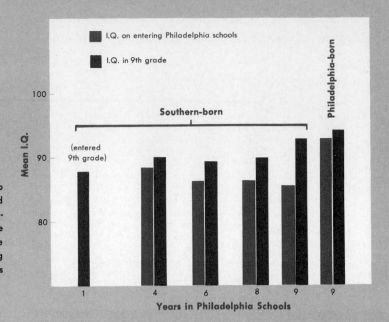

The mean scores are for Negro children born in Philadelphia and Southern-born Negro children reaching the Philadelphia schools at the grades indicated. Scores at the time of initial testing shortly after coming to the city are compared with scores at Grade 9A. (After Lee, 1951)

each time. Identical tests were given each year to Negro children who had moved to Philadelphia from the South. When they first entered school, these children averaged lower than the Philadelphia-born children, regardless of the year at which they entered. The number entering at each level studied varied from 109 to 219, providing an adequate sample for statistical treatment. Between entrance time and Grade 9A their intelligence tended to rise, and, in general, the improvement in their mean scores at Grade 9A corresponded with the number of years they had lived in Philadelphia, as shown in Figure 16–12 (Lee, 1951).

While the data are clear, we again face a problem of interpretation. The effects can hardly be attributed to schooling, for the Philadelphia-born were superior to the Southern-born even in the first grade.[4] Also, the local-born did not improve materially during their years in the Philadelphia schools. Apparently the ultimate level of intelligence was affected by the general

increase in environmental stimulation that came with the move to the large city.

Studies concerned with the results of repeated testing, I.Q. scores as related to schooling, and the influence of moving from rural to urban areas all show that there is nothing automatically constant about the I.Q. Such constancy as we find can be attributed to hereditary aspects (as we shall see in the next chapter) as well as to the fact that, in general, there is a uniformity of environment for the particular child in his home and community. When there are major changes in the environment, changes in the I.Q. also tend to be found, but some of these changes are not correlated with known aspects of environmental stimulation.

Present Status of Ability Tests

Among the various tests of ability, we have chosen to consider in greatest detail the intelligence test. Despite their limitations, intelligence tests provide what is perhaps the most useful quantitative tool that psychology has developed. The usefulness of such tests will continue, provided they are

[4] Those Philadelphia-born who had been to kindergarten had been eliminated in the tabulations from which Figure 16–12 was constructed.

kept in perspective and neither overvalued as telling more about a person than they actually measure nor undervalued because of their obvious defects. In what follows we shall try to view them in the perspective of other ability measures, and in relation to the social consequences of their use.

The blurred distinction between aptitude tests and achievement tests

We pointed out earlier that aptitudes have to be assessed on the basis of prior achievements. It is a mistake to assign aptitude to innate potential and achievement entirely to training; both are complex results of innate potential, generalized experience with the environment, and specific training. We shall deal in greater detail with the heredity-environment problem in the next chapter, but it is worth noting that the actual tests are always a result of heredity-environment interactions. Thus a scholastic aptitude test (the preferred name for an intelligence-type test that predicts school or college grades) has in it a lot of learned material, although it does not demand that the student have taken a particular course in mathematics or foreign language; an achievement test in a particular subject does presuppose special acquaintance with a body of material.

A useful illustration of the blurred distinction between the two types of tests is the National Merit Scholarship Qualifying Test (NMSQT), given annually to upwards of 800,000 high school students in the United States (Stalnaker, 1965). While this test is given to all students regardless of the school subjects they have studied, it is still a test of *educational development*, not of aptitude alone, and indicates both the contribution of the student's aptitude and the effectiveness of his schooling. The success of the test in predicting success in college is quite high; in terms of our definition of aptitude testing as designed for prediction, it reveals aptitude for college work, but of course achievement tests and high school grades also predict college work. For example, the first group of 520 Merit Scholarship recipients entered college in 1956. For those on whom records were

available in 1965 (94 percent of the original group), it was found that 96 percent had graduated from college, and advanced degrees had been obtained by more than half of the men and by 40 percent of the women.

For practical purposes of prediction the fact that test content reflects both individual potential and the results of good schooling is immaterial. From the point of view of understanding the nature of intelligence it does matter, however, whether or not good schooling actually raises intellectual potential. We shall face this again in the next chapter.

Public attacks on testing

Early in the 1960s a number of attacks were made upon psychological testing (e.g., Black, 1963; Gross, 1962; Hoffman, 1962). These were based on several objections, such as the invasion of privacy, the secrecy surrounding test scores, the types of talent selected by tests, and the unfairness of the tests to minority groups (Brim, 1965). These are all problems that have to be taken seriously by psychologists and others using tests, and indeed they do take them seriously (Goslin, 1963).

The problem of invasion of privacy is of the same order as a physical examination to qualify for participation in athletics. When the purpose is benign and the tests are used to help the individual to plan his own life and to avoid failure, it is no different, in principle, than advising the child with a heart ailment not to go in for long-distance running.

The secrecy surrounding test scores arose through the fear that parents might overvalue tests that indicated their child to be somewhat handicapped, whereas the psychologist would prefer to have repeated tests and to make all sorts of allowances. This generally good reason for withholding scores has backfired somewhat, however, through making it appear that the test scores are more important than they are. Actually the best that they do is predict school grades, and there is really no more damage in one's knowing that he has a low I.Q. than in getting a poor report card from school. Results of attitude studies show that children who were given their test scores more commonly raised their intelligence estimates than not (Brim, 1965). In other words, there are many indicators to the child, beyond intelligence test scores, that he is brighter or duller than the other children. The National Merit Scholarship Corporation gives full disclosures of its scores, with apparently beneficial results.

As to the types of talent selected by tests, this would indeed be a serious charge if school and college admissions were based on intelligence tests alone. There is a good deal of pressure within the psychological profession itself to place more emphasis on creativity and nonintellectual factors in academic selection (Getzels and Jackson, 1962; Gough, 1965). Psychologists know that the intelligence test is a limited predictor (as the study of gifted persons showed, p. 434), but this does not condemn it as useless.

The fairness of the tests to underprivileged and minority groups is also a complex problem, to which psychologists have devoted considerable study (Deutsch and others, 1964). A point that is overlooked is that ability tests provide objective criteria and, when properly used, may overcome some of the discrimination practiced against minority groups, thus increasing the opportunities of members of minority groups. This follows because the tests measure ability rather than social status. In some recent comparisons of white and Negro adult respondents, controlled for social class, it was found that lower-class Negroes were indeed more favorable to the use of tests in job selection and promotion than the white respondents (Brim, 1965).

The status of intelligence tests and unsolved problems

Intelligence tests are serviceable instruments. The best of these are the individual tests, such as the Stanford-Binet and Wechsler scales, rather than group tests. Because they require trained testers and take a long time to administer they permit supplementary observations to detect whether or not the tests are appropriate, and they furnish information beyond the mere score. Good group tests are convenient and timesaving, but subject to larger errors than individual tests. Tests repeated at intervals tell more than any single test can.

Because intelligence tests appear to stress verbal ability, they tend to handicap children from impoverished environments where the necessary verbal stimulation is not provided. Despite the appearance of performance scales depending less on words than the obviously verbal tests do, most of the performance scales are not free of dependence on verbal abilities, even when they do not require the ability to read.

Further improvement of intelligence tests can be expected, particularly as factor-analytic techniques are refined and as the results of factor analysis are used in the study of such problems as sex differences, age effects, and environmental influences on specific components of intelligence. It is unlikely that all abilities will be found equally influenced by growth or by environmental opportunities. Perhaps more inventiveness needs to be directed toward performance tests in order to eliminate the verbal factor more completely than at present.

SUMMARY 1. Men differ in all sorts of ways, and any one of these differences may affect how well they succeed in their work and in society.

2. The psychologist uses ability testing to study individual differences. *Aptitude tests* attempt to predict the success in some kind of performance not yet attained, as in judging how much an individual will profit by training before training is undertaken. *Achievement tests* measure present attainment, or what the subject has learned after the completion

of training. Both tests can use similar items. The difference between them lies in their purposes.

3. Achievement tests are very widely used. Most educational examinations, whether in elementary school, high school, or college, are of this kind, as are also most civil service examinations.

4. In order to make predictions from tests, tests must meet certain specifications. Studies of *reliability* tell us whether or not the test scores are self-consistent. Studies of *validity* tell us how well the tests measure what they are supposed to measure, how well they predict according to an acceptable criterion.

5. When tests meet the specifications, they can be applied in schools, in industry, in civil service, or in the armed forces. The pilot-selection program of the U.S. Army Air Forces during World War II illustrates the nature of a *test battery* and how the results of tests are used in prediction.

6. The simplest application of the results of studies in prediction is the *critical score,* so set that those who score below this point are disqualified, while those above it are accepted or permitted to continue. A correlation coefficient between the test and some *criterion* can also be used in prediction.

7. Intelligence tests are useful aptitude tests because they measure abilities important in school, in vocational success, and in other aspects of social adjustment.

8. The first successful intelligence tests were developed by Alfred Binet in France in 1905. To him we owe the concept of *mental age,* according to which we regard dull children as slow in their development, their responses being like those of children younger in age. Conversely, bright children are advanced beyond their years. This concept has been followed in later revisions of Binet's scales, the most widely used of which has been the Stanford-Binet. Terman, who was responsible for the Stanford-Binet, introduced the *intelligence quotient* (I.Q.) as an index of mental development, following a suggestion of Stern. The I.Q. is obtained by expressing intelligence as a ratio of mental age (M.A.) to chronological age (C.A.). The *deviation* I.Q. adopted in the most recent Stanford-Binet adjusts the obtained I.Q.'s so that at each chronological age they have a mean of 100 and a standard deviation of 16.

9. Efforts to improve the diagnostic value of intelligence tests have taken two chief forms. One is to divide the items of the test into more than one scale. This attempt is illustrated by the verbal and performance scales of the Wechsler Adult Intelligence Scale and the Wechsler Intelligence Scale for Children. The second method of improving the diagnostic value of intelligence tests is to arrange subtests according to the findings of *factor analysis.* The individual tests can then represent the factors found to determine the test intercorrelations. One such battery, the tests for Primary Mental Abilities developed by Thurstone, is proving to be a promising tool of research and prediction. However, Guilford has shown that there may be many more factors than Thurstone found.

10. By using deviation I.Q.'s, the Wechsler Adult Intelligence Scale makes it possible to use the concept of intelligence quotient with adults, and to interpret such an I.Q. approximately as it is interpreted earlier in life. The I.Q. is assigned an average of 100 for each adult age group, and the standard deviation is set arbitrarily at 15. When intelligence test scores are not adjusted in this way, it is found that verbal intelligence reaches its peak at the age level of 25–34, performance intelligence somewhat earlier. Intelligence test scores decline slowly thereafter, with the performance scores falling off more rapidly than the verbal ones.

11. The extremes of intelligence are represented by the *mentally subnormal* at one end of the scale and the *intellectually gifted* at the other. A final decision that a child is or is not subnormal depends on more than intelligence test scores; for example, with the same score one child may be classed as subnormal, another as normal. The subnormal are further classified as *mentally retarded* or *mentally defective.* Mental retardation is a deficiency present from birth, with no obvious brain damage. Mental defectiveness results from illness, injury, or a physical defect. Subnormal children can learn, and thus many of them can do socially useful work under supervision or even achieve a measure of social independence. The fact that the impairment in intelligence level persists throughout life means only that this condition imposes a special responsibility upon society to make provision for adequate care and training.

12. The mentally gifted as a group show superior attainments throughout childhood and early adult life. Their histories belie the notion that very highly intelligent people are sickly or poorly adjusted. Superior intelligence is of itself no assurance of success; some gifted children are misfits in adult life even though their intelligence scores remain high.

13. For groups of children selected as brighter and less bright by tests at age five, the differences in mental age persist; the relative constancy of the I.Q. is shown by high correlations between successive tests. However, this constancy is only relative, for the correlations tend to fall with greater time between tests, and some children show large changes in I.Q. between tests. Furthermore, there is some evidence for the influence of the stimulation of city life, I.Q.'s tending to rise with years in the city.

14. Public attacks upon testing are based on such objections as the invasion of privacy, the secrecy surrounding test scores, types of talent selected by tests, and unfairness of the tests to minority groups. Psychologists have answers to these criticisms. They recognize that ability testing carries with it social responsibility.

15. The intelligence test, cautiously used, is an important predictive device, although it does give undue weight to verbal ability. Factor analysis may help intelligence tests become more truly diagnostic.

SUGGESTIONS
FOR
FURTHER
READING

For general summaries of the present status of knowledge about individual differences, three useful books are Anastasi and Foley, *Differential psychology* (3rd ed., 1958); Tyler, *The psychology of human differences* (2nd ed., 1956); and Thorndike and Hagen, *Measurement and evaluation in psychology and education* (1961).

The general principles of test construction, problems of reliability and validity, and appropriate use of tests can be found in Cronbach, *Essentials of psychological testing* (2nd ed., 1960). The latest version of the Stanford-Binet is Terman and Merrill, *Stanford-Binet intelligence scale: manual for the third revision* (1960); of the Wechsler Adult Intelligence Scale, Wechsler, *The measurement and appraisal of adult intelligence* (4th ed., 1958).

The problems of subnormality are treated in an extensive review of the literature sponsored by the National Association for Retarded Children: Masland, Sarason, and Gladwin, *Mental subnormality* (1958). See also Robinson and Robinson, *The mentally retarded child* (1965). The last of several volumes on a group selected for high intelligence as children, and studied 35 years later, is Terman and Oden, *The gifted group at mid-life* (1959).

17 Behavior Genetics

Modern genetics, the science of heredity, shows how the physical characteristics of offspring derive from the characteristics of the parents. Behavior genetics is a newer branch of genetics concerned with the inheritance of behavior rather than of physical structure. There is an interesting question here, whether or not anything is added by studying behavior, for surely behavior (if inherited) must depend upon physical structures' and their related physiological and biological processes. That is, if intelligence is inherited, it is because the brighter person inherits a nervous system that is superior to the one inherited by the less bright person. While this sounds logical enough, even inherited structure is not observed directly; what is observed, even in such features as size and coloration, reflects the interaction of heredity and environment. Viewed in this way, a rat's ability to run a maze may be just as useful an indicator of heredity as the weight of its brain. Thus the inheritance of behavior can be studied in its own right, just as the inheritance of physical structure can be studied. Before examining the evidence for the inheritance of behavior, we shall review briefly the major principles of hereditary transmission.

Principles of Genetics

The science of genetics has made enormous strides within the last few years. The following brief introduction provides a background for our study of problems related to the inheritance of behavior.

Phenotypes and genotypes

While heredity in general produces resemblances between parents and offspring, the science of genetics teaches us to search beneath superficial resemblances; in fact, certain *lacks* of resemblance between parents and offspring give us our chief clues to the mechanism of heredity. For example, that the offspring of black guinea pigs are in the proportion of three black to one white illustrates a fundamental principle of heredity; that half the sons of parents who see colors normally may be color-blind illustrates another principle. To understand these illustrations we have to distinguish between the *phenotype*—the individual as he actually is (e.g., the black guinea pig or the parent who sees color normally), and the *genotype*—the individual as a carrier of genetic qualities that may or may not be manifested by him (e.g., a mother who may transmit color blindness to her sons).

Chromosomes and genes

An individual's *genotype* consists of the hereditary units that he has received from his parents and that he will transmit to his offspring. These units are carried by microscopic particles found within each cell of the body, known as *chromosomes*. A chromosome is composed of many individual determiners of heredity called *genes*. Each body cell in man has 46 chromosomes. At conception the human being receives 23 chromosomes from the father's sperm and 23 chromosomes from the mother's ovum. These 46 chromosomes form 23 pairs, which are duplicated in every cell of the body as the individual develops (Figure 17–1). It was thought until recently that man had 24 pairs of chromosomes, but the lower number is now established as typical, although there are some abnormal cases (Tjio and Levan, 1956).

Genes also occur in pairs—one gene of each pair comes from the sperm chromosomes and one gene from the ovum. We have no exact way of counting the genes, for unlike the chromosomes they do not show up under the microscope as separate particles. But we may be sure from what we know of other organisms that the total number of genes in each human chromosome is at least 1000, and perhaps much higher. Because the numbers of genes and chromosomes are so high, it is extremely unlikely that two human beings would have the same heredity, even with the same parents. One exception, however, is identical twins.

An important attribute of the gene is *dominance* or *recessiveness*. If both members of a gene pair are dominant, the individual will show the trait determined by the genes. If one is dominant and the other recessive, he will show the trait of the dominant gene, but he will also carry the recessive gene, which may show up as a trait in his offspring. A recessive trait shows up only if both genes are recessive.

One pair of chromosomes proves to be of particular interest, the pair that is associated with the sex of the individual and with the genes of certain traits that are "sex-linked." A normal female has two X-chromosomes, a normal male one X-chromosome and one Y-chromosome. The female inherits one X-chromosome from the mother, one from the father; the male inherits his X-chromosome from his mother, his Y-chromosome from his father. Because the Y-chromosome is a small and limited chromosome, it acts in heredity as though it carries only recessive genes. The X-chromosome may carry either dominant or re-

17–1

Chromosomes

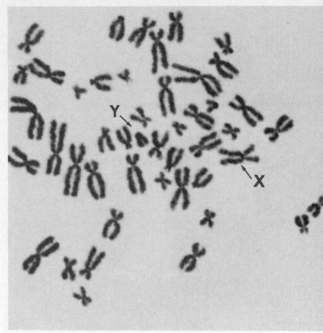

Dr. J. H. Tjio

A photo of all the human chromosomes; based on skin tissue, male (enlarged 1500 times actual size).

cessive genes. Hence a recessive characteristic in the male, such as color blindness, comes about only when the male inherits a recessive color-blindness gene from his mother; females are less often color-blind, because to be so they would have to have both a color-blind father and a mother who was either color-blind or carried a recessive gene for color blindness. Thus the X-chromosomes and Y-chromosomes have helped to unravel some of the puzzling problems of human hereditary traits.

The techniques that led to correcting the number of human chromosomes from 48 to 46 have also made possible other advances in human genetics, particularly the discovery of a chromosomal basis for some puzzling developmental difficulties.

One such condition is a form of mental subnormality known as mongolism. It turns out that the mongoloid individual has an extra small chromosome, probably one of his chromosomes reduplicated (Lejeune, Gautier, and Turpin, 1959).

Some complications within genetic determination

The notion that traits are determined by single gene pairs, the phenotype depending on whether or not one of the pair is dominant, applies only to a few unitary traits. When it does, the so-called *Mendelian ratios* apply, as named for Mendel, the founder of modern genetics. Thus when a pure black guinea pig, with two dominant genes for black (called *homozygous* because both members of the gene pair are alike) is mated with a pure white guinea pig with two recessive genes (also called *homozygous* because both genes are alike), then the offspring will all be black; though they are phenotypically indistinguishable from the black parent, they are genotypically different (called *heterozygous* because one member of the gene pair is dominant, one recessive). Now if two of these heterozygous guinea pigs mate, their offspring will be in the ratio of three black to one white, this three-to-one ratio being the most typical of the Mendelian ratios. One third of the black guinea pigs will be homozygous, the other two thirds heterozygous, and the white of course homozygous. The assumption here is that of complete dominance of the black, so that the heterozygous pigs are not distinguishable from the dominant homozygous ones.

In some cases, however, the heterozygote is intermediate between the two forms of the homozygote, in which case there is incomplete dominance. Furthermore, even when a trait is determined by only a single gene pair, there may be more than a single pair of gene types (called *alleles*) in the population, although of course one individual has only a single pair from among the several possible ones. Coat color in the mouse well illustrates these complexities. For example, some aspects of coat color in the mouse may be determined by any combination of two alleles selected from among three dominant alleles and two recessive ones. When two alleles are combined from among these five alleles we have color varying from a yellow-coated mouse to one agouti-colored (typical grizzled mouse-color) on the back but white below, or agouti on the back and gray below, as in the house mouse (Grüneberg, 1952). Note that these are all the result of this single gene pair, but a pair selected from among five possible alleles.

One point to be noted is that the laws of heredity do not require that "like beget like." In fact, the best evidence of heredity comes from the *unlikeness* of some of the offspring from the parents, as in the proportion of the white guinea pigs born to all-black heterozygous ones.

Biochemical genetics

Within the past few years the mechanism of heredity has come to be much better understood through biochemical researches. A very complex substance known as DNA (abbreviation for *deoxyribonucleic acid*) is known to be the material basis for gene action, and considerable ingenuity has been exercised in deciding how the genetic "code" succeeds in directing the development of the organism (Crick, 1962). The DNA must of course be quite stable, and yet capable of duplicating itself in all the cells of the body; this appears to be the case, thus making possible not only the development of the organism but the transmission of its hereditary characteristics to succeeding generations. The DNA must somehow direct the formation of amino acids which in turn form the proteins that are at the base of the cellular processes from which the organism is eventually constructed and by which it is controlled. The intermediate steps use another nucleic acid, RNA (for *ribonucleic acid*) which exists in several forms, of which *messenger* RNA and *transfer* RNA describe the different functions. Messenger RNA somehow reads the code from DNA (possibly by pairing itself with the DNA molecule of the nucleus), and then it leaves the nucleus. It activates the *transfer* RNA which combines with amino acids in a sequence dictated by the messenger RNA, thus forming the protein chains.

Because DNA somehow codes biological

memory, it is an inviting conjecture that RNA may code the memories arising in the lifetime of the individual. This possibility has been discussed in Chapter 12 (pp. 321–23).

Population genetics

The basic characteristics of a population of animals or of human beings depend upon the genes extant in that population. Because of various selective factors that occur through inbreeding (the death of the unfit, and the like) there is a "drift" in the genes available, so that, for example, some human groups differ markedly in their blood groups, although all share the same basic blood types. The study of the gene distribution throughout groups of individuals that mate with each other, and its consequences for these groups, is known as *population genetics.*

The principles that have been developed in connection with population genetics have an important consequence for the study of human genetics: since evidence can be obtained simultaneously on the characteristics of parents and children, it can be gathered in the lifetime of a single scientist, without requiring the gathering of family histories over several generations. The application of the method to problems of psychological interest has thus far been slight, but it is to be hoped that eventually more ways may be found to use this method in the study of psychological inheritance.

One interesting study of population genetics resulted in the discovery of a curious kind of taste deficiency in about 30 percent of the population. A substance with the chemical name of phenyl-thio-carbamide (abbreviated PTC) when taken into the mouth at low concentrations, tastes very bitter to 70 percent of the population. It is insipid or tasteless to the rest. There are some differences in threshold, but the resulting distribution has two modes,[1] as expected from a distribution composed of two "types" (Figure 17–2). Because taste is not a characteristic by which people choose their mates, the genetic determiners for PTC tasting are distributed at random throughout the population. That is, in any 100 people tested from a given intermarrying population, the proportion of tasters to nontasters will be relatively constant. Because the ratio is constant, it is possible to predict the taste deficiencies of the offspring of marriages of tasters and nontasters, according to the principles of genetic determination. The prediction is based on the assumption that nontasting is a sim-

[1] A distribution that has two modes, or two points of high frequency, is called a *bimodal distribution.* It tends to arise when there are two major types among the population. For a discussion of mode, see Chapter 15, p. 398.

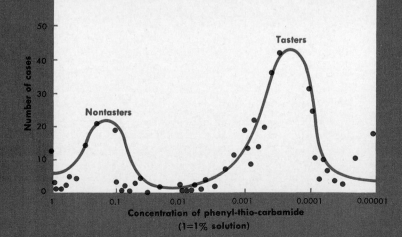

17–2

Bimodal distribution curve resulting from two population "types"

Distribution in the population of tasters and nontasters of phenyl-thio-carbamide. (After Cohen and Ogdon, 1949)

ple recessive trait, determined by one gene pair, and that tasting is dominant. Since all nontasters are assumed to be pure recessives (having two recessive genes), all the children of two nontasters should be nontasters. When both parents carry a dominant and a recessive gene, the offspring, according to the Mendelian ratio, should be in the proportion of 3 tasters to one nontaster. Whenever one parent is pure dominant, all children should be tasters. The results of a study of the inheritance of taste deficiency are given in Table 17–1. The data show how successful the prediction is: the phenotypes occur in the proportions expected from the inferred genotypes.

Most psychological characteristics do not lend themselves to as straightforward a study as that of tasting and nontasting of PTC. The greater complexity is in part due to the fact that psychological characteristics enter into the choice of mates, and hence a random distribution of genetic determiners cannot be assumed. In addition, it is unlikely that many psychological characteristics are determined by single gene pairs.

Heredity in Animal Behavior

Animal breeding experiments tell us something about the influence of heredity on behavior. Some strains of mice, for example, go into convulsions when they are exposed to high-pitched sounds, while others do not. When these strains are crossed, the susceptibility to seizures follows genetic rules as though the seizures were inherited as a dominant trait (Witt and Hall, 1949). Wildness and tameness in rats are hereditary. According to some authorities, change in a single gene pair will convert a wild strain into a tame one (Keeler and King, 1942).

Maze learning in rats

Several experiments have been directed to a study of the inheritance of learning ability in rats. By mating those that did poorly in maze learning with others that did poorly, a "dull" strain was produced; by mating those that did well with others that did well, a "bright" strain was produced (Heron, 1935, 1941; Tryon, 1940). Although separation of "bright" and "dull" strains was successfully achieved, the experiments were somewhat unsatisfactory on two counts: (1) the "brightness" and "dullness" were specific to maze learning (Searle, 1949), and (2) the strains were not genetically pure, so that it was difficult to infer the genetic determiners involved (Hall, 1951). A later experiment tended to meet these two objections by using a type of maze more analogous to a general intelligence test and by attempted control of the genotypes through brother-sister matings (Thompson, 1954). The experiment succeeded in a separation of bright and dull strains within a few generations (Figure 17–3).

Phototaxis in fruit flies

Experiments quite satisfactory from the point of view of genetics have been done with the fruit fly, Drosophila. The behavior selected was phototaxis, that is, the tendency to be attracted to a source of light. By mating those with a strong tendency with others showing the strong tendency and those with a weak tendency with others with a weak tendency, a segregation of types was attempted. The results over successive generations led to the same kind of separation as earlier found in the rat (Figure 17–4). The use of the fruit fly has two advantages over use of the rat for this kind

TABLE 17–1

Inheritance of taste deficiency to phenyl-thio-carbamide

Matings of parents	Children with taste deficiency	
	Predicted	Observed
Taster × taster (N = 425)*	12.4%	12.3%
Taster × nontaster (N = 289)	35.4	36.6
Nontaster × nontaster (N = 86)	100.00	97.9

SOURCE: Snyder (1932).

* N = number of families tested.

Inheritance of maze learning in rats

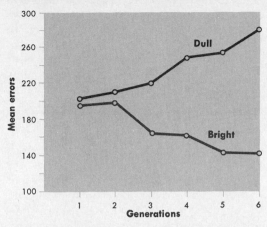

Mean error scores of "bright" and "dull" rats selectively bred for performance on the Hebb-Williams maze. (After Thompson, 1954)

of experiment: (1) it takes far less time to breed successive generations, and (2) the detailed mapping of genes and chromosomes has been carried out more successfully so that a genetic interpretation of the behavioral findings can be made more precise.

The carefully controlled breeding experiments carried out with animals are not possible with human beings for a number of reasons. Social obstacles prevent our making marriages to suit the convenience of the geneticist. Even if marriages could be planned, the long life span of human beings would make it difficult to follow several generations except by going back to old records, which are often incomplete. The difficulties do not, however, prevent our obtaining satisfactory evidence that the human inheritance of some characteristics does in fact follow the genetic principles established by studying other animal forms. The evidence is fairly satisfactory for eye color, hair color, and many body features. The evidence regarding the inheritance of psychological characteristics is much harder to evaluate.

Other evidence from animal behavior

Maze learning in rats and phototaxis in fruit flies serve merely as illustrations of many other experiments concerned with the inheritance of behavior (Fuller and Thompson, 1960; McClearn, 1962). The dog has served as a subject in a number of these studies. Thus, in the early work of James (1941), Basset hounds were found to be lethargic and German shepherds excitable; offspring of Basset hound-shepherd breeding were found to be intermediate. Later studies (e.g., Fuller, 1955; Scott, 1954) have shown other differences in emotionality among well-established dog

Selective breeding for phototaxis in the fruit fly

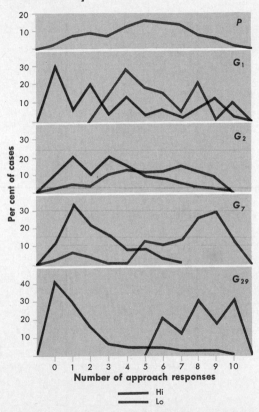

With ten opportunities to make approach responses to light, the offspring of parents selected for a high number of approaches average much higher in successive generations than the offspring of those selected for a low number of approaches. Vertical axis, percent of cases yielding each number of approaches. The original parent generation (P) is shown with the first (G_1), second (G_2), seventh (G_7), and twenty-ninth (G_{29}) offspring generation. (From Hirsch and Boudreau, 1958)

breeds, as well as differences in their trainability. These differences may be considered essentially hereditary, although environment always makes its contributions.

Heredity in Human Intelligence and Mental Illness

The familiar rules of genetics, as we have noted, are stated in terms of unitary traits determined by single gene pairs, but actually most traits for which the determiners are known are not so simple. Traits that vary along a dimension, as height does in man, tend to be determined by more than one gene. If there were only one pair, we would have one height for dominant men and one height for recessive men, just as the tasters and nontasters form separable groups. Intelligence varies, as height does, on a scale from subnormality to great brilliance, without the sharp break that would let us classify men into two groups—the bright and the stupid. Hence to the extent that intelligence (or any other complex trait) may be inherited, we would expect it to be controlled by a number of genes.

The problem of the inheritance of a psychological characteristic of man has been most thoroughly investigated in the field of intelligence. It turns out that the heredity-environment relations are very complex indeed. Hence much of the remainder of this chapter will be devoted to evidence about the inheritance of intelligence.

The hereditary component in intelligence

To study the possibility of hereditary determiners of a complex trait, we may begin by examining *resemblances* between parents and offspring or of offspring to each other. A convenient index of resemblance is the familiar coefficient of correlation. We turn now to some studies that use the coefficient of correlation to determine evidence for the inheritance of intelligence.

Parents and children. If parents contribute to the intelligence of their children through heredity, we would expect a correlation between the intelligence of parents and children. The earlier in the child's life this correlation is found, the more evidence it will give for heredity; for after the child has lived in a home for several years, the influence of environment cannot be ruled out. But the discovery of a correlation early in life depends upon the possibility that intelligence can be measured early.

While a number of scales have been prepared for measuring the psychological development of infants, we now know that these scales do not adequately predict the scores a child will later make on intelligence tests. At least up to the age of two, the I.Q. at age six can be better predicted from the educational level of the parents than from the test scores of the infant (Bayley, 1940a, 1940b).

This instability of the scores during the first years prevents us from obtaining an early estimate of intelligence free of the influence of home environment. Part of the reason for the low correlations between early and later tests lies in the shift in test content. Tests of very young infants are necessarily nonverbal, while verbal tests become very important later on. Not until the child becomes verbal (beginning at the age of two, so far as our test results indicate) is the I.Q. predictive of later I.Q.

If we wait until the school years, when the I.Q. can be satisfactorily measured, we find a positive correlation between the parents' and the child's I.Q. With a large parent-child sample (428 father-child scores and 534 mother-child scores) the score of either parent alone correlated .49 with that of the school-age offspring (Conrad and Jones, 1940). This correlation is about the same size as that obtained between parent and child for a physical characteristic such as height and gives some presumption of hereditary influence, although, of course, environment has now become a factor.

Foster parents. One way to isolate the influences of inheritance and environment is to study children raised by foster parents. A great many children are placed for adoption each year. Because adoptions are handled by social agencies, tests are usually given and records are kept so that the possibilities of follow-up studies are good.

Two main questions require answers:

1. Does the ultimate I.Q. of children adopted within the first few months of life correlate more highly with that of their *blood* parents or with that of their *foster* parents? [2] Does the I.Q. of foster children also correspond to the educational and occupational levels of their *foster* parents?
2. Does the generally favorable atmosphere of homes into which children are adopted raise the general *level* of intelligence, whether or not the correlation changes?

In answer to the two questions, we shall use the data from three studies:

1. One study done at Stanford University compared the relationships between legally adopted children and their foster parents with similar relationships between children and their blood parents. The group studied included 214 foster children and 105 control children living with their blood parents. The average age of adoption of the foster children was three months; all were adopted before the age of 12 months (Burks, 1928).
2. Another study done at the University of Minnesota after the California study repeated many of the same comparisons. The foster-child group consisted of 194 legally adopted children, all of illegitimate birth and all placed in the adoptive home before the age of six months. A like number of control children, living with their blood parents, furnished comparative data (Leahy, 1935).
3. A third study was made at the State University of Iowa, in which foster children were given repeated tests as they grew up, and their ultimate intelligence level was compared with the low intelligence level

[2] It is difficult to find a short word to designate the biological parent-child relationship. The notion of blood relationship is familiar, hence *blood parent* will be used to mean the biological parent as contrasted with a foster parent.

of their blood mothers. All the children had been placed for adoption before the age of six months. Several reports were published earlier, but a final report gives the test results for the foster children when they reached a mean age of 13 years (final test at ages 11 to 18) (Skodak and Skeels, 1949).

How do these studies answer the two questions that were posed? First we may consider the *correlational* data. Does the intellectual status of the child resemble that of the blood parents or that of the foster parents? Here the Iowa data are the most pertinent because test scores are available from the blood mothers, and some evidence is also available on the educational levels of the blood fathers. The data are given in Table 17–2. If parental education affects the child through environment,

---

TABLE 17–2

Correlations between blood-parent I.Q., blood-parent education, foster-parent education, and I.Q. of foster child *

	Number of cases	Coefficient of correlation (r)
Blood parents, with whom child has not lived		
Mother's I.Q. and child's I.Q.	63	.44
Mother's education in years, and child's I.Q.	92	.32
Father's education in years, and child's I.Q.†	60	.40
Foster parents, with whom child has lived at least 10 years		
Mother's education and child's I.Q.	100	.02
Father's education and child's I.Q.	100	.00

SOURCE: Skodak and Skeels (1949).
* All children were placed for adoption before the age of 6 months. Children's I.Q.'s used in correlations were obtained at ages 10–18 (mean age, 13).
† Not given in the report, but computed from the data given there. The blood father's education was unknown for the other 40 cases in the sample of 100.

then we would expect a correlation with the education of the foster parents, *with whom the child lives*. On the contrary, however, the correlations in Table 17–2 are significant only with the blood parent, with whom the child has *not* lived. The complete lack of correlation with foster-parent education is surprising. A small correlation between foster parent and foster child would be expected on the basis of selective placement, that is, on the basis of the fact that social agencies place children as often as possible in homes matching the anticipated ability level of the child. For example, in the Iowa study under discussion, the blood mother's I.Q. and the foster father's occupational status correlated .35 as a result of selective placement (McNemar, 1940).

In the Stanford and Minnesota studies we have the possibility of comparing parent-child resemblances of children living with their blood parents and of children living with foster parents. For those living with their blood parents we have, of course, the joint influence of heredity and environ-

ment. The main comparisons are in Table 17–3. In every comparison blood children resemble parents far more than foster children resemble foster parents.

Our first question is ready to be answered: Parent-child resemblances are greater with blood parents than with foster parents, *whether or not* the child has grown up with his blood parents.

The answer to the second question, however, requires other kinds of data, for we are now concerned with the *level* of intelligence rather than with the relative ranks reflected in correlation coefficients. Here two of the three studies agree that the intelligence level of foster children is *higher* than would be predicted from their hereditary backgrounds. How much higher is not too clear, but an average gain of 10 or more I.Q. points over predictions based on the blood mother's intelligence level is suggested by these two studies. This gain is to be attributed to the fact that homes selected for placement are above the average not only in socioeconomic level but also in general stability. An infant raised in a warmly affectionate and stable home where he is definitely welcomed, and often the only child, has an excellent opportunity for developing his capacities to the fullest—that is, beyond the development of the unselected children on whom test norms are based. This increase is a general pattern regardless of the attributes of the particular foster home, as is shown by the fact that the child's I.Q. bears little relation to the degree of intelligence of foster parents.

The most striking increases were reported in the Iowa study, in which mothers averaging low normal (I.Q. 91) produced children who scored at an average level of 109 or 117 I.Q.[3] at the average age of 13, after living in superior homes from early infancy.

We are justified in the broad conclusion that a good home environment beginning early in life has central importance for the development of the child, intellectually

TABLE 17–3

Parent-child resemblances: correlations between parents and blood and foster children

	Parent-child correlation	
	I.Q. of foster children	I.Q. of blood children
Mother's I.Q.		
Stanford study*	.19	.46
Minnesota study†	.24	.51
Father's I.Q.		
Stanford study	.07	.45
Minnesota study	.19	.51
Cultural index of home		
Stanford study	.25	.41
Minnesota study	.26	.41

* SOURCE: Burks (1928).
† SOURCE: Leahy (1935).

[3] The average was 109 on the 1916 Stanford-Binet, using divisors recommended in 1937, and 117 on the 1937 Stanford-Binet.

TABLE 17-4

Resemblance in height of children of the same parents

Pairs of children	Number of pairs	Coefficient of correlation (r)
Ordinary siblings (like-sexed)	52	.60
Fraternal twins (like-sexed)	52	.64
Identical twins	50	.93

SOURCE: Newman, Freeman, and Holzinger (1937), p. 75.

as well as socially. A good environment will not make all children alike, but it will give each a chance to develop fully his biological potentialities.

Twin studies. Study of heredity and environment in man is greatly furthered by the presence of *identical twins* among pairs of children born to the same parents. Consider, for example, family resemblances in height (Table 17–4). Ordinary brothers and sisters (known as *siblings*) show a moderate degree of resemblance, as represented by a correlation of $r = +.60$. *Fraternal twins*, who develop from separate ova, are no more alike genetically than ordinary siblings; they need not be of the same sex nor do they necessarily resemble each other. It is possible that the effects of a common intra-uterine environment and common diet after birth might make fraternal twins slightly more alike than ordinary siblings, but the greater similarity, if any, is not fully proved by the correlations of Table 17–4. The highest degree of similarity is found for identical twins ($r = .93$). *Identical twins* are so named because they are genetically identical, that is, they develop from the same ovum. They are always of the same sex and usually resemble each other very closely.

What can correlation coefficients tell us about the inheritance of intelligence? Again the study of twins provides us with the

most illuminating data (Table 17–5). We find the resemblances in the same order as those for height: ordinary siblings are least alike, fraternal twins more alike but close to siblings, and identical twins most alike.

The differences in correlation between identical and fraternal twin pairs have by now been shown in numerous studies done around the world. Thus Erlenmeyer-Kimling and Jarvik (1963) found 14 studies yielding an average correlation of .87 in intellectual resemblance between identical twins and 11 studies yielding a mean of .53 for fraternal twins. In a study based on an unusually large sample, Nichols (1965) found a correlation of .87 between 687 identical twin pairs and one of .63 for 482 fraternal twin pairs.

Most identical twins are reared in very similar environments. Hence further evidence on the contributions of both heredity and environment is provided by studies of identical twins reared apart.

Identical twins reared apart. After careful search, American investigators were able to locate 19 pairs of identical twins, all of whom had been separated early in life (Newman, Freeman, and Holzinger, 1937). A comparable search in England led to the finding of another 21 pairs (Burt, 1955). Hence we have two studies separated in time and in geography, yet both yield similar interpretations. The two chief

TABLE 17-5

Resemblance in Binet intelligence quotients of children of the same parents

Pairs of children	Number of pairs	Coefficient of correlation (r)
Ordinary siblings *	384	.53
Fraternal twins (like-sexed) †	52	.63
Identical twins †	50	.88

* SOURCE: McNemar (1942), p. 40.

† SOURCE: Newman, Freeman, and Holzinger (1937), p. 77.

findings so far as intelligence is concerned were as follows:

1. Despite the subjects being raised apart, the resemblance in intelligence of identical twin pairs remained higher than for fraternal twins who had been raised together. The coefficient of correlation between intelligence test scores for *separated* identical twins was .77 in the American study and .84 for the English study, to be compared with the figures for fraternal twins *reared together* of .63 in the American study and .53 in the English study. This greater resemblance in test scores for the identical twins, despite their separation, suggests the importance of heredity. The argument that they may still have had similar environments is scarcely an answer, for their environments could hardly have been as similar as those for fraternal twins reared together.

2. Nevertheless, the correlations between identical twins reared apart was lower than for identical twins reared together. The comparison correlations are for those together vs. those apart were .88 vs. .77 (American study) and .92 vs. .84 (English study). It appears, therefore, that some effect of environment is also demonstrable in these figures. In the American study the lower correlation for pairs of identical twins reared apart was produced chiefly by four pairs who were reared apart in the most contrasting environments. It follows that extremes of environment can influence intelligence-test performance.

Conclusions on heredity, environment, and intelligence. Putting all these findings on siblings and on twins together, we are led to the following conclusions with regard to the contributions of heredity and environment to measured intelligence.

1. Since *identical twins* are more alike in intelligence than *fraternal twins,* inheritance appears to play a part in the determination of intelligence. This conclusion is plausible, because the resemblance in intelligence corresponds to the known correspondence of identical twins in heredity. This greater resemblance in test scores

of identical-twin pairs as compared with fraternal-twin pairs persists until late in life. This has been confirmed for 51 pairs of female twins, all of whom were over 60 years of age. The 30 identical pairs showed significantly less difference from each other than did the 21 fraternal pairs on four of six tests (vocabulary, block designs, digit span, and digit-symbol substitution). Differences between the two types of twins were not significant on tests of recognition of similarities and on motor coordination, although here too the direction of difference favored greater similarity between the identical pairs (Kallmann and Sander, 1949).

We cannot be sure, however, that the greater resemblance of identical twins as compared with fraternal twins is due entirely to heredity. The environment of identical twins may be more alike than that of fraternal twins, because they look alike and tend to be dressed alike and otherwise treated as a pair. Fraternal twins may diverge from each other in physical characteristics and hence provide unlike environments for each other. Yet the additional finding that identical twins reared apart still resemble each other in intelligence more than fraternal twins reared together is a potent argument for the hereditary contribution.

2. Since *fraternal twins* are more alike in intelligence than *ordinary siblings,* we know that environment must also play a part in the determination of intelligence. The influence must be environmental, because from a genetic standpoint fraternal twins are no more alike than ordinary siblings. They do, however, share a common intra-uterine environment and are both subjected to any congenital effect due to the mother's nutritive or glandular condition during pregnancy. This prenatal condition is a potential environmental influence upon their development. They also share an environment after birth which is more alike than that for ordinary siblings. Brothers and sisters born singly are necessarily born into families of unlike size and to parents of unlike age and experience, and these differences in family pattern are undoubt-

edly an important environmental influence in the shaping of many psychological characteristics. Children born in pairs (i.e., as twins) have the same number of brothers and sisters, have parents of the same age and socioeconomic status, and are (usually) brought up under identical theories of diet and of child care. Thus while the social environments of two members of a fraternal-twin pair differ according to the way the twins differ from each other, their environments tend to be more alike than those of ordinary siblings and somewhat less similar than those of identical twins.

Again the fact that the mean differences between the identical-twin pairs reared apart were greater for those with most dissimilar environments supports the importance of the environment.

If we accept the correlations of Table 17–5 at their face value, along with the evidence from identical twins reared apart, we arrive at a compromise position on the nature-nurture issue. We are led to the conclusion that there is some contribution to psychological characteristics from heredity, some from environment.

Only careful study and better theoretical models will tell us how much environmental modification to expect of the various characteristics determined jointly by heredity and environment. In the studies of identical twins above, the authors came to the conclusion that physical characteristics are least modified by environment, intellectual characteristics somewhat more, and personality characteristics most of all.

Heated controversies have flared up from time to time among psychologists over the interpretation of data on heredity and environment, particularly some of the data from foster homes and twins that have just been reviewed. It turns out, in retrospect, that one source of disagreement arose through a failure to see that for a given body of data interpretations based on *correlation coefficients* might lead to one result, whereas interpretations based on *mean scores* might lead to another. As a general rule, correlation coefficients lead to results favoring the hereditary interpretation, while mean changes favor the environmentalist interpretation. Therefore those engaged in the debate have in the past tended to emphasize the kinds of data that supported their own preferences.

That correlations and means consider different aspects of the data is clear from a comparison of the Burks (1928) and Leahy (1935) studies. The results from the two studies, considering correlations only, were alike (Table 17–3). Results for means were different, however. The Stanford foster children had ultimate I.Q.'s below those of the blood children, while the Minnesota foster children had ultimate I.Q.'s equal to those of their blood-children siblings. Hence studies agreeing on correlations need not agree on means.

While the difference between correlational results and mean results is at first puzzling, another example takes away some of the mystery. Consider the heights of children as related to the heights of parents. Within the last several decades there has been a remarkable increase of height, owing to improved diet and control of disease, so that children now tend to be taller than their parents. If one were to argue that height is a matter of environment (nurture), he could point to the increase in the stature of Italians in New York City over their counterparts in Italy, the increase in height of the Japanese since World War II, as well as the gradual increase in height of American college students. If, however, one were to argue that height is a matter of heredity (nature) he would use correlation coefficients to show that taller parents still have taller children than shorter parents do, and that the correlation between parent and child height is now just what it was a century ago.

In these discussions the point needs repeated emphasis: if attention is paid to correlation coefficients, great weight will be given to heredity, while if attention is paid to changes in mean scoring level, weight will be given to environment. We shall consider again (p. 459) some attempts to find a solution to the relative importance of heredity and environment.

Heredity and mental illness

Because, as we shall see later (Chapter 21), mental illness is a social problem of great magnitude, a number of studies have been directed to determine the hereditary component in such illness. Particular attention has been given to the illness known as *schizophrenia*.

Here again the studies of twins have proved to be illuminating. If one member of a twin pair is diagnosed as schizophrenic, what are the chances that his co-twin will also be schizophrenic? If there is a hereditary component to the illness, it will be expected that among identical twins the chances will be much higher than among fraternal twins. This is indeed found to be the case in a number of studies, as summarized by Kallman (1953) in Table 17–6. The results for childhood schizophrenia (onset before age 15) are similar (Kallman and Roth, 1956).

These studies have been subjected to a number of criticisms, but the conclusion appears to be justified that there is a large hereditary component in the susceptibility to at least some forms of schizophrenia. The complexity of the issues involved is well illustrated by Rosenthal's reanalysis of some of Slater's data (Rosenthal, 1959; Slater, 1953). Rosenthal selected for care-

TABLE 17–7

Schizophrenic twins and family background of schizophrenic illness *

	Schizophrenic illness in family reported	No reported schizophrenic illness
Concordant pairs (both twins schizophrenic)	13	9
Discordant pairs (only one twin schizophrenic)	1	12

SOURCE: Rosenthal (1959).
* $P = .01$.

ful case study those identical-twin pairs in which both members had schizophrenia (concordant pairs) and those in which only one was affected (discordant pairs). On a number of indexes he was able to show a greater likelihood that the illness was hereditary when both twins were affected and essentially nonhereditary when only one was affected. For example, 60 percent of the 22 concordant pairs showed some schizophrenic illness in the family background, while only one of the 13 discordant pairs showed any family background of schizophrenia (Table 17–7). Rosenthal concludes that there may well be two broad classes of schizophrenia, one with a substantial hereditary component, one with the hereditary component absent or very slight.

The Interaction of Heredity and Environment

At best, heredity provides a *potential* for development; unless the environment is sustaining, this potential may never be realized. Accidents before, during, or following birth may modify development; dietary restrictions may stunt growth. We must always be aware of the *interaction* between

TABLE 17–6

Schizophrenic illness in co-twins of fraternal and identical twin pairs

	Fraternal twins		Identical twins	
Investigator	No. of pairs	Percent of affected co-twins	No. of pairs	Percent of affected co-twins
Luxenburger	60	3.3	21	66.6
Rosanoff	101	14.9	41	68.3
Essen-Möller	24	16.7	7	71.4
Slater	115	14.0	41	76.0
Kallman	685	14.5	268	86.2

SOURCE: Kallman (1953).

Interaction of heredity and environment upon eye development in fruit flies

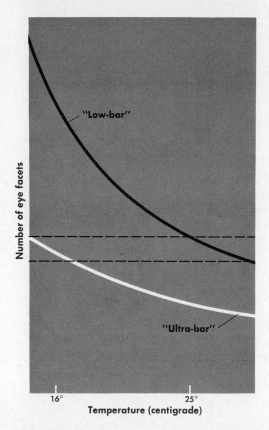

Those with "low-bar" heredity tend to develop more eye facets than those with "ultra-bar" heredity, but both groups develop fewer eye facets at higher temperatures. Note that between the parallel lines flies with very different heredity are alike in number of eye facets as a result of the environmental temperatures in which they develop. (Data from Krafka, 1919, as plotted by Hogben, 1933.)

heredity and environment if we are to understand individual differences.

Interaction in animal development

The fact that a trait is controlled by heredity does not mean that it is free from the influence of environment. The coat color of some species of rabbit, although predictable on the basis of heredity, is affected by the temperature of the cage in which the young rabbit develops (Sinnott, Dunn, and Dobzhansky, 1958). Animals that normally develop a black pigment fail to do so if they are kept in a warm cage. By artificially cooling a part of the skin area that is usually white, that area develops the black pigment. While we may think of skin color as determined by heredity, the actual appearance of the phenotype depends also on the environment, so that interaction is evident.

Another illustration comes from the effect of both heredity and environment (temperature) on the development of the eye of the fruit fly (Krafka, 1919; McClearn, 1962). Two genotypes ("low-bar" and "ultra-bar") have differing numbers of eye facets, as shown in Figure 17–5: the "low-bar" genotype tend to have more eye facets than the "ultra-bar" ones. Regardless of heredity, however, if fly larvae developed at high temperatures they would tend to have fewer eye facets than if they developed at low temperatures. Flies with "low-bar" heredity raised at high temperatures could have the same number of eye facets as "ultra-bar" flies raised at low temperatures, thus blurring the influence of heredity and environment. The relationships shown in Figure 17–5 illustrate the interaction.

Interaction in the development of intelligence

We have previously noted in the study of twins and of foster children (pp. 450–55) that intelligence can be accounted for only by taking into account *both* heredity and environment. Similar conclusions were implied in Chapter 16 (pp. 435–38) in considering factors influencing the stability of the I.Q. The problems created by this interaction are very great, and many of the disputes over intelligence arise because of some uncertainty as to how to weight the hereditary and environmental contributions.

One of the areas in which the issue arises is in considering the intelligence levels of different fractions of the population, by racial or national origin. Here the possibility of heredity looms large, but many environmental influences must also be considered.

Three problems make the determination of differences between such groups difficult: the problem of obtaining an adequate sample, the problem of assuring that test items are fair, and the problem of developing rapport in testing. When immigrant groups are tested, each group may represent a different fraction of its own native stock. It is generally conceded that in the period of most rapid immigration the northern-European immigrant into the United States represented a higher level of socioeconomic status within his native land than did most of the immigrants from southern Europe. Again, successive waves of immigration, as from Russia and Poland, came from different fractions of the native stock. When, therefore, a small group of Swedish-Americans or Italian-Americans or Russian-Americans is tested for purposes of determining national differences, selective migration becomes important as a possible cause of the results. The same difficulties appear in the study of racial differences. We have no way of knowing, for example, how representative the American Negro is of African Negroes.

The test items in today's intelligence tests represent primarily the language and culture of American public schools. Children from unassimilated cultural groups, even though they are attending these schools, may be handicapped by bilingualism at home. Or they may see the need for schooling differently, so that they do not use opportunities that the school offers in the same way as do native children. The assumption of a common exposure to the substance of the test items may be faulty.

Finally there is the problem of *rapport*. When an urban white experimenter tries to test a rural Negro in the South or visits an Indian school in the West, he may not be able to get representative results. Psychologists have used various methods to get around these difficulties, including training as psychological examiners some who belong to the groups being tested, but the difficulties continue to confuse efforts to establish intellectual differences among various groups of people.

The difficulties are reflected in efforts to assess the intelligence of the American Negro. Even under somewhat favorable circumstances the obtained Negro intelligence mean tends to remain below that of whites. Evidence for this conclusion comes, for example, from a settlement of Negroes in Kent County, Ontario, Canada, which dates back to 1812. Many Negro slaves found their way there before the Civil War and their descendants were accepted, went to good schools, and were treated on terms of equality. Still, over 100 years later, the mean intelligence of the Negroes in Kent County remained below that of the whites (Figure 17–6). As usual in such group comparisons, the two distributions overlap, and a number of Negro children score above the mean of the white children. The means, however, are different beyond chance expectation, suggesting a difference between the Negro stock and the white stock. These results were also influenced by socioeconomic differences. In rural areas of Kent County, where the circumstances of the Negroes are more nearly similar to those of the whites, the mean difference in I.Q. between Negroes and whites is 6 points, while in the cities, where their circumstances are less alike, the difference is 16 points.

The many difficulties in making a causal analysis of racial differences appear in the results of tests made during World War I. In some Southern states, the scores on the Army Alpha test obtained by members of the white draft were no higher than scores obtained by Negro draftees in some Northern states. In every state, however, the scores of the Negro draftees averaged below those of the white draftees. If we consider the two circumstances of being either white or Negro and being either from the North or from the South, the circumstances favorable to higher intelligence scores were being white and from the North; those unfavorable were being a Negro and from the South. Therefore, we ask whether the unfavored position of both the Northern and Southern Negro, rather than any inherent racial difference, may not have been responsible for his poor showing on the tests (Alper and Boring, 1944).

17–6

Distribution of I.Q. in one investigation of racial differences

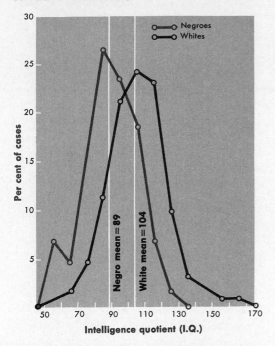

Distribution of I.Q. for Negro and white school children in Kent County, Ontario, Canada. (After Tanser, 1939)

The study of rising mean I.Q.'s of Southern-born Negroes who migrated to Philadelphia (p. 438) shows that gains can be expected with improved environment. The results of other studies have led to similar conclusions (e.g., Klineberg, 1935). But a difference in mean I.Q. still remains, though of course the distribution of I.Q.'s is such that racial membership alone can never tell us whether a given individual is bright or stupid. Even though according to intelligence tests very bright Negroes are fewer proportionately than very bright whites, there are, of course, many Negroes with high I.Q.'s. Research in seven Chicago public schools led to the identification of 103 Negroes possessing a Stanford-Binet I.Q. of 120 or above, and one girl who achieved an I.Q. of 200 (Witty and Jenkins, 1934).

Is there any consensus among psychologists on racial difference in intelligence? Results with other races lead to the same conclusions as do the studies of the Negro. Although some racial groups score consistently below whites on I.Q. tests, many of the differences are probably due to inadequacies in measurements or to inequalities in environmental opportunity, and many authorities believe that no racial differences have been demonstrated. Even if the obtained differences are taken at their face value, the results show so much overlap that membership in a racial group is no index of an individual's brightness.

CRITICAL DISCUSSION
Relative contribution of heredity and environment

The foregoing discussion has indicated some of the difficulties in making clear assertions about the relative contributions of heredity and environment, yet the fact that some kinds of behavior are more hereditary than others makes the possibility of assigning some kind of numerical value to heritability intriguing.

The statistical models that have been developed for assigning relative values to heredity and environment are all based on the contributions to variation in the traits studied. They ignore means, and thus tend to overemphasize the hereditary contribution relative to what it would be were changes in means taken into consideration (p. 455).

A convenient measure of variation used in these models is *variance*, the square of the standard deviation. The variance of the phenotypes in a population is made up of the variances of the genotype, the environment, and their interaction, as follows:

$$\sigma_p{}^2 = \sigma_g{}^2 + \sigma_e{}^2 + r_{ge}\sigma_g\sigma_e$$

where $\sigma_p{}^2$ = variance of the phenotypes in the population, $\sigma_g{}^2$ = variance due to differences in the genotype, $\sigma_e{}^2$ = variance due to environmental influences, and r_{ge} = correlation between hereditary and environmental effects. In practice, this basic formula is either simplified or made more complex before algebraic manipulations are made to solve the equation.

Complexities arise when special kinds of

matings are introduced (e.g., sibling matings), or when, in human studies, one has to recognize the various environments of family and community. A variety of models has been constructed, and the models are finding some uses in empirical studies of the relative contributions of heredity and environment (Vandenberg, 1965).

SUMMARY

1. The methods of the science of genetics are proving to be as applicable to behavior as to structure. The same distinctions are needed between the *phenotype* (i.e., the expressed characteristic) and the *genotype* (the underlying hereditary determiners that will be transmitted to the offspring) as are made when physical characteristics are under consideration. The *chromosomes* and *genes* must be responsible for hereditary components of behavior, as they are for inherited structures. Because some genes are *dominant,* some *recessive,* some *sex-linked,* various statistical predictions can be made about the traits of the offspring of particular kinds of matings. When these studies are conducted on whole populations, the methods become those of *population genetics,* a form likely to prove important in the study of the heredity of human behavior.

Important new knowledge is coming by way of *biochemical genetics,* which studies how genetic information is coded in DNA molecules and converted into proteins by way of RNA.

2. Selective breeding experiments in animals have resulted in convincing evidence that forms of behavior can be inherited. Illustrations include maze learning in rats, phototaxis in fruit flies, and temperament in dogs.

3. Because selective breeding is out of the question for human studies and many human characteristics are complexly determined, we are led to depend upon studies of resemblance as a function of blood relationship.

4. Studies of parent-child resemblance in intelligence are limited because the I.Q. of a child cannot be determined accurately before the age of two, when the influence of the home environment is already considerable. At later ages, parent-child resemblances in intelligence are of the same order of size as resemblances in height.

5. The study of foster children provides an opportunity to isolate the effect of home environment on intelligence. Three studies reviewed led to similar conclusions: (1) the *correlation* between the blood parents' intelligence and the child's intelligence remains higher than that between the foster parents' intelligence and the child's, even though the child moves into the adopted home within the first few months of life; (2) intelligence develops within the favorable environment of the foster homes to a *level* above that predicted from the blood-mother's intelligence and, on the average, to a level corresponding closely to that of children born into homes with the same characteristics as the foster homes.

6. In studies of resemblances of brothers and sisters, twins provide much useful information because there are two types of twins (*identical* and *fraternal*) with unlike degrees of genetic similarity. Studies based

on the correlations between the intelligence-test scores of ordinary siblings, fraternal twins, and identical twins (including identical twins reared apart) lead to the conclusion that both heredity and environment are important as determiners of individual differences in intelligence.

7. Studies of schizophrenia in fraternal and identical twins have found so much more correspondence for identical twin pairs that a strong hereditary component is very plausible. However, careful analysis of identical-twin data indicates that there may be two types of schizophrenia, one with a strong hereditary component, one with scarcely any contribution from heredity.

8. Interaction between heredity and environment is the rule, even for traits of known heredity. This interaction leads to much of the controversy surrounding such a problem as the development of intelligence.

9. Studies of ethnic and racial differences in intelligence show how difficult it is to construct tests that will lead to valid conclusions. Results indicating ethnic and racial differences, commonly found on the tests, do not justify propositions about fundamental differences between races. Three difficulties are hard to overcome: *representativeness* of the population tested, *fairness* of the tests to all groups, and *rapport* with those being tested. Overlap in I.Q. among the groups is so great that an individual's intelligence can never be judged on the basis of his membership in a given national or racial group.

SUGGESTIONS
FOR
FURTHER
READING

There are many good sources of information on genetics, of which an authoritative one is Stern, *Principles of human genetics* (2nd ed., 1960). There are now two good books on the genetic aspects of psychological characteristics in animals and man: Fuller and Thompson, *Behavior genetics* (1960), and Hirsch, *Behavior genetic analysis* (1967). For briefer introductions, two chapters by McClearn (1962, 1964) contain essential information on modern genetics and the evidence from behavior. Vandenberg (ed.), *Methods and goals in human behavior genetics* (1965), gives additional data on human twin studies and other aspects of human genetics.

For differences based on race, nationality, and class, useful summaries can be found in Anastasi and Foley, *Differential psychology* (3rd ed., 1958), and Tyler, *The psychology of human differences* (2nd ed., 1956).

For the special problems affecting the estimation of the ability of Negroes in the United States, see Pettigrew, *A profile of the Negro American* (1964).

18 Theories of Personality

Personality is one of the most familiar and at the same time one of the most difficult concepts in psychology. All of us use the term in our everyday conversation, but most of us would be hard put to provide an accurate statement of its meaning. The psychologist, for whom the concept is of central importance, cannot escape the need to attempt a precise statement.

In this text the term *personality* is used to mean the arrangement, or configuration, of individual characteristics and ways of behaving that determines an individual's unique adjustments to his environment. We stress particularly those personal traits that affect the individual's getting along with other people and with himself. Hence personality includes any characteristics that are important in the individual's personal adjustment, in his maintenance of self-respect. Any description of the individual personality must take into account appearance, abilities, motives, emotional reactivity, and the residues from experiences that have shaped the person as we find him. The term "personality" is thus widely inclusive, but it is not synonymous with all of psychology. It refers to the individual and the unique organization of traits that characterize him and his activities.

Personality Structure as a Unique Attainment

Because each individual is unique, the scientific description of a personality is bound to be difficult. We need to find some way to understand the enduring features of a person's behavior as they follow naturally from his developmental history, his goals, and the real-life problems that confront him. Our aim is to discover and describe, if we can, his *unique personality structure;* that is, how the various aspects of his personality fit together so that all are understandable in terms of some underlying pattern. If we succeed in this, we can understand superficial inconsistencies in his behavior. What he does will be consistent with his total personality structure, even though his actions may appear self-contradictory to those who do not understand him. He may be tender toward his family and cruel to his employees, of strong physique yet overly concerned about his health, sentimental about music and hard-boiled in politics. Even personal peculiarities and mannerisms (idiosyncrasies) can be seen as significant expressions of the deeper unity that is the total personality structure.

The possibility that we may comprehend personality in this way is opened up by clinical case studies. The clinical psychologist, as he tries to understand the conduct of his client, attempts to fit all aspects of the individual's behavior, including symptoms of disturbance, into a consistent pattern. Then what the client does is seen to follow from the kind of person he is. Once we understand his personality organization, we begin to understand him as a unique individual.

The shaping of personality structure

The broad outlines of personality formation are clear enough. We have already noted the importance of heredity, of maturation, of training in infancy, of social motives acquired through learning, and of ways of perceiving. What we are attempting now is a kind of summary of these many factors in development and socialization *as they have shaped the particular individual before us* and as they affect our understanding of him. As he stands before us now, he is an end product of his potentialities as they have been realized in the course of growing up. The problem that remains is for us to understand the patterning of these consequences of experience that gives the individual his uniqueness.

In surveying the origin of the personality structure we can begin with the infant's potentialities as established by his specific heredity and by whatever influences impinged upon him prior to birth. One infant does not start on equal terms with another. One may be born sturdy, another weak. One may be born more talented than another because of the kind of sense-organ equipment and nervous system he inherits. These potentialities are developed by the individual's experiences as he matures. Although all experiences are individual, we may distinguish between two broad classes: the *common experiences* shared by most individuals growing up in a given culture and *unique* or *individual experiences*, not predictable from the roles that the culture assigns the individual.

Experiences common to the culture

The process of growing up includes learning to behave in ways expected by our society. We usually accept group values without much reflection and without awareness that peoples of other cultures may not share these values. If our culture values cleanliness, promptness, and hard work, we also try to be clean, prompt, and industrious; we tend to think people admirable who exhibit these qualities, unless we are in some way alienated from the culture and thus protest against its values.

Conspicuous among the influences of the culture upon the individual are the *roles* that it assigns to him. He is born into some of these; for example, the boy is born into a masculine sex role and the girl into a feminine sex role. The demands of these roles vary from culture to culture, as we learned earlier (Chapter 4), but it is considered "natural" in any culture for boys and girls to have predictable differences in personality structure merely because they belong to one or the other sex.

Some roles are of our own choosing but are still patterned by the culture. Occupation is a conspicuous role of this kind. Occupational training involves more than learning the technical skills associated with the job; to be successful and comfortable in an occupation or profession requires that one also behave as others do in that occupation and be prepared to accept the status that his occupation brings. Sometimes the occupation has its visible sign: the artist's smock is not unlike the military uniform in that both are signs of a social role. Occupations may develop special attitudes and special speech forms as well as special types of dress. The counterman at the soda fountain dons not only a white jacket but also a special vocabulary which enables him to communicate swiftly and efficiently with his co-workers. An expression such as "combo wheat, hold the mayo" cannot be defined from the dictionary, but it is perfectly clear in its context.

Because adult behavior largely conforms to social roles, to some extent it is predictable. You know what behavior to expect of people at a formal tea or reception or at a football rally or a national political convention. At a Rotary Club meeting a naturally dignified or reserved man may act like his fellows, calling each by his first name, sharing the mood of open friendliness. When the meeting is over, he becomes again his usual self.

Because culture molds the individual, the suggestion has been made that each culture develops a somewhat characteristic personality structure; one culture may be typically more aggressive or more passive than another. Individuals then ring changes on this typical personality (Kardiner, 1939). This theory fits in with popular notions of "national character" whereby Italians differ characteristically from Germans or Irish, though caution is needed lest the basic truths be exaggerated (Inkeles and Levinson, 1954).

Even though cultural pressures impose some personality similarities, individual personality is not completely predictable from a knowledge of the culture in which the individual is raised, for two reasons: (1) the cultural impacts upon the person are not actually uniform because they come to him by way of particular people—parents and others—who are not all alike in their values and practices, and (2) the individual has some kinds of experiences that are distinctly his own.

Unique experiences

Each person reacts in his own way to the social pressures upon him. As Allport has so effectively put it: "The same fire that melts the butter hardens the egg." [1]

Personal differences in response may result from the biological equipment of the individual. As we noted earlier, no two individuals (except identical twins) are alike from a hereditary point of view. In addition to differences in size and intelligence, individuals may inherit all manner of subtle differences in sensitivity, reactivity, and endurance which bear upon ultimate personality development. When an individual is notably different (e.g., born with a club foot, a birthmark, or a hearing defect), we expect him to face problems out of the ordinary; but every individual, if we could only know everything about his inheritance, would appear "out of the ordinary" in his own way.

The biological potentialities of the individual are soon socialized under the influence of significant persons, such as his parents, his brothers and sisters, and others. It is these significant persons who transmit the culture in the precise form in

[1] Allport (1937), p. 102.

which it makes its impact upon the individual. They impose the social roles and provide the models which show how the roles are played. They give and withhold satisfaction of primitive impulses: they give food to satisfy hunger and use force to prevent biting. They approve and disapprove the child's behavior.

As the child comes to seek approval and to avoid disapproval, he becomes capable of hindsight and foresight and begins to see himself as a responsible agent. He develops a *conscience* whereby he judges his own conduct according to ideals he has acquired.

In the process of cultural transmission not all parents (or parent substitutes in the form of other significant persons) are equally successful. Some are incapable of providing the affection that the child needs in order to grow up a secure person. Others have themselves so resisted adopting conventional social roles that they transmit the roles badly to the new generation.

A child always shows the influences of his parents, though he need not resemble his parents. The contrasting possibilities are well described by two brothers in Sinclair Lewis' novel *Work of art*. Each of them ascribes his personality to his home surroundings.

> My father [said Oral] was a sloppy, lazy, booze-hoisting old bum, and my mother didn't know much besides cooking, and she was too busy to give me much attention, and the kids I knew were a bunch of foul-mouthed loafers that used to hang around the hoboes up near the water tank, and I never had a chance to get any formal schooling, and I got thrown on my own as just a brat. So naturally I've become a sort of vagabond that can't be bored by thinking about his "debts" to a lot of little shopkeeping lice, and I suppose I'm inclined to be lazy, and not too scrupulous about the dames and the liquor. But my early rearing did have one swell result. Brought up so unconventionally, I'll always be an Anti-Puritan. I'll never deny the joys of the flesh and the sanctity of Beauty.

> My father [said Myron] was pretty easygoing and always did like drinking and swapping stories with the boys, and my

mother was hard-driven taking care of us, and I heard a lot of filth from the hoboes up near the water tank. Maybe just sort of as a reaction I've become almost too much of a crank about paying debts, and fussing over my work, and being scared of liquor and women. But my rearing did have one swell result. Just by way of contrast, it made me a good, sound, old-fashioned New England Puritan.[2]

Beyond his unique biological inheritance and the specific ways in which the culture is transmitted to him, the individual is shaped by particular experiences. An illness with a long convalescence may provide satisfactions in being cared for and waited upon that profoundly affect the personality structure. Death of a parent may disrupt the usual identifications. Unusual successes or failures, accidents, opportunities for heroism, winning a contest, moving to another part of the country—there are countless such experiences that are relevant for development but not predictable from the culture, although of course their effects are partly determined by the culture.

Identity formation

The diverse influences of the common culture and experiences specific to the individual must become unified, or *integrated,* before the person has a recognizable personality structure. Erikson (1959) has described the process of achieving adult personality integration as *identity formation.* What are the steps through which the final adult identity comes about? An important series of steps results in the *identifications* of the child with significant people in his environment—with mother and father, with a brother or a sister, with a favorite neighbor or teacher. As long as these separate identifications remain, the personality is made up of parts, often not self-consistent. To be at once like a mother and a father, an older brother and a favored music teacher, is to be torn into a variety of roles—to experience what Erikson calls *role diffusion.* Such role diffusion, unless outgrown, may result in serious personality

[2] Lewis (1934), as quoted by Allport (1937), p. 102.

disturbance, as the following case illustrates.

Mr. Orchard, an advertising layout man for a department store, came to a mental hospital at the age of 35 because of increasing irritability and headaches which were associated with delusions that people were trying to take his job away from him and that they were trying to injure his 12-year-old son. He also had some religious preoccupations, and thought he was walking with God. He came to the hospital voluntarily.

In the course of growing up, Mr. Orchard had developed imperfect identifications with several people important to him, and he had been unable to achieve that kind of integration we describe as identity. His close attachment to his mother had been interrupted by her death when he was 12; he longed for closeness to his father, but his father was away from home a great deal until his early adult life. The third influence upon him was an aged, religious grandfather who took much responsibility for him after his mother's death, but who was too old to be a good identification figure. Who did Orchard think himself to be? He was like his mother in her hard-working, gentle ways. He was like his father in caring for artistic work, but with a certain debonair irresponsibility. His religious conflicts derived in part from his grandfather. Sometimes Orchard was a steady worker (like his mother), but at times, for no apparent reason, he would leave his job out of sheer restlessness (reminiscent of his picture of his father); at times he was full of religious devotion (like his grandfather), but occasionally he became religiously indifferent. Even when he was functioning at his best he showed a certain immaturity; with the increasing demands of parenthood, he was unequal to the crises that eventually brought him to the hospital. His identifications conflicted too greatly, and he could not settle upon a fixed image of himself.

Therapy was directed first toward a more realistic appraisal of his childhood. He had to give up being his mother's little boy; she had not deserted him, nor could any magic bring her back. His father had gone away to work as a salesman when work was hard to find; he had not deliberately failed his son, nor had he been as irresponsible as the son pictured him. As Mr. Orchard became clearer about his relationships with mother, father, and grandfather, his present problems came into sharper focus. After two months in the hospital he was well enough to return to home and job, and he appeared to have achieved a more satisfactory level of integration.[3]

Role diffusion is normally characteristic of early adolescence, when the youth has not yet "found himself" (not yet achieved identity), when he is both dependent and independent, loyal and defiant, daring and timid. He must master these divergent trends, give up being a carbon copy of other people (his identifications), and become himself (achieve identity).

The processes by which identity is finally achieved are various, but they all imply some experimentation with various experiences and roles. The adolescent characteristically seeks a range of subjective experiences, examines a number of philosophies of life (whether religious or political ideologies or both), commits himself temporarily (seriously or playfully) to occupational and other choices. Most societies allow a certain amount of freedom during the transition from childhood to adulthood, a period Erikson describes as a kind of *moratorium* (literally, a delayed period during which debts do not have to be paid; in this case, a period during which the adolescent does not have to assume full social obligations). If all goes well, the young adult emerges from that period prepared to make lifelong commitments. He has then achieved identity.

Theories of personality are attempts to account in a systematic and orderly way for personality structure. A successful theory must weave together the various strands descriptive of individuality into a fabric that has enduring, identifiable features, unique for each individual yet per-

[3] Case courtesy of Dr. Josephine R. Hilgard.

mitting individuals to be compared with one another. There are many theories— partly because personality is so loosely defined that all theories do not deal with the same subject matter, partly because the facts upon which a finished theory must rest are not yet well enough known. We shall consider four groups of theories: *type* theories, *trait* theories, *developmental* theories, and *dynamic* theories.

Type Theories

Theories of *personality* types are ancient in origin and they persist today, despite repeated rejections of type classifications by psychologists. The reasons for the prevalence of these theories are not hard to find. They represent a commendable effort to find some order in the midst of human diversity. Classification into *kinds* is the beginning of most sciences—kinds of rocks, kinds of weather, kinds of plants and animals; why not kinds of personalities? Furthermore, type theories build upon the common observation that there are at least *some* people whose personalities revolve about a cardinal or dominant characteristic, such as ambition, pride, adventure, bodily comfort. Thus it might be possible to classify all people into a few types if we could arrive at a short list of these central *themes* or *styles of life* that characterize some individuals so well. In the effort to do just this, students of personality have turned for clues to *physique* (body types), to *physiology* (body chemistry), and to *behavior* (psychological types).

Physique: body types

One kind of classification that goes far back in history is the theory of *body types* as determinants of personality. Bodily constitution, health, and vigor undoubtedly determine some manifestations of personality. The plausible relation between body and personality has led to the age-old tendency to assign traits on the basis of features of the body or face. As a rule, theories based on body type (or other constitutional attributes) tend to stress differences in general affective or emotional reactivity. Mothers of several children often report that their children seemed very different from birth: one was always lively, energetic, active, another was always placid, calm, quiet; one smiled readily, another was sober from the start. Many observers have noted such differences shortly after birth (e.g., Wolff, 1959; Bell, 1960). These general differences in reactivity are often referred to as differences in *temperament;* it is such differences that tend to be related to types of physique.

One attempt to develop a type theory based on bodily characteristics is that of Sheldon and his collaborators (Sheldon, Stevens, and Tucker, 1940; Sheldon and Stevens, 1942; Sheldon, 1954). They reject earlier theories, which divided individuals into distinct physical types (Kretschmer, 1925); instead they classify them according to three components. The terms used to describe the components derive from the names of the cell layers in the embryo from which different bodily tissues originate. The first or *endomorphic* component refers to the prominence of the intestines and other visceral organs. The obese individual is high in this component; his paunch indicates excess viscera. The second or *mesomorphic* component refers to bone and muscle. The athlete is predominantly mesomorphic, wide-shouldered and narrow-hipped, with rippling muscles. The third or *ectomorphic* component is based on delicacy of skin, fine hair, and sensitive nervous system. The ectomorphic person is tall, thin, stoop-shouldered; no one would confuse him with a mesomorph or an endomorph.

In rating a person, the system assigns one digit between 1 and 7 for each component in the order endomorph, mesomorph, and ectomorph, high numbers standing for more of the component. A man rated 3-6-2 might make a football fullback: low in respect to endomorphy, athletically powerful (with a 6 in mesomorphy), low in the delicate features of ectomorphy.

To each of these physical components is assigned a corresponding temperamental component. The predominantly endomorphic person tends to be classified temperamentally as one who loves to eat, seeks bodily comforts, and is sociable. The predominantly mesomorphic person is energetic, likes exercise, and is direct in manner. The ectomorph is sensitive and given to worry, fears groups, and needs solitude. He may or may not use his sensitive nervous system for artistic or scientific work.

The scheme satisfies all the appeals of a "type" theory of personality: it is biologically plausible because of its emphasis upon embryological origins, it dramatizes familiar extremes in physique, and it plays up familiar correspondences between the body and its activities.

Although Sheldon's types appeared plausible and were bolstered by impressive statistical data, once they were subjected to impartial scrutiny they met the fate of most of the older type systems. The dimensional scheme by which the three components of the body were selected turns out to be dependent on the statistical methods used; two dimensions would, in fact, cover the data equally well (Ekman, 1951; Lorr and Fields, 1954; Humphreys, 1957). The correlations between body type and temperament seem to reflect the contamination produced when one rater judges both type and temperament. Studies using *ratings* have usually given some small support to Sheldon's claims, but studies using *tests*, in which bias is excluded, have found few, if any, significant correlations between body build and personality (Tyler, 1956, p. 444).

Physiology: types based on body chemistry and endocrine balance

The ancient Greek classification of temperaments into four types was based on what was at that time accepted as body chemistry. The four types—*sanguine, phlegmatic, melancholic,* and *choleric*—were based on the prominence of one of the four "body fluids": the sanguine person, generally warmhearted and pleasant, had a prominence of blood; the phlegmatic person, listless and slow, had his qualities attributed to phlegm; the melancholic person, suffering from depression and sadness, had too much black bile; the choleric person, easily angered and quick to react, was influenced by his yellow bile. The modern counterpart of this theory would assign such functions to hormones, and at least one prominent contemporary biochemist has advocated a careful look at the chemistry of the body as a basis for temperament (Williams, 1956). While all of us have endocrine glands, they vary greatly in size from one person to another. It is found, for example, that one person's endocrine gland may weigh three times as much as the same gland in another person (without any enlargement due to disease); hence the relative prominence of one or another gland may give one person an excess of thyroid, another an excess of adrenal tissue. Williams concludes that each person has his own distinctive pattern of endocrine activity; according to this view, individual temperament is a kind of "endocrine symphony."

Some data exist that show a considerable stability in certain indicators of autonomic balance. Measures have been devised to determine whether the sympathetic or the parasympathetic responses are more active when stimuli call forth their antagonistic responses; in some individuals the sympathetic responses will be ascendant, in others the parasympathetic. When such measures

are taken as much as a year apart, children react very much alike on the two occasions, as indicated by a correlation of .70 in responsiveness from one time to the other (Wenger and Wellington, 1943). Individuals may demonstrate quite specific patterns of autonomic response; these patterns of physiological response have been demonstrated to bear some relationship to personality measures (Lacey and Van Lehn, 1952; Lacey, Bateman, and Van Lehn, 1952). The evidence is good enough that there is a constitutional (perhaps hormonal) basis for differences in temperament, but just how far we can go in appraising an individual in terms of his physiological functioning is not presently known.

It should also be noted that the results of accurate measurement do not actually yield "types," but continuities; individuals differ in their autonomic functioning in many ways and cannot be grouped into a few "types."

Behavior: psychological types

It is not necessary to turn to body types or to physiological types in order to hold to a theory of personality types. It is possible to look for types based on *behavior* or *psychological characteristics*, without recourse to other correlations. Perhaps the best known of the psychological type theories is the classification into *introverts*

18–1

Distribution of scores on an introversion-extraversion test

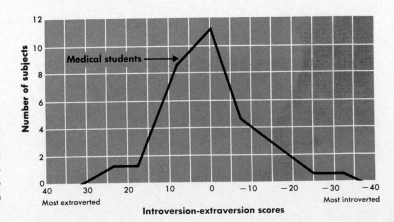

The distribution of scores is for 44 medical students. It follows the normal curve rather than showing a bimodal distribution, as would be expected if two separate types were being identified. (After Neymann and Yacorzynski, 1942)

and *extraverts* proposed by the Swiss psychologist Carl G. Jung (1875–1961). The introvert, especially in time of emotional stress or conflict, tends to withdraw into himself. Characteristics of introversion include shyness and a preference for working alone, for example, in libraries and laboratories rather than among people. The introvert may take to the speaking platform, as in the leading of a religious movement, but even there he is impelled from within. The extravert, by contrast, when under stress tends to lose himself among people. He is likely to be very sociable, a "hail fellow well met." He tends to choose occupations such as sales or promotional work where he deals with people rather than with things. He is likely to be conventional, orthodox, well-dressed, outgoing. It is not difficult for each of us to find among his acquaintances a "typical" introvert or a "typical" extravert. This gives such a classification plausibility and accounts for its popular appeal (Jung, 1923).

When we select traits that appear to belong to an introvert or an extravert, however, and construct tests on the basis of these traits, we make two discoveries. First, it develops that a test of general introversive or extraversive tendencies leads to a normal distribution of scores with a single mode, rather than to the bimodality that a type theory would call for (Figure 18–1); in other words, we discover that the introvert and extravert are merely extremes on a scale, not actually two distinct types.[4] They differ as do tall and short by departing in both directions from some middle condition: most people are *ambiverts*, neither introverts nor extraverts but sometimes one, sometimes the other. The second discovery is that the scale is complex. When tests of introversion-extraversion are analyzed by the method of factor analysis (see Chapter

16, pp. 427–28), as many as five factors can be identified (Guilford, 1940). These factors have been described as social introversion, thinking introversion, depression, tendency to mood swings, and happy-go-lucky disposition. Such results have made psychologists skeptical of otherwise plausible classifications into personality types.

There is an inherent appeal in the classification of individuals into types, and, despite the criticisms that are directed against type theories, the search for types continues to direct an appreciable amount of experimentation (e.g., Stein, 1963).

Estimate of type theories

Satisfactory type theories are not impossible. It may be that we shall eventually isolate men into types as distinctive as the blood types that so markedly affect the success of blood transfusions. There are no logical barriers against such theories. The fact is, however, that present theories have not produced the evidence needed to verify them. Even if the evidence were more satisfactory than it is now, two dangers in type theory would remain.

1. *The type description tends to assert too much about the individual.* As soon as a person is tagged according to a type theory, the assumption is that a great many assertions can safely be made about him. That is, he is expected to have all the characteristics belonging to that type; but the determiners of individual personality are too many, and they combine into something both too rich and too unusual to be described with a single general term.

The danger is that of assigning the person to a *stereotype.* We all too readily come to believe that Negroes are carefree and musical, Italians volatile, Scots thrifty, Swedes stolid. Such characterizations are stereotypes that ignore the individual differences among members of a group. A stereotype is, to be sure, a faulty type classification, but even a better type classification easily lends itself to abuse.

2. *The type description tends to hold to outmoded conceptions of personality and especially neglects cultural influences.* Stu-

---

[4] Dimensions such as introversion-extraversion may be useful in personality appraisal, although they do not yield sharp types. Even for such a clear type distinction as that of masculinity-femininity there are gradations shown by individual men and women (pp. 105–09). The point here is that *type theory* tends to exaggerate pigeon-holing.

dents of the development of the individual are aware of the enormous importance of childhood experiences and later opportunities in shaping personality. Type theories are sponsored primarily (though not exclusively) by those who see human characteristics as chiefly the result of biological inheritance. That is why many type theories refer to body form. The body is an important locus of personality, but personality is also interpersonal, that is, dependent on relations to other people. When one understands the richness and diversity of cultural influences, he loses faith in type theories.

Trait Theories

A *trait theory* is in some respects at the opposite extreme from a type theory; instead of grouping people according to a few types, it classifies people according to the degree to which they can be characterized in terms of a number of traits. According to trait theory, one can describe a personality by its position on a number of *scales,* each of which represents a trait. We may place the person on a scale of intelligence as indicating one personality trait, on a scale of emotional sensitivity as another trait, on a scale of ascendance-submission as a third. Because our language is very rich in trait names, a mere listing of specific traits is not enough; some sort of order has to be made of the countless ways in which a person can be characterized. We shall consider two subvarieties of trait theory: Allport's theory of personal dispositions and Cattell's theory of surface and source traits.

Allport's theory of dispositions

Gordon W. Allport (1937, 1961) accepts a kind of trait theory but distinguishes between *common traits* (those traits that are comparable among people) and *personal dispositions* (traits that are unique for the person). When we measure people according to trait scales we are measuring common traits. Thus Allport's *Scale of values* (Allport, Vernon, and Lindzey, 1960) is

designed to appraise common traits, comparing one person with another according to preferred values (theoretical, economic, esthetic, social, political, and religious). *Personal dispositions,* on the other hand, are traits that are unique for the person and hence cannot be used in an exact way in comparing one person with another. Thus two people may both be aggressive, but each will be aggressive in his own way, depending upon his individual experiences and capabilities.[5]

Allport views personal dispositions as being organized in a kind of hierarchy, some being much more important to the individual than others; for this purpose he distinguishes between *cardinal, central,* and *secondary* dispositions. A *cardinal disposition* is a characteristic so pervasive that it influences almost all aspects of behavior. Some individuals stand out because they are dominated by a single cardinal disposition; such persons often become "reference personalities" by which we describe others. If we say that someone is a Beau Brummell or a Don Juan or quixotic or narcissistic, we are classifying him by his resemblance to a reference personality whose characteristics we expect others to know. While few people are dominated by a cardinal disposition, many have a *few* dispositions that centrally describe their personalities. In a pilot study of 93 students, Allport asked each one to characterize someone he knew well in as many words, phrases, or sentences as were required. He found that the characterizations required an average of 7.2 essential characteristics, with a range of from 3 to 10 (Allport, 1960). This is support for the notion of a few central dispositions. Finally, there are many *secondary dispositions,* expressing relatively isolated interests or modes of responding; many of

[5] Strictly speaking, Allport would say that there is no such thing as a common trait because no two persons ever have exactly the same trait. But because individuals share a common culture there is a limited number of *roughly comparable* traits (common traits) that we can measure by tests and use as a crude prediction of what the person will do, even though they do not do justice to his unique individuality.

these are better characterized as "attitudes" than as "traits."

The essence of Allport's theory is that patterned individuality constitutes the subject matter of a science of personality. He therefore resists the tendency of others to reduce personality to the traits that are common to all men. He prefers to treat cardinal, central, and secondary "traits" as personal dispositions in describing individual uniqueness.

Cattell's theory of surface and source traits

Unless one has some sort of ordering principle, what comes out of a theory of common traits is simply a description of a person's position on a number of scales. If one could arrive at a *short* list of the main *common traits,* then one could characterize a person according to a *trait profile* or *psychograph* (Figure 18–2). The problem is to obtain a short list that is not arbitrary. One method that suggests itself is *factor analysis;* by obtaining a great many ratings or scores from the same people, we ought to be able to find those traits that cluster together so that we can use one name for the cluster.

While many investigators have used this approach, we may select the work of Ray-mond B. Cattell as illustrative, for it has represented a prodigious amount of data collection and analysis. In gathering his data, Cattell has used behavior observations and ratings, laboratory studies, and inventories, working with many different populations and age groups.

Allport and Odbert (1936) listed 17,953 words used in English to distinguish the behavior of one person from another. Cattell began his research with this list of trait names, adding the terms that psychologists have coined in their researches. By eliminating overlap of meanings, he came out with 171 personality or temperament variables describing the whole "personality sphere" (Cattell, 1946). Although some traits, such as ability, can be thought of as positions along a scale ranging from zero to a high value, most temperament variables can be expressed as polar opposites with the zero point lying between them (e.g., cheerful vs. gloomy). Cattell prefers such paired terms wherever possible. If many such variables are used to describe the same group of individuals, the variables can be examined for correlation; that is, it is possible to find out which are closely related to others and which are distinct.

Two main techniques of examining the

18–2

Trait profile (hypothetical)

If a standard set of common traits (such as A through H) could be agreed upon as giving a satisfactory characterization of a person, then an individual trait profile, such as the one shown here, would be as characteristic of the person as his fingerprints, provided the traits were stable and could be satisfactorily appraised.

interrelationships exist, leading to a distinction that Cattell makes between *surface* traits and *source* traits.

Surface traits are found by studying the *clusters* of the actually obtained correlations. For example, all traits that intercorrelate .60 or higher can arbitrarily be assumed to be a manifestation of one cluster or surface trait. Thus it is found that people judged on the three trait pairs of thoughtful vs. unreflective, wise vs. foolish, and austere vs. profligate tend to fall in similar positions on all three scales, at least to the extent of a correlation of .60; hence these three are clustered together (with others of similar sort) into the surface trait of disciplined thoughtfulness vs. foolishness. This and a few other surface traits are listed in Table 18–1. They are called *surface traits* because the similarity lies on the "surface" (i.e., is evident in the actual raw ratings), without any transformation

or process of inference leading to some less obvious underlying uniformity.

Source traits are found by another method, that of *factor analysis,* which is more subtle than *cluster analysis;* while it will show that traits that correlate highly with each other belong together, it may also assign to one factor some traits that correlate less highly with each other, and it will tell the extent to which each of the traits also reflects other factors. The traits that belong together as a result of factor analysis are called *source traits,* on the assumption that they reveal a deeper unity than that revealed through surface traits. The traits most representative of a source trait will also be highly correlated with each other as surface traits; the point is not that surface traits never reveal source traits, but rather that source traits help to explain the clustering of the surface traits and pick out those that are "purer" examples of a basic trait. Some of the chief source traits reported by Cattell are given in Table 18–2.

The ideal is clear enough: to find the few main source traits that turn up in a number of separate investigations. If these source traits can be identified, tests can be constructed to measure them; these test scores can then be weighted for any kind of personality assessment or prediction that may be desired. As we shall see later (Chapter 19, p. 491), Cattell has indeed constructed a test, the 16 PF Questionnaire, which is designed to assess 16 source traits (Cattell, 1957*b*).

A great deal of research has been stimulated by Cattell and his co-workers, yielding promising results in relation to anxiety and its physiological correlates, in educational prediction, in aspects of delinquency, and in occupational success. Owing to some unresolved problems in the use of factor analysis, the abstract aim to achieve an agreed-upon list of source traits to characterize personality has not been achieved.

Estimate of trait theories

What can we say about the success of trait theories as alternatives to type theories?

TABLE 18–1

Illustrative surface traits

The traits clustered together have all correlated at least $r = .60$ with each other within at least four investigations conducted with adults. The specific traits listed are examples from longer lists, and some liberties have been taken in shortening trait names as stated by Cattell.

Integrity, altruism vs. dishonesty, undependability
Honest vs. dishonest
Loyal vs. fickle
Fair-minded vs. partial

Disciplined thoughtfulness vs. foolishness
Thoughtful vs. unreflective
Wise vs. foolish
Austere vs. profligate

Heartiness vs. shyness
Sociable (forward) vs. shy
Sociable (gregarious) vs. seclusive
Intrusive vs. reserved

Thrift, tidiness, obstinacy vs. lability, curiosity, intuition
Habit-bound vs. labile
Thrifty vs. careless of property
Pedantic, tidy vs. disorderly

SOURCE: Cattell (1950), pp. 37–41.

TABLE 18–2

Illustrative source traits

A source trait has always been identified through factor analysis, and is said to determine the variability in measured surface traits. The examples are selected from a longer list.

Affectothymia vs. sizothymia

Good-natured vs. critical, grasping
Attentive to people vs. cool, aloof
Trustful vs. suspicious

Ego strength vs. emotionality and neuroticism

Mature vs. unable to tolerate frustration
Realistic about problems vs. evasive, avoids decisions
Absence of neurotic fatigue vs. neurotically fatigued

Dominance vs. submissiveness

Self-assertive, confident, vs. submissive, unsure
Boastful, conceited vs. modest, retiring
Aggressive, pugnacious vs. complaisant

Surgency vs. desurgency

Cheerful, joyous vs. depressed, pessimistic
Sociable, responsive vs. seclusive, retiring
Energetic vs. subdued, languid

SOURCE: Cattell (1965), pp. 66, 73, 90, 92.

1. The trait approach is a straightforward one, lending itself readily to experimentation. As a starting point there is scarcely any alternative to a trait approach; even contemporary type theories begin with trait appraisal. Hence the methods of trait appraisal are legitimate and merit additional careful investigation.

2. The trait profile that emerges from the scores of an individual is not an adequate description of his personality, even though it may be a true one. When behavior is broken down into traits, we have no way of knowing how the traits are ordered in the goal-seeking behavior of the individual. Thus a person characterized by the trait of compulsiveness may occupy himself merely with useless repetitive rituals, or, on the contrary, he may show dogged determination to stay with a productive task.

The trait profile, while it tells something about personality patterning, is not dynamic enough to show the interrelationships of the traits in the individual. One method proposed for meeting this objection is the use of *profile analysis*. It consists in appraising the trait patterns, stressing interrelationships as well as individual traits (Meehl, 1950).

3. An individual's traits are his ways of behaving under environmental provocation, and their existence depends upon this interaction between person and environment. There is some objection to assigning traits to an individual as though they were something he *possessed*. In some sense he does not possess shyness or forwardness: he acts (and feels) shy under some circumstances and acts forward (and does not feel shy) under other circumstances. Care is needed lest traits, like types, divert attention from the importance of the cultural surroundings in which behavior occurs.

A simple illustration of how environment elicits behavior is given by a study of aggressive behavior of boys in a camping situation. The total amount of aggressive interplay in the dining room so exceeded that observed elsewhere that a boy who might have been judged as lacking in aggression on the playing field might have been judged aggressive if observed only at the table (Gump and Kounin, 1959).

A theory of traits as characterizations of the person (dispositions that he possesses) lacks something in meaning, for traits will manifest themselves differently depending upon the environmental stresses upon the individual. Some sort of interactive theory is needed, in which what the person "possesses" is somehow appraised according to a range of situational circumstances in which these dispositions are called into play. We do not know how best to state such a theory, but the developmental theories and theories of dynamics about to be discussed make consideration of interaction a point of departure.

Developmental Theories

Theories that stress the importance of developmental history for personality need not deny the biological potentialities of the individual, as stressed in theories of physique or physiology, but they insist that this potential merely provides a set of limits within which personality takes shape. The relationship is comparable to that between maturation and learning: maturation provides a kind of ground plan of development; learning determines what the individual actually does with his matured capacities. Developmental theories tend to stress continuities: one can best predict what a person will do in a given situation by what he has done before in earlier situations that resemble the present. Thus environmental interaction finds a place in these theories, somewhat more firmly than in either type or trait theories. Three varieties of developmental theory will be considered: *psychoanalytic, learning,* and *role* theories.

Psychoanalytic theory of development

Psychoanalytic theory has both a developmental and an interactive aspect; that is, it is concerned both with the course of development from earliest childhood and with the motivational conflicts and crises that occur at any given time. At this point we shall be concerned primarily with the developmental aspects of the theory, returning later to the interactive (dynamic) aspects. Psychoanalysis, as we noted earlier (Chapter 3, pp. 73–74) stresses a continuity in growth: beginning in earliest childhood a shaping process goes on that results in a relatively enduring personality structure, one that changes slowly and is therefore characteristic of the mature individual at any given time. The steps, as we noted, could be defined either as those of psychosexual development (oral, anal, phallic, latency, genital), or as those of psychosocial stages, as designated by Erikson, each with a developmental crisis to be surmounted until identity is eventually achieved.

The fact that earlier modes of dealing with crises persist in the present is emphasized in the psychoanalytic concept of *fixation,* which refers to arrested development. An individual may in some sense have remained immature by being fixated or caught at one stage of development, so that there are excessive manifestations of that stage in his adult behavior. Such arrested development is partial only; in other respects such a person may be more fully grown up. Fixations lead to forms of character structure or personality structure associated with the stage at which the person is fixated. Two forms of personality structure that have been widely studied may serve to illustrate the psychoanalytic interpretation: the *compulsive* personality and the *authoritarian* personality.

The *compulsive* personality is characterized by excessive cleanliness, orderliness, obstinacy, and stinginess. In extreme cases, behavior becomes repetitive and ritualistic. Originally, psychoanalysts believed that this personality structure arose through excessive cleanliness training in the period of early infancy and therefore called it the "anal" character, after the developmental stage in which it presumably arose. In this view, if the crises associated with the anal stage are not successfully resolved, there will be residual fixations, that is, excessive residue from this stage operating in adult behavior. Later investigators have questioned this oversimplification of the origin of such a personality pattern. It is pointed out that the same parents who are excessive in cleanliness training are likely to make excessive demands for conformity, punctuality, and so on beyond early infancy, and that the personality structure may very well come about through such continued childhood training.

The existence of the compulsive personality received at least partial confirmation in one experiment in which 37 men living together in college fraternities rated each other on three traits. The ratings were made on a seven-point scale, and a pooled rating resulted for each of the men on each of the traits of stinginess, obstinacy, and orderliness. The reliabilities of these averaged ratings were found to be satisfactory, and they could thus be interpreted like test scores.

The test of the theory that the three traits form a pattern rests upon a correspondence among the traits. The correlations between trait ratings turned out as follows:

Stinginess and orderliness	.39
Stinginess and obstinacy	.37
Obstinacy and orderliness	.36

The correlations, while low, are all positive and in the expected direction. The results are all the more convincing when we recall that we consider orderliness a desirable trait, but both stinginess and obstinacy undesirable (Sears, 1936, 1943).[6]

The *authoritarian* personality is another personality structure for which there has been a series of studies (Adorno and others, 1950). It is said to arise out of extreme parental rejection or domination in childhood, leading to repressed hostility. This hostility finds expression in adult life in attacks on minority groups, as in anti-Semitism. The authoritarian personality pattern includes highly conventional behavior, superstition, destructiveness and cynicism, desire for power, concern over sex.[7]

Learning theories

Learning theories overlap with the psychoanalytic theories because they also stress the importance of early developmental experiences and the residues of earlier experience in later problem-solving. The differences between the two kinds of theories lie chiefly in the desire of the learning theorist to find specific experiences of reward and punishment that shape development, while the psychoanalyst (particularly of the more classical groups) seeks to explain development in terms of certain universal patterns that are to be found in all cultures. To the extent that both theories describe reality, they necessarily overlap.

Some of the learning theorists have indeed taken the Freudian theories as a starting point, but have translated these theories into learning terms. This is true of

---

[6] It may be noted that one of Cattell's surface traits includes thrift, tidiness, and obstinacy (Table 18–1). In theory, one might expect this to be a source trait because of the supposed common origin of these diverse manifestations.

[7] The tests for authoritarian personality have not escaped criticism, e.g., Christie and Jahoda (1954).

---

both Dollard and Miller (1950) and Whiting and Child (1953), although neither pair is committed to the psychoanalytic interpretation. For example, the motivational systems studied by Whiting and Child include the consequences of feeding, toilet training, management of sex and aggression, and dependency. While each of these aspects of behavior is for Whiting and Child an area of socialization, for a psychoanalyst each of them is an area also of psychosexual development. One wonders if, without the influence of psychoanalysis, the same areas would have been chosen; at the same time, the manner in which the development is studied differs greatly from that of the psychoanalyst. Cultural contrasts are studied, for example, where the classical analyst would have looked for similarities; and the later consequences of early experience are interpreted as generalized habits rather than the reflection of unconscious mechanisms.

It is instructive to consider the similarities and differences between the learning viewpoint and the psychoanalytic one. While the classical psychoanalyst considers the basic drives to be those of sex and aggression, the learning theorist adds hunger, thirst, and pain as drives in their own right. There are in psychoanalysis many derivative motives, established by way of some of the transformation mechanisms that we shall meet later (Chapter 20), but these transformations are stated largely in metaphorical terms; the learning theorists have worked out a more careful system of arriving at secondary motives through learning based on primary drives. The stages in development that the psychoanalyst calls psychosexual are recognized by the learning theorists but are held to depend upon aspects of maturation other than sex and to relate to the demands made by parents in a particular culture. In other words, the rewards and punishments administered by significant people in the culture are seen as important in forming habits, including those of anxiety. The mechanisms of fixation, displacement, and the like can be studied as habit phenomena. Fixation is likely to be a result of overlearning, not corrected by new learning; displacement follows principles of generalization by way of similarity. The distinction between conscious and unconscious is essentially that between the labeled and the unlabeled: if one can label and talk about an experience, it is conscious; if one is vague about it and cannot label and talk about it, then it has its effects "unconsciously." The learning of labels is itself a habit phenomenon.

What psychoanalysis and learning theories have in common is the explanation of the present in terms of the past. The past provides a residue of experiences and memories (habits, to the learning theorist) that can be tapped when a present problem comes up. We tend to relate new experiences to past ones similar to these new ones, and hence bring to bear the modes of behavior that have worked for us in the past; when past experiences have been unsatisfactory (frightening, anxiety-provoking), similar experiences in the present may give rise to similar responses of alarm or panic. Present personality is somewhat consistent and predictable because of this tendency to draw upon a long past in meeting the problems of the day.

Role theories

Closely related to the learning theories are the role theories, which describe personalities according to the manner in which the individual meets the various demands that society makes upon him in his role of child, parent, man, woman, worker, citizen. These theories are close to the learning theories in that they assume that the biological individual is adaptable enough to fit a variety of roles; he evidently has to *acquire* his role behavior through experience with his particular culture. The difference in emphasis between the two theories lies chiefly in that the continuity of behavior in learning theory is attributed to habit, whereas in role theory much of the continuity is contributed by the stability of the roles into which the individual is cast; thus the enduring fabric of society is as important as the enduring fabric of his habits (Newcomb, Converse, and Turner, 1964).

Role *behavior* depends first of all on the role *positions* that society establishes; that is, certain ways of behaving toward others are defined by different positions. According to Linton (1945), there are at least five kinds of positions in even the simplest societies: (1) age-sex positions, (2) occupational positions, (3) prestige positions (e.g., chief, slave), (4) family, clan, or household positions, and (5) positions in association groups based on congeniality or common interests (e.g., an orchestra member). Occupants of a given position are expected to fulfill the role by behaving in certain ways; some kinds of behavior are prescribed, some are permitted, and some are forbidden. A prescribed role makes a few firm demands and a number of permissive ones. Thus a mother, if she is to fulfill her role, must provide her children with enough to eat, and should not treat them cruelly or torture them; she has discretion, however, about how much she reads to her children or whether or not she sends them to Sunday school.

The possibility of studying personality through role behavior is a good one, in part because the samples of behavior to be studied are somewhat specified by the role. For a given woman, as a mother her behavior toward the child is relevant, as a wife her behavior toward the husband, as an employer her behavior toward the employee.

The role theory of personality development, in summary, may be demonstrated by the following example. An infant is born into certain prearranged roles (family, sex, nationality). His freedom is limited by these roles, in that many of his choices have been made for him before he is born: where he will live, what language he will learn, and so on. When he is still dependent, his parents (or other responsible adults) are obligated to teach him the behavior appropriate to these preestablished roles. Depending upon the society in which he is born, he will be able to make a number of role choices of his own: whether or not to take up music or to participate in athletics, what occupation to prepare for. There may be great pressures from his social environment that limit his choices even in these areas, but in any case he will begin to put a personal stamp upon the way in which he behaves in the roles. In the end, what we mean by his personality (from this point of view) is the consistency of the features of his role behaviors.

An interesting study of the changes in personality associated with role behavior was made following World War II in which the subjects were British soldiers who had spent several years in prisoner-of-war camps (Curle, 1947). Their habitual role behaviors were first disrupted by entering military life, with its new demands upon them; then they went overseas and had to learn new roles; finally they entered prison camp. At each stage their home ties became more remote and their new ways of life became more real. In the prison camp, where the men were separated from their officers, they had to participate vigorously to create a tolerable culture of their own; this new culture became social reality for them. Consequently they did not adjust well when transplanted later to their homes. Those who were helped to make the shift by living for a time in "transitional communities" adjusted much better than those who were returned directly to their homes (Curle and Trist, 1947). The point here is that some of the continuity of personality as we know it is provided by the continuity of the roles in our familiar communities; old habits are not enough to retain this continuity if circumstances are too drastically changed for too long.

Estimate of developmental theories

A developmental theory is certainly on sound ground in recognizing that man can and does learn and that he grows up in a culture in which he necessarily participates according to the rules and provisions of that culture. Hence any adult personality is a product of its development. But this does not solve the problem of selecting one developmental theory as most cogent.

Some of the unresolved issues are:

1. What is the relative importance of the earliest years compared with the later years of childhood? The psychoanalytic theories (and some of the learning theories as well) place great emphasis upon the very early years in the shaping of personality; we do not know how reversible these influences are.

2. What is the relative importance of constitutional factors as compared with learning? The same problem met with in intelligence (Chapter 17) is equally pertinent in the study of personality. If physique and endocrine balance are important, as some claim, just how important are they?

3. Is development a continuous process, in which gradual maturation interacts with gradually acquired habits, or is development discontinuous, with definite maturational *stages*, as implied in the psychoanalytic theory of psychosexual development, in Erikson's theory of psychosocial crises, and in some of Piaget's proposals?

4. To what extent is the continuity of personality maintained by the stability of social structure (role positions) rather than by continuities within the individual habit structure? This is the main issue between learning theories and role theories.

5. How, in a developmental theory, can personality best be appraised? The *case history* appears to be called for; but if this is constructed from a retrospective interview, it may be inaccurate. Perhaps present behavior can be sampled; but in that case our *measurements* conform to other theories, even though our *explanations* may take developmental forms.

Dynamic Theories

Because we seek a characterization of the enduring aspects of personality, we are led to characterizations according to types or traits or to personality structures of one kind or another as a result of developmental history. There is another way of looking at personality, however, and that is according to various strands that are in unstable equilibrium, so that present behavior is a result of the interplay of various dispositions, often in conflict; these conflicts always take place in the present, no matter what their origins in the past may have been, so that theories of *personality dynamics*—the theories concerned with these present conflicts—are inevitably *interactive* theories rather than developmental ones. This causes something of a problem, because many theories that are from one point of view developmental are from another point of view concerned with personality dynamics; this is certainly true of psychoanalysis and of learning theories. In any case, we need to consider those aspects of several theories that address themselves to personality dynamics.

Psychoanalysis as a dynamic theory

We have already considered psychoanalysis as a developmental theory, concerned with the historical origins of personality. It is also a theory of personality dynamics, concerned as well with features of contemporary personality organization and action.

As one way of approaching the problems of conflicting tendencies within the individual, Freud (1927) introduced the concepts of the *id, ego,* and *superego*. While each of these portions of the personality has its own developmental history, we are here concerned with the interactions that take place in the adult personality.

The *id* is the depository of the innate instinctual drives (sexual, aggressive), which in their bald form seek immediate expression when aroused. If unbridled, the id would always seek immediate gratification of primitive, irrational, pleasure-seeking impulses. The id is manifested at an early stage of development, but it is not outgrown; we are all our lives to some extent creatures of impulse, and it is this irrational, impulsive part of ourselves that is used to infer the id as part of the structure of the personality.

Classical psychoanalytic theory saw the *ego* as developing later out of the id, but modern ego theory within psychoanalysis postulates a primitive ego alongside a primitive id; in any case, the more fully developed ego, as the part of the personality responsible for controlling behavior in so-cially approved ways, comes into play later in life. The desire for immediate pleasure must be held in check; a long route may be necessary before the pleasure can be obtained in a proper manner. With maturity, the ego rules the id, but there are conflicts between them, and occasionally the id has its way. In dreams, for example, when the ego is relaxed, wish-fulfillment (an id function) may hold sway, and rational controls may be abdicated. The ego thus represents our ordinary social self, going about the work of the world, being as realistic and rational as possible, causing us to act in ways congenial with other people and to accept the social roles that are prescribed. If the id is in the service of the "pleasure principle" (implying immediate gratification), the ego is subservient to the "reality principle" (implying postponed gratification).

The third part of the personality, the *superego*, develops out of the ego's experiences with social reality and the rules laid down by parents. The inferred superego is most nearly synonymous with *conscience*. It keeps us working according to an ideal of the self arising in early childhood, especially through parental prohibitions.

From the point of view of a dynamic interpretation of personality, the key concept here is that these three inferred parts of the personality are often at odds: the ego postpones the gratifications that the id wants right away, and the superego wars with both the id and the ego because they fall short of the moral code that it represents. There is some danger in thinking of these inferred parts of the personality as three warring persons within the individual, but the threefold classification, if not overdone, usefully calls attention to discordant trends commonly found within the same person.

Learning theory and role theory as dynamic theories

Conflict also has its place in learning theories and role theories of personality, although in these theories the arena of conflict is not defined by the id, ego, and superego. In learning theory, the structural units are habits and drives, any of which may come into conflict with any other; in role theory, the demands of the various positions that an individual holds may produce conflicts in his role behaviors appropriate to these roles. The conflicts provide learning experiences out of which new habits and new role behaviors emerge. Since conflict is discussed in terms of habits in Chapter 20, further consideration will be omitted at this point.

Estimate of dynamic theories in relation to developmental theories

Theories of personality dynamics attempt to deal with the present manifestations of the results of development in a manner that gives due attention to the different strands of development, that recognizes the multiple demands upon the individual, and that allows for the fact that personality reveals itself in the interactions among people.

The *developmental* theory stresses the lines of influence from the early years to the later ones, postulating significant continuities, modified to be sure by maturation and new learning. These developmental continuities can be studied by correlational techniques, in which early influences (such as feeding, toilet training, sibling rivalry, parental discipline) are related to later behavior, either in the usual environment, as indicated, for example, by the relationship between feeding and food preferences as an adult, or in special test situations, as shown in the relationship between, say, early discipline and scores on an adult test for anxiety. To explain such relationships the course of development is *inferred;* that is why we call it a *theory* of development.

The *dynamic theory* deals with the same set of facts in another way. It is concerned with an inference about the personality structure as it exists at a given time. The infant personality, for example, is assumed to be less differentiated than the adult personality. Consider the adult personality structure. It cannot be studied directly but has to be *inferred* from its consequences. It may be inferred from

usual behavior, as a function of ordinary life situations, and from special examples of behavior elicited by tests. The kind of relationship commonly studied is that in which behavior in ordinary life situations is predicted from test scores. *If* this prediction is satisfactory, and *if* the test has been constructed in terms of some sort of theory of personality structure, then (and only then) can useful statements be made about the inferred personality structure of the individual. In this manner a theory of personality dynamics makes use of personality data.

If one accepts this analysis, it is evident that there is no conflict between developmental theories and dynamic theories. It is understandable that theories such as those of psychoanalysis, learning, and role behavior are almost necessarily concerned both with development and dynamics.

There is room for many individual variations of theories stressing developmental and dynamic aspects of personality, but it appears plausible that future developments in personality theory will find some way of eventually combining both aspects into an overall theory.

Personality Integration and the Concept of the Self

The search for personality structure is a search for some unifying principle or characterization that expresses the essential unity of the person, as well as his uniqueness. The belief that the personality is unified has a long history, including the conception of a soul regulating and unifying the body, and, in some forms of religious belief, surviving bodily death. On empirical grounds the concept of unity is strengthened from the outside by the fact that the locus of the person is a single body, and from the inside by the fact that we have continuous memories of ourselves as the "same" person.

Actually, the personality is perhaps not so highly unified. The fact of tensions and conflict within the person has long been recognized, and the tensions between id, ego, and superego were anticipated by the struggles within body, mind, and spirit emphasized within the Hebraic-Christian traditional beliefs. Modern role theory indicates that a person may play at once several roles and may vacillate between roles. The concept of *dissociation* is used to state the fact that there are sometimes split-off aspects of personality functioning, as found normally in dreams. Cases of multiple personality illustrate the problems involved in dramatic ways.

Multiple personality

An extreme case testing the notion of personality unity is that in which several "personalities" exist at once in the same person, so that the individual at one time behaves in accordance with one integrated behavior pattern, at other times in accordance with another. To the classical cases in the literature (e.g., Prince, 1906; Franz, 1933), there has been added the case of Eve White, with her alternate personalities known as Eve Black and Jane (Thigpen and Cleckley, 1954, 1957; Lancaster, 1958). The case has been of sufficient interest to provide the basis for a motion picture, *The three faces of Eve.*

Eve White was a serious-minded and conscientious young mother who came to a therapist for treatment of severe headaches. In the midst of one of her interviews, in which with considerable agitation she reported that she had occasionally been hearing hallucinatory "voices," she suddenly underwent a striking personality change and became a youthful, buoyant, flirtatious personality who called herself Eve Black. The personality Eve Black was completely aware of the thoughts and activities of Eve White, but Eve White did not even suspect Eve Black's existence, until they became "acquainted" in the therapist's office. Later on a third personality emerged, a more mature one who called herself Jane. The Eve White and Eve Black personalities had apparently been coexisting since early childhood, when Eve Black would get Eve White into trouble, only to withdraw, with Eve White denying everything and suffer-

ing more extreme punishment because she denied what Eve Black had caused her, unknowingly, to do. Some of these childhood incidents were substantiated by interviews with her parents. Recently Eve Black had gone on a clothes-buying spree and had then hidden the clothes at home. When the irate husband reprimanded Eve White, she could only deny that she had purchased the clothes, and she escaped her husband's further anger by her eagerness to take the clothes back to the store in order to replenish their bank account.

The major differences between Eve White and Eve Black have been summarized as follows:

Eve White	Eve Black
Demure, retiring, in some respects almost saintly.	Obviously a party girl. Shrewd, childishly vain, and egocentric.
Face suggests a quiet sweetness; the expression in repose is predominantly one of contained sadness.	Face is pixie-like; eyes dance with mischief as if Puck peered through the pupils.
Voice always softly modulated, always influenced by a specifically feminine restraint.	Voice a little coarsened, "discultured," with echoes or implications of mirth or teasing.
An industrious and able worker; also a competent housekeeper and a skillful cook. Not colorful or glamorous. Limited in spontaneity.	A devotee of pranks. Her repeated irresponsibilities have cruel results on others. More heedless and unthinking, however, than deeply malicious.[8]

The distinctiveness of the personalities of Eve White and Eve Black shows up on projective tests, on electroencephalograms, and in handwriting studies by experts. A "blind analysis" made from the case material by other workers (Osgood and Luria, 1954) by means of the semantic differential method (Chapter 14) also shows distinctive personalities and gives some cues as to the role diffusions involved. It is fairly evident that Eve White's primary identification is

[8] Quoted, but with some abbreviation, from Thigpen and Cleckley (1954), pp. 141–42.

with her mother, who had trouble with her husband when Eve was young, just as Eve now is having trouble with her husband. Eve Black's identification appears to be with her father; it is to be regretted that we do not know more about him. Those who studied the case find no good explanation for Jane. A possibility is that she represents the grandmother with whom Eve lived after her mother was separated from her father and went to earn a living in a distant city. In any case we appear to have here a case of extreme disparity of childhood *identifications* which prevent the achievement of a single *identity* for the various aspects of the one individual (see pp. 465–66).

What can we learn from this case? First of all, we should hesitate to make any effort to correlate personality strictly with the body, for here we have the quite discordant possibilities of an Eve White and an Eve Black in the same physique. Secondly, we see that the recognizable unity of an individual personality is based solely on its behavioral characteristics, for with the same body, the same physical and social history, personalities as different, yet as individually consistent, as Eve White and Eve Black emerge. Thirdly, what we find here dramatized is also true to a lesser extent of the normal person—that the typical personality integrates a number of strands which at different times and under different occasions may cause us to behave in ways that seem very different, and yet reflect certain basic personality needs. The unity of personality is at best precarious.

Self and personality

Because of some philosophical problems connected with it, the concept of the self has long been the business of philosophy rather than psychology. More recently, however, in recognition of the need for some kind of unifying principle or ground for the manner in which a person perceived himself, the concept of the self has become a proper sphere of inquiry for psychologists.

Although no complete agreement has yet been reached about the terms of the discussion, many psychologists accept the distinction between the inferred *personality structure,* with which this chapter has thus far been concerned, and the *self* of which the subject is aware (sometimes called the *phenomenal self*), the self of self-perception. The personality structure, which characterizes the individual and represents him as decision-maker, planner, and even as self-deceiver, can be understood by an external observer, who may infer unconscious processes of which the individual is unaware. The self, however, depends upon the person's perception of his own behavior; how he sees himself can, of course, be communicated to another and thus become part of psychological science.

Self-perception

A newborn child makes no distinction between himself and things outside himself. Self-perception is an achievement that comes through growth and experience. In time the child learns that his fingers are tied onto his body as his clothes are not; he learns that there are other people who treat him in special ways and whom he can influence. He learns to stand off and take a look at himself, to see his behavior in relation to others. The result is the complex awareness of self. Four aspects of self-awareness are worth noting.

Perceiving the self as an agent. We feel responsible for our acts; we pride ourselves on our achievements and blame ourselves for our failures. This feeling of responsibility implies an active someone who does things, an actor behind the activity. Because we tend to think primarily in concrete terms, we often identify this agent with our bodies. The body enters self-awareness because it is sensitive (the pains of the body are *my* pains) and because it is able to do things (it is *I* who chop the wood). Threats to the body are threats to me. But I and my body are not quite one and the same; in one sense the body belongs to me and as an agent I make use of it. The feeling of effort—that I have to force my body to do what I wish it to do—gives a subjective basis for the distinction between my body and me. One source of self-awareness is, then, the feeling of the self as in control of the body, as something that receives impressions and manages the body's affairs.

Perceiving the self as continuous. To the external observer the continuity of the bodily organism suffices to make John the same person today that he was yesterday. But to John himself his identity is maintained by his memories—continuous memories dated in his personal past. Multiple personalities (as in the Eve White case) persist only because some of the memories are not available.

The perception of the self as continuous makes possible a reflective self-evaluation that carries the burdens of the past into the present and projects them into the future. One becomes especially aware of self in uncertainties about the self, in doubts and self-criticism. The continuity of the self makes the self an object of permanent concern for the individual.

Perceiving the self in relation to other people. Just as the personality structure is largely the result of interpersonal relations, of social interaction with other people, so, too, self-perception is importantly influenced by other people. That is, our self-perceptions are formed largely by the acceptances and rejections of other people, although we may in self-defense deny what they see in us. Good mental health requires that our self-perceptions do in fact correspond in general to the perceptions others have of us; distortion of self-appraisal and of self-evaluation is always found in mental illness.

Perceiving the self as the embodiment of values and goals. Consider what we mean by ambition, jealousy, vanity, prestige, shame, guilt. Self-regard looms large in all of these. Detach them from a perception of the self, and the words have no meaning for the individual. A system of values and attitudes is built up around situations that have goal character, that can stir up feelings of self-enhancement or self-degradation. An *ideal self* (the self I

would wish to become) is developed, and a person judges his actual conduct against this ideal. The ideal and the judgments combine to give self-perception a central place in social motivation. There are those who believe the maintenance and enhancement of the self to be the central feature of social motivation (Combs and Snygg, 1959). The self is assuredly an object of primary value to us. Because we perceive the self as an object of value, its successes and failures are important to us.[9]

Measuring self-perception

The self as perceived by the person is a subjective experience, and yet it is not wholly inaccessible to objective study. The personality inventory, described in the next chapter, rests on self-ratings, and can be interpreted as one kind of report on self-perception. As ordinarily used, however, the personality inventory is scored against norms obtained from a larger population, and thus loses something of individual uniqueness.

Another promising method for the study of self-perception, which is finding increasing use, is known as the *Q-technique* (Stephenson, 1953). It resembles the personality inventories in that it depends on statements that the person accepts as applicable or inapplicable to him, but there the similarity ends. The subject, under instructions, sorts a large number of statements, perhaps 100, into a number of piles, so that the statements form a distribution from the few least applicable to him to the ones most applicable. The middle piles, which will be the largest, will contain the statements of ambiguous applicability ("sometimes yes, sometimes no"; "can't say"). Now each statement can be given a score according to the pile in which it is found. The subject is then asked to sort the same statements under different instructions. For example, he can sort statements bearing on introversion and extraversion as they apply to him in different kinds of social situations. "Consider your-

[9] The concept of the self is a difficult one, not yet fully assimilated within contemporary psychology (e.g., Lowe, 1961; Wylie, 1961).

self at a formal dinner where the guest of honor is a distinguished musician." "Consider yourself at a picnic with a few of your best friends." "Consider yourself in a committee meeting of a group of experts in a field in which you, too, are an expert." Each statement gets a score for each condition. These scores can be correlated for any two conditions, and the results factor-analyzed or treated by other appropriate statistical methods of analysis. What can be learned from such analyses? It is possible to determine which are the most persistent traits as perceived by the individual, and how they cluster. Some statements will be found to vary more than others in their applicability; that is, a person does not find himself equally introverted or extraverted in all social groups: he may be the life of the party among his intimates, but easily cowed in the presence of strangers (Stephenson, 1939). By the use of this method the interpersonal nature of traits is kept in the foreground.

Self-perception and self-evaluation are likely to have an increasing place in the psychology of personality. The individual as a planner and decision-maker, who knows what he is about and how he feels, is too important to ignore.

SUMMARY 1. *Personality* is defined as the configuration of individual characteristics and ways of behaving which describe an individual's unique adjustments to his environment.

2. *Personality structure* refers to the persistent unique features that give coherence to a personality. A man's personality structure arises through the roles that culture assigns to him and through individual experiences.

3. Out of the many experiences of growing up, a person moves through the stages of *identifications* with others toward the achievement of *identity* for himself.

4. The tendency to group personalities into a few *types* is a very old one. Some theories stress *body types,* others stress *physiology* (body chemistry and endocrine balance), some are based solely on *behavior* (e.g., Jung's classification into introverts and extraverts). Such evidence as exists tends to refute type theories; objective measures of temperament and personality show little relation to Sheldon's body types, and other measures tend to fall into normal distributions rather than into the bimodal distributions that type theories suggest.

5. Allport's theory of personal dispositions is a kind of *trait* theory that he sets against the notion of common traits shared by all people. He prefers to emphasize the inner organization of motives, traits, and personal styles, thus stressing patterned individuality. Within the individual there is a hierarchy of traits (or dispositions) from *cardinal* through *central* to *secondary* traits. A short list of central dispositions often suffices to describe an individual; the listed dispositions vary from person to person and are not common traits.

6. Cattell bases his trait theory on common traits, holding that sufficient uniqueness can be indicated through combinations of common traits present at different strengths. He distinguishes between *surface traits,* grouped together through cluster analysis (because they all correlate together), and *source traits,* arrived at through factor analysis. The hope is that a limited number of source traits might suffice to be

used in the satisfactory appraisal of all personalities, but that day has not yet arrived.

7. The trait principle is an essential starting point for an empirically grounded theory of personality, whatever the nature of that theory, but a *trait profile* is an insufficient characterization of an individual. Some kind of meaningful organization of traits is essential in order to characterize the person in his interaction with the strains of the environment.

8. *Developmental theories* stress the origins of personality in early life, and the continuities of development as growth proceeds.

9. *Psychoanalytic theory* stresses stages in development, called *psychosexual stages* in the classical theory (oral, anal, phallic, latency, and genital). Erikson has added *psychosocial crises* as a recognition of the environmental influences at each stage. The significance for personality development is that throughout life there are residues from each of these stages, especially through *fixation* (arrested development at one or another stage) or *displacement* (one object of gratification substituting for another). Two adult personality structures are representative: the *compulsive* and the *authoritarian* personality.

10. *Learning theories* also recognize the continuities in development, but emphasize the formation of *habits* which are then generalized to new situations.

11. *Role theory* is also a developmental theory, in that *role behavior* has to be acquired appropriate to the *role positions* that are ready-made for the individual, or which he chooses. The stability of personality structure is determined by the stability of social structure as well as by the stability of the individual's system of habits.

12. Theories of *personality dynamics* are concerned with contemporary manifestations of personality in interaction with the physical and social environment, particularly as *conflicts* arise because of discordant trends within the personality, or habit conflicts, or role conflicts.

13. The *psychoanalytic* theory of personality dynamics is given order by the concepts of *id, ego,* and *superego* as the persistent features of the personality that enter into conflict. The id is irrational and impulsive, seeking immediate gratification; the ego postpones gratification, so that it can be achieved realistically and in socially approved ways; the superego (conscience) imposes a moral code.

14. None of the present theories of personality dynamics has succeeded in formulating a way in which to characterize all personalities according to some common scheme, although the possibility of such a formulation clearly exists.

15. The search for personality structure is a search for some unifying principle or manner of describing the person so as to express his essential unity as well as his uniqueness. The person may not, in fact, be very highly unified; there may be conflicting substructures within the personality, dissociated trends, alternative roles. Such fragmented personality structures are well illustrated by cases of *multiple personality*, in

which several moderately consistent personalities appear in alternation in the same individual.

16. The concept of the *self* is increasingly being accepted in contemporary psychology, after having long been denied a place. The inferred personality structure is describable according to an external observer, but the *self* (sometimes called the *phenomenal self*) is the self of which the subject is aware, the self of self-perception. The self so defined is perceived as an agent, as continuous, as reflected in relations with other people, and as the embodiment of goals and values. Methods of measuring self-perception are being developed.

SUGGESTIONS FOR FURTHER READING

The best single source on personality theories is the book by Hall and Lindzey, *Theories of personality* (1957), in which a dozen theories are systematically but sympathetically set forth, with temperate criticisms. There is an accompanying book of readings, Lindzey and Hall (eds.), *Theories of personality: primary sources and research* (1965). Another useful source is a collection edited by Wepman and Heine, *Concepts of personality* (1963). See also Sarason, *Personality, an objective approach* (1966), and Byrne, *An introduction to personality* (1966). An introduction to Allport's theory is his small book, *Becoming* (1955), also available in a paperback edition. The major statement of his position is *Pattern and growth in personality* (1961).

Cattell has a number of books describing his researches and his orientation, of which a later one is *The scientific analysis of personality* (1965). Guilford, *Personality* (1959), gives an excellent review of personality dimensions, especially those arrived at by factor analysis, which allows his summaries to be compared with those of Cattell.

That learning theory does not necessarily lead to uniform conclusions about personality is illustrated by Dollard and Miller, *Personality and psychotherapy* (1950), in which the emphasis is upon learning but the cast is somewhat psychoanalytic, and Bandura and Walters, *Social learning and personality development* (1963), which is anti-psychoanalytic. Role theory tends to be emphasized by sociologists, for example, Nadel, *The theory of social structure* (1957).

Problems of the self have been reviewed by Wylie, *The self concept* (1961).

Lest the erroneous impression be left that the various theories are contradictory, rather than supplementary, a useful corrective can be provided by Allport, *Letters from Jenny* (1965), in which the case of an interesting but somewhat unusual woman is discussed from the viewpoint of several alternative theories.

19 Personality Appraisal

If the individual, as a result of his development and present interactions with his environment, has achieved some sort of enduring personality structure, there must be some way in which this structure can be characterized more precisely by means of measurement or other types of appraisal. The success of the intelligence test set the background for the development of personality tests that might serve as a measure of other aspects of individuality as intelligence tests have served as a measure of intellectual characteristics.

One difference between intelligence and personality is immediately apparent: intelligence can be measured according to whether or not the responses of the person correspond to truth and fact, so that all people can be measured against the same standard. But personality structure is unique to the individual; the question arises whether or not it is appropriate to attempt to measure personality against common standards or criteria. An extreme view would be to leave to the artist rather than to the scientist the attempt to describe the rich uniqueness of the individual. But to accept this position would be to give up a scientific psychology of personality, a step most psychologists would be reluctant to take.

The problem of uniqueness in personality is in essence no more difficult than the problem of biological uniqueness. Whenever the consequences of a very large number of antecedent variables (whether these are "genes" or "individual experiences") produce a composite effect, the result is unique chiefly because a repetition of any one combination is mathematically improbable. The uniqueness is not *unlawful* in relation to antecedent events; it is merely *unlikely* because of the many possible combinations. An example is provided by the uniqueness of individual fingerprints. Despite this uniqueness it is possible to find a number of signs by which to classify fingerprints, so that an individual can be identified according to a code. Thus the lawfulness of fingerprint design does not conflict with uniqueness. Correspondingly, we may grant the uniqueness of the individual and still proceed with an analysis according to single variables, multiple variables, or some complex type of patterning. How we proceed will depend in part on our preferences determined by theory: those seeking a *type* classification will search somewhat differently from those satisfied with *traits*, while those with developmental or dynamic conceptions will necessarily make appraisals that fit in (or put to the test) their particular point of view.

Personality Characteristics Subject to Appraisal

The present personality is of course a product of its development, but it is appraised or characterized by the way it is now expressed. Following the distinction we have made from time to time between the developmental and interactive viewpoints, we may say that the present personality can be *understood* according to its developmental history, but can be *assessed* according to its contemporary interactions. We are thus interested in how well a person gets along with others *now*, even though there may be various routes over which he could have traveled in becoming the person he now is.

Personality expression is so diverse that there are many ways of talking about it and many ways of characterizing an individual. Allport (1960) has listed ten kinds of units used in describing personality, ranging from "ideational schemes" to unconscious motives; Guilford (1959) writes of seven "modalities of traits," indicating that the kind of trait we see depends upon the direction from which we view personality (Figure 19–1). There are many overlapping terms in their lists, but the lack of agreement shows that some arbitrariness enters. Common properties that appear in various descriptive characterizations of personality can be summarized as follows:

1. *Physique.* A person's physical endowments of bodily size, strength, grace, and appearance become aspects of his personality; they influence the manner in which other people react to him, and these reactions, in turn, shape his image of himself as worthy or unworthy. More exact measurements are implied in those theories which stress body types (Chapter 18, pp. 466–67), but other theories call attention to the body also. For example, we noted earlier in the discussion of adolescence that early or late development had their influences on the developing personality (pp. 94–95).

2. *Temperament.* A person's characteristic mood is thought to be influenced by certain inherited physiological patterns, as, for example, by the general responsiveness of the autonomic nervous system or the activity levels of the various endocrine glands, as noted earlier (pp. 467–68). Concern over temperament is one of the ancient ways of viewing personality; we are prepared today to make better measurements

19–1

Modalities of traits representing different aspects of personality

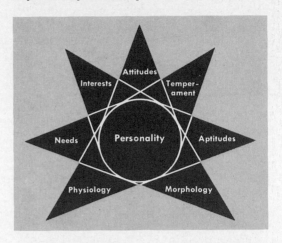

In this diagram, personality is shown as an integrated whole, which can be viewed from different directions: from one direction we see one kind of trait, from another we see another kind of trait. (From Guilford, 1959)

both at the level of physiology and at the level of overt behavior in order to enhance our knowledge.

3. *Intellectual and other abilities.* Personality really covers the whole field of individual differences, and it is important to bear in mind that intellectual abilities are also a part of personality, even though for convenience we may sometimes distinguish between "intelligence tests" and "personality tests." Other abilities, such as the skills involved in musical performance, are also relevant to personality. A developed sense of humor requires a quick appreciation of literary allusions; the detection of similarities and incongruities depends upon a high order of intelligence. It is evident that "personality" and abilities are intertwined in many ways.

4. *Interests and values.* Personality is in part reflected in the kinds of things one likes to do, what one enjoys, what one appreciates. Interests are usually defined according to objects or activities; that is, one may be interested in stamps or coins or old motor cars; in chemistry, biology, international affairs, reading, music, or sports. The list of potential interests is

practically limitless, but a sampling of these interests can clearly tell us something about the person who has them.

Values are related to interests in that they tend to place some sorts of involvement higher in a scale of preference than other sorts; when one says he prefers classical music to popular music he is telling you something about his values as well as about his interests. When men are classified according to their dominant values, larger classes of activities are usually specified than in the case of interests; the *Scale of values* (Allport, Vernon, and Lindzey, 1960) attempts to measure the extent to which one's values can be classified as theoretical, economic, esthetic, social, political, or religious.

5. *Social attitudes*. A person necessarily adopts attitudes toward features of his contemporary culture. He is likely to be either more conservative or more liberal in politics; he may feel strongly about racial equality, or academic freedom, or birth control. Expressed in personality terms, these attitudes toward particular features of life reveal such characteristics as authoritarianism, equalitarianism, or dogmatism. The problems of attitudes and opinions will be treated more fully in Chapter 23.

6. *Motivational dispositions*. We have already met attempts to assess individuals according to their achievement motives or their affiliative motives (Chapter 6, pp. 139–40). Other motivational dispositions have served in the description of individual personalities. Some of the motives implied may be unconscious.

7. *Expressive and stylistic traits*. Very often when we characterize a person we tell something about his style: politeness, talkativeness, consistency, hesitancy, sociability, criticalness. There are a great many such "personality traits" that seem somewhat independent of the content being expressed; that is, the traits will show themselves at home and at the office, in social groups and in professional meetings. These expressive and stylistic traits are commonly revealed in interaction with other people.

8. *Pathological trends*. Sometimes it is easier to characterize illness than health; one way of describing the normal person is to say that he differs from others in the direction of one or another mental illness. Thus an overexcited form of mental disturbance is known as a *manic* form, and a generally excited and vivacious person (not really in any danger of mental illness) may be called *hypomanic,* which means "undermanic" and which suggests that he resembles the manic but doesn't go that far. Another form of illness is known as *schizophrenia,* and a person who is withdrawn and introverted (again, not at all mentally ill) may be described as *schizoid*. Because these terms tend to take on value connotations, they are probably not to be encouraged; yet their convenience, in some instances, is not to be denied.

This listing of descriptive terms referring to personality suggests why it is difficult to find satisfactory brief descriptions of individual persons, and why some sort of theory is needed to bring order into the characterization of personality.

Personality Inventories

One way in which we size up a person is to ask him some questions about himself, which will prepare us to express some descriptive judgments about him. To do this more systematically we may have him answer a great many questions that others have also answered; from these answers about himself we can derive a sort of "score" by which to compare his answers with those of others and then arrive at a description of his personality in some standard form.

In one early test of this kind, the Thurstone Neurotic Inventory, the person was asked to answer questions of the following type:

Yes No ? Do you take responsibility for introducing people?

Yes No ? Are your feelings easily hurt?

Yes No ? Do you like to be with other people a great deal?

Yes No ? Do your interests change quickly?

The person taking the test checks whether his answer to each question is yes, no, or uncertain. From the total of the answers in which he indicates some sort of "trouble" he was scored (on this test) on a scale running from normal to neurotic. Other personality inventories, as we shall see, attempt to scale many other dimensions of personality.

The personality inventory has been developed on the model of the intelligence test and is often called a *personality test*. It should conform to the rules of reliability (self-consistency) and validity (correlation with a criterion) (pp. 418–20). Those constructing personality inventories commonly choose groups of well adjusted and groups of poorly adjusted persons whose scores serve as criteria for validating the test; that is, the test is tried out on both groups, and only those questions which the two groups answer differently are retained. The "purified" test (consisting of the best items) will then supposedly discriminate between well adjusted and poorly adjusted. But it is difficult to be sure that the groups really represent the qualities that the test proposes to distinguish.

A personality inventory may be designed to measure a single trait, a dimension of personality. Thus we have tests of ascendance-submission and tests of introversion-extraversion. Or the test may provide an overall estimate of personal adjustment in an attempt to distinguish between the adjusted and the neurotic. When a test seeks to measure at once several aspects of personality, it may come out with a *profile* of scores rather than a single score. Some illustrative personality inventories are described below.

Minnesota Multiphasic Personality Inventory

The Minnesota Multiphasic Personality Inventory (MMPI) illustrates a self-rating instrument following the eighth category cited above (pathological trends). The test is arranged in the form of 495 statements, sometimes with each printed on a separate card. The subject sorts the cards into three piles: the statements that he judges to be true, those that he judges to be false, and those about which he "cannot say."[1] Some of the items are:

> I have never done anything dangerous for the thrill of it.
> I daydream very little.
> My mother or father often made me obey even when I thought it was unreasonable.
> At times my thoughts have raced ahead faster than I could speak them.
> I like to read newspaper editorials.

Responses are scored according to the correspondence between the answers given by the subject and those given by patients with different kinds of psychological disturbances. The result is a profile of nine scores, each arranged as a standard score (see p. 404). Typical profiles are shown in Figure 19–2. One is for "normal" persons, the other for those classified as "neurotic."

In addition to the scales originally provided for the test, many new ones have been developed. The number of items is so large and the range of questions asked so great that it is possible to construct scales that reflect many dimensions of personality other than those for which the test was originally intended. At least 100 such scales have been constructed (Welsh and Dahlstrom, 1956).

Built into the scoring of the MMPI are a number of "control keys" to correct for types of responding that make the results invalid. For example, one control key counts the number of items skipped, or interpreted as "cannot say." If the subject has failed to reply to too many questions, his answers obviously cannot be compared with the statistical norms of those who answer many more of the questions. Another key provides an L ("lie")-score by detecting those who give many improbable answers, such as replying "false" to "I sometimes put off until tomorrow what I ought to do today." Another scale counts up the number of very rare answers that the subject gives, again a sign of falsification or carelessness if too many are given,

[1] In the booklet form he indicates merely whether each statement does or does not apply to himself; the "cannot say" is indicated only by omitting a reply.

Personality profiles

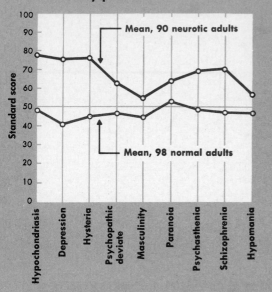

Profiles of normal adults and adults with neurotic tendencies on the Minnesota Multiphasic Personality Inventory. Each of the nine scores is arranged as a standard score, with mean of 50 and standard deviation of 10. The nine scales are based on scores of groups of patients showing the symptoms indicated. The beginning student need not attempt to understand the individual scales in order to understand what the test attempts to do. (After Schmidt, 1945)

while still another corrects for a tendency to deny symptoms. Thus various degrees of subtlety have been employed in improving the value of the test.

The foregoing brief account naturally raises some questions about the validity of such a test in general. How can a test as a whole be valid if we are skeptical about the answers to particular questions? Two points need to be made. First, as long as the subject is cooperating and answering conscientiously the factual basis of the answer may not be as important as what the reply reveals about the person. The answer to the question "Do you blush easily?" need not distinguish between those who blush frequently and those who blush less frequently. The one who answers "yes" is more concerned or sensitive about his blushing than the one who answers "no," and this is what we are interested in.

Second, the correction scales, used to detect careless or uncooperative subjects, are so designed as to pick up only the more absurd kinds of self-contradiction; they do not reject the unusual answers of the maladjusted person.

Edwards Personal Preference Schedule

While the MMPI represents the purely empirical method of test construction, in that a mass of items are weighted in accordance to the responses made to them by appropriate groups of subjects, the Edwards Personal Preference Schedule (EPPS) is constructed quite differently. The items were selected upon the basis of face validity; that is, Edwards (1954) chose his items to represent the content of 15 basic motivational dispositions or needs, as set forth by Murray (1938) (see p. 143). These include such needs as abasement, achievement, dominance, aggression, autonomy. The inventory consists of 225 items presented in pairs; it contains 30 statements bearing upon each of the 15 needs. The emphasis is not on psychopathology, as in the MMPI, but rather on motives found among all members of a normal population. Because the appraisal is of motivational dispositions, it illustrates the sixth of our descriptive categories of personality (p. 488).

Edwards built his scale in such a manner as to circumvent some of the biases of other inventories, chiefly the tendency to present oneself in a favorable light by replying in ways that may be considered socially desirable. He did this by arranging his items as *forced choices* between statements judged to be equally socially desirable. Thus the subject taking the test must answer either A or B of an item such as the following:

A   I like to be successful in things undertaken.
B   I like to form new friendships.

Both of these are statements that are socially acceptable, but one stresses more particularly achievement, while the other stresses affiliation with others. Of course some items require a choice between unfavorable statements:

A   I feel depressed when I fail at something.
B   I am nervous when talking before a group.

The point is that, for persons for whom the items are essentially inapplicable, their choices ought to be about 50/50, because they are equally desirable or undesirable so far as they could be made so.

The forced-choice method has a disadvantage, however, in that it gives only the *relative* preferences for one pattern of motive over another, but does not reveal the *absolute* level of that motive. That is, a relatively listless person might come out with a ranking of his motives similar to that of a highly energetic one; unless their hierarchies differed, there would be no way by which to distinguish their general arousal levels. However, if it is assumed that each person is strongly motivated in some direction (even to be fairly inactive and dependent on others), then a motive that is chosen consistently against others must fairly well characterize his motivational system.

Cattell's 16 PF Questionnaire

We noted in the previous chapter how Cattell had distinguished between surface traits and source traits (pp. 471–72). It was his hope that by analyzing a very large number of trait ratings and measurements, and then analyzing them by factor-analytic methods, he could come out with a picture representative of the whole personality sphere. An individual would be characterized according to his standing with respect to the most fundamental source traits.

Cattell's 16 PF ("personality factors") scales illustrate this approach. The result of an enormous amount of work in locating the main source traits, in selecting items to best represent them, and then in assembling them into a short and usable test is condensed into this final product (Cattell, 1957*b*). It yields scores on 16 relatively independent personality characteristics ("source traits") such as dominance, emotional stability, radicalism, and will control. In principle the test has certain advantages in that it is less arbitrarily related to pathology (as in the MMPI) or to a somewhat arbitrary list of needs (as in the EPPS); it represents a wide search for the most significant things to say about a personality. Unfortunately, however, the individual scales as subtests are too short to be very reliable, so that the test is not in fact very useful in giving a description of a single subject's personality.

The validity of personality inventories

The success of the intelligence test led to great hopes for similar success with personality inventories. The problems of the two kinds of tests turned out, however, to be quite different. Three major differences are worth mentioning:

1. Any single item on an intelligence test always has a correct answer. Hence, the main problem of the test constructor is to arrange the items according to their difficulty or representative quality. But a single item of the personality test has *no independent correct answer*. Some items may be answered in the affirmative by 80 percent of neurotic people and by 60 percent of normal people. Hence an item may be useful as one among many that help to distinguish the neurotic from the normal, but taken by itself it means little. It may have a neurotic *weight* in the test score, but it is scarcely a sign of neuroticism if 60 percent of non-neurotic people find it applicable to themselves. The single items in personality inventories thus have different status from those in intelligence tests.

2. A subject may deliberately give false answers to items in a personality inventory, thereby producing a score more indicative of either normal or neurotic adjustment than is actually the fact. False answering on an intelligence test leads only to lower scores, ordinarily against the subject's wishes, while false answers on a personality inventory can be made in the effort to give a picture of good or poor adjustment.

3. A third difficulty lies in the *additive*

assumption commonly made in testing. In intelligence tests it worked reasonably well to add up the number of correct answers in arriving at a score, because the more answers that correspond to truth and fact the more intelligent these answers are. When the same assumption is carried over to personality tests the result is not as satisfactory, because the total number of "adjusted" and "maladjusted" statements may not in fact index the degree of disturbance. One small area of severe disturbance may in fact be as serious for normal functioning as several of them, and some one strong positive characteristic may counterbalance a number of weaknesses.

The additive assumption has been questioned as a result of some efforts to measure personality characteristics predictive of hypnotic susceptibility (J. R. Hilgard, 1965). It was found that subjects who scored high in some *one* characteristic related to hypnotic susceptibility scored as high on the criterion of hypnosis as those who scored high on *several* of the characteristics. This led to the suggestion of *alternative* predictors, as contrasted with *additive* predictors. The possibility exists that this distinction may hold in the prediction of personality functioning in other areas.

Another way of meeting this same criticism of the additive assumption in personality tests is to use a *pattern analysis* or *configural scoring* of scores, rather than a mere sum. The assumption is that scores patterned in certain ways may be more diagnostic than the average or sum of these scores (Meehl, 1950). A little reflection will show that traits in combination have very different meanings from traits taken alone. Consider, for example, the difference in the meaning of "slow" in the combination "slow and accurate" and "slow and careless." In the first context the "slow" has the suggestion of deliberation and caution, while in the second it suggests stupidity or inattention. The MMPI is almost always interpreted according to the patterning of scores.

The consequence of these differences between the two types of test is that personality tests have not been as successful as intelligence tests, although they have been successful enough to be genuinely useful. The personality inventory results in errors of two kinds. The *false positives* classify one as disturbed or neurotic when he is not seriously in need of help. While one is unlikely to report troubles he does not have, the test items do permit exaggerated reporting of minor difficulties. The test becomes a kind of "cry for help," and it can in fact be used to detect those who welcome an opportunity for counseling. But the *false negatives* are more troublesome—they classify the disturbed individuals who are fighting to conceal their weaknesses and who are intelligent enough to falsify their self-estimates in the direction of social conformity. (This falsification need not be deliberate; the mechanisms of self-deception are sufficient to lead to faulty self-judgments even when the subject is trying to be honest.) Personality inventories, however, can be used successfully to pick out from a larger population those likely to become neuropsychiatric casualties. The tests can then be supplemented by interview.

To establish the validity of a test it is necessary to have some *criterion* against which to measure its predictions. Thus a scholastic aptitude test has school grades as its criterion. However, it is very difficult to secure appropriate criterion measures for personality tests. One method, mentioned above, is to consider the scores of extremely disturbed individuals as indications of what a disturbed score would look like. Then a "normal" individual is judged to be maladjusted if his scores resemble those of hospitalized patients. This method is not very satisfactory, however, because personality is more a matter of individual trait patterning than a sum of answers to test items. When the method was turned around and a search made for "sound" individuals, as judged by those who knew them best, these "sound" individuals were found to have a wide range of scores on personality inventories (Barron, 1954). Thus the method of item-sorting by correlation with a criterion, which works well for intelligence tests, is not as satisfactory for personality tests.

The fact, pointed out by Cronbach (1960), that we seek in personality tests a *characteristic* performance, rather than one at its *best*, means that valid personality tests are harder to develop than ability tests (which seek the performance at its maximum). Since it is not difficult to falsify a score on a personality inventory, there are always likely to be maladjusted people who score within the normal range on the test.

Personality inventories have provided us with useful information about trait distributions within the population and about the intercorrelations among traits. Nevertheless, these tests remain fallible instruments, and their improvement is one of the pressing tasks facing psychology.

CRITICAL DISCUSSION

Biasing factors in the responses to personality inventories

The interpretation of a personality inventory does not depend upon the accuracy of the answers, provided one subject makes answers that are consistently different from another. Thus if men answer a question consistently one way and women another, the question may be used in a masculinity-femininity scale regardless of its content. However, it is important that the answers do in fact reflect the content of the questions. That is, we hope that those who say "I sometimes feel just miserable" do actually feel depressed more frequently or more deeply than those who deny feeling miserable, although for some purposes of interpretation it would not matter exactly what the factual basis was, so long as it revealed a tendency to be aware of mood changes. Analysis of answers to personality inventories shows two very prevalent kinds of distortion, one of which is based on the general (but not the specific) content of the question, the other of which merely depends upon the way the question is asked.

The first of these, which has been called the *social desirability* variable by Edwards (1957), is a tendency to answer the questions in a manner that would be expected of well adjusted and acceptable people or of people who wish to deny illness and deviancy. The lower end of the social desirability scale is, of course, the exaggeration of anxiety, symptoms, and nonconformity to social expectations (as in the "just miserable" question cited above). A straightforward method of estimating social desirability in inventory responses is to count the number of agreements of a subject with items that the majority of a general population answer in a given direction. When Edwards constructed a key in this manner, with a social-desirability scale of 39 items, he found substantial correlations with many of the MMPI scales—for example, +.61 with Gough's status scale and −.84 with Taylor's manifest anxiety scale (Edwards, 1957, p. 33). Thus the tendency to conform to social expectations is certainly one feature in personality inventories; it is a feature that Edwards attempted to correct in the EPPS by forcing choices between items rated equal in social desirability. Other ways of studying social desirability are possible, leading to conclusions slightly different from those of Edwards, but the relevance of social desirability as a biasing variable is unquestioned (Wiggins, 1959; Crowne and Marlowe, 1964).

The second tendency found in personality inventories is an *acquiescence tendency* (Cronbach, 1942; Wiggins, 1962). This is a tendency to agree with the test item when no issue is at stake; the opposite extreme is that of caution, even when the issue is innocuous. Studies have shown that items relatively free of a consistently meaningful content may still distinguish between groups with identifiable personality characteristics, one study characterizing the "yeasayers" as contrasted with the "naysayers" (Couch and Keniston, 1960). It should be noted that the acquiescence tendency can be estimated regardless of the content of the test items; while the reply to a statement may therefore tell something about the subject, it does not necessarily describe him according to the content of the test item (Berg, 1959).

These tendencies are doubtless present, but further investigation shows that there are content aspects of the inventories that survive after the biasing tendencies are corrected (Eysenck and Eysenck, 1964; Rorer, 1965; Rundquist, 1966). Thus the advances in the understanding of response biases in personality inventories do not discredit the inventories, but they indicate that more so-

Projective Tests

If there is a unity of personality that expresses itself directly or indirectly through all that a person does, then there ought to be some way of characterizing this unity, this personality structure lying behind and giving direction to the individual act. Because this individual style of behavior ought to reveal itself most readily when expression is free, psychologists have selected imaginative productions as being perhaps the most revealing of personality. In imagination the individual is free to build his own world and to make himself the hero in whatever drama he chooses to construct; in this free play he may reveal unconscious tendencies, that is, tendencies of which he is unaware. These imaginative productions the psychologists obtain through *projective tests*. The personality inventories already described have fixed alternatives, so that the subject must reply by making a choice among ready-made answers. Projective tests are more ambiguous, less highly structured, and potentially more revealing. Because the subject puts more of himself into the answers, he is said to *project* his personality through them, as the movie camera projects the image on the screen. Hence the name projective tests.

Thematic Apperception Test

One kind of projective test consists of a series of pictures about which the subject tells stories. The subject usually becomes absorbed in the imaginative productions he is building around each picture and says things about the characters in the stories that really apply to himself. The somewhat forbidding name of the test, Thematic Apperception Test (abbreviated TAT) (Morgan and Murray, 1935; Stein, 1955) is intended to describe the fact that the test reveals basic "themes" that recur in the imaginative productions of a person. Apperception means a readiness to perceive

in certain ways, based on prior individual experience. Hence the test name implies that a subject interprets an ambiguous stimulus according to his individual readiness to perceive in a certain way and that he elaborates the stories in terms of preferred plots or themes that reflect his fantasies. We have already met the use of this kind of instrument in the assessing of achievement motivation (pp. 153–54).

When confronted with a picture similar to that in Figure 19–3, a 21-year-old patient told the following story.

> She has prepared this room for someone's arrival and is opening the door for a last general look over the room. She is probably expecting her son home. She tries to place everything as it was when he left. She seems like a very tyrannical character. She led her son's life for him and is going to take over again as soon as he gets back. This is merely the beginning of her rule, and the son is definitely cowed by this overbearing attitude of hers and will slip back into her well ordered way of life. He will go through life plodding down the tracks she has laid down for him. All this represents her complete domination of his life until she dies.[2]

[2] Arnold (1949).

19–3

A picture similar to one used in the Thematic Apperception Test

The pictures usually have elements of ambiguity in them, so that the subject can "read into" them something from his own experience or fantasy.

A group inkblot test

A group of subjects write down what they see in an inkblot thrown on the screen. The blot is similar to those used in the Rorschach test, but is not one of the series actually used in individual testing.

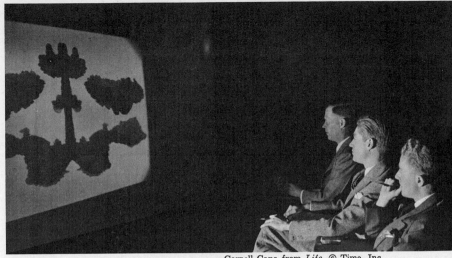

Cornell Capa from *Life*, © Time, Inc.

Although the original picture shows only a woman standing in an open door, the subject's readiness to respond with something about his relationship to his mother led to this story of a woman's domination of her son. The clinician whose patient told this story reports that facts obtained later fully confirmed the interpretation that the story reflected the subject's own problems.

In taking the TAT, the subject tells stories about 20 pictures. If special problems are preoccupying him, they may show up in a number of the stories. For that reason, the TAT in the hands of a skilled interpreter may make possible the discovery of personality patterns unique to the person being tested.

The subtlety of the TAT does not assure that the subject is in fact revealing himself in the stories that he tells. While various kinds of data have tended to support TAT interpretations (e.g., Henry, 1956), some negative evidence also exists. In one study, the relationship to parents represented in TAT stories failed to correspond to known relationships to parents revealed in the course of psychotherapy (Meyer and Tolman, 1955). However, some satisfactory results have been obtained with special scoring keys designed to measure such characteristics as achievement motivation (reported earlier, p. 156) or fear and aggression (Mussen and Naylor, 1954). Under such circumstances the test scores were found to relate significantly to nontest measures of the same variables.

Rorschach test

The Rorschach inkblot test is another of the many projective tests (Rorschach, 1942; first published in 1921). It consists of a series of cards, each displaying a rather complex inkblot (see Figure 19–4). If ink is spilled on a piece of paper that is then creased down the middle, a bilaterally symmetrical blot like that shown in Figure 19–4 will result. From many such designs, a few standard ones have been selected, and the experienced tester knows something about the responses to be expected from each. The subject tells what he sees on the card. He may see several different things on a single card, or he may see the same ambiguous shape as representing at once several figures. The test capitalizes on our familiar tendency to see imaginary faces, animals, battle scenes, or fairyland figures in cloud formations.

The subject's responses to the inkblot are in some ways more revealing than his replies to a personality inventory. The subject is much less self-conscious about those responses than when replying to questions about himself in a personality inventory, and what appear to him to be very matter-of-fact responses to what he sees in the

TABLE 19–1

Nature of interpretations of Rorschach responses

Example of response	Nature of scored response	Direction of interpretation
"Reminds me of a bat, the whole thing."	Location on card of described features	Suggests intellectual aspects of personality
"Two women with high-heeled shoes, trying to pull something apart."	Human movement	Related to creative capacity
"A pair of raccoons climbing."	Animal movement	Related to immaturity-maturity
"Here's a green grasshopper."	Color	Degree of contact with outer reality
"A pair of pliers."	Form	Degree of emotional control
"The darkness there may be clouds."	Shading and color	Expression of anxiety

SOURCE: Table courtesy of Frances G. Orr.

blots may be revealing of unconscious aspects of his personality. The TAT has a similar advantage over the personality inventory, but even in it the characters of the stories are often recognizable to the subject. The Rorschach is the more subtle of these tests.

How can Rorschach responses be scored and interpreted? It takes several months of training for a tester to learn to score the test and to interpret the results. Hence we can give here only the briefest hints as to the directions the scoring and interpretation take. The responses are classified by type according to a conventional system, with a minimum of interpretation, as in the column of Table 19–1 headed *Nature of scored response*. The response classes include detail, form, color, movement, and similar objective categories. The frequencies of these categories are then counted and used in interpretation. Some of the directions of interpretation are given in the last column of Table 19–1. The main point of the table is to show how remote the interpretation is from what the subject has reported. If the subject responds predominantly to a few features of the card and excludes the others, he presumably tells us something about himself.

Those skilled in the use of the Rorschach claim to obtain from it important information about the subject's personality structure. Because the test is more ambiguous in content than the TAT, it is said to get at deeper unconscious patterns. While the limits of what can be done with the Rorschach are a matter of debate at the present time, it remains popular in clinical practice.

Because the personality picture that results from the Rorschach is largely individual, the problem of validating the conclusions is a difficult one. Among the more appropriate methods of validation is that known as "blind matching." A judge has two sets of data about a group of individuals. One set of data consists of their Rorschach responses. The other set consists of biographical material giving characteristic behavior in life situations. The judge attempts to match the test results with the personality portrait given by the biography. The conditions for an experimental validation of this kind have to be set up very carefully to assure independence of the two sets of material, and few studies fully meet these demands. Unfortunately, satisfactory validation of the Rorschach by such methods is still lacking, and most careful studies are damaging to the test's reputation (Zubin, 1954; Cronbach, 1956).

Why should a test of doubtful validity remain popular? There are several answers. For one thing, the results, while not always dramatic, are usually beyond chance. A second reason is that the responses are judged in the context of other information about the person. The test serves the clinician as a kind of mirror to hold up to the patient, and the clinician has other information from the process than is found in the test scores alone. It is not surprising that for this reason clinicians tend to prefer the test more than psychologists whose interest is in test construction. A third point is that the responses to the test are highly varied and individual, so that it is possible to rescore them for a number of research purposes, often with useful results, as, for example, when the test is used in cross-cultural studies (Lindzey, 1961).

A systematic effort to improve the test has been made by Holtzman and others (1961), who have developed many new inkblots, with variations among them based on conjectures that have arisen in connection with research on Rorschach's original blots. This test, consisting of parallel forms of 45 cards each, yields interesting interrelationships with other personality measures, such as the MMPI (Moseley, Duffey, and Sherman, 1963).

The two tests, TAT and Rorschach, which we have described in some detail, suffice to introduce us to projective tests. They show in part how test devices can be selected (or invented) which are appropriate to analyzing personality as an organized whole, as a "structure."

Other Methods of Personality Assessment

Many appraisals of personality depend upon the judgment of skilled observers. While the foregoing accounts of personality inventories and of projective tests indicate efforts to parallel the successes of intelligence tests, in the end we must always return to observation of the person functioning in his environment if we are to know how successful our tests have been. In this section we shall be concerned with efforts to improve observation and judgment.

Rating scales

Many personality judgments are made by other people. The employer selects his employee; the jury decides the responsibility of the accused; the scholarship committee decides which students deserve aid; each of us decides whose friendship to cultivate. A rating scale is a device by which a rater can record his judgment of another person according to the traits defined by the scale. The preferred form of rating scale is that known as the *graphic rating scale*, an example of which is shown in Figure 19–5. Each trait is represented by a segmented line; one end indicates one extreme of the trait to be rated, and the other end represents the opposite extreme. The rater places a check mark at an appropriate place on the scale to represent the degree to which the subject possesses the trait. There are a number of other rating-scale devices, such as rankings and man-to-man comparisons (Tiffin, 1959).

The rater must understand the scale; he must be sufficiently acquainted with the person rated so that he can make useful judgments of him; and he must avoid the *halo effect* and other common errors in rating. (The halo effect is the tendency to rate a person high on all traits because he makes a very good impression on one or two or, conversely, to rate him low throughout because he makes a poor impression on one or two traits.) When used with proper care, the rating scale is a very helpful device for recording judgments of other people.

Sociometry

Sociometry deals with one very important aspect of personality: how the person affects others. William James once said that we have as many selves as there are people who recognize us (because our "self" is largely how we affect others), and a later psychologist, Mark A. May, once defined personality as "social stimulus value."

Sociometry is a word coined by Jacob L. Moreno, a psychiatrist much impressed by the importance of the individual's role among other people. The mutual attrac-

19–5 A graphic rating scale

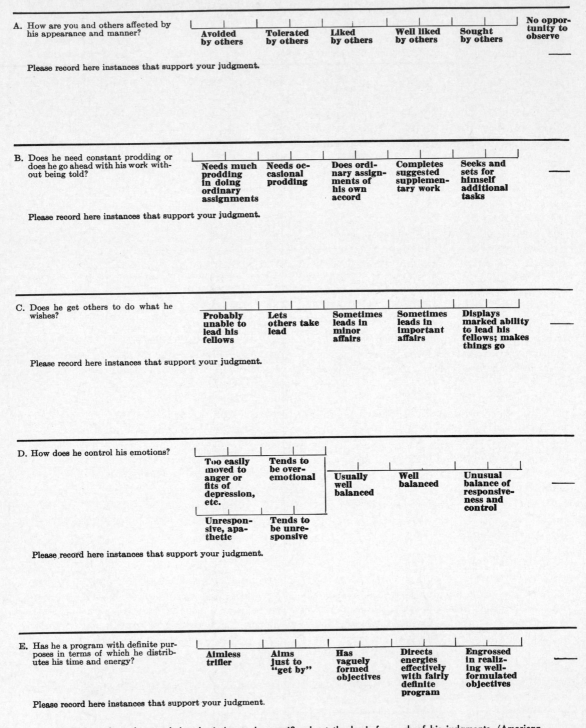

A. How are you and others affected by his appearance and manner?

Avoided by others	**Tolerated by others**	**Liked by others**	**Well liked by others**	**Sought by others**

No opportunity to observe

Please record here instances that support your judgment.

B. Does he need constant prodding or does he go ahead with his work without being told?

Needs much prodding in doing ordinary assignments	**Needs occasional prodding**	**Does ordinary assignments of his own accord**	**Completes suggested supplementary work**	**Seeks and sets for himself additional tasks**

Please record here instances that support your judgment.

C. Does he get others to do what he wishes?

Probably unable to lead his fellows	**Lets others take lead**	**Sometimes leads in minor affairs**	**Sometimes leads in important affairs**	**Displays marked ability to lead his fellows; makes things go**

Please record here instances that support your judgment.

D. How does he control his emotions?

Too easily moved to anger or fits of depression, etc.	**Tends to be over-emotional**	**Usually well balanced**	**Well balanced**	**Unusual balance of responsiveness and control**
Unresponsive, apathetic	**Tends to be unresponsive**			

Please record here instances that support your judgment.

E. Has he a program with definite purposes in terms of which he distributes his time and energy?

Aimless trifler	**Aims just to "get by"**	**Has vaguely formed objectives**	**Directs energies effectively with fairly definite program**	**Engrossed in realizing well-formulated objectives**

Please record here instances that support your judgment.

A scale such as this one helps the judge to be specific about the basis for each of his judgments. (American Council on Education; after Fryer and Henry, 1950)

tions and rejections among the members of a social group can be plotted, as done in Figure 19–6. Such a diagram is a *sociogram,* a chart of the relations within the group that tells us something about the more and less popular group members.

The method of sociometry is applicable to the study of any group of mutual acquaintances, whether in a club, a classroom, a housing project, or an office. The procedure is simple. There is some sort of vote in which each person expresses choices for or against other members of the group—for one to sit next to in class or to share a room with in the dormitory. Often a short list is called for, so that a preferential order is established for four or five group members. Preferably, from the standpoint of group morale, these are decisive choices; that is, they result in a shift of seating arrangements, partnerships, and so on. But the ballots also provide the necessary information for a sociometric mapping of the groups, from those with the highest votes who are the most admired or respected to those who remain unchosen by anyone. The resulting data can be used to make inferences about the socially significant aspects of personality, which lead on the one hand to individual acceptance and participation, on the other to isolation (Jennings, 1950).

Complex observations and judgments

A dissatisfaction with any partial approach to the measurement of personality has led to a number of studies in which very extensive records were kept. Subjects under study were assigned special field tasks to perform, for example, participating in house parties; then, after being under observation for many hours in "naturalistic" settings, they would have their test responses recorded and analyzed. This kind of procedure has come to be called "assessment," a familiar term that became used in this more specialized sense in the Office of Strategic Services during World War II, when such devices were used to select candidates for various hazardous missions (OSS Assessment Staff, 1948).

The major studies that have been carried on using this method are not very encour-

19–6

A sociometric diagram

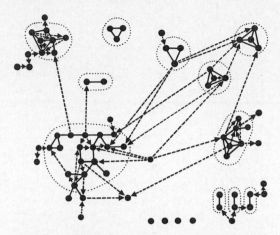

Mutual attractions among 15-year-old girls are shown here. Each dot represents one girl. Solid lines show mutual attractions; broken lines show one-way attraction in the direction of the arrow. Four of the girls are completely isolated from the group. (After Jones, 1943)

aging in their results. The most successful study was one of candidates for the British civil service (Vernon, 1950) in which there had been a careful job analysis; the future occupational tasks of the candidates were therefore clearly identified. Among the tasks assigned the candidates during a three-day "house party" were civil service paperwork, committee tasks, and group discussions. Correlations with later job performances were in the range of .50 to .65.

On the other hand, elaborate studies of trainees in clinical psychology (Kelly and Fiske, 1951) yielded little beyond what could have been predicted from material in the folders of the candidates before assessment began; similarly, a study of candidates for psychiatric training in the Menninger School of Psychiatry yielded very little (Holt and Luborsky, 1958). One of the most thorough studies was that of Air Force officers, conducted at the Institute for Personality Assessment Research at the University of California in Berkeley (MacKinnon, 1958). One hundred officers were brought for three-day assignments during which they lived with psychologists under almost continuous observation, and over 600 "scores" were obtained. However, almost no correlations rose above .30; the whole enterprise must be viewed as a failure of prediction, although there were some useful by-products.

In summarizing the assessment procedures that have shown most promise of success in prediction, Cronbach (1960) mentions three:

1. Peer ratings appear to be as useful as those of trained psychologists, probably because the peer knows more about the job requirements than the clinician.
2. Performance tests that are very near to the task to be performed have considerable validity.
3. The most important criterion for valid assessment is that the assessors have a clear understanding of the psychological requirements of the criterion task. This was true of the British civil servant study; it was also true of a study of officer candidates who were judged by recent graduates of Officer Candidate School (Holmen and others, 1956).

While personality tests are far from satisfactory, they appear to be as successful as judgments based on complex observations.

CRITICAL DISCUSSION
Clinical and statistical predictions

People experienced in the judging of other persons can often take advantage of slight clues and specific individual experiences that are lost to the test standardized on groups of people. Their judgments, which can be called *clinical*, are the alternatives to predictive scores arrived at by methods, which can be called *statistical*. How does the issue stand between the relative successes of clinical and statistical predictions?

A careful review by Meehl (1954), who has had abundant clinical and statistical experience, is informative. He found 20 studies that provided competent clinicians with information of a type that could also be expressed in mechanical formulas. With the same type of information available for judgment, in all but one of the studies the statistical predictions based on the formula were equal to or superior to the predictions made by the clinicians. In most cases if the clinician supplemented the statistical information by corrections made on the basis of his judgment, the prediction was weakened rather than improved.

This support for tests (which permit arriving at the scores that can be entered into formulas) must not be taken as an indictment of the clinical method, and is not so intended by Meehl, who points out that there are many times when a usable formula is not available (Meehl, 1957). Holt (1958), in a kind of reply and supplement to Meehl, points out that the clinicians were sometimes denied information and forced to guess in situations in which the statistical evidence was available, for example, the relation between high school and college grades. The discussion has been continued by Gough (1962) and Sawyer (1966).

In view of the tendency to be biased in favor of personal judgment (as in the desire to interview candidates for admission to a college or job applicants, rather than to rely on records), it is worth noting how fallible human judgment is when it comes to making predictions in fairly complex situations. One illustration, differing in substance from the kinds of studies reviewed by Meehl but leading to similar conclusions, is given by a study of the prediction of football game outcomes made by coaches as compared with a purely statistical prediction of the outcomes based on past team performances. The coaches were given the predictions, and asked to correct them on the basis of their knowledge of supplementary factors, such as injuries, home games, traditional rivalries, and so on. The corrections of the coaches almost invariably made the predictions worse than if reliance was on the formula alone (Harris, 1963).

It would be foolish to interpret studies showing the limitations of clinical prediction as denying the validity of the face-to-face relationships of the clinic. The purpose of the clinician is not so much to make predictions as to produce changes in desirable directions. As long as progress is made, it does not matter that a number of false leads (or false predictions) have had to be rejected in the course of clinical treatment.

SUMMARY   1. The uniqueness of the individual is not an obstacle to personality appraisal any more than the uniqueness of the biological organism is an obstacle to the scientific study of genetics.

2. There are many ways of characterizing an individual. At least eight classes of units can be used in personality appraisal: (1) *physique,* (2) *temperament,* (3) *intellectual and other abilities,* (4) *interests and values,* (5) *social attitudes,* (6) *motivational dispositions,* (7) *expressive* and *stylistic traits,* and (8) *pathological trends.*

3. The personality inventory is a device for self-characterization through replies to a large number of questions. Three examples include the Minnesota Multiphasic Personality Inventory (MMPI), basing its scales upon the empirical comparison of responses with those given by various deviant groups; the Edwards Personal Preference Schedule (EPPS), based on Murray's theory of needs and using a forced-choice technique; and Cattell's 16 PF Questionnaire, using 16 categories chosen according to the results of factor analysis.

4. The personality inventory, by contrast with an intelligence test, seeks to determine a characteristic performance rather than one at its best. Various biasing factors enter in to make personality testing by means of inventories difficult and to some extent uncertain.

5. Projective tests are more ambiguous and less highly structured than personality inventories, thus permitting the person to reveal his personality (including unconscious aspects of it) more freely. Examples are the storytelling picture test, known as the Thematic Apperception Test (TAT), and the Rorschach inkblot test. While results with these tests appear to be above chance levels, there are many difficulties in the interpreting of test scores derived from them.

6. Other methods of personality appraisal involve judgment by informed observers. Among these methods are *rating scales,* in which traits to be judged are specified, *sociometry,* in which social interaction is appraised, and *assessment,* the result of complex observations and judgments.

7. In comparisons between clinical and statistical predictions, greater success has usually been reported for the statistical predictions. In some sense, however, the tasks appropriate to the two methods are different, and the issues between them are not completely settled by appeal to specific prediction.

SUGGESTIONS FOR FURTHER READING   Cronbach, *Essentials of psychological testing* (2nd ed., 1960), has a number of chapters on personality appraisal; other books, specifically devoted to personality, are Allen, *Personality assessment procedures* (1958), and Sarason, *Personality: an objective approach* (1966).

The MMPI is probably the most worked-over of the personality inventories. Useful books about it are Welsh and Dahlstrom, *Basis readings on the MMPI in psychology and medicine* (1956), and Dahlstrom and Welsh, *An MMPI handbook: a guide to use in clinical practice and research* (1960). Edwards, *The social desirability variable in personality assessment and research* (1957), shows one of the biasing factors in self-inventories.

For the results of factor analysis in the personality sphere, the best summaries are Cattell, *Personality and motivation structure and measurement* (1957*a*), and Guilford, *Personality* (1959); a British variant, not dealt with in the text, is Eysenck, *The structure of human personality* (1959).

There are a number of books on the TAT, of which Kagan and Lesser, *Contemporary issues in thematic apperceptive methods* (1961), is a fair representative. Klopfer and others, *Developments in the Rorschach technique* (1954), and Rickers-Ovsiankina, *Rorschach psychology* (1960), are advanced books on the inkblot test. A supplementary development using a greater variety of stimulus cards is Holtzman and others, *Ink blot perception and personality* (1961). For projective tests in general, see Zubin, Eron, and Schumer, *An experimental approach to projective techniques* (1965), and Anderson and Anderson (eds.), *Introduction to projective techniques* (1951).

For more complex assessment and observational procedures, see OSS Assessment Staff, *Assessment of men* (1948), and Stern, Stein, and Bloom, *Methods in personality assessment* (1956). Note also Vernon, P. E., *Personality assessment: a critical survey* (1964).

CONFLICT, ADJUSTMENT, AND MENTAL HEALTH

We have completed a survey of the growth processes from infancy through adulthood and have considered the major topics of general psychology, culminating in the characterization of the individual personality. Now we are prepared to see what happens when the individual is placed under stress through conflict and frustration. When the ordinary methods of adjusting to the problems that arise are not adequate, we face threats to mental health and so become interested in psychotherapy and other methods of readjustment.

20 Conflict and Adjustment

No matter how resourceful we may be in coping with our problems, the circumstances of life inevitably involve stress. Our motives are not always easily satisfied; there are obstacles to be overcome, choices to be made, and delays to be tolerated. Each of us tends to develop characteristic ways of responding when our attempts to reach a desired goal are blocked. The nature of these characteristic response patterns to frustrating situations determines, to a large extent, the adequacy of our adjustment to life.

Conflict

In any individual there are always many motives active at a given time, and the goals to which they lead may be mutually exclusive. When two motives conflict the satisfaction of one leads to the frustration or blocking of the other. Often a student cannot be an outstanding college athlete and still earn the grades needed to enter graduate school. Even when only one motive is involved, there may be various ways of approaching the goal and conflict arises at the point where the paths to the goal diverge. For example, one can get an education at any one of a number of colleges, but choosing which one to enter presents a conflict situation. Even though the goal will eventually be reached, progress toward it is disrupted by the necessity for making a choice.

One way of viewing conflict situations is to classify them into the following three categories: approach-approach, avoidance-avoidance, and approach-avoidance (Lewin, 1935). These are defined as requiring a choice between two (or more) positive incentives, between two negative incentives, or between two aspects of an incentive at once positive and negative. The conflicts of real life often involve more than two alternatives; classifying the conflicts according to two alternatives is convenient but does not, of course, tell the whole story.

Approach-approach conflict

When a person has two or more desirable but mutually exclusive goals, he is temporarily torn between them. Two interesting classes may be scheduled for the same period; two attractive positions may become available at the same time; a menu may offer a choice among equally attractive entrees. When such acceptable alternatives occur (all positive incentives), the choice is usually made promptly after a brief period of vacillation. Sometimes, however, if the decision is important and the two goals have equally strong appeal, an approach-approach conflict can be a difficult one. This is especially true for children. If a youngster has to make a choice between a racing bicycle and a completely equipped camping tent for his birthday, he may spend a long period in uncomfortable vacillation before making his decision. In this case the conflict has an avoidant as well as an approach component: choosing the bicycle causes anxiety about losing the tent. This more complex situation has been called *double approach-avoidance* conflict.

Avoidance-avoidance conflict

Given a choice between two unattractive alternatives (both incentives negative), there is a strong tendency to escape the dilemma by doing something else. The child who is told to eat his spinach or go right to bed may play with his fork or stare out the window. If he is forced to choose, he takes longer to decide and vacillates more than he would in choosing between two attractive alternatives.

The approach-approach and avoidance-avoidance conflicts differ in the choice behavior they call forth, depending upon changes in the attractiveness (or repugnance) of the goal as it is approached. The nearer one gets to a positive incentive, the stronger the approach reactions; the nearer one gets to a negative incentive, the stronger the avoidance reactions. When there are two attractive goal objects (an approach-approach conflict), starting toward one of them increases the tendency to go toward it, at the same time reducing the tendency to go to the other, so that a return to the state of indecision is unlikely. When there are two unattractive goal-objects (an avoidance-avoidance conflict), starting toward one of them increases the tendency to withdraw and tends to force the individual back into indecision and vacillation. The spinach becomes more repugnant when it is on the fork than when it is on the plate, but the thought of bed keeps the child at the table.

Approach-avoidance conflict

Many incentives are at once desirable and undesirable, both positive and negative. The girl likes candy, but she does not want to get fat. Getting "high" at a party is fun, but the hangover the next morning is not. The attitude toward a goal at once wanted and not wanted, liked and disliked, is called an *ambivalent* attitude. Ambivalent attitudes are very common (Figure 20–1). The child runs away from home to escape parental domination, only to come running back to receive parental protection; his attitude toward his parents is ambivalent. Another child enjoys school but looks forward to vacation. The approach-avoidance conflict is one of the most important for us to understand, for many of the conflicts of ordinary life are of this sort.

A person confronted by a goal-object that is at once attractive and dangerous vacillates in his approach. The dangers seem less real when the goal is at a distance, so that the inviting character of the incentive leads to approach reactions. But the sense of danger increases as the goal is approached, so that nearer to the incentive one has a tendency to withdraw. This simultaneous tendency "to" and "from" leads to vacillation at some point near enough to the goal for one to be aware of the dangers but distant enough to be safe from them. When a man is about to ask the boss for a raise, he is drawn near the boss's door by the possibility of success, but his anxiety about possible rebuff, or even dismissal, mounts as he approaches. The result may involve several false starts before he either carries through his plan or abandons it.

We may illustrate by two experiments in which hungry rats were taught to run the length of an experimental alley to obtain food at a point made distinctive by the presence of a light; this training established approach reactions. Then the rats were given a brief electric shock while eating. The shock added avoidance tendencies to the approach tendencies and hence produced an approach-avoidance conflict, or ambivalence toward the food.

To test the resulting conflict behavior, the rats were placed at the start of the maze. The characteristic behavior corresponded to that predicted: the rat started in the direction of the food but came to a stop before reaching it. The place of stopping could be experimentally controlled by modifying the strength of either hunger or shock (Brown, 1942; Miller, 1959).

The behavior of the rats in this experiment can be better understood and ex-

Camera Clix

20–1

A case of ambivalence

The boy wants both to approach the goose and to back away from it. Such an approach-avoidance conflict results in a great amount of vacillation, as the attractiveness of the object keeps the child in the region of conflict, while fear is enhanced as he gets closer.

plained by using the concept of *gradients* of approach and avoidance. By a gradient we mean a change in the response strength as a function of the distance from the goal object. The pull of a magnet upon a piece of iron at a distance is an analogous (but simpler) gradient. The pull (or strength of the gradient) increases greatly as the distance between the piece of iron and the magnet is shortened.

The method devised for determining gradients was as follows. The rats wore a light harness so that the experimenter could restrain them briefly along the route. When they were restrained, the amount of pull on the harness could be recorded in grams, thus providing a measure of the approach tendency. When restrained near the goal, the rats pulled harder then when restrained farther from the goal. This increase in pull is shown (see Figure 20–2, *left*) by the slight rise in the line representing the gradient of approach between the far and the near test.

Other rats received a brief electric shock at the end of the alley. When placed at that end of the alley without shock, they tended to run away from the place where the shock had been received. When restrained nearer to the place of shock, the rats pulled away from the place of shock much harder than when restrained farther away from it. The difference between the test near shock and far from shock is shown in the gradient of avoidance (Figure 20–2, *right*).

Note also that the slope of the two lines differs: the line for avoidance is much steeper than the one for approach.

How do the results of this experiment on gradients of approach and avoidance help us understand the results of the experiment on ambivalence? If we examine the two plotted gradients, the one for approach represents a pull on the harness to the left, the one for avoidance represents a pull on the harness to the right. When a rat has been fed and shocked at the same point, both gradients are set up

Gradients of approach and avoidance

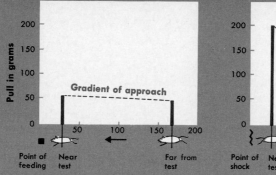

The strength of approach and avoidance is measured by the pull on the restraining harness. Note that the avoidance gradient (*right*) is steeper than the approach gradient (*left*). (After J. S. Brown, 1948)

at once. If we imagine the two gradients superimposed, they would cross at a point between 100 and 150 centimeters from the goal. At this point the two opposing tendencies would exactly balance. If the lines represented the true reaction tendencies, the rat in the experiment on ambivalence would be expected to stop at the point where the lines cross, and this is approximately what happened. This point of intersection can be moved either to the right or to the left by changing the strengths of either the approach or the avoidance tendencies. The effect of increasing the shock is to raise the avoidance gradient, thus placing the point of intersection farther from the place of being shocked. These predictions could be made from the experiment on gradients and were confirmed in the experiment on ambivalence.

The two foregoing sets of experiments, taken together, illustrate four principles important in the understanding of ambivalent behavior.

1. The tendency to approach a positive incentive is stronger the nearer the subject is to it.
2. The tendency to go away from a negative incentive is stronger the nearer the subject is to it.
3. The strength of avoidance increases more rapidly with nearness than does that of approach. In other words, the avoidance gradient is steeper than the approach gradient.
4. The strength of the tendency to approach or to avoid varies with the

20–3

Measuring approach and avoidance gradients

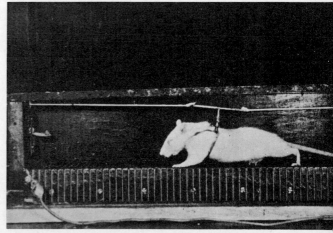

Dr. Neal E. Miller

The harness permits measurement of the amount of pull exerted by the rat, thereby yielding the results plotted in Figure 20–2.

strength of the drive upon which it is based. Increased drive tends to raise the height of the entire gradient of approach or avoidance (Miller, 1959).

For human beings the practical consequences of conflicts of the approach-avoidance type are very great. As we shall see in the next chapter, enduring approach-avoidance conflicts form the basis for serious behavior problems. The third principle helps explain how a person is drawn back into an old conflict situation by his own tendencies. He follows the pull, because at a distance the positive aspects seem more inviting than the negative ones seem forbidding. The young swimmer who wants to show off as a diver is led by his positive wishes to climb to the high platform. As he climbs, however, he begins to realize that it is a long way down to the water. His fears mount, and he may suffer the humiliation of climbing down again. He need not have placed himself in the conflict, but at a distance the desire to dive took precedence over the fear. Such conflicts are characteristic of ambivalence. They are not resolved smoothly: even though the conflict situation is avoidable, the approach tendencies draw the individual back into the zone where the avoidance tendencies begin to mount. Everyone knows of couples who go steady, break up, make up again, only to break up once more. Away from each other, their mutual attraction takes precedence because negative feelings are reduced; close to each other, the negative feelings drive them apart. To an outsider it appears irrational that people who get along so poorly attempt reconciliation. Once the ambivalence of their attitudes is recognized, however, their attempts at reconciliation become understandable, even if not reasonable.

Some complications result from the fact that the gradients of real life are usually multiple. A conflict over the use of alcohol usually involves more than a choice between the amount of liking for the taste of alcohol and the amount of dislike for the aftereffects; it can involve religious scruples, forgetting troubles, losing self-control, seeking companionship, escaping responsibility. Sometimes an approach-avoidance conflict is resolved by refusing to select either alternative and becoming ill or in some way evading the choice.

In our society the approach-avoidance conflicts that are most pervasive and difficult to resolve generally involve the following three areas (these are areas in which each of us has to make some sort of decision or compromise). (1) *Independence vs. dependence.* We may in times of stress want to resort to the dependency that is characteristic of childhood, to have someone take care of us and solve our problems for us. But we are taught that the ability to stand on our own two feet and assume responsibilities is a mark of maturity. (2) *Cooperation vs. competition.* In American life much emphasis is placed on competition and success; the Horatio Alger theme is a familiar one. Competition begins in early childhood among siblings, continues through school and college (both in the classroom and on the playing field), and culminates in business and professional rivalry. At the same time we are urged to cooperate and help our fellow men. The concept of "team spirit" is as American as the success story. Such contradictory expectations pave the way for potential conflict. (3) *Impulse expression vs. moral standards.* All societies have to place some degree of regulation upon impulse control. We noted in Chapter 3 that much of childhood learning involves imposing cultural restrictions upon innate impulses. Sex and aggression are two areas where our impulses most frequently conflict with moral standards, and violation of these standards may generate strong feelings of guilt.

These three areas then constitute the greatest potential for serious conflict. As we shall see in the next chapter, failure to find a workable compromise may result in mental illness.

Frustration

A continuing or unresolved motivational conflict is a source of frustration. We have mentioned frustration several times in our discussion thus far but have not given a precise definition. Because the term has developed several different connotations in everyday speech, it is important that we clarify its meaning before going on to consider the consequences of frustration and its relevance to mental health.

Whenever a person's progress toward a desired goal is blocked, delayed, or otherwise interfered with, we say he encounters *frustration*. The word *frustration* has sometimes been used to refer to an emotional state instead of to an event. That is, as a consequence of blocked goal-seeking a person becomes confused, baffled, and annoyed; if we were to ask him how he feels he would probably say he felt "angry and frustrated." He is thus equating frustration with an unpleasant emotional state. In this book, however, we shall hold to the meaning of frustration as the *thwarting circumstances* rather than their consequences.

We have discussed the various types of conflict at some length because they provide a major source of human frustration. But there are other barriers to drive satisfaction. The physical environment presents such obstacles as icy weather, rugged mountains, and arid deserts. The social environment presents obstacles through the restrictions imposed by other people and the customs of social living. Children are thwarted by parental denials, disapprovals, and postponements: Larry has the tricycle that David wants to ride; Father won't let John drive the car until he is 17; and Jane's parents insist that she is not old enough to marry. The list could be expanded endlessly.

Deficiencies in the environment prevent need-satisfaction quite as effectively as obstacles. A drought can be as frustrating to a farmer as a blizzard. Many of the deficiencies found to be frustrating are those within the individual himself. Some people are handicapped by blindness, deafness, or paralysis. Not everyone who wants to can become a distinguished painter or musician or can pass the examination necessary to become an engineer, physician, or lawyer. If one sets his goals beyond his ability, then frustration because of one's own deficiencies will be the inevitable result.

Immediate Consequences of Frustration

Frustration—whether it is the result of obstacles, deficiencies, or conflict—has both immediate and remote consequences. When blocked in his goal-seeking, the individual may react immediately or may develop attitudes toward uncertainty or risk-taking that have more enduring consequences. We shall first turn to a consideration of some of the immediate consequences of frustration. These consequences might equally well be called *symptoms* or *signs* of frustration.

An experiment on the effects of frustration in young children illustrates several of its immediate consequences. The subjects were 30 young children, ages two to five—that is, of nursery school and kindergarten age. The experiment will be described in the present tense, as though we were observing it.

The children came one at a time into a room that contains several toys, parts of which are missing—a chair without a table, an ironing board but no iron, a telephone receiver without a transmitter, a boat and other water toys but no water. There are also papers and crayons. Some of the children set about playing eagerly and happily. They make up for the missing parts imaginatively. They use paper as water in which to sail a boat or they substitute their fist for the telephone transmitter.

On the second day of observation we see a group of children who behave quite differently. Although they appear to be in the same general physical condition as the first group and their clothes show that they come from similar social and economic backgrounds, they seem unable to play constructively, unable to fit the toys into meaningful and satisfying activities. They play roughly with the toys, occasionally jumping on one and breaking it. If they draw with the crayons, they scribble like younger children. They whine and nag at the adult present. One of them lies on the floor, stares at the ceiling, and recites nursery rhymes, paying no attention to anyone else.

What accounts for the differences in behavior of these two sets of youngsters? Is the second group suffering from some sort of emotional disturbance? Have some of these children been mistreated at home? Actually, the children in this second group are the same as those in the first group; they are simply in a later stage of the experiment. They are showing the symptoms of frustration, frustration that has been deliberately created in the following way.

After playing happily with the half-toys, as described earlier, the children had been given an added experience. An opaque screen had been removed, allowing them to see that they were in a larger room containing not only the half-toys but other toys that were much more elaborate and attractive. This part of the room has a table for the chair, a dial and bell for the telephone, a pond of real water for the boat. When we see the unhappy children in the later stage of the experiment, a wire screen has been placed between them and their happy hunting ground. They are denied the "whole" toys and can use only the "part" ones. They are frustrated (Barker, Dembo, and Lewin, 1941).

Why was the half-toy situation satisfying the first time and frustrating the second? The answer is easy to find. Goal-seeking behavior was satisfied the first time, as the children played happily with the available toys; in the second stage they knew of the existence of the more attractive and satisfying toys, and so a new goal had been set up. The first day the goal was attainable; the second day, it was not. To play now with the half-toys is to be stopped short of a richer possible experience, and hence is frustrating.

This experiment illustrates a number of the immediate consequences of frustration. In discussing some of these consequences, we shall make reference to additional details of the experiment and draw further illustrations from related experiments and from the frustrating experiences of everyday life.

Restlessness and tension

In the toy experiment, one of the first evidences of frustration shown by the children was an excess of movement: fidgeting about and generally restless behavior. Drawings took the form of scribbling, because the muscles were tense and movements were thus jerky. This restlessness was associated with many actions indicating unhappiness: whimpering, sighing, complaining. Unhappy actions were recorded for only seven of the 30 children in the free-play situation but for 22 of the same 30 in the frustrating situation.

An increase in tension and in the level of excitement also occurs when adults are blocked and thwarted. They blush or tremble or clench their fists. Children under tension fall back upon thumb-sucking and nail-biting; adults also turn to nail-biting, as well as to smoking and gum chewing, as outlets for their restlessness.

Aggression and destructiveness

Closely related to increased tension and restless movements are the rage states that lead to destructiveness and hostile attacks. In the frustration experiment, kicking, knocking, breaking, and destroying were greatly increased following frustration. Only five children did any kicking or knocking in the original free-play situation, but 18 did so in frustration.

Direct aggression. Frustration often leads to aggression against the individual or object that is the source of the frustration. In the experiment just described, direct attack on the barrier was not uncommon. In ordinary play situations, when one small child takes a toy from another child, the second is likely to attack the first in an attempt to regain the toy. The victim of a slighting remark usually replies in kind—though for many adults the aggression may be verbal rather than physical. The anger engendered when one is blocked tends to find expression in some kind of direct attack. Because the obstacle or barrier was the source of the blocking in the experiment, the children's first attempt at problem-solving was to get by the barrier or remove it. Aggression of this kind need not be hostile; it may be a learned way of solving a problem. When the obstacle is another person, the first tendency is to attack that person, treating him as a barrier. But this may not be the only form aggression takes in response to frustration.

Displaced aggression. Frequently the frustrated individual cannot satisfactorily express his aggression against the source of the frustration. Sometimes the source is vague and intangible. Then he does not know what to attack, yet feels angry and seeks *something* to attack. At other times the person responsible for the frustration is so powerful that to attack him would be dangerous. When circumstances block direct attack on the cause of frustration, the result is what we call "displaced aggression." Displaced aggression is an aggressive action against an innocent person or object rather than against the actual cause of the frustration. The man who is bawled out by his boss may come home and take out his unexpressed resentment on his wife or children. The tongue-lashing Bill gives his quiet freshman roommate may be related to the poor grade Bill received on the midterm quiz. The child who is not getting along well with his playmates may come home and pull the kitten's tail.

The practice of "scapegoating" is an example of displaced aggression. An innocent victim is blamed for one's troubles and becomes the object of aggression. Prejudice against minority groups has a large element of displaced aggression or scapegoating. The fact that for the period from 1882 to 1930 the price of cotton in certain regions of the South was negatively correlated with the number of lynchings in the same regions (the lower the price of cotton the higher the number of lynchings) suggests that the mechanism of displaced aggression may have been involved. The greater the economic frustration, the greater the likelihood that aggression would be displaced

Displaced aggression

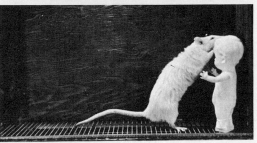

When the rat that has been the object of aggression is not present, the attacking rat displaces his aggression toward the doll. (From Miller, 1948b)

against the Negroes, a group serving as a scapegoat since they were not responsible for the price of cotton.

Displaced aggression can be demonstrated experimentally. One rat is taught to strike another by being rewarded for such aggression. When he strikes the other rat, the electric current that has been building up in the grid on which he stands is turned off, and he escapes the shock. This rewards the aggressive behavior. When another rat is no longer present, the trained rat directs his aggressive behavior toward the "innocent bystander," a rubber doll previously ignored (Figure 20–4). Thus aggression is transferred from an inaccessible to an accessible object (Miller, 1948b).

Apathy

One baffling feature of human behavior is the tendency for similar situations to lead to diametrically opposite behavior by different individuals. While a common response to frustration is active aggression, another response is its opposite—apathy, indifference, withdrawal, inactivity, inattentiveness (e.g., in the experiment, the child who lay on the floor staring at the ceiling). We do not know why one person reacts with aggression and another with apathy to the same frustrating situation, but it seems likely that learning is an important factor; reactions to frustration can be learned in much the same manner as other habits. The child who strikes out angrily when frustrated and finds that his need is then satisfied (either through his own efforts or because a parent rushes to placate him) will probably resort to the same type of behavior the next time his motives are thwarted. The child whose aggressive outbursts are never successful, who finds he has no power to satisfy his needs by means of his own behavior, may well resort to apathy and withdrawal when confronted with a frustrating situation.

When resistance is futile, the frustrated person may become sullen and detached instead of angry and defiant. Apathy often indicates that aggressive tendencies are being held in check or inhibited, but they may express themselves indirectly.

Studies of inmates in concentration or prisoner-of-war camps indicate that apathy may be the "normal" or typical reaction to extremely frustrating situations of long duration where there is no hope of escape. Bettelheim (1943) has described the behavior of prisoners exposed to the incredibly inhuman conditions of the Nazi concentration camps at Dachau and Buchenwald. He observed that many of them developed an attitude of detachment and extreme indifference in the face of continual deprivation, torture, and threats of death. Reports by American servicemen who were confined in Korean prisoner-of-war camps indicate a similar phenomenon. A large number of these men were interviewed and given psychological tests immediately following their repatriation. Almost all of them at some time during their imprisonment experienced a reaction characterized by listlessness, indifference to the immediate situation, lack of emotional expression, and complete absorption within themselves. Since these men could respond appropriately and rationally when spoken to and since the content of their speech and their behavior did not suggest depression or psychosis, the reaction seems best described as apathy. The severest of such "apathy reactions" frequently resulted in death. Two things seemed to save the man close to death: getting him on his feet and doing something, no matter how trivial, and getting him interested in some current or future problem. It was usually the efforts and support of a friend that helped the individual to snap out of a state of apathy (Strassman, Thaler, and Schein, 1956).

Fantasy

When problems become too much for us, we sometimes seek the "solution" of escape into a dream world, a solution through *fantasy* rather than on a realistic level. This was the solution of the child who lay on the floor reciting nursery rhymes in the frustration experiment (p. 510), and of other children in the experiment who crossed the barrier by talking about the whole toys on the other side. One little girl fished through the wire, imagining the floor on the other side to be the pond that was actually out of reach.

Unrealistic solutions are not limited to children. The pin-up girls in the soldiers' barracks symbolize a fantasy life that goes on when normal social life with women is frustrated. But experiments have also shown that men on a starvation diet lose their interest in women and instead hang on their walls pictures of prepared food cut from magazines (Guetzkow and Bowman, 1946).

As we shall see in the next chapter, severe and continuous frustration may produce such complete escape into fantasy that the individual loses his ability to distinguish between his fantasy world and the real one.

Stereotypy

Another consequence of frustration is *stereotypy* in behavior, that is, a tendency to blind, repetitive, fixated behavior. Ordinary problem-solving requires flexibility, striking out in new directions when the original path to the goal is blocked. When repeated frustration baffles a person, some of his flexibility appears to be lost, and he stupidly makes the same effort again and again, though experience has shown its futility.

For example, a white rat can be taught

20–5

Stereotypy

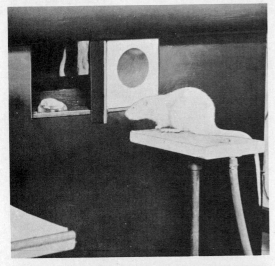

Dr. N. R. F. Maier

Shown here is the apparatus used in Maier's experiment on stereotypy. *Above:* The left window is open, the food exposed, and the frustrated rat seems to pay attention to it. *Below:* The rat's jump, however, remains fixated; that is, despite the open window the rat continues to jump to the right and to bump his nose and fall into the net below.

to jump to one of a pair of stimulus cards attached to windows by so arranging the cards that the rat finds food behind the positive card but is punished if he jumps to the negative card. The positive card may be one with a black circle on a white background, the negative one a white circle on a black background. The cards are so arranged that the rat knocks over the positive card when he hits it, opening the window that gives access to a platform where there is a food reward. If the rat jumps against the negative card, the card does not give way. Instead, the rat bumps against the card and falls into a net. By varying the positions of the cards, the experimenter can teach the rat to select the positive one and to jump consistently to it.

This discrimination experiment is converted into a frustration experiment by making the problem insoluble. That is, each of the two cards leads half the time to reward (positive reinforcement), half the time to punishment (negative reinforcement), regardless of its position at the left or the right. Hence, whichever choice the animal makes is "correct" only half the time. The result is that the rat, forced to jump, tends to form a stereotyped habit of jumping regularly to one side, either to the right or to the left, no longer paying attention to which card is exposed. The rat is still rewarded half the time and punished half the time after having adopted this stereotyped habit.

Once the stereotyped habit has been adopted, it is very resistant to change, so much so that it has been called an "abnormal fixation." For example, if the rat that has come to jump regularly to the right is now punished every time he jumps, he may continue to jump to the right for as many as 200 trials, even though the left window remains open as an easy and safe alternative (Figure 20–5). The behavior is so stereotyped that the alternative does not exist for the rat (Maier, 1949).

Further studies must be made before we know just what analogies are permissible between human behavior and these experimental results. It is quite possible, though not proved, that some forms of persistent behavior, such as thumb sucking in young children or stuttering, have become more firmly fixed (i.e., stereotyped) because punishment and repeated frustration in efforts to get rid of them have intensified the undesirable responses. The persistence of difficulties in arithmetic, reading, and spelling among bright children (and some adults) may be explained in part as a consequence of errors similarly stereotyped by early frustration.

Regression

Regression is defined as a return to more primitive modes of behavior, that is, to modes of behavior characterizing a younger age. There are two interpretations of regression. One is that in the midst of insecurity the individual attempts to return to a period of past security. The older child seeks the love and affection once bestowed upon him by behaving again as he did when younger: crying, seeking parental caresses, and so on. This type of regression is called *retrogressive* behavior, a return to behavior once engaged in.

The second interpretation of regression is that the childish behavior following frustration is simply a more primitive quality, but not actually a return to earlier behavior. This kind of regression, in contrast to retrogression, is called *primitivation*. Thus the adult accustomed to the restraints of civilized behavior may become so upset by frustration as to lose control and start a fistfight, even though he did no fistfighting as a child. Both forms of regression may, of course, occur together. In the frustration experiment with half-toys and restricted space discussed earlier, regression was shown through decrease in the constructiveness of play. We consider that this decreased constructiveness is a form of primitivation rather than retrogression because we do not ask whether the child returns to a mode of play characteristic of *him* at an earlier age. Without careful case studies we have no way of being sure, however, that the behavior was not retrogressive. It is a safe conjecture that it was in some instances. By means of a rating scale, each child's play in both the free and the frustrating situation was appraised as to its degree of constructiveness, that is, (1) according to its likeness to the well-thought-out and systematic play of older children, or (2) according to its similarity to the fragmentary play of younger children. As a consequence of frustration the play tended to deteriorate. Drawing became scribbling; instead of pretending to iron clothes on the ironing board, children would knock the board down. In this experiment the total loss in maturity shown amounted to 17.3 months of mental age; that is, the play of these children became like that of children about a year and a half younger.

The immediate consequences of frustration—the evidence that a person has been thwarted—are themselves ways of fighting the frustration. They are not merely signs of trouble but are also attempts at solution. If the solution is successful, the obstacles are overcome, the needs met, the conflicts resolved, and the frustrating episode is ended. However, some personal problems endure for a long time. They have continuing histories, and ways of dealing with them become habitual. These ways become so typical of the person that they help reveal what he is like. When we say that a person is aggressive or retiring, that he stands up for his rights, that he lets himself get pushed around, that he lives in a dream world, that he has a suspicious nature, we are talking about ways in which he habitually meets frustration.

Defense Mechanisms

The immediate reactions to frustration (restlessness, destructiveness, apathy, fantasy, stereotypy, regression) illustrate general techniques that young children adopt in order to solve their problems. These attempts at solution may become habitual, so that even at the nursery school age not all children react alike. In adults these habitual modes of meeting repeated or continuing conflict and frustration are highly individual and complex, but a few modes of adjustment occur so frequently that they have been sorted out and given names.

They are called *defense mechanisms* [1] because they protect the individual's self-esteem and defend him against excessive anxiety when faced with continuing frustrations.

When the fox in Aesop's fable rejected the grapes that he could not reach "because they were sour," he illustrated a defense mechanism known as rationalization. He escaped acknowledging his inability to reach the grapes by asserting that he did not really want them. In the following discussion we shall meet a number of other mechanisms, such as projection, in which we falsely attribute to others the undesirable traits that we possess, and repression, in which we conveniently forget what might otherwise be troublesome. Because nearly all these mechanisms distort reality in one way or another, we may well consider what purposes they serve.

We may describe the purposes of defense mechanisms both positively and negatively. Positively, they seek *to maintain or enhance self-esteem;* negatively, they seek *to escape or defend against anxiety.* The goal of seeing ourselves as commendable, admirable, and strong makes us enhance our self-respect as best we can, partly by denying any memory, impulse, or action that might be interpreted as self-belittling or self-degrading and partly by taking credit for whatever appears fine and noble in our behavior. The goal of reducing anxiety is a closely related one, for a good deal of anxiety has to do with security of status. In any case, a state of anxiety is unpleasant; we seek to avoid such states and to reduce them if they arise.

All defense mechanisms have in common the quality of *self-deception,* which may be evident in two chief forms—*denial* and *disguise.*

The clearest evidence for *denial* of impulses, memories, or actions that might cause us anxiety or might belittle us comes through *amnesia,* in which memory is temporarily lost. As we noted earlier (p. 326), the fact that such memories may be recov-

ered without relearning supports the interpretation that they are not "lost" but merely hidden by repressive mechanisms. That the lost memories tend to be personal, while impersonal memories are not lost, supports the interpretation that the repression in amnesia is often motivated by some form of anxiety or guilt.

Disguise is the second form of self-deception. Whenever impulses are falsified, as in rationalization, or traits inappropriately assigned, as in projection, the person's true motives are being masked. We shall meet other disguises in the mechanisms known as "reaction-formation" and "substitution."

Three precautions should be kept in mind during the discussion of individual defense mechanisms. (1) All of the mechanisms are to be found in the everyday behavior of normal people. Used in moderation, they increase satisfaction in living and are therefore helpful modes of adjustment. It is only when the mechanisms become the dominant modes of problem-solving that they indicate personality maladjustment. (2) The classification of the separate mechanisms is arbitrary, and the borderlines between them are not distinct and clearly marked. Often the reaction of an individual to a particular frustrating event can show characteristics of two or three different mechanisms. (3) Labeling behavior (e.g., as displaced aggression, rationalization, or substitution) may provide useful descriptive information, but it is never an explanation of the behavior involved. A full explanation requires understanding of the needs that make the person rely on defense mechanisms in his attempt to solve his problems.

Rationalization

Each of us wishes to act reasonably and on the basis of acceptable motives. If we act impulsively, or for motives that we do not wish to acknowledge even to ourselves, we often interpret what we have done in such a way that we seem to have behaved rationally. Assigning logical reasons or plausible excuses for what we do impulsively is known as *rationalization*. Rationalization does not mean "to act rationally"; it means to so justify conduct according to

[1] The defense mechanisms were first called to the attention of psychologists by Freud and other psychoanalytic writers.

personally desirable motives that we *seem* to have acted rationally.

In the search for the "good" reason rather than the "true" reason for what we do, we can bring forward a number of excuses. These excuses are usually plausible, and the circumstances they justify may be true ones; they simply do not tell the whole story. A few brief illustrations may serve to show how common rationalization is.

1. Liking or disliking as an excuse: The girl who was not invited to the dance said she would not have gone if asked because she did not like some of the crowd.
2. Blaming circumstances and other people: "Mother failed to wake me." "My tools were dull." (Note that in true rationalization as distinguished from deliberate falsifying, the actual situation would be that the mother had failed to do the waking or that the tools had been dull. But the mother may have expected the speaker to set the alarm clock as usual, and sharpening the tools may have been the responsibility of the one who used them.)
3. Necessity as an excuse: "I bought this new model because the old car would have had a lot of expensive repairs coming up before next summer."

While the foregoing examples show the person fooling himself instead of others, the excuses are of the sort that a person conceivably might use consciously to put himself in a favorable light with others. We therefore need a more convincing illustration to show us that rationalization may be used when the person is completely unenlightened about the reason for his conduct —when, in other words, rationalization is unconsciously motivated. Such an illustration is provided by the results of experiments on posthypnotic suggestion.

A subject under hypnosis is told that when he wakes from the trance he will watch the pocket of the hypnotist. When the hypnotist removes a handkerchief from the pocket, the subject will raise the window. The subject is told that he will not remember the hypnotist's telling him to do this.

Aroused from the trance, the subject feels a little drowsy, but presently circulates among the people in the room and carries on a normal conversation, all the while furtively watching the hypnotist's pocket. When the hypnotist in a casual manner removes his handkerchief, the subject feels an impulse to open the window, takes a step in that direction, but hesitates. Unconsciously he mobilizes his wishes to be a reasonable person; so, seeking for a reason for his impulse to open the window, he says, "Isn't it a little stuffy in here?" Having found the needed excuse, he opens the window and feels more comfortable (Hilgard, 1965).

Projection

All of us have undesirable traits or qualities that we do not acknowledge even to ourselves. One unconscious mechanism that protects us from acknowledging them we call *projection*. In projection we protect ourselves from recognizing our own undesirable qualities by assigning them in exaggerated amount to other people. Our own tendencies are thereby justified; we remove the stigma from our bad qualities by minimizing them in ourselves and by exaggerating them in others. Suppose I have a tendency to be critical of or unkind to other people, but would dislike myself if I recognized this tendency. If I am convinced that those around me are cruel or unkind, then any harsh treatment I give them is not based upon *my* bad qualities. I am simply giving them what they deserve. If I can assure myself that everybody else cheats in college examinations, my unacknowledged tendency to take some academic short-cuts is not so bad. Projection is really a form of rationalization, but the tendency to projection is so pervasive in our culture that it merits discussion in its own right.

Two experiments highlight the pervasiveness of projection. The first (Sears, 1936) deals with a group of university students, members of three college fraternities. The members of each fraternity were asked to rate the other members on four undesirable traits: stinginess, obstinacy, disorderliness, and bashfulness. The first three of these are strongly disapproved-of traits, while the fourth is mildly disapproved of. Each student was asked also to rate himself on each of these traits. In all, 97 fraternity members participated in the experiment.

Some members obviously possessed one or another of the traits to a high degree. Among these, some, as shown by their self-ratings, were aware of their traits; others were unaware of them. Those students who possessed an undesirable trait in a high degree and yet were unaware of possessing it tended to assign their own undesirable traits to others to a greater extent than did the rest of the students. While the correlations on which these interpretations are based were all low, they were consistently in the direction that would be expected if they were interpreted according to a projection mechanism.

The second experiment in projection was done in Vienna, with graduate students with whom the judges in the experiment were very well acquainted. The most striking finding of this study was a tendency on the part of the subjects to go so far in self-ratings as to convert bad traits to their opposite. The person who said of himself that he was "sincere under all conditions" was rated by the judges as lacking in sincerity. This subject, of course, found others full of sham and insincerity as compared with himself (Frenkel-Brunswik, 1939).

Reaction-formation

A person can often conceal a motive from himself by giving strong expression to its opposite. We have met this tendency, called *reaction-formation*, in the foregoing experiment on projection in which self-appraisals were occasionally completely the reverse of fact. The mother of an unwanted child may feel guilty about not welcoming her child, and so become over-indulgent and overprotective of the child in order to assure the child of her love and also, perhaps, to assure herself that she is a good mother.

One mother who wished to do everything for her daughter could not understand why the child was so unappreciative. At great sacrifice she had the daughter take expensive piano lessons. She sat beside the little girl to assist her in the daily practice sessions. While she thought she was being extremely kind to her child, she was actually demanding and, in fact, hostile. She was unaware of her own hostility, but, when confronted with it, she admitted that as a child she had hated piano lessons. Under the conscious guise of being kind, she was actually being unconsciously cruel to her daughter. The daughter, vaguely sensing what was going on, developed symptoms that brought her to the child-guidance clinic.

There is always the possibility that reaction-formation is present among those who engage in "anti" activities, such as censoring salacious literature or preventing cruelty to animals. The censoring individual may actually be fascinated by such literature. He wages a campaign against it in order to fight its fascination for him. Among the ardent antivivisectionists there are some who fear their own tendency toward cruelty so deeply that they become sentimental about protecting animals from the implied cruelty of others.

A good illustration of reaction-formation is found in the behavior of the missionary in W. Somerset Maugham's story, *Rain*. His zealous efforts to reform the prostitute Sadie Thompson represented a reaction against his strong sexual attraction to her.

The existence of reaction-formation in some people does not mean that motives can never be taken at their face values. Not all reformers are moved to action by veiled or hidden impulses. Real abuses need to be corrected: if a polluted water supply is spreading disease, rational men seek to get rid of the source of trouble. It would be foolhardy to say that those who take responsibility for correcting such an abuse are illustrating reaction-formation against their own unconscious desires to poison someone.

Dissociation

In the normal course of events, actions, feelings, and thoughts belong together. If you realize that someone is hurting you, you feel angry and strike back; your thought, your anger, and your muscular actions are all part of one harmonious whole. But such a unity of thinking, feeling, and doing is easily disrupted by the conflicts that early training produces. Then *dissociation,* or a splitting of the total activity, occurs. Although dissociation takes many forms, we shall consider here only two of its manifestations: *compulsive movements* and *excessive theorizing.*

Compulsive movements, actions that the person feels compelled to repeat over and over again, show the splitting off of movement from the feelings appropriate to them. Most people have a few such mannerisms, gestures, tics, or ritualistic movements (Krout, 1954).

For some people such compulsive movements are very important: one person avoids the lines on the sidewalk, another touches the telephone poles as he walks by, a third counts things. Folklore gives us a hint of what sort of impulse may be dissociated: "Step on a crack and you'll break your mother's back." Why, then, avoid cracks? When you avoid cracks, you avoid the impulse to injure someone. Your self-esteem is maintained because, through dissociation, your hostile impulses or fears are concealed (Figure 20–6).

Compulsive routines are carried out quite automatically and usually with little emotion, thus belying the depth of feeling that lies behind them. But the compulsive person may display excessive emotion when, for any reason, his ritualized behavior is interrupted. He thus shows, indirectly, that the behavior is actually strongly motivated. Why? In the first place, the ritualistic activity stands for something else, not recognized by the person himself. A twitching arm may substitute for the act of hitting in anger; blinking eyes may symbolize a wish to look at some forbidden scene, and at the same time express a conflict about looking; avoiding cracks may

symbolize avoiding temptation. In the second place, carrying out the ritual, without emotion, unconsciously assures the person that the dangerous or forbidden act for which the movement stands will not be

20–6

Compulsive behavior as a defense

LINES AND SQUARES

Whenever I walk in a London street,
I'm ever so careful to watch my feet;
   And I keep in the squares,
   And the masses of bears,
Who wait at the corners all ready to eat
The sillies who tread on the lines of the street,
   Go back to their lairs,
   And I say to them, "Bears,
  Just look how I'm walking
    in all of the squares!"

Compulsive behavior in both children and adults reduces anxiety by a magical, ritualistic protection against a worry or fear. The true basis for the anxiety is often unacknowledged, as indeed it is in the Milne poem. The child's fears are not really "the bears who wait at the corners." (From the book *When We Were Very Young,* by A. A. Milne, illustrated by Ernest H. Shepard. Copyright 1924 by E. P. Dutton Co., Inc. Renewal 1952 by A. A. Milne. Reprinted by permission of E. P. Dutton Co., Inc., and Methuen & Co., Ltd.)

carried out, and possible guilt is successfully warded off. We will see this defense mechanism carried to the extreme when we discuss obsessive-compulsive neurosis in the next chapter.

Excessive theorizing is another form of dissociation, in which talking or thinking about something becomes a substitute for action, and the person thereby avoids the feelings of self-depreciation which might otherwise result from the incapacity for action. A young psychologist, for example, found participation in group discussion very difficult. He then became interested in the theory of group discussion, took a notebook along to record what people did in discussion groups, and so protected himself from feeling inadequate as a group member. Adolescents, alarmed by the emotions accompanying newly intensified sexual impulses, sometimes go through a period when they scorn all emotions and try to make everything as impersonal, abstract, and theoretical as possible.

Repression

By this time we are prepared to see how each new mechanism is a method of protecting a person from full awareness of impulses that he (perhaps unconsciously) would prefer to deny. If the impulse is denied entirely, we have the mechanism of *repression*.

As we learned in the discussion of emotional control in Chapter 7, repression must be distinguished from suppression. The process of suppression is one of self-control —keeping impulses, tendencies, or wishes in check and perhaps holding them privately while denying them publicly. In such an instance, the person is aware of a suppressed impulse. In repression, the person himself is unaware of whatever it is that is repressed.

Repression, if completely successful, would mean a total forgetting—a total absence of awareness of the personally unacceptable motive and a total absence of behavior resulting from such a motive. Usually, however, repression is not completely successful, and impulses find indirect expression. Many of the defense

mechanisms already discussed serve repression, as they protect the individual (by means of the several disguises) from awareness of his partially repressed impulses.

Cases of *amnesia* illustrate some aspects of repression. In one case, a man was found wandering the streets of Eugene, Oregon, not knowing his name or where he had come from. Study by means of hypnosis and other techniques made it possible to reconstruct his history and to restore most of his memory. Following domestic difficulties he had gone on a drunken spree completely out of keeping with his earlier social behavior, and he had subsequently suffered deep remorse. His amnesia was motivated, first of all, by the desire to exclude from memory the mortifying experiences that had gone on during his spree. He succeeded in forgetting all the events before and after the spree that might remind him of the spree itself. Hence the amnesia spread, and he completely lost his sense of personal identity. When his memories returned, he could recall events before the drinking episode as well as subsequent happenings, but the deeper repression of the period of which he was most ashamed successfully protected him from recalling its disagreeable events (Beck, 1936).

As we saw earlier, experimental studies of memory have demonstrated some of the typical characteristics of repression. These studies, taken in conjunction with clinical observations, have contributed to our knowledge of the dynamics of motivated forgetting.

Substitution

The last defense mechanism we shall consider is the one that best succeeds in fulfilling its function, that is, solving a person's problems and reducing his tensions without exposing to him (or to the world) motives or tendencies of which he or his culture disapproves. This is the mechanism of *substitution*, whereby approved goals are substituted for unapproved ones, and activities that have possibilities of success are entered upon instead of activities that are doomed to failure.

Substitution is sometimes divided into two forms: *sublimation* and *compensation*. Both are incompletely understood, but the families of behavior to which they refer are familiar and important.

Sublimation is the process whereby socially unacceptable motives find expression in socially acceptable form. The desire for sexual gratification, if frustrated, may be sublimated in the writing of love letters or poetry or in painting. According to psychoanalytic theory, in the sublimation of the sexual impulse the energy of the original impulse finds expression through another means. The expression is disguised, but it is the original impulse that gains expression; hence successful sublimation reduces tension and leads to satisfying behavior. This is the theory, but it has been subjected to criticism. A study of 40 adult males suggests that the sublimation of sex is seldom fully successful: when normal sexual outlets are not used, some forms of residual sexual expression are usually present (Taylor, 1933). Whether or not direct sublimation takes place, substitute activities undoubtedly occur when a basic drive is thwarted. These may be called attempts at sublimation; even when they are not completely successful, they serve in part to reduce tension. Sexual behavior satisfies not only physiological needs, but needs centering around companionship, dependency, being mothered, and mothering. Some of these associated motives can be successfully satisfied by activities not satisfying primary sex needs.

Compensation is a strenuous effort to make up for failure or weakness in one activity through excelling in either a different or an allied activity. The boy who fails at games may compensate for the failure by excessive study in order to gain recognition in the classroom. Here, a completely different activity substitutes for the athletic ineffectiveness.

A peculiar form of compensation known as *overcompensation* comes in an attempt to deny a weakness by trying to excel where one is weakest. The weakness thus acts as a goad to superior performance. Such overcompensation was much stressed by Alfred Adler (1870–1937), one of the early psychoanalysts who broke with Freud and set up his own system of individual psychology (Adler, 1917; Ansbacher and Ansbacher, 1956). Illustrations are not hard to find. The power-driven dictators of recent times have been mostly men of short stature, who may have suffered a sense of physical powerlessness for which they overcompensated by a struggle for political might. Mussolini, Hitler, and Stalin were short, as was Napoleon before them. Theodore Roosevelt, a frail boy with weak eyes, took up boxing at Harvard and later led the Rough Riders during the Spanish-American War. Overcompensation is an energetic and effective (though not necessarily admirable) way of meeting weakness.

Our discussion has tended to emphasize the negative aspects of defense mechanisms. But some experts feel that not enough attention has been paid to the manner in which healthy, effective people handle their frustrations and conflicts. The behaviors we have been describing as defenses against anxiety can also be viewed as distorted adaptations of effective ways of coping with conflicts; that is, they are "potentially adaptive processes which have gone astray" (Kroeber, 1963). Thus most mechanisms have a positive or *coping* aspect as well as a defensive aspect. Denial, the refusal to face painful thoughts or feelings, is a form of selective awareness or attention. Its positive aspect is *concentration,* the ability to temporarily set aside painful thoughts in order to stick to the task at hand. Projection is an exaggerated and erroneous sensitivity to another person's unexpressed feelings or thoughts. A positive form of sensitivity would be *empathy,* the ability to appreciate how another person feels. Table 20–1 lists some basic processes or mechanisms, each followed by its defensive aspect and its coping aspect.

For any given conflict situation an individual might use one or more of these mechanisms in its defensive form, its cop-

TABLE 20-1

Mechanisms and their manifestations

Mechanism	As a defense	As a method of coping
Discrimination: ability to separate idea from feeling, idea from idea, feeling from feeling.	**Dissociation:** keeps apart ideas that emotionally belong together or severs ideas from their appropriate emotion.	**Objectivity:** separates ideas from feelings to achieve a rational evaluation or judgment where necessary.
Means-end symbolization: ability to analyze experience, to anticipate outcomes, to entertain alternative choices.	**Rationalization:** offers apparently plausible explanation for behavior to conceal nature of underlying impulse.	**Logical analysis:** analyzes carefully the causal aspects of situations.
Selective awareness: ability to focus attention.	**Denial:** refuses to face painful thoughts or feelings.	**Concentration:** temporarily sets aside painful thoughts in order to stick to task at hand.
Sensitivity: apprehension of another's unexpressed feelings or ideas.	**Projection:** unrealistically attributes an objectionable tendency of his own to another person instead of recognizing it as part of himself.	**Empathy:** puts himself in the other person's place and appreciates how the other fellow feels.
Time reversal: ability to recapture feelings and ideas from the past.	**Regression:** resorts to age-inappropriate behavior to avoid responsibility or demands from others and to allow self-indulgence.	**Playfulness:** utilizes feelings and ideas from the past to add to his solution of problems and enjoyment of life.
Impulse diversion: ability to modify aim or object of an impulse.	**Displacement:** temporarily and unsuccessfully represses unacceptable impulses. May displace to an inappropriate object.	**Sublimation:** finds alternate channels that are socially acceptable and satisfying for expression of primitive impulses.
Impulse restraint: ability to control an impulse by inhibiting expression.	**Repression:** totally inhibits feelings or ideas. Repressed material revealed only symbolically as in dreams.	**Suppression:** holds impulses in abeyance until the proper time and place with the proper objects.

SOURCE: Adapted with modifications from Kroeber (1963).

ing form, or a combination of both. An estimate of a person's mental health would be based on the extent to which he habitually uses these mechanisms in a coping rather than a defensive manner.

In a study designed to investigate the usefulness of this formulation of defense and coping behavior a large group of men and women were rated (on the basis of extensive interviews) as to the type of mechanisms they characteristically used in response to conflict and the degree to which they utilized the coping or defensive form. An attempt was then made to predict from these ratings the individual's behavior on a Rorschach test. An elaborate set of hypotheses was developed that specified how each of the mechanisms would be reflected in a specific Rorschach score. For example, use of the defense mechanism of dissociation should be positively related to a tendency to give part responses to inkblot areas that are commonly seen as wholes. A sufficient number of hypotheses were verified to suggest that this might be a fruitful model for describing human conflict behavior (Kroeber, 1963).

Defense Mechanisms and Adjustment

Man is capable of rational problem-solving; that is, he can face a problem squarely, weigh the alternatives according to their probable consequences, and take action guided by the results of deliberation. Our knowledge of the defense mechanisms tells us, however, that much behavior that appears to be activated by conscious reasoning is in fact directed by unconscious motives.

Limitations upon direct problem-solving

It is possible to attack and solve a personal problem as we do any other kind of problem—such as one in mathematics or science—by asking clear questions, assembling evidence, judging the possible consequences, and trying to verify in practice what we have concluded from the evidence. There are two chief reasons, however, why we are often not able to solve our personal problems in a straightforward, rational manner.

1. A person's motives or emotions may be so strongly involved that they distort the evidence or the problem itself, so that the person is incapable of direct problem-solving. The self-deceptive mechanisms that we have been considering tend to set up such obstacles. For example, the engineering or medical student who finds himself failing cannot admit to himself that he is not bright enough to pursue certain courses at the college of his choice; he must therefore find a rationalization instead of solving his academic problem. If he gets sick, he converts an academic problem into a health problem; if he becomes a subject for disciplinary action, he converts an intellectual problem into a moral one. When defense mechanisms hold sway, the person himself sets up obstacles that stand in the way of a rational solution to his problems.

2. Sometimes there are too many unknowns in the equation. The world in which we live is not sufficiently orderly to permit fully rational problem-solving. At best a man has to take risks based on his best estimates against the uncertainty of the future; while the most rational solution is to estimate probabilities, this may not satisfy, so he may relieve his anxiety

by adopting a superstitious or fatalistic solution.

Because of these limitations upon purely reasonable conduct—limitations both internal and external—man is often tempted to fall back on irrational mechanisms.

How mechanisms may contribute to satisfactory adjustment

How successfully can a person use defense mechanisms to avoid or reduce anxiety and to maintain self-esteem? If defense mechanisms were not partially successful, they would not persist as they do. They may provide a protective armor while we are learning more mature and realistic ways of solving our problems. When we no longer need the defenses, their importance fades, and we increasingly face our problems according to the demands of the total situation. The defense mechanisms thus help toward satisfactory adjustment in several ways.

1. *They give us time to solve problems that might otherwise overwhelm us.* If we are able to rationalize failures that would otherwise cause us to despair, or if we can find partial justification for conduct that would otherwise make us despise ourselves, such defense mechanisms sustain us until we can work out better solutions to our conflicts. They provide palliatives comparable to those drugs that reduce symptoms without curing disease. Some of the antihistamines, for example, get rid of the sneezing and itching and watering of eyes of the hayfever victim until he takes the pollen tests and allergy shots that will get at the cause of the hayfever. The temporary relief helps him to live more comfortably until he is cured. Ultimately, of course, he wants to find a cure so that he will no longer need the drugs. So, too, one should no longer need his defense mechanisms if he attains realistic ways of solving his personal problems.

2. *The mechanisms may permit experimentation with new roles and hence teach new modes of adjustment.* Even when we adopt new roles for faulty reasons, as in reaction-formation, or when we misjudge

people, as in projection, we expose ourselves to corrective experiences from which we may learn social techniques. We may judge someone to be unkind, but as we discover his genuine acts of kindness we may learn to correct our error in judgment. What begins as self-deception may provide occasions for modifying the self.

3. *Rationalization, by starting a search for reasons, may lead to rational conduct in the future.* The tendency to justify behavior that we have found satisfying may lead to false reasons, but it may also lead to a more careful analysis of cause-and-effect relationships. If the latter occurs, as pointed out earlier, a present rationalization may become a future reason.

4. *Behavior illustrative of a mechanism may be socially useful and even creative.* Romantic poetry or art, even though it is produced as a substitute for, or sublimation of, unfulfilled desires, may still be valuable art. So, too, compulsive tendencies may lead to concentrated effort on a task. The person who works hard toward well-defined objectives because of an excessive need for achievement may, in fact, achieve a great deal. Thus the defense mechanisms may get us over rough spots and give a motivational lift leading to better adjustment.

Why the defense mechanisms fail to provide satisfactory adjustment

Nearly all the statements just made about the usefulness of the mechanisms can also be reversed to point up their failures. The person who depends upon defense mechanisms for protection may never be forced to learn more mature ways of behaving; the roles adopted through the mechanisms may remain unrealistic, leading to withdrawal from social contacts rather than to improved relationships with people; rationalizations may take the form of useless rituals or wasteful compulsions instead of creative effort.

Even where such behavior is socially useful, it will not prove completely satisfying to the individual as long as it has its roots in irrational purposes. Tension reduction is incomplete because the incentives are inappropriate to the drive. Actions based on such defense mechanisms never reach their goals; the drive continues, and the resulting behavior, irrationally driven, is not fully tension-reducing.

SUMMARY 1. When two motives conflict the satisfaction of one leads to the blocking of the other. *Conflicts* are of three major types: *approach-approach, avoidance-avoidance,* and *approach-avoidance.* Behavior in a conflict situation can be understood according to four principles: the gradient of approach, the gradient of avoidance, the greater steepness of the avoidance gradient, and the heightening of the gradients with increased motivation.

2. *Frustration* arises whenever ongoing, goal-seeking activity is obstructed. The chief sources of frustration are motivational conflicts; obstacles—the opposition furnished by things or other people; and deficiencies in the environment or in the person himself.

3. Some of the immediate consequences of frustration are as follows: *restlessness* and *tension, destructiveness* and *aggression, apathy, fantasy, stereotypy,* and *regression.* They show us how important it is to understand the behavior of individuals when their goal-seeking behavior is blocked.

4. The *defense mechanisms* represent habitual efforts to meet more enduring conflicts. Among the defense mechanisms found in everyday behavior are: *rationalization, projection, reaction-formation, dissociation, repression,* and *substitution.* (This list is not complete, and there is much

overlap.) The defense mechanisms have two purposes in common: to protect the individual against excessive anxiety and to maintain his self-esteem. They serve these purposes and effect tension reduction by means of self-deception, denial of impulses, and disguise of motives.

5. Many personal problems can be solved rationally, that is, by taking into account the evidence, the alternatives, and the consequences of each of the alternatives. But clear, logical choice is difficult for two reasons: (1) the person's own emotions and prejudices often get in the way of such a choice; and (2) the future is always uncertain, so that there are always unknowns and risks have to be taken. Here defense mechanisms often enter. When defense mechanisms are employed in moderation and do not exclude more realistic facing and solving of problems, they may increase the sense of well-being and so serve a useful purpose, sometimes protecting the person until he can reach a realistic solution. But actions based on defense mechanisms can never be genuinely satisfying because they are impelled by motives irrationally related to the defensive behavior.

SUGGESTIONS FOR FURTHER READING

The experimental analysis of conflict has been best formulated by Miller in a chapter entitled "Liberalization of basic S-R concepts; extensions to conflict behavior, motivation, and social learning," in Koch, *Psychology: a study of a science*, vol. II (1959). The original discussion of the three types of conflict appears in Lewin, *A dynamic theory of personality* (1935). Some research on conflict behavior is included in Haber (ed.), *Current research in motivation* (1966).

Frustration as a source of aggressive behavior is documented in Dollard and others, *Frustration and aggression* (1939); as a source of stereotypy in Maier, *Frustration: a study of behavior without a goal* (1949). Both are now available in paperbound editions.

The classical account of the defense mechanisms is Anna Freud, *The ego and the mechanisms of defense* (1937); a thorough discussion of the many mechanisms that have been proposed is given by Sarnoff, *Personality dynamics and development* (1962). Several experiments relating preferred defenses to various background factors, including socioeconomic class, are reported in Miller and Swanson, *Inner conflict and defense* (1960).

21 Mental Health and the Behavior Disorders

In one way or another each of us is inevitably involved in conflict—all people are occasionally placed under stressful conditions where they experience strong feelings of anxiety. Some of us, however, by virtue of our biological make-up, the characteristic techniques we have developed to handle conflict, and the amount of support provided by our environment, are better able to withstand stress than others. But there is no such thing as an ideally adjusted person; we all resort to self-deception and mechanisms of defense at times. Nor is there complete agreement as to what characteristics would describe a hypothetical, ideally adjusted person. As we shall see later, the concept of adjustment and normality depends to some extent upon the cultural and social group to which the individual belongs. However, it is possible to conceive of a continuum of adjustment with positive, highly adaptive behavior at one end and complete helplessness and self-defeating behavior at the other. Most of us would fall somewhere between the middle and the well-adjusted end of the continuum. Below the middle are those individuals who experience such severe conflicts that their attempts to cope with the resulting anxiety seriously interfere with their ability to meet the problems of everyday life, although they can usually hold down a job and get along to some extent with their family and friends; such people are called *neurotic*. At the far end of the continuum are those individuals who are so burdened with conflicts and who

have resorted to such extreme methods of defense that they are helpless to deal with reality and may be dangerous to themselves or to others; such people are called *psychotic*.

Thus, psychosis, neurosis, and normal adjustment are considered as varying degrees along a continuum of mental health with no sharp dividing line separating any of the three. We will discuss first some of the characteristics considered to be indicative of "good adjustment" or "mental health" in our western culture, and then go on to discuss the various forms of behavior disorder, including neurosis and psychosis. These characteristics do not sharply distinguish between the mentally healthy and the mentally ill, but rather represent traits the well-adjusted person possesses to a greater degree.

Mental Health

The well-adjusted person is not without conflicts, but he is not unduly distressed by them. He attacks his problems in a realistic manner; he accepts the inevitable; he understands and accepts his own shortcomings and the shortcomings of those with whom he must deal. The maladjusted person, by contrast, is unduly disturbed by his conflicts. He often tries to solve his problems by denying reality. He commonly tends to take issue with other people over matters that cannot be helped, or he may withdraw from other people so that mutually satisfactory solutions are impossible.

It is not true that the well-adjusted person must be a social conformist. Adjustment through conforming may, and often does, result in less conflict than protesting. A person who lives comfortably under the rules of the group with which he associates is saved some of the problems that confront the social reformer. But a reformer can be as well adjusted as a conformer. The reformer may have a vision of the good society that he seeks, he may associate with others who agree with him, and he may accept on a realistic basis the clashes with those who disagree.

Productivity and zest

A mentally healthy or well-adjusted person is also a productive person. That is, he has a quality of spontaneity in work and in social relations that we recognize as creative, as using his potentialities and powers. He is able to use his endowments, whether meager or ample, in productive activity. A well-adjusted person has zest for living; he does not have to drive himself to meet the demands of the day, but enters into activities with enthusiasm. One of the frequent symptoms of poor mental health is a readiness to fatigue, a desire to avoid effort. Indeed, it is often difficult to distinguish between fatigue that is due to organic illness and fatigue that is due to emotional conflict.

It is sometimes argued that people who suffer from unresolved conflicts do creative work precisely because they suffer (see p. 389). Artists such as Van Gogh and Gauguin were artistically productive but emotionally disturbed, and one wonders if achieving mental health would have robbed them of creative power. The question is debatable, but it is clear from their lives that these artists achieved their artistic products at the cost of great pain to themselves, their families, and their friends. Although a few people somehow turn their troubles to advantage, many others are unable to use their creative abilities because of the conflicts that inhibit their productivity.

Ability to form affectionate relationships

The well-adjusted person is able to form satisfying relationships with other people. He is sensitive to the needs and feelings of others, does not make excessive demands for the gratification of his own needs, and is able to both give and receive affection. Often the mentally ill person is so lacking in self-esteem and so concerned with protecting his own security that he becomes extremely self-centered; he is preoccupied with his own feelings and strivings and can only seek affection, without being able to reciprocate.

Self-knowledge and acceptance

The well-adjusted person has some awareness of his own motives and feelings. Although, of course, no one fully understands why he behaves as he does or why he feels as he does toward certain people and situations, the mentally healthy person has considerably more self-awareness than one who is mentally ill. He is not trying to hide important feelings and motives from himself. He appraises fairly accurately his abilities and liabilities and does not grossly overestimate or underestimate what he is capable of doing. For this reason he does not try to achieve totally unrealistic goals and thus feel continually guilty when he fails; nor, on the other hand, does he shy from tasks of which he is capable because he lacks confidence in his ability to perform them.

We have listed only some of the traits that the well-adjusted individual possesses to a greater degree than the maladjusted. Other experts, particularly those from a country whose culture is quite different from ours, might emphasize different characteristics. Throughout our discussion of maladaptive or disordered behavior, we may gain some clues as to factors that predispose toward good adjustment by noting conditions that lead to maladjustment. At the end of the next chapter we will discuss some of the practices that can enhance mental health.

Behavior Disorders

Concept of abnormality

Before discussing the types of behavior that are classed as abnormal we might do well to consider what we mean by "abnormal." Even within psychology the terms "abnormal" and "normal" are not used consistently. One definition is based on *statistical frequency*. We noted in Chapter 15 that many characteristics of people, such as height, weight, and intelligence, follow a normal distribution when measured over a large population. Most people fall within the middle range of height, with a few who are abnormally tall or abnormally short. Abnormal by this definition is that which is statistically infrequent or deviant from the norm. But such a definition would also classify as abnormal the person who is extremely intelligent or extremely happy. Obviously in defining behavior that is maladjustive we consider more than statistical frequency.

The *society* in which we live classifies certain behavior as abnormal according to its standards. Usually, but not always, such behavior is also statistically infrequent within that group. But behavior that is considered normal or well-adjusted by one society may be considered abnormal by another. Among the Tchambuli, a New Guinea tribe, the men are shy, subservient, and engage in what we consider feminine activities such as dancing and weaving; the women are the dominant sex who choose their mates and manage the affairs of the tribe. In our society such behavior on the part of men would be considered an indication of insecurity and weakness. Among some American Indian tribes there is nothing unusual about "hearing voices" when no one is actually talking or "seeing visions," but we would consider such behavior abnormal. Even within our own society the different social classes hold divergent views as to what is considered abnormal or deviant sexual behavior. In his survey of *Sexual behavior in the human male*, Kinsey reports that among the working class masturbation as a sexual outlet is viewed as abnormal and a form of perversion; middle-class, college-educated men consider such behavior as acceptable, although not necessarily commendable.

A third, and perhaps most important, definition of maladjusted or abnormal behavior involves *degree of impairment* or *injury*. If a person is so immobilized by conflict and anxiety that he cannot meet his everyday responsibilities, or if his behavior threatens harm to himself or someone else, then he is considered to be behaving abnormally.

In most instances all three definitions—statistical, social, and degree of impairment—are used together in diagnosing maladjustment.

The normal person's quota of symptoms

Before we consider the symptoms of disordered behavior it might be well to reemphasize the point that there is no sharp distinction between adequate adjustment and mental illness. A person well within the range of normal physical health is seldom entirely free of the symptoms of sickness. How many people have no cavities, no skin blemishes, or no colds? Yet most people are healthy. Similarly, a person well within the range of normal mental health may have occasional outbursts of temper, may get a headache after an unpleasant argument, may lose his appetite or become nauseated because of an emotional crisis, or may become suspicious that someone is talking about him. As we go on to consider some of the symptoms of disordered behavior, we will do well to acknowledge that each of us has his quota of symptoms, and that to be free of mental illness does not require us to be symptom-free.[1]

Neuroses

The less severe forms of behavior disorder, troublesome enough to call for expert help

---

[1] A person with any doubts about the severity of his symptoms should not hesitate to seek professional psychological help.

and occasionally requiring hospitalization, are called *neuroses* (plural form of *neurosis*).[2] These disturbances are often merely more extreme forms of normal defense mechanisms used in an attempt to resolve a persistent conflict. We noted in the preceding chapter that conflicts of the approach-avoidance type are usually the most difficult to resolve satisfactorily, particularly if they stem from two equally strong motives. As one need becomes stronger and is about to be gratified, the opposing need, which is in danger of being frustrated, increases in strength, and a state of vacillation ensues. Such unresolved conflicts result in feelings of anxiety, tension, and helplessness. And if a realistic solution cannot be achieved, the individual either remains in a state of severe anxiety or resorts to one or more of the defense mechanisms in an attempt to reduce anxiety. In the neurotic individual this defense is seldom satisfactory for two reasons: it usually alleviates only a small part of the total anxiety; and it interferes with the person's daily functioning, thereby creating further problems.

The chief symptom of neurosis, then, is *anxiety*. Often the anxiety is obvious. The individual appears strained and tense; his increased tension may result in such symptoms as indigestion, diarrhea, loss of appetite, and insomnia. Sometimes the anxiety is not readily apparent, but we judge from the person's maladaptive behavior that he is defending against anxiety by the extreme use of one or more defense mechanisms.

We cannot attempt to cover all the various types of neurotic behavior but we will briefly describe four of the more common reactions. These include *anxiety reaction, obsessive-compulsive reaction, phobic reaction,* and *conversion reaction.* Traditionally, neurotic disorders have been classified according to symptoms rather than type of conflict involved. Such a classification is not completely satisfactory, however, because frequently a neurotic has symptoms of more than one reaction type.

[2] The terms "psychoneurosis" and "neurosis" are used interchangeably as are "psychoneurotic" and "neurotic."

Anxiety reactions

Although we have said that anxiety is the predominant characteristic of neurosis, in many of the neurotic reactions it is concealed by other symptoms. In *anxiety reactions,* however, it is very much in the open. The typical anxiety neurotic lives from day to day with a level of tension much greater than the normal individual. This chronic state of apprehension is often punctuated by *acute anxiety attacks* that may occur as often as several times a day or as infrequently as once a month. The acute attacks involve an overwhelming feeling that something dreadful is about to happen, usually accompanied by such physiological symptoms as heart palpitations, rapid breathing, perspiration, muscle tension, faintness, and nausea. These physiological symptoms result from excitation of the sympathetic division of the autonomic nervous system (see p. 49) and are the same symptoms that one may experience when extremely frightened.[3] The anxiety neurotic, however, usually has no idea why he is frightened. His anxiety is sometimes termed "free-floating" because it is not associated with a particular stimulus or object but occurs in a wide variety of situations. It is a function not of external stimulus events but of feelings and conflicts within the individual. Anxiety that is evoked by specific situations (e.g., speaking before a group or going out on a blind date) is called "bound" anxiety because it is bound to a specific situation. Bound anxiety is less incapacitating than free-floating anxiety but it can sometimes be troublesome enough to be classed as neurotic. Bound anxiety in a particularly irrational form will be discussed under the section on *phobic reactions.*

Anxiety reactions reflect feelings of helplessness and inadequacy in the face of

[3] There are several organic conditions such as overactivity of the thyroid gland, heart disease, hypoglycemia, and some endocrine disorders that can produce the same symptoms as an anxiety attack. For this reason it is always wise to rule out such possibilities by a thorough medical examination before assuming that the symptoms are of psychological origin.

threatening or stressful situations. Most of us have experienced anxiety and tension (and even some of the physiological symptoms to a milder degree) when confronted with a stressful situation. Such feelings are normal reactions to stress; they are considered neurotic only when they become habitual ways of responding to situations that most people can handle with little difficulty. Usually the anxiety neurotic is a person who has strong feelings of inadequacy and inferiority yet at the same time maintains unrealistically high standards of conduct and achievement and feels guilty when he fails to live up to his standards. No matter how successful he may be he cannot relax; he still feels apprehensive about his ability to meet the demands of the future. Any sudden stress in his life situation may precipitate an acute anxiety attack—the threatened loss of professional or social goals, the loss of a parent or other person upon whom he felt dependent, and the threatened breakthrough of unacceptable and dangerous impulses are all factors that may lead to an acute anxiety attack. The following is a case where the threatened breakthrough of hostile feelings was sufficient to trigger anxiety attacks.

An eighteen-year-old male student developed severe anxiety attacks just before he went out on dates. Analysis revealed that he came from a very insecure home in which he was very much attached to an anxious, frustrated, and insecure mother. He was not particularly attractive and had considerable difficulty getting dates, particularly with the girls of his choice. The girl he had been recently dating, for example, would not make any arrangements to go out until after 6:00 P.M. of the same day after her chances for a more preferable date seemed remote. This had increased his already strong feelings of inferiority and insecurity, and had led to the development of intense hostility toward the opposite sex which was mostly on an unconscious level. The symptoms of this repressed hostility, however, came out in obsessive thoughts on the part of the patient of choking the girl to death each time they were out together. As he put it, "When we are alone in the car, I can't get my mind off her nice white throat and what it would be like to choke

her to death." At first he put these thoughts out of his mind, but they returned on subsequent nights with increasing persistency. Then, to complicate the matter, he experienced his first acute anxiety attack. It occurred in his car on the way over to pick up his date and lasted only a few minutes, but the patient was panic stricken and thought that he was going to die. After that he experienced several additional attacks, strangely enough under the same conditions.

The relationship of the repressed hostility to the patient's obsessive thoughts and to the development of anxiety is quite obvious in this case. However, it was not at all obvious to him. He was at a complete loss to explain both his obsessive thoughts and the anxiety attacks.[4]

Obsessive-compulsive reactions

Next to anxiety reactions, *obsessive-compulsive reactions* are the most frequent of the neurotic disorders. Obsessive-compulsive reactions occur in three major forms: obsessive thoughts—those that recur persistently, often unwelcome and disturbing; compulsive acts—irresistible urges to repeat a certain stereotyped or ritualistic act; obsessive thoughts with compulsive acts—thoughts of lurking disease germs combined with the compulsion of excessive hand washing. All of us at times have persistently recurring thoughts ("Did I leave the gas turned on?") and urges to ritualistic behavior (knocking on wood after boasting), but with the obsessive-compulsive neurotic these obsessive thoughts and compulsive urges occupy so much time that they seriously interfere with his daily life. He recognizes the irrationality of his thoughts and behavior but is unable to control them. Often the attempt to stop produces anxiety.

Obsessive thoughts cover a wide variety of topics but most frequently involve aggressive or sexual impulses—the person has persistently recurring thoughts of pushing his mother down the stairs, drowning his infant son in the bathtub, throwing himself in front of a speeding car, walking naked down the aisle of the church, raping little children. The possibility of these thoughts being carried out in action is virtually nil

[4] Coleman (1964), p. 198.

but the individual feels no control over them, cannot understand why they persist, and fears not only that he will perform the act but that he is becoming insane.

Compulsive acts are frequently designed to counteract such unacceptable impulses (impulses of which the individual may or may not be aware). For example, a person who feels guilty about masturbation or other sexual behavior he views as sinful may feel compelled to wash his hands many times a day, thereby cleansing himself of immoral thoughts or behavior. A mother who has feelings of hostility and resentment toward her children may find herself continually compelled to check on their safety. Coleman (1964) cites the case of a woman whose repressed hostile feelings toward her daughter resulted in a compulsive urge to make the sign of the cross and repeat, "God protect my dearly beloved little daughter." The behavior seemed senseless to the woman, who had no idea why she felt compelled to say it.

Many obsessive-compulsives have very elaborate and time-consuming routines controlling their daily activities (for example, washing and dressing in a specified order, stirring their coffee exactly ten times, arranging their food in a set number of piles on the plate and consuming the piles in a certain order). This sort of methodical and ritualistic behavior seems designed to serve two purposes: it represents an attempt to establish order in a world that is confusing and threatening, and it guards against unacceptable impulses. (If one is continually busy and thinking of something else, there is less opportunity for improper thoughts or behavior.) Even when the dangerous impulses do enter consciousness they are dissociated from their normal emotion and appear in the form of obsessive thoughts which, although disturbing, are not felt by the individual to be really a part of himself. For example, our college student who had difficulty getting dates was upset by his thought of choking his dates but would have been considerably more disturbed had he realized the extent of his hostile feelings and destructive impulses toward females.

Phobic reactions

Phobic reactions are excessive fears of certain kinds of situations in the absence of real danger, or fears that are totally out of proportion to the amount of danger that a situation may involve. The person usually realizes that his fear is irrational but still feels anxiety (ranging from mild feelings of uneasiness to an acute anxiety attack), which is relieved only by avoiding the phobic situation. The list of objects or situations that can evoke phobic reactions is endless; some of the more common are fear of closed places (claustrophobia), fear of high places (acrophobia), fear of crowds (ocholophobia), fear of animals (zoophobia), and fear of the dark (nyctophobia). Since a scientific name can be constructed for any irrational fear simply by prefixing the word "phobia" by the Greek word for the object feared, some of the earlier literature on phobias is replete with impressive diagnoses.

Although most of us have some minor irrational fears, in phobic reactions the fears are so intense as to interfere with the person's daily living. Examples would be the person whose fear of closed places is intense enough to prevent him from traversing narrow hallways or entering small rooms, even though his daily activities require him to do so, or the individual whose fear of crowds prevents him from attending movies or walking when the sidewalks are congested. Occasionally a person may have one specific phobia and yet be quite normal in every other respect. But often a phobic individual shows other symptoms of neurotic disorder such as tenseness, feelings of inadequacy, and so on.

How do phobic reactions develop? When a person shows fear of something that he knows is harmless, we assume that the phobic object is associated with (or symbolizes) something else that is dangerous. Some phobic reactions are simply conditioned fear reactions. We saw in the chapter on emotions how Watson conditioned the boy Albert to fear a white rat when the appearance of the rat was paired with the noxious stimulus of a loud sound. This conditioned fear response then generalized to other furry objects. If in adult life Albert continued to show strong fear reactions to his wife's mink coat and (because he had forgotten the conditioning experience of his childhood) had no awareness of the source of this fear, we would say he had a phobic reaction. Some phobic reactions can be similarly traced to traumatic childhood experiences. Cameron and Magaret (1951) mention the case of a man who feared, among other things, red skies at evening. After extensive analysis he was helped to recall that as a boy he had been terrified by the red flames of a tenement fire in which he had erroneously thought that his mother was being burned to death. The red sky of the sunset symbolized the red flames he feared would destroy his mother, upon whom he was very dependent. Frequently, as in this case, the fear is displaced by means of stimulus generalization from the originally feared object to another object or idea, so that the person is unaware of the source of his anxiety.

Phobic reactions of a more pervasive nature may develop as a means of defending the individual from repressed impulses (usually aggressive or sexual) which he feels may become dangerous. A woman who had a phobic fear of walking down the street unless someone else was with her was found to be actually fearful of her own sexual feelings toward men (feelings which her strict upbringing had convinced her were sinful). By avoiding situations where she might encounter men alone she avoided the possibility of losing control of her sexual impulses. In one sense phobias have an advantage over anxiety states or obsessive-compulsive reactions. In phobic reactions the fear is directed toward a specific object and the person can reduce anxiety by avoiding this object. The obsessive-compulsive or the anxiety neurotic have no such easy out.

Conversion reactions

In *conversion reactions* (formerly called *hysteria* or *conversion hysteria*) physical symptoms appear without any underlying organic cause. The symptoms may be (1) sensory—loss of sensation in some part of the body (usually an arm or leg), blindness, or deafness; (2) motor—paralysis of a limb or entire side of the body, muscular tremors or tics, speech disturbances such as aphonia (inability to speak above a whisper) or mutism, and occasional convulsions or "fits" similar to epileptic convulsions; (3) visceral —including such symptoms as coughing or sneezing spells, persistent hiccuping, choking sensations, lump in the throat, and a variety of vague aches or pains. The presumption is that anxiety has been reduced or dispelled by being "converted" into symptoms that serve unconscious purposes of the patient. For example, if, through conversion reactions, a soldier's legs become paralyzed, he is protected from acknowledging his fear of battle, which would be belittling to him; he is likely to be sent away from the battlefront, so that the occasion for his fear will be removed; discharged from the army, he will probably recover the normal use of his legs, for he has no organic or structural injury.

It should be emphasized that the person with a conversion reaction is not faking; his disorder is quite real to him, and it usually is easy to distinguish him from a malingerer. In fact, in a sensory symptom where there is loss of pain sensitivity (analgesia) in some part of the body, the patient feels no pain when stuck with a pin. (Interestingly enough, this situation is similar to that of a hypnotized subject who, under instructions that he will feel no pain, shows no pain reaction when his skin is deeply pierced by a needle.) However, even though real, the disorder may be selective: a pilot whose conversion reaction of night blindness prevents him from flying at night may be able to drive a car; a person whose symptom is total blindness may be able to see well enough to dodge an object thrown at him; a person reacting with deafness may be able to hear instructions shouted in an emergency.

As in the case of the soldier with paralyzed legs, almost every conversion reaction can be traced to an attempt to avoid or solve a problem by means of illness. Most of us have at times pleaded illness to avoid some particularly unpleasant situation. However, the neurotic carries this tendency to the extreme when faced with a serious conflict to the extent that his daily life is seriously interfered with. In addition to avoiding the problem, the conversion symptom provides the secondary gain of eliciting sympathy and support from relatives and friends.

It is interesting to note that the more dramatic types of reactions, such as sudden paralysis or being struck blind or deaf, are becoming increasingly rare in civilian life; however, they are still relatively common among servicemen during wartime. It may be that with the increasing medical sophistication of our population such dramatic afflictions are no longer viewed as medically feasible, and patients seem to be developing instead vague aches and pains which are more difficult to distinguish from organic disorders. Conversion reactions in civilian life occur mainly among adolescents and young adults.

Concluding comments on neurotic reactions

We have discussed four types of neurotic reactions. As we mentioned at the onset the symptoms frequently overlap and it is not always clear how to categorize a particular patient. Our college student (p. 529) could be classified as an anxiety reaction or an obsessive-compulsive reaction, depending upon which symptoms seemed the most predominant. Actually he was using obsessive thoughts as a defense against anxiety, but this defense was not very successful, and the anxiety was breaking through in the form of acute panic reactions. The four neurotic reactions could be placed on a continuum in terms of the degree of observable anxiety. The person with an anxiety reaction exhibits the greatest amount of anxiety; indeed he has no successful defense against anxiety. The phobic individual comes next with his intense fear of one particular situation. The obsessive-compulsive shows less manifest anxiety than the phobic individual. And the person with a conversion reaction shows the least amount of anxiety, presumably

because his tension has been diverted into physical symptoms.

We have stressed the fact that neurotic reactions are exaggerated forms of normal defense mechanisms; neurotic symptoms are responses which the individual has learned to use to defend himself against anxiety and to increase his feelings of security. Initially these responses may be fairly successful in reducing anxiety and hence are reinforced and strengthened. However, under conditions of increased stress the individual redoubles his defensive efforts so that they reach maladaptive proportions (i.e., seriously interfere with his ability to cope with the problems of daily existence) and are only partially successful in reducing anxiety. He is thus stuck with a pattern of responding that not only fails to relieve his anxiety but also creates additional adjustment problems for him.

Since feelings of inadequacy and anxiety underlie all of the neurotic reactions we may well ask what determines the particular symptoms an individual develops. Why is one person plagued by obsessive thoughts while another develops paralysis of the arm in response to a conflict situation? We do not know the complete answer. The most plausible explanation is that neurotic symptoms are extreme forms of the reaction patterns a child learns in his early life through interaction with the important people in his environment. Often such reaction patterns are appropriate in the situation in which they were learned but are maladaptive when applied to situations in later life. For example, the parent who rewards the child with excessive fussing and attention when he is sick and who encourages him to stay home from school when there is the slightest sign of illness may predispose the youngster to retreat into illness whenever he encounters a difficult situation in later life. We can see where a person with this type of background might develop a conversion reaction when faced with a crisis situation. Or the parents who place great emphasis upon correct and proper behavior and instill feelings of guilt whenever the child deviates from their standards may be predisposing the child to an obsessive-compulsive reaction in adult life. Although such hypotheses are plausible they cannot be verified until we have more intensive studies of the family relationships of children who later become neurotic.

Psychoses

The person with a *psychotic disorder* (*psychosis,* plural *psychoses*) is more severely disturbed than one with a neurotic disorder. His personality is disorganized, and his normal social functioning is greatly impaired. Although in the past it was generally believed that neuroses and psychoses were two distinctly different kinds of disorders, most experts today believe that there is a continuity from normality through neurosis and psychosis, the differences being largely a matter of severity of the symptoms. Perhaps one of the chief distinctions is that while the neurotic is trying desperately to cope with his anxiety in order to function in the world, the psychotic has to some extent given up the struggle and lost considerable *contact with reality.* He may withdraw into his own fantasy world and fail to respond to things going on around him. Or he may respond with exaggerated emotions and actions that are inappropriate to the situation. Frequently his thought processes are disturbed to the extent that he experiences delusions (false beliefs) or hallucinations (sense experiences in the absence of appropriate external stimuli, such as imagining voices talking to him in abusive language). For these reasons the psychotic individual is more likely to require hospitalization and protective care than the neurotic.

It is customary to distinguish between two general categories of psychoses: *organic* and *functional. Organic psychoses* refer to psychotic symptoms that are the result of a known physiological cause. *Functional psychoses* are disorders of psychological origin without any demonstrable physiological cause. (This distinction will be considered in more detail later.) We will limit our discussion primarily to the functional psychoses since they are of great-

est interest to the psychologist. Two of the most prevalent functional psychoses are *manic-depressive reaction* and *schizophrenic reaction.*

Manic-depressive reactions

The *manic-depressive reactions* are characterized by recurrent and exaggerated deviations of mood from the normal mood to either the *manic phase* (strong excitement and elation), or the *depressive phase* (extreme fatigue, despondency, and sadness). A few patients exhibit the whole cycle, but most vary between the normal mood state and one of the extreme phases, depression being the most common.

In the milder form of the manic phase (hypomania) the patient shows great energy and enthusiasm. He talks continually, has unbounded confidence in his ability, rushes from one activity to another with little need of sleep, and makes grandiose plans with little attention to their practicality (but seldom puts these plans into action or completes them if he does). His behavior is similar in some respects to an individual who is mildly intoxicated.

In the more severe form of mania (hypermania) the patient behaves more like the popular notion of the raving maniac. He may be continually pacing about, singing, shouting obscene phrases, screaming. He is confused and disoriented and may experience hallucinations and delusions. In some hypermanic patients all moral inhibitions are abandoned, and they may exhibit unrestrained sexual behavior or violent assaultive behavior.

The intense excitement of the hypermanic state can be reduced by the use of sedatives and hydrotherapy so that the visitor to a neuropsychiatric ward seldom sees the violent ravings and uncontrolled behavior that were more common 30 years ago.

In the depressed phase the patient's behavior is essentially the opposite of what we have described in the manic phase. Instead of being overactive the individual's mental and physical activity is much slower than normal. Instead of feeling overconfident and boastful, his self-esteem is at its lowest ebb. He feels dejected and discouraged; life seems hopeless and not worth living. Feelings of worthlessness and guilt predominate, and it is not infrequent that patients in this condition will attempt suicide. In the most intense state of depression the patient is bedridden and indifferent to all that goes on around him. He refuses to speak or to eat, and he has to be fed intravenously and completely cared for by others.

As we have said, most patients experience either mania or depression with periodic recovery to more normal behavior, but some develop a cycle of alternating between manic and depressed phases. It is not clear what factors initiate the switch from one phase to the other, but despite the extreme dissimilarity of manic and depressive behavior, many experts conclude that they are psychologically related. They propose that the elatedness and energetic activity of the manic phase is a defense against underlying feelings of inadequacy and worthlessness which break through in the depressive phase. Such a reaction is not unlike that of a normal person who tries to escape from the anxiety of a stressful situation by throwing himself into a full round of gay and busy activities in an attempt to forget about his problems.

There is much we do not know about the etiology of manic-depressive psychosis. The fact that this type of reaction occurs much more frequently among the offspring of manic-depressives than in the general population suggests that there may be a genetic predisposition to the disorder (Kallman, 1959). Studies of individuals with depressive reactions indicate that two main psychological factors are involved: (1) high standards of achievement and feelings of extreme guilt and worthlessness when these standards are not attained, and (2) a rigid conscience that prohibits the outward expression of hostility so that the anger experienced in the face of frustration is turned inward against the self. Usually some crisis in the individual's life situation precipitates the disorder: the death of a loved one, failure in marriage, a severe setback in work (Arieti, 1959).

Some interesting information concerning the cultural determiners of depression has been obtained from a study of suicide in the Scandinavian countries (Hendin, 1964). Although Denmark, Sweden, and Norway have similar climates and social institutions, the suicide rate in the first two countries (approximately 20 per 100,000) is among the world's highest, while Norway has one of the lowest rates (7.5 per 100,000). The author of the study attempts to relate the difference in suicide statistics to differences in child-rearing practices and the values instilled during childhood. A point of interest to the present discussion is that although Denmark and Sweden have similar suicide rates, the reasons for committing suicide differ in the two countries. The Swedes, whose child-rearing practices tend to encourage competition, ambition, and early independence from parents, become depressed and attempt suicide when they experience failure in their work. The Danes, on the other hand, who are encouraged in childhood to remain dependent on their parents and to inhibit acts of aggression or even competition, become depressed when they experience, through death or divorce, the loss of a loved one upon whom they were dependent. In both countries depression results from failure to achieve a vitally important need. But the need differs depending upon the culture; for the Swedes it is achievement and for the Danes, dependency. The lower suicide rates for Norway is attributed to the fact that Norwegian children are encouraged to be neither overly ambitious nor overly dependent and are allowed more free expression of aggression than Swedish or Danish children. Because of this freedom of expressed aggression, the Norwegian does not have to turn it inward.

Schizophrenic reactions

Schizophrenia is by far the most common of the psychotic disorders. It has been estimated that 50 percent of all neuropsychiatric hospital beds are occupied by patients diagnosed as schizophrenic. The word *schizophrenic* is derived from the

Greek words *schizin* ("to split") and *phren* ("mind"). The split does not refer to multiple personalities as in the case of Eve White (see p. 480) or as in the famous fictional account of Dr. Jekyll and Mr. Hyde, but rather to a splitting of the thought processes from the emotions; one of the symptoms of schizophrenia is a blunting or dulling of emotional expression or the display of an emotion that is inappropriate to the situation or the thought being expressed. The symptoms of schizophrenia are many and varied, so much so that some experts believe that the term is currently being used to cover more than one type of disorder. The primary symptoms, however, can be summarized under the following headings (although not every schizophrenic will show all of the symptoms):

1. *Disturbances of affect.* The schizophrenic does not show emotion in a normal way. He usually appears dull and apathetic or he may react with emotions that are inappropriate to the situation, for example, speaking of tragic events without any display of emotion or while actually smiling.

2. *Withdrawal from active interchange with the realistic environment.* The schizophrenic loses interest in the people and events around him. In extreme cases the patient may remain silent and immobile for days (in what is called a *catatonic stupor*) and may have to be cared for as an infant.

3. *Autism.* Withdrawal from reality is usually accompanied by absorption in an inner fantasy life. Inappropriate emotional behavior can sometimes be explained by the fact that the schizophrenic may be reacting to what is going on in his private world rather than to external events. The schizophrenic may be so enmeshed in his fantasy world that he is disoriented in time and space; that is, he does not know what day or month it is or where he is.

4. *Delusions and hallucinations.* The most common delusions experienced by the schizophrenic are the beliefs that external forces are trying to control his thoughts and actions (delusions of influence) or that

certain people or groups are persecuting him (delusions of persecution). Auditory hallucinations are much more common than visual ones—the schizophrenic frequently hears voices. When persecutory delusions and/or hallucinations are predominant the person is called *paranoid.* He may become suspicious of his friends and relatives, fear that they are poisoning him, complain that he is being watched, followed, and talked about. Paranoid delusions can be understood as extreme forms of the defense mechanism of projection. Rather than face the anxiety generated by recognition of his own hostile impulses, the paranoid schizophrenic projects his hostility onto others; it is they who are unjustly trying to harm him.

5. *"Queer" behavior.* The schizophrenic's behavior may include peculiar gestures, movements, and repetitive acts that make no sense to the observer but are usually closely related to the schizophrenic's fantasy world.

6. *Disturbances of thought.* The schizophrenic's speech is frequently incoherent and disconnected. He makes associations that seem senseless to the observer and may even coin new words (*neologisms*) to express his peculiar thoughts. On word association tests he gives associations that deviate markedly from those of the normal individual (Broen and Storms, 1964). When the disorder is long-standing there is progressive deterioration of intellectual ability as measured by standard intelligence tests.

In most cases these symptoms do not develop overnight. They are the result of a gradual process of increasingly unsatisfactory interpersonal relationships and withdrawal from social contacts. The following case history illustrates this gradual process.

A. J. was always extremely shy and as a small child would run away and hide when visitors came to the house. He had one or two boy friends but as a teenager he never associated with girls and did not enjoy school parties or social functions. He had few interests and did not engage in sports. His school record was mediocre, and he left high school at the end of his sophomore year. The principal felt that he "could have done better" and remarked about his "queer" and seclusive behavior. Shortly before leaving school his shyness increased considerably. He expressed fears that he was different from other boys and complained that the other children called him names. He became untidy, refusing to wash or wear clean clothes.

After leaving school A. J. worked at a number of odd jobs but was irregular in performing his duties and never held any one job longer than a few weeks. He finally became unemployable and stayed home, becoming more and more seclusive and withdrawn from community and family life. He would sit with his head bowed most of the time, refused to eat with the family, and when visitors came would hide under the bed. He further neglected his appearance, refusing to bathe or get a hair cut. He occasionally made "strange" remarks and frequently covered his face with his hands because he felt he looked "funny."

The psychiatrist who interviewed the boy when he was brought to a local mental hygiene clinic at the age of 17 noted frequent grimacing and silly and inappropriate smiling but found that he was correctly oriented in terms of time and place and could answer questions coherently in a flat tone of voice. He complained of having recurring thoughts but denied any hallucinations or delusions. He expressed a wish for help so that he could go back to work.

A. J. was admitted to the state neuropsychiatric hospital with a diagnosis of schizophrenia. Testing with the Wechsler Adult Intelligence Scale showed that he had average intelligence (fullscale I.Q. 96) but indicated the beginnings of some intellectual impairment. The results of the Rorschach test reinforced the schizophrenic diagnosis.[5]

Attempts to classify schizophrenic reactions

Traditionally the schizophrenic reactions have been classified into nine different types based on the predominant clinical symptoms. This system of classification has not proved to be very satisfactory, however, because the symptoms overlap from one category to the next, and the diagnosis for a single patient may change from one

type to another during the course of his illness. More recently a two-dimensional classification has been proposed, based not on the schizophrenic's present symptoms but on his premorbid (pre-illness) adjustment and the prognosis for recovery. *Process schizophrenia* involves a history of long-term, progressive deterioration in adjustment with little chance of recovery. *Reactive schizophrenia* involves fairly adequate premorbid social development, with the illness being precipitated by some sudden stress, such as the death of a loved one, loss of job, and so on; the prognosis for recovery is good. A number of rating scales have been developed that attempt to evaluate the patient's premorbid personality and the nature of the onset of illness and to classify him accordingly. Some of these scales have shown good ability to predict a patient's speed of recovery. However, it appears that there is no clear-cut dichotomy between the two groups; rather there is a continuum of personality organization from the most process to the most reactive schizophrenic (Herron, 1962).

Once a classification has been made in terms of one set of criteria the next step is to examine the groups so classified in order to determine additional variables that distinguish between them. Hopefully such a procedure will add to our knowledge about etiological factors and types of treatment. Initially some experts thought that the two groups might be distinguished on a neurological basis. They hypothesized that process schizophrenia, which starts comparatively early in life, might be caused by some sort of brain damage or deficit; consequently, process schizophrenics might respond on certain tests in a manner similar to patients with diagnosed brain damage, while the reactive schizophrenics would not. Such studies have generally had negative results (McDonough, 1960). So far there is little empirical evidence to support the notion that process schizophrenia has an organic etiology and reactive does not (Herron, 1962). However, it has been possible to differentiate between process and reactive schizophrenics on some physiological and psychological measures. For

---

[5] Burton and Harris (1947).

example, reactive schizophrenics are more responsive physiologically (in terms of blood pressure response to a chemical stimulant) than process schizophrenics (King, 1958) and more responsive emotionally to anxiety-producing stimuli (Reisman, 1960). These results support the conclusion that the withdrawal of the process schizophrenic is of long duration, while the withdrawal of the reactive schizophrenic is in response to more recent environmental stress. The fact that the severity of the schizophrenic disorder (as measured by length of hospitalization) is positively correlated with the degree of withdrawal from interpersonal contacts during adolescence is indicated by Table 21–1.

A large-scale study aimed at classifying schizophrenia into more meaningful subgroups than those of either the traditional psychiatric classification or the process-reactive dichotomy was carried out at the University of Michigan over a period of seven years. More than 600 subjects were tested on about 400 biochemical, physiological, and psychological measures in an attempt to differentiate subgroups of schizophrenics which could then be studied further to obtain information regarding etiology, course of illness, treatment, and prognosis. Although the voluminous data from this project have not been completely analyzed, the investigators have found evidence for seven distinct subgroups that differ statistically from each other on certain biological and behavioral characteristics. Hopefully, future investigators will be able to use these subgroups as a base for further research into the nature of schizophrenia. Table 21–2 presents some of the variables in this study that were found to differentiate schizophrenic from normal subjects (Gerard, 1964).

Organic and Functional Illness

The neuroses and psychoses described in the preceding sections are classified as "psychogenic" or "functional," meaning that there is no identifiable organic change in the brain or nervous system associated with them. There are in addition to these reactions many kinds of mental disturbance associated with known organic changes in the brain or nervous system—with alcoholism, acute infections, syphilis, tumors, head injuries, epilepsy, and cerebral arteriosclerosis (hardening of the arteries). Usually the individual has shown normal adjustment prior to the disease or injury, and his subsequent peculiarities in behavior are attributed to damage of the nervous system.

However, the distinction between functional and organic mental disorders is not completely clear-cut. An already unstable individual might become psychotic following a brain injury, while a better-adjusted person might show little change in behavior. In the case of cerebral arteriosclerosis in an elderly person, for example,

TABLE 21–1

Adolescent peer interaction and length of hospitalization as an adult schizophrenic

	Percentage of cases in each interaction category		
Length of hospitalization	High inter-action	Medium inter-action	Low inter-action
Short term (6 months)	73	18	9
Relapsing (at least 2 separate admissions and total hospitalization 1–3 years)	9	36	55
Long term (3 years or more)	0	18	82

Adult hospitalized schizophrenics were categorized (on the basis of intensive interviews) as to amount of weekly interaction they had with their peers during mid-adolescence (ages 15–17). High interaction refers to social contact with at least one peer two or more times per week; medium interaction requires one contact per week; low interaction less than one contact per week. Each row of the table adds up to 100 and presents the percentage of cases classified as high, medium, and low for a given length of hospitalization. Those patients whose adolescence was characterized by high interaction clearly require a shorter term of hospitalization than those in the low category.

SOURCE: Pitt and Hage (1964).

TABLE 21–2
Differences between schizophrenic and nonschizophrenic patients

Schizophrenics have significantly

More or higher	Less, smaller, or slower
Childhood behavior	**Psychological test performance**
difficulty in peer relations	reaction time
brooding	manual speed
conformity and nonaggressiveness	concept formation and reasoning ability
maladjusted mothers	social understanding
Psychiatric characteristics	**Anthropometric characteristics**
withdrawal	chest girth
conceptual and mental disorganization	
motor disturbance	**Biochemical measurements**
anxiety (Gorham scale)	urine volume
	sodium
Physiological functions	potassium
body-core temperature (but lower skin temperature)	serum phosphorus
disturbed respiration at rest	
improvement in night vision after breathing oxygen	

SOURCE: Gerard (1964).

there appears to be little correlation between the degree of cerebral damage and the severity of the mental symptoms. One patient with extensive damage may show only mild intellectual impairment and be able to function quite adequately, whereas another with less damage may show signs of mental confusion, uncontrolled emotional outbursts, and such a lack of responsible behavior that he requires hospitalization. It is apparent that factors other than the actual physiological damage (such as the individual's pre-illness personality and the amount of stress to which he is subjected in his present environment) influence the person's reaction to his illness.

It also seems probable that some of the psychotic cases now classed as functional will ultimately be traced to physiological variables. General paresis, once classed as functional, was discovered in the early 1900s to be caused by the syphilis spirochete. Although not all syphilis victims develop general paresis (only about 5 percent of all untreated syphilitics become paretic), those that do show a wide variety of mental symptoms similar to those we have discussed in connection with the functional psychoses.

When we call an illness functional or psychogenic, we do not mean that there are no changes in the nervous system associated with it. There may indeed be some hereditary basis for susceptibility to the particular disturbance. We imply, however, that the changes are of the kind that take place in learning and habit formation, rather than the kind associated with bacterial infection or neural damage. If the changes are of the functional variety, the disorder is more likely to be reversible—more susceptible to cure through a process of reeducation—than is an organically based disorder.

Moreover, functional psychological illness may be associated with organic physical change in parts of the body other than the nervous system. These are the illnesses commonly called *psychosomatic*. A dramatic illustration is provided by experiments with monkeys on the induction of duodenal ulcers, colitis, and other gastrointestinal

Ulcers in executive monkeys

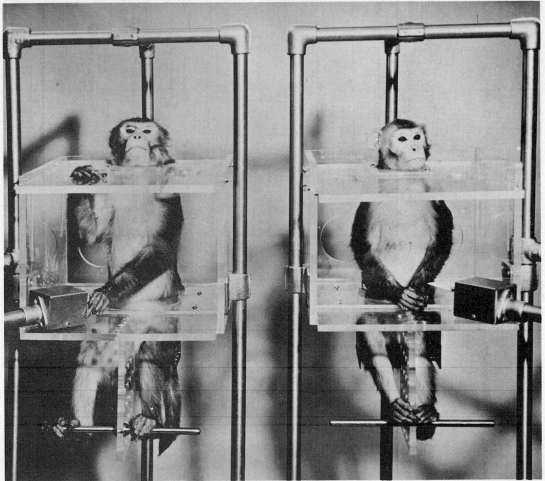

Medical Audio Visual Dept., Walter Reed Army Inst. of Research

Both animals receive brief electric shocks at 20-second intervals. The one at the left (the "executive") has learned to press its lever, thus preventing shocks to both animals, provided the lever is pressed at least once every 20 seconds; the lever for the monkey at the right is a dummy. Although both monkeys receive the same number of shocks, only the "executive" monkey develops the ulcers. (After Brady, 1958)

disturbances through a conditioning procedure (Brady and others, 1958). In one arrangement, monkeys participated in the experiment in pairs, each monkey being confined in a chairlike restraining device (Figure 21–1). An electric shock was delivered at intervals. One of the monkeys (whimsically called the "executive" monkey) had a lever that could be used to turn off or prevent the shock. When he pressed the lever, the shock was turned off for *both* monkeys. Thus both monkeys suffered identical shocks; if their physiological damage were due to shocks, it would affect both equally. What happened was that only the "executive" monkey developed the ulcers; apparently the constant alertness required to turn off or prevent the shock produced a continuing state of tension that resulted in the ulcers. The helpless monkey, who could only take the shocks as they came, was somehow less reactive and less disturbed (Brady, 1958).

While the psychogenic or functional origin of symptoms in neurotic reactions have been rather firmly established, the causative factors in the psychotic reactions are still the subject of intensive investigation.

CRITICAL DISCUSSION

Research on the causes of schizophrenia

Arguments over organic versus functional factors in the causation of mental disease currently center around schizophrenia, the most prevalent of the psychoses. The fact that schizophrenia is at present classified as a "functional" psychosis does not mean that it will necessarily remain in that category. Current research on schizophrenia can be classified into three groups, each group having a different point of view about cause.

Research stressing functional causation. The most prevalent theory of the functional type is that something in the early parent-child relationship, particularly the relationship with the mother, predisposes the individual to schizophrenia. Numerous studies have investigated the early home life of the schizophrenic by means of interviews with the parents and siblings and the patient himself. These studies have consistently found that one or both parents are seriously disturbed emotionally: either the home environment is one of intense conflict between the parents with each trying to dominate and devaluate the other and to win the child to his side, or the pathological approach to child rearing set by the dominant and most disturbed parent is passively accepted by the other (Lidz and others, 1965). Typically the mother is described as dominating, overdemanding, and overprotective—keeping the child close to her, making all his decisions for him, and limiting his involvement with other people. Yet underlying this overinvolvement is a basic rejection of the child (Clausen and Kohn, 1960; McCord and others, 1962). The father, on the other hand, is frequently little involved in the relationship with the child, either by virtue of his absence from home or his apathy and disinterest.

The question naturally arises as to why, if the family interactions are so pathological, do not all the children in the family become schizophrenic? Many do become seriously emotionally disturbed. Lidz and his colleagues (1965) found that among the 24 siblings of the 16 schizophrenics they studied intensively only three could, by the most lenient standards, be considered well adjusted; three were rated as adequately adjusted, eight as emotionally disturbed, seven as borderline schizophrenics, and three as actively schizophrenic. Those siblings who were adequately adjusted tended to remain aloof from the family and left home as early as possible. Further light on this question is provided by Lu (1962), who interviewed the parents of 50 hospitalized schizophrenics, all of whom had a nonschizophrenic sibling of the same sex and approximately the same age. In almost all of the cases it was found that the parents expected more obedience and submissiveness from the preschizophrenic child than from his normal sibling. The preschizophrenic child was more docile than his sibling and restricted his relationships to the family, while the sibling frequently was able to break away from parental control and establish broader social contacts.

Other studies have been concerned with disruptions due to parent-loss by death and to the influences at work as the home is reconstituted (Hilgard and Newman, 1961; Hilgard, Newman, and Fisk, 1960). We hope that with the increasing number of large-scale longitudinal studies concerned with patterns of child-rearing and family attitudes among different social groups, we will in the future have sufficient data to determine more accurately in what ways the family life of the schizophrenic does deviate from the normal. The ideal situation would be one in which we had available from birth onward developmental histories for a large population of individuals, and could compare the histories of those persons who later become schizophrenic with those who developed normally.

Research stressing heredity. Despite the fact that in many cases poor parent-child relationships do lead to schizophrenia, there are many individuals with an equally unfavorable childhood who do not develop the disorder. This fact convinced some investigators that there is a genetic predisposition to schizophrenia (see Chapter 17, p. 456).

Although there is evidence in favor of a hereditary causation for some cases of schizophrenia, we do not know how this susceptibility is transmitted by the genes. And even if future research does establish a firm hereditary basis for schizophrenia, it is probable that environmental factors (such as poor family relationships or other forms of stress) are important in determining whether the disorder will actually develop in a susceptible individual.

Research stressing biochemical factors. It may be that as a result of a hereditary defect, prenatal deficiency, or some other factor schizophrenics metabolize products that cause their mental symptoms. Some investigators have therefore searched for products in the blood or urine that differentiate schizophrenics from other persons.

The biochemical studies to be fully meaningful should provide the answer to the following questions. (1) If the kinds of chemical products found excessively in schizophrenics' blood or urine are injected into a normal person, will he develop symptoms resembling those of schizophrenia? (2) If known chemical antidotes to those products are injected, will the symptoms of schizophrenics be alleviated? While a clear answer cannot be given to these questions, partial evidence is encouraging to those who believe in a chemical basis for the symptoms. The drug LSD-25, if injected, produces hallucinatory symptoms in a normal person which somewhat resemble those in schizophrenics (Hoch, 1955). Drugs known to be antagonistic to LSD-25 sometimes have ameliorative effects in schizophrenia. All these drugs have chemical similarities with adrenalin, with the chemical products that result from its metabolism, or with its neutralizers. The drugs are marketed under many names, two of which are the so-called tranquilizers, chlorpromazine and reserpine. The results of research are not yet sufficiently established to provide a chemical explanation of schizophrenia. For a critique of such studies, see Kety (1959).

All of the developments we have discussed are promising, all are controversial, and none are mutually exclusive. The variety and complexity of schizophrenic symptoms suggest that we may be dealing not with a single disorder but with a group of disorders which have some symptoms in common. Thus we may be looking not for a single cause of schizophrenia but for a number of etiological agents. It may well be that in some cases physiological and biochemical factors are primarily responsible for the schizophrenic symptoms, while in others environmental factors play the major role.

Character Disorders

Character disorder is a diagnostic category which requires separate treatment. The reactions in this category differ from neuroses and psychoses in that they involve a life-long pattern of socially deviant or "acting-out" behavior, rather than mental or emotional symptoms, and the individual experiences little, if any, anxiety or distress. Although the category has not been well defined and includes a number of diverse disorders, such as delinquency and criminal behavior, alcoholism, drug addiction, and sexually deviant behavior, we will limit our discussion to one reaction known as *antisocial reaction* (also called *psychopathic reaction*). The disorder is a serious one, and may be more resistant to treatment than the typical neurosis.

The chief characteristic of the antisocial personality is a lack of moral development, or conscience, and an inability to abide by the laws and customs of his society. His behavior is determined almost entirely by his own needs, and he is largely oblivious to the needs of others. He behaves impulsively, seeks immediate gratification of his needs, and cannot tolerate frustration. Whereas the average child by the age of two realizes that there are some restrictions in his environment and that at times he must postpone his pleasures in consideration of his parents' needs, the psychopath seldom learns to consider any but his own desires. It is this need for immediate gratification with no thought for the consequences that frequently involves him in conflict with the law. Seldom is his crime a premeditated one. He behaves on impulse; indeed, his life seems to be a series of erratic and impulsive acts with no long-range goals or purpose in view.

Unlike the neurotic, the psychopathic personality shows few, if any, signs of anxiety. In fact several studies have indicated that he is at ease in situations that would make the average person tense and apprehensive. In a study by Lippert and Senter (1966) GSR measurements (p. 184) were taken on two groups of adolescent delinquents selected from the detention unit of a juvenile court: one group was diagnosed psychopathic reaction and the other was diagnosed "adjustment reaction of adolescence." The measurements were taken from each subject during successive periods of rest, stimulation by auditory and visual stimuli, stress, and adaptation following stress.

During the stress period pseudoelectrodes were attached to the subject's leg, and he was told that in 10 minutes he would be given a very strong but harmless shock. (A large clock was visible so that the subject could note the time when the shock was to occur; no shock was actually administered.) The results showed no difference between the two groups in GSR measures during rest or in response to auditory or visual stimulation. However, during the 10 minutes of shock anticipation the nonpsychopathic group showed significantly more tension than the psychopathic group, and, at the moment when the clock indicated shock was due, most of the nonpsychopathic delinquents showed an abrupt drop in skin resistance (indicating a sharp increase in anxiety); *none* of the psychopaths showed this reaction. The psychopathic group also returned to their resting GSR level much more rapidly than did the other group. These results support the clinical impression that the psychopathic individual has little anxiety concerning future discomforts or punishments. If this is the case, his impulsive acts become more understandable, since he is not deterred by fear of the consequences.

Often, the psychopath on first meeting appears to be an intelligent, pleasant, and well-mannered individual who gives the impression of frankness and honesty. It soon becomes apparent, however, that he feels no guilt concerning his antisocial acts (no matter how appalling) and has no compunctions about lying, which he does skillfully and convincingly. Unlike the nonpsychopathic delinquent, who may rebel against society but who still adheres to the code of his "gang," the psychopath seems to have few values—neither those of society nor of a gang—and he feels no alliance or loyalty to anyone but himself. Although superficially he may appear friendly, the psychopath is usually a lone wolf who is incapable of forming a close and warm relationship with another person. These two characteristics, guiltlessness and lovelessness, are so outstanding that they are considered the distinguishing features in the diagnosis of psychopathic personality disorder (McCord and McCord, 1964).

In the same way that neurotic reactions were discussed as exaggerated forms of normal defense mechanisms, the characteristics of the psychopath can be found in a much milder degree among normal persons. We all vary in our ability to postpone gratifications of our impulses, in the strictness of our conscience and feelings of guilt when we break social codes, and in our ability to be concerned with the welfare of other people. There is no sharp dichotomy between the normal individual and the psychopath. Individuals could be placed along a continuum in terms of the characteristics we have described; the psychopaths would be those persons who fell at the extreme end of the continuum.

Causative factors in psychopathic personality

What factors contribute to the development of the psychopathic personality? We might expect such individuals to come from homes where they received no discipline or training in moral behavior. But the answer is not that simple. Although some psychopaths do come from slum neighborhoods where antisocial behavior may actually be reinforced and where adult criminals may serve as models for personality development, many more come from "good" homes where their parents are prominent and respected members of the community.

Many theorists believe that the development of a mature conscience depends upon an affectionate relationship with an adult during the early childhood years. The normal child internalizes his parents' values (which generally reflect the values of his society) because he wants to be like them and because he fears the loss of their love if he does not behave in accordance with their values. When a child receives no love from either of his parents he does not fear its loss. Such a child does not identify with the rejecting parents and does not internalize their rules. Wrongdoing consists not in breaking rules, only in getting caught and punished. He experiences little or no anxiety or guilt and is classified as a psychopath. While this theory of the origin of psychopathic behavior has some plausibility, firm knowledge awaits further research.

CRITICAL DISCUSSION
Mental disorders and the law

Our discussion of character disorders leads us to consideration of a topic which is currently of great concern to social scientists, members of the legal profession, and to anyone who works with criminal offenders —what should our laws be with regard to treatment of a mentally disturbed person who commits a criminal act. The psychopath can be one of the most dangerous types of criminals; nevertheless, by our current legal definition he is not insane and, consequently, cannot be committed to a neuropsychiatric hospital for treatment. His treatment is based solely upon the determination of his guilt.

The idea that a person is not responsible for an act that is due to a mental disorder was first introduced into law in 1724, when an English court maintained that a man was irresponsible if "he doth not know what he is doing, no more than . . . a wild beast." Contemporary standards of legal responsibility, however, are based on the M'Naghten

decision of 1834. M'Naghten, a Scotsman, suffered the paranoid delusion that he was being persecuted by the English prime minister, Sir Robert Peel. In an attempt to kill Peel he mistakenly shot Peel's secretary. All involved in the trial were convinced by M'Naghten's senseless ramblings that he was insane. He was judged not responsible by reason of insanity and sent to a mental hospital, where he remained until his death 22 years later. The reigning monarch at the time, Queen Victoria, was not pleased by the verdict—apparently feeling that political assassinations should not be taken lightly— and called upon the House of Lords to review the decision. The decision was upheld and the rules were put into writing regarding the legal definition of insanity. The M'Naghten Rules state that a defendant may be found "not guilty" by reason of insanity only if he were so severely disturbed at the time of his act that he did not know what he was doing or, if he did know, did not know that it was wrong.

The distinction of knowing right from wrong has been the basis of decisions on legal insanity up to the present time. Many psychologists and psychiatrists who are called upon for expert testimony in such trials feel that the M'Naghten Rules are much too narrow. Frequently individuals who are clearly psychotic can still respond correctly when asked if a particular act is morally right or wrong. And a kleptomaniac knows that it is wrong to steal, but his compulsion to do so is so intense that such knowledge does not deter him. A few states, recognizing this situation, have added to their statutes the doctrine of "irresistible impulse"; in such states a defendant may be declared legally insane, even if he knew what he was doing and knew right from wrong, if the jury decides he was driven to his crime by a compulsion too strong to be resisted.

A more reasonable legal definition of insanity was provided by the U.S. Court of Appeals for the Second Circuit in 1966. The court adopted the definition of criminal responsibility that had been proposed by the American Law Institute after a careful 10-year study. It is: "A person is not responsible for criminal conduct if at the time of such conduct as a result of mental disease or defect he lacks substantial capacity either to appreciate the wrongfulness of his conduct or to conform his conduct to the requirements of the law." The word "substantial" suggests that "any" incapacity is not enough to avoid criminal responsibility; but "total" incapacity is not required either. The word "appreciate" rather than "know" implies that intellectual awareness of right or wrong is not enough; the person must have some understanding of the moral or legal consequences of his behavior before he can be held criminally responsible. This new rule is mandatory in all federal courts in New York, Connecticut and Vermont. But it is expected that the lower courts in these states will also follow the rule, and hopefully it will be adopted by other state and federal courts.

The problem of legal responsibility in the case of mentally disordered individuals is indeed complex. A revolutionary approach toward criminal law has been proposed by Sheldon Glueck (Glueck, 1962). His proposal would separate two functions of the law, determination of guilt and imposition of the sentence. The jury in a criminal case where sanity was in question would be asked only to determine whether the defendant is guilty of the crime with which he is charged. If he is convicted, the determination of treatment would be made by a tribunal of criminologists, psychologists, and psychiatrists who would evaluate the nature and causes of his behavior and decide whether the needs of society and the individual's chances for rehabilitation would be best served by treating him in a neuropsychiatric hospital or punishing him in a prison. The convicted individual's progress could be evaluated periodically and a decision made as to when he had made a sufficiently satisfactory adjustment so that he could be released. This procedure would be superior to a system under which the judge must prescribe in advance the minimum length of time the individual should be hospitalized.

Prevalence of Mental Disorders

Severe mental illness is an important social problem. At any given moment approximately 750,000 patients are being cared for in the mental hospitals of the United States, and they occupy more than half of all hospital beds.[6] This means that there are more people presently hospitalized for mental illness than for cancer, heart disease, tuberculosis, and all other diseases combined. Estimates indicate that one out of every 10 babies born today will be hospitalized for mental illness at some time during his life (Goldhammer and Marshall, 1953). If these statistics sound too depressing, we should hasten to add that half the patients admitted to mental hospitals are eventually discharged as improved or recovered, most of these within the first year of entering the hospital. The percentage is higher for well-staffed hospitals using modern treatment methods.

The approximate distribution of mental hospital admissions in terms of type of disorder is shown in Figure 21–2. As you can see, the most prevalent diagnosis is schizophrenic reaction; about 25 percent of first admissions to public mental hospitals are individuals classed as having one of the schizophrenic disorders. (The incidence in the general population is approximately 16 per year for every 100,000 people.) Because of the relative youth of schizophrenic patients and their comparatively low death rate, those who are not discharged accumulate over the years to make up half of the resident population of these hospitals. Older persons suffering from senile disorders related to cerebral arteriosclerosis and other physiological conditions of aging constitute 24 percent of first admissions; since their death rate is relatively high they make up only about 14 percent of the resident hospital population.

The admission rate for neurosis is low because many neurotics are treated as outpatients and therefore are not entered on hospital records. For this reason, and because the disorder is not clearly defined and merges with the normal, the prevalence of neuroses in the general population is hard to estimate. However, what data there

[6] This somewhat astonishing figure results from the fact that many mental patients are hospitalized for several months or even years while general medical patients require an average hospitalization of only two weeks.

21-2

First admissions to U.S. Public Mental Hospitals in 1965

In this figure senile disorders refer to cerebral arteriosclerosis and other physiological conditions of aging: organic brain disorders to infection, injury, epilepsy, and so on. (From data of the U.S. Public Health Service)

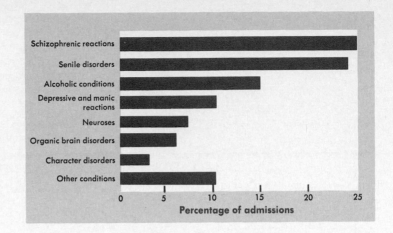

are suggest that neurotic disorders are far more prevalent than we might expect. Two community studies, one in New York City and another in a small town in Nova Scotia, give some measure of the extent of symptoms of disturbed mental health. The New York study estimates that 30 percent of the population have clinical symptoms sufficient to disturb their everyday lives. That this high figure is not due solely to the strains of urban life is indicated by the figure of 32 percent for the small town (Srole and others, 1962; Leighton and others, 1963).

Community surveys have begun to provide some interesting information concerning the distribution of the various disorders in different socioeconomic groups, although the reasons for the differences are not at all clear. Several studies have found that the neuroses are more prevalent in the upper and middle classes, while a disproportionate number of psychotic reactions occur in the lower class. In the New York study that covered all ranges of socioeconomic status, the incidence of psychotic disorders was found to be 13 percent in the lowest socioeconomic group, as compared with 3.6 percent in the upper class (Srole and others, 1962). A study in New Haven, Connecticut, found similar results and noted that even among the neurotics there were class differences in types of symptoms. The upper-class neurotics tended to experience

more subjective emotional discomfort—anxiety, dissatisfaction, and unhappiness with themselves—while the lower-class neurotics tended to show more somatic symptoms and unhappiness and friction with other people. The middle class showed both sorts of symptoms (Hollingshead and Redlich, 1958).

A number of different hypotheses have been offered to explain the class differences in incidence of psychoses. These include (1) movement downward in class status as the individual becomes more seriously disturbed and less able to hold a job, (2) class differences in child-rearing practices which may predispose the children to different kinds of defense mechanisms, and (3) the devastating effect of poverty which engenders a feeling of helplessness and a desire to withdraw from the harshness of reality. Much more information is needed before we can evaluate the contribution of these and other factors to the higher incidence of psychoses among the lower class.

The question has often been asked whether the conditions of modern life have increased the amount of mental illness. This is obviously an extremely difficult, if not impossible, question to answer. Although mental-hospital admission rates have increased more rapidly than the increase in population within the past 80 years, the difference can be largely explained by increased hospital facilities, a more enlightened attitude toward mental illness, and a major increase in the number of senile patients being cared for in hospitals. Careful consideration of these and other facts has led most experts to conclude that there was little if any increase in severe mental illness between the years 1885 and 1940. During World War II there was a noticeable increase in mental-hospital admission rates for males of service age. This increase could be explained by (1) increased facilities provided by the Veterans Administration Hospitals, (2) the possibility that induction examinations identified mentally ill who would otherwise have gone undetected, and (3) the possibility that war conditions and separation from home actually increased the severity and/or frequency of mental disorders (Pugh and MacMahon, 1962).

Since the year 1955, we have seen for the first time a slight decline in the number of patients in mental hospitals. Despite an increasing population there were 15,587 fewer patients in U.S. mental hospitals in 1959 than there were in 1955, and the decline appears to be continuing (see Figure 21–3). This encouraging trend can be attributed in part to the improved treatment techniques, including the use of tran-

21–3

Patients in mental hospitals

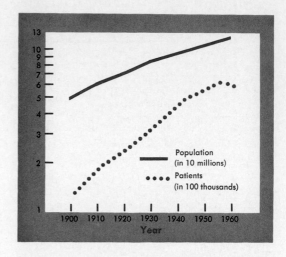

This figure compares the number of patients in mental hospitals with the total population (aged 15 and over) of the United States from 1900 to 1960. The solid curve measures the total population in units of 10 million. The dotted curve measures the number of mental patients per 100 thousand persons in the population. (After Pugh and MacMahon, 1962)

quilizing drugs, which will be discussed in the next chapter.

SUMMARY   1. We can think of a continuum of adjustment ranging from the well-adjusted individual—who is characterized by productivity, zest for life, ability to relate warmly to other people, and acceptance of his own motives and feelings—through the maladjusted *neurotic* and the more seriously disturbed *psychotic*. The diagnosis of abnormal behavior is based on statistical frequency, social values, and degree of impairment.

2. *Neurotic reactions*, characterized by anxiety, are usually extreme forms of normal defense mechanisms used in an unsuccessful attempt to resolve persistent conflicts. These include *anxiety reaction*, *obsessive-compulsive reaction*, *phobic reaction*, and *conversion reaction*.

3. *Psychotic reactions* involve a more serious disintegration of behavior, disturbance of thought processes, and a weakened contact with reality. Two common *functional psychoses* (those with no clear organic basis) are *manic-depressive reaction* (characterized by exaggerated deviations in mood) and *schizophrenic reaction* (which may include such symptoms as withdrawal, autism, delusions, hallucinations, and flattened or inappropriate affect). There are also mental disorders associated with definite organic causes (alcoholism, physical disease, and injury) and

psychosomatic illnesses in which there are physiological changes (such as ulcers) which accompany psychological conditions.

4. Research on the causative factors in schizophrenia has been concerned with pathology of the schizophrenic's early home life, evidence for a hereditary predisposition to the disorder, and the possibility that biochemical defects may cause schizophrenic symptoms.

5. Persons suffering from a type of *character disorder* called *psychopathic reaction* are impulsive, concerned only with their own needs, unable to form close relationships, free from anxiety or guilt, and frequently involved in trouble with the law. Severe rejection by both parents during childhood is postulated as the factor responsible for failure to develop a mature conscience.

6. Mental disorders constitute a serious social problem. It is estimated that one out of every 10 babies born today will spend some time in a mental hospital; community studies have shown as many as 30 percent of the population as having clinical symptoms of personality disturbance sufficient to interfere with their daily efficiency. Severity of mental disorder is inversely related to socioeconomic status, with psychosis occurring three times as often in the lower classes as in the upper.

SUGGESTIONS FOR FURTHER READING

For general treatments of mental disorders there are textbooks in psychiatry, such as Redlich and Freedman, *The theory and practice of psychiatry* (1966), and those in abnormal psychology, such as Coleman, *Abnormal psychology and modern life* (3rd ed., 1964), or White, *The abnormal personality* (3rd ed., 1964), or Maher, *Principles of psychotherapy: an experimental approach* (1966). Arieti, *American handbook of psychiatry,* 2 vols. (1959), is a useful reference source.

Problems of personal adjustment, especially as faced by college students, are treated in Heyns, *The psychology of personal adjustment* (1958), Lindgren, *Psychology of personal development* (1964), and McKinney, *Psychology of personal adjustment* (3rd ed., 1960).

An excellent review of research and theory on schizophrenia is provided by Jackson, *The etiology of schizophrenia* (1960). Some useful original papers dealing with research on abnormal behavior have been collected by Palmer and Goldstein in *Perspectives in psychopathology* (1966).

22 Psychotherapy and Related Techniques

In the last chapter we described the various types of behavior disorders. We shall now go on to discuss the kinds of treatment or therapeutic techniques that are being used in attempting to cure these disorders. These therapeutic techniques can be divided into two major classes: *somatotherapy*, which attempts to change the patient's behavior by physiological methods (drugs, shock treatment, or psychosurgery); and *psychotherapy*, which attempts to bring about behavior change through psychological methods, most frequently processes of communication between the patient and another person called the *therapist*. We shall mention the somatotherapies only briefly and devote most of our discussion to various types of psychotherapy. Before we do so, however, it is enlightening to consider briefly the history of treatment of the mentally ill.

Historical Background

Man's attitude toward and treatment of mental illness has varied throughout the ages as a function of his attitude toward himself and the world around him. The early Chinese, Egyptians, and Hebrews considered disordered behavior to be caused by demons or evil spirits which had taken possession of the body. The treatment then was to exorcise the demons by such techniques as prayer, incantation, magic, and the use of purgatives concocted from herbs. In the event that such treatment brought no improvement, more extreme measures were taken to insure that the body would be an unpleasant dwelling place for the evil spirit; flogging, starving, burning, even stoning to death were not infrequent forms of treatment. The Old Testament makes a number of references to demonology. In Leviticus (20:28) it is stated that "A man also or woman that hath a familiar spirit, or that is a wizard, shall surely be put to death: they shall stone them with their stones: their blood shall be upon them." Although in most cases possession was thought to be by evil spirits, instances where the behavior was of a mystical or religious nature were believed to result from possession by a good or holy spirit. Such people were therefore respected and worshiped. During this period treatment of the mentally ill was in the hands of the priests who had the power to perform the exorcism.

The first real progress in the understanding of mental disorders came with the Greek physician Hippocrates (c. 460–377 B.C.), who rejected the idea of demonology and maintained that mental disorders were the result of pathology of the brain.

He and the Greek and Roman physicians who followed him argued for a more humane treatment of the mentally ill. Instead of the primitive methods of exorcism they stressed the importance of pleasant surroundings, exercise, proper diet, massage, soothing baths, and some less desirable methods such as bleeding, purging, and mechanical restraints. Although there were no institutions as such for the mentally ill, many were cared for with great kindness by physicians in temples dedicated to the Greek and Roman gods.

Such progress did not last, however. The Middle Ages saw a growing revival of primitive superstition and demonology. The mentally ill were thought to be in league with Satan and to possess supernatural powers by which they could cause floods, pestilence, and all sorts of injuries to others. In the belief that by cruelly treating an insane person one was punishing the devil inside him, such measures as beating, starving, and branding with hot irons were considered justified. This type of cruelty reached its horrible culmination with the witchcraft trials that sentenced to death thousands of people (many of them mentally ill) during the 15th through 17th centuries.

To cope with the mentally ill who roamed the streets in the latter part of the Middle Ages, asylums were created. These were not treatment centers but simply prisons whose inmates were chained in dark and filthy cells and treated more like animals than human beings. It was not until after the French Revolution in 1792 when Philippe Pinel was put in charge of La Bicêtre (an asylum in Paris) that some improvement was made in the treatment of these unfortunate people. Pinel was allowed, as an experiment, to remove the chains from the inmates. Much to the amazement of the skeptics who thought he was mad to unchain "such animals," Pinel's experiment was a success. With release from restraint, placement in clean and sunny rooms instead of dungeons, and kind treatment, many who had been considered hopelessly mad for years improved sufficiently to leave the asylum.

The beginning of the 20th century brought great strides in medicine, the biological sciences, and experimental psychology. The discovery of the syphilis spirochete in 1905 demonstrated a physical cause for the mental disorder general paresis and encouraged those physicians who held an organic view of causation. The work of Sigmund Freud and his followers laid the groundwork for an understanding of mental illness as a function of environmental factors. And Pavlov demonstrated in his laboratory experiments on conditioning that a state similar to an acute neurosis could be produced in animals by requiring them to make discriminations beyond their capacities.

Despite these scientific advances the general public in the early 1900s still had no understanding of mental illness and viewed mental hospitals and their inmates as objects of fear and horror. The education of the public in the principles of mental health was begun through the efforts of Clifford Beers. Beers was a Yale graduate who as a young man developed a manic-depressive psychosis and was hospitalized for three years in several private and state hospitals. Although chains and other methods of torture had long since disappeared, the straightjacket was still widely used to restrain excited patients; lack of adequate funds made the average state mental hospital—with its overcrowded wards, poor food, unsympathetic and frequently sadistic attendants, and understaffing of doctors and nurses—a far from pleasant place to live. After his recovery Beers published his experiences in a now famous book entitled A mind that found itself (1908). This book did much to arouse the interest of the public. Beers worked ceaselessly in an effort to educate the public in an understanding of mental illness and in 1909 helped to organize the National Committee for Mental Hygiene. In 1950 this organization joined with two related groups to form what is now the National Association for Mental Health. The mental-hygiene movement played an invaluable role in educating the public and in stimulating the organization of child-guidance clinics and community mental-health clinics, which could aid in the prevention as well as the treatment of mental disorders.

Current treatment facilities

The past 25 years has seen a vast improvement in our facilities for treatment of the mentally disturbed. The neuropsychiatric hospitals established by the

Veterans Administration following the end of World War II were in most instances markedly superior to the average state-supported hospital (partly because of more adequate funds) and served as an impetus for the improvement of the state hospitals. Although some state hospitals are still primarily custodial institutions where inmates lead an idle and futile existence in run-down, overcrowded wards, most mental hospitals today are attractive, well-kept, and busy places, where trained, sympathetic personnel guide the patients through a wide range of activities designed to achieve maximum physical and mental health. Each patient's daily schedule is planned to meet his own needs and may perhaps include an hour with his individual therapist or in group psychotherapy or in occupational therapy designed to teach skills as well as provided relaxation. Treatment may also include "hydrotherapy" in the form of an hour in the swimming pool to help relieve tensions, other forms of physical recreation including team sports, and educational therapy, which prepares the patient to obtain a better job upon release from the hospital. Patients who are well enough may work part-time in the various hospital departments as patient-employees, thereby earning some money and a feeling that they are contributing to the welfare of the hospital community.

Whereas in the past mental hospitals have been fairly isolated institutions located away from the major cities, the current trend is toward building hospitals near universities and medical schools in our more populated areas. In this way there is closer contact with the latest research developments and much more interaction between the hospital staff and various specialists on the university or medical school faculty. Many mental hospitals serve as training centers for interns in psychiatry, psychology, and psychiatric social work as well as a means of experience for students in psychiatric nursing, occupational and physical therapy. In addition, some mental hospitals carry on large scale research projects of their own. Locating mental hospitals in or near the cities also makes the task of gradually integrating the patient back into community life much easier.

Other current developments include the trend toward smaller mental hospitals with a capacity of less than 1000 beds (some of the older state hospitals are gigantic, overcrowded structures housing as many as 6000 patients) and the emphasis on a *therapeutic community*. The concept of the therapeutic community implies that *all* aspects of the patient's hospital environment should be involved in his treatment. This concept, of course, underlies the various programs we have discussed as characteristic of the modern mental hospital (occupational and education therapy, patient-employee program, etc.), since all of these activities are designed to encourage the individual's skills and abilities. It goes even further, however, in suggesting that ideally all of the patient's activities and interactions with hospital personnel should be designed to help him understand and modify his behavior. This means that nurses and ward attendants must be well-trained and sensitive to the patient's problems. The benefits of one hour with an individual psychotherapist may be easily undone if the remainder of the day involves interaction with indifferent ward personnel. Thus the optimal situation is one where the staff members form a team in their treatment of the patient, consulting frequently as a group to evaluate his progress and make suggestions for further treatment.

In addition to the neuropsychiatric hospitals (federal, state, and private) an extremely important function is served by outpatient and mental-health clinics. A number of neuropsychiatric hospitals maintain outpatient clinics where discharged patients may be seen for follow-up treatment. Mental-health clinics supported by federal, state, and county funds are now available to service almost every community, as are a number of private clinics. Their part in preventing serious mental illness by treating emotionally disturbed individuals before their condition becomes acute enough to require hospitalization cannot be overemphasized.

A pattern of cooperation which has developed within mental health clinics has now come to be fairly widespread. In these clinics, a team of workers representing three professions works together on each case: a psychiatrist, a clinical psychologist, and a psychiatric social worker. Together they collect the pertinent facts, discuss a plan for treating the case, and agree on a division of responsibility. In any one clinic the division of labor among the members of the team may vary from case to case but is determined in part by the special competencies of the three professions.

A *psychiatrist* is a medically trained specialist whose experience covers both cases in mental hospitals and in outpatient clinics. In the team approach he takes medical responsibility in addition to any specific role he may have in an individual case. A *psychoanalyst* is a specialist within psychiatry who uses the methods and theories derived from Sigmund Freud. A psychoanalyst is today almost always a psychiatrist,[1] but a psychiatrist is often not a psychoanalyst.

A *clinical psychologist* has had graduate training in psychology, has usually earned his Ph.D., and has served special internships in the fields of testing and diagnosis, psychotherapy, and research. He tends mainly to administer and interpret the psychological tests used in the clinic, and to conduct psychotherapy. He usually is also active in research.

A *psychiatric social worker* usually has earned his M.A. at a graduate school of social work, including an internship, and has special training in interviewing in the home and in carrying treatment procedures into the home and community. Because of this special training, the social worker is likely to be called upon to collect information about the home and to interview relatives, in addition to carrying a share in the therapeutic procedures with the patient.

In mental hospitals a fourth professional person joins the team: the *psychiatric nurse*. Psychiatric nursing is a specialty within the nursing profession and calls for special training in the handling of mental patients —both those severely disturbed and those on the way to recovery.

In our discussion of psychotherapeutic techniques we will not specify the profession to which the psychotherapist belongs (except in the case of psychoanalysis, as mentioned above); the assumption is that he is a trained and competent member of any one of these professions.

The Psychotherapies

The term *psychotherapy* embraces a wide variety of techniques whose goal is to help the emotionally disturbed individual modify his behavior so that he can make a more satisfactory adjustment to his environment. As we shall see, some psychotherapists believe that modification of behavior is dependent upon the patient's understanding of his unconscious motives and conflicts, while others feel that patients can learn more adaptive ways of coping with their problems without necessarily exploring factors in the past that have led to the development of the problem. Despite differences in techniques all methods of psychotherapy have certain basic features in common. They involve communication between two individuals, the patient and the therapist, in which the patient is encouraged to express freely his most intimate fears, emotions, and experiences without fear of being judged or condemned by the therapist. The therapist, in turn, while being sympathetic and understanding of the patient's problems, does not become emotionally involved (as would a friend or relative) but maintains a detached objectivity, which enables him to view the patient's difficulties more clearly.

The techniques of psychotherapy have been used most successfully with the milder forms of mental disorder, the neuroses, although some therapists have reported success with psychotics (Fromm-Reichmann, 1948). The neurotic is usually aware that he has problems, is anxious for help, and is able to communicate with the therapist.

[1] There are a few "lay" psychoanalysts, that is, analysts without an M.D. degree.

The psychotic, on the other hand, is frequently so involved in his fantasy world and so unaware of reality that it is extremely difficult to communicate with him. The process of establishing contact (developing what is called "rapport") with the psychotic is a lengthy one which must be undertaken before psychotherapy can begin. Fortunately, some new drugs being used with psychotic patients make them more amenable to treatment by psychotherapy.

Psychoanalysis

The psychotherapeutic technique with which the average layman is most familiar is psychoanalysis, a method of treatment based on the concepts of Sigmund Freud. Psychoanalysis is not a large profession; in 1965 there were some 1,200 members of the American Psychoanalytic Association, the recognized organization for the fully accredited psychoanalysts in this country. But the influence of psychoanalysis is much more pervasive than the small number of practitioners would suggest.

Along with a method of treatment, Freud proposed a body of psychological theory that has, in one form or another, influenced much of modern thinking—in drama and literature as well as in psychology, medicine, and social science. While we shall be concerned chiefly with the nature of psychoanalytic therapy, it should be kept in mind that the observations made within this technique represent the basic data upon which Freud's theories rest.

Free association. The psychoanalyst ordinarily sees a patient for 50 minutes a visit several times a week for periods of from one to several years. Psychoanalytic therapy, in its original form, is thus not only intensive but extensive. In the introductory sessions the patient gives a description of his symptoms. He recounts relevant facts from his personal biography. He is then prepared to enter upon *free association,* one of the foundations of the psychoanalytic method. The purpose of free association is to bring to awareness and to put into words repressed thoughts and feelings of which the patient is unaware or which

ordinarily go unacknowledged if they come to awareness.

In free association, the patient is taught the "basic rule" that he is to say everything that enters his mind, without selection, without editing. This rule is a very difficult one to follow. The patient's lifetime has been spent in learning self-control, in learning to hold his tongue, in learning to think before speaking. Even the patient who tries conscientiously to follow the rule finds that he fails to tell many things. Some passing thoughts seem to be too unimportant to mention, some too stupid, others too indiscreet.

Suppose, for example, that a person's freedom is being hampered by the presence in his household of an invalid for whose care he is responsible. Under such circumstances, he may unconsciously wish for the relief that death of the invalid might bring. But he would disapprove of such a death wish because it would be a violation of his loyalty to the sick person. Actually, a death wish of this kind may be very near to awareness, but the habits of a lifetime make the patient deny the wish even to himself. He may show in his fantasies or in other ways a preoccupation with death; possibly he hums tunes that are played at funerals. By acknowledging these fleeting thoughts and feelings instead of repressing them, he becomes aware, first of all, of previously unrecognized ideas and feelings close to awareness. With practice, he gradually brings to consciousness ideas and feelings that he has more deeply repressed.

A person represses certain thoughts and feelings because he fears that to acknowledge them will threaten or degrade him. And he therefore resists their recall. The *resistances* must be overcome before he can associate freely. One of the tasks of the therapist is to aid the patient to overcome his resistances. Sometimes a patient has a free flow of associations until he comes to something that blocks him. Then his mind seems to go blank, and he can think of nothing to say. This blankness is judged to be resistance to the recall of something effectively repressed. Sometimes, after a particularly revealing session, the patient may forget his next appointment, another indication of resistance to revealing what is hidden. Because resistances are unconscious, they mean that the patient is unable to cooperate fully even though he consciously wishes to do so.

Interpretation. The psychoanalyst attempts to overcome resistance and to lead the patient to fuller self-understanding through *interpretation.* The interpretation is likely to take two forms. First, the analyst calls the attention of the patient to his resistances. The patient often learns something about himself when he discovers that a train of associations is suddenly blocked, that he forgets his appointment, that he wants to change the subject, and so on. Second, the analyst may privately deduce the general nature of what lies behind the patient's statements and by imparting a hint may facilitate further associations. The patient may say something that seems trivial to him and half-apologize for its unimportance. Here the analyst may point out that what seems trivial may in fact allude to something important. This hint may lead, if the interpretation is appropriately timed, to significant associations. It should be noted that the analyst is careful not to suggest *just what it is* that is important to the patient; this the patient must discover for himself.

The analyst gives somewhat different interpretations in the early and late stages of the analysis. Early in the analysis he is likely to give interpretations that help the patient to understand resistance. He may encourage free association by pointing out the importance of the seemingly trivial or by noting connections in the patient's associations between thoughts that at first seemed totally unrelated. But, as the analysis moves on, the analyst gives more complex interpretations of the content of the patient's associations. When the patient reports a dream, as he usually does, the analyst may encourage him to give associations to the dream in order to aid in its interpretation. Sooner or later the analyst himself figures in the patient's dreams or associations. The relationship between patient and analyst then becomes an occasion for interpretation. The patient's emotionalized attitudes toward the analyst are known as *transference,* a process that we need to discuss further.

Transference. Any psychotherapeutic relationship is social, involving a relationship between the patient and the therapist. In psychoanalytical treatment the attitudes of the patient toward the analyst become important in determining his progress. Sooner or later in analysis the patient develops strong emotional responses toward the psychoanalyst, perhaps admiring him greatly in one session only to despise him in the next. This tendency of the patient to make the therapist the object of emotional response is known as *transference,* and the interpretation of transference, although a controversial topic, is one of the foundations of psychoanalytic therapy. According to the theory, the patient sees the therapist as possessing attitudes like those of his parents or those of his brothers and sisters, though the therapist may be very unlike any of the people for whom he substitutes.

To cite one example: A young woman being treated by a woman psychoanalyst remarked one day as she entered the analyst's office, "I'm glad you're not wearing those lace collars you wore the last several times I was here. I don't like them on you." During the hour, the analyst was able to point out that she had not in fact worn any lace collars. During the preceding sessions the patient had assigned to the analyst the role of the patient's mother and had falsely pictured the analyst as dressing as the patient's mother had dressed when the patient was a child undergoing the emotionally disturbing experiences now being discussed in the analytic hours. The patient, while surprised, accepted the interpretation and thereby gained understanding of transference.

Transference does not always involve false perceptions; often the patient simply expresses feelings toward the analyst that he had felt toward figures important earlier in his life. On the basis of these expressed feelings, the analyst is able to interpret the nature of the impulses that have been displaced in his direction. For example, a patient who has always admired an older brother detects something in the analyst's attitude that reminds him of the brother. An angry attack upon the analyst may lead to the uncovering of hostile feelings toward his brother that the patient heretofore had never acknowledged. The analyst, by studying how the patient feels toward him, helps the patient to understand better his conduct in relation to others.

Abreaction, insight, and working through. The course of improvement during psychoanalytic therapy is commonly attributed to three main experiences: *abreaction,* gradual *insight* into one's difficulties, and the patient's repeated *working through* of his conflicts and his reactions to them.

A patient experiences *abreaction* when he freely expresses a repressed emotion or relives an intense emotional experience. The process is also called "catharsis," as though it were a kind of emotional cleansing. Such free expression may bring some relief, but by itself it does not eliminate the causes of conflict.

A patient has *insight* when he understands the roots of the conflict. Sometimes insight comes upon the recovery of the memory of a repressed experience, but the popular notion that a psychoanalytic cure typically results from the sudden recall of a single dramatic episode is mistaken. The patient's troubles seldom have a single source, and insight comes through a gradual increase in self-knowledge. Insight and abreaction must work together: the patient must understand his feelings and feel what he understands. The reorientation is never simply intellectual.

Even while on the road to recovery, the patient goes through a lengthy process of reeducation and problem-solving known as *working through.* By facing the same conflicts over and over again, the patient learns to react in more mature and problem-solving ways, to face rather than to deny reality, with the support of the analyst in the permissive situation of the interview. By working through, the patient becomes strong enough to face the threat of the full original conflict situation without distortion and to react to it without undue anxiety.

The end result claimed for a successful psychoanalysis is a deep-seated modification of the personality which will make it possible for the patient to cope with his problems on a realistic basis, without the recurrence of the symptoms that brought him to treatment, and which will lead to a more comfortable and richer life. In terms of the discussion in Chapter 20, instead of relying on defensive behavior he relies on coping behavior.

Client-centered psychotherapy

Client-centered or *nondirective* psychotherapy is a method developed by Carl Rogers and his associates (Rogers, 1951; Rogers and Dymond, 1954) that in some respects is markedly different from psychoanalysis. It is *client-centered* because its purpose is to have the client or patient arrive at the insights and make the decisions rather than the therapist. It is *nondirective* because the therapist does not try to direct the patient's attention to specific topics (such as his relationship with his wife or his early childhood experiences) but leaves the subjects to be discussed up to the patient. Unlike psychoanalysis, client-centered therapy does not attempt to relate the patient's problems to experiences in his early history. It is concerned with the patient's *present* attitudes and behavior; for this reason the client-centered therapist does not believe it necessary to obtain a case history or to spend the initial interviews gathering biographical material.

Client-centered therapy can be described rather simply, although in practice it requires great skill and is much more subtle than at first appears. The therapist begins by structuring the interview, by explaining the terms of agreement between him and the client: the responsibility for working out his problems is the client's; he is free to leave at any time, and it will be his choice whether or not to return; the relationship is a private and confidential one; the client is free to speak of intimate matters without fear of reproof or of having the information revealed to others. Once the interview is structured, the client does most of the talking. Usually he has a good deal to "get off his chest." The therapist is a patient but alert listener. When the client stops, as though expecting the therapist to say something, the therapist usually acknowledges and accepts the feelings the client has been expressing. For example, if the client has been telling about how he is nagged by his mother, the therapist may say: "You feel that your mother tries to control you." His effort is to *clarify* the feelings the client has been expressing, not to judge them or to elaborate on them.

What usually happens is that the client begins with a rather low evaluation of himself, but in the course of facing up to his problems and bringing his own resources to bear on them he turns to the positive. For example, one reported case began with statements such as the following:

> Everything is wrong with me. I feel abnormal. I don't do even the ordinary things of life. I'm sure I will fail on anything I undertake. I'm inferior. When I try to imitate successful people, I'm only acting. I can't go on like this.[2]

By the time of her 11th and final interview she expressed the following attitudes, contrasting strikingly with those of the first interview:

> I am taking a new course of my own choosing.
> I am really changing.
> I have always tried to live up to others' standards that were beyond my abilities.
> I've come to realize that I'm not so bright, but I can get along anyway.
> I no longer think so much about myself.
> I'm much more comfortable with people.
> I'm getting a feeling of success out of my job.
> I don't feel quite steady yet, and would like to feel that I can come for more help if I need it.

To see whether this kind of progress is typical, experimenters have carefully analyzed recorded interviews. When the client's

[2] From the case of Miss Tilden, reported by Snyder and others (1949), pp. 128–203. All names in reported cases have been changed to protect the subjects' privacy.

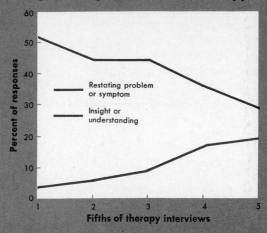

22–1

Changes during client-centered therapy

Results for 10 subjects and 60 interviews in client-centered therapy are shown here, with three to nine interviews per subject. Stating of the problem gradually gives way to increased frequency of statements indicating understanding. (Drawn from data presented by Seeman, 1949)

statements are classified and plotted, the course of therapy turns out to be fairly predictable. For example, in the early interviews the client spends a good deal of time talking about his difficulties, stating his problem, describing his symptoms. In the course of therapy, he increasingly makes statements showing that he understands the meaning for his personality of the topics being discussed, that he foresees a favorable outcome. By classifying all the client's remarks as either problem restatements or statements of understanding and insight, one can see the progressive increase in insight as therapy proceeds (Figure 22–1).

What does the therapist do to bring about these changes? First of all, he creates an atmosphere in which the client feels his own worth and significance. The atmosphere arises not as a consequence of technique but out of the therapist's conviction that every person has the capacity to deal constructively with his psychological situation and with those aspects of his life that can come into conscious awareness (Rogers, 1961).

In accepting this point of view, the therapist is not merely a passive listener, for if he were the client might feel that the therapist was not interested in him. So the therapist listens intently and tries to show in what he says that he can see things as the client sees them. In the beginning, Rogers, as the originator of client-centered therapy, laid great emphasis upon having the therapist try to clarify the feelings expressed by the client. Rogers now believes that method to be too intellectualistic; he currently places the emphasis upon the therapist's trying to adopt the client's own frame of reference, upon his trying to see the problems as the client sees them, although without becoming emotionally involved in them. To have therapeutic value, the change in the client must be a change in feeling, a change in attitude—not merely a change in intellectual understanding.

A great deal has been learned from those who advocate and practice client-centered therapy. It is too early to know with certainly what its range of usefulness will be and wherein its limitations lie. It does appear, however, that this method can function successfully only with individuals who want to discuss their problems and can verbalize their feelings with some degree of ease. With persons who do not voluntarily seek help, such as prisoners and juvenile delinquents, and with neurotics who are too inhibited to discuss their feelings spontaneously, more directive methods are usually necessary. The techniques of client-centered therapy have been used successfully, however, in areas such as play therapy with children, group therapy, and even classroom teaching. And client-centered therapists have made a very significant contribution in their attempts to analyze scientifically what takes place during the process of psychotherapy.

Psychotherapy based on learning theory

A more recent approach to psychotherapy attempts to apply the principles of learning (as discussed in Chapter 11) to the treatment of neurotic (and in some instances, psychotic) disorders. If maladaptive behavior is learned, then by employing some of the techniques developed in experimental work on learning we should be able to substitute new and more appropriate responses for the maladaptive ones. While some psychologists have attempted to interpret what takes place during psychoanalysis or client-centered psychotherapy in terms of learning principles (Dollard and Miller, 1950), others have gone further and attempted to devise new methods of treatment based on our knowledge of learning and motivation (Lazarus and Rachman, 1957; Wolpe, Salter, and Reyna, 1964; Ullman and Krasner, 1965).

One of the techniques frequently used is based on the principle of *counter-conditioning*: maladaptive responses (including responding to a situation with anxiety) can be weakened or eliminated by strengthening incompatible or antagonistic responses. Wolpe (1958) gives an experimental example of the creation of a "neurosis" in cats and its subsequent cure by counter-conditioning. Cats who received electric shocks in their feeding cages eventually refused to eat not only in their cages but anywhere in the experimental room. This reaction would be similar to the spread (or generalization) of anxiety in a patient. The conditioned anxiety conflicted with the normal eating response. Psychotherapy must then involve extinction of the anxiety response so that the normal response (i.e., eating) can occur. Wolpe found that he could inhibit the anxiety by a gradual process of feeding the animal elsewhere in the laboratory, at some distance from the room in which the shock had been administered. Although there might be incipient anxiety reactions these were overcome (inhibited) by the successful act of eating. Gradually the feeding was brought closer to the original place, but never at a pace too rapid to upset the eating. When the cat was able to eat in the room where it had become disturbed, it was soon also ready to eat in the cage where it had originally been shocked. Thus it was "cured" of its neurosis. Wolpe describes the cure as taking place by *reciprocal inhibition* (i.e., the strengthening of eating inhibits anxiety), but it is also an example of counter-conditioning.

22–2

Fear of snakes eliminated through counter-conditioning

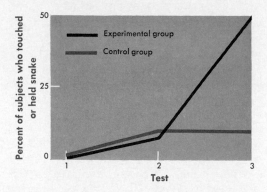

Subjects were college students who reported an intense fear of snakes. Subjects in both groups were first tested to see how closely they would approach a large, non-poisonous snake and whether they would actually touch or hold the snake upon request (Test 1). They then spent five sessions constructing an anxiety hierarchy regarding snakes and also receiving training in muscle relaxation, after which they were again tested to see if they would touch or hold the snake (Test 2). The control group received no further training. The experimental group was given 11 sessions of counter-conditioning in which progressively more disturbing items in the anxiety hierarchy were visualized in conjunction with relaxation. Both groups were then given a final test (Test 3). Comparing the results of Test 2 with those of Test 3 we see that the group who experienced counter-conditioning showed a marked change in their behavior toward snakes, while the control group showed only a slight change. The fact that there is little change between Test 1 and Test 2 for either group indicates that neither the effects of suggestion implicit in participating in the experiment nor relaxation training alone (where the relaxation is not specifically associated with the anxiety-producing stimuli) produced much modification in behavior. (After Lang, 1964)

In extending this process to the treatment of human patients Wolpe begins by discovering in interviews with the patient what sorts of situations are anxiety-producing for him. He then compiles a list of situations or stimuli to which the patient responds with anxiety; the stimuli are ranked in order from the least anxiety-producing to the most fearful (the list is termed the *anxiety hierarchy*). On the assumption that relaxation is antagonistic to anxiety, Wolpe trains the patient to relax (using a method of deep muscle relaxation, sometimes accompanied by hypnotic suggestion or tranquilizing drugs) and instructs him to visualize the least anxiety-producing situation. (This would correspond to feeding the cat in a remote room in the laboratory.) If the relaxation is not disturbed, the patient then goes on to imagine the next item on the list. This process continues through a series of sessions until the situation that originally provoked the most anxiety now elicits only relaxation. Thus the patient has been conditioned to respond with relaxation to situations that initially produced a response of anxiety. The anxiety response has been eliminated through the strengthening of an antagonistic or incompatible response—relaxation. The results of an experimental study using this technique to eliminate fear of snakes is shown in Figure 22–2.

Other responses antagonistic to anxiety which may be used with the counter-conditioning procedure are *assertive* or *approach* responses. An individual whose anxiety stems from the repressed resentment he experiences because of his inability to stand up to his mother may be taught to be gradually more and more assertive in situations involving his mother, first in visualized situations and later in actuality; mother then comes to evoke assertive behavior rather than submission and anxiety. Wolpe and other therapists employing counter-conditioning techniques have reported remarkable success in eliminating specific phobias as well as treating cases involving more general anxiety (Wolpe, 1958; Lazarus, 1963).

Although the method of counter-conditioning has been used most frequently in eliminating anxiety or fear reactions, it can also be used to eliminate maladaptive behavior that involves *approaching* a situation rather than avoiding it. For example, in the treatment of alcoholics it is possible to substitute an avoidance response for an approach response. By the use of nausea-producing drugs such as emetine, the sight and smell of alcohol become associated with feelings of nausea, and, hence, a stimulus (alcohol) that previously elicited an approach response now elicits an avoidance response. Although this method of curing alcoholics has been criticized because it does not change the underlying causes of the alcoholism, it has been used successfully with a large number of cases (Lemere and others, 1942). It is most effective when the avoidance-conditioning is followed by some attempt to deal with the anxiety that impels the individual to seek relief with alcohol, either by the relaxation method described above or by more traditional means of psychotherapy.

The *principle of reinforcement* has also been used as a technique for strengthening positive habits to replace maladaptive behavior. Frequently the habit the therapist wants to reinforce is one that has very low strength in the individual's repertoire of habits (occurs very infrequently) or may be one that he has never learned, such as talking in a mute child. In this case a technique similar to Skinner's "shaping" of behavior in operant conditioning (see p. 285) is used; responses that approximate or move in the direction of the desired behavior are reinforced, with the therapist gradually requiring closer and closer approximation until the desired behavior occurs. Reinforcement may consist of social rewards (such as praise, attention, and special privileges); with children and very withdrawn psychotics more primary forms of reinforcement (such as food or cigarettes) may be necessary.

Psychotherapy based on the principles of learning that we have been discussing has been given various titles; the one currently in greatest use is *behavior therapy,* so called because it is concerned with modifying the *behavior* of the patient rather than developing insight or resolving unconscious conflicts. Behavior therapists maintain that insight is not a prerequisite for and frequently does not result in behavior change; maladaptive behavior can be modified more directly by the use of learning principles. In addition, once certain "undesirable" aspects of an individual's behavior have been changed other persons react to him in a more positive way which, in turn, stimulates further behavior modification.

More traditional therapists and psychoanalysts have criticized behavior therapy as a superficial method of treatment because it deals only with symptoms and leaves the conflict unresolved. They maintain that what beneficial results are obtained with this method are a function of the relationship between the therapist and patient (the interest and attention given by the therapist with the possibility of transference) and not the specific techniques employed. The behavior therapists have responded with appropriate rebuttals to these criticisms and have countered by claiming that the success of traditional psychotherapy is based upon the unwitting use of learning principles in the therapy sessions (e.g., when a patient discusses behavior or impulses about which he feels guilt and the therapist does not reinforce these feelings with disapproval, the guilt feelings tend to *extinguish*). Such questions can only be answered by further research including studies designed to compare the effectiveness of behavior therapy and of traditional therapies in treating behavior disorders of various kinds. In the meantime it is clear that behavior theory has provided a challenge to some of the older concepts of therapeutic interaction and has opened up new possibilities for the use of scientific principles in the practice of psychotherapy.

CRITICAL DISCUSSION
"Mental illness" vs. "maladaptive habits"

Although the concept of "mental illness" was a great improvement over the medieval explanation that disordered behavior was the result of possession by demons, some psychiatrists and psychologists today question the appropriateness of the "illness" or "disease" analogy. Terms such as mental health, mental patients, and emotional illness imply that disordered behavior is a symptom of some underlying disease process. Yet we know that the neuroses do not involve any brain pathology or disease; and so far there is no clear evidence of the role of such factors in the development of the psychoses.

The disease concept is misleading for a

number of other reasons. It suggests that there is a sharp division between normality and abnormality. Yet we have seen that whether certain behavior is considered normal or a symptom of some underlying disturbance depends upon the social group to which the individual belongs, the situation in which the behavior occurs (overt aggression is normal on the football field but not in the classroom), and the age of the individual (bed-wetting and temper tantrums are normal for the two-year-old but not for the adolescent or the adult). In the case of physical pathology the treatment usually involves alteration or removal of the pathological agent (e.g., in tuberculosis, destroying the bacteria by means of antibiotics). In the behavior disorders it is usually not the underlying motivations that need to be altered but the manner in which the individual has learned to satisfy his needs (Rotter, 1954). In the treatment of a homosexual we do not remove the sexual motivation but try to direct it toward a socially more acceptable object.

Central to the illness concept is the controversy regarding the treatment of symptoms. If behavior disorders are analogous to physical disorders, then it is futile (and often dangerous) to treat the symptoms without removing the underlying pathology. (The medical man does not simply apply an ointment to the rash that develops as a symptom of syphilis, but destroys the syphilis spirochete by antibiotics.) Many psychotherapists, particularly psychoanalysts, believe that this concept is true for the behavior disorders. A specific phobia, for example, is only the surface expression of more complex emotional difficulties; removal of the phobia without treatment of the underlying difficulties will result in the appearance of another, perhaps more serious, symptom. Behavior therapy is criticized because it does not treat the inner conflicts but removes only the symptom, leaving the patient open to *symptom substitution*. Behavior therapists, on the other hand, maintain that there is no underlying conflict or illness. Neurosis consists of maladaptive habits formed through a process of conditioning; remove the habits (symptoms) by substituting more appropriate ones and you have "cured the illness" (Eysenck, 1960). So far this debate has not been resolved. In a survey of cases treated by behavior-

therapy methods, only three instances of symptom substitution have been found (Grossberg, 1964). This is not conclusive proof, however, since follow-ups of the patients over longer periods might have revealed new symptoms, and there may have been some subtle symptoms of which the investigators were unaware.

Despite the controversy, however, there does seem to be some advantage to discarding the disease concept of behavior disorders, especially as far as the neuroses are concerned. According to one psychiatrist, the phenomena now called mental illness should be removed from the category of illnesses and regarded instead as the expression of man's struggle with the problem of how he should live. As he sums up the problem: "Our adversaries are not demons, witches, fate, or mental illness. We have no enemy whom we can fight, exorcise, or dispel by 'cure.' What we do have are *problems in living*—whether these be biologic, economic, political, or sociopsychological." [3]

Group therapy

A majority of emotional problems stem from the individual's difficulties in relating to his fellow man—feelings of isolation, rejection, and loneliness; an inability to interact satisfactorily with others or form meaningful friendships. In addition to dealing with a patient's anxieties and conflicts, the psychotherapist attempts to help him achieve more satisfactory interpersonal relations. Although a number of aspects of the patient-therapist relationship produce progress toward the latter goal, the final test lies in how well the patient can apply the attitudes and responses he has learned during the therapy hour to personal relationships in his daily life. With this fact in mind we can see that there might be some advantage in *group therapy*, where the patient can work out his problems in the presence of others, observe how they react to his behavior, and try out new methods of responding when old ones fail.

Group therapy, in one form or another, has gone on informally for many years. Camp counselors have been able by group

[3] Szasz (1962), p. 118.

discussions to help children who come to summer camps. They have improved the child's relations to his fellow campers and raised the child's respect for himself as an accepted member of the group. Children have found help in scout troops and in other clubs under wise and friendly leadership. Alcoholics Anonymous, an organization founded by two ex-alcoholics to help other alcoholics give up the habit, employs a form of group therapy. By discussing their experiences and problems with alcohol in group meetings new members realize that they are not alone in their problems and are encouraged by the success other members have had in conquering alcoholism.

Psychologists and psychiatrists have come to recognize group therapy as a scientific, psychotherapeutic method to be planned and studied like any other acceptable method (Slavson, 1962; Rosenbaum and Berger, 1963). Therapists from various orientations (psychoanalytic, client-centered, and even behavior therapy) have modified their techniques to be applicable to therapy groups. Group therapy has been used successfully in a variety of settings—on hospital wards with both psychotic and neurotic patients, in mental-health clinics, with parents of disturbed children, and even with troubled business executives. Most typically the groups consist of a small number of individuals with similar problems. The therapist generally remains in the background allowing the members to exchange experiences, comment on each other's behavior, and discuss their own symptoms as well as those of the other members. While initially members tend to be defensive and uncomfortable about exposing their weaknesses, they gradually become more objective about their own behavior and more aware of the effect their attitudes and behavior have upon others. They gain an increased ability to identify and empathize with other members and a feeling of self-esteem when they are able to help a fellow member by an understanding remark or a meaningful interpretation. Group therapy has several advantages over individual therapy: (1) the method saves

time, because one therapist can help several people at once; (2) the patient becomes aware that he is not alone in his problem, that others have similar feelings of guilt, anxiety, or hostility; (3) the patient has the opportunity to explore his attitudes and reactions by interacting with a variety of people, not just the therapist. Individuals frequently receive a combination of group and individual therapy so that they can benefit from the advantages of both.

Psychodrama. A unique form of group psychotherapy is *psychodrama*, a method of acting out emotional situations in a stage setting, as shown in Figure 22–3 (Moreno, 1946). A specific situation is selected by the patient or the therapist (such as a son telling his mother that he intends to marry a girl of whom she disapproves), and the scene is spontaneously played with one or two patients taking the main roles and the others acting as supporting cast and audience. A number of different techniques are used: the patient may reenact a traumatic situation from his past life, thus achieving a certain amount of emotional release or catharsis; he may act out present situations that are anxiety-producing for him, thereby gaining some measure of control over his anxiety; he may learn new and more appropriate ways of responding by acting out situations in which he has reacted inappropriately in the past. Patients who are shy and inhibited may start out by being spectators and gradually work up through minor roles to major parts. In this way they learn to express themselves more freely and spontaneously and develop social skills in meeting new situations.

Role playing. A more informal type of psychodrama called *role playing* is sometimes used in hospitals to help the patient prepare for the type of situations he will encounter upon discharge. A therapist and one or two patients may enact a scene where the patient is being interviewed for a job. This gives the patient practice in presenting himself to the employer, answering the types of questions he may be asked, and deciding how to handle the reluctance

22–3

Psychodrama

Psychodrama is the technique of having the patient act out his problems on a stage in closely supervised situations. Above, an audience of patients and therapists watches patient-actors unfold a domestic situation on the stage.

J. R. Black

some employers still feel about hiring former mental patients.

Role playing is sometimes used as an aid in individual therapy also. One therapist, treating an adolescent boy who, among other problems, was fearful of calling girls for dates, decided to help him overcome this fear by role playing. With the therapist playing the role of the girl, they enacted numerous phone conversations, thus giving the boy practice in handling various responses the girl might make and particularly in coping with rejection, which had been one of his greatest concerns. The youngster became quite adept in these phone conversations, transferred this skill to real life situations, and, with additional role playing aimed at developing social behavior appropriate for actual dates, became much more relaxed and self-confident in his interactions with the opposite sex.

Family therapy. Another special form of group therapy which has recently received increased attention, particularly among those therapists working with schizophrenic patients, is *family therapy*. Here the therapy group is the patient and his immediate family. The group may consist of husband and wife or parents and children. On the assumption that the patient's problems reflect a more general maladjustment of the family, the therapy is directed toward helping the family members clarify and express their feelings toward one another, develop greater understanding of each other, and work out more effective ways of relating to each other and of solving their common problems.

An eclectic approach

A large number of psychotherapists, perhaps the majority, do not adhere strictly to any one of the therapeutic methods we have discussed so far. Instead they maintain an *eclectic approach,* selecting from the different methods those techniques they feel are most appropriate for the particular patient under treatment. Although their theoretical orientation may be more strongly toward a particular method or "school" (e.g., more psychoanalytic than client-centered), they feel free to discard those concepts they view as not especially helpful and to select techniques from other schools. In short, they are flexible in their approach to treatment. In dealing with an anxiety neurotic, for example, an eclectic psychotherapist might use tranquilizers and relaxation training to help reduce the patient's level of anxiety. (A psychoanalyst would not because he considers anxiety necessary to motivate the patient to explore his conflicts.) To help him understand the origins of his problems the eclectic therapist might discuss certain aspects of the patient's history (a client-centered therapist does no delving into the past) but might feel it unnecessary to explore childhood experiences to the extent that a psychoanalyst does. He might use other techniques that fall under the general heading of education. For example, he might provide information about sex and reproduction to help relieve the anxieties of an adolescent who has been badly misinformed and feels guilty regarding his sexual impulses, or he might explain the functioning of the autonomic nervous system to reassure an anxiety neurotic that some of his symptoms, such as heart palpitations and hand tremors, are not indications of a disease.

Another approach an eclectic psychotherapist might use, one we have not mentioned so far in our discussion of psychotherapy, involves changing the patient's environment. The therapist might feel, for example, that a young man who has serious conflicts in his relationships with his parents can make little progress in overcoming his difficulties while remaining in the home environment. In this instance he might recommend that the youth attend a preparatory school or college away from home or seek employment in another community. Occasionally, with a younger child, the home environment may be so seriously detrimental to the child's mental and physical health that the therapist may, with the help of welfare agencies and courts, see that he is placed in a foster home. Often a delinquent child from a poor home environment improves when placed in a good foster home.

Research on Psychotherapy

It is evident from the foregoing discussions that there are a number of approaches to psychotherapy and that they involve somewhat different presuppositions. Scientific status will eventually be achieved by the system that is most coherent with some established set of psychological principles and is so worked out that it is a feasible and efficient method for dealing with mental-health problems. It is not enough for the psychotherapist to treat a number of cases according to his particular methods and then cite the percentage of "cures" he has obtained. We need to know, in addition to the major problems of what is a cure and who makes the judgment, what variables the therapist manipulated in the therapy sessions and how they affected the patient's behavior. It may well be that the techniques the therapist consciously employed were not the ones that affected the changes observed in the patient; other variables, of which the therapist may not even have been aware, may have been the important ones. Only by systematically manipulating specific variables in the therapy relationship and observing their effect on the patient can psychotherapy approach the status of a scientific discipline.

Because of the large number of variables which interact during the therapeutic interview, research in psychotherapy presents a very difficult and complex problem. In addition to the various techniques the therapist employs there are factors in the therapist's personality that may influence the outcome of therapy; these are termed *therapist variables*. And, of course, no two patients bring the same attitudes, problems, and methods of handling their problems to the therapeutic session. These *patient variables* will influence not only how the patient responds to treatment but also how the therapist may respond to him. It has been shown that therapists react differently to different patients (Strupp, 1958) and, as we shall see, some therapists are more effective with certain types of patients than with others. The intermingling of therapist, patient, and technique or methodological variables in the psychotherapeutic process makes it extremely difficult to assess which variables are related to a successful outcome. For this reason, although much has been accomplished in the relatively short time in which scientific methods of investigation have been applied to the problems of psychotherapy, the major work is yet to be done.

We will not endeavor to summarize the research findings in the area of psychotherapy but will present a few experiments which will serve to illustrate the types of research presently being conducted. In an attempt to relate therapist variables to outcome of therapy with schizophrenic patients, Whitehorn and Betz (1960) analyzed the case records of 100 schizophrenics treated at a psychiatric clinic. Using ratings by the clinic staff and other measures of improvement, they isolated one group of therapists (Group A) whose patients had a fairly high improvement rate (75 percent rated as improved) and another group (Group B) whose patients showed little improvement (27 percent rated as improved). Both groups of therapists were comparable in terms of level of experience and number of patients treated, and both were equally successful in treating neurotic and depressed patients. Somehow they differed, though, in the way they related to the schizophrenic patients. Analysis of the therapists themselves revealed that the Group A therapists (the most successful) showed greater understanding of the patient's motivations, were concerned with understanding the patient as a *person* rather than a *case*, and were actively involved in helping the patient work out solutions to his problems rather than in improving his symptoms or his ward behavior. The Group B therapists, on the other hand, tended to be less actively and personally involved with the patient; their approach was more passive and pedagogical, that is, offering interpretations and instructions. These findings are consistent with other reports (Fromm-Reichmann, 1948) indicating that a high level of active involvement is necessary to establish a relationship of trust and confidence with schizophrenic patients. Further work established the fact that it was possible to distinguish between the A and B therapists on the basis of scores on the Strong Vocational Interest Inventory, a test that measures certain personal attitudes as well as vocational interests. A screening device, based on those test questions which were found to clearly differentiate between A and B therapists, was used successfully to predict with a new group of therapists from another clinic which ones would achieve a high rate of success in treating schizophrenic patients and which ones would not.

Much of the contemporary research on psychotherapy is concerned with the *process* of psychotherapy rather than with the *outcome,* that is, with what takes place between the therapist and patient in an individual therapy session and over a series of sessions. In one such investigation (Lennard and Bernstein, 1960) four therapists carried two patients each through eight months of psychotherapy, obtaining a tape recording of each session. Since the sessions occurred on an average of twice a week, some 500 sessions were involved in the study. From their records the investigators were able to determine the changes in the kinds of communications made over long periods, as well as typical changes within the session. Various kinds of comparisons could be made, such as that of Table 22–1, in which some consequences of greater or lesser activity on the part of the therapist are indicated. It appears within the limits of this study that patients preferred the more active therapists, as indicated by their more frequent willingness to remain in therapy when the research was over, by the infrequency of broken appointments, and by the fewer signs of strain indicated within sessions.

CRITICAL DISCUSSION
Computer simulation of psychotherapy

A new and rather revolutionary approach to psychotherapy research involves programming a computer to act as a therapist (Colby, Watt, and Gilbert, 1964). The process of developing such a program forces the therapist to specify the rules which determine his responses to the patient's verbalizations.

TABLE 22–1

Degree of therapist's activity and indications of strain in interaction between patient and therapist

	More active therapists		Less active therapists	
	A	B	C	D
Number of propositions offered by therapist per session	142	106	58	48
Kinds of propositions:				
Evaluative-prescriptive	32%	46%	18%	29%
High information specificity	47	44	24	32
Low information specificity	15	4	26	27
Unclassified	6	6	32	12
Total propositions	100%	100%	100%	100%
Signs of Strain:				
Patients who discontinued treatment although invited to continue at end of research	1	0	2	2
Broken appointments during first 25 sessions	0	0	3	7
Patients' complaints about strain	few	few	many	many

SOURCE: Lennard and Bernstein (1960), Table 15, p. 115. Each therapist treated two patients.

This research has just begun and the program developed so far only permits the computer to carry on a simple therapeutic dialogue which is similar to the interview a live therapist might conduct in his initial sessions with the patient. The subject sits at a teletype connected to the computer and types out anything he wishes to say. The computer sends back a typewritten reply. The rules for coding the program are complex but involve essentially the following process. The computer is programed to recognize several hundred key words or phrases, such as "I hate," "I worry," "my mother," and to select a response from a group of replies designated as appropriate for that key word or phrase. The response selected may involve adding certain appropriate words in the input sentence. For example, PERSON: "My mother dislikes me." PROGRAM: "Why do you feel your mother dislikes you?" The computer also keeps track of key topics for use in formulating future responses. If the input sentence does not contain any key words, the computer is pro-gramed to steer the person away from non-key topics or to return him to previous topics. For example, PERSON: "It is a nice day today." PROGRAM: "Let's go back and talk more about your mother." Table 22–2 presents an excerpt from an actual conversation between the computer and a volunteer subject. Except for the misunderstanding that occurs in line 4, the conversation is not unlike the information-gathering type of interview a therapist conducts in his first few sessions with a patient. Indeed, experienced therapists who were asked to evaluate a group of computer protocols without being told their source judged them to be quite adequate initial interviews.

So far the computer's responses are limited to questioning, clarifying, rephrasing, and only occasionally interpreting. Colby and his fellow investigators are now attempting to develop a program which can make causal interpretations based on an understanding of the patient's problems. If such a program can be developed satisfactorily, computer simulation of psychotherapy could serve a number of highly useful purposes. It could provide a unique research opportunity; for example, certain rules for responding could be changed and the effect on the subject observed. It could be helpful in training apprentice therapists. If it proved beneficial in the treatment of individuals with behavior disorders, it would provide a very efficient means of overcoming the shortage of therapists in hospitals, for one computer system could then handle several hundred patients an hour. And the program need not be completely automatic; it could be designed so that a human therapist could monitor the system, adding his own responses where he deemed appropriate or directing the computer to certain response groups.

Although the idea of a computer conducting psychotherapy may strike the reader as fantastic (and only time will tell whether it really is feasible), this is but another example of the tremendous impact the computer has had on current developments in psychology (see p. 351 and p. 381).

Relative success of psychotherapeutic techniques

No attempt will be made here to evaluate the relative success of the methods of psychotherapy that we have discussed: psychoanalysis, client-centered therapy, behavior therapy, group therapy, and the eclectic approach. Scientists will ultimately learn what kind of method will work best with what kind of client and what kind of therapist, but the problem is extremely complex.

In the first place, it is very difficult to determine how severe a person's problems are at the time he comes for treatment and how well he would get along without treatment. Even patients with severe mental illness sometimes recover spontaneously—without any clear therapy and with no striking environmental change.

In the second place, the criteria of benefit from treatment are very difficult to establish. Can we trust the client's statement that he feels better or that he is pleased with his therapist? Can we trust his family's statement that he is easier to live with? Sometimes a person who has become

---

TABLE 22–2

Excerpt from a "therapeutic" dialogue between a computer and a subject

PROGRAM	How can I help you?
PERSON	I don't know.
PROGRAM	What don't you understand?
PERSON	No.
PROGRAM	Can you elaborate?
PERSON	I am sick and tired today.
PROGRAM	Do you have any idea why?
PERSON	Yes, I'm old.
PROGRAM	Please go on.
PERSON	I seem to have lost interest in everything.
PROGRAM	Tell me more about such feelings.
PERSON	I have some idea why I feel this way, too.
PROGRAM	You have?
PERSON	It seems that I miss having a family.
PROGRAM	What makes you feel you miss having a family?
PERSON	There is a challenge about it.

SOURCE: Colby, Watt, and Gilbert (1964).

---

relieved from his burdens of conflict may seem even harder to live with, for he now fights back against the people who originally caused some of his troubles.

Finally, as we have already mentioned, the classification of success according to method of treatment cannot take into account the role of the individual therapist. We are dealing with subtle human relationships, and the sensitivity and understanding of the counselor or therapist are very important; no formal technique can make up for a lack of appropriate human qualities in the therapist.

These difficulties in appraising therapy do not leave us helpless. Experiments using before-and-after tests and recorded interviews have been performed chiefly by client-centered therapists (Rogers and Dymond, 1954) but also, as we have seen, by therapists using other methods. It is too early to assign relative values to the different approaches.

Much remains to be learned about the root of psychological disturbances and their improvement under therapy. The social problems of mental illness are so great that they deserve increasing investment of manpower and money. Although more is being spent on research than ever before (approximately 70 million dollars annually), the yearly sum is less than the cost of launching two Atlas missiles.

Somatotherapy

A great many psychiatrists and some psychologists have assumed that behavior disorders (particularly the psychoses) are caused by physiological, as opposed to environmental, factors (see research on causes of schizophrenia, p. 540), and can be treated most effectively by physiological or physical methods. Indeed, some notable successes have been achieved with somatotherapy. Vitamin treatment has reduced the prevalence of mental disturbances associated with pellagra; antibiotics, through curing syphilis, have reduced the once prevalent organic psychosis known as general paresis; barbiturates have alleviated the symptoms of epilepsy. However, some of the somatotherapies developed for treatment of the functional psychoses have proved less successful than anticipated. The use of electric shock to produce convulsive seizures and unconsciousness was a popular method of treatment 15 years ago. No one knew how the shock produced its effect, but it was thought to be particularly successful in curing severely depressed patients. Experience has shown, however, that the method is only moderately successful; and it is used less frequently today than it once was. Brain surgery to sever the nerve fibers connecting the hypothalamus and the prefrontal lobes in an attempt to reduce intense emotional behavior also proved unsatisfactory. The method of treatment that holds the most promise today is *chemotherapy*, the use of tranquilizers and other types of drugs to modify behavior.

Chemotherapy

Chemicals had been used to influence behavior for many years. Narcotics have been used to reduce pain; alcohol and sedatives such as the barbiturates, to lessen anxiety and induce sleep; stimulants such as caffeine, to relieve depression. However,

only within the past 15 years (with the introduction of the two major tranquilizers, reserpine and chlorpromazine) have chemicals been used extensively in the treatment of the behavior disorders. Reserpine is derived from the root of the rauwolfia plant, which has been used in India and Nigeria for many years as a sedative. It was first used in this country in 1954 after it was discovered to be effective in lowering high blood pressure and in calming extremely disturbed and agitated mental patients. Chlorpromazine is a synthetic drug, one of the phenothiazine compounds, which was first produced in France in 1952. Both of these drugs have the amazing capacity to calm and relax the individual without inducing sleep, although they may produce some degree of drowsiness and lethargy. They have been particularly effective in the treatment of schizophrenics. In addition to calming the intensely agitated schizophrenic, these drugs gradually alleviate or abolish his hallucinations and, to a lesser extent, delusions; even more important they frequently decrease the extent of emotional withdrawal so that the patient can be reached by psychotherapy. There have been a number of very spectacular cases where chronic schizophrenics, who had been considered hopeless cases for years, regained contact with reality following treatment with reserpine or chlorpromazine, were able for the first time to discuss and work through their problems, and were eventually discharged from the hospital. We noted in the preceding chapter that following the introduction of tranquilizing drugs the statistics on neuropsychiatric hospital populations indicated a decrease in total number of patients.

A great deal more research is needed before we know exactly how these tranquilizing drugs work—both in terms of their physiological and their behavioral effects. Their main effect on behavior seems to be the reduction of anxiety and fear responses. Experiments with rats have shown the chlorpromazine eliminates a previously learned avoidance response; phenobarbital does not (Miller, Murphy, and Mirsky, 1957). Reduction of fear may make the schizophrenic less susceptible to hallucinations and delusions and less apt to withdraw from his environment. He is consequently more amenable to psychotherapy.

Before we get too enthusiastic about the promising situation described so far, we should mention some of the drawbacks. All of the tranquilizers at times have undesirable side effects, such as liver problems, dermatitis, and occasionally convulsive seizures. Chlorpromazine seems to have fewer side effects than reserpine and to be more effective in controlling psychotic symptoms. Consequently, it and some of the other phenothiazine compounds are most frequently used at present. But none of these drugs really "cures" the behavior disorder. They are a very helpful part of the total treatment program: through their application, a number of patients, previously unresponsive to other forms of treatment, are able to leave the hospital and return to the community; others, though not sufficiently improved to be discharged, become much less of a management problem on the wards; and still others can be kept out of the hospitals by maintenance dosages of drugs on an outpatient basis. However, unless the chemotherapy is accompanied by some attempt to help the patient cope with his problems, either through psychotherapy or improvement of his environmental situation, the probability of a reoccurrence of the disorder is high. Furthermore, these drugs have not been in use long enough for us to be able to evaluate their long-range effects.

The treatment of behavior disorders by means of chemicals has made remarkable progress within a very brief period of time. The field of *psychopharmacology* (which combines the skills of the chemist, physiologist, and psychologist to study the effect of drugs on human behavior) is at present a rapidly growing area of intense research. New chemical compounds are being investigated daily, and there is every hope that the future will bring even greater progress in the treatment of the mentally disturbed by chemical means. However, in the view of most psychologists and psychiatrists, psy-chopharmacology can provide only a partial answer to the problem of mental illness. It seems unlikely that attitudes and response patterns which have developed gradually over the individual's lifetime can be suddenly changed by the administration of a drug.

CRITICAL DISCUSSION
The double-blind procedure in drug studies

The initial enthusiasm for a new treatment method is almost always dampened by the evidence from more adequately controlled research. This has been particularly true in the area of chemotherapy. The results of a drug study may be affected by a number of variables other than the therapeutic properties of the drug itself. One such variable is the hope and confidence the patient places in a new treatment. For example, it has been clearly demonstrated that the giving of a *placebo* (an inert substance that has no pharmacological properties and cannot affect the patient physiologically) can frequently bring about marked improvement in a patient's physical and mental condition, thus demonstrating that his improvement was the result of his attitude. Another variable is the confidence of the doctors and nurses in a new treatment method, which can also inadvertently affect their judgment of the results. And the extra attention focused on the patient because he is the subject of a research project can have beneficial effects. To control the first two variables the more stringent studies use what is called the *double-blind* procedure. Half the patients receive a placebo, the others receive the actual drug. Neither the patients nor the doctors and nurses who must judge the results of the treatment know who received the drug; thus in the ideally controlled study both patients and judges are "blind."

The importance of a well-controlled research design has been shown by a survey of 35 studies dealing with the effect of chlorpromazine on hospitalized schizophrenics (Glick and Margolis, 1962). Each study was classified according to the extent that awareness of medication was controlled: (1) double-blind—neither patient nor judges aware, (2) single-blind—only judges aware, and (3) nonblind—both patient and judges aware. The 35 studies taken as a whole showed a median of 52 percent of the patients judged as "improved." The 12 double-blind studies showed a median of 37.5 percent judged as improved; while the 23 single-blind studies showed a median of 59.7 percent improved. Thus we see that the more carefully controlled studies report considerably less improvement following treatment with chlorpromazine than do the studies that are less well controlled.

Although it seems probable that differences in adequacy of experimental control were partly responsible for the differences in results, the double-blind studies differed from the single-blind in another major respect: the average period of drug treatment was significantly longer for patients in the single-blind studies than in the double-blind. Hence the higher improvement rate for the single-blind studies may have resulted from the fact that the patients in these studies had a more extended period of treatment. The more control one requires in a study, the more difficult it is to sustain the procedures for a long period of time. And in a treatment setting where we are concerned with the welfare of the patient, there is the ethical problem of how long one should withhold potentially beneficial treatment by using the individual as a control.

Practices Enhancing Mental Health

Mental health is essentially a public health problem; that is, the ideal is to create circumstances for healthful living rather than to become preoccupied with the problems of disease. It is better to eliminate mosquitoes than to treat malaria, and to guard the water and milk supply than to treat typhoid fever. Similarly, it is better to provide for normal emotional development than to be concerned primarily with the therapy of neuroses.

Useful work

Absorption in useful work keeps an individual in touch with reality and enhances self-esteem, provided that he accepts the work as dignified and suited to his abilities and interests.

Experience during the depression of the early thirties showed the demoralizing effects of idleness and unemployment. Initially the unemployed were placed on a dole, because it is the cheapest kind of relief to administer. But experience taught the importance of work relief instead, for without work the individual tended to disintegrate (Watson, 1942). Work is not only a matter of livelihood; it provides in itself an important satisfaction and is usually essential to self-esteem. Then, too, many people find satisfaction outside the job in hobbies such as stamp-collecting, handicrafts, or gardening. These projects, because they are self-initiated and self-regulated, enhance the feeling of being a creative person.

Social participation

Man is a social animal and suffers when isolated from his fellows. The circumstances of modern life tend to produce loneliness for many people. As people move—and they move about a great deal these days—they lose contact with friends and relatives. Apartment dwellers today seldom know those who live across the hall; the child often has difficulty finding playmates. Social correctives have to be introduced, not as newfangled ideas but as a return to earlier social arrangements. For example, the nursery school substitutes for the large family and for association with neighborhood children; the community center takes the place of the neighborhood barn dance. Such substitutes must be found for people of all ages. Similar problems emerge also, as we saw in Chapter 4, for older people, as they become an increasing proportion of the population.

Self-understanding

To what extent may a person better his own health through self-understanding? This is a difficult question, because a preoccupation with personal problems may be worse than ignoring them and going about the business of living. A few helpful suggestions, nevertheless, emerge out of the experiences of therapists.

1. *A person can learn to accept his feelings as something natural and normal.* Sometimes the desire to face situations unemotionally leads to a false kind of detachment and imperturbability that has destructive consequences. The person begins to suspect emotion and loses the ability to accept as valid the joys and sorrows of the interplay with other people. In many emotion-arousing situations the disturbing emotion is in part a result of his feeling that he does not come up to expectations or that he falls short of his ideal. Even to experience such emotions is frightening, so he tries to escape them by denial. Actually, there are many situations in which one can accept unpleasant emotion as perfectly normal and not belittling. It is not necessary to be ashamed of being homesick, or of being afraid of a spirited horse one does not know how to ride, or of being angry at someone who has been a disappointment. These emotions are natural; civilized life permits them, and it is more wholesome to give them free play than to deny them. To be anxious about one's emotions often leads to a vicious circle. You are afraid that you will be afraid. You then discover that you are in fact mildly afraid. The discovery confirms your suspicion about yourself and then exaggerates the fear. It is better to be willing to accept the naturalness of your emotions as they arise.

2. *If blocked by circumstances from free emotional expression, a person can seek permissible outlets.* Civilized life puts restraints upon free emotional expression. A person may not be permitted to tell his boss or his mother just what his feelings are, but he may accept his own feelings as justified and still withhold their direct expression. But on the principle that such unexpressed feelings tend to persist as tensions, some indirect outlet is desirable. Sometimes an equivalent can be found in violent exercise —expressing hostility with an ax upon a woodpile. Who hasn't taken a rapid walk and eventually found both his pace and his emotion slowing down? Sometimes it helps to acknowledge felt emotion to a sympathetic person not involved in the crisis situation. If a person accepts his right to feel emotion, he may give expression to it in indirect or substituted ways if the direct channels of expression are blocked.

3. *By discovering the occasions that provoke emotional overreaction, a person can learn to guard against it.* Most people find some kinds of situations in which they tend to be more emotional than do other people. It may be that some small failures cause them undue chagrin; it may be that they find certain people excessively annoying. By learning to detect the situations that lead to emotional distortion, they sometimes learn to see the situations in new ways so that this undue emotion no longer arises. It occasionally happens that our exaggerated awarenesses of some shortcoming makes us unduly sensitive to criticism. This is one form that projection takes. If my work is so heavy that I have to return to the office at nights, I may get the feeling that I am neglecting my wife or family. If, however, my wife so much as mentions my return to the office, I may get angry—sure that she is accusing me of neglect. Then I will insist that my family makes too many demands upon me. If I can recognize my wife's remark for what it is, an expression of sympathy because I am so busy, then I should feel no anger at her.

Limitations of self-help

The person overwrought by emotional problems does well to seek the counsel of a psychiatrist, a clinical psychologist, or other trained therapist. The mechanisms of self-deception are so pervasive, and unconscious motivation so real, that it is difficult to solve a long-standing personal problem without help. The willingness to seek help is a sign of emotional maturity, not of weakness. The therapist should not be thought of only as the court of last appeal. We do not wait until our teeth are falling out before we go to a dentist. Obtaining psychological help when we need it can become as accepted a practice as going to a dentist. To have emotional or personality disturbances is no more reprehensible than to have a cavity in a tooth.

SUMMARY   1. The history of treatment of the mentally ill has progressed from the medieval notion that disordered behavior resulted from possession by evil spirits and should be punished accordingly, through custodial care in ill-kept and isolated asylums, to our modern concept of the *therapeutic community,* which employs a wide variety of activities designed to help the mentally ill patient understand and modify his behavior and improve his social and vocational skills.

2. *Psychotherapy* is the treatment of behavior disorders by psychological means. An extended type of psychotherapy is *psychoanalysis,* which is based on the concepts of Freud. Through the method of *free association* repressed thoughts and feelings are brought to awareness. By *interpreting* the patient's associations the analyst helps him to see the roots of his disturbance. Through the process of *transference* the patient uses the analyst as a substitute for another person as the object of many of his neurotic reactions. The analyst, in turn, attempts through the understanding of transference to use it as an aid to therapy. Through the processes of *abreaction, insight,* and *working through,* the neurosis may eventually be cured.

3. Other psychotherapeutic approaches include *client-centered psychotherapy* and *behavior therapy.* Behavior therapy applies such learning principles as *counter-conditioning* and *shaping of behavior* through reinforcement to modify maladaptive behavior. *Group therapy* provides an opportunity for the mentally ill individual to explore his attitudes and behavior in interaction with others who have similar problems.

4. Research on the various methods of psychotherapy is concerned both with the therapeutic *process* (i.e., how the patient changes as a result of what goes on within the therapeutic sessions) and with *outcome* (i.e., what percentage of patients are more or less permanently helped by treatment). Present evidence is ambiguous in evaluating the relative advantages of the different methods of treatment; there is a great need for further research to provide better understanding and more appropriate use of psychotherapy.

5. In the treatment of behavior disorders by physical methods (*somatotherapy*) the greatest advances have been made by *chemotherapy,* the use of various tranquilizing and energizing drugs to modify behavior.

6. Mental health is a serious national problem. It is desirable to place emphasis upon the *prevention* of maladjustment. Both useful work and satisfactory social participation are important in maintaining mental health. The individual can help himself through appropriate self-evaluation, by accepting his own emotions as natural, by finding channels for emotional expression, and by getting such understanding as he can on the occasions on which he overreacts. There are genuine limitations to self-help, however, and it is not a sign of weakness to seek professional help.

SUGGESTIONS FOR FURTHER READING

For those interested in the history of treatment of the mentally ill, fascinating material can be found in Zilboorg and Henry, *A history of medical psychology* (1941), and Veith, *Hysteria: the history of a disease* (1965).

A review of many different systems of psychotherapy is provided by Harper, *Psychoanalysis and psychotherapy* (1959). Ford and Urban, *Systems of psychotherapy* (1963), furnishes a detailed comparative analysis of 10 of the more widely used systems.

For an introduction to psychoanalytic theory, see Kubie, *Practical and theoretical aspects of psychoanalysis* (1950), and Menninger, *Theory of psychoanalytic technique* (1958). On client-centered therapy, see Rogers, *On becoming a person: a therapist's view of psychotherapy* (1961). The principles of behavior therapy are presented in Wolpe, Salter, and Reyna (eds.), *The conditioning therapies* (1964), Paul, *Insight vs. desensitization in psychotherapy* (1966), and Krasner and Ullman (eds.), *Research in behavior modification* (1965). On group therapy, see Slavson, *Practice of group therapy* (1962).

Problems of personal adjustment, especially as faced by college students, are treated in such books as Heyns, *The psychology of personal adjustment* (1958), Lindgren, *Psychology of personal development* (1964), and McKinney, *Psychology of personal adjustment* (3rd ed., 1960).

SOCIAL
BEHAVIOR

Man's life is inescapably social, and human psychology necessarily concerns itself with the relations between the individual and the group. Social psychology is that branch of psychology concerned especially with the problems that arise in the interactions among individuals: sensitivity to status, interpersonal relations of various kinds, attitudes and opinions and their change. Among the applications of psychology to human affairs lie many within the field of social behavior. Psychology offers no panaceas for social problems, but its developing research methods, joining forces with those of other behavioral sciences, give promise of great social usefulness.

23 Social Psychology

Individual behavior is always influenced by the social context in which it occurs. This is true for lower animals as well as for man, but man is preeminently social; he is born dependent upon other human beings, and his life is spent largely in interaction with other men. Other people are both stimuli for him and the occasions for his responses; their responses to him determine many of the things that he does and how he feels.

All of the chapters of psychology can be written around the "social" theme: the *development* of social behavior, social *motives*, the *learning* of social behavior, the *perception* of people. It is not possible to present an adequate account of general psychology without social references, and we have already met much that is social in earlier chapters. Social considerations figured particularly when we viewed behavior from the *developmental* point of view, as when we saw how early experiences led to the socialization of the child, the acquiring of language, and the other requisites for social life. In this chapter we shall be somewhat more concerned with the social behavior of man from the *interactive* point of view; that is, how the person behaves in the presence of others and is influenced by them.

Social Structure and Social Norms

When we study behavior in a social context we find that responses to stimuli show certain regularities that are the result of tacit agreements among those who live together. In a society in which automobiles are driven on the right side of the road, we respond to the steering wheel and other controls in such a manner as to keep the car on the right, and we expect other drivers to do the same.

When the many regularities, expectations, and rules of a society are studied in their interrelationships, we are concerned with *social structure*, particularly as behavior is affected by rank or position or role. When the totality of social arrangements is under examination we commonly refer to the *culture* (as in "the Samoan culture"), or, in still larger terms, to the *civilization* (as in "western civilization"). All these terms indicate that the behavior of man can be understood only in relation to the various demands and constraints made upon him which arise through the social context in which he lives, with its historical traditions and contemporary social organization.

Social stratification and social mobility

There are tendencies in both lower animals and man to arrange relationships in some sort of hierarchy, in which those higher in the hierarchy have some privileges over those lower in the hierarchy. In human societies, the most general aspect of these distinctions is found in *caste* and *class*.

A *caste* is a social group with boundaries which cannot be crossed without severe social punishment. The old caste system in India is most familiar, with caste grades ranging from the high-caste Brahman to the low-caste Untouchable. Where such a caste system flourishes it is hereditary, and it is unthinkable that a child should not grow up within his caste. In America, the color line has produced many of the characteristics of a caste system so far as the treatment of the Negro is concerned. The many laws forbidding intermarriage of white and Negro illustrate the idea of hereditary caste: Negroes shall marry within their own group, whites within their own group. Recent tendencies to improve the rights of Negroes are founded on the belief that the preservation of residues from a caste society is undemocratic.

A *class* is a social group with certain common characteristics, but the boundaries are much less firm between classes than between castes. We speak of the great middle class, with no implication that some middle-class people will not become upper class or that some lower-class people will not raise middle-class children. In a mobile society such as ours, the tradition of "log cabin to president" prevails, with its implication that social class positions are not fixed.

It is usually considered somewhat offensive to call attention to the class structure of American society. We pride ourselves on equal opportunities in America, on America as the great melting pot. The very doctrine of progress through individual initiative has made us competitive, but it is partly because we are so competitive with each other that a class structure has grown up. We are insistent that the opportunities for climbing the social ladder remain, but we also recognize the social ladder and define it. Studies have shown that it is possible to detect a class structure within American cities. Typical results from two such studies are given in Table 23–1 for the people of an old New England city (called "Yankee City") and for a small town in the midwestern part of the United States (called "Jonesville").

Except for societies with rigid caste divisions, there is always considerable

TABLE 23–1 Class structure in American cities		
Class	Yankee City	Jonesville
Upper-upper	2%	3%
Lower-upper	2	3
Upper-middle	10	11
Lower-middle	28	31
Upper-lower	33	41
Lower-lower	25	14
	100%	100%

SOURCE: Warner and Lunt (1941); Warner, Meeker, and Eells (1949).

mobility, both upward and downward despite a recognizable class structure. This has been true in Japan and Europe as well as in the United States (Table 23–2). The results for nonfarm workers in the various countries show that about one-fifth or more of the population in each country shifts from manual to nonmanual occupations (or the reverse) between generations. Comparable studies show intermarriages across class lines to be roughly equivalent in frequency in all these countries.

These facts might be described as sociological ones; they become more interesting as psychological facts when we think how the possibility of social climbing (or loss of status) may affect the individual. There are, of course, the positive aspects, in that the possibility of being rewarded for effort by more satisfactory status and esteem is motivating, thus encouraging striving and giving hope of success. The very possibility of change brings with it attendant anxieties, however, and social mobility is not without its costs. One evidence of this is the suicide rate among the well-to-do. This was noted by one of the earliest investigators, Durkheim, writing in 1897 (Durkheim, 1958). He found that the more people with independent means, the more suicides; wretchedly poor countries had little suicide. His findings have been confirmed by later studies (e.g., Henry and Short, 1954). The explanation usually given is that people high in social status have few restraints

TABLE 23–2

Social mobility: Changes in occupational class in succeeding generations in nonfarm population

Country	Mobile upward (Fathers manual workers; sons nonmanual)	Mobile downward (Fathers nonmanual; sons manual workers)	Total vertical mobility (Across the line between working and middle class)
United States	33%	26%	30%
Germany	29	32	31
Sweden	31	24	29
Japan	36	22	27
France	39	20	27
Switzerland	45	13	23

SOURCE: Lipset and Bendix (1959), p. 25.

to account for their frustrations and hence turn their aggressions against themselves.[1]

Intergroup tensions and prejudice

Achieving status has the desirable consequence of creating satitsfying relationships among individuals. At the same time the very attitudes of struggling to achieve status, to "belong," lead some people to reject those who are not within the group. The problem of antagonism among groups is of major concern because it is a threat to harmonious social living.

In-groups and out-groups. A perceptual structuring similar to a figure-ground relationship occurs in group identification, so that the group in which membership is held becomes a figure with fairly definite contours. The group to which a person belongs and with which he identifies himself is known as an *in-group.* Other people are identified as not belonging, or as members of *out-groups.* The boundaries are further sharpened if the interests of groups conflict so that the in-group and the out-group come into competition. Feuds between family groups and political battles between

the party in power and the party seeking power represent in-group–out-group conflicts. Caste and class distinctions are, of course, fundamentally based on in- and out-grouping.

The boundaries between groups are not all alike. Some boundaries are more permeable than others; that is, individuals can cross them and come into or go out of the group. On college and university campuses many clubs and societies are open to all or nearly all students who care to join them, and there is little coercion to remain in the group if interest lags. In other organizations, such as fraternities, admission is by way of special invitation and initiation, and the pressure is very strong against breaking group ties once they are established. The boundaries of fraternity membership are less permeable than those of the other clubs.

Assigning oneself to a group leads one to assign others to groups—even though the "others" may have group feelings entirely different from the groups to which one assigns them. One kind of arbitrary group classification leads to *stereotyping,* in which people attribute to an individual characteristics which they believe typical of the group to which they assign him.

An illustration of stereotyping is given in a study by Secord, Bevan, and Katz

---

[1] The problem of suicide is more complex than this; it is mentioned here solely to indicate that successful social position may have its costs. See also p. 534.

(1956), in which subjects whose attitudes toward Negroes were known were asked to rate a number of pictures according to 25 traits. The pictures included 10 Negro faces and five white faces, with the Negro faces selected to reflect a wide range of Negroid features. The traits listed were 10 physiognomic traits characteristic of Negroes, and 15 personality traits widely regarded as part of the stereotype of the Negro. Once a subject selected a picture as that of a Negro, he tended to assign categorically the personality traits characteristic of the Negro as he conceived them, paying no attention whatever to the individual differences in the pictures. The results held for the less prejudiced individuals as well as for the more prejudiced ones. Thus there is a strong tendency to assign traits to an individual on the basis of his group membership, even though individuals vary in the extent to which they show the characteristics of the group.

The nature of in-groups, out-groups, and stereotyping is well illustrated in an experiment conducted at a summer camp for 24 boys of about 12 years of age, selected from lower-middle income groups (Sherif, 1951). The boys were allowed to mix freely during the first days of the camping experience, and they formed a number of spontaneous friendships. Camp counselors and other unobtrusive observers

took note of these relationships. This period, known as *Stage 1*, provided the background for dividing the boys into two groups for *Stage 2*. For the most part, the budding friendships of Stage 1 were arbitrarily disrupted in forming the new groups, to be known as the "Red Devils" and the "Bulldogs." The purpose was to see whether or not the in-group feelings produced by the treatment in Stage 2 would violate the spontaneous friendship patterns of Stage 1. In Stage 2 the groups were separated spatially, lived in different places, and had their swimming at different times, so that every occasion presented an opportunity for each boy to feel that the group was "his" group. When given the opportunity at the end of this stage to name the boys from the whole camp whom he liked, each boy showed a striking shift toward preference for those *within* the group.

The shift in preference for those who had worked together and had come to belong together is well illustrated by the results shown in Table 23–3. It remained to be seen whether or not the other group was also perceived as an out-group, particularly to the extent that there would by rivalry and disparagement. This was tested in *Stage 3*, in which the two groups were pitted against each other in various activities (athletics, camp clean-ups, etc.). The groups were quite evenly balanced, so that

TABLE 23–3

Choices of friends at end of Stage 1 and at end of Stage 2 in a summer camp experiment on intergroup relations

		Choices received by	
	Choices made by	Eventual in-group	Eventual out-group
End of Stage 1	Eventual Red Devils	35%	65%
	Eventual Bulldogs	35	65
		In-group	Out-group
End of Stage 2	Red Devils	95	5
	Bulldogs	88	12

SOURCE: Sherif (1951).

with only minor manipulation by the authorities their competitive scores remained very nearly alike, each group being ahead for awhile—although in the end the Bulldogs won. Many observations showed extreme antagonism developing between the groups, with hostile name calling and unscheduled fights; the hostility was increased by the eventual victory of one side. Some evidence of *stereotyping* also occurred. While at first the athletic contests showed signs of good sportsmanship, after a time this changed, and the changes included distorted perceptions of the other group. In a tug-of-war, for example, the losers accused the winners first of having selected more favorable ground, and on another occasion of having "done something to the rope." Things began to get so out of hand at the end that the final days of camp were devoted to breaking down the intergroup antagonisms. One successful event in this connection was to have a "camp" team play a game against another camp, thus uniting the whole camp against the outsiders. The study showed very well, in miniature, many of the conditions for in-group and out-group behavior in ordinary social settings.

We wish now to examine further some of the ways in which in-group and out-group feelings create intergroup problems.

Scapegoating. The notion of a "scapegoat" derives from an ancient practice reported in the Old Testament. Periodically the sins of a tribe were transferred with appropriate ceremonies to a goat, which was then driven off into the wilderness. The innocent goat was made to suffer for the sins of the people.

The practice of finding a victim upon whom to place the blame for our troubles and hence to make the object of our aggressions is a familiar one. The child may retaliate against a pet when frustrated by parents or playmates; Hitler found it convenient to blame the Jews for Germany's plight; industrialists blame labor unions for rising prices; labor unions blame capitalists for causing depressions; farmers blame politicians for hard times connected with crop failures. We have already discussed scapegoating as the mechanism of displaced aggression.

How do group phenomena enter into the selection of objects for scapegoating? In an analysis of scapegoating, Allport (1944) pointed out the following characteristics that make some people easy victims.

1. Members of the group to receive the aggression must be easily identifiable. The dark skin color of the Negroes makes them much more vulnerable to attack than if they looked like whites. A perceptible difference is enough to favor the separation of figure and ground, and to serve as a reminder of the possibility of difference between in-group and out-group. Sometimes identifiability is enforced, as when Hitler required Jews to wear special insignia.

2. Members of the out-group must be accessible. The mechanism of displacement requires that we substitute for the inaccessible target an accessible one (see p. 511). When Hitler had to find an enemy to attack before Germany rearmed, he turned to the Jews within Germany. In the South, although in times of economic hardship the preferred targets of blame might have been Northern industrialists, it was easier to give vent to feeling against the Negroes, who were accessible, than against the absent industrialists.

3. Those selected as scapegoats must be unable to retaliate. If aggression is in danger of punishment, it swerves away and finds another victim unable to strike back. In an authoritarian situation—that is, one in which there is a strong leader—the leader may be responsible for much of the frustration of group members. But since the leader is in a protected and powerful position, the aggression is taken out on some lesser individual or individuals.

4. The scapegoats usually will have been scapegoats before. People and nations usually manage to justify their aggressions self-righteously. The current inciting incident is often too trivial or the responsibility of the scapegoat too remote to justify the extent of the aggression except on the basis of previous antagonism. A very small incident is often the excuse for new aggression, be-

cause an undercurrent of hostility persists from the past. The Turk may attack the Armenian in his midst or the Japanese the Korean, partly because they have attacked these people before.

If a community wants to protect a group habitually chosen as scapegoats, it must invoke the usual sanctions that protect individual liberty as well as counteract the four conditions that have been outlined above. The changes are a matter of degree. Racial characteristics which make some members of a group identifiable cannot be erased. But habits of dress and gesture which make ethnic groups different from others can be modified so that the minority group conforms more nearly to the practices of the dominant group, with a consequent reduction in social distance.

The accessibility of the target groups is lessened when segregation is lessened. Rioting against Negro minorities in the North has occurred almost exclusively in cities in which a high degree of segregation exists, as in Chicago, where a mob can find a Negro community to attack. In some more recent rioting by Negroes, the existence of an unfavored Negro area in the midst of a surrounding white community has a similar effect once there has been an incitation to hostile action. Boundary phenomena are enhanced when the boundaries are visible geographically.

The law must increase the retaliatory strength of the victims of aggression. We can check the displacement mechanism only by making aggression toward the out-group punishable in the same way as in-group aggression.

The fourth condition can be met chiefly through education. The more people become aware of the irrationality of group action and of past injustices in the blame assigned to minority groups, the more they will resist future abuses.

Racial prejudice. By "racial prejudice" we mean expressions of disapproval toward members of given ethnic groups, whether racial in a biological sense or merely of the same cultural or national origins. Such prejudices in America are commonly expressed against Negroes, Jews, Orientals, Italians, Mexicans, Puerto Ricans, and other groups considered more or less "foreign," even though, like the American Indians, they are frequently as native as the groups showing the prejudice.

One study of women college students showed an excessive amount of racial prejudice (especially prejudice against Jews) among those who were members of sororities, those of upper-income levels, and those who were politically conservative. While sororities often communicate race prejudice through their procedures of selecting members, the anti-Semitic attitudes did not follow simply from the group identifications of these girls. More careful study revealed many basic personality needs which were finding disguised expression in hostile feelings toward Jews.

A test designed to discover the degree of anti-Semitism was administered to a group of University of California women. Those with extreme anti-Semitic scores were interviewed and tested more intensively to determine what, if any, qualities they had in common. It was found that most of those high in anti-Semitism showed high conformity on socially acceptable characteristics such as respect for parents, neatness, self-control, and lack of sensuality. When the girls were studied with such devices as the Thematic Apperception Test, however, a great deal of repressed hostility was detected. It was inferred that many of their natural impulses to express their likes and dislikes directly were being repressed. Through the distortions of the defense mechanisms, especially projection, they were attributing bad qualities and impulses to minority groups, thereby justifying their feelings of antipathy (Frenkel-Brunswik and Sanford, 1945; Adorno and others, 1950).

Three methods of attacking the problem of race prejudice are possible. One is to try to improve the mental health of children as they grow up so that they do not need to indulge in scapegoating in order to maintain status or to excuse their inadequacies. The second is to reduce social supports given to prejudice by community arrangements, such as segregation in residence, in schools, or on the job. And, finally, it is possible to reduce the teaching of prejudice which goes on subtly through the stereotypes of comic strips, radio programs, and motion pictures.

The problem will not be fully solved until adults become aware of the degree to which they pass on to their children their own attitudes, often without intended malice. Probably the unintentional transmission of prejudice through casual remarks, anecdotes, and innuendoes accounts for more prejudice than direct efforts of agencies promoting hatred.

Values in social psychology

The limits of responsibility of the social psychologist in the study of value-laden fields, such as prejudice, are not entirely clear.

As a research scientist he must of course remain objective in his study of the facts as they exist, not selecting or distorting the phenomena in accordance with his own preferences. He can study prejudice exactly as he studies sensory thresholds or the learning curves of laboratory rats. On this much of his task there is agreement (Marquis, 1948).

The social scientist can also remain objective in evaluating programs whose policy direction is in the hands of someone else. If a school system has decided to try to reduce prejudice among its pupils, he can arrange the before-and-after tests to see how well the program has worked. Here, too, his role can be detached, though now the temptation is strong for him to offer suggestions to correct obvious defects in the program. As soon as he does that, his personal values are being joined with those of the policymakers, even though the advice he gives comes out of his scientific background.

It is almost inevitable that in our society the social scientist, in some of his roles at least, will use his techniques and knowledge to influence policy. He will fight for the right to be as rational as possible in the study of irrational social processes—a right that would be denied him in authoritarian countries. When he tries to influence policy, he is perhaps exercising his rights as a citizen rather than as a scientist, but these two functions are not always clearly distinguishable. We would not think well of an electrical engineer who was willing to take orders from a town council to install a direct-current system if he knew that an alternating-current system was better adapted to the community's needs. We would expect him to use his expertness to influence relevant policies. So, too, if the social psychologist were sure that one kind of treatment of offenders was better than another in reducing juvenile delinquency, we would expect him to advocate it. In these illustrations there is no conflict over the values: the community wants an efficient electrical system and wants to reduce delinquency. Therefore the scientist's advice on policy is acceptable. When the values are themselves the subject of debate, however, the role of the scientist is more difficult. Perhaps in these situations we can distinguish between his two roles, that of *investigator* and that of *advocate*, permitting both roles but not confusing the two (Allport, 1954b, pp. 515–19).

Social norms and compliance behavior

By a *social norm* of conduct is meant a type of social behavior whose regularity can be understood only in reference to the group to which the person belongs. Eating when hungry does not represent a social norm, but holding the knife and fork in a certain way while eating does. Obviously behavior in groups runs more smoothly when people observe the expected norms, so that they come to appointments at the time agreed upon, stop their cars for red lights, remain appropriately quiet during concerts, and so on. While this is all fairly obvious, it is equally evident that some people are nonconformists and do not like to accept the general norms of conduct. As we shall see, there is a good deal of social pressure favoring compliance, and we turn now to some experimental studies of how social influence is exerted.

Conformity to social influences. How much pressure does a group put upon its

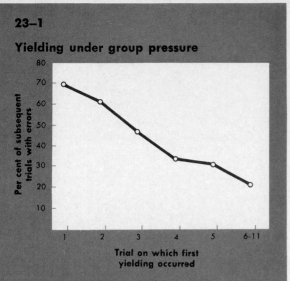

Yielding under group pressure

Per cent of subsequent trials with errors

Trial on which first
yielding occurred

Those who yield early tend to continue to yield, thus making many errors of judgment on the later trials. See text for explanation. (After Asch, 1956)

members to conform to the ideas of the majority? We all know the appeal of the expression, "When in Rome, do as the Romans do." Conformity is not only a good way to get along, it is also for most people a congenial way. The question remains whether group pressures operate in ways beyond mere congeniality in order to influence a person's judgment.

In an experiment designed to study the effect of majority opinion, even when it is contrary to fact, small groups of subjects observed a standard straight line, and then judged which of three other lines equaled it in length. One of the other lines was longer, one shorter, one equal to the standard; the differences were great enough that threshold judgments were not involved. All but one member of each group had been instructed to agree upon a wrong answer for a majority of the trials. The experimental subject was thus pitted against a majority, and his problem was whether to report what he would have reported if he had been alone, and hence to disagree with the majority, or to doubt his own judgment and agree. Many subjects refused to change and continued to hold to their independent appraisals. But a substantial number yielded

under pressure from the others' apparent judgments. The amount of yielding depended upon (1) the clarity of conditions (lack of clarity led to conformity to majority opinion), (2) individual differences, and (3) the size and unanimity of the opposition. With the opposition of only one other person there was very little yielding; with two against one the amount of yielding became pronounced; and a majority of three was nearly as effective as larger majorities against the lone dissenter.

The importance of some factor within the individual is suggested by the ease of yielding. Those who yielded early in the experiment showed greater willingness to conform than those who yielded late (Figure 23–1).

Questioning of the subjects showed that for the most part they respected the genuineness of the judgments expressed by the majority and that they had great doubt about their own judgments when they disagreed with the majority. In other words, the subjects agreed not merely for the sake of agreement, but because they had rejected their original beliefs as being caused by some sort of optical illusion or some previously unsuspected trouble with their eyes (Asch, 1956).

Thus the mere assertion of majority opinion, without any effort to persuade, may lead susceptible individuals to agree with the majority even on a factual matter on which individual judgment would lead to opposite conclusions.

The beliefs and practices of a social group are passed on from one generation to the next. It is of interest to know whether the norms arrived at in a laboratory context can similarly be passed on. In these experiments it is usually a confederate of the experimenter who has set up the norms. The question now becomes: Will the victim of this confederate act as if he were a confederate, passing on the acquired norms to new subjects? In this case a "generation" is very short; each new laboratory group can be considered a new generation, if the "passing on" is done by those who have just acquired their norms. Such an experiment was devised by Jacobs and Campbell (1961).

A confederate, in the first generation, by example influences his associates to perceive more movement of a stationary light than he would otherwise perceive. Such movement, known as the *autokinetic phenomenon,* has been much studied in a social context since the pioneering work of Sherif (1936), and this first phase of the work is similar to the results of the Asch experiment just reported. The simplest arrangement is to use a two-person group, beginning with one confederate and one naive subject. When the confederate leaves, the now experienced subject is left with a new naive subject. The more experienced subject then leaves and is replaced by another naive subject, and so on. By the sixth generation there is no longer a significant difference between those whose responses were derived from the confederate and the responses of the control subjects. The experiment succeeded in showing how naive respondents unknowingly became conspirators in passing on a cultural distortion of reality. However, as the authors point out, the distortions are eroded quite rapidly compared with the persistence of various superstitions in real life. It appears, therefore, that the laboratory studies lack something of the kind of support given in actual life for bizarre beliefs. The results through nine such "generations" are plotted in Figure 23–2.

Circumstances favoring compliance. A great deal of social behavior is regulated by group "norms" to which the group members are expected to comply. Thus closely knit groups come to share common attitudes and opinions on many topics. When a member is assimilated into a group, his perceptions tend to change to conform to the group norms. Studies have shown that the more strongly a member is attracted to a group, the more he tends to conform to the group norms (Kelley and Volkart, 1952). Moreover, a member who is not fully acceptable to a group tends to be more sensitive to majority group opinion than fully accepted members, who are freer to deviate and to hold opinions of their own (Jackson and Saltzstein, 1958).

23–2

Transmission of artificial norms in two-person groups

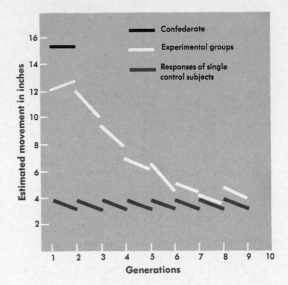

(After Jacobs and Campbell, 1961)

While for the most part these changes of opinion in conformity to group pressure take place without great strain, sometimes compliance is forced. A study by Festinger and Carlsmith (1959) bears on the consequences of forced compliance. Subjects placed in an extremely boring experiment were offered various amounts of money to persuade prospective subjects for the same experiment that the experience had been interesting and exciting. According to the authors' theories, two results should occur on the basis of the following principles:

1. When a person is forced to do or say something discordant with his privately held opinion, that opinion will tend to change in such a way as to make it correspond more closely to the act performed.
2. The greater the pressure used to induce the discordant act (in this case, the amount of money), the *smaller* will be the tendency to change the original opinion.

The first effect follows from Festinger's concept of *dissonance reduction* (i.e., the reduction of incongruity between opinion and action), a concept we have already met (p. 158). This result was found: subjects who complied in telling others that the task was interesting changed their own reports on how interesting the task had been.

The second effect is not so obvious, although it is also predicted from the theory. If one yields to a great pressure, the dissonance is reduced by the pressure, so that there is less incongruity in telling a fib for a large sum of money than for a small one. One doesn't tell a fib for a small sum; one changes one's opinions. The experimental results confirmed this prediction.

A person's behavior in any situation is often very much influenced by what someone else has just done. For example, Helson, Blake, and Mouton (1958) found that they could influence the number of signatures on a petition both by the strength of the request made to sign and by the reaction of others, say, by the number of signatures already on the petition when it was circulated.

A related experiment (Freed and others, 1955) studied the circumstances under which students would violate a sign prohibiting entry of a building. The signs had three degrees of "strength," the stronger signs pointing to alternatives:

STRONGEST: "Absolutely No Admittance— Use Another Entrance"
NEXT: "You Are Requested to Enter by Another Entrance"
WEAKEST: "Absolutely No Admittance"

The subjects of the experiment were those who approached the entrance in the normal course of their lives; in other words, they did not know they were participating in an experiment. The accomplice, when he saw someone approaching, walked up to the door and read the sign; half the time he obeyed the instruction, half the time he disobeyed and entered. In the control condition, no accomplice was present.

Results were in the predicted direction. The highest conformity was found with the strongest sign and a compliant social model; the lowest conformity (greatest violation of the prohibition) with the weakest sign and a nonconforming model. Interviews with the inadvertent subjects showed that they were usually unaware of the background that determined their conformity or nonconformity.

Social conformity and independence of judgment are obviously both essential to the smooth running of social life and to progress. The foregoing studies, while dealing with small-scale social processes, are relevant to social behavior of broader significance.

Attitudes and Opinions

In ordinary social interchange the attitudes, preferences, and prejudices that sway people affect the satisfactions of living together. In a political democracy, sensitive to the wishes of the people, the molding and expressing of public opinion are of the essence of the political process. In an international situation in which the sensitivities of peoples are easily injured and antagonisms aroused, the understanding of attitudes and opinions may mean the difference between war and peace. Hence attitudes and opinions—who holds them and how they change—are topics for serious study.

Attitudes

A precise definition of attitude is difficult because attitudes overlap with other kinds of psychological preparation for response. We may accept the following definition, recognizing that it will become clearer when placed in the context of the following studies: an *attitude* represents both an *orientation* toward or away from some object, concept, or situation and a *readiness to respond* in a predetermined manner to these or *related* objects, concepts, or situations.[2] Both orientation and readiness to respond have emotional, motivational, and intellectual aspects, and they may in part be unconscious ("I do not like thee, Dr. Fell, the reason why I cannot tell. . . .").

[2] The definition combines features of Allport's definition (1954a), p. 43, and that of Hovland, Janis, and Kelley (1953), p. 7.

Enduring attitudes develop through many learning experiences related to other people. Allport (1935) has suggested four common conditions for the formation of attitudes:

1. The accretion and integration of responses learned in the course of growing up. For example, being raised in a home in which the mother defers to the father and in which the sons are valued above the daughters will affect general attitudes regarding male supremacy.

2. The individuation, differentiation, or segregation of experiences. Experiences do not merely accumulate; they become sharpened and patterned, so that some attitudes become more specific as the individual grows up.

3. The influence of some dramatic experience or trauma. Sometimes a single experience may have a lasting influence and may generalize to related stimuli. Nausea following the eating of a strange food may generalize to a distaste for all related dishes. A bad experience with a single member of some ethnic group may lead to a distrust of all members of that group.

4. The adoption of ready-made attitudes. Sometimes attitudes are picked up intact through imitation of the attitudes of parents or others.

Because attitudes are so interwoven with affective and highly motivated experiences, they become abiding personality characteristics. On the other hand, attitudes as components of personality cannot be separated from the objects or events in the social context to which they refer. Thus a "conforming" person is not necessarily socially conservative; a member of a left-wing group may have conforming tendencies that make him go along with his group. An extended study of 10 men by Smith, Bruner, and White (1956) showed a good deal of correspondence between their individual life histories and their attitudes toward Russia, but the relationships were by no means one-to-one. It was clear, however, that their attitudes toward Russia were dictated only in part by the facts as they saw them; the attitudes were also expressions of other aspects of the individual personalities. For example, men who were more likely to blame others than themselves when things went wrong in their personal lives were also more likely to place the burden of blame on Russia for the worsening of United States-Soviet relations.

Attitude scales. Attitude scales can be constructed in a manner similar to personality inventories. The questions, instead of dealing with personal problems and troubles, deal with preferences and beliefs about social issues. Such scales attempt to measure attitudes toward political parties, religions, Negroes, labor unions, international organizations. Once a satisfactory scale has been prepared, those who take it as a test can be scored for the degree to which they hold a favorable or unfavorable attitude, and any changes in their attitudes will show up in their scores on repeated tests.

One of the very early uses of such attitude scales was made in testing the effect of a motion picture on changing the attitudes of school children. After a large group of high school students had taken an attitude test to determine how favorable or unfavorable their attitudes were toward the Chinese, they witnessed a motion picture giving a sympathetic portrayal of Chinese life. When they took the attitude test again the following day, the scores showed a distinct shift in the favorable direction. Some of the students took the test again five months later, and others 19 months later. Results showed that 62 percent of the students retained the improved attitude as long as a year and a half after they had seen the picture (Peterson and Thurstone, 1932).

Social psychologists have given a great deal of attention to constructing attitude scales and to developing theories about attitude measurement. Many investigators, among them those who conducted the study described above, have made use of Thurstone's method (Thurstone and Chave, 1929). Thurstone constructed his attitude scales by assembling a large number of statements concerning a topic, some mildly favorable and mildly unfavorable, others strongly favorable and strongly unfavorable. A hundred or more judges sorted these statements into a number of piles, indicating their judgments as to the degree to which the statement was favorable or unfavorable. For example, a judge, whether personally pro- or anti-union, would sort the following statement as extremely favorable to unions: "All industrial workers should belong to unions." Similarly, he would sort the following as unfavorable: "Labor unions should be forbidden by law." He might have more trouble knowing just where to put statements such as: "Labor leaders do not represent rank-and-file membership," or "Workers have a right to organize, but the closed shop, in which all workers have to belong to the union, should be prohibited." Studies have shown, however, that judges who differ greatly in their own attitudes agree quite well in their estimation of the degree of favorableness or unfavorableness of individual items (Hinckley, 1932). Those who use Thurstone's method then construct the scale to be used as a test by selecting items upon which the judges are in substantial agreement. These will represent fairly equal intervals along the scale from favorable to unfavorable. Each item receives a number to indicate its scale position. When a subject takes the test, he indicates which statements he can endorse. His score corresponds to the average scale position of the items he endorses.

Another method, that of Likert (1932), eliminates the use of judges by having each subject give his answers along a 5-point scale: *strongly approve, approve, undecided, disapprove, strongly disapprove.* Although there are some differences, the results of the Thurstone and Likert methods agree rather well in discriminating between those with favorable and unfavorable attitudes on a given issue.

The quantitative techniques of Thurstone, Likert, and others have made it possible to study changes in attitudes through various influences and to study the persistence of changes through time.

Technical developments in attitude appraisal during and since World War II deserve more than the passing mention they have received thus far, even though an introductory discussion cannot do justice to them because they are complex and involve advanced statistical and mathematical assumptions.

Guttman's *scalogram* method seeks to find "pure" scales along a single dimension, so that a subject who answers any one question favorably will answer favorably *all* items to which a favorable reply is more commonly given. We can imagine a table of favorable $(+)$ and unfavorable $(-)$ responses as follows, question 1 being the easiest to answer in a favorable direction (and therefore the "least" favorable), question 6 being the most extreme, that is, requiring the most favorable attitude possible in order to yield an agreeing answer.

Sub-ject	*Questions in scaled order from least to most favorable*					
	Least					Most
	1	2	3	4	5	6
A	+	+	+	+	+	+
B	+	+	+	+	+	−
C	+	+	+	+	−	−
D	+	+	+	−	−	−
E	+	+	−	−	−	−
F	+	−	−	−	−	−
G	−	−	−	−	−	−

With a scale that worked this way we would be sure that Subject A was the most favorable in attitude toward the given object or situation and Subject G the least favorable. Note that one who has an in-between attitude, such as Subject D, expresses his attitude not merely as "favorable on three of the six questions" but "favorable on *only* the three questions that are most commonly answered in the direction of a a favorable attitude." If the scale worked according to theory, the responses of Subject D would be the only kind of response pattern with three favorable answers out of six. The scale thus seeks an ideal of internal consistency. But this ideal is not actually found, and statistical devices have to be developed to determine how close the actual scale comes to it.

For instance, in scaling 12 questions on attitudes toward the army, the question that was most easily answered in the favorable direction, and which therefore fell at the *least* favorable end of the scale, was: "In general, how interested do you think the army is in your welfare?" (A series of possible replies was included for checking.)

The question at the *most* favorable extreme of the scale, which according to expectations would be answered favorably only if all other answers were favorable, was: "On the whole, do you think the army gives a man a chance to show what he can do?"

The test of the scale comes when one determines how consistent with the ideal the replies actually are. This particular scale had a "coefficient of reproducibility" of $r = .89$ (a perfect scale would yield $r = 1.00$), so it was fairly successful in meeting the criteria set up (Guttman, 1950).

Opinions

Attitudes grade into opinions, and there is no sharp difference between them. We may attempt, however, to hold to a difference proposed by Hovland, Janis, and Kelley (1953). An attitude, as indicated earlier, represents an orientation or preference and may be in part unconscious. An *opinion,* according to the above authors, always involves some kind of *expectation* or *prediction* (not merely a preference), and can always be put into words. The subject may avoid putting his opinions into words, or what he says may not express his true opinion, but according to this definition an opinion *can* always be *verbalized.*

No matter how we separate attitudes and opinions by definition, they are closely related. If you hate a person (expressing an *attitude* of hatred), you are likely to expect bad behavior of him (expressing an *opinion* about his behavior). If he behaves better than predicted (thus changing your *opinion*), you may like him better (thus changing your *attitude*).

Another rather practical distinction be-

tween attitude measurement and opinion measurement can be made: attitude measurement tends to deal primarily with the *individual* (where he stands on a scale of favorable or unfavorable attitudes), while opinion measurement tends to deal with *subgroups* (e.g., the fraction of the population most likely to vote in a school-bond issue). These differences bear some relation to the Hovland, Janis, and Kelley definitions because opinion studies, more often than attitude studies, deal with predicted action. The distinction is of some interest because investigators tend to be concerned with *private* attitude but *public* opinion.

The public opinion survey. The public opinion poll first attained national interest with the presidential election of 1936. Using the "straw-vote" technique then accepted, the *Literary Digest* incorrectly predicted the election of Landon over Roosevelt, while the better-designed polls, of which the Gallup poll is the best known, predicted Roosevelt's reelection. The success of the public opinion polls brought them into prominence.

The public opinion survey is not to be identified only with the election poll, for many surveys have purposes other than predicting election outcomes. It is true, however, that newspaper and magazine polls grew out of the election-prediction polls, so that the public opinion "ballot" tended at first to be modeled largely after an election ballot. People were asked to state what side of an issue they were on, and the percentage of answers was then reported.

We now know that the simple "yes-no" answer to a question about a public issue is likely to be very misleading. For one thing, the form of the question may produce a great variation in the number answering one way or the other.

Here are two questions asked of a sample of the public early in 1945: [3]

"After the war would you like to see the United States join some kind of world organization, or would you like to see us stay out?" (National Opinion Research Center, January, 1945)

[3] Quoted by Cartwright (1946), p. 28.

Join	64%
Stay out	26
Undecided	10
	100%

"Do you think the United States should join a world organization with police power to maintain world peace?" (American Institute of Public Opinion, April, 1945)

Yes	81%
No	11
No opinion	8
	100%

There is no reason to suppose that the difference between 64 percent and 81 percent is a reflection of any change in international attitudes between January and April. The phrase "to maintain world peace" in the second question no doubt raised the percentage of affirmative answers.

One of the chief difficulties with the opinion ballot is that it is hard to know how firmly the respondent holds his convictions, a problem met also in attitude scaling. The answers to "yes-no" questions may be given as casually as they sometimes are to the questions in a college "true-false" examination. The vagueness or firmness of answers is partly dependent on the extent to which public opinion has crystallized on an issue. Often people are asked to give opinions about highly technical matters, such as the influence of atomic energy on the future of civilization. In response to such questions there is often a high percentage of "No opinion." Interpretations of the opinions offered then have to be made with extreme caution.

Even though the ballot form is used, many refinements in questioning are possible. One device is to use a number of *fixed alternatives* instead of a mere "yes-no" reply. Often a printed card with four or more possible replies is handed to the person being interviewed. He is asked to select the one which most nearly represents his own opinion. Another device is that of the "filter" question, used to determine what question should be asked next. The follow-

ing illustration [4] shows how a stereotyped reply can be broken down by asking a second question of those who answer in a conventional manner:

Do you believe in freedom of speech?

Yes	97%
No	1
Don't know	2
	100%

If "Yes," do you believe in it to the extent of allowing Fascists and Communists to hold meetings and express their views in this community?

Yes	23%
No	72
No opinion	5
	100%

Because answers depend on the context in which the questions are asked and because they depend so much upon both the form and the wording of the question, a single percentage can never be interpreted unambiguously. Successive polls repeating identical questions do indicate trends, however, and these are often very revealing.

The alternative to the ballot form of question is that known as the *free-answer* or *open* question, that is, a question to which the the respondent must reply in his own words. This method has genuine advantages, although it requires somewhat more skilled interviewers (who are asked to record answers as nearly verbatim as possible), and it makes statistical analysis more difficult. For one thing, the free answer makes it easier to interpret the meaning of the question to the respondent. It also makes possible an understanding of the meaning of the reply. "Yes-no" answers often conceal meaning.

Many public opinion surveys now make use of both free-answer and fixed-alternative questions. One suggestion is that the free-answer question should be used in the pretest to determine what answers are desirable as fixed alternatives in the main

[4] American Institute of Public Opinion, November, 1940. Quoted by Cantril (1944), p. 22.

study. Then the findings of the main survey should again be studied through more detailed interviewing (Lazarsfeld, 1944).

The problem of sampling. A properly conducted public opinion survey is like any other scientific investigation. It has to be carefully designed in order to yield unambiguous results. We have considered some of the pitfalls in the form of the poll question. It is important that we know what the respondent understands by our questions, how thoughtful and informed his opinion is, with what conviction he states his answer, and what he intends by it. It is also important that we ask our questions of the right people. The selection of those whose replies we seek constitutes the problem of *sampling*. While we have made great advances in selecting a sample, our sampling methods are still not foolproof.

The logic of sampling is fundamentally very simple. Ideally, once we have defined the total group to be sampled (e.g., registered voters, males of draft age, owners of motor vehicles), we should so design the sample that each person in the group has an equal chance of being represented.[5] If we could give every person in the country a number chosen at random, and then make our sample by drawing, say, every thousandth person, we would have a simple random sample. The cost of doing this would, of course, be prohibitive, so that methods have to be devised of achieving a compromise that lies near this ideal.

Let us examine two methods commonly used. The first is that of *quota control*. In the past this was the method of sampling most widely used by the commercial polls, but it is a method that has led them into error. On the basis of census data, pollsters choose communities to represent the nation; within these communities they assign each

interviewer a quota of persons to be interviewed. These quotas, when added up, should represent the population of the country in miniature. The quota is developed not only according to the number of people from each community but according to certain characteristics or controls. These ordinarily include sex, age, and economic level, with separate quotas for whites and Negroes. While the intended sample may be fairly representative according to these characteristics, the actual sample tends to be unrepresentative. The interviewer, by selecting the people to meet the quota requirements, introduces his personal biases into the sample. For example, many interviewers are middle-class housewives, who hesitate to go into dingy houses on dirty streets. The sample thus tends to be short of the lowest economic groups, with the better-educated groups too well represented. One analysis of two polling samples showed 20 percent more people polled in the better-educated group than there should have been according to U.S. Census reports (Cantril, 1944).

In order to avoid the bias introduced by the method of quota control, an alternative method known as *area sampling* has been developed. In this method, whether applied on a national or local basis, interview assignments are usually made according to residence units. The interviewer has no choice; he is told exactly where to go and whom to interview. No substitutions are allowed, for the person hard to reach may be the very one needed to assure the representativeness of the sample. Not all desired respondents will be reached, but with this method the number not reached can be ascertained, and something about them can be known from the neighborhoods in which they live.

Area sampling is really only one variation of the broader method of *probability sampling*, in which the probability that each member of the population is included in the sample is determined in advance so that sampling statistics can be accurately applied. There are other ways of obtaining the specific assignments required by probability sampling. In a wartime study of

---

[5] Instead of *equal chance* of being represented, it would be more accurate to say *known probability* of being represented. Thus we could sample 1 in 100 in a large city and 1 in 10 in a small city, and still arrive at an unbiased estimate for the whole population represented; in order to do so, the results would of course have to be weighted according to the number of persons each reply represented.

small manufacturing plants, for example, a representative sample was drawn from the social security files, and assignments were made by name and address of the plant.

Surprising accuracy can be achieved with small samples if they are carefully designed. The confidence limits can be determined by appropriate statistical formulas, so that the degree of accuracy can be known in advance and the sample size determined in accordance with the needed accuracy for the purposes at hand.

The study of voting behavior

The study of elections has served well as a testing ground for public opinion measurement, and the substance is interesting because of its social psychological importance. Elections are significant in a democracy, the issues and candidates are widely publicized, and accurate records are kept. The initial interest in studying voting behavior—the projection of election results —has come to be supplemented by many other interests related to the sources of political affiliation, such as the effects of income, education, and social class upon loyalty to a party, or the nature of those who switch allegiance.

The fact that a poll result does not agree perfectly with the election result does not necessarily detract from the usefulness of the poll as a method of studying voting behavior. A poll reflects voting behavior at a given time; since elections are held at another point in time, the results may have been influenced in the meantime by several factors beyond the pollster's control. One of these factors is that voters change their minds. Even though they answer honestly about how they plan to vote, they may hear a speech or have a talk with friends and decide to vote differently. Then, too, not all of those interviewed will vote, so that the interview sample may not represent the voting sample. In states that discourage voting by Negroes, a representative sample of Negroes and whites would not be a good election sample. Bad weather may affect the farm and urban vote differently, since farmers find it harder than city residents to get to election booths in

bad weather. Also, the system of electoral votes means that the polls analyzing national elections have to work state by state, lest slight errors in borderline states with large electoral votes throw off the prediction. The difficulty of dealing with national elections was indicated in 1960, when even the modern computing machines, fed all the information from prior elections, were unable to make satisfactory projections from the votes as they came in on election night.

However, polls and opinion surveys do provide a more accurate estimate of popular feelings than do other methods. For example, in an effort to understand how the Goldwater strategy in 1964 could have gone so wide of the realities of the political situation, a University of Michigan survey group suggests that perhaps too much attention was paid to opinions expressed by letter writers instead of to survey results. People who are fond of writing letters often write over and over again and tend to get counted more than once in any tabulation; two-thirds of the letters are written by 3 percent of the population. As a consequence, the politician who relies on counts of letters received may have a very biased picture of actual voter preference. Some differences between mass opinion, as revealed by a count of persons surveyed, and "letter" opinion within the same sample are shown in Figure 23–3 (Converse, Clausen, and Miller, 1965).

The actual process by which a voter decides how to vote and the issues which may influence him vary from election to election. Some voters have no trouble at all in making up their minds how they will vote: their party affiliations, their social class or economic group interests, their liking for the party's candidate—all are in harmony. But other voters are in conflict: they like the candidate, but do not like the party's policies; they like the domestic policy, but are out of sympathy with the foreign policy. They then have trouble in making up their minds and often decide late. Thus, in the elections of both 1952 and 1956, partisan attitudes readily predicted how those who decided early would

Mass opinion vs. letter opinion during the election year of 1964

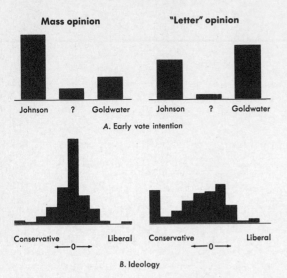

Mass opinion   **"Letter" opinion**

Johnson   ?   Goldwater   Johnson   ?   Goldwater

A. Early vote intention

Conservative ← 0 → Liberal   Conservative ← 0 → Liberal

B. Ideology

The early vote intention (A) is predominantly in favor of Johnson according to a count of people in the survey, but favors Goldwater according to the letter count among the same sample. While the ideological positions (B) are rather evenly divided between conservatives and liberals according to the people count, with most voters not taking a stand between liberalism and conservatism, the letter writers tend to sharpen the conservative-liberal distinction. (After Converse, Clausen, and Miller, 1965)

vote, but did not predict for the late deciders, as shown in Figure 23–4 (Campbell and others, 1960). When their conflicting attitudes were studied, it was found that those with more conflicts were indeed the ones who represented the highest proportion of late deciders (Figure 23–5).

The 1964 elections provided a special type of conflict for one group of voters. In that year, the extremely conservative wing of the Republican party captured the nomination, leaving liberal Republicans and some independents without a candidate. The Democratic party could then move to capture these votes without any loss of support from the more extreme liberals in their own ranks. The consequence was a landslide for the Democrats.

Influencing Attitudes and Opinions

While the discussions of attitudes and opinions in the foregoing account could not avoid some mention of how attitudes and opinions are formed and changed, we wish now to look more specifically at the problems of how changes come about.

Consistency in attitude change

In addition to knowing what attitudes people hold, psychologists are interested in how these attitudes change. We shall study later some of the attempts to alter what people believe through persuasive communications (pp. 593–96), but at this point it is appropriate to discuss a theory that has occupied many social psychologists over the last decade. This theory, in most general terms, states that a person likes his beliefs and his behavior to be consistent, and if he finds them inconsistent he maneuvers in one way or another to reduce the discrepancy—by altering his beliefs, by changing his behavior, or both. Hence we may follow Brown (1965) in calling this a *consistency* theory. Actually, there are three closely related variants of the theory: *balance, congruity,* and *cognitive dissonance*.

The *balance model* has several forms. It was originally proposed by Heider (1946, 1958), again on the assumption that we like consistency between what we believe and how we (and others) behave.

We may look at Heider's theory from the point of view of one person perceiving two others, and hence also perceiving some sort of relationship between them. If he likes them both, he expects them to like each other; if he likes one and not the other, he expects them to dislike each other. A *balanced state* is one in which the perceived relationships are harmonious and internally consistent. For example, if A likes B and A also likes C, then A's perception will be in balance if he finds that B and C also like each other; but his perception will be imbalanced if he notes that B

Unpredictability of late deciders

Within two elections it was found that the decisions of those who made up their minds late could not be predicted as well from their partisan attitudes as the decisions of those who made up their minds early. This is interpreted as due to conflict. (After Campbell and others, 1960)

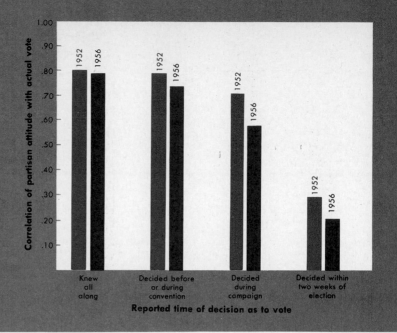

23–5

Conflict and delayed voting decision

and C dislike each other. The tendency is for one's perception to move in the direction of balance; thus imbalance leads to motivation to change in the direction of cognitive balancing (Figure 23–6).

The *congruity* theory (Osgood and Tannenbaum, 1955) assumes that we can scale our attitudes toward people and proposals along a scale from very positive (+3) to very negative (−3). While similar to the balance theory, it adds quantities by which changes can be measured. If a person is the source of a pronouncement about something, we suffer no sense of incongruity if he is a liked person who likes what we like or if he is a disliked person and approves something we dislike. Conversely, there is incongruity when a liked person dislikes something we like or a disliked person likes something we like. Where there is some incongruity, the theory proposes that something will be done to restore equilibrium. For example, if a liked person supports something we dislike, our tendency is to like him less and to favor the disliked proposal more, thus correcting the discrepancy. The amount of movement will depend, according to the theory, on the amount of polarization, that is, on how

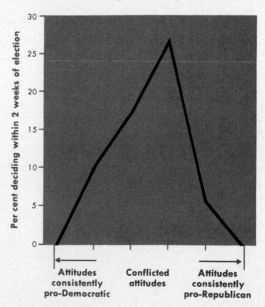

Of those with consistently pro-Democratic or pro-Republican attitudes, none waited until two weeks before the election to decide how to vote. For other voters, the more conflict in attitude, the greater the delay in deciding how to vote. Based on a scale of five partisan attitudes, election of 1956. (After Campbell and others, 1960)

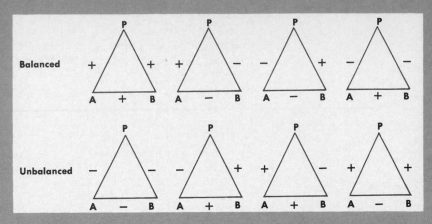

Balanced

Unbalanced

The states refer to the perceptions (cognitions) of the perceiver (P) as he observes the two persons A and B. A plus (+) sign means that the persons connected by the line are perceived to like each other; a minus (—) sign means that they dislike each other. The top four triangles represent balanced states, the bottom four unbalanced ones, according to the theory of Heider (1958).

extreme our views are either about the person or about the proposition. Thus if our state senator, whom we admire, comes out in support of farm prices, which we do not favor, we are likely to change our views on support of farm prices if we are great admirers of the senator. If, however, we are only moderate supporters of the senator and feel very strongly about farm price supports, the discrepancy will lead to a less favorable attitude toward the senator. The theory has been moderately successful in describing the shifts in attitude that do indeed occur when there is incongruity (Osgood, 1960).

The third of the consistency theories, that of *cognitive dissonance*, was originated by Festinger (1957), and has led to a great amount of subsequent experimentation (Brehm and Cohen, 1962; Festinger and others, 1964). While this theory is in many ways closely related to the other theories, it places a great deal of attention upon the aftereffects of decision-making, so as to reduce any discrepancy between what was believed and what was done. Thus any good clothing salesman knows that it is wise to keep on selling after the deal is closed: "I am glad you chose that one, because I was hoping all along you would choose it. It is such a fine value, looks so

good on you." The purchaser may have a momentary fear that he made a wrong choice or that he paid too much, and he needs to have his cognitive dissonance reduced through reassurance. There is of course conflict prior to choice, but at that stage, according to Festinger, the person is more open to a realistic appraisal of alternatives; it is after he has committed himself that his dissonance is most felt, and he then begins to alter his cognitions in such a way as to reduce the dissonance. This is the mechanism earlier cited whereby the belief in the association between tobacco smoking and lung cancer depended upon the subject's decision to smoke or not to smoke, and whereby the willingness to be bribed into changing an opinion depends on the size of the bribe. The theory also bears upon the resistance to extinction of behavior learned with minimal incentives (Lawrence and Festinger, 1962), and it therefore has quite wide generality.

The three consistency theories (congruity, balance, and cognitive dissonance) represent some of the most significant theorizing within the field of attitude change. That they predict many of the same findings is encouraging; that there are some disagreements among them is to be expected in scientific research.

The effectiveness of communications

How are people influenced to change their attitudes, opinions, and beliefs? The answer is found in part through ordinary learning experiences and through the rewards and punishments the individual receives from the culture. Attempts to influence people in large numbers come mainly by way of channels of communication: through the spoken word over the radio; through the printed word in newspapers, books, and magazines; audiovisually through motion pictures and television; and through oral presentations before audiences. We turn now to a consideration of the effectiveness of some of these many varieties of communication.

The *mass media* of communication are those whose messages reach millions of people: newspapers and magazines, motion pictures, radio, television. Many studies are concerned with the type and size of audience reached by the mass media and with their influence upon such audiences. Only a few selected examples can be given here.

While the newspaper is not as important as it once was because of other sources of news reports, it has many features (in addition to news coverage) that make it an important part of the daily lives of a great many people. A 17-day newspaper strike in New York City provided the occasion for a study of what "missing the newspaper" meant to people (Berelson, 1954). People felt that they did not know as well what was going on in the world because they did not have the paper, and they also reported missing the satisfaction provided by the act of reading, without primary concern in some cases for the content being read. The paper was a source of security, providing an indirect social contact with important people and a feeling of intimacy and serving satisfying "ritualistic" values.

A striking case of the influence of the radio occurred some years ago in a broadcast of an "invasion from Mars." What happened was the subject of a study by Cantril, Gaudet, and Herzog (1940). Some six million people listened to a radio play on the evening of October 30, 1938. Orson Welles, as Professor Richard Pierson reported what purported to be an invasion by men from Mars, an invasion that threatened our whole civilization. So skillfully was the dramatization done that at least a million of the listeners were frightened or disturbed. Most of these thought they were listening to a news broadcast. Before the broadcast ended, people were packing their belongings, driving their cars into the country at high speeds, crying, praying, seeking to rescue their loved ones. Later, detailed interviews were conducted with 135 persons, of whom over 100 were known to have been upset by the broadcast. The purpose of the interviews was to get at the psychological bases for the widespread panic that the broadcast caused.

It was found that the people had great faith in radio commentators. That faith made the people who thought they were listening to a news broadcast completely credulous. They were confirmed in their fears when they found their neighbors as disturbed as they and saw the congestion of traffic in the streets. The fear spread; the people coalesced into a panic-stricken mob, for there was nothing they could do to stem the power of these invaders from another world.

Although a comparative newcomer on the scene, television has become so widespread that its relative recency is easily forgotten. A dramatic illustration of its impact was provided by the Kennedy-Nixon debates in the election of 1960.

One study of the debates was based on interviews with 95 New Yorkers before the first debate, immediately after, and again after the fourth (and last) debate (Table 23–4). While the sample is not generally representative of voters, the results confirmed the findings of a wider sample, as reported in the Gallup poll release of October 12, 1960. According to the national poll, about twice as many thought Kennedy did better in the debates than thought Nixon did better; the results in the small sample showed a switch to Kennedy by 10 of the 95 voters and a

TABLE 23-4

Shifts in voting decisions following the viewing of the Kennedy-Nixon television debates in the campaign of 1960: a panel of 95 New Yorkers

	Decided for Kennedy	Undecided	Decided for Nixon
Before first debate	37	27	31
After first debate	47	20	28
After fourth debate	52	12	31

SOURCE: Lang and Lang (1961).

loss of three Nixon voters after the first debate. More careful analysis, however, showed that Kennedy's gain in favorable impression was more pronounced than his gain in votes; most of the shifts came from undecided voters who already were leaning in the direction of a vote for Kennedy. After the fourth debate, Nixon had held his original supporters, while Kennedy had gained solely from the undecided group (Lang and Lang, 1961). In any case, there was some impact from the televised debates, and in an election so close any influence can be significant.

The importance of TV in the lives of contemporary school children is brought out strikingly by some studies reported by Schramm (1960). Of a sample of 508 fifth- and sixth-grade San Francisco children, 74 percent viewed TV on any one day, with the average viewing time being two and a half hours, about the same as the amount of time spent in free play. Very little of the viewing was of educational programs.

A large-scale study in England of viewing by children (Himmelweit, Oppenheim, and Vince, 1958) showed that viewing was negatively correlated with intelligence; the higher a child's intelligence, the less time he spent before the TV screen. While children can learn from TV, there appears to be no net gain because TV replaces other experiences, such as reading. Television does not appear to lead to action; for example, few children proceeded

to make anything even though a model for so doing was shown on television.

Influencing opinion in experimental audiences

Some suggestions were made earlier about social conformity (pp. 580–83). We are here concerned with the influences received by a member of a particular kind of group, an *audience*. An audience receives some kind of *communication* from a speaker or other leader around whom the audience is *polarized*, that is, to whom the members of the group pay more or less continuous attention. To illustrate the many studies of experimental audiences, we shall examine three specimens.

1. *One-sided vs. two-sided arguments.* A study by Hovland, Lumsdaine, and Sheffield (1949) was arranged to establish which method of presentation was more effective: giving only one side of an argument or giving both sides but favoring one. Near the end of World War II, radio transcriptions were prepared that were aimed at preventing the American soldier from expecting the war with Japan to be over shortly after the war ended in Europe. These transcriptions took two forms. The first program presented only the arguments indicating why the war in the Pacific would be drawn out. The second program presented "both sides"; that is, in addition to arguments for a long war, it pointed out

factors that might enable the United States to end the war quickly, especially if it could concentrate upon the Japanese when the war in Europe drew to a close.

In a preliminary survey, troops were first given a chance to estimate the probable length of the war, so that their changes in opinions and estimates could be appraised later after they had listened to the radio programs in orientation sessions.

The programs succeeded in doing what they attempted. The percentage of soldiers who expected the war to last at least another year and a half increased from 37 percent before the programs to 59 percent after them. A control group showed little change over the same period of time, thus proving the programs to have been effective. While the two programs appeared about equally effective, further analysis showed a curious difference in their effects upon men holding different views before hearing them.

Men who originally thought the war would be short showed a greater net change from hearing the "both sides" program; those who originally thought that the war would be long showed a greater net change in expecting the war to last even longer from hearing the "one side" program.

The investigators suggest, plausibly enough, that the men who were unfavorably disposed to the basic message of the program (i.e., that the war would be long) already knew the arguments on their side (favoring a short war). By rehearing the arguments they already believed, they gained confidence in the speaker and became ready to listen to the opposing arguments.

2. *Credibility of the source.* Whether or not an opinion will be changed by a communication depends in part on the confidence the listener has in the speaker. In one experiment, three groups of high school students, who had been invited to a studio, were addressed on juvenile delinquency by a guest speaker who favored extreme leniency in the treatment of delinquents. The speaker was introduced to each group in a different way:

POSITIVE: As an authority; a judge of a juvenile court.
NEUTRAL: As an unidentified member of the studio audience.
NEGATIVE: As a member of the studio audience who had been a delinquent and was now out on bail on a charge of dope peddling.

The opinions on leniency of treatment of juvenile offenders which resulted from the talk varied according to the order of credibility of the speaker, the "positive" speaker having most effect, the "negative" speaker least. The differences between the group who heard the positive speaker and those who heard the negative were highly significant statistically (Kelman and Hovland, 1953).

A retest three weeks later produced an important finding: those exposed to the communication from a negative source showed more opinion change in the direction of the content of the communication now than they had immediately after the communication, while those exposed to the positive source showed a reduced effect after three weeks (Figure 23–7). The communicator and the message apparently became dissociated, and the people remem-

23–7

Effect of credibility of speaker upon opinion change

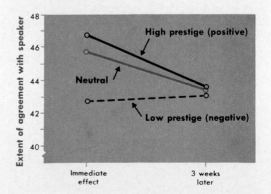

The high-prestige speaker caused more immediate changes in opinions than did the other two. After three weeks, however, the results were quite different. The three-weeks effect for the neutral source is inferred from the report. (After Kelman and Hovland, 1953)

bered what was said without thinking about who said it.

3. *Effect of fear arousal.* The appeal to fear is familiar in persuasive communications, whether in lectures on health, in religious revivals, or in political campaigns. How effective are such appeals? One experiment, an illustrated lecture on dental hygiene in which all the members of a freshman class in a Connecticut high school participated, dealt with several degrees of fear arousal (Janis and Feshbach, 1953). Although results showed that the communications were fear-arousing, as intended, the change in conformity to the recommended dental practices was in an order *inversely* related to the amount of fear appeal (Table 23–5).

The conclusion from the experiment is that a nonfrightening appeal is more likely to lead to conformity than a frightening one, at least if the threats are not relieved by reassurances contained in the communication. If unrelieved, the audience becomes motivated to ignore or minimize the importance of the threats. This interpretation relates the results to the mechanism of repression (p. 519).

CRITICAL DISCUSSION
Opinion changes within fear-arousal experiments

The negative relationship between fear arousal and opinion change as reported by Janis and Feshbach in the experiment just cited has not gone unchallenged. While some experiments have supported their findings, others have yielded a positive relationship between the fear arousal and the change in behavior. For example, Berkowitz and Cottingham (1960) found that they could produce more favorable attitudes toward the use of automobile seatbelts when they used greater appeal to fear. In studies of intentions regarding inoculations against tetanus, Leventhal, Singer, and Jones (1965) found high fear arousal more effective than low fear arousal. McGuire (1966) has attempted to resolve the dilemma produced by these disagreements through postulating that at low levels of initial anxiety or concern, fear arousal will make the subject more receptive to the message and hence will enhance opinion change; however, as the initial level of anxiety becomes very high, further fear arousal would mobilize defenses and thus produce a resistance to change.

TABLE 23–5

Conformity to recommended dental-hygiene practices after illustrated lecture

Nature of appeal used in lecture	Net change in direction of conformity *
Minimum fear appeal ($N = 50$)	+36%
Moderate fear appeal ($N = 50$)	+22%
Strong fear appeal ($N = 50$)	+ 8%
Control (other lecture)($N = 50$)	0%

SOURCE: Janis and Feshbach (1953).

* Net change is the total number who changed toward conformity less those who changed in the opposite direction. For the difference between the minimum fear appeal and the strong fear appeal, $P = .03$; for the difference between the minimal appeal and control, P less than .01. Other differences, P greater than .05.

Coercive persuasion: brainwashing

The term "brainwashing" was introduced by Hunter (1951) as a translation of a Chinese term meaning "cleansing of the mind," used in reference to ridding the Chinese of old beliefs in order to become reeducated for life in a Communist state. The word has come to be applied to various efforts to change the outlook of prisoners, both military and civilian, through various persuasive techniques used while the authorities have control over the lives of the prisoners and hence can use coercive measures. The expression "coercive persuasion" is favored by Schein and others (1961).

The possibility of controlling men's minds came strongly to attention in the purge trials of the Soviet Union, in which former leaders in the Communist movement confessed their crimes publicly before they were executed. The confessions seemed so out of character that the Western world assumed that some special psychological methods (or perhaps drugs) had been used to produce the confessions. Later examination of the evidence (e.g., Leites and Bernaut, 1954) shows a complex set of historical and situational as well as psychological factors to be involved. Smith (1954) found some parallels in English treason trials in the 16th century and interpreted the confessions to mean that in some strange way the prisoners confessed in order to prove that the regime was more important than their own lives. The Russians traditionally isolated the prisoner from others and, through repeated interrogation, extracted a confession from him. The Chinese methods tend to be quite different, with the objective being to make the individual a useful member of the Communist community rather than to liquidate him.

Detailed information on Chinese methods of "thought reforms" have come through two main sets of interviews, the first with American war prisoners who were returned from Chinese prisons during the exchange of prisoners after the Korean fighting ended in 1953 (Lifton, 1954; Schein, 1956), the second with civilian Westerners—doctors, missionaries, students, and businessmen—who were returned from Chinese prisons to Hong Kong (Lifton, 1956). In the exchange of military prisoners it was found that a few Americans had collaborated with the Chinese Communists, and 21 refused repatriation; in view of the very great number of prisoners held by the Western forces who refused repatriation, this was not a very significant validation of the Chinese indoctrination methods. The civilians actually proved in some ways more interesting, because among them were those who showed definite signs of change as a result of their experiences. Two books (Lifton, 1961; Schein and others, 1961) give the reflections of those who have done the most to try to understand what happened.

One unique feature of the Chinese method was the absence of any use of torture to extract confessions. There were discomforts, some arising out of such inevitabilities as the Westerners' dislike of Chinese prison food, and there were some manacles and chains, although these were used more for psychological effect than for their production of pain. That is, manacles were used to show that the crimes that the person was about to confess were serious ones. A second feature was the use of the group pressures of cellmates to enhance the indoctrination program. Cellmates further along in their sympathies with the Communist regime were used to persuade their lagging cellmates to come along also, and they reported on their progress to an interrogator. There were repeated lectures and, of course, individual interrogation, with various rewards for good behavior and with deprivation of privileges as punishment for nonconformity.

The aim of the prison "reform" was to obtain a confession of past transgressions, and then to produce "conversion" to Communist ideals and programs. This, according to Schein and others (1961), took place in three major steps: *unfreezing, changing,* and *refreezing.* The unfreezing consists in one's beginning to doubt one's past standards to the point of desire to change or to abandon that belief. Lifton (1956) quotes a European priest, describing how he saw things at this stage in his "reform":

> And now, like a monster out of the abyss, the most fearful realization dawns: You, the missionary, the herald of the gospel, are not you a messenger of the imperialist conquerors, their pioneer, on account of your ethnological and industrial reports on your missionland? And after the occupation of your missionland you go on rendering the conquerors many different services. And take your mission as a whole: Does it not now prove as a big, long and heavy sin? And the question whether your mission activity has been of more harm or good to the people answers itself. But because you grew up in imperialistic ideologies, it has never until now occurred to you how much you have been of help in the enslaving and the exploitation of a people which formerly enjoyed liberty . . .

The *unfreezing,* which ended in the confession of capitalistic sins against the people, was not permitted to come easily. Fabricated confessions, designed to ease the pressures of prison life, were detected and punished; one of the frustrating features of the experience was that the prisoner knew that he had to confess something but he did not know what he was to confess, and if he tried to guess he was detected. In the end, he had to find something that was plausible to him, as in the priest's statement just quoted.

The process of *changing* came about as the prisoner began to see merit in the points of view of those who were teaching him about Communism, as he began to learn from his cellmates and to adopt some of their positions to replace those of his own he had now distrusted and discarded. Finally, the *refreezing* consisted in consolidating the new position in such a way as to find it congenial. That is, others were pleased with the subject because of the views he held; he could see himself as an upright, sensitive, and forward-looking person, whose new beliefs fitted into his own conception of his love for his fellow man. If this phase was successful, he would be a changed person when released to the non-Communist world.

The study of the released civilians in Hong Kong showed that the process was not very successful, if by success is meant the turning out of devoted Communists. Some showed no discernible effects at all, as illustrated in the case report of Father Phillips (Becker, 1958); some complied under duress, but they were in no sense "broken men" and had not fundamentally changed their attitudes; others who com-

plied showed various degrees of attitude change accompanying their behavioral compliance. Among the more striking changes were those who felt a strong "sense of commitment," as though they had not previously cared enough about the plight of man; such a case is reported by Rickett and Rickett (1957). According to Schein and others (1961), such committed people felt some sympathy for the plight of the Chinese, but were not, in fact, committed Communists.

A number of theories have been proposed to account psychologically for the changes that take place under these circumstances. Some theories consider physiological stress along with the psychology of learning. One of these, for example, shows how "debility, dependency, and dread" could be used, according to what we know about learning, to produce the kinds of changes found (Farber and others, 1957); others suggest that psychoanalytic mechanisms can account for the change, especially various aspects of guilt, dependency, identification, and identity struggles (Moloney, 1955). Still others make use of the concepts familiar in the social psychology of attitude change (Kelman, 1958). While it is possible to interpret the results in these ways, it is widely conceded that those responsible for the indoctrination programs in the prisons of China were probably little influenced by any academic theory, basing their methods much more on such Confucian concepts as "sincerity," "self-cultivation," and "harmony," combined with the practices and the theories of Marxist-Leninist doctrine (Lifton, 1961).

SUMMARY

1. Social behavior in man is influenced by the physical environment and the environment of other people. *Social norms* represent expected regularities in conduct and tacit agreements about how to behave. *Social structure* refers to the interrelationships of these norms with other prescriptions of the society regarding roles and status. Larger aspects of these arrangements for group living are referred to as the *culture* or the *civilization* of which the individual is a part.

2. Social stratification occurs according to *caste* or *class*, the caste having boundaries that cannot be crossed (e.g., by way of intermarriage), while the class permits changes. Moving across class lines is called *social*

mobility, and such mobility is found in most societies. The opportunity for upward mobility is motivating because it provides the hope of improved status, but it also has its attendant costs in the way of anxiety. One extreme expression of this is the increased suicide rate among the well-to-do.

3. Intergroup tensions arise because of boundaries between *in-groups* and *out-groups.* Racial prejudice is an illustration of the ways in which *scapegoating* and *stereotyping* operate.

4. Individual behavior tends to be influenced by the group of which the individual is a member. Resistance to change can be overcome by *group process,* in which participation by members of the group is used to make the change acceptable. The degree to which the individual is attracted to the group—how cohesive the group is—may affect the amount of conforming behavior. The behavior of others provides a kind of standard for us; studies of petition-signing and of violation of prohibitions show that the strength of the invitation or the prohibition is but one determiner of conduct; what someone else has done in the situation is equally important.

5. An *attitude* can be described as an *orientation* favorable or unfavorable to some object, concept, or situation, and a *readiness to respond* in some predetermined manner to these or related objects, concepts, or events. Attitudes can be *scaled* by several methods, of which those of Thurstone and Likert are representative.

6. *Opinions* deal with *expectations* or *predictions* about the consequences of certain courses of action; while attitudes may in some cases be unconscious, opinions are always conscious, and can be put into words.

7. The public opinion survey has found many uses in government and in industry beyond the prediction of election results.

8. One problem in conducting surveys is the use of *fixed-alternative* vs. *free-answer* questions. The free-answer questions have the advantage of revealing how the respondent interprets the question and what he intends by his answer, but the difficulties of interviewing are increased. Another problem is that of obtaining the *sample.* The choice lies between the *quota-control* method and the *area* method, a form of the method *probability sampling,* favored because it eliminates interviewer bias.

9. The study of voting behavior is now aimed at understanding characteristics of the voter and considerations affecting his choices, with the prediction of election outcomes a secondary matter. It is possible to study, for example, how conflicts over issues delay the voter's decision.

10. Attitude and opinion changes have led to several theories based on the notion that a person prefers to have his attitudes, beliefs, and behavior internally consistent. When they are found inconsistent, he tends to shift something in order to bring them more nearly into balance. Three related theories emphasizing *cognitive consistency* are the *balance* theory of Heider, the *congruity* theory of Osgood and Tannenbaum, and the *dissonance* theory of Festinger.

11. The mass media (newspapers and magazines, motion pictures, radio, television) affect the attitudes, opinions, and beliefs of a large audience. Some representative studies of radio and television indicate how influential appeals over these media can become. Television is being studied also for its more specific role in educating the young.

12. Studies of the effects of communications on experimental audiences give partial answers to three questions, chosen as representative of other questions asked in such studies: Is a one-sided or a two-sided argument more persuasive? What is the influence of credibility of the source of the communication? How effective is an appeal to fear in changing behavior?

13. *Coercive persuasion* ("brainwashing") refers to the efforts to convert the thinking of prisoners (both military and civilian) to a point of view favorable to the regime of the captors by coercive techniques that include environmental control (physical or social), deprivation, reward, and confession—techniques ordinarily not considered "educational" because of the extreme uses of the power residing in the hands of those attempting to produce the changes. The steps of change can be described as *unfreezing* of familiar attitudes, beliefs, and values, *changing* these attitudes, beliefs, and values, and then *refreezing,* or consolidating the new position.

SUGGESTIONS FOR FURTHER READING

For a general orientation to social psychology, there are a number of good textbooks. Representative ones are Brown, *Social psychology* (1965), Krech, Crutchfield, and Ballachey, *Individual in society* (1962), Newcomb, Converse, and Turner, *Social psychology* (1964), and Secord and Backman, *Social psychology* (1964). Proshansky and Seidenberg (eds.), *Basic studies in social psychology* (1965), and Steiner and Fishbein (eds.), *Current studies in social psychology* (1965), provide a well-selected collection of studies. For looking up special topics, Lindzey and Aronson (eds.), *Handbook of social psychology* (rev. ed., 1967), is a good resource.

Interpersonal behavior is dealt with more fully in Cartwright and Zander (eds.), *Group dynamics* (2nd ed., 1960), and Bennis and others (eds.), *Interpersonal dynamics* (1964). For responses to group pressure, see Berg and Bass, *Conformity and deviation* (1961). On prejudice, see Allport, *The nature of prejudice* (1954), and Pettigrew, *A profile of the American Negro* (1964).

For various systematic approaches to the understanding of attitudes and their change, see Rosenberg, Hovland, McGuire, Abelson, and Brehm, *Attitude organization and change* (1960), and Cohen, *Attitude change and social influence* (1964).

The public opinion literature bulks large. For an introduction to methods by which surveys are conducted, see Hyman, *Survey design and analysis* (1955). Results of surveys, and other issues in connection with public opinion, are found in Katz, Cartwright, Eldersveld, and Lee (eds.), *Public opinion and propaganda* (1954). On election studies there is a book of readings, Burdick and Brodbeck (eds.), *American voting behavior* (1959), and a careful restudy of the attitudes and other characteristics that have determined the presidential votes, Campbell and others, *The American voter* (1960).

Two books on "brainwashing" are Lifton, *Thought reform and the psychology of totalism* (1961), and Schein and others, *Coercive persuasion* (1961). See also Biderman and Zimmer (eds.), *The manipulation of human behavior* (1961).

24 Psychology as a Profession

Science is essentially a technique for solving problems by way of understanding based on data. In its pure science aspects, any science stresses the search for general principles and laws that yield this understanding of its data; in its applied aspects, it seeks to use the understanding that has been achieved in order to solve practical problems. Many pure and applied sciences can be thought of in pairs—astronomy and navigation, physics and engineering, biology and agriculture, biochemistry and pharmacology, anatomy and surgery; both members of the pair have important problems of their own to solve, and the task of the applied scientist is not merely that of a broker or middleman advising the practical consumer how to use the products of pure science. The navigator, the engineer, the agriculturist, the pharmacologist, and the surgeon have to develop techniques and instruments of their own, and conduct their own researches in the same scientific spirit as that of the scientist working on the more abstract or purer problems.

The same considerations apply within psychology. Some of its search for general principles of development and interaction is clearly in the spirit of basic science; yet its efforts to solve problems of child rearing, of the management of learning, or of psychotherapy are applications to practical problems. While the earlier chapters have emphasized the basic science aspects of psychology, applications have not been overlooked, especially when studies in the field of application have also enriched the knowledge of general psychology—as is often the case. Thus practical studies in the testing of school children have led to a better understanding of individuality, and efforts to overcome resistance to change in an industrial plant have contributed to our understanding of group processes generally. The usefulness of a scientific experiment is determined not by the substance on which it works, or the practical significance of the problems it attacks, but by the precision of its methods and the relevance of its results to theory; applied science can serve pure science, just as pure science also serves the applied field.

Through many applications psychologists have gone beyond their teaching and research positions in universities to become of service in a variety of fields. Psychology as a profession has grown up within the span of a single lifetime. Hence the public generally has a rather vague notion about what psychologists do, tending to associate psychology mostly with interest in abnormal behavior.

Fields of Specialization Within Psychology

Psychology has been growing by leaps and bounds, as shown by the increase in membership of the national association of psychologists, the American Psychological Association (Figure 24–1). This accelera-

Membership in the American Psychological Association

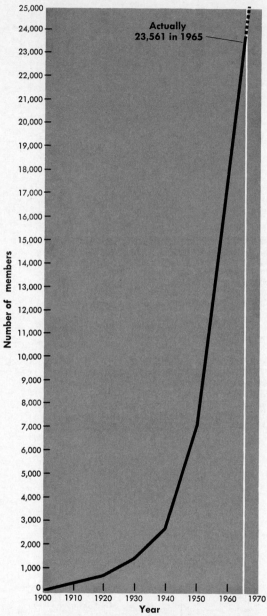

APA membership has more than tripled since 1950.

ties) account for barely half the psychologists. Next in order come governmental agencies, with the federal government employing as many psychologists as state and local governments combined. Next come private agencies: business, industry, clinics, and guidance centers. The psychologists who practice privately, offering their services to the public for a fee, represent a small minority.

What a psychologist does is not, of course, determined solely by who pays his salary. A psychologist working in a government laboratory may be doing exactly the same sort of work that he would do in a university. A psychologist at work in a Veterans Administration clinic may be doing just what he would do if he were working privately with a group of professional colleagues. One answer to what kinds of psychologists there are, and how many there are of each, is provided by a study conducted by the National Science Foundation (Table 24–1). An analysis relating the type of employer to the field of specialization is given later in Table 24–2 (p. 608).

Experimental psychologists

The traditional field of general psychology, which is devoted to research in the principles of psychology as they apply to men in general or to organisms in general, is best supported by our institutions of higher learning, where the bulk of research in the basic problems of psychology goes on. Most university psychologists are also teachers of psychology, although, with funds for research increasingly available, some psychologists are devoting themselves to full-time research. Since World War II experimental psychologists have been increasingly drawn into applied experimental research, in which their training in sensory psychology is brought to bear on problems of communication, dial reading, and the development of detection devices. Laboratory studies of learning are used in developing training aids for the armed services and selection devices for duties requiring a high order of motor skill. For those who are drawn to psychology as a laboratory science, who like to use apparatus and find

tion has come about in part because of the increasing employment of psychologists outside colleges and universities. At present the academic positions (teaching, research, and administration in colleges and universi-

TABLE 24–1

Fields of specialization
within psychology

Specialty	Males	Females	Total	Per-cent
Clinical	2912	1312	4,224	38.1
Counseling	1056	269	1,325	12.0
Developmental	181	199	380	3.4
Educational	635	218	. 853	7.7
School	113	162	275	2.5
Experimental, comparative, and physiological	957	135	1,092	9.9
Human engineering	149	6	155	1.4
Industrial	266	21	287	2.6
Personnel	766	70	836	7.5
Personality	306	51	357	3.2
Social	468	71	539	4.9
Quantitative (statistics, tests, and measurements)	332	65	397	3.6
General and non-specialized	151	61	212	1.9
Nonpsychological	113	24	137	1.2
Totals	8405	2664	11,069	99.9

SOURCE: Ogg (1955), p. 5. Based on the replies of 11,069 psychologists to a questionnaire from the National Science Foundation.

satisfaction in precise measurement, experimental psychology offers many opportunities.

Clinical and counseling psychologists

The largest single interest among professional psychologists is now in *clinical psychology*. The typical clinical psychologist works in an agency giving care or treatment—a mental hospital, an institution for the mentally subnormal, a prison, a juvenile court, a mental-health clinic, a college or university health service, or a child-guidance clinic. He may also practice privately, alone or in affiliation with other professional colleagues. His affiliations with the medical profession are close, especially with psychiatry, as we learned in Chapter 22.

After the clinical psychologist has had sufficient experience, he is eligible upon examination to qualify for a diploma in Clinical Psychology awarded by the American Board of Examiners in Professional Psychology, a body created by psychologists to certify the competence of psychologists working at high levels of professional responsibility.

The close affiliation of the clinical psychologist with mental health problems draws him largely into hospitals and clinics. This leaves an enormous amount of psychological work for guidance centers handling normal people whose problems are typically those of vocational and educational guidance or minor difficulties in social adjustment. Advisement and guidance workers, who have come to think of themselves as *counseling psychologists* rather than as clinical psychologists, secure a thorough training of a somewhat different kind from that of the clinical psychologist. They need to know much more than the clinical psychologist about occupations, about requirements for admission to professional schools and other training institutions, and about aids to study. The differences between the counselor and the clinical psychologist are, of course, not sharp, for the counselor has to be alert to the person who seems merely upset about a superficial problem but who is really deeply disturbed. The counselor refers such a person to clinical services, confining himself to problems not classifiable as illness. A diploma is provided by the American Board of Examiners in Professional Psychology for psychologists with top qualifications in counseling and guidance.

Clinical and counseling psychologists together account for half the psychologists in Table 24–1.

Social psychologists

Social psychologists are best known for their work in public opinion and attitude surveys, audience measurement, and market research. The survey method is now widely used for a variety of purposes by newspapers, magazines, radio and television networks, as well as by agencies of the government, such as the Census Bureau, Department of Labor, Department of Agriculture, Treasury Department, Federal Reserve System, and the armed forces. The technical skills required are sampling, interviewing, questionnaire construction, the interpretation of survey data, and knowledge of group dynamics.

In view of continuing international tensions and the efforts to meet them by propaganda and counterpropaganda, propaganda analysis is important for social psychologists. More generally, all problems of psychological warfare fall within the province of social psychology; we considered earlier some aspects of coercive persuasion (Chapter 23).

New developments in methods for studying small groups and for modification of group attitudes have brought social psychologists more actively into community work where they attempt, for example, to modify attitudes that produce intergroup tensions. Thus a kind of clinical social psychology is developing which may do for communities what clinical psychology now does for the individual.

Social psychology has both its basic-science and its applied-science aspects. As a basic science it is concerned with such problems as the influence of the culture upon personality development, social motives, language and communication, the influence of the group upon individual performance, problems of identification, imitation, and role-playing. We have treated these topics as part of general psychology, where indeed they belong. As an applied science social psychology is concerned with studying existing attitudes and preferences and how they are influenced. A division of the American Psychological Association, known as the Society for the Psychological Study of Social Issues, is especially interested in the possible services of social psychology in the solution of pressing public problems.

Industrial psychologists

An industrial society makes available many goods which add to the comforts and satisfactions of living, but it also creates a number of problems. The high degree of division of labor calls for careful vocational guidance and training to assure some measure of success and satisfaction on the job, and the conditions of work raise many problems for those responsible for maintaining morale. The responsibilities of employee selection and training, of work satisfaction and morale, fall to the personnel or industrial psychologist.

Human factors research. World War II saw the development of many complex instruments, such as radar devices used for aircraft detection and sonar devices for submarine detection. The airplane cockpit became a mass of instrument dials, almost too many for one man to keep track of. Designers recognized that machines must take account of the human operator, and a number of research laboratories were set up to work specifically upon the problem of better machine design in relation to the men who were to use the machines (Figure 24–2). Such research has continued and has come to be known as *human factors research;* its problems are shared by the engineer familiar with the machinery and by the psychologist familiar with the human operator.

Space technology. The great interest in manned space travel has led to a careful consideration of the psychological problems involved. A man traveling in a projectile must be able not only to survive, but also to carry out the necessary operations to make his presence in the spaceship scientifically useful. He therefore has to be protected from both excessive physical stress and the psychological stress of confinement, isolation, and weightlessness.

The operant-conditioning methods developed by psychologists (Chapter 11) made it possible to train chimpanzees to perform both continuous and discrete tasks while traveling through space with both high acceleration and weightlessness. Their satisfactory performances under these conditions demonstrated the feasibility of human flights (Rohles, Grunzke, and Reynolds, 1963).

In noting the tasks that were to lie ahead, Melton and Briggs (1960) stated:

Indeed, the space age should be both a challenge and a source of satisfaction to engineering psychologists. Since the space vehicle will have radically different control characteristics and requirements, as compared to present-day aircraft, there should be considerably less resistance to instrumentation which conforms to human requirements more than to tradition.

The year 1961 saw what had been fantastic plans actually beginning to be realized with the initial flight of a Russian cosmonaut and the later suborbital flights of the American astronauts. The developments since then have, of course, been very rapid, with longer flights, rendezvous in space, and space walks all bringing us closer to a manned flight to the moon.

Statisticians

A knowledge of statistics is essential to all psychologists, but some specialize in statistical methods and the application of statistics to test construction.

Tests are important tools for the research psychologist generally, as well as for the clinical psychologist, the counselor, the educational psychologist, the industrial psychologist, and the social psychologist. Hence whenever any large-scale research enterprise is undertaken, at least one statistical expert is needed.

While statisticians in psychology earlier were associated largely with test construction and the interpretation of test results, their duties now are much wider. They are called upon as experts in sampling theory to design samples for public opinion or market surveys. They are called upon as experts in experimental design to help experimental psychologists or other research psychologists arrange their procedures for gathering and analyzing data in the best possible manner.

Psychology and Other Professions

It is characteristic of applied problems that they belong to more than one field of inquiry. The social problems with which psychologists are concerned are usually

24–2

An application of psychological research

NASA

The complex instrument panel of this simulated space capsule has been carefully designed to accommodate the abilities and perceptions of the operator, so that even under stress of space travel he will be able to operate the instruments.

problems within medicine, education, law, political science, sociology, and social welfare. Hence as psychology begins to offer professional services, there are many opportunities for collaboration with other professions.

Psychology and the law

Legal psychology—the application of psychology to problems of lawmaking, law enforcement, the examination of witnesses, and the treatment of the delinquent and criminal—offers much promise for the future (see p. 543).

The study of *testimony* and *evidence* is one field of interest, opened up in the earliest application of psychology to the law in a book by Hugo Münsterberg entitled *On the witness stand* (1908). The heavy dependence upon the testimony of eyewitnesses in criminal trials may lead to miscarriages of justice; experimental research shows how fallible human perception and memory are, even when witnesses are attempting to report honestly. One law professor, noting the abuses of testimony, collected a whole volume of cases in which innocent people were convicted, largely on the basis of such faulty testimonial evidence (Borchard, 1932). An empirical study of 154 rules of evidence, participated in by both lawyers and psychologists, suggested that a number of these rules should be revised or discarded (Britt, 1940).

Another psychological problem is that of the *individual offender*. Who is likely to commit crimes? What are the chances of restitution to society? One question that arises is the relationship between intelligence and criminality. While it is frequently found that lower I.Q.'s are associated with crimes of violence (homicide, assault, and sex crimes) and higher I.Q.'s with crimes such as forgery and embezzlement, interpretation is difficult. For example, only the more intelligent members of the population are exposed to the temptations of embezzlement. Perhaps, with respect to crimes of violence, the more intelligent criminals escape detection or (because of social status) are more likely to receive suspended sentences. Studies of juvenile delinquency show that intellectual deficiency cannot be the primary cause for delinquency, for the range of intelligence is wide and overlaps greatly with the intelligence distribution of a control population. Other psychological contributors to delinquency were considered earlier (Chapter 4).

Finally, there are many psychological problems within the *broader aspects of the law,* aspects having nothing to do with crime and punishment as we ordinarily think of them. Many problems coming before lawyers have psychological aspects: patent and trademark disputes, divorce, taxation, and social legislation. Social scientists are occasionally called upon as expert witnesses to determine the consequences of certain social practices. Thus, in the hearings on desegregation leading to the Supreme Court decision, a brief was prepared by psychologists and other social scientists and was accepted in evidence by the Supreme Court (Clark, 1953).

Only a few of the fields of possible interaction between psychology and the law have thus far been developed. Law schools, unlike medical schools, have not made a practice of adding psychologists to their faculties. Thus the area is one in which developments may be expected in the future.

Psychology and education

General psychology and educational psychology are closely related, partly because of the magnitude of the task confronting educators: providing appropriate learning experiences for all children—rural and urban, bright and dull—and extending learning opportunities upward into the adult years. The central topics within educational psychology (individual differences, learning and memory, motivation, group behavior, mental health, and personality) are merely the topics of general psychology placed in the context of the schools. In this context the topics become *applied:* when to begin the teaching of reading or arithmetic and how best to go about it; how to meet the problems of the slow and fast learner; which activities are best carried out individually, which in groups; how to train teachers; and so on. To some extent education has become the major technological outlet for psychology. The relationship of education to experimental psychology is conceivably similar to that between engineering and physics.

As a scientific specialty *educational psychology* is concerned with psychological research applied to any and all aspects of educational practices. Educational psychologists have their places on the faculties of universities and teachers colleges and play a part in the training of teachers. The psychologists employed by high schools and elementary schools are more likely to be called *school psychologists* (instead of educational psychologists), for they have specific tasks: giving psychological tests, making special provisions for the handicapped or for children in need of remedial work, dealing with special guidance problems that require relationships with child-guidance clinics or community social agencies. Because we have already discussed the central topics of educational psychology, and because we have seen some educational applications in the earlier chapters, we shall not go further into the special problems of educational and school psychologists.

Psychology and medicine

Clinical psychologists work closely with psychiatrists, social workers, psychiatric nurses, and others, particularly in child-guidance clinics, mental-health services of various kinds, and hospitals for the mentally ill. We have seen how psychology bears on these problems in several chapters.

While psychology is itself a nonmedical science, its connections with medicine are very close, as are those of other basic sciences such as biochemistry and physiology. Medical science is interested in health as well as in disease; psychology's concern with the growth and development of the total functioning individual brings it into relationship with the health emphasis within medicine. As a behavioral science the ramifications of psychology are, of course, much broader than those of medicine.

The psychologist's role in society

Because so many personal and public problems are at the root psychological, the role of the psychologist in society is likely to become increasingly important. One of the present difficulties is that psychology has not yet developed sufficiently to assume some of the responsibilities already asked of psychologists. A science can handle only problems that have become manageable. To have people seek the advice of a psychologist on problems for which his instruments are inadequate may be flattering to the psychologist, but it is also embarrassing to him. He must restrict himself to what he can do lest the public become disappointed in his answers. While the psychologist is wisely modest about what has been achieved thus far, he need not blind himself to the importance his work may achieve if he builds soundly.

Who Becomes a Psychologist?

Because psychology is a rather new profession, growing very rapidly, it attracts to itself many who have started out to train for other fields. Psychologists have been interested in this matter and have done a number of self-studies of their profession. The American Psychological Association, under a grant from the National Science Foundation, conducted one such study. The professional aspects, having to do with personnel and training, were reported in a book by Kenneth E. Clark, chairman of the committee in charge of that part of the survey (Clark, 1957).

The study concerned itself in part with the differences among the various psychological specialties. Thus the areas of specialization in 1954 were found to vary with the type of employment, as shown in Table 24–2.

The psychologist's vocational-interest pattern

How does the psychologist compare in vocational interests with those in other professions? One answer is provided by scores on the Strong Vocational Interest Blank, a test widely used in vocational guidance.

It consists of 400 items, most of which are answered by circling one of the three letters *L*, *I*, and *D* that appear with the item: *L* for like, *I* for indifferent, and *D* for dislike. The items in the men's blank include 100 occupations, 36 school subjects, 49 amusements and hobbies, 48 miscel-

TABLE 24–2

Type of employer in 1954 of psychologists within various specialties who received their doctoral degrees from 1930 to 1944

	Specialization within psychology					
Employer	General	Exper. & Physiol.	Pers. & Social	Clinical	Educ. & Develop.	Industrial
College or university	71%	83%	73%	48%	83%	35%
Other educational institution	3	2	—	5	8	—
Federal government	11	8	8	18	7	9
Private industry, self-employed	1	1	1	11	—	8
Private industry, employee	5	2	7	—	—	37
Nonprofit organizations, including hospitals	4	4	10	10	1	11
State and local government	5	—	1	8	1	—
	100%	100%	100%	100%	100%	100%
	$N = 77$	$N = 158$	$N = 101$	$N = 276$	$N = 177$	$N = 97$

SOURCE: Clark (1957).

laneous activities, 47 peculiarities of people, 40 activities to be ranked by groups of 10 according to their order of preference, 40 paired items between which a choice is to be made, and 40 items consisting of self-ratings of abilities and personal characteristics.

The test has been given to large groups of men and women engaged in representative occupations. An individual who takes the test is scored according to the resemblance of his answers to those of people successfully employed in the given occupation. Thus, if he answers in the manner typical of life insurance salesmen, he is scored high in life insurance interest; if he answers in the manner typical of engineers, he is scored high in engineering interest. Separate scoring keys are available for a large number of occupations. The individual gets a separate score for each of the occupations for which the test is scored.

Occupational interests tend to run in groups, so that some simplification is obtained by scoring for occupational groups instead of for individual occupations.

The groups for men are:

GROUP I Artist, psychologist, architect, physician, dentist.

GROUP II Mathematician, physicist, engineer, chemist.

GROUP III Production manager.

GROUP IV Aviator, farmer, carpenter, mathematics-physical science teacher, printer, policeman, forest service.

GROUP V YMCA secretary and physical director, personnel manager, city school superintendent, minister, social science teacher.

GROUP VI Musician.

GROUP VII Certified public accountant.

GROUP VIII Purchasing agent, office worker, accountant, banker.

GROUP IX Real estate salesman, life insurance salesman, sales manager.

GROUP X Lawyer, author-journalist, advertising man.

GROUP XI President of manufacturing concern.

The first point to be noted is that psychologists fall into a group which is both esthetically sensitive and scientifically interested in man; that is, psychologists score along with artists and architects on the one hand, and physicians and dentists on the other. The interests of Group II are not very different; these are the more strictly quantitative scientific interests of the mathematician, physicist, engineer, and chemist. Many psychologists score higher on Group II than on Group I occupations. As a whole, psychologists do not score as high in the welfare professions of Group V.

One way of noting the relationship between appropriate interests and success in the profession has been to study the vocational-interest scores of those elected to the presidency of the American Psychological Association by their fellow members (Campbell, 1965). Scores were available for 50 presidents and for 1,024 psychologists in general. The presidents tended to score higher on the scientific occupations of Groups I and II, and lower on the social welfare occupations of Group V (Table 24–3).

What these results appear to mean is that professional psychologists are research-oriented and respect scientific activity somewhat more than they do helping other people on a face-to-face basis.

The psychologist's values

Psychology is too diverse to be characterized simply—for example, by typical scores on an interest test. In order to get a clearer picture of the divergences among psychologists, Thorndike (1954) developed a scale by which to test their preferences for one kind of psychologist over another. He did this by preparing, first of all, a list of well-known psychologists representing such diverse activity patterns within psychology as global theorizing, laboratory experimenting, providing non-laboratory substantive data (as in intelligence testing), developing techniques for analyzing data, disseminating psychological knowledge. The notion was that, if psychologists were called upon to indicate which persons had made the most important contributions to psychology, they would show by their choices what they most valued. After some preliminary tests to be sure that his list of names was appropriate, Thorndike grouped the names into triads, and the person taking the test was asked to rank the three names in the order of their importance as contributors to psychology. Thus one triad consisted of the following three names (the statement in

TABLE 24-3

Differences in scores on the Strong Vocational Interest Blank between presidents of the American Psychological Association and psychologists in general

Occupational scale	APA presidents mean scores (N = 50)	Psychologists in general median scores (N = 1,024)	Difference
Groups I and II			
Physician	45	39	+6
Physicist	40	31	+9
Mathematician	43	35	+8
Engineer	41	34	+7
Chemist	47	41	+6
Group V			
Personnel manager	33	41	−9
Social science teacher	25	32	−7
YMCA physical director	22	28	−6

The standard scores are so arranged that scores of 30–34 are interpreted as B−; 35–49 as B; 40–44 as B+; 45 and up as A. Scores of B and above mean considerable resemblance in interests to those who continue in the named occupation.

SOURCE: Campbell (1965), p. 643.

parentheses indicates what the name is expected to stand for):

Karl Pearson   (techniques of data analysis)

John Dewey   (dissemination of ideas through teaching and writing)

Hermann Ebbinghaus   (laboratory experimentation)

The scores were arranged into nine scales, which were then intercorrelated and factor analyzed. Two main factors emerged, one stressing the contrast between the laboratory and the clinic, the other the contrast between a verbal or typological approach and a quantitative or psychometric one.

Cronbach (1957) reanalyzed the same data with comparable findings, and came out with the conclusion that psychology as a science consists essentially of two disciplines. One is committed to the experimental laboratory method, in which it is possible to control conditions and observe their consequences. The other studies the correlations presented in nature, whether these rely on test procedures or upon field observations. Cronbach notes that if you consider only this contrast, Thorndike's data show that the psychologist's esteem for experimenters is correlated $-.80$ with his esteem for psychologists who use the correlational method. Cronbach detected many signs of convergence of the two disciplines, and, of course, his recommendation was that they be combined and not merely run along in parallel. It is evident that psychology as a profession has found room for those with quite divergent conceptions of science.

Where Psychology Is Going

At any one period in its history there are always centers of excitement in a science where new problems are being worked upon and older issues reformulated in ways that revitalize them. In order to see the present and future in perspective, it is worthwhile to note some of the changes in emphasis that have taken place in psychology in the past.

Psychology broke off from philosophy by establishing itself as an experimental science in the latter part of the nineteenth century. As noted earlier, the first chair in psychology in America was established in 1888 at the University of Pennsylvania for J. McKeen Cattell, who had received his Ph.D. under Wundt at Leipzig. His laboratories, and the many others that were established at about that time, were concerned chiefly with sensory thresholds, reaction time, emotion, and memory. Their importance was in proving that a laboratory science of psychology was possible.

World War I broadened psychology by drawing the most vigorous psychologists into the war efforts, where, called upon to develop tests and to validate various devices, many of them learned statistics for the first time. The public acceptance of the intelligence test was very important, and individual differences became a respectable topic within the core of psychology. After World War I there came a flurry of tests and test theories, including the developments within factor analysis.

World War II gave a second forward boost to psychology. If World War I may be said to have launched ability testing, World War II promoted clinical and social psychology, on the one hand, and human factors research, on the other. Within clinical psychology there came the development of interest in projective tests, personality assessment, psychodynamics, and psychotherapy. The Veterans Administration and the National Institute of Mental Health seized upon these developments and encouraged them in the postwar years by subsidizing psychological training centers and by granting financial aid to those who wished to become trained as clinical psychologists. The best-known of the sociopsychological developments during World War II were those in the survey field (consumer surveys, attitude-opinion studies, propaganda analysis) and studies of group dynamics, including small-group behavior and the study of experimental audiences. Human factors research drew psychologists from the fields of sensory psychology and learning—the basic-science fields that had remained largely confined to the laboratory and aloof from applications. These psychologists preferred the expression "applied experimental psychology" to the older "applied psychology"; the older industrial psychology had fitted man to the machine, while the newer approach required the machine to be designed with the human operator in mind. Soon these psychologists were at work in studies of specialized training, in designing dials, headphones, radar screens, and in studying "trouble-shooting" (diagnosing and repairing defective equipment).

All of this research settled down a little after World War II. The results were carefully recorded (19 volumes on psychology in the air forces, four volumes on the sociopsychological studies in the army, and a number of others); some of the new material came to be used in textbooks for instructional purposes. Some disillusionment set in: things that had seemed very exciting and promising in the heat of war no longer seemed quite as profound, and some of the leads turned out not to hold up very well when carefully tested. Much of the substance remains, however, and now the settling down has finally taken place, and many new ways of looking at things have begun to emerge. It is always hard to identify the important developments that are taking place in the present, for while many possible lines of investigation are opened up, only a few catch on; the historian's task is much easier than the prophet's. It is possible, however, to note some of the problems that represent the growing edge of psychology today, recognizing that other less dramatic features are also being investigated and may at any time produce some new forward thrust. Psychology is a complex field and its trends are more likely to be divergent than convergent.

Comparative psychology, behavior genetics, and evolutionary theory

Although the evolutionary interests of psychologists have always been strong, and

animal laboratories have been a standard part of a psychology department, the investigations of the animal laboratory have tended to focus on topical questions (aspects of learning and discrimination, the effects of drugs, the role of parts of the brain), and the experiments have tended to be carried out on a limited number of species, with considerable emphasis upon the white rat. There are two ways in which animal studies can be of use. The first, and in the past the more typical, is the kind of study in which lower animals are used to throw light on problems arising in human psychology, much as animals are used in the medical school in the study of treatments intended later to be used on man. The second is that in which the psychologist studies animals in their own right in order to comprehend their behavior and the interrelationships between species, recognizing what Frank Beach calls "the equality of organisms," that is, the equal significance of the worm, the octopus, the spider, and the porpoise for purposes of comparative behavior study. This second kind of comparative psychology is having a forward surge, partly through the influence of the European ethologists who showed how much was overlooked if animals were not carefully studied in their natural habitats. These naturalistic studies and related studies in the laboratory contribute to the study of genetics and evolution by producing behavioral evidence of species relationships that supplement the morphological (i.e., structural) comparisons, which have thus far been the chief sources of evidence for both genetics and evolutionary theory.

Physiological psychology

For a time, especially in the 1930s, there was a kind of declaration of psychology's independence from physiology, as there had been earlier from philosophy. This came about because of the discovery that many previously held notions of brain action were in fact faulty, that there was much less localization of function in the brain than had previously been thought, and that we knew virtually nothing about the action of the brain in relation to higher mental processes. It was argued that it does not matter whether the brain acts like a telephone switchboard or like a complex field of forces; in either case habits will still be acquired as they are now acquired, sensory thresholds will be what they are, and memory functions will remain as we know them. The position was that psychologists could set the problems for the physiologists to solve, that psychology was sounder in its facts than students of brain physiology were in theirs, and that psychology could not wait for the physiologist but had to go ahead on its own. This position has its merits even today, for there always is enough independence of one science from another for each to go its own way, even though there may be interconnections that will facilitate the advance of both.

This attitude began to change about 1950. Hebb's influential book on *The organization of behavior* appeared in 1949; while highly speculative, it made a good deal of sense and proposed a kind of neuropsychology that offered promise. Concurrently a number of exciting developments had taken place in neurophysiology itself, and these have continued. The knowledge of the arousal mechanism, operating via the reticular formation, led to new interpretations of sleep, wakefulness, and energetic action. The knowledge that some efferent fibers could modulate afferent processes brought renewed interest to the physiology of sensory processes and of attention. The discovery that eye movements correlated with EEG patterns signified dreaming opened a whole field of research. Locating a "pleasure center" in the brain fitted in with an emerging neo-hedonism, or emphasis on the importance of pleasure in motivation. The brain enzymes began to be related to adaptive behavior; the discovery of new types of responses in the dendrites and an interest in the glia cells opened further lines of inquiry. The possibility that memory is stored by RNA changes is but one of the exciting possibilities.

Psychologists are participating in all of these developments, and the prospects are better than ever for solving some of the age-old problems on the relation between brain and behavior. Here is a dramatic illustration of the interrelationships of science: modern electronics and modern chemistry combine with anatomy, physiology, and psychology to make possible what no one science could do alone.

Mathematical and computer models

There have been many attempts in the past to use mathematics in biology and social sciences, but here, too, recent forward strides make the present different from the past. With a background of the game-theory model of the economists, the decision-theory model of the political scientists, and the information-theory model of the communications theorists and cyberneticists, psychologists have gone forward with their own mathematical model-building, the most advanced work being done in probabilistic models concerned with learning and perception. The high-speed computer provides a tool that supplements the mathematical model, although the mathematical model and the computer are essentially one, in that the program that is fed into the computer is itself a mathematical model. The most exciting development of computer models is in the simulation of cognitive processes, that is, of problem-solving and creative thinking. Computers are more than elaborate playthings, and there is a serious interaction that goes both ways: careful studies of human learning and thinking help in the design of the machines, but once the machine is built and we find what it can (or cannot) do, then we are likely, through correcting the instructions to the machine, to gain a better understanding of what the human being does. There are practical applications, too, as programed instruction is adapted to the computer, so that more classrooms can be monitored at once, even though each pupil proceeds at his own rate. No one can yet tell just where all of this activity is leading, but a young psychologist who wants to know what is happening in his field will be excluded from much of it if he cannot read the literature using the nomenclature of probability theory and modern mathematics.

Learning, motivation, and the technology of instruction

The psychology of learning has been an ascendant field of interest in psychology ever since William James gave prominence to the concept of habit, but more particularly following the work of Thorndike and Watson early in this century and the influence of Pavlov's studies of the conditioned reflex. The careful systematic formulations of Hull, with exciting controversies stirred up by Tolman, Lashley, Köhler, Skinner, and others, gave this topic unusual prominence over the last three decades. Interest in learning, as a theoretical and experimental topic, continues unabated, although the complexities that have turned up have reduced many psychologists' confidence in the general formulations and have diverted interest to motivation and other related topics.

While motivation has always interested some psychologists, the approach to the topic shifts; as it shifts, psychologists of different background and persuasion pick it up. For a time, early in the century, the problems of *instinct* were studied; later, *drives* induced by deprivation (especially hunger, thirst, sex) came under study; the psychoanalysts contributed *anxiety* and *guilt* as motivating forces. The newer developments, chiefly over the last decade, have emphasized such topics as the group of drives formerly neglected (exploration, curiosity, manipulation, frustration-induced drives), the influence of needs and values on perception, the expression of motives in fantasy (e.g., achievement and affiliation motives), and in values and value systems. The topic of motivation has become so broad that many psychologists have become uneasy about it; this uneasiness is a sign that the subject matter is taken seriously but that there are many unsolved problems.

A burst of criticism of the public schools, following the Russian launching of the satellite Sputnik, has challenged psychologists to apply whatever principles they have discovered in their laboratory investigations of learning and motivation to problems of improving actual instruction. For historical reasons that would take too much space to recount here, an earlier rapport between psychology and education, especially in the fields of learning and memory, was all but lost between 1940 and 1960.[1] The laboratory had moved farther and farther away from relevant content, choosing its materials for the study of learning chiefly on the basis of convenience in relation to theoretical issues. Thus the laboratory drifted away from the problems of instruction, and the school found it increasingly difficult to make any use of the results of learning experiments.

One immediate consequence of the interest in revitalizing education since 1960 has been substantial aids to research through the Office of Education of the Department of Health, Education, and Welfare and through the National Science Foundation. Many large-scale research endeavors have brought in subject-matter specialists (mathematicians, linguists, physical and biological scientists) to work alongside psychologists and educators in developing new materials and methods of instruction. Thus the separation between what is actually to be taught and the psychology of learning has been narrowed.

One technological advance came in the form of *programed learning* and the computer-based teaching machine. This new development has brought the attention and services of many very well-trained experimental psychologists to education. The programing technique has forced attention to the problems of organization of knowledge and has led the experimenter on learning to deal with subject matter relevant to schooling. But programed learning is only one illustration of emphasis upon the content of learning studies. The motivational side of learning is not being neglected, and studies of anxiety in school children, for example, consider the actual

[1] The schools continued to use the technical services of psychologists in the fields of testing and counseling, but curriculum and instruction made little or no use of psychological services.

test situations to which the child is exposed in school. This renewed interest in the applied problems of learning and motivation, coming at a time when there is also a renewed interest in cognitive processes generally, is likely to have an important feedback to the psychology of learning and motivation. That is, when attention is paid to relevant learning content, features such as the organization of knowledge come to the fore and add dimensions that may have been neglected in laboratory studies in which meaning was a more artificial variable.

Behavior and subjective phenomena

Behaviorism, the theory that makes behavior the only legitimate subject matter of psychology, has had a somewhat undulating history since its influence was first strongly felt in the years after its announcement by John B. Watson in 1913. For many psychologists in the early years, and for many today, behaviorism keeps psychology within the family of sciences, with data that can be recorded with instruments, open to study and repetition by competent scientists. The data of science, the behaviorist says, must be open and public, subject to measurement, prediction, and control. With these desirable goals nearly all psychologists agree.

But what is the price to be paid? Do we have to throw away the kinds of experiences that are not easily translated into these terms? Although the behaviorist soon recognized that nothing had to be left out (because you could always talk about "verbal responses" when reporting subjective states), in a subtle way the more "subjective" problems, such as those raised by dreams and hallucinations, tended to be neglected because the "you mustn't say" attitude toward subjective experiences easily became translated into "you mustn't study." This was not a necessary consequence of the behaviorist position, but it was an inadvertent by-product.

That form of strident behaviorism which is at present the most confident, represented by B. F. Skinner and his followers, still very much reflects this earlier position, and doubts the existence of any "inner life," and emphasizes the study of overt behavior (including speech) to the neglect of problems tainted with subjectivity. This group is strongly influential, not only in experimental psychology but in applied fields as well, particularly programed learning, for the popularity of which Skinner is largely responsible, and the form of psychotherapy that uses verbal operant conditioning.

Within behaviorism itself there are many more moderate forms. Thus Edward C. Tolman's cognitive psychology was called by him "purposive behaviorism"; while it had no place within it for "raw" subjective experience, it was broadly tolerant of many problems others thought of as subjective. A disciple of Edwin Guthrie's form of behaviorism has added *perceptual responses* to the muscular and glandular responses that were once the only legitimate substance of a strict S-R behaviorism (Sheffield, 1961). If perceptual responses are accepted as *central responses,* then the peripheralism of classical (and Skinnerian) behaviorism is rejected. Sheffield is willing to say, for example, that a watchmaker looking at the outside of a familiar watch "sees" the works inside as a learned perceptual response; this is a genuine central response, and not merely a form of talking to himself about the works.

There are those who have no sympathy with behaviorism, and they reject it rather than try to modify it. Among the points of view are various forms of phenomenology, existentialism, and humanistic psychology. Existentialism and humanistic psychology tend to reject the biological approach that has been characteristic of American psychology, seeing the problems of psychology rather in terms of human values, human concerns, individual uniqueness, and the individual meaning of life and destiny. Adherents to humanistic psychology sometimes refer to it as a "third movement," the first being the experimental tradition culminating in behaviorism, and the second being psychoanalysis, which came closer to the human problem but is viewed by the humanistic psychologists as too deterministic and pessimistic.

With these divergent trends, what can we predict for the future? It is doubtful that Skinner's form of behaviorism, despite its successes, will ever take over the field. Its technological successes are very great indeed, and psychology is much the richer for them; operant conditioning brings many forms of behavior under stimulus control. At the same time Skinner's behavioristic approach is too dogmatic, too antiphysiological, too antisystematic to wholly satisfy man's curiosity about himself. As in other sciences, psychologists will continue to seek for explanations both in reductive terms (i.e., in terms of physiology and biochemistry) and in systematic terms (e.g., hierarchical structures and mathematical models with interchangeable constants). Even though at present the varied and somewhat eclectic approaches by the non-Skinnerians lack the confidence of the Skinnerians, the alternative approaches will doubtless continue to flourish.

The main stream of psychology in the years ahead is more likely to remain within the broadly biological tradition rather than to be diverted into any extreme form of phenomenalism or of humanistic psychology. The more tolerant forms of biological psychology permit a free interest in cognitive processes of all kinds—in dreams, in hypnotic phenomena, in intention, in problems of self-perception, planfulness, and "will." It is of interest that while the behaviorism of Skinner is attracting many followers there is at the same time an increased interest in cognitive processes of all kinds and in the formulations of Jean Piaget, who would be most surprised were he to be called a behaviorist.

Phenomenalism and humanistic psychology serve a useful critical function by warning against triviality and the neglect of important issues, and the present developments may again serve in this way. However, one cannot make a science of human behavior merely by standing in awe of it and marveling at it; such a position drifts into a more and more obscure account of the nature of man. But as soon as phenomenal description becomes at all clear and systematic, it partakes of the very science that phenomenology opposes and, in fact, becomes assimilated into it. To the extent that the phenomenologists call attention to the whole man in his environment, they provide the same sort of corrective that the ethologists have provided for comparative psychology: they see that the right questions are asked, whether or not we approve of the answers.

One of the genuine problems that the humanistic psychologists pose is the need for a better understanding between a biological psychology and the position of the humanistic disciplines, a conflict that in other spheres has led to the distinction between our two cultures, scientific and nonscientific (Snow, 1959). Psychology has probably kept its distance from the humanities in part because of its eagerness to establish itself as a science and in part because of its still-too-recent divorce from philosophy. Nevertheless psychologists study esthetics, language (psycholinguistics, communication), values, and meanings. We can hope that understanding between psychology and the humanities will increase—to their mutual advantage.

Human development and mental health

Nowhere do the problems of pure science and of applied science overlap more than in the study of human development, for adults are responsible for the decisions that are made in the course of a child's development, and if these decisions are guided by scientific knowledge they are illustrations of applied science. These are old problems, but new knowledge and techniques will help in obtaining new answers.

The older longitudinal studies of the past (following a group from birth onward) tended to bog down in data; because the time span is so great, observations that are recognized as needed today were not made when the studies were begun, and trying to answer today's questions with data collected yesterday has not proved very satisfactory. Undoubtedly new longitudinal studies will use methods of group overlap, so that data covering a span of years can be collected more quickly. With modern sampling methods it is possible to study several age groups simultaneously (e.g., studying the age groups from birth through 5, 5 through 10, 10 through 15, and 15 through 20), thereby doing the equivalent of 20 years' observations in five.

One practical reason for proposing methods of child rearing is to achieve good mental-health outcomes, that is, to bring up children who can cope with their problems and can face crises without breakdown. This is one facet of the general problem of personality development, from the point of view of its social significance; clinical psychology must concern itself with the prevention of mental illness as well as with its diagnosis and treatment.

The research tasks before a developmental psychology include the study of normal development and the factors that affect it, given the raw materials provided by heredity and prenatal development; the prediction of outcomes (successful adjustment, delinquency, personality disturbances); diagnostic procedures along the way; and remedial practices, including psychotherapy.

A comprehensive social psychology

Nothing is more pressing than an understanding of human social life and institutions that will permit more rational solutions to the problems of human civilization than those we now attempt. War as an instrument of policy is recognized on all sides as stupid and dangerous to human survival; the armaments race has no equilibrium point and hence must run eventually to destructive encounter, unless some other policy intervenes. These are sober facts of human social behavior, about which we somehow feel helpless because we have not yet been able to accept scientific processes in the control of human affairs. It is a paradox that the highest developments of science are used in weapon development but that the makers of these advanced weapons do not know how to control their use or even their reduction.

A comprehensive social psychology must deal with group behavior at all levels, including the international level, but this does not mean that social psychology now has the answers to the problems that international issues create. Where does it now stand? Systematic social psychology has tended to go back to the individual and to small groups to discover the forms of social perception and social interaction that are at the root of large social institutions; even larger social decisions (e.g., the declaration of war by a nation's cabinet) can be simulated by a "game" in which the relevant information is given to the participants and they are set the task of arriving at a decision. Decisions by leaders are, after all, the decisions of individuals.

To what extent the social institution acts like an organism is an old question, to which the answer is not entirely clear. There are kinds of "institution morality" that appear different from individual morality; thus nations are "insulted" and retaliate with a violence that would not characterize individual reactions; the people of two nations may declare their liking for each other and yet fight over issues that are largely ceremonial in character.

It is the task of social psychology of the future to understand the rational and irrational in human social behavior and institutions. This understanding, if applied in such a way as to make human relations more humane, could turn out to be science's greatest contribution to mankind.

SUMMARY   1. Psychology began as a small profession within the lifetime of some still living. It surged ahead after the two world wars, until by 1965 it numbered over 23,000 members in its national society, the American Psychological Association, and its rapid growth is continuing.

2. Colleges and universities are still the largest employers of psychologists; many members of the profession now work for government agencies or private organizations. Relatively few are in private practice.

3. Of the numerous specializations within psychology, *clinical psychology* is now the largest; the two specialties of *clinical* and *counseling* psychology account for half the professional psychologists. Other specialties include *experimental psychology, social psychology,* and *statistics.*

4. Psychology is also applied within other professions, such as law, education, and medicine. *Legal psychology* has dealt with testimony and evidence, the examination of witnesses, study of the individual delinquent and criminal, and with some broader problems of the law. *Educational psychology* deals with the applications of principles of learning, motivation, personality, and group behavior to the schools, while the school psychologist has special functions within the school system. The relationships with *medicine* are close, through clinical psychology and the psychologist's interest in early childhood and in developmental problems.

5. The interests of psychologists lie close to those of physical scientists, although their interests also have something in common with those of artists, architects, and physicians. A distinction can be made between those psychologists whose interests lead them to use experimental techniques and those who are interested in correlational techniques, but there are some indications that these interests are coming closer together.

6. In attempting to see where the problems of psychology lie in the years ahead, it is possible to note important developments in these areas: *comparative psychology,* particularly in relation to genetics and evolutionary theory; *physiological psychology,* particularly the study of the brain in relation to behavior; *mathematical and computer models,* in learning and the simulation of cognitive processes; *learning, motivation,* and the *technology of instruction,* with an emphasis on the *content* of learning; a freer study of perceptual, cognitive, and other *subjective phenomena* through a lessening of the influence of a narrow behaviorism; *human development* and *mental health;* and a comprehensive *social psychology.* These developments in both basic and applied science make possible an eventual significant contribution of psychology to human understanding and to human welfare.

SUGGESTIONS
FOR
FURTHER
READING

There are a number of textbooks in applied psychology that cover in detail the topics suggested by this chapter. A useful one is Anastasi, *Fields of applied psychology* (1964). For human factors and managerial psychology, see Leavitt, *Managerial psychology* (2nd ed., 1964), McCormick, *Human factors in engineering* (2nd ed., 1964), and Schein, *Organizational psychology* (1964).

Space technology, from the psychologist's viewpoint, is summarized in Sells and Berry (eds.), *Human factors in jet and space travel* (1961), and Brown (ed.), *Physiology of man in space* (1963).

For psychology as a profession, see Clark, *America's psychologists: a survey of a growing profession* (1957). The beginning student who may be interested in psychology as a career will find the following pamphlets helpful: Ross and Lockman, *A career in psychology* (1965), and Webb, *The profession of psychology* (1962).

For a picture of contemporary psychology as a science with the best available guesses as to where it is going, the following work provides the thinking of recognized experts, written not for beginners but for other psychologists: Koch (ed.), *Psychology: a study of a science.* (This work is eventually to be in seven volumes, the first six of which appeared between 1959 and 1963.)

Glossary

The glossary defines technical words appearing in the text and some common words when they are used in psychology with special meanings. No attempt is made to give the range of variations of meaning beyond those used in the text. For fuller definitions and other shades of meaning, consult any standard dictionary of psychology, such as English and English, *A comprehensive dictionary of psychological and psychoanalytical terms* (1958).

ability. Demonstrable knowledge or skill. Ability includes aptitude and achievement (cf. *aptitude, achievement*).

abnormal fixation. A stereotyped habit very resistant to change (cf. *stereotypy*).

abreaction. In psychoanalysis, the process of reducing emotional tension by reliving (in speech or action or both) the experience which caused the tension (syn. *catharsis*).

absolute threshold. The intensity or frequency at which a stimulus becomes effective or ceases to become effective, as measured under experimental conditions (cf. *threshold, difference threshold*).

achievement. Acquired ability, e.g., school attainment in spelling (cf. *aptitude*).

achievement motive. The social motive to accomplish something of value or importance, to meet standards of excellence in what one does.

achromatic colors. Black, white, and gray (cf. *chromatic colors*).

acquiescence. A biasing variable in personality inventories, leading some subjects to reply more frequently in the affirmative, regardless of the content of the test item (cf. *social desirability variable*).

acquisition. The stage during which a new response is learned and gradually strengthened.

adaptive behavior. Behavior that brings the organism into adjustment with its variable environment (cf. *behavior*).

additive mixture. The mixture of lights; two spotlights focused on the same spot yield additive mixture; colored sectors of paper rotated on a color wheel also yield additive mixture (cf. *subtractive mixture*).

adolescence. In human beings, the period from puberty to maturity, roughly the early teens to the early twenties (cf. *puberty*).

adrenal gland. One of a pair of endocrine glands located above the kidneys. The medulla of the gland secretes the hormones adrenalin and noradrenalin. The cortex of the gland secretes a number of hormones, collectively called the adrenocortical hormones, which include cortisone (cf. *endocrine gland*).

adrenalin. One of the hormones secreted by the adrenal medulla, active in emotional excitement (syn. *epinephrine;* cf. *noradrenalin*).

affective-arousal theory. A theory of motivation that accounts for the tendency for behavior to be directed according to anticipated pleasure or pain (McClelland).

affective experience. An emotional experience, whether pleasant or unpleasant, mild or intense (cf. *emotional state*).

afferent nerve. A bundle of nerve fibers transmitting impulses into the central nervous system from the periphery. Receptors connect directly with afferent nerves (usually synonymous with *sensory nerve;* cf. *efferent nerve*).

affiliative motive. In man, the tendency to depend upon another person or persons, to associate with them, to form friendships or other attachments (syn. *dependency motive*).

afterimage. The sensory experience that remains when a stimulus is withdrawn. Usually refers to visual experience, e.g., the negative afterimage of a picture, or the train of colored images that results after staring at the sun.

age-mates. Other children of the same age with whom a child associates and from whom he commonly derives some of his standards (syn. *peer group*).

aggression. (1) Destructive activity of any sort. (2) Activity undertaken in order to do harm to another person either through actual physical injury or through some kind of belittling or malicious ridicule (this is the usual text usage).

agoraphobia. Fear of open places (cf. *phobic reaction*).

algorithm. A fixed routine for finding a mathematical solution, an exact procedure, as in extracting square root. A computer commonly uses algorithmic methods, but may use other methods (cf. *heuristic method*).

ambivalence. Simultaneous liking and disliking of an object or person; the conflict caused by an incentive that is at once positive and negative (cf. *conflict*).

amnesia. The partial or total loss of memory for past experiences. The memories lost in amnesia have not been completely destroyed, for the forgotten events may again be remembered without relearning when the person recovers from his amnesia (cf. *repression*).

anal stage. The second stage according to the psychoanalytic theory of psychosexual development, following the oral stage. The sources of gratification and conflict have to do with the expulsion and retention of feces (cf. *psychosexual development*).

androgen. The collective name for male sex hormones, of which testosterone, secreted by the testes, is best known (cf. *sex glands, estrogen*).

antagonistic muscles. Muscles arranged in pairs, so that when one contracts, the other stretches, e.g., the biceps and triceps muscles of the upper arm (cf. *reciprocal innervation*).

anthropology. The science that studies chiefly nonliterate ("primitive") societies. Its main divisions are archaeology (the study of the physical monuments and remains from earlier civilizations), physical anthropology (concerned with the anatomical differences among men and their evolutionary origins), and social anthropology (concerned with language, social institutions, and behavior) (cf. *behavioral sciences*).

anticipation method. A method of rote memorization, appropriate to either serial memorization or paired-associates learning, in which the subject learns to respond to a stimulus item with the response item next to appear in the aperture of the memory drum. The method permits scoring successes and failures throughout memorization.

antisocial reaction. Cf. *psychopathic reaction*.

anxiety. A state of apprehension or uneasiness, related to fear. The object of anxiety (e.g., a vague danger or foreboding) is ordinarily less specific than the object of fear (e.g., a vicious animal).

anxiety reaction. A form of neurotic reaction characterized by a diffuse dread, often accompanied by tenseness, palpitation, sweating, nausea (cf. *neurotic reaction*).

apathy. Listlessness, indifference; one of the consequences of frustration (cf. *frustration*).

aphasia. Impairment or loss of ability to articulate words or to comprehend speech.

appetitive behavior. Seeking behavior (cf. *aversive behavior*).

aptitude. The capacity to learn, e.g., typing aptitude prior to practice on a typewriter. Aptitude tests are designed to predict the outcome of training, hence to predict future ability on the basis of present ability (cf. *achievement*).

area sampling. A method used in making surveys of attitudes and opinions, the respondents being selected according to their place of residence; one form of probability sampling (cf. *quota control, probability sampling*).

aroused motive. A motive that is inferred from behavior actually occurring (cf. *motivational disposition*).

artificial intelligence. The performance by a computer of tasks that have hitherto required the application of human intelligence.

association areas. Portions of the cerebral hemispheres other than the projection areas. Because their function is unknown, the assumption is made that these areas serve some sort of integrative ("association") function (cf. *intrinsic cortex*).

association psychology. A pre-experimental psychology, whose basic explanatory principle was the association of ideas (cf. *faculty psychology*).

associative thinking. Relatively uncontrolled and undirected thinking as in free association, reverie, and dreams (cf. *directed thinking*).

asymptote. The stable level to which a variable tends over the course of time; e.g., in learning, the final response strength after an extended period of acquisition. The asymptote is the point at which the learning curve levels out.

attention. The focusing of perception leading to heightened awareness of a limited range of stimuli.

attitude. An orientation toward or away from some object, concept, or situation; a readiness to respond in a predetermined manner to the object, concept, or situation (cf. *attitude scale, opinion, prejudice*).

attitude scale. A scale for the quantitative appraisal of attitudes (cf. *scalogram*).

authoritarian personality. A personality syndrome said to be common to those whose attitudes are authoritarian instead of democratic. The syndrome is characterized by highly conventional behavior, concern over sex, superstitiousness, destructiveness, and cynicism (cf. *personality syndrome*).

autistic thinking. A form of associative thinking, controlled more by the thinker's needs or desires than by reality; wishful thinking (cf. *daydreaming, rationalization*).

autism. Absorption in fantasy to the exclusion of interest in reality; a symptom of schizophrenia.

autonomic nervous system. A system of nerve cells and nerve fibers regulating smooth muscle and glandular activities. While the system is closely integrated with the brain and spinal cord, it has some cell bodies and synapses lying outside the brain and spinal cord (syn. *vegetative nervous system;* cf. *parasympathetic division, sympathetic division*).

average. A value representative of a frequency distribution, around which other values are dispersed, e.g., the mean, median, or mode of a distribution of scores (syn. *measure of central tendency*).

aversive behavior. Avoidance behavior (cf. *appetitive behavior*).

avoidance learning. A form of learning controlled by the threat of punishment. The learning is motivated by the anxiety raised by the threat and the reduction of anxiety when the punishment is avoided (cf. *escape learning*).

axon. That portion of a neuron that transmits impulses to other neurons (cf. *neuron, dendrite*).

basal mental age. In individual tests of the Binet type, the highest age level at which, and below which, all tests are passed (cf. *mental age*).

basilar membrane. A membrane of the ear within the coils of the cochlea, supporting the organ of Corti. Movements of the basilar membrane stimulate the hair cells of the organ of Corti, producing the neural effects of auditory stimulation (cf. *cochlea, organ of Corti*).

behavior. Those activities of an organism that can be observed by another organism or by an experimenter's instruments. Included within behavior are verbal reports made about subjective, conscious experiences (cf. *conscious processes*).

behavior therapy. A method of psychotherapy based on learning principles. It uses such techniques as counter-conditioning, reinforcement, and shaping to modify behavior.

behavioral sciences. The sciences concerned in one way or another with the behavior of man and lower organisms; especially social anthropology, psychology, and sociology, but including some aspects of biology, economics, political science, history, philosophy, and other fields of study (cf. *anthropology, psychology, sociology*).

behaviorism. A school or system of psychology associated with the name of John B. Watson; it defined psychology as the study of behavior and limited the data of psychology to observable activities. In its classical form it was more restrictive than the contemporary objective (behavioral) viewpoint in psychology (cf. *school of psychology*).

bimodal distribution. A frequency distribution with two points at which there are a high number of cases, hence two modes (cf. *mode*).

binocular cues. Cf. *distance cues*.

binocular disparity. Cf. *retinal disparity*.

blood pressure. The pressure of the blood against the walls of the blood vessels. Changes in blood pressure following stimulation serve as one indicator of emotion (cf. *emotional indicator*).

blood volume. The volume of the blood in a bodily member (e.g., hand, finger) due to dilation or constriction of blood vessels. Changes in volume serve as one indicator of emotion (cf. *emotional indicator*).

body-sense area. A projection area of the cerebral cortex lying behind the fissure of Rolando. Electrical stimulation of the area commonly results in the report of sensory experiences, e.g., "It feels as though I am moving my finger" (syn. *somesthetic area*; cf. *motor area*).

brain stem. The structures lying near the core of the brain; essentially all of the brain with the exception of the cerebral cortex and the cerebellum and their dependent parts.

brainwashing. Cf. *coercive persuasion*.

brightness. The dimension of color that describes its nearness in brilliance to white (as contrasted with black). A bright color reflects more light than a dark one (cf. *hue, saturation*).

brightness constancy. The tendency to see a familiar object as of the same brightness, regardless of light and shadow that change its stimulus properties (cf. *color constancy, object constancy*).

Broca's speech area. A portion of the left cerebral hemisphere said to control motor speech.

CAI. A common abbreviation for computer-assisted instruction, i.e., instruction carried out under computer control.

cardiac muscle. A special kind of muscle found only in the heart (cf. *smooth muscle, striate muscle*).

cardinal disposition. An outstanding disposition that dominates an individual personality, often making that person a "reference personality" according to which others are judged, e.g., a Beau Brummell or Don Juan (cf. *central disposition, secondary disposition*).

case history. A biography obtained for scientific purposes; the material is sometimes supplied by interview, sometimes collected over the years.

caste. Social stratification in which boundaries are sharply defined and not to be crossed (cf. *class*).

castration. Surgical removal of the gonads; in the male, removal of the testes; in the female, removal of the ovaries.

center. A place within the nervous system where impulses in activated neurons can produce impulses in other neurons across synapses. A center contains numerous cell bodies of neurons; while most centers are within the brain and spinal cord, some lie outside (syn. *central processes*; cf. *ganglion*).

central nervous system. In vertebrates, the brain and spinal cord, as distinct from the nerve trunks and their peripheral connections (cf. *autonomic nervous system*).

central disposition. One of a few dispositions sometimes sufficient to characterize an individual (Allport) (cf. *cardinal disposition, secondary disposition*).

centralist position. A theoretical position held by certain psychologists who believe that thinking can best be explained as processes going on inside the brain or nervous system, with muscular movements as mere accompaniments or facilitators of the central processes (cf. *peripheralist position*).

cerebral cortex. The surface layer of the cerebral hemispheres in higher animals, including man. It is commonly called gray matter because its many cell bodies give it a gray appearance in cross section, in contrast with the nerve fibers that make up the white matter.

cerebral hemispheres. Two large masses of nerve cells and fibers constituting the bulk of the brain in man and other higher animals. The hemispheres are separated by a deep fissure, but connected by a broad band of fibers, the corpus callosum (syn. *cerebrum*; cf. *cerebral cortex*).

character disorder. A general category of behavior disorders involving a life-long pattern of socially deviant behavior rather than mental or emotional symptoms. It includes such diverse disorders as alcoholism, criminal behavior, drug addiction, sexually deviant behavior, and psychopathic reaction (syn. *personality disorder*; cf. *psychopathic reaction*).

chemical integration. Bodily organization for harmonious or unified action through chemical substances transmitted via the bodily fluids, especially the hormones (cf. *hormones, mechanical integration, neural integration*).

chemotherapy. The use of drugs in the treatment of mental disorders (cf. *somatotherapy*).

chlorpromazine. Cf. *tranquilizer*.

chromatic colors. All colors other than black, white, and gray, e.g., red, yellow, blue (cf. *achromatic colors*).

chromosome. Small particles found in pairs in all the cells of the body, carrying the genetic determiners (genes) that are transmitted from parent to offspring. A human cell has 46 chromosomes, arranged in 23 pairs, one member of each pair deriving from the mother, one from the father (cf. *gene*).

chronological age (C.A.). Age from birth; calendar age (cf. *mental age*).

clairvoyance. A form of extrasensory perception in which the perceiver is said to identify a stimulus that is influencing neither his own sense organs nor those of another person (cf. *extrasensory perception, telepathy, precognition*).

class. A level of social stratification, e.g., upper, middle, and lower class, but without the rigid boundaries characterizing caste, so that mobility between classes is possible (cf. *caste*).

class interval. In statistics, a small section of a scale according to which scores of a frequency distribution are grouped, e.g., heights grouped into class intervals of a half inch (cf. *frequency distribution*).

classical conditioning. Conditioned-response experiments conforming to the pattern of Pavlov's experiment. The main feature is that the originally neutral conditioned stimulus, through repeated pairing with the unconditioned one, acquires the response originally given to the unconditioned stimulus (syn. *stimulus substitution*; cf. *operant conditioning*).

claustrophobia. Fear of closed places (cf. *phobic reaction*).

cleanliness training. A euphemism for teaching the infant to control urination and defecation.

client. A synonym for *patient*, the term used by counselors who wish to avoid the medical connotations of the patient-physician relationship (cf. *client-centered therapy*).

client-centered therapy. A method of psychotherapy designed to let the client learn to take responsibility for his own actions and to use his own resourcefulness in solving his problems (syn. *nondirective counseling*).

clinical psychologist. A psychologist, usually with a Ph.D. degree, whose training involves hospital and clinic experience. His techniques include testing, diagnosis, interviewing, psychotherapy, and conducting research (cf. *counseling psychologist, psychiatrist*).

cluster analysis. An analysis of trait (or item) inter-correlations, based on grouping together those traits (or items) that show similar patterns of inter-item correlation. The method is more superficial than factor analysis, for which it sometimes substitutes (cf. *factor analysis, surface trait*).

cochlea. The portion of the inner ear containing the receptors for hearing (cf. *basilar membrane, organ of Corti*).

coefficient of correlation. A numerical index used to indicate the degree of correspondence between two sets of paired measurements. The most common kind is the product-moment coefficient designated by r.

coercive persuasion. Influencing the thought patterns of prisoners whose lives are completely under the control of those seeking to influence them, thereby permitting kinds of influence not ordinarily possible (syn. *brainwashing*).

cognitive dissonance. The condition in which one has beliefs or knowledge that disagree with each other or with behavioral tendencies; when such cognitive dissonance arises, the subject is motivated to reduce the dissonance through changes in behavior or cognition (Festinger).

cognitive theory. A point of view contrasted with stimulus-response (S-R) theory, more concerned with "knowing" and "perceiving" than with "movement-responses" (cf. *stimulus-response psychology*).

color blindness. Defective discrimination of chromatic colors (cf. *monochromatism, dichromatism, red-green color blindness*).

color circle. An arrangement of chromatic colors around the circumference of a circle in the order in which they appear in the spectrum, but with the addition of nonspectral reds and purples. The colors are so arranged that those opposite each other are complementaries in additive mixture.

color constancy. The tendency to see a familiar object as of the same color, regardless of changes in illumination on it which alter its stimulus properties (cf. *object constancy*).

color-mixing primaries. Three hues chosen to produce the total range of hues by their additive mixture. A spectral red, green, and blue are usually selected (cf. *psychological primaries*).

common trait. An aspect of personality in respect to which most people within a culture can be profitably compared (Allport) (cf. *disposition*).

comparative psychology. The study of the behavior of lower organisms in their interrelationships with each other and with man.

compensation. A form of defense mechanism by which one attempts to cover up or balance failure in, or lack of talent for, one activity by a strenuous effort to excel in either a different or an allied activity (cf. *substitution, sublimation, overcompensation*).

complementary hues. Two hues which in additive mixture yield either a gray or an unsaturated color of the hue of the stronger component.

compulsive movements. Repetitive actions which a person feels driven to make and which he is unable to resist; ritualistic behavior; a form of dissociation (cf. *dissociation*).

compulsive personality. A personality syndrome characterized by cleanliness, orderliness, and obstinacy. In the extreme, behavior becomes repetitive and ritualistic (syn. *anal character*; cf. *personality syndrome*).

concept. The properties or relationships common to a class of objects or ideas. Concepts may be of concrete things, e.g., the concept "poodle dog" referring to a given variety of dog, or of abstract ideas, e.g.,

equality, justice, number, implying relationships common to many different kinds of objects or ideas.

concurrent validity. Validity determined by the internal consistency of the parts of a test, all scores obtained at the same testing (cf. *construct validity, content validity, predictive validity*).

conditioned emotion. An emotional response acquired by conditioning, i.e., one aroused by a stimulus that did not originally evoke it (cf. *conditioning*).

conditioned response. The learned or acquired response to a conditioned stimulus, i.e., to a stimulus that did not evoke the response originally (cf. *classical conditioning, unconditioned response*).

conditioning. The process by which conditioned responses are learned (cf. *classical conditioning, operant conditioning*).

cone. In the eye, an element of the retina found predominantly in the fovea and more sparsely throughout the retina. The cones mediate both chromatic and achromatic sensations (cf. *retina, rod, fovea*).

confidence limits. In statistics, upper and lower limits derived from a sample, used in making inferences about a population; e.g., from the mean of a sample and its standard error one can determine limits which permit a statement that the probability is 95 in 100 that the population mean falls within these limits (cf. *statistical inference, statistical significance*).

conflict. The simultaneous presence of opposing or mutually exclusive impulses, desires, or tendencies.

connotative meaning. The suggestions and emotional meanings of a word or symbol, beyond its denotative meaning. Thus naked and nude both refer to an unclothed body (denotative meaning), but they have somewhat different connotations (cf. *denotative meaning, semantic differential*).

conscience. An internal recognition of standards of right and wrong by which the individual judges his own conduct (cf. *superego*).

conscious processes. Events such as perceptions, after-images, private thoughts, and dreams, of which only the person himself is aware. They are accessible to others through verbal report or by way of inference from other behavior (syn. *experience, awareness*; cf. *unconscious processes*).

construct validity. Validity determined by a process of inference more complex than that involved in predicting a specific criterion. The inference is usually in hypothetical form; e.g., if this is a good measure of achievement motivation, it should relate to scores on a learning task, even though that task is not itself a measure of achievement motivation (cf. *concurrent validity, content validity, predictive validity*).

control group. In an experimental design contrasting two groups, that group not given the treatment whose effect is under study (cf. *experimental group*).

consummatory behavior. Cf. *goal activity*.

controlled association. The process in word-association experiments in which the subject is instructed to give a specific kind of associated word, e.g., one opposite to that of the stimulus word (cf. *free association*).

conversion reaction. A form of neurotic reaction in which the symptoms are paralysis of the limbs, insensitive areas of the body (anesthesias), uncontrolled emotional outbursts, or related bodily symptoms. The presumption is that anxiety has been "converted" into a tangible symptom (syn. *hysteria*; cf. *neurotic reaction*).

corpus callosum. A large band of fibers (white matter) connecting the two cerebral hemispheres.

correlation. Cf. *coefficient of correlation*.

counseling psychologist. A trained psychologist, usually with a Ph.D. or Ed.D. degree, dealing with personal problems not classified as illness, such as academic, social, or vocational problems of students. His skills are similar to those of the clinical psychologist, but his work is usually in a nonmedical setting (cf. *clinical psychologist*).

counter-conditioning. The replacement of a particular response to a stimulus by the establishment of another (usually incompatible) response.

creative thinking. A form of directed thinking in which the subject seeks to discover new relationships, to achieve new solutions to problems, to invent methods or devices, or to produce new artistic objects or forms (cf. *critical thinking*).

criterion. (1) A set of scores or other records against which the success of a predictive test is verified. (2) A standard selected as the goal to be achieved in a learning task, e.g., the number of runs through a maze to be made without error as an indication that the maze has been mastered.

critical flicker frequency. If the rate of alternation between light and dark phases of stimuli is increased, there comes a point at which flicker disappears and a steady light is perceived; this fusion rate is known as the critical flicker frequency (syn. *critical fusion frequency*).

critical period. A stage in development during which the organism is optimally ready to learn certain response patterns. It is closely related to the concept of maturational readiness.

critical ratio. A mean, mean difference, or coefficient of correlation, divided by its standard error. Used in tests of significance (cf. *statistical significance*).

critical scores. Scores based on experience with tests used for a given purpose, so that persons scoring below the critical level are rejected as unlikely to succeed; e.g., a critical score on a scholastic aptitude test for college students is one below which no candidate is accepted for admission.

critical thinking. A form of directed thinking in which the subject seeks to arrive at judgments of truth or value (cf. *creative thinking*).

cues to distance. Cf. *distance cues*.

cue-stimulus theory. A theory of motivation that gets along without the concept of drive by assuming that behavior comes exclusively under the control of stimuli (cf. *drive*).

culture-fair test. A type of intelligence test that has been so constructed as to minimize bias due to the differing experiences of children raised in a rural rather than an urban culture or in a lower-class rather than in a middle-class or upper-class culture (syn. *culture-free test*).

cybernetics. The study of regulatory mechanisms, such as thermostats and governors. One of the several models used in theory construction (cf. *model*).

dark adaptation. The increased sensitivity to light when the subject has been continuously in the dark or under conditions of reduced illumination (cf. *light adaptation*).

daydreaming. Reverie; free play of thought or imagination. Because of self-reference, usually a form of autistic thinking (cf. *autistic thinking*).

decibel. A unit for measuring sound intensity, which has a logarithmic relation to the amplitude.

defense mechanism. An adjustment made, often unconsciously, either through action or the avoidance of action in order to escape recognition by oneself of personal qualities or motives which might lower self-esteem or heighten anxiety (cf. *rational problem-solving*).

delayed-response experiment. An experiment used with both subhuman animals and man as a test of memory. The subject observes the experimenter place an incentive under one of two or more containers. Then a shield is placed between the subject and the containers for a period of delay before the subject chooses the proper container. Accuracy of his choice tests his memory for the placing of the incentive.

delusion. False beliefs characteristic of some forms of psychotic disorder. They often take the form of delusions of grandeur or delusions of persecution (cf. *paranoid schizophrenia*).

dendrite. The specialized portion of the neuron which (together with the cell body) receives impulses from other neurons (cf. *axon*).

denial. Cf. *self-deception*.

denotative meaning. The primary meaning of a symbol, something specific to which the symbol refers or points; e.g., my street address is denotative; whether or not I live in a desirable neighborhood is a connotative meaning secondary to the address itself (cf. *connotative meaning*).

deoxyribonucleic acid (DNA). Large molecules found in the cell nucleus and primarily responsible for genetic inheritance. These molecules manufacture various forms of RNA which are thought by some to be the chemical basis of memory (cf. *ribonucleic acid*).

dependency motive. A motive based on the need to be taken care of by someone, to gain support through affiliation (syn. *affiliative motive*).

dependent variable. The variable whose measured changes are attributed to (or correspond to) changes in the independent variable. In psychological experiments, the dependent variable is often a response to a measured stimulus (cf. *independent variable*).

depth perception. The perception of the distance of an object from the observer or the distance from front to back of a solid object (cf. *distance cues*).

descriptive statistics. Simplifying or summarizing statements about measurements made on a population. Strictly speaking, descriptive statistics should apply solely to populations, rather than to samples, but the term is used loosely for summarizing statements about samples when they are treated as populations (cf. *statistical inference*).

developmental explanation. An explanation of behavior that stresses the historical roots of present activity, focusing on accumulating experience as the individual grows and learns (cf. *interactive explanation*).

deviation I.Q. An intelligence quotient (I.Q.) computed as a standard score with a mean of 100 and a standard deviation of 15 (Wechsler) or 16 (Stanford-Binet), to correspond approximately to traditional intelligence quotient (cf. *intelligence quotient*).

dichromatism. Color blindness in which either the red-green or the blue-yellow system is lacking. The red-green form is relatively common; the blue-yellow form is the rarest of all forms of color blindness (cf. *monochromatism, red-green color blindness*).

difference equation. An equation used in probabilistic treatments of learning to express the change in probability of response from one trial to the next (syn. *linear operator*).

difference threshold. The minimum difference between a pair of stimuli that can be perceived under experimental conditions (cf. *threshold, absolute threshold, just-noticeable-difference*).

digital computer. A computer that performs mathematical and logical operations with information, numerical or otherwise, represented in digital form.

dimension. A scale from one extreme to another along which orderly variations occur, e.g., pitch as a dimension of tone, brightness as a dimension of light, length as a size dimension, the degree of favorableness as a dimension of attitude (cf. *scale*).

direct aggression. Aggression against the person or object producing frustration (cf. *aggression, displaced aggression*).

directed thinking. Thinking directed toward a goal or toward the solution of a problem (cf. *creative thinking, critical thinking, associative thinking*).

discrimination. (1) In perception, the detection of differences between two stimuli. (2) In conditioning, the differential response to the positive (reinforced) stimulus and to the negative (nonreinforced) stimulus (cf. *generalization*). (3) In social psychology, prejudicial treatment, as in racial discrimination.

discriminatory stimulus. A stimulus that becomes an occasion for an operant response, e.g., the knock that leads one to open the door. The stimulus does not elicit the operant response in the same sense that a stimulus elicits respondent behavior (cf. *operant behavior*).

disguise. Cf. *self-deception*.

displaced aggression. Aggression against a person or object other than that which was (or is) the source of frustration (cf. *direct aggression*).

displacement. In psychoanalysis, the substitution of one object for another as a source of gratification.

disposition. A personal trait to be distinguished from a common trait because of its uniqueness (Allport) (cf. *common trait*).

dissociation. A defense mechanism in which there is splitting of aspects of behavior or experience which normally would occur together. Thus dissociated movements occur without their appropriate emotional accompaniments, or dissociated thoughts occur without appropriate action (cf. *compulsive movements, defense mechanism, multiple personality*).

dissonance. (1) In music, an inharmonious combination of sounds; contrasted with consonance. (2) In social psychology, Festinger's term for a perceived inconsistency between one's own attitudes and one's behavior (cf. *cognitive dissonance*).

distance cues. (1) In vision, the monocular cues according to which the distance of objects is perceived—such as superposition of objects, perspective, light and shadow, and relative movement—and the binocular cues used in stereoscopic vision (cf. *stereoscopic vision*). (2) In audition, the corresponding cues governing perception of distance and direction, such as intensity and time differences of sound reaching the two ears (cf. *stereophonic hearing*).

distributed practice. An arrangement of learning trials in a task in which there is time intervening between trials, as opposed to immediately consecutive trials (syn. *spaced practice*; cf. *massed practice*).

DNA. Cf. *deoxyribonucleic acid*.

dominance. The higher status position when social rank is organized according to a dominance-submission hierarchy; commonly found in human societies and in certain subhuman animal groups.

dominant gene. A member of a gene pair, which, if present, determines that the individual will show the trait controlled by the gene, whether or not the other member of the pair is the same or different, that is, recessive (cf. *recessive gene*).

double blind. An experimental design, often used in drug research, in which neither the investigator nor the patients know which subjects are in the treatment and which in the nontreatment condition until the experiment has been completed.

drive. (1) An aroused condition of the organism based upon deprivation or noxious stimulation, including tissue needs, drug or hormonal conditions, and specified internal or external stimuli, as in pain (text usage). (2) Loosely, any motive (cf. *motive*).

drive-reduction principle. The principle that a motivated sequence of behavior can be best explained as moving from an aversive state of heightened tension (i.e., drive) to a goal state in which the drive is reduced. The goal of the sequence, in other words, is drive reduction.

dualism. The assumption that psychic (mental) and physical (body; brain) phenomena are both real but fundamentally different in nature.

duct gland. A gland, such as the tear gland or salivary gland, that secretes its product on the surface of the body or into the body cavities but not directly into the blood stream (cf. *endocrine gland*).

dynamometer. An instrument used in measuring strength of grip.

eardrum. The membrane at the inner end of the auditory canal, leading to the middle ear (cf. *middle ear*).

ectomorphic component. The third of the three components of physique in Sheldon's type theory. It comprises delicacy of skin, fine hair, and ultrasensitive nervous system (cf. *endomorphic component, mesomorphic component, type theory*).

educational psychologist. A psychologist whose research interest lies in the application of psychological principles to the education of children and adults in schools (cf. *school psychologist*).

EEG. Cf. *electroencephalogram*.

effector. A bodily organ activated by motor nerves; a muscle or gland (cf. *receptor*).

efferent nerve. A bundle of nerve fibers transmitting impulses from the central nervous system in the direction of the peripheral organs. Efferent nerve tracts commonly end in muscles or glands (usually synonymous with *motor nerve*; cf. *afferent nerve*).

ego. In Freud's tripartite division of the personality, that part corresponding most nearly to the perceived self, the controlling self which holds back the impulsiveness of the id in the effort to delay gratification until it can be found in socially approved ways (cf. *id, superego*).

ego involvement. Commitment to and absorption in a task so that success in it becomes important to self-esteem and failure leads to chagrin (cf. *level of aspiration*).

ego theory. The theory in psychoanalysis that stresses functions of the ego, as against almost exclusive preoccupation with libido (cf. *ego, libido theory*).

electroconvulsive shock therapy. A form of shock treatment for mental illness in which high-voltage current is passed briefly through the head, producing temporary unconsciousness and convulsions, with the intention of alleviating depression or other symptoms (cf. *shock therapy*).

electroencephalogram (EEG). A record obtained by attaching electrodes to the scalp (or occasionally to the exposed brain) and amplifying the spontaneous electrical activity of the brain. The EEG is useful in studying some forms of mental disturbance (e.g., epilepsy) and in research on brain function.

emergency reactions. The physiological accompaniments of intense emotional excitement interpreted (by Cannon and others) as a method of preparing the organism to meet emergencies.

emotional indicator. A sign or symptom of the activity going on in an emotional state. Physiological indicators that can be continuously recorded are commonly selected for experimental purposes.

emotional state. The condition of the organism during affectively toned experience, whether mild or intense (cf. *affective experience*).

endocrine gland. A ductless gland, or gland of internal secretion, that discharges its products directly into the blood stream. The hormones secreted by the endocrine glands are important chemical integrators of bodily activity (cf. *duct gland, hormones*).

endomorphic component. The first of three components of physique in Sheldon's type theory. It comprises prominence of intestines and other visceral organs, including a prominent abdomen, as in the obese individual (cf. *mesomorphic component, ectomorphic component, type theory*).

envy. The emotional and motivational consequence of rivalry with another person, based on some desired characteristic or possession of that person (cf. *jealousy*).

equilibratory senses. The senses which give discrimination of the position of the body in space and of the movement of the body as a whole (cf. *kinesthesis, semicircular canals, vestibular sacs*).

errors of measurement. That part of the variation in a distribution of scores, or in statistics derived from them, attributable to the fallibility of the measuring instrument, errors in observation, etc. (cf. *sampling errors*).

escape learning. A form of learning controlled by actual painful stimulation. Escape from the punishment brings an end to the unpleasant or painful situation and is therefore rewarding (cf. *avoidance learning*).

estrogen. The collective name for female sex hormones secreted within the ovary (syn. *ovarian hormones; cf. sex glands, androgen*).

estrus. The sexually receptive state in female mammals. It is a cyclical state, related to menstruation in the primates and man (syn. *heat; cf. menstruation*).

ethologist. One of a group of zoologists and naturalists particularly interested in kinds of behavior that are specific to a species. More of their work has been on insects, birds, and fishes than on mammals (cf. *instinct*).

evoked potential. An electrical discharge in some part of the nervous system produced by stimulation elsewhere. The measured potential is commonly based upon response averaging by a computer.

existentialism. A philosophical viewpoint emphasizing that man is not a ready-made machine, but rather that he has the freedom to make vital choices and to assume responsibility for his own existence. It emphasizes subjective experience as a sufficient criterion of truth.

expectation. An anticipation or prediction of future events based on past experience and present stimuli (cf. *sign learning*).

expectation-value theory. A theory of motivation and decision-making that accounts for choices on the basis of values (or utility) and the risks involved, e.g., the probability that such values will be attained.

experimental design. A plan for collecting and treating the data of a proposed experiment. The design is evolved after preliminary exploration, with the aims of economy, precision, and control, so that appropriate inferences and decisions can be made from the data.

experimental group. In an experimental design contrasting two groups, that group of subjects given the treatment whose effect is under investigation (cf. *control group*).

experimental psychologist. A psychologist whose research interest is in the laboratory study of general psychological principles as revealed in the behavior of lower organisms and man.

explicit movements. Movements easily observed and measured; overt movements (cf. *implicit movements*).

exploratory behavior. Behavior leading to inferences concerning the curiosity motive (cf. *investigatory response, locomotor response, orienting reflex*).

extinction. (1) The experimental procedure, following either classical or operant conditioning, of presenting the conditioned stimulus without the usual reinforcement. (2) The reduction in response that results from this procedure (cf. *reinforcement*).

extrasensory perception (ESP). A controversial category of experience consisting of perception not mediated by sense-organ stimulation (cf. *clairvoyance, precognition, telepathy, psychokinesis*).

extravert. One of the psychological types proposed by Jung. The extravert is more preoccupied with social life and the external world than with his inward experience (cf. *introvert, type theory*).

extrinsic motivation. The motivational control of behavior through the possibility of reward or punishment external to whatever satisfactions or annoyances reside in the behavior itself, e.g., working for a prize rather than the satisfactions in the task (cf. *intrinsic motivation*).

factor analysis. A statistical method used in test construction and in interpreting scores from batteries of tests. The method enables the investigator to compute the minimum number of determiners (factors) required to account for the intercorrelations among the scores on the tests making up the battery.

factors of advantage. The bases for favoring one stimulus pattern over another in attention. They include factors in the perceiving person (set, interest, habit) and factors in the stimuli (size, intensity, frequency, vividness) (cf. *attention, selectivity*).

faculty psychology. A pre-experimental psychology that viewed the mind as composed of a number of separate powers or faculties, including intellect, feeling, will, and many others (cf. *association psychology*).

family therapy. Psychotherapy with the family members as a group rather than treatment of the patient alone (cf. *group therapy*).

fantasy. Daydreaming, "wool gathering," imagination; sometimes a consequence of frustration. It is used as a personality indicator in projective tests (cf. *projective tests*).

feedback. The returning to a control center of the information regarding events under its control; in psychology, the sensory return from the periphery used in the control of movement and analogous processes (cf. *cybernetics*).

feeling tone. The pleasantness or unpleasantness of an affective experience (cf. *affective experience*).

field properties. In Gestalt psychology, the properties of organized wholes that influence the interpretation or action of the parts. The term derives by analogy to fields of force in physics (cf. *Gestalt psychology*).

field theory. That form of Gestalt psychology associated particularly with Kurt Lewin (cf. *Gestalt psychology*).

figure-ground perception. Perceiving a pattern as foreground against a background. Patterns are commonly perceived this way even when the stimuli are ambiguous and the foreground-background relationships are reversible.

fissure of Rolando. The central fissure of each cerebral hemisphere, lying between the frontal and parietal lobes (syn. *central fissure*).

fissure of Sylvius. A deep fissure at the side of each cerebral hemisphere, below which lies the temporal lobe.

fixation. In psychoanalysis, arrested development through failure to pass beyond one of the earlier stages or to change the objects of attachment (e.g., fixated at the oral stage, or fixated upon the mother).

fixed-alternative question. A question asked on a test, an examination, or a survey, requiring the answer to be selected from alternatives provided by the questioner (syn. *multiple-choice question; cf. free-answer question*).

flow chart. A diagrammatic representation of the sequence of choices and actions in an activity.

forebrain. The portion of the brain evolved from the foremost of the three enlargements of the neural tube, consisting of the cerebrum, thalamus, hypothalamus, and related structures (cf. *hindbrain, midbrain*).

formal discipline. An older interpretation of transfer of training, justifying the study of a subject not for its own sake but for the training it supposedly gives the mental faculties, e.g., studying Latin not to learn Latin but to improve judgment and reasoning (cf. *faculty psychology, transfer of training*).

fovea. In the eye, a small area in the central part of the retina, packed with cones; in daylight, the most sensitive part of the retina for detail vision and color vision (cf. *retina, cone*).

fraternal twins. Twins developed from separate eggs. They are no more alike genetically than ordinary brothers and sisters and can be of the same or different sexes (cf. *identical twins*).

free-answer question. A question asked on an examination or in a survey, requiring a reply in the form of a comment, sentence, or longer discourse (syn. *open question; cf. fixed-alternative question*).

free association. (1) The form of word-association experiment in which the subject gives any word he thinks of in response to the stimulus word (cf. *controlled association*). (2) In psychoanalysis, the effort to report without modification everything that comes into awareness.

frequency distribution. A set of scores assembled according to size and grouped into class intervals (cf. *class interval, normal distribution*).

frequency theory. A theory of hearing that assumes that neural impulses arising in the organ of Corti are activated by the basilar membrane of the ear in accordance with the frequency of its vibration rather than with the place of movement (cf. *place theory, traveling wave theory, volley theory*).

frontal lobe. A portion of each cerebral hemisphere, in front of the central fissure (cf. *occipital lobe, parietal lobe, temporal lobe*).

frustration. (1) As an event, the thwarting circumstances that block or interfere with goal-directed activity. (This is the usage in the text.) (2) As a state, the annoyance, confusion, or anger engendered by being thwarted, disappointed, defeated.

functional autonomy. The theory that motives may become independent of their origins, e.g., the miser may come to value money for its own sake rather than for the motive-satisfying things that originally gave it reinforcing value.

functional fixedness. The entrenchment of meaning which comes about through using a tool or object in a familiar way, so that the user finds it difficult to employ that tool or object in novel ways.

functional psychosis. A psychotic disorder of psychogenic origin without clearly defined structural change (cf. *organic psychosis*).

functionalism. Cf. *stimulus-response psychology*.

galvanic skin response (GSR). Changes in electrical conductivity of, or activity in, the skin, detected by a sensitive galvanometer. The reactions are commonly used as an emotional indicator (cf. *emotional indicator*).

ganglion (pl. ganglia). A collection of nerve cell bodies and synapses, constituting a center lying outside the brain and spinal cord, as in the sympathetic ganglia (cf. *center*).

gastrointestinal motility. Movements of parts of the digestive tract caused by contraction of smooth muscle; one form of emotional indicator (cf. *emotional indicator*).

gene. The unit of hereditary transmission, localized within the chromosomes. Each chromosome contains many genes. Genes are typically in pairs, one member of the pair being found in the chromosome from the father, the other in the corresponding chromosome from the mother (cf. *chromosome, dominant gene, recessive gene*).

general adaptation syndrome. Selye's term for the typical sequence of events when the body is subjected to severe stress, moving from the alarm reaction through resistance, to exhaustion.

generalization. (1) In concept formation, problem-solving, and transfer of training, the detection by the learner of a characteristic or principle common to a class of objects, events, or problems. (2) In conditioning, the principle that once a conditioned response has been established to a given stimulus, other similar stimuli will also evoke that response (cf. *gradient of generalization, discrimination*).

general aptitude. The aptitude for acquiring proficiency in many activities rather than in a special set of activities. An intelligence test is designed to measure general aptitude; a typing test is designed to measure special aptitude (cf. *special aptitude*).

general factor. (1) A general ability underlying test scores, especially in tests of intelligence, as distinct from special abilities unique to each test (Spearman). (2) A general ability with which each of the primary factors correlates (Thurstone) (cf. *factor analysis*).

genetics. That branch of biology concerned with heredity and the means by which hereditary characteristics are transmitted (cf. *population genetics*).

genital stage. In classical psychoanalysis, the final stage of psychosexual development, culminating in sexual union with a member of the opposite sex (cf. *psychosexual development*).

genotype. In genetics, the characteristics that an individual has inherited and will transmit to his descendants, whether or not he manifests these characteristics (cf. *phenotype*).

Gestalt psychology. A system of psychological theory emphasizing pattern, organization, wholes, and field properties. It permits a form of introspection known as phenomenology (cf. *behaviorism, field properties, phenomenology*).

glia cells. Supporting cells (not neurons) composing a substantial portion of brain tissue; recent speculation suggests that they may play a role in the storage of memory.

goal. (1) An end state or condition toward which the motivated behavior sequence is directed and by which the sequence is completed. (2) Loosely, the incentive (cf. *incentive*).

goal activity. The activity in the presence of the incentive that reduces the drive or in other ways completes the motivated sequence of behavior (syn. *consummatory behavior;* cf. *preparatory activity*).

gradient. (1) Any regular change correlated with a change in some dimension such as distance; often plotted as a curve (cf. *gradient of texture*). (2) A change in the tendency to respond in relation to a systematic change in distance, time interval, or other dimension of stimulation (cf. *gradient of approach, gradient of avoidance, gradient of generalization*).

gradient of approach. The increase in the strength of the tendency to move toward a positive incentive the nearer the subject is to the incentive (cf. *gradient of avoidance*).

gradient of avoidance. The increase in the strength of the tendency to withdraw from a negative incentive the nearer the subject is to the incentive (cf. *gradient of approach*).

gradient of generalization. The orderly decrease in strength of the generalized conditioned response with decreasing similarity of the stimuli used in testing to the original stimulus used in conditioning; often plotted as a curve (cf. *gradient, generalization*).

gradient of texture. If a surface is perceived visually as having substantial texture (hard, soft, smooth, rough, etc.) and if the texture has a noticeable grain, it becomes finer as the surface recedes from the viewing person, producing a gradient of texture which is important in judgments of slant and of distance (cf. *distance cues*).

graphic rating scale. One of several kinds of scales used when one person rates another. The rater records his judgment by placing a mark at some point along a printed line, one end of which indicates the lowest degree of the trait, and the other, the highest degree (cf. *rating scale*).

group test. A test administered to several people at once by a single tester. A college examination is usually a group test (cf. *individual test*).

group therapy. A group discussion or other group activity with a therapeutic purpose participated in by more than one client or patient at a time (cf. *psychotherapy*).

GSR. Cf. *galvanic skin response.*

habit. A learned stimulus-response sequence (cf. *conditioned response, sensorimotor task*).

hallucination. A sense experience in the absence of appropriate external stimuli; a misinterpretation of imaginary experiences as actual perceptions (cf. *illusion, schizophrenic reaction*).

halo effect. The tendency to rate an individual improperly as high or low on a wide range of traits because we have prior information that he is high or low on one or a few of these traits.

hedonism. The theory that man seeks pleasure and avoids pain; an extreme form of the theory (in philosophy) is that pleasure or happiness is the highest good.

heterosexuality. Interest in or attachment to a member of the opposite sex; the normal adult outcome of psychosexual development.

heuristic method. A nonrigorous method for discovering the correct solution to a problem through obtaining approximations to the correct answer, through using analogies and other methods of search, without the painstaking exploration of all possibilities. Computing machines can be programed to use such methods (cf. *algorithm*).

hindbrain. The portion of the brain evolved from the final one of the three enlargements of the primitive neural tube, consisting of the cerebellum, the medulla, and related structures (cf. *forebrain, midbrain*).

homeostasis. An optimal level of organic function, maintained by regulatory mechanisms known as homeostatic mechanisms, e.g., the mechanisms maintaining a uniform body temperature (cf. *homeostat*).

homeostat. A particular portion of the brain that regulates the equilibrium point of some bodily system, similar to the regulation of temperature by a thermostat (cf. *homeostasis*).

homosexuality. (1) In psychoanalytic theory, a normal stage of psychosexual development, in which attachment is to members of one's own sex. (2) The adoption in adult life of the cultural role appropriate to a member of the opposite sex. (3) Engaging in sexual relations with a member of the same sex.

hormones. The internal secretions of the endocrine glands which are distributed via the blood stream and affect behavior (cf. *chemical integration, endocrine gland*).

hue. The dimension of color from which the major color names are derived (red, yellow, green, etc.), corresponding to wave length of light (cf. *brightness, saturation*).

human factors research. An applied science participated in jointly by engineers and psychologists, concerned with the design of equipment and the arrangement of work conditions to provide the most effective combination of man and machine (syn. *applied experimental psychology, biomechanics, human engineering*).

hunger drive. A drive based on food deprivation (cf. *drive, hunger pangs, specific hunger*).

hunger pangs. The twinges of pain experienced during stomach contractions.

hypnotic trance. The dreamlike state of heightened suggestibility induced in a subject by a hypnotist (cf. *post-hypnotic suggestion*).

hypnotism. The process of inducing the hypnotic trance (syn. *hypnosis*).

hypothalamus. One of the structures at the base of the brain, portions of which are significant in sleep and in emotional and motivational behavior.

hypothetical construct. One form of inferred intermediate mechanism. The construct is conceived of as having properties of its own, other than those specifically required for the explanation, e.g., the memory trace, which is inferred to explain the retention curve, is assumed to have electrochemical properties, localization in the nervous system, etc. (cf. *intervening variable*).

id. In Freud's tripartite division of the personality, that part reflecting unorganized, instinctual impulses. If unbridled, it seeks immediate gratification of primitive needs (cf. *ego, superego*).

identical components theory. A theory of transfer of training which proposes that a new task is learned more easily the more it consists of the same components as tasks already mastered (E. L. Thorndike) (cf. *transfer of training*).

identical twins. Twins developed from a single egg. They are always of the same sex and commonly very much alike in appearance, although some characteristics may be in mirror-image, e.g., one right-handed, the other left-handed (syn. *uniovular twins;* cf. *fraternal twins*).

identification. (1) The normal process of acquiring appropriate social roles in childhood through copying, in part unconsciously, the behavior of significant adults, e.g., the child's identification with his like-sexed parent. (2) A defense mechanism by which an individual enhances self-esteem through behaving, in fantasy or in actual conduct, as if he were another person—the one with whom he identifies himself (cf. *imitation*). (3) Close affiliation with others of like interest, e.g., identifying with a group.

identification figures. Adult models copied, partly unconsciously, by the child, especially the child's parents (cf. *identification*).

identity formation. The process of achieving adult personality integration, as an outgrowth of earlier identifications and other influences (cf. *identification, role diffusion*).

idiot savant. A mentally subnormal individual (of any grade, but usually not classifiable as an idiot) who has unusual ability in one or more specialized activities.

illumination. The third of the four stages in creative thought proposed by Wallas, in which the solution suddenly appears or previously disconnected aspects suddenly are seen in relationship (cf. *preparation, incubation, verification*).

illusion. In perception, a misinterpretation of the relationships among presented stimuli, so that what is perceived does not correspond to physical reality; especially, but not exclusively, an optical or visual illusion (cf. *delusion, hallucination*).

imitation. Behavior that is modeled upon or copies that of another (cf. *identification*).

immediate memory span. The number of items (digits, letters, words, etc.) that can be repeated after a single presentation.

implicit movements. Movements that can be detected only with sensitive measuring instruments; covert movements (cf. *explicit movements*).

imprinting. A term used by ethologists for a species-specific type of learning that occurs within a limited period of time early in the life of the organism and is relatively unmodifiable thereafter; e.g., young ducklings learn to follow one adult female (usually the mother) within 11 to 18 hours after birth. But whatever object they are given to follow at this time they will thereafter continue to follow (cf. *ethologist*).

incentive. (1) A tangible goal object which provides the stimuli that lead to goal activity. (2) Loosely, any goal (cf. *goal*).

incubation. The second of the four stages in creative thought proposed by Wallas, during which, by a process not fully understood, the preparation leads to the emergence of creative thought (cf. *preparation, illumination, verification*).

independent variable. The variable under experimental control with which the changes studied in the experiment are correlated. In psychological experiments, the independent variable is often a stimulus, responses to which are the dependent variables under investigation (cf. *dependent variable*).

individual differences. Relatively persistent unlikenesses in structure or behavior between persons or members of the same species.

individual test. A test designed to be administered to one person at a time. Binet intelligence tests are individual tests (cf. *group test*).

infancy. The period of helplessness and dependency in man or other organisms; in man, roughly the first two years (cf. *childhood, adolescence*).

infant debility. A condition of retarded development found among some institutionalized infants, attributed to the lack of affectionate care.

information-processing model. A model based on assumptions regarding the flow of information through a system; usually best realized by a computer program.

in-group. A group to which a person belongs and with which he identifies himself (cf. *out-group*).

inner ear. The internal portion of the ear containing, in addition to the cochlea, the vestibular sacs and the semicircular canals (cf. *cochlea, semicircular canals, vestibular sacs*).

insight. (1) In problem-solving experiments, the perception of relationships leading to solution. Such a solution can be repeated promptly when the problem is again confronted. (2) In psychotherapy, the discovery by the subject of dynamic connections between earlier and later events, so that he comes to recognize the roots of his conflicts.

instinct. The name given to unlearned, patterned, goal-directed behavior, which is species-specific, as illustrated by nest-building in birds or by the migration of salmon.

insulin. The hormone secreted by the pancreas (cf. *hormones, insulin shock*).

insulin shock. A state of coma resulting from reduced blood sugar when insulin is present in excessive amounts. Insulin shock is used as one form of shock therapy in treating mental illness (cf. *shock therapy*).

integration. The organization of parts into a harmoniously operating whole, as in the expression "integrated personality" (cf. *chemical integration, mechanical integration, neural integration*).

intelligence. (1) That which a properly standardized intelligence test measures. (2) According to Binet, the characteristics of an individual's thought processes that enable him to take and maintain a direction without becoming distracted, to adapt means to ends, and to criticize his own attempts at problem solution (cf. *mental age*).

intelligence quotient (I.Q.). A scale unit used in reporting intelligence test scores, based on the ratio between mental age and chronological age. The decimal point is omitted, so that the average I.Q. for children of any one chronological age is set at 100 (cf. *chronological age, mental age, deviation I.Q.*).

intensity. One of the dimensions of sensory experience; a quantitative measure of strength or degree, e.g., a bright light has a high intensity, a soft tone a low intensity. A change in intensity is distinguished from a change in quality, which is a change in kind (cf. *dimension, quality, quantity*).

interactive explanation. An explanation of behavior that deals with the arousal and control of behavior in the present, according to stimuli that are currently responded to, motives that are active, and possibilities of response that are open; nonhistorical explanation (cf. *developmental explanation*).

interest. A persisting tendency to pay attention to and to enjoy some activity or content, especially a vocational interest.

intermittent reinforcement. Cf. *partial reinforcement.*

interpretation. In psychoanalysis, the analyst's calling attention to the patient's resistances in order to facilitate the flow of associations; also his explanation of symbols, as in dream interpretation (cf. *resistance*).

interpretive therapy. A form of psychotherapy, used with children as well as with adults, in which the therapist helps the subject to put his conflicts into words, to understand their symbolic meanings, and through this process to solve his problems (cf. *psychotherapy*).

intervening variable. A process inferred to occur between stimulus and response, thus accounting for one response rather than another to the same stimulus. The intervening variable may be inferred without further specification, or it may be given concrete properties and become an object of investigation.

interview. A conversation between an investigator (the interviewer) and a subject (the respondent) used for gathering pertinent data either for the subject's benefit (as in the psychotherapeutic interview) or for information-gathering (as in a sample survey).

intracerebral processes. Inferred processes in the brain used to account for response classes including perceptions, images, and thoughts that are incompletely specified in terms of movement (cf. *intervening variable*).

intrinsic cortex. Term used by Pribram for the so-called association areas, on the assumption that they have integrative functions in handling complex activities but that this handling does not necessarily involve learned associative links (cf. *association areas*).

intrinsic motivation. Motivation in which the action and the ends served by the action are organically or inherently related, as distinct from action motivated by promise of reward or threat of punishment, e.g., assembling a model airplane in order to fly it, composing a sonnet to give expression to a mood (cf. *extrinsic motivation*).

introspection. (1) A specified form of introspection (trained introspection) describing mental content only, without the intrusion of meanings or interpretations. (2) Any form of reporting on subjective (conscious) events or experiences (cf. *phenomenology*).

introvert. One of the psychological types proposed by Jung, referring to the individual who, especially in time of emotional stress, tends to withdraw into himself and to avoid other people (cf. *extravert, type theory*).

investigatory response. The form of exploratory behavior which involves the manipulation of an unfamiliar object, picking it up, tearing it apart, etc. (Berlyne) (cf. *exploratory behavior, locomotor exploration*).

item. Any single unit of test or experimental materials, e.g., a single question in a test composed of many questions or a single nonsense syllable in a list of syllables to be memorized (cf. *test, test battery*).

James-Lange theory. A classical theory of emotion, named for the two men who independently proposed it. The theory states that the stimulus first leads to motor responses, and then the awareness of these responses constitutes the experience of emotion.

J-curve. A distribution curve of the behavior of individuals, in the form of an inverted J. It appears when social controls are placed upon behavior, e.g., at an intersection when traffic is regulated by a stop sign.

jealousy. A special form of anxiety arising from fear of loss of a loved one's affection to a rival, with both emotional and motivational consequences (cf. *envy*).

just-noticeable difference (j.n.d.). A barely perceptible physical change in a stimulus; a measure of the difference threshold. The term is used also as a unit

for scaling the steps of sensation corresponding to increase in the magnitude of stimulation (cf. *difference threshold*).

kinesthesis. The muscle, tendon, and joint senses, yielding discrimination of position and movement of parts of the body (cf. *equilibratory senses*).

latency. (1) A measure of response, referring to the delay between the occurrence of the stimulus and the onset of the response. (2) In psychoanalysis, a period in middle childhood, roughly the years from six to twelve, when both sexual and aggressive impulses are said to be in a somewhat subdued state, so that the child's attention is directed outward, and his curiosity about the environment makes him ready to learn (cf. *psychosexual development*).

latent content. The underlying significance of a dream, e.g., the motives or wishes being expressed by it, as interpreted from the manifest content (cf. *interpretation, manifest content*).

latent learning experiment. A type of experiment in which opportunity for learning spatial relationships is given under conditions of inappropriate drive or absent incentive; e.g., a rat is permitted to explore a maze without food in the goal box. The learning is later tested under changed drive-incentive conditions. The experiment, when successful, is used to support the sign learning theory (cf. *sign learning*).

law of effect. Thorndike's principle that the consequences of an activity determine whether or not it will be learned. In its later forms stress was placed on the influence of reward. Hence learning under the law of effect is virtually synonymous with operant conditioning (q.v.).

learning. A relatively permanent change in behavior that occurs as the result of practice. Behavior changes due to maturation or temporary conditions of the organism (e.g., fatigue, the influence of drugs, adaptation) are not included.

learning curve. A graph plotting the course of learning, in which the vertical axis (ordinate) plots a measure of proficiency (amount per unit time, time per unit amount, errors made, etc.), while the horizontal axis (abscissa) represents some measure of practice (trials, time, etc.).

learning set. A case in which an animal's rate of learning gradually improves over a series of problems of the same general type; in essence, the phenomenon of learning-to-learn.

level of aspiration. A goal that the individual sets as something he expects to achieve or strives to achieve. Reaching the goal is interpreted by him as success, falling short as failure (cf. *achievement motive*).

libido theory. The theory within psychoanalysis that human development and motivation are best understood by studying the manifestations of the libido—the energy of the sexual instinct—which throughout life becomes attached to new objects and expressed through various types of motivated behavior (cf. *ego theory, neo-Freudian theory*).

lie detector. An apparatus using one or more of the emotional indicators in order to determine guilt of a subject through his emotional responses while answering questions in a false or unintentionally revealing manner (cf. *emotional indicator*).

light adaptation. The decreased sensitivity of the eye to light when the subject has been continuously exposed to high levels of illumination (cf. *dark adaptation*).

limbic system. A set of structures in and around the midbrain, forming a functional unit regulating motivational-emotional types of behavior, such as waking and sleeping, excitement and quiescence, feeding, and mating.

linear operator. Cf. *difference equation*.

linguistics. The investigation of problems of language; linguistics has been a branch of social anthropology, but psychologists have been participating increasingly in studies of language (syn. *psycholinguistics*).

localized functions. Behavior controlled by known areas of the brain; e.g., vision is localized in the occipital lobes (cf. *projection area*).

location constancy. The tendency to perceive the place at which a resting object is located as remaining the same even though the relationship to the observer has changed (cf. *object constancy*).

locomotor exploration. That form of exploratory behavior which consists in running about, inspecting the environment (Berlyne) (cf. *exploratory behavior, investigatory response*).

loudness. An intensity dimension of hearing correlated with the amplitude of the sound waves that constitute the stimulus. Greater amplitudes yield greater loudnesses (cf. *pitch, timbre*).

LSD-25. Cf. *lysergic acid derivatives*.

lysergic acid derivatives. Chemical substances derived from lysergic acid, the most important of which is LSD-25. When taken by a normal person, it produces symptoms similar in some respects to those of the schizophrenic reaction (cf. *schizophrenic reaction*).

manic-depressive reaction. A psychotic reaction characterized by mood swings from the normal in the direction either of excitement and elation (manic phase) or of fatigue, despondency, and sadness (depressive phase). Many patients do not show the whole cycle.

manifest content. The remembered content of a dream, the characters and their actions, as distinguished from the inferred latent content (cf. *latent content*).

masochism. A pathological desire to inflict pain upon oneself or to suffer pain at the hands of others (cf. *sadism*).

mass media. The instruments of communication which reach large numbers of people simultaneously, including the press, radio, television, and motion pictures.

massed practice. Practice in which trials are continuous or closely spaced (cf. *distributed practice*).

maternal drive. The drive, particularly in subhuman animals, induced in the female through bearing and nursing young, leading to nest-building, retrieving, and other forms of care (cf. *drive*).

mathematical model. A model formulated in mathematical terms (cf. *model*).

maturation. Growth processes in the individual that result in orderly changes in behavior, whose timing and patterning are relatively independent of exercise or experience though they may require a normal environment (cf. *training*).

maze. A device commonly used in the study of animal and human learning, consisting of a correct path and blind alleys.

mean. The arithmetical average; the sum of all scores divided by their number (cf. *average*).

mean deviation. The average amount by which each score departs from the mean of all the scores (cf. *measure of variation*).

measure of central tendency. Cf. *average*.

measure of response. A quantitative index of response strength, such as amplitude, latency, probability, and rate of response.

measure of variation. A measure of the dispersion or spread of scores in a frequency distribution, e.g., the range, the mean deviation, the standard deviation (q.v.).

mechanical integration. Bodily organization for harmonious action through the mechanical arrangements of bones, joints, and muscles (cf. *chemical integration, neural integration*).

median. The score of the middle case when cases are arranged in order of size of score (cf. *average*).

membership group. A social group to which an individual belongs (cf. *reference group*).

memory drum. A mechanical device used to present verbal materials in rote-learning experiments.

memory trace. The inferred change in the nervous system which persists between the time that something is learned and the time that it is recalled.

menarche. The first menstrual period, indicative of sexual maturation in a girl (cf. *menstruation*).

menstruation. The approximately monthly discharge from the uterus (cf. *menarche*).

mental age (M.A.). A scale unit proposed by Binet for use in intelligence testing. If an intelligence test is properly standardized, a representative group of children of age six should earn an average mental age of six, those of age seven a mental age of seven, etc. A child whose M.A. is above his chronological age (C.A.) is advanced; one whose M.A. lags behind is retarded (cf. *chronological age, intelligence quotient*).

mental health. Absence of mental illness; more positively, a state characterized by adjustment, a productive orientation, and zest (cf. *mental illness*).

mental illness. Emotional, motivational, and social maladjustment severe enough to interfere with the ordinary conduct of life (cf. *mental health, neurotic reaction, psychotic disorder*).

mentally defective. A descriptive term applied to a mentally subnormal individual whose deficiency is based on some sort of brain damage or organic defect (cf. *mentally retarded*).

mentally gifted. An individual with an unusually high level of intelligence, commonly an I.Q. of 140 or above.

mentally retarded. A mentally subnormal individual whose problems lie in a learning disability with no evident organic damage (cf. *mentally defective*).

mentally subnormal. An individual whose intelligence is below that necessary for adjustment to ordinary schooling; the more intelligent among the subnormal are classified as *educable* in special classes, the next level as *trainable*, while the lowest group classifies as more severely retarded (syn., but now obsolete, *feeble-minded*; cf. *mentally defective, mentally retarded*).

mesomorphic component. The second of three components of physique in Sheldon's type theory. Refers to the prominence of bone and muscle, as in the typical athlete (cf. *endomorphic component, ectomorphic component, type theory*).

method of approximations. A variation of operant conditioning in which the desired performance is encouraged by reinforcing "approach" responses, i.e., responses approximating the correct performance (cf. *operant conditioning, shaping of behavior*).

midbrain. The second of the three enlargements of the neural tube, upon which later structures of the brain have evolved. The midbrain in the fish consists chiefly of the optic lobes ("eye brain"); in man this portion has not been greatly increased in relative size, the most pronounced evolutionary changes having taken place in the forebrain (cf. *forebrain, hindbrain*).

middle ear. The portion of the ear containing the hammer, anvil, and stirrup bones, which connect the eardrum to the oval window of the inner ear.

miniature system. A set of interconnected laws and principles designed to account for a limited sphere of psychological activities, e.g., a theory of rote learning, a theory of hearing.

mirror drawing. A laboratory learning task in which the skill under study is that of tracing the contour of a star or other figure while viewing it in a mirror.

modality. A separate sense or sensory department, e.g., vision, audition. Experiences within a single modality can be arranged along continuous dimensions, with intermediate values. There is no simple way of moving across from one modality to another, e.g., to find the experience lying midway between a given odor and a given color.

mode. The most frequent score in a distribution, or the class interval in which the greatest number of cases fall (cf. *average*).

model. Miniature systems are often constructed according to a logical, mathematical, or physical model. That is, the principles according to which data are organized and made understandable parallel those of the model; e.g., the piano keyboard is a model for understanding the basilar membrane; the speed-regulating governor is a model for the feedback principle of cybernetics (cf. *miniature system*).

monochromatism. Total color blindness, the visual system being achromatic. A rare disorder (cf. *dichromatism*).

monocular cues. Cf. *distance cues*.

mood. A state of emotional susceptibility, enduring for some minutes or hours, in which most of the person's emotional responses tend to be similar, e.g., cheerful mood, morose mood (cf. *temperament*).

motivated forgetting. The theory that forgetting can be explained according to the motives of the learner (cf. *repression*).

motivation. A general term referring to the regulation of need-satisfying and goal-seeking behavior (cf. *motive*).

motivational disposition. A persistent tendency to the arousal of a specific motive; the tendency exists even though the motive is not being expressed. Most classifications of motives refer to motivational dispositions (cf. *aroused motive*).

motivational sequence. A sequence of behavior which begins with a motive, continues in preparatory or goal-directed activity, and ends in goal activity in the presence of an incentive.

motive. Any condition of the organism that affects its readiness to start upon or continue in a sequence of behavior (cf. *motivational sequence, physiological motive, social motive*).

motor area. A projection area in the brain lying in front of the fissure of Rolando. Electrical stimulation commonly results in motor responses (cf. *body-sense area*).

multimodal distribution. A distribution curve with more than one mode (cf. *mode*).

multiple personality. An extreme form of dissociation in which the individual's personality is split into separate personalities often alternating with each other. The memories of one of the split-off personalities commonly are not accessible to the other (cf. *dissociation*).

multiple-response learning. The acquiring of patterns or sequences of responses in mastering a task, e.g., in learning a skill or memorizing a poem (cf. *sensorimotor task, rote memorization*).

muscle. The effectors through which motion is produced. Muscles are of three types: smooth muscle, striate muscle, and cardiac muscle (q.v.).

muscle tone. A state of slight contraction that keeps muscle in a readiness to respond. A tense person may have an exaggeration of muscle tone (syn. *muscle tonus*).

myelin. The fatty sheath surrounding certain nerve fibers known as myelinated fibers. Impulses travel faster and with less energy expenditure in myelinated than in unmyelinated fibers.

narcissism. Self-love; in psychoanalytic theory, the normal expression of pregenital development (cf. *pregenital stages*).

naturalistic observation. Observation of events as they occur in nature, without experimental control of behavior, e.g., studying the nest building of birds or observing the sleeping postures of a newborn human infant.

nature-nurture issue. The problem of determining the relative importance of the hereditary component (nature) and the result of up-bringing in the particular environment (nurture) upon mature ability; such a determination is especially important in relation to intelligence.

need. A physical state involving any lack or deficit within the organism (cf. *motive, drive*).

negative incentive. An object or circumstance away from which behavior is directed when the object or circumstance is perceived or anticipated (cf. *positive incentive*).

negativism. A type of defiant behavior in which there is active refusal to carry out requests. Common in early childhood but met occasionally at all ages (syn. *negativistic behavior*).

neo-Freudian theory. The views of psychoanalytic theorists and practitioners which, while related to those of Freud, have departed from his in important ways. Most neo-Freudians in interpreting personality development give more weight than Freud did to the influence of the specific culture as contrasted with inherited instinctual tendencies (e.g., libido). Some prominent neo-Freudians are Fromm, Horney, Kardiner, and Sullivan (cf. *libido theory*).

nerve cell. Cf. *neuron*.

nerve net. A nervous system characteristic of lower organisms, in which impulses are transmitted in all directions from the point of stimulation (cf. *synaptic nervous system*).

neural integration. Bodily organization for harmonious or unified action through the brain and nervous system (cf. *chemical integration, mechanical integration*).

neural quantum theory. A theory of psychophysical phenomena that views the sensory system as a discrete, step-wise process (cf. *signal detectability theory*).

neuron. The nerve cell; the unit of a synaptic nervous system. Man's brain contains billions of neurons (cf. *polarized synaptic transmission*).

neurosis. Cf. *neurotic reaction*.

neurotic reaction. A form of maladjustment in which the individual is unable to cope with his anxieties and conflicts and develops abnormal symptoms. The disturbance is not so severe as to produce a profound personality derangement, as with the psychotic reactions (syn. *psychoneurosis, neurosis*; cf. *anxiety reaction, conversion reaction, phobic reaction, obsessive-compulsive reaction*).

nonliterate society. A society or culture without written records, formerly called a primitive society (cf. *anthropology*).

nonparametric statistics. Statistics computed without the assumption of an underlying distribution of known form. The formulas of nonparametric statistics commonly make use of ranked data, as in rank-difference correlation (syn. *distribution-free statistics*).

nonsense syllable. An item used in rote memorization experiments, usually consisting of two consonants with a vowel between, e.g., PUV, GEB. The combination of letters must not form a word in familiar languages.

noradrenalin. One of the hormones secreted by the adrenal medulla, whose action is in some, but not all, respects similar to adrenalin (syn. *norepinephrine;* cf. *adrenalin*).

norm. An average, common, or standard performance under specified conditions, e.g., the average achievement test score of nine-year-old children or the average birth weight of male children (cf. *test standardization*).

normal curve. The plotted form of the normal distribution (q.v.).

normal distribution. The standard symmetrical bell-shaped frequency distribution, whose properties are commonly used in making statistical inferences from measures derived from samples (cf. *normal curve*).

null hypothesis. A statistical hypothesis that any difference observed among treatment conditions occurs by chance and does not reflect a true difference. Rejection of the null hypothesis means that we believe the treatment conditions are actually having an effect.

nystagmus. Involuntary eye movements characterized by slow and quick phases in opposite directions; one of the consequences of bodily rotation.

object achievement. Perceiving an object as enduring and permanent, e.g., when the subject recognizes the object he now sees as the same object he saw before (cf. *object constancy*).

object constancy. The tendency to see objects as relatively unchanged under widely altered conditions of illumination, distance, and position (cf. *color constancy, location constancy, shape constancy, size constancy*).

object size. The size of an object as determined from measurement at its surface. When size constancy holds, the observer perceives a distant object as near its object size (cf. *perspective size, size constancy*).

objective science. A science whose data are open to observation by any competent observer, as in the physical and biological sciences. Behaviorism sought to eliminate subjectivity from psychology, hence to make it an objective science (cf. *subjective science*).

objective scoring. Scoring done according to a code so that all competent scorers arrive at the same score for the same test, e.g., the scoring of fixed-alternative (multiple-choice) questions (cf. *subjective scoring*).

obsessive-compulsive reaction. A neurotic reaction taking one of three forms: (1) recurrent thoughts, often disturbing and unwelcome (obsessions); (2) irresistible urges to repeat stereotyped or ritualistic acts (compulsions); (3) both of these in combination (cf. *neurotic reaction*).

occipital lobe. A portion of the cerebral hemisphere, behind the parietal and temporal lobes (cf. *frontal lobe, parietal lobe, temporal lobe*).

occupational therapy. A form of help to a patient suffering from personality maladjustment or mental illness, whereby he is kept busy in constructive work.

Oedipal stage. In psychoanalysis, an alternative designation of the phallic stage of psychosexual development, because it is at this stage that the Oedipus complex arises (cf. *psychosexual development, Oedipus complex*).

Oedipus complex. In psychoanalytic theory, sexual attachment to the parent of the opposite sex, originating as the normal culmination of the infantile period of development.

operant behavior. Behavior defined by the stimulus to which it leads rather than by the stimulus that elicits it, such as behavior leading to reward (syn. *emitted behavior, instrumental behavior;* cf. *respondent behavior, voluntary action*).

operant conditioning. The strengthening of an operant response by presenting a reinforcing stimulus if, and only if, the response occurs (syn. *instrumental conditioning, reward learning;* cf. *classical conditioning*).

opinion. A judgment or belief involving an expectation or prediction about behavior or events (cf. *attitude*).

oral behavior. Behavior deriving from the infant's need to suck or, more generally, to be fed through the mouth.

oral stage. In psychoanalysis, the first of the stages of psychosexual development, in which pleasure is derived from the lips and mouth, as in sucking at the mother's breast (cf. *psychosexual development*).

organ of Corti. In the ear, the actual receptor for hearing, lying on the basilar membrane in the cochlea and containing the hair cells where the fibers of the auditory nerve originate (cf. *basilar membrane, cochlea*).

organic motive. Cf. *physiological motive.*

organic psychosis. A psychotic disorder caused by disease, injury, drugs, or other definable structural change (cf. *functional psychosis, psychotic disorder*).

organism. In biology, any form of plant or animal life. In psychology, the word is used to refer to the living individual animal, whether human or subhuman.

orienting reflex. (1) A nonspecific response to change in stimulation involving depression of cortical alpha rhythm, galvanic skin response, pupillary dilation, and complex vasomotor responses (a term introduced by Russian psychologists). (2) Head or body movements which orient the organism's receptors to those parts of the environment in which stimulus changes are occurring.

otoliths. "Ear stones" (cf. *vestibular sacs*).

out-group. Persons outside the in-group, especially if they belong to a group with which the in-group is in conflict (cf. *in-group*).

ovarian hormones. Cf. *estrogen.*

overcompensation. A form of compensation in which extreme effort is made to overcome feelings of weakness or inferiority by excelling where one is weakest. Thus a sickly youngster may try to become an athlete or a professional dancer (cf. *compensation*).

overlearning. Any learning beyond bare mastery.

overtone. A higher frequency tone, a multiple of the fundamental frequency, which occurs when a tone is sounded by a musical instrument (cf. *timbre*).

pacing. The principle that tasks to be learned can be presented to the learner in an order of difficulty corresponding to his natural developmental rate (cf. *maturation, readiness to learn*).

pain drive. The drive aroused by noxious stimulation, revealed by agitated behavior or behavior directed toward removing or escaping from the painful stimulus (cf. *drive*).

paired-associate learning. The learning of stimulus-response pairs, as in the acquisition of a foreign language vocabulary. When the first member of a pair (the stimulus) is presented, the subject's task is to give the second member (the response).

pancreas. A bodily organ situated near the stomach. As a duct gland it secretes pancreatic juice into the intestines, but some specialized cells function as an endocrine gland, secreting the hormone insulin into the blood stream (cf. *endocrine gland*).

parameter. Any of the constants in a function that defines the form of the curve. It ordinarily differs when experimental conditions or subjects are changed.

paranoid schizophrenia. A schizophrenic reaction in which the patient has delusions of persecution (cf. *schizophrenic reaction*).

parasympathetic division. A division of the autonomic nervous system, nerve fibers of which originate in the cranial and sacral portions of the spinal cord. Active in relaxed or quiescent states of the body, and to some extent antagonistic to the sympathetic division (q.v.).

parathyroid glands. Endocrine glands adjacent to the thyroid gland in the neck, whose hormones regulate calcium metabolism, thus maintaining the normal excitability of the nervous system. Parathyroid inadequacy leads to tetany (cf. *endocrine gland, tetany*).

parietal lobe. A portion of the cerebral hemisphere, behind the central fissure and between the frontal and occipital lobes (cf. *frontal lobe, occipital lobe, temporal lobe*).

part learning. Learning a multiple-response task in piecemeal fashion, then combining the acquired parts (cf. *whole learning*).

partial reinforcement. Reinforcing a given response only some proportion of the times it occurs (syn. *intermittent reinforcement*).

passive decay. A theory of forgetting which implies that the memory trace fades with disuse (cf. *memory trace*).

percentile scale. Cf. *centile scale*.

perception. The process of becoming aware of objects, qualities, or relations by way of the sense organs. While sensory content is always present in perception, what is perceived is influenced by set and prior experience, so that perception is more than a passive registration of stimuli impinging on the sense organs.

perceptual patterning. The tendency to perceive stimuli according to principles such as proximity, similarity, continuity, and closure. Emphasized by Gestalt psychologists (cf. *figure-ground perception*).

performance. Overt behavior, as distinguished from knowledge or information not translated into action. The distinction is important in theories of learning.

peripheralist position. A view held by some psychologists that all thinking goes on in action (in speech or other movements) (cf. *centralist position*).

personal disposition. Cf. *disposition*.

personality. The individual characteristics and ways of behaving which, in their organization or patterning, account for an individual's unique adjustments to his total environment (syn. *individuality*).

personality assessment. (1) Generally, appraisal of personality by any method. (2) More specifically, personality appraisal through complex observations and judgments, usually based in part upon behavior in contrived social situations.

personality dynamics. Theories of personality that stress personality dynamics are concerned with the interactive aspects of behavior (as in conflict resolution), with value hierarchies, with the permeability of boundaries between differentiated aspects of personality, etc. Contrasted with developmental theories,

though not incompatible with them (cf. *interactive explanation*).

personality inventory. An inventory for self-appraisal, consisting of many statements or questions about personal characteristics and behavior which the person judges to apply or not to apply to him (cf. *projective test*).

personality structure. The inferred unifying pattern underlying individual ways of behaving, giving consistency to otherwise contradictory traits and meaning to otherwise inexplicable mannerisms and eccentricities.

personality syndrome. An acquired personality type; a combination of characteristics which, though unique in its individual expression, bears a resemblance to the personality structures of others who have shared somewhat similar problems and have adopted somewhat similar solutions to their problems (cf. *compulsive personality, authoritarian personality*).

perspective size. The size of an object according to the geometry of perspective, i.e., its size diminishes directly in proportion to its distance (cf. *object size, size constancy*).

phallic stage. In psychoanalysis, that stage of psychosexual development in which gratification is associated with sex organ stimulation and the sexual attachment is to the parent of the opposite sex (cf. *Oedipal stage, psychosexual development*).

phenomenology. Naive report on conscious experience, as by a child, as contrasted with trained introspection; the study of unanalyzed experience (cf. *Gestalt psychology*).

phenotype. In genetics, the characteristics that are displayed by the individual organism, e.g., eye color, intelligence, as distinct from those traits which he may carry genetically but not display (cf. *genotype*).

phi phenomenon. Stroboscopic motion in its simpler form. Commonly produced by successively turning on and off two separated stationary light sources; as the first is turned off and the second turned on, the subject perceives a spot of light moving from the position of the first to that of the second (cf. *stroboscopic motion*).

phobic reaction. Excessive fear in the absence of real danger (cf. *agoraphobia, claustrophobia, neurotic reaction*).

phrenology. The doctrine that specific mental faculties are localized in definite cerebral regions. Included are such vague and complex faculties as truthfulness, love, curiosity, and musical ability. The convolutions of the skull are presumed to indicate the strength of the faculties located beneath.

physical sciences. Those sciences, such as astronomy, chemistry, mineralogy, and physics, dealing chiefly with laws and relationships derived from study of the inanimate world, rather than with laws and relationships peculiar to living things.

physiological motive. A motive based upon an evident bodily need, such as the need for food or water (syn. *organic motive*; cf. *social motive*).

physiological psychology. That branch of experimental psychology concerned with the relationship between physiological functions and behavior.

physiology. That branch of biology concerned primarily with the functioning of organ systems within the body.

pilomotor response. The response of muscles in the skin in which the hairs stand on end, giving a roughened appearance to the skin known as "goose flesh" or "goose pimples." May result either from cold or as part of an emotional state (cf. *emotional indicator*).

pitch. A qualitative dimension of hearing correlated with the frequency of the sound waves that constitute the stimulus. Higher frequencies yield higher pitches (cf. *loudness, timbre*).

pituitary gland. An endocrine gland located centrally in the head. It consists of two parts, the anterior pituitary and the posterior pituitary. The anterior pituitary is the more important part because of its regulation of growth and of other endocrine glands. One of its hormones, ACTH (adrenocorticotropic hormone), has become medically important (syn. *hypophysis;* cf. *endocrine gland*).

place-learning experiment. A variety of animal maze experiments designed to test whether or not what is learned is the location of the goal in space rather than the movements required to reach the goal (cf. *sign learning*).

place theory. A theory of hearing that associates pitch with the place on the basilar membrane where activation occurs (cf. *frequency theory, traveling wave theory, volley theory*).

placebo. An inert substance used in place of an active drug; given to the control group in an experimental test.

plateau. In a learning curve a period of no improvement, preceded and followed by improvement (cf. *learning curve*).

polarized synaptic transmission. The transmission of nervous impulses across synapses in one direction only (from axon to dendrite or cell body); characteristic of higher nervous systems, beyond the stage of the nerve net.

population. The total universe of all possible cases from which a sample is selected. The usual statistical formulas for making inferences from samples apply when the population is appreciably larger than the sample, e.g., five to ten times larger than the sample (cf. *sample*).

population genetics. That branch of genetics concerned with the distribution of genetic determiners throughout the population (cf. *genetics*).

positive incentive. An object or circumstance toward which behavior is directed when the object or circumstance is perceived or anticipated (cf. *negative incentive*).

post-hypnotic suggestion. A suggestion made to a hypnotized subject that he will perform in a prescribed way after coming out of the trance. The activity is usually carried out without the subject's awareness of its origin in a specific suggestion (cf. *hypnotism*).

precognition. A claimed form of extrasensory perception in which a future event is perceived (cf. *extrasensory perception, clairvoyance, telepathy*).

predictive validity. Validity determined by how well a test predicts a criterion (cf. *concurrent validity, content validity, construct validity*).

pregenital stages. In psychoanalysis, the oral, anal, and phallic stages of psychosexual development (cf. *psychosexual development*).

prejudice. An attitude that is firmly fixed, not open to free and rational discussion, and resistant to change (cf. *attitude*).

preparation. The first of four stages of creative thinking proposed by Wallas. In the preparation stage, the thinker obtains appropriate information, skills, and techniques which later come to fruition in what he creates or invents (cf. *incubation, illumination, verification*).

preparatory activity. Goal-directed or goal-seeking activity aroused by a drive or by external stimuli when the drive is active.

preparatory set. Cf. *set*.

primary abilities. The abilities, discovered by factor analysis, that underlie intelligence test performance (cf. *factor analysis*).

primary colors. Cf. *color-mixing primaries, psychological primaries*.

primary sex characteristics. The structural or physiological characteristics that make possible sexual union and reproduction (cf. *secondary sex characteristics*).

primitive society. Cf. *nonliterate society*.

proactive inhibition. The interference of earlier learning with the learning and recall of new material (cf. *retroactive inhibition, transfer of training*).

probability sampling. A general method of sampling, applicable to attitude and opinion surveys, in which the probability that any one member of the population will be included in the sample is known. The actual selection of cases is random so that inferences based on sampling statistics can be made (cf. *area sampling*).

probability value. A probability statement associated with a statistical inference, e.g., "The probability (P) is .05 that a difference of this size between the sample means would have occurred even though the population means were the same" (cf. *statistical inference, statistical significance*).

product-moment correlation. Cf. *coefficient of correlation*.

program. (1) A plan for the solution of a problem; often used interchangeably with "routine" to specify the precise sequence of instructions enabling a computer to solve a problem. (2) In connection with teaching, a set of materials arranged in sequences of units, called frames, so that learning can proceed with a minimum of error. The program can be presented in book form as well as in a form suitable for use with a teaching machine (cf. *teaching machine*).

projection. A defense mechanism by which a person protects himself from awareness of his own undesirable traits by attributing those traits excessively to others (cf. *defense mechanism*).

projection area. A place in the cerebral cortex where a function is localized; e.g., the visual protection area is in the occipital lobes.

projective test. A personality test in which the subject reveals ("projects") himself through his imaginative productions. The projective test gives much freer possibilities of response than the fixed-alternative personality inventory. Examples of projective tests are the Rorschach test (ink blots to be interpreted) and the Thematic Apperception Test (pictures that elicit stories) (cf. *personality inventory*).

prolactin. A pituitary hormone associated with the secretion of milk (cf. *hormones*).

psi. The special ability said to be possessed by the subject who performs successfully in experiments on extrasensory perception and psychokinesis (cf. *extrasensory perception, psychokinesis*).

psychedelic drugs. An alternate name for "consciousness-expanding" drugs (cf. *psychotomimetic drugs, LSD-25*).

psychiatric nurse. A nurse specially trained to deal with patients suffering from mental disorders.

psychiatric social worker. A social worker trained to work with patients and their families on problems of mental health and illness, usually in close relationship with psychiatrists and clinical psychologists (cf. *psychiatrist, clinical psychologist*).

psychiatrist. A medical doctor specializing in the treatment and prevention of mental disorders both mild and severe (cf. *psychoanalyst, clinical psychologist*).

psychiatry. A branch of medicine concerned with mental health and mental illness (cf. *psychiatrist, psychoanalyst*).

psychoactive drugs. Drugs that affect man's behavior and consciousness (cf. *tranquilizers, psychedelic drugs, psychotomimetic drugs, LSD-25*).

psychoanalysis. (1) The method developed by Freud and extended by his followers for treating neuroses. (2) The system of psychological theory growing out of experiences with the psychoanalytic method.

psychoanalyst. A psychotherapist, now usually trained as a psychiatrist, who uses methods related to those originally proposed by Freud for treating neuroses and other mental disorders (cf. *psychiatrist, clinical psychologist*).

psychodrama. A form of spontaneous play acting used in psychotherapy.

psychogenic. Caused by psychological factors (e.g., emotional conflict, faulty habits) rather than by disease, injury, or other somatic cause; functional rather than organic.

psychograph. Cf. *trait profile*.

psychokinesis (PK). A claimed form of mental operation said to affect a material body or an energy system without any evidence of more usual contact or energy transfer, e.g., affecting the number which comes up in the throw of dice by a machine through wishing for that number (cf. *extrasensory perception*).

psychological primaries. Hues that appear to be pure, i.e., not composed of other hues. Most authorities choose a particular red, yellow, green, and blue. (The red-green and blue-yellow pairs chosen in this way are not complementary colors.) (cf. *color-mixing primaries*).

psychology. The science of the behavior of man and other animals (cf. *behavior*).

psychopathic reaction. A type of character disorder marked by impulsivity, inability to abide by the customs and laws of society, and lack of anxiety or guilt regarding behavior (syn. *antisocial reaction;* cf. *character disorder*).

psychopharmacology. The study of the effects of drugs on behavior.

psychophysical function. A curve relating the likelihood of a response to the intensity of the presented stimulus.

psychophysical methods. Experimental and statistical methods for determining absolute thresholds, difference thresholds, and scale values for stimuli that can be arranged along a physical continuum (cf. *threshold*).

psychophysics. A name used by Fechner for the science of the relationship between mental processes and the physical world. Now usually restricted to the study of the sensory consequences of controlled physical stimulation (cf. *psychophysical methods*).

psychosexual development. In psychoanalysis, the theory that development takes place through stages (oral, anal, phallic, latency, genital), each stage characterized by a zone of pleasurable stimulation and appropriate objects of sexual attachment, culminating in normal heterosexual mating (cf. *oral stage, anal stage, phallic stage, latency, genital stage, psychosocial crises*).

psychosocial crises. A modification by Erikson of the psychoanalytic theory of psychosexual development, giving more attention to the social and environmental problems associated with the various stages of development, and adding some adult stages beyond genital maturing (cf. *psychosexual development*).

psychosomatic disorders. Ailments with organic symptoms attributable to emotional or other psychological causes.

psychotherapy. Treatment of personality maladjustment or mental illness by psychological means, usually, but not exclusively, through personal consultation (cf. *somatotherapy*).

psychotic disorder. Mental illness in which the patient shows severe change or disorganization of personality, often accompanied by depression, delusions, hallucinations; commonly requires hospitalization (syn. *psychosis,* pl. *psychoses;* cf. *functional psychosis, organic psychosis*).

psychotomimetic drugs. Drugs that produce psychotic symptoms (cf. *LSD-25*).

puberty. The age at which secondary sex characteristics appear and sex functioning begins to mature (syn. *pubescence;* cf. *adolescence*).

public opinion. Widely shared beliefs, including common plans for action, chiefly in respect to problems of governmental policy (cf. *attitude, opinion*).

punctiform distribution. The arrangement of sensitive areas of the skin; a distribution of sensitive spots with insensitive areas between them.

punishment. A negative incentive, capable of producing pain or annoyance (cf. *reward*).

pupillary response. The constriction or dilation of the pupil of the eye, brought about either by changes in illumination or as an emotional accompaniment (cf. *emotional indicator*).

purpose. A goal that can be stated in words and toward which action is directed (cf. *unconscious motive*).

pursuit learning. A laboratory task in which the subject learns to keep the point of a hinged stylus in contact with a small metal target mounted on a rotating phonograph-like turntable.

quality. A characteristic denoting differences in kind, rather than differences in intensity or amount; e.g., a light and a sound differ in quality; red and blue, and the notes A and B♭, differ in quality (cf. *quantity*).

quantity. Amount or intensity (cf. *quality*).

quota control. A sampling method used in attitude and opinion surveys, in which the interviewer is instructed to select respondents with certain defined characteristics, e.g., of stated age, sex, economic level (cf. *area sampling*).

range. The variation of scores in a frequency distribution from the lowest to the highest. A value that grows larger as the number of cases increases, hence to be used with extreme caution (cf. *measure of variation*).

rank correlation (ρ). A correlation computed from ranked data. The coefficient is designated by the small Greek letter rho (ρ) to distinguish it from the product-moment correlation (r), of which it is an approximation (cf. *coefficient of correlation*).

rapid eye movements (REM). Eye movements that usually occur during dreaming and that can be measured by attaching small electrodes laterally to and above the subject's eye. These register changes in electrical activity associated with movements of the eyeball in its socket.

rapport. (1) A comfortable relationship between the subject and the tester, insuring cooperation in replying to test questions. (2) A similar relationship between therapist and patient. (3) A special relationship of hypnotic subject to hypnotist.

rating scale. A device by which a rater can record his judgment of another person (or of himself) on the traits defined by the scale (cf. *graphic rating scale*).

rational problem-solving. Arriving at a solution by sound reasoning on the basis of the best available evidence; realistic problem-solving (cf. *defense mechanism*).

rationalization. A defense mechanism in which self-esteem is maintained by assigning plausible and acceptable reasons for conduct entered upon impulsively or for less acceptable reasons (cf. *defense mechanism*).

reaction-formation. A defense mechanism in which a subject denies a disapproved motive through giving strong expression to its opposite (cf. *defense mechanism*).

reaction time. The time between the presentation of a stimulus and the occurrence of a response (cf. *latency*).

readiness to learn. The state of the learner that makes a given task an appropriate one for him to master because (1) he is sufficiently mature physiologically, (2) he has the appropriate preparatory training, and (3) he has an aroused interest or desire to learn (cf. *maturation, pacing*).

recall. The form of remembering in which the subject demonstrates retention by repeating what was earlier learned, e.g., demonstrating recall of a poem by reciting it (cf. *recognition, redintegrative memory, relearning*).

receptor. A specialized portion of the body sensitive to particular kinds of stimuli and connected with sensory nerves, e.g., the retina of the eye. Used more loosely, the organ containing these sensitive portions, e.g., the eye or the ear (cf. *effector*).

recessive gene. A member of a gene pair which determines the characteristic trait or appearance of the individual only if the other member of the pair is recessive. If the other member of the pair is dominant, the effect of the recessive gene is masked (cf. *dominant gene*).

reciprocal inhibition. (1) The relationship between muscles that are controlled through reciprocal innervation (Sherrington). (2) A variety of psychotherapy in which symptoms are decreased through presenting their occasion under circumstances in which response in inhibited (Wolpe).

reciprocal innervation. A form of neural integration in which one of a pair of antagonistic muscles is actively inhibited when the other member of the pair contracts (cf. *antagonistic muscles*).

recognition. That form of remembering indicated by a feeling of familiarity when something previously encountered is again perceived (cf. *recall, redintegrative memory, relearning*).

red-green color blindness. The commonest form of color blindness, a variety of dichromatism. In the two subvarieties, red-blindness and green-blindness, both red and green vision are lacking, but achromatic bands are seen at different parts of the spectrum (cf. *color blindness, dichromatism*).

redintegrative memory. Remembering the whole of an earlier experience on the basis of partial cues; recollection of events in the personal history of the subject, with their attendant circumstances (cf. *recall, recognition, relearning*).

reduction screen. A screen containing a small aperture so that a restricted area of a surface can be viewed through it. With a reduction screen brightness constancy (and other constancies) tends to be lessened (cf. *object constancy*).

reference group. The group with which an individual compares himself when he makes self-estimates of status. Most people have several reference groups. A reference group may or may not be a membership group (cf. *membership group*).

reflex action. A relatively simple response largely under the control of a specific stimulus, occurring rather mechanically, such as the pupillary response to light or the knee-jerk from a tap on the tendon below the knee. Other examples of reflex action are sneezing, perspiring, and the beating of the heart (cf. *respondent behavior*).

refractory phase. The period of temporary inactivity in a neuron after it has once fired.

regression. A return to more primitive or infantile modes of response, either (1) retrogression to behavior engaged in when younger, or (2) primitivation, i.e., more infantile or childlike behavior, but not necessarily that which occurred in the individual's earlier life.

reinforcement. (1) In classical conditioning the experimental procedure of following the conditioned stimulus by the unconditioned stimulus. (2) In operant conditioning the analogous procedure of following the occurrence of the operant response by the reinforcing stimulus. (3) The process which increases the strength of conditioning as a result of these arrangements (cf. *classical conditioning, operant conditioning, extinction*).

reinforcing stimulus. (1) In classical conditioning, the unconditioned stimulus. (2) In operant conditioning, the stimulus that reinforces the operant (typically, a reward).

relearning. That form of remembering in which the subject demonstrates memory for something previously learned through the saving in time or trials required for learning the material again (cf. *recall, recognition, redintegrative memory*).

releaser. A term used by ethologists for a stimulus that sets off a cycle of instinctive behavior (cf. *ethologist, instinct*).

reliability. The self-consistency of a test as a measuring instrument. Reliability is measured by a coefficient of correlation between scores on two halves of a test, alternate forms of the test, or retests with the same test, a high correlation signifying high consistency of scores for the population tested (cf. *validity*).

REM. Cf. *rapid eye movements*.

reminiscence. In psychology a term for the occasional rise in a curve of retention before it falls, e.g., when under some circumstances more may be retained after an interval than immediately upon completion of learning (cf. *retention curve*).

repression. (1) A defense mechanism in which an impulse or memory which might provoke feelings of guilt is denied by its disappearance from awareness (cf. *defense mechanism, suppression*). (2) A theory of forgetting (cf. *motivated forgetting*).

reserpine. Cf. *tranquilizer*.

resistance. In psychoanalysis, a blocking of free association; a psychological barrier against bringing unconscious impulses to the level of awareness. Resistance is part of the process of maintaining repression (cf. *repression, interpretation*).

respiration rate. The rate of breathing. When respiration rate is used in the study of emotion, an additional measure is commonly used, known as the inspiration-expiration ratio. This is computed as a ratio between the time spent in inspiration and the time spent in expiration (I/E) (cf. *emotional indicator*).

respondent. (1) One who responds; used chiefly to refer to those interviewed in public opinion surveys. (2) A class of responses (cf. *respondent behavior*).

respondent behavior. A type of behavior corresponding to reflex action, in that it is largely under the control of, and predictable from, the stimulus (syn. *elicited behavior;* cf. *operant behavior*).

response. (1) The behavioral result of stimulation in the form of a movement or glandular secretion. (2) Sometimes, any activity of the organism, including central responses (such as an image or fantasy), whether or not the stimulus is identified and whether or not identifiable movements occur. (3) Products of the organism's activity, such as words typed per minute.

retention curve. A curve plotted with some measure of remembering on the vertical axis and the elapsed time since learning on the horizontal axis. The curve tends to fall rapidly at first, then more slowly, though this is not invariable (cf. *reminiscence*).

reticular formation. A system of ill-defined nerve paths and connections within the brain stem, lying outside the well-defined nerve pathways, and important as an arousal mechanism.

retina. The portion of the eye sensitive to light, containing the rods and the cones (cf. *rod, cone*).

retinal disparity. The fact that an object projects slightly different images on the two retinas due to the different positions of the right and left eyes (syn. *binocular disparity*).

retroactive inhibition. (1) The interference in recall of something earlier learned by something subsequently learned. (2) The theory of forgetting which proposes that much, or most, forgetting is due to the interference by new learning with the recall of the old (cf. *proactive inhibition, transfer of training*).

retrograde amnesia. The inability to recall events that occurred during a period of time immediately prior to a shock or functional disturbance, although the memory for earlier events remains relatively unimpaired.

retrogression. Cf. *regression*.

reverberating circuit. A loop of neurons that may continue to fire without external stimulation; one of the speculative mechanisms to account for the persistence of memories.

reward. A positive incentive capable of arousing pleasure or satisfying a drive; a reinforcing stimulus (cf. *punishment*).

rhodopsin. Cf. *visual purple*.

ribonucleic acid (RNA). Complex molecules that control cellular functions; theorized by some to be the chemical mediator of memory.

RNA. Cf. *ribonucleic acid*.

rod. In the eye, an element of the retina mediating achromatic sensation only; particularly important in peripheral vision and night vision (cf. *retina, cone*).

role. By analogy with an actor's role, the kind of behavior expected of an individual because of his place within social arrangements, e.g., the male role, the mother's role, the lawyer's role. Any one person fulfills or adopts numerous roles on varied occasions.

role diffusion. A stage of development said by Erikson to characterize many adolescents (and others) in which various identifications with others have not been harmonized and integrated (cf. *identification, identity formation*).

role playing. A method for teaching principles affecting interpersonal relations by having the subject assume a part in a spontaneous play, whether in psychotherapy or in leadership training (cf. *psychodrama*).

rote memorization. Verbatim learning, as in learning a poem "by heart" (cf. *paired-associates learning, serial memorization, substance memorization*).

saccule. Cf. *vestibular sacs*.

sadism. A pathological motive that leads to inflicting pain upon another person (cf. *masochism*).

salivary secretion. Secretion of the salivary glands, elicited by food or chemical substance in the mouth or by conditioned stimuli, or occurring as an emotional accompaniment (cf. *emotional indicator*).

sample. A selection of scores from a total set of scores known as the "population." If selection is random, an unbiased sample results; if selection is nonrandom, the sample is biased and unrepresentative (cf. *population*).

sampling errors. The variation in a distribution of scores, or of statistics derived from them, to be attributed to the fact that measurements are made on a variable sample from a larger population. Thus sampling errors persist even though all measurements are accurate (cf. *errors of measurement, sample*).

saturation. The dimension of color that describes its purity; if highly saturated it appears to be pure hue and free of gray, but if of low saturation it appears to have a great deal of gray mixed with it (cf. *brightness, hue*).

scale. A set of ascending or descending values used to designate a position or an interval along a dimension. Thus a ruler may have a scale in inches, a test a scale in I.Q. units (cf. *interval scale, ordinal scale, ratio scale*).

scaling. Converting raw data into types of scores more readily interpreted, e.g., into ranks, centiles, standard scores (cf. *attitude scale*).

scalogram. A scale for measuring favorability or unfavorability of attitudes constructed according to Guttman's method. The intent is to arrive at a "pure" scale, so that a subject with a specified attitude who answers a certain question favorably will be favorable to all questions less extreme, and unfavorable to all questions more extreme (cf. *attitude scale*).

scapegoating. A form of displaced aggression in which an innocent but helpless victim is blamed or punished as the source of the scapegoater's frustration (cf. *displaced aggression*).

schizophrenic reaction. A functional psychotic disorder in which there is a lack of harmony or split between aspects of personality functioning, especially between emotion and behavior. Symptoms may include autism, hallucinations, and delusions (syn. *schizophrenia,* formerly *dementia praecox;* cf. *psychotic disorder*).

school of psychology. An all-embracing system designed to encompass the data of psychology according to a limited set of principles and procedures. Such schools are not as prominent today as they once were (syn. *system of psychology;* cf. *behaviorism, Gestalt psychology, psychoanalysis, S-R psychology*).

school psychologist. A professional psychologist employed by a school or school system, with responsibility for testing, guidance, research, etc. (cf. *educational psychologist*).

secondary reinforcer. A stimulus that has become reinforcing through prior association with a reinforcing stimulus (cf. *reinforcing stimulus*).

secondary sex characteristics. The physical features distinguishing the mature male from the mature female, apart from the reproductive organs. In man, the deeper voice of the male and the growth of the beard are illustrative (cf. *primary sex characteristics*).

secondary disposition. A minor disposition, aroused by a narrow range of stimuli, and resulting in a narrow range of equivalent responses (Allport) (cf. *cardinal disposition, central disposition*).

second-order conditioning. Conditioning in which what was previously the conditioned stimulus now serves as the unconditioned or reinforcing stimulus (cf. *secondary reinforcer*).

selectivity. The perceptual response to parts of incoming stimuli and the ignoring of others (cf. *attention*).

self. The subject's personality as perceived by the subject (cf. *personality*).

self-consciousness. A form of heightened self-awareness when an individual is especially concerned about reactions of others to him.

self-deception. Behavior whose motives are unconscious or inadequately perceived by the person himself because of (1) denial of the true motives, or (2) disguise of these motives (cf. *defense mechanism*).

self-demand schedule. A flexible arrangement for feeding in which the time an infant is fed is determined according to his behavior. It replaces a four-hour or other rigid schedule (syn. *self-schedule, demand schedule*).

self-perception. The individual's awareness of himself; differs from self-consciousness because it may take the form of objective self-appraisal (cf. *self-consciousness*).

self-recitation. In memorization, the method of spending some fraction of the study time in attempted recall.

semantic differential. A method developed by Osgood for using rating scales and factor analysis in studying the connotative meanings of words (cf. *connotative meaning*).

semicircular canals. Three curved tubular canals, in three planes, which form part of the labyrinth of the inner ear and are concerned with equilibrium and motion.

sensorimotor task. A multiple-response task in which muscular movement is prominent, e.g., riding a bicycle, playing a piano. Laboratory sensorimotor tasks include mazes, mirror drawing, pursuit learning, etc. (cf. *multiple-response learning*).

sensory adaptation. The reduction in sensitivity that occurs with prolonged stimulation and the increase in sensitivity that occurs with lack of stimulation; most noted in vision, smell, taste, and temperature sensitivity (cf. *dark adaptation, light adaptation*).

septal area. A portion of the brain deep in the central part, between the lateral ventricles, which when stimulated electrically (in the rat, at least) appears to yield a state akin to pleasure.

serial memorization. That form of rote memorization in which a list of items, or a passage of prose or poetry, is learned in sequence from beginning to end, so that each item or word is a cue to the one that follows it (cf. *paired-associate learning*).

serial position effect. The difficulty in memorization and recall resulting from position of items within a list to be learned and remembered. The point of maximum difficulty is just after the middle of the list.

set. (1) A preparatory adjustment or readiness for a particular kind of action or experience, usually as a result of instructions, e.g., the set to respond with a word opposite in meaning to the stimulus word in an experiment on controlled association. (2) A habitual tendency to respond in a particular manner.

sex gland. As duct glands, the sex glands are active in mating behavior, but as endocrine glands their hormones affect secondary sex characteristics as well as maintaining functional sexual activity. The male hormones are known as androgens, the female hormones as estrogens (syn. *gonads;* cf. *endocrine gland*).

sex-linked trait. A trait determined by a gene transmitted with the same chromosomes that determine sex, e.g., red-green color blindness (cf. *X-chromosome, Y-chromosome*).

shape constancy. The tendency to see a familiar object as of the same shape regardless of the viewing angle (cf. *object constancy*).

shaping of behavior. Modifying operant behavior by reinforcing only those variations in response that deviate in a direction desired by the experimenter; the whole population of responses thus reinforced then drifts in the desired direction (Skinner) (syn. *method of approximations*).

shock therapy. A form of treatment of mental illness, especially in the relief of depression (cf. *electroconvulsive shock therapy, insulin shock*).

sibling. A brother or a sister.

sibling rivalry. Jealousy between siblings, often based on their competition for parental affection.

sign learning. An acquired expectation that one stimulus (the sign) will be followed by another (the significate) provided a familiar behavior route is followed. This interpretation of learning, by Tolman, is considered by him an alternative to the interpretation of learning as habit formation (cf. *latent learning experiment, place-learning experiment*).

signal detectability theory. A theory of psychophysical phenomena that views the sensory system as an analog process (cf. *neural quantum theory*).

simulation. The representation of the essential elements of some phenomenon, system, or environment to facilitate its study (often by or involving an automatic computer).

sine wave. A cyclical wave which when plotted corresponds to the plot of the trigonometric sine function. The sound waves of pure tones yield this function when plotted.

size-age confusion. The tendency to judge age by size, e.g., perceiving as awkward those adolescents who are large for their ages.

size constancy. The tendency to see a familiar object as of its actual size regardless of its distance (cf. *object constancy*).

skewed distribution. A frequency distribution that is not symmetrical. It is named for the direction in which the tail lies; e.g., if there are many small incomes and a few large ones, the distribution is skewed in the direction of the large incomes (cf. *frequency distribution, symmetrical distribution*).

smooth muscle. The type of muscle found in the digestive organs, blood vessels, and other internal organs. Controlled via the autonomic nervous system (cf. *cardiac muscle, striate muscle*).

social desirability variable. A biasing variable in personality inventories, leading some subjects to reply in the direction of socially approved responses, whether or not their answers are descriptive of themselves (cf. *acquiescence*).

social femininity. The tendency to answer questions on a masculinity-femininity test as women do rather than as men do.

social masculinity. The tendency to answer questions on a masculinity-femininity test as men do rather than as women do.

social motive. A motive serving group life, involving particularly interactions with other organisms of the same species (cf. *ego-integrative motive, survival motive*).

social psychologist. A psychologist whose research interest lies in the behavior of the individual as he influences and is influenced by other individuals in a social environment (cf. *anthropologist, sociologist*).

socialization. The shaping of individual characteristics and behavior through the training that the social environment provides.

sociogram. A social map or diagram showing interactions, usually of mutual attraction or antagonism, among group members (cf. *sociometry*).

sociology. The behavioral or social science dealing with group life and social organization in literate societies (cf. *behavioral sciences*).

sociometry. A method of social mapping to indicate relationships of attraction and rejection among members of a social group. Each member expresses his choices for or against other members. The social map is constructed from the data provided by these choices (cf. *sociogram*).

somatotherapy. Treatment of personality maladjustment or mental illness by drugs, electric shock, surgery, or other methods directly affecting bodily processes (cf. *psychotherapy, chemotherapy*).

source trait. A trait derived by the method of factor analysis; all traits loaded heavily on a common factor belong together (Cattell) (cf. *surface trait*).

spastic paralysis. A condition of excessive isotonic muscular contraction, commonly due to a brain injury at birth (syn. *cerebral palsy*).

special aptitude. The degree of aptitude to learn a specific activity, e.g., musical aptitude, clerical aptitude (cf. *general aptitude*).

specific hunger. Hunger for a specific food incentive, such as a craving for sweets (cf. *hunger drive*).

split-brain preparation. A deep vertical incision through the corpus callosum in an animal's brain that separates most of the two hemispheres. It is used to study the bilateral transfer of training (cf. *corpus callosum*).

spontaneous recovery. The return in strength of a conditioned response after a lapse of time following extinction (cf. *extinction*).

S-R psychology. Cf. *stimulus-response psychology*.

standard deviation. The square root of the mean of the squares of the amount by which each case departs from the mean of all the cases (syn. *root mean square deviation;* cf. *measure of variation, standard error, standard score*).

standard error. The standard deviation of the sampling distribution of a mean and of certain other derived statistics. It can be interpreted as any other standard deviation (cf. *standard deviation*).

standard error of estimate. The standard error of the differences between predicted values and true values of some measure; used, for example, in interpreting a coefficient of correlation.

standard score. (1) A score that has been converted to a scale of measurement with a mean of zero and a standard deviation of 1.0, based on a distribution of scores used in calibration. (2) A score based on standard scores but converted to another scale for convenience, e.g., with a mean of 50 and a standard deviation of 10.

stanine score. A U.S. Air Forces type of standard score (originally, "standard nine"), with a mean of five

and standard deviation of two. Scores range from one through nine (cf. *standard score*).

statistical inference. A statement about a population or populations based on statistical measures derived from samples (cf. *descriptive statistics*).

statistical significance. The trustworthiness of an obtained statistical measure as a statement about reality, e.g., the probability that the population mean falls within the limits determined from a sample. The expression refers to the reliability of the statistical finding and not to its importance (cf. *confidence limits, critical ratio, probability value*).

statistician. An applied mathematician; in psychology, one especially trained in the statistical tools useful in test construction and the interpretation of test data and in the design of experiments.

status motives. Motives related to one's established or desired position relative to others (cf. *dominance, achievement*).

stereophonic hearing. The binaural perception of the distance and direction of a sound source owing to the difference in reception by the two ears.

stereoscopic vision. (1) The binocular perception of depth and distance of an object owing to the overlapping fields of the two eyes. (2) The equivalent effect when slightly unlike pictures are presented individually to each eye in a stereoscope (cf. *distance cues*).

stereotype. A biased generalization, usually about a social or national group, according to which individuals are falsely assigned traits they do not possess. Thus a person may have a stereotyped conception of the Italians or Scots which distorts his perception of any individual Italian or Scot.

stereotypy. The continued repetition of behavior which appears to serve no realistic purpose and may, in fact, be punished; inflexible behavior, which may be a consequence of frustration (cf. *frustration*).

steroids. Complex chemical substances, some of which are prominent in the secretions of the adrenal cortex and may be related to some forms of mental illness (cf. *adrenal gland*).

stimulus (pl. **stimuli**). (1) Some specific physical energy impinging upon a receptor sensitive to that kind of energy. (2) Any objectively describable situation or event (whether outside or inside the organism) that is the occasion for an organism's response (cf. *response*).

stimulus-response psychology. A psychological view that all behavior is in response to stimuli and that the appropriate tasks of psychological science are those identifying stimuli, the responses correlated with them, and the processes intervening between stimulus and response. There are several varieties of stimulus-response (S-R) theory, depending on the kind of intervening processes inferred (cf. *intervening variables*).

stimulus-sampling theory. A theory of behavior, with primary emphasis on learning, that views the organism as an essentially probabilistic process.

stimulus substitution. Cf. *classical conditioning*.

striate area. Cf. *visual area*.

striate muscle. Striped muscle; the characteristic muscles controlling the skeleton, as in the arms and legs. Activated by cerebro-spinal nervous system (cf. *cardiac muscle, smooth muscle*).

stroboscopic motion. An illusion of motion resulting from the successive presentation of discrete stimulus patterns arranged in a progression corresponding to movement, e.g., motion pictures (cf. *phi phenomenon*).

subjective science. A science limited to self-observation, so that its data are not public. Psychology based solely on introspection is subjective in that its raw data are limited to the observations of the subject on his own conscious processes. However, the report of these experiences provides objective data, so that introspection does not have to be excluded from objective psychology (cf. *objective science*).

subjective scoring. Test scoring requiring complex judgments by the scorer, as in the grading of essay examinations (cf. *objective scoring*).

sublimation. A form of the defense mechanism of substitution, whereby socially unacceptable motives find expression in socially acceptable forms; most commonly applied to the sublimation of sexual desires (cf. *substitution, compensation*).

submission. Cf. *dominance*.

substance memorization. The learning of the message, plot, or events in a passage in contrast to learning its exact words (cf. *rote memorization*).

substitution. A defense mechanism whereby the person maintains self-esteem by substituting approved goals for unapproved ones and activities that can be carried out successfully for activities doomed to failure (cf. *sublimation, compensation, overcompensation*).

subtractive mixture. Color mixture in which absorption occurs, so that results differ from additive mixture obtained by rotating colors on a color wheel or by mixing projected lights. Subtractive mixture occurs when transparent colored filters are placed one in front of the other, and when pigments are mixed (cf. *additive mixture*).

superego. In Freud's tripartite division of the personality, that part corresponding most nearly to conscience, controlling through moral scruples rather than by way of social expediency. The superego is said to be an uncompromising and punishing conscience (cf. *id, ego*).

suppression. A process of self-control in which impulses, tendencies to action, wishes to perform disapproved acts, etc., are in awareness, but not overtly revealed (cf. *repression*).

surface trait. A trait derived by the method of cluster analysis; all traits that intercorrelate above some predicted value (e.g., above $r = .60$) can be considered to have something in common (Cattell) (cf. *source trait*).

survival motive. A motive closely related to maintaining the life of the organism in its environment; thus motives related to bodily needs for food, water, air, moderate temperatures, etc. (cf. *ego-integrative motive, social motive*).

symmetrical distribution. A frequency distribution in which cases fall equally in the class intervals on either side of the middle; hence the mean, median, and mode fall together (cf. *frequency distribution, skewed distribution*).

sympathetic division. A division of the autonomic nervous system, characterized by a chain of ganglia on either side of the spinal cord, with nerve fibers originating in the thoracic and lumbar portions of the spinal cord. Active in emotional excitement and to some extent antagonistic to the parasympathetic division (q.v.).

synapse. Cf. *synaptic nervous system*.

synaptic nervous system. A nervous system characteristic of all higher organisms, in which nerve cells are distinct and conduction is polarized, that is, occurs only in one direction across the junction between nerve cells called a synapse (cf. *nerve net*).

systematic distortion. A theory of forgetting which implies that memory is distorted through orderly changes in the memory trace other than fading or dropping out of details.

taboo. Something strongly prohibited or banned within a culture, usually with severe penalties for violation.

tachistoscope. An instrument for the brief exposure of words, symbols, pictures, or other visually presented material; sometimes called a T-scope.

taste deficiency. A trait used in the study of population genetics. Nontasting of certain substances, such as phenyl-thio-carbamide, is a recessive characteristic in man, while tasting is a dominant characteristic (cf. *dominant gene, recessive gene, population genetics*).

teaching machine. A device to provide self-instruction by means of a program proceeding in steps following each other at a rate determined by the learner; the machine is arranged to provide knowledge about the correctness or incorrectness of each reply (cf. *programing*).

telepathy. The claimed form of extrasensory perception in which what is perceived depends upon thought transference from one person to another (cf. *extrasensory perception, clairvoyance, precognition*).

temperament. That aspect of personality revealed in the tendency to experience moods or mood changes in characteristic ways; general level of reactivity and energy (cf. *mood*).

temporal lobe. A portion of the cerebral hemisphere, at the side below the fissure of Sylvius and in front of the occipital lobe (cf. *frontal lobe, occipital lobe, parietal lobe*).

test. A collection of items (questions, tasks, etc.) so arranged that replies or performances can be scored and the scores used in appraising individual differences (cf. *item, test battery*).

test battery. A collection of tests whose composite scores are used to appraise individual differences (cf. *item, test*).

test method. A method of psychological investigation. Its advantages are that it allows the psychologist to collect large quantities of useful data from many people, with a minimum of disturbance of their routines of existence and with a minimum of laboratory equipment (cf. *test, experimental method*).

test profile. A chart plotting scores from a number of tests given to the same individual (or group of individuals) in parallel rows on a common scale, with the scores connected by lines, so that high and low scores can be readily perceived (cf. *trait profile*).

test standardization. The establishment of norms for interpreting scores by giving a test to a representative population and by making appropriate studies of its reliability and validity (cf. *norm, reliability, validity*).

tetany. A physiologically disturbed state of the organism marked by widespread intermittent muscular contractions and muscular pain; may be caused by calcium deficiency as a consequence of defective parathyroid secretion (cf. *parathyroid glands*).

theory. A set of assumptions (axioms) advanced to explain existing data and predict new events; usually applicable to a wide array of phenomena and experimental situations.

thinking. Behavior carried on in terms of ideas (representational or symbolic processes); ideational problem-solving as distinguished from solution through overt manipulation (cf. *associative thinking, directed thinking*).

threshold. The transitional point at which an increasing stimulus or an increasing difference not previously perceived becomes perceptible (or at which a decreasing stimulus or previously perceived difference becomes imperceptible). The value obtained depends in part upon the methods used in determining it (cf. *absolute threshold, difference threshold, psychophysical methods*).

thyroid gland. An endocrine gland located in the neck, whose hormone thyroxin is important in determining metabolic rate (cf. *endocrine gland*).

thyroxin. The hormone of the thyroid gland (cf. *thyroid gland*).

timbre. The quality distinguishing a tone of a given pitch sounded by one instrument from that sounded by another. The differences are due to overtones and other impurities (cf. *overtone*).

tip-of-the-tongue phenomenon. The experience of failing to recall a word or name when we are quite certain we know it.

T-maze. An apparatus in which an animal is presented with two alternative paths, one of which leads to a goal box. It is usually used with rats and lower organisms (cf. *maze*).

token learning. An arrangement within operant conditioning in which a token (e.g., a poker chip) as a secondary reinforcer can be exchanged for a primary reinforcing stimulus (e.g., food).

trained introspection. Cf. *introspection*.

training. Learning that is guided by another individual, such as a parent or teacher, or, as in self-training, learning that is deliberately undertaken to shape behavior in particular directions (cf. *maturation*).

trait. A persisting characteristic or dimension of personality according to which individuals can be rated or measured (cf. *trait profile, type theory*).

trait profile. A chart plotting the ratings of a number of traits of the same individual on a common scale in parallel rows, so that the pattern of traits can be visually perceived (syn. *psychograph*; cf. *trait, test profile*).

trait theory. The theory that human personality is most profitably characterized by the scores that an individual makes on a number of scales, each of which represents a trait or dimension of his personality (cf. *type theory*).

tranquilizer. A drug such as chlorpromazine or reserpine used to reduce anxiety and relieve depression; hence useful in the therapy of mental disorders.

transfer of training. The effect of prior learning on present learning. If learning a new task is facilitated, transfer is positive; if the new learning is interfered with, transfer is negative (cf. *formal discipline, proactive inhibition, retroactive inhibition*).

transfer through principles. A theory of transfer of training which proposes that new learning is facilitated by detecting the applicability of principles or generalizations discovered in prior learning (cf. *transfer of training*).

transference. In psychoanalysis, the patient's unconsciously making the therapist the object of emotional response, thus transferring to him responses appropriate to other persons important in the life history of the patient.

traveling wave theory. A modification by Békésy of the place theory of hearing. The theory states that when a sound of given frequency enters the ear, a wave travels along the basilar membrane and displaces it a maximum amount at a certain point, the point depending on its frequency (cf. *basilar membrane, frequency theory, place theory, volley theory*).

trial-and-error learning. An expression characterizing multiple-response learning, in which the proper response is selected out of varied behavior through the influence of reward and punishment. Variously described as approximation and correction, fumble and success, etc. (cf. *multiple-response learning, operant conditioning*).

trichromatism. Normal color vision, based on the classification of color vision according to three color systems: black-white, blue-yellow, and red-green. The normal eye sees all three; the color-blind eye is defective in one or two of the three systems (cf. *dichromatism, monochromatism*).

type theory. The theory that human subjects can profitably be classified into a small number of classes or types, each class or type having characteristics in common which set its members apart from other classes or types (cf. *trait theory*).

unconditioned response. The response given originally to the unconditioned stimulus used as the basis for establishing a conditioned response to a previously neutral stimulus (cf. *conditioned response*).

unconscious motive. A motive of which the subject is unaware, or aware of in distorted form. Because there is no sharp dividing line between conscious and unconscious, many motives have both conscious and unconscious aspects.

unconscious processes. (1) Processes, such as wishes or fears, that might be conscious but of which the subject is unaware. (2) Less commonly, physiological processes of the body (circulation, metabolism, etc.) that go on outside of awareness (cf. *consciousness*).

utricle. Cf. *vestibular sacs*.

validity. The predictive significance of a test for its intended purposes. Validity can be measured by a coefficient of correlation between scores on the test and the scores which the test seeks to predict, i.e., scores on some criterion (cf. *criterion, reliability*).

variable. One of the stimulus, response, or background items undergoing study in an experiment (cf. *dependent variable, independent variable*).

variance. The square of a standard deviation or standard error.

variation. Cf. *measure of variation*.

verbal report. A statement in words by a subject; often an account of his subjective, conscious experiences, thus making them accessible for study (cf. *behavior*).

verification. The final step in creative thought proposed by Wallas. For the mathematician or scientist, verification is in the form of logical or experimental proof. For the artist, verification consists in a review, to determine whether or not the artistic creation expresses what is intended (cf. *preparation, incubation, illumination*).

vestibular sacs. Two sacs in the labyrinth of the inner ear, called the saccule and utricle, which contain the otoliths ("ear stones"). Pressure of the otoliths on the hair cells in the gelatinous material of the utricle and saccule gives us the sense of upright position or departure from it (cf. *equilibratory senses*).

visual area. A projection area lying in the occipital lobe. In man, partial damage to this area produces blindness in portions of the visual field corresponding to the amount and location of the damage (syn. *striate area*).

visual field. The total visual stimuli acting upon the eye when it is directed toward a fixation point.

visual purple. A light-sensitive substance contained in the rods of the eye (syn. *rhodopsin*).

volley theory. A modified frequency theory of hearing proposed by Wever and Bray which suggests that the frequency of the stimulus may be represented in bundles of fibers in the auditory nerve responding somewhat independently, so that the frequency is represented by the composite volley, even though no single fiber carries impulses at that rate (cf. *frequency theory, place theory, traveling wave theory*).

voluntary action. Self-initiated action (cf. *operant behavior*).

Weber's law. A law stating that the difference threshold is proportional to the stimulus magnitude at which it is measured. It is known to be accurate only over limited stimulus ranges (cf. *difference threshold*).

weighted items. If one item (or a single test in a battery of tests) has been found to predict better than another, it is assigned a higher weight, so that it will influence a composite score more than the item (or test) of lower predictive value.

whole learning. Learning a multiple-response task as a unit, e.g., memorizing a long poem from beginning to end without separate practice of the parts (cf. *part learning*).

word-association experiment. An experiment designed for studying associative processes in which the subject responds to a stimulus-word by saying as promptly as possible the first word that he thinks of (cf. *free association, controlled association*).

working through. In psychoanalytic therapy, the process of reeducation by having the patient face the same conflicts over and over again in the consultation room, until he can independently face and master the conflicts in ordinary life.

X-chromosome. A chromosome which, if paired with another X-chromosome, determines that the individual will be a female. If it is combined with a Y-chromosome, the individual will be a male. The X-chromosome transmits sex-linked traits (cf. *chromosome, sex-linked trait, Y-chromosome*).

Y-chromosome. The chromosome which, combined with an X-chromosome, determines maleness. Its role in sex-linked traits is as though it carried only recessive genes (cf. *chromosome, sex-linked trait, X-chromosome*).

zest. In mental health, the ability to take a hearty interest in living, to seek out opportunities for useful activity, recreation, good fellowship; to be distinguished, however, from frenzied overactivity (cf. *mental health*).

References and Index to Authors of Works Cited

The numbers in **bold face** following each reference give the text pages on which the paper or book is cited. Citations in the text are made by author and date of publication.

ABELSON, J., *see* Douvan and Abelson (1966).

ABELSON, R. P. (1964) Mathematical models for the distribution of attitudes under controversy. In Frederiksen, N., and Gulliksen, H. (Eds.) *Contributions to mathematical psychology.* N. Y.: Holt, Rinehart and Winston, 41–160. — **384**

ABELSON, R. P., *see also* Rosenberg and others (1960).

ADAMS, J. A., *see* Reynolds and Adams (1953).

ADAMSON, R. E., and TAYLOR, D. W. (1954) Functional fixedness as related to elapsed time and set. *J. exp. Psychol.,* 47:122–26. — **379, 380**

ADLER, A. (1917) *Study of organ inferiority and its psychical compensation.* Washington, D. C.: Nervous and Mental Disease Publishing Co. — **520**

ADOLPH, E. F. (1941) The internal environment and behavior: water content. *Amer. J. Psychiat.,* 97:1365–73. — **124**

ADORNO, T. W., FRENKEL–BRUNSWIK, E., LEVINSON, D. J., and SANFORD, R. N. (1950) *The authoritarian personality.* N. Y.: Harper. — **475, 579**

AGNEW, H. W., JR., *see* Williams, Agnew, and Webb (1964).

AINSWORTH, M. D., *see* Klopfer and others (1954).

ALDRICH, C. A., and NORVAL, M. A. (1946) A developmental graph for the first year of life. *J. Pediat.,* 29:304–08. — **63**

ALLEN, R. M. (1958) *Personality assessment procedures.* N. Y.: McGraw-Hill. — **501**

ALLPORT, F. H. (1955) *Theories of perception and the concept of structure.* N. Y.: Wiley. — **245**

ALLPORT, G. W. (1935) Attitudes. In Murchison, C. (Ed.) *Handbook of social psychology.* Worcester, Mass.: Clark Univ. Press, 798–844. — **584**

ALLPORT, G. W. (1937) *Personality.* N. Y.: Holt. — **136, 464, 465, 470**

ALLPORT, G. W. (1944) *ABC's of scapegoating.* Chicago: Central Y.M.C.A. College. — **578**

ALLPORT, G. W. (1954a) The historical background of modern social psychology. In Lindzey, G. (Ed.) *Handbook of social psychology.* Reading, Mass.: Addison-Wesley, 3–56. — **583**

ALLPORT, G. W. (1954b) *The nature of prejudice.* Reading, Mass.: Addison-Wesley. — **580, 600**

ALLPORT, G. W. (1955) *Becoming.* New Haven, Conn.: Yale Univ. Press. — **485**

ALLPORT, G. W. (1960) *Personality and social encounter.* Boston: Beacon Press. — **470, 487**

ALLPORT, G. W. (1961) *Pattern and growth in personality.* N. Y.: Holt, Rinehart and Winston. — **470, 485**

ALLPORT, G. W. (1965) *Letters from Jenny.* N. Y.: Harcourt, Brace & World. — **485**

ALLPORT, G. W., and ODBERT, H. S. (1936) Trait-names: a psycho-lexical study. *Psychol. Monogr.,* 47, No. 211. — **471**

ALLPORT, G. W., VERNON, P. E., and LINDZEY, G. (1960) *A study of values: a scale for measuring the dominant interests in personality* (3rd Ed.). Boston: Houghton Mifflin. — **470, 488**

ALPER, T. G., and BORING, E. G. (1944) Intelligence test scores of northern and southern white and Negro recruits in 1918. *J. abnorm. soc. Psychol.,* 39:471–74. — **458**

ALPERT, R., *see* Sears, Rau, and Alpert (1965).

AMES, A., JR. (1951) Visual perception and the rotating trapezoidal window. *Psychol. Monogr.,* 65, No. 324. — **220**

ANASTASI, A. (1964) *Fields of applied psychology.* N. Y.: McGraw-Hill. — **617**

ANASTASI, A., and FOLEY, J. P., JR. (1958) *Differential psychology* (3rd Ed.). N. Y.: Macmillan. — **443, 461**

ANDERSON, G. L., *see* Anderson and Anderson (1951).

ANDERSON, H. H., and ANDERSON, G. L. (Eds.) (1951) *An introduction to projective techniques.* N. Y.: Prentice-Hall. — **502**

ANDERSON, R. C., and AUSUBEL, D. P. (1965) *Readings in the psychology of cognition.* N. Y.: Holt, Rinehart and Winston. — **393**

ANDERSSON, B. (1953) The effect of injections and hypertonic solutions in parts of the hypothalamus of goats. *Acta Physiol. Scand.,* 28:188–201. — **124**

ANGELL, G. W. (1949) The effect of immediate knowledge of quiz results on final examination scores in freshman chemistry. *J. educ. Res.,* 42:391–94. — **342**

ANKLES, T. M. (1939) *A study of jealousy as differentiated from envy.* Boston: Bruce Humphries. — **179**

ANSBACHER, H. L., and ANSBACHER, R. R. (Eds.) (1956) *The individual psychology of Alfred Adler.* N. Y.: Basic Books. — **520**

ANSBACHER, R. R., *see* Ansbacher and Ansbacher (1956).

APPLEY, M. H., *see* Cofer and Appley (1964).

ARCHER, E. J., *see* Bourne and Archer (1956).

ARIETI, S. (Ed.) (1959) *American handbook of psychiatry.* (2 vols.) N. Y.: Basic Books. — **534, 547**

ARKIN, A. M., HASTEY, J. M., and REISER, M. F. (1966) Post-hypnotically stimulated sleep-talking. *J. nerv. ment. Dis.,* 142:293–309. — **257**

ARNOLD, M. (1949) A demonstration analysis of the TAT in a clinical setting. *J. abnorm. soc. Psychol.,* 44:97–111. — **494**

ARNOLD, M. (1960) *Emotion and personality.* (2 vols.) N. Y.: Columbia Univ. Press. — **173, 174**

ARNOLD, M., *see also* Kuhlen and Arnold (1944).

ARONSON, E., *see* Lindzey and Aronson (1967).

ASCH, S. E. (1956) Studies of independence and submission to group pressure: 1. A minority of one against a unanimous majority. *Psychol. Monogr.,* 70, No. 416. — **581**

ASERINSKY, E., and KLEITMAN, N. (1953) Regularly occurring periods of eye motility, and concomitant phenomena, during sleep. *Science,* 118:273–74. — **254**

ATKINSON, J. W. (1953) The achievement motive and recall of interrupted and completed tasks. *J. exp. Psychol.,* 46:381–90. — **327**

ATKINSON, J. W. (1957) Motivational determinants of risk-taking behavior. *Psychol. Rev.,* 64:359–72. — **341**

ATKINSON, J. W. (1964) *An introduction to motivation.* Princeton, N. J.: Van Nostrand. — **138, 156, 162**

ATKINSON, J. W., *see also* McClelland, Atkinson, Clark, and Lowell (1953); Moulton, Raphelson, Kristofferson, and Atkinson (1958).

ATKINSON, J. W., and FEATHER, N. T. (Eds.) (1966) *A theory of achievement motivation.* N. Y.: Wiley. — **162**

ATKINSON, J. W., and LITWIN, G. H. (1960) Achievement motive and test anxiety conceived as motive to approach success and motive to avoid failure. *J. abnorm. soc. Psychol.,* 60:52–63. — **156, 157**

ATKINSON, R. C. (1957) A stochastic model for rote serial learning. *Psychometrika,* 22:87–95. — **341**

ATKINSON, R. C. *see also* Groen and Atkinson (1966).

ATKINSON, R. C., BOWER, G. H., and CROTHERS, E. J. (1965) *An introduction to mathematical learning theory.* N. Y.: Wiley. — **308, 313, 415**

ATKINSON, R. C., and ESTES, W. K. (1963) Stimulus sampling theory. In Luce, R. D., Bush, R. R., and Galanter, E. (Eds.) *Handbook of mathematical psychology,* Vol. II. N. Y.: Wiley, 121–268. — **308, 344**

ATKINSON, R. C., and HANSEN, D. N. (1966) Computer-assisted instruction in initial reading: the Stanford Project. *Reading Res. Quart.,* 2:5–25. — **352**

ATKINSON, R. C. and SHIFFRIN, R. M. (1967) Mathematical models for memory and learning. In Kimble, D. P. (Ed.) *Learning, remembering and forgetting,* Vol. III. N. Y.: *N. Y. Acad. Sci.* — **328**

AUSUBEL, D. P., *see* Anderson and Ausubel (1965).

AX, A. F. (1953) The physiological differentiation between fear and anger in humans. *Psychosom. Med.,* 15:433–42. — **169, 170**

AZRIN, W. H., HOLZ, W. C., and HAKE, D. F. (1963) Fixed-ratio punishment. *J. exp. anal. Behav.,* 6:141–48. — **357**

BABICH, F. R., JACOBSON, A. L., BUBASH, S. and JACOBSON, A. (1965) Transfer of a response to naive rats by injection of ribonucleic acid extracted from trained rats. *Science,* 149:656–57. — **322**

BABICH, F. R., *see also* Jacobson, Babich, Bubash, and Jacobson (1965).

BACKMAN, C. W., *see* Secord and Backman (1964).

BAER, P. E., *see* Fuhrer and Baer (1965).

BAILEY, L. L., *see* Marquart and Bailey (1955).

BAKER, C. T., *see* Sontag, Baker, and Nelson (1958).

BAKER, K. E., *see* Gagné and Baker (1950).

BALDWIN, B. T., and STECHER, L. I. (1922) Mental growth curves of normal and superior children. *Univ. Ia. Stud. Child Welf.,* 2, No. 1. — **436**

BALL, E. S., *see* Bossard and Ball (1955).

BANDURA, A. (1962) Social learning through imitation. In Jones, M. R. (Ed.) *Nebraska symposium on motivation.* Lincoln, Nebr.: Univ. of Nebraska Press, 211–69. — **83**

BANDURA, A. (1965) Vicarious processes: a case of no-trial learning. In Berkowitz, L. (Ed.) *Advances in experimental social psychology,* Vol. II. N. Y.: Academic Press. — **372**

BANDURA, A., and WALTERS, R. H. (1959) *Adolescent aggression.* N. Y.: Ronald Press. — **91**

BANDURA, A., and WALTERS, R. H. (1963) *Social learning and personality development.* N. Y.: Holt, Rinehart and Winston. — **485**

BARBER, T. X. (1965) Experimental analysis of "hypnotic" behavior: review of recent empirical findings. *J. abnorm. Psychol.,* 70:132–54. — **263**

BARKER, C. H., *see* Schein, Schneier, and Barker (1961).

BARKER, L. S., *see* Barker and Barker (1963).

BARKER, R. G., *see* Stone and Barker (1937).

BARKER, R. G., and BARKER, L. S. (1963) Sixty-five and over. In Williams, R. H., Tibbitts, C., and Donahue, W. (Eds.) *Processes of aging,* Vol. I. N. Y.: Atherton Press, 246–72. — **104**

BARKER, R. G., DEMBO, T., and LEWIN, K. (1941) Frustration and regression: an experiment with young children. *Univ. Ia. Stud. Child Welf.,* 18, No. 386. — **510**

BARRON, F. (1954) *Personal soundness in university graduate students.* Berkeley, Calif.: Univ. of California Press. — **492**

BARRON, F. (1963) *Creativity and psychological health.* Princeton, N. J.: Van Nostrand. — **388, 389**

BARRON, F., *see also* Taylor and Barron (1963).

BARRON, J. N., *see* Kelsey and Barron (1958).

BASS, B. M., *see* Berg and Bass (1961).

BATEMAN, D. E., *see* Lacey, Bateman, and Van Lehn (1952).

BATEMAN, F., *see* Soal and Bateman (1954).

BAYER, E. (1929) Beiträge zur Zweikomponententheorie des Hungers. *Z. Psychol.,* 112:1–54. — **129**

BAYLEY, N. (1932) A study of the crying of infants during mental and physical tests. *J. genet. Psychol.,* 40:306–29. — **175, 176**

BAYLEY, N. (1940a) Mental growth in young children. 39th Yearbook, Part II, National Society for the Study of Education. Chicago: Univ. of Chicago Press. — **450**

BAYLEY, N. (1940b) Factors influencing the growth of intelligence in young children. 39th Yearbook, Part II, National Society for the Study of Education. Chicago: Univ. of Chicago Press. — **450**

BAYLEY, N., and TUDDENHAM, R. D. (1944) Adolescent changes in body build. 43rd Yearbook, National Society for the Study of Education. Chicago: Univ. of Chicago Press. — **95**

BEACH, F. A. (1944) Relative effects of androgen upon the mating behavior of male rats subjected to pre-brain injury or castration. *J. exp. Zool.,* 97:249–85. — **126**

BEACH, F. A. (1956) Characteristics of masculine "sex drive." In Jones, M. (Ed.) *Nebraska symposium on motivation.* Lincoln, Nebr.: Univ. of Nebraska Press, 1–32. — **126**

BEACH, F. A., *see also* Ford and Beach (1951).

BEARDSLEE, D. C., and WERTHEIMER, MICHAEL (Eds.) (1958) *Readings in perception.* Princeton, N. J.: Van Nostrand. — **245**

BECK, L. F. (1936) Hypnotic identification of an amnesia victim. *Brit. J. med. Psychol.,* 16:36–42. — **519**

BECK, W. S., *see* Simpson and Beck (1965).

BECKER, K. (1958) *I met a traveller: the triumph of*

Father Phillips. N. Y.: Farrar, Strauss, and Cudahy. — **598**

BECKER, R. F., KING, J. E., and MARKEE, J. E. (1962) Studies on olfactory discrimination in dogs. II. Discriminatory behavior in a free environment. *J. comp. physiol. Psychol.*, 55:773–80. — **209**

BEERS, C. W. (1908) *A mind that found itself*. N. Y.: Doubleday. — **549**

BEIDLER, L. M. (1961) Mechanisms of gustatory and olfactory receptor stimulation. In Rosenblith, W. A. (Ed.) *Sensory communication*. N. Y.: Wiley. — **210**

BÉKÉSY, G. V. (1930) Über das Fechner'sche Gesetz und seine Bedeutung für die Theorie der aukustischen Beobachtungsfehler und die Theorie des Hörens. *Ann. Phys.*, 7:329–59. — **192**

BÉKÉSY, G. V. (1960) *Experiments in hearing*. N. Y.: McGraw-Hill. — **208, 216**

BELL, H. M. (1950) Retention of pursuit rotor skill after one year. *J. exp. Psychol.*, 40:648–49. — **296**

BELL, R. Q. (1960) Relations between behavior manifestations in the human neonate. *Child Develop.*, 31:463–77. — **467**

BENDIX, R., *see* Lipset and Bendix (1959).

BENEDICT, R. (1934) *Patterns of culture*. Boston: Houghton Mifflin. — **155**

BENNETT, E. L., and CALVIN, M. (1964) Failure to train planarians reliably. *Neurosci. res. Prog. Bull.*, 2, No. 4:3–24. — **322**

BENNIS, W. G., SCHEIN, E. H., BERLEW, D. E., and STEELE, F. I. (Eds.) (1964) *Interpersonal dynamics*. Homewood, Ill.: Dorsey Press. — **600**

BENSLEY, M., *see* Heidbreder, Bensley, and Ivy. (1948).

BENZINGER, T. H. (1961) The human thermostat. *Sci. Amer.*, 204:134–47. — **41, 42**

BERELSON, B. (1954) What "missing the newspaper" means. In Schramm, W. (Ed.) *The process and effects of mass communication*. Urbana, Ill.: Univ. of Illinois Press, 36–47. — **593**

BERG, I. A. (1959) The unimportance of test content. In Bass, B. M., and Berg, I. A. *Objective approaches to personality assessment*. Princeton, N. J.: Van Nostrand, 83–89. — **493**

BERG, I. A., and BASS, B. M. (Eds.) (1961) *Conformity and deviation*. N. Y.: Harper. — **600**

BERGER, M., *see* Rosenbaum and Berger (1963).

BERGER, R. J. (1963) Experimental modification of dream content by meaningful verbal stimuli. *Brit. J. Psychiat.*, 109:722–40. — **257**

BERKOWITZ, L., and COTTINGHAM, D. R. (1960) The interest value and relevance of fear arousing communications. *J. abnorm. soc. Psychol.*, 60:37–43. — **596**

BERLEW, D. E., *see* Bennis and others (1964).

BERLYNE, D. E. (1966) Curiosity and exploration. *Science*, 153:25–33. — **131**

BERLYNE, D. E., and SLATER, J. (1957) Perceptual curiosity, exploratory behavior and maze learning. *J. comp. physiol. Psychol.*, 50:228–32. — **131**

BERNAUT, E., *see* Leites and Bernaut (1954).

BERNSTEIN, A. (1955) Some relations between techniques of feeding and training during infancy and certain behavior in childhood. *Genet. Psychol. Monogr.*, 51:3–44. — **76**

BERNSTEIN, A., *see also* Lennard and Bernstein (1960).

BERRY, C. A., *see* Sells and Berry (1961).

BERRY, P. C., *see* Taylor, Berry, and Block (1958).

BERSH, P. J. (1951) The influence of two variables upon the establishment of a secondary reinforcer for operant responses. *J. exp. Psychol.*, 41:62–73. — **284**

BEST, C. H., and TAYLOR, N. B. (1955) *The physiological basis of medical practice*. Baltimore, Md.: Williams and Wilkins. — **51**

BETTELHEIM, B. (1943) Individual and mass behavior in extreme situations. *J. abnorm. soc. Psychol.*, 38:417–52. — **512**

BETZ, B. J., *see* Whitehorn and Betz (1960).

BEVAN, W., *see* Helson and Bevan (1967); Secord, Bevan, and Katz (1956).

BEXTON, W. H., HERON, W., and SCOTT, T. H. (1954) Effects of decreased variation in the environment. *Canad. J. Psychol.*, 8:70–76. — **54**

BIDERMAN, A. D., and ZIMMER, H. (Eds.) (1961) *The manipulation of human behavior*. N. Y.: Wiley. — **600**

BIRCH, H. G., and RABINOWITZ, H. S. (1951) The negative effect of previous experience on productive thinking. *J. exp. Psychol.*, 41:121–25. — **379**

BIRDSALL, T. G., *see* Swets, Tanner, and Birdsall (1961).

BIRNEY, R. C., *see* Teevan and Birney (1961) (1964a) (1964b).

BIRNEY, R. C., and TEEVAN, R. C. (Eds.) (1961) *Reinforcement*. Princeton, N. J.: Van Nostrand. — **313**

BIRNEY, R. C., and TEEVAN, R. C. (Eds.) (1962) *Measuring human motivation*. Princeton, N. J.: Van Nostrand. — **162**

BIRREN, J. E., *see* Fisher and Birren (1947).

BISHOP, G. H., and CLARE, M. H. (1952) Sites of origin of electric potentials in striate cortex. *J. Neurophysiol.*, 15:201–20. — **38**

BLACK, H. (1963) *They shall not pass*. N. Y.: Morrow. — **439**

BLAKE, R. R., *see* Freed and others (1955); Helson, Blake, and Mouton (1958).

BLAKESLEE, P., *see* Gunter, Feigenson, and Blakeslee (1965).

BLANCHARD, M. B., *see* Jones, Conrad, and Blanchard (1932).

BLOCK, C. H., *see* Taylor, Berry, and Block (1958).

BLOCK, J. (1957) Studies in the phenomenology of emotions. *J. abnorm. soc. Psychol.*, 54:358–63. — **172**

BLOOM, B. S. (1956) Report on creativity research at the University of Chicago. In Taylor, C. W. (Ed.) *The 1955 University of Utah Research Conference on the Identification of Creative Scientific Talent*. Salt Lake City, Utah: Univ. of Utah Press, 182–94. — **388**

BLOOM, B. S. (1964) *Stability and change in human characteristics*. N. Y.: Wiley. — **90**

BLOOM, B. S., *see also* Stern, Stein, and Bloom (1956).

BLUM, R., and Associates (1964) *Utopiates: the use and users of LSD–25*. N. Y.: Atherton Press. — **265, 268**

BOGEN, J. E. *see* Gazzaniga, Bogan, and Sperry (1965).

BORCHARD, E. M. (1932) *Convicting the innocent: 65 actual errors of criminal justice*. New Haven, Conn.: Yale Univ. Press. — **606**

BOREN, J. J., *see* Brodie and others (1960).

BORING, E. G. (1950) *A history of experimental psychology* (2nd Ed.) N. Y.: Appleton-Century-Crofts. — **29**

BORING, E. G., *see also* Alper and Boring (1944); Holway and Boring (1941); Herrnstein and Boring (1965).

BOSSARD, J. H. S., and BALL, E. S. (1955) Personality roles in the large family. *Child Develpm.*, 26:71–78. — **84**

BOUDREAU, J. C., *see* Hirsch and Boudreau (1958).

BOURNE, L. E., JR. (1966) *Human conceptual behavior.* Boston: Allyn and Bacon. — **393**

BOURNE, L. E., JR., and ARCHER, E. J. (1956) Time continuously on target as a function of distribution of practice. *J. exp. Psychol.*, 51:25–33. — **337, 338**

BOWER, G. H. (1961) Application of a model to paired-associate learning. *Psychometrika*, 26:255–80. — **299**

BOWER, G. H. (1966) A descriptive theory of human memory. In Kimble, D. P. (Ed.) *Learning, remembering and forgetting*, Vol. II. N. Y.: New York Academy of Science. — **299, 301, 328**

BOWER, G. H., *see also* Atkinson, Bower, and Crothers (1965); Hilgard and Bower (1966).

BOWER, G. H., and TRABASSO, T. R. (1964) Concept identification. In Atkinson, R. C. (Ed.) *Studies in mathematical psychology*. Stanford, Calif.: Stanford Univ. Press, 32–94. — **301**

BOWMAN, P. H., *see* Guetzkow and Bowman (1946).

BOYD, E. (1952) *An introduction to human biology and anatomy for first year medical students.* Denver, Colo.: Child Research Council. — **92**

BRADY, J. V. (1958) Ulcers in "executive" monkeys. *Sci. Amer.*, 199:95–100. — **539, 540**

BRADY, J. V., PORTER, R. W., CONRAD, D. G., and MASON, J. W. (1958) Avoidance behavior and the development of gastroduodenal ulcers. *J. exp. Anal. Behav.*, 1:69–73. — **539**

BRECKINRIDGE, E. L. (1953) *Effective use of older workers.* Chicago: Wilcox and Follett. — **114**

BREHM, J. W., *see* Rosenberg and others (1960).

BREHM, J. W., and COHEN, A. R. (1962) *Explorations in cognitive dissonance.* N. Y.: Wiley. — **592**

BRELAND, K., and BRELAND, M. (1966) *Animal behavior.* N. Y.: Macmillan. — **286**

BRELAND, M., *see* Breland and Breland (1966).

BRELSFORD, J. W., JR., *see* Theios and Brelsford (1966).

BRIGGS, G. E., *see* Melton and Briggs (1960).

BRIM, O. G., JR. (1965) American attitudes toward intelligence tests. *Amer. Psychologist*, 20:125–30. — **439, 440**

BRITT, S. H. (1940) The rules of evidence: an empirical study in psychology and law. *Cornell Law Quart.*, 25:556–80. — **606**

BROADBENT, D. E. (1958) *Perception and communication.* N. Y.: Pergamon Press. — **249**

BROADBENT, D. E. (1963) Flow of information within the organism. *J. verb. Learning verb. Behav.*, 4:34–39. — **328**

BROADBENT, D. E. (1965) Information processing in the nervous system. *Science*, 150:457–62. — **330, 393**

BRODBECK, A. J., *see* Burdick and Brodbeck (1959); Davis and others (1948).

BRODIE, D. A., MALIS, J. L., MORENO, O. M., and BOREN, J. J. (1960) Nonreversibility of appetitive characteristics of intracranial stimulation. *Amer. J. Physiol.*, 199:707–09. — **293**

BROEN, W. E., JR., and STORMS, L. H. (1964) Schizophrenic behavior disorganization from the standpoint of psychological behavior theory. *Calif. ment. Hlth. Dig.*, 2:14–15. — **535**

BROGDEN, W. J., *see* Roessler and Brogden (1943).

BROWN, D. G. (1957) Masculinity-femininity development in children. *J. consult. Psychol.*, 21:197–202. — **83**

BROWN, J. F., and VOTH, A. C. (1937) The path of seen movement as a function of the vector field. *Amer. J. Psychol.*, 49:543–63. — **230**

BROWN, J. H. U. (Ed.) (1963) *Physiology of man in space.* N. Y.: Academic Press. — **617**

BROWN, J. S. (1942) The generalization of approach responses as a function of stimulus intensity and strength of motivation. *J. comp. Psychol.*, 33:209–26. — **505**

BROWN, J. S. (1948) Gradients of approach and avoidance responses and their relation to motivation. *J. comp. physiol. Psychol.*, 41:450–65. — **507**

BROWN, P. K., and WALD, G. (1964) Visual pigments in single rods and cones of the human retina. *Science*, 144:45–52. — **201**

BROWN, R. (1962) Models of attitude change. In Brown, R., and others (Eds.) *New directions in psychology*. N. Y.: Holt, Rinehart and Winston, 1–85. — **158**

BROWN, R. (1965) *Social psychology.* N. Y.: Free Press. — **590, 600**

BROWN, R., and HILDUM, D. C. (1956) Expectancy and the identification of syllables. *Language*, 32:411–19. — **371**

BROWN, R. W., and LENNEBERG, E. H. (1954) A study in language and cognition. *J. abnorm. soc. Psychol.*, 49:454–62. — **375, 410**

BROWN, R. W., and MC NEILL, D. (1966) The "tip-of-the-tongue" phenomenon. *J. verb. Learning verb. Behav.*, 5:325–37. — **319**

BROZ, W., *see* Lemere, Voegtlin, Broz, O'Hollaren, and Tupper (1942).

BRUCE, R. W. (1933) Conditions of transfer of training. *J. exp. Psychol.*, 16:343–61. — **344**

BRUNER, J. S. (1960) *The process of education.* Cambridge, Mass.: Harvard Univ. Press. — **68**

BRUNER, J. S. (1966) *Toward a theory of instruction.* Cambridge, Mass.: The Belknap Press of Harvard Univ. Press. — **363**

BRUNER, J. S., *see also* Smith, Bruner, and White (1956).

BRUNER, J. S., BUSIEK, R. D., and MINTURN, A. L. (1952) Assimilation in the immediate reproduction of visually perceived figures. *J. exp. Psychol.*, 44:151–55. — **320**

BRUNER, J. S., and GOODMAN, C. C. (1947) Value and need as organizing factors in perception. *J. abnorm. soc. Psychol.*, 42:33–44. — **240**

BRUNER, J. S., and POSTMAN, L. J. (1949) On the perception of incongruity: a paradigm. *J. Pers.*, 18:206–23. — **240**

BUBASH, S., *see* Babich, Jacobson, Bubash, and Jacobson (1965); Jacobson, Babich, Bubash, and Jacobson (1965).

BÜHLER, C. (1933) The social behavior of children. In Murchison, C. (Ed.) *Handbook of child psychology*. Worcester, Mass.: Clark Univ. Press, 374–416. — **98, 99**

BUGELSKI, B. R. (1956) *The psychology of learning.* N. Y.: Holt. — **313**

BUGENTAL, J. F. T. (1963) Humanistic psychology: a new breakthrough. *Amer. Psychologist*, 18:563–67. — **7**

BURDICK, E., and BRODBECK, A. J. (Eds.) (1959) *American voting behavior.* Chicago: Free Press of Glencoe, Ill. — **600**

BURGESS, E. W., and COTTRELL, L. S. (1939) *Predicting success or failure in marriage.* Englewood Cliffs, N. J.: Prentice-Hall. — **109**

BURGESS, E. W., and WALLIN, P. (1953) *Engagement and marriage.* Philadelphia: Lippincott. — **109**

BURKE, C. J., *see* Estes and Burke (1953).

BURKS, B. S. (1928) The relative influence of nature and nurture upon mental development: a comparative study of foster parent-child resemblance and true parent-child resemblance. 27th Yearbook, Part I, National Society for the Study of Education. Chicago: Univ. of Chicago Press. — **451, 452, 455**

BURLINGHAM, D., see Freud and Burlingham (1943) (1944).

BURT, C. (1955) The evidence for the concept of intelligence. *Brit. J. educ. Psychol.*, 25:158–77. — **453**

BURTON, A., and HARRIS, R. E. (1947) *Case histories in clinical and abnormal psychology*. N. Y.: Harper. — **536**

BURTT, H. E. (1941) An experimental study of early childhood memory. *J. genet. Psychol.*, 58:435–39. — **316**

BUSH, R. R., see Luce, Bush, and Galanter, Vol. I (1963), Vol. III (1965).

BUSIEK, R. D., see Bruner, Busiek, and Minturn (1952).

BUTLER, R. A. (1953) Discrimination learning by rhesus monkeys to visual-exploration motivation. *J. comp. physiol. Psychol.*, 46:95–98. — **131**

BUTTENWIESER, P. (1935) *The relation of age to skill of expert chess players*. Unpublished Ph.D. dissertation, Stanford University. — **110**

BUXTON, C. E., and ROSS, H. V. (1949) Relationship between reminiscence and type of learning technique in serial anticipation learning. *J. exp. Psychol.*, 39:41–46. — **338**

BYRNE, D. (1966) *An introduction to personality*. Englewood Cliffs, N. J.: Prentice-Hall. — **485**

BYRNE, W. L., and others (1966) Memory transfer. *Science*, 153:658 — **322**

CALDWELL, B. M. (1964) The effects of infant care. In Hoffman, M. L., and Hoffman, L. W. (Eds.) *Review of child development research*, Vol. I. N. Y.: Russell Sage Foundation, 9–87. — **76**

CALVIN, M., see Bennett and Calvin (1964).

CAMERON, N., and MAGARET, A. (1951) *Behavior pathology*. Boston: Houghton Mifflin. — **531**

CAMPBELL, A., CONVERSE, P. E., MILLER, W. E., and STOKES, D. E. (1960) *The American voter*. N. Y.: Wiley. — **590, 591, 600**

CAMPBELL, B. A., and SHEFFIELD, F. D. (1953) Relation of random activity to food deprivation. *J. comp. physiol. Psychol.*, 46:320–22. — **120**

CAMPBELL, D. P. (1965) The vocational interests of American Psychological Association presidents. *Amer. Psychologist*, 20:636–44. — **609**

CAMPBELL, D. T., see Jacobs and Campbell (1961); Segall, Campbell, and Herskovitz (1963).

CANNON, W. B. (1927) The James-Lange theory of emotion. *Amer. J. Psychol.*, 39:106–24. — **173**

CANNON, W. B. (1929) *Bodily changes in pain, hunger, fear, and rage* (2nd Ed.). N. Y.: Appleton-Century-Crofts. — **166**

CANNON, W. B. (1934) Hunger and thirst. In Murchison, C. (Ed.) *Handbook of general experimental psychology*. Worcester, Mass.: Clark Univ. Press, 247–63. — **122**

CANNON, W. B. (1939) *The wisdom of the body* (Rev. Ed.). N. Y.: Norton. — **55**

CANNON, W. B. (1945) *The way of an investigator: a scientist's experiences in medical research*. N. Y.: Norton. — **386**

CANTRIL, H. (1944) *Gauging public opinion*. Princeton, N. J.: Princeton Univ. Press. — **587, 588**

CANTRIL, H., GAUDET, H., and HERZOG, H. (1940) *The invasion from Mars*. Princeton, N. J.: Princeton Univ. Press. — **593**

CANTRIL, H., and HUNT, W. A. (1932) Emotional effects produced by the injection of adrenalin. *Amer. J. Psychol.*, 44:300–07. — **168**

CARLSMITH, J. M., see Festinger and Carlsmith (1959).

CARMICHAEL, L. (1926) The development of behavior in vertebrates experimentally removed from the influence of external stimulation. *Psychol. Rev.*, 33:51–58. — **211**

CARMICHAEL, L. (1954) The onset and early development of behavior. In Carmichael, L. (Ed.) *Manual of child psychology* (2nd Ed.). N. Y.: Wiley, 60–185. — **61**

CARMICHAEL, L., HOGAN, H. P., and WALTER, A. A. (1932) An experimental study of the effect of language on the reproduction of visually perceived form. *J. exp. Psychol.*, 15:73–86. — **321**

CARMICHAEL, L., ROBERTS, S. O., and WESSEL, N. Y. (1937) A study of the judgment of manual expressions as presented in still and motion pictures. *J. soc. Psychol.*, 8:115–42. — **172**

CARMICHAEL, L., and SMITH, M. F. (1939) Quantified pressure stimulation and generality of response in fetal life. *J. genet. Psychol.*, 54:425–34. — **61**

CARROLL, J. B. (1964) *Language and thought*. Englewood Cliffs, N. J.: Prentice-Hall. — **375**

CARTWRIGHT, D. (1946) Public opinion polls and democratic leadership. *J. soc. Issues*, 2:23–32. — **586**

CARTWRIGHT, D., see also Katz and others (1954).

CARTWRIGHT, D., and ZANDER, A. (Eds.) (1960) *Group dynamics: research and theory* (2nd Ed.). Evanston, Ill.: Row, Peterson. — **600**

CATTELL, J. MC K. (1903) A statistical study of eminent men. *Pop. Sci. Mon.*, 62:359–77. — **106–07**

CATTELL, R. B. (1946) *Description and measurement of personality*. Yonkers, N. Y.: World Book. — **471**

CATTELL, R. B. (1949) *The culture free intelligence test*. Champaign, Ill.: IPAT. — **422**

CATTELL, R. B. (1950) *Personality*. N. Y.: McGraw-Hill. — **472**

CATTELL, R. B. (1957a) *Personality and motivation structure and measurement*. Yonkers, N. Y.: World Book. — **502**

CATTELL, R. B. (1957b) *The Sixteen Personality Factor Questionnaire* (Rev. Ed.). Champaign, Ill.: IPAT. — **472, 491**

CATTELL, R. B. (1963) The personality and motivation of the researcher from measurements of contemporaries and from biography. In Taylor, C. W., and Barron, F. (Eds.) *Scientific creativity: its recognition and development*. N. Y.: Wiley, 119–37. — **389**

CATTELL, R. B. (1965) *The scientific analysis of personality*. Baltimore, Md.: Penguin Books. — **473, 485**

CHAMBERS, R. M., see Coppock and Chambers (1954).

CHANDLER, P. J., see Freed and others (1955).

CHAPLIN, J. P., and KRAWIEC, T. S. (1960) *Systems and theories of psychology*. N. Y.: Holt, Rinehart and Winston. — **29**

CHAPMAN, D. W. (1932) Relative effects of determinate and indeterminate *Aufgaben*. *Amer. J. Psychol.*, 44:163–74. — **237**

CHAVE, E. J., see Thurstone and Chave (1929).

CHERRY, E. C. (1953) Some experiments on the recognition of speech, with one and with two ears. *J. acoust. Soc. Amer.*, 25:975–79. — **250**

CHILD, I. L. (1954) Personality. *Annu. Rev. Psychol.*, 5:149–70. — **361**

CHILD, I. L., see also Whiting and Child (1953).

CHOMSKY, N. (1964) Current issues in linguistic theory. In Fodor, J. A., and Katz, J. J. (Eds.) *The structure of language: readings in the philosophy of language.* Englewood Cliffs, N. J.: Prentice-Hall. — **373**

CHRISTIE, R., and JAHODA, M. (Eds.) (1954) *Studies in the scope and method of "The authoritarian personality."* Chicago: Free Press of Glencoe, Ill. — **475**

CLARE, M. H., *see* Bishop and Clare (1952).

CLARK, B., and GRAYBIEL, A. (1949) Linear acceleration and deceleration as factors influencing nonvisual orientation during flight. *J. Aviat. Med.,* 20:92–101. — **214**

CLARK, K. B. (1953) Desegregation: an appraisal of the evidence. *J. soc. Issues,* 9:2–76. — **606**

CLARK, K. E. (1957) *America's psychologists: a survey of a growing profession.* Washington, D. C.: Amer. Psychol. Assn. — **607, 608, 617**

CLARK, R. A. (1952) The projective measurement of experimentally induced levels of sexual motivation. *J. exp. Psychol.,* 44:391–99. — **150**

CLARK, R. A., *see also* McClelland and others (1953).

CLARK, R. A., and SENSIBAR, M. R. (1956) The relationship between symbolic and manifest projections of sexuality with some incidental correlates. *J. abnorm. soc. Psychol.,* 53:182–86. — **150**

CLAUSEN, A. R., *see* Converse, Clausen, and Miller (1965).

CLAUSEN, J. A., and KOHN, M. L. (1960) Social relations and schizophrenia. In Jackson, D. (Ed.) *The etiology of schizophrenia.* N. Y.: Basic Books. — **540**

CLAYTON, K. N. (1964) T-maze choice-learning as a joint function of the reward magnitudes of the alternatives. *J. comp. physiol. Psychol.,* 58:333–38. — **288, 289**

CLECKLEY, H. M., *see* Thigpen and Cleckley (1954) (1957).

CLEMES, S. R. (1964) Repression and hypnotic amnesia. *J. abnorm. soc. Psychol.,* 69:62–69. — **326**

COFER, C. N., and APPLEY, M. H. (1964) *Motivation: theory and research.* N. Y.: Wiley. — **138, 162**

COFER, C. N., and MUSGRAVE, B. S. (Eds.) (1963) *Verbal behavior and learning.* N. Y.: McGraw-Hill. — **335**

COHEN, A. K. (1955) *Delinquent boys: the culture of the gang.* Chicago: Free Press of Glencoe, Ill. — **99**

COHEN, A. R. (1964) *Attitude change and social influence.* N. Y.: Basic Books. — **600**

COHEN, A. R., *see also* Brehm and Cohen (1962).

COHEN, J., and OGDON, D. P. (1949) Taste blindness to phenyl-thio-carbamide and related compounds. *Psychol. Bull.,* 46:490–98. — **447**

COLBY, K. M., and GILBERT, J. P. (1964) Programming a computer model of neurosis. *J. math. Psychol.* 1:405–17. — **384**

COLBY, K. M., WATT, J. B., and GILBERT, J. P. (1964) A computer program which conducts psychotherapeutic dialogue. Unpublished preliminary communication., Computation Center, Stanford University. — **563, 565**

COLEMAN, J. C. (1961) *The adolescent society.* N. Y.: Free Press of Glencoe. — **99, 103**

COLEMAN, J. C. (1964) *Abnormal psychology in modern life* (3rd Ed.). Chicago: Scott, Foresman. — **529, 530, 547**

COLEMAN, W., and WARD, A. W. (1955) A comparison of Davis-Eells and Kuhlmann-Finch scores of children from high and low socioeconomic status. *J. educ. Psychol.,* 46:465–69. — **423**

COMBS, A. W., and SNYGG, D. (1959) Individual behavior (Rev. Ed.). N. Y.: Harper. — **482**

CONGER, J. J., *see* Mussen, Conger, and Kagan (1963); Sawry, Conger, and Turrell (1956).

CONRAD, D. G., *see* Brady and others (1958).

CONRAD, H. S., *see* Jones and Conrad (1933); Jones, Conrad, and Blanchard (1932).

CONRAD, H. S., and JONES, H. E. (1940) A second study of familial resemblance in intelligence. 39th Yearbook, Part II, National Society for the Study of Education. Chicago: Univ. of Chicago Press. — **450**

CONVERSE, P. E., *see* Campbell, Converse, Miller, and Stokes (1960); Newcomb, Converse, and Turner (1964).

CONVERSE, P. E., CLAUSEN, A. R., and MILLER, W. E. (1965) Election myth and reality: the 1964 election. *Amer. political Sci. Rev.,* 59:321–36. — **589, 590**

COPPOCK, H. W., and CHAMBERS, R. M. (1954) Reinforcement of position preference by automatic injection of glucose. *J. comp. physiol. Psychol.,* 47:355–57. — **291**

COREN, S., *see* Eichengreen, Coren, and Nachmias (1966).

CORNELISON, A., *see* Lidz, Fleck, and Cornelison (1965).

CORNSWEET, J. C., *see* Riggs and others (1953).

CORNSWEET, T. N., *see* Riggs and others (1953).

COSTA, L. D., *see* Vaughan, Costa, Gilden, and Schimmel (1965).

COTTINGHAM, D. R., *see* Berkowitz and Cottingham (1960).

COTTRELL, L. S., *see* Burgess and Cottrell (1939).

COUCH, A., and KENISTON, K. (1960) Yeasayers and naysayers: agreeing response set as a personality variable. *J. abnorm. Soc. Psychol.,* 60:151–74. — **493**

COULSON, J. E. (Ed.) (1962) *Programmed learning and computer-based instruction.* N. Y.: Wiley. — **364**

COULSON, J. E., and SILBERMAN, H. F. (1960) Results of an initial experiment in automated teaching. In Lumsdaine, A. A., and Glaser, R. (Eds.) *Teaching machines and programmed learning,* 452–68. — **356**

COURTS, F. A. (1939) Relations between experimentally induced muscular tension and memorization. *J. exp. Psychol.,* 25:235–56. — **10**

COWLES, J. T. (1937) Food-tokens as incentives for learning by chimpanzees. *Comp. Psychol. Monogr.,* 14, No. 71. — **136**

CRAIGHILL, P. G., *see* Sarason, Mandler, and Craighill (1952).

CRICK, F. H. C. (1962) The genetic code. *Sci. Amer.,* 207:66–74. — **446**

CRONBACH, L. J. (1942) Studies of acquiescence as a factor in the true-false test. *J. educ. Psychol.,* 33:401–15. — **493**

CRONBACH, L. J. (1956) Assessment of individual differences. *Annu. Rev. Psychol.,* 7:173–96. — **496**

CRONBACH, L. J. (1957) The two disciplines of scientific psychology. *Amer. Psychologist,* 12:671–84. — **610**

CRONBACH, L. J. (1960) *Essentials of psychological testing* (2nd Ed.). N. Y.: Harper. — **426, 443, 493, 500, 501**

CROTHERS, E. J., *see* Atkinson, Bower, and Crothers (1965).

CROTHERS, E. J., and SUPPES, P. C. (1967) *Some experiments on learning Russian.* N. Y.: Academic Press. — **298, 373**

CROWNE, D. P., and MARLOWE, D. (1964) *The approval motive.* N. Y.: Wiley. — **493**

CRUCHFIELD, R. S., *see* Krech, Cruchfield, and Ballachey (1962).

CULLEN, C., *see* Li, Cullen, and Jasper (1956).

CUMMINGS, E., DEAN, L. R., NEWELL, D. S., and MC CAFFREY, I. (1960) Disengagement—a tentative theory of aging. *Sociometry,* 23:23–35. — **114**

CURLE, A. (1947) Transitional communities and social reconnection, Part I. *Hum. Relations*, 1:45–68. — **477**

CURLE, A., and TRIST, E. L. (1947) Transitional communities and social reconnection, Part II. *Hum. Relations*, 1:240–88. — **477**

CURREN, J. F., *see* Grant and Curran (1953).

DAHLSTROM, W. G., *see* Welsh and Dahlstrom (1956).

DAHLSTROM, W. G., and WELSH, G. S. (1960) *An MMPI handbook: a guide to use in clinical practice and research.* Minneapolis, Minn.: Univ. of Minnesota Press. — **501**

DALLENBACH, K. M., *see* Jenkins and Dallenbach (1924); Minami and Dallenbach (1946).

D'AMATO, M. R., and JAGODA, H. (1960) Effects of extinction trials on discrimination reversal. *J. exp. Psychol.*, 59:254–60. — **18**

DASHIELL, J. F. (1925) A quantitative demonstration of animal drive. *J. comp. Psychol.*, 5:205–08. — **119**

DAVID, H. (1965) *Manpower policies for a democratic society.* N. Y.: Columbia Univ. Press. — **435**

DAVIES, J. T. (1962) The mechanism of olfaction. In *Biological Receptor Mechanisms.* 16th Symp. Exptl. Biol., Univ. Birmingham, England, Sept. 1962. Cambridge: Cambridge Univ. Press. — **209**

DAVIS, A., *see* Eells and others (1951).

DAVIS, A., and DOLLARD, J. (1940) *Children of bondage.* Washington, D. C.: Amer. Coun. Educ. — **148**

DAVIS, A., and EELLS, K. (1953) *Davis-Eells games.* Yonkers, N. Y.: World Book. — **422**

DAVIS, H., *see* Stevens and Davis (1938); Stevens, Davis, and Lurie (1935).

DAVIS, H. V., SEARS, R. R., MILLER, H. C., and BRODBECK, A. J. (1948) Effects of cup, bottle and breast feeding on oral activities of newborn infants. *Pediatrics*, 2:549–58. — **76**

DAVIS, J., *see* Restle and Davis (1962).

DEAN, L. R., *see* Cummings, Dean, Newell, and McCaffrey (1960).

DEESE, J. E., and HULSE, S. (1967) *Psychology of learning* (3rd Ed.). N. Y.: McGraw-Hill. — **313**

DELGADO, J. M. R., ROBERTS, W. W., and MILLER, N. E. (1954) Learning motivated by electrical stimulation of the brain. *Amer. J. Physiol.*, 179:587–93. — **133, 292**

DE MARTINO, H. A., *see* Stacey and De Martino (1958).

DEMBER, W. N. (1960) *The psychology of perception.* N. Y.: Holt, Rinehart and Winston. — **245**

DEMBO, T., *see* Barker, Dembo, and Lewin (1941).

DEMENT, W. (1960) The effect of dream deprivation. *Science*, 131:1705–07. — **258**

DEMENT, W. (1965) An essay on dreams: the role of physiology in understanding their nature. In Barron, F., and others (Eds.) *New directions in psychology*, II. N. Y.: Holt, Rinehart and Winston, 135–257. — **255**

DEMENT, W., and KLEITMAN, N. (1957) The relation of eye movements during sleep to dream activity: an objective method for the study of dreaming. *J. exp. Psychol.*, 53:339–46. — **254, 376**

DEMENT, W., and WOLPERT, E. (1958) The relation of eye movements, bodily motility, and external stimuli to dream content. *J. exp. Psychol.*, 55:543–53. — **256**

DENNIS, M. G., *see* Dennis and Dennis (1940).

DENNIS, W. (1935) The effect of restricted practice upon the reaching, sitting, and standing of two infants. *J. genet. Psychol.*, 47:17–32. — **64**

DENNIS, W. (1954a) Bibliographies of eminent scientists. *Sci. Mon.*, 79:180–83. — **111, 113**

DENNIS, W. (1954b) Predicting scientific productivity in later decades from records of earlier decades. *J. Gerontol.*, 9:465–67. — **113**

DENNIS, W. (1955) Variations in productivity among creative workers. *Sci. Mon.*, 80:277–78. — **113, 387**

DENNIS, W. (1958) The age decrement in outstanding scientific contributions: fact or artifact? *Amer. Psychologist*, 13:457–60. — **113**

DENNIS, W., and DENNIS, M. G. (1940) The effect of cradling practices upon the onset of walking in Hopi children. *J. genet. Psychol.*, 56:77–86. — **64**

DENNY, J. P., *see* Spielberger, Weitz, and Denny (1962).

DEUTSCH, J. A. (1960) *The structural basis of behavior.* Chicago: Univ. of Chicago Press. — **124**

DEUTSCH, J. A., and JONES, A. D. (1959) The water-salt receptor and preference in the rat. *Nature*, 183:1472. — **124**

DEUTSCH, J. A., FISHMAN, J. A., KOGAN, N., NORTH, R., and WHITMAN, M. (1964) Guidelines for testing minority group children. *J. soc. Issues*, 22:127–45. — **440**

DISTLER, L., *see* Mussen and Distler (1959).

DOANE, B. K., MAHATOO, W., HERON, W., and SCOTT, T. H. (1959) Changes in perceptual function after isolation. *Canad. J. Psychol.*, 13:210–19. — **54**

DOBELLE, W. A., *see* Marks, Dobelle, and MacNichol (1964).

DOBZHANSKY, T., *see* Sinnott, Dunn, and Dobzhansky (1958).

DOLLARD, J., *see* Davis and Dollard (1940).

DOLLARD, J., and MILLER, N. E. (1950) *Personality and psychotherapy.* N. Y.: McGraw-Hill. — **475, 485, 556**

DOLLARD, J., and others (1939) *Frustration and aggression.* New Haven, Conn.: Yale Univ. Press. — **148, 524**

DONAHUE, W., *see* Williams, Tibbitts, and Donahue (1963).

DOUVAN, E., and ABELSON, J. (1966) *The adolescent experience.* N. Y.: Wiley. — **116**

DOWNING, J. J., and WYGANT, W., JR. (1964) Psychedelic experience and religious belief. In Blum, R., and associates, *Utopiates.* N. Y.: Atherton Press, 187–98. — **265**

DROLETTE, M. E., *see* Funkenstein, King, and Drolette (1957).

DU BOIS, P. H. (Ed.) (1947) The classification program. *AAF Aviat. Psychol. Program Res. Rep.*, No. 2. — **418, 420**

DUFFEY, R. F., *see* Moseley, Duffey, and Sherman (1963).

DUFFY, E., (1962) *Activation and behavior.* N. Y.: Wiley. — **173**

DUNBAR, F. (1955) *Mind and body: psychosomatic medicine* (2nd Ed.). N. Y.: Random House. — **183**

DUNCKER, K. (1945) On problem-solving (Trans. by Lynne S. Lees). *Psychol. Monogr.*, 58, No. 270. — **379**

DUNN, L. C., *see* Sinnott, Dunn, and Dobzhansky (1958).

DUNN, W. L., JR. (1954) Visual discrimination of schizophrenic subjects as a function of stimulus meaning. *J. Pers.*, 23:48–64. — **361**

DURKHEIM, E. (1958) *Suicide* (original date, 1897). Chicago: Free Press of Glencoe, Ill. — **575**

DUSENBURY, D., and KNOWER, F. H. (1939) Experimental studies of the symbolism of voice and action: II. A study of the specificity of meaning in abstract tonal symbols. *Quart. J. Speech*, 25:67–75. — **172**

DYMOND, R. F., *see* Rogers and Dymond (1954).

EBBINGHAUS, H. (1885) *Memory* (Trans. by H. A. Ruger and C. E. Bussenius). N. Y.: Teachers College (1913). — **307, 318, 335**

EBNER, F. F., and MYERS, R. E. (1960) Inter- and intra-hemispheric transmission of tactile gnosis in normal and corpus callosum-sectioned monkeys. *Fed. Proc.*, 19:292. — **349**

ECCLES, J. C. (1953) *The neurophysiological basis of the mind; the principles of neurophysiology.* N. Y.: Oxford Univ. Press. — **58**

ECCLES, J. C. (1958) The physiology of imagination. *Sci. Amer.*, 199:135–46. — **37, 44**

ECCLES, J. C. (1964) *The physiology of the synapses.* Berlin: Springer. — **58**

EDWARDS, A. L. (1954) *Edwards Personal Preference Schedule* (Manual). N. Y.: Psychological Corporation. — **490**

EDWARDS, A. L. (1957) *The social desirability variable in personality assessment and research.* N. Y.: Dryden. — **493, 501**

EDWARDS, A. L. (1960) *Experimental design in psychological research* (Rev. Ed.). N. Y.: Holt, Rinehart and Winston. — **415**

EELLS, K., *see* Davis and Eells (1953); Warner, Meeker, and Eells (1949).

EELLS, K., DAVIS, A., HAVIGHURST, R. J., HERRICK, V. E., and TYLER, R. W. (1951) *Intelligence and cultural differences.* Chicago: Univ. of Chicago Press. — **422**

EGYBÂZI, E., *see* Hydén and Egybâzi (1963).

EICHENGREEN, J. M., COREN, S., and NACHMIAS, J. (1966) Visual-cliff preference by infant rats: effects of rearing and test conditions. *Science*, 151:830–31. — **237**

EKMAN, G. (1951) On the number and definition of dimensions in Kretschmer's and Sheldon's constitutional systems. In Ekman, G., Husen, T., Johansson, G., and Sandstrom, C. I. (Eds.) *Essays in psychology dedicated to David Katz.* Uppsala, Sweden: Almqvist & Wiksells, 72–104. — **467**

ELDERSVELD, S., *see* Katz and others (1954).

ELKIN, F., and WESTLEY, W. A. (1955) The myth of adolescent culture. *Amer. Sociol. Rev.*, 20:680–84. — **91**

ELLIOTT, M. H. (1928) The effect of change of reward on the maze performance of rats. *Univ. Calif. Publ. Psychol.*, 4:19–30. — **129**

ELLIOTT, O., *see* Freedman, King, and Elliott (1961).

EMERSON, P. E., *see* Schaffer and Emerson (1964).

EMMONS, W. W., and SIMON, C. W. (1956) The nonrecall of material presented during sleep. *Amer. J. Psychol.*, 69:76–81. — **257**

EMSLIE, A. G., *see* Hainer, Emslie, and Jacobson (1954).

ERICKSEN, S. C. (1942) Variability in attack in massed and distributed practice. *J. exp. Psychol.*, 31:339–45. — **339**

ERIKSEN, C. W. (Ed.) (1962) *Behavior and awareness.* Durham, N. C.: Duke Univ. Press. — **192, 268**

ERIKSON, E. H. (1959) Identity and the life cycle. *Psychol. Issues*, 1, No. 1. — **74, 465**

ERIKSON, E. H. (1963) *Childhood and society* (2nd Ed.). N. Y.: Norton. — **60, 73, 74**

ERLENMEYER-KIMLING, L., and JARVIK, L. F. (1963) Genetics and intelligence: a review. *Science*, 142:1477–79. — **453**

ERON, L. D., *see* Zubin, Eron, and Schumer (1965).

ESPENSCHADE, A. (1940) Motor performance in adolescence. *Monogr. Soc. Res. Child Develpm.*, 5, No. 24. — **96**

ESTES, W. K. (1944) An experimental study of punishment. *Psychol. Monogr.*, 57, No. 263. — **357, 358**

ESTES, W. K. (1949) A study of motivating conditions necessary for secondary reinforcement. *J. exp. Psychol.*, 39:306–10. — **285**

ESTES, W. K. (1950) Toward a statistical theory of learning. *Psychol. Rev.*, 57:94–107. — **308**

ESTES, W. K. (1955) Statistical theory of distributional phenomena in learning. *Psychol. Rev.*, 62:369–77. — **308**

ESTES, W. K. (1959) The statistical approach to learning theory. In Koch, S. (Ed.) *Psychology: a study of a science*, Vol. II. N. Y.: McGraw-Hill, 380–491. — **308, 311**

ESTES, W. K. (1960) Learning theory and the new "mental chemistry." *Psychol. Rev.*, 67:207–23. — **299**

ESTES, W. K. (1964a) Probability learning. In Melton, A. W. (Ed.) *Categories of human learning.* N. Y.: Academic Press. — **299, 300**

ESTES, W. K. (1964b) All-or-none processes in learning and retention. *Amer. Psychologist*, 19:16–25. — **308**

ESTES, W. K., *see also* Atkinson and Estes (1963).

ESTES, W. K., and BURKE, C. J. (1953) A theory of stimulus variability in learning. *Psychol. Rev.*, 60:276–86. — **308**

ESTES, W. K., and SUPPES, P. C. (1959) Foundations of linear models. In Bush, R. R., and Estes, W. K. (Eds.) *Studies in mathematical learning theory.* Stanford, Calif.: Stanford Univ. Press, 137–79. — **308**

EVANS, J. L., GLASER, R., and HOMME, L. E. (1960) A preliminary investigation of variation in the properties of verbal learning sequences of the "teaching machine" type. In Lumsdaine, A. A., and Glaser, R., *Teaching machines and programmed learning.* Washington, D. C.: NEA., 446–51. — **355–56**

EVANS, R. M. (1948) *An introduction to color.* N. Y.: Wiley. — **216**

EYSENCK, H. C., *see* Eysenck and Eysenck (1964).

EYSENCK, H. J. (1959) *The structure of human personality.* London: Methuen. — **502**

EYSENCK, H. J. (Ed.) (1960) *Behavior therapy and the neuroses.* N. Y.: Pergamon Press. — **559**

EYSENCK, S. B. G., and EYSENCK, H. C. (1964) "Acquiescence" response set in personality inventory items. *Psychol. Reports*, 14:513–14. — **493**

FADIMAN, J., *see* Savage, Savage, Fadiman, and Harman (1964).

FARBER, I. E. (1954) Anxiety as a drive state. In Jones, M. R. (Ed.). *Nebraska symposium on motivation.* Lincoln, Nebr.: Univ. of Nebraska Press, 1–46. — **360**

FARBER, I. E., HARLOW, H. F., and WEST, L. J. (1957) Brainwashing, conditioning, and DDD. *Sociometry*, 20:271–85. — **598**

FEATHER, N. T., *see* Atkinson and Feather (1966).

FECHNER, G. (1860) *Elements of psychophysics* (Trans. by H. E. Adler). N. Y.: Holt, Rinehart and Winston, 1966. — **191**

FEIGENBAUM, E. A. (1959) An information processing theory of verbal learning. P-1817 (October). Santa Monica, Calif.: RAND Corp. — **384**

FEIGENBAUM, E. A. (1967) Elements of an information processing theory of memory. In Kimble, D. P. (Ed.) *Proceedings of the third conference on learning, remembering and forgetting.* N. Y.: New York Academy of Science. — **384**

FEIGENBAUM, E. A., and FELDMAN, J. (Eds.) (1963) *Computers and thought.* N. Y.: McGraw-Hill. — **383, 393**

FEIGENSON, L., *see* Gunter, Feigenson, and Blakeslee (1965).

FELDMAN, J., *see* Feigenbaum and Feldman (1963).

FELDMAN, J., and HANNA, J. F. (1966) The structure of responses to a sequence of binary digits. *J. math. Psychol.*, 3:371–87. — **384**

FELEKY, A. (1922) *Feelings and emotions.* N. Y.: Pioneer Press. — **171**

FERSTER, C. B., and SKINNER, B. F., (1957) *Schedules of reinforcement.* N. Y.: Appleton-Century-Crofts. — **283**

FESHBACH, S., *see* Janis and Feshbach (1953).

FESTINGER, L. (1942) Wish, expectation, and group standards as affecting level of aspiration. *J. abnorm. soc. Psychol.*, 37:184–200. — **152, 153**

FESTINGER, L. (1957) *A theory of cognitive dissonance.* Evanston, Ill.: Row, Peterson. — **158, 592**

FESTINGER, L., *see also* Lawrence and Festinger (1962).

FESTINGER, L., and CARLSMITH, J. M. (1959) Cognitive consequences of forced compliance. *J. abnorm. soc. Psychol.*, 58:203–10. — **582**

FESTINGER, L., RIECKEN, H. W., JR., and SCHACHTER, S. (1956) *When prophecy fails.* Minneapolis, Minn.: Univ. of Minnesota Press. — **158**

FESTINGER, L., and others (1964) *Conflict, decision, and dissonance.* Stanford, Calif.: Stanford Univ. Press. — **158, 592**

FIELDS, P. E. (1932) Studies in concept formation: I. The development of the concept of triangularity by the white rat. *Comp. Psychol. Monogr.*, 9, No. 2. — **368**

FIELDS, V., *see* Lorr and Fields (1954).

FINDLAY, A. (1948) *A hundred years of chemistry* (2nd Ed.). London: Duckworth. — **386**

FISHBEIN, M., *see* Steiner and Fishbein (1965).

FISHER, C. (1965) Psychoanalytic implications of recent research on sleep and dreaming. *J. Amer. psychoanal. Assn.*, 13:197–303. — **256, 258**

FISHER, M. B., and BIRREN, J. E. (1947) Age and strength. *J. appl. Psychol.*, 31:490–97. — **110**

FISHMAN, J. A., *see* Deutsch, Fishman, Kogan, North, and Whitman (1964).

FISK, F., *see* Hilgard, Newman, and Fisk (1960).

FISKE, D. W., *see* Kelly and Fiske (1951).

FISKE, D. W., and MADDI, S. R. (Eds.) (1961) *Functions of varied experience.* Homewood, Ill.: Dorsey Press. — **90**

FJERDINGSTAD, E. J., NISSEN, T., and RØIGAARD-PETERSEN, H. H. (1965) Effect of ribonucleic acid (RNA) extracted from the brain of trained animals on learning in rats. *Scand. J. Psychol.*, 6:1–6. — **322**

FLANAGAN, J. C. (1963) The definition and measurement of ingenuity. In Taylor, C. W., and Barron, F. (Eds.) *Scientific creativity: its recognition and development.* N. Y.: Wiley. — **390**

FLECK, S., *see* Lidz, Fleck, and Cornelison (1965).

FODOR, J. A. (1965) Could meaning be an r_m? *J. verb. Learn. verb. Behav.*, 4:73–81. — **373**

FODOR, J. A., and KATZ, J. J. (Eds.) (1964) *The structure of language: readings in the philosophy of language.* Englewood Cliffs, N. J.: Prentice-Hall. — **393**

FOLEY, J. P., JR. (1940) An experimental investigation of the effect of prolonged inversion of the visual field in the rhesus monkey. *J. genet. Psychol.*, 56:21–51. — **222**

FOLEY, J. P., JR., *see also* Anastasi and Foley (1958).

FOORD, E. N., *see* Hebb and Foord (1945).

FORD, C. S., and BEACH, F. A. (1951) *Patterns of sexual behavior.* N. Y.: Harper. — **94, 95**

FORD, D. N., and URBAN, H. B. (1963) *Systems of psychotherapy.* N. Y.: Wiley. — **571**

FOREMAN, S., *see* Greenspoon and Foreman (1956).

FORGUS, R. H. (1966) *Perception: the basic process in cognitive development.* N. Y.: McGraw-Hill. — **245**

FORLANO, G. (1936) School learning with various methods of practice and rewards. *Teach. Coll. Contr. Educ.*, No. 688. — **332**

FORWALD, H. (1961) A PK experiment with die faces as targets. *J. Parapsychol.*, 25:1–12. — **241**

FOULKES, D. (1966) *The psychology of sleep.* N. Y.: Scribners. — **268**

FOULKES, D., *see also* Monroe, Rechtschaffen, Foulkes, and Jensen (1965).

FRANCK, K., and ROSEN, E. (1949) A projective test of masculinity and femininity. *J. consult. Psychol.*, 13:247–56. — **108**

FRANZ, S. I. (1933) *Persons one and three.* N. Y.: McGraw–Hill. — **480**

FREED, A., CHANDLER, P. J., BLAKE, R. R., and MOUTON, J. S. (1955) Stimulus and background factors in sign violation. *J. Pers.*, 23:499. — **583**

FREEDMAN, D. G., KING, J. A., and ELLIOT, O. (1961) Critical period in the social development of dogs. *Science*, 133:1016–17. — **64**

FREEDMAN, D. X., *see* Redlich and Freedman (1966).

FREEMAN, F. N., *see* Wood and Freeman (1932); Newman, Freeman, and Holzinger (1937).

FRENCH, E. G. (1958) Effects of the interaction of motivation and feedback on performance. In Atkinson, J. W. (Ed.) *Motives in fantasy, action, and society.* Princeton, N. J.: Van Nostrand, 400–08. — **140, 141**

FRENCH, T. M. (1952) *The integration of behavior.* Vol. I. Chicago: Univ. of Chicago Press. — **179**

FRENCH, T. M., and FROMM, E. (1963) *Dream interpretation: a new approach.* N. Y.: Basic Books. — **258**

FRENKEL-BRUNSWIK, E. (1939) Mechanisms of self-deception. *J. soc. Psychol.*, 10:409–20. — **517**

FRENKEL-BRUNSWIK, E., *see also* Adorno and others (1950).

FRENKEL-BRUNSWIK, E., and SANFORD, R. N. (1945) Some personality factors in anti-Semitism. *J. Psychol.*, 20:271–91. — **579**

FREUD, A. (1937) *The ego and the mechanisms of defense.* London: Hogarth Press. — **524**

FREUD, A., and BURLINGHAM, D. (1943) *War and children.* N. Y.: Internat. Univ. Press. — **80**

FREUD, A., and BURLINGHAM, D. (1944) *Infants without families.* N. Y.: Internat. Univ. Press. — **80**

FREUD, S. (1900) *The interpretation of dreams.* (Standard edition, 1953), Vols. IV and V. London: Hogarth Press. — **257**

FREUD, S. (1927) *The ego and the id.* London: Hogarth Press. — **478**

FREUD, S. (1933) *New introductory lectures on psychoanalysis.* N. Y.: Norton. — **257**

FRIEDENBERG, E. Z. (1959) *The vanishing adolescent.* Boston: Beacon Press. — **103**

FROMM, E., *see* French and Fromm (1963).

FROMM-REICHMANN, F. (1948) Notes on the development of treatment of schizophrenics by psychoanalytic psychotherapy. *Psychiatry*, 11:263–73. — **551, 563**

FRYER, D. H., and HENRY, E. R. (Eds.) (1950) *Handbook of applied psychology* (2 vols.). N. Y.: Rinehart. — **499**

FUHRER, M. J., and BAER, P. E. (1965) Differential classical conditioning: verbalization of stimulus contingencies. *Science*, 150:1479–81. — **278**

FULLER, J. L. (1955) Hereditary differences in trainability of purebred dogs. *J. genet. Psychol.*, 87:229–38. — **449**

FULLER, J. L. (1962) *Motivation, a biological perspective.* N. Y.: Random House. — **138**

FULLER, J. L., and THOMPSON, W. R. (1960) *Behavior genetics.* N. Y.: Wiley. — **449, 461**

FUNKENSTEIN, D. H. (1955) The physiology of fear and anger. *Sci. Amer.,* 192:74–80. — **170**

FUNKENSTEIN, D. H., KING, S. H., and DROLETTE, M. E. (1957) *Mastery of stress.* Cambridge, Mass.: Harvard Univ. Press. — **171**

FURTH, H. G. (1966) *Thinking without language: psychological implications of deafness.* N. Y.: Free Press. — **374**

GAGNÉ, R. M., and BAKER, K. E. (1950) Stimulus pre-differentiation as a factor in transfer of training. *J. exp. Psychol.,* 40:439–51. — **345**

GALANTER, E. (1962) Contemporary psychophysics. In Brown, R., and others (Eds.). *New Directions in Psychology.* N. Y.: Holt, Rinehart and Winston, 89–156. — **189**

GALANTER, E., *see also* Luce, Bush, and Galanter (1963), (1965); Luce and Galanter (1963); Miller, Galanter, and Pribram (1960).

GALLOWAY, A., *see* Wallach and Galloway (1946).

GARMEZY, N. (1952) Stimulus differentiation by schizophrenic and normal subjects under conditions of reward and punishment. *J. Pers.,* 20:253–76. — **361**

GARMEZY, N., *see also* Kimble and Garmezy (1963).

GARRETT, H. E. (1940) Variability in learning under massed and spaced practice. *J. exp. Psychol.,* 26:547–67. — **339**

GATES, A. I. (1917) Recitation as a factor in memorizing. *Arch Psychol.,* N. Y., No. 40. — **332**

GATES, G. S. (1923) An experimental study of the growth of social perception. *J. educ. Psychol.,* 14:449–61. — **175**

GATES, G. S. (1926) An observational study of anger. *J. exp. Psychol.,* 9:325–36. — **181**

GAUDET, H., *see* Cantril, Gaudet, and Herzog (1940).

GAUTIER, M., *see* Lejeune, Gautier, and Turpin (1959).

GAZZANIGA, M. S., BOGEN, J. E., and SPERRY, R. W. (1965) Observations on visual perception after disconnexion of the cerebral hemispheres in man. *Brain,* 88:221–36. — **349**

GERARD, R. W. (1964) The nosology of schizophrenia: a co-operative study. *Behav. Sci.,* 9:311–33. — **537, 538**

GESELL, A., and THOMPSON, H. (1941) Twins T and C from infancy to adolescence: a biogenetic study of individual differences by the method of co-twin control. *Genet. Psychol. Monogr.,* 24:3–122. — **66**

GETZELS, J. W., and JACKSON, P. W. (1962) *Creativity and intelligence: explorations with gifted students.* N. Y.: Wiley. — **389, 390, 440**

GEWIRTZ, J. L., *see* Rheingold, Gewirtz, and Ross (1959).

GIBSON, E. J., and WALK, R. D. (1956) The effect of prolonged exposure to visually presented patterns on learning to discriminate them. *J. comp. physiol. Psychol.,* 49:239–42. — **24**

GIBSON, E. J., and WALK, R. D. (1960) The "visual cliff." *Sci. Amer.,* 202 (IV):64–71. — **236**

GILBERT, J. P., *see* Colby and Gilbert (1964); Colby, Watt, and Gilbert (1964).

GILDEN, L., *see* Vaughan, Costa, Gilden, and Schimmel (1965).

GIRDEN, E. (1962) A review of psychokinesis. *Psychol. Bull.,* 59:353–88. — **244**

GLADWYN, T., *see* Masland, Sarason, and Gladwyn (1958).

GLASER, R. (Ed.) (1965) *Teaching machines and programmed learning, II: Data and directions.* Washington: NEA. — **364**

GLASER, R., *see also* Evans, Glaser, and Homme (1960); Lumsdaine and Glaser (1960); Taber, Glaser, and Schaefer (1965).

GLICH, B. S., and MARGOLIS, R. (1962) A study on the influence of experimental design on clinical outcome in drug research. *Amer. J. Psychiat.,* 118:1087–96. — **567**

GLICKMAN, S. E. (1961) Perseverative neural processes and consolidation of the neural trace. *Psychol. Bull.,* 58:218–33. — **330**

GLUECK, E., *see* Glueck and Glueck (1964).

GLUECK, S. (1962) *Law and psychiatry.* Baltimore, Md.: Johns Hopkins Press. — **544**

GLUECK, S., and GLUECK, E. (1964) Potential juvenile delinquents can be identified: what next? *Brit. J. Criminol.,* 4:215–26. — **100**

GOLDENWEISER, A. A. (1937) *Anthropology.* N. Y.: Appleton-Century-Crofts. — **155**

GOLDHAMER, H., and MARSHALL, A. W. (1953) *Psychosis and civilization.* Chicago, Free Press of Glencoe, Ill. — **544**

GOLDIAMOND, I. (1958) Indicators of perception: I Subliminal perception subception, unconscious perception: an analysis in terms of psychophysical indicator methodology. *Psychol. Bull.,* 55, 373–411. — **192**

GOLDSTEIN, K., and SCHEERER, M. (1941) Abstract and concrete behavior: an experimental study with special tests. *Psychol. Monogr.,* 53, No. 239. — **370**

GOLDSTEIN, M. J., *see* Palmer and Goldstein (1966).

GOODENOUGH, D. R., *see* Rechtschaffen, Goodenough, and Shapiro (1962).

GOODENOUGH, D. R., SHAPIRO, A., HOLDEN, M., and STEINSCHRIBER, L. (1959) A comparison of dreamers and nondreamers: eye movements, electroencephalograms and the recall of dreams. *J. abnorm. soc. Psychol.,* 59:295–302. — **256**

GOODENOUGH, F. (1931) Anger in young children. *Univ. Minn. Inst. Child Welf. Monogr. Ser.,* No. 9. — **183**

GOODENOUGH, F. (1932) Expression of the emotions in a blind-deaf child. *J. abnorm. soc. Psychol.,* 27:328–33. — **175**

GOODMAN, C. C., *see* Bruner and Goodman (1947).

GORDON, J. E. (Ed.) (1966) *Handbook of hypnosis.* N. Y.: Macmillan. — **268**

GOSLIN, D. A. (1963) *The search for ability: standardized testing in social perspective.* N. Y.: Russell Sage Foundation. — **439**

GOUGH, H. G. (1957) *California Psychological Inventory.* Palo Alto, Calif.: Consulting Psychologists Press. — **108**

GOUGH, H. G. (1962) Clinical vs. statistical prediction in psychology. In Postman, L. (Ed.) *Psychology in the making.* N. Y.: Knopf, 526–84. — **100, 500**

GOUGH, H. G. (1965) Misplaced emphases in admissions. *J. College Student Personnel,* 6:130–35. — **440**

GRAHAM, C. H. (Ed.) (1965) *Vision and visual perception.* N. Y.: Wiley. — **216, 245**

GRAHAM, C. H., *see also* Hsia and Graham (1965).

GRANT, D. A., and CURRAN, J. F. (1953) Relative difficulty of number, form, and color concepts of a weight-type problem using unsystematic number cards. *J. exp. Psychol.,* 43:408–13. — **370**

GRAYBIEL, A., *see* Clark and Graybiel (1949).

GREEN, B. F. (1963) *Digital computers in research.* N. Y.: McGraw-Hill. — **382, 393**

GREEN, D. M., and SWETS, J. A. (1966) *Signal detection theory and psychophysics*. N. Y.: Wiley. — **192, 216**

GREENSPOON, J. (1955) The reinforcing effect of two spoken sounds on the frequency of two responses. *Amer. J. Psychol.*, 68:409–16. — **341**

GREENSPOON, J., and FOREMAN, S. (1956) Effect of delay of knowledge of results on learning a motor task. *J. exp. Psychol.*, 51:226–28. — **342**

GREGORY, R. L., (1966) *Eye and brain: the psychology of seeing*. N. Y.: McGraw-Hill. — **216, 245–46**

GRINDER, R. E. (Ed.) (1963) *Studies in adolescence*. N. Y.: Macmillan. — **116**

GROEN, G. J., and ATKINSON, R. C. (1966) Models for optimizing the learning process. *Psych. Bull.*, 66:309–320. — **356**

GROSS, M. L. (1962) *The brain watchers*. N. Y.: Random House. — **439**

GROSSBERG, J. M. (1964) Behavior therapy: a review. *Psychol. Bull.*, 62:73–85. — **559**

GRÜNEBERG, H. (1952) *The genetics of the mouse*. The Hague, Netherlands: Martinus Nijhoff. — **446**

GRUNZKE, M. E., see Rohles, Grunzke, and Reynolds (1963).

GUETZKOW, H. (1951) An analysis of the operation of set in problem-solving behavior. *J. gen. Psychol.*, 45:219–44. — **378**

GUETZKOW, H., and BOWMAN, P. H. (1946) *Men and hunger*. Elgin, Ill.: Brethren Publishing House. — **512**

GUILFORD, J. P. (1940) An inventory of factors *STDCR*. Beverly Hills, Calif.: Sheridan Supply Co. — **469**

GUILFORD, J. P. (1954a) A factor analytic study across the domains of reasoning, creativity, and evaluation I: Hypotheses and description of tests. *Reports from the Psychology Laboratory*. Los Angeles, Calif.: Univ. of Southern California. — **390**

GUILFORD, J. P. (1954b) *Psychometric methods* (2nd Ed.). N. Y.: McGraw–Hill. — **415**

GUILFORD, J. P. (1959) *Personality*. N. Y.: McGraw–Hill. — **485, 487, 502**

GUILFORD, J. P. (1961) Factorial angles to psychology. *Psychol. Rev.*, 68:1–20. — **429**

GUILFORD, J. P. (1963) Potentiality for creativity and its measurement. In *Proceedings of the 1962 invitational conference on testing problems*. Princeton, N. J.: Educational Testing Service, 31–9. — **389**

GUILFORD, J. P., and HOEPFNER, R. (1966) *Structure-of-intellect factors and their tests*, Los Angeles, Calif.: Reports from the Univ. of Southern California, No. 36. — **428**

GUMP, P. V., and KOUNIN, J. S. (1959) Issues raised by ecological and "classical" research efforts. *Merrill-Palmer O. Beh. Develop.*, 6:148–52. — **473**

GUNTER, R., FEIGENSON, L., and BLAKESLEE, P. (1965) Color vision in the cebus monkey. *J. comp. physiol. Psychol.*, 60:107–13. — **369**

GUTHRIE, E. R. (1940) Association and the law of effect. *Psychol. Rev.*, 47:127–48. — **292**

GUTTMAN, L. (1950) The basis for scalogram analysis. In Stouffer, S. A., and others, *Measurement and prediction*. Princeton, N. J.: Princeton Univ. Press, 60–90. — **586**

HABER, R. N. (Ed.) (1966) *Current research in motivation*. N. Y.: Holt, Rinehart and Winston. — **138, 162, 524**

HADAMARD, J. (1945) *The psychology of invention in the mathematical field*. Princeton, N. J.: Princeton Univ. Press. — **387**

HAGE, J., see Pitt and Hage (1964).

HAGEN, E., see Thorndike and Hagen (1961).

HAINER, R. M., EMSLIE, A. G., and JACOBSON, A. (1954) An information theory of olfaction. *Annals N. Y. Acad. Sciences*, 58:164. — **212**

HAKE, D. F., see Azrin, Holz and Hake (1963).

HALL, C. S. (1934) Emotional behavior in the rat: I. Defecation and urination as measures of individual differences in emotionality. *J. comp. Psychol.*, 18:385–403. — **167**

HALL, C. S. (1951) The genetics of behavior. In Stevens, S. S. (Ed.) *Handbook of experimental psychology*. N. Y.: Wiley, 304–29. — **448**

HALL, C. S. (1953) *The meaning of dreams*. N. Y.: Harper. — **258**

HALL, C. S., see also Lindzey and Hall (1965); Witt and Hall (1949).

HALL, C. S., and LINDZEY, G. (1957) *Theories of personality*. N. Y.: Wiley. — **485**

HALL, J. F., (1966) *The psychology of learning*. Philadelphia, Pa.: Lippincott. — **313**

HAMBURGER, V., see Willier, Weiss, and Hamburger (1955).

HAMILTON, M. A., see Laidlaw and Hamilton (1937).

HANNA, J. F., see Feldman and Hanna (1966).

HANSEL, C. E. M. (1966) *ESP: a scientific evaluation*. N. Y.: Scribners. — **246**

HANSEN, D. N., see Atkinson and Hansen (1967).

HARDING, J. S., see Leighton, Harding, Macklin, Macmillan, and Leighton (1963).

HARLOW, H. F. (1949) The formation of learning sets. *Psychol. Rev.*, 56:51–65. — **346, 347**

HARLOW, H. F. (1951) Primate learning. In Stone, C. P. (Ed.) *Comparative psychology* (3rd Ed.). N. Y.: Prentice-Hall. 183–238. — **347**

HARLOW, H. F. (1953) Mice, monkeys, men and motives. *Psychol. Rev.*, 60:23–32. — **132**

HARLOW, H. F. (1958) On the meaning of love. *Amer. Psychologist*, 13:673–85. — **79**

HARLOW, H. F., see also Farber, Harlow, and West (1957); Moon and Harlow (1955).

HARLOW, H. F., and HARLOW, M. K. (1966) Learning to love. *Amer. Scientist*, 54:244–72. — **80**

HARLOW, H. F., HARLOW, M. K., and MEYER, D. R. (1950) Learning motivated by a manipulation drive. *J. exp. Psychol.*, 40:228–34. — **130**

HARLOW, H. F., and ZIMMERMAN, R. R. (1959) Affectional responses in the infant monkey. *Science*, 130:421–32. — **79**

HARLOW, M. K., see Harlow and Harlow (1966); Harlow, Harlow, and Meyer (1950).

HARMAN, W., see Savage, Savage, Fadiman, and Harman (1964).

HARMS, E. (Ed.) (1960) Fundamentals of psychology: the psychology of thinking. *Ann. N. Y. Acad. Sci.*, 91:1–158. — **393**

HARPER, R. A. (1959) *Psychoanalysis and psychotherapy: 36 systems*. Englewood Cliffs, N. J.: Prentice-Hall. — **570–71**

HARRIMAN, A. E., see Ross and Harriman (1949).

HARRIS, C. S. (1965) Perceptual adaptation to inverted, reversed, and displaced vision. *Psychol. Rev.*, 72:419–44. — **223**

HARRIS, F. R., JOHNSTON, M. K., KELLEY, C. S., and WOLF, M. M. (1965) Effects of positive social reinforcement on regressed crawling of a nursery school child. In Ullman, L., and Krasner, L. (Eds.) *Case studies in behavior modification*. N. Y.: Holt, Rinehart and Winston, 313–19. — **288**

HARRIS, I. D. (1961) *Emotional blocks to learning*. N. Y.: Free Press of Glencoe. — **364**

HARRIS, J. G., JR. (1963) Judgmental versus mathematical prediction: an investigation by analogy of the clinical versus statistical controversy. *Behav. Sci.*, 8:324–35. — **500**

HARRIS, R. E., *see* Burton and Harris (1947).

HARRISON, M. (1964) *The story of the Initial Teaching Alphabet.* N. Y.: Pitman. — **68**

HARVEY, E. N. (1922) Some recent experiments on the nature of the nervous impulse. *J. nerv. ment. Dis.*, 55:503–05. — **35**

HASTEY, J. M., *see* Arkin, Hastey, and Reiser (1966).

HASTINGS, W. W. (1902) *A manual for physical measurements.* Springfield, Mass. Privately published. — **92**

HATHAWAY, M. L. (1957) Heights and weights of children and youth in the United States. *U. S. Dept. Agr. Home Econ. Res. Rpt. 2.* — **92**

HAVIGHURST, R. J. (1957) The social competence of middle-aged people. *Genet. Psychol. Monogr.*, 56:297–375. — **114**

HAVIGHURST, R. J., *see also* Eells and others (1951).

HAYS, W. L. (1963) *Statistics for psychologists.* N. Y.: Holt, Rinehart and Winston. — **401, 410, 413, 415**

HEBB, D. O. (1946) On the nature of fear. *Psychol. Rev.*, 53:259–76. — **176**

HEBB, D. O. (1949) *The organization of behavior.* N. Y.: Wiley. — **58, 224, 612**

HEBB, D. O., and FOORD, E. N. (1945) Errors of visual recognition and the nature of the trace. *J. exp. Psychol.*, 35:335–48. — **320**

HECHT, S., and SHLAER, S. (1938) An adaptometer for measuring human dark adaptation. *J. opt. Soc. Amer.*, 28:269–75. — **196**

HECHT, S., and WILLIAMS, R. E. (1922–23) The visibility of monochromatic radiation and the absorption spectrum of visual purple. *J. gen. Physiol.*, 5:1–34. — **201**

HEIDBREDER, E. (1946) The attainment of concepts: I. Methodology and terminology. *J. gen. Psychol.*, 35:173–89. — **369**

HEIDBREDER, E. (1948) The attainment of concepts: VI. Exploratory experiments on conceptualization at perceptual levels. *J. Psychol.*, 26:193–216. — **369**

HEIDBREDER, E., BENSLEY, M., and IVY, M. (1948) The attainment of concepts: IV. Regularities and levels. *J. Psychol.*, 25:299–329. — **370**

HEIDER, F. (1946) Attitudes and cognitive organization. *J. Psychol.*, 21, 107–12. — **590**

HEIDER, F. (1958) *The psychology of interpersonal relations.* N. Y.: Wiley. — **590, 592**

HEINE, R. W., *see* Wepman and Heine (1963).

HELD, R. (1965) Plasticity in sensory-motor systems. *Sci. Amer.*, 213:84–94. — **223**

HELSON, H., and BEVAN, W. (Eds.) (1967) *Contemporary approaches to psychology.* Princeton, N. J.: Van Nostrand. — **29**

HELSON, H., BLAKE, R. R., and MOUTON, J. S. (1958) Petition-signing as adjustment to situational and personal factors. *J. soc. Psychol.*, 48:3–10. — **583**

HENDIN, H. (1964) *Suicide in Scandinavia.* N. Y.: Grune and Stratton. — **534**

HENDRICKSON, G., and SCHROEDER, W. H. (1941) Transfer of training in learning to hit a submerged target. *J. educ. Psychol.*, 32:205–13. — **347**

HENNEY, K. (1938) *Principles of radio* (3rd Ed.). N. Y.: Wiley. — **204**

HENRY, A. F., and SHORT, J. F. (1954) *Suicide and homicide: some economic, sociological and psychological aspects of aggression.* Glencoe, Ill.: Free Press. — **575**

HENRY, E. R., *see* Fryer and Henry (1950).

HENRY, G. W., *see* Zillboorg and Henry (1941).

HENRY, W. E. (1956) *The analysis of fantasy.* N. Y.: Wiley. — **495**

HERNÁNDEZ-PEÓN, R. (1961) Reticular mechanisms of sensory control. In Rosenblith, W. A. (Ed.) *Sensory communication.* N. Y.: Wiley, 497–520. — **239**

HERNÁNDEZ-PEÓN, R., SCHERRER, H., and JOUVET, M. (1956) Modification of electric activity in the cochlear nucleus during "attention" in unanesthetized cats. *Science*, 123:331–32. — **238, 239**

HERON, W., *see* Bexton, Heron, and Scott (1954); Doane and others (1959).

HERON, W. T. (1935) The inheritance of maze learning ability in rats. *J. comp. Psychol.*, 19:77–89. — **448**

HERON, W. T. (1941) The inheritance of brightness and dullness in maze learning ability in the rat. *J. genet. Psychol.*, 59:41–49. — **448**

HERRICK, C. J. (1924) *Neurological foundations of animal behavior.* Chicago: Univ. of Chicago Press. — **36**

HERRICK, V. E., *see* Eells and others (1951).

HERRNSTEIN, R. J., and BORING, E. G. (1965) *A source book in the history of psychology.* Cambridge, Mass.: Harvard Univ. Press. — **29**

HERRON, E. W., *see* Holtzman and others (1961).

HERRON, W. C. (1962) The process-reactive classification of schizophrenia. *Psych. Bull.*, 59:329–42. — **536**

HERSKOVITZ, M. J., *see* Segall, Campbell, and Herskovitz (1963).

HERZOG, H., *see* Cantril, Gaudet, and Herzog (1940).

HESS, E. H. (1956) Space perception in the chick. *Sci. Amer.*, 195:71–80. — **222, 231**

HESS, E. H. (1957) Effects of meprobamate on imprinting in water-fowl. *Ann. N. Y. Acad. Sci.*, 67:724–32. — **64**

HESS, E. H. (1959) Imprinting. *Science*, 130:133–41. — **64**

HESS, E. H., *see also* Ramsay and Hess (1954).

HESS, E. H., and POLT, J. M. (1960) Pupil size as related to the interest value of visual stimuli. *Science*, 132:349–50. — **193**

HESS, R. D. (1955) Controlling cultural influence in mental testing: an experimental test. *J. educ. Res.*, 49:53–58. — **423**

HEYNS, R. (1958) *The psychology of personal adjustment.* N. Y.: Holt. — **547, 571**

HILD, W. (1964) Electrophysiological phenomena observed in single neurons and neuroglia cells in cultures of central nervous tissue. In Brazier, M. A. B. (Ed.) *Brain function,* Vol. II: *RNA and brain function; Memory and learning.* Los Angeles, Calif.: Univ. of California Press, 109–34. — **43**

HILDUM, D. C., *see* Brown and Hildum (1956).

HILGARD, E. R. (1961) Hypnosis and experimental psychodynamics. In Brosen, H. (Ed.) *Lectures on experimental psychiatry.* Pittsburgh, Pa.: Univ. of Pittsburgh Press. — **27**

HILGARD, E. R. (1962) What becomes of the input from the stimulus? In Ericksen, C. W. (Ed.) *Behavior and awareness: a symposium of research and interpretation.* Durham, N. C.: Duke Univ. Press, 46–72. — **192**

HILGARD, E. R. (Ed.) (1964) *Theories of learning and instruction.* 63rd Yearbook, Part I, National Society for the Study of Education. Chicago: Univ. of Chicago Press. — **363**

HILGARD, E. R. (1965) *Hypnotic susceptibility.* N. Y.: Harcourt, Brace & World. — **260, 261, 268, 516**

HILGARD, E. R., *see also* Weitzenhoffer and Hilgard (1959).

HILGARD, E. R., and BOWER, G. (1966) *Theories of learning* (3rd Ed.). N. Y.: Appleton-Century-Crofts. — **313, 335, 363**

HILGARD, E. R., JONES, L. V., and KAPLAN, S. J. (1951) Conditioned discrimination as related to anxiety. *J. exp. Psychol.*, 42:94–99. — **361**

HILGARD, E. R., SAIT, E. M., and MAGARET, G. A. (1940) Level of aspiration as affected by relative standing in an experimental social group. *J. exp. Psychol.*, 27:411–21. — **152**

HILGARD, E. R., and TART, C. T. (1966) Responsiveness to suggestions following waking and imagination instructions and following induction of hypnosis. *J. abnorm. Psychol.*, 71:196–208. — **259**

HILGARD, E. R., WEITZENHOFFER, A. M., LANDES, J., and MOORE, R. K. (1961) The distribution of susceptibility to hypnosis in a student population: a study using the Stanford Hypnotic Susceptibility Scale. *Psychol. Monogr.*, 75, No. 512. — **259**

HILGARD, J. R. (1933) The effect of early and delayed practice on memory and motor performances studied by the method of co-twin control. *Genet. Psychol. Monogr.*, 14, No. 6. — **67**

HILGARD, J. R. (1951) Sibling rivalry and social heredity. *Psychiatry*, 14:375–85. — **84**

HILGARD, J. R. (1965) Personality and hypnotizability: inferences from case studies. In Hilgard, E. R., *Hypnotic susceptibility*. N. Y.: Harcourt, Brace & World, 343–74. — **492**

HILGARD, J. R., and NEWMAN, M. F. (1961) Evidence for functional genesis in mental illness: schizophrenia, depressive psychoses, and psychoneuroses. *J. nerv. ment. Dis.*, 132, 3–16. — **540**

HILGARD, J. R., NEWMAN, M. F., and FISK, F. (1960) Strength of adult ego following childhood bereavement. *Amer. J. Orthopsychiat.*, 30, 788–98. — **540**

HILL, W. F. (1956) Activity as an autonomous drive. *J. comp. physiol. Psychol.*, 49:15–19. — **130**

HIMMELWEIT, H. T., OPPENHEIM, A. N., and VINCE, P. (1958) *Television and the child*. N. Y.: Oxford Univ. Press. — **594**

HINCKLEY, E. D. (1932) The influence of individual opinion on construction of an attitude scale. *J. soc. Psychol.*, 3:283–96. — **585**

HINDE, R. A. (1959) Some recent trends in ethology. In Koch, S. (Ed.) *Psychology, a study of a science*, Vol. II. N. Y.: McGraw-Hill, 561–610. — **127**

HIRSCH, J. (1967) *Behavior genetic analysis*. N. Y.: McGraw-Hill. — **461**

HIRSCH, J., and BOUDREAU, J. C. (1958) Studies in experimental behavior genetics: I. The heritability of phototaxis in a population of *Drosophila melanogaster*. *J. comp. physiol. Psychol.*, 51:647–51. — **449**

HIRSH, I. J. (1952) *The measurement of hearing*. N. Y.: McGraw-Hill. — **216**

HOCH, P. H. (1955) Experimental psychiatry. *Amer. J. Psychiat.*, 111:787–90. — **541**

HOCHBERG, J. (1964) *Perception*. Englewood Cliffs, N. J.: Prentice-Hall. — **245**

HOELZEL, F. (1927) Central factors in hunger. *Amer. J. Physiol.*, 82:665–71. — **121**

HOEPFNER, R., *see* Guilford and Hoepfner (1966).

HOFFMAN, B. (1962) *The tyranny of testing*. N. Y.: Crowell-Collier. — **439**

HOFFMAN, L. W., *see* Hoffman and Hoffman (1964).

HOFFMAN, M. L., and HOFFMAN, L. W. (Eds.) (1964) *Review of child development research*, Vol. I. N. Y.: Russell Sage Foundation. — **90**

HOGAN, H. P., *see* Carmichael, Hogan, and Walter (1932).

HOGBEN, L. (1933) *Nature and nurture*. London: Allen and Unwin. — **457**

HOLDEN, M., *see* Goodenough and others (1959).

HOLLINGSHEAD, A. B., and REDLICH, F. C. (1958) *Social class and mental illness: a community study*. N. Y.: Wiley. — **545**

HOLMEN, M. G., KATTER, R. V., HONES, A. M., and RICHARDSON, I. F. (1956) An assessment program for OCS applicants. *Hum RRO tech. Rep. 26*. — **500**

HOLT, R. R. (1958) Clinical and statistical prediction: a reformulation and some new data. *J. abnorm. soc. Psychol.*, 56:1–12. — **500**

HOLT, R. R., *see also* Klopfer and others (1954).

HOLT, R. R., and LUBORSKY, L. (1958) *Personality patterns of psychiatrists*. N. Y.: Basic Books. — **499**

HOLTZMAN, W. H., THORPE, J. S., SWARTZ, J. D., and HERRON, E. W. (1961) *Inkblot perception and personality*. Austin, Tex.: Univ. of Texas Press. — **497, 502**

HOLWAY, A. H., and BORING, E. G. (1941) Determinants of apparent visual size with distance variant. *Amer. J. Psychol.*, 54:21–37. — **221**

HOLZ, W. C., *see* Azrin, Holz, and Hake (1963).

HOLZINGER, K. J., *see* Newman, Freeman, and Holzinger (1937).

HOMME, L. E., *see* Evans, Glaser, and Homme (1960).

HONES, A. M., *see* Holmen, Katten, Hones, and Richardson (1956).

HONIG, W. K. (Ed.) (1966) *Operant behavior: areas of research and application*. N. Y.: Appleton-Century-Crofts. — **313**

HONZIK, C. H., *see* Tolman and Honzik (1930).

HOPPE, F. (1930) Erfolg und Misserfolg. *Psychol. Forsch.*, 14:1–62. — **152**

HOSTELLER, R. C., *see* McGaugh and Hosteller (1961).

HOVLAND, C. I. (1937) The generalization of conditioned responses: I. The sensory generalization of conditioned responses with varying frequencies of tone. *J. gen. Psychol.*, 17:125–48. — **277**

HOVLAND, C. I., *see also* Kelman and Hovland (1953); Morrisett and Hovland (1959); Rosenberg and others (1960).

HOVLAND, C. I., JANIS, I. L., and KELLEY, H. H. (1953) *Communication and persuasion*. New Haven, Conn.: Yale Univ. Press. — **583, 586**

HOVLAND, C. I., LUMSDAINE, A. A., and SHEFFIELD, F. C. (1949) *Experiments on mass communication*. Princeton, N. J.: Princeton Univ. Press. — **594**

HSIA, Y. (1965) Photochemistry of vision. In Graham, C. H. (Ed.) *Vision and visual perception*. N. Y.: Wiley. — **200**

HSIA, Y., and GRAHAM, C. H. (1965) Color blindness. In Graham, C. H. (Ed.) *Vision and visual perception*. N. Y.: Wiley, 395–413. — **200**

HUBEL, D. H., and WIESEL, T. N. (1959) Receptive fields of single neurones in the cat's striate cortex. *J. Physiol.*, 148:574–91. — **46**

HUBEL, D. H., and WIESEL, T. N. (1963) Receptive fields of cells in striate cortex of very young, visually inexperienced kittens. *J. Neurophysiol.*, 26:994–1002. — **46**

HUBEL, D. H., and WIESEL, T. N. (1965) Receptive fields and functional architecture in two nonstriate visual areas (18 and 19) of the cat. *J. Neurophysiol.*, 28:229–89. — **46**

HUDSPETH, W. J., MC GAUGH, J. L., and THOMPSON, C. W. (1964) Aversive and amnesic effects of electroconvulsive shock. *J. comp. physiol. Psychol.*, 57:61–64. — **331**

HULL, C. L. (1943) *Principles of behavior.* N. Y.: Appleton-Century-Crofts. — **132**

HULL, C. L. (1951) *Essentials of behavior.* New Haven, Conn.: Yale Univ. Press. — **307, 309**

HULL, C. L. (1952) *A behavior system.* New Haven, Conn.: Yale Univ. Press. — **132**

HULSE, S., *see* Deese and Hulse (1967).

HUMPHREY, B. M., *see* Rhine and Humphrey (1944).

HUMPHREY, E. M., and ZANGWILL, L. O. (1952) Dysphasia in left-handed patients with unilateral brain lesions. *J. Neurol. Neurosurg. Psychiat.,* 15:184–93. — **48**

HUMPHREYS, L. G. (1957) Characteristics of type concepts with special reference to Sheldon's typology. *Psychol. Bull.,* 54:218–28. — **467**

HUNT, E. B. (1962) *Concept learning: an information processing problem.* N. Y.: Wiley. — **384, 393**

HUNT, W. A., *see* Cantril and Hunt (1932).

HUNTER, E. (1951) *Brainwashing in Red China.* N. Y.: Vanguard. — **596**

HURLOCK, E. B. (1966) *Adolescent development* (3rd Ed.). N. Y.: McGraw-Hill. — **116**

HUXLEY, A. (1954) *The doors of perception.* N. Y.: Harper and Row. — **265**

HYDÉN, H. (1959) Biochemical changes in glial cells and nerve cells at varying activity. In *Biochemistry of the central nervous system. Proceedings of the Fourth International Congress of Biochemistry.* Vol. III. London: Pergamon Press, 64–89. — **322**

HYDÉN, H., and EGYBÁZI, E. (1963) Glial RNA changes during a learning experiment in rats. *Proc. Nat. Acad. Sci. U. S.,* 49:618–24. — **322**

HYMAN, H. H. (1955) *Survey design and analysis.* Glencoe, Ill.: Free Press. — **600**

INBAU, F. E., *see* Reid and Inbau (1964).

INHELDER, B., *see* Piaget and Inhelder (1941).

INHELDER, B., and PIAGET, J. (1958) *The growth of logical thinking from childhood to adolescence.* N. Y.: Basic Books. — **393**

INKELES, A., and LEVINSON, D. J. (1954) National character: the study of modal personality and sociocultural systems. In Lindzey, G. (Ed.) *Handbook of social psychology.* Reading, Mass.: Addison-Wesley, 977–1020. — **464**

IRION, A. L., *see* McGeoch and Irion (1952).

IRWIN, O. C. (1952) Speech development in the young child: II. Some factors related to the speech development of the infant and young child. *J. speech hearing Disorders,* 17:269–79. — **372**

ISAACSON, R. L. (Ed.) (1964) *Basic readings in neuropsychology.* N. Y.: Harper and Row. — **58**

IVY, M., *see* Heidbreder, Bensley, and Ivy (1948).

JACKSON, C. M. (1928) Some aspects of form and growth. In Robbins, W. J., and others. *Growth.* New Haven, Conn.: Yale Univ. Press. — **95**

JACKSON, D. D. (Ed.) (1960) *The etiology of schizophrenia.* N. Y.: Basic Books. — **547**

JACKSON, D. D., *see also* Savage, Terrill, and Jackson (1962).

JACKSON, J. M., and SALTZSTEIN, H. D. (1958) The effect of person-group relationships on conformity processes. *J. abnorm. soc. Psychol.,* 57:17–24. — **582**

JACKSON, P. W., *see* Getzels and Jackson (1962).

JACKSON, T. A. (1942) Use of the stick as a tool by young chimpanzees. *J. comp. Psychol.,* 34:223–35. — **303**

JACOBS, R. C., and CAMPBELL, D. T. (1961) The perpetuation of an arbitrary tradition through several generations of a laboratory microculture. *J. abnorm. soc. Psychol.,* 62:649–58. — **581, 582**

JACOBSON, A., *see* Babich, Jacobson, Bubash, and Jacobson (1965); Hainer, Emslie, and Jacobson (1954); Jacobson, Babich, Bubash, and Jacobson (1965).

JACOBSON, A., KALES, A., LEHMANN, D., and ZWEIZIG, J. R. (1965) Somnambulism: all-night EEG studies. *Science,* 148:975–77. — **257**

JACOBSON, A. L., *see* Babich, Jacobson, Bubash, and Jacobson (1965).

JACOBSON, A. L., BABICH, F. R., BUBASH, S., and JACOBSON, A. (1965) Differential approach tendencies produced by injection of ribonucleic acid from trained rats. *Science,* 150, 636–37. — **322**

JACOBSON, E. (1932) Electrophysiology of mental activities. *Amer. J. Psychol.,* 44:677–94. — **376, 377**

JACOBSON, R., *see* Zelman, Kabat, Jacobson, and McConnell (1963).

JAGODA, H., *see* D'Amato and Jagoda (1960).

JAHODA, M., *see* Christie and Jahoda (1954).

JAMES, W. (1897) *The will to believe.* N. Y.: Longmans, Green. — **265**

JAMES, W. (1902) *The varieties of religious experience.* N. Y.: Longmans, Green. — **251**

JAMES, W. T. (1941) Morphological form and its relation to behavior. In Stockard, C. R. (Ed.) *The genetic and endocrinic basis for differences in form and behavior.* Philadelphia, Pa.: Wistar Institute, 525–643. — **449**

JANIS, I. L., *see* Hovland, Janis, and Kelley (1953).

JANIS, I. L., and FESHBACH, S. (1953) Effects of fear-arousing communications. *J. abnorm. soc. Psychol.,* 48:78–92. — **596**

JARVIK, L. F., *see* Erlenmeyer-Kimling and Jarvik (1963).

JASPER, H., *see* Li and others (1956); Penfield and Jasper (1954).

JASTROW, J. (1935) *Wish and wisdom.* N. Y.: Appleton-Century. — **243**

JENKINS, J. G., and DALLENBACH, K. M. (1924) Oblivescence during sleep and waking. *Amer. J. Psychol.,* 35:605–12. — **323, 324**

JENKINS, M. D., *see* Witty and Jenkins (1934).

JENNINGS, H. H. (1950) *Leadership and isolation* (2nd Ed.). N. Y.: Longmans, Green. — **499**

JENSEN, J., *see* Monroe, Rechtschaffen, Foulkes, and Jensen (1965).

JENSEN, S. E., and RAMSEY, R. (1963) Treatment of chronic alcoholism with lysergic acid diethylamide. *Canad. psychiat. Assn. J.,* 8:182–88. — **264**

JERNEGAN, H. W. (1927) Productivity of doctors of philosophy in history. *Am. Hist. Rev.,* 33:1–22. — **113**

JERSILD, A. T. (1963) *The psychology of adolescence,* (Rev. Ed.). N. Y.: Macmillan. — **116**

JOHN, E. R. (1967) *Mechanisms of memory.* N. Y.: Academic Press. — **335**

JOHNSTON, M. K., *see* Harris, Johnston, Kelley, and Wolf (1965).

JONES, A. D., *see* Deutsch and Jones (1959).

JONES, A. W., *see* Pressey and Jones (1955).

JONES, H. E. (1943) *Development in adolescence.* N. Y.: Appleton-Century-Crofts. — **499**

JONES, H. E., *see also* Conrad and Jones (1940).

JONES, H. E., and CONRAD, H. S. (1933) The growth and decline of intelligence. *Genet. Psychol. Monogr.,* 13, No. 3. — **430**

JONES, H. E., CONRAD, H. S., and BLANCHARD, M. B. (1932) Environmental handicap in mental test performance. *Univ. Calif. Publ. Psychol.,* 5:63–99. — **437**

JONES, L. V., *see* Hilgard, Jones, and Kaplan (1951).

JONES, M. C., *see* Mussen and Jones (1958).

JONES, M. C., and MUSSEN, P. H. (1958) Self-conceptions, motivations, and interpersonal attitudes of early- and late-maturing girls. *Child Develop.*, 30:491–501. — 95

JONES, S., *see* Leventhal, Singer, and Jones (1965).

JOUVET, M., *see* Hernández-Peón, Scherrer, and Jouvet (1956).

JUDD, C. H. (1908) The relation of special training and general intelligence. *Educ. Rev.*, 36:42–48. — 347

JUDD, D. B. (1952) *Color in business, science, and industry.* N. Y.: Wiley. — 216

JUNG, C. G. (1923) *Psychological types.* N. Y.: Harcourt, Brace & World. — 469

KABAT, L., *see* Zelman, Kabat, Jacobson, and McConnell (1963).

KAGAN, J. (1958) The concept of identification. *Psychol. Rev.*, 65:296–305. — 83

KAGAN, J. (1964) Acquisition and significance of sex typing and sex role identity. In Hoffman, M. L., and Hoffman, L. W. (Eds.) *Review of child development research*, Vol. I. N. Y.: Russell Sage Foundation, 137–67. — 82, 151

KAGAN, J., *see also* Mussen, Conger, and Kagan (1963).

KAGAN, J., and LESSER, G. S. (1961) *Contemporary issues in thematic apperceptive methods.* Springfield, Ill.: Thomas. — 502

KAGAN, J., and MOSS, H. A. (1962) *Birth to maturity.* N. Y.: Wiley. — 87, 88

KAHN, F. (1943) *Man in structure and function* (2 vols.). N. Y.: Knopf. — 234

KALES, A., *see* Jacobson, Kales, Lehmann, and Zweizig (1965).

KALLMANN, F. J. (1953) *Heredity in health and mental disorder.* N. Y.: Norton. — 456

KALLMANN, F. J. (1959) The genetics of mental illness. In Arieti, S. (Ed.) *American handbook of psychiatry.* N. Y.: Basic Books, 175–234. — 534

KALLMANN, F. J., and ROTH, B. (1956) Genetic aspects of preadolescent schizophrenia. *Amer. J. Psychiat.*, 112:599–606. — 456

KALLMANN, F. J., and SANDER, G. (1949) Twin studies on senescence. *Amer. J. Psychiat.*, 106:29–36. — 454

KAMIYA, J. (1961) Behavioral, subjective, and physiological aspects of drowsiness and sleep. In Fiske, D. W., and Maddi, S. R. (Eds.) *Functions of varied experience.* Homewood, Ill.: Dorsey Press. — 257

KAPLAN, M. F., and SINGER, E. (1963) Dogmatism and sensory alienation: an empirical investigation. *J. consult. Psychol.*, 27:486–91. — 159

KAPLAN, S. J., *see* Hilgard, Jones, and Kaplan (1951).

KARDINER, A. (1939) *The individual and his society.* N. Y.: Columbia Univ. Press. — 464

KARSH, E. B. (1962) Effects of number of rewarded trials and intensity of punishment on running speed. *J. comp. physiol. Psychol.*, 55:44–51. — 357

KATTER, R. V., *see* Holmen, Katter, Hones, and Richardson (1956).

KATZ, BERNARD (1952) The nerve impulse. *Sci. Amer.*, 185:55–64. — 37

KATZ, BRENDA, *see* Secord, Bevan, and Katz (1956).

KATZ, DANIEL, CARTWRIGHT, D., ELDERSVELD, S., and LEE, A. MC C. (Eds.) (1954) *Public opinion and propaganda.* N. Y.: Dryden. — 600

KATZ, DAVID (1937) *Animals and men: studies in comparative psychology.* N. Y.: Longmans, Green. — 129

KATZ, J. J., *see* Fodor and Katz (1964).

KEELER, C. E., and KING, H. D. (1942) Multiple effect of coat color genes in the Norway rat, with special reference to temperament and domestication. *J. comp. Psychol.*, 34:241–50. — 448

KELLEY, C. S., *see* Harris, Johnston, Kelley, and Wolf (1965).

KELLEY, H. H., *see* Hovland, Janis, and Kelley (1953).

KELLEY, H. H., and VOLKART, E. H. (1952) The resistance to change of group-anchored attitudes. *Amer. sociol. Rev.*, 17:453–65. — 582

KELLY, E. L. (1939) Concerning the validity of Terman's weights for predicting marital happiness. *Psychol. Bull.*, 306:202–03. — 109

KELLY, E. L., and FISKE, D. W. (1951) *The predictability of performance in clinical psychology.* Ann Arbor, Mich.: Univ. of Michigan Press. — 499

KELMAN, H. C. (1958) Compliance, identification, and internalization: three processes of attitude change. *Conflict Resolution*, 2:51–60. — 598

KELMAN, H. C., and HOVLAND, C. I. (1953) "Reinstatement" of the communicator in delayed measurement of opinion change. *J. abnorm. soc. Psychol.*, 48:327–35. — 595

KELSEY, D., and BARRON, J. N. (1958) Maintenance of posture by hypnotic suggestion in patient undergoing plastic surgery. *Brit. Med. J.* 5073:756–57. — 262

KENDERDINE, M. (1931) Laughter in the preschool child. *Child Develpm.*, 2:228–30. — 180

KENISTON, K., *see* Couch and Keniston (1960).

KEPPEL, G., *see* Underwood and Keppel (1962).

KESSEN, M. L., *see* Miller and Kessen (1952).

KESSEN, W. (1965) *The child.* N. Y.: Wiley. — 90

KESSEN, W., *see also* Mandler and Kessen (1959).

KESSEN, W., and MANDLER, G. (1961) Anxiety, pain, and the inhibition of distress. *Psychol. Rev.*, 68:396–404. — 178

KETY, S. (1959) Biochemical theories of schizophrenia. *Science*, 129:1528–32, 1590–96. — 541

KIERKEGAARD, S. (1944) *The concept of dread.* (Trans. by W. Lowrie.). Princeton, N. J.: Princeton Univ. Press. — 179

KILPATRICK, F. P. (Ed.) (1961) *Explorations in transactional psychology.* N. Y.: New York Univ. Press. — 246

KIMBLE, D. P. (Ed.) (1965) *Learning, remembering, and forgetting*, Vol. I. *The anatomy of memory.* Palo Alto, Calif.: Science and Behavior Books. — 335

KIMBLE, D. P. (1967a) *Learning, remembering, and forgetting*, Vol. II. *Organization of recall.* N. Y.: New York Academy of Sciences. — 335

KIMBLE, D. P. (1967b) *Learning, remembering, and forgetting*, Vol. III. *Readiness to remember*, N. Y.: New York Academy of Sciences. — 335

KIMBLE, G. A. (1955) Shock intensity and avoidance learning. *J. comp. physiol. Psychol.*, 48:281–84. — 24

KIMBLE, G. A. (1961) *Hilgard and Marquis' Conditioning and learning* (2nd. Ed.). N. Y.: Appleton-Century-Crofts. — 313

KIMBLE, G. A., and GARMEZY, N. (1963) *Principles of general psychology* (2nd Ed.). N. Y.: Ronald Press. — 276

KING, G. F. (1958) Differential autonomic responsiveness in the process-reactive classification of schizophrenia. *J. abnorm. soc. Psychol.*, 56:160–64. — 537

KING, H. D., *see* Keeler and King (1942).

KING, J. A., *see* Freedman, King, and Elliott (1961).

KING, J. E., *see* Becker, King, and Markee (1962).

KING, S. H., *see* Funkenstein, King, and Drolette (1957).

KINSEY, A. C., POMEROY, W. B., and MARTIN, C. E. (1948) *Sexual behavior in the human male.* Philadelphia, Pa.: Saunders. — 97, 527

KIRK, S. A. (1958) *Early education of the mentally retarded.* Urbana, Ill.: Univ. of Illinois Press. — **433**

KLEEMEIER, R. W. (Ed.) (1961) *Aging and leisure: a research perspective into the meaningful use of time.* N. Y.: Oxford Univ. Press. — **116**

KLEIN, S. P., *see* Skager, Schultz, and Klein (1965).

KLEITMAN, N. (1939) *Sleep and wakefulness.* Chicago: Univ. of Chicago Press. — **253**

KLEITMAN, N. (1963) *Sleep and wakefulness* (2nd. ed.). Chicago: Univ. of Chicago Press. — **252, 268**

KLEITMAN, N., *see also* Aserinsky and Kleitman (1953); Dement and Kleitman (1957).

KLINEBERG, O. (1931) A study of psychological differences between "racial" and national groups in Europe. *Arch. Psychol., N. Y.,* No. 132. — **437**

KLINEBERG, O. (1935) *Negro intelligence and selective migration.* N. Y.: Columbia Univ. Press. — **459**

KLINEBERG, O. (1938) Emotional expression in Chinese literature. *J. abnorm. soc. Psychol.,* 33:517–20. — **175**

KLOPFER, B., AINSWORTH, M. D., KLOPFER, W. G., and HOLT, R. R. (1954) *Developments in the Rorschach technique.* Yonkers, N. Y.: World Book. — **502**

KLOPFER, W. G., *see* Klopfer and others (1954).

KNAPP, P. H. (Ed.) (1963) *Expression of the emotions in man.* N. Y.: Internat. Univ. Press. — **186**

KNAPP, R. R. (1965) Relationship of a measure of self-actualization to neuroticism and extraversion. *J. consult. Psychol.,* 29:168–72. — **160**

KNIEF, L. M., and STROUD, J. B. (1959) Intercorrelations among various intelligence, achievement, and social class scores. *J. educ. Psychol.,* 50:117–20. — **423**

KNOWER, F. H., *see* Dusenbury and Knower (1939).

KOCH, H. L. (1956*a*) Children's work attitudes and sibling characteristics. *Child Develpm.,* 27:289–311. — **84**

KOCH, H. L. (1956*b*) Sissiness and tomboyishness in relation to sibling characteristics. *J. genet. Psychol.,* 88:231–45. — **84**

KOCH, S. (Ed.) (1959–1963) *Psychology: a study of a science,* Vols. I–VI; one volume in preparation. N. Y.: McGraw-Hill. — **618**

KÖHLER, W. (1925) *The mentality of apes.* N. Y.: Harcourt, Brace & World. — **302, 313**

KOESTLER, A. (1965) *The act of creation.* N. Y.: Macmillan. — **181**

KOGAN, M., *see* Deutsch, Fishman, Kogan, North, and Whitman (1964).

KOGAN, N., *see* Wallach and Kogan (1965).

KOHLBERG, L. (1963) The development of children's orientations toward a moral order: I. Sequence in the development of moral thought. *Vita Humana,* 6:11–33. — **85, 86**

KOHLBERG, L. (1964) Development of moral character and moral ideology. In Hoffman, M. L., and Hoffman, L. W. (Eds.) *Review of child development research,* Vol. I. N. Y.: Russell Sage Foundation, 383–431. — **86**

KOHLER, I. (1962) Experiments with goggles. *Sci. Amer.,* 206:62–72. — **222**

KOHN, M. L. (1959) Social class and parental values. *Amer. J. Sociol.,* 64:337–51. — **83**

KOHN, M. L., *see also* Clausen and Kohn (1960).

KOLB, L. C., *see* Noyes and Kolb (1958).

KOOISTRA, W. H. (1963) Developmental trends in the attainment of conservation, transivity, and relativism in the thinking of children. Unpublished Ph.D. dissertation, Wayne University. — **71, 72**

KOUNIN, J. S., *see* Gump and Kounin (1959).

KRAFKA, J. (1919) The effect of temperature upon facet number in the bar-eyed mutant of drosophila. Part I. *J. genet. Physiol.,* 2:409–32. — **457**

KRASNER, L., *see* Ullman and Krasner (1965).

KRASNER, L., and ULLMANN, L. P. (Eds.) (1965) *Research in behavior modification.* N. Y.: Holt, Rinehart and Winston. — **571**

KRAWIEC, T. S., *see* Chaplin and Krawiec (1960).

KRECH, D., CRUCHFIELD, R. S., BALLACHEY, E. L. (1962) *Individual in society.* N. Y.: McGraw-Hill. — **600**

KRETSCHMER, E. (1925) *Physique and character.* N. Y.: Harcourt, Brace & World. — **467**

KRIS, E. (1952) *Psychoanalytic explorations in art.* N. Y.: Internat. Univ. Press. — **389**

KRISTOFFERSON, A. B., *see* Moulton, Raphelson, Kristofferson, and Atkinson (1958).

KROEBER, T. C. (1963) The coping functions of the ego mechanisms. In White, R. W. (Ed.) *The study of lives.* N. Y.: Atherton Press, 178–98. — **520, 521**

KROUT, M. H. (1954) An experimental attempt to determine the significance of unconscious manual symbolic movements. *J. genet. Psychol.,* 51:121–52. — **518**

KRUEGER, W. C. F. (1929) The effect of over-learning on retention. *J. exp. Psychol.,* 12:71–78. — **333**

KUBIE, L. S. (1950) *Practical and theoretical aspects of psychoanalysis.* N. Y.: Internat. Univ. Press. — **571**

KUBIE, L. S. (1958) *Neurotic distortion of the creative process.* Lawrence, Kans.: Univ. of Kansas Press. — **389**

KUENNE, M. R. (1946) Experimental investigation of the relation of language to transposition behavior in young children. *J. exp. Psychol.,* 36:471–90. — **374**

KUHLEN, R. G., *see* Pressey and Kuhlen (1957).

KUHLEN, R. G., and ARNOLD, M. (1944) Age differences in religious beliefs and problems during adolescence. *J. genet. Psychol.,* 63:291–300. — **103**

LACEY, J. I., BATEMAN, D. E., and VAN LEHN, R. (1952) Autonomic response specificity and Rorschach color responses. *Psychosom. Med.,* 14:256–60. — **468**

LACEY, J. I., and VAN LEHN, R. (1952) Differential emphasis in somatic response to stress. *Psychosom. Med.,* 14:71–81. — **468**

LAIDLAW, R. W., and HAMILTON, M. A. (1937) A study of thresholds in apperception of passive movement among normal control subjects. *Bull. Neurol. Inst., N. Y.,* 6:268–73. — **213**

LAMBERT, W. W., SOLOMON, R. L., and WATSON, P. D. (1949) Reinforcement and extinction as factors in size estimation. *J. exp. Psychol.,* 39:637–41. — **241**

LANCASTER, E. (1958) *The final face of Eve.* N. Y.: McGraw-Hill. — **480**

LAND, E. H. (1959) Color vision and the natural image. *Proc. natl. Acad. Sci.,* 45:115–29, 636–44. — **202**

LANDAUER, T. K. (1964) Two hypotheses concerning the biochemical basis of memory. *Psychol. Rev.,* 71:167–79. — **323**

LANDAUER, T. K. (1967) *Readings in physiological psychology.* N. Y.: McGraw-Hill. — **58**

LANDAUER, T. K., and WHITING, J. W. M. (1964) Infantile stimulation and adult stature of human males. *Amer. Anthropol.,* 66:1007–28. — **69, 70**

LANDES, J., *see* Hilgard, Weitzenhoffer, Landes, and Moore (1961).

LANDIS, C., ZUBIN, J., and METTLER, F. A. (1950) The functions of the human frontal lobe. *J. Psychol.,* 30:123–38. — **167**

LANDIS, J. T. (1942) What is the happiest period of life? *Sch. & Soc.,* 55:643–45. — **104, 105**

LANG, G. E., *see* Lang and Lang (1961).

LANG, K., and LANG, G. E. (1961) Ordeal by debate: viewer reactions. *Pub. Opin. Quart.*, 25:277–88. — **594**

LANG, P. J. (1964) Experimental studies of desensitization psychotherapy. In Wolpe, J., Salter, H., and Reyna, L. J. (Eds.) *The conditioning therapies.* N. Y.: Holt, Rinehart and Winston. — **557**

LANGNER, T. S., *see* Srole and others (1962).

LANTZ, B. (1945) Some dynamic aspects of success and failure. *Psychol. Monogr.*, 59, No. 271. — **182**

LAWRENCE, D. H., and FESTINGER, L. (1962) *Deterrents and reinforcement: the psychology of insufficient reward.* Stanford, Calif.: Stanford Univ. Press. — **592**

LAZARSFELD, P. F. (1944) The controversy over detailed interviews: an offer for negotiation. *Publ. Opin. Quart.*, 8:36–60. — **588**

LAZARUS, A. A. (1963) The results of behavior therapy in 126 cases of severe neurosis. *Behav. Res. Ther.*, 1:69–79. — **557**

LAZARUS, A. A., and RACHMAN, S. (1957) The use of systematic desensitization in psychotherapy. *S. Afr. med. J.*, 32:934–37. — **556**

LEAHY, A. M. (1935) Nature-nurture and intelligence. *Genet. Psychol. Monogr.*, 17:235–308. — **451, 452, 455**

LEAVITT, H. J. (1964) *Managerial psychology* (2nd Ed.). Chicago: Univ. of Chicago Press. — **617**

LEE, A. MC C., *see* Katz and others (1954).

LEE, E. S. (1951) Negro intelligence and selective migration: a Philadelphia test of the Klineberg hypothesis. *Amer. sociol. Rev.*, 16:227–33. — **438**

LEEPER, R. W. (1935) A study of a neglected portion of the field of learning: the development of sensory organization. *J. genet. Psychol.*, 46:41–75. — **227**

LEGGITT, D. (1934) Measuring progress in working skills in ninth-grade civics. *School Review*, 42:676–87. — **348**

LEHMAN, H. C. (1938) The most proficient years at sports and games. *Res. Quart. Amer. Assn. Hlth & phys. Educ.*, 9:3–19. — **111**

LEHMAN, H. C. (1953) *Age and achievement.* Princeton, N. J.: Princeton Univ. Press. — **107, 111, 112, 113**

LEHMAN, H. C. (1960) The age decrement in outstanding scientific creativity. *Amer. Psychologist*, 15:128–34. — **113**

LEHMANN, D., *see* Jacobson, Kales, Lehmann, and Zweizig (1965).

LEIGHTON, A. H., *see* Leighton, Harding, Macklin, Macmillan, and Leighton (1963).

LEIGHTON, D. C., HARDING, J. S., MACKLIN, D. B., MACMILLAN, A. M., and LEIGHTON, A. H. (1963) *The character of danger: psychiatric symptoms in selected communities.* N. Y.: Basic Books. — **545**

LEITES, N., and BERNAUT, E. (1954) *Ritual of liquidation.* Glencoe, Ill.: Free Press. — **597**

LEJEUNE, L., GAUTIER, M., and TURPIN, R. (1959) Les chromosomes humains en culture de tissus. *C. R. Acad. Sci.*, Paris, 248, 262. — **446**

LEMERE, F., VOEGTLIN, W., BROZ, W., O'HOLLAREN, P., and TUPPER, W. (1942) The conditioned reflex treatment of chronic alcoholism: VIII. A review of six years' experience with this treatment of 1526 patients. *J. Amer. med. Assn.*, 120:269–70. — **558**

LENNARD, H. L., and BERNSTEIN, A. (1960) *The anatomy of psychotherapy.* N. Y.: Columbia Univ. Press. — **563, 564**

LENNEBERG, E. H. (1961) Color naming, color recognition, color discrimination: a reappraisal. *Perceptual and Motor Skills*, 12:375–82. — **375**

LENNEBERG, E. H., *see also* Brown and Lenneberg (1954).

LENNEBERG, E. H., and ROBERTS, J. M. (1956) *Indiana U. Pubs. in Anthrop. and Linguistics*, Memoir 13. — **375**

LESSER, G. S., *see* Kagan and Lesser (1961).

LEUBA, C. (1941) Tickling and laughter: two genetic studies. *J. genet. Psychol.*, 58:201–09. — **180**

LEVAN, A., *see* Tjio and Levan (1956).

LEVENTHAL, H., SINGER, R., and JONES, S. (1965) Effects of fear and specificity of recommendation upon attitudes and behavior. *J. Pers. soc. Psychol.*, 2:20–29. — **596**

LEVIN, H., *see* Sears, Maccoby, and Levin (1957).

LEVINE, S. J. (1962) Psychophysiological effects of infantile stimulation. In Bliss, E. L. (Ed.) *Roots of behavior.* N. Y.: Hoeber. — **69**

LEVINSON, B., and REESE, H. W. (1963) Patterns of discrimination learning set in preschool children, fifth graders, college freshmen, and the aged. *Final Report, Cooperative Research Project No. 1059*, U. S., Dept. of Hlth., Educ., and Welf. — **346**

LEVINSON, D. J., *see* Adorno and others (1950); Inkeles and Levinson (1954).

LEWIN, K. (1935) *A dynamic theory of personality.* N. Y.: McGraw-Hill. — **504, 524**

LEWIN, K., *see also* Barker, Dembo, and Lewin (1941).

LEWIS, D. (1960) *Quantitative methods in psychology.* N. Y.: McGraw-Hill. — **415**

LEWIS, D. J., and MAHER, B. A. (1965) Neural consolidation and electroconvulsive shock. *Psychol. Rev.*, 72:225–39. — **331**

LEWIS, D. J., and MAHER, B. A. (1966) Electroconvulsive shock and inhibition: some problems reconsidered. *Psychol. Rev.*, 73:388–92. — **331**

LEWIS, H. B. (1963) Individual differences among non-reporters in failure to recall dreams. Paper presented at Association for Psychophysiological study of Sleep. — **256**

LEWIS, S. (1934) *Work of art.* N. Y.: Doubleday, Doran. — **465**

LI, C. L., CULLEN, C., and JASPER, H. H. (1956) Laminar microelectrode analysis of cortical unspecific recruiting response and spontaneous rhythms. *J. neurophysiol.*, 19:131–43. — **38**

LIDZ, T., FLECK, S., and CORNELISON, A. R. (1965) *Schizophrenia and the family.* N. Y.: Internat. Univ. Press. — **540**

LIFTON, R. J. (1954) Home by ship: reaction patterns of American prisoners of war repatriated from North Korea. *Amer. J. Psychiat.*, 110:732–39. — **597**

LIFTON, R. J. (1956) "Thought reform" of Western Civilians in Chinese Communist prisons. *Psychiatry*, 19:173–95. — **597**

LIFTON, R. J. (1961) *Thought reform and the psychology of totalism.* N. Y.: Norton. — **597, 598, 600**

LIKERT, R. (1932) A technique for the measurement of attitudes. *Arch. Psychol.*, N. Y., 28, No. 194. — **585**

LINDGREN, H. C. (1964) *Psychology of personal development.* N. Y.: American Book. — **547, 571**

LINDSLEY, D. B. (1951) Emotion. In Stevens, S. S. (Ed.) *Handbook of experimental psychology.* N. Y.: Wiley, 473–516. — **173**

LINDZEY, G. (Ed.) (1958) *Assessment of human motives.* N. Y.: Rinehart. — **162**

LINDZEY, G. (1961) *Projective techniques and cross-cultural research.* N. Y.: Appleton-Century-Crofts. — **497**

LINDZEY, G., *see also* Allport, Vernon, and Lindzey (1960); Hall and Lindzey (1957).

LINDZEY, G., and ARONSON, E. (Eds.) (1967) *Handbook of social psychology* (Rev. Ed.). Reading, Mass.: Addison-Wesley. (In press). — **600**

LINDZEY, G., and HALL, C. S. (Eds.) (1965) *Theories of personality: primary sources and research*. N. Y.: Wiley. — **485**

LIPPERT, W. W., and SENTER, R. J. (1966) Electrodermal responses in the sociopath. *Psychonomic Science*, 4:25–26. — **542**

LIPSET, S. M., and BENDIX, R. (1959) *Social mobility in industrial society*. Berkeley, Calif.: Univ. of California Press. — **576**

LIPSITT, L. P., and SPIKER, C. C. (Eds.) (1963) *Advances in child development and behavior: I*. N. Y.: Academic Press. — **90**

LITWIN, G. H., *see* Atkinson and Litwin (1960).

LIVINGSTON, R. B. (1958) Central control of afferent activity. In *Reticular formation of the brain* (Henry Ford International Symposium). Boston: Little, Brown, 177–86. — **54**

LOCKMAN, R. F., *see* Ross and Lockman (1965).

LOEWENSTEIN, W. R. (1960) Biological transducers. *Sci. Amer.*, 203:98–108. — **52**

LOGAN, F. A. (1959) The Hull-Spence approach. In Koch, S., *Psychology: a study of a science*, Vol. II. N. Y.: McGraw-Hill, 293–358. — **307**

LOGAN, F. A. (1964) The free behavior situation. *Nebr. Symp. Motivation*, 12:99–134. — **129**

LORGE, I. (1930) Influence of regularly interpolated time intervals on subsequent learning. *Teach. Coll. Contr. Educ.*, No. 438. — **295**

LORR, M., and FIELDS, V. (1954) A factorial study of body types. *J. clin. Psychol.*, 10:182–85. — **467**

LOWE, C. M. (1961) The self-concept: fact or artifact? *Psychol. Bull.*, 58:325–36. — **482**

LOWELL, E. L. (1950) A methodological study of projectively measured achievement motivation. Unpublished M.A. thesis, Weslevan Universitv. — **154**

LOWELL, E. L., *see also* McClelland and others (1953).

LU, Y. C. (1962) Contradictory parental expectations in schizophrenia. *Arch. Gen. Psychiat.*, 6:219–34. — **540**

LUBORSKY, L., *see* Holt and Luborsky (1958).

LUCE, G. G., and SEGALL, J. (1966) *Sleep*. N. Y.: Coward-McCann. — **268**

LUCE, R. D. (1963) Detection and recognition. In Luce, R. D., Bush, R. R., and Galanter, E. (Eds.) *Handbook of mathematical psychology*, Vol. I. N. Y.: Wiley, 103–90. — **192**

LUCE, R. D., BUSH, R. R., and GALANTER, E. (Eds.) (1963) (1965) *Handbook of mathematical psychology*, Vols. I, III. N. Y.: Wiley. — **216, 313**

LUCHINS, A. S. (1942) Mechanization in problem solving: the effect of *Einstellung*. *Psychol. Monogr.*, 54, No. 248. — **378**

LUCHINS, A. S., and LUCHINS, E. H. (1959) *Rigidity of behavior*. Eugene, Ore.: U. of Oregon Press. — **393**

LUCHINS, E. H., *see* Luchins and Luchins (1959).

LUH, C. W. (1922) The conditions of retention. *Psychol. Monogr.*, 31, No. 142. — **318**

LUMSDAINE, A. A. (1959) Teaching machines and self-instructional materials. *Audio-visual commun. Rev.*, 7:163–72. — **354**

LUMSDAINE, A. A., *see also* Hovland, Lumsdaine, and Sheffield (1949).

LUMSDAINE, A. A., and GLASER, R. (Eds.) (1960) *Teaching machines and programmed learning*. Washington, D. C.: NEA. — **364**

LUNT, P. S., *see* Warner and Lunt (1941).

LURIA, Z., *see* Osgood and Luria (1954).

LURIE, M. H., *see* Stevens, Davis, and Lurie (1935).

LUTTGES, M., and others. (1966) An examination of "transfer of learning" by nucleic acid. *Science*, 151:834. — **322**

MC ARTHUR, C. (1956) Personalities of first and second children. *Psychiatry*, 19:47–54. — **84**

MC CAFFREY, I., *see* Cummings, Dean, Newell, and McCaffrey (1960).

MC CLEARN, G. E. (1962) The inheritance of behavior. In Postman, L. (Ed.) *Psychology in the making*. N. Y.: Knopf, 144–252. — **449, 457, 461**

MC CLEARN, G. E. (1964) Genetics and behavior development. In Hoffman, M. L., and Hoffman, L. W., *Review of child development research*, Vol. I. N. Y.: Russell Sage Foundation, 433–80. — **461**

MC CLELLAND, D. C. (Ed.) (1955) *Studies in motivation*. N. Y.: Appleton-Century-Crofts. — **154, 162**

MC CLELLAND, D. C. (1961) *The achieving society*. Princeton, N. J.: Van Nostrand. — **162**

MC CLELLAND, D. C. (1965) Toward a theory of motive acquisition. *Amer. Psychologist*, 20:321–33. — **155**

MC CLELLAND, D. C., ATKINSON, J. W., CLARK, R. A., and LOWELL, E. L. (1953) *The achievement motive*. N. Y.: Appleton-Century-Crofts. — **153**

MC CONNELL, J. V. (1966) Comparative physiology: learning in invertebrates. *Ann. Rev. Physiol.*, 28:107–36. — **322**

MC CONNELL, J. V., *see also* Zelman, Kabat, Jacobson, and McConnell (1963).

MC CONNELL, R. A., *see* Schmeidler and McConnell (1958).

MC CONNELL, R. A., SNOWDON, R. J., and POWELL, K. F. (1955) Wishing with dice. *J. exp. Psychol.*, 50:269–75. — **242**

MC CORD, J., *see* McCord and McCord (1964); McCord, McCord, and Zola (1959); McCord, Porta, and McCord (1962).

MC CORD, W., and MC CORD, J. (1964) *The psychopath: an essay on the criminal mind*. Princeton, N. J.: Van Nostrand. — **542**

MC CORD, W., MC CORD, J., and ZOLA, I. K. (1959) *Origins of crime*. N. Y.: Columbia Univ. Press. — **100**

MC CORD, W., PORTA, J., and MC CORD, J. (1962) The familial genesis of psychosis. *Psychiatry*, 25:60–71. — **540**

MC CORMICK, E. J. (1964) *Human factors in engineering* (2nd Ed.). N. Y.: McGraw-Hill. — **617**

MC DONOUGH, J. M. (1960) Critical flicker frequency and the spiral after effect with process and reactive schizophrenics. *J. consult. Psychol.*, 24:150–55. — **536**

MC GAUGH, J. L. (1966) Time-dependent processes in memory storage. *Science*, 153:1351–58. — **330**

MC GAUGH, J. L., *see also* Hudspeth, McGaugh, and Thompson (1964); Thiessen and McGaugh (1958).

MC GAUGH, J. L., and HOSTETTER, R. C. (1961) Retention as a function of the temporal position of sleep and activity following waking. Unpublished manuscript. — **338, 339**

MC GAUGH, J. L., and PETRINOVICH, L. F. (1966) Neural consolidation and electroconvulsive shock re-examined. *Psychol. Rev.*, 73:382–87. — **332**

MC GEOCH, J. A., and IRION, A. L. (1952) *The psychology of human learning* (2nd Ed.). N. Y.: Longmans, Green. — **335, 340, 363**

MC GRAW, M. B. (1940) Neural maturation as exemplified in achievement of bladder control. *J. Pediat.*, 16:580–90. — **66**

MC GRAW, M. B. (1943) *The neuromuscular maturation of the human infant.* N. Y.: Columbia Univ. Press. — **67**

MC GUIRE, W. J. (1966) Attitudes and opinions. *Ann. Rev. Psychol.*, 17:475–514. — **596**

MC GUIRE, W. J., *see also* Rosenberg and others (1960).

MC KINNEY, F. (1960) *Psychology of personal adjustment* (3rd Ed.). N. Y.: Wiley. — **547, 571**

MAC KINNON, D. W. (1958) An assessment of Air Force officers. Part V: Summary and applications. *WADC Technical Report 58–91 (V).* Wright Development Center. — **499**

MAC KINNON, D. W. (Ed.) (1962) *The creative person.* Berkeley, Calif., Univ. of California General Extension. — **388, 393**

MAC KINNON, D. W. (1965) Personality and the realization of creative potential. *Amer. Psychologist,* 20:273–81. — **388**

MC LEAN, P. D. (1950) Psychosomatic disease and the "visceral brain"; recent developments bearing on the Papez theory of emotion. *Psychosomat. Med.,* 11:338–53. — **41**

MAC MAHON, B., *see* Pugh and MacMahon (1962).

MC NEILL, D., *see* Brown and McNeill (1966).

MC NEMAR, Q. (1940) A critical examination of the University of Iowa studies of environmental influences upon the I.Q. *Psychol. Bull.,* 37:63–92. — **452**

MC NEMAR, Q. (1942) *The revision of the Stanford-Binet scale.* Boston: Houghton Mifflin. — **423, 437, 453**

MC NEMAR, Q. (1962) *Psychological statistics* (3rd Ed.). N. Y.: Wiley. — **415**

MAC NICHOL, E. F., JR., *see* Marks, Dobelle, and MacNichol (1964).

MAAS, H. (1963) The young adult adjustment of twenty wartime residential nursery children. *Child Welf.,* 42:57–72. — **80**

MACCOBY, E. E., *see* Sears, Maccoby, and Levin (1957).

MACKLIN, D. B., *see* Leighton, Harding, Macklin, Macmillan, and Leighton (1963).

MACKWORTH, N. H. (1950) Researches in the measurement of human performance. *Med. Res. Counc. Special Report Ser.,* No. 268. London: H. M. Stationery Office. — **250**

MACLAY, H., and WARE, E. E. (1961) Cross-cultural use of the semantic differential. *Behav. Sci.,* 6:185–90. — **368**

MACMILLAN, A. M., *see* Leighton, Harding, Macklin, Macmillan, and Leighton (1963).

MADDI, S. R., *see* Fiske and Maddi (1961).

MAGARET, A., *see* Cameron and Magaret (1951); Hilgard, Sait, and Magaret (1940).

MAGOUN, H. W. (1963) *The waking brain* (2nd Ed.). Springfield, Ill.: Thomas. — **41**

MAHATOO, W., *see* Doane and others (1959).

MAHER, B. A. (1966) *Principles of psychotherapy: an experimental approach.* N. Y.: McGraw-Hill. — **547**

MAHER, B. A., *see also* Lewis and Maher (1965) (1966).

MAIER, N. R. F. (1932) The effect of cerebral destruction on reasoning and learning in rats. *J. comp. Neurol.,* 54:45–75. — **304**

MAIER, N. R. F. (1949) *Frustration: a study of behavior without a goal.* N. Y.: McGraw-Hill. — **513, 524**

MAIER, N. R. F., and SCHNEIRLA, T. C. (1935) *Principles of animal psychology.* N. Y.: McGraw–Hill. — **304**

MALINOWSKI, B. (1929) *The sexual life of savages in northwestern Melanesia.* N. Y.: Liveright. — **97**

MALINOWSKI, B. (1935) *Coral gardens and their magic* (2 vols.). N. Y.: American Book Co. — **155**

MALIS, J. L., *see* Brodie and others (1960).

MALTZMAN, I. (1960) On the training of originality. *Psychol. Rev.,* 67:229–42. — **388**

MANDLER, G. (1962) Emotion. In Brown, R., and others (Eds.). *New directions in psychology.* N. Y.: Holt, Rinehart and Winston, 269–343. — **186**

MANDLER, G., *see also* Kessen and Mandler (1961); Sarason, Mandler, and Craighill (1952).

MANDLER, G., and KESSEN, W. (1959) *The language of psychology.* N. Y.: Wiley. — **19**

MANDLER, G., and SARASON, S. G. (1952) A study of anxiety and learning. *J. abnorm. soc. Psychol.,* 47:166–73. — **360, 361**

MARCUSE, F. L. (Ed.) (1964) *Hypnosis throughout the world.* Springfield, Ill.: Thomas. — **262**

MARGOLIS, R., *see* Glick and Margolis (1962).

MARKEE, J. E., *see* Becker, King, and Markee (1962).

MARKS, W. B., DOBELLE, W. H., and MAC NICHOL, E. F., JR. (1964) Visual pigments of single primate cones. *Science,* 143:1181–82. — **202**

MARLOWE, D., *see* Crowne and Marlowe (1964).

MARQUART, D. I., and BAILEY, L. L. (1955) An evaluation of the culture free test of intelligence. *J. genet. Psychol.,* 86:353–58. — **423**

MARQUIS, D. G. (1948) Research planning at the frontiers of science. *Amer. Psychologist,* 3:430–38. — **580**

MARQUIS, D. P. (1941) Learning in the neonate: the modification of behavior under three feeding schedules. *J. exp. Psychol.,* 29:263–82. — **75**

MARROW, A. J. (1938) Goal tensions and recall. *J. genet. Psychol.,* 19:3–35, 37–64. — **327**

MARSHALL, A. W., *see* Goldhamer and Marshall (1953).

MARTIN, C. E., *see* Kinsey, Pomeroy, and Martin (1948).

MARTIN, W. E., and STENDLER, C. B. (1959) *Child development: the process of growing up in society* (2nd Ed.). N. Y.: Harcourt, Brace & World. — **90**

MASLAND, R. L., SARASON, S. B., and GLADWYN, T. (1958) *Mental subnormality.* N. Y.: Basic Books. — **431, 432, 443**

MASLOW, A. H. (1954) *Motivation and personality.* N. Y.: Harper. — **142, 159**

MASLOW, A. H. (1959) Cognition of being in the peak experiences. *J. genet. Psychol.,* 94:43–66. — **160, 251**

MASLOW, A. H. (1962) *Toward a psychology of being.* Princeton, N. J.: Van Nostrand. — **159, 162**

MASON, J. W., *see* Brady and others (1958).

MAX, L. W. (1935) An experimental study of the motor theory of consciousness: III. Action-current responses in deaf-mutes during sleep, sensory stimulation, and dreams. *J. comp. Psychol.,* 19:469–86. — **376**

MAY, R. (1950) *The meaning of anxiety.* N. Y.: Ronald. — **179**

MEAD, M. (1935) *Sex and temperament in three primitive societies.* N. Y.: Morrow. — **97, 106**

MEAD, M. (1949) *Male and female.* N. Y.: Morrow. — **106**

MEDNICK, S. A. (1962) The associative basis of the creative process. *Psychol. Rev.,* 69:220–32. — **390**

MEEHL, P. E. (1950) Configural scoring. *J. consult. Psychol.,* 14:165–71. — **473, 492**

MEEHL, P. E. (1954) *Clinical vs. statistical prediction.* Minneapolis, Minn.: Univ. of Minnesota Press. — **500**

MEEHL, P. E. (1957) When shall we use our heads instead of the formula? *J. counsel. Psychol.*, 4:268–73. — **500**

MEEKER, M., *see* Warner, Meeker, and Eells (1949).

MELTON, A. W. (Ed.) (1964) *Categories of human learning.* N. Y.: Academic Press. — **363**

MELTON, A. W., and BRIGGS, G. E. (1960) Engineering psychology. *Annu. Rev. Psychol.*, 11:71–98. — **604**

MELZACK, R., and SCOTT, T. H. (1957) The effects of early experience on the response to pain. *J. comp. physiol. Psychol.*, 50:155–61. — **69**

MENNINGER, K. (1958) *Theory of psychoanalytic technique.* N. Y.: Basic Books. — **571**

MENZIES, R. (1937) Conditioned vasomotor responses in human subjects. *J. Psychol.*, 4:75–120. — **276**

MERRILL, M. A. (1938) The significance of I.Q.'s on the revised Stanford-Binet scales. *J. educ. Psychol.*, 26:641–51. — **425**

MERRILL, M. A., *see also* Terman and Merrill (1937) (1960).

METTLER, F. A., *see* Landis, Zubin, and Mettler (1950).

MEYER, D. (1965) *The positive thinkers: a study of the American quest for health, wealth and personal power from Mary Baker Eddy to Norman Vincent Peale.* Garden City, N. Y.: Doubleday. — **160, 265**

MEYER, D. R., *see* Harlow, Harlow, and Meyer (1950).

MEYER, M. M., and TOLMAN, R. S. (1955) Correspondence between attitudes and images of parental figures in TAT stories and in therapeutic interviews. *J. consult. Psychol.*, 19:79–82. — **495**

MICHAEL, S. T., *see* Srole and others (1962).

MILES, C. C., *see* Terman and Miles (1936).

MILLER, D. R., and SWANSON, G. E. (1960) *Inner conflict and defense.* N. Y.: Holt-Dryden. — **109, 524**

MILLER, G. A., GALANTER, E., and PRIBRAM, K. H. (1960) *Plans and the structure of behavior,* N. Y.: Holt. — **151, 250, 373**

MILLER, H. C., *see* Davis and others (1948).

MILLER, J. G., *see* Uhr and Miller (1960).

MILLER, N. E. (1948*a*) Fear as an acquired drive. *J. exp. Psychol.*, 38:89–101. — **134, 135**

MILLER, N. E. (1948*b*) Theory and experiment relating psychoanalytic displacement to stimulus-response generalization. *J. abnorm. soc. Psychol.*, 43:155–78. — **511**

MILLER, N. E. (1959) Liberalization of basic S-R concepts: extensions to conflict behavior, motivation, and social learning. In Koch, S. (Ed.) *Psychology: a study of a science,* Vol. II. N. Y.: McGraw-Hill, 196–292. — **505, 508, 524**

MILLER, N. E. (1961) Analytic studies of drive and reward. *Amer. Psychologist,* 16:739–54. — **120**

MILLER, N. E., *see also* Dollard and Miller (1950); Delgado, Roberts, and Miller (1954); Myers and Miller (1954).

MILLER, N. E., and KESSEN, M. L., (1952) Reward effects of food via stomach fistula compared with those of food via mouth. *J. comp. physiol. Psychol.*, 45:555–64. — **291**

MILLER, R. E., MURPHY, J. V., and MIRSKY, I. A. (1957) Persistent effects of chlorpromazine on extinction of an avoidance response. *Arch. Neurol. and Psychiat.*, 78:526. — **566**

MILLER, W. E., *see* Campbell and others (1960); Converse, Clausen, and Miller (1965).

MILNE, A. A. (1924) *When we were very young.* N. Y.: Dutton. — **518**

MILNER, B. (1958) Psychological defects produced by temporal lobe excision. In *The brain and human behavior.* Res. Publ. Assn. Nerv. Ment. Dis., 244–57. — **42**

MILNER, P. M. (1966) *Physiological psychology.* N. Y.: Holt, Rinehart and Winston. — **58**

MILNER, P. M., *see also* Olds and Milner (1954).

MINAMI, H., and DALLENBACH, K. M. (1946) The effect of activity upon learning and retention in the cockroach. *Amer. J. Psychol.*, 59:1–58. — **324**

MINTURN, A. L., *see* Bruner, Busiek, and Minturn (1952).

MIRSKY, I. A., *see* Miller, Murphy, and Mirsky (1957).

MOLONEY, J. C. (1955) Psychic self-abandon and extortion of confession. *Int. J. Psychoanal.*, 36:53–60. — **598**

MONROE, L. J., RECHTSCHAFFEN, A., FOULKES, D., and JENSEN, J. (1965) The discriminability of REM and NREM reports. *J. pers. soc. Psychol.* (In press). — **255**

MONTAGU, M. F. A. (1946) *Adolescent sterility.* Springfield, Ill.: Thomas. — **94**

MOON, L. E., and HARLOW, H. F. (1955) Analysis of oddity learning by rhesus monkey. *J. comp. physiol. Psychol.*, 48:188–94. — **369**

MOORE, O. K. (1965) From tools to interactional machines. In *New approaches to individualizing instruction,* 5–12. Princeton, N. J.: Educational Testing Service. — **68**

MOORE, R. K. *see* Hilgard, Weitzenhoffer, Landes, and Moore (1961).

MORENO, J. L. (1946) *Psychodrama.* N. Y.: Beacon House. — **560**

MORENO, O. M., *see* Brodie and others (1960).

MORGAN, C. D., and MURRAY, H. A. (1935) A method for investigating fantasies: the thematic apperception test. *Arch Neurol. Psychiat.*, 34:289–306. — **494**

MORGAN, C. M. (1937) The attitudes and adjustments of recipients of old age assistance in upstate and metropolitan New York. *Arch. Psychol.*, N. Y., 30, No. 214. — **105**

MORGAN, C. T. (1965) *Physiological psychology* (3rd Ed.). N. Y.: McGraw-Hill. — **58**

MORGAN, C. T., and MORGAN, J. D. (1940) Studies in hunger: II. The relation of gastric denervation and dietary sugar to the effect of insulin upon food-intake in the rat. *J. genet. Psychol.*, 57:153–63. — **122**

MORGAN, J. D., *see* Morgan and Morgan (1940).

MORGULIS, S., *see* Yerkes and Morgulis (1909).

MORLOCK, H. C., JR., *see* Williams, Morlock, and Morlock (1963).

MORLOCK, J. V., *see* Williams, Morlock, and Morlock (1963).

MORRISETT, L., and HOVLAND, C. I. (1959) A comparison of three varieties of training in human problem solving. *J. exp. Psychol.*, 58:52–55. — **348**

MOSELEY, E. C., DUFFEY, R. F., and SHERMAN, L. J. (1963) An extension of the construct validity of the Holtzman Inkblot Technique. *J. clin. Psychol.*, 19:186–92. — **497**

MOSS, H. A., *see* Kagan and Moss (1962).

MOULTON, R. W., RAPHELSON, A. C., KRISTOFFERSON, A. B., and ATKINSON, J. W. (1958) The achievement motive and perceptual sensitivity under two conditions of motive-arousal. In Atkinson, J. W. (Ed.) *Motives in fantasy, action, and society.* Princeton, N. J.: Van Nostrand. — **154**

MOUTON, J. S., *see* Freed and others (1955); Helson, Blake, and Mouton (1958).

MOWRER, O. H. (1960) *Learning theory and behavior.* N. Y.: Wiley. — **179**

MOWRER, O. H., *see also* Whiting and Mowrer (1943).

MUELLER, C. G. (1965) *Sensory psychology*. Englewood Cliffs, N. J.: Prentice-Hall. — **216**

MÜNSTERBERG, H. (1908) *On the witness stand*. N. Y.: McClure. — **606**

MUNN, N. L. (1940) The effect of knowledge of the situation upon judgment of emotion from facial expressions. *J. abnorm. soc. Psychol.*, 35:324–38. — **171**

MURDOCK, G. P. (1937) Comparative data on the division of labor by sex. *Social Forces*, 15:551–53. — **106**

MURPHY, G. (1949a) *Historical introduction to modern psychology* (Rev. Ed.). N. Y.: Harcourt, Brace & World. — **29**

MURPHY, G. (1949b) The place of parapsychology among the sciences. *J. Parapsychol.*, 13:62–71. — **241**

MURPHY, G., *see also* Solley and Murphy (1960).

MURPHY, J. V., *see* Miller, Murphy, and Mirsky (1957).

MURRAY, E. J. (1964) *Motivation and emotion*. Englewood Cliffs, N. J.: Prentice-Hall. — **138, 162, 186**

MURRAY, E. J. (1965) *Sleep, dreams, and arousal*. N. Y.: Appleton-Century-Crofts. — **268**

MURRAY, H. A., and others (1938) *Explorations in personality*. N. Y.: Oxford Univ. Press. — **142, 143, 490**

MURRAY, H. A., *see also* Morgan and Murray (1935).

MUSGRAVE, B. S., *see* Cofer and Musgrave (1963).

MUSSEN, P. H. (Ed.) (1960) *Handbook of research methods in child development*. N. Y.: Wiley. — **90**

MUSSEN, P. H. (1963) *The psychological development of the child*. Englewood Cliffs, N. J.: Prentice-Hall. — **90**

MUSSEN, P. H., *see also* Jones and Mussen (1958); Payne and Mussen (1956).

MUSSEN, P. H., CONGER, J. J., and KAGAN, J. (1963) *Child development and personality* (2nd Ed.). N. Y.: Harper and Row. — **90**

MUSSEN, P. H., and DISTLER, L. (1959) Masculinity, identification, and father-son relationships. *J. abnorm. soc. Psychol.*, 59:350–56. — **83**

MUSSEN, P. H., and JONES, M. C. (1958) The behavior-inferred motivations of late- and early-maturing boys. *Child Develpm.*, 29:61–67. — **95**

MUSSEN, P. H., and NAYLOR, H. K. (1954) The relationships between overt and fantasy aggression. *J. abnorm. soc. Psychol.*, 49:235–40. — **495**

MUUSS, R. E. (1962) *Theories of adolescence*. N. Y.: Random House. — **116**

MYERS, A. K., and MILLER, N. E. (1954) Failure to find a learned drive based on hunger; evidence for learning motivated by "exploration." *J. comp. physiol. Psychol.*, 47:428–36. — **135**

MYERS, G. C. (1928) The price of speed pressure. *Educ. Res. Bull.*, 7:265–68. — **67**

MYERS, R. E., *see* Ebner and Myers (1960).

NACHMIAS, J., *see* Eichengreen, Coren, and Nachmias (1966).

NADEL, S. F. (1957) *The theory of social structure*. Glencoe, Ill.: Free Press. — **485**

NAGEL, E., *see* Wolman and Nagel (1965).

NAKAMURA, C. Y. (1958) Conformity and problem solving. *J. abnorm. soc. Psychol.*, 56:315–20. — **389**

NAYLOR, H. K., *see* Mussen and Naylor (1954).

NELSON, V. L., *see* Sontag, Baker, and Nelson (1958).

NEUGARTEN, B. L., and others (1964) *Personality in middle and late life*. N. Y.: Atherton Press. — **114, 116**

NEWCOMB, T. M., CONVERSE, P. E., and TURNER, R. H. (1964) *Social Psychology*. N. Y.: Holt, Rinehart and Winston. — **476, 600**

NEWELL, A., *see* Simon and Newell (1964).

NEWELL, A., SHAW, J. C., and SIMON, H. A. (1958) *The processes of creative thinking*. Paper P–1320. Santa Monica, Calif.: The RAND Corp. — **383**

NEWELL, A., and SIMON, H. A. (1956) The logic theory machine: a complex information processing system. *Transactions on information theory*. Institute of Radio Engineers, IT–2, No. 3, 61–79. — **382**

NEWELL, D. S., *see* Cummings, Dean, Newell, and McCaffrey (1960).

NEWMAN, E. B. (1939) Forgetting of meaningful material during sleep and waking. *Amer. J. Psychol.*, 52:65–71. — **323**

NEWMAN, H. H., FREEMAN, F. N., and HOLZINGER, K. H. (1937) *Twins: a study of heredity and environment*. Chicago: Univ. of Chicago Press. — **453**

NEWMAN, M. F., *see* Hilgard and Newman (1961); Hilgard, Newman, and Fisk (1960).

NEYMANN, C. A., and YACORZYNSKI, G. K. (1942) Studies of introversion-extroversion and conflict of motives in the psychoses. *J. genet. Psychol.*, 27:241–55. — **468**

NICHOLS, R. C. (1965) The National Merit Twin Study. In Vandenberg, S. G. (Ed.) *Methods and goals in human behavior genetics*. N. Y.: Academic Press, 231–43. — **453**

NISSEN, T., *see* Fjerdingstad, Nissen, and Røigaard-Petersen (1965).

NORMAN, D. A., *see* Waugh and Norman (1965).

NORRIS, E. B., *see* Spence and Norris (1950).

NORTH, R., *see* Deutsch, Fishman, Kogan, North, and Whitman (1964).

NORVAL, M. A., *see* Aldrich and Norval (1946).

NOWLIS, V., *see* Sears and others (1953).

OAKES, W. F. (1956) Latent learning in the three-table apparatus. *J. exp. Psychol.*, 51:287–89. — **304**

OCHS, S. (1965) *Elements of neurophysiology*. N. Y.: Wiley. — **58**

O'CONNELL, D. N., *see* Shor, Orne, and O'Connell (1966).

ODBERT, H. S., *see* Allport and Odbert (1936).

ODEN, M. H., *see* Terman and Oden (1947) (1959).

OGDEN, D. P., *see* Cohen and Ogdon (1949).

OGG, E. (1955) Psychologists in action. *Publ. Affairs Pamph.*, 229. N. Y.: Public Affairs Committee, Inc. — **603**

O'HOLLAREN, P., *see* Lemere, Voegtlin, Broz, O'Hollaren, and Tupper (1942).

OLDS, J. (1956) Pleasure centers in the brain. *Sci. Amer.*, 193:105–16. — **133, 292**

OLDS, J., and MILNER, P. M. (1954) Positive reinforcement produced by electrical stimulation of septal area and other regions of rat brain. *J. comp. physiol. Psychol.*, 47:419–27. — **133**

OLDS, J., and OLDS, M. E. (1965) Drives, rewards, and the brain. In Barron, F., and others (Eds.) *New directions in psychology II*. N. Y.: Holt, Rinehart and Winston, 329–410. — **3, 292, 293**

OLDS, J., and SINCLAIR, J. (1957) Self-stimulation in the obstruction box. *Amer. Psychologist*, 12:464. — **292**

OLDS, M. E., *see* Olds and Olds (1965).

OPLER, M. K., *see* Srole and others (1962).

OPPENHEIM, A. N., *see* Himmelweit, Oppenheim, and Vince (1958).

OPTICAL SOCIETY OF AMERICA (1953) *The science of color*. N. Y.: Crowell. — **216**

ORNE, M. T. (1959) The nature of hypnosis: artifact and essence. *J. abnorm. soc. Psychol.*, 58:277–99. — **263**

ORNE, M. T. (1962) On the social psychology of the psychological experiment: with particular reference to demand characteristics and their implications. *Amer. Psychologist*, 17:776–83. — **263**

ORNE, M. T., *see also* Shor and Orne (1965); Shor, Orne, and O'Connell (1966).

OSBORN, A. F. (1963) *Applied imagination* (3rd Ed.). N. Y.: Scribner's. — **381**

OSBORNE, M. F. (1959) Brownian motion in the stock market. *Operations Research*, 7:145–73. — **191**

OSGOOD, C. E. (1949) The similarity paradox in human learning: a resolution. *Psychol. Rev.*, 56:132–43. — **344**

OSGOOD, C. E. (1952) The nature and measurement of meaning. *Psychol. Bull.*, 49:197–237. — **367**

OSGOOD, C. E. (1953) *Method and theory in experimental psychology*. N. Y.: Oxford Univ. Press. — **226, 335**

OSGOOD, C. E. (Ed.) (1954) Psycholinguistics: a survey of theory and research problems. *J. abnorm. soc. Psychol.*, 49:4, Part 2, Suppl. — **367**

OSGOOD, C. E. (1960) Cognitive dynamics in the conduct of human affairs. *Pub. Opin. Quart.*, 24:341–65. — **592**

OSGOOD, C. E. (1963) On understanding and creating sentences. *Amer. Psychologist*, 18:735–51. — **373**

OSGOOD, C. E., and LURIA, Z. (1954) A blind analysis of a case of multiple personality using the semantic differential. *J. abnorm. soc. Psychol.*, 49:579–91. — **480**

OSGOOD, C. E., and SEBEOK, T. A. (Eds.) (1965) *Psycholinguistics*. Bloomington, Ind.: Indiana Univ. Press. — **393**

OSGOOD, C. E., and TANNENBAUM, P. H. (1955) The principle of congruity in the prediction of attitude change. *Psychol. Rev.*, 62:42–55. — **591**

OSS ASSESSMENT STAFF (1948) *Assessment of men.* N. Y.: Rinehart. — **499, 502**

PALMER, J. O. and GOLDSTEIN, M. J. (1966) *Perspectives in psychopathology*. N. Y.: Oxford Univ. Press. — **547**

PALOLA, E. G., *see* Sarason and Palola (1960).

PANTIN, C. F. A. (1952) The elementary nervous system. *Proc. Roy. Soc.*, London, Series B, 140:147–68. — **35**

PAUL, G. L. (1966) *Insight vs. desensitization in psychotherapy*. Stanford, Calif.: Stanford Univ. Press. — **571**

PAVLOV, I. P. (1927) *Conditioned reflexes*. N. Y.: Oxford Univ. Press. — **275, 313**

PAYNE, D. E., and MUSSEN, P. H. (1956) Parent-child relations and father-identification among adolescent boys. *J. abnorm. soc. Psychol.*, 52:358–62. — **83**

PENFIELD, W. (1958) *The excitable cortex in conscious man*. Liverpool, Eng.: Liverpool Univ. Press. — **48**

PENFIELD, W., and JASPER, H. (1954) *Epilepsy and the functional anatomy of the human brain*. Boston: Little, Brown. — **48**

PENFIELD, W., and RASMUSSEN, T. (1950) *The cerebral cortex of man*. N. Y.: Macmillan. — **47**

PENFIELD, W., and ROBERTS, L. (1959) *Speech and brain mechanisms*. Princeton, N. J.: Princeton Univ. Press. — **377**

PERIN, C. T. (1942) Behavior potentiality as a joint function of the amount of training and the degree of hunger at the time of extinction. *J. exp. Psychol.*, 30:93–113. — **307**

PETERSON, L. R., and PETERSON, M. J. (1959) Short-term retention of individual verbal items. *J. exp. Psychol.*, 58:193–98. — **328**

PETERSON, M. J., *see* Peterson and Peterson (1959).

PETERSON, R. C., and THURSTONE, L. L. (1932) *The effect of motion pictures on the social attitudes of high school children*. Ann Arbor, Mich.: Edwards Bros. — **584**

PETRINOVICH, L. F., *see* McGaugh and Petrinovich (1966).

PETTIGREW, T. F. (1964) *A profile of the Negro American*. Princeton, N. J.: Van Nostrand. — **461, 600**

PFAFFMANN, C. (1964) Taste, its sensory and motivating properties. *Amer. Scientist*, 52:187–206. — **210, 211**

PIAGET, J. (1932) *The moral judgment of the child*. N. Y.: Harcourt, Brace & World, Inc. (Republished, Glencoe, Ill.: Free Press, 1948). — **85**

PIAGET, J. (1952) *The origins of intelligence in children*. N. Y.: Internat. Univ. Press. — **132**

PIAGET, J., *see also* Inhelder and Piaget (1958).

PIAGET, J., and INHELDER, B. (1941) *Le développement des quantités chez l'enfant*. Neuchâtel, Switzerland: Delachaux et Niestle. — **71, 72**

PITT, R., and HAGE, J. (1964) Patterns of peer interaction during adolescence as prognostic indicators in schizophrenia. *Amer. J. Psychiatry*, 120:1089–96. — **537**

PLUTCHIK, R. (1962) *The emotions: facts, theories, and a new model*. N. Y.: Random House. — **164, 186**

POINCARÉ, H. (1913) *The foundations of science*. N. Y.: Science Press. — **387**

POLT, J. M., *see* Hess and Polt (1960).

POLYA, G. (1945) *How to solve it*. Princeton, N. J.: Princeton Univ. Press. — **383**

POLYA, G. (1954) *Mathematics and plausible reasoning*. Princeton, N. J.: Princeton Univ. Press. — **383**

POLYAK, S. L. (1941) *The retina*. Chicago: Univ. of Chicago Press. — **195**

POMEROY, W. B., *see* Kinsey, Pomeroy, and Martin (1948).

PORTA, J., *see* McCord, Porta, and McCord (1962).

PORTER, R. W., *see* Brady and others (1958).

POSTMAN, L. (1962*a*) The temporal course of proactive inhibition for serial lists. *J. exp. Psychol.*, 63:361–69. — **325, 333**

POSTMAN, L. (Ed.) (1962*b*) *Psychology in the making*. N. Y.: Knopf. — **29**

POSTMAN, L. (1963) One-trial learning. In Cofer, C. N., and Musgrave, B. S. (Eds.) *Verbal behavior and learning*. N. Y.: McGraw-Hill. — **301**

POSTMAN, L., *see also* Bruner and Postman (1949); Underwood and Postman (1960).

POWELL, K. F., *see* McConnell, Snowdon, and Powell (1955).

PRATT, J. G., *see* Rhine and Pratt (1957).

PREMACK, D. (1962) Reversibility of the reinforcement relation. *Science*, 136:255–57. — **291**

PREMACK, D. (1965) Reinforcement theory. *Nebraska symposium on motivation*. Lincoln, Nebr.: Univ. of Nebraska Press, 123–88. — **291**

PRESSEY, S. L. (1926) A simple apparatus which gives tests and scores—and teaches. *Sch. and Soc.*, 23:373–76. — **350**

PRESSEY, S. L., and JONES, A. W. (1955) Age changes in moral codes, anxieties, and interests, as shown by the "X-O" tests. *J. Psychol.*, 30:485–502. — **101**

PRESSEY, S. L., and KUHLEN, R. G. (1957) *Psychological development through the life span*. N. Y.: Harper. — **116**

PRIBRAM, K. H. (1958) Neocortical function in behavior. In Harlow, H. F., and Woolsey, C. N. (Eds.) *Biological and biochemical bases of be-*

havior. Madison, Wis.: Univ. of Wisconsin Press, 151–72. — **41**

PRIBRAM, K. H. (1960) A review of theory in physiological psychology. *Annu. Rev. Psychol.,* 1–40. — **41, 48**

PRIBRAM, K. H., *see also* Miller, Galanter, and Pribram (1960).

PRINCE, M. (1906) *The dissociation of a personality.* N. Y.: Longmans, Green. — **480**

PRITCHARD, R. M. (1961) Stabilized images on the retina. *Sci. Amer.* 204:72–77. — **196, 197**

PROKASY, W. F. (Ed.) (1965) *Classical conditioning.* N. Y.: Appleton-Century-Crofts. — **313**

PRONKO, N. H., *see* Snyder and Pronko (1952).

PROSHANSKY, H. M., and SEIDENBERG, B. (Eds.) (1965) *Basic studies in social psychology.* N. Y.: Holt, Rinehart and Winston. — **600**

PUGH, T. F., and MAC MAHON, B. (1962) *Epidemiologic findings in United States mental hospital data.* Boston: Litte, Brown. — **546**

RABINOWITZ, H. S., *see* Birch and Rabinowitz (1951).

RACHMAN, S., *see* Lazarus and Rachman (1957).

RADLER, D. H., *see* Remmers and Radler (1957).

RAMSAY, O. A., and HESS, E. H. (1954) A laboratory approach to the study of imprinting. *Wilson Bull.,* 66:196–206. — **64**

RAMSEY, R., *see* Jensen and Ramsey (1963).

RAND CORPORATION (1955) *A million random digits.* Glencoe, Ill.: Free Press. — **243**

RAPAPORT, D. (1950) *Emotions and memory.* N. Y.: Internat. Univ. Press. — **326**

RAPHELSON, A. C. (1957) The relationship between imaginative, direct, verbal, and physiological measures of anxiety in an achievement situation. *J. abnorm. soc. Psychol.,* 54:13–18. — **154**

RAPHELSON, A. C., *see also* Moulton, Raphelson, Kristofferson, and Atkinson (1958).

RASMUSSEN, T., *see* Penfield and Rasmussen (1950).

RATLIFF, F., *see* Riggs and others (1953).

RATLIFF, F., and RIGGS, L. A. (1950) Involuntary motions of the eye during monocular fixation. *J. exp. Psychol.,* 40:687–701. — **196**

RAU, L., *see* Sears, Rau, and Alpert (1965).

RAWCLIFFE, D. H. (1959) *Illusions and delusions of the supernatural and occult.* N. Y.: Dover. — **243**

RAYNER, R., *see* Watson and Rayner (1920).

RECHTSCHAFFEN, A., *see* Monroe, Rechtschaffen, Foulkes, and Jensen (1965).

RECHTSCHAFFEN, A., GOODENOUGH, D. R., and SHAPIRO, A. (1962) Patterns of sleep talking. *Arch. gen. Psychiat.,* 7:418–26. — **257**

REDLICH, F. C., and FREEDMAN, D. X. (1966) *The theory and practice of psychiatry.* N. Y.: Basic Books. — **547**

REDLICH, F. C., *see also* Hollingshead and Redlich (1958).

REESE, H. W., *see* Levinson and Reese (1963).

REID, J. E., and INBAU, F. E. (1964) *Lie detection.* Baltimore, Md.: Williams and Wilkins. — **186**

REIFF, R., and SCHEERER, M. (1959) *Memory and hypnotic age regression.* N. Y.: Internat. Univ. Press. — **315**

REISER, M. F., *see* Arkin, Hastey, and Reiser (1966).

REISMAN, J. M. (1960) Motivational differences between process and reactive stimuli. *J. Pers.,* 28:12–25. — **537**

REITMAN, W. R. (1965) *Cognition and thought.* N. Y.: Wiley. — **384, 393**

REMMERS, H. H., and RADLER, D. H. (1957) *The American teenager.* Indianapolis, Ind.: Bobbs-Merrill. — **98**

RENNIE, T. A. C., *see* Srole and others (1962).

RESTLE, F. (1965) Significance of all-or-none learning. *Psychol. Bull.,* 64:313–25. — **301**

RESTLE, F., and DAVIS, J. (1962) Success and speed of problem solving by individuals and groups. *Psychol. Rev.,* 69:520–36. — **380**

RETHLINGSHAFER, D. (1963) *Motivation as related to personality.* N. Y.: McGraw-Hill. — **162**

REYNA, L. J., *see* Wolpe, Salter, and Reyna (1964).

REYNOLDS, B., and ADAMS, J. A. (1953) Motor performance as a function of click reinforcement. *J. exp. Psychol.,* 45:315–20. — **342**

REYNOLDS, H. H., *see* Rohles, Grunzke, and Reynolds (1963).

RHEINGOLD, H. L., GEWIRTZ, J. L., and ROSS, H. W. (1959) Social conditioning of vocalizations in the infant. *J. comp. physiol. Psychol.,* 52:68–73. — **372**

RHINE, J. B. (1942) Evidence of precognition in the covariation of salience ratios. *J. Parapsychol.,* 6:111–43. — **243**

RHINE, J. B., and HUMPHREY, B. M. (1944) The PK effect: special evidence from hit patterns: I. Quarter distributions of the page. *J. Parapsychol.,* 8:18–60. — **242**

RHINE, J. B., and PRATT, J. G. (1957) *Parapsychology, frontier science of the mind.* Springfield, Ill.: Thomas. — **241**

RIBBLE, M. A. (1943) *The rights of infants.* N. Y.: Columbia Univ. Press. — **76**

RICHARDSON, I. F., *see* Holmen, Katten, Hones, and Richardson (1956).

RICHTER, C. P. (1943) The self-selection of diets. In *Essays in biology.* Berkeley, Calif.: Univ. of California Press, 500–05. — **123**

RICKERS-OVSIANKINA, M. A. (Ed.) (1960) *Rorschach psychology.* N. Y.: Wiley. — **502**

RICKETT, A., and RICKETT, A. (1957) *Prisoners of liberation.* N. Y.: Cameron Associates. — **598**

RICKETT, ADELE, *see* Rickett and Rickett (1957).

RIECKEN, H. W., JR., *see* Festinger, Riecken, and Schachter (1956).

RIESEN, A. H. (1950) Arrested vision. *Sci. Amer.,* 183:16–19. — **69, 235**

RIESEN, A. H. (1961) Stimulation as a requirement for growth and function in behavioral development. In Fiske, D. W., and Maddi, S. R. (Eds.) *Functions of varied experience.* Homewood, Ill.: Dorsey Press, 57–80. — **235**

RIGGS, L. A., *see* Ratliff and Riggs (1950).

RIGGS, L. A., RATLIFF, F., CORNSWEET, J. C., and CORNSWEET, T. N. (1953) The disappearance of steadily fixated visual test objects. *J. opt. soc. Amer.,* 43:495–501. — **197**

RILEY, D. A. (1962) Memory for form in Postman, L. (Ed.) *Psychology in the making.* N. Y.: Knopf, 402–65. — **320**

ROBERTS, J. M., *see* Lenneberg and Roberts (1956).

ROBERTS, L., *see* Penfield and Roberts (1959).

ROBERTS, S. O., *see* Carmichael, Roberts, and Wessel (1937).

ROBERTS, W. W., *see* Delgado, Roberts, and Miller (1954).

ROBINSON, H. B., and ROBINSON, N. M. (1965) *The mentally retarded child.* N. Y.: McGraw-Hill. — **443**

ROBINSON, N. M., *see* Robinson and Robinson (1965).

ROCK, I. (1957) The role of repetition in associative learning. *Amer. J. Psychol.,* 70:186–93. — **299**

ROE, A. (1963) Personal problems and science. In Taylor, C. W., and Barron, F. (Eds.) *Scientific creativity.* N. Y.: Wiley, 132–38. — **391**

ROESSLER, R. L., and BROGDEN, W. J. (1943) Conditioned differentiation of vasoconstriction to subvocal stimuli. *Amer. J. Psychol.*, 56:78–86. — **277**

ROGERS, C. R. (1951) *Client-centered therapy.* Boston: Houghton Mifflin. — **554**

ROGERS, C. R. (1961) *On becoming a person: a therapist's view of psychotherapy.* Boston: Houghton Mifflin. — **160, 555, 571**

ROGERS, C. R., and DYMOND, R. F. (Ed.) (1954) *Psychotherapy and personality change.* Chicago: Univ. of Chicago Press. — **554, 565**

ROHLES, F. H., JR., GRUNZKE, M. E., and REYNOLDS, H. H. (1963) Chimpanzee performances during the ballistic and orbital Mercury flights. *J. comp. physiol. Psychol.*, 56:2–10. — **604**

RØIGAARD-PETERSEN, H. H., *see* Fjerdingstad, Nissen, and Røigaard-Petersen (1965).

ROKEACH, M. (1960) *The open and closed mind.* N. Y.: Basic Books. — **393**

RORER, L. G. (1965) The great response-style myth. *Psychol. Bull.*, 63:129–56. — **493**

RORSCHACH, H. (1942) *Psychodiagnostics.* Berne, Switzerland: Hans Huber. — **495**

ROSEN, E., *see* Franck and Rosen (1949).

ROSENBAUM, M., and BERGER, M. (1963) *Group psychotherapy and group function.* N. Y.: Basic Books. — **560**

ROSENBERG, M. (1965) *Society and the adolescent self-image.* Princeton, N. J.: Princeton Univ. Press. — **101, 102**

ROSENBERG, M. J., HOVLAND, C. I., MC GUIRE, W. J., ABELSON, R. P., and BREHM, J. W. (1960) *Attitude organization and change.* New Haven, Conn.: Yale Univ. Press. — **600**

ROSENTHAL, D. (1959) Some factors associated with concordance and discordance with respect to schizophrenia in monozygotic twins. *J. nerv. ment. Dis.*, 129:1–10. — **456**

ROSENTHAL, R. (1966) *Experimenter effects in behavioral research.* N. Y.: Appleton-Century-Crofts. — **29**

ROSENZWEIG, M. R. (1954) Cortical correlates of auditory localization and of related perceptual phenomena. *J. comp. physiol. Psychol.*, 47:269–76. — **232**

ROSENZWEIG, M. R. (1962) The mechanisms of hunger and thirst. In Postman, L. (Ed.) *Psychology in the making.* N. Y.: Knopf, 73–143. — **124**

ROSS, H. V., *see* Buxton and Ross (1949).

ROSS, H. W., *see* Rheingold, Gewirtz, and Ross (1959).

ROSS, S., and LOCKMAN, R. F. (1965) *A career in psychology.* Washington, D. C.: Amer. Psych. Assn. — **617–18**

ROTH, B., *see* Kallmann and Roth (1956).

ROTTER, J. B. (1954) *Social learning and clinical psychology.* N. Y.: Prentice-Hall. — **559**

ROTTER, J. B., *see also* Schroder and Rotter (1952).

RUGER, G. J., *see* Thorndike and Ruger (1923).

RUNDQUIST, E. A. (1966) Item and response characteristics in attitude and personality measurement: a reaction to L. G. Rorer's "The great response-style myth." *Psychol. Bull.*, 66:166–77. — **493**

RUSSELL, B., *see* Whitehead and Russell (1925).

RUSSELL, W. A., and STORMS, L. H. (1955) Implicit verbal chaining in paired-associate learning. *J. exp. Psychol.*, 49:287–93. — **345**

SAIT, E. M., *see* Hilgard, Margaret, and Sait (1940).

SALTER, A., *see* Wolpe, Salter, and Reyna (1964).

SALTZSTEIN, H. D., *see* Jackson and Saltzstein (1958).

SANDER, G., *see* Kallmann and Sander (1949).

SANFORD, R. N., *see* Adorno and others (1950); Frenkel-Brunswik and Sanford (1945).

SARASON, I. G. (1960) Empirical findings and theoretical problems in the use of anxiety scales. *Psychol. Bull.*, 57:403–15. — **359**

SARASON, I. G. (1966) *Personality: an objective approach.* N. Y.: Wiley. — **485, 501**

SARASON, I. G., and PALOLA, E. G. (1960) The relationship of test and general anxiety, difficulty of task, and experimental instructions to performance. *J. exp. Psychol.*, 59:185–91. — **360**

SARASON, S. B., *see* Mandler and Sarason (1952); Masland, Gladwyn, and Sarason (1958).

SARASON, S. B., MANDLER, G., and CRAIGHILL, P. G. (1952) The effect of differential instructions on anxiety and learning. *J. abnorm. soc. Psychol.*, 47:561–65. — **359, 360**

SARBIN, T. R. (1950) Contributions to role-taking theory: I. Hypnotic behavior. *Psychol. Rev.*, 57:255–70. — **259**

SARBIN, T. R. (1956) Physiological effects of hypnotic stimulation. In Dorcus, R. M. (Ed.) *Hypnosis and its therapeutic applications.* N. Y.: McGraw-Hill, 4/1–4/57. — **263**

SARBIN, T. R. (1965) Hypnosis as a behavior modification technique. In Krasner, L., and Ullmann, L. P. (Eds.) *Research in behavior modification.* N. Y.: Holt, Rinehart and Winston, 341–64. — **259, 263**

SARNOFF, I. (1962) *Personality dynamics and development.* N. Y.: Wiley. — **524**

SAVAGE, C., SAVAGE, E., FADIMAN, J., and HARMAN, W. (1964) LSD: therapeutic effects of psychedelic experience. *Psychol. Reports*, 14:111–20. — **264**

SAVAGE, C., TERRILL, J., and JACKSON, D. D. (1962) LSD, transcendence, and the new beginning. *J. nerv. ment. Dis.*, 85:425–39. — **265**

SAVAGE, E., *see* Savage, Savage, Fadiman, and Harman (1964).

SAWRY, W. C., CONGER, J. J., and TURRELL, R. B. (1956) An experimental investigation of the role of psychological factors in the production of gastric ulcers in rats. *J. comp. physiol. Psychol.*, 457:143. — **276**

SAWYER, J. (1966) Measurement *and* prediction, clinical *and* statistical. *Psychol. Bull.*, 66:178–200. — **500**

SCHACHTEL, E. G. (1959) *Metamorphosis.* N. Y.: Basic Books. — **315**

SCHACHTER, S. (1959) *Psychology of affiliation.* Stanford, Calif.: Stanford Univ. Press. — **146, 147**

SCHACHTER, S., *see also* Festinger, Riecken, and Schachter (1956).

SCHACHTER, S., and SINGER, J. E. (1962) Cognitive, social and physiological determinants of emotional state. *Psychol. Rev.*, 69:379–99. — **168, 169**

SCHAEFER, H., *see* Taber, Glaser, and Schaefer (1965).

SCHAFFER, H. R., and EMERSON, P. E. (1964) The development of social attachments in infancy. *Monogr. soc. res. child Dev.*, 29, Serial No. 94. — **77, 78**

SCHEERER, M., *see* Reiff and Scheerer (1959); Goldstein and Scheerer (1941).

SCHEIN, E. H. (1956) The Chinese indoctrination program for prisoners of war. *Psychiatry*, 19:149–72. — **597**

SCHEIN, E. H. (1964) *Organizational psychology.* Englewood Cliffs, N. J.: Prentice-Hall. — **617**

SCHEIN, E. H., *see also* Bennis and others (1964); Strassman, Thaler, and Schein (1956).

SCHEIN, E. H., SCHNEIER, I., and BARKER, C. H. (1961) *Coercive persuasion.* N. Y.: Norton. — **596, 597, 598, 600**

SCHER, J. M. (Ed.) (1962) *Theories of the mind.* N. Y.: The Free Press of Glencoe. — **268**

SCHERRER, H., see Hernández-Peón, Scherrer, and Jouvet (1956).

SCHIFF, M. (1867) Leçons sur la physiologie de la digestion, Vol. I. Florence and Turin, Italy: H. Loescher. — **125**

SCHIMMEL, H., see Vaughan, Costa, Gilden, and Schimmel (1965).

SCHLOSBERG, H. (1952) The description of facial expressions in terms of two dimensions. *J. exp. Psychol.*, 44:229–37. — **171**

SCHLOSBERG, H. (1954) Three dimensions of emotion. *Psychol. Rev.*, 61:81–88. — **171, 173**

SCHLOSBERG, H., see also Woodworth and Schlosberg (1954).

SCHMEIDLER, G. R., and MC CONNELL, R. A. (1958) *ESP and personality patterns.* New Haven, Conn.: Yale Univ. Press. — **242**

SCHMIDT, H. O. (1945) Test profiles as a diagnostic aid: the Minnesota Multiphasic Inventory. *J. appl. Psychol.*, 29:115–31. — **490**

SCHNEIER, I., see Schein, Schneier, and Barker (1961).

SCHNEIRLA, T. C., see Maier and Schneirla (1935).

SCHRAMM, W. (1960) Television in the life of the child: implications for the school. In Schramm, W. (Ed.) *New teaching aids for the American classroom.* Stanford, Calif.: Inst. for Comm. Res., 50–70. — **594**

SCHRODER, H. M., and ROTTER, J. B. (1952) Rigidity as learned behavior. *J. exp. Psychol.*, 44:141–50. — **380**

SCHROEDER, W. H., see Hendrickson and Schroeder (1941).

SCHULTZ, W., see Skager, Schultz, and Klein (1965).

SCHUMER, F., see Zubin, Eron, and Schumer (1965).

SCOTT, J. P. (1954) The effects of selection and domestication upon the behavior of the dog. In Russell, E. S. (Ed.) Symposium on 25 years of progress in mammalian genetics and cancer. *J. Nat. Cancer Inst.*, 15:739–58. — **449**

SCOTT, T. H., see Bexton, Heron, and Scott (1954); Doane and others (1959); Melzack and Scott (1957).

SEARLE, L. V. (1949) The organization of hereditary maze-brightness and maze-dullness. *Genet. Psychol. Monogr.*, 39:279–325. — **448**

SEARS, P. S. (1940) Levels of aspiration in academically successful and unsuccessful children. *J. abnorm. soc. Psychol.*, 35:498–536. — **154**

SEARS, P. S., see also Sears and others (1953).

SEARS, R. R. (1936) Experimental studies of projection: I. Attribution of traits. *J. soc. Psychol.*, 7:151–63. — **475, 516**

SEARS, R. R. (1943) Survey of objective studies of psychoanalytic concepts. *Soc. Sci. Res. Coun. Bull.*, 51. — **475**

SEARS, R. R. (1961) Relation of early socialization experiences to aggression in middle childhood. *J. abnorm. soc. Psychol.*, 63:466–92. — **149**

SEARS, R. R., see also Davis and others (1948).

SEARS, R. R., MACCOBY, E. E., and LEVIN, H. (1957) *Patterns of child rearing.* Evanston, Ill.: Row, Peterson. — **81, 82, 146**

SEARS, R. R., RAU, L., and ALPERT, R. (1965) *Identification and child rearing.* Stanford, Calif.: Stanford Univ. Press. — **86**

SEARS, R. R., WHITING, J. W. M., NOWLIS, V., and SEARS, P. S. (1953) Some child rearing antecedents of aggression and dependency in young children. *Genet. Psychol. Monogr.*, 47:135–234. — **146, 148**

SEBEOK, T. A., see Osgood and Sebeok (1965).

SECORD, P. F., and BACKMAN, C. W. (1964) *Social psychology.* N. Y.: McGraw-Hill. — **600**

SECORD, P. F., BEVAN, W., and KATZ, B. (1956) Perceptual accentuation and the Negro stereotype. *J. abnorm. soc. Psychol.*, 53:78–83. — **576–77**

SEEMAN, J. (1949) A study of the process of nondirective therapy. *J. consult. Psychol.*, 13:157–68. — **555**

SEGALL, J., see Luce and Segall (1966).

SEGALL, M. H., CAMPBELL, D. T., and HERSKOVITZ, M. J. (1963) Cultural differences in the perception of geometrical illusions. *Science*, 139:769–70. — **228**

SEIBERT, L. C. (1932) A series of experiments on the learning of French vocabulary. *Johns Hopkins Univ. Stud. Educ.*, No. 18. — **332**

SEIDENBERG, B., see Proshansky and Seidenberg (1965).

SELLS, S. B., and BERRY, C. A. (Eds.) (1961) *Human factors in jet and space travel: a medical-psychological analysis.* N. Y.: Ronald. — **617**

SELYE, H. (1956) *The stress of life.* N. Y.: McGraw-Hill. — **55, 58**

SEM-JACOBSEN, C. W., and TORKILDSEN, A. (1960) In Ramey, E. R., and O'Doherty, D. S. (Eds.) *Electrical studies on the unanesthetized brain.* N. Y., Hoeber, 280–88. — **293**

SENDEN, M. V. (1932) *Raum- und Gestaltauffassung bei operierten Blindgeborenen vor und nach Operation.* Leipzig, Germany: Barth. — **224, 234**

SENSIBAR, M. R., see Clark and Sensibar (1956).

SENTER, R. J., see Lippert and Senter (1966).

SEVERIN, F. T. (Ed.) (1965) *Humanistic viewpoints in psychology.* N. Y.: McGraw-Hill. — **7**

SHAFFER, L. F. (1947) Fear and courage in aerial combat. *J. consult. Psychol.*, 11:137–43. — **165**

SHAPIRO, A., see Goodenough and others (1959); Rechtschaffen, Goodenough, and Shapiro (1962).

SHAW, J. C., see Newell, Shaw, and Simon (1958).

SHEEHAN, M. R., see Woodworth and Sheehan (1964).

SHEER, D. (Ed.) (1961) *Electrical stimulation of the brain.* Austin, Tex.: Hogg Foundation and Univ. of Texas Press. — **58**

SHEFFIELD, F. D. (1961) Theoretical considerations in the learning of complex sequential tasks from demonstration and practice. In Lumsdaine, A. A. (Ed.) *Student response in programed instruction: a symposium.* Washington, D. C.: National Academy of Sciences–National Research Council. — **614**

SHEFFIELD, F. D. (1965) Relation between classical conditioning and instrumental learning. In Prokasy, W. F. (Ed.) *Classical conditioning: a symposium.* N. Y.: Appleton-Century-Crofts, 302–22. — **292**

SHEFFIELD, F. D., see also Campbell and Sheffield (1953); Hovland, Lumsdaine, and Sheffield (1949).

SHELDON, W. H. (1954) *Atlas of men: a guide for somatotyping the adult male at all ages.* N. Y.: Harper. — **467**

SHELDON, W. H., and STEVENS, S. S. (1942) *The varieties of temperament.* N. Y.: Harper. — **467**

SHELDON, W. H., STEVENS, S. S., and TUCKER, W. B. (1940) *The varieties of human physique.* N. Y.: Harper. — **467**

SHEPPARD, J. J., JR. (1966) *A critical review of the experimental foundation of human color perception.* Santa Monica, Calif.: The RAND Corp. — **194, 202**

SHERIF, C. W., see Sherif and Sherif (1964).

SHERIF, M. (1936) *The psychology of social norms.* N. Y.: Harper. — **467**

SHERIF, M. (1951) A preliminary study of inter-group relations. In Rohrer, J. H., and Sherif, M., *Social psychology at the crossroads.* N. Y.: Harper, 388–424. — **577**

SHERIF, M., and SHERIF, C. W. (1964) *Reference groups: exploration into conformity and deviation of adolescents.* N. Y.: Harper and Row. — **100**

SHERMAN, L. J., *see* Moseley, Duffey, and Sherman (1963).

SHIFFRIN, R. M., *see* Atkinson and Shiffrin (1967).

SHLAER, S., *see* Hecht and Shlaer (1938).

SHOR, R. E., and ORNE, M. T. (Eds.) (1965) *The nature of hypnosis.* N. Y.: Holt, Rinehart and Winston. — **268**

SHOR, R. E., ORNE, M. T., and O'CONNELL, D. N. (1966) Psychological correlates of plateau hypnotizability in a special volunteer sample. *J. pers. soc. Psychol.*, 3:80–95. — **260**

SHORT, J. F., *see* Henry and Short (1954).

SHUTTLEWORTH, F. K. (1939) The physical and mental growth of girls and boys age six to nineteen in relation to age at maximum growth. *Monogr. Soc. Res. Child Develpm.*, 46, No. 210. — **93**

SIDOWSKI, J. B. (Ed.) (1966) *Experimental methods and instrumentation in psychology.* N. Y.: McGraw-Hill. — **29**

SIGEL, I. E. (1964) The attainment of concepts. In Hoffman, M. L., and Hoffman, L. W. (Eds.) *Review of child development research*, Vol. I. N. Y.: Russell Sage Foundation, 209–48. — **71**

SIIPOLA, E. M. (1935) A study of some effects of preparatory set. *Psychol. Monogr.*, 46, No. 210. — **240**

SILBERMAN, H. F., *see* Coulson and Silberman (1960).

SIMON, C. W., *see* Emmons and Simon (1956).

SIMON, H. A., *see* Newell, Shaw, and Simon (1958); Newell and Simon (1956).

SIMON, H. A., and NEWELL, A. (1964) Information processing in computer and man. *American Scientist*, 52:281–300. — **384, 393**

SIMPSON, G. G., and BECK, W. S. (1965) *Life: an introduction to biology.* N. Y.: Harcourt, Brace & World. — **35, 36, 39**

SINCLAIR, J., *see* Olds and Sinclair (1957).

SINGER, E., *see* Kaplan and Singer (1963).

SINGER, J. E., *see* Schachter and Singer (1962).

SINGER, J. L. (1966) *Daydreaming: an introduction to the experimental study of inner experience.* N. Y.: Random House. — **268**

SINGER, R., *see* Leventhal, Singer, and Jones (1965).

SINNOTT, E. W., DUNN, L. C., and DOBZHANSKY, T. (1958) *Principles of genetics* (5th Ed.). N. Y.: McGraw-Hill. — **457**

SJOBERG, B. M., JR. (1965) *The effect of drugs upon suggestibility and susceptibility to hypnosis.* Ph.D. dissertation, Stanford University. — **264**

SKAGER, R. W., SCHULTZ, W., and KLEIN, S. P. (1965) Quality and quantity of accomplishments as measures of creativity. *J. educ. Psychol.*, 56:31–39. — **388**

SKEELS, H. M., *see* Skodak and Skeels (1949).

SKINNER, B. F. (1938) *The behavior of organisms.* N. Y.: Appleton-Century-Crofts. — **280, 282, 313**

SKINNER, B. F. (1950) Are theories of learning necessary? *Psychol. Rev.*, 57:193–216. — **283**

SKINNER, B. F. (1954) The science of learning and the art of teaching. *Harvard educ. Rev.*, 24:86–97. — **350**

SKINNER, B. F. (1957) *Verbal behavior.* N. Y.: Appleton-Century-Crofts. — **372**

SKINNER, B. F., *see also* Ferster and Skinner (1957).

SKODAK, M., and SKEELS, H. M. (1949) A final follow-up of one hundred adopted children. *J. genet. Psychol.*, 75:3–19. — **451**

SLATER, E. (1953) *Psychotic and neurotic illnesses in twins.* London: Her Majesty's Stationery Office. — **456**

SLATER, J., *see* Berlyne and Slater (1957).

SLATER, P. (1961) Toward a dualistic theory of identification. *Merrill-Palmer Quart.*, 7:113–26. — **83**

SLAVSON, S. R. (1962) *Practice of group therapy.* N. Y.: Internat. Univ. Press. — **560, 571**

SLOAN, L. L., and WOLLACH, L. (1948) A case of unilateral deuteranopia. *J. opt. Soc. Amer.*, 38:502–09. — **200**

SLUCKIN, W. (1965) *Imprinting and early learning.* Chicago: Aldine. — **90**

SMEDSLUND, J. (1961) The acquisition of conservation of substance and weight in children. *Scand. J. Psychol.*, 2:11–20; 71–84; 85–87; 153–55; 156–60; 203–10. — **72, 73**

SMITH, K. U., and SMITH, W. M. (1962) *Perception and motion.* Philadelphia, Pa. Saunders. — **223**

SMITH, L. B. (1954) English treason trials and confessions in the sixteenth century. *J. Hist. Ideas*, 15:471–98. — **597**

SMITH, M. B., BRUNER, J. S., and WHITE, R. W. (1956) *Opinions and personality.* N. Y.: Wiley. — **584**

SMITH, M. F., *see* Carmichael and Smith (1939).

SMITH, W. M., *see* Smith and Smith (1962).

SNOW, C. P. (1959) *The two cultures and the scientific revolution.* N. Y.: Cambridge Univ. Press. — **615**

SNOWDON, R. J., *see* McConnell, Snowdon, and Powell (1955).

SNYDER, F. W., and PRONKO, N. H. (1952) *Vision with spatial inversion.* Wichita, Kans.: McCormich-Armstrong. — **222**

SNYDER, L. S. (1932) Studies in human inheritance: IX. The inheritance of taste deficiency in man. *Ohio J. Sci.*, 32:436–40. — **448**

SNYDER, W. U., and others (1947) *Casebook of nondirective counseling.* Boston: Houghton Mifflin. — **555**

SNYGG, D., *see* Combs and Snygg (1959).

SOAL, S. G., and BATEMAN, F. (1954) *Modern experiments in telepathy.* New Haven, Conn.: Yale Univ. Press. — **241, 242, 243, 244**

SOKOLOV, E. N. (1963) Higher nervous functions: the orienting reflex. *Ann. Rev. Physiol.*, 25:545–80. — **131**

SOLLEY, C. M., and MURPHY, G. (1960) *Development of the perceptual world.* N. Y.: Basic Books. — **246**

SOLOMON, P., and others (Eds.) (1961) *Sensory deprivation.* Cambridge, Mass.: Harvard Univ. Press. — **58**

SOLOMON, R. L., *see* Lambert, Solomon, and Watson (1949).

SONTAG, L. W., BAKER, C. T., and NELSON, V. L. (1958) Mental growth and development: a longitudinal study. *Monogr. Soc. Res. Child Develop.*, 23, Serial No. 68. — **436, 437**

SPEARMAN, C. (1904) General intelligence objectively determined and measured. *Amer. J. Psychol.*, 15:201–93. — **427**

SPENCE, K. W. (1956) *Behavior theory and conditioning.* New Haven, Conn.: Yale Univ. Press. — **132**

SPENCE, K. W. (1964) Anxiety (drive) level and performance in eyelid conditioning. *Psychol. Bull.*, 61:129–39. — **359, 360**

SPENCE, K. W., and NORRIS, E. B. (1950) Eyelid conditioning as a function of the inter-trial interval. *J. exp. Psychol.*, 40:716–20. — **337**

SPERRY, R. W. (1951) Mechanisms of neural maturation. In Stevens, S. S. (Ed.) *Handbook of experimental psychology.* N. Y.: Wiley, 236–80. — **213**

SPERRY, R. W. (1961) Cerebral organization and behavior. *Science,* 133:1749–57. — **349**

SPERRY, R. W. (1964) The great cerebral commissure. *Sci. Amer.,* 210:42–52. — **349**

SPERRY, R. W., *see also* Gazzaniga, Bogen, and Sperry (1965).

SPIELBERGER, C. D. (1962) The effects of manifest anxiety on the academic achievement of college students. *Ment. Hyg.,* 46:420–26. — **361**

SPIELBERGER, C. D. (Ed.) (1966) *Anxiety and behavior.* N. Y.: Academic Press. — **364**

SPIELBERGER, C. D., WEITZ, H., and DENNY, J. P. (1962) Group counseling and the academic performance of anxious college freshmen. *J. counsel. Psychol.,* 9:195–204. — **361**

SPIES, G. (1965) Food versus intracranial self-stimulation reinforcement in food-deprived rats. *J. comp. physiol. Psychol.,* 60:153–57. — **292**

SPIKER, C. C., *see* Lipsitt and Spiker (1963).

SPITZ, R. A. (1946) The smiling response: a contribution to the ontogenesis of social relations. *Genet. Psychol. Monogr.,* 34:57–125. — **78**

SPITZER, H. F. (1939) Studies in retention. *J. educ. Psychol.,* 30:641–56. — **334**

SROLE, L., LANGNER, T. S., MICHAEL, S. T., OPLER, M. K., and RENNIE, T. A. C. (1962) *Mental health in the metropolis: the midtown Manhattan study.* N. Y.: McGraw-Hill. — **545**

STACEY, C. L., and DE MARTINO, M. F. (Eds.) (1963) *Understanding human motivation* (Rev. Ed.). Cleveland, O.: Howard Allen. — **162**

STALNAKER, J. M. (1965) Psychological tests and public responsibility. *Amer. Psychologist,* 20:131–35. — **439**

STECHER, L. I., *see* Baldwin and Stecher (1922).

STEELE, F. I., *see* Bennis and others (1964).

STEIN, M. I. (1955) *The Thematic Apperception Test* (Rev. Ed.). Reading, Mass.: Addison-Wesley. — **494**

STEIN, M. I. (1963) Explorations in typology. In White, R. W. (Ed.) *The study of lives.* N. Y.: Atherton Press, 280–303. — **469**

STEIN, M. I., *see also* Stern, Stein, and Bloom (1956).

STEINER, I. D., and FISHBEIN, M. (Eds.) (1965) *Current studies in social psychology.* N. Y.: Holt, Rinehart and Winston. — **600**

STEINSCHRIBER, L., *see* Goodenough and others (1959).

STELLAR, E. (1954) The physiology of motivation. *Psychol. Rev.,* 61:5–22. — **167**

STENDLER, C. B. (Ed.) (1964) *Readings in child behavior and development* (2nd Ed.). N. Y.: Harcourt, Brace & World. — **90**

STENDLER, C. B., *see also* Martin and Stendler (1959).

STEPHENSON, W. (1939) Methodological consideration of Jung's typology. *J. ment. Sci.,* 85:185–205. — **483**

STEPHENSON, W. (1953) *The study of behavior: Q-technique and its methodology.* Chicago: Univ. of Chicago Press. — **482**

STERN, C. (1960) *Principles of human genetics* (2nd Ed.). San Francisco, Calif.: Freeman. — **461**

STERN, G. G., STEIN, M. I., and BLOOM, B. S. (1956) *Methods in personality assessment.* Glencoe, Ill.: Free Press. — **502**

STEVENS, C. F. (1966) *Neurophysiology: a primer.* N. Y.: Wiley. — **58**

STEVENS, S. S. (Ed.) (1951) *Handbook of experimental psychology.* N. Y.: Wiley. — **216**

STEVENS, S. S. (1957) On the psychophysical law. *Psychol. Rev.,* 64:153–81. — **191**

STEVENS, S. S. (1966) Metric for the social consensus. *Science,* 151:530–41. — **191**

STEVENS, S. S., *see also* Sheldon and Stevens (1942); Sheldon, Stevens, and Tucker (1940).

STEVENS, S. S., and DAVIS, H. (1938) *Hearing.* N. Y.: Wiley. — **205**

STEVENS, S. S., DAVIS, H., and LURIE, M. H. (1935) The localization of pitch perception on the basilar membrane. *J. genet. Psychol.,* 13:297–315. — **208**

STEVENSON, H. C. (Ed.) (1963) *Child psychology.* 62nd Yearbook, Part I, National Society for the Study of Education. Chicago: Univ. of Chicago Press. — **90**

STOKES, D. E., *see* Campbell and others (1960).

STOLZ, H. R., and STOLZ, L. M. (1951) *Somatic development of adolescent boys.* N. Y.: Macmillan. — **116**

STOLZ, L. M., *see* Stolz and Stolz (1951).

STONE, C. P., and BARKER, R. G. (1937) Aspects of personality and intelligence in postmenarcheal and premenarcheal girls of the same chronological age. *J. comp. Psychol.,* 23:439–55. — **97**

STORMS, L. H., *see* Broen and Storms (1964); Russell and Storms (1955).

STRASSMAN, H. D., THALER, M. B., and SCHEIN, E. H. (1956) A prisoner of war syndrome: apathy as a reaction to severe stress. *Amer. J. Psychiat.,* 112:998–1003. — **512**

STRATTON, G. M. (1897) Vision without inversion of the retinal image. *Psychol. Rev.,* 4:341–60, 463–81. — **222**

STRAUSS, A. A., *see* Werner and Strauss (1941).

STROUD, J. B., *see* Knief and Stroud (1959).

STRUPP, H. H. (1958) The psychotherapist's contribution to the treatment process. *Behav. Sci.,* 3:34–67. — **562**

SUCI, G. J. (1960) A comparison of semantic structures in American Southwest culture groups. *J. abnorm. soc. Psychol.,* 61:25–30. — **368**

SULLIVAN, H. S. (1949) The theory of anxiety and the nature of psychotherapy. *Psychiatry,* 12:3–13. — **179**

SUPPES, P. (1966) The use of computers in education. *Sci. Amer.,* 215:206–23. — **5, 352**

SUPPES, P., *see also* Crothers and Suppes (1967); Estes and Suppes (1959).

SUTCLIFFE, J. P. (1960) "Credulous" and "skeptical" views of hypnotic phenomena: a review of certain evidence and methodology. *Int. J. clin. exp. Hyp.,* 8:73–101. — **263**

SUTCLIFFE, J. P. (1961) "Credulous" and "skeptical" views of hypnotic phenomena: experiments on esthesia, hallucination, and delusion. *J. abnorm. soc. Psychol.,* 62:189–200. — **263**

SWANSON, C. E., *see* Miller and Swanson (1959).

SWARTZ, J. D., *see* Holtzman and others (1961).

SWETS, J. A. (1964) *Signal detection and recognition by human observers.* N. Y.: Wiley. — **216**

SWETS, J. A., *see also* Green and Swets (1966).

SWETS, J. A., TANNER, W. P., JR., and BIRDSALL, T. G. (1961) Decision processes in perception. *Psychol. Rev.,* 68:301–40. — **192**

SZASZ, T. (1962) *The myth of mental illness: foundations of a theory of personal conduct.* N. Y.: Hoeber-Harper. — **559**

TABER, J., GLASER, R., and SCHAEFER, H. (1965) *Learning and programmed instruction.* Reading, Mass.: Addison-Wesley. — **364**

TANNENBAUM, P. H., *see* Osgood and Tannenbaum (1955).

TRAISMAN, A. S., and TRAISMAN, H. S. (1958) Thumb-and finger-sucking: a study of 2,650 infants and children. *J. Pediat.*, 52:566–72. — **76**

TRAISMAN, H. S., *see* Traisman and Traisman (1958).

TRIST, E. L., *see* Curle and Trist (1947).

TRYON, R. C. (1940) Genetic differences in maze-learning ability in rats. 39th Yearbook, Part I, National Society for the Study of Education. Chicago: Univ. of Chicago Press, 111–19. — **448**

TSANG, Y. C. (1938) Hunger motivation in gastrectomized rats. *J. comp. Psychol.*, 26:1–17. — **121**

TUCKER, W. B., *see* Sheldon, Stevens, and Tucker (1940).

TUDDENHAM, R. D., *see* Bayley and Tuddenham (1944).

TUPPER, W., *see* Lemere, Voegtlin, Broz, O'Hollaren, and Tupper (1942).

TURIEL, E. (1966) An experimental test of the sequentiality of developmental stages in the child's moral judgments. *J. Personal soc. Psychol.*, 3:611–18. — **86**

TURNBULL, C. M. (1961) Some observations regarding the experiences and behavior of the BaMbuti Pygmies. *Amer. J. Psychol.*, 74:304–08. — **221**

TURNER, R. H., *see* Newcomb, Converse, and Turner (1964).

TURPIN, R., *see* Lejeune, Gautier, and Turpin (1959).

TURRELL, R. B., *see* Sawry, Conger, and Turrell (1956).

TYLER, F. T. (1964) Issues related to readiness to learn. In Hilgard, E. R. (Ed.) *Theories of learning and instruction*. 63rd Yearbook, Part I, National Society for the Study of Education. Chicago: Univ. of Chicago Press, 210–39. — **68**

TYLER, L. E. (1956) *The psychology of human differences* (2nd Ed.). N. Y.: Appleton-Century-Crofts. — **443, 461, 467**

TYLER, R. W., *see* Eells and others (1951).

UHR, L., and MILLER, J. G. (Eds.) (1960) *Drugs and behavior*. N. Y.: Wiley. — **268**

ULLMANN, L. P., *see* Krasner and Ullmann (1965).

ULLMANN, L. P., and KRASNER, L. (Eds.) (1965) *Case studies in behavior modification*. N. Y.: Holt, Rinehart and Winston. — **556**

UNDERWOOD, B. J. (1957) Interference and forgetting. *Psychol. Rev.*, 64:49–60. — **324, 325**

UNDERWOOD, B. J. (1961) Ten years of massed practice on distributed practice. *Psychol. Rev.*, 68:229–47. — **339**

UNDERWOOD, B. J. (1966) *Experimental psychology* (2nd Ed.). N. Y.: Meredith. — **29, 335**

UNDERWOOD, B. J., and KEPPEL, G. (1962) One-trial learning? *J. verb. Learn. verb. Behav.*, 1:1–13. — **301**

UNDERWOOD, B. J., and POSTMAN, L. (1960) Extra-experimental sources of interference in forgetting. *Psychol. Rev.*, 67:73–95. — **325**

URBAN, H. B., *see* Ford and Urban (1963).

VANDENBERG, S. G. (Ed.) (1965) *Methods and goals in human behavior genetics*. N. Y.: Academic Press. — **460, 461**

VAN LEHN, R., *see* Lacey and Van Lehn (1952); Lacey, Bateman, and Van Lehn (1952).

VAUGHAN, H. G., JR., COSTA, L. D., GILDEN, L., and SCHIMMEL, H. (1965) Identification of sensory and motor components of cerebral activity in simple reaction-time tasks. *Proc. 73rd Ann. Conv. Amer. Psychol. Assn.*, 179–80. — **45**

VEITH, I. (1965) *Hysteria: the history of a disease*. Chicago: Univ. of Chicago Press. — **570**

VERNON, P. E. (1950) The validation of civil service selection board procedures. *Occup. Psychol.*, 24:75–95. — **499**

VERNON, P. E. (1961) *Intelligence and attainment tests*. N. Y.: Philosophical Library. — **430**

VERNON, P. E. (1964) *Personality assessment: a critical survey*. N. Y.: Wiley. — **502**

VERNON, P. E., *see also* Allport, Vernon, and Lindzey (1960).

VERPLANCK, W. S. (1955) The control of the content of conversation: reinforcement of statements of opinion. *J. abnorm. soc. Psychol.*, 51:668–76. — **287**

VINCE, P., *see* Himmelweit, Oppenheim, and Vince (1958).

VOEGTLIN, W., *see* Lemere, Voegtlin, Broz, O'Hollaren, and Tupper (1942).

VOEKS, V. (1964) *On becoming an educated person* (2nd Ed.). Philadelphia, Pa.: Saunders. — **363**

VOLKART, E. H., *see* Kelley and Volkart (1952).

VOLKOVA, V. D. (1953) On certain characteristics of conditioned reflexes to speech stimuli in children. *Fiziol. Zh. SSSR*, 39:540–48. — **277**

VOTH, A. C., *see* Brown and Voth (1937).

WALD, G., *see* Brown and Wald (1964).

WALK, R. D., *see* Gibson and Walk (1956) (1960).

WALKER, E. L. (1964) Psychological complexity as a basis for a theory of motivation and choice. *Nebr. Symp. Motivation*, 12:47–95. — **131**

WALLACH, H., and GALLOWAY, A. (1946) The constancy of colored objects in colored illumination. *J. exp. Psychol.*, 36:119–26. — **219**

WALLACH, M. A., and KOGAN, N. (1965) *Modes of thinking in young children*. N. Y.: Holt, Rinehart and Winston. — **390, 393**

WALLAS, G. (1921) *The art of thought*. N. Y.: Harcourt, Brace & World. — **385**

WALLIN, P., *see* Burgess and Wallin (1953).

WALLS, G. L. (1960) "Land! Land!" *Psychol. Bull.*, 57:29–48. — **202**

WALTER, A. A., *see* Carmichael, Hogan, and Walter (1932).

WALTERS, R. H., *see* Bandura and Walters (1959) (1963).

WANG, G. H. (1923) The relation between "spontaneous" activity and oestrous cycle in the white rat. *Comp. Psychol. Monogr.*, 2, No. 6. — **125**

WARD, A. W., *see* Coleman and Ward (1955).

WARDEN, C. J. (1931) *Animal motivation*. N. Y.: Columbia Univ. Press. — **120, 121**

WARE, E. E., *see* Maclay and Ware (1961).

WARNER, W. L., and LUNT, P. S. (1941) *The social life of a modern community*. New Haven, Conn.: Yale Univ. Press. — **575**

WARNER, W. L., MEEKER, M., and EELLS, K. (1949) *Social class in America*. Chicago: Science Research Associates. — **575**

WATSON, G. (1942) Morale during unemployment. In Watson, G. (Ed.) *Civilian morale*. Boston: Houghton Mifflin. — **568**

WATSON, J. B. (1913) Psychology as the behaviorist views it. *Psychol. Rev.*, 20:158–77. — **17, 614**

WATSON, J. B. (1925) *Behaviorism*. (Rev. Ed., 1930). N. Y.: Norton. — **17**

WATSON, J. B., and RAYNER, R. (1920) Conditioned emotional reactions. *J. exp. Psychol.*, 3:1–14. — **176**

WATSON, P. D., *see* Lambert, Solomon, and Watson (1949).

WATT, J. B., *see* Colby, Watt, and Gilbert (1964).

WAUGH, C., and NORMAN, D. A. (1965) Primary memory. *Psychol. Rev.*, 72:89–104. — **328, 329**

WEBB, E. (1961) Weber's law and consumer prices. *Amer. Psychologist*, 63:450. — **191**

WEBB, W. B. (Ed.) (1962) *The profession of psychology*. N. Y.: Holt. — **618**

WEBB, W. B., *see also* Williams, Agnew, and Webb (1964).

WECHSLER, D. (1949) *Wechsler intelligence scale for children*. N. Y.: Psychological Corp. — **426**

WECHSLER, D. (1955) *The Wechsler Adult Intelligence Scale manual*. N. Y.: Psychological Corp. — **427, 430**

WECHSLER, D. (1958) *The measurement and appraisal of adult intelligence*. (4th Ed.). Baltimore, Md.: Williams and Wilkins. — **426, 443**

WEISS, P. A., *see* Willier, Weiss, and Hamburger (1955).

WEISSMAN, P. (1957) Conscious and unconscious autobiographical dramas of Eugene O'Neill. *J. Amer. psychoanal. Assn.*, 5:432–60. — **391**

WEITZ, H., *see* Spielberger, Weitz, and Denny (1962).

WEITZENHOFFER, A. M., *see* Hilgard, Weitzenhoffer, Landes, and Moore (1961).

WEITZENHOFFER, A. M., and HILGARD, E. R. (1959) *Stanford hypnotic susceptibility scales, forms A and B*. Palo Alto, Calif.: Consulting Psychologists Press. — **261**

WELLINGTON, M., *see* Wenger and Wellington (1943).

WELSH, G. S., *see* Dahlstrom and Welsh (1960).

WELSH, G. S., and DAHLSTROM, W. G. (Eds.) (1956) *Basic readings on the MMPI in psychology and medicine*. Minneapolis, Minn.: Univ. of Minnesota Press. — **489, 501**

WENDT, G. R. (1951) Vestibular functions. In Stevens, S. S. (Ed.) *Handbook of experimental psychology*. N. Y.: Wiley, 1191–223. — **214**

WENGER, M. A., and WELLINGTON, M. (1943) The measurement of autonomic balance in children: method and normative data. *Psychosom. Med.*, 5:241–53. — **468**

WEPMAN, J. M., and HEINE, R. W. (Eds.) (1963) *Concepts of personality*. Chicago: Aldine. — **485**

WERNER, H., and STRAUSS, A. A. (1941) Pathology of figure-ground relation in the child. *J. abnorm. soc. Psychol.*, 36:236–48. — **433**

WERTHEIMER, MAX (1912) Experimentelle Studien über das Sehen von Bewegungen. *Z. Psychol.*, 61:161–265. — **19**

WERTHEIMER, MAX (1923) Untersuchungen zur Lehre von der Gestalt. *Psychol. Forsch.*, 4:301–50; portions trans, in Ellis. W. D. (1938) *A source book of Gestalt psychology*. N. Y.: Harcourt, Brace & World. — **225**

WERTHEIMER, MICHAEL, *see* Beardslee and Wertheimer (1958).

WESSEL, N. Y., *see* Carmichael, Roberts, and Wessel (1937).

WEST, L. J., *see* Farber, Harlow, and West (1957).

WESTLEY, W. A., *see* Elkin and Westley (1955).

WEVER, E. G. (1949) *Theory of hearing*. N. Y.: Wiley. — **208, 216**

WHEATLEY, M. D. (1944) The hypothalamus and affective behavior in cats. *Arch. Neurol. Psychiat.*, 52:298–316. — **167**

WHITE, R. W. (1959) Motivation reconsidered: the concept of competence. *Psychol. Rev.*, 66:297–333. — **130, 159**

WHITE, R. W. (1964) *The abnormal personality*. (3rd Ed.). N. Y.: Ronald Press. — **547**

WHITE, R. W., *see also* Smith, Bruner, and White (1956).

WHITEHEAD, A. N., and RUSSELL, B. (1925) *Principia mathematica* (2nd Ed.). (Original date, 1910–13). Cambridge, England: Cambridge Univ. Press. — **383**

WHITEHORN, J. C., and BETZ, B. J. (1960) Further studies of the doctor as a crucial variable in the outcome of treatment with schizophrenic patients. *Amer. J. Psychiat.*, 117:215–23. — **563**

WHITING, J. W. M., *see* Landauer and Whiting (1964); Sears and others (1953).

WHITING, J. W. M., and CHILD, I. L. (1953) *Child training and personality: a cross-cultural study*. New Haven, Conn.: Yale Univ. Press. — **144, 150, 475**

WHITING, J. W. M., and MOWRER, O. H. (1943) Habit progression and regression—a laboratory investigation of some factors relevant to human socialization. *J. comp. Psychol.*, 36:229–53. — **358**

WHITMAN, M., *see* Deutsch, Fishman. Kogan, North, and Whitman (1964).

WHORF, B. L. (1950) *Four articles on metalinguistics*. Washington, D. C.: Foreign Service Institute. — **374**

WHORF, B. L. (1956) In Carroll, J. B. (Ed.) *Language, thought, and reality*. N. Y.: Wiley. — **374**

WIESEL, T. N., *see* Hubel and Wiesel (1959) (1963) (1965).

WIGGINS, J. S. (1959) Interrelationships among MMPI measures of dissimulation under standard and social desirability instructions. *J. consult. Psychol.*, 23:419–27. — **493**

WIGGINS, J. S. (1962) Strategic, method, and stylistic variance in the MMPI. *Psychol. Bull.*, 59:224–42. — **493**

WILLIAMS, H. L., MORLOCK, H. C., JR., and MORLOCK, J. V. (1963) *Discriminative responses to auditory signals during sleep*. Paper presented at American Psychological Association, Philadelphia, Pa. — **257**

WILLIAMS, R. E., *see* Hecht and Williams (1922–23).

WILLIAMS, R. H., TIBBITTS, C., and DONAHUE, W. (1963) *Processes of aging*, Vol. I. N. Y.: Atherton Press. — **116**

WILLIAMS, R. J. (1956) *Biochemical individuality*. N. Y.: Wiley. — **468**

WILLIAMS, R. L., AGNEW, H. W., JR., and WEBB, W. B. (1964) Sleep patterns in young adults: an EEG study. *EEG clin. Neurophysiol.*, 17:376–81. — **254**

WILLIER, B. H., WEISS, P. A., and HAMBURGER, V. (1955) *Analysis of development*. Philadelphia, Pa.: Saunders. — **90**

WINER, B. J. (1962) *Statistical principles in experimental design*. N. Y.: McGraw-Hill. — **415**

WINTERBOTTOM, M. R. (1958) The relation of need for achievement to learning experiences in independence and mastery. In Atkinson, J. W. (Ed.) *Motives in fantasy, action, and society*. Princeton, N. J.: Van Nostrand, 453–78. — **154**

WITKIN, H. A. (1959) The perception of the upright. *Sci. Amer.*, 200:50–56. — **225**

WITT, G. M., and HALL, C. S. (1949) The genetics of audiogenic seizures in the house mouse. *J. comp. physiol. Psychol.*, 42:58–63. — **448**

WITTY, P. A., and JENKINS, M. D. (1934) The educational achievement of gifted Negro children. *J. educ. Psychol.*, 25:585–97. — **459**

WOLF, M. M., *see* Harris, Johnston, Kelley, and Wolf (1965).

WOLF, S., and WOLFF, H. G. (1942) Evidence on the genesis of peptic ulcer in man. *J. Amer. Med. Assn.*, 120:670–75. — **173**

WOLFF, H. G., *see* Wolf and Wolff (1942).

WOLFF, P. H. (1959) 0bservations on newborn infants. *Psychosom. Med.*, 21:110–18. — **467**

WOLFF, P. H. (1966) The causes, controls, and organization of behavior in the neonate. *Psychol. Issues*, 5, Monograph 17. — **250**

WOLLACH, L., *see* Sloan and Wollach (1948).

WOLMAN, B. B., and NAGEL, E. (Eds.) (1965) *Scientific psychology*. N. Y.: Basic Books. — **29**

WOLPE, J. (1958) *Psychotherapy by reciprocal inhibition*. Stanford, Calif.: Stanford Univ. Press. — **556, 557**

WOLPE, J., SALTER, A., and REYNA, L. J. (Eds.) (1964) *The conditioning therapies*. N. Y.: Holt, Rinehart and Winston. — **556, 571**

WOLPERT, E., *see* Dement and Wolpert (1958).

WOOD, B. D., and FREEMAN, F. N. (1932) *An experimental study of the educational influences of the typewriter in the elementary school classroom*. N. Y.: Macmillan. — **66**

WOODROW, H. (1927) The effect of type of training upon transference. *J. educ. Psychol.*, 18:159–72. — **348**

WOODWORTH, R. S. (1938) *Experimental psychology*. N. Y.: Holt. — **171**

WOODWORTH, R. S. (1958) *Dynamics of behavior*. N. Y.: Holt. — **130**

WOODWORTH, R. S., and SCHLOSBERG, H. (1954) *Experimental psychology* (Rev. Ed.). N. Y.: Holt. — **231, 335**

WOODWORTH, R. S., and SHEEHAN, M. R. (1964) *Contemporary schools of psychology* (3rd Ed.). N. Y.: Ronald Press. — **29**

WRIGHT, R. H. (1964) Odor and molecular vibration: the far infrared spectra of some perfume chemicals. *Ann. N. Y. Acad. Sci.*, 116:552–58. — **209**

WULF, F. (1922) Über die Veränderung von Vorstellungen (Gedächtnis und Gestalt). *Psychol. Forsch.*, 1:333–73. — **320**

WYGANT, W., JR., *see* Downing and Wygant (1964).

WYLIE, R. C. (1961) *The self concept*. Lincoln, Nebr.: Univ. of Nebraska Press. — **482, 485**

YACORZYNSKI, G. K., *see* Neymann and Yacorzynski (1942).

YARROW, L. J. (1954) The relationship between nutritive sucking experiences in infancy and non-nutritive sucking in childhood. *J. genet. Psychol.*, 84:149–62. — **76**

YERKES, R. M., and MORGULIS, S. (1909) The method of Pavlov in animal psychology. *Psychol. Bull.*, 6:257–73. — **272**

YOUNG, P. T. (1937) Laughing and weeping, cheerfulness and depression: a study of moods among college students. *J. soc. Psychol.*, 8:311–34. — **180**

Index

Day residues, and manifest content of dream, 257
Decibel, defined, 205
Decision theory, 155
Defense mechanisms, 514–21; and adjustment, 521–23; purposes of, 515; self-deception in, 515 ff.
Deficiency motives, 159
Déjà vu, 315
Delinquency, juvenile, 91, 99–100, *100*, 542, 606
Delirium, 251, 320
Delusion, 251, 535
Dendrites, 36, 37
Denial, as form of self-defense, 515, *521*
Denotative meaning, 366
Deoxyribonucleic acid (DNA), 322, 446
Dependency motive, 144; behavior related to, *145*, 145–47, *146*
Dependent variable, 9, 10, 19, 24
Depression, cultural determiners of, 534
Depth perception, 229–33, *233*, 234, 235–37
Descartes, René, 13, 14, 234, 248, 386
Descriptive linguistics, 371
Descriptive statistics, 396
Design, experimental, 23–25, 414
Destructiveness, as consequence of frustration, 510
Development, 3, 60–70; cognitive, stages in, *71*, 71–73; critical periods in, 60, 62, 70, 74; emotional, 174–78; infant, orderly behavior patterns in, 62–64, *63*; and mental health, 615–16; moral, *85*, 85–87, *86*; psychosexual, 73; psychosocial, 73–74, *74*; of social attachments, 77–80, *78*; stages in, 61, 70–74; *see also* Growth; Maturation
Developmental explanation, 22, 23
Developmental theories, of personality, 473–77
Deviation I.Q., 425; mean, 399, 400, *400*; standard, 399, 400, 401, *401*
Diary of development, in case history, 12
Diet, self-selection of, by animals, 122–23, *123*
Difference equation, in stimulus-sampling theory of learning, 310
Difference threshold, 190–91
Difference tone, 206
Differential forgetting theory, of distributed practice, 337–38
Digit memory, training in, 66, 67, *67*
Digit span test, 426
Digit-symbol learning, 359, *360*
Digit-symbol test, 427
Dimension of color, 198, 199, 206
Direct aggression, 510–11
Directed thinking, 365
Discipline, 81; formal, doctrine of, 343–44
Discovery, scientific, 385–87
Discrimination: in conditioning, 278, *278*, 279, 280; inferior perceptual, 361; learning curves for, 346, *347*; manifestations of, *521*; tactile, 349, *349*
Disengagement, in old age, 114
Disguise, as form of self-deception, 515
Disgust, 164, 167
Displaced aggression, 511, *511*
Displacement: as defense mechanism, *521*; as dream mechanism, 257
Disposition(s): Allport's theory of, 470–71; motivational, 139–40, 141, 142, 156, 488
Dissociation, 480, 518, *521*
Dissonance reduction, 158, *158*, 582–83, 592
Dissonant tones, 206
Distance, monocular cues to, 232–33, *233*
Distortion, systematic, of memory trace, 320–23, *321*, 327
Distributed practice, in learning skills, 295, 336, *337*, 337–40, *338*, *339*
Distribution: bimodal, 447 *n.*, *447*; frequency, 397, 397–99, *398*; normal, *403*, 403–04; skewed, 398, 399, *399*; symmetrical, 398
Disuse theory of forgetting, 319–20, 324, 327
Divorce rate, 109
D-motives, 159
DNA (deoxyribonucleic acid), 322, 446
Dog(s): conditioned responses in, 271–73, *272*, 274; experiments with, on insensitivity to pain, 69; heredity of, 449; and thirst drive, 123–24

Dogfish, brain of, 38, 39
Dogmatism scale, 159
Dominant gene, 445, 446
Double approach-avoidance conflict, 505
Double-aspect theory, in monism, 248
Double-blind procedure, in drug studies, 567–68
Dream(ing), 248, 252, 255–58; *see also* Sleep
Drive(s): acquired, 134–35; as emotions, 173, 178–79; fear, *see* Fear; hunger, *see* Hunger drive; maternal, 126; measurement of, *120*, 120–21; and needs, 119–20, 128; pain-avoidance, 127, 133–34; sex, *125*, 125–26, 150; thirst, 123–24; *see also* Behavior; Emotion(s); Motivation (motives)
Drive-incentive relationship, 128–29
Drive-reduction theory, of reinforcement, 291
Drug addiction, 541
Drugs, psychoactive, 263–65
Dualism, and mind-body problem, 247–48
Duckling, imprinting in, 64, 65
Duct glands, 32
Ductless glands, *see* Endocrine glands
Duke University, 243
Duplex theories, of forgetting, 328–32, *329*
Dynamic theories, of personality, 477–79
Dynamometer, 10, *10*, 182

Ear, *202*, 203, *203*, 214; *see also* Auditory sense
Eardrum, *202*, 203
Ebbinghaus, Hermann, *15*, 296, 317
Ecology, 8
ECS (electroconvulsive shock), 331
Ecstasy, 164, 251
Ectomorphy, 467
Education: and psychology, 606–07; transfer of training applied to, 348
Edwards Personal Preference Scale (EPPS), 490–91, 493
EEG (electroencephalogram), 44, *44*, 254, *254*, 255, 258, 612
Effectors, in nervous system, 51, 53, *53*
Efferent nerves, 53, *53*, 54
Ego, in Freudian theory, 150, 478, 480
Ego involvement, 152
Einstein, Albert, 159, 385, 386, 387
Elections, study of, 586, 589–90, *590*, *591*, 593–94
Electric shock, in somatotherapy, 566
Electrical stimulation, of brain, 3, 43, *43*, 45, 46, 48, 292–93, *293*, 377
Electroconvulsive shock (ECS), 331
Electrodes: attached to outside of skull, *44*; implanted in brain of rat, 3, *4*, 43, *43*, 133, 292–93, *293*
Electroencephalogram (EEG), 44, *44*, 254, *254*, 255, 258, 612
Electromyograph, *45*
Electronic computer, *see* Computer, electronic
Electrophysiology, 211
Embeddedness of lines, illusions based on, 227, *227*
Embryo, 42, 61
Embryology, 8, 42
Emergency reactions, 166–67
Emergency theory, of emotions, 386
Emotion(s), 4, 163–85; activation theory of, 173; adaptive significance of, 182, 183; adrenal medulla active in, 32; and behaviorism, 17–18; bodily changes in, 164–66; Cannon-Bard theory of, 173; catharsis of, 184, 554; conditioned, 176; control of, 183, 184, 185; development of, 174–78; disruptive, 182, 183; distinguishing among, 168–73, *170*; as drive, 173, 178–79; emergency theory of, 386; as incentive, 179–80; intensity of, 163, *164*, 168, 182; James-Lange theory of, 173; as judged from photographs, *171*, 171–72; learning how to express, 175; learning occasions for, 175–76; maturation of, 171, 174–75; in mental health, 569; and motivated behavior, 178–82; physiological differentiation of, 172–73; physiological mechanisms in, 166–67; pleasant, 163, 172; and problem-solving, 182; and psychosomatic disorders, 55, 183; rejection-attention axis of, 172, *172*; release of, 183; repression of, 184; and sex, 178; suppression of, 183, 184, 519, *521*;

8
9
0
E   1
F   2
G   3
H   4
I   5
J